Incomprehensible Certainty

INCOMPREHENSIBLE CERTAINTY

Metaphysics and Hermeneutics of the Image

THOMAS PFAU

UNIVERSITY OF NOTRE DAME PRESS
NOTRE DAME, INDIANA

For my students,

also my teachers

Tout ce qui est incompréhensible ne laisse pas d'être.

—Blaise Pascal, *Pensées*

CONTENTS

ILLUSTRATIONS

PREFACE

What follows is a sustained reflection on images, taking that term in its widest compass, and on the kinds of knowledge uniquely opened up by their experience. Throughout this book, the concept of the image (*imago, eikōn*) is distinguished from (though not opposed to) its historically and materially contingent instantiation as "picture" (Gk. *eidolon*; Lat. *pictura*; Ger. *Gemälde, Kunstbild*), that is, an artifact designed to produce an optical illusion of sorts or simulate an extraneous object or scene. Whereas the *eidolon* rests on a logic of illusion or simulation, with the picture substituting itself *for* "its" object, talk of an image or icon presupposes an awareness of the ontological difference between the visible image and what it brings into our presence. Being squarely focused on the latter, this book is not, at least not primarily, concerned with pictorial techniques and their historical permutation. Rather, it means to explore the ontological status of images, as well as the hermeneutic challenges posed by their multilayered (visual, affective, reflective, and articulate) experience. Hence, even as the readings and arguments here advanced frequently draw on conceptual models and individual accounts developed by art history, this study is not conceived as an intervention in that discipline but, at most, as a reflection supplemental to it. The same can be said of the book's complementary relation to other fields of humanistic inquiry, including phenomenology, philosophical and theological aesthetics, and literary studies. All of these pursuits rely, often unwittingly, on an implicit understanding of visuality and our complex and subtly creative response to the myriad images in which our ambient world continually gives itself to us.

During the years I worked on this book, it became gradually more apparent how profoundly images and their experience are implicated in both metaphysical realism and modern phenomenology. As regards the former, this book primarily draws on Plato's metaphysics, as articulated in his later writings, which by many twists and turns ended up informing both the long Neoplatonist tradition and a great deal of Christian writing from its very beginnings all the way to the present. Though never a seamless and uncomplicated affair, the relationship between the Platonism and Christian theology extending from pseudo-Dionysius to Nicholas of Cusa all the way to writers such as Hans Urs von Balthasar in our time nevertheless exhibits some fundamental points of convergence, specifically as regards the unique capacity of images for mediating noncontingent, metaphysical truths. Hence, in what follows my concern is not with the image as an artifact contingently fashioned so as to convey discrete anthropomorphic meanings in mimetic or illusionist, pictorial form; nor for that matter is it the image understood as the material correlate of value-neutral perception or formal-aesthetic connoisseurship such as it flourished in the later Renaissance and in eighteenth-century philosophical aesthetics. Rather, my focus is on the image as a *medium*, a fulcrum of truth that by its very nature transcends the fluctuating affective states and epistemic concerns of its finite beholder. The principal hypothesis, to be probed in a variety of historical contexts, traditions of inquiry, and genres of writing, runs something like this: wherever we perceive organized visible form *as an image* we have become aware of how the order of the visible is always ontologically—or, more precisely, analogically—linked to a numinous, and as such *in*visible, domain. For ultimately, it is that domain which constitutes both the image's true source and the proper telos to which it orients its beholder. Simply (perhaps too simply) put, it is *in* and *through* the medium of the image that Being (*Sein*) manifests itself to human experience as something incontrovertibly real and intrinsically good, which is to say, not as a fleeting aggregation of optical "data" but as *logos*.

Such a formulation, hazarded in the intellectual and cultural situation of today's anthropocentric humanities, may well scandalize, as indeed it should, with its unrepentant openness to metaphysical questions and its implicit rejection of a hermeneutics of suspicion in favor of a phenomenology and hermeneutics of constructive discernment. As for the plausibility of my argument or, if the phrase be still permitted, its truth-value, that naturally depends on whether the interpretations marshaled on its behalf will be judged persuasive. Time will tell. For now, suffice it to say that the hypothesis developed throughout this book approaches the image as the medium through which we are presented with a noncontingent and nonpropositional type of knowledge. To close in on what specifically such knowledge consists of, three levels—metaphysics, phenomenology, and hermeneutics—have to be constantly kept in play. Drawing generously and gratefully on a wide array of arguments and insights concerning images offered from within multiple humanistic disciplines, this study eschews methodical (let alone professional) allegiance to any one of them. Instead, the

objective throughout is to scrutinize the ontological place of images, the phenomenology of their experience, and the way that such experience came to be successively
articulated in philosophical, theological, and literary writing from Plato to Rilke.

In the course of some twenty-five hundred years, the dynamics of what Husserl
calls "image-consciousness" (*Bildbewußtsein*), however enigmatic and resistant to
conceptualization, had time and again emerged as a flashpoint for philosophical,
theological, and literary *writing*. In spite of such difficulties, the originally Platonic
surmise never faded: namely, that visual intuition and a focused articulation of its
import are altogether indispensable for human beings to achieve orientation in the
world; furthermore, that the order of image and word, though ontologically distinct
from one another, are not incommensurable (as Lessing, for one, had claimed); and,
finally, that orders of *logos* and appearance are essentially complementary and mutually constitutive. For in its essence, all appearance is, potentially, a case of *manifestation*. By contrast, to discredit the visible as mere deception or illusion amounts
but to a secondary and contingent judgment—aimed not at what appears but at notions we may have (often mistakenly) formed about it. To entertain this quintessentially Realist hypothesis of the visible as the manifestation of its invisible source
necessarily means rejecting, or at least suspending, the deterministic axioms and reductionist methodologies that for several decades have been increasingly, and sometimes carelessly, embraced by humanistic inquiry. In fact, human cognition is far too
complex in its formal and affective bearings, and far too rich in its implications, as
to accommodate itself to an analytic parsing of propositions or a historicist retrieval
of its material "determinants" and discursive contexts.

Even less plausible would be attempts to "explain" the intuitive depth and force
of visual experience by means of naturalistic algorithms about neurological input-
output ratios. Like D. B. Hart, whose hard-hitting polemic in this regard I fully endorse, I consider the latter approach a monumental category error and a lamentable
relapse into a quasi-Spinozist "mechanical monism." At the very least, one ought to
pause at the wholly question-begging manner in which such explanatory schemes
reduce consciousness to "an emergent result or epiphenomenon of unguided physical
events," and by default supplant the very concept of significant *experience*, including
the experience of images, with a wholly contentless and invariant concept of bio-
chemical *processes*.[1]

By contrast, Plato, John of Damascus, and Husserl, to name but a few, always
understood that any inquiry into the nature of images presupposes that the visible

1. Hart 2013, 162; there being "an absolute qualitative abyss between the objective facts of
neurophysiology and the subjective experience of being a conscious self," it follows that "electro-
chemical events are not thought, even when they may be inseparably associated with thoughts"
(157, 159). For a critique of similarly reductionist tendencies in "contextualism" or some version of
New Historicism, see Gordon 2014.

form in question is experienced *as* an image. It is the distinctive "appresentation" (Husserl) of the visible world in the medium of the image that allows us to speak of "experience" (*Erlebnis*) in the first place. For insofar as a muddy stream of optical data indifferently traverses our gaze and ends up imperceptibly percolating into consciousness, there is as yet no proper warrant for speaking of experience at all, or for that matter of consciousness. For that to happen, experience must be suffused by a palpable excess—both as regards the distinctive nature of the phenomenon giving itself to our gaze and the quality of attention it elicits in the beholder. Put differently, unlike garden-variety acts of "perception" (*Wahrnehmung*), the "experience" (*Erlebnis*) of an image properly so called constitutes a distinctive "event" (*Ereignis*). Here the visible does not so much "fulfill" (*erfüllen*) as exceed the intentionality with which we approach it. In so doing, the image that, in Jean-Luc Marion's phrase, is "characterized by an excess of intuition, and thus of givenness, over the intention, the concept, and the aim" does not yield "information" of a discursive and notional kind but, instead, issues in what in an astute turn of phrase G. M. Hopkins calls an "incomprehensible certainty."[2] A decade earlier, Hopkins's onetime spiritual adviser, J. H. Newman, had used the term "certitude" to characterize this intuitive fusion of sight and insight, which by its very nature exceeds the explanatory scope and authority of available conceptual schemes and methods.

Undergirding this book as a whole is this numinous event of "super-abundant [*überzähliges*] *Dasein*" made manifest in the medium of the image and consummated "in our saturated gaze, in our speechless heart [*im überfüllteren Blick und im sprachlosen Herzen*]," as Rilke was to put it. Contrary to the by now commonplace, not to say complacent, distinction between metaphysical, "premodern" frameworks and the professed anti- or indeed postmetaphysical habits of post-Kantian inquiry, a philosophically and theologically informed study of visual experience strongly suggests that image-consciousness is essentially and indelibly entwined with metaphysics and, thus, resists conceptual or otherwise determinative reflection. Yet while making that case more fully, the final section of the introduction below also cautions that such a sweeping claim must guard against mystical obfuscation and free-floating speculation. Whatever claims are to be advanced about the transformative encounter with the visible image must always be borne out in phenomenological description and hermeneutic practice. This complementarity of metaphysics, phenomenology, and hermeneutics will subsequently be developed further in the book's first two chapters, which take up the concept of the image in Platonic and early Christian thought, respectively.

Considering how from their very beginnings—in the cave paintings found at Lubang Jeriji Saléh (Borneo), Chauvet (France), or Teruel (Spain)—images have

---

2. Marion 2008, 33.

always straddled the borders between cult object, religious symbol, and illusory artifact, any accounting for their historical constancy and enduring appeal ought to begin with a phenomenological description of our shifting response to them. In his magisterial 1989 study, David Freedberg thus thought it "clear that the basic divisions would have to be by classes of response rather than by classes of images."[3] By contrast, a glance at the titles of chapters 3 through 8 in the present study might initially suggest that it has reverted to an older, quasi-Linnéan system of formal classifications. In fact, the conceptual grid organizing the chapters (e.g., forensic, liturgical, epiphanic) does not propose an objective categorization of certain *kinds* of images but, instead, seeks to highlight their specific cognitive *function*. At the same time the present argument also moves beyond functionalism by conceiving the encounter of image and consciousness as a unique type of "event" (*Ereignis*), one whose deeper significance cannot be contained by a vocabulary of sharply demarcated pictorial functions and kinds of intentionality. For what transpires or "eventuates" in the encounter of consciousness and image, what is partially unveiled or disclosed, are noncontingent, metaphysical truths that categorically exceed the purview of any given conceptual scheme and methodological protocol, and which consequently can be limned only in the form of phenomenological description and hermeneutic reflection.

It is for this reason that, starting with the introduction, this book attempts to secure its claims inductively by proceeding from focused interpretations of specific images and of writings alternately unfolding an image theory or sifting the import of a particular visual experience. Above all, what follows is a work of hermeneutics—variously philosophical, theological, art historical, and literary in its bearings, yet always in focused dialogue with a complex tradition comprising many voices, each of which begs, first and foremost, to be listened to rather than dominated by critical methods of our own devising. Like all dialogue, hermeneutic practice hinges on our capacity for patient, undesigning attention and our generous responsiveness to the unfathomable eloquence of forms, both visual and verbal, wherein being discloses itself to us. Put differently, unlike the hermeneutics of suspicion or "critique" that has arguably proven the Enlightenment's most vexing and ambivalent legacy, the approach cultivated throughout this study amounts less to a method than an ethos. Rather than premise that phenomena and their experience must be conformed to, and redeemed by, conceptual schemes of our own devising, a hermeneutics of discernment views the phenomenon as the site where the *logos*—the good and the true—is always offering itself, is extended toward us as a gift whose fulfillment, however, requires nothing less than our utmost powers of discernment. At bottom, all thinking originates in such listening, beholding, and responding to the "calling"

3. Freedberg 1989, xxi.

(*kalein*) of the visible, experienced as mediating the true and, consequently, also as "beautiful" (*to kalon*).

And yet, our encounter with appearance always entails an element of "crisis" (Gk. *krinein*). We constantly struggle to disentangle what is contingently, albeit conspicuously, visible in appearance from its noncontingent, per se invisible import or truth. Every encounter with an image carries within it the possibility of epistemic error and idolatrous confusion, which are bound to leap to the fore the very instant when the beholder fails to distinguish between appearance-*of* and appearance-*as*. Still, the predicament cannot be avoided in the way Descartes had famously proposed, namely, by summarily discrediting appearance as inherently deceptive. For to do so would preemptively disenchant the phenomenon, denude it of its gift character, its power of mediating, manifesting, and revealing the true. To open ourselves to the presence of the phenomenon, to attend to it, endure it, and thus allow it to crystallize into an image that temporarily envelops us in an "incomprehensible certainty" rather than contingent and fallible "proof," necessarily means taking a risk. To behold an image, in other words, is ultimately to encounter ourselves, less as epistemic than as moral agents. Starting out on this note, and in keeping with the inductive approach followed throughout this study, the introduction opens by considering a moment in Dostoevsky's *The Idiot*, which presents us with a vivid parable of the abyss of meaning opened up by a failed, idolatrous gaze and a more successful, though acutely risk-fraught iconic vision.

The beginnings of this book date to an Andrew W. Mellon postdoctoral seminar on the history of the image that I coorganized with David Womersley (Oxford University) at the National Humanities Center in 2013 and, the year after, in Berlin. The many fruitful and congenial exchanges with the seminar participants at the time impressed on me the exceptionally rich and variegated, as well as daunting, dimensions of the topic. As I continued to grapple with how to structure a book on the subject of images and the distinct forms of knowledge arising from their experience, a stroke of good luck intervened when I was invited to join two weeklong seminars on the topic "Image as Theology" sponsored by the University of Notre Dame, King's College, and the Manfred Lautenschläger Foundation in London during the unsettled "Brexit" summer of 2016 (betokening worse upheavals soon to come) and then again a year later in Rome. The many conversations at these meetings, further enriched by excursions to local museums and churches, proved invaluable for clarifying the intentions for my still evolving book. I am particularly grateful to Ben Quash, Mark McInroy, Robin Jensen, and Judith Wolfe for their constructive input and their numerous suggestions of further reading and art historical materials.

Since then, exchanges with other colleagues have continued to inspire and focus my thinking and writing. I am especially indebted to John Betz, James Simpson, Fr.

Thomas Joseph White, and Judith Wolfe for their counsel on some of the theological, historical, and philosophical aspects of the present argument. Closer to home, I have for many years had the good fortune of extended, searching conversation with learned and brilliant colleagues about all manner of books and ideas relevant to this project. For their intellectual and personal comradeship, I particularly thank David Aers, Sarah Beckwith, Kavin Rowe, Stanley Hauerwas, Paul Griffiths, and Tom Ferraro. A very special debt of gratitude goes to Reinhard Hütter. In our weekly conversations, for several years held in our home offices and, as a result of the current pandemic, during socially distanced strolls around the neighborhood, Reinhard has been the very embodiment of intellectual friendship: unfailingly generous with his inexhaustible learning while also gently probing my ongoing attempts at clarifying my book's conceptual architecture and overall objectives. Another word of thanks goes to Stephen Little for his generous and effective guidance of the book from its very beginnings; like so many authors who have had the good fortune of working with Stephen at the University of Notre Dame Press, I was sad to see him leave his position, and I wish him well in his new endeavors. Also, I thank Heidi Madden and Lee Sorensen at Duke Libraries for sharing their expertise and helping to resolve obscure queries concerning library matters and image permissions over the past couple of years. A generous grant from Duke's Arts & Sciences Research Council helped cover costs associated with image rights and reproduction of images and is hereby gratefully acknowledged.

Without question my most extensive intellectual debt is to my many students for their unflagging engagement and perceptive questioning of readings and arguments I first tried out in various undergraduate and graduate seminars. Whether it was a text by Plato, Dionysius, or Maximus, or a poem by Goethe, Hopkins, or Rilke, or various permutations of modern phenomenology, my students' persistent, fittingly Socratic questioning did much to help sharpen and clarify many of the arguments that have since found their way into this book. In so doing, they continually deepened my love of learning and taught me most of what I know. One of them deserves special mention. During the "plague year" of 2020, Aaron Ebert generously agreed to a first copyediting of the entire manuscript, a daunting task he discharged altogether brilliantly. Aside from paying meticulous attention to philological, stylistic, and formatting issues, Aaron also queried occasional turns of argument and in so doing helped me clarify it on multiple occasions. He truly embodies everything that over the past decade has made teaching in Duke's Divinity School such a rewarding experience for me. Thanks are also due to Sheila Berg for her efficient and careful final review of the manuscript.

The final push toward finishing this book happened over the past twelve months, which for people all over the world have brought insecurity, isolation, and often suffering and agonizing loss to an extent not seen in several generations. If ever the work of reading, writing, and teaching has felt like a privilege and a refuge, it has been during this past year. And even though personal loss also intruded, my daughters and my wife, Sandra Cotton, have been an inexhaustible source of love, hope, and joy.

Durham, NC
July 2021

ACKNOWLEDGMENTS

A short version of my reading of Julian of Norwich in chapter 3 was first published by the *Hedgehog Review* (2017); portions of chapter 5 first appeared in *Studies in Romanticism* (2010) and are here reprinted in greatly revised form; short sections on Nicholas of Cusa and G. M. Hopkins were previously published in *Logos* 22.4 (2018); an earlier version of my reading of Hopkins's "Hurrahing in Harvest" was first included in an essay collection, *Judgment & Action*, edited by Viv Soni and Thomas Pfau; and some of the materials included in chapter 8 first appeared in *Phenomenology to the Letter*, ed. P. Haenssler, K. Mendicino, and R. Tobias, and in an issue of *Salmagundi* (2017). I thank all the publishers for their permission to reprint a revised version of these materials. Along the way, some of the book's arguments were first tried out at invited lectures I gave at Harvard, Yale, Vanderbilt, the Jagiellonian University in Krakow, the Catholic University of America, the Institute for the Arts & Culture at UVA, Bard College, Brown University, and at a special seminar on phenomenology and literature convened at the Annual Meeting of the German Studies Association. As always, the ensuing discussions generated insights and accumulated intellectual debts far too numerous to recall.

ABBREVIATIONS

A Maximus the Confessor, *On Difficulties in the Church Fathers: The Ambigua*, 2 vols., trans. and ed. Nicholas Constas (Cambridge, MA: Harvard University Press, 2014)

AT Nicholas of Cusa, *De Apice Theoriae*†

BT Martin Heidegger, *Being and Time*, trans. Joan Stambaugh (Albany: SUNY Press, 1996)

CD Augustine, *De Civitate Dei* (*The City of God Against the Pagans*)

CH pseudo-Dionysius, *Celestial Hierarchy**

CMC Maximus the Confessor, *On the Cosmic Mystery of Jesus Christ: Selected Writings from Maximus the Confessor*, trans. Paul M. Blowers and Robert Louis Wilken (Crestwood, NY: St. Vladimir's Press, 2003)

Comp. Nicholas of Cusa, *Compendium*†

Conf. Augustine, *The Confessions*, trans. Philip Burton (New York: Knopf, 2001)

DB Nicholas of Cusa, *De Beryllo*†

DC Nicholas of Cusa, *De Coniecturis*†

DI Nicholas of Cusa, *De docta ignorantia*†

DN pseudo-Dionysius, *Divine Names**

DP Nicholas of Cusa, *De Principio*†

EH   pseudo-Dionysius, *Ecclesiastical Hierarchy**

EP   pseudo-Dionysius, *Epistolae**

GHA   Johann W. von Goethe, *Werke*, Hamburger Ausgabe, 14 vols., ed. Erich
        Trunz (Munich: Beck, 1981)

GL   *On Genesis* (*De Genesi ad Literam*), trans. Edmund Hill, O.P. (Hyde Park,
        NY: New City Press, 2002)

HCW   Gerard Manley Hopkins, *The Collected Works of Gerard Manley Hopkins*,
        8 vols., gen. ed. Lesley Higgins and Michael J. Suarez, S.J. (Oxford: Oxford
        University Press, 2006–)

HMW   Gerard Manley Hopkins, *Gerard Manley Hopkins: The Major Works*, ed.
        Catherine Phillips (Oxford: Oxford University Press, 1986)

IM   Nicholas of Cusa, *Idiota de Mente*[†]

KA   Rainer Maria Rilke, *Werke: Kommentierte Ausgabe*, 4 vols., ed. Manfred
        Engel and Ulrich Fülleborn (Leipzig: Insel, 1996)

KBD   *Nikolaus von Kues: Briefe und Dokumente zum Brixner Streit*, ed. Wilhelm
        Baum and Raimund Senoner (Vienna: Turia & Kant, 1998)

LPG   Charles Lyell, *Principles of Geology*, ed. James A. Secord (Harmondsworth:
        Penguin, 1997)

MSW   Maximus the Confessor, *Selected Writings*, trans. George C. Berthold (New
        York: Paulist Press, 1985)

MT   pseudo-Dionysius, *Mystical Theology**

NA   Nicholas of Cusa, *De li non aliud*[†]

PG   *Patrologia Graeca*, 110 vols., ed. Jacques-Paul Migne (Paris: Imprimerie
        Catholique, 1857–66).

PL   *Patrologia Latina*, 221 vols., ed. Jacques-Paul Migne (Paris: Imprimerie
        Catholique, 1841–55).

PNF   *Post-Nicaean Fathers*, 14 vols., ed. Philip Schaff and Henry Wace (Peabody,
        MA: Hendrickson Publishers, 2012)

QD   Nicholas of Cusa, *De Quaerendo Deum*[†]

R   Julian of Norwich, *A Revelation of Love*, in *The Writings of Julian of Nor-
        wich*, ed. Nicholas Watson and Jacqueline Jenkins (Philadelphia: University
        of Pennsylvania Press, 2006).

RB   Rainer Maria Rilke, *Briefe in zwei Bänden*, ed. Horst Nalewski (Leipzig: Insel, 1991)

RCW   John Ruskin, *The Works of John Ruskin*, 39 vols., ed. E. T. Cook and Alexander Wedderburn (London: George Allen, 1903–12)

ST   Thomas Aquinas, *Summa Theologiae*

TP   Nicholas of Cusa, *Trialogus de Possest*[†]

V   Julian of Norwich, *A Vision of a Devout Woman*, in *The Writings of Julian of Norwich*, ed. Nicholas Watson and Jacqueline Jenkins (Philadelphia: University of Pennsylvania Press, 2006).

VD   Nicholas of Cusa, *De Visione Dei*[†]

VS   Nicholas of Cusa, *De Venatione Sapientiae*[†]

---

[*] In pseudo-Dionysius, *The Complete Works*, trans. Colm Luibheid (New York: Paulist Press, 1987).

[†] In Nicholas of Cusa, *Complete Philosophical and Theological Treatises of Nicholas of Cusa*, 2 vols., trans. Jasper Hopkins (Minneapolis: Arthur J. Banning Press, 2001). Latin references follow Karl Borman's 2002 edition of Cusa's *Philosophisch-theologische Werke*, 4 vols. (Hamburg: Felix Meiner).

INTRODUCTION

Writing the Image

> *Can something that has no image come as an image? . . . In my room a little lamp is always lighted before the icon at night—the light is dim and negligible, but nevertheless you can see everything.*
>
> —Ippolit, in Fyodor Dostoevsky, *The Idiot*

READING

Ippolit's stray observation about the Christ icon, found in his "Testament" halfway through Dostoevsky's *The Idiot* (1869), throws into relief an issue that is of concern throughout this book. Supposing that the "image" (*obraz*) is not dismissed as something altogether illicit—a case of deception, simulation, or an idol—can it be anything other, and possibly more, than one more object among countless others? Or is a wooden panel covered with a tenuously illuminated, painted form but another entity within an economy of things and signs adventitiously fashioned and readily consumed? Is the image but another object rendered visible by natural light? Or might it be a source of light, of knowledge attainable only by way of visible mediation rather than abstract reasoning? In a book featuring in-depth discussions of several paintings (and allusions to yet more), what are we to make of Ippolit's surprising affirmation that the image has unique powers of disclosure, that it potentially allows

1

us "to see everything"?[1] Does the icon merely reflect whatever "negligible" physical light has been shed on it, or does it have powers of manifestation that altogether transcend naturalistic conceptions of knowledge? And, if the latter premise were to be granted, is the icon but a special *kind* of image, or does it reveal the very essence of the images and, thus, show them to be ontologically distinct from mundane objects and commodities?

As we shall find, merely to pose such questions opens up the possibility that human knowledge might rest on metaphysical foundations after all, foundations concerning which modern skeptical, critical, and naturalistic epistemologies have been pointedly uncurious, if not openly dismissive. In fact, if we are to inquire into the scope and depth of images and to scrutinize the intuitive certitude to which they give rise we will have to suspend, at least temporarily, our commitment (however dear and seemingly "natural") to a strictly immanent frame of inquiry. As variously mapped by Descartes, Hume, Kant, Hegel, and modern reductionist thinkers, such a commitment is anchored in a *cogito* scrupulously detached from appearances and intent on mastering them by means of some universal *method*, even as doing so may come at the price of ever-increasing levels of conceptual abstraction and a consequent loss of intuitive kinship with the so-called world of experience. While my aim in what follows is not to contest such epistemological models, neither are they to circumscribe and constrain the proposed study of images and the phenomenology of their experience. Rather than venture some a priori hypothesis about possible metaphysical entanglements of human knowledge—a hypothesis likely to be shaped by abstract axioms of a skeptical, critical, dialectical, or naturalistic kind—let us for the time being continue in inductive fashion, namely, by examining how Dostoevsky's novel frames for us the relation between image and cognition, seeing and ethical responsibility, epistemic claims and human love. Conceptual gains are bound to reveal themselves, but they will likely prove more persuasive, more concrete, more *felt*, if we allow them to arise from the concrete dynamics of a specific presentation, in this case Dostoevsky's dramatic depiction of what it means to behold an image, rather than be introduced as abstract hypotheses up front.

To the moribund nihilist Ippolit, who finds himself inexplicably consumed by metaphysical questions, the icon's radiance is a source of both epistemic perplexity and spiritual reassurance. Poignantly worded, Ippolit's remark acknowledges an incontrovertible fact, namely, that the *experience* of this humble icon manifestly exceeds its material and formal cause; and it is this unresolved tension between the icon's epistemic and experiential dimensions that reflects an overarching, psycho-

---

1. For a discussion of painting, photography, and ekphrastic writing in *The Idiot*, see Brunson (2016), who reads the novel as "Dostoevsky's impassioned attempt . . . to harness the power of the verbal and the visual in order to transcend the limits of both" (449).

Figure I.1. Hans Holbein, *Body of the Dead Christ in the Tomb*, 1521–22. Basle, Öffentliche Kunstsammlung

logical and spiritual disorientation at the heart of Dostoevsky's later fiction. Dostoevsky's *Idiot* is structured around this fundamental antithesis between icon and idol, as crystallized by two images that reappear at key moments in the narrative: Holbein's painting *Body of the Dead Christ in the Tomb* (fig. I.1) and a fictional photographic portrait of the novel's wounded heroine, Nastasya Filippovna. These contrasting images mark the divide between a premodern, contemplative vision and the modern, libidinal gaze, between apprehending the visible image as the portal to numinous, invisible truths or, conversely, asserting epistemic dominion over the subject depicted. Indeed, it is tempting to map the antithesis onto a more elemental one between a metaphysical conception of life as truly fulfilled only in posthumous eternity and a naturalistic one that defines life *ex negativo* as concluding, irrevocably, in death. Yet Dostoevsky's juxtaposition of these two kinds of gaze blurs that antithesis to the point of almost, paradoxically, inverting it. Thus the pallid and fatally mangled body of Holbein's *Dead Christ* seems to confound any prospect of his resurrection and the promise of eternal life it holds for humankind. By contrast, the photographic portrait of Nastasya (the short form for the Russian *anastasia* = "resurrection") appears to be the very embodiment of triumphant and self-sufficient human life.

While the finer points of this antithetical image pairing remain to be sifted, we will not be able to trace in detail the many ways in which their antinomy structures Dostoevsky's novel as a whole. Instead, let us begin by homing in on Nastasya's photographic portrait, which reinforces the polarity just sketched by eliciting two diametrically opposed responses. From Ganya and Rogozhin, it draws a crudely possessive, indeed hateful gaze that eventually culminates in Rogozhin murdering the unattainable object of his desires. By contrast, Prince Myshkin in his study of Nastasya's photographic portrait not only acknowledges her stunning beauty but also, with troubled empathy, picks up on an unsettling contrast of pained defiance and naive simplicity in her face. Under his searching gaze, the photo does not "represent" a physical being. It is no idolatrous substitute for her body, that fulcrum of Ganya's and Rogozhin's psychosexual coveting and loathing. Instead, by focusing so attentively on Nastasya's face, the Prince apprehends her portrait as a medium or "true image" (*vera icon*) capable of unveiling contradictory truths about her and, in so doing, establishing a spiritual bond between the beholder and the human being thus made manifest.

> It was as if he wanted to unriddle something hidden in that face which had also struck him earlier. The earlier impression had scarcely left him, and now it was as if he were hastening to verify something. The face, extraordinary for its beauty and for something else, now struck him still more. There seemed to be a boundless pride and contempt, almost hatred, in that face, and at the same time something trusting, something surprisingly simple-hearted; *the contrast even seemed to awaken some sort of compassion* as one looked at the features. The dazzling beauty was even unbearable, the beauty of the pale face, the nearly hollow cheeks and burning eyes—strange beauty! The prince gazed for a moment, then suddenly roused himself, looked around, hastily put the portrait to his lips and kissed it. (*DI* 79–80; emphasis mine)

We can see here why, in Dostoevsky's iconography, the real is never reducible to a representational object or to a subject's contingent projections. Rather, it is experienced (often in the medium of an image) as the distillation of life's "most profoundly unbearable questions."[2] Indeed, the Prince's study of Nastasya's image throws into relief a central motif of this book, namely, that seeing is not a case of unmasking but of participation, and that its ethos is one of communion between the beholder, the image, and what is mediated in the latter rather than of critical detachment and epistemic doubt. As Rowan Williams so thoughtfully puts it, "To see the truth in someone is not only to penetrate behind appearances to some hidden static reality. It also has to be, if it is not to be destructive, a grasp of the motors of concealment, a listening to the specific language of a person hiding himself. It is perhaps the difference between 'seeing through' someone and understanding [her]."[3] With the furtive kiss he bestows on the portrait the Prince confirms that his reverential and empathic gaze seeks to discern Nastasya's humanity in her icon. That said, the long-standing, Eastern Orthodox practice of kissing an icon here seems strangely out of place, considering that the image in question is a photograph rather than an icon "written" in accordance with a rich and deep iconographic tradition and that it depicts not a saint, let alone Christ or Mary, but a woman of altogether questionable moral and social standing. Most likely, these incongruities account for the Prince's furtive veneration of the icon. Yet that he does so anyway shows that what he affirms is not Nastasya's embattled public persona but, on the contrary, her longing for redemption, which

2. Gattrall 2004, 5.
3. Williams 2008, 51.

her haughty demeanor cannot conceal from Myshkin. It is this invisible telos rather than Nastasya's conspicuous physical presence that her portrait mediates for him.

The second scene, early in Book II, features one of the more famous descriptions of a painting found in modern literature. It begins with Myshkin being received with consternation by his adversary Rogozhin, who proceeds to lead the Prince deep into the recesses of his strangely meandering, ominous home. Resembling a Kafkaesque burrow, the house may have been built in the ruins of a collapsed church and, through a web of carefully embedded allusions, is vaguely associated with the "Old Believers," a schismatic group that had formed in opposition to liturgical and textual reforms forced through under Patriarch Nikon of Moscow beginning in 1652. Yet by the mid-nineteenth century, whatever spiritual fervor may have once been fomented in this building has been supplanted by an aura of physical violence and impending death. Not by accident Ippolit will later compare Rogozhin's house to a "graveyard" (*DI* 407); and the Prince, too, immediately upon entering "felt very oppressed" (*DI* 218). In contrast to various indistinct paintings "of bishops and landscapes" lining a reception hall, the painting hanging over a doorway into a private room immediately draws Myshkin's uneasy attention, both on account of its uncommon format ("around six feet wide and no more than ten inches high") and because it triggers a sense of déjà vu ("as if recalling something").[4] As Rogozhin eagerly points out, it is "an excellent copy" of Holbein's *Dead Christ* (see fig. I.1) for which someone had recently offered him five hundred rubles.

Rogozhin's crude appraisal of the image as no more than a marketable commodity contrasts with its disquieting impact on the Prince, who recalls having seen the painting abroad and, ever since, being "unable to forget it." Myshkin's distressed response to Rogozhin's stray and indifferent observation ("I like looking at that painting") sets the stage for the Prince's precarious meeting with his adversary: "'At that painting!' the prince suddenly cried out, under the impression of an *unexpected* thought. 'At that painting! A man could *even* lose his faith from that painting!'— 'Lose it he does,' Rogozhin suddenly [*vdrug*] agreed *unexpectedly* [*neozhidanno*]." In ways so characteristic of Dostoevsky's incisive psychology, the Prince's emphatic protest is yet tinged with a hint of equivocation: "'What,' the prince suddenly stopped. 'How can you! I was *almost* joking, and you're so serious! And why did you ask me whether I believe in God?" (218; emphasis mine). An echo of his earlier "even" ("A man could *even* lose his faith"), the meaning of "almost" here is hard to parse. I take

---

4. As Dostoevsky's wife, Anna Grigorievna, records in her memoirs, Dostoevsky chose to stop in Basel, where Holbein had worked as a young artist between 1519 and 1526 and again between 1528 and 1532, specifically to view Holbein's *Dead Christ*. In the event, the painting "made an overwhelming impression on my husband, and he stood before it as if dumbstruck. . . . There was in his agitated face that expression as of fright which I had seen more than once in the first moments of an epileptic fit" (quoted in *ID* xiii).

it to suggest that the encounter with a painting as powerful as Holbein's *Dead Christ* is bound to *reveal* the beholder's true spiritual condition, which is not to suppose (as Rogozhin readily does) that the painting has the power of *causing* someone's loss of faith. It does not. In fact, to suggest that "Holbein's Christ lacks resurrection and redemption" is to overlook that the *Dead Christ* by definition signifies against the background of fifteen hundred years during which scripture, liturgy, and an evolving iconographic tradition had continually affirmed Christ's resurrection by drawing on key episodes in the Gospels (the Last Supper, the Stations of the Cross, the Crucifixion, Christ's Deposition, the Pietà, etc.).[5]

Several factors speak against a mechanistic interpretation of Holbein's painting as positively inducing a loss of faith. For one thing, as Robert Jackson notes, "*obraz* is the axis of beauty in the Russian language; it is 'form,' 'shape,' 'image'; it is also the iconographic image, or icon—the visible symbol of the beauty of God." Precisely this spiritual integrity and formal self-sufficiency of the image shows it to be imbued with a unique kind of agency—not causal in any efficient sense but diagnostic and revelatory. The image "transfigures the person who comes into contact with it."[6] At first blush, however, none of this seems to be borne out by the copy of Holbein's *Dead Christ* that so viscerally unsettles Myshkin. Indeed, considered from a formal perspective, Holbein's painting presents itself as "a kind of anti-icon, . . . a nonpresence or a presence of the negative" that strengthens its association with Rogozhin's feral persona.[7] As Rowan Williams reminds us, "In classical Orthodox iconography, the only figures shown in profile are demons and—sometimes—Judas Ischariot." Yet even as Rogozhin's Holbein copy presents us with "an image of Christ that is—in Orthodox terms—no image at all," it would be misleading to say that what we see is but a "painting of a Christ 'emptied of divine content.'" In fact, as Williams later points out, at its core the icon stages for the beholder "the coexistence of infinite abundance with historical limitation."[8] As such, the icon never simply affirms spiritual meanings but, as any material thing marooned in a disordered world, remains susceptible to abuse—being trampled or spat upon, as happens elsewhere in Dostoevsky's oeuvre –to trivialization, and also to illicit appropriation. To view Holbein's *Dead Christ* as pictorial evidence of naturalism's triumph over faith, of finitude over the life that Christ had said to embody (Jn 14:6) seems misguided, not least because

---

5. "Dostoevsky uses Holbein's iconography to morally implicate the reader in the tempting experience of such purely human emotions as anguish, compassion and passionate doubts about the possibility of Christ's resurrection—the emotions and temptations of which Christ himself partook" (Meerson 1995, 208, 209).

6. Jackson 1966, 47, 53.

7. Williams 2008, 53.

8. Ibid., 53–54, 207.

such an interpretation would implicitly align itself with the naturalistic and predatory sensibility of the novel's most dissolute character, Rogozhin.

Instead, as we shall find time and again, the true aim of iconic seeing is to guide its beholder toward heightened self-recognition, which begins with a humbling reminder concerning the utter fragility and vulnerability of the good and the true in us. While such spiritual self-awareness may have often eluded Dostoevsky's late nineteenth-century readers, it was arguably the foundation for Holbein's early fifteenth-century contemporaries. As Bätschmann and Griener note in their study of Holbein, the grim naturalism of the *Dead Christ* in no way prevented viewers at the cusp of the Reformation from understanding the image as "a work of piety." Like Grünewald's Isenheim Altarpiece, Holbein's painting "sought to instill deep feelings of guilt and empathy. . . . 'Martyrizing' the feelings of the beholder through such graphic and repugnant details" as the clotted blood in his chest wound and the postmortem discoloration of bodily extremities was part of a profoundly Christ-centered theological aesthetic of suffering. It had risen to prominence along with new forms of lay piety known as the *devotio moderna*, which had swept across the Low Countries during the fifteenth century.[9] In this context, the materiality of painting functions as a metonym for Christ's physical suffering, which in turn is visualized as an analogue for a self-humbling and profoundly empathetic conception of piety.

Notably, it was Basel's most famous citizen at the time, Erasmus, who had condemned the fast-spreading destruction of sacred images by that city's increasingly rabid iconoclasts and, in his writings of the mid-1520s, sought to make a measured case for a "rational use of cult images."[10] Many of Erasmus's arguments also surface in what may well be the period's most eloquent and lucid defense of images, Thomas More's *Dialogue Concerning Tyndale* (1528–29). Just as for More the image is truly itself only as a mental vision, for which words or pictures provide the necessary, albeit imperfect medium, so some 350 years later Dostoevsky's art also posits "the inseparability of the ideal (beauty) from its incarnation (Christ)."[11] To give due "reverence to an image," More had written, does not mean "fixing [one's] final intent in the image" but responding to it "as the figure of the thing framed with imagination, and so conceived in the mind."[12] Likewise, Dostoevsky's theological poetics traverse a vast "moral-aesthetic spectrum . . . [that] begins with *obraz*—image, the form and embodiment of beauty—and ends with *bezobrazie*—literally that which is 'without

---

9. Bätschmann and Griener 1997, 138; though at the time Holbein was in Basel, the "city was a powder keg of religious and political tension," which finally erupted on 9 February 1529 (Ash Wednesday), when mobs of militant iconoclast reformers stormed the city's Cathedral and purged it of all images and artworks, an action the city council was forced to accept (Eire 2016, 239–41).

10. Bätschmann and Griener 1997, 145.

11. Jackson 1966, 56.

12. More 1927, 20 (*Dialogue Concerning Tyndale*, bk. I, ch. 2).

image.'" As is the case with More or mystics such as Julian of Norwich and Nicholas of Cusa, whose visual theology I consider later, Dostoevsky understands this condition of being "without image" as a state of disgrace and disfigurement, "a deformation, finally, of the divine image" itself.[13] Notably, the Russian *obraz* can also mean "face," which further underscores its proximity to the Orthodox icon. To be "without image" thus means being spiritually de-faced or inwardly disfigured, and it is this condition that Holbein's painting of Christ's mangled body exposes in Rogozhin.[14] The latter's vacillating response shows the visible image to relate to the beholder's invisible (spiritual) condition in the same way that the theological concept of *figura* (Gk. *typos*) is fulfilled and consummated in an ultimately imageless meaning, one that no beholder could ever have anticipated or intended.

Yet even as the "imageless" (*bezobrazie*) condition is associated with spiritual disfigurement, it is not the result of an encounter with visible ugliness or corruption that, for Rogozhin's naturalistic gaze, remains the only take-away from Holbein's *Dead Christ*. The painting's grim aspect does not cause the loss of (spiritual) beauty but, instead, exposes it. Hence, in the present scene, Holbein's painting reveals Rogozhin's utter incapacity for love and faith. He truly cannot *see* Christ's image in Holbein's painting because his gaze never advances beyond what is plainly visible. He thus fails to actuate the deeper meaning of the imageless, which is to access, through the medium of the visible, an invisible beauty and truth that can only be attained on a foundation of faith. While Rogozhin owns a copy of Holbein's *picture*—with the Russian *kartina* emphasizing the tableau's material nature—he is "without *image*" (*bez-obraz*), itself a figural expression for being faithless and disgraced. Spiritual beauty eludes him who can only ever see what is literally and transparently visible in front of him. By contrast, if "the perception of beauty is inseparable for Dostoevsky from the leap of faith," apprehending the spiritual dimension of visible things, the iconic truth within the material picture, always requires an antecedent faith ("the evidence of things not seen" [Heb. 11:1]).[15] Consequently, the visible image is but the medium that will reveal faith, or its absence, but can never causally bring about either condition. The point is underscored by the fact that the Holbein painting is a copy, with the copyist's name not known, and that it hangs over a threshold rather than being placed, as an icon would be, illuminated by a candle in a corner.[16] Dostoevsky, that is, takes care not to invest the material image with a primitive talismanic

---

13. Jackson 1966, 58.

14. See Gatrall 2004, 3–4; and Apollonio 2009a, which notes that, "in order to unite spirit and flesh," icons in Dostoevsky's fiction "must offer at least two levels of meaning. On the surface . . . they are mimetic, representing fictional characters leading their physical lives on earth, but at the same time they embody timeless, divine images" (29).

15. Jackson 1966, 38.

16. See Apollonio 2009b, 95.

or magical aura, notions often unthinkingly deployed by theoreticians and historians of art.[17]

Time and again, Dostoevsky's narrative draws attention to this revelatory power of the image by stressing the "sudden" and "unexpected" turns of thought that Holbein's *Dead Christ* occasions both in the Prince and Rogozhin. Holbein's unsparingly naturalistic depiction of Christ's battered body subtly aligns with Rogozhin's quite possibly murderous intentions vis-à-vis the Prince, whom he regards as a competitor for Nastasya Filippovna. Indeed, the wound that Christ's Roman executioners inflicted with their lances, so prominently featured in Holbein's painting, appears metonymically related to the fixed-blade knife with a "staghorn handle" that, in the preceding chapter, had prompted the Prince to question its purpose and, in turn, draw irritable and increasingly defensive rejoinders from Rogozhin. Meanwhile, in the scene just quoted, Rogozhin's affirmation that Holbein's dead Christ may well have caused those who have seen the painting to have lost their faith, voiced so "unexpectedly" (to whom?—the reader or possibly Rogozhin himself) shows that his spiritual condition is on the cusp of being decided.

The central challenge posed by Holbein's image of the dead Christ will be expressly formulated only much later, and then not by the Christlike Myshkin but by his double, the committed nihilist Ippolit, who at this point also happens to be mortally ill. His description of Holbein's painting is embedded in an extended and searching spiritual testament of sorts, which Ippolit reads out to various parties assembled at a soirée. Ippolit's characterization of the painting makes clear just how much is at stake for the viewer confronting the image of the dead Christ. To be sure, at first glance Holbein's unsparing pictorial naturalism offers nothing that could distract from Christ's maimed physicality, as is also confirmed by Ippolit's opening, detailed ekphrasis of the painting that he, too, had seen "in one of the gloomiest rooms of [Rogozhin's] house."

This picture portrays Christ just taken down from the cross. It seems to me that painters are usually in the habit of portraying Christ, both on the cross and taken down from the cross, as still having a shade of extraordinary beauty in his face; they seek to preserve this beauty for him even in his most horrible suffering. But in Rogozhin's picture there is *not a word about beauty*; this is in the fullest sense the corpse of a man who endured infinite suffering before the cross, wounds, torture, beating by the guards, beating by the people as he carried the cross and fell down under it, and had finally suffered on the cross for six hours (at least according to my calculation). True, it is *the face of a man* who has *only*

17. On the uncritical use of "picture-magic," see Freedberg 1989, 78–81.

just been taken down from the cross, that is, retaining in itself a great deal of life, of warmth; nothing has had time to become rigid yet, so that the dead man's face shows suffering as if he were feeling it now (the artist has caught that very well); but the face has not been spared in the least; it is nature alone, and truly as the dead body of any man must be after such torments. (*DI* 407–8; emphasis mine)

Both Ippolit and the Prince intuitively feel the profound hermeneutic and spiritual challenge posed by Holbein's painting, even as their responses turn out to be diametrically opposed. For Ippolit, the challenge can be distilled into a single, all-encompassing question: Can something that has no image come as an image? Can the visible presence of Holbein's image positively unveil the invisible? Can it mediate a numinous truth, or will its flagrant naturalism and oppressive visibility invalidate Christ's transcendent spiritual authority? Can the image truly disclose the divine, or does it only ever amount to some illicit substitution, simulation, or impersonation of its putative referent?

Both for the saintly Prince and the nihilist Ippolit, responding to Holbein's painting exposes a profound and seemingly insoluble hermeneutic and spiritual crisis that, as evidenced by how they verbalize it, goes to the very heart of modern existence. Even for the nihilist and religious skeptic Ippolit, Holbein's image surprisingly exposes the limits of a purely naturalistic worldview rather than simply reinforcing it. Thus, he recalls how the early Christian church had "established that Christ suffered not in appearance but in reality, . . . and that his body, therefore, was fully and completely subject to the laws of nature" (*DI* 408). Hence, a strictly naturalistic view ought to be understood not as the end but only as the beginning of a genuine hermeneutic engagement with Holbein's image. Noting furthermore how the painting does not feature those assembled on Golgotha—"who surrounded the dead man . . . [and] must have felt horrible anguish and confusion"—Ippolit suspects that the painting's present-day beholder will experience similar feelings of doubt and distress. For given that many of those present at Christ's torture and execution had previously witnessed him performing miracles, also mentioned by Ippolit, his suffering and death seem utterly incongruous with his life. In its gruesome physicality, Christ's maimed body "at once smashed all their hopes and *almost* their beliefs" (*DI* 408; emphasis mine). The naturalistic image of death thus stands in sharpest contrast to the transcendent beauty and dignity of the life that had preceded it; and it is this conflict that Holbein's picture restages some fifteen hundred years later. Like those assembled at Golgotha, the modern beholder of Holbein's painting will also "go off in terrible fear, though each carried within himself a tremendous thought that could never be torn out of him" (*DI* 409).

Just what that "tremendous thought" might be about emerges in four brief recollections with which Prince Myshkin responds to Rogozhin's religious skepticism. Yet again, the memory of "four different encounters in the last week" surfaces "unexpectedly [*neozhidanno*]" (*DI* 219). Holbein's image here is complemented by four narrative vignettes that have the effect of bringing about a fragile communion between the Prince and Rogozhin. There is his brief encounter with an atheist, which leaves the Prince convinced that professed atheists always seem to be talking about something else (their own, typically undiagnosed despair?) rather than their avowed unbelief. Then there is the story of a man murdering his friend over something as trivial as a watch, though not until he has first prayed to God and sought his forgiveness for the deed he is about to commit. Next comes the story of a petty swindler trying to sell the Prince a "silver crucifix," which both parties know is made of cheap tin: "I took out twenty kopecks, gave them to him, and put the cross on at once." As he does so, the Prince knowingly plays his part in this petty deception because what matters to him is not to "condemn this Christ-seller," lest he fail to honor some good there may yet be "locked away in these drunken and weak hearts" (*DI* 220). The final scene, fleeting though full of humble spirituality, has the Prince query a young mother who, upon seeing her infant smile for the first time, crosses herself. Asked why, she responds that her response mirrors God's who "rejoices each time he . . . sees a sinner standing before him and praying with all his heart" (*DI* 221).

Rendered with painterly concision, each scene captures the moment where finite, sinful human beings inexplicably transcend their condition, or at least have revealed their latent ability to remember and aspire to the *imago Dei* that is indelibly inscribed in them. Moreover, while the individual encounters exhibit a tableau-like, gestural quality, they comprise an anagogical sequence of sorts, with each successive scene marking an increase in spiritual purity. Cumulatively, they show that "the values of Christian love and religious faith . . . are too deep a necessity of the Russian spirit to be negated by his practical failure, any more than they are negated by reason, murder, or sacrilege."[18] The chapter closes with Rogozhin proposing that he and the Prince exchange crucifixes. As the Prince asks that the two embrace, Rogozhin "no sooner raised his arms than he lowered them again at once. He could not resolve to

18. Frank 2010, 582. Frank's point is powerfully echoed by Sergius Bulgakov, who, writing in 1916, recalls the transformative experience of seeing Raphael's *Sistine Madonna* in Zwinger in Dresden nearly two decades earlier, when he found himself vacillating between Marxism and Orthodoxy: "This was not an aesthetic emotion, no; it was *an encounter*, new knowledge, *a miracle*. . . . I involuntarily called this contemplation *a prayer*, and every morning, . . . I ran there, 'to pray' and to weep before the face of the Madonna. . . . I did not need a 'philosophical' idea of Divinity but a living faith in God, in Christ and the Church" (Bulgakov 2012b, 10).

do it; he turned away so as not to look at the prince. . . . 'Never fear! Maybe I did take your cross, but I won't kill you for your watch!' he murmured unintelligibly, suddenly laughing" (*DI* 223). Rogozhin's abortive gesture of Christian brotherhood, suffused with symbolic meaning, as well as his muttered words of self-recognition suggest that the Prince's meditation on Holbein's painting and on humankind's suspension between doubt and redemption has made him profoundly aware of his own perilous spiritual condition.

REFLECTION

As Dostoevsky fully understood, "nothing can be more difficult than . . . to portray a perfectly good man." Indeed, if "there is only one positively good figure in the world—Christ—so that the phenomenon of a boundlessly, infinitely good figure is already in itself an infinite miracle," then Prince Myshkin categorically precludes those who meet him either in the novel or as its readers from identifying with his imago.[19] Yet it does not follow that the vast majority of modern individuals struggling to get ahead in our volatile and disordered world therefore resemble, as it were by default, the feral and homicidal Rogozhin. Far more likely, today's predominant sensibility will turn out to be a version of Ippolit: alternately reluctant to affirm any belief in a transcendent (noncontingent) reality, presumably for fear of being deemed wrong, naive, and biased; or defiantly rejecting all belief, so as to mask their inward despair with an outward show of resolve. And yet the modern individual also resembles Ippolit in this: it finds its defensive cocoon recurrently punctured by sights, such as Holbein's painting, that it experiences as profoundly, albeit ineffably, meaningful. Even in a world "seared with trade; bleared, smeared with toil," Hopkins writes, "there lives the dearest freshness deep down things." Time and again, that is, we find ourselves brought up short by fleeting moments that, requiring no external confirmation, ever impress themselves on us, such as when "tumbled over rim in roundy wells, / Stones ring" or when a kestrel soaring high above us performs its visible "mastery." Such scenes infuse consciousness with a certitude at once incomprehensible and indubitable, simply by dint of the formal clarity and mesmerizing pres-

---

19. Dostoevsky 1987, 262, 269–70. Still, Dostoevsky's artistic intentions, as sketched in his notebooks and correspondence, evidently underwent significant change in the course of writing the novel itself, where "the pressure of writing is pushing [Dostoevsky's] intention out of shape" (Williams 2008, 50). Thus, Myshkin appears conspicuously vague in his grasp of Orthodox theology and notably evasive when asked whether he believes in God, and overall quite reticent; see also Frank 2010, 557–63, who remarks on the constantly fluctuating "plans" for the novel and notes that the letter to Maikov, in which the idea of Myshkin as a "perfectly beautiful man" is mentioned, remains a "nebulous outline" even as the novel is well under way (quote from 562).

ence with which reality manifests itself in them.[20] Like the character of Leo Naphta in Mann's *Magic Mountain*, to be considered later, Ippolit's psyche appears divided between a total negation of the world and instances of visual plenitude, between his professed nihilism, a seemingly logical if unbearable position to hold, and moments of intuitive fullness and clarity that echo the Platonic triad of the beautiful, the good, and the true. It is this internal division that renders Ippolit paradigmatic of modernity's agonized outlook on existence. Still, as the writers to be considered in part 2 of this study argue in a variety of ways, perched somewhere on the spectrum between agnosticism and skepticism the modern individual finds itself regularly unsettled by images that have the power to let "you see everything." It is this "incomprehensible certainty" (as G. M. Hopkins calls it in a letter from 1883), this charism of the image as infinitely "more-than"—more than a token of private, ephemeral desire and more than a mere tool of representation—that fuels the 2,500-year-old philosophical and theological tradition that this book selectively considers.

At the conclusion of *Minding the Modern*, which this study is intended to complement, I hinted at what I take to be a fundamental predicament of intellectual history over the past two centuries. On the one hand, modern subjectivity appears marked, indeed wounded, by a profound estrangement or "dissociation of sensibility" brought about by the rise of skeptical and naturalistic epistemologies since the seventeenth century. Responding to Weber's claim that modernity's progressive "disenchantment of the world" had drained lived existence of intuition, meaning, and purpose, both humanistic and theological inquiry after 1918 began to sift the past for religious and aesthetic resources that might allow it to recover a sense of individual and communal flourishing. Yet in so doing, modern thought found itself daunted by the monumental challenge of retrieving a Christian-Platonist tradition that, as Coleridge for one believed, stood the best chance of healing the wounds inflicted by the successive regimes of theological voluntarism and nominalism, epistemological skepticism, and mechanist-reductionist conceptions of nature. In the event, Coleridge's inability to complete such a synthesis of Athens and Jerusalem, Platonism and Christianity, in accessible and coherent form aptly illustrates the vexed condition of modern thought—suspended between a reductionist epistemology it cannot endure and a Christian-Platonist synthesis it cannot reclaim.

Still, as writers such as Goethe, Novalis, Hölderlin, and Coleridge and some of their modernist heirs understood, any retrieval of the human being as a responsible and self-aware agent required a fusion of intuitive and rational cognition that could never be accomplished by ratiocinative and abstract methods alone. More variegated, free-flowing, and experimental forms of writing (poetry, essays, florilegia, notebooks, sketches, and all kinds of "musings") were needed to delineate what

---

20. Hopkins 1986, 128, 129.

Husserl, a far less complex writer to be sure, would term the "principle of principles: that each intuition affording [something] in an originary way is a legitimate source of knowledge."[21] Husserl's assertion that "originary intuition" (*ursprüngliche Anschauung*) is not only a legitimate, but an indispensable source of knowledge was but the latest iteration of similar claims that had animated philosophical and theological inquiry extending from Plato and Plotinus via pseudo-Dionysius, Bernard, Bonaventure, and Nicholas of Cusa into the modern era. Like some of the poets of his own time, Rilke and the young T. S. Eliot in particular, Husserl felt justified to start from the world's "absolute givenness" in intuition, quite simply because the latter constitutes its own incontrovertible *Evidenz*.[22] For what is unconditionally and immediately given in "pre-predicative" intuition must not be mistaken for a "conclusion" produced in syllogistic form, nor does its reality depend on some extraneous and a posteriori method for its verification. Instead, Husserl's "principle of principles" asserts that human cognition—both in interpretive and empirical fields—can succeed only if, and only insofar as, reflective thought lets itself be guided by the dynamic structure of "appearance" (*Erscheinung*). Reflection can never be a "founding" or self-grounding act. Rather, it is the main technique whereby consciousness comes to discern its own "pre-predicative" immersion in the phenomenal world.[23] Far from being the antagonist of appearance, reflection can succeed only if, with the utmost attention and humility, it allows its observations, descriptions, and questionings to be guided by what is given in intuition. Knowledge, that is, does not get under way by preemptively resisting, let alone discrediting, phenomena; its foundation cannot be an all-consuming skepticism claiming epistemic authority by compulsively reenacting an in essence parasitical gesture of doubt. Rather, knowledge begins by an act of assent to the reality of the world as it gives itself in intuition. As John Henry Newman had remarked decades before Husserl was to formulate his concept of eidetic intuition, to assent to an image as it registers in intuition is not the same as making a claim about the reality of the thing depicted in the image: "the fact of the distinctness of the images, which are required for real assent, is no warrant for the existence of the objects which those images represent." Yet, for precisely this reason, our "real assent" to the presence of the image as such cannot be subject to doubt, for to "meddle with the springs of thought and action is really to weaken them."[24]

---

21. Husserl 2014, 44 (§ 24).

22. Husserl 1997, 11 / 1991, 13.

23. On the concept of the "pre-predicative," see Romano (2015, 66–88), who earlier notes that "the 'pre-linguistic' with which phenomenology is concerned . . . can be recognized as such only by a being who is able to speak, and which remains always expressible in principle *without remainder* by such a being" (15; original emphasis). All subsequent emphases in quoted material are in the original, unless noted otherwise.

24. Newman 1979, 80, 177–78.

Consequently, what is thus given in intuition must not be misconstrued as the "efficient" cause of a knowledge that supposedly exists separately from it. Contrary to the axioms of Lockean empiricism, intuition is not reducible to "sensation," indeed, categorically differs from it. Conversely, intuition must not be understood as *concluding* the process of experience and cognition, as various strands of Sentimentalism, Romanticism, and post-Romantic antirationalism would maintain. Rather, what is given in intuition begs to be fleshed out by hermeneutic practice, an art (*subtilitas*) that, always keeping the phenomenon in view, seeks to distill its deeper significance by discerning its underlying formal and contextual parameters (rhetorical, intellectual, religious, aesthetic, economic, etc.). More than anything, hermeneutics is informed by a distinctive ethos of respecting, listening-to, and valuing the phenomenon as it *in*forms and subtly *re*forms consciousness itself. By contrast, where reflection is construed as a mere technique for *overcoming* appearances, thus treating what is given in intuition as merely provisional or positively deceptive matter, it risks losing itself in self-certifying, empty speculation and is liable to end up worshipping intellectual idols of its own making. In fact, "world" is ever the correlate of experience, and experience thrives on engagement and participation rather than doubt and detachment. It is constituted by numberless acts of intuition, discernment, and judgment whose full import stands to be sifted in dialogue with other members of the interpretive communities we inhabit. Phenomenological reflection of the kind that Husserl insisted was needed to grasp the reality and significance of our intuitions is neither monolithic in form nor monologic in practice. Rather, it enjoins the subject of experience to be maximally responsive to the structure of appearance, as well as careful and caring when seeking to articulate the meaning of its intuitions for others. Put differently, experience pivots on our *shared* hermeneutic commitment to the world's incontrovertible and abundant givenness qua phenomenon—be it a human face, a natural form, an image, or, indeed, the written word. This ongoing dialogue with the phenomenal world positively "forms" (*bilden*) the human subject by ceaselessly prompting it to cultivate its powers of attention (seeing, listening, reading) and, thereby, learning to embrace the world of visible things as intrinsically saturated with meaning or "form." Yet this process can succeed only if we learn to participate in the phenomenon and to accept its intrinsic form as our principal guide.

Virtually all the writers and artists considered in this book share this fundamental premise—that reflection can never fully emancipate itself from the phenomenon *by* which it was summoned and *to* whose experiential reality it responds, just as conversely the world of appearances would remain opaque and unfulfilled were it not for our communal, hermeneutic involvement in it. Thus, what Husserl calls our intuitive "apprehension" (*Auffassung*) of the phenomenal world—not to be confused with "perception" (*Wahrnehmung*)—furnishes reflection with both its incontrovertible point of departure and the formal and material specificity that allows thought to issue in meaningful and communicable knowledge rather than losing itself in hermetic abstractions or arid speculation. "To the thinking soul," writes Aristotle, "images serve as if they were contents of perception. . . . That is why the soul never thinks without an image."[25] It follows that reflection does not fashion images of the world in an occasional and discretionary sense but, on the contrary, responds to the world as it is antecedently given in the medium of an image. For the visible world is not simply a random concatenation of disjointed objects that we may choose to perceive and represent (or ignore). There is no view from nowhere, no neutral vantage point outside our "lifeworld" (Husserl's *Lebenswelt*) that would allow us to do so. Rather, we are always already "thrown into" and, thus, "in-the-world" (what Heidegger calls *Geworfenheit* and *in-der-Welt-sein*). Yet if the reality of the world given in intuition is never something "merely subjective," our image of the world cannot be understood as a function of self-expression or projection. Instead, precisely because the world always crystallizes in a specific image such as founds an "originary intuition" (Husserl), "interpretation is not an occasional, post facto supplement; rather understanding is always interpretation."[26]

What at first blush seems a somewhat abstract claim, plausible but lacking texture, is cashed out once we attend to the different genres of writing concerned with tracing how the world registers in "image-consciousness" (as Husserl calls it). For, as Plotinus and Maximus the Confessor had noted long ago, the phenomenon can give itself in intuition and be experienced as indelibly real only because, and to the extent that, it is organized or, as Hopkins puts it, "inscaped." Only its formal organization allows it to register in consciousness at all and, thus, summons us to discern its deeper import. Put differently, the phenomenon does not register in intuition as a random "occurrence," but, as a case of *manifestation*, it elicits and focuses the beholder's attention. Prefigured in the event of sight is thus a future insight that by definition exceeds the scope of what is plainly and transparently visible. By its very nature, that is, phenomenality is experienced as the disclosure of something that does not, indeed, *cannot*, appear per se—though not because the invisible other of appearance is somehow defective or pathologically self-enclosed. On the contrary, what does *not* appear as such but instead becomes manifest *in* and *by means of* a specific appearance is itself the very source or (metaphysically speaking) the *logos* that brings forth the visible. Were it otherwise, eye and mind would lack all coordination, there being then no reason to suppose that the deliverances of sight are in any way intelligibly structured, and that they seek to guide us to a truth beyond (though never opposed

---

25. Aristotle 1984, 1:685 (*De Anima* 431a15).

26. Gadamer 2006, 306. As Robert Sokolowski puts it, "The mind cannot be separated [from the world] in this way; the mind is a moment to the world and the things in it; the mind is essentially correlated with its objects," and the principal defect of modern skeptical epistemologies is "to introduce a separation where we should simply make a distinction" (2000, 25–26).

to) appearance. Instead, failing to understand the difference between appearance-*of* and appearance-*as*, between the visible and what it makes manifest, we would thus neither truly "see" nor seek to "know" (both meanings being encompassed by the Greek *eidō*).

All this is to say that in its very essence phenomenality stands for a dynamic event rather than an ephemeral happening. It has agency insofar as it mediates a reality that, depending on our powers of vision, always exceeds the merely perceptible. To be sure, the sheer "givenness" of the image in the modality of what Jean-Luc Marion calls a "saturated phenomenon" may, and often will, entail its material objectivation as an artifact, a picture evidently made by human hands. Thus, the mosaics in Hagia Sophia and at St. Catherine's Monastery, medieval prayer icons, or, for that matter, Cézanne's bathers were obviously all made by hands painstakingly engaged with various types of matter (wooden panels, canvas, tempera, siccative oil, etc.). Even so, from eighth-century Byzantine iconographers and their theological defenders all the way to painters and intensely visual writers such as Ruskin, Hopkins, Cézanne, Rilke, or T. S. Eliot, the insight consistently voiced is the same: the image realized in pictorial form is not a garden-variety product but, on the contrary, the *response* to an intuitive vision whose invisible substance it seeks to realize and communicate in visible form. Far from contriving some idolatrous appearance or other, the true image attests to the fact that the visible scene or face it depicts has *found* the iconographer or artist. Hence, true visualizing of reality such as takes objective form in graphic or verbal images can never be governed by an ego or cogito: "The landscape . . . becomes conscious in me," Cézanne remarks; "What you *look* hard at seems to *look* hard at *you*," Hopkins writes in his notebooks.[27] If the maker of images finds himself enthralled "sur le motif," as Cézanne likes to put it, this is precisely because "making" here involves an active and creative response to the incontrovertible givenness of the world qua image. The act of artistic "making" and "creating" of a picture always bears witness to the anterior presence and call of an image, itself the medium through which metaphysical truth, invisible per se, is disclosed to us in the first place. Hence, what truth there is in an image is bound up with its sheer givenness—which a naturalistic epistemology can neither account for nor call into question ex post facto.

To proceed from this hypothesis, which this book's chapters aim to consolidate by and by, is to accept that the visible world cannot be mechanistically "explained" (away) as either the efficient cause or contingent effect of strictly anthropomorphic perception. Close consideration of the structure of appearance, which is consummately embodied in the medium of the image, ends up exposing modernity's strictly

---

27. Cézanne, as reported by Joachim Gasquet, in Doran 2001, 111; Hopkins, *HCW* III:504 (emphasis mine).

immanent frame as a literally groundless and logically incoherent fantasy. For the very manner in which the phenomenon gives itself in intuition, its "incomprehensible certainty," sets consciousness on a hermeneutic journey at the end of which "we will arrive where we started / And know the place for the first time." Only a patient and dedicated hermeneutic engagement with what is given in intuition can lead the individual toward greater self-recognition, that is, to finding itself "renewed, transfigured, in another pattern."[28] To participate in the phenomenal world thus means to find oneself caught up in an anagogical progression. It begins once consciousness ceases to focus on the *what* of appearance and instead scrutinizes *how* a visible thing registers in intuition. In so shifting from a "natural stance" to a phenomenological one, consciousness learns to see itself as participating *in* the world rather than standing agnostically or skeptically apart *from* it. Once the relation of mind and world is understood as reciprocal, not oppositional, it becomes possible to respond to phenomena as instances of mediation, visible beacons that help orient consciousness toward something that does not show itself per se, yet of which we can only become aware and which we can only seek to understand on the basis of what *does* appear.

Throughout this book, we shall find that what is mediated *by* the phenomenon can be actualized only as an image, whose experience in intuition is logically anterior to perception. For what is ordinarily understood by "object-perception" (*Dingwahrnehmung*) presupposes, rather than produces, an image. From this follows a further point (developed in chapter 2), namely, that the image is always both obstruction and manifestation, a screen barring the beholder from gaining "immediate" access to the numinous source of all appearance and yet offering itself as a quasi-anagogical conduit toward that source. Stressing the essential mediacy and opacity of image and phenomenon, Gadamer observes that "it is of decisive importance that 'Being' does not display itself totally in its self-manifestation; rather it withholds itself and withdraws itself with the same primordiality with which it manifests itself."[29] Put in modern theoretical terms, image and phenomenon are always forms of mediation, are "medial" and, hence, never wholly transparent in their very essence. Or, to draw on the alternative terminology of classical metaphysics and Byzantine theology, the visible world can reveal its invisible truth only through an "image" (*eikōn*) that always remains, to an extent, a "screen" (*iconostasis*). The initial formulation of a coherent image concept, a process spanning from Plato to the Byzantine iconodules, is a complex story that is selectively traced in the first two chapters. For now, suffice it to say that to speak of an image always means to posit—but is never reducible to—a

---

28. Eliot 2015, 1:208, 206 ("Little Gidding," V, 28–29, and III, 16). As Gadamer writes, "Understanding what an artwork tells one is surely an encounter with oneself [*Selbstbegegnung*]" (1993a, 6).

29. Gadamer 2007, 162.

concrete visible depiction (*mimēsis*). By its very nature, the image can be no more reduced to a mundane perception of pictures than it can exist independent of the latter.

Far from simulating or "copying" a reality accessible and intelligible by discursive or conceptual means, the image amounts to a "depiction" (*Darstellung*) of what discursive "representation" (*Vorstellung*) can neither attain nor contain. As Hans Belting notes, "Only a reality that can solely subsist in the image protects the latter from being confused with reality."[30] It follows that "learning to see," a process in which Goethe, Ruskin, Hopkins, and Rilke found themselves caught up just as much as their Neoplatonist forebears, pivots on learning to respond to the visible world as *imago* rather than allowing it to calcify into a settled inventory of perceived "objects." To see thus means prima facie to respond to the distinctive, charismatic presence of the visible, to participate in the phenomenon as it gives itself in experience rather than attempt to *fore*see or *pre*dict its meaning. Well before Marion's recent, influential account of "givenness" and "saturated phenomena," Maurice Merleau-Ponty had remarked how our encounter with the visible requires an undesigning, essentially kenotic stance of contemplation: "Seeing is not a certain mode of thought or presence to self; it is the means given me for being absent from myself, for being present from within at the fission of Being."[31] As virtually all the writers explored in this study understood, by participating in the visible qua image and learning to see it as the manifestation of the invisible, numinous source that sustains it in being, the beholder also comes to discern the outlines of her own moral persona. It is this agency-like nature of the image, its capacity to mediate a knowledge not owned but received by its beholder, and hence capable of transforming her, that this book means to trace across a wide array of figures and epochs.

Arguably, retrieving a tradition of iconic seeing as a form of knowing runs counter to the anthropomorphic certainties of modern culture, in particular its seizure of the image as a digital artifact—produced, manipulated, and consumed with abandon. All those either embodying a broadly speaking Neoplatonist or Christian metaphysics, from Plato to Nicholas of Cusa, yet also their modern descendants (including Goethe, Ruskin, Hopkins, Bulgakov, and von Balthasar), would undoubtedly have been bewildered and dismayed by contemporary culture's "bulimic need for . . . icons" and its reigning phenomenology of distraction rather than attention, compulsion rather than reflection.[32] Over the past century, in particular since the meteoric rise of digital technologies, the postindustrial worlds of Western and Central Europe, North America, and most of East Asia have taken on an intensely visual character. Ours is a world of visibility without phenomenality, of pictures and all manner of

---

30. Belting 2006, 22.
31. Merleau-Ponty 1993, 146.
32. Sarah 2017, 37.

visual simulacra disseminated with unprecedented efficiency and without physical or mental effort on countless digital platforms (TikTok, Snapshat, Instagram, We-Chat, Tumblr, Reddit, Twitter, WhatsApp, Facebook, etc.) and colonizing every facet of life. From journalism's instant coverage of natural disaster and war, police violence and street protests, ecological devastation and human suffering; from building-sized images hawking luxury goods in commercial districts and airports to celebrities compulsively posting selfies so as to reaffirm their coveted iconic status; from graffiti and 3-D street painting to digital art reshaping and expanding the range of our visual experiences; from browsing the greatly changed faces of former childhood friends to retrieving high-resolution art images, all available with a few keystrokes via Google Images or ArtStor; from controversial cartoons to photographic evidence of suffering, violence, or beauty either natural or man-made: the image is at our *command* as never before. Functioning as quasi-prosthetic extensions of the postmodern subject and attesting to its seemingly boundless sway, images in the digital age tend to reinforce the prevailing naturalistic view of human existence as a function of personal preference, volition, desire, or, indeed, sheer compulsion. Casually disseminated as an ephemeral commodity, yet imbued with the latent power of instantly generating political, cultural, and religious controversy, the "image" today is conceived above all as an *object* and commodity, that is, as a "picture" to be instantaneously summoned, consumed, and, eventually, discarded at will.

At the same time, it may be objected that our contemporary situation merely reflects a timeless human proclivity toward idolatry whose perils had been flagged again and again over the past 2,500 years: beginning with Plato and the Old Testament prohibitions, continuing in the writings of, among many others, Eusebius, Constantine V, Cramner, Calvin, and Knox, and enduring into the present, both in the crude iconoclasm of the Afghan Taliban and in the high-theory idiom of, say, Emmanuel Levinas's "Reality and Its Shadow." That much is certainly true, just as there is no denying that iconodulia and iconoclasm have maintained an oddly symbiotic relation almost from the beginning, rather in the spirit of Blake's proverb that "opposition is true friendship." In the event, we shall consider iconoclasm only in passing since its historical persistence is mostly a result of its unexamined, logically flawed image concept. For the iconoclast prejudges the image as wanting to substitute itself for its prototype; on this view, the image seeks to usurp and displace (rather than mediate) the invisible in some determinate, visible form. Yet to argue thus is to impugn the image a priori for its alleged scandalous aspiration to total visibility and total congruence with what it depicts, a view that is misguided on at least two counts. First, it presupposes that truth, specifically religious truth, can and must be accessed immediately. Second, it posits that the written word (and it alone) is capable of achieving such immediacy, which is to say, that scripture is literally self-interpreting and transparent as to its meaning.

Ultimately, it is not so much the image per se but the specter of mediation, of whatever kind, that vexes the iconoclast. That is, iconoclasm's antinomian view of image and word as supposedly locked in competition for the same epistemic space assumes that by its very nature mediation amounts to a betrayal of truth rather than its fulfillment. According to this line of reasoning, the "word" (*logos*) is conceived as strictly aniconic and, consequently, as incompatible with figural speech and indeed mediation of any kind whatsoever. It is, finally, this *rhetorical* dimension undergirding the production and articulation of meaning in general at which the iconoclast demurs. To be sure, Christian humanists such as More and Erasmus in the sixteenth century subjected this aniconic view to withering critique.[33] In time, eighteenth-century scholars such as Robert Lowth and Johann Gottlieb Herder, adopting a less polemical tone, likewise sought to unravel the enduring hostility to images (by Calvinists, Methodists, and Pietists) by demonstrating how much the visual and metaphoric richness of modern poetry and art owes to the figural and imagistic splendor of the Hebrew scriptures, particularly the prophetic books.[34] Still, though incisive and learned, their arguments never quite succeeded in dislodging the iconoclast's categorical prejudice against mediation. Instead, and most paradoxically, he (for the iconoclast voice is conspicuously, aggressively masculine) repudiates the image either because it cannot succeed or because it succeeds all too well. That is, the image either scandalizes by differing too much from its ostensible referent and thus devaluing it—such as cartoon drawings of the prophet Mohammad by Kurt Westergaard—or it transgresses by purportedly substituting itself for what cannot (or must not?) be depicted at all.

While closer scrutiny of either position's underlying, logical fallacy will have to wait until chapter 2, there is no denying that idolatry—being the apotheosis of a "representationalism" that aspires to the total fusion of image and object—has always been looming, and never more so than in today's image-saturated world. As Simone Weil notes, "L'idolâtrie vient de ce qu'ayant soif de bien absolu, on ne possède pas l'attention surnaturelle et on n'a pas la patience de la laisser pousser." As a result of our refusal to let the "power of supernatural attention" develop, the image is swal-

33. As More insists in his *Dialogue concerning Tyndale* (1529), "All the words that be either written or spoken be but images representing the things that the writer or speaker conceiveth in his mind: likewise as the figure of the thing framed with imagination, and so conceived in the mind, is but an image representing the very thing that a man thinketh of." Indeed, as More provocatively continues to argue, "image painted, graven, or carved may be so well wrought, and so near to the quick and to the truth, that they shall naturally, and much more effectually represent the thing than shall the name either spoken or written. . . . Nor these two words *Christus Crucifixus*, do not so lively represent (to) us the remembrance of his bitter passion, as doth the blessed image of the crucifix, neither to a layman nor to a learned (man)." More 1927, 20–21 (bk. 1, ch. 2).

34. See Robert Lowth's *Lectures on the Sacred Poetry of the Hebrews* (Latin, 1753; English, 1787); Johann Gottlieb Herder, *Vom Geist der hebräischen Poesie* (1782–83).

lowed up by the *libido dominandi*, turns into its idolized other, and as visual artifice and simulacrum floods and devalues our contemporary lifeworld to an unprecedented degree. Frantically consumed and disgorged as a visual stimulus, or deployed as an ideological cudgel of sorts, the idol enables and entices the mind to seek refuge from itself—from thought, from ideas—in distraction. What distinguishes both the idolatrous and the iconoclast subject is its manic, feverish preoccupation with doing at the expense of reflection and contemplation. Again, Simone Weil captures the salient point particularly well: "L'activité doit être continue, tous les jours, beau-coup d'heures par jour. Il faut donc des mobiles de l'activité qui échappent aux pensées, donc aux relations: des idoles."[35] It is this relentless downward transposition of the image into idol, into a visual distraction, that shows idolatry and iconoclasm to share the same psychic causation. In both cases, the same manic fashioning and bulimic consumption of visual simulacra serves to fend off what Weil calls our power of "supernatural attention [*l'attention surnaturelle*]." This defeat of contemplation by distraction, reflection by compulsion, thinking by doing, is not an accidental by-product of idolatry and iconoclasm but, on the contrary, its covert aim. As Belting notes, "Images have been so denuded of our faith that they amount to no more than mere pictures; consequently, we no longer need to reject them. Idolatry thus has mutated into iconoclasm in a new key.... Meanwhile, the abuse of images has become invisible."[36]

To accept Belting's view, as I do, is to understand that the central flaw of iconoclasm never truly rested with its opposition to idolatry. Rather, it stemmed from the iconoclast's misguided assumption that a fetishizing, idolatrous gaze is the *only* conceivable response to images. As Marion has remarked, "Iconoclasm criticizes the supposed idolatrous derivation of icons, because it persists in interpreting according to the logic of similitude and mimetic rivalry, without ever suspecting—or accepting—that the *túpos* has categorically broken away from any imitation of an original. The icon does not represent; it presents ... in the sense of making present the holiness of the Holy One."[37] That there has been something of a resurgence of iconoclast polemics over the past thirty years should not surprise considering how the postmodern, antimetaphysical gaze tends to claim images as a kind of virtual property, fetishizing them for sexual pleasure or weaponizing them for ideological ends, yet always treating the image as a mere picture: exhaustively visible and seemingly transparent as regards its meaning or, if not, to be so rendered by digital manipulation and

---

35. "Idolatry comes from the fact that, while thirsting for absolute good, we do not possess the power of supernatural attention and we have not the patience to allow it to develop"; and "[Activity] has to continue each day and for many hours each day. Motives for our activity are therefore needed which shall be independent of our thoughts, hence of our relationship [to ideas]: idols" (Weil 1999, 60).
36. Belting 2006, 26, 29.
37. Marion 2004, 77.

tendentious captioning.[38] This downward transposition of the image from a medium of disclosure to the picture as a commodity and fetish has decisively altered the quality of the gaze that it institutes. Joseph Pieper speaks of a shift from seeing as the "apprehension of the real" (*Wirklichkeitsgewahrung*) to a gaze of measureless *curiositas*. Riveted on all manner of visible ephemera, such unbridled "lust of the eyes" (2 Jn 2:16) deracinates the beholder's psychological and spiritual persona, which now finds itself immured in a world strictly "fashioned in its own image and likeness." Where "impressions and sensations incessantly chase one another outside the windows of our eyes, . . . the human person's unique power of apprehending the real is being suffocated."[39] To the extent that a purely immanent, sensational, and covetous gaze has become the norm in our image-saturated world, pictures can only be experienced as *emblems* like those found in groups of four on the pages of Caesare Ripa's *Iconologia* (1603) (fig. I.2)—consumed rather than seen, prized for their glaring visibility, and subject to instantaneous decoding and strong, affective evaluation.[40]

Appearing at the very threshold of modernity's anthropocentric turn, Ripa's book attests to the emergence of what, writing in 1938, Heidegger calls "the age of the world-picture" (*Zeit des Weltbildes*). In the wake of Copernicus and Galileo, that is, the image stakes a totalizing claim on the world as an aggregate of discrete things to be rendered utterly visible and to be aggregated into a single, all-encompassing "world-picture" (*Weltbild*). Whereas the premodern icon, and the vision whereby it registers in consciousness, is received as a spiritual gift, the modern picture is conceived as a material product. Unlike the image, it does not mediate the invisible in the form of a visible analogue but aspires to total dominion over the visible by disputing the reality of anything that resists this quest for total transparency of the world. Furthermore, this "world-picture," which aggregates countless representations of visible particulars, categorically breaks with the ethos of humility and patience so central to the phenomenology of image-consciousness in Neoplatonist and Byzantine thought. The rupture represented by the emergence of the world-picture is considered in more depth in chapter 4, which juxtaposes Nicholas of Cusa's mystical

---

38. See Koerner 2002; Barber and Boldrick 2013; Freedberg 1989, 378–428; Besançon 2000, 183–226; Bredekamp 2010, 192–230; Simpson 2010, 1–48.

39. Pieper 2006, 191–93 (trans. mine).

40. A different scenario involves scientific "imaging," a subject briefly taken up in chapter 6. Though understandably invested in maximizing the visibility of the image, the forensic gaze of, say, a molecular biologist or an electrical engineer crucially does not fetishize visibility as a quasi-totemic good and possession for its own sake. Rather, she will prize the visible image as a medium enabling her to grasp complex causal relationships or the basic organization of matter, thus allowing her to participate more fully in the *ratio* or *logos* that underwrites the specificity and intelligibility of the material world qua form.

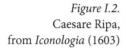

Figure I.2.
Caesare Ripa,
from *Iconologia* (1603)

anthropology to Leon Battista Alberti's theory of linear perspective. Once it is accepted that "man is the scale and measure of all things," as Alberti (echoing Protagoras) so bluntly puts it, the invisible is either demoted to the not-*yet*-visible or written off as epistemically irrelevant. Conversely, the new concept of "correct," linear perspective not only legitimates the modern picture in a formal sense; it also furnishes a warrant for modernity's boundless epistemic ambition, its unleashing of *curiositas* as not only justifiable but as the stance needed for remaking the totality of the visible world in our own image. Unsurprisingly, where "the painter is not concerned with things that are not visible," as Alberti puts it, the metaphysical and theological underpinnings of the *eikōn* are first dismissed and eventually forgotten, the result being that the image (now equated with the visible "picture") appears entirely fungible with the mundane objects that it claims to represent.[41]

---

41. Alberti 2004, 72 (II.36).

Henceforth, it is mere "picture" (*pittura*), a material artifact unilaterally manufactured and consumed by human beings; and as such it aspires to depict all visible reality on a single, two-dimensional surface. Whatever cannot be rendered visible within the matrix of the world-picture, whatever eludes the imperative of total visibility, will be dismissed as unreal, a mere phantasm bereft of all philosophical standing. Grounded in a logic of strict immanence and unlimited epistemic ambition, this new world-picture institutes an entirely new gaze. Proprietary and libidinal in nature, this gaze no longer responds to the phenomenal, visible world as a gift and visible analogue of invisible truths. Instead, being committed to capturing the world as an objective and all-encompassing picture, it must reject and discredit the inherited concept of the image (*eikōn*) as gift and intercession. However, this seeming triumph of the world-picture also entails serious liabilities. For if the anthropomorphic and scientific world-picture should fail to capture the totality to which it lays exclusive claim, it is liable to disintegrate into a multitude of competing pictures, each lodging the same totalizing claim, yet also proving incommensurable with all other such pictures.

Such creeping fragmentation can already be observed during the long Enlightenment (ca. 1650–1815), whose cherished dream of a *mathesis universalis* subsequently dissolves into an array of specialized disciplines operating independent of one another. Yet while such a pattern of progressive subspecialization in the natural sciences appears to an extent a function of their respective subject matter, a similar fragmentation of interpretive disciplines (the study of classical philology, national literatures, theology, history) into subfields and their embrace of quasi-scientific methodologies threatens to corrode the intuitive experience of meaning long considered to be the substance of humanistic inquiry. With the gap between normativity and objectivity steadily widening in the second half of the nineteenth century, the perhaps inevitable result was a surge of antihumanist, pessimist, and existentialist polemics extending from Schopenhauerian antirationalism, Nietzschean perspectivism, and Spengler's cultural pessimism all the way to the rampant "denialism" characterizing our dystopian present. For ours is a world of countless, mostly incommensurable world-pictures, each of which purports to render the world and our place in it exhaustively and authoritatively visible while being locked in insoluble conflict with all other such constructs. Visceral confrontation rather than joint reasoning, and the fetishizing of social divisions rather than a commitment to searching dialogue, has been the inevitable legacy of a strictly anthropomorphic gaze.

Heidegger's thesis of modernity as the "age of the world-picture" arguably holds even more true for our present moment than for the totalitarian era in which he formulated it. Never before has it been so difficult to distinguish between reality and its counterfeit than in our digitally hyperconnected and algorithmically engineered present. Every social interaction and public space appears pictorially overdetermined, forever inundating eye and mind with visual prompts, to say nothing of the myriad pictures (in the form of montages, gifs, holographs, and advertising banners crawling down the margins of our computer screens) pervading our waking lives and saturating every imaginable public space, both physical and virtual, with commercial stimuli. What Walter Benjamin had famously described as the "shock-character" of the moving image, a sensation that in the early 1930s was mostly confined to the cinema, has since engulfed the public sphere as a whole. Both on account of its ubiquity and its aggressive optical designs on the beholder's subconscious, the postmodern image overwhelms the subject's sensorium and, consequently, tends to be effortlessly *absorbed* rather than becoming a focus of hermeneutic scrutiny. As evidenced by the recent, dramatic surge of conspiracy theories opposing historical, political, and scientific reality with "alternative facts," a growing segment of today's distracted and dissociated, global citizenry appears on the verge of entering a terminally postliterate and in tendency sociopathic condition. Gazing and knowing, addictive spectatorship and articulate reflection, respectively, have fundamentally parted ways or, worse yet, are increasingly misconstrued as being one and the same. Thus, in the ecologically and spiritually devastated, neoliberal dystopia deforming and imperiling human life around the globe, images for the most part seek to tap and unleash deep reservoirs of collective desire or aggression. An idol in all but name, the postmodern image has become instrumentalized, and often is weaponized, as a "prediscursive," quasi-totemic tool prized mainly for its ability to elicit either instant approval or visceral condemnation. It is this atrophying of hermeneutic responsibility in our dealings with the visible world that prompts Marion, adopting uncharacteristically strong language, to speak of "the universal blasphemy of spectacles . . . [and] the disaster of the image."[42]

In this era of self-incurred hermeneutic indigence brought about by commercialized visual simulacra, the image (*eikōn*) is no longer experienced as it had been for a tradition extending from Plato and pseudo-Dionysius to Florensky and Bulgakov: a call to humble, attentive, and undesigning exegesis, that is, the focal point of hermeneutic discernment and, thus, a source of transformative dialogic engagement with others. Prized instead for its instantaneous and glaring visibility, the image has been reduced to a visual commodity designed to stimulate reflex-like, addictive types of response bound to deprive today's global, digital citizenry of the hermeneutic skills needed for any meaningful interaction with images and, by extension, blind the modern individual to the infinity that, as Levinas argues, is found in the face of the human being across from us. Here, then, we have a prima facie instance of how classical liberalism's fantasy of the world as a wholly immanent sphere—an all-

---

42. Marion 2004, 68, 83.

encompassing, deregulated marketplace of self-interested subjects incessantly pursuing and exchanging fungible commodities—ends up denuding the visible world of its very texture and, ultimately, its reality. Thus, the boundless and instantaneous availability of images for voyeuristic consumption stands in exactly inverse relation to the degree of hermeneutic care and responsibility with which they are received and used, respectively. As a growing tide of research into cyber-bullying, internet pornography, "deep-fake" videos, graphic violence in online games, and the paralyzing effects of social media addiction has shown, such hermeneutic indigence comes at a steep price.[43] For inasmuch as the image, today more than ever, is treated as but another commodity placed at our disposal, the hubris and narcissism that fuel its casual deployment ends up eroding and disrupting community. Alternately wielded as an incendiary tool or a coveted possession—in short, as an idol rather than a medium begging attentive contemplation and patient discernment—the image exposes just how opaque human beings have become to one another. In a world incessantly disgorging and consuming opinions, yet quietly distrustful or openly dismissive of factual knowledge, individuals more than ever have been conditioned to see only what conforms to the picture already fashioned of the subject at hand; and where that subject is a human person, those belonging to the so-called generation Z that came of age in the internet era are found to have greatly diminished powers of empathy. Having been inundated from early childhood by millions of images depicting the physical and psychological abuse of human beings, this latest generation often appears to lack to an alarming extent the gift of empathetic vision that allows one human being to see in another the image (*imago Dei*) of who she truly is and may yet become.

ARGUMENT

So much by way of a Jeremiad, "not very satisfactory," it must be admitted, and leaving us "still with the intolerable wrestle / With words and meanings."[44] And wrestle we must, in the face of the epistemic hubris and hermeneutic indigence that characterize postmodern culture's consumptive stance vis-à-vis the visible world. Yet the aim of what follows is not one of polemic but of retrieval, specifically of a Neoplatonist and Christian conception of the image as the medium granting us

---

43. A Google-Scholar search of "research on cyber-bullying" returned more than 16,000 articles since 2019; running an inquiry into "research on social media addiction" produces more than 20,000 scholarly citations for the same period. The search string "internet pornography—use—motivation" yields over 5,000 citations of scholarly publications since 2019 [14 July 2020]; and "violence in video games effect" turns up 17,000 scholarly references.

44. Eliot 2015, 1:187 ("East Coker," II, 18–21).

access to noncontingent (or "pre-predicative") meaning—a conception that against increasing odds has endured into the modern era. Particularly in the Neoplatonic tradition, yet also in patristic, Byzantine, and high medieval, mystical accounts of "spiritual" and "intellectual" vision that evolved from it, the image was understood as mediating an ultimately invisible reality in visible form. It constitutes a portal to truths that categorically exceed the scope of strictly immanent, ratiocinative notions, the latter remaining forever liable to succumb to skeptical questioning or mutate into conceptual idols of our own making. A first, fundamental aim of what follows is to show why the image cannot and must not be conflated with a quotidian understanding of "picture"—neither in its older, material nor in its contemporary, digital realization. For unlike the picture, the image is the correlate of an intuition, not a perception. It thus stands categorically apart from the order of embodied or virtual (i.e., manipulable) objects, just as the Neoplatonist concept of intuition or "mental vision" (*visio intellectualis*) cannot be reduced to naturalistic theories of sight and perception. Instead, as already noted, the image is a medium, not an object or an instrument, whose power inheres in manifesting the real rather than appropriating the useful.

Still, an image typically depicts (*darstellen*) a particular "visible object" (Husserl's *Bildobjekt*), which naturally requires a material scaffolding (Husserl's *Bildträger*) of sorts. Given this entanglement of image (*eikōn*) and matter (*hylē*), the possibility always remains that the "image" may be deformed into a visual fetish (*eidōlon*) and, as such, be instrumentalized for strictly affective or ideological ends. Where this happens, the resulting idol traps both its maker and beholder within a cocoon of fluctuating desires and interests; and where large numbers of such hermetic individuals converge around an idol—be it a visible emblem, an incendiary picture, or a domineering and empty persona wielding political power, a mask rather than a face—the result will not be community but its counterfeit. Instilling in its beholder both a "lust of the eyes" (*concupiscentia oculorum* [1 Jn 2:16]) and a "lust for dominion" (Augustine's *libido dominandi*), the idol by its very nature blocks the passage from experience to love. Hence, it can never bring about an authentic community—which pivots on an ethic of love, humility, and forgiveness—but at most a state of agitated finitude such as may discharge itself in bouts of greed, hate, rage, and pride. Whatever its specific *Gestalt*, the idol remains but a cultural pathogen that induces blindness, not knowledge.

By contrast, where we find ourselves in the presence of a "true image" (*vera icon*), consideration of its metaphysical, phenomenological, and hermeneutic implications proves both inexhaustible and enriching. The chapters that follow seek to show in a variety of contexts how, by its very nature, the image manifests a reality that transcends subjective desire or intention while also exceeding the scope of mono-causal explanation. Yet if the image stands ontologically apart from the domain of objects and the propositional knowledge we seek of them, then a different kind of response to the image is called for. No longer, that is, can we default to an Enlightenment (in origin Pyrrhonist) methodology of critical detachment, warranted assertibility, and generalized suspicion of appearance that has long constricted the scope and diminished the relevance of humanistic inquiry. Instead, the approach implicitly called for by a study of image and image-consciousness, and which this study will follow throughout, unfolds on three distinct but related plateaus. There is, first, the metaphysical aspect, always to be kept in view, which (in the absence of any plausible, competing explanation) maintains that the event of visibility and the reality of what, in the medium of the image, becomes manifest cannot be accounted for as mere visual contingencies but are integral to Being. Second, there is the fact that any metaphysical argument remains incomplete or, at least, risks remaining formulaic unless it is complemented by a phenomenological description of how the image, understood as event and manifestation, undergirds and enlarges the scope of our conscious awareness, thereby inviting us to develop a perspective on our very existence. Third, such a phenomenological account of "image-consciousness" (Husserl's *Bildbewußtsein*) must in turn be supplemented by a historically informed hermeneutics that will attend to the diverse traditions of inquiry and genres of writing wherein visual experience has been variously articulated.

Metaphysics

One of this book's central aims is to make the case for both the centrality and persistence of metaphysics.[45] Following a loosely chronological order, the four chapters that comprise part 1 argue that a coherent theory of the image cannot do without metaphysical foundations. Thus, chapter 1 begins by tracing the development of the image concept in Plato, from its rather contradictory formulation in Books 4, 6, 7, and 10 of the *Republic* to the more probing metaphysical account offered in the *Sophist*. There, at last, Plato works out a coherent understanding of the image whose legacy extends into the modern era. For no longer does he conceive the image as a case of illicit representation, that is, a simulacrum that would substitute itself for Being (*to on*). Instead, building on his critique of Parmenidean monism, the *Sophist* gradually works out why mediation is itself integral to Being. "The One" of the Eleatic school cannot be thought at all unless it becomes manifest in "the many" that comprises the order of appearance. Conversely, the realm of phenomena will remain unintelligible as long as it is either conflated with or diametrically opposed to Being. Hence we must learn to think the order of appearances as essentially related (*pros alla*) to the One *of* which they are manifestations. Simply put, the world of

---

45. On the question, "Is there metaphysics after critique?," see Desmond, 2012, 89.

phenomena does not betray but, on the contrary, fulfills Being. To be sure, every appearance *in* and *through* which Being discloses itself also amounts to an epistemic constraint or condition of sorts. Yet such "conditionality [*Bedingtheit*]," Gadamer points out, "is not a diminution of historical cognition but an integral feature of truth itself." For it is "the Reason intrinsic to things as such [*Vernunft der Dinge selber*]" that discloses itself in phenomena in such a way as to prompt us "to present and communicate [*darstellen und mitteilen*] it in a specific mode of speech." What Plato and his patristic descendants call *logos* is the source of our understanding of phenomena, which fulfills the deliverances of intuition in the form of articulate speech (*logoi*) whose "purpose . . . is to make something manifest" (*Offenbarmachen ist der Sinn der Rede*).[46]

Drawing on the pioneering work of Emmanuel Alloa, the readings that follow aim to develop a "medial phenomenology," with the principal focus placed on the metaphysical underpinnings of mediation and mediality. What, we ask, is always presupposed when we speak of a text or image as a medium? What allows it to function as such, and what is the relation between the medium itself and the reality that, however ineffable per se, can only reach us in mediated form? As we shall find, the very possibility of mediation rests on a metaphysical foundation long known by the name *analogia*. Indeed, more than anything it is a shared commitment to the concept of analogy that links all the principal writers considered in this study, not just those of the premodern era whose metaphysical commitments may seem unsurprising (though they are hardly uncomplicated), but also modern figures like Goethe, Ruskin, and Rilke. At its heart, the principle of *analogia* posits a noncontingent relation between the visible and the invisible, between time-bound, visible being and the supra-temporal, invisible form that (partially) manifests itself through the phenomenon. *Analogia* names "the point of intersection of timelessness / With time . . . the unattended / Moment, the moment in and out of time, / The distraction fit, lost in a shaft of sunlight."[47] Meticulously calibrated as ever, Eliot's phrasing not only echoes the metaphysical, speculative status of analogy but also alerts us to how this "intersection" registers in concrete experience. Analogy, in other words, is not something merely notional and abstract but, on the contrary, is borne out by the distinctive texture and quality of how we experience the visible world as both a "moment in and out of time." Far from some random occurrence, Eliot's "distraction fit, lost in a shaft of sunlight" is an instance of what Husserl calls *Evidenz*, that is, an intuitive warrant for grasping the visible as the manifestation of something beyond mere perceptibility. Indeed, were it not for this metaphysical principle of *analogia*, visible

---

46. Gadamer 1993b, 40, 47.
47. Eliot 2015, 1:199 ("Dry Salvages," V, 18–25).

particulars could never be discerned as significant forms, that is, as harbingers of knowledge not yet realized but, instead, would remain so much perceptual flotsam. No more than disjointed and opaque sensation, the welter of perceptual data engulfing consciousness at any moment could at most be arranged in some classificatory system of our own devising, such as we find in Carl Linné's *Systema Naturae* (1735). Yet such an approach inevitably remains arbitrary, incomplete, and excessively static in contrast to the dynamic and teleological character exhibited by natural forms as unfolded and observed in time. As Goethe and Ruskin were to argue, knowledge of such forms does not consist in the imposition of abstract conceptual schemes *on* their appearance. Rather, it requires that the observer discern the intrinsic organization of a specific natural entity (Goethe's plant, Ruskin's cloud) as disclosed by its continually changing appearance. That is, inquiry into natural forms must be guided by their distinctive ways of manifesting themselves to the beholder. To understand the reality and *logos* of a given species thus begins by "seeing the idea," as Goethe had put it to a skeptical Schiller, in the way that it manifests itself in a specific visible form.

Once this much is accepted and honored in practice, further reflection reveals that there has to be an ontological bond, between the visible thing and its invisible form. Beginning with Plato and pseudo-Dionysius and continuing through Aquinas, Nicholas of Cusa, all the way to Goethe, von Balthasar, and Przywara, this relation is known by the name *analogia*. It bears stressing that *analogia* is neither a theoretical concept nor a scientific hypothesis. Rather, it is presupposed, and justifiably so, because of the way that we experience the visible as our principal conduit toward the intelligible. The visible, in other words, is never mere sensory "noise" or an ephemeral "occurrence," since the dynamic presence and intuitive reality of form furnishes the ontological condition absent which we could not even enter into an epistemic relationship with the world of phenomena. Were it not for these Platonic ideas or Aristotelian, substantial forms, the visible could never be experienced as phenomenon but would amount to no more than a contingent, isolated apparition devoid of any actual or potential meaning. We thus could never see, or seek to understand, a particular X *as*, say, a gazelle, a rose, or a windhover. Yet in premising that the visible is also potentially intelligible—namely, by dint of its very being rather than as a result of social or scientific convention—we implicitly posit an analogy between the necessarily circumscribed phenomenon and its numinous source. That said, it bears remembering that the concept of *analogia* only posits a noncontingent *relation* between the visible and the invisible. It cannot be reduced to a monistic identity, nor can the ontological difference that it implies be overcome by a dialectical process. For the "relation" (Plato's *pros alla*) at issue is ontologically real rather than an abstract notion or heuristic fiction of our own devising. Being a metaphysical principle, that is, analogy is not a temporal or "historical" concept and, hence, cannot be dialectically resolved into outright identity or sheer heterogeneity. Instead, it enables us to navigate between the Scylla of pure immanence, which in idolatrous fashion would posit the *identity* of image and object, and the Charybdis of a radically disjunctive, iconoclast framing of the visible and the invisible as positively antagonistic.[48]

Though he does not employ the term itself, Augustine, in the following, eloquent passage from one of his sermons, adumbrates the central role of *analogia*, not only for those adhering to a specifically Christian concept of creation, but, like most natural philosophers before Augustine and since, crediting the world of natural phenomena as imbued with reason (*logos*) and, therefore, as potentially intelligible.

> Question the beauty of the earth, question the beauty of the sea, question the beauty of the air, amply spread around everywhere, question the beauty of the sky, question the serried ranks of the stars, . . . question all these things. They all answer you, 'Here we are, look; we're beautiful.' Their beauty is their confession.[49]

Like Plato before him and Cusa, Goethe, Ruskin, and Hopkins later on, Augustine here posits that phenomena have agency; they speak or, more precisely, they "answer" us by focusing and enriching our gaze. Their figural eloquence and abundant beauty, which the beholder will intuit in sky, stars, and so much more, leave no doubt that seeing is, at its best, our way of entering into dialogue with the invisible *logos* and of participating in it by responding and honoring its myriad visible forms. Hence, what we call "image" is not a special case of the visible but, instead, names its very essence. Far from being a derivative of material things, a second-tier kind of "representation" (*mimēsis*) as Plato still argues in Book 10 of the *Republic*, the image offers the most vivid concretion of the metaphysical principle of analogy. It mediates for us a reality with which it is inextricably entwined, yet with which it can never fully coincide. As so often, Pascal puts the matter most succinctly when observing, "La nature a des perfections, pour montrer qu'elle est l'image de Dieu; et des défauts, pour montrer qu'elle n'est que l'image"[50] Given its timeless quality, the analogical relation of the image vis-à-vis what it depicts can neither harden into a logical antinomy nor dialectically resolve into an identity; for either "resolution" would once again place it in finite time. Instead, being implicitly premised on the metaphysical principle of analogy, the image keeps the visible and the invisible in an ontological

---

48. For a fuller discussion of the principle of *analogia*, particularly in the context of Goethe, Ruskin, and Maximus the Confessor, see chs. 5–7 below. On the concept of *analogia*, see especially Betz, in Przywara 2014, 30–114; White 2011, 246–79; von Balthasar 1991, 613–27.

49. Augustine 1993, 71 (Sermon 241).

50. "Nature has perfections, to show that it is the image of God; and it has flaws, to show that it is but the image" (Pascal 1954, 1200; #416).

and productive *tension* (not an opposition), a tension that expresses itself at all times in the beholder's "consciousness of difference" between image and object.

That said, we shall also find that in most of the writers here considered (pseudo-Dionysius, Cusa, Ruskin, Hopkins, Rilke, among others), the image will forever strive to overcome its felt distance and estrangement from the invisible reality that it mediates. Yet this the image can never definitively accomplish, as any attempt of that kind would set it on a path toward idolatry, namely, by attempting to *simulate* or *substitute* itself for its object. Indeed, the only way that the ontological difference between image and object can be effectively bridged is for the image to suspend itself by slowly gravitating toward an aniconic condition and, as it were, asymptotically approaching the numinous. Byzantine icon theorists such as John of Damascus and Theodore the Studite understood this very well, though the same gravitational pull of the image toward the imageless can also be traced in the intellectual and artistic development of Ruskin, Hopkins, and Rilke.

Phenomenology

As already noted, the languages of metaphysics and phenomenology ought to be viewed as complementary. For just as being discloses itself, however fleetingly and imperfectly, in the order of appearance, so phenomenological talk of "appearances" whose essence consists in their being "experienced" (Husserl: *die Erscheinungen erscheinen nicht, sie werden erlebt*) only signifies if *what* appears is the manifestation of something *beyond* all appearance. Thus, an analysis of the world's "immediate givenness in intuition" rests on certain metaphysical presuppositions that phenomenological reflection is uniquely positioned to help us draw out. One such presupposition already mentioned and of overriding significance for this book's argument concerns the principle of *analogia*. Yet this principle of a qualified analogy between the visible and the invisible ought not be conceived as something merely notional but, instead, must disclose itself in the phenomenology of visual experience. A metaphysical postulate par excellence, the analogy between the visible and the invisible must register as a kind of intuitive certitude, that is, in the specific and significant manner in which the givenness of the world registers in experience. Tracing the latter dynamic is, of course, what phenomenological description is all about; or, in Robert Sokolowski's pithy formulation, "*phenomenology is reason's self-discovery in the presence of intelligible objects.*" What manifests itself in appearance is never raw unorganized matter but, always, a distinctively organized form. It is this conjunction of appearance and form that carries both metaphysical and phenomenological implications. Thus "'Being' is not just 'thing-like' . . . [but] involves disclosure or truth, and phenomenology looks at being primarily under its rubric of being truthful." It bears recalling that the Greek word for "form" (*eidos* = "that which is seen") is directly related to the act of "seeing" (*eidō*) and, proximately, to the older Greek word for "image" (*eidōlon*). The experiential reality of sight thus presupposes a metaphysical concept of form, since it is only on this premise that seeing can be phenomenologically understood as a significant *act* rather than a random occurrence; or as Sokolowski puts it, "'form' is the principle of disclosure in things."[51]

Absent some phenomenological description of our encounter with form, and of consciousness and phenomenon as mutually constitutive realities, metaphysical speculation about Being would remain just that, speculation. The present study thus regards the discursive traditions of metaphysics and phenomenology as substantially interdependent and historically continuous. Indeed, as is by now well understood, the phenomenological tradition spanning from Husserl via the early Heidegger and Merleau-Ponty to its (mostly French) inflection in the work of Chrétien, Henry, and Marion constitutes a unique development in modern thought. For it is the only philosophical movement whose mode and aims of inquiry sharply diverge from modernity's otherwise dogmatic commitment to a language of strict immanence reflected in the many competing -isms (skepticism, empiricism, historicism, materialism, psychologism, positivism, reductionism) that have dominated the past two centuries in particular.[52] That modern phenomenology should so explicitly have parted ways with virtually every other epistemological approach reflects its underlying metaphysical commitments. For even as Husserl for one often professes himself agnostic about such matters, the very possibility of phenomenological reflection rests on the *logos* principle; that is, it premises that "experience . . . has its own structure. It is what is present here that is in unity with what is not present, both are indispensable, and we simultaneously know about both, about this unity. This

---

51. Sokolowski 2000, 4, 65. This is not the place to delve into Husserl's shifting and equivocal position vis-à-vis metaphysical realism. For a balanced discussion of the issue, see Zahavi (2003), who, cautiously, "favors" a reading of Husserl as "conced[ing] that metaphysical problems are real problems. Even after introducing the concept of "bracketing" (*epochê*) in 1907 and, henceforth, professing himself agnostic about things as "real existents" outside of intentionality, Husserl's project remains caught up in metaphysical issues. In fact, "phenomenology is not a theory about the *merely* appearing, . . . [for] appearances are not *mere* appearances. For how things appear is an integral part of what they really are" (27, 55).

52. It is in Husserl's 1935 Prague lectures published as *Crisis of European Sciences* that modern phenomenology is for the first time differentiated from other philosophical and intellectual movements. Portraying it as a third way of sorts, Husserl there seems rather less anxious to eschew classical metaphysics than to point out the dangers of the strictly immanent and instrumental concept of knowledge ushered in by the scientific revolutions of the seventeenth century; see Husserl 1970, 3–100 (§§ 1–27). For subsequent meta-reflections on the aims and underpinnings of modern phenomenology by some of its eminent representatives, see Gadamer 1987, 105–46; Marion 2002b, 1–29; and for a sharply critical reflection on French phenomenology's "theological turn," Janicaud's wide-ranging introduction (Janicaud 2000, 3–103); for a historical genealogy of early twentieth-century phenomenology in relation to modern Catholic thought, see Baring 2019, 23–147.

unity cannot come from experience; rather, it is the 'structure' that precedes it." As Jan Patočka goes on to note, "In what manifests itself we always have, in some way, the whole, and manifesting itself . . . constantly points to some kind of whole. We are, so to speak, embedded within this manifesting." Whereas the majority of modern epistemological projects seeks to produce conceptual warrants for knowledge based on the assumption that mind and world, taken as such, belong to essentially distinct domains, phenomenology takes the obverse approach. Premising an ontological co-ordination of consciousness and object, its descriptive and reflective practice aims to draw out that antecedent, metaphysical fact in the domain of experience. Not fragmentation but integration is its aim, or, as Patočka writes, phenomenology "wants to derive results . . . that are metaphysical."[53]

Nevertheless, the mere fact that the coordination of mind and world needs to be retrieved and made explicit at all also indicates that consciousness is fundamentally estranged from the fullness of meaning so unexpectedly revealed to it in intuition. For intuition delivers infinitely more than what quotidian "natural consciousness" takes itself to be perceiving; or, as Marion notes, the "happening phenomenon" is marked by an "excess" of givenness over and above what we foresee or predict it to contain.[54] The underlying motif here is evidently Platonic in origin, involving a primal sense of "wonder" (*thaumazein* [*Theaetetus* 155d]), which in turn issues in the soul's estrangement from Being and its eventual retrieval of the idea that had brought forth the "happening phenomenon" in the first place. Hence it is that Plato characterizes the moment of genuine thought as a case of "remembering" (*anamnein*), as something that wells up within us rather than being produced by an intellect supposedly free of any metaphysical presuppositions whatsoever. As William Desmond puts it, properly speaking,

> we do not think; we are startled into thinking, as an access of light or understanding, or fresh astonishment or perplexity, comes to flare up in us. We cannot "project" ourselves into such startlement. . . . The best thought always surprises, and less by its own self as thinking [than] by what is being given to selving for thought. Thought is a being overcome by what is thought-worthy, a being struck into mindfulness: the thought-worthy comes over us first, and we are called beyond ourselves. And, of course, that at all we are called into this porosity in thinking can itself become an occasion of astonishment.[55]

The underlying quality of thought thus has us open ourselves to what until now has neither been thought nor indeed imagined. Put differently, thought is both the cause

---

53. Patočka 2002, 23, 20, 33.
54. See Marion 2002b, 30–53.
55. Desmond 2012, 106.

of a certain estrangement of mind from its comfort zone and, by dint of its responsive discernment of what is "thought-worthy," also remedies that condition. The same archetypal pattern of withdrawal and return (*exitus/reditus*) characteristic of thought extends from the writings of Plato and Plotinus via patristic writers into the medieval mystical tradition where it becomes enmeshed with a conception of eschatological vision that is considered in chapter 3. From there, the pattern extends to Nicholas of Cusa and the fifteenth-century Platonist revival into the writings of Goethe and, indeed, modern phenomenology. The continuity in question, yet also its challenge, is provocatively stated in Patočka's *Plato and Europe*, where he notes how "man as the exponent of phenomenon pays dearly for this privileged position in the whole universe. He pays dearly, for while he is conscious of the whole, that this totality shows and manifests itself to him, he also sees his own eccentricity, that he has fallen out from the center, that he . . . as the caretaker of the phenomenon is at the same time the only creature who knows that its phenomenal domain has an end." Startling here is Patočka's appraisal of our confrontation with the phenomenon as a burden insofar as we find ourselves overwhelmed by its abundant nature, which he suspects will ultimately prove both inexhaustible and inescapable. For it is this very "awareness that man is a creature of truth—which means of the phenomenon— and that this is his *damnation*."[56]

Still, those very phenomena that infuse the beholder's consciousness with a profound sense of its "eccentricity" and estrangement from the very truth that is our ultimate telos are never mere symptoms of "damnation." They are also, always, a source of potential redemption. Not only, that is, may consciousness respond to the gift that is the "happening phenomenon," but inasmuch as intuition allows itself to be absorbed by a phenomenon's abundant givenness, consciousness is freed to participate in the visible, not as an inventory of inert objects or conceptual "positings" (*Setzungen*), but as the self-manifestation of their invisible, numinous source. The phenomenological project of retrieving consciousness as always already absorbed *in* the phenomenal world, rather than diffidently looking *at* it from outside, bears a close affinity to what Orthodox Christianity terms *kenôsis*. Here "to be conscious is not to be in time," as Eliot puts it in *Four Quartets*. Likewise, his attention drawn by blades of grass evenly bent by the weight of "crisp, gritty snow," G. M. Hopkins writes in his notebook: "I saw the inscape freshly, as if my eye were still growing."[57] Such elision of subjective desires, fears, and projections is by no means anti- or irrational. Indeed, "intuition" (*Anschauung*) in the way that phenomenology from Husserl to Marion tends to deploy the term is the very apotheosis of consciousness, not its antonym. What the phenomenological, theological, and literary voices considered in

---

56. Patočka 2002, 34–35.
57. Eliot 2015, 1:181 ("Burnt Norton," II, 38); Hopkins, *HCW* III:544.

this study always reject, then, are not consciousness and reason but their illicit conflation with finite, discursive practice, which causes the reality of experience to be reduced to whatever conceptually warranted assertions we feel entitled to make about it. In fact, as Gadamer observes, "experience in its deeper sense . . . is never merely a confirmation of expectations [*Erfahrung ist niemals bloße Bestätigung*]." Or, to quote Eliot again, all merely discursive "knowledge imposes a pattern, and falsifies, / For the pattern is new in every moment, / And every moment is a new and shocking / Valuation of all we have been."[58]

By now, we begin to see why a medial phenomenology of the image of the kind here proposed cannot be guided by a modern concept of the "art image" as it arose in the Renaissance and was consolidated by Enlightenment and Romantic aesthetics in whose long shadow we still find ourselves today. What renders such a framework inapposite and, ultimately, misleading is its construal of beauty as an *effect* of the aesthetic work rather than its source, which in turn results in a creeping disaggregation of the beautiful from the true and the good or, at most, a qualified (Hegelian) construal of beauty as but the provisional scaffolding of a truth properly "realized" (*verwirklicht*) only in conceptual form. Indeed, Hegel's systematic account of art in its successive historical permutations also reveals how, from the extrinsic perspective of speculative dialectics, "aesthetic consciousness is always secondary to the immediate truth-claim that proceeds from the work of art itself. . . . This alienation [*Entfremdung*] into aesthetic judgment always takes place when we have withdrawn ourselves and are no longer open to the immediate claim of that which grasps us."[59] Not only does a formal aesthetic or art historical approach estrange us from the truth-value of the artwork, but it also obscures the spiritual intuition absent which the work would never have come into being in the first place. Indeed, like their (Neo)Platonist and patristic forebears, the writers considered in part 2 (Goethe, Ruskin, Hopkins, Cézanne, and Rilke) all understand the beautiful as real because and insofar as it is indexed to the true rather than to ephemeral aesthetic ideals or conventions of taste. Beauty, Plato insists, is not, at least not principally, a function of *what* appears but, rather, is entwined with the event of phenomenality as such. It is in "beautiful colors and shapes," not the representational contents they mediate, that the beautiful inheres; and inasmuch as the beautiful mediates the true and the good, Plato takes care to disaggregate beauty from pictorial mimesis: "By the beauty of a shape [*skematōn*], I do not mean what the many might presuppose, namely, that of a living being or of a picture [*zōgraphēmatōn*]." As we shall see, the later Plato quite emphatically considers mediation—that is, the self-manifestation of the idea in visible form—as

---

58. Gadamer 2007, 200; Eliot 2015, 1:187 ("East Coker," II, 34–37).

59. "What is the *aesthetic* consciousness when compared to the fullness of what has already addressed us" (Gadamer 1976, 5, 8 / 1993b, 220, 223).

ontologically warranted rather than as a metaphysical defect: "We notice that the force of the good has taken refuge in an alliance with the nature of the beautiful."[60]

If the beautiful pivots on what Plato calls the "coming-into-being" (*genesis eis ousian*) of the good and the true *in* a specific appearance, then our encounter of the image holds significance only insofar as we intuit it as manifestation rather than representation; which in turn invalidates the persistent attempts of Enlightenment and Romantic aesthetics to assimilate the image to the order of semblance and to dilute the ontological truth that it mediates either in the discourse of sensation, expressivity, or in historical and sociological analyses of styles and tastes.[61] Profoundly aware that "art is not an alternative to the natural world but an intensification of its operations," Goethe, Ruskin, Hopkins, Cézanne, and Rilke all understand their art, not as the production of pictures, but as their way of responding to the summons of the image as it has given itself in intuition.[62] Far from an anthropocentric contrivance, the work of art (*ergon*) acknowledges and preserves the charism of the phenomenon in objective form. Goethe's botanical sketches, his aphorisms and didactic lyrics (e.g., "The Metamorphosis of Plants"), Ruskin's writings on Turner or his drawings of rocks and ferns, and Hopkins's nature sonnets of the late 1870s all bear witness to the real as it discloses itself in the image *seen* rather than a picture or verbal artifact contingently *envisioned*. Witnessing here takes the form of heightened attention to the "happening" phenomenon and, thus, honoring the visible things whose beauty, as Augustine had put it, is also their confession. Such attention is no more a mere coefficient of optics, image resolution, and acuity of sight than it is a function of the will. Instead, as Simone Weil so poignantly argues, attention pivots on the maximal suspension of desire and will: "Attention consists in suspending our thought, leaving it detached, empty, and ready to be penetrated by the object." Like the practice of humility, patience, and empathy, attention is prima facie cultivated as a habit, for "we do not obtain the most precious gifts by going in search of them but by waiting for them."[63] Noting the myriad distinct phenomena that come forth

---

60. Plato 1997, 454 (*Philebus* 51b–c, 64e).

61. Plato 1997, 414 (*Philebus* 26d). "*Aletheia* does not simply mean unconcealment. Certainly, we say that 'it' comes forth, but the coming forth itself has something peculiar about it. This peculiarity consists in the fact that the work of art presents itself in such a way that it both conceals itself and at the very same time authenticates itself" (Gadamer 2007, 214). On the vexed relation of modern (Kantian) aesthetics to the Platonic tradition, see Pfau 2021.

62. Alloa 2017, 65.

63. Students in school will succeed to the extent that they exclude all extraneous concerns ("good marks, pass[ing] examinations," etc.) from their mental space and "apply[] themselves equally to all their tasks, with the idea that each one will help to form in them the habit of that attention which is the substance of prayer" (Weil 1977, 46, 49). On the mystical undertow of Weil's concept of attention, see Chevanier 2012, 46–51; Hellman 1982, 82–89.

during Spring—"Thrush's eggs [that] look little low heavens" and "glassy peartree leaves"—Hopkins emphasizes the need to see and participate in these things *before* the image offered to intuition has been obscured by conceptual schemes and socio-cultural filters: "Have, get before it cloy / Before it cloud."[64] Thus, where we seek to know, both the world and ourselves, we must have first seen; and whatever we may come to know will have been decided in advance by the quality of our visual attention to the real as it gives itself in phenomenal form.

Insofar as the experience of images issues in fundamental ("eidetic") intuitions of being, it also reveals the lineaments of the beholder's intellectual and spiritual constitution, both present and future. A recurrent motif throughout this book thus is that, ultimately, any encounter with an image reveals something about its beholder rather than the latter passing "aesthetic judgment" on the image. While tracing the subtle and complex interplay of visuality and cognition across a spectrum of different genres of writing, disciplines of inquiry, and within distinct conceptual and disciplinary traditions, my argument also attends to another aspect of "image-consciousness" often ignored by modern inquiry, namely, its essential incommensurability with Cartesian or Kantian models of consciousness as self-possession. In fact, both theological and phenomenological accounts of visual cognition from Plato and Plotinus via Dionysios and Bonaventure to Husserl, Merleau-Ponty, and Marion have time and again emphasized that *how* an image registers *in* consciousness proves inseparable from its transformative impact *on* that consciousness. Transformation, be it in the Platonic sense of *metanoia*, the Augustinian sense of *conversio*, or the Ovidian-Goethean sense of metamorphosis or *Verwandlung*, always unveils a hidden and essential potentiality within being as such. Unlike externally induced, mechanical "alteration," transformation is essentially "a transformation into the true," as Gadamer calls it. To say that transformation unveils the truth of a given being is not, however, to oppose such truth to a thing's contingent appearance. On the contrary, the numinous dimension of being, its truth and reality, positively demands that it manifest itself *in* or, rather, *through* the play of appearance. The true is always enmeshed with the infinite fecundity of what it means for being to "appear" (Gk. *phainesthai*; Ger. *erscheinen*) and manifest itself in the first place. Yet by the same token, our grasp of truth and reality necessarily remains precarious and incomplete. This volatility at the heart of all appearance, the way it oscillates between illusion or revelation, becomes apparent wherever philosophical, theological, and literary writing reflects on how consciousness tends to be both informed and transformed by its interaction with images.

---

64. *HCW* 130–31. As the German lyricist Eduard Mörike had put it, "Now my soul is like a crystal / That, *as yet*, no false ray of light has struck [Einem Kristall gleicht meine Seele nun, / Den noch kein falscher Strahl des Lichts getroffen]" (Mörike 1997, 2:665; emphasis mine).

It is this emphatically constructive aspect of transformative vision that would have us push back against Patočka's one-sided appraisal of phenomenality as evidence of the human being's calamitous estrangement from Being, indeed its "damnation." For what is crystallized in the medium of the image (*eikōn*) also constitutes a source of the beholder's transformation and potential redemption. At its best, where our gaze receives the image with gratitude and humility, attending to the visible precisely as it gives itself in intuition, it ends up releasing consciousness from the thralldom of time distended by desire. This holds true not only for the artist's intuitive encounter with the phenomenal world but also for the beholder of the visual or verbal artwork capturing that very encounter, as well as the reflections to which it gave rise. Merleau-Ponty's lucid phenomenological description of what it is like to see a painting resonates with Ruskin's and Rilke's accounts of their transformative encounters with Turner and Cézanne, respectively: "I would be hard pressed to say *where* the painting is I am looking at. For I do not look at it as one looks at a thing, fixing it in its place. My gaze wanders within it as in the halos of Being. Rather than seeing it, I see according to, or with it."[65] At the heart of the arguments here unfolded, then, is not "the image" as a specialized form of representation but as a catalyst of focused attention and a source of open-ended reflection. As Dostoevsky's juxtaposition of a covetous and a transformative gaze clearly means to teach us, the image is prima facie not an object but an agent. It not only confronts but, potentially, also reconstitutes and transforms its beholder in ways liable to emerge as focal points for a second-order reflective awareness and interpretive practice.

Hermeneutics

The last observation also indicates that a phenomenology of visual attention, however exacting, can account for the intuitive knowledge wrought by our interaction with images only formally but not for its specific contents. For what is given in intuition and subsequently worked through by the gaze as it "wanders . . . in the halos of Being" must in turn be fulfilled in articulate speech or writing, which is always contextually embedded. A phenomenology of image-consciousness cannot remain neutrally descriptive, as Husserl appears to think, but must be complemented by hermeneutic practice. Yet to insist that "the so-called givenness cannot be detached from its interpretation" and, consequently, to stress the "universality of hermeneutics" is not at all to expose givenness as a myth, as Sellars had argued. On the contrary, a leitmotif taken on from phenomenology and hermeneutics and underpinning this book's entire argument holds that interpretation is itself a response to the world's

---

65. Merleau-Ponty 1993, 126.

givenness in intuition, the latter being an ontological datum impervious to analytic second-guessing. Far from a secondary, remedial procedure, interpretation is positively "called for" by the phenomenon's distinctive mode of self-manifestation. Just as literary and scriptural figuration is fulfilled, not invalidated, in exegetical practice, so hermeneutic practice "serves [*dient*]" the phenomenon by seeking to draw out its intrinsic reality and significance.[66] When understood as a response to the call of the phenomenon's "givenness," interpretation can neither supplant what is given in intuition, nor can it expose and "deconstruct" it as a false origin. On the contrary, interpretation takes on faith that the word is not opposed to but continuous with the phenomenal world of experience—both being manifestations of one and the same *logos*—and that whatever meanings interpretation may attain are not imposed *on* phenomena but, on the contrary, have been discerned *in* and by means of them.

Fundamentally, then, all interpretation is a drawing-out of a reality antecedently given and a (necessarily partial and incomplete) attempt at its typological fulfillment. As a variously discursive or creative effort at making-explicit the *logos* that is intrinsic to the world of phenomena, hermeneutic practice responds to that world as a gift rather than claiming conceptual dominion over it. To the extent that hermeneutic practice yields communicable meanings, those engaged in it will have participated in what was given in intuition and will have been enriched and transformed by that encounter. As sight issues in insight, the phenomenal world is recognized as a gift, which by its very nature is honored only when shared with others in writing or speech. As we shall see, iconic vision begs to be fulfilled in hermeneutic practice, for only so can its import be properly shared with others and, ultimately, unite individual beholders in a community of knowledge. For the truth mediated by the image can be achieved only if and when it is *shared* in articulate and notably impersonal speech. In its iconic realization, therefore, an image must not be understood as a projection of the self but, instead, demands a form of *kenôsis*, of self-suspension. On that premise, the icon institutes and reaffirms a human (liturgical and spiritual) community that in the Eastern Orthodox and Catholic tradition was always understood as more than, and as ontologically prior to, any contingent agglomeration of individuals, be it a "society," a "movement," or a "collective." In the presence of the image, and in undesigning and reverential contemplation of it, the principle of individuation is fundamentally transcended, though not negated, as strictly immanent (and incipiently totalitarian) ideologies would have it. Rather, selfhood is suspended on behalf of a knowledge that by definition is never a private but always a communal achievement. The visible image's essential orientation toward communicability and

---

66. Gadamer 1993b, 339, 350. As Gadamer has often noted, his concept of philosophical hermeneutics seeks to elaborate Heidegger's analyses of the basic structure of "understanding" and "interpretation" (*Verstehen und Auslegung*); see Heidegger 1996, 134–44 (*BT* §§ 31–32).

community (still tenuously reaffirmed in Kant's third *Critique*) is aptly reflected in the conciliatory embrace that Prince Myshkin offers to Rogozhin, just as the latter's refusal of it embodies the modern skeptic's prevaricating stance and his consequent, existential isolation.

What, then, are some of the implications of the hermeneutic approach taken in this study? A first one, drawn from the foundational arguments of (Neo)Platonist, patristic, and Byzantine image theory, shows image and word to be continuous and complementary. The philosophical and theological tradition extending from Plato to Nicholas of Cusa consistently maintains that what the visible image mediates infinitely exceeds the scope of both pictorial and discursive representation. Rather than competing with transcendent Being, the experiential quality of image and vision attests to the gift and event of the real as it is given (but not yet fulfilled) in intuition. Anchoring the entire Neoplatonist tradition is the incontrovertible if also incomprehensible reality of a lifeworld abounding with specific forms given in experience and received as tokens of a knowledge yet to be achieved. What may be legitimately placed in doubt, then, is not the ontological fact of givenness but only the representations and concepts the finite intellect seeks to impose on it. A phenomenological and hermeneutic exploration of image-consciousness thus is not, at least not primarily, concerned with *what* is seen but fundamentally builds on the grace and gift *that* things continually appear to us as distinctly "inscaped" presences. The latter reveal an essential relation between the *logos* expressed in appearance as such and the *logoi* of discursive and creative speech concerned with its elucidation.

From this follows a second implication that will be of concern throughout the following pages, namely, that as we respond to the event of phenomenality, our interpretation can do justice to what is given in intuition only if and for as long as it tarries with the specific form whose call it answers. To see is to honor the visible, not to supplant it with intellectual notions (or idols) of our own devising. It is here that the question of dialectics arises, which has shadowed modern thought for the past two centuries. What does it mean to say that the image is "fulfilled"? How do speech or writing relate to what Husserl calls "originary intuition" and "image-consciousness"? Can a phenomenology of image-consciousness "fulfill" the image without thereby "superseding" (*aufheben*) it in the Hegelian sense? Put differently, can phenomenological and hermeneutic inquiry be pursued without turning into an immanent, dialectical narrative? For two reasons, the answer to the last question can and should be "yes." Readers of the *Phenomenology of Spirit* (1807) will recall how, early on in the preface, Hegel not only inveighs against the naturalistic and skeptical epistemologies of the Enlightenment, but, just as forcefully, against the obverse tendency "in our time, [one] as prevalent as it is pretentious": namely, to claim an "immediate knowledge of the Absolute" that his Romantic contemporaries term "intuition" (*Anschauung*). For Hegel, navigating between the Scylla of an Enlightenment materialism according to which "sense is so fast rooted in earthly things" and the Charybdis of Romantic intuitionism, which seeks "to shroud in a mist the manifold variety of his earthly existence and of thought," is possible only if we learn to grasp history as a dialectical progression. On this view, there is no ontological given, no "fixed point, . . . no being, or essence, or a universal in general" that philosophy might claim as its Archimedean center. Rather, there is only a continuously evolving *Subjekt* inseparable from its discrete historical instantiations, a subject whose reality is incrementally "realized" (*verwirklicht*) by means of its continual "self-movement" (*Selbstbewegung*). The first half of Hegel's strangely shaped book thus traces a recurrent antinomy between a particular object bound up with contingent sensation and conscious but unreflected perception and the empty universality of thinking that has not yet accounted for its own genesis. As it unfolds the dialectical reconciliation of this antinomy across many stages of increasing complexity, Hegel's *Phenomenology* continually reiterates its founding premise, namely, that "Truth has only the concept [*Begriff*] as the element of its existence."[67]

Consequently, whatever does not accommodate itself to the determinate economy of the Hegelian concept is expunged as literal non-sense, "a mystery without portfolio." It is this "kataphatic reduction into history, proposition or sign" of *all* human experience and meaning that the following exploration of image and image-consciousness rejects.[68] For whereas dialectics stages the progressive emancipation of the "concept" (*Begriff*) from the realm of historically contingent phenomena and discursive practices, a hermeneutics of the image must remain true to the fact that *what* is mediated by the image—be it the Platonic triad or the apophatic God of Christianity—forever transcends time-bound, human cognition. That is, the relation between the visible and the invisible is ever qualified by the principle of *analogy*, rather than being speculatively framed as an *identity* accomplished in history. Hence, the image as it gives itself in intuition does not contest but, rather, attests to the absolute transcendence of (divine) being. At stake here is the relationship between intuition and time, an issue thrown into relief in chapter 3, which focuses on the relation between the visible image and eschatological vision. Hegel, of course, is fully aware of this relation and, early in his preface, recalls how long ago people "had a heaven adorned with a vast wealth of thoughts and imagery. . . . Instead of dwelling in this world's presence, men looked beyond it, . . . to an other-worldly presence. . . . [They] give themselves up to the uncontrolled ferment of [the divine] substance," imagining that "God gives [them] wisdom in sleep." In the event, "what they receive . . . is nothing but dreams." Where Neoplatonists and medieval mystics speak of experiences

---

67. Hegel 1977, 5–6, 13, 4.
68. O'Regan 2014, 137.

involving their "spiritual senses" and issuing in a distinctive "intellectual vision" (*visio intellectualis*), Hegel sees but an illusory transcendence arising from a failure of dialectical thinking. Visions of transcendence are but so much "rapturous haziness," illicit projections ventured by forms of consciousness that have not yet grasped their contingent historical situatedness, or immanence.[69]

Yet this account is overdrawn. In fact, Hegel's critique "applies only to unrestricted and not christologically regulated apophasis."[70] That is, it only bears on the remote, impersonal God of Enlightenment deism, natural theology, and perhaps also Schelling's absolute. Indeed, Hegel can dismiss the image received in intuition as hazy and devoid of a conceptual warrant only because he has chosen to elide from the outset how that image can be, and indeed has been, realized with the utmost focus and clarity by Christ's human face. Hence, writers such as Julian of Norwich, Cusa, Hopkins, or von Balthasar can credibly argue that Christ's "iconic status does not remove mystery so much as focus it."[71] By contrast, Hegel's dialectical economy tends to frame the image as locked in competition with the concept and, thus, as lacking determinacy (*Bestimmung*) and necessarily provisional. Given his commitment to philosophy as a self-authenticating, systemic endeavor, Hegel cannot accept the possibility of the image as having separate ontological standing, let alone the possibility of an "incomprehensible certainty" mediated solely by the image and inaccessible to conceptual and discursive reason. Instead, both image and intuition for Hegel can only signify as transitional phases within a dialectical progression confirming the anthropomorphic and immanent constitution of Reason (*Vernunft*) and Spirit (*Geist*). As he writes in the *Encyclopedia* (1818), "For itself, the image is transitory [*Das Bild ist für sich vorübergehend*]." Once sublated into the realm of pure "intelligence," the image henceforth subsists only as something "internalized / remembered" (*erinnert*) and preserved in quasi-fossilized form in the "subconscious" (*bewußtlos aufbewahrt*). Resembling the nineteenth-century institution of the museum, Hegelian "intelligence" is only prepared to commemorate the image as something "no longer existing" (*nicht mehr existierend*), that is, only as a type of cultural "property" (*Eigentum*) and intellectual "capital" (*Besitz*).[72] Speculative knowledge can only be attained at the expense of intuitive experience, just as the space of phe-

---

69. Hegel 1977, 5–6. See Desmond 2012, 3–21, 64–86, on Hegel's insistent foreclosure of Platonic "wonder" or "astonishment," a seemingly inevitable consequence of Hegel's axiom that "the intelligibility of being . . . is unthinkable apart from determinacy" and its implicit "predilection for the univocity of being" (14).

70. O'Regan 2014, 137.

71. Balthasar, quoted in O'Regan 2014, 137. As O'Regan goes on to remark, "Although an absolute necessity of Christian discourse, apophasis is constrained" (137).

72. Hegel 1970, 3:259–61 (*Encyclopedia*, pt. III, §453); for an incisive reading of this section from the *Encyclopedia*, see Derrida 1982, 207–72.

nomenality is wholly circumscribed by the dominion of the concept. Arduously fashioned by the ceaseless "labor of the spirit" (*Arbeit des Geistes*), the "concept" (*Begriff*) is said to pass through myriad discursive forms and conceptual schemes and, in so doing, gradually takes possession of transcendence. On such dialectical reasoning, knowledge *eo ipso* lodges a claim to ownership and dominion over the thing known, rather than understanding itself as participating in it.

Unlike speculative dialectics, hermeneutic practice of the kind also pursued throughout this book constitutes more of an ethos than a method. It pivots on our receptivity to phenomena *as they give themselves in intuition*, rather than being seized by conceptual means and extruded as a dialectical sequence of "reflexive determinations." At its heart, hermeneutic practice acknowledges that, far from being self-evident and univocal, "the meaning of the determinate has to be interpreted."[73] Put differently, hermeneutics does not so much reject Hegel's conception of Reason (*Vernunft*) as self-regulating, and of Being's speculatively self-determinations, as it reminds us of the dialogic nature of all philosophical insight. For knowledge does not arise out of a play of mutually exclusive, monologic claims and incommensurable standpoints. Rather, it presupposes an essential porousness and receptivity presupposed by the very notion of rational, specifically *human* agency, that is, a "willingness to let something communicate itself to us [*sich etwas sagen lassen zu wollen*]."[74] As a practice that, to an extent, always contains an aleatory element, hermeneutics turns on the cultivation of epistemic humility, somewhat analogous to the "cloud of unknowing" into which medieval contemplatives seek to enter. On this model, the visible forms that give themselves in intuition mediate a reality that is only ever accessible *per analogiam* and can never be claimed "in and for itself," as Hegel would have it.

Phenomenology and hermeneutics thus do not conceive of mediation as a matter of historical contingency, that is, as provisional scaffolding waiting to be disassembled once speculative reason, having parsed being and appearance, pronounces the world as exhaustively "determined" (*bestimmt*). The drama of phenomenality, of manifestation as an irreducible event, reminds us that we must not "identify intelligibility, indeed being at all, with determinacy" and that appearance is an integral, not

---

73. Desmond 2012, 35; as Desmond puts it later on, the "point is not to deny the necessity of concepts, it is to question whether Hegel's concept as self determining thought can be the last word, or indeed the first" (73).

74. Gadamer 1993a, 6. Recently, Rita Felski has argued for the value of "remaining on the same plane as my object of study," for learning to discern the limitations built into a modern "hermeneutics of suspicion" by complementing it with a "hermeneutics of trust, of restoration, of recollection." Doing so, she notes (in ways echoing Simone Weil's ethics of attention), means to cultivate our powers of "receptivity, . . . to allow ourselves to be marked, struck, impressed by what we read" and, thus, to learn to embrace the text as "cofactor" (Felski 2015, 6, 9, 12).

an accidental, feature of "the intimate strangeness of being." Transposed into a theological language that will feature prominently throughout this book, this is to say, an apophatic account of divine self-concealment in the order of images and, more generally, appearances, far from constituting an *obstacle* to be remedied by dialectics, furnishes the very *source* that calls forth and guides all hermeneutic reflection.[75] Hence, when understood as a necessary extension of phenomenological description, hermeneutics amounts to a "showing of its own kind; it is a showing-at. . . . Speaking is connected fundamentally with perceptual manifesting, for speech after all points to things.[76] Moreover, only if hermeneutic speech understands itself as responding to something antecedently given, as the recipient of a gift rather than claiming possession of an object, will it be able to give back what it has received from tradition in augmented form.[77]

Finally, a word may be in order as regards this book's somewhat fluid interdisciplinary approach. Prompting this book's persistent back-and-forth movement between phenomenological description, literary and art historical, as well as theological and philosophical, reflection is the fact that the dynamism of images manifestly exceeds the scope of any one of these disciplinary formations. For one thing, to probe intuitive or "pre-predicative" (Husserl) forms of experience, such as the call-and-response relationship between image and consciousness, is to realize that no single method is ever adequate to the task at hand. For by its very nature, method is a *discursive* construct, whereas visual cognition is always tinged with (though not reducible to) a pre- or extralinguistic, intuitive dimension or what patristic authors such as Gregory of Nyssa or pseudo-Dionysius call "spiritual senses." To reject that prediscursive aspect as a priori unreal, simply because it does not accommodate itself to the conceptual schemes and methodological protocols of Cartesian and post-Cartesian rationality, would obviously beg the question of the image on a grand scale. In fact, there always remains in humanistic inquiry, taking that phrase in its widest sense, an aleatory and improvisational element that shows the knowledge produced to be as much a function of grace and discernment as of some particular method. Avoiding the equivocal Greek term *technē*, which blurs the boundaries between methodical "making" and inspired "creating," Hans-Georg Gadamer instead opts for the Latin *subtilitas* so as to distinguish between three distinct yet contiguous levels of hermeneutic practice: explication, interpretation, and application. Far from considering this state of affairs a predicament, I regard it as an opportunity for her-

---

75. Desmond 2012, xxi–xxii.

76. Patočka 2002, 25.

77. "Interpreters do not simply pass on (*traditio*) but in and through interpretation reveal new facets of the phenomenon of Christ and thus 'give back' (*redditio*). This giving back is what makes the tradition ever new" (O'Regan 2014, 135); on the concept of tradition, see also MacIntyre 1990, 170–95; Pfau 2013a, 53–75; Pfau 2017b.

meneutic discernment and creative reflection that is entirely apposite to this book's topic and, more generally, as something to be embraced rather than resisted. Hence, too, this book does not purport to offer a systematic "theory of the image," nor for that matter does it attempt to outline a Neoplatonist or theological account of beauty. Instead, theological and philosophical insights are meant to arise more organically from a series of focused hermeneutic studies of images and their unique power and efficacy.

A Preview (and Some Disclaimers)

Uniting virtually all the writers considered in the following pages is a commitment to elucidating the image's dynamic manifestation rather than taking possession of its presumptive contents. It is a commitment to be honored in hermeneutic practice, namely, by listening in (empathetically, though not uncritically) on a variety of literary, philosophical, and theological writings as they parse the visual experience of images and symbolic forms. Ranging from Plato to Rilke, the works here considered are themselves a form of hermeneutic practice rather than the subjective "expression" (*Ausdruck*) of a contingent, inward experience. For they seek to formulate a "statement" (*Aussage*) about the numinous import of Being as it gives itself—at once excessively and incomprehensibly—in intuition. It is no accident, then, that most of the writers considered in what follows found that giving *voice* to the specific image and vision that so utterly captured their attention required that they free themselves from the dominant formal and rhetorical conventions of their respective times. Only if we accept that, say, Julian's *Vision of a Devout Woman*, Ruskin's account of Turner in *Modern Painters I*, or Rilke's lyric emulation of Cézanne's impersonal style originates in an intuitive experience at once ineffably and incontrovertibly *true* can we disentangle the many layers of meaning alternately converging in a given visual experience and subsequently parsed in contemplative, lyric, or critical writing. For if it were otherwise, and if not only the forms of writing of, say, Maximus, Goethe, Hopkins, or Rilke but also the underlying, intuitive experience were merely a function of constantly shifting historical and psychological parameters, interpretation would find itself confronting outright entropy, not just contingency, and thus would prove impossible. In the event, for hermeneutics to approach specific forms as intrinsically meaningful and potentially intelligible it must have premised a noncontingent *logos* that specifically reveals itself by means of (contingent) appearance.[78]

---

78. Heraclitus's insight that "although the logos is common to all, the many live as though they had a private understanding" (Kirk, Raven, and Schofield 1983, 187 [Heraclitus, Fragment # 195]) still resonates in Wittgenstein's arguments against private language. Nevertheless, a great deal of modern epistemological skepticism, positivism, and reductionism continues to entangle itself

This much hermeneutics shares with Hegelian dialectics. Yet unlike the latter, hermeneutic practice views understanding as an open-ended enterprise whereby a finite intelligence may participate *in* the *logos*, namely, by dialogically sifting how it continually manifests itself in intelligible (visible or textual) forms. As noted before, such "participation" (*methexis*) is inherently aleatory and constantly self-revising, ever responsive to the intrinsic richness of the phenomena it engages, rather than in-strumentalizing its findings for immanent, systemic purposes. Unlike the modern conception of method employed in the service of a philosophical system, that is, her-meneutic practice constitutes an "art" (*subtilitas*) whose scope of vision is necessarily larger, less shrewdly selective than the dialectician's withering gaze, which considers the excess and splendor of phenomena as an obstacle to be cleared and contained by increasingly abstract conceptual schemes. By contrast, a hermeneutic engagement of past forms of expression and cognition specifically requires us to be maximally alert to the phenomenon's many-layered texture: how it is informed by questions of genre, rhetorical convention, pictorial technique, and scriptural, theological, and intellec-tual subtexts, not to mention its socioeconomic and political embeddedness. Just how to calibrate the relative significance of all these factors remains itself a matter of judgment, an art honed by practice and informed by experience and, as such, uncon-strained by methodological or systemic imperatives.

As I had previously argued in *Minding the Modern*, humanistic inquiry never ought to content itself with abstract generalizations and high-altitude surveys of complex intellectual terrain.[79] Likewise, the present study also aims to show rather than tell, in the sense just sketched, how different genres of writing (poetic, aes-thetic, theological, and philosophical) evolving at different points in history respond in their own distinctive ways to an ineffable plenitude of meaning manifesting itself in the medium of the image. Doing so, however, requires a prismatic, or robustly cross-disciplinary, perspective—on art historical, philosophical, theological, literary, and more broadly historical matters—that is hard to cultivate and arguably impos-sible to balance and flesh out to every reader's satisfaction. While historical develop-ments and specific debates, as well as ambient "contextual" forces, are intermittently flagged throughout this book, my main focus will be on theological and intellectual traditions as these inform attempts at conceptualizing the image and accounting for its distinctive phenomenology. To that end, the organizing principle of this book

---

in a performative contradiction by disavowing a noncontingent *logos*, which at the same time such discourse must presuppose if it is to meet with uptake as an intelligible argument. The metaphysical *logos* principle is a precondition of human inquiry, not its contingent product.

79. Pfau 2013a, 64–66, 420–27, 456–60; among the most comprehensive reflections on the limits of "method" in scientific and humanistic inquiry are Polanyi 1962 and Gadamer 2006, esp. 228–35.

fuses historical and paradigmatic argument. While the initial two chapters sketch the philosophical and theological parameters of image theory in Platonic and Byzantine thought, chapters 3–8 overlay the book's chronological sequence with a paradigmatic approach by successively focusing on the image's eschatological, speculative, symbolic, forensic, liturgical, and epiphanic dimensions. There are several reasons for proceeding in this way. Most important, just as metaphysics must be complemented by phenomenology, so the latter must be differentiated by a hermeneutic alertness to different genres of writing and their formal and historical bearings. Thus, rather than front-load the argument with some a priori, monolithic "theory of the image," the first two chapters trace the gradual, at times agonistic evolution of a coherent and enduring image concept in Platonic, Neoplatonic, and Byzantine writing. As chapter 1 argues, in his prolonged wrestling with questions of image and mimesis, Plato not only discovered their metaphysical underpinnings but also realized that the numinous Being at the heart of metaphysical inquiry necessarily implies mediation, that it must be thought as eternally self-manifesting and self-revealing. Drawing on Plotinus, more than Plato, patristic, and Byzantine thought, extends this insight, now reframed in fourth- and fifth-century Christological debates that provide earlier speculation about image and representation with the emergent motif of the Christ icon. Chapter 2 offers a compressed survey of the material and conceptual evolution of icon theory, culminating in a robust defense of images during the era of Byzantine iconoclasm (AD 726–843) and, finally, in the icon's formal institution, consecration, and integration into liturgical practice during the ninth century.

Starting in chapter 3, we begin to explore the first of the six paradigms here presented as a loosely historical sequence, with each one seeking to throw into relief a particular set of functions served by images, as well as the specific types of response they tend to elicit. In exploring the image under the heading of eschatology, my principal concern is with the way that eschatological vision, mediated by images of Christ crucified and the pietà motif, stages the irruption of numinous, timeless meanings into human, time-bound existence. The chapter begins with a discussion of Augustine's understanding of time and anagogy. It then considers how the Augustinian view of all temporal being as an *imago* prefiguring its eventual fulfillment *beyond* time is taken up in the mystical writings of Bernard and the Victorine School and, a century later, in the writings of Bonaventure. From there, the chapter proceeds to consider how the image of Christ crucified focuses eschatological expectancy in Julian of Norwich's *Vision of a Devout Woman*, the so-called short text in which she recalls and reflects on her intense vision of Christ at her deathbed. While the motivic range of images informing mystical and contemplative writing of the fourteenth century tends to be narrow, involving mainly the Man of Sorrows in painted or sculpted form, it considerably expands during the fifteenth century. Tracing the shift from icons serving communal and liturgical purposes to the emergent genre of the private, "devotional image" (*Andachtsbild*) in the work of van Eyck, we find the spiritual clarity and urgency so characteristic of Julian's eschatological vision become noticeably blurred and attenuated. A new type of pictorial realism now weakens the image's capacity of mediating transcendence and, instead, shows the visible and the invisible to be competing for the same epistemological space. In what is a momentary break with the book's chronological order, the chapter's final section considers the afterlife and final disintegration of the devotional image in the work of Thomas Mann during the first quarter of the twentieth century. His early short story, "Gladius Dei," still frames the collapse of eschatological vision as a grotesque-comical encounter, pitting a Savonarola-like iconoclast against the hedonistic and decadent culture of turn-of-the-century Munich. A decade later, farce turns into tragedy, as Mann's *Death in Venice* (1912) traces the nefarious impact of fin-de-siècle symbolism and its confused metaphysics on the novella's protagonist, von Aschenbach, whose descent into voyeurism and idolatry reflects an unprecedented level of eschatological despair. Closing the chapter is a brief discussion of an early thirteenth-century wooden pietà in *The Magic Mountain* (1924), a fitting symbol of grief for Europe's moribund civilization on the eve of World War I.

At the center of chapter 4 stands Nicholas of Cusa, arguably the dominant philosophical and theological figure of the fifteenth century, whose oeuvre is widely regarded as marking the transition from late Scholasticism to Renaissance Platonism. A fundamental question recurring throughout Cusa's writings and culminating in his most popular work, *De Visione Dei* (1453), concerns the nature of mystical vision, specifically as mediated by an iconic presentation of Christ. Overall, Cusa's oeuvre seeks to move beyond the static antinomy of a rigidly aniconic ideal of piety then gaining support among various monastic orders and the laity and the arid abstractions of an increasingly defensive Scholasticism mainly entrenched in the universities. As he attempts to reconcile practical piety and speculative reason, Cusa draws on the Platonic idea of "participation" (*methexis*) to develop a model of intellectual vision wherein the Christ icon effects a quasi-phenomenological shift of focus, away from the picture seen and toward ascertaining the spiritual quality informing one's own gaze. If, in Cusa's well-worn phrase, "seeing and being-seen coincide," the resulting vision is not merely an individual act, let alone a projection of private (likely irrational) spiritual longing, but, instead, founds a spiritual community. For even though the icon is uniquely experienced by each individual beholder, its transformative power will be found to have always extended equally to all those who have submitted to its "omnivoyant" gaze. From the standpoint of hermeneutic reflection, the *imago* seen in the present is transmuted into the *figura* of a hoped-for spiritual community, just as empirical vision is by definition *provisional*, *prefiguring* an aniconic and timeless spiritual fulfillment. To underscore Cusa's integrative, rather than disjunctive, conception of empirical sight and spiritual vision, the chapter's final two sections juxtapose his speculative image concept to Leon Battista Alberti's outline of a theory of linear perspective, widely understood to have instituted a distinctly modern gaze that aspires to total epistemic dominion over the visible while professing utter agnosticism concerning all things invisible.

With part 2, our exploration of the image and its phenomenology shifts to the modern era. Of the principal figures considered—Goethe, Ruskin, Hopkins, and Rilke—the first two share a concern with the rise of naturalistic epistemologies and the role of visual cognition in the natural sciences. Thus, at the center of chapter 5 stand the botanical writings and associated maxims and reflections of Goethe. Some three hundred years after Cusa, Goethe's theory of visual intuition, organic process, and symbolic form reinstates core elements of Platonism, albeit in a context now greatly changed by the rise of mechanist theories of causality and taxonomic models of natural form during the Enlightenment. The chapter first considers Goethe's rehabilitation of "appearance" (*Erscheinung*) and "intuition" (*Anschauung*) as indispensable sources of knowledge, as well as his relational rather than oppositional understanding of morphological "difference" exhibited by all organic form. As is the case for Plotinus, Goethe conceives the observer's experience of dynamically evolving, natural forms as a case of highly involved "participation" (*methexis*) rather than analytic detachment. As he never tires to stress, apprehending visible form as a process of continual self-differentiation or metamorphosis means participating in the invisible idea of which such form is a specific and dynamic manifestation. The continuity between Cusa and Goethe is palpable here, as are the ways, also considered, in which Goethe's organicism stands apart from Hegelian dialectics. Still, Goethe's model of visual cognition and form qua metamorphosis remains incomplete unless the idea purportedly seen can also be "presented" (*dargestellt*) in analogous, symbolic form. Thus, the chapter's final section cross-references Goethean metamorphosis with Ovid, and the Goethean symbol with the competing theories of Cassirer and Bulgakov, the aim being to draw out the objective and metaphysical (rather than subjective-aesthetic) implications of "presentation" (*Darstellung*). Particularly in Goethe's late *Maxims and Reflections*, the classical principle of *analogia*—"a primordial metaphysical kinship" (*metaphysische Urverwandtschaft*) between symbol and *logos*—resurfaces as the indispensable, ontologically real foundation for aesthetic and scientific cognition alike.[80]

Chapter 6 frames the discussion of image and image-consciousness in the context of early Victorian models of scientific and aesthetic realism. Unlike what

---

80. Gadamer 2006, 64.

happens on the Continent, where social and political concerns shape a new, post-Romantic aesthetic, English and Scottish conceptions of realism are closely linked to the consolidation of natural science (biology and geology in particular) as a rigorously inductive, observation-based pursuit. The first section thus traces how Lyell and the young Charles Darwin came to understand what Michael Hanby calls "the ontological primacy of intelligible things," that is, form as the indispensable foundation for gaining access to the real.[81] As it turns out, for the scientist to visualize a given particular as warranting investigation, the visible thing must already have been grasped as the instantiation of its underlying *form*. Strictly speaking, that is, one cannot ever "see" the particular as such, for in the absence of a wider pattern of similar kinds, an isolated particular would only confront and confound our gaze with unorganized, optical "noise." As the young Darwin and Ruskin came to realize, reality can be seen and understood only as the concrete manifestation of a noncontingent pattern, that is, as the visible manifestation of its *species*. The concept of a species, in other words, is not something imposed *on* empirically visible forms. Rather, it is the ontological precondition absent which eye and mind could never engage in joint and purposeful observation. It is this central, albeit frequently ignored tension between a mimetic and a metaphysical notion of "realism"—that is, between the image understood as either *homologous with* or *analogous to* truth—that the next two sections explore in Ruskin's *Modern Painters I* (1843) and in his controversial lectures on Pre-Raphaelite aesthetics a decade later. Inexorably and painstakingly, Ruskin finds himself edging away from a naive concept of pictorial realism (as sheer illusionism or hypersimulation) and from the dead end of ekphrastic writing to which it would confine the art critic. This evolution correlates with Ruskin's growing interest in the phenomenology of seeing a given image, which he gradually realizes is never fungible with the perception of a given object. Seeing constitutes an "event," a witnessing of visual appearance as the manifestation of an invisible, substantive form, which Ruskin, ever the passionate defender of Turner's late works, finds preeminently realized in the modality of color and texture.

Reflecting Ruskin's enduring influence, while also developing a theologically far more profound understanding of the essential affinity between pictorial and metaphysical realism, is the central figure of chapter 7, Gerard Manley Hopkins. Yet whereas a great deal of criticism has framed Hopkins's unique if often hermetic writings in relation to various influences (Scotus, Ignatius, Newman, Darwin, and Ruskin being the most prominent), the reading attempted here foregrounds Hopkins's conceptual, rather than biographical or philological, kinship with two distant theological forebears (pseudo-Dionysius and Maximus the Confessor), as well as with phenome-

---

81. Hanby 2013, 212.

nological arguments formulated only during the decades following his death in 1889. Accounting for Hopkins's intensely visual idiom is his exceptional alertness to the distinctive organization and dynamic presentation of natural forms. Poetry for him does not fashion images so much as it responds to the intrinsic charism of natural phenomena, which his notebooks and poetry tend to present as *acheiropoietai*, images not wrought by human hands. Echoing a long-standing distrust of abstraction and generalization that runs through English letters—we think of Locke, Blake, Wordsworth, Darwin, Newman, and Ruskin—Hopkins conceives poetic form as a verbal analogue of the "inscape" to whose abundant givenness it bears witness. With its distinctive cadence, pitch, and ("sprung") rhythm, lyric speech thus attests to, and formally seeks to emulate, the visual experience that had drawn it forth to begin with. What allows a visible thing to become the focal point of poetic writing is a realization, formulated long before Husserl's concept of "eidetic intuition" by Duns Scotus: namely, that "a thing which is true can be known before its truth is known."[82] The chapter's first two sections focus on the formal and phenomenological implications of Hopkins's poetic idiom, which seeks to capture the reality with which a visible thing elicits and shapes our attention and, in time, issues in a lyric form "written expressly for the image's sake."[83] As it turns out, the concept of form and experience that, starting with his studies at Balliol College and later confirmed by his readings of Duns Scotus, Hopkins steadily refines anticipates a major shift in modern phenomenology, namely, from a modal to an eidetic concept of necessity. No longer, that is, does a thing's essence consist in the "general properties" (*Wesensallgemeinheiten*) that we may predicate of it by relying on logical categories. Instead, the essentiality of a thing inheres in its unique way of giving itself in intuition, what Husserl will term "eidetic necessity" (*Wesensnotwendigkeit*). Pivoting from philosophical to theological concerns, the final two sections explore deep affinities between Hopkins's liturgical conception of seeing the natural world and the strict apophaticism of pseudo-Dionysius and Maximus the Confessor. Of particular concern here is their reliance (shared by Hopkins) on *analogia* as the principle by which to avoid framing the relation between divine being and finite appearance either in antinomian terms (Gnosticism) or as one of outright identity (Pantheism).

The book's final chapter takes up a phase in European thought and culture, roughly between 1905 and 1912, when the image concept underwent a profound revaluation in early modernist painting and poetry, just as Husserl begins to formulate his comprehensive outline of phenomenology as a new philosophical method. Uniting these developments is a shared concern with accessing the very foundations of sensory and intuitive experience that, as representatives of high modernism argued,

---

82. Scotus 1987, 99.
83. *HCW* II:559.

had been occluded by late Romantic, realist, and fin-de-siècle symbolist aesthetics: namely, sound, rhythm, color, and texture. Undergirding modernism's guarded
quest for an epiphanic image concept is a concern with unveiling both being and
its experience as a holistic *event* rather than as an inert "object" or a contingent
psychological "state." The chapter's first section examines Husserl's 1905 lectures on
"image-consciousness," arguably the ground zero for phenomenology's proposed
shift of focus, away from the "perception of things" (*Dingwahrnehmung*) and toward
the experience of perception itself (*Erlebniswahrnehmung*). Not by accident, it was
this scrutiny of image and "image-consciousness" (*Bildbewußtsein*) that allowed
Husserl to formulate his concept of phenomenology between 1905 and 1907, just as
exploring the charism of visible things enabled Rilke to overcome his residual symbolist allegiances and evolve the pointedly objective style of his *New Poems* (1907/8).
What Rilke calls "the quiet redemption of the thing's very being" (*des Dingseins leise
Erlösung*)—to be achieved by a new "plainspoken" poetic idiom (*sachliches Sagen*)—
was in large measure the fruit of his encounter with the works of Rodin and Cézanne.[84] Particularly the latter's oeuvre modeled for Rilke a "new" conception of the
image whose premodern, metaphysical, and theological underpinnings he had first
glimpsed during his travels in Russia.[85] Rather than being framed as the willed production of visible novelties, the "image" at the heart of Rilke's "Thing-Poems" (*Dinggedichte*) constitutes itself in our pre-predicative response to the world's abundant
phenomenality and absolute givenness in intuition. Grounded in what Merleau-
Ponty will later call "perceptual faith," early modernist sculpture, painting, and lyric
thus evolve forms aimed at stabilizing this givenness of the world qua image.[86] The
chapter's final section picks up on a shift in Rilke's lyric oeuvre starting around 1912
that closely resembles a dynamic previously observed in Julian, Cusa, and Hopkins:
namely, the gradual evolution of the image from a visible mediation of the invisible
toward its outright self-suspension. Increasingly ill at ease with "an intellectual appropriation of the world that so utterly relies on the eye," Rilke after 1912 begins to
detach the (lyric) image from its perceptual moorings in three-dimensional, Euclidian space and, instead, outlines an increasingly aniconic poetics situated in a non-
Euclidian, imaginary space that he calls *Weltinnenraum*.[87]

     While this study covers a fair amount of ground in mostly chronological
fashion, it does not purport to offer a linear survey of a theological, philosophical, let

---

84. *KA* 4:424, 624.
85. On the formative impact of Russian icon theology on Rilke's "pre- and post-revelatory
poems" and poetics, see Cushman 2002 (quote from 88).
86. Merleau-Ponty 1968, 28.
87. *KA* 2:504.

alone art historical kind. Instead, it is conceived as a study of paradigmatic image concepts, their diverse material and medial realization, and likewise changing accounts of image experience variously advanced in discursive (philosophical and theological) and creative writing. By concentrating on the eschatological, speculative, symbolic, forensic, liturgical, and epiphanic dimension of images, this book leaves a sizable gap extending from the Renaissance to the Enlightenment, an omission for which at least some rationale ought to be tendered. The main reason for this lacuna is a near-inverse ratio between that period's immense formal innovation and technical proficiency as regards the painted *picture* and its pointedly uncurious and often antimetaphysical conception of the *image*. James Simpson has written insightfully on eighteenth-century aesthetic theory as a crypto-iconoclast practice aimed at neutralizing the image's metaphysical and theological dimensions. Thus, the period's emergent practice of collecting art "is in part produced as a place of asylum from iconoclasm. It offers the secular space in which we are permitted to contemplate images. Even as that asylum was being shaped, however, it registered, and attempted to neutralize, the dangers of the image." Remarking on the Protestant origins of Enlightenment aesthetic theory, Simpson further observes how "taste, with its focus on form, is a strategy . . . designed to look at Rome again. But one could only look at Rome by neutralizing its power to enthrall. Focus on the form, ignore the content. . . . The category of the aesthetic is itself, in sum, a historical product of iconoclasm."[88] While approaching the issue from a nearly obverse position, Georges Didi-Huberman ends up telling a similar story of the art image's progressive asphyxiation by theories of painting and academic art history from Vasari to Panofsky. Summarizing his critique of Panofsky, he notes that

> "humanism" . . . acts . . . like a magic and pacifying word. It passes triumphantly from the status of object of study to that of theoretical program—congruent with that object. . . . The history of art, when it calls itself a "humanistic discipline," does nothing but appeal to synthesis, but conjure away all the violence, deception, and "inhumanity" that images are—and always have been—able to foment. The history of art as a "humanistic discipline" does nothing but trace a magic circle, within which it . . . recreates images in the image of its own thought: its humanistic *Idea* of art.[89]

---

88. Simpson 2010, 116–54 (quotes from 120, 133).

89. Didi-Huberman 2005, 85–138; quote from 117. As Adorno had remarked, in the wake of Renaissance humanism and Enlightenment aesthetics, "artworks are neutralized and thus qualitatively transformed epiphanies" from which "apparition, the heavenly vision . . . has been driven out without a trace" (1997, 80).

Few works better exemplify this quarantining of the image within a strictly immanent and sharply circumscribed pictorial rhetoric than Shaftesbury's essay, "Historical Draught or Tablature," and his accompanying "Letter concerning Design" (1712), intended as commentary on a large drawing, *The Judgment of Hercules* (fig. I.3). Tellingly, the drawing was produced (by Paolo de Matteis of Naples) in accordance with Shaftesbury's precise written specifications; in other words, the picture Shaftesbury conceives as the ideal embodiment of Enlightenment art and taste strictly aims to complement an anthropocentric concept of "design" first conceived in discursive and only then rendered in pictorial form. With intellection now preceding intuition, a wedge has been driven between vision and perception, image and picture. The visible no longer mediates the invisible but, in merely pictorializing an antecedent concept, actually means to safeguard against the possibility that images might open vistas on nonconceptual, numinous meanings. Such confident repurposing of the visible for strictly immanent ends also resonates in Shaftesbury's urbane prose style, which does much to domesticate the Enlightenment image within a preestablished pictorial rhetoric ("the heroick Style") and a likewise settled, neoclassical ideal of spatiotemporal finitude ("Unity of Time and Action").

On Shaftesbury's account, an image is legitimated *only* insofar as it reflects an antecedent design and, being wholly cleansed of all visual excess, reinforces strictly anthropocentric symmetries. There is to be nothing "contrary to Order, contrary to the History, and to the *Decorum*, or Decency of Manners." Indeed, in its rigid formal and rhetorical organization, Shaftesbury's ideal "Tablature" seems above all designed to purge phenomenality of all excess; and the artist shall "do his utmost to diminish and reduce the excessive Gaiety and Splendor of . . . Objects, which wou'd otherwise raise such a Confusion, Oppugnancy, and Riot of Colours, as wou'd to any judicious Eye appear absolutely intolerable." Insofar as the objective of the "Tablature" is to reinforce anthropomorphic conceptions of virtue and propriety by pictorial means, allegorical painting merely reconfirms notions extrinsic to it. Thus, Shaftesbury's opening definition of *tablature* underscores how a highly stylized ideal of verisimilitude, formal symmetry, and total visibility means to fend off any lingering metaphysical dimensions that might reveal the visible image as an *eikōn* of the invisible: "In Painting we may give to any particular Work the Name of *Tablature*, when the Work is in reality 'a *Single Piece*, comprehended in one *View*, and form'd according to *one single* Intelligence, Meaning, or Design; which constitutes a *real* WHOLE, by a mutual and necessary Relation of its Parts."[90]

90. Shaftesbury 2001, 228, 217, 222, 229, 214.

Figure I.3. Anthony Ashley Cooper, 3rd Earl of Shaftesbury, *The Judgment of Hercules* (design by Paolo de Matteis)

This is not the place to show how William Hogarth, arguably the sharpest critic of Shaftesbury's neoclassical aesthetics, far from overturning his predecessor's downward transposition of the symbolic image into allegorical "Design," actually reinforces and expands that paradigm with his brilliant visual satires of everyday urban life. Likewise (to stay within the parameters of English painting), it would be the subject of another discussion to show how Thomas Gainsborough's landscapes continue to consolidate the Enlightenment's image concept within a strictly immanent matrix. Suffice it to say that, even as the Enlightenment's depotentiation of image and intuition into pictures and percepts advances, a note of sadness begins to surface, as though realist painting were quietly mourning the very demise of vision that it itself had, perhaps inadvertently, brought about. We might think here of the peculiar contrast of spiritual desolation and unearned material confidence displayed by upper-class "propertied" subjects, such as Gainsborough's *Mr. and Mrs. Andrews* (1750) (fig. I.4). Three decades later, that tension erupts into the open as the late Gainsborough sheds unsparing light on the pervasive material and spiritual immiseration that is the price inevitably paid for an urban political economy and the material blandishments

Figure I.4. Thomas Gainsborough, *Mr. and Mrs. Andrews*, 1750

accumulated by an emerging middle class.[91] Between Hogarth's midcentury social satires and Gainsborough's wistful depictions of the nameless poor straggling at the margins of Britain's "progressive" political economy, Enlightenment aesthetics bears out what in *On Naïve and Sentimental Poetry* (1795) Schiller analyzes as a "sentimental" cast pervading all modern art, alternately expressed in satiric or elegiac form. What, in perhaps overly generalizing ways, Adorno remarks about art as a whole fittingly describes not only the trivialization of the image under the heading of the "Picturesque" but also the consequent, melancholic sense of loss arising from the confinement of the image within a matrix of pure immanence mapped out in advance by Enlightenment aesthetics: "Because meaning, whenever it is manifest in an artwork, remains bound up with semblance, all art is endowed with sadness; art grieves all the more, the more completely its successful unification suggests meaning. . . . In the utopia of its form, art bends under the burdensome weight of the empirical world from which, as art, it steps away."[92]

---

91. See Gainsborough's various realizations of the "Cottage Door" motif from 1778, 1780, and 1786; on the increasing physical and spiritual destitution of Gainsborough's late subjects, see John Barrell (1980, 35–88), who also notes how, by way of subtle scriptural allusion, Gainsborough intimates a relation between Christ's sufferings and those of the rural poor in his own time. For an example, see *The Harvest Wagon* (1767), whose choreography of figures is widely seen as alluding to Rubens's 1617 version of *Christ's Deposition from the Cross*, and Barrell's discussion of that connection (1980, 59–62); see also Pfau 1997, 17–82.

92. Adorno 1997, 105.

Another kind of subject excluded from this study concerns the moving image and, with a couple of exceptions, photography. As regards the latter, the reason for this nonengagement ultimately comes down to limits of both expertise and space in a book already quite long. That said, there is ample evidence to suggest that, like painting, photography is capable of transcending conceptions that would confine the image within a restrictive economy of perception, verisimilitude, and verification—which is to say, a framework in which the visible picture may only duplicate meanings already established by other, presumably discursive or syllogistic, means. In fact, photography's distant kinship to the acheiropoietic (uncreated) image so vigorously defended by the Byzantine iconodules often seems palpably echoed by its modern practitioners (think of Dorothea Lange, W. Eugene Smith, André Kertész, Henri Cartier-Bresson, or Robert Doisneau) who so often insist on the image having *found them*, rather than vice versa, and who fundamentally understand their medium to reveal what Merleau-Ponty calls "the lived perspective, that which we actually perceive."[93] Still, it would be the subject of another book, to be written by someone more knowledgeable on the subject, to show how the medium of photography might (or might not) support what is a central claim of the present book: namely, that our response to images tends to become more profound and acute if the formal and material organization of pictorial space—including the chromaticism and saturation of color, deviation from single viewpoint optical expectation, and a recalibration of proportions in accordance with *how* things are experienced rather than *what* is seen—is *not* circumscribed by perceptual conventions but, instead, invites eye and mind to respond to what is visibly given in a holistic and intuitive manner that comports with the image's total integration and continuity of shape, color, texture, and perspective. In what follows, then, my concern is with how our response to images may, under optimal conditions, enable us to pinpoint nonpropositional or, to use Husserl's term of art, "pre-predicative" modes of cognition. That said, the claim here is not that image and vision constitute some mystical alternative to propositional knowledge. Rather, it is the *image*—whose experiential reality and hermeneutic potential often far surpasses its material realization as a *picture*—that alone can mediate for us the reality that we may subsequently seek to render discursively explicit.[94] Where we hope to know we must already have seen, a point gradually embraced by Plato whose evolving conception of the image we shall now consider.

---

93. Merleau-Ponty 1993, 64; rather incongruously, Merleau-Ponty claims that this lived perspective, so richly achieved by Cézanne, is unattainable for the photographic image.

94. Whether similar claims might be lodged for nonvisual kinds of sensory experience, in particular hearing/listening, is beyond the purview of this study and will not be addressed. The increasingly lively field of sound studies has much to say about it.

Part I

IMAGE THEORY AS
METAPHYSICS AND THEOLOGY

The Emergence of a Tradition

1

———

A BRIEF METAPHYSICS
OF THE IMAGE

Plato—Plotinus

Mute is the Delphian god, and desolate, long now deserted
Lie the pathways where once, while hopes would gently escort him
Up walked the questioning man to the town of the truth-loving seer.
But the light above speaks kindly to mortals as ever,
Full of promises, hints, and the great Thunderer's voice, it
Cries: do you think of me?

[Stumm ist der delphische Gott, und einsam liegen und öde,
Längst die Pfade, wo einst, von Hoffnungen leise geleitet,
Fragend der Mann zur Stadt des redlichen Sehers heranstieg.
Aber droben das Licht, es spricht noch heute zu den Menschen,
Schöner Deutungen voll und des großen Donnerers Stimme
Ruft es: denket ihr mein?]

—Friedrich Hölderlin, "The Archipelago"

OF IDOLS AND ANICONICISM: THE ONTOLOGICAL AMBIVALENCE
OF THE IMAGE IN PLATO'S *REPUBLIC*

Any inquiry into how images, and visible phenomena more generally, bear on human cognition will have to begin with Plato. For his dialogic exploration of the nature and function of images fundamentally breaks with the way that archaic and early

63

Athenian Greek culture had conceived of visual appearance and presentation. Prior to the fourth century, as Jean-Pierre Vernant has shown, the image is not yet conceived in terms of "imitation" (*mimēsis*) but as a form of simulation, be it in the form of a mime's theatrical performance, an *eidōlon* conjuring an apparition or optical illusion, or a totemic substitute for the absent god (what Pausanias refers to as a *choanon*). Exemplary in this regard is Odysseus's encounter with his mother, Anticlea, in the underworld: "And I, my mind in turmoil, how I longed / to embrace my mother's spirit, dead as she was! / Three times I rushed toward her, desperate to hold her, / three times she fluttered through my fingers, sifting away / like a shadow, dissolving like a dream."[1] The visual phenomenon here is presented as entirely unreal, a mere "shadow" (*skia*) whose illusory nature is confirmed by Odysseus's failed attempts to embrace it. Hence, insofar as such "pure 'semblance' . . . has no other reality than this similitude in relation to what it is not," we are not yet presented with an image, either in the archaic sense of an idol or in the philosophical sense of the icon. Whereas in Homer moments of conspicuous visuality remain apparitional or shadowy, thus suggesting that the image in question lacks any objective correlate, the situation in Plato's dialogues is fundamentally changed. Here the stress is consistently and "emphatically put on the relationship between the image and the thing of which it is the image, on the relationship of resemblance that joins and yet distinguishes the two."[2] Indeed, as we proceed through relevant passages in his dialogues, it becomes apparent that during some twenty-five hundred years of pondering the image's legitimacy (or lack thereof) the debate has remained fundamentally within the orbit of Platonic thought.

That this should be so is due, at least in part, to Plato's deeply equivocal and gradually evolving understanding of how "appearances" (*ta phainomena*) relate to concrete "beings" (*ta onta*), to Being (*to on*), and, ultimately, to that which "lies beyond Being" (*epekeina tēs ousias, Rep.* 509b)—namely, the Good (*to agathon*). Given the indirect, often ironic, and performatively self-aware nature of Socratic dialogue, the following discussion of Plato's theory of the image will have to dwell on various paradoxes arising from his deceptively forthright rejection of images (*ta eidōla*) in Book 10 of the *Republic*, paradoxes left unresolved until Plato succeeded in working out a comprehensive dialectical account of Being and non-being (*mē on*) in his *Parmenides* and, especially, in the *Sophist*.[3] A first, fairly obvious paradox concerns the

---

1. Homer 1996 (11:233–37), Fagles translation; the corresponding Greek lines in the Chicago Homer (http://homer.library.northwestern.edu) are 11:204–8.
2. Vernant 1991, 154, 166.
3. The chronological order of Plato's dialogues, as well as the criteria on which such ordering may legitimately draw, has been a contested issue for centuries. For a philological review of different schemes proposed since the mid-nineteenth century, see Brandwood 1990. For a meta-reflection on the hermeneutic presuppositions and likely pitfalls facing any proposed chronology of Plato's

fact that, for all his professed hostility to images and mere appearance, Socrates throughout Plato's writings makes copious and often highly inventive use of images, including conventional rhetorical tropes such as the statesman piloting the ship of state or the commonplace figure of the sun as an image of the good, though also other, elaborately constructed and highly self-reflexive images, such as the winged charioteer in the *Phaedrus*, the sophist portrayed as angler, the allegory of the cave, or the divided line as an image of our knowledge. Often intricate, such verbal images not only confirm Glaucon's observation that "words are more malleable than wax and the like" (*Rep.* 588d) but also reveal "a fine line between the role of words in the *formation* of a verbal image and their role in the *interpretation* of that image."[4] Indeed, late antiquity frequently takes Plato's view of images to have been affirmative, such as his contention in the *Timaeus* that the entire physical and perceptible universe (*to pan*), far from being a random assemblage of particulars, constitutes an overarching "order [*kosmos*] . . . modeled after that which is changeless" (29a), for which reason Plato insists that sensible matter is best viewed as a time-bound image of the original form as it obtains in the divine maker's mind. Hence it cannot surprise to find eighth- and ninth-century Byzantine iconodules resting their defense of images on Platonic motifs even as their iconoclast opponents also invoke his authority to buttress their position.

At least in part, Plato's equivocal role in this interminable debate stems from the fact that the image's true valence reveals itself in the hermeneutic presuppositions the beholder brings to it, which more often than not will cause the deeper import of the visible to be misconstrued or missed altogether. As Plato notes in the *Phaedrus*, while "the soul of every human being has seen reality, . . . not every soul is easily reminded of the reality there by what it finds here." And even those "fortunate few . . . whose memory is good enough" to recognize and be "startled when they see an image of what they saw up there" will ultimately find that "their experience is beyond their comprehension because they cannot fully grasp what it is that they are seeing" (250b). It is the image's inherent plenitude, not its alleged deficiency, that accounts

writings, see Poster (1998), who sums up her principal conclusions thus: "1. The ordering of Platonic dialogues has significant hermeneutic consequences for Platonic philosophy, and the types of order assumed by any given interpreter and the specific arrangements of the dialogues within those general types of order construct Platonic interpretations. 2. That the orders of Platonic dialogues used by various interpreters of Plato are not pre-existent objective orders which supply absolute independent criteria by which it is possible to judge interpretive theories, but rather narratives constructed by various hermeneutic assumptions" (294).

4. Patterson 2013, 433. For a discussion of "Socrates as Poet," see Zuckert 2009, 352–64. The images mainly serve inspirational and didactic purposes: "The most [Socrates] can do with the images he draws is to arouse the desires of his interlocutors; he cannot make them philosophers. To become philosophers, he states, they would have to undertake arduous studies in dialectics," for which only mathematics can provide a feasible analogue (Zuckert 2009, 353).

for this almost universal failure of visual comprehension. Time and again, Plato's critique of images reveals that the central problem of *mimēsis* arises from ignorance of the productive tension in which the image stands vis-à-vis both its beholder and the object depicted. The confusion is further exacerbated by the fact that it appears to have taken Plato some time to work through the implications of image and the world of appearances. Thus, the strident critique of "images" (*ta eidōla*) advanced in Book 10 of the *Republic* entangles itself in contradictions whose gradual resolution in later dialogues (*Timaeus*, *Sophist*, *Parmenides*) paradoxically gives rise to the first truly comprehensive theory of the image in Western thought. As a result of the earlier argument's productive miscarriage—as fine a demonstration of philosophical dialectics as one could ask for—Platonic thought ends up yielding the conceptual groundwork for most future thinking about images. Referencing *Republic* 10 (598b), Emmanuel Alloa comments that "the entire history of aesthetics . . . could be read as a single hypertrophic footnote to Plato's original dichotomy," namely, whether the image seeks to imitate being or its appearance. "In responding to [this dichotomy], aesthetics can either (in Hegelian fashion) frame semblance as the mode of access to Being or, conversely (in a vulgar Nietzschean approach), can unilaterally affirm the omnipotence of semblance."[5]

As we shall see, Plato ends up demonstrating that the image can never be written off as a self-contained object but, instead, is ontologically (not just functionally) bound up with the very being *of* which it is the image. As we read in the *Timaeus*, "Since that for which an image has come to be is not at all intrinsic to the image, which is invariably borne along to picture something else, it stands to reason that the image should therefore come to be *in* something else, somehow clinging to being" (52c). Having no reality or being independent of the specific relation to both that which it depicts and, no less crucially, its addressee, the image thus mediates for the beholder the real being, which, in turn, furnishes the ontological warrant for such acts of *mimēsis* to begin with. Hence, as Plato appears to have realized only after completing the *Republic*, images must not be lumped together with other discrete objects (*ta onta*); for they are not fungible with what they depict but, instead, have independent ontological standing. In ways that remain to be scrutinized further, the image is relational (*pros alla*), for which reason "the measure by which we may appraise its valence must be sought in the being that it depicts. When measured against what has been depicted, it becomes evident that the image is *other than*, though not *the other of* what it depicts."[6]

---

5. Alloa 2011b, 39 (trans. mine).

6. "Jenes Maß, an dem sich das Sein des Bildes misst, ist das Seiende, das es abbildet. Am Abgebildeten gemessen zeigt sich, dass das Bild *anders* ist, ohne aber darum bereits *das Andere* des Abgebildeten zu sein" (Alloa 2011b, 22; trans. mine).

It is this decisive qualification, consistently overlooked by iconoclasts through the ages, that takes us to another paradox. For insofar as images neither stand autonomously apart from what they depict nor simply coincide with it, they demand of their beholder a commitment to interpretation that, even as it originates in an act of visual apprehension, can be brought to conclusion only in rational speech (*logos*). An image, then, is never a correlate of perception alone but, instead, a fusion of intuition, perception, and judgment: "To lend [images] an essence is to interpret them as the appearance of a coherent but non-appearing sense; to lend them existence is to interpret them as the index of existing things. Images crave this double interpretation, without which they would be incomprehensible. They cannot interpret themselves." Hence, the reality of images is inextricably bound up with hermeneutic labor, that is, with a process of discernment ultimately consummated in some kind of articulate, meaningful, and revelatory speech or writing; and as Plato discovers, to meet this hermeneutic challenge is to concede that the image cannot be dismissed as mere "non-being" but, instead, possesses incontrovertible reality: "Images are altogether manifest. To deny them is impossible." And yet "it is scarcely possible to describe their reality: they are not nothing, since they occur as images." Instead, they "float without fixity between being and nothingness."[7]

As the relation between visible things (*ta onta*) and their imitation in images (*ta eidōla*) is being rethought in the *Sophist*, it emerges that the image—the *eikōn* rather than *eidōlon*—never truly competes with Being for the same epistemological space. Rather, images are dialectically entwined with being (*to on*); they mediate its numinous essence for finite intellects and, in so doing, lay the very foundation for empirical and philosophical knowledge alike. Far from constituting a static and insurmountable antinomy, Being and non-being turn out to be part of a single, all-encompassing dialectic. Thus, "non-being" (*mē on*) cannot simply be written off as the sheer negation of Being, a pure "nothing" (*ouk on*), any more than it can be validated as an entity of wholly independent standing. For in either scenario it would already have to *be* and, in apparent illogic, would be invested with a reality of its own. Instead, "non-being" (*mē on*) is intelligible only within a dialectic of revelation and concealment; and as the "visitor" from Elea will demonstrate to Theaetetus in the *Sophist*, nowhere does this dialectic manifest itself more clearly than in the medium of the image and the unique hermeneutic practice to which it gives rise.

Yet another of Plato's many paradoxes has to do with the fact that what began as a thoroughgoing critique and refutation of the image ends up yielding an enduring and capacious metaphysical framework for our understanding of it. To that end, Plato's *Sophist* not only has to dismantle the Sophists' approach to knowledge, but, no less crucially, must also exhibit the incoherence of Parmenides's strictly *aniconic*

---

7. Balthasar 2001, 132–34.

conception of knowledge. Neither the physicists' radical empiricism, nor the Eleatics' monistic idealism, nor the Sophists' habit of nominalist equivocation can furnish an adequate model for philosophical inquiry. For each of these positions subverts the possibility of true knowledge of the world. In the case of the Eleatics, the dogmatic claim "that the all is one" denudes Being of all dialectical movement and, in effect, quarantines it from manifest "beings" (*ta onta*) susceptible of meaningful predication.[8] Whereas Parmenides asserts that the One encompasses all and therefore cannot be subject to propositions (true or false) that would link it to the many, the Sophists take the obverse stance by maintaining that there can be no such a thing as a truly false proposition; for any such statement, simply taken as an act and event independent of whether its predicate can be verified or not, has already performatively established itself as a reality in its own right. Parmenidean monism fails in that the truth it posits can never become the property of consciousness. Thus, "Being is a phenomenon only when it is at a distance from itself," when it has been imaged by consciousness; and the task of *mimēsis* "is precisely to institute the interval whereby Being can appear to itself." The requirement of phenomenological distance qua presentation, moreover, is not a contingent or elective one but names the condition under which alone Being can become an object of philosophical awareness. Hence, "the dualism of Being and its proper image, which comes to be thought of as the phenomenal condition of Being, cannot be limited in its scope."[9]

Yet philosophy's essential task of surpassing monism cannot be solved by the Sophists' obverse approach either; for to construe Being as merely epiphenomenal to representation, an equivocal mirage projected by the unlimited free play of rhetoric, is not to have explained reality but to have explained it away. "Non-being" (*mē on*) turns into sheer "nothingness" (*ouk on*). Hence, for Plato to succeed in forging a middle passage between Parmenides's hermetic monism and the Sophists' performative relativism, "our becoming better dialecticians generally" (*Statesman* 285d) is of vital importance. As early as Book 2 of the *Republic* (377e–386c), Socrates characterizes images and stories alike, particularly those of gods and demigods in Homeric narrative and Attic tragedy, as blaspheming and corrupting. This they do whenever "a story gives a bad image of what the gods and heroes are like, the way a painter does whose picture is not at all like the thing he's trying to paint" (377d–e). Reflecting the influence of the Eleatics, Socrates's argument here appears to turn on a strict antinomy of essence and appearance. Put as a rhetorical question to Adeimantus, the fun-

---

8. See *Parmenides* 128a–b, 137b. For the corpus of Parmenides's philosophical statements, including their summary in Diogenes Laertius's *Lives* (Book IX), see Kirk, Raven, and Schofield 1983, 239–62. As Besançon writes, "Parmenidean Being cannot be plural. It is unique: *to on*. Reason, the logos, shows 'being' but never 'Being.' . . . Thus, appearance and *physis* are on one side, truth and metaphysics on the other" (2000, 22).

9. Henry 1973, 66, 68.

damental issue appears to be this: "Do you think that a god is a sorcerer, able to appear in different forms at different times, sometimes changing himself from his own form into many shapes [*phantazesthai allote en allais ideais*], sometimes deceiving us by making us think that he has done it? Or do you think he's simple and least of all likely to step out of his own form?" (380d). With Adeimantus still dithering, Socrates sharpens the point: "If [the god] steps out of his own form, mustn't he either change himself or be changed by something else [*heautou methistasthai ē hyp' allou*]?" Being and appearance here stand vis-à-vis one another as categorically "other" (*allos*). Alterity is not understood as a function of Being's internal differentiation and dynamic becoming but, instead, is conceived as its categorical antonym. Framed as something externally and mechanistically induced, alteration (*alloiōsis*) is squarely the *other of* identity, which again is understood as a timeless cocoon.

For reasons that will become clear in my discussion of the *Sophist*, it bears juxtaposing the concept of alteration to that of transformation. Whereas alteration thus betokens a defect, indeed a kind of declension within being itself, "transformation means that something . . . has become its true being, in comparison with its earlier being." A concept of transformation, which Parmenides's philosophy notably lacks, necessarily requires a medium *in* and *through* which Being can realize its essence more fully. All transformation thus will necessarily involve the transmutation of Being "into an apparent structure [*Verwandlung ins Gebilde*]."[10] For the time being, however, Socrates's argument remains within the purview of Parmenides's aniconic monism, as evidenced by his stipulation that "the best things are least liable to alteration or change" (380e). Implicitly, then, all visible appearance or manifestation is interpreted as the "alteration" (*alloiōsis*) of a timeless essence and, hence, as a lapse or distortion (381c) that genuine philosophical inquiry must avoid.

Where an appearance imposes itself on a listener in the form of an image or a story, the resulting "imitation" (*mimēsis*) is construed as doubly derivative, illicit, and thus as a transgression on the part of the image maker, or indeed as a self-betrayal of the god himself. Already we confront the paradox, not resolved until the

---

10. Gadamer 2006, 111; naturally, the overarching term for the medial "structures" (*Gebilde*) wherein this transformation is realized is art itself. Yet precisely because its core function inheres in this transformative drawing-out of the essence of beings, art cannot be understood in a purely internalist manner, that is, as "aesthetics." As von Balthasar notes, "It is no surprise, then, that the knower is inclined to rest, as it were, in the image world and its signification. He need only give himself to the appearances, need only read them with understanding, in order to be flooded by a wealth of significance. Since this revelation bestows on him more than he can ever lay hold of, he sees no reason to raise himself above the sphere of images. This, then, is how the aesthete lives and views the world. He correctly apprehends that there is such a thing as significance. Yet he falls into another, albeit more subtle, form of detaching the phenomenal image from the core of being as if it were a thing in its own right. Because the image world really shows on its surface the whole self-expressing depth, the aesthete believes that he can dispense with the depth itself" (2001, 143–44).

Sophist, that the imitation in question cannot be a mere "nothing" because, simply qua appearance, it already proves incontrovertibly real. Far from a mere chimera or illusion to be explained away as an aery nothing, mimetic forms instead expand our sense of the real, of Being itself. It is this elemental power of images that prompts Socrates to speak of the *eidōlon* as a "true falsehood" (*alēthōs pseudos*). The phrase hints at the transitional status of the idol, its lingering archaism. Thus, to the extent that it "manifests both a real presence and an irremediable absence at the same time, . . . the archaic *eidōlon* [is] less an image in the sense in which we understand it today than a double."[11] It is this residual, totemic function, this enigmatic and seemingly uncontainable efficacy of the idol, rather than its epistemic deficiency, that constitutes the true target of Socrates's critique of image and imitation. Far from invalidating and dispelling the reality of the image, its being twice removed from the realm of forms only underscores its seemingly boundless adaptivity. Hence, when speaking of imitation as "a kind of game and not to be taken seriously" (*Rep.* 10, 602b), Socrates may well be pushing back against growing evidence that the image, far from being derivative and deficient, actually works *too well*.

While no comprehensive account of Plato's image theory can possibly bypass *Republic* Book 10, there are good reasons to be weary of the exemplary status that the book's dialogue has long been accorded in this regard. Hence, the following brief consideration of how, in his dialogue with Plato's older brother, Glaucon, Socrates here resumes his earlier critique of Homeric mimesis in Book 3 (395c–397c), ultimately treats this final book of the *Republic* as deeply problematic. It is so either because it falls significantly short of the probity with which Plato treats of the central issue elsewhere or, alternatively, because it remains unclear whether Socrates's oddly dogmatic rejection of images might not in the end have to be read as surreptitiously self-ironizing. Both interpretive scenarios will have to be given at least some consideration before we can move on to the *Sophist*, which arguably features Plato's most profound discussion of the image and its metaphysical underpinnings.

For now, let us recall Socrates's major charge against Homer, which concerns the way that his poetry forever vacillates between direct narrative and the speech of characters evidently impersonated by the poet. A subsidiary critique, building on Book 3 of the *Republic* (386a–401d), holds that Homer's listeners are bound to imitate the characters and actions imitated in his poetry. Yet this indictment of Homeric *mimēsis* features an incongruous mix of hyperbole and ambiguity. Who, after all, is responsible for the alleged miscarriage of Homeric imitation? Is it the poet, the performer, or the listener? And what are the specific formal traits that allegedly cause *mimēsis* to impose on the credulity of the beholder/listener in ways that rhetoric— whose practitioners are notably *not* banned from the polis—presumably does not? In

---

11. Vernant 1991, 168.

passing, we note that Socrates's distinction between *mimēsis* as narrative art and as copy-making, respectively, will a millennium later sponsor an at least partial defense of the use of religious images. Thus, in two letters to Bishop Serenus of Marseille from July 599 and October 600, Pope Gregory the Great addresses the increasingly contested theological issue of images depicting Christ's human form or that of saints and the question of what kind of reverence if any they ought to be accorded. His defense of images pivots on their ability to stimulate a lively memory of scripture among the preponderantly illiterate congregants of his time, which is to say, to function as metonyms of biblical narrative: "Pictorial representation is made use of in Churches for this reason; that such as are ignorant of letters may at least read by looking at the walls what they cannot read in books."[12]

Returning to the *Republic*, let us now consider Socrates's well-known charge that "everything mimetic" (*hapantas tous mimētikous*) tends to "distort the thought of anyone who hears it" (595b). Imitation supposedly does this by overwhelming the listener/beholder with its sheer charisma, which causes a shift in focus from the "form" or "idea" (*tēn idean*) of being to its appearance. "What does painting do in each case?," Socrates asks. "Does it imitate that which is as it is, or does it imitate that which appears as it appears? Is it an imitation of appearances or of truth [*ē pros to phainomenon, hōs phainetai, phantasmatos ē alētheias ousa mimēsis*]?" (598a–b). Imitation here is construed as entirely parasitical, devoid of any reality; far from serving as a conduit to the truth of being (*ē alētheias ousa*), it is portrayed as its antagonist. It is quintessentially *non-being* masquerading as Being, a point to be explored with far more nuance in the *Sophist*. Socrates's earlier analogy of the mirror (596d),

---

12. Epistles, Book IX, Letter 105 (*PNF* 13:23); a subsequent, more severely worded epistle to Serenus reiterates the point while also stressing that the issue was never the "adoration" (*adoratio*) of saints depicted, let alone of the image as such, but rather a venue for the faithful to participate in the truth of scriptural narrative: "To adore a picture is one thing, but to learn through the story of a picture what is to be adored is another. For what writing presents to readers, this picture presents to the unlearned who behold it, since in it even the ignorant see what they ought to follow; in it the illiterate read. Hence, and chiefly to the nations, a picture is instead of reading" (Epistles, Book XI, Letter 13 [*PNF* 13:53]); naturally, Gregory's defense presupposes that the images in question reinforce already existing catechetical practice: "Pictures could not be 'live writing' for someone who did not know what the writing said." At the same time, Gregory does not address the practices in which the *adorantes* engaged, which might have legitimately troubled Serenus: "Were people kissing these images, or scraping bits of paint off them, or prostrating themselves before them?" (Noble 2009, 43); see also the landmark 1954 essay by Kitzinger, who traces the growing opposition to religious images during the second half of the sixth century. Drawing on criticisms previously voiced by the Monophysites, that opposition subsequently extends from Bishop Serenus of Marseille in the West to "rebellious priests in Armenia" and Paulician heretics in the East. It is here that doctrinal, in particular Christological, concerns move to the center of a debate that, some one hundred twenty years later will result in the first major wave of Byzantine iconoclasm under Leo III (see Kitzinger 1954, 132–34).

by means of which "you could quickly make the sun, the things in the heavens, the earth, yourself" appear, had already established the antinomian line of argument for Book 10. By their very nature, imitations (*mimētai*) can only ever simulate real beings (*ta onta*), which in turn instantiate their respective ideas in a necessarily imperfect manner.

According to Socrates, images will only ever imitate appearances, not truth, simply because the painter "knows nothing about the crafts" required for making the things that painting depicts. Still, there is something perplexing about his decision to situate painting, a craft whose popularity had lately been surging, in relation to other crafts whose productions it allegedly imitates. Why does Socrates suppose that the painter "attempts to imitate . . . the works of craftsmen" rather than "looking to the thing itself in nature" (598a)? Why not posit instead that, like any other craft, painting also looks to the form of what it depicts rather than to the object wherein that form has been contingently realized? Here the legitimacy and quality of a given image is said to depend entirely on whether it verifiably imitates its "image object" (Husserl's *Bildgegenstand*). Yet once imitation is appraised solely with a view to its success in copying, or mirroring, a material reality, failure will be the only option. For in that case the image either falls short of copying particular being or, where it succeeds in the trompe l'œil sense of Zeuxis's painted grapes and curtains, it can no longer be distinguished from its object referent and, thus, effectively obliterates itself.[13] Either way, Socrates is only prepared to credit the image (*eidōlon*) with an ethos of fabrication or simulation, thereby defining it as the contrary of (though curiously also as parasitical on) real existent objects. It has no intrinsic dimension, does not participate in the reality it depicts, and, as a result, lacks all symbolic power. Perhaps, as Lambert Wiesing has argued, the incoherence addling Socrates's critique of the image stems from a lexical imprecision introduced by Plato's modern translators. As he notes, "*Depiction* is a mistranslation of *mimesis*. . . . For 'mimesis' is a genus; it corresponds to a wide concept of imitation," of which "depiction" and "copying or replication" are the two principal ones.[14] Even so, in strange contrast to arguments found earlier in the *Republic* and in the later dialogues, Book 10 appears committed to denying the image any truth-bearing capacity.

Indeed, Socrates in Book 10 of the *Republic* never seems to entertain the possibility that images might possess intrinsic significance. Hence, as he resumes his argument ("Therefore [*porrō*] imitation is far removed from the truth" [598b]), his deductive confidence rests on the assumption that truth is incommensurable with

---

13. Ultimately, these competing paradigms of the image as sheer illusion and as simulacrum of the real, respectively, collapse into one another, thereby in effect dissolving the image as a distinct reality. Plato acknowledges as much in the *Cratylus*, with Socrates observing that "an image cannot remain an image if it presents all the details of what it represents" (432b).

14. Wiesing 2010, 106.

the realm of appearances. Yet this rigid antinomy of truth and appearance, Being and manifestation, remains something of an outlier even within Plato's own oeuvre; indeed, Gadamer considers it a "crass absurdity," one whose illogic Plato himself gradually analyzes and overcomes.[15] There can be no question that just about every other discussion of image and appearance in Plato's corpus proves more searching and incisive as regards both their ontological underpinnings and the phenomenology of their experience. In trying to account for the sheer incongruity of Book 10, which he considers a somewhat "artificial addition" to the *Republic*, Wiesing has noted that Plato's use of "mimesis" covers two fundamentally incompatible forms of visualization: "depiction" and "copying." Only the former truly qualifies as an "image" (*eikōn*) insofar as here "it is not something actual that resembles something else but something appears to a viewer to resemble something else." By contrast, where we speak of a "copy, . . . a material object is to possess physical resemblance to another material object." Yet in that case, we are no longer looking at an instance of mediation but, instead, are presented with an instance of outright substitution or simulation that effectively strips mimesis of any symbolic and noetic dimension. In the event, though, Wiesing is forced to concede that in Book 10 "an equivocal concept [*mimēsis*] is not yet recognized and reflected on its equivocality; it belongs to an early phase of philosophical argumentation in which necessary differentiations have not yet been completed.[16] Even so, it is odd that in the final book of the *Republic* Socrates the consummate dialectician should still not have sought to clarify his premised antinomy of truth and appearance, nor, where mimesis is concerned, have made a serious attempt to sift its conceptual implications. As a result, Socrates's sharp "divide" (*chōrismos*) between form and mimesis threatens to undermine the reality and significance of his doctrine of ideas, rendering the latter impossibly remote, indeed conjectural, and in so doing inviting the type of critical treatment that Platonic "form" and "idea" receive in the early books of Aristotle's *Metaphysics*.[17]

There remains, however, the possibility of an alternate reading, one that would view Book 10 as the culmination of Socratic irony. On this account, the *Republic*, the first and possibly greatest political utopia, winds up on a note of extreme structural irony. Socrates's conspicuously doctrinaire rejection of mimesis and his proposed

---

15. Gadamer 1986, 16.

16. Wiesing 2010, 107–8.

17. Unlike Vernant, and more in sync with Pollitt (*The Ancient View of Greek Art*, 1974) and Joly (*Le renversement platonicien*, 1974), I do indeed posit a structural tension or "a conflict between the discussion in the *Sophist* and that in the *Republic*" (Vernant 1991, 169). Book 10 seems the outlier, not only in view of the far more nuanced discussion found in the *Sophist* and in Books 6 and 7 of the *Republic*, but because even in the (putatively earlier) *Cratylus*, Socrates expressly distinguishes— as in Book 10 he curiously fails to do—between an imitative "craft [*technē*] . . . concerned with imitating qualities" such as "sound and shape" and the craft "of someone who imitates the being or essence of things" (423d, 431d).

expulsion of all imitators from the polis, rather than being taken at face value, might be read as a reductio ad absurdum. The draconian measures here so unceremoniously urged in that most inconclusive of genres, Socratic dialogue, thus might be read as grotesquely overstating the "chasm" (*chōrismos*) separating idea from appearance and, by implication, parodying the certainties to which a philosophical culture dominated by the Sophists habitually lays claim. At the very least, there is a grim irony in the fact that Socrates, who in Book 10 accuses the painter of "deceiving the children" (598c), had been sentenced to death for this very crime some nineteen years before Plato writes the *Republic*. Just like Socrates's hectoring indictment of all "imitators," the charge had been contrived in bad faith back then and, resurfacing two decades later in Plato's text, once again comes across as inflated and lacking a clear warrant. Perhaps by the time readers have reached Book 10, it is expected that they have mastered the art of structural irony so characteristic of Socrates's performance throughout the preceding books.[18] Or, alternatively, the concluding book's peculiarly rigid argumentation is part of Socrates's strategy of "holding back" knowledge for which he considers his interlocutors to be as yet unprepared. "What prevents Socrates from sharing the medicine [*pharmakon*] of knowledge is an oath . . . to pass on the 'things of superior value' only if the cognitive and ethical conditions for their adequate reception exist."[19]

In at least one respect, however, Book 10 anticipates the far more nuanced appraisal of images found elsewhere in Plato and, indeed, prepares the ground for their defense in the writings of the Byzantine iconodules—John of Damascus, Theodore of Stoudios, and the patriarchs Nicephoros and Photios—a millennium later. Thus, Socrates concedes "that all poetic imitators, beginning with Homer, imitate

18. According to Wiesing (2010, 111), Plato "criticizes what he criticizes as if it were a copy. Yet this, precisely, is the decisive point: he criticizes something that is not a copy but presents itself as a copy for doing so—and this something, for him, is the image." For to contend that "Plato treats all forms of mimesis as if they were copies even though some—images, precisely—are not copies" is to overlook the terminological shift from *eidōlon* to *eikōn*, as well as Plato's later concern with situating *mimēsis* vis-à-vis a metaphysics of "participation" (*methexis*). Precisely the image's participation *in*, and manifestation *of*, the reality of forms, however, lies at the heart of Plato's later dialogues. Were it not for this concept of participation, Plato could not navigate between the equally self-defeating notions of imitation either as an outright duplication of beings or as encroaching on a Parmenidean concept of Being and Truth as wholly numinous and impenetrably self-contained.

19. Szlezàk 1993, 90 (trans. mine); Socrates "often makes it explicit that he has more to say about a topic currently being explored yet is not prepared to do so at this time" (29). Plato's critique of writing (see *Phaedrus*, 274b–278e; *Seventh Letter*, 344c–d) in any event underscores the provisional nature of all philosophical inquiry. Remarking on the essential incompleteness of Platonic dialogue, Pieper observes that, "by its very nature, dialogic form is best suited to demonstrate that the 'most profound' knowledge and wisdom, what is 'ultimate' and 'essential' [*das Letzte, das Eigentliche*] is *not* the property of the author" (2002, 224; trans. mine).

images of virtue [*tous poiētikous mimētas eidōlōn aretēs*]" (600e). What may at first glance seem a stray remark turns out to break with the founding assumptions of Book 10. For here at last the image is construed not as parasitical on ectypal beings but as looking directly to the archetypal forms (of virtue) themselves. Such a position also chimes far better with the *Republic*'s overarching focus on what lies "beyond being [*epekeina tēs ousias*]," namely, the Good (*to agathon*) and "its image [*tēn eikona autou*]" (509a–b). Socrates' analogy, according to which the sun is to the visible world what the Good is to the intelligible world (508c), hints at the ontological filiation of the visible with the Good. A further corollary of the nexus between the visible and the intelligible realms is that between visible beings ("animals, plants, . . . manufactured things") and their images (*phantasmata*), on the one hand, and that between knowledge and opinion, on the other: "as the opinable is to the knowable, so the likeness is to the thing that it is like [*homoiōthen pros to hō hōmoiōthē*]" (510a). In effect, Plato here is premising an ontological coordination of the visible with the numinous, that is, an analogy of being and participation, that will eventually be worked out in philosophical theology from Aquinas to Erich Przywara. Were it not for this *analogia entis*, human beings would remain forever unable to account for their intuitively meaningful encounter with sensible, in particular visible, phenomena, while, conversely, whatever notions and concepts abstract thought happens to yield could never be intuitively cashed out. Hence the idea of knowledge that emerges in Plato's dialogues is not that of an impermeable cocoon but, rather, a progressive understanding of how the numinous truth of forms is continually mediated by the realm of appearances, which in turn are experienced as significant precisely because we intuit their relatedness to that truth. Thus, once a visible impression is recognized as manifesting a concrete reality, it becomes the "stepping stone to take off from, enabling [reason] to reach" the form itself, what Socrates calls the "unhypothetical principle." Far from being the antonym of the intelligible, visible appearance—distilled in the medium of the image—furnishes the indispensable fuel for reason's progression toward the Good.

That said, to speak of the "image" (in contrast to the material artifice of the "picture") as a *medium* requires further clarification. To begin with, we need to acknowledge that Socrates does not have a concept of the "medium" in the way that modern, art historical, and anthropological inquiry understands the materiality of pictures (e.g., color, texture, tonal shading, size, proportions) and their medial character. Whereas a modern anthropology of images regards "the picture [as] the image with a medium," arguing that the latter "helps us to see that the image neither equates with living bodies nor with the lifeless object," Socrates considers the material scaffolding whereby *eidos* is transposed into *phantasma* as being in direct competition with the material object that is being depicted. As Belting notes, "The image always has a mental quality, the medium always a material one."[20] For the purposes of reading Plato, then, "medium" does not refer to the material realization of the image qua "picture" but to the way that the reality and truth of forms (*eidē*) is entwined with their phenomenalization as "images" (*eikones*). The Platonic image essentially names an action of the mind, a specific kind of mental striving, such as the focused activity of remembering or some other reaching toward insight. As Socrates remarks in the *Phaedo*, "Our sense perceptions . . . surely make us realize that all that we perceive through them is striving to reach that which is Equal [*ison*] but falls short of it." For an image to be experienced as such, "we must have possessed knowledge of the Equal itself if we were about to refer our sense perceptions of equal objects to it" (*Phaedo* 75b). For Plato, the image thus mediates an antecedent (divinely infused?) knowledge. Insofar as it facilitates the "remembering" (*anamnēsis*) that is the very foundation of human knowing, the Platonic image shows itself to be essentially noetic. Its sensory dimension remains strictly subordinate to its intellectual function, with *eikōn* enabling mind to grasp the relation between a given appearance and its form. That the image is capable of "mirroring the essence in the appearance" at all presupposes moreover the subject's elemental receptivity to it, which "occurs in an immediately more than sensory, indeed intellectual space." The Platonic *eikōn* thus throws into relief the essential complementarity of intellect and sensible being that prompts Socrates to remark "how lavish the maker [*dēmiourgon*] of our senses was in making the power to see and be seen" (507c). As such, the Platonic image bears witness to that metaphysical coordination or "ordering" (*kosmos*) of mind and world by presenting itself as "a suspended middle [*schwebende Mitte*] between the appearance and the thing that appears."[21] Indeed, were it not for the mediation of the "image" (*eikōn*), finite reasoners could never even begin to "grasp the power of dialectic [*tē tou dialegesthai dynamei*]" (511b).

At the same time, no image can ever overcome the ontological difference separating appearances from forms. Hence, when taking Socrates to "mean what happens in geometry [*hypo tais geōmetriais*] and related sciences" (510d–511b), Glaucon identifies geometry as the art (*technē*) uniquely suited to distill "clear" images from the shadowy and inchoate realm of appearances below. The reduction of the image to lawful forms could be read as a philosophical rationale for the geometric abstractions of Malevich, Feininger, and Mondrian some twenty-five hundred years later.

---

20. "Within the triad image-medium-body, medium refers to the technology or artisanship that transmits the image to whatever it is that gives visibility to the image" (Belting 2011b, 9, 11, 15, 20); see also Alloa's incisive discussion of Aristotle's use of *diaphanēs*, which he reads as a first outline of a theory of the image as constitutively "transparent" medium (2011b, 91–101); on Plato's discrimination between the neuter *eidos* and the feminine *idea*—with the latter being consistently chosen in reference to the Good—see Schindler 2008, 140.

21. Balthasar 2001, 153, 138; trans. modified.

Indeed, Socrates's example of geometry raises a fundamental question: Do the visible forms presented by the geometrician merely serve to "illustrate" abstract concepts of his art? Or are those concepts themselves, as worked out by Euclidian geometry, merely ex post facto clarifications of a knowledge intuitively acquired by seeing the forms in question? Be that as it may, the purpose of Socrates's own bit of modernist abstraction—the "divided line" of 509d—reinforces two fundamental points: (1) the "intelligible relations of geometric similarity do not encompass all the particular beings and their distinctive characteristics" and (2) the realm of appearances, though ever irreducible to that of forms, remains nevertheless at all times analogically related to them.[22] Hence, as Socrates acknowledges, dialectics is bound up with "terms of relative clarity and opacity," beginning with that "subsection of the visible [which] consists of images." Its only fuel is "imagination" (*eikasia*), the power of making images (*eikones*). Hence, the ectypal realm of images or likenesses is never outright *opposed to* though always *distinct from* the realm of forms or ideas. Unlike the Sophists, who err by always construing difference as a static antinomy, Socratic dialectics regards the apparent tension between the realm of visible appearance and that of forms as generating all "thought" (*dianoia*) and, thus, guiding the mind toward a vision of the Good.

Arguably the *Republic*'s most prominent discussion of images—ironically presented in what turns out to be a "strange image" (*atopon eikona* [515a]) in its own right, producing an abundance of ironies and paradoxes—is the allegory of the cave (Bk. 7, 514a–530a). Most obviously, there is the structural irony of arguing the deficient nature of the ectypal realm by means of an elaborate image on which Socrates bestows an equally elaborate interpretation, thus revealing the image as precisely the kind of dialectical stimulant that Book 10 claims no imitation can ever be. Yet for Socrates's interpretive outline of the allegory to take hold and for his listeners not to succumb to the cave dwellers' idolatrous conflation of image (shadow) and reality, the reader must achieve hermeneutic distance vis-à-vis both the world of appearances and the verbal allegory that seeks to draw out their epistemic limitations. For the philosophical task at hand is not to reject the image as mere shadow play or some derivative (and hence illicit) projection but, instead, to recognize and dialectically harness its hermeneutic potential. "This is why we can say that in an image it is not something actual that resembles something else but something appears to a viewer to resemble something else."[23] Or, as Allan Bloom remarks, "only the awareness that an image is an image makes it possible to judge its true character."[24] Hence, too, it is

---

22. Zuckert 2009, 360; "reflections or images may be more or less accurate, but none is simply false" (360).

23. Wiesing 2010, 107; "depiction is concerned with creating an object on which an image object appears for the viewer, an image object that, in a physical sense, is not present at all" (108).

24. Bloom 1968, 404.

that in unfolding his allegory Socrates continually draws on the faculty of human sight as the very foundation for philosophical insight. These interlocking and evolving modalities of seeing and comprehension, then, ensure the allegory's dialectical progression toward "the form of the good, [which] is the last thing to be seen, and . . . reached only with difficulty" (517b). In charting this movement toward the good, the parable must continually recalibrate the traveler's respective epistemological "situation" (*topos*) and the relative degrees of knowledge it will support. Indeed, "there is a great deal of progress to be made before one arrives at the sublime height of pure reflection, and the use of images—similes, analogies, parables, myths . . . — can in a variety of ways play a constructive role in the development of one's understanding of important issues and ideas."[25] For the overarching objective, which is to exit the cave rather than illuminate it, necessarily requires of the learner "time to get adjusted before he could see things in the world above" (516a).

While visible things necessarily stand in ectypal relation to forms, the practice of imaging them here is not disparaged but, on the contrary, identified as the terrain *through which* and *by means of which* alone human cognition can advance. Were Socrates to institute a sharp antinomy between the sensible and the intelligible, readers of the allegory would be unable to identify in it any narrative progression or philosophical yield. The image itself would remain forever opaque. Foreshadowing the same narrative pattern of *exitus-reditus* found in Plotinus's *Enneads*, Augustine's *Confessions*, Bonaventure's *Itinerarum Mentis in Deum*, and Nicholas of Cusa's *De Venatione Sapientiae*, Plato's "upward journey of the soul to the intelligible realm [*eis ton noēton topon*]" (517b) outlines a visual catechesis, an education *into* the senses rather than the rejection of sense-based cognition as idolatrous and false.[26] What defines a philosophically sound and ethical vision is, first, that the things seen are grasped as realities distinct from the images by which they are mediated for the intellect; and, second, that the resulting knowledge must be articulated for a community. By contrast, what invalidates the idol is its purely private, proprietary, and hermetic nature, which amounts to no more than the isolated cave dweller's projection. Intrin-

---

25. Patterson 2013, 438–39. As Plato's allegory puts it, "When someone sees a soul disturbed and unable to see something, . . . he'll take into consideration whether it has come from a brighter life and is dimmed through not having yet become accustomed to the dark or whether it has come from greater ignorance into greater light and is dazzled by the increased brilliance" (518a); hence Bloom notes, the philosopher can only ever function as "a guide, not a torchbearer. The attempt to illuminate the cave is self-defeating: a part of man craves the shadows" (1968, 403).

26. On the tradition of the "spiritual senses," see the essays in Gavrilyuk and Coakley 2012. Naturally, in the millennium separating Plato's writings from the Byzantine iconoclastic struggles, Platonic thought came to be inflected by writers of various backgrounds: pagan (Plotinus, Porphyry, Proclus), Jewish (Philo), and Christian (Basil of Caesarea, Gregory of Nyssa, Augustine, and, perhaps most crucially, in the corpus Dionysiacum); invariably, then, Plato must be understood as naming a complex and internally fractious interpretive tradition rather than as a single voice.

sic to the idolatrous gaze is, further, its fetishizing of beauty as coming first in the order of experience. In fact, as Jean-Louis Chrétien notes while recalling the etymological link between "beauty" (*to kalon*) and a "calling" (*kalein*), "the Platonic tradition . . . has thought beauty to be, in its very manifestation, a call, a vocation and provocation. . . . Things and forms do not beckon us because they are beautiful in themselves, for their own sake, as it were. Rather, we call them beautiful precisely because they call and recall us." Taking Chrétien's "us" in its strict, plural sense, we note that what Socrates calls "education" (*paideia*) is by definition a dialogic and communal practice, a "turning around" (*metastrephō*). It "takes for granted that sight is there but that it isn't turned the right way or looking where it ought to look" (518d). Arising from such redirection, sight becomes alert and responsive to meanings that are not privately asserted but communally received. For meaning that cannot be shared is no meaning at all; or, as Chrétien puts it, "visible beauty calls for spoken beauty."[27]

IMAGE THEORY AS METAPHYSICS: DIALECTICS OF BEING AND NON-BEING IN PLATO'S *SOPHIST*

As we turn from the *Republic* to Plato's later discussion of the image in the *Sophist*, two interlocking terminological shifts need to be considered. The first concerns Plato's introduction of the concept of "participation" (*methexis*), in the *Parmenides* and the *Sophist*, where the term serves to balance his as yet unstable notion of mimesis. The second shift, already hinted at, involves Plato's parsing of image as "idol" and "icon," respectively. Let us start with the first.

In a landmark essay from 1978, Gadamer revisited the age-old question of whether Plato did "at first really . . . teach that the ideas were apart for themselves until one day he recognized that the problem of participation entailed in the postulation of such ideas for themselves was altogether insoluble? Or do both postulations belong together: the ideas being for themselves, the so-called *chōrismos* (separation), and the difficulty, to which one is thereby exposed, concerning participation, or *methexis*, as it is called." Ultimately, as Gadamer persuasively argues, the "*chōrismos* is not a doctrine that must first be overcome [but] . . . an essential component of true dialectic," which in turn must not be "advanced as evidence against the *chōrismos* and is not a remedy for it."[28] As we shall see, no other concept is more consequential for understanding the ontological valence of images in relation to the truth of Being than that of *methexis*. Indeed, in coining the neologism *methexis* (a compound of *meta-* and *echein* = "to have/share with"), Socrates furnished a conceptual blueprint

---

27. Chrétien 2004, 3, 11.
28. Gadamer 1986, 9–10, 19–20.

for arguments that centuries later would underwrite the Trinitarian and incarnational doctrines gradually refined between the Councils of Nicaea (AD 325) and Chalcedon (AD 451), as well as the *imago Dei* conception of the human being.[29] As regards the latter, its Platonic undertow clearly shows in Gregory of Nyssa's *On the Making of Man*, written around Easter 379 when, commenting on Genesis 1:27 ("in the image of God" / *kat' eikona theou*), he remarks, "Image is *not in part* of our nature, nor is the grace in any one of the things found in that nature, but this power extends equally to all the race: and a sign of this is that mind is implanted alike in all. . . . Our whole nature, then, extending from the first to the last, is, so to say, one image of Him Who is."[30] Absent an ontology of participation (of the finite human being in divine Being) human sensory experience could never transcend its contingent nature, a predicament addressed in Gregory's doctrine of the "spiritual senses" and, much later and in a very different key, in Hegel's critique of "sense-certainty" in the *Phenomenology of Spirit*.[31] An implication of the concept of participation that, unlike Gregory, Plato has not yet drawn out involves the concept of creation, in contradistinction to material production or biological reproduction. For *methexis* posits that visible being—both in all its particulars and as a whole—has reality and is intelligible only insofar as it manifests its invisible "form" (*eidos*). Participation and creation thus are two sides of the same coin, for only by participating in its form can a thing manifest itself as a *distinct* and *specific* appearance susceptible of perception and understanding. This convertibility of being and intelligibility implied in Plato's concept of participation will occupy us again later. For now, let us recall the central passage in which Plato unfolds that concept in the *Parmenides* as the older, eminent philosopher puts the key question to the "young Socrates" thus:

> PARMENIDES: "Is it your view that, as you say, there are certain forms from which these other things, by getting a share of them, derive their names—as, for instance, they come to be like by getting a share of likeness, large by getting a share of largeness, and just and beautiful by getting a share of justice and beauty?"
> "It certainly is," Socrates replied.
> PARMENIDES: "So does each thing that gets a share get as its share the form as a whole or a part of it. . . . Do you think, then, that the form as a whole—one thing—is in each of the many? Or what do you think?"

---

29. See especially the decrees from the Council of Rome (AD 382), Denzinger 2012, nos. 163–76; letter from Cyril of Alexandria to Nestorius during the Council of Ephesus (AD 431), no. 250; for the anathemata pronounced against Nestorius at the time, nos. 252–57.

30. *PNF* 5:406 (*On the Making of Man*, XVI.17); emphasis mine.

31. "By the very operation of our senses we are led to conceive of the reality and intelligence which surpasses the senses." *Of the Soul and Resurrection*, quoted in Coakley 2012, 48; see Coakley's discussion of Gregory's conception of the "spiritual senses" (36–55); see also Hegel 1977, 58–67.

"What's to prevent its being one, Parmenides?" said Socrates.

PARMENIDES: "So being one and the same, it will be at the same time, as a whole, in things that are many and separate; and thus it would be separate from itself."

"No it wouldn't," Socrates said. "Not if it's like one and the same day. That is in many places at the same time and is nonetheless not separate from itself. If it's like that, each of the forms might be, at the same time, one and the same in all." (131a–b).

To Parmenides's objection that if the many were to participate in the One, they would themselves have to be "composed of thoughts" and thus become pure "mind" (*nous*), Socrates replies, "That isn't reasonable. . . . These forms [*eidē*] are like patterns [*paradeigmata*] set in nature, and other things resemble them and are likenesses; and this partaking of the form [*hē methexis hautē tois allois gignesthai tōn eidōn*] is, for the other things, simply being modeled on them" (132d). Discussing this passage, Gadamer emphasizes that "Plato is obviously fully aware of the paradox in a participation or taking part [*Teilhabe*] that does not take *a* part, but participates in the whole."[32]

Now, while *methexis* posits an ontological continuum between appearance and idea, it no more asserts their substantive *identity* than it concedes their outright *antinomy*. Instead, the term asserts an essential relatedness between the Platonic forms and the contingent realities said to share in them. In ways that, as we shall see, will prominently resurface in Goethe's theory of the symbol, the concept of "difference" here does not operate disjunctively but, through the medium of the image, affirms the ontological relatedness of form and appearance. Hence it is a category error to reify the image as but one more entity among others. In fact, the one essential trait of the image (*eikōn*)—in contrast to its many contingent, formal, and material permutations—is precisely this: it stands in dialectical relation (*pros alla*) to the respective form or being *of* which it is the image, and it has no reality independent of this relation.[33] In his *Lives and Opinions of Eminent Philosophers*, written sometime during the third century AD, Diogenes Laertius distinguishes between "things

---

32. Gadamer 1986, 11.

33. On this point, Gadamer's claim that "the logical connection of the man to the one" brought out by the concept of "participation" (*methexis*) "was not implied in *mimēsis*" seems overdrawn. It is hard to find a warrant for his claim of a "change from *mimēsis* to *methexis*" and its constituting a "decisive turn" on Plato's part such as "renders *mimēsis* an inappropriate expression" (1986, 11–12). Gadamer qualifies his point, however, when he remarks on the complementarity between the two terms, with *mimēsis* emphasizing the nature of that which participates in the idea and *methexis* "starting from the other side, . . . and in so doing, leav[ing] the ontological status of what participates undefined" (12–13).

absolute [*kath' heauta*]" and "those which are relative [*pros ti*]." While the former require no external criteria for their explanation, "those which are called relative . . . stand in need of some explanation, as that which is greater than something or quicker than something, or more beautiful and the like. For the greater implies a less, and the quicker is quicker than something. . . . And in this way, according to Aristotle, Plato used to divide the primary conceptions also."[34]

It is precisely this relational or "relative" kind of being that defines the image as both distinct from and essentially related to the reality it depicts. As Alloa puts it, "For the image to be valid *as an image* and function as a presentation [*in seiner Darstellungsfunktion*], it must be the image *of something* and, thus, be ordered *pros alla*."[35] In the event, Diogenes blurs his distinction by using the Aristotelian *pros ti* rather than Plato's *pros alla*. The shift matters in that Aristotle's formula "de-ontologizes" the relation in question, construing it as strictly a matter of ascription and convention. By contrast, Plato's *pros alla* posits an intrinsic "resemblance" (*homoiōsis*) of image and being not subject to an external act of institution or definition. By contrast, where the metaphysical kinship between being and appearance has been suspended, the concept of participation quickly loses all relevance, and the "question concerning the image's ontological valence [*Frage nach dem Sein des Bildes*] is supplanted by a concern with the image's referent and its addressee [*wovon es ein Bild und wem es ein Bild ist*]."[36] Pushing back against Aristotle's immanent and contingent view of the image-archetype relation, von Balthasar stresses that "the image is an original expression [*ein ursprünglicher Ausdruck*]. It is a creation, not an imitation. . . . It expresses something that it is not, because it itself is only the expression *of* something [*von etwas*]. Though it is not that something, the image does contain it in the form of expression. Indeed, it is precisely what the image is not—being's power to give an image of itself—that enables the image to be an image in the first place."[37]

Far from being quarantined from the realm of appearances, the reality of forms is visibly and recognizably accomplished in the domain of the many. Appearances participate in being by rendering its totality and order comprehensively manifest. They share in a numinous reality from which they nevertheless differ without, however, being its diametrical other. Parmenides's dilemma has to do with the fact that within his idealist monism there is no place, no function for appearances at all. Here the image is viewed as altogether "bereft of truth or as a pallid copy that is irrelevant

---

34. Diogenes Laertius, *Lives* III.109 (www.perseus.tufts.edu/hopper/text?doc=D.%20L; accessed 30 July 2019).

35. Alloa 2011b, 26 (trans. mine).

36. Ibid., 27. Curiously, it is the *pros ti* of Aristotle's *Categories*, rather than the Platonic idea of *methexis*, that will provide the foundation for Patriarch Nikephoros's defense of icons in the early ninth century; see the incisive discussion by Mondzain (2005, 86–92).

37. Balthasar 2001, 140 (trans. modified).

for knowledge." Hence, for Parmenides to clarify the role of images and appearance in general means "dissolving them into a concept or immediate intellectual intuition, as if the appearances were merely a mist that dissipates in the rising sun. The substantiality of the world's existence in itself triumphs over the inessentiality of mere appearance. And so, in the end, it becomes incomprehensible why there is any appearance at all."[38] Yet precisely this failure to account for the image, which is incontrovertibly given in experience and real per se, exposes the blind spot in Parmenides's philosophical framework. For his part, Plato will solve the dilemma by having Socrates dialogically work out that manifold appearance is itself an integral trait of being, not its antonym. Insofar as the relation between form and appearance is one of participation (*methexis*) it presupposes their ontological consubstantiality (*homoousia*). Indeed, once this dialectical relation is properly grasped, yet only then, it becomes clear why the ontology of participation must be complemented by a phenomenology of the image.

There is another sense, though not made fully explicit by Plato, in which the concept of participation bears on our understanding of the image. For not only does the image mediate contingent being with the form that it imperfectly realizes; the image thereby also institutes a community whose members share in the knowledge thus mediated. As we shall see in Bonaventure and Nicholas of Cusa, not only does the image visibly reveal how contingent being participates in the truth of form. The image itself is also the object of a different kind of participation, that of the beholder witnessing this self-manifestation of the truth of being qua beauty—"this radiant property of truth, . . . thanks to which every encounter with truth is a new event," as von Balthasar puts it.[39] This impulse to share the truth of the image, which is experienced as the gift of beauty, turns out to be one of several Platonic motifs strongly present in Kant's aesthetics. Hence, as Kant rightly notes, even as the content of aesthetic experience cannot be captured by a determinative judgment, the *experience* of the beautiful is inextricably entwined with its "communicability" (*Mitteilbarkeit*). Thus, the meaning of the "aesthetic-reflective judgment" is validated by the degree to which a community can participate in that judgment. It is this capacity of the image to bring into existence a spiritual community, in which truth has been communally received rather than privately conceived, that also features prominently in the writings of late medieval contemplatives such as Julian of Norwich and Nicholas of Cusa.

Let us now take up the second shift, mentioned above, which concerns the bifurcation in Plato's nomenclature of the image as *eidōlon* and *eikōn*, respectively.

---

38. Ibid., 136; in speaking of "the essence of truth," which a strict rationalism or idealism fails to grasp, as "the revelation in the appearance of the very being that does not itself appear" (*erscheindende Offenbarung des nichterscheinenden Seienden selbst*) (137), von Balthasar hews conspicuously close to Heidegger's analysis of the concept of phenomenon in *Being and Time* (§ 7).

39. Ibid., 141–42.

Throughout Plato's writings, discussions of *mimēsis* and images are almost always associated with the figure of the Sophist as "copy-maker" (*eidōlopoion* [*Sophist* 239d]) or the "maker of likenesses" (*tēn eikastikēn . . . technēn* [*Sophist* 235d]). Now, the later Plato's preferred term for "image," *eikōn*, is not attested prior to the fifth century, and its emergence has been linked to a wider cultural development, unfolding between the seventh and fourth centuries BC, that saw the focus of the image shift from a representation of the invisible to an imitation of appearance.[40] The older term, *eidōlon*, thus tends to foreground the ephemeral visibility and apparitional character of appearance, for which reason Allan Bloom frequently renders it as "phantom," a decision justified by the Greek use of the diminutive (*-ōlon*). By contrast, the relatively new coinage *eikōn* places stress on the image's constitutive relatedness to (*pros alla*) real being, its participation in it and, hence, its capacity to manifest that reality in the medium of an image.[41] Notably, the new word *eikōn* places greater stress on the image's adequation to that *of which* it is the image while rejecting the possibility that visuality and appearance are intrinsically significant.

The stated purpose of the *Sophist* is, of course, to ferret out its eponymous figure, that most elusive public persona of fourth-century Greek culture. Probably so as to avoid framing the dialogue as but another rhetorical contest that, for the Sophists, had proven such lucrative business around Athens, Plato here silences Socrates altogether. The true nature of philosophy and those practicing it must not be indexed to some particular individual but, instead, is to be impersonally unfolded between the unnamed stranger from Elea and Theaetetus, with Socrates present but *silent* throughout. Plato thus "suggests that we ought not to look for the philosopher somewhere else, but instead ought to look more closely at what is already in front of us."[42] Where the very nature of reality, of Being and non-being, is at stake, knowledge stands to be drawn out from within each participant because it is common to all; it is part of their very being rather than a discrete intellectual "position" temporarily held by a rhetorically skilled reasoner seeking to persuade others. Using the "method of division" first sketched in the *Phaedrus* (265d–266b), the stranger from Elea offers a preliminary characterization of the Sophist "as the money-making branch of expertise in debating, disputation, controversy, fighting, combat, and acquisition" (226a). Soon afterward, the stranger introduces a fundamental analogy between the painter

---

40. See Vernant, "From the 'Presentification' of the Invisible to the Imitation of Appearance" (1991, 151–63) and "The Birth of Images" (164–85).

41. Alloa (2011b, 18) points out that *eikōn* derives from the Indo-Germanic root *ṛeid* or *id-*, "which points to a primordial fusion of seeing and cognition" subsequently reflected in the Greek *idein* ("to see") and *eidenai* ("to discriminate, know") and, ultimately, *eidos* and *idea* ("aspect, Gestalt, form").

42. Schindler 2008, 221.

and the Sophist, arguing that both fraudulently claim "expertise to make and do everything" (*technē sunapanta epistasthai pragmata* [233d]). In fact, their pretended "making" turns out to involve nothing more than an impressive facility in "the game of imitation" (234b). Thus, the Sophist is depicted as a kind of word painter or "wizard" (*goēs*) who imposes on his gullible listeners with "spoken copies [*eidōla legomena*] of everything, so as to make them believe that the words are true" (234c). He is a "cheat and imitator [*goēta . . . kai mimētēn*]" (235a) who produces false appearances.

While all that may seem straightforward enough, it turns out to pose a major problem, not least for a self-identified member of the Eleatic school of Parmenides and Zeno (216a). For according to Parmenides's teachings, there is only one thing—Being/Truth—and "nothing" (*ouk on*) else. Such a monism simply leaves no room for "non-being" (*to mē on*) or "false" appearances such as those allegedly disseminated by the Sophists. Hence, in order to prove his case against the latter, the stranger from Elea will paradoxically have to dismantle the philosophical framework of his revered teacher from Elea. "What," he asks, "should the name, *that which is not*, be applied to?" (237c). The analogy between the purely logical notion of "non-being" and the phenomenology of *mimēsis* is palpable enough; and the basic question ("Can non-being be predicated?") evidently pertains as much to the perceptible world of the "many" as to the numinous "One" (238e). This "One" is neither a number, as it will be for Aristotle, nor some logical singularity from which multiples might be deduced. Rather, it is the "source" or primal "cause" (*aitia*) of *all* being. Parmenides's error stems from the fact that by characterizing "non-being" as "unthinkable" (*adianoēton*), "unsayable" (*arrēton*), "unutterable" (*aphthegkton*), and "unformulable" (*alogon*), he implicitly invests it with grammatical and formal-logical identity while at the same time insisting that no reality corresponds to it. Yet, the stranger concedes, "what is not in any way would not even be capable of being pronounced."[43] Hence, as he leads Theaetetus to conclude, the negations at the heart of Parmenides's strict apophaticism end up affirming the very reality they would disavow.

---

43. Natorp 2004, 263; "Hence what is not, conceived as such and without qualification (*auto kath' auto*), cannot legitimately be pronounced or said or thought. . . . The critique of the concept of non-being is partly directed . . . against the sophist, who supposes that, in showing that non-being—understood in an absolute sense (which in reality is no sense at all)—is indeed in every way impossible, he has reduced the concept of non-being itself to absurdity. On the other hand, however, . . . the critique is directed against Parmenides' thesis that only being is and that non-being is not in any way, hence is unthinkable and unsayable. This claim proves to be self-contradictory. . . . The central paradox leads to a conclusion of foundational importance for understanding the logic of appearance and the ontological valence of the image. For it shows that 'Being' itself is something different from what it is predicated of [*das Sein selbst ist etwas Andres als wovon es ausgesagt wird*]" (264, 267).

It is in the context of clarifying the logical relationship between Being and non-being, or reality and appearance, that Plato introduces the corollary distinction between "two types of copy-making[,] . . . likeness-making and appearance-making [*eikastikēn kai phantastikēn*]" (236c). Whereas "likenesses" are subject to verification and cross-referencing with the thing from which they allegedly derive, "appearances" (*phantasmata*) seem, if anything, harder yet to locate within a general epistemology. For the very attempt to do so "involves the rash assumption that that which is not is, since otherwise falsity would not come into being" (237a). To make matters worse, the notion of "likeness" itself soon begins to unravel as well, it proving seemingly impossible to parse likeness and copy.

> THEAETETUS: What in the world would we say a copy is, sir, except something that's made similar to a true thing and is another thing that's like it [*heteron de legeis toiouton alēthinon*]?
> VISITOR: You're saying it's another *true* thing like it? Or what do you mean by *like it*?
> THEAETETUS: Not that it's *true* at all, but that it resembles the true thing.
> VISITOR: Meaning by *true*, really being?
> THEAETETUS: Yes.
> VISITOR: And meaning by *not true*, contrary of true?
> THEAETETUS: Of course.
> Visitor: So you're saying that that which is like is not really that which is, if you speak of it as not true.
> THEAETETUS: But it *is*, in a way.
> VISITOR: But not truly, you say.
> THEAETETUS: No, except that it really is a likeness.
> VISITOR: So it's not really what is, but it really is what we call a likeness [*hēn legomen eikona*].
> THEAETETUS: Maybe *that which is not* is woven together with *that which is* in some way. It's quite bizarre. (240a–c)

In the end, "likeness" turns out to be just "another true thing." By dint of its incontrovertible reality qua appearance, what Husserl will eventually call the "absolute givenness" of the phenomenon, likeness confirms that non-being is not the "contrary of true [*enantion alēthous*]" but a specific manifestation of it. In the event, the distinction between a true likeness and sheer semblance cannot be sustained. For the very notion of a "likeness" can neither be reduced to a mirror-style "phantom" or "copy" (*eidōlon*) nor simply disaggregated from the being to which it relates and which it makes appear. Hence, the alleged nothingness of "semblance" (*phantastikē*) turns out to be an integral component of Being. As Paul Natorp puts it, "Appearing is just as much something positive as is . . . non-being."[44] Still, to put it thus remains too defensive a formulation. For not only has the dialogue by now established the distinct reality of image and appearance, and by extension the dialectical bond between Being and non-being. It has also made clear that unconditional, self-enclosed, numinous Being (*to on*) cannot even be thought without its dialectical other: the image.

Important here is the terminological shift, in the exchange just quoted, from a positively unreal "appearance" (*phantasma*) to a simulation or "copy" (*eidōlon*) of being to an actual "likeness" (*eikōn*), which latter is neither a mere duplicate of being nor a reality separate from it. Hence, the initial distinction between the making of appearances and likenesses, respectively, does not amount to a hard-and-fast opposition but can only serve heuristic purposes. Plato's metonymic progression from *phantasma* to *eikōn* shows that the relation between form and appearance, Being and non-being can no longer be construed as an opposition. As Natorp observed long ago, non-being, when "understood in the sense of negative positing and not in the sense of absolute annihilation and nothingness," furnishes the essential complement to the Parmenidean concept of Being as self-identity and non-relationality. As such, non-being is "not the contrary [*Gegenteil*], but the obverse aspect of being [*Gegenseite des zunächst unbezüglich gedachten Seins*]." Indeed, the ontological valence of non-being as this "obverse aspect" of Being itself, and hence its phenomenalization in the medium of the "image" or "likeness" (*eikōn*), is an *essential* feature of Being. It is not a contingent predicate of Being but unveils the latter's dialectical constitution. "Non-being," that is, "belongs just as much, or almost more, to being as does the non-relational (i.e., pre-relational aspect [of being]). For being . . . signifies, in the most fundamental sense, relation [*Sein besagt . . . grundwesentlich Beziehung*]." Hence, Natorp concludes, "non-being *is*, by virtue of partaking in being [*das Nichtsein ist, indem es am Sein teilhat*]."[45] This indeed is what the visitor summarizes (258d–e), once again emphasizing the relational and essentially dialectical nature of Being while also cautioning that "to dissociate each thing from everything else is to destroy totally everything there is to say. The weaving together of forms is what makes speech possible for us" (259e).

In opposing the Sophists' view of reality as consisting of nothing but equivocal and endlessly contestable propositions, Plato commits himself to a philosophical

---

44. Ibid., 262; "non-being does not mean what is 'contrary' (*enantion*) to being, but only being different."

45. Ibid., 279–80 (trans. modified). While Wiesing (2010, 117–20) is right to note that in the *Sophist* Plato recognizes that not all imitation strives for "likeness" (*Ebenbildnerei* in Schleiermacher's translation), his reading unhelpfully abides within the antinomy of "likeness-making" and "appearance-making," which must not be taken in an ontological sense, since doing so would ignore the entire and pivotal analysis of the dialectic bond between being and non-being. In fact, the antinomy serves only heuristic purposes.

framework in which statements acquire meaning and significance only because (and insofar as) they are *about* something that has independent reality. As the *Phaedo* had shown, the *logoi* that reveal truth about beings constitute judgments, not concepts. The *Sophist* affirms as much when pointing out that intelligible speech, whether true or false, concludes a process of "thinking" ("the soul's conversation with itself"), "belief" ("the conclusion of thinking") and "appearing," which the stranger characterizes as "the blending of perception and belief" (264b). Judgments rendered in the form of intelligible propositions are therefore intrinsically bound up with the reality of appearances. They are defined by their "aboutness," by their characterizing X *as* Y and, hence, not reducible to mere names referring to an isolated "this." For "to try to separate everything from everything else is the sign of a completely unmusical and unphilosophical person" (259d–e). Intelligible speech (*ho logos*) thus proceeds integratively, moving as it does from discrete beings (*ta onta*) to their true being (*to on*) or form (*eidos*). In its constitutive "aboutness" or relational quality, intelligible speech (*logoi*) presupposes a reality whose order (*logos*) transcends the contingency of the things with which such speech is concerned. A judgment thus does not simply *name* but properly *mediates* being. At the same time, even as it is in the very nature of propositional speech to *transcend* a given phenomenon, it can do so only *by not losing sight* of the latter, that is, of how its subject gives itself in experience. For with the exception of mathematics, what we call judgment "doesn't happen on its own but arises for someone through perception," and precisely where this is the case we speak of "appearance [*phantasia*]" (264a).

Once more, the dialogue takes up the nature of "image-making" and the earlier distinction (236c) between the making of "likenesses" (*mimēsis eikastikēn*) and that of "appearances" (*phantastikēn*). Ostensibly, "appearance-making" is explicit about its status in that here "falsity appear[s] truly to be falsity [*pseudos ontōs on pseudos*]" (266e). Such a seemingly paradoxical notion of an imitation whose semblance-like nature "truly appears to be a falsity" paves the way for a fundamental shift in Plato's thinking about images. For where imitation employs illusionist techniques, the artist is either conscious of doing so or not (267b); and where the material and perspectival choices underlying the making of an "appearance" have been made with full awareness, they will have been shaped not only by the *object* of imitation but also by consideration of the *addressee* to whom the image or sculpture is directed. We recall how, when first introducing the distinction between likeness- and appearance-making, the former was defined in sculptural terms as the kind of imitation where the maker "keeps to the proportions of length, breadth, and depth of his model" while also adhering "to the appropriate colors of its parts." In response to Theaetetus's sensible question ("But don't all imitators try to do that?"), the stranger had pointed out that, particularly with "very large works," individual parts of a sculpture have to be adjusted based on the beholder's viewpoint.

In what is often thought to be an allusion to Phidias's famous *Athena Parthenos*, erected in 438 BC in the Parthenon temple on the Acropolis and reputedly measuring almost forty feet in height, the stranger suggests that mimetic fidelity is observer-dependent. Whereas in Book 4 of the *Republic*, Socrates had insisted that the proportion of a statue's individual parts is answerable to the whole, the stranger now appears to take the obverse position.[46] For sculptors simply to "reproduce the true proportions of their beautiful subjects," with no concern for the beholder's viewpoint, would end up distorting the object as perceived by the observer.

> STRANGER: The upper parts would appear smaller than they should, and the lower parts would appear larger, because we see the upper parts from farther away and the lower parts from closer.
> THEAETETUS: Of course.
> STRANGER: So don't those craftsmen say goodbye to truth, and produce in their images the proportions that seem to be beautiful instead of the real ones?
> THEAETETUS: Absolutely. (235e–236a)

It is tempting to read this exchange as a key moment in the passage beyond semblance or illusion and thus as confirmation of the gradual shift that, on Vernant's account, "starting from idols that functioned as symbolic actualizations of different models of the divine, . . . finally arrived at the image, properly speaking: that is, the image conceived as an imitative artifice reproducing in the form of a counterfeit the external appearance of real things."[47]

Yet to speak with such ease of artifice and counterfeit is to overlook the fact that, certainly in the *Sophist*, such "making of appearances" is interwoven with Plato's dialectics of being and truth. To be sure, the religious cult of archaic seventh-century Greece appears to have effectively collapsed by the time Plato is writing, such that

---

46. "Suppose, then, that someone came up to us while we were painting a statue and objected that, because we had painted the eyes . . . black rather than purple, we had not applied the most beautiful colors to the most beautiful parts of the statue. We'd think it reasonable to offer the following defense: 'You mustn't expect us to paint the eyes so beautifully that they no longer appear to be eyes at all, and the same with the other parts. Rather you must look to see whether by dealing with each part appropriately, we are making the whole statue beautiful'" (*Rep.* 420c–d). For discussions of this issue, see Wiesing 2010, 112–21; Alloa 2011b, 40–49.

47. As Vernant goes on to argue, "The symbol that actualizes, that makes present in this world below a power from the world beyond (a fundamentally invisible being) is now transformed into an image that is the product of an expert imitation, which, as a result of skillful technique and illusionist procedures, enters into the general category of the 'fictitious'—that which we call art" (1991, 152). The thesis effectively reproduces Hans Belting's magisterial account of a shift from cult image to art image, albeit at a period much earlier than the one in which Belting locates this development.

"the statue is no longer required to operate in the world as an efficacious force." Its totemic power and its ritualized cycles of presentation and concealment have been supplanted by consciously wrought imitations whose "task [it] is to act on the eyes of spectators, to translate for them in a visible way the invisible presence of the god and communicate some lesson about divinity." Inasmuch as "the statue is 'representation' in a really new sense," Vernant concludes, by "bringing out the body's properly human dimension, sculpture initiated a crisis for the divine image . . . [that] must have also aroused a distrustful reaction." Indeed, he finds evidence of these misgivings specifically in "the work of Plato: nostalgia for ancient divine symbols, attachment to the most traditional forms of representing the gods, and reservations about all kinds of figuration of the divine."[48] Still, even as the unease in question may well account for Plato's ambivalence about *mimēsis*, the dialectical line pursued throughout the *Sophist* and also in Books 6 and 7 of the *Republic* works against conventional readings of Plato according to which images and appearances are inherently false. In fact, Plato gradually realizes that by their nature images are both related to and ontologically distinct from the invisible forms that they render visibly manifest.

Likewise, Plato's argumentation shows that, far from an inauthentic semblance imposed on a credulous viewer, the image's true valence is properly realized only in the beholder's hermeneutic engagement with it. It is only by reflecting, sifting, speaking, and writing about the image that its ontological status, as well as philosophy's own dependence on *mimēsis*, is properly revealed. The scrutiny brought to bear on the image, then, is not adversarial in nature but, on the contrary, is integral to "realizing" (in the Hegelian sense of *verwirklichen*) its full import. Hence, too, a hermeneutic of the image may legitimately focus either on the discrete illusionist techniques employed, its foregrounding of certain aspects of its referent, or the imitation's ability to elicit variously affective or intellectual responses. Yet all of these discrete foci can be cultivated only if the image's reality qua appearance has been unconditionally accepted and, along with it, the image's ontological relation (*pros alla*) to the truth of being that it makes appear. Fundamentally, *mimēsis* must always be considered from both an ontological and a phenomenological perspective. In this regard, Plato's admission that judging the "true proportions" (*Sophist* 235e) of a sculpture or image pivots on the relation between image and beholder constitutes a major advance in Western image theory. Henceforth, "the stage, . . . where the conflict between the legitimate and the illegitimate *pros alla*, between *eikōn* and *eidōlon* (and thus between philosophy and sophistry) plays out is none other than the space of manifestation [*nichts anderes als der Raum des Erscheinens*]."[49]

---

48. Ibid., 159, 163.
49. Alloa 2011b, 44.

As noted before, appearances qua appearances are incontrovertibly *given*. Moreover, they are inevitably limited in scope, and their very mode of self-manifestation always raises the possibility that we may be deceived about them or, at the very least, will grasp their depth only in part and imperfectly. Still, even for that to happen we must not only have accepted their givenness as such, but, in our evolving appraisal of appearances as "likenesses," must receive them as conduits to a reality that does not show itself per se. Indeed, "the *Sophist* marks the point where *the question of being can no longer be posed outside the space of its phenomenality [jenseits des Raums der Phänomenalität].*"[50] Yet Plato's insight into the dialectical bond of Being with non-being, form with appearance, also means that in responding to the image's reality and presence we are not asked to choose between an ontological and a phenomenological approach. For, as the *Sophist* makes clear, the image can be apprehended *as an image* only if the beholder understands it to be at once essentially related to what it makes manifest and at the same time belonging to a different order of being. Furthermore, this dialectic whereby the image has being only by dint of "relating to" (*pros alla*) a reality that essentially differs from its own must not be misconstrued as a mere philosophical proposition, let alone an aesthetic convention. On the contrary, the dialectic in question encompasses every configuration into which form and appearance can conceivably enter. For both being and image must share in one and the same ontology, the very notion of multiple ontologies being an absurdity. Consequently, a robust concept of the image (*eikōn*), understood neither as a mere simulacrum nor as a quasi-discursive signifier, requires a robust concept of transcendence.

As we saw, the *Sophist* establishes that to conceive the image as but one more "object" inter alia would be a category error. Rather, the image is medial in its very essence, revealing to the beholder not only that the self-manifestation of being unfolds in the realm of appearances (*phantasmata*), but, conversely, that the truth of appearance is consummated in the medium of the image. Hence, contrary to what a straightforward reading of *Republic* 10 suggests, the image (*eikōn*) is not parasitical on actual beings (*ta onta*) but participates, albeit only in medial form, in their very being. The point is brought out late in the *Sophist*, where the stranger hints that the true source of images is not found in the finite (human) "maker of likenesses" but, instead, is of a transcendent, divine nature. Thus, as philosophy presses its inquiry into the essence of appearance, it invariably confronts what von Balthasar calls "being's power to give an image of itself [*die Macht des Seins, von sich selbst ein Bild zu geben*]."[51] As remains to be seen when turning to twentieth-century phenomenological accounts of the image, to speak of an "appearance" or "phenomenon"

---

50. Ibid., 46.
51. Balthasar, 2001, 140.

is to be confronted with a complex structure, a "self-showing" (Heidegger), a logic of "manifestation" (M. Henry) or "self-giving" (Marion) wherein visible things, prior to becoming the focus of determinative inquiry, must have been intuitively apprehended as disclosures of a numinous and invisible *logos*. Groping toward a proto-phenomenological framework of this kind, the closing exchange between Theaetetus and the stranger or "visitor" (*xenos*) reads thus:

> VISITOR: There are copies of . . . things, as opposed to the things themselves, that also come about by divine workmanship.
> THEAETETUS: What kind of things?
> VISITOR: Things in dreams, and appearances that arise by themselves during the day. They're shadows when darkness appears in firelight, and they're reflections when a thing's own light and the light of something else come together around bright, smooth surfaces and produce an appearance that looks the reverse of the way the thing looks from straight ahead.
> THEAETETUS: Yes, those are two products of divine production [*tauta theias erga poiēseōs*]—the things themselves and the copies corresponding to each one." (266b–c)

To say that things and their copies, that is, appearances (*phantasmata*) and the images (*eikones*) mediating them, are the results "of divine production" is to hint at a fundamental analogy between numinous Being and visible phenomena. Beyond that, Theaetetus's conclusion also implies that whereas the finite human agent can "make" the material "picture," the image (*eikōn*) that is its true noetic correlate is by its very nature something received, not made. Where a depiction (*Darstellung*) is to be produced, an image must have already disclosed itself, and the source of that disclosure necessarily transcends the mind that receives it. Moreover, even as human picture-making mediates an image so inexplicably and incontrovertibly received—a gift begging fulfillment by what Cézanne calls *réalisation*—the process does not end here. For the material picture is itself but a first attempt to grasp the implications of the intuitive vision of which the image is the *noēma*. Ultimately, human beings' enduring fascination and hermeneutic struggle with images is a way of responding to the "incomprehensible certainty" (as Hopkins calls it) of the transcendent irrupting into the order of finitude. It is no accident, then, that a great deal of modern phenomenology, arguably the one strand in post-Enlightenment philosophy most responsive to questions of transcendence and metaphysics, came to constitute itself specifically as a prolonged meditation on the nature and import of visual experience. In so doing, phenomenology (not just in Husserl) proves most directly and enduringly responsive to Plato's rich and controversial reflections on the metaphysical and ethical dimensions of the image.

"MIND RETURNING INTO ITSELF":
METAPHYSICS OF VISUAL COGNITION AFTER PLATO

The focus, in this chapter as throughout the book, is on how images are experienced and how, in turn, their phenomenology is articulated in writing. How, that is, does philosophical, theological, and literary writing variously grasp the image's medial function and, in so doing, help unveil its metaphysical implications? Considering modernity's confidence that metaphysical questions could be, and by and large had been, settled on exclusively immanent terms, it cannot surprise that post-Cartesian thought sought to frame the image mainly as an epistemological challenge. Henceforth, the image will be construed as essentially convertible with other instances of matter (*res extensa*), that is, as one more entity begging to be propositionally explained and verified rather than as a call to be answered. In true Nominalist fashion, post-Kantian aesthetics thus tends to frame verbal expression either as supervening on the image or as outright incommensurable with it. The contrast with classical thought is palpable, in particular with Plato's painstakingly developed notion of a dialectical bond between image and reality according to which the *eikōn* derives its very being from its relation (*pros alla*) to the reality it mediates, a reality that would forever abide in monistic occlusion were it not for the image *in* and *through* which it becomes phenomenally manifest. That said, Plato's concept of appearances "participating" in the realm of ideas remains fundamentally speculative. It is not amplified into a theory of (aesthetic) judgment because for him participation is not the discrete act of an individual human agent but a metaphysical given. According to Plato, that is, acts of judgment cannot *instantiate* the bond between appearances and ideas; they can only make it *explicit*. The "relation" whereby an image is substantially bound up with the being of which it is the image is not itself a product of discursive convention or taste. Rather, the relation at issue forms part of an essential dialectic that, we have seen, shows the being of forms to be ontologically entwined with the "non-being" of appearances.

By contrast, Aristotle is no longer prepared to conceive of the "relation" between appearance and idea as intrinsic to their very being. Instead, there is a general push in Aristotle toward a conceptualist reframing of the metaphysical questions he inherits from Plato, questions he does not reject, yet whose scope, he insists, can be extracted from the performative vagaries of Platonic dialogue and reframed in a more ratiocinative idiom. Whereas Gadamer had maintained that "from early on Aristotle was critical of Plato's doctrine of the ideas but nonetheless was, and remained, a Platonist in his works," Alloa finds Aristotle consistently reinterpreting Plato in pointedly "de-ontologizing" ways.[52] Thus, in his *Metaphysics* (1088a26–30), Aristotle

---

52. Gadamer 1986, 14; Alloa 2011b, 27.

abandons the Platonic conception of the image as ontologically related to (*pros alla*) the being it makes visible. Instead, that relation now becomes one of contingent ascription (*pros ti*) or definition rather than a case of transcendent disclosure. In the event, Aristotle's finite reconception of the image produces tensions of its own. For once "*mimēsis* is no longer grounded in the reality of depiction [*Abbildlichkeit*], nor in that which is being depicted [*im Abgebildeten*]," the original question concerning the ontological status of the image has to be reformulated. "No longer do we ask *what* an image is but, instead, *to what extent x is an image of y*."[53] Thus begins the image's slow and steady migration from transcendent revelation to finite artifact.

Even so, Plato and Aristotle concur that an image's essential purpose can only be realized by hermeneutic practices that extend far beyond a merely passive gaze. Only if the image's powers of disclosure—that is, its capacity for manifesting the reality of forms for an attentive and reflective intelligence—have been made explicit and realized in a community of dialogue, only then will the image truly have accomplished its essential mission. To respond to an image is to embark on a trajectory of progressively more articulate, dialogic reasoning and, in so doing, to allow the meaning of an image to be consummated in acts of human, "ensouled" speech. Hence Aristotle defines "voice" (*phōnē*) not only physiologically ("the impact of inbreathed air against the windpipe"), but insists that "what produces the impact must have soul in it." And for that to happen, voice "must be accompanied by an act of imagination" (*phantasia*).[54] Elsewhere, he remarks how "spoken sounds are symbols of affections in the soul," with "written marks" (*graphomena*) in turn being "symbols of spoken sounds." Inasmuch as all of these signs arise from "affections in the soul," they presuppose an antecedent, shared field of reference: "But what these are in the first place signs of— affections of the soul—are the same for all; and what these affections are likenesses [*homoiōmata*] of—actual things—are also the same."[55] Whether *phantasma* is to be translated as "image" or, more generically, as "mental representation"—in the Kantian sense of *Vorstellung*—remains uncertain and contested. Not in doubt, however, is Aristotle's claim that human ("ensouled") speech and its interpretation arise from sensory, often visual impressions of the world, and that articulate and purposeful speech is essentially contiguous with these impressions or, at the very least, seeks to establish itself in continuity with them.

At the same time, the continuity in question ought not to be conceived in terms of efficient causation, that is, of images as it were mechanically "triggering" speech. Rather, spoken and written discourse constitutes itself in considered response to "likenesses" (*homoiōmata*) that, Aristotle insists, are also experienced by others. To

---

53. Alloa 2011b, 27.
54. *De anima* 420b28–32.
55. *De Interpretatione* 16a3–7.

articulate the import of a given image presupposes, and in turn seeks to consolidate, an interpretive community for which a shared image and the "affectations"
(*pathēmata*) it calls forth may become a founding presence. To write and "interpret"
(*hermēneuein*) an image thus means to acknowledge and honor it, not as an isolated
object, let alone as a private experience, but as a presence summoning the beholder
to bear articulate witness to the *logos* made manifest in the "image-appearance"
(*phantasma*). An integral feature of all image-consciousness, as Husserl calls it, thus
concerns the hermeneutic activity to which an image summons its beholder; and
as the latter struggles to discern and articulate its import, she may come to embrace
the image as the conduit toward a community of knowledge. Phenomenologically,
it matters to keep such "discerning" separate from "judging" the appearing image
in the form of a determinate proposition. As Alloa has shown, William Moerbeke's
thirteenth-century rendition of a key passage in *De Anima* (426^{b}10), according to
which sensory perception (*aisthēsis*) already implies a type of cognitive "discrimination" (*krinein*), has sown much confusion. For by translating *krinein* as "judging" (*iudicare*), Moerbeke foreclosed on the possibility that visual perception as such
might set in motion an open-ended process of nonpropositional, gradual discernment rather than expire in an instantaneous and definitive act of predication. Crucial
for Alloa's account and, also, for the readings developed throughout this chapter
(and indeed my entire argument) is precisely the possibility that Moerbeke's restrictive translation forecloses on—namely, that "the aesthetic opens up onto the transcendent *logos* without being outright congruent with it."[56]

To appreciate the integrative and disclosive power of images, we must keep in
view the logical distinction between sense perception and judgment, albeit without
causing it to harden into an outright dualism between raw "sense data" (*aisthēta*) and
"concepts" (*noēmata*). Our hermeneutic engagement with visual phenomena and
with images in particular, far from framing them as pre- or irrational "stuff," apprehends them as intrinsically and holistically meaningful entities not fungible with ordinary objects in the world. Images or, as Marion calls them, saturated phenomena,
appear imbued with meanings that not only logically precede, but, as regards their
experience, exceed the scope of propositional and discursive speech. Inasmuch as
the meaning of images seems synthetic rather than analytic, integrative rather than
disjunctive, their ultimate significance rests with bringing about a community of
knowledge rather than some contingent and ephemeral revelation in the individual
beholder. As Plotinus will note, "Since all souls derive from the same from which the
soul of the Whole derives too, they have a community of feeling."[57] Linking visual

---

56. Alloa 2011b, 65–67; quote from 67 (trans. mine).
57. *Ennead* IV.3.8; citations of Plotinus follow the Armstrong (Loeb) text, identifying the text
group (Roman numerals), followed by the treatise and chapter numbers (Arabic numerals).

sensation with the implicit *logos* made explicit in speech and writing is the notion of form. As we shall see, the Neoplatonist tradition views image (*eikōn*) and form (*eidos*) as profoundly entwined and, ultimately, as ordered toward an internal, nonpictorial (mental) vision whereby the intellect returns to the One of which it is the supreme emanation. As Plotinus will insist time and again, such a mental vision transcends, yet is not opposed to, discursive reasoning and propositional knowledge. Its distinctive intentionality, known as "contemplation" (*theōria*), requires a capacity for self-transcendence, a stance of sheer receptivity and humility that, under the heading *Gelassenheit*, the later Heidegger will once more summon against the domineering ethos of modern instrumental rationality.[58]

As remains to be seen, the Neoplatonist legacy will resurface in Husserl's account of image-consciousness, which likewise identifies a purely "apprehensive" (*auffassendes*) rather than "determinative" (*bestimmendes*) consciousness as the image's proper locus. Thus, the meaning and significance of images (*Bildsujet*)—though crucially mediated by the depicted "image object," which in turn is premised on the material "image scaffolding" (*Bildträger*)—are of an ideational nature. To be sure, image-consciousness cannot arise independent of the material concreteness of sight and its visible "object." Yet, as Aristotle had argued, we must distinguish between the sheer sensory apprehension of a particular thing and its being *taken-as* an image. Hence, he distinguishes between "proper sensibles," that is, primitive and unfiltered sensory impressions, and perception, which begins to identify raw data by parsing *accidens* and *forma*. The result is a third, inductive stage wherein the beholder achieves "a full conceptual grasp of external particulars by abstracting the *intelligibilia* from their perceptible representations."[59] Crucially, whatever meanings are abstracted from sense data are, on Aristotle's account, "drawn *from*" those data rather than projected *onto* them: "Thus, while concepts give true, deep significance to sensible particulars, sensible particulars truly imply their deeper significance. Concepts are immanent in objective reality for Aristotle, shrouded, yet somehow implied."[60] Hence, the Aristotelian concept ratifies and explicates, but does not contest, the ontological priority of Platonic "form" (*eidos*). Indeed, insofar as the concept makes the reality of forms explicit, Aristotle's realist account of cognition hews close to Plato's view of knowing as remembering (*anamnēsis*) whereby the mind is (re)turned to the transcendent source of the forms, just as the image is ontologically related to its archetype. The more fully a sensible appearance is being worked through and internalized in the form of *veridical*, as opposed to gratuitously "constructed," meanings,

---

58. Heidegger 2014, 27–71.

59. See *De Anima*, II.6 (418a); and for a compact discussion of Aristotle's epistemology, Smith 1981, 571–75.

60. Smith 1981, 571.

the more its perceptible scaffolding recedes into the background as but the image's material cause. Concurrently, attention shifts to the formal cause of the image, which consists of whatever is recognizably depicted on a wood panel, a clay or plaster wall, or a canvas.

Ultimately, the true locus of the "image," as opposed to its material and formal conditions of possibility, remains the apprehending consciousness itself, which honors the reality contained in all transient appearance by distilling the "species" in a form of mental sight. Hence Aristotle, no less than Plato, emphasizes the pivotal role of mental images (*phantasiai*) and, not infrequently, mines the complex etymological affinities of the Greek *eidos* (form), *eidon* (aorist: "I saw"), and *oida* (to know), which resonates in the Latin root *spec-* that ties together intro*spec*tion, *spec*ulation, and per*spec*tive. As Mark Smith notes, Aristotle's "theory of cognition by abstraction, once understood in terms of visual metaphor," shows how in the realist framework concrete visualization and abstract knowing (by means of mental imagery) are contiguous and commensurable. Just as it is true that in Aristotle's account, "apperception has been subtly transformed into an act almost of *seeing* the world intelligibly," so the materiality of sight and the ideality of mental vision are integral and mutually sustaining components—act and potency—of a single ontology.[61] There cannot be an objective *eikōn* absent an internal, "fulfilling intention," that is, without a form (*eidos*) apprehended as intrinsically significant and subject to hermeneutic scrutiny. Only if the formal aspects of what is visually apprehended trigger some kind of "focal awareness" (Polanyi) can a visible phenomenon be apprehended as an instance of symbolic "presentation" (*mimēsis*), that is, as an image. There has to be a marked shift in "perspective" (Husserl's *Einstellung*) such as will cause the beholding consciousness to reframe the "percept" (*aisthēton*) as an "image" (*eikōn*). For only where the depicted object is intuited as mediating an "image-subject" (Husserl's *Bildsujet*), will the noetic act of "image-consciousness" (*Bildbewusstsein*) truly stand apart from ordinary "object-consciousness" (*Gegenstandsbewusstsein*).[62] Only then is the mind's relation to the visible no longer one of unilateral appropriation but of reciprocal transformation.

Hence, if in Aristotle's visual theory of knowledge "action is invariably 'interaction,' . . . it is not enough to say that the external object or inherent color causes sight. The medium and the eye are causes too."[63] Thus, whatever is found to be of significance in the image pivots on the mind's willingness to suspend empirical certainty in favor of an open-ended process of hermeneutic discernment; and as an

---

61. Ibid., 574.
62. For a fuller discussion of Husserl's phenomenology of image-consciousness, see ch. 8 below.
63. Smith 1981, 577.

ethos of verification yields to an interpretive quest, the strong possibility arises that the beholding subject may itself emerge substantially transformed from its engagement with the image. In the case of ordinary perception, the "fulfilled intention" involves the verification (or falsification) of meanings taken to be available independently and beforehand. By contrast, the shift from percept to image, and from *visus* to *visio*, leaves behind the ostensibly self-contained realm of facts for the conspicuously fluid domain of values and goods. Among other things, a unifying feature of the next several chapters—on Plotinus, Nicholas of Cusa, and Goethe—will be precisely this reciprocal transformation of both image and beholder.

Once recognized as ontologically distinct from object perception, the image nudges its beholder to devise hermeneutic strategies no longer premised on Aristotelian formal logic and hemmed in by the law of contradiction. Instead, the image is conceived as the fruit of an interior vision, that is, as a "mental image" unveiled rather than a human contrivance. It mediates a process of insight or, in Plotinian terminology, an ascent to a plateau of mystical darkness and unknowing, a realm of contemplation essentially distinct from any anthropocentric domain of total visibility. Whereas garden-variety objects confront the perceiving subject as an epistemological puzzle of sorts awaiting a solution, things are quite otherwise in the domain of the image. For the interior, contemplative vision of the (Plotinian) One, the Trinitarian God of Dionysius and Cusa, or the *Urbild* about which Goethe finds himself corresponding with Schiller constitutes a mystery that, in grasping the world in its entirety as a parable, marks not the beginning but the culmination of a spiritual-cum-intellectual progression.[64] Here as in later chapters, the pattern remains the same, namely, that as it prompts us to discern its import, the image ends up abolishing itself as an objective entity and, instead, resolves itself into a strictly mental, indeed virtual reality.

Unsurprisingly, the complementary relation between a Platonist and an Aristotelian understanding of mental imagery, interior vision, and the knowledge associated with them did not go uncontested. Thus, a proto-reductionist approach to Aristotle's visual epistemology can already be observed in some thirteenth-century writers, such as Roger Bacon (1214–92), John Pecham (1230–92), Robert Grosseteste (1175–1253), and Witelo (1220–78). Focusing almost exclusively on the physiology and mechanics of sight, now understood as a purely optical, a-semantic occurrence, these "perspectivists" (as Mark Smith calls them) strip sight and vision of their speculative dimension. Increasingly, the metaphysical reality of *light* is dis-

---

64. Goethe's closing lines to *Faust II* capture this Neoplatonist conception of the world-as-parable and, hence, as an irresistible mystery with all due simplicity and clarity: "Alles Vergängliche / Ist nur ein Gleichnis; / Das Unzulängliche, / Hier wird's Ereignis" (lines 12,104–7).

placed by an anthropocentric and geometric concept of perspective, which in time will be treated as the sole cause determining the material nature and epistemic reach of sight. By the early fifteenth century, theories of linear, single-viewpoint perspective pioneered in the writings of Brunelleschi, Alberti, Vitruvius (on architecture), Ghiberti, Piero della Francesca, and their underappreciated precursor, Biagio Pelacani, further intensify the perspectivists' proto-naturalist reading of Aristotle. The result is a progressive elision, and at times an open contestation, of Aristotle's metaphysical realism. Not until the fifteenth-century rediscovery of Platonist and Neoplatonist thought in the work of Cusanus, Ficino, and Mirandola will a robust challenge be mounted to this reduction of vision to mere sight, and to the anthropomorphic construal of perspective as "a system and not just an intention," an approach that sought to curtail the validity of images to their mathematically "correct proportion."[65]

Much of this book will trace this Neoplatonist and unapologetically metaphysical conception of the image, both in its pagan (Plotinian) and post-Enlightenment (Goethean) instantiation, between which stands Nicholas of Cusa's luminous fusion of Neoplatonism with late medieval mystical theology. Extending far into the modern era, Neoplatonist thought appraises the image mainly in relation to contemplative states that fundamentally alter the way that mind relates to the ambient world. Such a contemplative appraisal of the perceptible world—of plants, fossils, and faces no less than of visual artifacts—causes the visible image (*eikōn*) to be assimilated to the notional realm of form (*eidos*). The writings of Plotinus, pseudo-Dionysius, Bonaventure, Cusanus, and Goethe all share this concern with the image's ideality and transformative powers. Insofar as the image has been internalized, and its eidetic potential fulfilled, it facilitates a type of contemplative self-awareness, a "joining of the contemplator and the contemplated," as Porphyry phrases it.[66] Here mind confronts the ethos informing its own gaze, that is, the pivotal moment when, in Plotinus's words, "the soul moves from its own content to itself" (IV.4.2).

On this account, the (mental) image is not, as it later will be for the British empiricist tradition from Hobbes to Priestley, a derivative of perception, just as ideas are not considered mere epiphenomena of sensation. In stark contrast to the Neoplatonist account, Hume considers ideas to be no more than "faint images of [sensory impressions] in thinking and reasoning," set apart from actual sense impressions

---

65. Belting 2011a, 136, 152. Smith (1981) offers an exceptionally detailed and compelling account of the incipient naturalism and scientism animating the Aristotelianism of Galen, Bacon, and Witelo in particular; see also Lindberg 1976, esp. 87–121, and the discussion of Cusanus below, 360–80.

66. Porphyry 2014, *On Abstinence*, I.29.

solely by the "degrees of force and liveliness with which they strike upon the mind, and make their way into our thought or consciousness."[67] Where, in characteristically Nominalist fashion, ideas are construed as mere vestiges of concrete sense perceptions, it follows (as Hume and, more stridently yet, Thomas Reid were to argue) that there simply cannot be such things as "general ideas" or Aristotelian, substantial forms. In time, the epistemological function of "form" appears increasingly denuded of its quasi-visual presence in consciousness. Instead, the notion of form, especially in Kant, becomes increasingly assimilated to the abstract and purely intellectual function of the "concept" (*Begriff*), even as it persists in the subterranean form of Kant's "transcendental schematism," absent whose mysterious yet indispensable operations no synthesis of the sensible and the intelligible would ever be possible.[68] By contrast, the Neoplatonist tradition considers sensations and ideas as ontologically distinct, though not unrelated, let alone opposed. Failure to grasp their distinctness is, ultimately, a function of a defective ethos of being in and visually engaging the world. Hence, whatever distrust Plato had expressed about images resolves itself into a critique not of images per se but of an idolatrous and unreflective mentality incapable of grasping the visible as the trace of, as well as our best conduit toward, the triad of the Good, the Beautiful, and the True. *Eidōlon*, not *eikōn*, is the target of Plato's disapproval.[69] His misgivings will be echoed by Augustine, who laments as "a terrible slavery of the soul this taking of symbols for reality, this inability to raise the eyes of the mind beyond the physical creation and take in the eternal light" (Ea demum est miserabilis animae servitus, signa pro rebus accipere; et supra creaturam corpoream, oculum mentis ad hauriendum aeternum lumen levare non posse).[70]

Born in AD 204/5 in Lycopolis, Egypt, Plotinus takes up his studies with Ammonius Saccus in Alexandria starting in 232 and by 243 leaves for an expedition to Persia, to study Persian and Indian philosophy. According to some scholars, certain linguistic and stylistic peculiarities in his writings place him in proximity to Coptic Christians. His participation in Emperor Gordian III's campaign against the Persians is cut short, however, when Gordian is murdered, most likely by his successor. Plotinus escapes first to Antioch and, by 245, to Rome, where he establishes himself as a

---

67. Hume 2007, *Treatise* I.i.1.

68. Indeed, to a significant degree modern philosophical and psychological work can be read as an "untiring endeavor to relegate mental images to a merely secondary place" or, indeed, invalidate their existence and/or role in human cognition. Nyiri, describing Wittgenstein's efforts, quoted in *Stanford Encyclopedia of Philosophy*, entry "Mental Imagery" (https://plato.stanford.edu/entries/mental-imagery/; accessed 19 April 2018). On Kant's account of the "transcendental schematism," see his *Critique of Pure Reason* (A 137–47), in Kant 1965, 180–87. For a discussion of the schematism's relevance to image theory, see Didi-Huberman 2005, 130–38; Pfau 2021.

69. See Plato, *Sophist*, esp. 259c–267d.

70. Augustine 1997, 74 (III.9).

highly respected man of learning with good connections to the imperial court and as a teacher of choice to the political elite until his death in 270. The years of Plotinus's adulthood coincide almost exactly with what is known as "the crisis of the third century" (235–84), a fifty-year period of extreme turmoil precipitated by the assassination of Emperor Alexander Severus. With more than twenty emperors often violently dispatching and rapidly succeeding one another during the next fifty years, the empire descends into constant internecine struggle. Economic upheaval, rebellions in faraway provinces, and tribal invasions are a regular occurrence, at times compounded by outbreaks of the plague. As Rome's political and civic ethos continues to unravel during the usually short-lived tenures of its ambitious military strongmen, the so-called barrack emperors, its political and legal institutions begin to fray and disintegrate.

Even more than the practical ethic of the later Stoics, Plotinus develops a philosophical framework that transcends the volatility and depravity of life in the empire.[71] Grouped in six books of nine each (hence *Enneads*), the fifty-four treatises were written between AD 255 and 270. Their definitive arrangement is the fruit of Plotinus's most famous student, Porphyry, who also wrote an uncommonly detailed biographical account of his teacher. It is widely agreed that, significant differences notwithstanding, Plotinus understood himself above all as reviving, reinterpreting, and transmitting Plato's philosophy, which he saw fundamentally in harmony with Aristotelian thought. Famously, Plotinus declares that his "statements are not new, [and] do not belong to the present time, but were made long ago" and that, consequently, his philosophy is "but an interpretation of them, relying on Plato's own writings" (V.1.8). However, the tone of the *Enneads* differs strikingly from Plato's idiom. Gone are the structural irony, the temperamental diversity of Socrates's interlocutors, and the alternately playful or sharply analytic quality of Platonic dialogue. Instead, a distinctly meditative tone pervades the *Enneads* as Plotinus considers the relationship between the three hypostases anchoring his entire thought: the One (*hen*), Intellect (*nous*), and the soul (*psyche*). Even so, Porphyry's account not only remarks on his teacher's "tone of rapt inspiration" and "real feeling" (*ta polla enthousiōn kai ekpathōs phrazōn*) but also notes that, for Plotinus, anything to be put in the form of a treatise had to be the fruit of dialectical clarification achieved through question and answer.[72]

Given the present, limited concern with Plotinus's influential understanding of internal vision and mental imagery, the broader contours of his sophisticated philosophical system can only be briefly touched on. The source of all being, and of every-

71. On the conceptual grammar of Stoic self-cultivation, see Hadot 1995, 81–87; Nussbaum 1994, 316–401; Pfau 2013a, 100–107.

72. Porphyry, "Life of Plotinus," chs. 13 and 14 in Plotinus, *Enneads*, vol. 1.

thing that can be predicated about the cosmos, as well as the goal toward which all material and intellectual being finds itself striving, is the "One." Recalling the Aristotelian God (*noēsis noēseōs*) in whom intellectual activity and its objects are one, Plotinus's One is characterized by absolute simplicity. Wholly ineffable, the One is logically anterior to all distinction, thought, and representation. "This unattainable generative mystery," as von Balthasar calls it, at once furnishes philosophy with its central task and its ultimate boundary.[73] For not only is the *ens metaphysicum* of the One logically presupposed by its particular "emanations"—intellect, soul, nature—but it is also the source that contains and reconciles all particularity, distinction, and opposition. More than a millennium after Plotinus, Nicholas of Cusa will speak of it as the *coincidentia oppositorum*. As such, the One is both antecedent to and beyond all thought; "it does not 'think' [and] it cannot be thought." For as Plotinus realizes, "the unity by which any particular thing is what it is, and is at once part of and distinct from the greater whole, is always logically prior to that thing." The infinitely various and textured reality of visible things, indeed the very possibility of Being manifested as *complexity*, must always be preceded (logically, not temporally) by "a more eminent 'act' of simplicity." Consequently, mind or thought (*nous*) cannot coincide with its source, cannot possess or reclaim the One, but instead can only participate in numinous Being insofar as it has exfoliated into infinite multiplicity.[74] This secondary status of the Plotinian *nous*, enacted as contemplation (*theōria*), also explains the substantive affinity of thinking and seeing throughout Plotinus's writings, as well as the deep-seated affinities between the One and the tradition of Christian apophaticism, such as we find it articulated by pseudo-Dionysius, John Scotus Eriugena, the Victorine School, and Cusanus, among others. Not without justification, Hans-Georg Gadamer considers Plotinus the "Father of negative theology."[75]

Utterly transcendent to mind, thought, and contemplative vision, Plotinus's One is their ontological source. Once acknowledged as "that from which Intellect and the intelligible with it come" (III.8.9), the One naturally falls outside the scope of human ratiocination and predication, and Plotinus remains firmly on guard against allowing it to be obscured by the fog of unbridled speculation. On the contrary, the One "holds all things distinctly and not in a vague general way," for anything less would entail an imperfection. Likewise, even as the One is the First Cause of everything, it is so not in the sense of time-bound, efficient causation but as the eternal ground or

---

73. Balthasar 1986, 282.

74. D. B. Hart 2017, 144–45.

75. Gadamer 1991, 413; rather less persuasive is Gadamer's attempt, likely inspired by Hans Jonas, to assimilate Plotinus's system to that of the Gnostics: "Not the power of revelation of a transcendent God [*eines jenseitigen Gottes*] but the power of an immanent, spiritualized earthly existence [*des eigenen irdisch-menschlichen Seins*] opens the path to redemption" (417).

source of all particularity and universality, all discrete action and experience, all feeling and cognition, all multiplicity and its underlying unity; for "multiplicity would not have existed, if what was not multiplicity had not existed before the multiplicity" (III.8.10).[76] For Plotinus, it thus follows that the One, or pure and undiluted, numinous Being, is synonymous with the Good (*to agathon*). For the principal mark of the Good is its eternal fecundity (Blake will later speak of the "prolific"), that is, its eternal and unquantifiable self-diffusion. Whereas "there is opposition in the quantitative" (VI.3.12), the One is characterized by an "endlessness forever welling up in it. . . . It boils over with life" (VI.5.12). In one of Plotinus's many arresting images, the One is said to resemble "a spring which has no other origin, but gives the whole of itself to rivers, and is not used up by the rivers but remains itself at rest, but the rivers that rise from it, before each of them flows in a different direction, remain for a while all together" (III.8.10). That the One has the character of the Good stems, for Plotinus, above all from the fact that it is eternally generative, that in it being and becoming, reality and potentiality, appear to coincide. Because the One diffuses itself throughout *all* and in each *particular* being, it has "given the trace of itself . . . to Intellect to have by seeing" (III.8.11). The essence of the One thus lies in its inexhaustible capacity for self-manifestation, a ceaseless self-giving that is in turn witnessed by those hypostases (intellect, soul) that have emanated from it. As such, intellect is at a first remove from the One, is *its* other, is the *thinking* image of the One that, because it transcends all relationality (including that of identity and difference), does not itself think. The Plotinian intellect relates to the One in the same way that the Platonic image stands vis-à-vis the reality *of* which it is the image; it establishes in reflection the complementarity of the one and the many that, from the perspective of the One, are eternally identical.[77]

Whereas in his critique of Platonic Form as the metaphysical cause of discrete being Aristotle had proposed the alternative concept of sequential and time-bound *generation*, Plotinus speaks of *emanation* or *begetting* (*gennēsis*). The latter implies a process whose inner logic transcends time, such that the emanations in no way detract from, let alone supplant, the One that is their Source. Emanation, then, is not to be understood as the production of discrete things *in time*. Rather, it affirms their ontological dependency on an eternally operative cause. The first such emanation is

---

76. As Beierwaltes notes, "The emphasis placed on the absolute difference or transcendence [of the One] makes clear, that the supreme reality of the One, . . . its formlessness and boundlessness, does not amount to a diffuse, chaotic amalgam [*Einerlei*] (such as 'the night in which all cows are black')" ([1985] 2016, 46–47; all translations from Beierwaltes's works are mine).

77. Analogously, the soul is the "image" or "trace" of the intellect; as time-bound and discursively constituted particularity, the soul (*psychē*) strives to "become conscious of the enduring *nous* that is operative within it, while also transcendent to it: both *in* and *through* the image, then, it 'realizes' its own archetype [*Urbild*]—i.e., the intellect" (Beierwaltes [1985] 2016, 82).

"intellect" (*nous*), "the essential act of pure thinking."[78] If "in the intelligible world is true being, [then] Intellect is the best part of it" (IV.2.1). It is the locus of forms or, rather, of the knowledge of forms and their extraordinary variety and distinctness. Still, by its very nature such knowledge will remain incomplete and, to an extent, fragmented: "For when it contemplates the One, it does not contemplate it as one: otherwise it would not become intellect. But beginning as one it did not stay as it began, but, without noticing it, became many, as if heavy [with drunken sleep], and unrolled itself because it wanted to possess everything" (III.8.8). By its very nature, intellect (or "mind," as *nous* is also rendered) is something of a paradox: as operative thought, or reflection, it unfolds in time even as its formal self-identity and its total identification with its subject matter appear to render it timeless (*achronos noēsis*). Changeless and dynamic qualities (*stasis* and *kinēsis*) coincide within it. "Time is present *in* intellect as non-time, that is, as something intelligible or something 'thought' (*noēton*) and, thus, is identical with *nous* itself."[79] Or, as T. S. Eliot will put it some seventeen hundred years later, "to be conscious is not to be in time, / But only in time can the moment in the rose-garden, . . . be remembered."[80]

Consequently, the divine intellectual vision in which contemplation seeks to participate does not unfold as a sequence of partial and incomplete "aspects" (Husserl's *Abschattungen*), for the latter are but symptoms of the soul's temporally distended and defective condition. For even though the soul struggles to attain a condition of timeless unity characteristic of the intellect, "it is in its nature to be divided . . . [by] departing from the Intellect and coming to be in a body" (IV.2.1). Hence, "discursive reasoning enters [the soul] here below, when it is already in perplexity and full of care" (IV.3.18). Well aware that such "perplexity" and "care" inform *all* sensory perception, Plotinus acknowledges that the perception of a thing will register in consciousness only insofar as its correlate fits into a "web of relevant concerns."[81] Put differently, a sense impression will result in a corresponding intentionality only if it corresponds to an anterior and interior *imago* of sorts: "It is not necessary to keep stored up in oneself what one sees. When what is perceived makes no difference, or the perception [*aisthēsis*] is not at all personally relevant, but is provoked involuntarily by the difference in the things seen, it is only the sense perception which has this experience and the soul does not receive it into its interior" (IV.4.8). Properly speaking, then, seeing as a conscious "event," as opposed to ephem-

78. Balthasar 1989b, 292.
79. Beierwaltes [1985] 2016, 99 (trans. mine).
80. Eliot 2015, 1:81 ("Burnt Norton," lines 38–42).
81. "Things at hand are always already understood in terms of a totality of relevance" (Zuhandenes wird immer schon aus der Bewandtnisganzheit her verstanden). Heidegger 1996, 140 (§ 32).

eral and mindless gazing, involves a mental attending-to that is distinct from the mere physiology of "sight" (*opsis*). Being focused not on matter but on the form of matter, focalized "perception does not belong to flesh." For it is not the soul that needs a body to exist, but a soul needs to be given "to the body so that the body may exist and be kept in being" (IV.4.22). Consequently, genuine sight for Plotinus is always a case of insight: "Perception of sense-objects is for the soul or the living being an act of apprehension, in which the soul understands the quality attaching to bodies and takes the impression of their forms [*ta eidē*]" (IV.4.23).[82]

The overriding concern of the *Enneads*, then, is to awaken the intellect from its inadvertent slumber and persistent dispersal into the many and to infuse it with contemplative habits needed for its longed-for "return" (*epistrophē*) to the One: "One must become Intellect and entrust one's soul to and set it firmly under Intellect, that it may be awake to receive . . . and may by this Intellect behold the One" (VI.9.3). At times, Plotinus's characterization of such an awakening and "return" bears a striking resemblance to Pauline Christianity's understanding of resurrection and rebirth, such as his opening affirmation, "I have woken up out of the body [*ek tou sōmatos*] to my self and have entered into myself, going out from all other things[,] . . . and come to identity with the divine" (IV.8.1). Again, Plotinus's language hews close to Paul's letters when he remarks that "the activity of sense-perception is that of the soul asleep; . . . but the true wakening is a true getting up from the body [*alēthinē apo sōmatos*], not with the body[,] . . . a rising altogether away from bodies, which are of the opposite nature to soul and opposed in respect of reality" (III.6.6). Vacillating between contingency and eternity, the many and the One, Plotinus's *nous* embodies this tension in its very operation.

As the principle or source of intelligibility, the One allows human beings to "know" being within the boundaries of predication, that is, by venturing propositions about a being's "whatness" or quiddity. Yet underpinning predication and syllogistic discourse is an inescapable dualism, such that for the mind to know anything always means knowing it in terms of something else (to know X *as* X^1). Knowledge is constitutively *dis*cursive (Lat. *discurrere* = "running to and fro") in the sense that much later Heidegger will speak of the ordinary thinking's "circuitousness" (*Umwegigkeit*).[83] For cognition to become *re*cognition, and for sight to become *in*sight, there

---

82. Plotinus's subsequent remark on how a "third thing" is needed to mediate between soul and external object bears startling resemblance to the "schematism" that, in Kant's first *Critique*, mediates between the "strictly heterogeneous" domains of the pure concepts of the understanding (the categories) and the "sense data" (*Sinnesempfindungen*) begging their application; on the relation of Kant's "transcendental schematism" to image theory and its particular deformation in modern philosophical aesthetics, see Pfau 2021.

83. Heidegger 1996, 71–77 (*BT* § 17). Bereft of intrinsic meaning ("a sign is not really 'comprehended' [*erfaßt*] when we stare at it"), the sign only "originates when something already at

must be an antecedent, numinous reality that is mediated by the intellect while, in turn, mediating the intellect with itself: "for this reason [intellect] is not the first, but what is beyond it must exist" (III.8.9), and inasmuch as "intellect exists in its thinking, . . . the best intellect" will turn not to external matters but "thinks what is before it; for in turning to itself it [re]turns to its principle [*eis auton gar epistrephōn eis archēn epistrephei*]" (VI.9.2). Werner Beierwaltes calls "this return of thought into itself [*Rückgang des Denkens in sich selbst*] the condition for its self-transformation into the timeless, absolute mind that manifests itself in thought."[84] At the same time, the orientation of *nous* toward knowledge (*epistēmē*) rather than opinion (*doxa*) shows that at stake "is not the intellect of one individual, but is universal" (III.8.8), even as the ultimate goal of its striving—the eternity and absolute simplicity of the One—remains unattainable for it qua intellect. Hence, as von Balthasar notes, an element of "self-seeking" or "yearning" (*eros*) informs the intellect, which thus "needs only itself, in distinction from the One which does not 'need' even itself."[85]

For Plotinus, it is not matter that constrains mind but, rather, the intellect's constitutively discursive, internally divided, and mediated form of operation. Contrary to the Gnostics of his time, whom he regards with a mix of fear and repugnance, Plotinus is careful not to cast aspersions on matter and nature or argue for its purported separation from the One.[86] Not coincidentally, many of the *Enneads'* most luminous images are premised on the beauty and inner perfection of natural beings (sun, stars, the sea, plants, etc.). Not embodied being is evil but the soul's potentially idolatrous attachment to it, which reflects a fundamentally disordered structure of desire. The latter may indeed constitute an insurmountable obstacle to the soul's longed-for return to the One; for only *minded*, self-conscious entities can choose to persist in their attachment to embodied being, rather than grasping and embracing the One as their true telos. Hence, in sharp opposition to the Gnostics, Plotinus maintains that "[God] will be present to all and will be in this universe, whatever the manner of his presence; so that the universe will participate [*methexei*] in him" (II.9.16).[87] Not only, then, is "our world . . . not separated from the spiritual world"

hand [*Zuhandenes*] is *taken as a sign*" (79–80). Hence the sign remains parasitical on the antecedent disclosure of being.

84. Beierwaltes 2001, 12.

85. Von Balthasar 1989b, 292. As Plotinus puts it, "The One, as it is beyond Intellect, so is beyond knowledge, and as it does not in any way need anything, so it does not even need knowing; but knowing has its place in the second nature" (V.3.12).

86. On Plotinus's rejection of Gnosticism, see Hadot 1993, 35–47; for a compelling refutation of Hans Jonas's ill-judged attempt to assimilate Plotinus to Gnosticism, see also Beierwaltes [1985] 2016, 93–95.

87. On Plotinus's view of the Gnostics, most fully worked out in *Ennead* II.9, see also Hadot 1993, 35–47. Plotinus's far more nuanced understanding echoes Plato's premise that "the body, as body [*sōma*], is neither good nor bad" (Plato 1997, 701 [*Lysis* 217a]).

(II.9.16), but the high degree of formal organization that defines all sensible particulars compels us to think of an indissoluble nexus between the One and the visible cosmos: "We have not, then, departed from being, but are in it, nor has it departed from us: so all things are one" (VI.5.1). By invoking two types of sensory experience, Plotinus means to reject the Gnostic view of a fallen, because material, universe wholly at odds with its transcendent creator-god (*dēmiourgos*).

> For how could there be a musician who sees the melody in the intelligible world and will not be stirred when he hears the melody in sensible sounds? Or how could there be anyone skilled in geometry and numbers who will not be pleased when he sees right relation, proportion and order with his eyes? For indeed, even in their pictures [*en tais graphais*] those who look at the works of art with their eyes do not see the same things in the same way, but when they recognize an imitation on the level of sense of someone who has a place in their thought they feel a kind of disturbance and come to a recollection [*anamnēsin*] of the truth. (II.9.16)

Plotinus's quarrel with the Gnostics here concerns not only their misguided assertions, but, more important, their very method of reasoning. For they appear unable (or, perhaps, unwilling) to consider how in its very givenness sensory experience itself is already structured by the *logos* that is the One. The Gnostics have no phenomenology but, instead, are committed to wholly abstract views about God and cosmos from the outset. For his part, Plotinus remains deeply attuned to the ways in which the *logos* of the One discloses itself through an infinite array of perfected forms (*logoi*), each of which enjoins the finite individual's soul and intellect to participate in it.

Given how intimately the experience of beauty and the knowledge of forms are entwined in Plotinus's writings, it cannot surprise that he should accord images an indispensable role. The transcendent realm of the good and the true can only be accessed through our active, visual encounter with beauty; and it is the quality of contemplative vision (*theōria*) and of its objective correlate, the image qua form (*eidos*), that now stands to be considered. While Plotinus retains some of Plato's ambivalence regarding the visible world and the status of images in particular, he places greater stress on the revelatory and transformative impact of beauty. "Beauty" (*to kalon*) gives heightened reality to the world and puts us in touch with its sheer, incontrovertible givenness: "He who sees [beautiful things] cannot possibly say anything else except that they are what really exists. What does 'really exists' mean? That they exist as beauties [*ti onta ontōs; ē kala*]" (I.6.5). For Plotinus, "being, insofar as it is encountered in thinking, is *form*: the concepts of *ousia* and *eidos* or *morphē* are coextensive. . . . All being is beautiful because it is form in its encounter with the

Intellect."[88] The fruit of a seemingly effortless fusion of "sight" (*opsis*) with knowledge, beauty consists in our "participating in form [*metochē eidous*]" and "sharing in a formative power [*logou . . . koinōnia*]" (I.6.2); and the encounter with beauty, according to Plotinus, defines the arc and substance of a human being's entire life, which consists in a progressively fuller attention to the good. Even as our encounter with beauty is both intuitive and instantaneous, its phenomenology appears plotted like a kind of spiritual exercise, to be pursued and cultivated for the entirety of one's life. Indeed, Porphyry's overall arrangement of the *Enneads* presents Plotinus's texts as a staged sequence guiding the student's philosophical progress. It commences with a "first glance [*tē prōtē aisthēton*]" (I.6.2) wherein seeing the form implies a certain knowledge of it ("the soul speaks of it as if it understood it"). It does so because, like Plato, Plotinus views understanding as a case of "recognition." In it the soul first has the experience, at once unsought and irresistible, of an ontological kinship with what it beholds: "The soul, since it is by nature what it is and is related to the higher kind of reality in the realm of being, when it sees something akin to it or a trace of its kindred reality, is delighted and thrilled and returns [*anapherei*] to itself and remembers [*anamimnēsketai*] itself" (I.6.2).

The physical event of "sight" (*opsis*) matters only insofar as the subject engaged in it is also "mindful" of it, namely, by grasping form as that which mediates between the material event of sight and its import for the ultimate spiritual goal of a knowledge no longer constrained by the contingencies of selfhood and discrete visible beings. Once correlated with the (Stoic) intellectual virtue of "attention" (*prosochē*), "form" thus reveals the visible world's ineffable kinship with the soul. Echoing Plato (*Phaedrus* 247c6), Plotinus thus speaks of an experience in which soul encounters its own ineffable reality: "not shape or color or any size, but soul, without color [*achrōmaton*] itself" (I.6.5). Empirical perception, then, can only ever be of legitimate concern to philosophy because it reveals mind and the material world, *psychē* and *physis*, to be ontologically ordered toward one another. Transfixed by this indelible nexus between sight and form, the soul has a tendency to tarry with, and actively scrutinize, the event of seeing itself. Plotinus's term of art for this phenomenological turn is "contemplation" (*theōria*), an activity altogether central to the ethical formation of the human being. Indeed, the encounter with beauty is, for Plotinus, the very goal of human striving only insofar as it elicits and guides the practice of contemplation. Once again alluding to the *Phaedrus* in what is chronologically the first of his treatises, Plotinus thus characterizes the encounter with the beauty of visible forms as "the greatest, the ultimate contest . . . set before our souls; all our toil and trouble is for this, not to be left without a share in the best of visions. The man

---

88. Balthasar 1989b, 294; trans. modified.

who attains this is blessed in seeing that 'blessed sight', and he who fails to attain it has failed utterly" (I.6.7).

Still, if mental vision is to be purged of all hedonistic or idolatrous attachments, the question of its proper execution remains as yet unanswered: "But how shall we find the way? What method [*tis mēchanē*] can we devise? How can one see the 'inconceivable beauty' [*kallos amēchanon*] which stays within the holy sanctuary and does not come out where the profane may see it?" (I.6.8). The kind of contemplative seeing Plotinus has in mind experiences the visible as so many "images, traces, [and] shadows [*eikones kai ichnē kai skiai*]" of something *beyond* vision. Hence, Plotinus insists, the soul must cultivate a form of attention untroubled by desire. It must learn to see and attend to visible beauty not as an object of desire but as the manifestation of a truth that will unveil itself only where mind has been purged of all volition and desire: "When he sees the beauty in bodies he must not run after them; we must know that they are images, traces, shadows, and hurry away to that which they image. For if a man runs to the image and wants to seize it as if it was the reality . . . [he] will . . . in soul, not in body, sink down into the dark depths where intellect has no delight, and stay blind in Hades, consorting with shadows" (I.6.8).

Yet even as the image is only ever the conduit to "form," it remains an indispensable feature of the beholder's moral formation, which ideally unfolds as a passage from *eikōn* to *eidos*.[89] The movement toward the One necessarily progresses, not against, but, rather, *by means of*, *through*, and *beyond* visible beauty. For inasmuch as soul and intellect remain estranged from the One, they must submit to this dialectic of working through material, visible beauty so as, ultimately, to transcend it: "The soul must be trained . . . just as someone making a statue which has to be beautiful cuts away here and polishes there and makes one part smooth and clears another, so you too must . . . never stop 'working on your statue' till the divine glory of virtue shines out on you" (I.6.9). The true artifact resulting from such effort is, of course, the human soul; for its beauty will be realized in proportion as it forgoes imposing its desires and conceptions on perceptible things and, instead, allows itself to be enfolded in a realm of visibly mediated, beautiful forms. In one of his most rhapsodic closing paragraphs that will be quoted time and again by writers from Augustine to Goethe, Plotinus informs us how we must come to the sight with a seeing power made akin and like to what is seen:

No eye ever saw the sun without becoming sun-like, nor can a soul see beauty without becoming beautiful. You must become first all *godlike* [*theoeidēs*] and all

---

89. We cannot here examine Plotinus's most comprehensive discussion of form, considered ontologically rather than as regards how intellect and soul participate in it, which is found in *Ennead* VI.7, the longest and, quite possibly, the most ambitious of his treatises.

beautiful if you intend *to see God* [*theasasthai theon*] and beauty. First the soul will come in its ascent to intellect and there will know the Forms, all beautiful, and will affirm that these, the Ideas, are beauty; for all things are beautiful by these, by the products of intellect and essence. That which is beyond this we call the nature of the Good, which holds beauty as a screen before it. (I.6.9; emphasis mine)[90]

Plotinus's conception of "becoming godlike" as a prerequisite for seeing god will return in patristic and Byzantine writing under the heading *theōsis*, a conceptual innovation arguably lacking a clear scriptural warrant that will be introduced by Gregory Nazianzen a century later.[91] Meanwhile, Plotinus's notion of the individual soul seeking to become "deiform" (*theoeidēs*), an early instance of the *visio Dei* motif that will pervade Augustinian and Scholastic thought for a full millenium, not only fuels speculation about his possible upbringing within a community of Egyptian Copts. It also goes to the very heart of future debates about images. Is their mediating function to be rejected on theological grounds as a case of hubris, it being premised that finite and sinful human beings are irremediably excluded from any participation in divine transcendence? Or, against such a static view, is the image being credited with the power of mediating finite and transcendent being and, thus, functioning as the catalyst for a dynamic conception of the spiritual life?

There can be no doubt that Plotinus inclines to the latter view, all the more because he is careful to distinguish between merely hedonistic gazing and a kind of contemplative seeing. Provided the act of seeing is governed by a truly impersonal or kenotic ethos, what eventuates is a "contemplation of the world of Forms" wherein we may experience "the pure fact" of form in its incontrovertible givenness. Whereas consciousness remains forever "split into two and, occupied by calculations and projects, believ[ing] that nothing can be found until it has been searched for," con-

---

90. Plotinus here capitalizes on the etymological link between God (*theos*) and "seeing" (*theaomai*), later also explored by Nicholas of Cusa. Augustine repeatedly quotes *Ennead* I.6.8f.; see *Confessions* I.18 and VIII.8; and *De Civitate Dei* IX.17. Having extensively studied the *Enneads* in 1805, Goethe adapted Plotinus's trope of the "sunlike" (*hēlioeidēs*) eye in a late epigrammatic poem of that year (later incorporated into his *Theory of Colors* [*Farbenlehre*] of 1810: "Wäre nicht das Auge sonnenhaft, / Die Sonne könnt' es nie erblicken; / Läg' nicht in uns des Gottes Kraft, / Wie könnt' Göttliches uns erzücken?" (*GHA* 1:367).

91. See Maslov (2012), who notes that Gregory, who never cites the most likely biblical warrant for *theōsis* (2 Pet 1:4), appears aware of the concept's dangerous proximity to pagan ideas of apotheosis; see Gregory, oration "On the Son" (*PNF* 7:301–9). Maslov sees the concept of *theōsis* "belonging firmly in the context of fourth-century debates on the nature of the philosophical life" (446) waged between Christians and pagans, which also explains the concept's proximity to the Stoic notion of "familiarity with the beautiful" (*oikeiōsis pros to kalon*) and what Maslov labels the "para-Christian" notion of *sympatheia*.

templation opens up a domain of experience free of any such divisions.[92] It is "the twofold activity of, on the one hand, a total absorption in the perception of being as *noēma*, so fully surrendered to what it beholds that the beholder forgets himself in what is beheld . . . and yet, on the other, also of a return to oneself, an encountering oneself in the object." The goal is "for the seer to become the seen."[93] "Seeing the form" (von Balthasar's "Schau *der Form*"), then, is not primarily a *material, optical* event. Rather, it demands our responsiveness to the phenomena as they give themselves to us in intuition—that is, to the unsought and indisputably real advent of form as the manifestation of truth. In his great treatise "The Forms and the Good," Plotinus probes this intrinsic perfection and integrative totality of form, whose timelessness removes it beyond the scope of "reasoning" (*logizesthai*): "for it is not possible to reason in what is always," simply because it is complete: "for this is what form is, being everything [*touto gar kai eidos ta panta*]" (VI.7.3). If "correctness" depends on the intellect's analytic and syllogistic powers, contemplative truth pivots on the mind's intuitive recognition of, and assent to, the timeless reality and incontrovertible presence of forms. Hence, Plotinus insists, "we must . . . not assume that the Form is spatially separate and then the Idea is reflected in matter as if in water." Rather, "matter, from every side grasping . . . the Idea, receives from the Form, over the whole of itself, by its drawing near to it all that it can receive, with nothing between" (VI.5.8).

Tellingly, the Platonic trope of "shadows" has been supplanted by the Plotinian language of mirrors, which seems to open up at least tentative prospects of self-recognition: "the souls of men see their images as if in the mirror of Dionysius" (IV.3.12). In what may be an echo of his earlier allusion to the figure of Narcissus (see *Ennead* I.6.8), Plotinus's image of water mirroring appearance draws attention to the far superior, integrative powers of forms. Even so, the trope of the mirror remains provisional and ambivalent, at once conjuring up scenarios of authentic self-recognition and the ever-looming specter of a purely narcissistic and idolatrous gaze—a polarity that pervades a great deal of ancient philosophical and patristic writing, from Plato, Plotinus, and Proclus forward to Gregory of Nyssa, pseudo-Dionysius, and the eighth- and ninth-century iconodules (John Damascene, Nikephoros, Theodore the Studite, Photios). As we shall see, the same tension also structures the conflict between the modern, anthropocentric, single-viewpoint theory of vision developed in Alberti's *On Painting* (1435) and opposing arguments, worked out in deeply considered Neoplatonist terms, by Nicholas of Cusa.[94]

---

92. Hadot 1993, 41.

93. Balthasar 1989b, 299.

94. See below, ch. 4. On images of reflection in Plotinus, see Schroeder, 1992, 52–65; Clark 2016, 83–90. Clark notes that the efficacy of the mirror (and of the soul as a mirror) depends on its surface remaining undisturbed. For Cusa, see the discussion below; and esp. Hoff 2013, 33–75.

"THE TRUEST LIFE IS BY THOUGHT":
IMAGE AND CONTEMPLATIVE VISION IN THE *ENNEADS*

To return to Plotinus, we find how, mediated by the visible "image," form is not an ideal opposed to the realm of appearances but, instead, actively discloses what he calls the "forming principle" (*logos*) visibly imprinted on matter (*hylē*). To know is to let oneself be guided *by* appearance rather than overleap it in a fit of idealist speculation or self-consciously disengage from it in Pyrrhonist fashion. The challenge, put in loosely Kantian terms, remains the same for Plotinus as for modern epistemology: namely, to understand "how the appearance, which in and of itself contains no trace of universality and necessity, can nonetheless lay the groundwork for universal and necessary knowledge." And here it won't do to simply assert that "knowledge that transcends the reach of the senses is solely the product of the subject's spontaneity." For such a position would amount to little more than "a kind of conjuror's trick." In fact, the Kantian appeal to "spontaneity" ultimately masks the fact that, by knowing in-accordance-with appearance, consciousness finds itself in the position of a respondent to the call of the phenomenon. Here knowing is not a "determinative" (*bestimmend*) act of imposing a conceptual scheme on the world of appearance. On the contrary, knowledge eventuates as an aleatory process, an improvisational chain of call and response whereby the subject experiences the ontological coordination of being and appearance within itself. Hence, von Balthasar continues, "the only possible basis for knowledge of the truth . . . is the subject's primary ability immediately to mirror—in the intrinsic interconnection between sense and intellect within itself—the mirroring of the essence in the appearance."[95]

Likewise, for Plotinus, mind or intellect (*nous*) stands not so much for a *subject* but, instead, names the *medium* through which nature becomes present to itself as an object of contemplation. For unlike Descartes's *res extensa*, Plotinian nature (*physis*) is not an antonym of reason (*logos*) but is essentially infused with it. It is *onto-logos*, Reason, by dint of its very being rather than in any contingent, notional sense arising "from reasoning" (*ek logou*) and "research" (*skopeisthai*). Hence, Plotinus notes, for the intellect to actively intervene in an object "means not yet possessing" and to conceive nature as "a life and a rational principle and a power which makes [*dynamis poiousa*]. Making, for it, means being what it is. . . . So by being contemplation [*theōria*] and object of contemplation [*theōrēma*] and rational principle [*logos*], it makes in so far as it is these things. So its making [*poiēsis*] has been revealed to us as contemplation" (III.8.3).

Contemplation is not an occasional kind of practice, let alone an esoteric or idiosyncratic pursuit. Rather, it is the telos of life as Plotinus conceives of it, the highest

---

95. Balthasar 2001, 153.

form of participation in the Good; and, as such, promises to release the human being from the thralldom of desire, dominion, and the bondage of subjectivity. Being geared toward comprehensive wisdom rather than particular knowledge, contemplation "is not situated merely on the cognitive level, but encompasses the self's very being. It is a progress which causes us to *be* more fully, and makes us better."[96] Contemplation enables the finite soul to understand itself as a medium for "nature . . . at rest in contemplation of the vision of itself" (III.8.4). In it, beholding and being beheld coincide (*videre et videri coincidunt*), as Nicholas of Cusa will later put it, quoting Eckhart of Hochheim. For Plotinus, it follows that "contemplation and vision [*to theōrēma*] have no limits" (III.8.5) but, by their very nature, exceed the scope of intellect and discourse. Not by accident, Plotinian contemplation aspires to a condition of total silence. Like the figure of Ottilie in Goethe's *Elective Affinities* (1809), whose utter silence links her to nature's mute and timeless fecundity, Plotinus's self-contemplating nature is also enveloped by eternal silence, even if, as a result, it appears "somewhat blurred [*amydrotera*]." At the same time, nature can be raised to a superior level of explicitness by another form of contemplation, "clearer for sight," wherein it constitutes itself as "the image of another contemplation [*eidōlon theōria allēs*]" (III.8.4).[97]

According to Plotinus, in contemplation the rational principle is no longer "outside but . . . [is] united with the soul of the learner." Hence, "soul" (*psychē*) must not be confused with some form of Romantic subjectivity, private revelation, or moral sentiment. Instead, having "become akin to . . . the rational principle," the Plotinian soul has evolved into a dis-individuated extension of the *logos* principle. It "utters and propounds it—for it did not possess it primarily—and learns it thoroughly and by its proposition becomes other than it, and looks at it" (III.8.6). Plotinus is careful here not to blur the line between soul and the perfection, eternity, and simplicity of the One to which it draws close in mental vision. Yet neither does he suggest that their distinctness entails an ultimate opposition or incommensurability. Instead, he often speaks of seeing the light "with" and "by means of" the object, which throws light itself into relief. Schroeder has remarked on this striking "complex of ontological (*sunousia*) and epistemological (*sunoran, sunaisthēsis, sunesis*) vocabulary, each of which is initiated by the prefix *sun-* (with) so as to convey "an elastic inven-

---

96. Hadot 1995, 83.

97. On Plotinus's trope of silence and its proximity to "begetting" (in contrast to "making"), see Schroeder 1992, 40–65. Plotinus is well aware, however, that human beings may not only surpass nature's silent contemplation by means of mental vision, but, conversely, may fall well short of it by "making action [*praxis*] a shadow of contemplation." Insofar as the "doer or maker [of action] had nothing in view beyond the thing done," action amounts to "a weakening of contemplation" (III.8.4). Properly speaking, action must be "for the sake of contemplation and vision [*heneka theōrias kai theōrēmatos*]," which is the true "goal [*telos*]" (III.8.6).

tory of presence and dependence, describing the mutual presence of source and product without confusing the one with the other."[98]

This ontological difference, which keeps the finite soul and the transcendent One at once distinct and related, is itself a constant focus of awareness. In apprehending and mediating the two realms in their very relatedness, thought (*noēsis*) overcomes its own internal division, recognizing and returning to the One as its own source; and as it does so, the temporally distended operation of syllogistic and discursive thought is supplanted by an atemporal, mental vision. Here "intellect . . . sees by another light the things illuminated by that first nature, and sees the light in them. . . . If it abandons the things it sees and looks at the medium by which it sees them, it looks at light and the source of light" (V.5.7). As such, mental vision fulfills what the soul could not yet apprehend. For even as "soul, too, was a rational principle and a sort of intellect, [albeit] an intellect seeing something else, . . . it is not full, but has something wanting in relation to what comes before it; yet it itself sees also quietly what it utters. For what it utters, . . . it utters because of its deficiency, with a view to examining it" (III.8.6).

If "the intellectual act is without parts and . . . remains unobserved within, verbal expression unfolds its contents and brings it out of the intellectual act into the image-making power [*ek tou noēmatos eis to phantastikon*], and so shows the intellectual act as if in a mirror." As it ensures "apprehension and persistence and memory of [thought]" (IV.3.30), discourse "brings forth [*propherō*] in words" something as yet unrealized, indeed unrealizable as *knowledge* but adumbrated in contemplation (*theōria*). Indeed, the relationship of speech to vision remains, for Plotinus, inherently ambivalent. On the one hand, articulate, meaningful speech always ought to clarify the deliverances of sensory perception. As such, language is itself a gift of, and a covenant with, the One. To understand it thus is to arrive at "a partial answer to the question why we should undertake to discuss the One if we already know that we may not disclose it. The very fact that language belongs to the creation and is the gift of the One to us carries with it the mandate and even the imperative of theological discourse. Language, especially theological language, is not altogether our own project."[99]

Still, given that "all activity (*poiēsis*) happens for the sake of contemplation," spoken discourse remains something "secondary, a necessary expedient." Indeed, inasmuch as the word stands in the service of knowledge, it tends toward apophatic self-negation and a condition of silence the closer it draws to the ineffable transcen-

---

98. Schroeder 1992, 52.

99. For a discussion of Plotinus's understanding of word, discourse, poetry, and the powers of disclosure encoded in them, see Schroeder 1992, 66–90; quote from 69.

dence of the One.[100] Silence marks the mind's attempted return to a condition that for the intellect, being distended in time, is only imperfectly attainable: "For if it was not in every way and forever varied, in so far as it was not varied, Intellect would stand still. But if it stands still, it does not think." Yet because it manifests itself as thought, intellect is at all times "all movement filling all substance." At the same time, this very mode of activity also shows intellect to be "always the same, journeying through the things which are not the same, because it does not change" (VI.7.13). In ways later echoed by Cusanus and Hegel, Plotinus considers thought both phenomenologically, as manifest in its restless "journeying" through a cosmos filled with objects of interest, and ontologically, as striving toward total self-recognition by participating in the One and the Good: "So intellect came to be by being filled, and when it was filled it was, and simultaneously it was perfected and saw [*apetelesthē kai heōra*]" (VI.7.16).[101] Contemplation does not so much supersede intellect as it fulfills its innermost goal (telos), namely, to recognize the One as its cause, in the twofold sense of origin and end; and such recognition will, phenomenologically speaking, unfold as a condition of complete stillness that, more than a millennium and a half later, T. S. Eliot's *Four Quartets* captures in words of crystalline, haunting simplicity.

> Words, after speech, reach
> Into the silence. Only by the form, the pattern,
> Can words or music reach
> The stillness, as a Chinese jar still
> Moves perpetually in its stillness.
> Not the stillness of the violin, while the note lasts,
> Not that only, but the co-existence,
> Or say that the end precedes the beginning,
> And the end and the beginning were always there
> Before the beginning and after the end.
> And all is always now.[102]

---

100. Balthasar 1989b, 298–99.

101. See also Plotinus's later, twofold characterization of the intellect, which "has one power for thinking, by which it looks at the things in itself, and one by which it looks at what transcends it by a direct awareness and reception, *by which also before it saw only, and by seeing acquired intellect and is one*" (VI.7.35; emphasis mine).

102. Eliot 2015, 1:183 ("Burnt Norton," lines 3–13). See also Robert Cardinal Sarah's observation, "Silence is not the exile of speech. It is the love of the one Word. Conversely, the abundance of words is the symptom of doubt. . . . [T]he most defective human relationship is precisely one in which the silence of attention is absent" (2017, 80–81).

Just so, Plotinus regards contemplation as the very apotheosis of intellect, a moment of self-transcendence wherein sequential, time-bound knowledge unexpectedly opens up onto a state in which sight appears to merge with what is seen, where knower and known no longer communicate across a divide, where knowing merges with *participating-in* the Good—which, as Plotinus notes, "must be desirable, but must not become good by being desirable" (VI.7.25). It is the moment of realization "that what comes into being is what I see in my silence, an object of contemplation which comes to be naturally, and that I, originating from this sort of contemplation have a contemplative nature. And my act of contemplation makes what it contemplates" (III.8.4). Conversely, embodied sight and discursive speech always risk succumbing to epistemological hubris, that is, to becoming instruments of cupidity and interested action. Hence, "in men of action the soul fits what it possesses to the things outside of it" (III.8.6) by conflating what it seeks with known beings. For Plotinus, silence does not so much disrupt ratiocination and discourse as it supersedes them. For silence arises from insight into realities unattainable for human predication: "The truly good and wise man, therefore, has already finished reasoning when he declares [*apophainei*] what he has in himself to another; but in relation to himself he is vision. For he is already turned to what is one, and to the quiet which is not only of things outside but in relation to himself, and all is within him" (III.8.6).

The silence of contemplative vision thus completes the figure that, more than anything, links Plotinus to his Christian successors (pseudo-Dionysius, John Scotus Eriugena, Cusanus)—namely, a pattern of withdrawal (*exodus*) and return (*reditus*). Corresponding to the *noēsis* known as contemplation, the *noēma* of "form" mediated by the mental image (*phantasma*) promises to overcome the fragmented, temporally distended condition of the soul. It aims to see the *all* and, to do so, must overcome selfhood and recover the intellect's primal bond with divine thought, of which it is an emanation. That the movement of the soul toward intellect runs parallel to the shift from externally conditioned perception to internal, self-emptying (kenotic) vision reflects "the special pathos" of Plotinian metaphysics. For "so long as being is discriminated from the transcendent principle of unity," mind remains enclosed by an unrelenting temporal "dialectic of identity and negation." To quote David B. Hart's lucid summation:

> If the truth of all things is a principle in which they are grounded and by which they are simultaneously negated, then one can draw near to the fullness of truth only through a certain annihilation of particularity, . . . a sort of benign desolation of the soul, progressively eliminating—as the surd of mere particularity—all that lies between the One and the noetic self. . . . The pathos to which I refer is a sadness residing not within Plotinus the man, but within any logically dialectical metaphysics of transcendence. For transcendence, so understood, must also be

understood as a negation of the finite, and a kind of absence or positive exclusion from the scale of nature. . . . For so long as one dwells in the realm of finite vision, one dwells in untruth.[103]

Embedded in contemplative vision there is always an element of renunciation, "a journey of the alone to the alone" (as Hart puts it).[104] For not only does such vision reflect insight into the inescapable transience of all distinctly visible things, but it has grasped their irremediable estrangement qua things from the numinous One. Inasmuch as contemplation seeks to bridge the chasm separating finite and eternal being, reflective consciousness will search to pass into a state of vision anchored in (mental) images that are no longer made or written in the literal sense of *eikonographein* but, instead, are revealed—partially and fleetingly—as pure "form" (*eidos*): "Just as he who wishes to see the intelligible nature will contemplate what is beyond the perceptible if he has no mental image of the perceptible, so he who wishes to contemplate what is beyond the intelligible will contemplate it when he has let all the intelligible go; he will learn that it is by means of the intelligible, but what it is like by letting the intelligible go" (V.5.6). Hence, as von Balthasar notes, "the ascent of the *nous* towards identity is indeed profitable for knowledge of the One; and yet again, it is also useless."[105] Ultimately, the entire progression or, rather, return "from nature to soul, and soul to intellect" (III.8.8), pivots on the cultivation of what Hadot calls "the highest state [of] complete passivity."[106] Plotinus's *Enneads* lays out, in so many ways, a program of spiritual exercises aimed at helping the disciple attain a state of complete "self-emptying" (*kenōsis*).[107] Fueling that quest is the realization that true knowledge ultimately exceeds the domain of reference, predication, and discourse that is the intellect's proper domain. For the life of the intellect, which to be sure Plotinus in no way disparages, nevertheless is constitutively exiled from the One: "for when [thought] contemplates the One, it does not contemplate it as one: otherwise it would not become intellect." Hence, even as there are degrees of knowledge, only contemplation can close the gap between intellect and its ultimate object. Here indeed "the truest life is life by thought [*hē zōē hē alēthestatē noēsei zōē estin*]," the stage where "living and life . . . are one" (III.8.8).

---

103. D. B. Hart 2017, 146.
104. Ibid., 146.
105. Balthasar 1989b, 304.
106. Hadot 1993, 8.
107. As Hadot remarks about the philosophical schools in imperial Rome, "The work, even if it is apparently theoretical and systematic, is written not so much to inform the reader of a doctrinal content but to form him, to make him traverse a certain itinerary in the course of which he will make spiritual progress" (1995, 64).

Yet seen from below, this ascent, which is also, metaphysically speaking, a return of the finite emanation to its source, requires some form of mediation. For the Good (*to agathon*) cannot be captured as an abstract, transcendent idea but must be realized in lived practice. Hence the question arises: "By what sort of simple intuition could one grasp this which transcends the nature of intellect?" Plotinus's answer—"it is by the likeness in ourselves [*tō en hēmin homoiō*]" (III.8.9)—sets up one of the most arresting passages in *Ennead* III.8.

> What is it, then, which we shall receive when we set our intellect to it? Rather, the intellect must return, so to speak, backwards, and give itself up, in a way, to what lies behind it (for it faces in both directions); and there, if it wishes to see that First Principle, it must not be altogether intellect. . . . For all things [together, the totality of being] are not an origin, but they came from an origin [*ex archēs*], and this is no more all things, or one of them. . . . For that which generates is always simpler than what is generated. If this [Origin], then, generated Intellect, it must be simpler than Intellect. (III.8.9)

One can see Plotinus here establishing several motifs that will occupy philosophical and theological reflection in the centuries to come. To begin with, the intellect's "return" (*epistrophē*) hinges on relinquishing, once and for all, any claim to self-sufficiency. In time, Proclus's *Elements of Theology* will identify this return of mind to the very cause from which it sprang as defining the essential movement of thought. The movement of thought will have run its course only when it has recognized both the necessity and the ultimate futility of its own, errant constitution. Only then will the intellect have reached its terminus in the simplicity of the One from which it had temporarily strayed.[108] This apotheosis of thought, which entails suspending its claim to self-possession, presages Augustine's concern with epistemological humility ("when mind knows itself it does not excel itself with its knowledge"), studiousness, and a self-awareness undiluted by externalities: "So when [mind] is bidden to know itself, it should not start looking for itself as though it had drawn off from itself, but should draw off what it has added to itself."[109] Likewise, Plotinus's narrative conception of philosophy, involving the intellect's "return" and self-surrender to "what lies behind it" foreshadows Augustine's understanding of the human person's gradual "conversion" and overcoming of sinful self-absorption (*homo incurvatus in se*) and consequent turning toward its ultimate "source" and "origin" (*fons et origo*).

Furthermore, Plotinus thinks of the One in strictly normative and apophatic terms rather than in the notional and dialectical ways in which modern philosophy

---

108. "All things proceed in a circuit, from their causes to their causes again" (Proclus 1963, D, prop. 31–39; quote from D 33).

109. Augustine 1991, 273, 295 (IX.1.4; X.3.11).

(and a good bit of modern theology) struggles to acknowledge and delimit God's transcendence. Thus, the One, for Plotinus, *eo ipso* coincides with "the Good which brings fulfillment to the sight of Intellect. . . . Therefore, when you have said 'The Good' do not add anything to it in your mind, for if you add anything, you will make it deficient by whatever you have added. Therefore you must not even add thinking, in order that you may not add something other than it and make two, intellect and good. For Intellect needs the Good, but the Good does not need it" (III.8.11). The simplicity and eternity of the transcendent One is not to be conceived dialectically, that is, as the contrary of immanence in its finitude and multiplicity. In fact, transcendence in both the Neoplatonist and Augustinian-Thomist traditions, *contains* immanence rather than being its other. It is the source of all otherness, the "non-Other" (*non-aliud*), as Cusanus will put it, in which simplicity and multiplicity, identity and heterogeneity, being and becoming coincide, and from which all oppositions have emanated. Any attempt to think the One thus has to begin by acknowledging it as ontologically anterior to all predication and, consequently, as wholly ineffable.

Still, even as Plotinus restricts the intellect to a strict apophaticism that in time will be worked out by his greatest Christian exegete, pseudo-Dionysius, he realizes that there must be some positive intuition, some palpable hint that at once summons the intellect to participate in the One even as it enjoins us to cultivate a stance of epistemic humility: "The Good, therefore, has given the trace of itself [*ichnos autou*] . . . to Intellect to have by seeing [*horōnti . . . echein*], so that in Intellect there is desire . . . and a movement to convergence with its form" (III.8.11). Plotinian "form" (*eidos*), as attained by contemplative vision, is that trace; and if "form is the trace left by what is formless," then Neoplatonist ontology must be complemented by a phenomenological account of how form manifests itself within the finite intellect (*nous*).[110] For Plotinus no less than for any variety of modern thinkers (Husserl, Weil, Iris Murdoch), such an account takes for its point of departure the cultivation of attention, something the later Stoics, Epictetus in particular, had been arguing since the first century.[111] For a philosophy aimed at spiritual perfection requires that the student not only give timely "attention" (*prosochē*) to the right kind of concern. It also demands that, in so doing, mind detach itself—in a kind of *epochē* or Husserlian

---

110. Balthasar 1989b, 308; "Keine einzelne Form stillt die Sehnsucht der Seele: *ichnos tou amorphou morphē*: die Gestalt ist Spur eines Gestaltlosen."

111. Epictetus views attention as the type of awareness (and self-awareness) that ought to accompany *every action in the fullest possible manner at all times*: "there is no part of life to which attention does not extend," just as there is no activity that can be performed "better by not attending." Likewise, attention should govern not only the performance but also the selection of practical tasks. For if "to defer things is advantageous, it is still more so to give them up altogether." Inasmuch as "relaxing attention" is never warranted, the concept becomes virtually synonymous with the ideal state of mental action. Epictetus 1995, 181–82.

bracketing—from the ambient world's myriad distractions.[112] Following a Platonist line of argument, Murdoch sees a strong link between attention and virtue. Inasmuch as attention "imperceptibly builds up structures of value round about us," it constitutes a habit that, with due care, can flourish into authentic virtue. Such care or cultivation, Murdoch suggests, specifically involves "focusing our attention upon things which are valuable: virtuous people, great art," and, thus, experiencing beauty as "an occasion for 'unselfing.'"[113] Like his twentieth-century Platonizing heirs, Plotinus ponders what quality of attention needs to be cultivated for the contemplative mind to ascend from predicating being as sheer existent to apprehending it as a "trace" of the One. Can there be a type of intellectual action that does not effect change within its object? Is there a form of nonconstructivist knowledge, one that does not subsume the order of being to that of the concept but, instead, unfolds as a lucid witnessing of how being gives itself? Simply put, can there be a knowing without any making (or unmaking) of its object?

It is in *Ennead* V.8 that Plotinus most fully addresses these concerns. Adjusting Plato's distinction between "natural things" and works of art and, indeed, anticipating the Renaissance antinomy of *creare* and *facere*, Plotinus here fundamentally rethinks "making" (*poiein*). Rather than a strictly secondary manipulation of matter—"an inferior thing that consorts with another inferior thing to produce an inferior offspring," as Plato had put it (*Rep.* 603b)—Plotinian "art" (*technē*) seeks to retrace the principle of creation itself. Its true focus is on the creative process rather than on imitating its products. Art makes "the work beautiful according to the forming principle of what it is making." Hence, imitation (*mimēsis*) is no longer considered derivative of nature but, on the contrary, participates in (and makes acutely visible) the creative force (*energeia*) whereby nature brings forth its individual products. While agreeing with Plato that "natural things are imitations too," Plotinus in-

---

112. For the role of attention in modern thought, see Husserl, *Ideen I* (1913), § 92; and especially his searching discussion in *Ding und Raum* (1907), §27, §41. There, Husserl's attempt to capture attention descriptively, namely, as a distinctly focused "attitude" (*Einstellung*) ends up confronting Husserl with the enigma of consciousness per se. Thus, he speaks of attention as "a certain 'attitude,' an ineffable characteristic [*eine gewisse 'Einstellung,' ein unsagbares Charakteristikum*]," that seemingly originates in "the lived experience of an appearance [*Erlebnis einer Erscheinung*]." Such an intentional experience yields nothing more than an "animated sensuous datum [*beseeltes Datum*], ineffably suffused by the attentive intentionality [*eine unsagbare Durchtränkung mit der aufmerkenden Intention*]" (Husserl 1997, 122–23/1991, 146–47 [§41]).

113. Murdoch 1970, 36, 54–55, 82. Elsewhere, Murdoch remarks how "art demands moral effort and teaches quiet attention" (1997, 453). Murdoch's debt not just to Plato but to the writings of Simone Weil is palpable here; see especially Weil's "Reflections on the Right Use of School Studies" (1999, 44–52). Unlike Murdoch, however, Weil regards attention as not only an achievement, but a gift, an instance of grace: "No true effort of attention is ever wasted, though it may never have any visible result" (1999, 91). On Weil's mystical account of attention, see Chenavier 2012, 46–51.

sists that, contrary to arguments developed in Books 3 and 6 of the *Republic*, "the arts do not simply imitate what they see, but they run back up to the forming principles from which nature derives" (V.8.1). Far from duplicating contingently embodied forms, works of art participate in the creative *logoi* of their respective objects. Indeed, to the extent that artistic creation allows "the rational forming principle" (*logos*) to register in the soul, the resulting form or mental image proves "more beautiful than that in nature" (V.8.3).

To experience beauty, therefore, is to become co-creator of dynamic being rather than passively react to an alien object or manufactured proposition whose very nature remains parasitical on being itself. Plotinus's overarching concern, then, is to delineate contemplation as a form of attention that is no longer contingent on some fluctuating object presentation or on a "self" asserting dominion over the world of appearances. As he insists, "We do not yet see a thing while it is outside, but when it comes within, it influences us. But it comes in through the eyes as form alone" (V.8.2). Form (*eidos*) alone renders a thing visible and, thus, real "within" us. Consequently, both form and beauty must be understood as *internal* and eternal rather than extensional and contingent, for "beauty does not lie in magnitude." Hence, "the beauty present in the matter which is the soul" has the status of an agent rather than a product: "It is not an expressed forming principle at all, but is the maker of the first forming principle" (V.8.3). So understood, beauty mediates the beholder's intellect (*nous*) with the One and the Good, which mind it recognizes as ontologically inaccessible. Elicited by and uniquely responsive to the beautiful, Plotinian contemplation (*theōria*) is the one form of attention uniquely capable of linking nature, soul, and intellect in a single virtuous state: "Contemplation ascends from nature to soul, and soul to intellect, and the contemplations become always more intimate and united to the contemplators, and in the soul of the good and wise man the objects known tend to become identical with the knowing subject. . . . [For] the truest life is life by thought [*hē zōē hē alēthestate noēsei zōē estin*]" (III.8.8).[114]

To be sure, Plotinus's thought, like that of his contemporary philosophical schools (Stoics, Academics, Epicureans), cannot eschew what Pierre Hadot calls the "perpetual conflict between the philosopher's efforts to see things as they are from the standpoint of universal nature and the conventional vision of things underlying human society."[115] Yet in the case of Plotinus in particular, that fundamental tension is itself embedded in the structure of his arguments, namely, as the antagonism between the telos of pure contemplation for which Plotinus's spiritual exercises seek to

---

114. As Plotinus's disciple and "editor," Porphyry, was to put it, "Beatific contemplation does not consist of the accumulation of arguments or a storehouse of learned knowledge, but in us theory must become nature and life itself" (Porphyry, *On Abstinence* I.29; as quoted in Hadot 1995, 60).

115. Hadot 1995, 58.

prepare us and their dependency on being mediated by finite, visible matter: "What image of [the intellect], then, could one take? For every image will be drawn from something worse. But the image must be taken from Intellect, so that one is not really apprehending it through an image, but it is like taking a piece of gold as a sample of all gold" (V.8.3). Unlike the gods, human beings will only ever experience the convertibility of beauty and intellect, of perfected form and perfected self-awareness, to a certain degree but never completely; for "we are not accustomed to see any of the things within and do not know them, pursue the external and do not know that it is that within which moves us: as if someone looking at his image and not knowing where it came from should pursue it" (V.8.2).

Still, the ultimate goal of Plotinian virtue is to liberate human vision from being merely reactive to, and circumscribed by, contingent and external appearance. In the first of his treatises, Plotinus still appears to believe in a dramatic and definitive conversion of sorts, as per his blunt enjoinder to "shut your eyes, and change to and wake another way of seeing, which everyone has but few use" (I.6.8). Yet by the time of Treatise 30 (*Ennead* V.8), the argument has become more nuanced and its account of contemplative vision more fully fleshed out. Those who have achieved genuine intellectual vision, the gods, "do not grow weary of contemplation." Furthermore, in the "fullness" (*plērōma*) of inner vision, all subjective considerations have melted away and the quality of attention has achieved a certain universality: "Things are not different from each other so as to make what belongs to one displeasing to another with different characteristics." Hence, too, time no longer degrades the fullness of intellectual vision, for the latter is not here indexed to proprietary desire but has become infinitely giving and expansive: "Fullness does not cause contempt for that which has produced it: for that which sees goes on seeing still more, and, perceiving its own infinity and that of what it sees, follows its own nature. Life holds no weariness for anyone when it is pure. . . . This life is wisdom" (V.8.4).

The last point is crucial and bears further consideration. Insofar as knowledge transcends the occasional and discursive kind diffused among individual souls, it falls within the domain of wisdom (*sophia*), "which is true substance" (V.8.5). As such, wisdom is "the most intensive mode of divine being following the One."[116] Hence, "one must not then suppose that the gods or the 'exceedingly blessed spectators' in the higher world contemplate propositions, but all the Forms we speak about are beautiful images [*kala agalmata*] in the world, . . . images not painted but real" (V.8.5). It is precisely this "non-discursiveness of the intelligible world," which Ploti-

---

116. Beierwaltes 2001, 52; he goes on to remark that Plotinian wisdom is "contiguous [*anschlußfähig*] with the Christian conception of wisdom, provided it is understood as identical with the divine word or spirit [*Geist*]" (52).

nus finds embodied in the picture language of the Egyptians, that attests to the onto-logical nexus between form, image, and mental vision. More than a millennium and a half later, Schelling will reclaim that form of knowledge (from, among others, Kant) under the heading "intellectual intuition." Discursive speech is itself summoned by the imagistic fullness of that intuition. Hence, "if we see intuition as giving birth to speech and speech as the attempt to recapture intuition, then we must surely see the relation between intuition and speech as dialectical." Even as discursive speech is the gift enabling the mediation of thought (*noēsis*) qua representation and reflection, all speech is already teleologically ordered toward the One. For the intuition that calls forth speech is itself "a function of silence."[117] Hence, the "cult image" (*agalma*), which Plotinus credits with fusing the totality of a thing's aspects into a single and complete visible presence, constitutes both the very foundation of discourse and the threshold beyond which discursive thought cannot advance: "Every image is a kind of knowledge and wisdom and is a subject of statements, all together in one, and not discourse or deliberation. But [only] afterwards [others] discovered, starting from it in its concentrated unity, a representation in something else, already unfolded and speaking it discursively" (V.8.6). Time-bound discursive and propositional reason-ing (*epistēmas theōrēmata*) is by definition incapable of grasping and articulating its own enabling conditions.[118] At the same time, inasmuch as spoken and written dis-course takes itself to be concerned with a reality from which it stands forever at a re-move, it feeds off the anterior presence of forms. If "all this universe is held fast by forms from beginning to end," the very "archetype" (*paradeigma*) of form originates in unfathomable eternal silence ("done without noise and fuss") (V.8.7).

Intelligible beauty, for Plotinus, explains why the form in its sheer manifestation or self-disclosure is not only recognized as a Truth but also compels our assent to it as a Good: "For the human being, the beautiful image of the absolutely beautiful is to become the incentive for a return into himself, and for a cognitive ascent toward the One [*erkennender Aufstieg zum Prinzip*]." As it entwines phenomenon and observer in a qualitative bond, form manifests itself, not as some value-neutral perception, but as "a reality met by 'marveling' (*thaumazein*) and the question concerning the

---

117. Schroeder 1992, 76.

118. In his great treatise on the soul, Plotinus elaborates why human beings habitually assume that the soul depends on the body: "It is because the soul is not visible, but the body is, so we see the body and are aware that it is ensouled because it moves and perceives, and so say that it has soul. It would then be a natural consequence for us to say that the soul is actually in the body. But if the soul was visible and perceptible . . . we should not have said that the soul was in the body, but that the unimportant was in the more important." Yet the categories of thought available in his time seem to preclude just that: "For none of the ways of a thing's being in anything which are currently spoken of fits the relationship of the soul to the body" (IV.3.20–21).

'why' of such beauty."[119] Yet that question cannot be settled by discursive means but, instead, enjoins the beholder to achieve a state of undesigning attention. To encounter form as it manifests itself in the medium of visible beauty is to know qua witnessing rather than proposition. Form here is manifested not as an object but as the event (*Ereignis*) of numinous reality unveiled in the modality of the image. It is the advent of truth itself "beautifully disposed: as if the conclusion was there before the syllogism." The luminous, clear disposition of the phenomenal world is no mere predicate of intellect but, rather, its ontological ground. If, as Plotinus remarks, intelligible beauty "is before consequential and purposive thinking," its irresistible hold on contemplation attests to something unconditionally given or, indeed, revealed. Unlike some effect conspicuously wrought or a desire serendipitously gratified, beauty ratifies the transformative advent of form within the soul, which cannot but recognize that "the power in the intelligible world has nothing but its being and its being beautiful" (V.8.7).

For Plotinus, this convertibility of beauty and sheer being attests to their coincidence and perfection ("for in deficiency of beauty it would be defective also in reality" [V.8.9]). Beauty thus fulfills what Gadamer considers the defining trait of the image: it brings about "an increase in being [*ein Zuwachs an Sein*]."[120] Or, in Plotinus's words, "it is more reality in so far as it is beautiful [*mallon gar ousia ē kalē*]" (V.8.9). Hence, even as "beauty is not primarily an *aesthetic* . . . but an ethical norm, it may become aesthetically significant for a theory of art only because it has to be understood as an ontological principle subtending sensible reality overall."[121] As it infuses the beholder with the silent and contemplative knowledge of form, visible beauty emerges as the medium by which the intellect—forever perched on the threshold between time and eternity, the One and the many—may participate in the true.

Still, every image naturally is the image of something, of a being that constitutes its ground and *in* which the image participates; and, as our discussion of Plato had established, participation involves a dialectical tension between a certain similarity and a (greater) difference between image and archetype. The relation is one of *analogia* rather than outright identity, an insight that we will find undergirding Nicholas of Cusa's conception of the image and its role in late medieval mystical theology. Thus, the essential difference separating the image from its archetype (the Plotinian

119. Beierwaltes [1985] 2016, 90.

120. Gadamer 2006, 135.

121. On Plotinus's conception of beauty, see Beierwaltes 2001, 53–70; quote from 54 ("daß <Schönheit> als ein ontologisches Strukturmoment der sinnfälligen Wirklichkeit insgesamt zu denken ist").

One) is not a deficiency of the former; rather, it throws into visible relief the eternal and ineffable self-identity of the latter. The archetype can only ever come into focus for the intellect in virtue of being subject to "presentation" (*Darstellung*) in the medium of the image. If the original is first in the order of being, the image is first in the order of apprehension. Its constitutive difference vis-à-vis its original does not negate, let alone supplant, the latter's essential identity. Rather, it opens it to partial view, "through a glass darkly." The interplay of identity and difference in the way that the image relates to the archetype involves not a collision of incommensurables but a productive, dialectical tension. Only in and through the image does mind release or "realize" (in what Hegel will eventually call *verwirklichen*) the positive essence of the being of which it is the image. As Werner Beierwaltes puts it, this "'realization of the image' [*Realisierung des Bildes*] is above all a releasing [*Freisetzen*] of the *positive* potential in the image, a mobilization of the identity, unity, or resemblance that prevails within it. Hence it can be the negation of the negative [*Negation des Negativen*], such that the pictorial reality brings about a return and ascent: from the many images to the one archetype [*Urbild*]." At the same time, to maintain that, by its very nature, every image stands to its original in a "relation of dependency" (*Bedingungsverhältnis*) necessarily presupposes an ontological framework.[122] For only where identity and difference are grasped as dialectically entwined features of reality, rather than as an antinomy, can we speak of images at all. Only where there is a timeless and unchanging One sustaining the dialectical to-and-fro of identity and difference and promising its ultimate reconciliation can an image and its archetype ever enter into a distinct and constructive relationship.

For Plotinus and those extending his legacy for the next millennium (Proclus, pseudo-Dionysius, John Scotus Eriugena, Meister Eckhart, Bonaventure, Nicholas of Cusa, among others), a dialectical movement of resemblance and otherness structures the relation of the image not only vis-à-vis the being of which it is the image but also vis-à-vis the One or absolute *logos* that guarantees the possibility of such a relation in the first place. For if being was bereft of all internal structure and continuity-in-becoming, it could never be meaningfully set in relation to anything else. Absent this Plotinian One, or what Cusa will call the *non-aliud*—the Being that is never "other" vis-à-vis any particular being (yet therefore is also never identifiable with any single being)—the intellect would find itself adrift in a Nominalist universe of terminally disaggregated singularities. In that case, there would be no *eidos* (Lat. *species*), no form, and hence no image, which always presupposes the ontological relatedness of the One and the many. There would be no intelligible beauty but only ephemeral pleasure, no essential knowledge but only contingent acts of quantification. As we

---

122. Beierwaltes [1985] 2016, 78. See also Gadamer 2006, 130–38.

shall see in chapter 4, it is no coincidence that the most comprehensive assimilation of Neoplatonism by Christian theology should have begun at the beginning of the fifteenth century, at a time when the elaborate arguments and claims of late Scholastic Nominalism were increasingly deemed unpersuasive on both intellectual and affective grounds.

2

THEOLOGY AND PHENOMENOLOGY OF THE BYZANTINE ICON

O sages standing in God's holy fire
As in the gold mosaic of a wall,
Come from the holy fire, perne in a gyre,
And be the singing-masters of my soul.
Consume my heart away; sick with desire
And fastened to a dying animal
It knows not what it is; and gather me
Into the artifice of eternity.

—W. B. Yeats, "Sailing to Byzantium"

"EVIDENCE OF THINGS NOT SEEN": PRE-NICAEAN THEOLOGIES OF IMAGE AND SPIRITUAL VISION

Eighth- and ninth-century Byzantium is a rare case where a conflict lasting nearly 120 years produced not only violence and destruction but also, surprisingly, a significant intellectual advance. For it was out of the struggle over the legitimacy of image veneration in the Eastern Church that "perhaps for the first time in Western thinking—a consistent and comprehensive image concept . . . developed."[1] Leaving

---

1. Alloa 2013, 6. As Pelikan notes, "The conflict over Iconoclasm was always much more than a political struggle; at the same time, it was certainly never less than political" (2011, 7); while

aside for the moment the conflict's political dimension—a growing rift between the emperor and a Phrygian episcopacy largely co-opted by him, on the one hand, and the provincial church and the monasteries, on the other—the issues underlying and shaping the iconoclast debate are fundamentally theological in kind.[2] When framed in both a theological and a phenomenological matrix, as this chapter argues it ought to be, iconoclasm appears the fulcrum of numerous, concurrently unfolding debates in Mediterranean late antiquity. They include (1) the challenge of reconciling the gradualism of Hellenistic thought and Neoplatonist notions of spiritual "ascent" with Pauline Christianity's radical idea of spiritual "conversion" (*metanoia*) and transformation; (2) the conflicting approaches to imagining the relation of Creator to creation in kataphatic and apophatic terms, respectively; (3) the growing role of material objects, and of images in particular, not only in liturgical practice but also in emergent forms of private devotion that by the seventh century have taken on a life of their own, rather apart from the Eastern Church and the Divine Liturgy formulated by St. John Chrysostom; (4) attempts at the start of the eighth century to develop an (in essence phenomenological) distinction between two kinds of intentionality vis-à-vis the icon: a misguided, idolatrous worshipping of visible matter, on the one hand, and the "veneration" (*proskynēsis*) of visible images and relics insofar as they mediate and focalize the "worship" (*douleia*) of the invisible Triune God, on the other; (5) the growing ecclesial and political divide between Byzantium and Rome; and (6) within the Byzantine empire itself, a struggle, rapidly intensifying after AD 700, over whether monastic communities in the empire's far-flung provinces or a preponderantly urban episcopacy ought to be the arbiters of the true faith. Underlying all these conflicts and debates, however, is the ongoing quest for a Christology that would meet the theological requirements of the learned class (the *arcani*) and, at the same time, could be effectively reconciled with diverse forms of popular piety that had established themselves in the eastern Mediterranean and the Byzantine empire's rural interior.[3] In the event, it is this last concern that overarches all the

Schönborn concurs that "the icon controversy is primarily a religious phenomenon, . . . a dispute about the 'true religion,' the purity of the Church" (1994, 144), he also notes that iconoclasts and iconophiles alike seemed at times to operate without a coherent and clearly articulated image concept. John of Damascus for one never actually produces a definition of the icon and surprisingly omits distinguishing "between *natural and artificial image*" (194).

    2. On the historical background, see the magisterial survey by Brubaker and Haldon (2011), as well as Brown's landmark essay from 1973. As Schönborn points out, "At the [iconoclast] council of A.D. 754 *all* the bishops obeyed the will of the emperor and became iconoclasts, and thirty years later . . . once again *all* the bishops unanimously signed the decrees of the iconophile Council of A.D. 787" (1994, 187), including some of the *same* bishops.

    3. Peter Brown's claim that "on the whole, the discussion of the Christological issues involved in the worship or rejection of icons was remarkably desultory throughout the eighth century" (1973, 3) misses the salient point, namely, that none of the other issues could be coherently addressed, let

others and bears out George Florovsky's view that iconoclasm "was an integral phase of the great Christological dispute" that had been unfolding since the first Council of Nicaea (AD 325).[4]

As regards the very heart of the faith, questions concerning Christology continued to loom since its initial, notably contrasting, articulation in the writings of Irenaeus and Origen; and with every new generation these questions demanded to be answered anew and, it seemed, with steadily increasing urgency. If upon appearing in this world, Christ retained "the form of God [*morphē theou*]" while at the same time taking "upon him the form of a servant [*morphēn doulou*]" by being "made in the likeness [*homoiōmati*] of men" (Phil. 2:7), how is his dual nature to be reconciled with the strict invisibility of God (Ex 33:20; Jn 1:18)? How could he, who walked among men in Galilee, be declared "consubstantial with the Father," as in time the Nicene Creed will do? What quality of vision, what spiritual intentionality, is required to make both *experiential* and *theological* sense of Christ's affirmation that "he that hath seen me hath seen the Father" (Jn 14:9)? Already forty-five years old, Augustine's lingering perplexity in this regard seems acute and representative: "As for the mystery of *The Word Made Flesh*, at that I could not even guess."[5] The challenge presented by the Incarnate God is not solved, only intensified, by the uncompromising language in which Paul's letters frame it. Here, every trace of Platonic and Hellenistic gradualism appears eclipsed by the dramatic events of Christ's crucifixion and resurrection. Gone is any echo of a second Platonic hypostasis, and there is no hint as yet of monarchist views of God or subordinationist views of Christ as a "secondary God" (*deuteros theos*), such as will surface in Origen and, another century later, in the arguments put forward by the bishops of Caesarea and Nicomedia at the Council of Nicaea.

If, as Eusebius of Caesarea for one was to suggest, monarchism, subordinationism, and modalism all served the purpose of making Christ's dual nature more readily communicable to the faithful, Paul's letters would seem to have none of it.[6] Indeed, rarely is his uncompromising outlook more fully on display than where the question

---

alone resolved, without confronting yet again the fundamental choice: either to accept the proposition that visible, material things serve as conduits toward the invisible or, by rejecting the Hellenistic idea of the *logos* encompassing finite and divine being, to relapse into a Manichaean or Gnostic doctrine of sorts. As John of Damascus was to argue so stridently, everything turns on how to understand the Incarnation of the Lord. On problems with construing iconoclasm "as a 'Semitic' objection against the 'Hellenistic' re-paganization of the Church," see Florovsky, who notes that the Phrygian "higher Clergy and other intellectuals" supportive of the emperor's push for the destruction of images were themselves often Hellenistic in their formation and sympathies (1950, 82, 83).

    4. Florovsky 1950, 79.

    5. Augustine 2001, 153 (*Conf.* 7.19.25).

    6. Besançon 2000, 84–86.

of the *imago Dei* is concerned, with Paul adjusting the concept of the image in at least two ways. For one, his antinomy of icon and idol is uncompromising, with the latter categorically proscribed as an illegitimate and sinful substitution or simulation: "Do I mean then that food sacrificed to an idol is anything, or that an idol is anything?" (1 Cor 10:19). Beyond that, however, Paul also distinguishes between image (*eikōn*) and likeness (*homoion*), crediting each with its own efficacy and legitimacy.[7] Thus, "likeness" pertains less to the act of vision than to that of cognition or, more precisely, to the *recognition* of what has already been seen. It accredits a visual representation with a specific identity and significance, such as the emperor's likeness found on coins. Recalling the Platonic idea of *mimēsis*, likeness signifies strictly within the context of finite, earthly existence and, thus, lacks the transcendent and eschatlogical connotations of *eikōn*. Like Dostoevsky's "image" (*obraz*), Paul's icon positions the beholder on a trajectory that will "transform" her into an image of God. Hence, Paul's puzzling reference to Christ as "the image of the invisible God" (*hos estin eikôn tou theou tou aoratou / qui est imago Dei invisibilis* [Col 1:15]) hints at his emergent understanding of the image as mediation rather than representation and "manifestation" rather than simulation. If the metamorphosis of Paul's faithful "into the same image" (i.e., of Christ [2 Cor 3:18]) is best visualized as a form of ascent, the language of "manifestation" implies a descent of sorts. The apostles understand themselves not as independent agents "walking in craftiness . . . but by manifestation of the truth [*phanerōsei tēs alētheias*]," so that "the life also of Jesus might be made manifest [*phanerōthē*] in our mortal flesh" (2 Cor 4:2, 4:11).[8]

We have come a long way from Plato, who, even in his most trenchant account of the image in the *Sophist*, still invests *eikōn* with an apparitional, unreal quality. Such residual connotations of inferiority or insubstantiality have altogether disappeared in Paul's letters. Not only have *eikōn* and *eidōlon* been firmly desynonymized, but henceforth their opposition will be an integral feature of Paul's antinomian pars-

---

7. See Rom 8:3 (God sent "His own Son in the likeness [*homoiōmati*] of sinful flesh"), whereas the human being is "the image [*eikōn*] and glory of God" (1 Cor 11:7). "The general rule seems to be that earthly representations have 'likeness' while divine similitude and future transformations are spoken of in terms of 'image'" (Jensen 2005, 13).

8. On this passage, see Heath 2013, 194–96, who offers a partial defense of Reitzenstein's controversial reading in *Die hellenistischen Mysterienreligionen* (1927) of Paul's notion of seeing as a simultaneously corporeal and spiritual act effecting a form of *theōsis*—what he called *Verwandlung durch Schau*—by transforming the beholder into "the image of the Lord" (*eikōn kyriou*). Predictably, Reitzenstein's interpretation drew opposition on account of both its putative Hellenism and its Catholicism, such as in Frances Back's dissenting reading in her programmatically titled *Verwandlung durch Offenbarung* (Transformation by Revelation). Still, even as "the grammatical/syntactical structure of 2 Cor 3:18 does underline the agency of the spirit empowering transformation *while we look*, it is misleading to press this to the point of driving a wedge between *Verwandlung durch Offenbarung* and *Verwandlung durch Schau*" (Heath 2013, 185–86).

ing of spirit and letter, faith and law, new and old covenant. In the absence of any cross-contamination between icon and idol, seeing the *eikōn* becomes for Paul a way of gauging the scope and durability of the true faith. Having "returned to the Hellenic theme of transformative vision," the Letter to the Hebrews positions the *eikōn* as the very linchpin for supplanting the regime of the flesh with that of an unconditional faith that, reminiscent of Plato, its author characterizes as "the evidence [*elenchos*] of things not seen" (Heb. 11:1).[9] Just as for the later Socrates the true aim of dialogue involves not the gratuitous, skeptical questioning of his interlocutors but, rather, the joint excavation of an underlying truth, so Paul's *elenchos* attests to an antecedent, unconditional "faith" (*pistis*) in a truth that had to be logically presupposed for dialogic action and syllogistic demonstration to be pursued at all. At the same time, Paul's faith in "things unseen" (*ou blepomenōn*) attests to a fundamentally new conception of vision and image. What the icon points to, the metanoia it is to bring about in the beholder, is an essentially imageless, spiritual vision no longer tinged by the material contingencies and spiritual hazards associated with embodied "sight" (*opsis*).

Of particular relevance in this regard is 2 Corinthians 3:18, which throws into relief the visible image's implacable drive toward its own self-suspension, a pattern we shall have occasion to observe time and again in other writers throughout this study: "But we all, with open [unveiled; *anakekalymmenō*] face beholding as in a glass [*katoptrizomenoi*] the glory of the Lord, are changed into the same image [*tēn autēn eikona*] from glory to glory, even as by the Spirit of the Lord." Yet again, the underlying motif is the passage of "flesh" (*sarx*) into "spirit" (*pneuma*), which here correlates with a faithful removing of the "veil" (*kalymma*) and passing "into the same image" that Christ's *imago Dei* has modeled for them. As Paul writes just before the passage in question, "the veil is done away [*anakalyptomenon*] in Christ" (2 Cor 3:14), who thus functions dually as the visible, incarnate image of God *and* as the invisible eschaton, "the glory of the Lord" *into which* the faithful are to be transformed. By analogy, integrating two distinct (though never opposed) dimensions, Paul's "image" (*eikōn*) encompasses and promises to reconcile visible appearance and its invisible fulfillment. The Pauline image thus ought to be understood as the indispensable *medium* (not an "object") of finite vision and, as such, retains affinity with Paul's "veil." Yet inasmuch as the visible icon is no mere ephemeral appearance but, instead, manifests a substantive truth, it prefigures the invisible telos into which it is to transform the beholder. In the Incarnate Lord, then, the order of the visible both attains its consummate presence and is decisively transfigured. On Paul's account, Christ supremely models for the faithful the icon's true meaning, namely, as both the apotheosis and the ultimate self-suspension of the visible.

---

9. Besançon 2000, 86.

As we shall see, the capacity of the image to "transform" (*metamorphoumetha*) its beholders into "the same image," that is, into the truth that Christ's image has made manifest, is a recurrent Pauline motif. Time and again, empirical "sight" (*opsis*) is presented less as a self-contained visual experience than as the catalyst for the beholder's inward transformation. Commenting on 2 Corinthians 3:18, Origen identifies as true beholders those "for whom the Lord is always present to the eyes of the mind [*dianoias ophthalmōn*]."[10] Once we understand that the "divine image" (*eikōn theou*) is both source and telos of vision, it becomes clear that spiritual sight is never unilaterally accomplished by a finite individual. Rather, such sight adumbrates, however tentatively, a spiritual community—the "we" or, rather, "all of us" (*pantes*), that is, the ideal of Christian brotherhood as the template for a truly ethical community.[11] For Paul, seeing the "divine image" means above all opening oneself to being seen, to behold one's own spiritual condition "with open [unveiled; *anakekalymmenō*] face . . . as in a glass." This speculative fusion of "seeing" with "being seen" will recur again in Nicholas of Cusa's *De Visione Dei* (1453), and we will also find it echoed, perhaps more faintly, in G. M. Hopkins's observation that "what you look hard at seems to look hard at you" (*HCW* 1:504).

Paul's unusual choice of the middle form (*katoptrizesthai*), "to behold in a mirror," underscores his association of "mirrors with indirect" and, consequently, incomplete "vision." Governing both the preceding clause and the one following, the verb form points to "what Moses does not want to see (the created images) *and* [to] what he does want to see (the very form)."[12] Reminiscent of 1 Corinthians 13:12 ("through a glass darkly"), the image in the Second Letter to the Corinthians likewise aims to reconcile a veiled "now" with a fully transparent future. Still, the kind of spiritual sight of which Paul here speaks is no mere instance of ephemeral speculation. Rather, it constitutes a positively transformative event in that in such seeing God manifests himself to the beholder in the medium of the image, thereby justifying her eschatological hopes. Frances Back speaks of a "prophetic 'seeing' of revelation" (*prophetisches 'Sehen' der Christusbotschaft*), with her use of quotation marks qualifying "seeing" as but a trope for spiritual cognition; Rabens amends the reading by suggesting that "Christ himself could be interpreted as the mirror" that brings

---

10. Quoted by Mark J. McInroy ("Origen of Alexandria"), in Gavrilyuk and Coakley 2012, 32.

11. "When Jesus calls his disciples 'brothers' . . . it is a decision for the future, for in these twelve the new People of God is being addressed; in them it is being designated as a people of brothers. . . . This community is far more public than a mystery group. It sees itself . . . in analogy with the people of Israel—indeed, with humanity" (Ratzinger 1993, 26, 34). Rabens reads "being changed" or "transformed" in 2 Cor 3:18 as indicative of a strong "ethical dimension," akin to the "transformation" and "renewal" of which Paul speaks in Col 3:10 (Rabens 2013, 197, 199).

12. Heath 2013, 220; Heath also notes that *katoptrizein* in its middle form (*katoprizesthai*) is "otherwise unattested in this sense at this period" (218). For a comprehensive discussion of 2 Cor 3:18, see Rabens 2013, 171–203.

about a more "personal encounter" and self-recognition in the individual. Overall, his reading of "*katoptrizomenoi* as beholding the glory of God on the face of Jesus [as] the more likely reading of 3:18" seems more persuasive in that it balances *what* is revealed, God's glory, with the visible presence *through* which it is revealed, Christ's human face and form. Not only is "seeing" not reduced to a conventional synonym for "knowing," but Paul's use of the present tense also frames contemplative seeing as an ongoing process rather than as an instantaneous and definitive "conversion" (*metanoia*).[13]

Significant in this regard is Paul's characterization of those beholding the Lord with an "open" or "unveiled" face, which clearly recalls Exodus 34:29–35. There Moses removes his veil while speaking to God but, upon returning to his people, "put the veil upon his face again" because its new radiance instilled fear in them. Alluding to how Moses stood unveiled before God, who had just called for the breaking of idols (Ex 34:13), Paul specifically links the eschaton of unmediated vision to the removal of the "veil," that is, to moving beyond the visible image: "Seeing then that we . . . use great plainness of speech: And not as Moses, [*who*] put a veil over his face" (2 Cor 3:12–13). In time, Paul's trope of the veil will be seized upon as a scriptural warrant of sorts for the Byzantine icon and the iconostasis as they become formalized in the seventh century. Related to the dialectic of veiling and unveiling is Paul's characterization, in Hebrews 1:3, of Christ as "the brightness of his glory, and the express image of his person [hos ōn apaugasma tēs doxēs kai charaktēr tēs hypostaseōs autou]." Paul here introduces a key concept, *hypostasis*, that has significant bearing on the theology of the icon as *imago Dei*. The concept is subsequently pondered in an important patristic text, Basil of Caesarea's Thirty-Eighth Letter, now widely thought to have been written by his brother, Gregory of Nyssa. In it, Gregory shows that there is an ontological difference between Being (*ousia*) and its self-realization in the persons (*hypostaseis*) of the Trinity. Put differently, *hypostasis* must not be conceived abstractly; it is "not the indefinite conception of the essence . . . but the conception which by means of the expressed peculiarities gives *standing* and circumscription to the general and uncircumscribed."[14] Just as "person" is not the equivalent of the abstract concept "man" but its concrete, visible instantiation, so *hypostasis* amounts to a concretion or specification of being. As we shall see, some fifteen hundred years later, the distinction between *ousia* and *hypostasis* will recur, once again as part of an effort to conceptualize the image, in John Ruskin's distinction between the "general" and the "specific" and in the young Charles Darwin's attempts at visualizing the

---

13. Back, quoted in Rabens 2013, 180; as Rabens notes, "*katoptrizomenoi* . . . suggests a continuous activity" (183).

14. Basil, Epistle 38, *PNF* 8:137 f.; on this letter and the founding role of hypostasis for later theologies of the icon, see Schönborn 1994, 17–33. On the concept of hypostasis, see also Ratzinger 2013, 103–19.

specificity of a given "species" without becoming bogged down in random particularity or empty abstraction.[15] For if the specificity of being cannot be accessed inferentially or by a process of abstraction, then it must manifest and reveal itself to human sight. Hence, in Paul's Letter to the Hebrews, the concept of *charaktēr* forms a corollary of *hypostasis*, connoting both "person" in that it "specifies 'a certain man,'" as Gregory notes, and also "image, engraving, and imprint."[16] Paul's concept of *hypostasis*, in the way that Gregory draws out its implications, thus serves two intimately entwined purposes: first, it preserves the distinctness of the image as such, by ensuring that it is not conflated with what it depicts; and second, the specificity implied by the concept of *hypostasis* ensures that the God who achieves presence in the *imago* of the Son is apprehended not as a purely transcendent, notional Being (*ousia*) but as He who has mediated and reconciled immanence and transcendence.

How are the faithful to prevent the ontological predicate of God's invisibility from being misconstrued as his effective absence? How is the apophatic theology of most Fathers, later enshrined in the writings of pseudo-Dionysius, to be reconciled with affirmations of God's eternal and unconditional presence both *in* and *to* creation? How are the faithful to move beyond a merely passive expectancy of their Lord and Redeemer by imagining themselves as active respondents to the "enabling grace" of their eventual salvation?[17] While not contesting God's invisibility in the least, Paul in his letter to the Corinthians nevertheless posits a movement of visible and embodied being toward the transcendent and uncreated God. As his syntax suggests, the image (*eikōn*) mediates between the two realms by positing, in effect, an analogical relation between them: "And as we have borne the image of the earthy, we shall also bear the image of the heavenly" (1 Cor 15:49). Likewise, Paul's affirmation that "the invisible things of him from the creation of the world are clearly seen, being understood by the things that are made" (Rom 1:20), posits an analogy between visible creation and the invisible God. It is this concept of analogy that, some four centuries after Paul, allows his putative student on the Areopagus, Dionysius, to lay the groundwork for a theological aesthetics. Especially his *Celestial Hierarchy* succeeds to a degree not seen before in aligning the two dimensions of the image that Paul had first distinguished: its ability, as *homoion*, to produce a "likeness" of visible, earthly authority and simultaneously, as *eikōn*, to render Christ's divine nature intuitable to the spiritual senses of the faithful. Dionysius's view had been adumbrated in

---

15. See below, ch. 5.

16. As Schönborn notes, "Each Person's own *property* . . . is nothing else but the specific way in which this Person relates to the *other* Persons." To the question, "How is it possible for the Person of the Son . . . to be the image of the Father?," the "preliminary" answer thus will be: "It is the particular property of each of the Divine Persons to reveal each other" (1994, 28–29); Schönborn offers a fuller discussion of *charaktēr* in the context of early Byzantine iconoclasm under Leo III later on (181–85).

17. See Aquinas, *ST* I-II 109–14; and the discussion in Wawrykow 2005, 192–221.

Basil of Caesarea's much-quoted remark "that the honor rendered to the image passes to the prototype."[18] Yet already in Paul, the genitive construction ("image *of* the invisible God") no longer conceives of Christ as a second hypostasis in Neoplatonist fashion. There is no hint of subordination here, and *eikōn* consequently does not denote some derivative or subsidiary imitation but, instead, functions as the coequal medium *in* and *through* which God has freely chosen to manifest himself.

Yet for that conception to appear plausible, it is necessary to distinguish between the image as a *visible* likeness and the phenomenology—the quality of its experience—to which it gives rise, which centers on an *interior*, or spiritual, vision. Where the beholder apprehends Christ as the *eikōn theou*, the intentional object of such vision is not something external to the beholder but, instead, concerns the beholder's own spiritualization (*theōsis*). In what follows, my principal focus is on the icon as a "living" image: not an inert "representation" (*mimēsis*) but a dynamic medium experienced by the faithful beholder as imbued with a unique agency and presence perhaps best captured by the modern concept of performativity.[19] Of particular interest are hieratic depictions of Christ, the Virgin Mary, and/or saints; a discussion of images depicting scenes from scriptural narrative is deferred until much later. The form of the icon that apparently evolved in the Mediterranean East during the second half of the sixth century institutes an entirely new kind of gaze. To behold it means not only to see, but, simultaneously, to find oneself as the focus of a gaze from beyond. Integral to the *eikōn* is this capacity for eliciting a formalized or ritualized response—of veneration, prayer, meditation, and/or contemplation—absent which the meaning of the icon would remain substantially unfulfilled. As such, the *eikōn* stands in sharp contrast to the finite idol (*eidōlon*) that purports to simulate, and thus substitute itself for, some reality external to it. As its Byzantine defenders will in time vigorously maintain, the *eikōn* instead mediates Christ's numinous reality and presence, from which, moreover, it draws its legitimacy as such; and it never seeks to negate the ontological gap separating it from that reality, which is why Basil specifically notes that "the honor rendered to the image *passes to* [*diabainei*] the original." Inasmuch as a theological grammar of the icon is inseparable from its experience in liturgical and devotional practice, we have here a prima facie case of image theory *as*

---

18. *On the Holy Spirit*, 18:45 (*PNF* 8:137–41); echoing Basil, Theodore the Studite writes that "the copy shares the glory of its prototype, as a reflection shares the brightness of the light" (1981, I.8). Regarding Basil's much-quoted statement, see also Besançon 2000, 84 f.; and Ladner (1953, 4), who points out Basil's "noteworthy . . . distinction of an image by nature (*physikōs*) or generation (*genetōs*)—as in the Father-Son relationship—from an image as *mimēma*, as an imitation by art."

19. On the performative or "animist" character of icons, see Freedberg 1989, 74–76; see also Pentcheva, who considers "iconicity [to be] defined as a ceaseless action" (2017a, 61); and also Kartsonis, for whom "the icon manifests its prototype alive and capable of presence, thought, will, action, interaction, and dialogue with the viewer" (1998, 65).

phenomenology; that is, the icon's very being is accessible only in an *experiential*, as opposed to a *notional*, sense. Hence, intertwining an exploration of the image with twentieth-century phenomenology helps draw out its "visual efficacy" throughout this study. It is also meant to buttress the overarching thesis, namely, that the conceptual depth and import of images is never abstract (though the visual presentation itself may well be) but emphatically practical in nature, and that images open up forms of cognition that remain categorically inaccessible to inferential and propositional reasoning.

It is one of the great paradoxes of religious history that, of all things, an era of religious and political conflict ended up significantly advancing our understanding of the image. While "image doctrine was born and developed under the pressure of a political crisis," as Mondzain notes, defending the icon quickly outgrew its immediate occasion and became "a broader plea concerning the conditions and modalities of thought itself."[20] Not until the polemics and counter-polemics of the early eighth century had anyone formulated so poignantly what, for the purposes of this study, is a foundational claim: namely, that the image does not seek to depict a verifiable entity but, rather, to mediate a numinous and invisible, presence. To the Byzantine defenders of religious images, the icon's noetic correlate is not a contingent perception but a spiritual truth. Consequently, the icon's aim is not to produce a verifiable representation but to induce in its beholder either a state of focused remembrance (e.g., of Christ's Passion or other moments of biblical narrative) or a similarly concentrated, prayerlike attention to an invisible, spiritual presence as mediated by depictions of Christ's or a particular saint's human face. Seeing the hieratic icon thus is intimately bound up with the beholder's longed-for conversion when, as Dionysius puts it, "the soul becomes divinized" as a result of having learned to focus "on the most unambiguous perceptions . . . on the things most distinctly seen."[21] Dionysius's outline in his *Celestial Hierarchy* of a supremely concentrated visual intentionality helps explain the emergence, in the second half of the sixth century, of a new style of iconic portraiture that notably excludes all extraneous scenic or decorative elements and, shorn of all visual distraction, brings its beholder face-to-face with Christ or the saints. As George Florovsky argued in 1950, iconoclasm was "a doctrinal controversy . . . [and] an integral phasis of the great Christological dispute" that had been unfolding since the first Council of Nicaea (AD 325).[22] With the exception of Sergei Bulgakov, whose defense of the icon employs a substantially different logic

---

20. Mondzain 2005, 76.

21. Pseudo-Dionysius 1987, 80 (*Divine Names*, 709a); henceforth cited parenthetically as *DN*.

22. Florovsky 1950, 78, 79. On the "Trinitarian Foundations" of the icon, see Schönborn 1994, 3–43; Constas 2014, 61–79; Mondzain 2005, 25–34; see also Ostrogorsky 1929.

from what we find in the writings of John Damascene and other eighth- and ninth-century iconodules, most theologians have concurred with Florovsky's appraisal.[23]

In contrast, a historicist approach to iconoclasm, concurrently pursued throughout the twentieth century and into the present, maintains that the icon's conceptual challenge and theological import is at best peripheral to what were fundamentally political, military, and ecclesial power struggles that came to a head with the ascent of Leo III in AD 717. This historicist line was put forward in particularly uncompromising fashion early on by Henri Grégoire, and since the 1970s it has been echoed and elaborated by Peter Brown, John Haldon, and Leslie Brubaker.[24] Brown's landmark 1973 essay, while richly informed, encapsulates historicism's question-begging approach to religious and aesthetic phenomena, namely, to "explain" a specific phenomenon such as the icon in exclusively functional ways while paying no attention to the specific form or "mode of being" (Gadamer's *Seinsweise*) that uniquely enables such forms to fulfill these specific functions to begin with. Rather than situate the Byzantine icon in relation to the relic, and to some extent as its successor, as Kitzinger had done, Brown mainly associates it with the figure of the "holy man" in seventh-century Byzantium, a monastic, saintly figure whose authority "as an intercessor with God" was not conferred by the bishops but instead appears to have been a function of his spiritual charism. The icon, Brown contends, was Byzantine culture's solution for extending the spiritual presence of this holy man beyond his natural life span. Icons, that is, were "*merely* thought to be holy; and "*merely* fill[ed] the gap left by the physical absence of the holy man." Yet "merely" begs the central question regarding the intrinsic capacity of the image to achieve a unique *presence*, as opposed to serving as but a pictorial sign that simply "refers to" the holy man. Pressing the functionalist argument further, Brown imagines the icon to have served the hermit's "desperate *need* . . . to focus his attention on some enduring and resilient figure," a need that, he claims, could only have "found a resolution in the icon hanging in his monastic cell." At the same time, Brown surmises that "icons were invested with holiness in the late sixth and seventh centuries because they *still* expressed the continuing *needs* of the ancient city," and generally imagines religious images to have served other unspecified "psychological *needs*."[25] From a historicist's vantage point, that is, the icon is only *functionally* intelligible, namely, as a talismanic expedient rather than as a medium whose capacity to manifest truths beyond the realm of contingent appearance holds profound metaphysical implications. The problem with such anthropocentric and functionalist accounts is their inherently reductionist

---

23. See Schönborn 1994, 1–134; Mondzain 2005, 69–118; Alloa 2013.

24. See Florovsky's sharply critical engagement of Grégoire's 1948 study, *Byzantium* (in Florovsky 1950, 77–78).

25. Brown 1973, 12–13, 6, 19 (my emphasis).

drift, which in the present case means that the icon is not so much explained as it is explained away as a "mere" makeshift solution for various anthropological and cultural "needs." Paradoxically, the very fact that some such "explanation" is called for at all, even in the eyes of a historian, already attests to the icon's distinctive excess and unique efficacy.

By now, it should be clear that a genuine phenomenology of image-consciousness must take seriously the icon's grounding in a metaphysics of presence. Thus, as von Balthasar stipulates, "when a being reveals itself in the world of images, the images while not, of course, the being itself, are also not some additional, extraneous element alongside it. Rather, they are nothing other than its self-revelation and impartation. The being that manifests itself in the images has no language other than that of the images. It has such *need* of these images that without them it simply could not fully realize its very being."[26] Whereas Brown's account of the icon as serving historically contingent "needs" implies that some other material entity could have served these needs equally well, von Balthasar traces the icon back to the ontological "need" of being to manifest itself, to disclose and give itself as appearance. Yet this it can do only if the *form* that visibly appears is experienced as ontologically entwined with the being that it makes manifest. An image sensu strictu can neither be a matter of mere contingency nor of outright consubstantiality. Rather, as Plato's late dialogues had first shown, the *eikōn* essentially relates to *and* differs from the being that it unveils. Like the Incarnation, to which its early Byzantine defenders (John of Damascus in particular) connect it time and again, the "image is everywhere a figure of immanence, absolute in the one case relative in the other. In one it concerns a presence, in the other an absence. . . . It is what Nikephoros calls *symbol*."[27] Inasmuch as historicist methodologies conceive of "explanation" as a strictly contingent and occasional undertaking, and consequently suspend (or outright reject) the very possibility of an essential relationship between observable phenomena and their invisible source, a historical approach to the icon plainly cannot succeed.

Instead, what is called for is a hermeneutic that at least temporarily suspends the skeptical axioms of modern epistemology. For the first step of humanistic inquiry is to capture the *how*, not the *what*, of experience—that is, to attend to the icon's experiential dimensions as these are unfolded for us in patristic and Byzantine image theory, as well as in the gradual consolidation of the Byzantine icon's distinctive form and function. A first step in this direction will be to consider the competing image concept found in the writings of Origen and Dionysius, arguably two figures whose divergent appraisal of embodied being, visible matter, and the "image" had lasting

---

26. Von Balthasar 2001, 148 (emphasis mine).
27. Mondzain 2005, 77. "This is why the model of every relation is that of father and son: it is a donation of life" (78).

impact on the eighth- and ninth-century iconoclast controversy. Likewise, a few representative examples of pre-iconoclast religious imagery will have to be considered so as to adumbrate the significant formal shift that the medium undergoes, particularly in the wake of Dionysius's antirealist image concept. Still, what follows does not purport to constitute a "history" or even a "prehistory" of the icon but, at most, a compressed and selective outline of its theological and formal bearings. In the event, the major pre-Nicaean theologians—Irenaeus, Clement of Alexandria, Origen, Tertullian—who take up questions of the image and art do so against the background of proliferating heresies, pagan cults, and the looming threat of Gnostic intellectualism.[28] We can by and large bypass a discussion of their writings because pre-Nicaean Christian thought, to the extent that it takes up the question of images at all, mainly does so as part of its ongoing effort at demarcating the true faith from pagan opposition and heretical distortions. That an objection to images is prompted chiefly by the persistence of pagan cults is forcefully brought home in an exasperated outburst found in Origen's *Against Celsus*: "And they too are not less insane who think that images, fashioned by men of worthless and sometimes most wicked character, confer any honour upon genuine divinities."[29] Of particular concern here is Gnosticism's rejection of one of Christianity's core beliefs, affirmed time and again by Irenaeus—that the God of creation and the God of salvation are one and the same. It is only as part of ongoing confrontation with pagan and Gnostic belief systems, and not as an unresolved issue intrinsic to the Christian faith itself, that the image constitutes a theological challenge prior to the first Council of Nicaea.

The one exception in this regard may be Origen (AD 184–253), whose spiritualism, though firmly opposed to Gnostic thought, is sometimes portrayed as sharing in Gnosticism's antinomian view of spirit and matter and, thus, as having "cast the question of the divine image onto a path leading to iconoclasm."[30] Such a view seems problematic, not least because it fails to distinguish sufficiently between Origen's own writings, which feature "an enormous range of sensory terms" and the far more equivocal, albeit enduring, legacy of Origenism, which far more than its progenitor tends to frame sensory and spiritual cognition in antinomian terms.[31] In fact, Origen's distinction between "the Word in the eternity of heaven" and its manifestation

---

28. These pre-Nicaean discussions of religious art are beyond the scope of this chapter. For particularly relevant texts, see the following: Irenaeus (AD 130–202), *Against Heresies* (Besançon 2000, 86–92; Jensen 2005, 74–77); Tertullian (AD 155–240), *On Idolatry*; Clement of Alexandria (AD 150–211), *Stromateis* (Jensen 2005, 9–11); Origen (AD 184–253), *Against Celsus*.

29. Origen 1872, 2:155 (*Against Celsus*, III, 76). As Jensen notes, "Clearly, Origen worries more about the worshipping of idols than about the making of images" (2005, 12).

30. Besançon 2000, 94; underlying Besançon's claim is Florovsky's influential 1950 essay on Origen and Eusebius.

31. McInroy, in Gavrilyuk and Coakley 2012, 21.

on earth "by means of shadows, likenesses, and images" does not construe the two realms as incommensurable.[32] It would be more accurate to speak of a complementarity in Origen's writings between the eternal, supra-sensible, and hence invisible *logos*, on the one hand, and God's temporal, sensory, and abundantly visible manifestation, on the other. Thus, even as "all material and corporeal things . . . have the nature of a fleeting and frail shadow," they nevertheless furnish the indispensable point of departure for the human being's anagogical movement "from things visible to things invisible." Inasmuch as the "advance" toward the invisible God does not *negate* but *fulfill* the import of sensible things, it unveils within the finite human being a potentiality that, referencing Solomon, Origen calls a spiritual or "divine sense."[33] In taking this view, Origen joins a long genealogy of writers, "extending from Plato to Philo and St. Paul, and from Plotinus and Proclus to Pseudo-Dionysios the Areopagite and John of Damascus," all of whom appear instrumental in what Ladner calls "the transfer of the image concept from the sensible to the intellectual realm."[34]

What, then, are we to make of Origen's recurrent claim of "perceiving God"? Is it merely a metaphor, rhetorical hyperbole, or does such "spiritual sight" intuitively confirm the metaphysical premise of an analogy between the spiritual (invisible) and the creaturely (visible) realms? Though Origen's "intermingling" of the two modes causes his writings to remain frustratingly ambivalent in this regard, "sharpening the distinction between analogy and metaphor is necessary" for understanding his "doctrine of the spiritual senses."[35] Still, how are we to appraise the early Origen's catachrestic expressions, such as "seeing with the eyes of the heart [*oculis cordis*]"?[36] McInroy's observation that it is "precisely when an author speaks of detecting an immaterial presence that he or she is using sensory language in a 'non-metaphorical' manner" is key here. For Origen's notion of spiritual senses, including what he refers to as the hearing of "unspeakable words" (2 Cor 12:4), ultimately rests on the distinction between "non-being" (*mē on*) and "nothing" (*ouk on*) developed in Plato's *Sophist*. Thus, what is unspeakable, and yet is spiritually "heard," and what is invisible, and yet is subject to spiritual perception, are not mere phantasms or nothings. Rather,

---

32. Still, Origen's Christology remains problematic inasmuch as it "sees the earthly life of Jesus mostly as a shadowy image of the hidden truth of the Eternal Word" (Schönborn 1994, 51); this aspect of Origen's theology will haunt iconophile arguments half a millennium later as they once again wrestle with "the temptation of Docetism, which made of the living flesh a phantomlike or transitory appearance" (Mondzain 2005, 81).

33. Origen 1984, #25 (*De principiis* IV.4.10), quoted by McInroy, in Gavrilyuk and Coakley 2012, 31.

34. Ladner 1953, 5; "that the image-likeness was something spiritual-intellectual was to remain the almost unanimous opinion of the Fathers of the Church from Clement of Alexandria and Origen" (11).

35. McInroy, in Gavrilyuk and Coakley 2012, 25, 30.

36. Origen 1984 (*De principiis*, I.1.9).

the noetic correlate of Origen's spiritual sense—the transcendent reality or *logos* on which it is focused—is antecedently and incontrovertibly real. It constitutes what Husserl calls an "absolute givenness" (*absolute Gegebenheit*), a numinous *presence* that is spiritually "sensed" as manifesting itself in the analogous medium of the audible word and the visible form. As Origen writes, "One cannot say that, because the sensible is not true, the sensible is therefore false; for the sensible can have an analogy to the actual."[37] Contrary to the self-mystification of modern, and specifically Romantic, notions of "immediacy," the concept of *analogia* that tentatively emerges in Origen manages to distinguish between the *how* and *what* of experience, between the immediate or absolute "givenness" of the sensible world in experience and an awareness that appearance is the *medium*, not the essence, of the invisible *logos* that it brings before us.

Where Origen's refers to "eyes of the mind [*dianoias ophthalmōn*]" and to a "bodiless voice [*phōnē mē sōmati*]," the spiritual senses in question are neither opposed to the *logos* nor identical to it. Rather, their operation furnishes material evidence of the way that intuition is anagogically ordered toward a supersensible meaning (*plēroma*). The ascent in question is not a function of the subjective will but responds to the phenomenal world's indisputable and abundant givenness in intuition, thus intimating to the finite human being that "the true image of God is within!"[38] That said, Origen's theology is marked by a peculiar imbalance between his committed (albeit abstract) Trinitarianism and his weak concept of the Incarnation. To be sure, when he speaks of Christ as "the image by which we come to the knowledge of the Father," *eikōn* does not imply a derivative or subordinate status for the image. Rather, it denotes a kind of "pattern" in the sense of Christ's substantive identity with the Father. Yet as is the case in his exegesis of John 14:9 ("He that hath seen me hath seen the Father"), Origen simply posits this identity "without any reference to the Incarnation."[39] Whether Origen's heirs consider the "shadow" of corporeality, including Christ's human form, as *compensating for* the finite human being's deficient powers of cognition, as Eusebius would argue, or, alternatively, regard such shadowy appearances as positively *detracting from* the "spiritual" truth of the Trinitarian God, they sometimes appear curiously reluctant to develop a robust account

---

37. Origen 1984, #30; referencing Paul (Rom 1:20 and 2 Cor 4.18), Origen notes "that this visible world contains instruction about the invisible world and that this earthly condition contains 'images of the heavenly things' (cf. Heb. 9:24), so that from the things that are below we can ascend to the things which are above" (#33).

38. Origen, *In Psalm* 4.4 (quoted by McInroy, in Gavrilyuk and Coakley 2012, 24, 32); Schönborn 1994, 51.

39. Schönborn 1994, 50. Origen's schematic Trinitarianism is echoed a century later by Hilary of Poitiers. Sharpening the antinomian implications of Origen's writings, Hilary insists (1) that "an image must express the form of Him whose image it is" and (2) that no image can be adequate to "the Son of the invisible Father" (Thiessen 2004, 20).

of the Incarnation. Instead, the focus is on the anagogical role of visible forms, such as when Ephrem the Syrian in a letter to Publius speaks of beauty and the "natural mirror [of creation] as a foreshadowing of the Gospel."[40]

On Origen's account, man's quest for "divinization" (*theōsis*) invariably pivots on the gradual transfiguration of physical sight into contemplative seeing. In *Against Celsus*, he thus insists that the phrase "in the image" (*kat eikona/ad imaginem*) of Genesis 1:26 is not to be construed as positing an anthropomorphic resemblance between God and man but, instead, as unveiling the man as teleologically ordered *toward* God.

> Celsus, who fails to see the difference between "being the image of God," and "being created after the image of God," pretends that we said, "God made man His own image, and gave him a form like to His own." . . . It remains, therefore, that that which is "after the image of God" must be understood to be in our "inner man," which is also renewed, and whose nature it is to be "after the image of Him who created it," when a man becomes "perfect," as "our Father in heaven is perfect," and hears the command, "Be ye holy, for I the LORD your God am holy."[41]

Such a drive toward an imageless, spiritual vision pervades Origen's writings, and it explains why "instead of the all-too-physical concept of 'seeing,' [he] prefers the more spiritual concept of 'contemplating' (*theōrein*)."[42] Seeing here is not understood as "sense perception" along the lines of Lockean empiricism but, rather, as a form of embodied cognition. Hence, the imageless state toward which Origen sees mankind constitutively ordered in no way demands stripping away or overcoming our physical sensorium. Spiritual knowledge for Origen is not achieved by subtracting or repudiating the sensible. Rather, imageless cognition must be understood as the eschaton toward which human, embodied cognition is constitutively ordered; I say "constitutively" because there is nothing gratuitous or contingent about the way that what is present *to* the senses must already be "sensed" in an essentially intellectual or spiritual way, namely, as begging fuller comprehension. To "see" (as opposed to mindlessly "gazing") is to have already understood, albeit in an implicit manner, that things visually apprehended contain a knowledge whose integrity and perfection is total, even as it remains unfulfilled due to the natural imperfection of human, sense-bound cognition. Just as scriptural exegesis, the fulcrum of Origen's theology, entails

---

40. Thiessen 2004, 22.

41. Origen 1872, 487, 405 (*Against Celsus*, VII.66; VI.63); "man was created only to or after the image, whereas Christ was Himself *the* image of God" (Ladner 1953, 10).

42. Schönborn 1994, 50.

a gradual spiritualizing of the word, so bodily sight challenges the beholder to distill sense from the sensible, a manifest truth from what is plainly visible.

By its very mode of self-disclosure, the visible world calls upon its beholder not merely to be *seen*, but, ultimately, to be *known*. Far from inert and dumb "matter" (*hylē*), everything visible is *eo ipso* apprehended only as created and incarnate "form" (*morphē*); and as such it sets in motion a dialectic of call and response, sight and insight, that incrementally allows the beholder to grasp visible being as a "figure" (*typos*) mediating the *logos* that is its source. For Origen, seeing constitutes an essentially spiritual act; it instantiates a "perceptual faith" (as Merleau-Ponty will eventually call it) that embraces the visible as the evidence of things unseen: "The methods of *proof* and of *cognition* invented by a thought already established in the world, the concepts of *object* and *subject* it introduces, do not enable us to understand what the perceptual faith is." In fact, far from overcoming the intuitive certitude of seeing, reflection "retains everything contained in the perceptual faith: the conviction that there is something, that there is the world, the idea of truth, the true idea given." By contrast, the modern project of a philosophy of unremitting skepticism goes astray the moment it "makes of [perceptual faith] a belief among others." For Merleau-Ponty, the blind spot of the modern rationalist's "methodic doubt" concerns its irrational refusal of givenness—indeed, Grace might not be too strong a word; that is, it falters precisely to the extent that "it resists a factual evidence, represses an involuntary truth which it acknowledges to be already there and which inspires the very project of seeking an evidence that would be absolute." Ultimately, there is something gratuitous and metaphysically dishonest about the way that modern rationalism conflates reflection with negation and, thus, fails "to mention the borrowings it makes from Being."[43]

For all his talk about an anagogical progression from visible things to the invisible, Origen does not exhibit any proto-Hegelian tendencies; and his focus on the spiritual does not imply superseding, let alone expunging, the sensible world's integrity and dignity. Indeed, those who would reject embodied reality as a betrayal of the divine *logos*, and hence devalue visible things and destroy images, fail to grasp and honor the Incarnation as "God's pedagogical adaption to the level of our human capacities."[44] Such a stance does nothing to bring man closer to the eschaton but, on the contrary, risks a Gnostic disfigurement of creation while also revealing man's sinful desire to engineer his own salvation by laying waste to creation tout court. With good reason, Schönborn cautions that in studying the reception of Origen, "we

---

43. Merleau-Ponty 1968, 28, 30, 50, 106.

44. Schönborn 1994, 48; notably, the legitimacy of the Second Council of Constantinople (AD 553) would be contested by iconoclasts, which in turn prompted attempts to revalidate it at the Seventh Ecumenical Council (AD 787); see Barber 2002, 40–42; Brubaker and Haldon 2011, 260–76.

witness a tendency that every now and then will reappear during the following centuries: the tendency to see what is visible *only* as shadows of what is invisible, to emphasize in the image primarily the *shortcomings* in relation to the original, and to deemphasize its function of being *revelation* of the original."[45]

A particularly telling case of how the legacy of Origenism impinged on the iconoclast debate is an epistle allegedly written by Eusebius (AD 264–340) to the empress Constantia.[46] Eusebius's putative response to the empress's request for a Christ icon unfolds as a barrage of rhetorical, often hectoring questions whose irreverent tone casts further doubt on the letter's authenticity: "What did you have in mind, and of what kind should this icon of Christ be, as you call it? . . . Which icon of Christ are you looking for? The true, unchangeable image that by nature shows the likeness of Christ, or rather the other image that he has taken on for our sake when he clothed himself with the form of a servant?" In characterizing Christ as "the other image" of God made manifest in enfleshed, human form, Eusebius reveals both his heterodox (subordinationist) Christology and also his concept of the image as strictly derivative of, and thus inferior to, its prototype.[47] Assuming that the icon requested is to depict Christ in "his form as a servant," Eusebius emphasizes the fact that, in his human form, Christ's "flesh . . . is intermingled with the glory of God, that what is mortal has been swallowed up by life."[48] This last formulation in particular will later run afoul of Chalcedon's characterization of the relation between Father and

---

45. "It is a misrepresentation when Origen, time and again, is seen as one of the spiritual Fathers of iconoclasm, or else, of a form of Christianity opposed to rituals and ceremonies, to images and sacramentals, and advocating an exclusively spiritual cultus" (Schönborn 1994, 53–54).

46. Preserved only in Patriarch Nikephoros's anti-Origenist polemic *Contra Eusebium*, the letter bears many of the telltale signs of a forgery from a later period. While the epistle's authenticity may ultimately prove impossible to determine, a number of facts speak against it: first, none of Eusebius's other writings echo its concern with the Christ icon; second, there is little material evidence of Christ icons, such as is allegedly being requested by Empress Constantia, having been produced early in the fourth century; third, the letter in question surfaces only during the iconoclast era; and, fourth, it closely echoes rhetorical strategies and terminological choices only found at that point. All these considerations strongly suggest that the epistle is but another case of iconophiles fabricating "weak" arguments in favor of iconoclasm; such positions could then be included (and soundly refuted) in florilegia such as we find appended to the last of John Damascene's three treatises, *On the Holy Icons*, or, as in the present case, could be subject to an entire work devoted to dismantling iconoclast claims. Florovsky (1950, 84–86) considers Eusebius's letter authentic, a view disputed by Jensen (2005, 25); on the context of Eusebius's epistle, see Brubaker and Haldon 2011, 40–50; for a detailed reading of the epistle, see Schönborn 1994, 57–80.

47. Eusebius, quoted in Schönborn 1994, 63. As Schönborn continues, "The subordination of the Son is shown through the proper names given the Son, and the characterization as 'image', listed first, is thought to indicate this subordination with special clarity: the Logos is not consubstantial with the father, he is *only* his image. . . . The Son is image because he is *second* to the Father" (63; emphasis mine).

48. Eusebius, quoted in Schönborn 1994, 58–59.

Son as being free of "confusion or change, without division or separation." Paul's understanding of Christ as "the image of the invisible God" (Col 1:15) is here slanted in subordinationist ways that recall the real, fourth-century Eusebius's *Demonstratio Evangelica*. Here Christ is strictly secondary to, not consubstantial with, God the Father; and any icon of Christ, who himself is "the image of the ineffable and inscrutable Godhead," will inevitably attest to both Christ's subordination to the Father and the icon's standing at an ontological remove from that which it seeks to depict. Furthermore, and once again like Christ, the image's legitimacy is strictly temporal and provisional. For just as Christ's Incarnation is effectively canceled by his resurrection, when "the flesh has lost its own subsistence, [and] has been . . . 'swallowed up' by his divinity," so the icon's material scaffolding is voided by its ineffable prototype.[49] Also telling in this regard is Eusebius's terminology; rather than speak of Christ as the *eikōn* of the Father (*imago Dei*), his preferred term, *agalma*, connoting a human figure sculpted, painted, or verbally described, emphasizes the contingent and extrinsic relationship between the divine *logos* and embodied, human form.

Recalling this enduring and problematic aspect of Origenism, the Quinisext Council of Constantinople (AD 691–92) went on to reject allegorical representations of Christ as Lamb. Instead of such "ancient types and shadows . . . 'that which is perfect' [ought to] be delineated to the eyes of all, at least in colored expression," such that "Christ our God be henceforth exhibited in images, instead of the ancient lamb." Doing so will bring the faithful closer to the "humiliation of the Word" in the passion.[50] The council's pronouncement amounts to an implicit rebuttal of Origenism's understanding of the resurrection as effectively canceling out and sublating the Incarnate Christ, a position strongly associated with the subordinationism of Eusebius.[51] Meanwhile, Schönborn's remarks above evidently draw on Florovsky's earlier characterization of "Origen's Christology [as] utterly inadequate and ambiguous" and as unable to "integrate the Incarnation as a unique event into the general scheme of Revelation." With that premise in place, one could not but conclude that Origen's "whole system of symbols was something provisional, to be ultimately done away. One had to penetrate behind the screen of symbols. This was the major principle or postulate of Origen."[52] To be sure, that the interpretation of scripture, and, at a more quotidian level, the understanding of perceptible things, is informed by a

---

49. Eusebius, quoted in Schönborn 1994, 73.

50. Canon LXXXII, in *PNF* 14:401.

51. See Schönborn (1994, 57–72), who notes how, for Eusebius, Christ prior to the Resurrection is but the "instrument" (*organon*) of the Father, subordinate and indeed ontologically inferior to the *logos*. The construction of Christ's flesh as a sign of his as yet unrealized divinity is, of course, part and parcel of Eusebius's subordinationism.

52. Florovsky 1950, 87; it bears noting that in Origen's *Commentary on John* (II:61), symbols seem, in the end, to remain in some fashion.

strong eschatological component seems as true for Origen as for St. Paul, Philo, or any other number of patristic writers. Yet in suggesting that for Origen visible matter is but a "screen," Florovsky, perhaps inadvertently, opens the door for a more complex figural understanding of the image, namely, as both a barrier *from* and a conduit *toward* the divine. In time, this figure of the screen will be literalized as the iconostasis and retable that, starting in the late sixth century, becomes an established feature of Byzantine church interiors.

Though himself firmly opposed to Gnosticism's antinomy between a demiurge-creator and a redeeming god, Origen hews worrisomely close to the Gnostic view of "matter" (*hylē*) as inherently deficient and lapsed. Even before Origen, it had been above all Irenaeus (ca. AD 130–200) who insisted that God not be conceived in strictly numinous terms but also as authentically entwined with sensory and historical being. Irenaeus's God is continually "manifested and . . . shows forth," just as his "voice from the beginning to the end is present with His Handiwork." Whereas "in times long past, it was *said* that man was created after the image of God, . . . it was not [actually] *shown*; for the Word was as yet invisible."[53] Confronting the "immoderate Hellenism" of the Gnostics, Irenaeus "rehabilitate[s] history" as the domain of divine manifestation, though Besançon may overstate the case when arguing that for the bishop of Lyon "salvation comes about in history."[54] More accurately, for Irenaeus it is Christ's *imago Dei* that transmutes history from the pagans' anguished *durée* into a *figura* of Christian salvation, with visible being no longer expiring in its mundane occurrence but, for Irenaeus and even more for Tertullian, unveiling "a deeper meaning that suggests something in the future." Insofar as a new level of committed interpretation allowed "shadowy similarities in the struct of events . . . to make the *figura* recognizable," the emergence of a theological aesthetics is already preprogrammed in the earliest Church Fathers.[55]

Still, Gnosticism's devaluation of matter and all manner of visible, embodied being continues to influence early Christian thought throughout the third century and beyond. Arguably, its strongest imprint concerns the Arian and Eusebian view of Christ's *imago Dei* as inherently subordinate to God the Father and, consequently, inferior in Being. Lurking behind this subordinationist conception of God we detect Hellenism's enduring influence, particularly that of Neoplatonist emanationism; and it is this legacy that, less than two decades prior to Nicaea, once more prevailed when the Synod of Elvira (AD 304–5) issued in a rather vaguely worded injunction against "hanging pictures in churches, lest what is painted on the walls be venerated and

---

53. Irenaeus, quoted in Thiessen 2004, 17.
54. Besançon 2000, 89–90.
55. Auerbach 2014, 83, 79. As Besançon notes, "An aesthetics can find a place within Irinaeus' thinking" (2000, 90).

worshipped [placuit picturas in ecclesia esse non debere, ne quod colitur et adoratur in parietibus depingatur]." Not until the affirmation of Christ as the "perfect image" in the writings of Athanasius of Alexandria (ca. AD 296–373) is the lingering appeal of both Plotinian emanationism and Arius's subordinationism decisively checked. Embracing Paul's *imago Dei* as the foundation for his Trinitarianism, Athanasius may have been "the first to use . . . the simile of the Emperor's image," arguing that "in the image there is the idea [*eidos*] and form [*morphē*] of the emperor . . . [whose] likeness is unchanged in the image, so that who sees the image, sees the emperor in it, and again who sees the emperor, recognizes him to be the one in the image. The image might well say: 'I and the emperor are one,' 'I am in him and he is in me.'"[56] Alluding to John 10:30 ("I and my Father are one"), Athanasius here draws on the Hellenistic, in origin Platonic, concept of "participation" (*methexis*), according to which the image shares in the reality of that whose image it is and, in so doing, renders its archetype more fully present. The image here does not "refer to" God or emperor but, instead, manifests their very person both as an embodied, visible being and as an archetypal, invisible authority.

"CREATING TYPES FOR THE TYPELESS": FORMALIZING THE ICON AND ITS THEOLOGY AFTER NICAEA

The struggle over religious imagery has often been portrayed as a conflict between Athens and Jerusalem, between a Hellenizing, iconophile position and a Jewish, uncompromising rejection of the image as intrinsically idolatrous; and up to a point this way of framing the matter retains a certain plausibility. Still, as the case of Origen suggests, it would be more accurate to speak of two competing versions of Hellenism, "an unreformed and uncompromising Hellenic position" and a slowly advancing "Christianization of Hellenism."[57] Particularly during the first two centuries, Christianity struggled to distinguish its creed and practice from an ambient world awash in pagan idols. Consequently, "the typical early Christian theological position on visual art was less an objection to art as such than an attack on *non-Christian* images that invited worship and activities that drew the faithful into the values and practices (both religious and secular) of the surrounding culture."[58] The danger

---

56. Quoted in Ladner 1953, 8. The fusion of imperial and divine power in the icon first hinted at by Athanasius explains the enormous impact of the Kamoulianai portrait (~AD 555) and the Edessa Mandylion, "images not wrought by human hands" (*acheiropoietai*) that would eventually be credited with the military triumphs of Byzantium defending itself against Avar, Bulgar, and Persian invaders during the 620s. On these two icons, see Brubaker and Haldon 2011, 53–56; Belting 1994, 49–57; Belting 2006, 45–85.

57. Florovsky 1950, 96.

58. Jensen 2005, 14.

Figure 2.1. Torah niche, synagogue in Dura-Europos, Syria

lurking in images as perceived by early Christians was that of a pagan, sensuously alluring world forever threatening to disrupt the spiritual vision that the early church fathers regarded as the very apex of Christian teaching.[59] At the same time, monotheism had long featured its own visual culture, as evidenced by the ornamental imagery and common representation of Old Testament figures, as well as the menorah, the ark, and other liturgical implements found in Jewish temples. The central prohibition, "Thou shalt not bow down to [graven images] nor serve them" (Ex 25:5), was not felt to preclude enhancing sacred spaces with visual forms. Solomon's temple had been decorated with images of cherubim (1 Kgs 6:23–29) and with depictions of "oxen carrying the Molten Sea" (1 Kgs 7:24–26); and God had commanded that two cherubim with extended wings and made of gold be placed above the ark of the covenant, though obviously not for purposes of veneration.[60] A synagogue discovered

---

59. On early Christian opposition to religious images, see Jensen 2005, 1–20; Besançon 2000, 81–96; Belting 1994, 30–46; Kitzinger 1954.

60. See Weitzmann 1979, 366–89.

Figure 2.2. Mosaic floor, synagogue, Hamat Tiberias, ca. AD 300

only in 1932 in the Parthian and Roman border town of Dura-Europos (present-day eastern Syria) features extensive tempera-on-plaster paintings depicting episodes from the Old Testament. Surrounding the Torah niche (fig. 2.1), these scenes consist of a haphazard arrangement of midrashic elements taken from the Aramaic Targumim. Though at first blush surprising, such visual representation of episodes from the Old Testament reflects a widely observed increase in "narrative and didactic images . . . enter[ing] Christian assembly rooms and cemeteries in the third century."[61] Likewise, a synagogue floor mosaic in Hamat Tiberias, Israel, dating to about AD 300, features not only symmetrical ornaments but also a representation of the ark and signs of the zodiac inscribed in Hebrew, which in turn surround the sun god Helios in his chariot (fig. 2.2). As this rather bewildering blend of Jewish, Hellenistic, and imperial Roman motifs and styles suggests, the boundaries separating religious and aesthetic culture were porous and susceptible of much local variety well into the fourth century.[62]

---

61. Kitzinger 1954, 89.
62. See the discussion in Weitzmann 1979, 372–75.

Let us briefly return to the status of the image in pre-Nicene and early post-Nicene Christianity. As we already saw, a reductionist "explanation" of the rise of religious imagery in late antiquity in strictly functionalist and historicizing fashion seems unsatisfactory, if for no other reason than because it does not attend to the icon's formal specifics. More plausible, though still unsatisfactory, would be to conceive religious images as formal prompts for the kind of spiritual attention that liturgical action seeks to cultivate; doing so avoids reducing the *eikōn* to a mere expedient any more than the Eucharist is to be considered a mere substitute for, or symbol of, Christ's body. In both instances, visible matter occupies an ontological position entirely distinct from its place in ordinary perception and communication. In fact, like the Eucharist, the icon serves a dual function, at once an expression of memory and of hope. It is "a pledge and image of the reality to come. It does not only reproduce, [but] it also anticipates: *pre-signs, pre-figures, pre-demonstrates.*"[63] Even so, the icon also serves more pragmatic functions. For with the gradual fading of apostolic testimony and with Christianity's expanding imperial and cultural footprint in the wake of Constantine's momentous conversion and the legal reforms following the Edict of Milan (AD 313), new ways of mediating the faith for increasingly diverse and far-flung communities began to open up, and it was imperative that they be seized expeditiously. Thus, as pagan deities disappeared from imperial coinage during Constantine's later reign, Christianity's attitude to religious images was less haunted by the specter of paganism, and, following the Edict of Thessalonica (AD 380), it ceased to be the divisive topic it had once been.[64] By contrast, given the successive waves of persecution suffered by Christian religious communities prior to Constantine's reign, it is only natural that early Christians would have desisted from public "representations" of a faith that, for its adherents simply to survive, had to keep a low profile. In fact, most Christian images until about AD 350 would have been literally underground, restricted mainly to funereal art and occasional murals found on the walls of catacombs. At the same time, the decades leading up to the imperial toleration and eventual embrace of Christianity in the early fourth century witnessed an intensification of Christian, specifically narrative, imagery. Sarcophagi now routinely featured "a multiplicity of distinct events" for which there is "no real precedent in ancient funerary culture. . . . What ties these scenes together is . . . , broadly speaking, the message of deliverance through divine intervention."[65]

---

63. De Lubac 2006, 66 (quoting Augustine, Ratramus, and the Roman Missal).

64. "It was not before the second half of the fourth century that any writer began to speak of Christian pictorial art in positive terms. . . . Defense lagged behind attack, as attack had lagged behind practice" (Kitzinger 1954, 86–87).

65. Commenting on this "almost frenetic piling up of content and messages," Kitzinger remarks that "never in the history of the sculptured sarcophagus had there been an attempt to say so much in so little space" (1995, 23–24).

Figure 2.3.
Fragment of a sarcophagus
depicting Christ Blessing the
Loaves and Fish, AD 320.
Dumbarton Oaks Collection

What little pre-Nicene religious imagery has been preserved tends to feature representations of Old Testament scenes, mostly in stone ornamentation found on sarcophagi and occasionally juxtaposed to New Testament scenes, such as in the typological arrangement found on the Arles Sarcophagus dating to the very beginning of Constantine's reign (AD 306).[66] The abbreviated scriptural motifs dominating pre-Constantinian Christianity have been preserved mainly on sarcophagi, which is unsurprising given their durable material. Due to the more perishable nature of religious wall painting, tapestries, and mosaics, and not even factoring in the devastation wrought by eighth- and ninth-century iconoclasm in the eastern Mediterranean, gauging how prominently icons and visual representations of biblical narrative might have featured in ecclesial spaces until the sixth century has been very difficult. Even so, some fundamental shifts in Christian imagery prior to the start of iconoclasm can be observed and should here be noted. Characteristic of early fourth-century depictions of Christ is his representation as a beardless youth, such as in the fragment of a sarcophagus depicting Christ Blessing the Loaves and Fish (ca. AD 320) (fig. 2.3). Little is left of the scene recounted in Mark 6:39–41, though the cylindrical container under Christ's right hand and comparison with other sarcophagi have made it possible to identify its scriptural reference.[67] As yet missing is the iconic

---

66. See Weitzmann 1979, 400 (no. 55).
67. The fragment is now in the Dumbarton Oaks Collection; see Bühl 2008, 38–39.

face of the mature, bearded Christ that emerges in the fifth century and will find its most influential realization in the mid-sixth-century Pantocrator icon at St. Catherine's Monastery. Among the earliest images of Christ, the fragment's disproportionately large faces, in particular that of Christ who is facing both toward and beyond the viewer, already point to the strong nexus that will eventually associate "image" (*eikōn*) and "face" (*prosōpon*). Even so, its formal and material aspects remain palpably Roman, such as the deep grooves depicting the toga folds that, in theologically questionable ways, associate Christ with wealthy upper-class society.

As Christian imagery emerges from the catacombs into the worldly light of late imperial Rome, the function of images shifts from "shorthand pictographs" to a more complex and hermeneutically more challenging Christian iconography that is "equivalent to the mythological imagery of pagan sepulchral art."[68] However, throughout the fourth century a distinctly Roman, and secular, visual aesthetic leaves its imprint on these images. A case in point is the mid-fourth-century wall painting, *Christ Healing the Woman with the Issue of Blood* (fig. 2.4). Drawing on the story told by Matthew (9:20–22), Luke (8:43–48), and Mark (5:25–34), this image dates to the reign of Constantine or just after. Depicting Christ as an elegant, Roman youth, the mural's emphatic gestural language and its emphasis on Christ's flowing garment with which the suffering woman makes contact and thereby is healed creates a markedly dramatic situation. In foregrounding Christ's graceful posture and noble gesture toward the sufferer, the image presents us with a public, as it were oratorical, event rather than drawing attention to Christ's supernatural, spiritual persona. Following the shift of the capital from Rome to Constantinople by Constantine (324–30) and the initial, dogmatic Christology pronounced at the Council of Nicaea, the iconography of imperial power on coins, buildings, and other paraphernalia begins to be mirrored in depictions of Christ, who "no longer sat like a teacher on a chair, but like an emperor on a jewel-studded throne." Incrementally, "religious images began to receive marks of veneration analogous to the imperial images in the sixth century or even earlier," a development sanctioned by the Eastern Church in particular when, starting around AD 600, it "allowed icons of Christ and of the Virgin to stand in the place of the imperial images."[69]

The evolution of religious imagery from the Constantinian era to the partitioning of the Roman Empire in the wake of Theodosius (AD 379–92), who in 380 had decreed Nicene Christianity the official state religion, is vividly illustrated by the oldest preserved apse mosaic, located at the Church of Santa Pudenziana in Rome (ca.

---

68. Kitzinger 1995, 25–26.
69. Weitzmann 1979, x; Brown 1973, 10.

Figure 2.4. "Christ Healing the Woman with the Issue of Blood," ca. AD 340, catacombs of SS. Peter and Marcelllinus, Rome

AD 402) (fig. 2.5). No longer the upper-class, beardless Roman youth, Christ is here depicted, in a far more familiar manner, as a bearded, mature, and indeed regal presence. The mosaic shows him conspicuously enthroned above his disciples from whose more worldly attire his gold-colored robe sets him well apart, even as it links him with Mary to the right. Moreover, the semicircular ecclesial meeting space in which Christ and his apostles gather is conspicuously walled off from the public buildings in the distance. The mosaic's visual separation of sacred from worldly spaces and its strong symmetrical arrangement of human figures and architectural forms hint at a shift, then just getting under way, whereby the Christ icon becomes positively constitutive of the sacred domain. That said, we need to bear in mind that

Figure 2.5. Apse mosaic, Santa Pudenzia, Rome, AD 402

many of the early mosaics found at Santa Pudenzia or Santa Maria Maggiore would have been nearly impossible to decode for the faithful seeing them "from a distance of 14–25 meters" and, moreover, unprepared to identify the motifs without "an extremely well-informed guide." Add to that the fact that the execution of the mosaic decorations starting to appear in fifth-century churches tended to be delegated by the bishops to the artists, and it becomes "clear that there was no 'unité de doctrine' at all."[70]

Indeed, as Kitzinger has shown in great detail, the sumptuous floor decorations and vault mosaics that begin to adorn churches in Ravenna, Rome, Milan, and Thessaloniki throughout the fifth century remain heavily indebted to the academic classicism and pictorial realism favored by the Roman nobility. Only gradually do "proportions become ponderous, attitudes stiff and wooden, faces mask-like with big lifeless eyes staring into the void, [as] rounded relief gives way more and more to sharp incisions and hard schematic lines."[71] Perhaps the gradual formalization of hieratic images and the strict obeisance they appeared to command can be traced back to Constantine, who in his later years liked to have his image carried in processions through the streets of the city; it was expected that those present should "bow" be-

---

70. Brenk 2005, 149–50.

71. Kitzinger 1995, 47. See also Brenk (2005, 144), who notes that the second commandment placed the fourth- and fifth-century Church "under enormous pressure because Roman imagery was omnipresent in the cities . . . and was still greatly appreciated by the wealthy upper classes whose members had all suddenly converted to Christianity."

fore it as a sign of "respect," a gesture that faintly anticipates John of Damascus's distinction, in the middle of the eighth century, between prayerful "reverence" (*proskynēsis*) accorded to icons and "worship" (*douleia*) due to the invisible Triune God. Be that as it may, following Constantine's death (AD 337), it was to take nearly another century for Christian, and specifically Byzantine, iconography to settle into the forms in which it is familiar to us today. Significantly advanced by the Christology of Cyril of Alexandria (AD 376–444), this process of artistic and theological consolidation culminates during the reign of Justinian I (525–67), when the Christ icon came to derive its legitimacy from its association with the face of the emperor, a dynamic that by the beginning of the seventh century shows signs of being reversed.[72]

Yet my objective here is not to trace the formal evolution of religious icons or the fluctuating ecclesial and imperial controversy surrounding their veneration. Rather, it is to uncover in what ways the evolving theological rationale for the use of holy images was itself informed by the embodied experience of the icon in ecclesial spaces, liturgical practice, and personal prayer. Arguably, no other Christian writer of late antiquity did more to pave the way for the incorporation of the icon into theological reflection than pseudo-Dionysius. Though relatively small, the corpus of Dionysius's writings may justly be seen as having inaugurated a line of inquiry that some fifteen hundred years later was to be magisterially unfolded by Hans Urs von Balthasar under the heading of theological aesthetics. In outlining the integrative and generative relationship between visible things and the ineffable, divine *logos*, Dionysius time and again invokes the mediating power of the symbol. "We use whatever appropriate symbols we can for the things of God," he writes, referencing his as yet unwritten (never written? or lost?) *Symbolic Theology*.[73] Meanwhile, in his ninth

---

72. On the formalization of the hieratic image in sixth- and seventh-century Byzantium and Antioch, see Kitzinger 1954, 90–92, 125; 1995, 81–112; as well as the detailed study by Mainoldi (2020). On the political and economic background of this development, see Brubaker and Haldon (2011, 9–68), who maintain that the main theological concerns of the pre-iconoclast era were not "about visual representation, but about the epistemology of the divine: how could one know, and, therefore, in what ways could one describe, God?" (40). As Ladner notes, "The Greek Christian concept of the image was elaborated, not in the sphere of art, but in close contact with the development of the most fundamental dogmas about God and man" (1953, 4–5). On that theological debate, particularly in the Greek Fathers, see also Barber 2002, 13–37; and Schönborn 1994, 80–101, who focuses on Cyril of Alexandria's significant move beyond Origen and Eusebius. Whereas in Eusebius "the reality of the image is necessarily a lesser reality," Cyril premises his entire theology on the Incarnation: "Once the Incarnation is accepted as reality, it follows that 'the flesh assumed by the Word does not remain foreign and accidental to this word but becomes one with it'. The flesh is not 'an extrinsic cover' but belongs to the very identity of the Logos" (Schönborn 1994, 80–81).

73. All citations of the pseudo-Dionysian corpus follow the marginal pagination in *The Complete Works* (1987), which corresponds to vol. 3 of the *PG* edition of pseudo-Dionysius's writings. The English titles are given in abbreviated form, thus: *Divine Names* = DN; *Mystical Theology* = MT; *Celestial Hierarchy* = CH; *Ecclesiastical Hierarchy* = EH; *Letters* = EP [*Epistolae*]. Cited here, DN 592c.

letter, addressed to the hierarch Titus, we do find Dionysius elaborating on the sym-bol's dual structure and mediating function. The "sacred symbol" is to be understood as "the protective garb of the understanding of what is ineffable and invisible." What warrants such "protection" is an entrenched habit of the common man's "childish imagination" to reify the numinous by identifying it with some aspect of visible, three-dimensional reality. As a safeguard against such tendencies, "theological tra-dition has a dual aspect, the ineffable and mysterious on the one hand, the open and more evident on the other. The one resorts to symbolism and involves initiation. The other is philosophic and employs the method of demonstration" (*EP* 1105c–d). Symbolic theology thus serves as a "screen" in much the same way that symbols and images already do in Origen and, a century after Dionysius, in the iconostasis then beginning to establish itself as both a material and a spiritual screen in Byzantine church architecture. While defending against "mass prejudice," sacred symbols also facilitate a process of sensory-cum-spiritual initiation, a visual catechesis of sorts, aimed at infusing in the faithful "the simplicity of mind and the receptive, contem-plative power to cross over to the simple, marvelous, transcendent truth" (*EP* 1105c). As remains to be seen, the symbol's gnoseological and, more particularly, anagogical function requires that its material and formal presentation be distinguished from crudely Platonizing conceptions of mimesis as mere "copy-making" and a naive con-ception of pictorial realism.

At the same time, Dionysius's symbolic theology extends a project begun by Gregory of Nyssa and Basil of Caesarea a century and a half earlier, namely, to push back against Origenism's more rigid antinomies. Thus Mainoldi views the Corpus Dionysiacum as an "answer to the impasse which affected biblical exegesis as a result from the opposition between the schools of Alexandria and Antioch, . . . [and] in re-action to Alexandrian allegorism and to the wide influence exerted by Origen."[74] Like his Cappadocian precursors, Gregory of Nyssa and Basil of Caesarea in par-ticular, Dionysius frames the theological issues of beauty, appearance, and the good by drawing on the rich legacy of Neoplatonism. Since we will have occasion to return to Dionysius later, in the context of Gerard Manley Hopkins's conception of the lyric image as a kind of sacrament, the discussion here will be more circumscribed and somewhat different in its aims. Where Origen, and particularly his more radically minded successors (e.g., Eusebius), interprets the realm of the visible, of appearance, and of images as evidence of an ontological declension of sorts, Dionysius advances a fundamentally different view. Thus, even as he emphasizes the ontological differ-ence between "angelic," disembodied and "blessed conceptions," on the one hand, and human, sense-bound perception (*DN* 868b), on the other, Dionysius refuses to

---

74. Mainoldi 2020, 6–7. On the Platonist legacy in Dionysius's writings, see Boulnois 2020, 102–8.

construe the latter as merely defective or illegitimate: "Nevertheless, on account of the manner in which [human souls] are capable of concentrating the many into the one, they too, in their own fashion and as far as they can, are worthy of conceptions like those of the angels. Our sense perceptions also can be properly described as echoes of wisdom" (*DN* 868c). Just as the fact that God's lack of "mind and perception" (*nous* and *aisthēsis*) "is to be taken in the sense of what he has in superabundance and not as a defect," so conversely the human sensorium should be appraised not as obstructing but as teleologically ordered toward the *visio Dei*. Dionysius's Neoplatonist theology of spiritual ascent, while committed to "purifying [*anakathairesthai*] . . . the forms and shapes of all otherness, so that they may express what is holy," departs from its pagan intellectual forebears in one decisive respect. For it resists pushing the concept of spiritual ascent "to the point where one altogether abandons the relationship between the form and what it expresses, because viewed from above the relation of likeness and beauty between spirit and the sensible is itself a reflection of the relationship between God and the world (the *analogia entis*)."[75] Because it is distinguished by its specific form and thus stands forth and calls on the beholder's response and attentive engagement, the visible phenomenon is experienced as mediating a truth *beyond* it, though attainable only ever *through* and *by means of* the specific form that so irresistibly focuses our perceptual faith, not passively but dynamically, not as inert *res extensa* but as a manifest presence.

Dionysius's principal task is how to cultivate a contemplative, spiritual vision that arises from our interaction with the sensible realm rather than being opposed to it in antinomian fashion. With much greater emphasis than Origen, and exhibiting some affinity with the writings of Gregory of Nyssa, Dionysius thus frames sensory perception as an intrinsically significant event rather than as a theologically neutral fact. Capitalizing on the etymological connection between "beauty" (*to kalon*) and "calling" (*kalein*), he distinguishes between the *object* of perception and the *event* of how sense-based experience registers in consciousness. The former concerns the *quiddity* or "whatness" of perception, while the latter pertains to the *quality* of how the phenomenal world is experienced. Dionysius's name for that quality is "beauty." Echoing Plotinus's distinction between visible colors and the invisible light that enables us to discriminate between them, he observes how "like a light [beauty] flashes onto everything. . . . Beauty 'bids' all things to itself (whence it is called 'beauty') and gathers everything into itself."[76] To see, then, involves mind both directing itself

---

75. Balthasar 1984, 168.

76. *DN* 701c–d; see also Chrétien (2004, 14–16), who interprets this "calling" of the beautiful as a sign of "election," of grace visibly and indisputably received. Regardless of whether we hold religious views of some kind or other, or not at all, not to respond to the beautiful tends to be inwardly experienced as a spiritual lapse on our part.

outward and, when reflecting on the charismatic beauty of the visible world, understanding its own participation in the beautiful as "the source of all things, . . . the great creating cause [*aitia*] which bestirs the world and holds all things in existence by the longing inside them to have beauty" (*DN* 704a). Beauty and manifestation, then, are ontological corollaries. For if the manifestly beautiful were not experienced as the medium and portal opening upon a numinous truth beyond it, "it would not be the beautiful and would not awaken reverence."[77]

For Dionysius, it all comes down to this: "If God cannot be grasped by mind or sense-perception, if he is not a particular being, how do we know him?" (*DN* 869c); or, as he puts it earlier, "How can we speak of the divine names? How can we do this if the Transcendent surpasses all discourse and all knowledge, if it abides beyond the reach of . . . any perception, imagination, opinion, name, discourse, apprehension, or understanding?" (*DN* 593a–b). To be clear: Dionysius is not posing a rhetorical question but, instead, is addressing apophaticism's central challenge. The invisible God at the heart of apophatic theology is not a figure of sheer, insurmountable negation. To take that view risks instituting an ontological chasm, a terminal (in origin Gnostic) antinomy between Creator and Redeemer, between visible creation and its invisible source and telos. Apophaticism does not stand for such an insoluble conflict that, for those who let themselves be drawn into it, can spell only intellectual and, ultimately, spiritual defeat. Indeed, Dionysian "negation" or "suppression (*aphaeresis*) must not be taken in a defective or privative sense, but in a sense of eminence, of excess."[78] His apophaticism thus does not name an epistemic impasse but, instead, outlines a spiritual challenge: how to calibrate and sequence our various powers of cognition in such a way that they will bring us closer to something that, admittedly, always lies beyond the reach of conceptual thought and predicative language. In confronting that challenge, Dionysius largely adheres to the Christology formalized at Constantinople (AD 381), itself significantly anticipated in a letter by Gregory of Nyssa, long misattributed as Epistle 38 to his older brother, Basil of Caesarea. Concluding what was to become an influential brief for future icon theology, Gregory writes:

> Just as he who in a polished mirror beholds the reflection of the form as plain knowledge of the represented face, so he, who has knowledge of the Son, through his knowledge of the Son receives in his heart the express image of the Father's

---

77. Von Balthasar 1984, 164.

78. "It is an anonymous copyist who has inserted the concept of 'negative theology', in order to give a symmetrical title to the third chapter [of *The Divine Names*]: 'What the affirmative and the negative theologies are.' There is therefore no negative theology articulated to affirmative theology in Dionysius, and one can even less summarize his theology of divine names as 'negative theology'" (Boulnois 2020, 105–6).

Person. For all things that are the Father's are beheld in the Son, and all things that are the Son's are the Father's; because the whole Son is in the Father, and has all the Father in Himself. Thus the hypostasis of the Son becomes as it were form and face of the knowledge of the Father, and the hypostasis of the Father is known in the form of the Son, while the proper quality which is contemplated therein remains for the plain distinction of the hypostases.[79]

In bringing two ontologically distinct, though not opposed, domains or hypostases into alignment, Gregory's (and eventually Dionysius's) apophaticism furnishes the blueprint for a metaphysics of mediation, a mode of learning to discern *within* visible beauty its analogical affinity with its transcendent source: "It is a matter always and above all of vision, of looking and striving after vision, but ever only . . . of vision through veils that protect and conceal."[80] As Dionysius puts it:

> Everything is, in a sense, projected out from Him, and this order possesses certain images and semblances [*eikonas kai homoimata*] of His divine paradigms. We therefore approach that which is beyond all as far as our capacities allow us and we pass by way of the denial and the transcendence of all things and by way of the cause of all things. God is therefore known in all things and as distinct from all things. He is known through knowledge and through unknowing. (*DN* 869d–872a)

Such a dialectic of "knowing and unknowing" will continue to inform a great deal of Christian theology thereafter—from Maximus to John Scotus Eriguena, Meister Eckhart, St. Bonaventure, and Cusanus all the way to St. John of the Cross. Unsurprisingly, it will also furnish the foundation for arguments developed by the Byzantine defenders of icons in the eighth and ninth centuries. For Dionysius, the tension between mystical and corporeal vision, between a nonrepresentational and a determinative knowing, is something to be endured, not overcome; and what allows human beings to endure it is the dual nature of visible forms as both medium and veil, conduit toward the invisible God and yet, by dint of their strictly analogical status, reminder of the beholder's infinite distance from him. Dionysian contemplation thus understands God as the source of being, at once wholly immanent and wholly transcendent to it. Hence, contemplative vision is in its very essence an experience of mediation, with the beholder of *visibilia* simultaneously the agent and the product of

---

79. For a translation of the letter, see *PNF* 8:137–41; quote from 141. On Gregory's conception of the "person" (*hypostasis*) of the Son as icon of the Father, see Schönborn's incisive reading (1994, 28–41).

80. Von Balthasar 1984, 173; for a much fuller engagement with Gregory of Nyssa's conception of beauty, see von Balthasar's 1942 *Présence et pensée* and the discussion by Carnes (2014, 167–82).

such vision: "For it is quite impossible that we humans should, in any immaterial way, rise up to imitate and to contemplate the heavenly hierarchies without the aid of those material means capable of guiding us as our nature requires. Hence, any thinking person realizes that the appearances of beauty are signs of an invisible loveliness" (*CH* 121d).

It is the "immense contemplative capacity of the mind" that enables the finite intellect to grasp visible phenomena as materially constituted realities and as manifestations, that is, as signs indicating the relative place of embodied being within an infinitely gradated cosmological arrangement: "Order and rank here below are a sign of the harmonious ordering toward the divine realm" (*CH* 121c–d). Such a "celestial hierarchy," whose cosmological origins are found in Plato's *Timaeus* a millennium earlier and whose imprint will still register in Bonaventure's *Itinerarium* nearly a millennium later, furnishes the precondition absent which contemplative vision (*theōria*) would simply be impossible. According to this metaphysical principle of analogy, everything that *is* also *indicates* or *manifests* that *in* which it seeks to participate, namely, the divine source *from* which it derives its being, to which it seeks to return, yet *relative to* which it necessarily falls short in varying degrees. Corporeal (sensible) beings can never be reduced to an inert and value-neutral *res extensa* in the modern, Cartesian sense. Rather, by virtue of having a specific formal and material constitution or "nature," they are always already *signs*. Unlike the shadowy existence to which Origen had confined them, visible things and images are to be understood as "gifts . . . granted to us in a symbolic mode." For Dionysius, nothing can ever justify dismissing visible being as metaphysically neutral, let alone lapsed and inchoate matter. Instead, he argues, the material scaffolding presupposed in varying degrees by the manifestation of a specific form should be understood as a divine concession to the finitude and limitations of human cognition. For Dionysius, the nexus between the visible and the invisible that discharges itself in the eventlike character of manifestation attests to an ontology that falls outside what can be accounted for in causal terms. At this level of reflection, "there is no sort of link of natural necessity."[81] Hence, everything that is subject to sensory experience, including even "the beautiful odors which strike the senses [as] representations of a conceptual diffusion" (*CH* 121d), must be seen in analogical relation to the ultimate gift of the Incarnation, which the liturgy recalls by inviting us to "the reception of the most divine Eucharist" (*CH* 124a).

Dionysius thus outlines a generous way of reading *visibilia* (*effigia*) as gifts whose very mode of manifestation contains the seeds for their "anagogical" (*anagōgas*) (*CH* 121c) interpretation. Like "the sacred pictures of the scriptures," the entire visible realm ought to be approached as a meaningfully ordered and comprehensive cosmos

---

81. Von Balthasar 1984, 169.

of "sacred shapes and symbols [*tōn hieroplastōn symbolōn*]" (*CH* 124a). Ernesto Mainoldi sums up Dionysius's theological framework as follows:

> To the Origenian concept of spiritual perfection as intellectual (noetic) illumination, Pseudo-Dionysios opposes a historical and immediate spiritual achievement through sacramental and ecclesial life which entails deification in proportion to the proper capacity of each one (*kat' oikeian analogian*). Pseudo-Dionysian deification is accomplished through the anagogical movement entailed in the three steps on which all the structure of the hierarchical order depends: "purification" (*katharsis*), "illumination" (*ellampsis/photismos*), and "perfection" (*teleiōsis*). This progression indicates unambiguously that the apex of deification transcends intellectual (noetic) knowledge. . . . The Pseudo-Dionysian hierarchical and ecclesiastical framework therefore implies that the symbol is not merely a sign from which an intelligible truth has to be extrapolated, but it is the truth itself.[82]

Inasmuch as for Dionysius visible things (including images) are not reducible to mere human percepts but, instead, constitute divine gifts made manifest in symbolic form, his theological aesthetics appears immune to the charge of pagan idolatry: "We cannot, as mad people do, profanely visualize these heavenly and godlike intelligences. . . . They are not shaped to resemble the brutishness of oxen or to display the wildness of lions" (*CH* 137a). Instead, to apprehend being as an image is to have learned to see it rightly, that is, as a manifestation not merely of itself, but of the *logos* that allowed it to "stand forth" in all its significant specificity and, in so doing, elicit our sensory-cum-spiritual participation in it.

What makes the visible a "gift" is that, in its distinctive self-manifestation, it shows God to have made "a concession to the nature of our own mind" (*CH* 137b). The very "shape" (*morphē*) wherein matter becomes visible as a particular being also shows it to be the manifestation of an invisible "form" (*eidos*). What appears thus does not merely represent itself, but, as a trace of that "form," links what has thus manifested itself to its invisible source. All "appearing" (*phainesthai*) is the self-manifestation *of* something (invisible) *as* something (visible); manifestation is mediation in its very essence. More than a concession, this dialectic of veiling and unveiling that defines manifestation is, for Dionysius, integral to all Being and evidence of its divine nature. As Theodore the Studite will put it three centuries later, "If merely mental contemplation were sufficient, it would have been sufficient for Him to come to us in a merely mental way; and consequently we would have been cheated by the

---

82. Mainoldi 2020, 9.

appearance both of His deeds, if He did not come in the body, and of His sufferings, which were undeniably like ours."[83] Already for Dionysius, naturalistic attempts at explaining human sight as but a case of passive and value-neutral, psychophysiological occurrence are doomed to fail. For human sight belongs to the order of acts; it actively responds to the visible shape of being, which it apprehends as the conduit toward its numinous, invisible form. In the act of seeing, human agents experience phenomena as saturated with anagogical meaning. For Dionysius, then, visible being is essentially symbolic. In von Balthasar's formulation, the visible is "not simply the occasion for his seeing God; rather, he sees God *in* things. Colors, shapes, essences and properties are for him immediate theophanies."[84] As sight evolves into a contemplative visualizing, all visible matter is recast as a *medium* anagogically linking the human intellect with the divine; it is not a surrogate for the latter any more than a representation of it.

The question thus becomes what specific role the image (*eikōn*) might play within Dionysius's outline of a visual catechesis for the faithful. What image might there be that is not only compatible with, but positively conducive to apophaticism's "way of negation" (*CH* 141a)? What would an image look like that self-consciously disavows any claim to being a copy or substitute for the ineffable, transcendent God? What positive function is there that can be served only by a kind of image (*eikōn*) no longer circumscribed by a mimetic framework? Now, as Dionysius argues, "there are two reasons for creating types for the typeless [*tōn atypōn hoi typos*]," a phrase later echoed by John Damascene.[85] First and foremost, the kind of image at stake must in its very presentation defeat any temptation of the uneducated (*hoi polloi*) to identify the icon with what it makes present. Put differently, the iconographer's formal choices must emphatically resist a naive pictorial realism that, even in Dionysius's era, remains deeply entrenched in imperial Roman culture. Both the icon and scriptural writing, "far from demeaning the ranks of heaven, actually pay them honor by describing them with dissimilar shapes so completely at variance with what they really are. . . . Incongruities are more suitable for lifting our minds up into the domain of the spiritual than similarities are." In its formal presentation, that is, the icon must enact its own "way of negation." It must perform, as it were, an act of iconoclasm on itself by visibly disavowing any mimetic allegiances, which is why "the pious theologians so wisely and upliftingly stooped to incongruous dissimilarities" (*CH* 141b).

---

83. Theodore 1981, I.7.

84. Von Balthasar 1984, 179; emphasis mine.

85. "If forms for formless things and shapes for shapeless things are proposed, not the least reason is because our analogies are not capable of raising us immediately to intellectual contemplation but need familiar and natural points of reference" (John of Damascus 2003, III:21; henceforth cited in text as *JDI*).

Inscribed within the icon's very form, then, is its dissent from the naturalistic logic of pagan mimesis and pictorial realism. Inasmuch as "form in the icon is exceeded by its function," the lines and shapes that comprise it do not impose finitude but reveal an indelible nexus between the visible flesh and the invisible Word: "To draw is not to delimit. Christ is not the prisoner of the icon; *the iconic graph is neither a prison nor a tomb.* . . . To be seen is not its aim, and visibility does not belong within its essential definition. . . . Neither expressiveness nor the sign are part of its definition. Being one only with the economic figure of the divine procession, it is its manifestation and configuration, first in the invisible figure of similitude, then in the display of carnal visibility."[86]

To be sure, Dionysius does not offer an express account of the icon's formal design or execution but, instead, tackles the broader question of whether and under what conditions visible things may legitimately serve to draw the beholder closer to their divine source. Even so, while "the Neoplatonic writings of Pseudo-Dionysios in the late fifth century were not meant to describe the relationship of pictorial representation to its prototype, they helped stimulate the development of iconic images, especially in the post-Justinian period. One drew closer and was uplifted toward the holy prototype itself by contemplation of the holy image."[87] Formally speaking, Dionysius's brief remarks on religious art in his *Celestial Hierarchy* all converge in this: henceforth the icon will set itself apart from scenic, decorative, or otherwise "representational" art, simply because, in its essence, the icon is never a proper human artifact but the visible response to a gift of divine origin. Mainoldi may well be right to note that "*eikōn* is here correctly rendered by 'portrait', rather than referring to an abstract image in the theoretical sense." Inasmuch as "likeness" (*homoiōsis, homoiotēs*) "implies a causal relationship between the hypostasis and its image," what legitimates the image is not its mimetic correctness but its power of infusing the beholder with the real presence of its subject (*hypostasis*).[88] All extraneous, "scenic" elements associated with Roman (pagan) realism are jettisoned in favor of an exclusive pictorial focus on the human face. Already during the decades following Dionysius's writings, a new style of iconic portraiture begins to surface in which the beholder comes face-to-face with a particular saint or with Christ. The new form excludes all extraneous, potentially distracting features, as evidenced by some of the oldest surviving icons—which escaped the fury of eighth- and ninth-century iconoclasm—those found at

---

86. Mondzain 2005, 93, 80–81. See also Ivanovic, who understands Dionysius's "preference for dissimilar 'types of the typeless'" as a sensible prompt to the viewer that all theologically defensible images necessarily "require interpretation and explanation" and, hence, as a safeguard against the mimetic fallacy of interpreting potentially "less astonishing representations in a literal way" (2020, 82).

87. Margaret Frazer, in Weitzman 1979, 515.

88. Mainoldi 2020, 16.

St. Catherine's Monastery on the Sinai Peninsula. In sketching what should be read as a theological rationale for nonrepresentational images, Dionysius also happens to provide some of the weightiest arguments on which, two centuries later, the Byzantine defenders of icon veneration will gratefully draw. The formalization of the icon in Eastern Orthodoxy during the centuries following the end of iconoclasm—its increasingly self-conscious rejection of Western notions of verisimilitude, linear perspective, and coloristic realism—can all be traced back to Dionysius's pioneering arguments in the early sixth century. Yet beyond its defensive, apophatic line of argument, Dionysius's reasoning also exhibits a profoundly constructive dimension. The icon's conspicuously antirealist formalism, he insists, brings about an "uplifting" to which the "illiterate masses" (*hoi polloi*) can respond affirmatively, albeit without claiming to understand; for, "as scripture says, knowledge is not for everyone" (*CH* 140a–b). To the increasingly adversarial climate of the seventh century, Dionysius's writings furnished a vital resource for those, including Maximus the Confessor, who sought to push back against a resurgent Origenism whose "spiritualist" and antimaterial thrust seemed to preclude any form of mediation. The polarity of a Dionysian and Origenist theology subtends much of the iconoclast controversy that gets under way with Leo III's iconoclast edict of AD 726, followed by his decision to remove the Christ icon from the Chalce Gate of the imperial city. The latter act in particular confirms the extent to which, "at the latest from the 7th century onwards, images had become proper historical protagonists" whose interpretation had grown "increasingly precarious."[89]

ICONS IN THEOLOGICAL APOLOGETICS AND LITURGICAL PRACTICE FROM DIONYSIUS TO JOHN DAMASCENE

The concern in this chapter is not to retrace the historical and political back-and-forth of Byzantine iconoclasm, which others have done in minute and vivid detail. Rather, it is to formulate something like a theological grammar of the icon in close relation to the phenomenology of its experience. To that end, I will consider arguments by John Damascene, Nikephoros, and Theodore the Studite, aimed at producing a theological warrant for icon veneration, as well as ekphrastic accounts by Paulus Silentiarius and Patriarch Photios who, writing in the sixth and ninth century, respectively, furnish quasi-phenomenological accounts of the icon's operation in ecclesial space. Seen in the aggregate, these Byzantine defenders of icons outline a comprehensive account of the institution, function, form, and ontology of the image that,

---

89. Alloa 2013, 8.

as remains to be seen, will resurface in markedly different contexts (epistemological, scientific, aesthetic, poetic) over the next fifteen hundred years. Animating most eighth- and ninth-century iconodules is the ongoing metaphysical quest for a Christology whose previous formulation at the Council of Chalcedon (AD 451) had furnished mainly an institutional, political, and, up to a point, theological resolution of questions fundamental to the Christian faith.[90] Yet it is one thing to address these questions in exacting dogmatic language and quite another to cash out the meaning of such teachings in ways to which the faithful could intuitively respond. As is so often the case, the competing imperatives of theological coherence and political consent could be reconciled only in precariously abstract formulations. How, then, were Christian communities in East and West to make experiential sense of the council's stipulation that "one and the same Lord Jesus Christ, the only begotten Son, must be acknowledged in two natures [*en dyo physesin*], without confusion or change, without division or separation"?[91] Furnishing a dogmatic formulation for which there was as yet no corresponding phenomenology, the Chalcedonian definition seemed to "lack . . . charismatic impact" and, thus, even risked weakening the faith it meant to strengthen.[92] Of the many voices arising in the wake of Chalcedon's Trinitarian formula, Dionysius's seems most concerned with strengthening the link between dogma and experience, the invisible *logos* and its infinitely variegated manifestation.

> The truth we have to understand is that we use letters, syllables, phrases, written terms and words because of the senses. But when our souls are moved by intelligent energies in the direction of the things of the intellect, then our senses and all that go with them are no longer needed. And the same happens with our intelligent powers which, when the soul becomes divinized, concentrate sightlessly and through an unknowing union on the rays of "unapproachable light."

---

90. On Chalcedon's decisive influence on Trinitarian and Christological thought, extending well beyond the era of iconoclasm, see Beeley 2012, 256–84; and the essays by Gwinn, Price, and Herrin, in Price and Whitby 2009.

91. "The distinction between the two natures was never abolished by their union but rather the character proper to each of the two natures was preserved as they came together in one Person and one hypostasis [*hen prosōpon kai mian hupostasin*]. He is not split or divided into two Persons, but he is one and the same only begotten Son." The authoritative text in Denziger's *Enchiridion symbolorum* (#302) stresses that *en*, not *ek*, is the crucial preposition here—that is, *in* rather than *from* two natures, as Cyril of Alexandria had written and as the Miaphysites favored. Part of the reason Chalcedon proved so divisive is that not only "Nestorians" but also followers of *Cyril* felt betrayed by it. Writing against Nestorius, Cyril tended to favor more "singular" expressions of Christ's unity (Word-flesh) and the precise wording "*ek duo physeōn*" comes, in fact, from him (see his "First Letter to Succensus," §6). Beeley's (2012) treatment of Cyril and Chalcedon helpfully draws out the tensions. I am grateful to Aaron Ebert for some of these clarifications and suggestions.

92. Meyendorff 1983, 33.

When, as a result of the workings of perception, the mind is stirred to be moved up to contemplative conceptions, it sets a particular value on most unambiguous perceptions, on the clearest words and on the things most distinctly seen. (*DN* 708d–709a)

The numinous reality to which human perception points should be understood, Dionysius argues, not as the repudiation or antithesis of the senses but as their fulfillment. If the soul is to "become divinized," sensory perception must be rightly trained; it must learn to become focused "on the most unambiguous perceptions[,] . . . on the things most distinctly seen." Yet for that to happen, a specific kind of image is required, one from which all scenic and decorative elements have either been stripped altogether or, alternatively, have been so configured as to intensify the focus on a spiritual presence that is not merely to be "looked at," but is meant to effect in the beholder a transformative self-recognition. Let us consider three examples, all taken from around the middle of the sixth century, at a time when Christian iconography appears to be undergoing rapid formal consolidation and geographic expansion.

Among the more famous objects in the Dumbarton Oaks collection in Washington, DC, is the so-called Riha Paten (second half of sixth century) (fig. 2.6), a beautifully crafted and well preserved silver *diskos* on which the host is placed during the celebration of the Eucharist. What had long before started as Christian imagery on sarcophagi and wall painting in catacombs had by the early fifth century firmly established itself above ground in the form of apse mosaics, wall paintings, and ivory-carved plaques. As this sixth-century paten suggests, Christian images had also become an integral feature of liturgical practice. Adorning the paten on which the Eucharist is presented to the communicants during the celebration of the liturgy (*synaxis*), the Christian image here appears both functional and emblematic, fusing as it does the act of receiving communion with beholding a depiction of the Last Supper. Seeing and "remembering" have merged in a single act of embodied visualization. As Theodore the Studite will comment, when asking his disciples to "do this in memory of me," Christ was "obviously implying that He cannot be represented otherwise than by being remembered."[93] Woven into the very structure of the liturgy, the visual catechesis that Dionysius outlines in his *Celestial Hierarchy* undoubtedly was meant to reinforce the words of Institution and, more generally, passages from scripture that, with the exception of a few literate congregants, those assembled could only ever assimilate by hearing. Even then, further qualifications remain to be made. For one thing, "images can be interpreted in different ways, the ordinary people remaining standing in front of the symbols while the priests and the

---

93. Theodore 1981, I.10.

Figure 2.6.
Riha Paten, depicting the
Communion of the Apostles,
ca. AD 565–78. Dumbarton
Oaks Collection

contemplatives penetrate more deeply to their spiritual meaning; but a more penetrating (*optikōteros*) gaze could discern in the same images something still deeper
and more revealing." Aside from the fact that the spiritual knowledge facilitated by
the images embedded in liturgical practice comes in different degrees, there is the
more fundamental fact that "between manifestation and what is manifest there is no
sort of link of natural necessity . . . so [that] the more it reveals the more it conceals."
As von Balthasar sums up the metaphysical paradox at stake here, "The same knowledge of God demands both a deeper penetration *into* the image and also a more sublime transcendence *beyond* it, and the two are not separated one from another but
are the more fully integrated, the more perfectly they are achieved."[94]

Dating from the same period (mid-sixth century) is the icon of Christ and Abbot
Menas found at the Monastery of Apollo at Bawît, Egypt, some hundred miles south
of Cairo (fig. 2.7). A series of circular or semicircular shapes structures the image,
including the rounded chins of both figures, their ample halos, the unnaturally
enlarged and wide-open eyes, and the gentle curvature of what may be hills in the
background. The formal resemblance is further strengthened by the fact that Christ,
by now presented in his more familiar, bearded form, has put his right arm around
the abbot, whose right hand in turn affirms the Triune God here made manifest.[95]

---

94. Balthasar 1984, 169.

95. The position of the abbot's fingers evokes, though does not execute perfectly, the iconographic symbol for the tri-unity of Father, Son, and Holy Spirit. The hand gesture reappears frequently, including in the famous Deësis mosaic in the Hagia Sophia (thirteenth century), and each

Figure 2.7.
Christ and Abbot Menas,
Monastery of Apollo at
Bawît, Egypt,
sixth century. Paris, Musée
du Louvre, Section Copte,
X 5178

Cumulatively, these formal and symbolic devices confer theological weight and legitimacy not only on the figure next to Christ but also on the icon itself. The saints in question, or in this case the abbot, are depicted as Christ's *symmorphoi* in much the same way that Paul speaks of them in Romans 8:29: "For whom he did foreknow, he also did predestinate to be conformed to the image [*symmorphous tēs eikonos*] of his Son." Implicitly, then, the icon is part of a reciprocal economy wherein Christ confers institutional legitimacy and spiritual authority on the abbot just as the icon bears witness to that event and, in so doing, receives theological legitimacy *from* the spiritual authorities whom it depicts. Decisive in this regard and signaling the shift to a hieratic type of image that will soon become the stylistic norm of Byzantine icon-writing is the symmetry of Christ's and the abbot's unwavering gaze. Firmly directed at the beholder, that gaze denies the viewer the comforting illusion of inhabiting an ontologically different space from that of the icon, that is, of merely *looking at* a picture qua representation. Some twelve hundred years later, Manet will deploy the same technique so as to expose the detached gaze underlying modern pictorial realism, the petit-bourgeois assumption of distractedly gazing *at* a "picture" rather than

---

time it appears designed to strengthen continuity between Christ as the second Person of the Trinity, Christ as the visible *imago Dei*, and also the saints depicted on his side.

being in the presence of, and implicated in, the image. Reflecting the growing influence of the Corpus Dionysiacum during the sixth century, the icon enjoins the beholder to achieve the same clarity and directedness of spiritual vision here modeled by the "seeing" icon of Christ and Abbot Menas.

Arguably, no icon instantiates this conception of seeing as witnessing a presence more powerfully than the Christ Pantocrator icon from St. Catherine's Monastery on the Sinai Peninsula (established in AD 565) (fig. 2.8). Given the icon's formal resemblance to the solidus minted under Emperor Justinian II sometime around AD 695 (fig. 2.9), it may have been produced in Constantinople.[96] More certain than its provenance is the icon's dating, widely agreed to be the early sixth century. Most likely, the Pantocrator icon and other depictions of Christ from the later sixth and early seventh century would have furnished the template for the Christ image as we find it reproduced in Justinian's coins. Clearly, by the end of the seventh century the Christ icon was sufficiently established to be recognized as such. Why else place it on a coin whose design, after all, means to reinforce the metonymic relation between imperial and divine authority? Yet which side of the coin was to be considered the front? At first glance, the coin's inscription (*IesusCristosRex Regnantium*) seems to answer the question, with the reverse side identifying the emperor as the "servant of Christ" (*DNIustinian Usserus Christi*). After all, even as imperial assent was needed for Christ's face to appear on coins, the emperor's authority was understood to rest on divine support made visible by the Christ icon. Yet by being circulated on a coin also featuring the imperial image and, more generally, by allowing "icons of Christ and the Virgin to stand in the place of the imperial images," it was all but certain that the holy image would end up receiving "the same frankly pagan worship as their own images always had received."[97] The susceptibility of the Pantocrator's image and authority to shifting political winds was brought home when Christ's face abruptly disappeared from Byzantine coins following Justinian II's death (AD 711), only to reappear following the triumph of Orthodoxy and the end of iconoclasm in March 843. The ambiguity of worldly and spiritual meanings resulting from their uneasy entanglement in the pre-iconoclast era is further intensified by the sheer ubiquity of the Justinian solidus. It was here that "the age of mechanical reproduction of the image commences." Prior to the end of the iconoclast era, however, Alloa's claim that this new "ability to reproduce [the image] is . . . not a loss but, in fact, guarantees the aura" seems less persuasive.[98] That the authority of the Christ icon not only underwrote but also, up to a point, depended on imperial power emerges from the fact that

---

96. Constas 2014, 47; see also Schönborn 1994, 154–56. On portraits of Christ in late antiquity, see Jensen 2005, 131–72.

97. Brown 1973, 10.

98. Alloa 2013, 11.

Figure 2.8. Christ Pantocrator, ca. AD 550, Monastery of St. Catherine, Mount Sinai, Egypt

Figure 2.9. Solidus, minted ca. AD 695 under Emperor Justinian II

Justinian's coins were issued just three years after the Quinisext Council of Constantinople (AD 691). The decision to associate the imperial image with the Christ icon reflects imperial support for (or approval of?) the council's decree that henceforth Christ was to be depicted not as a lamb but in "human form." Notably, just three decades later, in 726, that support was to evaporate with the start of Leo III's iconoclast policies.[99] In any event, the Quinisext Council's decree appears to have given belated official approval to depictions of Christ's human form that, for more than a century, had become a firmly established feature in churches and at other holy sites across the eastern Mediterranean.

---

99. "Embracing therefore the ancient types and shadows as symbols of the truth and patterns given to the Church, we . . . order therefore that 'that which is perfect' may be delineated to the eyes of all, at least in colored expression; we decree that the figure in human form of the Lamb who taketh away the sin of the world, Christ our God, be henceforth exhibited in images, instead of the ancient lamb" (Canon 82).

Turning to the Pantocrator icon, then, we begin with a trait frequently over-looked because largely invisible in digital or print reproductions: its material, known as encaustic. It is a medium in which "colored pigments are suspended in heated beeswax," yielding a "warm, luminous transparency, along with a soft, smooth tex-ture not unlike the appearance of human flesh."[100] Specifically, the right half of Christ's face and body appear markedly naturalistic, with the shoulder more pronounced and fleshy, in contrast to its receding and downward-sloping, left counterpart; fur-thermore, the drooping left eye and raised eyebrow on the right individualize the face in ways consistent with late Roman pictorial realism. Furthermore, hints of ar-chitectural forms in the background and the elaborately ornamented book of scrip-ture that, paradoxically, Christ himself is already holding—presumably so as to sug-gest its divine provenance—constitute additional vestiges of a realist aesthetic, as does the bulging fleshiness of Christ's right hand and his elaborate clothing of tunic and mantle. Even so, a Roman aesthetic of pictorial verisimilitude governs only the right half of the icon. For as numerous commentators have pointed out, the icon's arguably most distinctive feature concerns the asymmetry of Christ's face, which is widely thought to reflect both the polarity of Christ as agent of divine justice and mercy and his human and divine natures. Following Kitzinger, who had remarked on the juxtaposition of classical and non- or anticlassical elements in early Byzantine iconography, and also building on subsequent work by Kurt Weitzmann, Maximos Constas has recently offered a finely grained analysis of "the icon's compelling du-ality" of (human) mercy and (divine) judgment.[101] As Constas insists, however, the icon's twofold aspect ought not be construed as an antinomy but, instead, as fusing "two divergent portrait types: a naturalistic image of a frail young man, and a colos-sal, almost non-human figure rendered in a style that is comparatively abstract, hier-atic, and symbolic."

The icon thus presents us with "a kind of bipolar structure informing God's self-manifestation, with an emphasis on the coming together in such a way that they con-tinue to coexist."[102] Not yet defining of the icon as a whole, though shaping its left,

---

100. Constas 2014, 42–43. Hints of an architectural backdrop remain ambiguous, though speculation about space and time (e.g., "the 'hour' depicted in our icon *may be* the 'dawn,' which is one of the names of the Messiah" [Constas 2014, 44]) is best avoided.

101. Kitzinger, quoted in Constas 52 nn. 34 and 35. If the Pantocrator icon furnished the domi-nant visual template for depictions of Christ ever after, its distinctive asymmetry is no longer ob-servable in later iterations, such as Dürer's famous self-portrait from 1500 or copies of the *vera icon* of van Eyck's studio from the late 1430s. As regards "the mutation of the icon into the portrait [*Wan-del von der Ikone zum Porträt*]," whose aesthetic corollary is a shift from a concern with "authen-ticity" (*Echtheit*) to the pursuit of mimetic "resemblance" (*Ähnlichkeit*), see Belting 2014, 148–56.

102. Constas 2014, 68, 54, 69; for Constas, the icon's dual structure consummately embodies the "Justiniac synthesis" (85). A similar bifurcation can be found in the Apse Mosaic from Sinai, with

otherworldly half, is a hieratic, almost abstract flatness that in time will establish itself as the norm for Byzantine icon writing, at which point "Christ's images became distilled to their most quintessentially iconographic . . . [and] postures were progressively stabilized into set types."[103]

It would be an overstatement, however, to claim of early Byzantine icons that these "new images resolutely break away from the mimetic portraits of the Roman *effigies*."[104] Indeed, the presence of Christ's distinct (though not opposed) human and divine natures in a single image, whose fusion of a realist and (for lack of a better word) abstract aesthetic reflects Chalcedonian Christology, is further reinforced by Christ's gaze. The pupil on the left points ever so slightly upward, whereas the one on the "realist" right side looks squarely at the beholder. Most likely, whoever "wrote" the Pantocrator icon was well aware of a dilemma confronting those writing icons in the still unsettled aftermath of Chalcedon, especially when depicting the crucifixion. For "if such images depicted Jesus with open eyes, they risked casting doubt on his physical death. Conversely, if they depicted him with closed eyes," as is the case with an eighth-century icon also from St. Catherine's Monastery, "they risked calling into question his divine nature, which naturally could not suffer corporeal death."[105] This uneasy coexistence of Christ's two natures has prompted Christoph Schönborn to situate the Pantocrator icon in the context of the protracted Christological debates that continued in the wake of Chalcedon. While this line of argument is persuasive as far as it goes, it does not clarify the relationship between notions yielded by theological reflection and their instantiation in specific pictorial form. Such contextualist embedding of the icon in some theological controversy or other only implies, but rarely ever demonstrates, a causal relationship between ambient (historical, economic, theological, or other "cultural") vectors and the particular *explanandum*, in this case, the strangely bifurcated Pantocrator icon.

While not confronting that methodological challenge outright, Constas's recent interpretation offers some valuable pointers. Unlike Schönborn, he maintains that to emphasize the dual nature of Christ in the Pantocrator icon fails to consider "Chalcedon's emphasis on unity." In fact, he goes on, Schönborn misconstrues the icon as "evidence for the production of theological art by proponents of the 'two natures' theology, which lends support to the 'Chalcedonian' interpretation of the Sinai Christ." Against such a view, Constas recalls Cyril of Alexandria's caveat "not to

---

Moses naturalistically depicted as firmly anchored on the ground, whereas Christ's hieratic image appears to float in a virtual space above and at the center of the image.

103. Carr, in Evans 2004, 149.

104. Alloa 2013, 5.

105. Belting 2006, 95.

divide the one Christ into two, [by] picturing a two-faced Emmanuel."[106] To "know" the two natures of the one Christ separately or, alternatively, to grasp their "hypostatic union" by physical sight is, for Cyril, equally impossible. Just as pure intuition cannot yield the theological knowledge at stake, so a wholly abstract model of cognition cannot reconcile what is *distinct* (two natures) with what is manifestly *unified* in Christ's one Person or "face" (*prosōpon*). For this structural impasse to be resolved, a different kind of seeing is required, one neither fungible with propositional knowing nor reducible to a purely material, optical event.[107] Drawing on a long lineage of Hellenistic writers, Cyril thus mobilizes the idea of spiritual or "contemplative" seeing (*theōria*). Foreshadowing what we will encounter again in figures as disparate as Nicholas of Cusa, Goethe, Hopkins, Cézanne, and Rilke, such contemplative or spiritual sight places great emphasis on the contiguity of the visual with the verbal, that is, on the way in which what may be known must first have been mediated in some visible form just as, conversely, the true import of having seen such a form will only ever be fulfilled in the medium of the word. Indeed, the very fact that we wish for the deliverances of intuition to be fulfilled in articulate speech also tells us that the act of seeing is latently conceptual, a case of active uptake rather than passive intake. Emphasizing the essential complementarity of *eikōn* and *logos* in contemplation, Cyril notes that "the line that separates word and image is erased, [and] the difference between them collapses."[108]

Yet by positing that seeing and knowing, image and word, are part of a complex reciprocal economy, writers from Cyril and Dionysius forward to the Byzantine iconodules effectively revive a Neoplatonist conception of the image that had always persisted alongside more functional, representational image models found in impe-

---

106. Cyril, quoted in Constas 2014, 67; while acknowledging the distinctness of Christ's divinity and humanity ("flesh is flesh and not Divinity . . . and likewise the Word is God and not flesh"), Cyril "resists the idea that there are two natures after the incarnation." For at that point, Christ's two "natures cannot properly be distinguished because, like a human soul and body, they now combine to make up a single living thing (*zōon*)" (Beeley 2012, 262). As Mondzain puts it, the "true saga of the image . . . is nothing other than the saga of the incarnation itself" (2005, 93).

107. The claim will resurface in Kant's first *Critique*: "Thoughts without content are empty, intuitions without concepts are blind" (*Gedanken ohne Inhalt sind leer, Anschauungen ohne Begriffe, sind blind*) (Kant 1965, 93 [A 51]). Kant's famous remark makes sense only as a statement on the fundamental *complementarity* of intuition and concept rather than their formal antinomy. On such "nonconceptual content" as is implied by, though not yet fulfilled in, intuition, see McDowell 1996, 46–65: "We must insist that the understanding is already inextricably implicated in the deliverances of sensibility themselves. Experiences are impressions made by the world on our senses, products of receptivity; but those impressions themselves already have conceptual content" (46).

108. Cyril, quoted in Constas 2014, 67; Cyril's argumentation, however, seemed to court the equally problematic, Miaphysite position; see Meyendorff, who notes that "Cyrillian Christology could easily be, and actually was, interpreted in a Monophysite sense by Eutyches and his followers," a scenario remedied only by Chalcedonian definition (1983, 33).

rial Roman culture. No longer, then, is the *eikōn* framed as an instance of raw, as it were, mythical representation, perhaps to be superseded and obviated by the abstract discriminations of conceptual thought. For the kind of theological knowledge that purports to dispense with contemplative seeing altogether by treating the image as, at most, some provisional scaffolding to be dispensed with sooner or later fails to honor the *logos* that seeks to realize itself in both patristic Christology and the Byzantine image. Instead, the challenge to which the Pantocrator icon so influentially responds is to navigate between the Scylla of a purely abstract conceptualization of Chalcedonian Christology and the Charybdis of diluting the dogma of Christ's two natures into an undifferentiated, mystical intuition. For both theological and formal reasons, the Byzantine icon cannot be mapped onto either a conceptualist or a representationalist grid. With remarkable alacrity, sixth- and seventh-century iconographers understood that for the icon to realize or make manifest Christ's Person as presence, both the nonidentity and the inseparability of his two natures, of the visible and the invisible understood as distinct yet complementary realities, had to be inscribed in the icon itself. No longer is the icon to be treated as but an ex post facto visualization or reflection of a theological framework. Instead, it will henceforth seek to *mediate* the reality of the Incarnation in an intuitively accessible image, albeit with the crucial qualification that to attentively contemplate the icon and fully internalize the presence it mediates amounts to an open-ended process in which seeing and knowing are no more in opposition than image and word or, indeed, Christ's human and divine natures.

What such contemplative seeing brings home is that for the Chalcedonian formula that Christ be "acknowledged in two natures . . . without confusion or change, without division or separation," to signify that all the faithful must have left behind the stranglehold of binary logic. The human and the divine, the visible and the invisible, are to be thought as both ontologically distinct and related. Neither a Hellenistic emanationism nor some Gnostic, antinomian disaggregation of Creator and Redeemer, nor any other opposition between the numinous and the visible captures the both/and logic of Chalcedonian consubstantiality where Christ's two natures, rather than being "split or divided into two Persons," are fully integrated "in one Person and one hypostasis." In rendering visible the Chalcedonian paradox of Christ's distinct natures ("without confusion or change, without division or separation"), the icon enables the faithful to participate in a metaphysical reality that transcends the domains of intuition and conceptualization alike. To that end, the icon initially summons features associated with Roman pictorial realism, only to expose them as inadequate to what it ultimately seeks to convey. Insofar as "the icon sought not to fall into the categories of representation, fiction, or illusion at all," it fundamentally alters both the concept of what an image is and the phenomenology of its experience; because the icon "institutes a gaze and not an object," its truth is no longer limited to rendering exhaustively visible what *can* be seen.[109] Rather, the icon enjoins the beholder to apprehend its internal, formal contradictions as traces (or Plotinian "shadows") of a reality that lies categorically beyond physical sight and empirical visibility. Soon, we will consider the ways in which the fusion of Christ's two natures in the icon shapes Byzantine image theory while also distilling from the iconodules' writings a phenomenology of how images operated and were experienced in liturgical and devotional practice. Yet before doing so, some additional background on the Christology underlying and framing Byzantine image theory is in order.

Though officially "resolved" by the doctrinal pronouncements at Chalcedon, the dual specter of Arianism (and Miaphysitism) and Nestorianism (or Dyophysitism), predictably lingers on and, indeed, will be reignited by the iconoclast debate in the eighth century. At first blush, the theological foundation of the arguments advanced by iconoclast bishops and emperors, beginning with Leo III, appear sound and compelling. To begin with, a qualified defense of the icon as depicting solely Christ's *human* form opens itself to the charge of pagan idolatry. Beyond that, such a defense of the icon hazards either reducing his reality to a single nature and, thus, reviving the miaphysite heresy or, alternatively, unduly splitting the second person of the Trinity into two seemingly unrelated natures in the manner of Nestorian dyophysitism. In either case, restricting the icon's scope to depicting Christ's human face ends up violating either the "major premise" (Bulgakov) of God's ineffability (cf. Jn 1:18), thus drawing the charge of attempting to circumscribe (*perigraphein*) the uncircumscribable.[110] Alternatively, it incurs the (Christological) objection that icons, in evident violation of Chalcedonian dogma, "mix and confuse" Christ's divine and human natures. As the iconoclast emperor Constantine V (AD 741–75) will insist, "1) Christ's '*prosōpon*' or hypostasis cannot be separated from his two natures. 2) One of the two natures, his divinity, cannot be depicted; it cannot be 'circumscribed.' 3) It is, therefore, impossible, to paint or 'circumscribe' the *prosōpon* of Christ."[111] Anxious to "purify Christianity [so as] to enable it better to withstand the challenge of Islam," Leo III's iconoclast policy had previously identified the cross as the only theologically legitimate and visible symbol of the faith.[112] To cement that claim, those assembled at the iconoclast synod of AD 815 appealed to the authority of the fourth-century Cypriote bishop Epiphanius of Salamis, who was said to have insisted "that

---

109. Mondzain 2005, 70—likely echoing Marion: "the icon does not result from a vision but provokes one" (1991, 17).

110. Bulgakov 2012a, 14; see also Mondzain 2005, 25–34.

111. Schönborn 1994, 173. As the iconoclast council of AD 754 had stipulated, "If anyone depicts in an icon the flesh which was deified by the union with the divine Logos, let him be anathema, because he separates the flesh from the divinity that assumed and deified it, and as a consequence he renders it unedified" (in Sahas 1986, 159).

112. Meyendorff 1983, 43.

our fathers painted nothing except the sign (*semaion*) of Christ, the cross," and that images "painted in colors on the walls should be whitewashed."[113]

About the primacy of the cross as the symbol of the Christian faith, and as the banner (*in hoc signo*) under which emperors ever since Constantine I were said to have triumphed over their adversaries, there could be little doubt. Still, the question remained as to what precisely set an image apart from a symbol and why the depiction of a human face (*prosōpon*) should only ever be understood mimetically rather than symbolically. Conversely, under what conditions might a visible image function as an instance of mediation, that, like the cross, is experienced as *typos* rather than as *eidōlon*? What specific property of the icon would allow the beholder to participate in the prototype (*epi to prōtotypon*), as Basil (or, more likely, Gregory of Nyssa) had famously put it in Epistle 38? It is this question that occupies John of Damascus in his three treatises against the iconoclasts, the last of which likely dates from around AD 741, just at the beginning of the reign of Constantine V, whose strident iconoclasm John so vigorously opposes.[114] Hewing close to the Christology of Chalcedon, John insists that, in venerating the icon,

> I do not venerate the creation instead of the creator, but I venerate the Creator, created for my sake, who came down to his creation without being lowered or weakened, that he might glorify my nature and bring about communion with the divine nature. . . . For the nature of the flesh did not become divinity, but as the Word became flesh immutably, . . . so also the flesh became the Word without losing what it was, being rather made equal to the Word hypostatically. Therefore, I am emboldened to depict the invisible God, not as invisible, but as he became visible for our sake, by participation in flesh and blood. (*JDI* III:6)

---

113. Barber 2002, 83–105 (quote from 87). As Brubaker and Haldon point out, the authenticity of Epiphanius's seemingly iconoclast position seems doubtful. Most likely it is one of a number of cases, famously including Eusebius's letter to the empress Constantia, where patristic documents supporting iconoclast policy were retroactively forged (2011, 45–47). An obverse case, where an icono*phile* position may have been belatedly crafted and attributed to a late patristic "authority," would be that of Hypatius, archbishop of the important see of Ephesus in AD 531–38. Anticipating a similar (and authenticated) exchange between Gregory the Great and Serenus of Marseille in AD 599, Hypatius is said to respond to Julian of Atramytium's more circumscribed concerns about the use of religious sculpture, a use the bishop expressly sanctions as an expedient for the illiterate: "We permit simpler people . . . to learn by way of initiation about such things by [the sense of] sight. . . . Divine wisdom in saving love of men sometimes remit[s] the strictness [of the injunction against graven images] for those souls which still need guidance." See Alexander 1952 (quote from 179–80).

114. On John's *Defense of Icons*, see Brubaker and Haldon 2011, 183–86; Louth 2002, 193–222; Schönborn 1994, 192–98; Tsakiridou 2013, 193–205. See also Ostrogorsky's earlier essay (1929); and Ouspensky 1992, I:119–50.

In his crude, though at the time hardly uncommon, supersessionist opening chapters, John maintains that the orthodox faith is no longer constrained by the Old Testament prohibition of graven images, which he insists had specifically applied to "the Jews on account of their sliding into idolatry."[115] Ultimately, what not only justifies, but positively compels the veneration of icons is a fundamental deficiency of human cognition; for "it is impossible for us to reach what is intelligible apart from what is bodily" (*JDI* III:11). Rather than being understood as an artifact gratuitously contrived, the icon proves to be an integral feature of John's theological anthropology. Perched on the line separating what is made from what is revealed, the icon is teleologically ordered toward truth and not, as the iconoclasts would have it, a manipulation of matter for merely contingent, finite purposes. To conceive the icon as a medium rather than an object is to come face-to-face with its indisputable, if also ineffable and indispensable, powers of disclosure: "Every image makes manifest [*ekphantorikē*] and demonstrates something hidden. . . . The image was devised to guide us to knowledge and to make manifest and open what is hidden, certainly for our profit and well doing and salvation" (*JDI* III:17). Ultimately, the centrality of the Incarnation, of "Christ [having become] visible in the flesh[,] made his representation in icons not only possible, but also ... [reflected] the need to affirm the continuing saving link between man and God that the incarnate Christ embodied."[116]

Yet to put it thus tells only half the story. For the icon qua medium serves also to shelter the human gaze from a divine presence and light that, were it not for the icon's semipermeable "veil" or "screen," would annihilate its finite beholder outright. Mindful of this dialectic of revelation and veiling, John takes care to remark on the ontological difference between an image and what it depicts: "An image is . . . a likeness [*homoiōma*] and pattern [*paradeigma*] and impression [*ektypōma*] of something, showing in itself what is depicted; however, the image is certainly not like the archetype, that is, what is depicted, in every respect—for the image is one thing and what it depicts is another—and certainly a difference [*diaphora*] is seen between them" (*JDI* III:16). Yet even as the difference in question can never be resolved into a formal and material identity of image and object, it must not be construed as an antinomy either. For inasmuch as the icon mediates that which it depicts, it is constitutively *related* to the depicted being vis-à-vis which it remains at an ontological remove. Already in his first treatise, John had referenced St. John Chrysostom's discussion of Paul's Letter to the Hebrews, in which the order of icon and prototype appears to be curiously reversed: "In a certain way, the first is an image of the second, Melchisedek [an image] of Christ, just as one might say that a sketch of a picture is a

---

115. Louth 2002, 207; *JDI* III:8.
116. Barber 2002, 80–81.

premonitory shadow [*proskiasma*] of the true icon in colors."[117] In the order of being, the *logos* obviously comes first; yet in the order of cognition, finite being functions like "the underpainting which precedes the colored picture."[118] The true fulfillment of the image that by its very nature abides between the ectypal and its numinous source is here figured as a lustrous, chromatically superabundant presence. Thus, "color animates the content of a picture in the same way that the human voice animates the text that is being read."[119] Here it is important to remember that, like everything else about the icon, the phenomenon of color, too, does not expire in its sheer visibility. Rather, it intimates a plenitude that can be conveyed only in the domain of the visible, yet which the beholder can realize only by discerning an anagogical charge within sensible phenomena of any kind, that is, by apprehending them as *typoi* rather than self-contained, finite matter.

Once again, then, we find that relationality and difference are not contingent but ontological predicates of the icon. They are *logical* corollaries of the icon's "mode of being" (*Seinsweise*), just as revelation and veiling are *phenomenological* corollaries delineating how an icon is experienced. Within the taxonomy of different kinds of images and their respective function and meaning, which John outlines in his third treatise (*JDI* III:18–23), the fourth one in particular emphasizes the dynamic operation of difference and relatedness in the icon.[120] At stake here are "shapes and forms and figures" (*schēmata kai morphas kai typous*) abounding throughout scripture that furnish "forms for formless things and shapes for shapeless things [*tōn atypōntōn hoi typoi*], . . . not least . . . because our analogies are not capable of raising us immediately to intellectual contemplation but need familiar and natural points of reference." Whereas a naive concept of representation would have the image expire once its putative referent has been identified and verified, the icon is fundamentally proleptic in its function. We recall how John, drawing on the authority of Gregory Nazianzen and pseudo-Dionysius, affirms that the ground and justification for icons are

---

117. *JDI* I:53; the argument is included in the florilegium for the later treatise (*JDI* III:51), with the passage in John Chrysostom uncertain, though possibly alluding to the latter's *Homily 12* (on Hebrews).

118. Ladner 1953, 19.

119. Tsakiridou (2013, 201) also quotes John Chrysostom: "For as long as somebody traces the outline as in a drawing, there remains a sort of shadow; but when he paints over it brilliant tints and lays on colors then an image appears."

120. As Louth notes, John's taxonomy here furnishes "not just a list; it is an evocation of the multitude of ways in which reality echoes reality, from the Father imaging forth the Son and the Son the Spirit in the life of the Trinitarian God, through the patterns of providence, humanity as an image of God, the way in which the visible world finds its reality in the spiritual world and images it forth, . . . the image, in its different forms, *is always mediating*, always holding together in harmony" (2002, 216; emphasis mine).

found in mankind's innate cognitive limitations. What legitimates and necessitates the icon is the fact that "we cannot behold the bodiless without using shapes that bear some analogy to us" (*JDI* III:21). Yet the economy within which the icon serves such compensatory purposes is not that of finite *mimēsis*. Rather, it concerns the relatedness between Creator and creation, between the infinite and invisible ground of being and its self-manifestation *in* and *as* visible form. Just as in Melchizedek's prophetic "shadow-writing" (*skiagraphē*) the written word anticipates its divine fulfillment, so in iconog*raphy* the visible word is intrinsically prefigurative and cannot be reduced, in naturalistic fashion, to a merely horizontal and immanent mode of signification. Hence the icon, particularly of the crucifixion and the Theotokos, manifests the depicted person as *typos*. It allows the beholder visually to approximate the numinous being of Christ or the saints in their respective specificity rather than seek to take mimetic possession of a contingent and finite particular. For that reason, the icon is both categorically *other* and *more* than the image (*eidōlon*). It "does not reproduce its original according to degrees of similitude" but, instead, "accomplishes first and perfectly the trait that distinguishes a type from, for example, an image." Instead of competing with the cross for the same epistemological space, the icon expands on the possibility, first and foremost embodied by the cross, that it might be "possible for an image to be bound under a ruled relation to a prototype without having to obey the laws and demands of the mimetic."[121]

Running through John's defense of images is this consistent emphasis on understanding the image as *typos*, which in turn explains his tendency "to present painting as a form of writing" and "his abundant use of *ekphrastic* writing in the *Defence*."[122] All this comports with the iconophile's understanding that icons are written (iconog*raphy*), not painted, and consequently partake of the word's inexhaustible fecundity rather than subject the *logos* to illicit circumscription. By contrast, the iconoclast

---

121. Marion 2004, 70–72. Notably, this capacity of iconic, as opposed to mimetic, presentation to open up access to the "typical" will resurface in Darwin's notebooks and Ruskin's *Modern Painters*. For both, the legitimacy of the visual is decisively bound up with its capacity to manifest the "specific," rather than the randomly particular, in visible nature. Both the biologist and the art historian are invested in the visible image precisely insofar as it promises to unveil a form, rather than duplicate matter, and thus reveals to the beholder "the possibilities of the typical" (Marion 2004, 69); see below, ch. 5; see also Mondzain 2005, 98–99.

122. Tsakiridou 2013, 197–98; rather question begging, however, is Tsakiridou's subsequent claim that in John's core argument ("I do not depict the invisible divinity, but I depict God made visible in the flesh") "the distinction is mute [sic! moot?]. Of course we paint what we see and we paint physical things" (199). Yet a theological defense of icons cannot but rest on the obverse premise, namely, that "seeing" cannot be reduced to a naturalistic conception of optics, horizontal visibility, and epistemic dominion. On the contrary, like Dionysius and Maximus before him, John operates within a tradition of the "spiritual senses" that, as this book contends throughout, had always persisted alongside more reductionist epistemologies of the kind that, rather unhelpfully, here subvert Tsakiridou's argument.

polemic of his imperial adversary, Constantine V, is compromised not only by its reductive image concept but also by the same anemic Christology that can be observed in Origen and his heirs. His contention that in depicting or "delineating" Christ's human face the icon has thereby also circumscribed his divine nature doubly fails to grasp the key points of Chalcedonian dogma, namely, that Christ's two natures be understood as neither confused or mixed nor separate, let alone opposed, but, rather, as essentially distinct *and* related.[123] Leaving aside Constantine's "fundamental error of confusing the incarnation with materialization," the emperor's iconoclast case is further weakened in that he misconstrues the *distinctness* of Christ's two natures as a positive *opposition*.[124] To do so not only reduces Christ's ensouled body, or "flesh" (*sarx*), to mere "matter" (*hylē*) but also revives an (in origin Gnostic) construal of matter as secondary, fallen, and ontologically *other* than God. For Constantine in particular, matter is not divinely *in*formed; it is not hypostasis but, instead, languishes in disorganized estrangement vis-à-vis a God who resembles more the *dēmiourgos* of the Gnostics than the God of Genesis, let alone the *logos* of John's Gospel. In marked contrast to the Hellenic concept of "form" (*eidos*), the iconoclasts conceive visible being as ephemeral, derivative, and ontologically illegitimate "matter" (*hylē*).[125] Following Basil of Caesarea's *On the Six Days of Creation* and exhibiting "a remarkable fusion of biblical and classical learning," John of Damascus rejects this account of matter as effectively disaggregating divine *logos* from visible being.[126] As he exhorts his opponents, "Do not abuse matter; for it is not dishonorable; this is the view of the Manichees" (*JDI* I:16).

Ultimately, what causes the iconoclasts' polemic to go astray is their failure to distinguish between physical matter and Christ's living form. In contrast, John takes pains to refer to Christ's visible being not as "matter" but as "flesh": "As the Word became flesh immutably, remaining what it was, so also the flesh became the Word without losing what it was, being rather made equal to the Word hypostatically. Therefore I am emboldened to depict the invisible God, not as invisible, but as he became visible for our sake, by participation in flesh and blood. I do not depict the

---

123. As Schönborn notes, Constantine's position would be refuted by Nikephoros and Theodore the Studite (1994, 176, 178).

124. Mondzain 2005, 94.

125. "This contempt for matter is one of the most striking traits of iconoclasm" (Schönborn 1994, 151). Likewise, Bulgakov remarks on the iconoclast's distorted, or reductive, concept of the body as a mere "collection of bones, muscles, nerves, etc." Yet unlike Schönborn, Bulgakov rejects the established defense of icons, advanced by John Damascene and Theodore the Studite, according to which Christ's divinity remains "unportrayable because It is imageless; in reality, It has Its image in man and is therefore portrayable. . . . Having *one hypostasis*, though in two natures, Christ also has *one image*, though it is disclosed *doubly*, in the two natures: invisibly and spiritually in one nature and visibly and bodily in the other nature" (2012a, 57, 62–63).

126. Louth 2002, 130.

invisible divinity, but I depict God made visible in the flesh."[127] Echoing the icono-clast council of 754, the synod that Leo V convened at Hagia Sophia in 815, with a temporary patriarch filling in for Patriarch Nikephoros, whose opposition to the em-peror's iconoclast policies remained unwavering, would yet again reject images on account of their taking on the form of "unworthy matter," thus resulting in "lifeless, dead, even contemptible" depictions.[128] Both Constantine V's iconoclast polemics and Leo V's more conciliatory and theologically more nuanced arguments suffer from a now familiar conceptual defect: they cannot conceive the difference between image and that which it depicts, between Being and non-being (Plato), in terms of a *relation* but only as a *logical contradiction*. Hence, too, Constantine routinely de-fines the icon as "the image of a person [*prosōpon*]," with evident stress on the icon's mimetic efficacy in rendering the human "countenance exactly *as it is*."[129] Once it is premised that "the icon is *only* that which can be seen," it naturally follows that it can never manifest a reality beyond itself, no matter how much it "presumes to be some-thing other than wood and paint." Confined within a matrix of duplication or simu-lation, it cannot possibly "depict" or "reveal" Christ's joint human and divine natures in the second person (*hypostasis*) of the Trinity.[130] What Constantine's iconoclasm fails to grasp is that, like Christ's distinct yet related natures, an image participates in *and* differs from that of which it is the image. We recall John's definition of the image as "a likeness depicting an archetype, but having some difference from it; the image is not like the archetype in every way" (*JDI* I:9). The iconoclast's twofold charges—namely, that the icon simulates a being with which it is ontologically incommensu-rable and that it would substitute itself for such a being—collapses the image into the idol. It thereby further posits a single phenomenology, imbued with a desire for ap-propriation and dominion, to govern all visual experience.

A shoddy Trinitarianism and an all but nonexisting Christology are the hall-mark of Byzantine iconoclast thought, which fundamentally fails to grasp the divine "economy" (*oikonomia*) so painstakingly worked out between Nicaea and Chalce-don. The aim of that economy was to "manage thinking, life, and history . . . by

---

127. *JDI* I:4. As Pelikan notes, already for Athanasius "the doctrine of the Incarnation had given a new meaning to the entire world of created matter, which had now been blessed by the presence of the material flesh in which the very logos of God had become truly human. . . . Therefore Athanasius insisted that the body of the Logos had to be a real human body 'not in mere appearance or fantasy but in reality' [*mē phantasiai alla alēthōs*]" (2011, 106).

128. Quoted in Schönborn 1994, 152. On the Synod of AD 815, see Brubaker and Haldon 2011, 366–83; Leo's attempt at dividing and winning over many of his iconophile opponents bore consid-erable fruit, as "virtually the whole Constantinopolitan clergy adopted the imperial position," as well as a considerable number of monasteries (Brubaker and Haldon 2011, 376–77).

129. Quoted in Schönborn 1994, 172. See also Ostrogorsky, who correctly notes that what sepa-rated iconoclasts and iconophiles were incommensurable concepts of the image (1929, 40–43).

130. Alloa 2013, 17.

combin[ing] all the effects of both pedagogical strategies and church doctrine." For that to happen, however, "an instrument had to be found whose message was unambiguous and allowed no further contradictions, a universal instrument that ignored the barrier of languages. . . . This instrument would have to be a holy and divine ruse, taking into account our body, our elementary adherences, and our emotions. This rational and magical instrument, it will be clear, is the iconic image."[131] As we have seen, this new type of image is distinguished by its essential *relatedness* vis-à-vis its prototype, as opposed to its putative *identity* with the person depicted. The very possibility of such an icon thus extricates visual representation from the reductionist logic of illusionism, animism, and simulation, overlapping conceptual frameworks all premised on the assumption that visual presentation centrally involves a quasi-totemic substitution of the image for its object. By contrast, navigating between either illicitly "mixing" Christ's visible and the invisible, embodied and ineffable natures or wholly disaggregating image and prototype, the Byzantine icon opens up an entirely new epistemic and spiritual domain of visual experience. In the writings of John of Damascus, Nikephoros, and Theodore the Studite, that is, "a kind of image emerges that cannot be properly addressed by the notion of aesthetic judgment and not even by [its] referentiality." Instead, from here on "it is not the perceived similarity that legitimizes images but their alleged indexical character: these images have a form (*typos*) that reproduces itself and leaves an imprint on any material that comes into contact with it." Paradoxically, this very "ability to reproduce is . . . not a loss but, in fact, guarantees the [icon's] aura."[132] Reproduction here must not be construed as mechanistic duplication but, instead, refers to the continuity of an emergent iconographic *tradition*, which understands likeness not as "optical illusionism" but as "accuracy of definition" guaranteed by a stable "range of signs that included the clothing, the attributes, the portrait type, and the inscription."[133]

By and large, the image concept distilled from otherwise heterogeneous disciplines of inquiry and genres of writing throughout this book largely comports with the iconophile view while also tracing its vastly underappreciated historical reach and conceptual force. Certainly, there is something impressive about the political courage and argumentative cogency exhibited by John of Damascus, Nikephoros, and Theodore the Studite, whose writing, "in spite of being a reaction to a specific historic situation, . . . exhibits an extraordinary argumentative richness which, in terms of complexity and range, greatly exceeds the contemplation of classic Attic philosophy."[134] Nevertheless, the prolonged iconoclast debate remains unsatisfactory

---

131. Mondzain 2005, 65.
132. Alloa 2013, 4, 13, 11.
133. Maguire 1996, 16; see also Barber 2002, 107–23.
134. Alloa 2013, 12.

and, ultimately, inconclusive mainly because of the polemical way in which it was conducted. Even more than the crudity of Constantine's image theory and the "massive Caesaropapism" supported by his hand-picked bishops, what frustrates is the static antinomy of "two positions poised in irreconcilable confrontation." To be sure, Schönborn's suggestion that the iconodules and iconoclasts might have "underst[ood] each other as complementary viewpoints" is not what is being argued here; and given how he characterizes each party's argumentative overreach, it is all but impossible to conceive of a theologically and conceptually sound resolution.[135] In the end, no amount of conceptual sophistication could adequately determine the ontological status of holy images and the reverence to be accorded to them. In fact, underlying the metaphysical realism presupposed by both parties in this conflict is the notion, typically unexamined, that what an image is can never be ascertained by categorial definition but only by "thick description" (Geertz) of how it performs. Anterior to any claims about the icon's ontological status or "essence," a quest already well under way in Plato's *Sophist*, a robust phenomenological account of its experience is needed. It is in the ninth century, particularly in the writings of Patriarch Photios and the iconodule Theodore the Studite that this shift in focus takes place, away from a priori definitions of the icon to materially and phenomenologically specific accounts of its distinctive mode of agency and the liturgical and institutional practices governing its institution and reception.

THE ICON PERFORMED IN ECCLESIAL SPACE: NAMING, CONSECRATION, VENERATION, EKPHRASIS

Within everyday secular culture, pictures may serve any number of functions—contemplative, scientific, documentary, legal, propagandistic, and so forth. For pictures to be efficacious in some such capacity, usually no formal authorization is ex-

---

135. "Do not the iconophiles all too readily infer, from the fact of the Incarnation, the necessity of images depicting the One incarnated? And do not the iconoclasts all too quickly make the ban of images into a total rejection of any earthly manifestation of things divine?" (Schönborn 1994, 191–92). It bears recalling that with very few exceptions the arguments of the iconoclasts have reached us only in the (no doubt opportunistic) redaction by their iconophile opponents. Thus, the *horos* containing the resolutions from the first iconoclast council (AD 754) was destroyed sometime after the (temporary) relegitimation of icon veneration at the Second Council of Nicaea (AD 787) and can only be partially reconstructed from selective and likely unreliable quotations found in iconophile writings of the ninth century. As for the ubiquity of invective and polemic that pervades the entire debate—and, if anything, resurfaces in even more virulent form in sixteenth- and seventeenth-century English iconoclasm and Dutch *Beeldenstorm*—it is most vividly on display in Theodore the Studite's three *Refutations* (*Antirrhetikoi*) and in the proliferating hagiography of icon defenders after the "Triumph of Orthodoxy" in AD 843. See the edition of sources by Talbot (1998), esp. the "Life of St. Theodosia" and the "Life of Patriarch Nikephoros I."

pected, though much contextual awareness, as well as formal and hermeneutic discernment, is necessary, it being understood that not all beholders will equally meet these requirements. Still, no specific rite of institution is required for most pictures to be recognized as such, and the vast majority of art images and emblems that confront us, certainly since the sixteenth century, are simply part of a vast inventory of "things" (*Dinge*) that, in Heidegger's phrase, happen to be objectively "at hand" (*vorhanden*) and pragmatically "ready-to-hand" (*zuhanden*).[136] Like a piece of wood or the chair that has been fashioned from it, such pictures accommodate any number of purposes to which the beholder/user may wish to put them, ranging from the decorative to the fantastic and the illicit. Or so it would seem at first glance. In fact, the notion of an entirely mundane image that operates within a strictly horizontal or immanent frame proves strangely elusive. Thus, a contingent and unassuming pattern of movement, say, of a falcon in midair, the foliar structure of ash boughs, or the ephemeral materiality of, say, a humble wood table covered with a patterned cloth and holding assorted fruit, or again a bouquet of blue hydrangeas—they all turn out to be imbued with unfathomable epiphanic potential. When absorbing, as these phenomena variously do, the attentive and undesigning gaze of a Goethe, Hopkins, Cézanne, Rilke, or Eliot, it is precisely their abundant presence and insistent "thereness" that captivates the beholder with a radiance at once ineffable and irresistible. This capacity of *natura* to suddenly manifest itself as *figura*, that is, of an apparent form (*morphē*) transposed into a symbolic or anagogical cue (*typos*) and intimating an as yet unfulfilled truth slumbering within visible matter, is no more a case of subjective projection than it is a random occurrence. Rather, this power of disclosure lies at the very heart of the being of images.

Take the case of scientific or documentary photography. At first, the pictures in question would appear at the farthest possible remove from the logic of the icon sketched above. Thus, documentary photographs are understood to serve

---

136. See Heidegger's distinction in *Being and Time* (1996), 66–76 (§§15–16). In his "On the Origin of the Work of Art" (1935/36), Heidegger specifically applies the distinction to art: "Works of art . . . are as naturally present as things. The picture hangs on the wall like a hunting weapon or a hat. A painting—for example van Gogh's portrayal of a pair of peasant shoes—travels from one exhibition to another. Works are shipped like coal from the Ruhr or logs from the Black forest. . . . Beethoven's quartets lie in the publisher's storeroom like potatoes in a cellar" (Heidegger 2002, 2–3). A decade and a half earlier, the Russian aesthetician, icon theorist, and mathematician Pavel Florensky had reached diametrically opposed conclusions: "A work of art is artistic precisely by virtue of the completeness of the conditions essential for its existence." When exiled from the ecclesial space with its irregular lighting and multisensory dynamics, however, the icon "grows numb and distorted . . . [in] the even, calm, cold and strong lighting of the museum." Thus, the presence of gold on icons "which by the diffused light of day is barbaric, heavy and devoid of content, comes to life in the flickering light of the icon lamp or candle, . . . conveying a presentiment of other, unworldly lights, filling a heavenly space" (Florensky 2004, 105, 107–8).

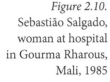

Figure 2.10.
Sebastião Salgado,
woman at hospital
in Gourma Rharous,
Mali, 1985

evidentiary purposes only; and they may do so only if the circumstances of their production and their actual image contents can be independently authenticated, say, as
evidence in an experimental process or in a legal proceeding. The documentary authority of a picture thus appears to depend on its verifiability within a determinate,
spatiotemporal setting. The event or scene that such pictures make present, and what
in turn authenticates them, seems to be a reality altogether extrinsic to the image's
formal and material constitution. Still, while documentary images—say, Sebastião
Salgado's photographs of the 1984–85 famine in the Sahel zone—must permit independent verification, this requirement hardly explains their visceral, unsettling impact on the viewer. Depicting (as per Salgado's notes) "a malnourished, dehydrated
woman wait[ing] her turn in the hospital in Gourma Rharous. Mali, 1985," one such
photograph vacillates between the documentary and the emblematic (fig. 2.10). In
focusing on a nameless woman's wrinkled and emaciated face cradled by her bony
hands, this photographic record of a human being in extremis has nothing spectacular or "scenic" about it. Instead, the true locus of human suffering is as much spiritual
as it is physical, an impression reinforced by the woman's downcast and inward-
looking eyes and by her head and torso enfolded in a plain cloth resembling those
worn by Mary in Carlo Crivelli's 1476 Pietà (fig. 2.11). As is the case in ninth-century
iconography, whose formal organization still reverberates in Crivelli's conservative
Italo-Byzantine aesthetic, contextual features are entirely missing. Moreover, Salgado's decision to relegate date, location, and description of his subject to the end of his
book rather than have them printed below the photograph suggests that such identi-
fiers are not meant to authenticate the picture in question. For the same reason, none
of his photographs of human subjects, including a figure as solitary and distinctive as
this woman, are ever identified by name. For doing so would inevitably distance the
viewer from a subject now perceived as wholly other, an unknown individual we will

Figure 2.11. Carlo Crivelli, Pietà, 1476. London, National Gallery

never know and marooned in a place we will never see. Where empathetic identification with a previously unknown person is the aim, a proper name or even a more generic inscription (e.g., "Woman in X, 1987") will only interfere by magnifying the
distance between beholder and subject. Instead, documentary photography instills
in the beholder a craving for a narrative such as might help explain the particular
scene of human devastation that so unsparingly confronts and focuses an otherwise
distracted gaze.

By contrast, the icon's ability to draw in its beholder is not forestalled by the
proper name, provided it features only the name, and no spatiotemporal markers, of
the saint depicted. For on its own, a proper name does not produce cognition but can
serve only as a token of *re*cognition; and for that to happen, some antecedent narrative must already be in place. Such narrative context, of course, is what scripture
and hagiography, as well as their elaboration and exegesis in weekly homilies, provided in such abundance for Christ and the Virgin, as well as for the saints whose

names appear beneath their icon. Unlike the underdetermined documentary image, the icon's phenomenological and spiritual efficacy is grounded in sacred and hagiographic narrative, for which reason the icon requires that its subject be recognizably identified by name. The religious cult image's very mode of being pivots on its formal institution whereby the relation of the visible image to the person depicted is affirmed in the twin rituals of naming and consecration. Inasmuch as the icon's consecration validates and legitimates the image as a presence, the ritual in question will necessarily draw on what Arthur Danto calls the mythic "power delivered to someone who learns one's name." For to name the icon does not *identify* an otherwise anonymous subject but ensures *recognition* of an anterior and incontrovertible spiritual presence made manifest through this particular medium. With good reason, Danto thus supposes that "the relationship between names and nameholders must have been construed as mystically as that between pictures and things pictured."[137] Only where this formal instauration has taken place will an icon be considered a truly sacred and efficacious depiction of Christ's (or a particular saint's) human form.

Naturally, the proposition that the icon could achieve sacred status in virtue of such rites was vigorously contested by Byzantine iconoclasts, who consistently held that "there were only three such [holy] objects: the Eucharist, . . . the church building, . . . [and] the sign of the Cross." To the Phrygian bishops assembled at the iconoclast council of 754, "icons could not be holy because they had received no consecration from above . . . [but] only illegitimate consecration from below."[138] While this does indeed appear to have been the position of iconoclast emperors and bishops, it comes with hazards of its own. For one thing, it risks undermining the spiritual authority of priests and bishops who, while serving in their respective ecclesial functions here "below," nevertheless were understood to hold not just another temporal office, but to function as true intercessors of God. In consecrating icons no less than administering the sacraments, priests and bishops were thought to mediate the faith in ways analogous to Christ, the incarnate *logos*, who in turn mediates the numinous, invisible God (Jn 14:9). The specific Eastern rite of consecration (*kathierōsis*)—of altars, icons, and church buildings—is premised on a divine economy in which matter and spirit, far from being contraries, are reconciled in the visible form of the flesh. For "the doctrine of the Incarnation had given a new meaning to the entire world of created matter, which had now been blessed by the presence of the material flesh in which the very Logos of God had become truly human."[139] Under the penumbra of a resolutely incarnational theology such as we

---

137. Danto 1982, 6–7.
138. Brown 1973, 5–6.
139. Pelikan 2011, 106. For a detailed description of the rite of consecration in Byzantium, with particular attention to the way sound and sight reinforce each other, see Pentcheva 2017a, 47–75.

find it in the writings of the Cappadocians, Dionysius, and Maximus the Confessor, visible being exceeds the perceptible matter inasmuch as it elicits a form of spiritual attention rather than expiring in transient sensation. Just as animate flesh (*sarx*) cannot be reduced to inert matter (*hylē*), visualization involves being ensouled or inspirited; it involves dynamic "inspiration" (*empsychōsis*) and, for that reason, resists naturalistic reduction to a case of mere passive sensation (*aisthēsis*). Where we speak of inspired seeing, the visible is apprehended as manifestation, that is, as the appearance *of* something that does not show itself *as and by means of* something that does.[140]

Unlike "perception" (*Wahrnehmung*), which is liable to error insofar as it treats the visible as a quasi-conceptual entity independent of its "apprehension" (*Auffassung*) in intuition, the gaze called forth by the icon responds to the image-appearance as a medium rather than object. Here seeing eventuates as "pure apprehension" (*reine Auffassung*), an intentional act whose phenomenal correlate proves incontrovertible, simply because what is seen is not subjected to predication or verification. Rather than seek to verify and master visible phenomena by means of deductive reasoning, the embodied subject kneeling before and praying to (*proskynein*) the icon is infused with epistemic humility. Beholding here does not assert epistemic dominion over what is seen any more than over the act of seeing. Put differently, to behold the icon is not to seek cognition of it but to pray for recognition by the being whose *typos* is manifested in the icon. Closely entwined with the phenomenology of prayer, to which we will return in chapter 3, the iconic gaze notably unfolds in a space that engages the subject's entire sensorium. Embedded in the complex sensory nature of Byzantine devotional and liturgical practice, iconic vision partakes of Orthodoxy's underlying view of matter as susceptible of "inspiration" (*empsychōsis*) and as "incarnate pneuma." Along with sight, "sound and smell give spatial and temporal dimension to [the] experience" at issue. The resulting fusion of sound and sight attenuates the seeming fixity of visual signs. Dissolving amid clouds of incense that themselves are moved by the soundwaves of chant, the icons adorning the walls and domes of Byzantine churches appear both unstable and endlessly animated, thereby affirming the transient and medial status of the visible. The resulting partial destabilization of visible matter is matched by the concurrent "blurring of semantic word chains," of spoken and chanted words gradually losing their phonetic contour as they

---

140. "Inspiriting denotes the process by which Holy Pneuma descends into and activates matter; it is targeted by the *kathierōsis* and activated by sacerdotal *epiklēsis*" (Pentcheva 2017a, 45). Ultimately, the consecration of icons is modeled on the words of institution during the celebration of the Eucharist, which transubstantiates bread and wine without, however, annihilating their physical reality. So consecrated, the Host—and likewise the icon—is known on the basis of what Merleau-Ponty calls "perceptual faith," rather than being confined within a disjunctive modern epistemology of sensory perception and abstract conceptualization.

reverberate between the vast arches and domes of, say, Hagia Sophia or St. Mark's Cathedral.[141]

A first description of this unique fusion of sensory and spiritual qualities in the image-saturated space of Byzantine churches can be found in Paulus Silentiarius's sixth-century ekphrasis of Hagia Sophia. Combining panegyric and description, this long poem was written during the building's (re)consecration between 24 December 562 and 6 January 563 and publicly recited for the emperor and leading officials soon thereafter; and with it, Paulus Silentiarius inaugurated an ekphrastic tradition that was to extend all the way to Yeats's Byzantium poems of the late 1920s. Known for the sensuous imagery of his more than eighty erotic poems, Paulus was well positioned when it came to conveying the overwhelming physical experience of this "newly accomplished miracle, a wonder scarcely to be believed when seen or heard." Everything here converges to produce an utterly "inspirited" (*empsychos*) space, beginning with the church's dome, unprecedented in scale: "Like a sphere and, radiant as the heavens, it bestrides the roof of the church, . . . like the firmament which rests on air," decorated with "the sign of the cross . . . within a circle by means of minute mosaic." Abounding throughout the vast building is masonry of seemingly inexhaustible variety of color and texture: "Curious designs glitter everywhere. . . . The joining of the cut marbles resembles the art of painting for you may see the veins of the square and octagonal stones meeting so as to form devices: connected in this way, the stones imitate the glories of painting."[142]

Perhaps not until Ruskin's *Stones of Venice* would there be a writer so alert to the ways that variety and shrewd juxtaposition of form, texture, aspect, and color reveal seemingly inert physical matter to be profoundly animated and visually absorbing. Miner's tools

> have cleft the speckled Phrygian stone, sometimes rosy mixed with white, sometimes gleaming with purple and silver flower. . . . The eye is absorbed by the bright green stone of Laconia and the glittering marble with wavy veins found in the deep gullies of the Iasian peaks, exhibiting slanting streaks of blood-red and livid white; the pale yellow with swirling red from the Lydian headland; the glit-

141. Pentcheva 2017a, 5. Another case of multisensory experience is that of the relief icon in the beholding of which "the eye seeks the tactility of textures and reliefs. Sight is understood and experienced as touch" (Pentcheva 2006, 631).

142. http://projects.mcah.columbia.edu/medieval-architecture/htm/or/ma_or_gloss_essay_paul.htm (accessed 26 March 2020). For a detailed account of Paulus's poem, its rhetorical organization, political aims, and seemingly minimalist theological underpinnings, see Macrides and Magdalino 1988; on the architectural form as Paulus would have encountered it in AD 562, see Kostenec and Dark 2011.

tering crocus-like golden stone which the Libyan sun, warming it with its golden light, has produced on the steep flanks of the Moorish hills; that of glittering black upon which the Celtic crags, deep in ice, have poured here and there an abundance of milk; the pale onyx with glint of precious metal . . . so that in one stone various beauties mingle.[143]

And yet, for all his sensuous prose, Paulus's ekphrases of the Theotokos ("Mother of Christ, the vessel of eternal life, whose holy womb did nourish its own Maker") and the Christ icon, the latter featured on an ellipsoid likely mounted above the chancel door, prove firmly orthodox: "A skilled hand has artfully . . . engraved the figure of the immaculate God who, without seed, clothed himself in human form. Elsewhere it has carved the host of winged angels bowing down their necks, for they are unable to gaze upon the glory of God, though hidden under a veil of human form He is still God, even if He has put on the flesh that removes sin."[144] When seen amid the flicker of hundreds of candles and during the shifting light of the matins (*orthros*) or vespers (*hesperinos*), the icons suspended in this sumptuously textured and polychrome ecclesial space transfigure sight into vision. In sharp contrast to the "dispersed light of the artist's studio or the museum gallery,

> the icon's power of mediating between the visible and the invisible is rendered palpable by its incalculably supple responsiveness to the play of a flickering flame that moves with every breath of wind, making allowance ahead of time for the effects of colored reflections from the bundles of light passing through colored, sometimes faceted glass, . . . this flood of light fragmenting, uneven, seeming to pulsate, rich in warm prismatic rays— a light which all perceive as alive, warming the spirit, emitting a warm fragrance. . . . The finest blue veil of incense dissolved in the air brings to the contemplation of icons and frescoes a softening and deepening of aerial perspective.[145]

Contrast this account of visual experience with modernity's concept of the art image as a facsimile of single-viewpoint, linear perception, dissected by academic criticism and expelled from liturgical space and practice into the agnostic space of museum and gallery where it languishes in monochrome electric twilight,

---

143. http://projects.mcah.columbia.edu/medieval-architecture/htm/or/ma_or_gloss_essay_paul.htm (accessed 26 March 2020).

144. http://projects.mcah.columbia.edu/medieval-architecture/htm/or/ma_or_gloss_essay_paul.htm (accessed 26 March 2020); see also the partial translation, with an introduction, by Bell (2009, 189–212).

145. Florensky 2004, 107–8.

an enigmatic artifact encased in a glass box. It is no accident that, in recoiling from the aesthetic conventions of nineteenth-century pictorial realism and the institutionalization of art as bourgeois property, writers such as Rilke, Mann, and Yeats and artists such as Kandinsky and Chagall found themselves inspired by the abundant sensuousness of the Byzantine icon and the Orthodox liturgy, if also bewildered by their inability to frame such visual experience in mimetic terms. We recall Thomas Mann's morally and visually impaired protagonist, von Aschenbach, standing "on the fissured mosaic floor" during Mass at St. Mark's in Venice, as "incense rose up, clouding the weak little flames of the altar tapers."[146] At once the apotheosis and an ironic critique of fin-de-siècle symbolism, Mann's 1912 novella stages the moral and intellectual bankruptcy of bourgeois "culture" (*Bildung*) in von Aschenbach's idolatrous, homoerotic gaze evidently disoriented in a liturgical space whose deeply reasoned theological integration of sensory and spiritual experience, of *aisthēsis* and *kenōsis*, ultimately eludes him. Likewise, Yeats's 1928 ekphrasis of the mosaics in Hagia Sophia, of "sages standing in God's holy fire / As in the gold mosaic of a wall, / . . . the singing-masters of my soul," reflects his search for a spiritual poetics grounded in the patristic idea of the spiritual senses rather than his native Catholic culture, and evidently also drawing on the legacy of Byzantine icon theory.[147] Budding modernists both, Mann and Yeats register a deep affinity between their own poetics and Byzantine forms of embodied and non-mimetic modes of cognition, even as they are also disturbed by their inability to describe and contain the multisensory forms that envelop and threaten to overwhelm them.

While this is not the place to explore in detail what constitutes ekphrasis, or whether ekphrastic writing is even a possibility, as Lessing's *Laokoön* would famously deny, clarification is needed on at least one point: namely, in ekphrasis the written word is not lodged in competition with the image, nor does it seek to substitute itself for a visible form. Lessing's construal of the temporal medium of writing and the spatial forms of the visual arts as outright incommensurable, which itself is premised on an antinomy of the visible and the intelligible, of spatial matter and temporal

---

146. Mann 1995b, 44; for a fuller discussion, see below, ch. 3, 305–16.

147. Yeats 1997, 197–98; the icon transcends natural form ("I shall never take / My bodily form from any natural thing, / But such a form as Grecian goldsmiths make / Of hammered gold and gold enamelling / To keep a drowsy emperor awake"); see also "Byzantium" (1929), in particular the reference to ornamental imagery ("Miracle, bird or golden handiwork / More miracle than bird or handiwork" [252]). Yeats, who in *A Vision* offers a fuller description of the city's religious buildings and objects, unwittingly echoes Silentiarius's ekphrasis, which likewise rates Hagia Sophia's inexhaustible visual riches higher than the beauty of the natural world: "Every mortal who has directed his eye to the glorious heaven has not long endured watching, with back-bent neck, the circling meadow clad with dancing stars; . . . But if anyone plants his step inside the holy precincts, he is unwilling to withdraw his foot again, but, with enchanted eyes, he bends and twists his neck hither and thither" (in Bell 2009, 204).

meanings, amounts to one more instance of the "principles" or axioms of Enlightenment thought creating the very problems that philosophical and aesthetic discourse subsequently struggles to solve. Thus, Lessing's arguments against the very possibility of ekphrasis are unsurprising if we view modern aesthetic formalism as but a remote descendant of Christian iconoclasm, often unwittingly recycling positions found in Eusebius and Constantine V and the pronouncements at the Councils of Hieria (AD 753) and Constantinople (AD 815). Far from an inevitable, logical premise, modern thought's antinomy of depiction and description, of spatial and temporal forms, attests to the visceral unease of "pure" faith and thought in the presence of the image and a deep-seated desire to quarantine the image. Where the image is considered as coarse and provisional scaffolding for spiritual and philosophical meanings that will be consummated only insofar as they have stepped out from underneath its shadow, ekphrasis is bound to be dismissed as a "minor genre" confronting its "semiotic 'others,' those rival, alien modes of representation called the visual, graphic, plastic or 'spatial' arts."[148]

Modern thought's discomfort with ekphrasis is part and parcel of its overarching attempt at containing the image's numinous implications—a project carried out in two successive phases. The first replicates the iconoclasm of Leo III and Constantine V, once again spanning a period of roughly 120 years (from 1530 to 1650).[149] Still, for all its sound and fury, both English iconoclasm and its Dutch counterpart known as *Beeldenstorm* proved, like most such ideological convulsions, an inconclusive affair. For no matter how thorough and extensive the material destruction of religious images and other artifacts, their expurgation could never be more than a crude first step toward a utopia whose contours remained terminally elusive: namely, a theology shorn of any forms of mediation. Hence, as James Simpson notes, "a more painful, unjoyful second sequence (c. 1558–1625)" was to follow, aimed at instituting "iconoclastic hygiene" that incrementally "worked its way into the liturgy, . . . but also into the most intimate recesses of the soul, breaking visual imagination, and breaking the idols of false doctrine." Yet if anything, this second, conspicuously intellectual phase of iconoclasm made it even more apparent that, being confronted with an antagonist

---

148. Mitchell 1994, 156.

149. The history of early modern iconoclasm will not be addressed in this book; for classic instances of Reformation iconoclasm, see Tyndale, *Answere to More* (1531); Calvin, *Institutes*, esp. I:11–12 (1536/2011); Foxe, *Actes and Monuments* (1563); and Salteren, *Treatise against Images and Pictures in Churches* (1641). For historical and art historical accounts of major disputes in sixteenth- and seventeenth-century image breaking, see the landmark studies by Aston 1990; Clark 2009, 161–203; Koerner 2004, 83–168; Latour and Weibel 2002 (esp. the essay by Koerner, 164–213); Barber and Boldrick 2013 (esp. the essays by Williams, 48–73; Barber, 74–91; and Sullivan, 92–113); as well as Simpson 2019, 159–97. For a curious instance of iconoclast polemic in twentieth-century thought, see Levinas 1987.

as fecund and Protean as the human imagination, "the iconoclast's job is never finished."[150] Starting in the early eighteenth century, the iconoclast's energy shifts from
material destruction to formal containment insofar as images of any variety are increasingly subject to formal-aesthetic description and an oblique economy of "taste"
constantly fine-tuned in a vast array of essays and reviews found in newspapers,
magazines, pamphlets, and the occasional treatise. It is this domestication of iconoclast fervor by the emergent grammar of aesthetic connoisseurship and Enlightenment philosophical aesthetics that ultimately brings the image into full and explicit
conformity with Neoclassicism's depoliticized, theologically neutered, and quasi-
rational ideal of beauty.

A millennium earlier, however, the relation of image and word and the spiritual
purposes served by the rhetorical genre of ekphrasis were being appraised in starkly
different terms. Thus, apophatic theology across the Mediterranean, from Dionysius
on, had not only understood images as fundamentally contiguous with inspired
speech, but had often conceived language itself primarily in terms of vision. Thus, for
writers like Paulus Silentiarius, Theodore the Studite, and the influential patriarchs
Nikephoros and Photios, the gravitational pull of the image toward the word, and
vice versa, is neither confined to the seemingly rarefied subgenre of ekphrasis nor felt
to require extraneous, philosophical legitimation. On the contrary, the very complementarity of visual and verbal forms attests to the integrative powers of the divine
logos. For Theodore, icon and *logos* both are forms of remembrance, with the word
no less than the image constituting "His corporeal appearance on paper . . . [in] the
divinely-written Gospels. He nowhere told anyone to write down the 'concise word'
[Rom 9:28; Is 10:23], yet His image was drawn in writing [*charattetai*] by the apostles."[151] In its strict formal sense, then, ekphrasis draws our attention to that complementarity by showing how inspired vision is both the source and the telos of religious
language, and how the word is premised on the image as an antecedent, ontologically
distinct, and charismatic reality. Taking up the question of ekphrastic poetry, Sigurd
Burckhardt, in an essay with the intriguing title "The Poet as Fool and Priest," thus
seeks to draw the underlying, central distinction.

> The painter's tree *is* the image but if the poet writes 'tree,' he does not create an
> image. He *uses* one; the poetic 'image' is one only in a metaphorical sense. Actu-
> ally it is something that evokes an image, a sign pointing to a certain preestab-
> lished configuration in our visual memory. . . . The so-called poetic image

---

150. Simpson 2019, 161–62.

151. Theodore 1981, I.10. A more precise translation of the Greek (*alla mên charattetai apo tōn
apostolōn mechri tou deuro*) might be, "but nevertheless it [the concise logos] is marked down by the
apostles to this day."

achieves its effect only by denying its essence; it *is* a word, but it functions by making us aware of something other than it is.[152]

While this is helpful as far as it goes, Burckhardt's distinction ultimately proves misleading. For in parsing the word/image distinction as a productive *relation* rather than a static antinomy, he posits the image itself as a metaphysical essence of sorts, that is, as an entity achieving a kind of consubstantiality with the being it depicts. Here it helps to recall Plato's mature conception of the image in his late dialogues, especially in the *Sophist*, discussed in the previous chapter. As Plato there shows, for something to be (and be apprehended as) an image, it has to be both constitutively *related to* and also *different from* the being *of* which it is the image. What Burckhardt fails to see is how his apt characterization of the ekphrastic word ("it functions by making us aware of something other than it is") turns out to hold equally true for the image. Both image and ekphrastic speech, and not just the latter, constitute forms of *mediation*. As such, both are inherently related to the numinous reality and integrity of Being, in which they participate to the extent that they successfully mediate it for us, something they can do only because they are *not* identical to what they depict. Still, in at least one respect, Burckhardt's point remains valid. For the ekphrastic word bears witness to the anterior reality of the visible (albeit still ectypal) world as it has gratuitously and abundantly given itself to the beholder. While the visible image can never *be* (identical to) the essence, it alerts the beholder to a possible encounter with numinous Being, a possibility, to be sure, that will never be definitively realized, yet that can also never be definitively foreclosed. Moreover, it is in the nature of this encounter that the mediation of the invisible by the visible will not be experienced simply as a logical possibility but as a metaphysical summons. For wherever Being accomplishes itself as a distinctive phenomenal presence, the myriad forms that comprise the domain of visible beauty will be experienced as both "beauty" (*to kalon*) and a "calling" (*kalein*), which is to say, as an event suffused with metaphysical significance rather than as a merely optical happening.

We are now in a better position to consider the question of how ekphrastic writing relates to the religious image, as expressed in the rite of icon consecration and the richly descriptive and at times rhapsodic language framing that rite. In ekphrastic writing no less than in homiletic speech, such as the one by Patriarch Photios extolling the splendor of the restored icons in Hagia Sophia (to which we will turn momentarily), the icon's sacred status is not predicated of it; sacredness is not a secondary quality ascribed to the icon any more than it is a magical power conjured by a priest's speech act. There is not first the icon, which then will be instituted as

---

152. Burckhardt 1956, 280.

a "holy image." Rather, the sacred is integral to the icon's very being, a fact that the language of institution and consecration merely makes explicit; hence what W. J. T. Mitchell terms "ekphrastic hope," namely, the quest for "vision, iconicity, or a 'still moment' of plastic presence through language."[153] Far from being incommensurable, then, image and word in Byzantine thought tend to be seen as complementary, as can be seen in the ekphrastic and homiletic writings of Paulus Silentiarius, Photios, and, eventually, Nikolaos Mesarites. They all understand the written and spoken word as fulfilling, not dialectically superseding, the spiritual vision mediated by the icon, which for that very reason is considered a timeless communal good worthy of veneration (*proskynēsis*).

We will return to the icon's spiritualization of visible matter momentarily. For now, let us recall that in guiding the sense- and time-bound human being to progress from "sight" (*opsis*) to "spiritual vision" (*theōria*), the icon furnishes a concrete phenomenological template for the beholder's ultimate, hoped-for "divinization" (*theōsis*). Indeed, "the notion of a divine plan with the aim of administering and managing fallen creation, and thus of saving it, makes the economy interdependent with the whole of creation from the beginning of time." Hence, insofar as the divine "economy is as much nature as it is providence," it adds an entirely new dimension to the aniconic spiritualism of the Origenists. For "the difference between theology and economy is the difference between believing without seeing and believing while seeing."[154] It would appear that "the consecration of an image makes it work, or at the very least, effects a change in the way it works," and that ultimately "consecration is a ritual act, and not merely a ceremonial one."[155] Once again, a strictly immanent and functionalist approach to the icon, which construes the icon's consecration and putative sacredness merely as a case of human-engineered ceremonial and "projection," begs the central question: Is the icon's sacred status but a function of its having been consecrated, or does consecration affirm the icon's intrinsic powers of mediating the sacred and the invisible? Drawing on Gadamer's account of the image, Freedberg sensibly rejects the functionalist and, in tendency, reductionist explanation. Instead, he regards consecration as a "completion rite" that formalizes and "publicly heightens" the icon's anterior, ontological power.[156] Far from a case of conjury or magic, the rite of consecration acknowledges the icon's antecedent and incontrovertible power, namely, to unveil and intensify the presence of the person depicted and, in so doing,

---

153. Mitchell 1994, 156.

154. Mondzain 2005, 21–22.

155. Freedberg 1989, 83.

156. Ibid., 86. Likewise, Bulgakov regards the icon's sanctification or "ecclesial naming [as] necessary for its completion" (2012a, 81).

to dramatize how spiritual meanings are mediated in the distinctive form of visible things.[157]

Hence, even as consecration "has an aim, a scope," and, consequently, "can only be defined in terms of the way it makes images efficacious," this does not mean that it "makes an image effective or operational. It may work before consecration, but in a different manner from the way it works after the ceremonies and rites."[158] Consecration affirms, but does not bring about, the image's ontology *as a medium* bridging the order of visible things with their invisible source. Were it not for the latter, the finite beholder would only ever confront raw, unorganized matter, which logically speaking could not even be a correlate of perception, much less become an object of knowledge. For that to happen, being must present itself as antecedently and distinctly *in*-formed, that is, as a *specific* form (*morphē*) that is intuitively grasped as "significant" and that elicits from the beholder what Merleau-Ponty calls "perceptual faith." It follows that not every image is sacred, just as conversely the sacred is not a precondition for something to be experienced as an image. Indeed, consecration offers a first hint at why it is important to distinguish between an *eikōn* in the strict sense and the much broader and more diffuse concept of religious art and imagery. As we shall see in the next chapter, the latter may serve any variety of mnemonic, dramatic, or emotive functions without, however, claiming any ontological kinship between image and prototype. For that to be the case, a second ritual act is required, that of *naming* the icon. It is this additional "completion rite," to recall Freedberg's phrase, that truly sets the icon apart from "religious" genre painting such as, beginning in the thirteenth century, begins to constitute itself as a distinct aesthetic practice in the West.[159] In the act of naming, both the icon's power of intercession and its distinctness from the One whom it depicts are expressly affirmed: "When one considers the likeness to the original by means of a representation, it is both Christ and

---

157. In ways that cannot be pursued here, Freedberg helpfully distinguishes between the totemic view of Theurgy and the "intermediary role of images" in Neoplatonist thought between the second and fourth centuries. Echoes of the talismanic function persist in Christianity (and also in Buddhism), such as when a relic is inserted into an image or sculpture of the deity (Freedberg 1989, 87, 95).

158. Ibid., 96. Likewise, Gadamer, also quoted by Freedberg, had previously remarked how an "act of institution [*Stiftung*] or . . . the public act of consecration or unveiling that assigns [the image] its purpose does not give it its significance [*Bedeutung*]" but, instead, merely makes explicit the image's intrinsic, "signifying function" (*Bedeutungsfunktion*), which is integral to its "mode of being" (*Seinsweise*) (Gadamer 2006, 148).

159. For this shift, see Belting 1994, 330–76. For Bulgakov, the icon must be understood as the visible predicate of the "name-subject," which alone underwrites the icon as a whole. This "unification of name and image," reinforced by the sprinkling of holy water on the icon or anointing it with myrrh, establishes the icon's sanctity "by the Grace of the Holy Spirit" and, thus, affirms its mode of being as fundamentally other than that of "a mere religious picture" (Bulgakov 2012a, 79, 81).

the image of Christ. It is Christ by the identity of name, but the image of Christ by its relationship. For the copy is a copy of its original, just as a name is the name of that which is named."[160] Though adopting a more cautious formulation, the bishops assembled at the Seventh Ecumenical Council at Nicaea (AD 787) had likewise recommended naming an icon "so that the intention of him who venerates it may be the more easily fulfilled." However, they did not yet formalize consecrating and naming as rites altogether necessary for the icon's completion and validation. Yet just two generations later, with the iconoclast era concluded, that step was taken.[161]

Until the seventh century, Christian iconography often appeared to intersect with a crypto-pagan, talismanic image concept, as evidenced by the widespread "employment of portraits of the saints as direct remedies against demons." Well aware of the charge of idolatry bound to be drawn by religious imagery deployed mainly for the purpose of defending one's physical well-being against envy and evil, John Chrysostom (AD 349–407) had already rejected any "incorporation of Christian imagery into household magic." Still, such talismanic use of icons would persist up to the beginning of the iconoclast era, with Christ's face mechanically reproduced on the solidus minted under Justinian II as the most conspicuous instance. If prior to the start of "iconoclasm, the saints were frequently left unnamed by inscriptions," the situation appeared fundamentally changed after AD 843, at which point the icon's legitimacy and practical uses came to be governed by more explicit theological rationales. As the manifestation of a unique spiritual presence, the icon's "essential purpose . . . was recognition," and it is the consequent "need to define and to name . . . [that] differentiates post-iconoclastic Byzantine portraiture from earlier practice." Henceforth, it was "ineffective to have multiple identical copies of the same image in one context, in one area of a church, or on one garment, because the individual viewer could reach the prototype only through one image at a time." In making explicit the icon's relation to the prototype whom it depicts, the rites of consecration and naming that become established and constitutive features of icon theology by the middle of the ninth century confirm a fundamental shift, from superficially Christian portraits

---

160. Theodore 1981, I.11. "What is there, of all the things before our eyes, that is nameless? How can the thing which is named be separated in honor from its appellation, so that we may offer veneration to the one and deprive the other of it? These are relationships, for a name is by nature . . . a sort of natural image of that to which it is applied [*kai hoion tis physikē eikōn tou kath' hyper legetai, pephyken*]" (I.14).

161. *PNF*, vol. 14, 554 (Quaestio LV); for a full translation of the council's proceedings, and a detailed historical introduction, see also Sahas 1986. Bulgakov's claim that "the sanctified icon becomes the place of *the presence in the image of the One who is imaged*, and in this sense . . . boldly identifies itself with Him" (2012a, 85), seems conceptually unsound. For it revives the substitutive and totemic notion of the image from which the Byzantine theory of "intercession" (*paraklēsis*) had taken such pains to set itself apart.

and motifs (found on amulets, jewelry, textiles, and pottery) "repeated and unnamed to images that were identified and presented singly."[162]

At the same time, the now-central rite of naming the icon also modifies Plato's ontological requirement according to which an image is truly such only if it stands in "relation to" (*pros alla*) that of which it is the image. To be sure, the icon's relational status per se remains unchallenged, indeed, at first glance appears to have been strengthened by the rites in question. Yet the nature of this relation has now decisively changed. For insofar as the name has become an integral feature of the icon, along with its consecration, the image's relation to its prototype is rendered explicit and particular. No longer, that is, does the "relation" in question emerge vicariously from the icon's performance, just as the category "relation" is no longer understood ontologically. Instead, the relation of image and prototype now pivots on its consecration and inscription, objectively rendered by the name affixed on or just below the image itself. Consequently, the relation of icon and the person whom it depicts *and* names has become a contingent, essentially a case of ascription of the kind that, in his *Categories*, Aristotle calls *pros ti*. The stated "formal resemblance" (*homoiōsis*) of image and prototype has supplanted any previous claims regarding their apparent "consubstantiality" (*homoousia*); or, as Mondzain puts it, "Christ is not in the icon; the icon is toward Christ."[163]

Not least because of this conceptual shift, the divisive issue of the icon's ontological status and theological legitimacy begins to fade, a development further accelerated by the end of iconoclast policy under Emperor Michael III in AD 843. Once the icon's relation to its prototype is understood as formally and institutionally sanctioned by the twin rites of naming and consecration, the salient question is no longer the epistemological one ("What is an image?") but, rather, the one directed at the icon's mode of being: "In what way and to what extent can X be an image of Y."[164] Reframed as an ontological predicate, as the *typos* rather than *mimēsis* of the prototype whose name is inscribed below it, the icon no longer exposes itself to the charge of "reification," that is, of aspiring to corporeal identity with the being it depicts in the manner of a totem or idol. In fact, precisely because the name of its prototype is inscribed on or below it in the distinct medium of letters, it has become impossible to conflate the icon with its prototype or impute to it any intention to do so. We recall how in totemic representation the material scaffolding of representation, what Husserl calls "image carrier" (*Bildträger*), is absorbed into the visible "image object"

---

162. Maguire 1996, 101, 137, 103, 106.

163. See Mondzain 2005, 83–92; quote from 88. On the underlying "contrast between *thesis* and *physis*, between imitation by art and natural or supernatural generation" in Platonic and patristic thought, see also Ladner 1953, 18–22; Alloa 2011b, 27 ff.

164. Alloa 2011b, 27–28.

(*Bildgegenstand*). The resulting, idolatrous gaze thus fails to distinguish between the ontological status of the appearing image and the "image subject" (*Bildsujet*) that it depicts.[165] By contrast, the twin rites of consecration and naming ensure that both the ontological difference and the relatedness of essence and appearance inform the icon's conscious experience. Just as René Margritte's *Ceci n'est pas une pipe* (1929) mocks the petit-bourgeois spectator's lingering attachment to pictorial illusionism, so the ritual of naming and consecrating the icon foregrounds the ontological *relation* of image and prototype precisely by disavowing their *identity*.

Embedded in the celebration of the divine liturgy, specifically in the homily, the naming and consecrating of an icon would typically feature an ekphrasis of its visible *Gestalt* or, in the event, a prolonged description drawing attention to the carefully wrought choreography of multiple icons. Perhaps the most celebrated document of icon consecration is found in a sermon by Photios, who, following the accession of Empress Theodora (regent for her son Michael III from 842 to 855), had been elevated to patriarch of Constantinople. In his sermon of 29 March 867, the date that since 843 had been celebrated as the "Triumph of Orthodoxy" feast day, Photios introduced a vast congregation to the icons that had been "restored" in Hagia Sophia.[166] Alternating between the language of consecration, reverence, ekphrasis, and theological polemic, Photios's sermon dwells mainly on these restored or re-created icons, whose defacement during successive waves of iconoclasm had left "this celebrated and sacred church look[ing] sad with its visual mysteries scraped off." Given the violence recently perpetrated against icons, that visible fruit of a "splendid piety erecting trophies against belief hostile to Christ," the images once more adorning the walls, columns, and domes of the largest building in the world demand a robust theological defense, just as their beholders, no longer accustomed to the presence of icons, require an imaginative visual catechesis.[167] Constructed with impressive rhetorical skill, Photios's sermon thus combines the formal institution and consecration of icons with reflections on their centrality to both liturgical action and a fully realized Christology. Predictably, such an approach will stress the contiguity between sensory perception, spiritual vision, and the telos of "deification" (*theōsis*) toward which the liturgy seeks to orient the celebrants.

---

165. On Husserl's phenomenology of "image-consciousness" (*Bildbewußtsein*), see below, ch. 8, 641–67.

166. On the tangled history of Hagia Sophia's construction and reconstruction under Justinian I, see Mainstone 1988, 9–65; Aksit 2012, 29–51.

167. Photios 1958, 291, 289. On Photios's sermon, see Nelson 2007, 146–54; also Belting (1994, 171), who notes how similar homilies, "delivered at the occasion of the consecration of churches" and seized as an "opportunity to defend the policy on images," were also given by Emperor Leo VI (886–912) and by Leo's father-in-law, Stylanos Zaoutzas. Astute and evocative in its rhetorical construction, Photios's sermon had quickly become recognized as a model of fusing theological, aesthetic, and political argument.

At the heart of Photios's homily is an ekphrasis of the Theotokos in the great dome of the Hagia Sophia, the icon that may have been consecrated on this particular occasion, a rite formalized only with the conclusion of the iconoclast era. Thus, under the reigns of Michael III (842–67) and Basil I (867–86), the formal consecration of icons after 843, which still was not regarded as obligatory by the Seventh Ecumenical Council, came to be embraced as the restitution of a tradition. More than ever, the icon's theological legitimacy and spiritual power seemed to pivot on its being instituted in public ceremonies whose ecclesial and political dimension now appeared wholly entwined. The religious images of the post-iconoclast era also underwent formal change, both in the large-scale iconography found in Byzantine churches and on coins minted under Basil I; thus, Christ and the Virgin were now typically presented as "enthroned." In the wake of iconoclasm's defeat, the motif of the Virgin assumed a unique function within Byzantine iconography, becoming "an inexhaustible source of new inventions and allusions."[168] Indeed, its new identification as the Theotokos (later: *mētēr theou*) was designed to reinforce Orthodox Christology against the alleged subordinationism of the iconoclasts. In addition, the Theotokos motif served to recall military triumphs against the Avars and Bulgars under the banner of the Virgin and Christ icon, which had also been painted on the gates of Constantinople during the siege of AD 626.[169]

Meanwhile, Photios's remarks on the dual origins of faith in speech and sight, with form either "transmitted by hearing" or visually "imprinted upon the tablets of the soul," draw on a long tradition of patristic writers committed to the sanctification of the senses that extends from Athanasius, John Chrysostom, and Gregory of Nyssa to Dionysius, Maximus the Confessor, and, in the patriarch's own time, Theodore the Studite.[170] For the latter, the premise of the iconoclasts and their Origenist forebears is palpably absurd: "If merely mental contemplation were sufficient, it would have been sufficient for Him to come to us in a merely mental way."[171] Such a purely notional conception of the faith, Theodore insists, plainly contradicts the embodied reality of creation as a whole and human beings in particular. Likewise, when directing those assembled to turn their eyes to the Theotokos icon in the great dome of Hagia Sophia (fig. 2.12), Photios takes pains to distinguish between seeing as a case of sensuous indulgence and as an intensely focused act of spiritual vision: "with such

---

168. Belting 1994, 30.

169. See Belting 1994, 35–41; Brubaker and Haldon 2011, 61–68.

170. Photios 1958, 294. The theological legitimation of the senses is indispensable for Pelikan (2011, 99–120), who notes that the Pauline ideal of "reasonable worship" (*logikē latreia*—Rom. 12:1) had to be balanced against the central event of the Incarnation, in which Christ had taken on a real human body "not in mere appearance or fantasy but in reality [*mē phantasiai alla alēthōs*]" (Athanasius, quoted in Pelikan 2011, 106).

171. Theodore 1981, I.7.

Figure 2.12. Apse mosaic with Theotokos icon, Hagia Sophia, Istanbul, ninth century

a welcome does the representation of the Virgin's form cheer us, inviting us to draw not from a bowl of wine, but from a fair spectacle, by which the rational part of our soul, being watered through our bodily eyes and given eyesight in its growth towards the divine love of Orthodoxy, puts forth in the way of fruit the most exact vision of truth. Thus, even in her images does the Virgin's grace delight, comfort and strengthen us!"[172]

Such visual directives aim to prepare the audience for Photios's lengthy ekphrasis of the "restored" (*anastēlōseōs*) Theotokos mosaic, which to judge by some details in his homily was not altogether the same as the one seen today. His rhetoric here works hard to nudge the faithful toward an imaginative mode of vision that, ideally, will have them participate in the prototype rather than tarry exclusively with its visible depiction. Provided that embodied sight (*visus/opsis*) and spiritual vision (*visio/theōria*) are brought into full alignment,

> the faithful will see the virgin mother carrying in her pure arms for the common salvation of our kind, the common Creator reclining as an infant. . . . A virgin mother, with a virgin's and a mother's gaze, dividing in indivisible form her temperament between both capacities, yet belittling neither by its incompleteness. With such exactitude has the art of painting, which is a reflection of inspiration from above, set up a lifelike imitation [*houtōs akribō eis physin tēn mimēsin estēsen*]. For, as it were, she fondly turns her eyes on her begotten Child in the affection of her heart, yet assumes the expression of a detached and imperturbable mood at the passionless and wondrous nature of her offspring and composes her gaze accordingly.[173]

The virgin's serene balancing of maternal love and "passionless" recognition of her child's divine provenance, of motherhood and virginity, exemplifies the both-and logic with which the church frames the icon: at once an embodied, vivid, and visible presence, it is also experienced as an ineffable and mysterious gift, written by human hands even as these hands are moved by divine inspiration.

Still, Mary's equanimity eludes Photios, who, in elaborating an analogy between the Orthodox faith, its material expression in church architecture, and the Virgin ("Christ's bride"), finds himself angrily reminiscing about the devastation wrought

---

172. Photios 1958, 290. The Theotokos described, either a painting or a mosaic, the location of which within the church building Photios's description also leaves uncertain, was "not in all probability the image that we see there today" (284). Indeed, Photios's claim that the Virgin has been reclaimed from "oblivion" to which the iconoclasts had temporarily consigned her may well imply that an entirely new mosaic icon had been created after 843; on this sermon and its context, see Nelson 2007, 143–68; Belting 1994, 167–72.

173. Photios 1958, 290.

by more than a century of iconoclasm. All too present for him is the specter of icons despoiled, leaving "the Church, Christ's bride, [stripped] of her own ornaments," a theological and aesthetic evil perpetrated against the faith and the church, "wantonly inflicting bitter wounds on her, . . . herein emulating Jewish folly."[174] Two successive phases of iconoclast violence had left the church "looking sad with its visual mysteries scraped off." In particular, the "restoration" of the Theotokos offers visible evidence of a long hoped-for retrieval of the Orthodox faith. Once consecrated, that is, the icon presents the faithful with "a complete and perfect image of piety."[175] The analogy is reinforced by Photios's carefully positioned references to scripture, specifically to the image of the anticipated Jerusalem "portrayed" or "graven" (*ezōgraphēsa*) "upon the palms of my hands; thy walls are continually before me" (Is 49:16). Yet the image of Jerusalem has not been engraved on the hands of his despairing servant, Zion. Rather, in a striking inversion, it is the Lord who assures Zion that his, Zion's, graven portrait is "continually before me." Just as the servant's name is written on the master's hand, so the icons once again displayed on the literal "walls" (*teichē*) of the church train their gaze onto the faithful assembled below, assuring them of the New Jerusalem that is their true eschaton. On Photios's telling, then, the walls of Hagia Sophia and the icons that enliven them are not, strictly speaking, of this world. Rather, they function like a screen or veil, at once reminding the faithful of their distance from the life to come and orienting them firmly toward it: "A mouth that has no moisture and no breath / Breathless mouths may summon," as Yeats was to put it.[176] The Theotokos in particular captures this anagogical relationship between the order of visible things and the transcendent God in whom it will be consummated.

Likening the restored paintings and mosaics adorning the walls of Hagia Sophia to the resurrection ("the image of the Mother rises up from the very depth of oblivion"), Photios presses the scriptural warrant for the veneration of icons: "Christ came to us in the flesh, and was borne in the arms of His Mother. This is seen and confirmed and proclaimed in pictures, the teaching made manifest by means of personal eye-witness, and impelling the spectators to unhesitating assent."[177] The sermon takes care to anchor the consecration of the Theotokos in a considered epistemology of the icon and of spiritual sight. Echoing his iconophile precursors (John, Nikephoros, Theodore), Photios thus posits a metaphysical analogy between the audible *logos* and the visible *eikōn*, between taking in Christ's word and receiving "a form through sight." Yet his allusion to Moses taking God's dictation (Ex 34:27) also shows how in

---

174. On the strident, at times anti-Jewish tone of Photios's sermon, see Nelson 2007; on similar outbursts in Theodore's *Refutations* and the visual polemic of the mid-ninth-century Chludov Psalter, see Brubaker and Haldon 2012, 368–82.

175. Photios 1958, 291–92.

176. "Byzantium," in Yeats 1997, 252.

177. Photios 1958, 293.

Photios's spiritual epistemology sight ultimately wins out. For while it is true that the media of both word and image allow "a form [to be] imprinted upon the tablets of the soul," it is sight rather than hearing that leaves the stronger impression and, in fact, is indispensable for drawing the beholder "to emulation" of the prototype. Thus, even as the faithful overwhelmingly *hear* the Gospels, their ability to register and internalize the meaning of scripture presupposes some mental image. A century before, John of Damascus had argued that "everywhere we use our senses to produce an image of the Incarnate God himself, and we sanctify the first of the senses (sight being the first of the senses), just as by words hearing is sanctified." Still, John regards sight and hearing, image and word, as fully equivalent, with either medium serving essentially mnemonic purposes: "For an image is a memorial, [and] what the book does for those who understand letters, the image does for the illiterate" (*JDI* I:17).

For his part, Photios takes a stronger view in which the image becomes foundational for all discursive understanding. Anticipating J. H. Newman's distinction between notional and real assent, he thus argues that for a verbal message to meet with real "uptake" it must draw on an antecedent, pre-discursive image for support.[178] Hence, as he ponders the phenomenology of listening, say, to particular narratives in scripture, Photios asks, "Has [the listener's] intelligence visualized and drawn to itself what he has heard? . . . Much greater [than hearing] is the power of sight." True understanding, Photios insists, is impossible without visualization, which differs from hearing by not being temporally distended, and which alone "sends the essence of the thing seen on to the mind, letting it be conveyed from there to the memory for the concentration of unfailing knowledge." Only where the mind has "seen, . . . comprehended [*katalēpsis*], . . . [and] visualized" can it be said to properly have assimilated spiritual meanings.[179] Photios's terminology here shows him relying on the ancient, so-called extramission theory of vision, also favored by Plato, Galen, the

---

178. While assent is "in its nature simply one and indivisible, and thereby essentially different from Inference," Newman also shows that assent takes essentially two forms, one nested within the other. "Notional assent," wherein we embrace a proposition as true, "seems like Inference because the apprehension which accompanies acts of Inference is notional also. . . . [Hence] we may call it the normal state of Assent to apprehend propositions as things." Yet forms of notional assent (e.g., Profession, Credence, Opinion, Speculation, Presumption) retain a solipsistic quality in that here "mind contemplates its own creations instead of things." Yet in "real assent, or belief, as it may be called," mind responds to the very realities that underlie the notions and inferences it has subsequently constructed. And here, just as Photios argued a millennium earlier, we are challenged to grasp that "the Divine Word speaks of things, not merely of notions. . . . Reading, as we do, the Gospels from our youth up, we are in danger of becoming so familiar with them as to be dead to their force." While Newman remains cautious about the theological value of images, and says nothing at all about their formal composition, he acknowledges that "the images in which [real assent] lives, representing as they do the concrete, have the power of the concrete upon the affections and passions (Newman 1979, 50–51, 76, 79, 86).

179. Photios 1958, 294.

Stoics, and Euclid among others, according to which the eye emits rays that capture the thing seen. These rays eventually return to the beholder, whose mind generates and stores the image composed by such quasi-tactile rapport between eye and object.[180] On this model, sight is a case of active seeking rather than passive recipiency, an embodied, haptic involvement with the phenomenal world whereby what is seen is also, at least implicitly, judged. Speaking of God and the saints, John of Damascus a century earlier had affirmed that, mediated by their icons, "all these we venerate and embrace and kiss with eyes and lips."[181]

Yet who is the beholder, and who is seen here? Photios's sermon suggests that, particularly where the Pantocrator and Theotokos are concerned, it is the icon whose gaze emits rays that will touch and release what spiritual goodness there is in the finite, human subjects assembled in the pews below. Quoting a passage from Nikolaos Mesarites's description of the Christ icon in the dome of the Holy Apostles Church in Constantinople (destroyed in 1462), Nelson characterizes that icon as "a figure leaning past the rim of heaven and down into our space." Christ, that is, enters into "the actual space and eye of the beholder," who thus experiences her own gaze as, ideally, responding with all possible fullness and commitment to the experience of being seen by the One depicted in the icon.[182] Encircled by the apostles, framed by chromatically varied decoration, the Theotokos in the Parekklesion of the Chora Church in Constantinople, whose present-day interior was completed in 1321, hews close to Mesarites's account. Here, too, what stands out is the iconic saints' downward gaze into the church interior, where it would meet and concentrate the raised eyes of the faithful (fig. 2.13). In this liturgical space, where alone "the unpurged images of day recede," human sight is at last able to extricate itself from the thralldom of sheer visibility.

Still, the phenomenology of beholding as it emerges from Photios's ekphrasis of the Hagia Sophia Theotokos appears to be contradicted in some of its details by what can actually be seen. Neither the direction of Mary's gaze nor Photios's description of her as standing quite comports with the icon now before us. Yet these empirical in-

---

180. See Nelson 2007, 151–54; Lindberg 1976, 18–57.

181. *JDI* II:10.

182. Nelson 2007, 156. On Photios's sermon, see also Belting 1994, 167–73. Born in 1163, Mesarites produced his lengthy description of the Church of the Holy Apostles sometime between 1198 and 1205; his ekphrasis of the Pantocrator icon is arguably the most detailed work in this genre, extending for several pages. In Downey's 1957 translation, it reads as follows: "This dome shows in pictured form the God-Man Christ, leaning and gazing out as though from the rim of heaven, at the point where the dome begins, toward the floor of the Church and everything in it, but not with His whole body or in His whole form. . . . One can see Him, to use the words of the Song (Cant. 2:9) looking forth at the windows, leaning out as far as His navel through the lattice at the summit of the dome like an earnest and vehement lover" (Downey 1957, 869–70).

Figure 2.13. Parekklesion, Chora Church, Istanbul, 1321

consistencies resolve themselves once we understand ekphrasis itself as part of the icon's phenomenology, of the way it is experienced in the dual modality of seeing the visible icon and actively visualizing its prototype; this is what Yeats means by the encounter with "Those images that yet / Fresh images beget."[183] Ekphrasis, in other words, is no mere ex post facto summary of a given image's form and contents.[184] Articulating *what* is seen, and *how* the visible image mediates the beholder with the truth beyond it, is itself an integral feature of the unfolding, visual-cum-spiritual

---

183. Yeats 1997, 253.

184. On tensions intrinsic to the concept of ekphrasis, see Mitchell 1994, 151–81, who remarks on its paradoxical status as "a minor and rather obscure literary genre," on the one hand, and its appearing "paradigmatic of a fundamental tendency in all linguistic expression," on the other. What Mitchell terms "ekphrastic fear," that is, the genre's seemingly animist capacity for "giving voice to the mute art object" (155), recalls anxieties voiced nearly a millennium and a half earlier by Byzantine iconoclasm. For an expansive account of ekphrasis that affirms it as an integral feature of poetry, see Krieger 1967.

experience. In the act of seeing the icon, the beholder is enjoined to gauge and re-flect on her spiritual distance vis-à-vis the icon's eternal and perfect gaze. An integral feature of the Byzantine icon's phenomenology thus concerns the beholder's self-recognition: "You measure your own soul by your interpretation of the image before you, a lifelike figure that you touch and grasp through your eye's optical rays." Such seeing is essentially "active and determinative, and hence the opposite of the passive, value-neutral optical process, assumed by modern science and its positivistic sub-sidiaries, antiquarianism and art history."[185] If Photios's stress on the "lifelike" im-pression contradicts our modern sense of pictorial realism, this only underscores our estrangement from the Byzantine icon's operative theo-logic. Once denuded of the spiritual agency that lies at the heart of Photios's sermon, the icon will be sup-planted by the Renaissance concept of the art image, a metaphysically agnostic con-ception wherein religious themes appear increasingly subordinate to concerns with stylistic innovation, political patronage, and the individual artist's professional ambi-tion, not to mention fluctuating notions of connoisseurship and public "taste."

Against the background of pictorial realism and its underlying mathematical concept of linear perspective as Western culture's dominant "symbolic form," under-standing the visual grammar of the Byzantine icon becomes an uphill struggle.[186] Considering the Byzantine icon's restrictive formal economy, its emphasis on nu-ance, minimal variations of posture, and gesture and its seemingly abstract presen-tation of bodies and faces, understanding the theological aims and spiritual effects of this form would seem to demand a type of "period eye" that may be all but impos-sible to reconstitute.[187] Yet its true challenge to the modern beholder stems not from a lack of historical erudition but spiritual commitment. For the phenomenology pre-supposed by the icon, which is implicit in the formal and material choices and aims of Byzantine iconography, is characterized by a palpably premodern ethos of search-

---

185. Nelson 2007, 159.

186. The classic formulation of linear perspective as the dominant symbolic form of visual culture since the Renaissance is Panofsky's eponymous study of 1937. In it, he juxtaposes ancient models of perspective, which he argues had defined perceptual truth via the beholder's contingent vantage point, to the modern (Renaissance) ideal of perceptual truth bound up with the viewer's "mental image" (*Sehbild*) of the object in question. Yet in so doing, Panofsky effectively presup-poses the modern, mathematical conception of linear perspective whose origins he means to trace, and which he prizes because it "described the world according to a rational and repeatable proce-dure . . . [and thus] overrode the distinctions of the idiomatic" (Panofsky 1997, Introd. 13). For an in-cisive critique of Panofsky's conception of art history as a "humanist," neo-Kantian discipline aspir-ing to bring past "symbolic forms" to total intelligibility, see Didi-Huberman 2005, esp. 117–32; the neo-Kantian assumptions underwriting Panofsky's account had already been vigorously challenged in Pavel Florensky's remarkable essay "Reverse Perspective," presented as a series of lectures in 1920 but, given the political turmoil of the time, not published in the Soviet Union until 1967 (Florensky 2004, 198–272); on twentieth-century Russian icon theory, see also Antonova 2010, 23–62.

187. On the notion of the "period eye," see Baxandall 1972, 29–108.

ing participation rather than hermeneutic suspicion. To behold the icon means, first and foremost, to achieve maximal attention and stillness, the sort of patient, humble, and undesigning *noēsis* that John of Damascus and the iconodules following him call "veneration." To our present intellectual culture, caught up in methodological one-upsmanship and unceasing critical "intervention," such an ethos—not to mention its metaphysical foundations and spiritual aims—appears all but unintelligible. Indeed, if we are to reclaim the icon as the paradigmatic case of what an image is—a case not of immanent representation but of numinous mediation—a mandatory first step will be to suspend modernity's commonplace approach to knowledge as the decisive *overcoming* and *supplanting* of intuition or "perceptual faith." Called for, instead, is a thick phenomenological description of the multilayered response that the icon elicits in its beholder. Without ignoring the icon's formal and material aspects, such phenomenological description will once again have to learn to embrace value terms, such as gift, gratitude, and self-recognition, as well as their theological corollaries, such as consecration, naming, prayer, and, above all, veneration (*proskynēsis*).

While there are hints that the veneration of images may date to the late fourth century, the practice had become firmly established by the first half of the sixth century, which witnessed "a tremendous increase and intensification of the cult of images."[188] A principal feature of this gradual development concerns the transfer of devotional attention from relics to icons, which also explains why early religious imagery, dating to the late second century, is found almost exclusively on funerary objects (sarcophagi, gravestones, portraits of the deceased, etc.).[189] As it gradually evolved into a "virtual relic in the absence of actual remains," the icon's spiritual authority would sometimes be enhanced by "deliberately inserting relics within images."[190] Unsurprisingly, this contiguity of icons with relics also prompted stress to be placed on the mnemonic function of images; echoing Gregory the Great, John of Damascus notes, "The image is a memorial. What the book does for those who

---

188. Kitzinger 1954, 115. Still, even as evidence for "the actual worship of religious images . . . and beliefs involving images prior to the middle of the sixth century [is] incontrovertible," it remains "scattered and spotty" (95).

189. The fact that early religious imagery tends to be found on objects of particularly durable material (stone, marble) naturally favored the preservation of funereal images and explains why "third-century Christian art in the West is preserved only as funerary art, at least until the fourth century" (Dinkler, in Weitzmann 1979, 396). As a result, our sense today of Christian imagery's initial distribution across a variety of media and locations is bound to be distorted.

190. Jensen 2005, 50; Freedberg 1989, 95. In his landmark study *Martyrium* (1946) André Grabar had established the veneration of images as a process wherein the icon superseded the relic as the main object of devotion in the Eastern Church. Following Grabar, Kitzinger holds that insofar as "sensual perception of the living form is the devout's primary need, it is obvious that the work of the painter and sculptor can be of greater assistance to him than a handful of dust and bones. . . . Hence the pictorial rendering of the living form was able to inherit the virtues of the relic" (1954, 116).

understand letters, the image does for the illiterate."[191] Still, the mere fact (if we accept it to be such) that the icon is uniquely able to operate in this way, while no longer being physically linked to the person remembered, only confirms the insufficiency of a strictly naturalistic explanation. In fact, historical genealogies such as those unfolded by Grabar, Kitzinger, and, more recently, Jensen tacitly presuppose an underlying, metaphysical dimension according to which "we find images always already charged with . . . spiritual functions," that is, we find "the spirit already imaged, and the image already spiritualized."[192] In Peter Brown's vivid surmise, with the saints seen "standing on the cool walls of the churches, pictures were more permanent reminders to the passer-by than were the liturgy and reading of the gospels of the story of Jesus and the passions of the saints."[193] While not wrong as far as it goes, such a characterization does not factor in the icon's unique phenomenology, which involved "not merely a visual reproduction and reminder of the events and persons depicted, [but] beyond their representation and reenactment . . . vouch[ed] for the absolute, uncompromised divine truth."[194] Yeats's characterization of the Byzantine icon as "the artifice of eternity" hints at this profound interpenetration of human making and divine creation, of the productions of time and those of eternity.

In fact, if the icon's efficacy had served exclusively pragmatic, and specifically mnemonic purposes, as the *Libri Carolini* and, eventually, the Council of Trent were to assert, its consecration and veneration should have been dismissed as pointless rituals.[195] Still, the soft iconoclasm getting under way by the end of the eighth century in the West will gradually grow in influence and enter into an oblique partnership with the rise of modern, naturalistic image theories in the mid-fifteenth century. For now, it suffices to recall its origins in Augustine's discrimination between bodily, spiritual, and intellectual sight, as well as the functional distinctions of the *ratio triplex*. Cumulatively, these discriminations underwrite the heavily qualified account of the image found in the *Libri Carolini*, the iconoclast polemic prepared at Charlemagne's behest and most likely written by Alcuin and Theodulf of Orléans for the 794 Synod in Frankfurt. Against the backdrop of the (as it would turn out, shortlived) reinstatement of icon veneration in Byzantium under Empress Irene at the Council of Constantinople (787), the *Libri* took a notably diffident view of the role of images in liturgical practice and theological reflection. Of lasting influence was the

---

191. *JDI* I:17; see also Bk. IV, ch. 16, in *Of the Orthodox Faith*, John of Damascus 1958, 370–73.
192. Balthasar 2001, 162.
193. Brown 1973, 7.
194. Kartsonis 1998, 76.
195. Bulgakov (2012a, 89). Bulgakov thus considers the Catholic position "a step back that in essence subverted" the very concept of *proskynēsis*. Regarding the Latin mistranslation of *proskynēsis* from the acts of Nicaea II (AD 787) in the *Libri Carolini*, see Alloa 2013; Noble 2009, 158–206.

Libri's mistranslation of *proskynēsis* (veneration) and *latreia* (worship) with the same Latin word, *adoratio*. Encouraged by Charlemagne himself, the authors of the *Libri* thus oppose as scandalous what they took to be the Byzantine empress's reinstatement of image *worship*.

Even so, the response set forth in the *Libri* does not follow the militant and conceptually flat-footed iconoclast polemics of Leo III and Constantine V. Instead, the Carolingian scholars formulate a program of "soft" iconoclasm according to which the written word stabilizes, legitimates, and ultimately supersedes the image's spiritual intention. Thus "only the inscription [*titulus*] is able to clearly distinguish between the holy and the profane."[196] The proper name inscribed under the portrait of a saint, or an instance of biblical exegesis aimed at elucidating the spiritual import of vivid, often sensual imagery, thus shows the written word to be less the antagonist of the image than its fulfillment. Conversely, the fact that the Byzantine church had always resisted a purely instrumental view raises the question of how eighth- and ninth-century Orthodoxy understood the "veneration" (*proskynēsis*) of icons and why "veneration" should prove so inextricably entwined with prayer.

Once again, John of Damascus offers us initial orientation: "Strangled with thoughts, as if with thorns, I come into the common surgery of the soul, the church; the luster of the painting draws me to vision and delights my sight like a meadow and imperceptibly introduces my soul to the glory of God." Certainly, the illiterate, but not they alone, will vigorously respond to icons "promoting the glory of God and his saints, . . . and honor them as images and copies and likenesses and books and a memorial for the illiterate, and to venerate and kiss them with eyes and lips, and cleave to them in [their] hearts, as a likeness of God incarnate, or of his Mother" (*JDI* III:9). Putting the matter thus confirms that, whatever the spiritual particulars of "veneration" may turn out to be, beholding the icon is wholly incommensurable with the modern ideal of objective, value-neutral perception. On the contrary, the very act of "seeing" the icon originates in a "seeking" for spiritual wholeness. In the liturgical context, that is, seeing an image is less a case of finite perception than the attempt to visualize of divine plenitude that is not only *guided by* the visible icon itself, but

---

196. See Alloa 2013, 24 ff.; for a detailed account of the *Libri Carolini*, see Noble 2009. Alloa shows that the effects of the *Libri*'s misconstrual of "veneration" (*proskynēsis*) as "adoration" linger well into the thirteenth century, such that Aquinas's discussion of the adoration of Christ (*ST* III. Q25) invokes the authority of John of Damascus to argue, in evident misconstrual of John's arguments in *De fide orthodoxa*, that "referentiality is not a property inherent to the image but to the sign" only (Alloa 2013, 25; trans. mine). See also Besançon (2000) on the "attitude of neutrality" that the *Libri* maintained toward images. Deemed incapable of forging a passage (*transitus*) from the material form to the divine prototype, "the sacred image keeps one foot in the profane world. It is by nature secularized or secularizable," which in due course revealed itself as a boon to the artist's freedom (Besançon 2000, 152).

ultimately seeks to move *beyond* it. In a liturgical context, therefore, to see the icon is also to acknowledge one's unfathomable distance vis-à-vis the prototype. That is, where I claim to "see" (*eidō*) the visible image I also "know" (*oida*) myself as "unknowing," that is, recognize myself as suspended between a temporal "not yet" and the hoped-for, eternal "now."

Seeing the icon thus begins with surrendering any claim to epistemic dominion and, instead, assuming a stance and pose of humility. "Veneration" (*proskynēsis*) of the icon entails a self-humbling, for which reason John of Damascus notes how the beholder's "bowing down is a symbol of submission and honor [*timē*]" (*JDI* I:14, 21). Both in its physical and spiritual sense, veneration involves the beholder in a progression *through* and *by means of* the icon and *toward* the prototype depicted in it. As we had seen, this contiguity was formalized in the rite of consecration, itself an indispensable precondition of all icon veneration.[197] Henceforth, "seeing" the icon means, fundamentally, submitting to its gaze as an "intercession" for God's judgment. Indeed, the intentional act known as veneration never addresses the icon itself but, moving through and beyond it, seeks to reach the *imago* of Christ, the Virgin, or a particular saint whom the icon makes present. As John of Damascus writes, "We must ascribe honor to the living tabernacles of God," the saints. While their natural bodies have passed, their *imago* remains present and deserving of reverence: "In psalms and hymns and spiritual songs, in contrition and in pity for the needy, let us believers worship the saints, as God also is most worshipped in such wise. Let us raise monuments to them and visible images, and let us ourselves become, through imitation of their virtues, living monuments and images of them."[198] Properly to behold the icon is to visualize and let oneself be absorbed by its prototype.

The visible image per se can only ever furnish the focal point for a unique case of *noēsis*, which can be no more reduced to an instance of perception than prayer can be construed as a case of propositional speech. Instead, when "praying before the icon, we pray directly to Him," the prototype of the visible image.[199] The completion or ultimate "realization" of the visible icon thus involves its transfiguration in prayer—which is more a unique intentionality than audible speech, wherein, "when it is ardent and inspired . . . [the subject] receives the Transcendent as the immanent" in the sense that the beholder seeks to become the beheld by petitioning God to see her.[200] In praying, the petitioner implores the iconic presence before her for the

---

197. "It is *not possible* to venerate icons in the same way one venerates sanctified icons" (Bulgakov 2012a, 85).
198. John of Damascus 1958, 367–70 (bk. IV, ch. 15).
199. Bulgakov 2012a, 85.
200. Bulgakov 2012b, 24.

grace of full self-recognition, which is to say, for the subject to be released from all sinful attachment to self. Release here requires that the praying subject achieve self-recognition, something made possible insofar as she conceives herself as "being seen" by the prototype mediated in the icon.[201]

Praying *to* an icon—that is, to the image serving as "intercessor" (*paraklētos*) for a saint, the Virgin, or Christ—thus is altogether central to what Byzantine image theory calls "veneration" (*proskynēsis*). Leaving aside the initial gesture of kissing the icon, performed by the priest, veneration can truly express itself only in the form of prayer, for which reason Bulgakov notes that "however high a value one places on the icon, its significance is nonetheless limited: i.e., it serves as a place for the meeting in prayer with God."[202] Far more than an instance of submission on the part of the faithful to the higher authority of the saints and the supreme figure of Christ, veneration involves the subject in a call-and-response dynamic that in Byzantine church architecture is visibly modeled by the way icons interact with one another across liturgical space. Again, Brown gets it partly right when noting how the early "monastic church may well have been the first milieu in which . . . the icon gained meaning through being part of the liturgy, and became a chosen vehicle for expressing the majestic rhythms of the divine plan of salvation." Yet the vertical logic whereby a "majestic" and "divine" soteriological scheme is visibly mediated for the frail congregant below—"but a paltry thing, / A tattered coat upon a stick"—tells only half the story.[203] The other, equally important half concerns the lateral communion of saints, the Virgin, and Christ with one another across ecclesial space and, in so doing, modeling for the finite human beholder the kind of visualization to which to aspire. Placed in apses, transepts, lunettes, and domes, as well as on the pillars, the walls, and the iconostasis at the heart of the Byzantine church, a given icon tends to be part of an ensemble of images whose choreography affirms the "ability of images to . . . physically communicate with each other in an environment that bridges the space and time of the images and the beholder." It is this modeling of call and response *among* icons that exemplifies for the beholder the summons encapsulated by all spiritual sight and enacted in veneration and prayer: namely, to emulate the icon's capacity for "presence, thought, will, action, interaction, and dialogue."[204] Moreover, the symmetrical

---

201. On prayer, see Turner 2011, 135–66; Maritain (1953, 27) quotes St. Anthony Abbot's saying that "prayer is not perfect if the monk knows he is praying." The same could be said about "seeing" the icon to which one prays.

202. Bulgakov 2012a, 91.

203. Brown 1973, 20; Yeats 1997, 197.

204. Kartsonis 1998, 71, 65. On the "pictorial program" of icons conceived both singly "and at the same time form[ing] part of a sequence following the architectural structure," see Belting 1994, 173–83 (quote from 178).

arrangement of icons within ecclesial space, as well as the rotation of movable portraits depending on a particular saint's feast day, helped "dispel the magical fascination that certain images exerted as physical objects."[205]

St. John Chrysostom's characterization of prayer (*proseuchē/oratio*) as "a link
mediating between God and man" aptly captures the fusion of seeking and seeing at
the heart of it: "As our bodily eyes are illuminated by seeing the light, so in contemplating God our soul is illuminated by him."[206] A form of intercessory speech, prayer,
or "beseking" as Julian of Norwich will call it, ought to be understood "as distinct
from contemplation, [just] as seeking is distinct from beholding." For in prayer, the
subject voices the hope that, figurally speaking, her silent speech will be heard and
her gaze, focused by the medium of the icon yet moving beyond it, may be returned.[207] Unlike declarative speech, prayer is principally informed by a longing that
it may be received and validated by the One whom the one praying ultimately seeks
to behold "face-to-face." It is the quintessential expression of the subject's longing for
self-recognition. It petitions God to affirm that the one praying is, and always has
been, seen and loved by him. Just as beholding the icon cannot be understood as an
act of perception, so the prayer wherein "veneration" (*proskynēsis*) phenomenalizes
itself must not be construed as a case of propositional speech. For in prayer the subject confesses "not being the origin of every good and every gift," that is, recognizes
her essential self-*in*sufficiency. Were we to take recourse to Aristotelian categories,
prayer would be an instance of the kind of speech (*logos*) that "is neither true nor
false [*logos apophantikos*]."[208] Whatever its specific contents, in its very form prayer
attests to the absolute subalterity, the "wounded" condition, of the one praying.

For this reason, too, prayer resists being defined as an audible or, for that matter,
inaudible mode of speech. As Teresa of Avila notes, prayer is "not simply an issue of
keeping one's mouth closed" any more than it "is made only with one's lips."[209] In fact,
the distinctive "noetic doing" involved in prayer constitutes an absolute rupture, a
miraculous "discontinuity in the immanent," that renders prayer categorically immune to syllogistic parsing in terms of true or false propositional utterances (*apo-
phansis*).[210] Yet if, in T. S. Eliot's compact formulation, "prayer is more / Than an
order of words, the conscious occupation / Of the praying mind, or the sound of the
voice praying," neither is it mere Hamlet-like soliloquy.[211] In fact, the obverse seems

---

205. Belting 1994, 183.

206. Homily VI; the Greek *euchē* denotes a wish, a desire, or vow. Combined with the prefix
pros- (toward), it takes on strong directional and aspirational connotations.

207. Turner 2011, 150.

208. Chrétien, in Janicaud 2000, 153; Aristotle 1984, 1:26 (*De Interpretatione* 17a4–5).

209. Quoted by Chrétien, in Janicaud 2000, 148.

210. Bulgakov 2012a, 160.

211. Eliot 2015, 1:202 ("Little Gidding," lines 46–48).

to be the case: namely, prayer understood as a form of inward speech in which the one praying seeks to be wholly divested of her subjectivity by God's response, by being heard, seen, and recognized. It is this self-consummation of the subject in the act of praying that is also reflected in prayer's distinctively *embodied* and *choreographed* form. Thus, prayer "concerns our body, our bearing, our posture, our gestures," as well as particular "gestures and movements such as raising the hand or kneeling."[212] For by kneeling or prostrating herself, the person praying physically seeks to surrender any claim to "see" or "know" the addressee of her prayer, confessing herself instead to be wholly dependent on being seen and recognized by God's "thou." Not coincidentally, the Greek word for "adoration on one's knees" (*proskynein*), which occurs eleven times in the Gospel of John (see esp. Jn 4:19–24), will also be the preferred term for the veneration of icons in the writings of John of Damascus and Theodore the Studite.

In a 1923 essay, Karl Holl sought to trace the origins of the iconostasis in the Eastern Church. Though very few references to this feature of Orthodox church architecture can be found prior to the tenth century, Holl shows that it had to have been well established by AD 600, which not coincidentally is also when the hieratic icon's distinctive form and function had separated itself from the broader and liturgically neutral phenomenon of devotional icons and religious illustrations of scriptural narrative.[213] Among the small number of references to the iconostasis, two in particular stand out. First, there is Paulus Silentiarius's ekphrasis of Hagia Sophia from AD 563, after it had been repaired following three earthquakes (in 553, 557, and 558) that had severely damaged it, exposing the main dome's faulty construction. Reconsecrated on 24 December 562, the building as described by Paulus just weeks later makes reference to "the middle panels of the sacred screen which form a barrier round the sanctified priests." Here, we learn, "the carver's tool has incised one symbol that means many words, for it combines the names of the empress and the emperor: It is like a shield with a boss in whose middle part has been carved the sign of the cross. And the screen gives access to the priests through three doors. For on each

---

212. Chrétien, in Janicaud 2000, 150; on the posture of prayer, see Basil, *On the Spirit* XXVII, in *PNF* 8:42; Gregory of Nyssa, *On the Holy Spirit: Against Macedonius*, in *PNF* 5:325. On the liturgical function of kneeling, and on its pagan (Aristotle, Theophrastus, Plutarch) and modern neopagan detractors, see Ratzinger 2000, 184–94, who remarks how "spiritual and bodily meanings of *proskynein* are really inseparable" (190).

213. Holl's thesis (1923, 227 ff.) proceeds inferentially by tracing Greek orthodoxy's development in juxtaposition to that of peripheral ecclesial communities (*Nebenkirchen*), in particular the Armenian and the Coptic church. Thus, he notes that since the iconostasis is a feature of Coptic church architecture, it had to have been in existence prior to the Copts splitting from the Eastern Church, a process essentially definitive by AD 600. By contrast, the Armenian church, which constituted itself during the decades following its rejection of Chalcedon (AD 451), did not yet know this architectural feature.

side the workman's hand has made a small door."[214] Perched between the nave and the sanctuary, the iconostasis constitutes a semipermeable membrane of sorts between the congregants and the sanctuary to the east. At its very center is the Christ icon, typically placed to the right of the Holy Doors leading to the sanctum surrounding the altar and allowing the faithful to visually grasp the threshold between the Incarnation and the Second Coming. Over time, the placement of icons came to follow certain conventions, with the Theotokos icon placed to the left of the Holy Doors, a Deësis icon above it, and the archangels Michael and Gabriel depicted on the north (entrance) and south (exit) doors, where they represent the "defender" and the "messenger" of the holy, respectively. Icons of still other apostles and saints appear on higher tiers, or "rubrics," of the iconostasis. Overall, the church's "sacred space is reorganized around the distinction between that which is given to visibility and that which is not, or cannot be, given to vision and knowledge."[215] Always, that is, the icon functions as both medium and veil.

For our purposes, particulars of icon arrangement are less important than understanding the theological rationale for the iconostasis, which on Holl's reading of Silentiarius's description of Hagia Sophia had become an established feature of Byzantine church architecture already during the reign of Justinian I. Most important, the iconostasis does not divide but, on the contrary, visibly links the profane and sacred spaces. As Maximus the Confessor writes, "The nave is the sanctuary in potency, by being consecrated by the relationship of the sacrament toward its end." In its dual aspect, then, the church building with the iconostasis at its very center mirrors "the entire world of beings produced by God in creation, [which] is divided into a spiritual world filled with intelligible and incorporeal essences and into this sensible and bodily world which is ingeniously woven together of many forms and natures." The church's spatial organization is wholly symbolic, allowing us "to perceive what does not appear by means of what does."[216] Crucially, what connects the two realms is a dual movement flanking the celebration of the liturgy, beginning with the "entrance of the holy mysteries" (*prōtē eisodos*), which takes place between the closing of the doors after the gospel reading and the kiss of peace, when the priests enter

---

214. http://projects.mcah.columbia.edu/medieval-architecture/htm/or/ma_or_gloss_essay
_paul.htm (accessed 1 May 2020). It bears pointing out, at the time of Silentiarius's description no human figures were depicted on the mosaics and that, in all probability, the Theotokos, the Deësis, and other iconic portraits were only added following the end of the iconoclast era in 843.

215. Constas 2014, 213.

216. Maximus 1985 [*MSW*], 188, 189. "God's holy church is in itself a symbol of the sensible world as such, since it possesses the divine sanctuary as heaven and the beauty of the nave as earth. Likewise the world is a church since it possess heaven corresponding to a sanctuary, and for a nave it has the adornment of the earth" (189); the relationship between the "sanctuary as symbol of the intelligible world and the nave as symbol of the world of sense" is reiterated in the closing chapter of the *Mystagogy* (208).

into the nave and through the north door of the iconostasis into the sanctuary, followed by their egress from behind the iconostasis (*eisodos tōn hagiōn mystēriōn*) at the culmination of the mass.

While it is not possible to determine how early the wall between the columns of the church came to be adorned with images and, thus, took on the now-familiar aspect of the iconostasis, the latter evidently functions in ways entirely consistent with the hieratic icons that in time came to be displayed on it. Far from being an inert, purely material feature of Eastern Church architecture, the iconostasis encapsulates the fundamental ontology of the image. That is, it functions as both medium and veil, a boundary designed to focus the attention and reverence of the faithful, yet also, by dint of the icons that adorn it, a bridge or window into the beyond. Important here is that the symbol, from Dionysius and Maximus forward to Gregory of Palamas and Symeon of Thessaloniki, never claims to *reveal* divine meanings but only ever to *mediate* them in forms proportionate to the intellectual and spiritual capacity of those who behold them. Every symbol is a veil, a screen at once ordering the beholder toward things divine and sheltering her from a fullness of vision that exceeds "this heavy load of fallen flesh."[217] Straddling nave and sanctuary, the visible and the invisible, icons and the screen they compose thus reflect the dual structure or "inward-outward character . . . distinctive of every sacrament." The metaphysical *paradeigma* underlying all reality as simultaneously its visible, empirical self and its divine, invisible source is, of course, the Incarnation wherein "God has visibly 'appeared among us,' traversing and thereby abolishing the opposition of 'above' and 'below.'" A millennium later, Goethe will still be wrestling with the fact that the symbol's intuitive power and manifest efficacy cannot be accounted for without, at the very least, committing oneself to a Neoplatonist metaphysics.[218]

It bears recalling here that in the evolving theological and liturgical context of late antiquity and Byzantine culture of the eighth and ninth centuries, the phenomenology of "seeing" increasingly parted ways with conceptions and the practice of everyday perception. The quality of spiritual sight to be attained in the encounter of a subject both beholding and praying to a consecrated icon was found to be enhanced by the multisensory nature of the liturgy, by its distinctive order and its familiar rhythms of speech and chant; by the fact that it unfolded within a space filled with luminous colors, elaborate ornaments, and the awe-inspiring attire of the priests; and by the fact that the sensorium of the faithful was enveloped by the sound of ancient hymns already mentioned in the acts of Chalcedon and also in Maximus's *Mystagogy*, and still sung today, as well as by the ubiquitous smells of myrrh and

---

217. Symeon, quoted in Constas, 2014, 211.

218. Constas 2014, 210; see below, ch. 5, 452–78; and on symbol and its metaphysics of *analogia*, see the discussion of Dionysius and Maximus in ch. 7, 591–640.

frankincense visibly wafting through the nave and billowing up from behind the iconostasis.[219] Thus, for Maximus the "entrance [*eisodon*] of the people" through the narthex into the nave of the church symbolizes "the conversion [*epistrophēn*] of the unfaithful from faithlessness to faith and from sin and error to the recognition of God [*epignōsin theou*]." At the conclusion of the liturgy, "the closing of doors [effects] the passage and transfer of the soul in its disposition from this corruptible world to the intelligible world, whereby having closed its senses like doors it renders them cleansed of the idols of sin."[220] With Hebrews 10:19–20 commonly cited as a scriptural warrant for the iconostasis and, more generally, for the dual function of the visible icon as both veil and medium, "the icon screen and its veiled portal were symbolic expressions of the Christian belief that the invisible God had been revealed to the world through paradoxical concealment in a veil of flesh" (*katapetasmatos tout' estin tēs sarkos*).[221] Two millennia later, Pavel Florensky will echo this conception of the image as a "veil" summoning the beholder to a vision that both begins in and exceeds perception. "*Iconostasis is the saints themselves*" in that it mediates what cannot be seen "face-to-face," and it is precisely in kenotic, prayerful, and attentive beholding that the consummation of sight in spiritual vision as the true telos of human life will be experienced. Hence, too, the iconostasis "does not conceal from the believer . . . [but] on the contrary . . . points out to the half-blind the Mysteries of the altar." The icon is neither a case of sheer obfuscation nor of effortless substitution. It "does not, in itself, take the place of the living witnesses, existing *instead* of them; rather, it *points toward* them—a concentration of attention that is essential to the developing of spiritual sight."[222] The true metonym of an image concept that had gradu-

---

219. A scene late in Thomas Mann's *Death in Venice* foregrounds the sensuous aspect of the Byzantine liturgy, as von Aschenbach follows Tadzio's family into St. Mark's Cathedral in Venice, where he finds himself standing "on the jagged mosaic floor, among kneeling, murmuring people crossing themselves and the compact splendor of the Oriental-looking temple, [which] rested heavily on his senses [*lastete üppig auf seinen Sinnen*]. In the front, the ornate priest was singing and wielding his utensils, incense was in the air, encompassing the weak flames of the candles on the altar" (Mann 1995b, 44). Estranged from the austere piety of his native Lutheran northern Germany, von Aschenbach appears overwhelmed by the pungent sensuality and illegible symbolism of the Catholic mass celebrated in this sumptuous, Italo-Byzantine church. He is bewildered by the liturgical structure, yet also senses the emptiness of his literary fame, associated with a decadent fin-de-siècle aesthetic, as well as his own and his culture's accelerating exhaustion and impending catastrophe.

220. *MSW*, 198, 207. For a detailed description, see Holl 1923, 234, whose proposed date for the origins of the iconostasis pivots on initial descriptions of this dual "procession" around AD 574, it "being evident that the ceremony of the *eisodos* only makes sense if the sanctuary was completely closed off [from the nave] by a solid wall" (235).

221. Constas 2014, 203; while his discussion centers on St. Symeon of Thessaloniki's (d. 1429) theological elaboration of the iconostasis, Constas notes how Symeon's account "is deeply rooted in an ancient tradition of liturgical, mystagogical and theological commentaries," including especially Dionysius and Maximus (206).

222. Florensky 1996, 62–63.

ally and arduously been evolved in the Eastern Mediterranean over the course of half a millennium, the material-cum-theological reality of the iconostasis encompasses a knowledge that the model of linear, single-viewpoint perspective rising to prominence in the West around 1450 will either forget or outright disavow: namely, that by its very ontology, image (*eikōn*) cannot achieve, and should not aspire to, total visibility and transparency; that epistemic and perspectival dominion over, and ultimate depletion of, visible creation was never its aim. Rather, it aims to induce in the beholder a fusion of prayerful seeking and epistemic humility, of seeing-*in* and seeing-*beyond* whose eschatological implications now stand to be considered.

3

THE ESCHATOLOGICAL IMAGE
Augustine—Bonaventure—Julian of Norwich

Omnis mundi creatura
quasi liber et picture
nobis est in speculum:
nostrae vitae, nostrae mortis,
nostri status, nostrae sortis
fidele signaculum.

[All the world's creatures
As a book and a picture
Are to us as a mirror;
in it our life, our death,
our present condition and our passing
are faithfully signified.]
     —Alain de Lille

THE IMAGE BETWEEN TIME AND ETERNITY: ANAGOGY AND ESCHATOLOGY FROM AUGUSTINE TO BONAVENTURE

Eschatology, or, as it was known until the nineteenth century, the discourse treating of "last things" (*de novissimis*), not only encompasses many of theology's foundational concepts but also tends to reveal their lingering instability. As the focal point of the theological virtue of hope, Christian eschatology holds that everything created and sustained in its finite existence in historical time not only will not be annihilated and lost, but, instead, will be reconciled with God and, thus redeemed, will participate in his eternal life. Such at least seemed to be the promise of the Gospels, even as early Christians gradually came to realize that its fulfillment not only was impossible to predict, but quite possibly not even conceivable in ordinary temporal categories.[1] Hence, even as eschatological hope was altogether central to the idea of a Christian community, there always remained the possibility that such "hope would be hope for the wrong thing" and that the epistemic humility befitting Christians would reduce the theological virtues to a generic expectancy wherein "the faith and the love and the hope are all in the waiting."[2] Eschatological speech is not—at least not in the first instance—about who will be redeemed and how; rather, it concerns the question of how to conceive the relation between our existence in distended time and our hoped-for redemption. For any speculation about, or hope for, the redemption of all beings (*apokatastasis*) already presupposes some understanding of how time and eternity are (or are not) related. For a liberation theologian like Gustavo Gutiérrez, "the growth of God's dominion is accomplished as a process in history . . . and without historical initiatives of liberation God's dominion cannot be realized." Using more restrained terms, Jürgen Moltmann concurs, suggesting that the Anselmian view of God as the "wholly other" (*der ganz Andere*) *beyond* history ought to be reinterpreted as "the wholly altering" (*der ganz Ändernde*) presence *in* history. On this view, the eschaton is to be realized incrementally, by using finite and historically contingent subjects as its instrument insofar as these engage in a critical questioning of all those historical forces actively opposing God's "absolute future."[3]

Opposing this conception of the eschaton as immanent to historical time and (in Pelagian or semi-Pelagian fashion) advanced by finite human agents is a radically disjunctive view according to which historical time and divine eternity are entirely discontinuous. Exemplary of this position is the young Karl Barth who in his *Römerbrief* (1922) holds that eschatological speech can pronounce God's sovereignty and transcendence only vis-à-vis the creature's utter contingency and nullity. On his reasoning, "the end of which the New Testament speaks is no temporal event, no legendary 'destruction' of the world; it has nothing to do with any historical, 'telluric', or cosmic catastrophe."[4] In time, however, Barth realized that his reading of Romans

---

1. "If I go and prepare a place for you, I will come again, and receive you unto myself, that where I am, there ye may be also" (Jn 14:3); "Christ was once offered to bear the sins of many; and unto them that look for him shall he appear the second time without sin unto salvation" (Heb. 9:28); "So also is the resurrection of the dead. It is sown in corruption; it is raised in incorruption" (1 Cor 15:42); see also Matt. 25:46; Heb. 9:28; 1 Jn 2:28.

2. Eliot 2015, 1:189 ("East Coker," lines 24–26).

3. Quoted in "Eschatologie," in Kasper 1993–2001, 3:864.

4. Barth 1968, 500.

13:11 had overstated the case and "that with all this art and eloquence I missed the distinctive feature of the passage, the teleology which it ascribes to time as it moves towards a real end." Intent on dislodging "the optimism of the Neo-Protestant conception of time," he had compromised his own true objectives by affirming a "one-sided supra-temporal understanding of God."[5] Barth's self-critique helps delineate the two interconnected issues to be explored in this chapter: first, that eschatological speech cannot succeed when framed as wholly antithetical to time and history any more than when construed as fully contiguous with them; and second, that to approach the productions of time as imbued with teleological significance requires a distinctive kind of eschatological vision and, thus, a specific image concept that allows time-bound subjects and communities to intuit and transcend their historically contingent situation.

The objective of this chapter is to trace a tradition in philosophical theology and theological aesthetics that extends from Augustine via Bernard, Richard of St. Victor, and Bonaventure to Julian of Norwich. According to this tradition, eschatological reflection must neither negate nor overleap the temporal and perceptual constraints attendant on all human knowledge. Rather, it considers such finite and material constraints as the point of departure for an intellectual and spiritual progression that takes the finite human person to the very threshold of eternity precisely by acknowledging, and actively harnessing, the visible productions of time. Any telling of such a story must begin by reexamining Augustine's revolutionary conception of time, that "most complex enigma [aenigma]" (Conf. XI.22.28) of the human mind (mens).[6] For it is time that reveals to the finite being its internal division between "focus" (attentio) and "dispersal" (distentio), leaving it endlessly perplexed by phenomena incessantly rushing toward it from an as yet unreal future, only to vanish into a past where the reality of experience and, indeed, time itself once again appear obliterated. A first step in this chapter is to recall how Augustine's "ontological paradox" (Ricoeur) of time carries profound eschatological implications that, far from devolving into idle speculation about God, condition the very image human consciousness has of itself. Not only is Christianity's visual-cum-narrative imagination eschatologically constituted from late antiquity until the threshold of the Reformation, but a resurgent eschatological dynamic also informs a wide spectrum of secular-humanist, existentialist, and postliberal Christian voices, both Protestant and Catholic, as they sift the cultural and spiritual wasteland of pre– and post–World War I Europe.[7]

---

5. Barth 2004, 635.

6. Augustine 2001, 276 (*Confessions* XI.22.28; henceforth cited parenthetically as *Conf.*).

7. The classical account here is by Löwith (1957); for a critique of Löwith's conception of modern historical consciousness (e.g., in Burckhardt, Marx, Hegel, Comte, Vico et al.) as a secularization of Augustinian eschatology, see Blumenberg 1983, 27–52.

While we shall return to those developments later in this chapter, a number of steps have to be taken before then. To begin with, we must briefly retrace how, in Book XI of his *Confessions*, Augustine draws out the eschatological dimension nested within our *experience* of time, even as no conceptual framework of our own devising can ever fully account for the reality of that experience. A second step has us follow Augustine as he moves from the paradoxical phenomenology of "inner-time consciousness" (to recall Husserl's phrase) to reflections about death, dying, and last things, particularly in Book XIII of *De Civitate Dei*. It is at this point that we reach our third and final plateau of inquiry, which returns us to this book's central theme: namely, the relation between image and logos, between the intuitive, timeless certitude of vision and the hermeneutic sifting of its implications in the temporal medium of speech or writing. While that dynamic pervades this book as a whole, the more particular objective of this chapter is to trace the changing relation between eschatological vision and narrative forms seeking "to apprehend / The point of intersection of the timeless / With time."[8] And it is this link between visual cognition and eschatological expectation that we shall then consider in a number of figures, including Richard of St. Victor, St. Bonaventure, and Julian of Norwich, followed by some reflections on the destabilization of eschatological vision in Jan van Eyck and its final disintegration in Tolstoy and Thomas Mann.

Turning at last to Augustine, we find him opening his discussion with the first of many paradoxes that, it turns out, cannot be solved within the anthropocentric terms in which they are framed: "What, then, is time. As long as no one asks me, I know; but if someone asks me and I try to explain, I do not know." In confronting us with an excess of intuition over conception, of experience over ratiocination, certitude over certainty, time presents itself as an "ontological paradox [that] opposes language not only to the skeptical argument but to itself."[9] What is habitually used as a tool for measuring motion turns out to be distressingly unreal, a self-consuming heuristic fiction that, far from ensuring continuity of minds embedded in the world, seemingly unravels all our conceptions: "How, then, do these two times exist, past and future, when the past no longer exists and the future does not yet exist[,] . . . the result being that we cannot truly say time exists except because it tends toward non-existence?" (*Conf.* XI.14.17). Still, even as time appears forever unlocalizable and infinitely divisible, its phenomenology—its certitude *within* and *for* consciousness—proves incontrovertible and real: "And yet, O Lord, we do perceive intervals of time," and past and future "exist in some way in the soul" (*Conf.* XI.16.21, 20.26). While conceding that time defies our conceptual grasp, Augustine affirms the absolute certitude of how we experience time: "But this I do know: we generally premeditate our

---

8. Eliot 2015, 1:199 ("Dry Salvages," lines 17–19).
9. Ricoeur 1984, 7; for a detailed reading of Book XI, see Kennedy 2003, 167–84.

future actions, and that premeditation is present, whereas the action which we pre-meditate does not yet exist, being in the future" (*Conf.* XI.18.23).

What turns out to be ill-judged, then, is not our experience of time but our at-tempt to reduce its phenomenology to some antecedent conceptual scheme. Hence, Augustine rejects the Aristotelian, chronometric view propounded by "some learned man" (*Conf.* XI.23.29), which considers time subsidiary to physical movement, a strictly quantitative tool used to calculate the revolution of planets or predict the hour of sunset. This won't do, Augustine insists, noting that the question to be an-swered, after all, is not "'What is a day?' but 'What is time?'" (*Conf.* XI.23.30). Yet if Augustine rejects the cosmological approach and expressly states that "time is not physical motion" (*Conf.* XI.2.31), neither does he accept the Skeptics' psychologizing view of time as a case of wholly subjective experience. For however variable time may feel, its phenomenology, how it registers in and positively shapes consciousness, transcends all historical, cultural, and psychological contingency. If anything, Augus-tine's account hews close to Plato's speculative and elliptical characterization of time as "the moving image of eternity."[10] Yet even that is only a point of departure for what, in *Confessions* XI, becomes a phenomenological account of time on which, as Husserl was to remark in 1905, philosophy had not substantially improved during the next fifteen hundred years. In one fell swoop, that is, Augustine establishes what twentieth-century phenomenology (in its variously Platonizing, existentialist, and metaphysical inflections) will only be able to restate: time (*tempus*) circumscribes the totality of existence for finite, rational animals, including all their attempts at achieving orientation in the world. Our fundamental disposition vis-à-vis the world and our own existence is temporal through and through. Time itself undergirds this "disposition" (*Befindlichkeit*) and "attunement" (*Stimmung*), as Heidegger will term it, such that *how* it registers *in* consciousness circumscribes all knowledge and every imaginable mode of self-awareness. Time's ineffable flux thus mirrors the constitutive restlessness of "mind" (*mens*) itself, which in turn exhibits the strict convertibility of *esse* and *actus*. Mind is both the virtual locus of time and its sole phenomenological *Evidenz*: "It is in you, my mind, that I measure time" (*Conf.* XI.27.36).

Opting for an unusual Latin word, Augustine famously states that "time is noth-ing other than distension; but of what? I do not know; but it would be wondrous were it not of the spirit itself [mihi visum est nihil esse aliud tempus quam distentio-

---

10. Plato 1997, 1241 (*Timaeus* 37d). "Augustine's vision can less than ever be said to be inde-pendent of the polemic whose long history stretches from Plato's *Timaeus* and Aristotle's *Physics* to Plotinus's *Enneads* III.7" (Ricoeur 1984, 14). On Augustine's Platonic debt, see Wetzel 2013, 117–32. See also Augustine's discussion of Platonism in *De Civitate Dei*, VIII.4–9.

nem; sed cuius rei, nescio, et mirum, si non ipsius animi]" (*Conf.* XI.26.33). Forever remembering or anticipating, noting and extrapolating, preserving and desiring, mind is both defined and lacerated by time: "in the mind . . . there are three things: expectancy, attention, and memory [*expectat et attendit et meminit*]. What the mind expects passes through what it gives attention to into what it remembers. Who would deny that the future does not yet exist? But there is in the mind the expectancy of things future [quis igitur negat futura nondum esse? sed tamen iam est in animo expectatio futurorum]" (*Conf.* XI.28.37).

In all its mental doings—remembering and desiring, dreading and hoping, feeling and calculating, and so forth—mind bears witness to its temporal "distention" even as its intellectual acts (not to be confused with psychological "states") continually fend off the looming threat of its temporal dispersal. By its very nature, that is, consciousness "shares in [time's] extension, but at the same time pays constant attention, so that it can gather together what rushes past in the present."[11] Indeed, whether by embracing Augustine's eschatological conception of time or, alternatively, by pledging itself to an immanent explanatory scheme such as naturalism, nihilism, or existentialism, modern thought over the past three hundred years or so has unfolded in the shadow of Augustine's understanding of time as distention. For (pace Spinoza) there simply was no possibility of returning to Plotinus's atemporal monism. In fact, Plotinus himself had already wrestled with the incommensurability of Platonic "eternity" (*aiōn*) and Aristotelian "time" (*chronos*); and here the Plotinian understanding of time as "the existential distance between departure and return, but distance within the same continuum" appears to have won out over Aristotle's motional cosmology.[12]

Nevertheless, time in Plotinus remains for the most part notional or apparitional, a heuristic fiction devised to gauge the ontological distance between the numinous One and its dispersal into the ideality of mind and the many contingent states of soul. As such, Plotinian time lacks texture. Only with the rise of a Christian metaphysics grounded in scriptural exegesis and benefiting from the seemingly inexhaustible fecundity of the parables and narratives of the Gospels could the central question—"whence comes the distance between the eternal and the temporal, and what is its measure?"—be posed with the desirable specificity, vividness, and

---

11. Augustine invites us "to see the whole structure of extended time as something essentially *past*, and to distinguish the striving toward that which is in front and above . . . from a future which is in time [*zu unterscheiden von einer zeithaften Zukunft*]" (von Balthasar 1967, 7–8).

12. Balthasar 1967, 20–21. See Plotinus, *Ennead* III.7.7: "What understanding could there be of eternity if we were not in contact with it? . . . We too, then, must have a share in eternity. But how can we, when we are in time?"

intuitive urgency.[13] Only in a world conceived in terms of specific narratives rather than abstract speculation can human beings grasp their temporal condition in concrete, quasi-visual form. Hence, time cannot be conceived in Gnostic terms, that is, as an abyss ever yawning between creation and redemption, an ontological void that should never have been. Instead, Augustine's realization that time is integral to creation in ways that can be approximated only in narrative form constitutes a momentous intellectual advance that the many stories and the overarching plot of his *Confessions* stage with unrivaled brilliance. The ultimate instance of a narrative extracting spiritual meanings from onrushing time is, of course, found in the parables of Jesus, for whom "any attempt to seize eternity either by escaping time or halting its flow is totally foreign." Henceforth, both "the conversion of the individual [and] the wanderings of the *Civitas Dei* through the medium of transient time will . . . be historical."[14] Put differently, the ontological gap separating *exitus* and *reditus* manifests itself in the distinctive, highly variable textures of historical experience, it being understood that "experience" here is not something human beings merely undergo passively but that they also coauthor insofar as they refine their powers of attention and narration. At every moment, historical time *may* contribute to the longed-for perfection of the human *imago Dei*, its "divinization" (*theōsis*), though the obverse scenario of a progressive falling-away from God and into sin remains—more for Augustine than for Gregory of Nyssa or Athanasius—an ever-present possibility. Still, reflecting the influence of the patristic accounts of *theōsis*, as developed for example in Athanasius's *On the Incarnation*, Augustine affirms the dynamic, temporal nature of the image and its intended "stretching-forth" toward the eschaton.[15]

It is in this context that Augustine's insistence on the convertibility of mind and time, *attentio* and *distentio*, turns out to pay real dividends. For by attending to and working through its temporal condition in a dialectic of vision and narration, human existence gradually raises itself above the existential predicament of *distentio*. As von Balthasar puts it, "Man exists in a transcending extension beyond himself, not only toward some things and his environment, but toward the world, toward being in general."[16] While at first blush echoing Heidegger's notion of a "clearing" (*Lichtung*), von Balthasar's argument reaches diametrically opposed conclusions. Thus he emphasizes that human existence is not haplessly circumscribed by the horizon of temporality but, being constitutively *aware of* its temporal constitution, has, to an extent,

---

13. Balthasar 1967, 21.

14. Ibid., 25.

15. See Greer 2001, 133–60, who remarks specifically on Augustine's qualified acceptance of the "redeemer myth" according to which "the redeemed become 'as like God as possible, [a] likeness [that] involves both spiritual and moral conformity to God" (142).

16. Balthasar 1967, 219.

always already transcended the brute facticity of this existential condition.[17] As a dynamic act rather than an inert state, consciousness is *eo ipso* imbued with an eschatological dimension, an expectancy of how, without negating the predicament of temporality, it is never wholly circumscribed by it: "Where being is illuminated [*gelichtet*] . . . there is his humanity, and he becomes illuminated to himself as spirit." Echoing Augustine's ingenious exploration of speech as a temporal flux of phonetic and lexical markers giving rise to a "sense" that is itself unconstrained by time, von Balthasar concludes that

> this paradoxical unity of oneness and distance is the miracle of language. . . . Language, as the expression of the existent world and of man, can only live in the resonance of this dual motion. It must not harden into a crystallizing "image" or "symbol" halfway between heaven and earth, spirit and instinct, and, thus, attribute to itself a false divinity (to which especially literature is prone). Language must, in the animated descent of the concept into the example, of pallid generality into the individual case of flesh and blood, and in the rising out of the limitations of a single instance into the breadth of the universal, remain close to its origins. *In this movement it will cross again and again the point of image and symbol, but each time create it anew, enrich it, confirm it.* . . . This crosswise movement can proceed, in suggestion and without ultimate radicality, where matter and logos are seen in their contrariety, but are ultimately related to *the image center of language*, as in the myths and parables of ancient peoples.[18]

It bears noting that von Balthasar does not privilege word over image, let alone view them as an antinomy. Instead, each medium completes the other and safeguards it against the kind of excess to which both word and image remain constantly

---

17. For *Dasein* even to be aware of "being-in-the-world" requires some illumination that raises existence above its brute facticity, that is, a "disclosedness of being-in in *clearing* [*Lichtung*] of Dasein in which something like sight first becomes possible" (Heidegger 1996, 170 [§36]). In seeking to outline a strictly immanent conception of Dasein as "Being-in," Heidegger notably struggles to avoid transcendent commitments, in particular when drawing on " what is traditionally called the "*lumen naturale* in [the] human being, [which] . . . means nothing other than . . . that it is 'illuminated' [*erleuchtet*][,] . . . that it is cleared [*gelichtet*] in itself *as* being-in-the-world, not by another being, but in such a way that it is itself the *clearing* [*Lichtung*]" (133 [§28]). It bears recalling that Descartes, to whom Heidegger alludes here, unhesitatingly attributes this light to God: "The light of nature [*lumen naturae*] or faculty of knowledge which God gave us [*a Deo nobis datam*] can never encompass any object which is not true in so far as it is indeed encompassed by this faculty, that is, in so far as it is clearly and distinctly perceived" (Descartes 1677, 8 [*Principia Philosophiae* I, Art. 30]); see also *Meditations* III, where Descartes expressly concludes that God "cannot be a deceiver, since it is manifest *by the natural light* that all fraud and deception depend on some defect" (Descartes 2017, 41; emphasis mine).

18. Balthasar 1967, 219–20, 24; emphasis mine.

susceptible, that is, the "pallid generality" of abstract language and the "false divinity" of the image. Inasmuch as the word responds to an antecedent vision, it also fulfills the latter's import by striving to make explicit the deliverances of intuition. Conversely, to the extent that the visible exceeds quotidian perception and "refuses to let itself be looked at as an object," it enjoins the beholder to confront this excess in the medium of the *image*. Here the visible will be experienced as "a phenomenon in which intuition would give *more, indeed immeasurably more*, than intention would ever have intended or foreseen."[19] Put differently, the very being and reality of an image is bound up with its power of inducing in the beholder an expectation of its eventual fulfillment, an encryption of significant meanings to be consummated in the temporal order of narrative and discursive speech. Yet if the *logos* is to fulfill what is made manifest in the medium of the image, such speech must unfold in accordance with (not in opposition to) the original vision. Within the tradition of mystical and contemplative writing to be explored in this and the next chapter, word and image thus realize their full potential only when seen as complementary rather than locked in opposition.

Ultimately, it is a precondition of all narrative—if not for the characters depicted within it, then certainly for the reader responding to it—that the subject not only *attend* to its fragmented, temporal condition, but, up to a point, also *transcend* it. Indeed, the human propensity to tell stories about all manner of things, thereby giving "sense" to what would otherwise seem an inchoate welter of not-yet and no-longer, shows human reason and speech (*logos*) to be neither wholly circumscribed by the horizon of finite time nor capable of transcending it outright. Instead, speech unfolds in constant dialectical tension with the finitude from which it springs, yet which it continually seeks to infuse with a sense of significant direction and from which, qua narrative, it aims to discern its ultimate end. For Augustine, at least, this very "distention of the mind, by which we create narratives and discover meaning in our individual and collective lives, is evidence of the divine image in us."[20] Hence his categorical assurance, a rarity in a book otherwise filled with intellectual paradoxes, that "there is in the mind the expectancy of things future" (*Conf.* XI.28.37). Language, and narrative form in particular, is what imparts direction and "sense" to

---

19. Marion 2008, 43, 32.

20. Throughout his meditation on time, Augustine repeatedly "exemplifies the temptation of concluding that we make our own lives." In fact, the ordering and directing of temporal flux is not to be confused with modern, "constructivist" models of inquiry. Yet neither is the *cor inquietum* to be considered "a regrettable limitation." Rather, it is a constant "source of creativity . . . [that] drives us to make meaning and reveals our transcendence" (Kennedy 2003, 180, 181). Overall, Augustine's decision to incorporate philosophical reflections on memory and time into the genre of confession shows that, "speculation on time is an inconclusive rumination to which narrative activity alone can respond" (Ricoeur 1984, 6).

time. Noting how "the Indo-European root *sent* means 'to go in a certain direction,'" von Balthasar observes how "language establishes an intimate connection between sense, direction, and time."[21] For Augustine, narrative is the very essence of the spiritual life, at once a continual gauging of the distance separating "sinful time" from the "time of Grace" while also mining time's fluctuating and inchoate productions for their hidden eschatological potential. Like the image and its prototype, human (sinful) time and divine eternity are not antagonists in the way that Gnosticism had taken them to be. On the contrary, that these two "cities, . . . the earthly and the heavenly, . . . are in this world mixed together and, in a certain sense, entangled with one another" (*CD* XI.1) is itself part of God's ineffable creation. Were it otherwise, not only would all attempts at giving narrative "sense" to human time come to nothing, but faced with the futility of such efforts human existence would contract into displays of spasmodic and inarticulate groveling that, for a while, had made Beckett's and Ionescu's plays appear so riveting—until audiences concluded that repetitive demonstrations of the death of meaning seemed a poor substitute for the life that, even if not expressly honored as a gift, nevertheless demanded both faith in and commitment to the possibility of meaningful narrative.

For his part, Augustine can be as unsparing as the most committed Heideggerian when it comes to acknowledging the precariousness of human existence. Long before Heidegger was to pronounce time as Dasein's condition of total immanence and its confinement within time understood as sheer "extension" (*Erstreckung*), Augustine had summarily characterized "my life is a distention [*ecce distentio est vita mea*]."[22] Pressing the gloomy line of argument further, he muses that "if a man in whose body death is already at work should rather be called dying, and if no one can be living and dying simultaneously, I do not know when he is living . . . . [Every man] surely is in death from the very beginning of his existence in this body. . . . He is in life and death simultaneously—in life, that is, which he lives until it is entirely taken away, but in death also, which he dies as his life is being diminished."[23] Yet even as Augustine unequivocally links human (sinful) time to "the finiteness of creaturely being," frequently reminding his readers of the "immanence of death in every moment of corrupted time," this is only ever half the

---

21. He goes on to note how "the Germanic word *sinda* means 'journey' or 'way,'" from which the modern "send" (to get someone started on a voyage) also derives, itself etymologically connected to the Old High German *sinnan* (to strive, go, or journey); von Balthasar 1991, 49.

22. *Conf.* XI.29.39. For this post-Augustinian formulation of time as "stretching-along" (*Erstreckung*), now shorn of any transcendent point of reference, see Heidegger 1996, 338–40 (§71) and his exploration of "boredom" in *Fundamental Concepts of Metaphysics* (1929–30); for a discussion, see Pfau 2018b.

23. *CD* XIII.9–10. Augustine's formulations here will be echoed, almost verbatim, by Georg Simmel in his 1910 essay, "The Metaphysics of Death." See also below.

story.[24] For temporal finitude does not circumscribe existence in toto, just as consciousness never reduces to an inert "state" but by its very nature entails a "sense" of temporal direction, expectancy, and discernment.

Augustine develops this point toward the end of his *Literal Commentary on Genesis* (*De Genesi ad litteram* [AD 401–16]). There, in what seems like a prescient refutation of Hobbes's and Locke's mechanistic accounts of perception, he unfolds a tripartite distinction between corporeal, spiritual, and intellectual vision. In fact, he insists, strictly speaking there is no such thing as bodily vision. For vision always includes a moment of discernment—not just a seeing-*of* X but seeing it *as* Y. In order to pass from sheer apprehension of what is literally visible to recognizing it as a specific and potentially significant reality, some degree of hermeneutic skill is required. Indeed, "there can be no bodily vision without the spiritual," simply because "it is not the body that senses but the soul through the body, using it as a kind of messenger [*quo velut nuntio utitur*]" (*GL* XII.24.51). Augustine's distinction between three kinds of vision, "with the eyes, . . . with the human spirit, . . . and with the attention of the mind" (*GL* XII.6.15), ought to be taken in an integrative, not disjunctive, sense. Since what is corporeally seen, if it is to be recognized at all, must have been *seen as* something specific, all bodily sight has to be infused with a latent spiritual vision, a mental image of some kind. Physical sight presupposes some kind of intellectual vision, an essentially aniconic form of knowledge that "touches on things which do not have any images" (*GL* XII.6.15). Of Augustine's three kinds of vision, spiritual sight is the most immediately significant. For in conjuring up things not yet, or no longer, present to the bodily senses, such a *visio spiritualis* effectively fuses memory with anticipation; past experiences are either reconfirmed by the present state of insight or will be revised in light of an emergent, more compelling pattern that more fully integrates these experiences and allows them to reveal their deeper, previously untapped significance.

Augustine's conjunction of memory and image is deeply intriguing, if also full of elusive implications. For one thing, his account at times almost suggests that *mens* and *memoria* are coextensive. Yet in the case of *mens*, we are presented with a type of active, deliberative thinking, whereas memories often impose themselves, seemingly unbidden, as writers from Plato to Marcel Proust have noted time and again. Moreover, by its very nature memory involves a form of "recognition"—more on the order of Plato's *anamnēsis* than Aristotle's (tragic) *anagnōrisis*—which not merely revives an event in the medial form of images, but in so doing unveils, for the first time, that event's truth-value. Recognition is not so much repetition or reca-

---

24. Balthasar 1967, 28. "From the very beginning of our existence in this dying body, there is never a moment when death is not at work in us. For throughout the whole span of this life—if, indeed, it is to be called life—its mutability leads us towards death" (*CD* XIII.10).

pitulation of things past as it makes their import and significance fully known for the first time. Unlike tragic recognition, however, where the insight gained is too late and cannot stave off an impending catastrophe, Platonic/Augustinian recognition is generative and transformative. For a phenomenological description shows memory not to refer to the past but, rather, to irrupt into the present, which it both *in*forms and thereby *trans*forms, often subtly and sometimes momentously. Hence, where physical sight yields a mental image that, in turn, brings about recognition, what has been literally visible now is being fulfilled; only now its latent significance has revealed itself. Augustinian *visus* is never obvious but always unveils a truth experienced as disquieting, inspiring, or outright transformative, respectively. Thus, when Belshazzar "saw the fingers of a hand writing on a wall," the import of physical sight revealed itself only once the king "understood it to be a sign" (*GL* XII.11.23). With the full import of visible things revealed only in the medium of the *image*, sight (*visus*), and along with it the beholding subject, is transformed into a spiritual act (*visio*).

It is here that Augustine's conception of vision links up with his account of time. For the image's operative structure is intrinsically anagogical in that it intimates, though never realizes outright, the possibility of its semantic fulfillment. The Augustinian *imago* is only ever *medium* and *conduit* to an original revelation, not that revelation itself. Conversely, even as spiritual vision supersedes and fulfills bodily sensation, the knowledge that eventuates remains circumscribed by the medial nature of the image. Carefully parsing *ratio essendi* and *ratio cognoscendi*, Augustine notes that even though "the image of a body comes *after* the body, still nevertheless, because that which is last in time comes to be in that which is first in nature, the image of a body in the spirit outclasses the actual body as it is in itself."[25] At the same time, Augustine is careful not to construe the image as merely a derivative of bodily vision: "It is not the body that makes its own image in the spirit, but the spirit itself which makes it in itself with a wonderful swiftness . . . [and] without the slightest interval of time in the spirit of the person seeing [*in spiritu videntis nullius puncti temporalis interpositione formatur*]." A strong link thus emerges between spiritual sight and figural interpretation. For as soon as the deliverances of corporeal vision are *taken as* images suffused with as yet unrealized meanings, it becomes clear that spiritual sight is a form of hermeneutic activity. And while such hermeneutic practice necessarily unfolds in time, the meanings it yields intrinsically strive to overcome temporality. Not coincidentally, Augustine's account of spiritual vision draws

---

25. *GL* XII.16.33 (emphasis mine); "cum prior sit corpore spiritus, et *posterior* corporis imago quam corpus, tamen quia illud quod tempore posterius est, fit in eo quod natura prius est, praestantior sit imago corporis in spiritu, quam ipsum corpus in substantia sua" (*Patrologia Latina* [henceforth *PL*] 34:467).

on the prophetic Book of Daniel. Having "seen in spirit and not . . . understood" the image formed by his bodily sight ("the fingers of a hand writing on the wall"), Belshazzar knows that the image contains something he has not yet grasped, for "he still understood it to be a sign, it being the mind's task to tell him so [*jam tamen signum esse intelligebatur, id habens ex mentis officio*]." When summoned to assist the king with bridging the gap between the image and its fulfillment,

> Daniel came forward, and as his mind was enlightened by the spirit of prophecy he revealed to the anxious king what that sign portended. Thus it was he who was really the prophet by this kind of vision, . . . rather than the man who both saw with bodily vision the sign produced in a bodily way, and when it was finished still perceived its image in his spirit by thinking about it, and yet was able to do nothing with his intellect except know that it was a sign and inquire what it signified. (*GL* XII.11.23)

So far, so good. Yet the scenario becomes more complicated, since "excessive concentration" (*nimia cogitationis intentione*) may cause "images of bodily realities [to impress themselves] on the spirit as strongly as if the bodies themselves were being presented to the senses" (*GL* XII.12.25). In such cases of "what is more usually called ecstasy" (*tunc magis ecstasis dici solet*), the image presents itself as a (potentially significant) simulacrum of sensory awareness. Where this is the case, memory can no longer cross-reference the image with the deliverances of bodily sight. As a result, discerning the meaning of such an ecstatic vision and judging its import as either pernicious or benevolent becomes "extremely difficult" (*discretio sane difficillima est*). Acknowledging the vexed proximity of inspired vision to his (often lurid) dreams, Augustine understandably "refuses to identify the preternatural with the supernatural or to conflate even truthful predictions with the grace of God."[26]

Augustine's two stages of rapture (*raptus animae duplex*), of spiritual and intellectual vision, respectively, in which the soul is "rapt away to sights perceived by the spirit as being like bodies" (*GL* XII.26.53), point to an eschatological dimension undergirding visual experience. It is this temporal movement from image to writing, from visuality toward articulacy, that figures prominently—while also creating significant tensions of its own—in the works of Christian mystics from the eleventh through the late fourteenth century. Underlying the spiritual ideal of an *unio mystica* is a deep ambivalence regarding images and "corporeal" visions that Bernard of Clairvaux was to outline in his *Sermons on the Song of Songs*. Filled with expansive commentary, the eighty-six sermons abound with carefully wrought imagery. Ever attentive to the sensuous imagery of his biblical source text, Bernard is also alert to

---

26. Newman 2005, 7.

the dangers posed by "the inrushing flood of ideas and images belonging to this world, which are very difficult indeed to banish [quae difficilius amoventur, irruentia imaginum corporearum phantasmata]."[27] The specific challenge here involves drawing out the spiritual implications of the tropes and figures in the Song of Songs while safeguarding against (though not denying) the sensuous nature of the images in question. Thus, the mystical union that, on an allegorical reading, is either consummated between God and the Church, or Christ and the faithful, or (in the twelfth century) God and Mary, has the reader withdraw "from the remembrance of things present." Yet paradoxically, it is the same intensely eroticized imagery that, throughout the Song of Songs, furnishes the indispensable catalyst for the reader's spiritual progression toward an aniconic state wherein the faithful shall be "divested not only of desire for, but also of the haunting ideas and images of, things corporeal and inferior [ut praesentium memoria excedens, rerum se inferiorum corporearumque non modo cupiditatibus, sed et similitudinibus exuat]."[28]

Central to Bernard's mysticism is the dialectic whereby the very images that perennially tempt the beholder into an attachment to transient and "inferior" things also furnish the concrete trial situations allowing finite human being to recognize and conquer such idolatrous desire. It is in the guise of focused images that visible things perennially challenge the beholder to sift the sensation of sight as an occasion for reflection and potential conversion. Hence, even as the image's sensuous presence threatens to occlude its allegorical, spiritual dimension, it is to be received above all as a providential gift. By pointing, in anagogical fashion, toward "pure relations with those [i.e., the saints] in which is the image and likeness of purity," the image enjoins its beholders to reconcile their finite, affective condition with their spiritual longing. Meanwhile, those who in their commerce with images have prevailed over their "desires for things material" will at least have attained "human virtue," which, Bernard concedes, is all one can and should seek for in this world. For to have altogether transcended "the sphere of material forms and ideas is a privilege of angelic purity [corporum vero similitudinibus speculando *non* involvi, angelicae puritatis est]."[29]

Sermon XLI offers just one of many instances where Bernard considers a specific, sensual image in the Song of Songs. The passage at issue is Songs 1.10 ff. (Solomon: "Thy cheeks are comely with rows of jewels, thy neck with chains of gold." The Friends: "We will make thee borders of gold with studs of silver".) Bernard seems perhaps too eager to construe gold as "denot[ing] the splendor of Divinity, and the wisdom which is from above [Aurum divinitatis est fulgor, aurum sapientia quae desursum est]." In any event, such allegorical reading is no straightforward affair. For

---

27. Bernard of Clairvaux 1895, 142 (no. XXIII) / *PL* 183:893b–c.
28. Ibid., 316 (no. LII) / *PL* 183:1031c–d.
29. Ibid.

it won't suffice simply to *assert* what the image in question (supposedly) denotes. Bernard must also account for why the spiritual meaning at stake should have taken the specific form of *this* image. In addition, he will have to ensure that the image— visual or verbal—will support, but not supervene on, its primary signification. If allegory is to yield the spiritual meaning at issue without substituting itself for it, the image that brings such meaning into focus will ultimately have to surpass and suspend its purely visual character.

> It is this gold which the celestial workers, to whom that ministry is committed, promise to fashion into glittering signs (so to speak) of truth [*fulgentia quaedam quasi veritatis signacula spondent*], and to insert them into the inward ears of the soul [*internis animae auribus inserturos*]. That signifies, I believe, nothing else than to connect the similitudes of certain spiritual realities [*texere spirituales quasdam similitudines*], and to bring the purest intuitions of the Divine wisdom before the perception of the soul absorbed in contemplation, so that it may behold, at least darkly and as in a glass, what it is not yet equal to beholding face to face.[30]

For these "glittering signs" and "similitudes" to evoke the "spiritual realities" in question, it is vital that images be apprehended not as human contrivances but as tokens of divine grace and as legitimate "seals of truth" (*veritatis signacula*). Legitimating the image is its transcendent origin as a *gift* mediating a knowledge beyond itself and, consequently, standing ontologically apart from any matrix of efficient causation. "The gift depends only on itself to give *itself*," and the more fully it does so, the less it can be equated with "the object that conventionally represents it. In fact, the more the gift delivers a considerable, indeed immeasurable, largesse, the less it succeeds in becoming visible as an objective thing."[31] Fittingly, Bernard's commentary brackets the image's materiality in the catachrestic trope of the "inward ears of the soul," and he reinforces the point with the well-worn allusion to St. Paul (1 Cor 13:12). The deeper purpose of mediation—that is, of parsing truth into appearance-*of* and appearance-*as*—is "to temper the exceeding brilliance of a light too penetrating to be endured. Hence . . . there present themselves to our imagination images and figures of lower (that is, earthly) things [*adsunt imaginatoriae quaedam rerum inferiorum similitudines*], to which the truths revealed from above are accommodated."[32] For the image to mediate an inherently aniconic truth, it cannot simply substitute itself *for* that truth as a contingent production wrought by a finite human

---

30. Ibid., 257 (no. XLI) / *PL* 183:896a–b.
31. Marion 2002a, 102, 104.
32. Bernard 1895, 257.

intellect. Rather, the contiguity of image and message must be—and must be experienced as—something transcendently ordained. At once memorial and prefiguration, mediating God as both the source and the telos of all finite experience, scriptural imagery facilitates the passage beyond distended, human time toward envisioning the eschaton.

A generation after Bernard, in a *Commentary on Revelation* (*In Apocalypsim Joannis Libri Septem*), Richard of St. Victor (1110–73) inflects the Augustinian scheme of corporeal and spiritual vision in ways that reinforce the aniconic thrust of twelfth-century mysticism.[33] Situated on the ground floor of Richard's hierarchical edifice, corporeal vision initially is purely object centered and thus of "the lowest, uncertain . . . and narrow [*infima et infirma . . . angusta*]" kind. A superior mode of vision takes figurally things that are corporeally present, that is, discerns within visible being a "meaning of great mystical power [*et intus magna mysticae significationis virtus continetur*], such as the grace of the holy spirit received by way of a flame [*Quid accepimus per flammam, nisi Spiritus sancti gratiam*]."[34] Echoing Bernard's trope of "inward ears," Richard's appeal to the "eyes of the heart" (*oculis cordis*) reflects the deep-seated apophaticism at the heart of the Victorine School's concept of *visio*. No longer is spiritual meaning conceived in straightforward allegorical fashion, in which modality remains both premised on and categorically distinct from empirical sight. Instead, the world of visible things on which allegorical interpretation depends is now also taken as infused with anagogical meanings, as mediating God who is the transcendent reality toward which material sight and spiritual vision are ordered in (narrative) time.[35] Thus "the mind, illumined by the holy spirit, by formal resemblance of visible things, and by images presented as certain figures and signs, is led to knowledge of the invisible." Finally, Richard specifies the fourth and highest type of vision, one "no longer mediated by the figures of visible things [*nullis mediantibus rerum visibilium figuris*]." Invoking pseudo-Dionysius, Richard speaks of symbolic and anagogical vision as the "gathering of visible forms pointing to the invisible" and as "the ascent or elevation of the mind to the heavenly things to be contemplated [*ascension sive elevatio mentis ad superna contemplanda*]."[36] What had

---

33. Richard's "typology of vision . . . differs significantly from the Augustinian one. It is not triadic but dyadic in nature, distinguishing corporeal from spiritual vision" (Fraeters 2012, 181–82).

34. Richard of St. Victor 2012, 344–45.

35. An early instance of the image's anagogical function can be found in Origen's characterization of Christ (via Jn 14:9) as "the image by which we come to the knowledge of the Father" (Origen 1869, 24 [*De Principiis*, Bk. I, ch. 2]). See also Hilary of Poitiers, who in *De Trinitate* asks "whether God can be brought together in an image so that He is visible through the image of a limited form" (Thiessen 2004, 21), and Ephrem the Syrian, who speaks of beauty and the "natural mirror [of creation] as a foreshadowing of the Gospel" (22). On anagogical and eschatological interpretation, see de Lubac 2000b, II:179–226; Auerbach 2014 ("*Figura*").

36. Richard of St. Victor 2012, 344–45 / *PL* 196:686b–687a.

been formally distinguished as corporeal, spiritual, and intellectual vision in Augustine is here recast as a narrative sequence, with each of Richard's four types of vision anagogically ordered toward the one by which it is to be superseded.

Each instance of visualization amounts to both a concrete hermeneutic act and to an *imago* of meanings unwittingly aimed at, albeit as yet unconsummated by, exegetical practice; and the "highest form of spiritual vision is, according to Richard, anagogic in nature."[37] With epigrammatic concision, Alain of Lille (ca. 1128–1202) points out the complementarity of Richard's distinctions, noting how "every creature in the world is, for us, like a book and a picture and also a mirror [*quasi liber est pictura nobis est, et speculum*]."[38] If for the Victorine theologians "the visible world represents no more than the first stage in the mind's ascent to God," it nevertheless, "in a fundamental shift, . . . now represents an indispensable stepping-stone along the way."[39] Far from being merely one of several "senses" of scripture, anagogy encompasses the inherently narrative thrust of all theological speech. Ever aimed at a "lifting up of the mind" (*mentis sublevatio*), as Richard of St. Victor calls it, exegesis mines scriptural imagery and parables for their proleptic (figurative) and transformative potential. At every point, that is, the word (*verbum*) functions both as an instance of literal reference and as foreshadowing its figurative *sensus*. For the Victorine School and most theologians up until the late fifteenth century, these two senses are never mutually exclusive. Indeed, discerning the "meaning" (*sensus*) of scripture is never reducible to an act of cross-referencing the *verbum* at stake with already established, antecedent notions. Spiritual meaning is not something to be decoded but fulfilled, and its discernment begins by engaging the visible world as a cornucopia, not of things, but of goods capable of inspiring in their beholder a potentially transformative, eschatological vision. The exegetical practice that is the foundation of Victorine and, as we shall see, Franciscan theology thus unfolds as a progressive sifting of both visual and verbal forms, which are understood as essentially contiguous and as affirming in so many ways a divine covenant between what is made corporeally manifest and its ultimate redemption.[40]

VISUALIZING THE ESCHATON THROUGH AND BEYOND THE IMAGE: BONAVENTURE AND HIS MYSTICAL HEIRS

A century after Richard of St. Victor, this anagogical conception, for which Romans 1:20 often serves as the proof-text ("For the invisible things of him, from the creation

---

37. Fraeters 2012, 181.
38. Quoted in Hamburger 2012, 289.
39. Hamburger 2012, 288.
40. Richard of St. Victor, quoted in de Lubac 2000b, III:190.

of the world, are clearly seen, being understood by the things that are made"), finds its fullest expression in Bonaventure's *Itinerarium Mentis in Deum* (1259), a work that did much to shape late medieval concepts of visuality. Central to Bonaventure's theology is the image of the Man of Sorrows, Christ's tortured and crucified human body, a motif of fairly recent provenance signaling the growing divide between Eastern Orthodox portrayals and the emergent realism of Western, especially Northern European, religious painting after 1400. Christ's visible presence on panel painting, on ornamented crucifixes, and in the elevated Host during the celebration of the Eucharist attests to the metaphysics of *analogia*—linking the visible and the invisible—that undergirds Christian liturgical and sacramental practice. For Bonaventure, faith is modeled on Augustine's narrative of conversion and restitution (*reparatio*) of man—opaque, fallen, and disfigured by sin—to his original state as the *imago Dei*. The six stages of that progression, at times modeled on the six days of creation, raise human beings from their lowest state, wounded by sin, to where "they shall see his face: and his name shall be on their foreheads" (Rv 22:4). The narrative begins with reviving God's likeness in the soul by means of the infused virtues (*recreatio*) and then moves on to raising the disfigured soul (*rectificatio*), to purging it of spiritual and physical defects (*sanatio*), to ensuring (through the Holy Spirit) the soul's spiritual progress (*expeditio*), to raising it to its ultimate goal (*perfectio*). What is conceived as an overall movement of return (*reditus*) and spiritual ascent also informs Bonaventure's cosmology. At the pinnacle of a process of progressive "balancing" (*secundum conciliationem*) stands the "human body . . . disposed to receive the noblest form, the rational soul, . . . through which . . . every nature may be led back, as if in an intelligible circle to its beginning [*quasi ad modum circuli intelligibilis reducatur ad suum principium*], in which it is perfected and beatified."[41]

As will be the case in Julian of Norwich's *Vision of a Devout Woman*, the temporal subject of this spiritual narrative can never be, or consider herself, its author. Mystical vision is no merely subjective "state," nor can it be understood as a special case of individual, discretionary action. In fact, the finite, temporal being neither owns nor controls the mental vision (*visio*) that guides her spiritual ascent. Rather, it is sanctifying grace that has *in*formed all material remnants (*vestigia*) to begin with and now operates through the images formed of them. In Bonaventure's theology, the image furnishes the beholder with a mirror (*speculum*) needed to achieve contemplative self-recognition (*speculatio*), which in turn unfolds in three successive stages: as purgative self-examination, as illumination realized in prayer and

---

41. Bonaventure 2005, 70–71 (Lat. Quaracchi, V:221). As Arthur O. Lovejoy remarked, the underlying principle of the intrinsic connectedness of all things (*connexio rerum*), which is also (albeit more cautiously) affirmed by Aquinas, "tended . . . to soften, though . . . not overcome, the traditional sharp dualism of body and spirit" (1964, 80).

meditation, and as the ultimate or "perfective" phase of loving contemplation.[42] Notably, it was his celebrated vision (*visio*) on Mount Alverna that instantaneously (*statim*) revealed to Bonaventure (*visum est mihi*) the narrative sequence of "six levels of uplifting illuminations through which the soul is prepared, as it were by certain stages or steps, to pass over to peace through the ecstatic rapture [*ad pacem per ecstaticos excessus*] of Christian wisdom."[43] Clearly indebted to Augustine and pseudo-Dionysius, Bonaventure understands the soul to advance both by means of and beyond the "vestiges" (*vestigia*) of embodied creation, which "serve as a ladder by which we can ascend into God." It is by gathering and distilling the visible world into the medium of the image that the Augustinian "*peregrinus*, this resident alien from his homeland, can at least see the road to his true country."[44] For the person first embarking on this trajectory, the "whole world of sense-objects" thus becomes reconfigured as "a mirror [*tanquam speculum*] through which we may pass to God, the highest creative Artist [*opificem summum*]."[45] Bonaventure's "figural" (*tanquam*) characterization of "visible realities" as a vast "mirror" (*speculum*) accentuates the link between vision and speculation, the charismatic image and the narrative outlining its gradual fulfillment.

Yet even as within that temporal sequence sensory perception comes first, the material vestiges that are its focus must have already been transmuted into "mental representations" or "likenesses" (*similitudines*). For, as Bonaventure notes elsewhere, "no sense object can stimulate the cognitive faculty except by means of a similitude [*nisi mediante similitudine*] which proceeds from the object as a child proceeds from its parent." Such similitude, moreover, is not strictly dependent on the object being present to the senses. Reminiscent of Plato's conception of *anamnēsis* (*Meno* 81b–86d), Bonaventure insists that "the supreme Mind can be known by the inner senses of our mind, [because] from all eternity there has emanated a Similitude, an Image [*Imago*], and an Offspring."[46] As Hegel will also argue in the opening chapter of his *Phenomenology* (1807), all sense data must be apprehended *by* (and thus be *for*) con-

---

42. On Hugh of St. Victor's introduction, in his *Tractatus super invisibilia*, of "speculation" as a way of circumnavigating St. Paul's argument against image worship (esp. in Rom 1:20), see Hamburger 2012, 288–89; see also Hugh's discussion "Three Ways of Seeing," in Hugh of St. Victor 1962, 182–86 (cf. *PL* 175:6–18).

43. Bonaventure 2002, 37.

44. Greer 2001, 116.

45. Bonaventure 2002, 47, 53. Freedberg sees in Bonaventure's oeuvre "a widening of the anagogical view by making plain the equation between artistic production and divine production." Yet he also detects in the *Itinerarium* "the initial stages of the collapse of the strictly anagogical view" whereby the mind's encounter with real images is supplanted by an "instantaneous kind of ascent, such that images are not just traces of [God], *vestigia*, [but] *simulacra*—divinely given signs" (1989, 166).

46. Bonaventure 1996, 47.

sciousness—that is, must register "in the medium" (*in medio*) of perception, which takes a certain sensory being *as a known* entity. That sensation can register in consciousness only as a mental image confirms that material things as such cannot be invested with "a degree of perfection altogether superior to that which bodies in fact possess." Hence, there always remains an "aspect of things in which their character as vestiges does *not* appear. Far from being divine resemblances in a pure state, they are only the reflection of this resemblance projected on the matter which constitutes them."[47] Indeed, the very deficiency intrinsic to perceptible things also haunts the images we form of them. For insofar as "in the object all remains foreseen in advance," thus allowing it to register in consciousness merely as an "anticipated phenomenon, . . . the object remains a fallen [*déchu*] phenomenon, . . . as always already *expired* [échu]." In this sense, both the object and its image appear bereft of all anagogical power. "Nothing new can happen to it anymore," and at most it may detain, distract, or seduce its beholder.[48]

The impasse reaches deeper, however, in that, in the absence of some generative and dynamic vision, meaningful perception cannot truly occur. As we shall see when considering the antinomies of pictorial realism in Ruskin's *Modern Painters*, where an image conforms to "its" object without any residue or excess, neither will ever be properly seen. Augustine had already affirmed as much when noting that "no bodily vision can occur unless spiritual vision also occurs simultaneously," though as he hastens to point out, "they are not told apart except when the sense is withdrawn from the bodily object."[49] Hence, the mind's capacity to apprehend material things as bona fide *vestigia* of their divine origin pivots on reflectively grasping corporeal being as "real" only insofar as it has been *taken as* some particular, identifiable thing; and for that to happen, it must register in consciousness as an image at the very instant of "corporeal" sight. Echoing Augustine, Bonaventure notes that "if it is in the nature of all knowable things to generate a likeness of themselves, they clearly proclaim that in them as in mirrors we can see the eternal generation of the Word, the Image, and the Son eternally emanating from God the Father [. . . in illis tanquam in speculis videri potest aeterna generatio Verbi, Imaginis et Filii a Deo Patre aeternaliter emanantis]."[50] For Bonaventure as for Augustine, the image is never a simple duplicate of some mind-independent, material reality. On the contrary, it is by dint of its "likeness" (*similitudo*) to an ineffable form that an image enables mind to become aware of material being in the first place and to respond to it

---

47. Gilson 1965, 195–96.
48. Marion 2002b, 36.
49. *GL* 492 (XII.24.51); "Non potest itaque fieri visio corporalis, nisi etiam spiritualis simul fiat: sed non discernitur, nisi cum fuerit sensus ablatus a corpore" (*PL* 34:475).
50. Bonaventure 2002, 71.

as the manifestation of a reality beyond it rather than expire in banal visibility: "The creature is nothing if not some kind of presentation or sculpture of God's wisdom."[51] It is through its empirical commerce with embodied creation, rather than by gratuitously superimposing metaphysical notions on it, that mind discovers "creatures [to be] shadows, echoes, and pictures [*umbrae, resonantiae, et picturae*] of that first, most powerful, most wise, and most perfect Principle. . . . They are vestiges, images, and spectacles proposed to us for the contuition of God [*ad contuendum Deum*]."[52]

Simply put, for sensible things to be properly experienced at all, they must be apprehended as "resemblances" (*similitudines*), "copies" (*effigia*), and "signs" (*signa*) that visibly mediate the very source of their being. Yet such mediation is never an instantaneous occurrence but, instead, unfolds as a hermeneutic act in time. Incrementally, that is, the beholding mind learns to see itself as not only *perceiving* discrete things, but as being inwardly transformed by the way it learns to distill such things as bearers of significant meanings. It recognizes itself as the subject of an anagogical narrative in which "every copy is a sign of its exemplar; and the road is a sign of the goal to which it leads." Once it has been apprehended as "a sign of its exemplar" (*exemplatum exemplaris*), each sensible form thus has a dual status as the material correlate of conscious awareness and as an image revealing something not apparent per se and, in so doing, unveiling for consciousness its own supersensible destiny.[53] In laying bare the anagogical structure of human cognition, images for Bonaventure effectively compel the inference of an omnipotent divine (or First) cause. Far from distorting a purely notional truth, as Descartes will eventually argue, the realm of visible "appearance" (*Erscheinung*) serves as the indispensable conduit to that truth.

Bonaventure's *Itinerarum* here anticipates a key insight of modern phenomenology, namely, that speaking of "the appearance 'of something' thus precisely does *not* mean that something shows itself; rather, it means that something makes itself known which does not show itself. It makes itself known through something that does show itself."[54] Hence, we can never truly speak of "pure appearing [because] all

---

51. "Item est vestigium sapientiae Dei. Unde creatura non est nisi sicut quoddam simulacrum sapientiae Dei et quoddam sulptile" (Lat. Quaracci, V:386). As Gilson puts it, "A creature is the shadow of God by those of its properties which are related to Him without specification of the class of cause under which it is considered; the vestige is the property of a created being related to God as to its efficient, exemplary or final cause; the image lastly is every property of the creature which implies God not only as cause but as object" (1965, 192).

52. Bonaventure 2012, 77.

53. Ibid., 79.

54. "Appearing is a *not showing itself*. But this 'not' must by no means be confused with the privative not which determines the structure of semblance [*die Struktur des Scheins*]. What does *not* show itself, in the manner of what appears, can also never seem [*Was sich in der Weise nicht zeigt, wie das Erscheinende, kann auch nie scheinen*]" (Heidegger 1996, 26).

appearance [*Erscheinen*] involves a diaphanous moment [*Durchscheinen*]," as Emmanuel Alloa puts it, a moment of both relatedness and divergence between the domain of the visible and what it makes manifest.[55] This ontological difference at once ensures that the image will remain *distinct from*, without being *opposed to*, the invisible being *of* which it is a manifestation. As Plato had come to realize by the time he wrote the *Sophist*, "the image is *other*, without thereby being already *the other of* what has been depicted."[56] Otherness in this context does not denote the categorical incommensurability of the image and its object. Rather, it affirms the image's contiguity with real existent being precisely insofar as it presents such being in the *medium* of an image. As such, the image differs not just formally but ontologically from the myriad objects it can "make present" (*darstellen*).

Following a trajectory outlined long before by Augustine, chapters 3 and 4 of Bonaventure's *Itinerarium* chart the progression "by means of the visible toward the Invisible [*per visibilia ad invisibilia*]." *Visio* now shuttles back and forth between what is present to the senses and a transcendent reality that, though not visible per se, can be disclosed only *through* the visible. A corollary of this distinction is that between the eye of the flesh and that of reason (*oculo carnis* and *oculo rationis*); and inasmuch as the mind is able to discern significant meanings encrypted in the domain of material *vestigia* by learning to interpret *visibilia* as *signa*, it will learn to see itself as the subject of an anagogical narrative and its underlying eschatological framework. In each instance, the image not only manifests the being it depicts but also furnishes the "mirror" (*speculum*) needed for the beholder's eventual speculative self-recognition.[57] It is this inner transformation arising from the beholder's hermeneutic scrutiny of visible things that helps cultivate what, following Hugh of St. Victor, Bonaventure calls "the eye of contemplation" (*oculum contemplationis*). The archetype for this stage is undoubtedly found in Book IX of Augustine's *Confessions*, as the young bishop of Hippo and his mother, reconciled at last ("forgetful of the past"), jointly reflect on "what manner of eternal life awaited the saints." Leaving behind everything visible ("sun, moon, and stars"), they muse on the possibility of a "vision [that] were to enrapture and swallow up and hide the beholder in itself." It would be a state wherein "one's very soul were to fall silent, [and] . . . all dreams and revelatory images, all tongues and symbols, all that comes to be by passing away were to fall silent" (*Conf.* IX.10.25).

---

55. Alloa 2013, 12.

56. Ibid., 22. At stake is the distinction (not an opposition) between the image's indicative or referential orientation (Aristotle's *pros ti*) and its instantiation, qua appearance, of a domain immune to critical or verificationist epistemologies; see Alloa 2011b, 22–61. On the distinctive "mode of being" (*Seinsweise*) of the image, see Gadamer 2006, 130–52, esp. 133–34; see also ch. 2 above, 147–64.

57. Bonaventure 2012, 81.

Just so, Bonaventure envisions a type of contemplation wherein the material "vestiges" previously reconstituted as images and subsequently distilled into "signs" will be embraced as gifts manifesting their Creator and directing the beholder's eyes to "the things that are above them [*oculo contemplationis ea quae sunt supra se*]."[58] Ultimately, "the image that is our soul [*imago nostri mentis*]" finds itself to have been guided all along by the deliverances of its spiritual or "interior senses [*sensibus interioribus*], . . . [which] have been restored to see what is most beautiful, to hear what is most harmonious, to smell what is most fragrant."[59] The "reformation of the image" that is man turns out to depend, so Bonaventure argues, on the three theological virtues, which he correlates with the "three main parts of Scripture: the Mosaic law, . . . the prophetic revelation, and the teaching of the Gospel" and with the ascending hierarchy of "threefold spiritual meaning: 1) the tropological which purges for an upright life; 2) the allegorical which enlightens for clarity of understanding; and 3) the anagogical which leads to perfection through spiritual ecstasies." Undergirding Bonaventure's spiritual progression is the image in its anagogical function, bringing about by "intermediate steps . . . the contemplation of God within us as in the mirrors of created images."[60] In his Commentary on Peter Lombard's *Sentences*, Bonaventure describes this speculative vaulting of the mind into God as an *anagogicus excessus*, later restated in his *Breviloquium* (1257) as the movement whereby the mind, by a "a certain learned ignorance, . . . is carried beyond itself into darkness and ecstasy [verum etiam quaedam ignorantia docta supra se ipsum rapitur in caliginem et excessum]."[61] The transformative impact of vision on the beholder also emerges in the *Collations on the Ten Commandments*, where Bonaventure characterizes this ecstatic and contemplative state as "immediate and therefore superior to mediated vision" and as involving "man's suspension beyond himself."[62]

Several questions now arise, some of which relate to the early fifteenth-century disputes concerning the nature of mystical vision to be explored in chapter 4. Is "ecstatic and contemplative vision" part of a narrative movement still unfolding within ("distended") time? Or does such vision amount to an instantaneous (seemingly noncognitive) epiphany that overleaps the temporal realm altogether? To rephrase the question in a different key: Does Bonaventure's "ecstatic vision" amount to a case of anagogical knowledge? Or does the "uplifting" (*suspensio*) at issue imply that the subject has attained an eschatological vision that takes it altogether beyond the bounds of human time? To pose the question is to inquire into the metaphysical

---

58. Bonaventure 2005, 98 (Lat. Quaracchi, V:230).

59. Bonaventure 2002, 101.

60. Ibid., 105–7.

61. Quaracchi II, 546 (*Commentary* Bk. 2, dist. 23, art. 2, quest. 3). Bonaventure 2005, 196.

62. "Quia causa immediata nobilior est quam mediata. . . . Hoc antem videre non est nisi hominis supsensi ultra se in alta visione" (*Collationes* 13.10–11, in Lat. Quaracchi, V: 386).

grounds on which anagogical conceptions of image and vision rest. "True anagogy," de Lubac remarks, "is always eschatological" and, for that reason, cannot be reduced to a merely subjective aspiration or expectation.[63] Instead, anagogy posits that the myriad things encountered within the finite realm may be apprehended as visible tokens, *figurae*, of Christ's promise fulfilled. To see visible being as infused with anagogical meaning is not a matter of subjective wishing, aspiring, or expecting but to receive it in its objective givenness, as a gift. From Plato and Plotinus through Augustine, Dionysius, and Maximus and all the way to Bonaventure and Nicholas of Cusa, both intellectual and spiritual cognition share the same metaphysical foundation: namely, human intuition affirms that, simply in virtue of how it elicits and conforms "sight" (*visus*) to itself, visible being already anticipates its eventual consummation in some form of quasi-conceptual "insight" (*visio*). Properly to see is to find oneself responding to the anagogical potential slumbering in what gives itself to be seen. Always more than inert matter, Bonaventure's *visibilia* engage the mind of the beholder precisely insofar as they are structured, specific, and self-manifesting beings. Their specificity causes them to be *for* an observing consciousness rather than inertly languishing in its vicinity; and in so phenomenalizing or manifesting themselves *for* consciousness, effectively calling out *to* it, Bonaventure's *vestigia* are transfigured into images. That is, rather than being mindlessly gazed at, they will be properly seen as objectively embodying the meanings that the observer learns to discern in them. The meaning of Bonaventure's *signa* is not subjectively ascribed to, let alone arbitrarily imposed on, visible being but, instead, is unveiled and discerned as both a metaphysical reality and a divine gift.

Yet if in Bonaventure's theology it is the concrete image, rather than an abstract notion, that bridges the ontological chasm between finite, historical time and eternity, on what side of the ontological divide does this place the beholder? Again de Lubac offers a cautionary and valuable distinction, noting that even as anagogy implies eschatology, it remains firmly anchored within a finite and temporal economy of meaning.

> One ought to avoid confusing the passage of time to eternity, which is always at the horizon of Christian thought, with escape into the atemporal. To assign to history, as indeed one must, a term that no longer belongs to history is quite a different thing than to deny history, or at least its role, its value, its fruitfulness; it is just the opposite. No longer being "historical," the "heavenly" and "spiritual" things are, in relation to us who have to live in time, "future things." . . . "Mystic, dogmatic, and solid speech" . . . does not establish him who holds it or who hears

---

63. De Lubac 2000b, II:197.

it within the mysteries of the future age. It is one thing to theorize about the final ends, and quite another to be carried off in ecstasy.[64]

While it is grounded in eschatological certitude, and hence never fungible with ordinary representation, the anagogical sign neither negates the domain of history and referential speech nor simply abides within it. Instead, anagogical speech confronts mind with the "almost unbearable strain" of its medium, language, and with a "linguistic estrangement" that is properly constitutive of all theology.[65] As it wrestles with the incommensurability of finite discourse and eternal truth, the anagogical *sign*—neither a mere sign nor ever wholly freed from the sign's shadow—no longer answers to an epistemology of doubt and verification. Rather, in wedding the visible image and its numinous fulfillment, anagogical speech infuses in the reader/beholder what John Henry Newman calls "certitude" and what Merleau-Ponty eventually develops under the heading "perceptual faith."

For Merleau-Ponty, such certitude is the prerogative of the "visible, [which] can thus fill me and occupy me only because I who see it do not see it from the depths of nothingness, but from the midst of itself." Mapping an *itinerarium* not unlike that traced by Bonaventure, Merleau-Ponty insists that, against the injunctions of modern skeptical epistemologies, one "must suspend the faith in the world only so *as to see it*, only so as to read in it the route it has followed in becoming a world for us." Reflective thought "must seek in the world itself the secret of our perceptual bond with it. It must use words not according to their pre-established signification, but *in order to state* this pre-logical bond."[66] Likewise, anagogy in Bonaventure is premised on the possibility of an experience wherein temporal sight and transcendent vision are not antagonistic but complementary. The finite and the numinous are fused into a single image rather than languishing in a state of asynchrony and logical contradiction of the kind premised by classical Pyrrhonism and modern skepticism.

Nevertheless, the fact remains that any image capable of reconciling the two domains remains bound to a particular *medium*. Hence the images calling for anagogical interpretation can only intimate their eschatological fulfillment but cannot themselves accomplish it. By contrast, as the doctrine concerning ultimate matters, eschatology no longer refers to a final point *in* time but involves a decisive break with Augustinian "memory-time." In positing the resurrection and immortality of the soul as a matter of absolute "certitude," eschatological speech does not designate some apocalyptic end *of* time but, at least until the thirteenth century, is strictly focused on what lies *beyond* time. Concurrently, on the subjective side, the intention-

---

64. Ibid., II:186, 188.
65. Griffiths 2016, 16.
66. Merleau-Ponty 1968, 113, 38.

ality corresponding to the objective (metaphysical) reality of the eschaton is the virtue of hope; and even as that virtue is necessarily practiced by finite subjects caught up within distended, mundane time, what it envisions falls categorically outside the domain of desire and history.

Still, starting in the thirteenth century, a rather different theological conception frames the eschaton as the culmination of a process unfolding in historical time that foreshadows the political utopias that surface at the threshold of the seventeenth century and, more recently, have become established under the rubric "political theology." While the latter is not our concern here, it is important to demarcate the eschatological image from modernity's concept of a human-engineered, political utopia. First flourishing at a time when eschatology's hold on theological reflection and religious practice begins to look tenuous, political theology gradually begins to supplant the normative structure of metaphysical realism with a constantly shifting calculus of economic, social, and political practices. As Hans Blumenberg has argued, early modern culture found itself confronted with the "untranslatability" of New Testament eschatology "into any concept of history, however defined." It responded "not by explain[ing] away the delay" but by evolving speculative philosophies of history aimed at "demonstrat[ing] the trustworthiness of its God to an unbelieving surrounding world not by the fulfillment of His promises but by the postponement of this fulfillment." What Blumenberg calls "the energy of the eschatological 'state of emergency'" begins to fuel a process of theoretical curiosity that ends up "taking the edge off of the biblical testimony of expectation of the end with allegorical interpretations, transposing it into expansive long-term speculations." Such a "historicization of eschatology" in turn spawned a new concept of "worldliness" (*Weltlichkeit*) that could no longer be understood as an antonym of un- or otherworldliness. Rather, it announced the arrival of a new epoch, that of the "world-picture" (*Weltbild*), wherein "the world [is] released to itself from the grip of its negation, [and] abandoned to its self-assertion."[67]

In time, political theology will not only *envision* a future shorn of sin and suffering, but will claim that future as the subject of a narrative demonstration and material realization within the bounds of historical time. Transposing the eschaton into a definitive future state, utopian conceptions henceforth serve to legitimate, implement, and enforce all concrete policies meant to bring it about, often at a staggering human cost. In essence, all political theology is secularized eschatology, grounded in anthropomorphic assumptions about shaping the course of future time and ensuring

---

67. Blumenberg 1983, 43–46, evidently echoing Heidegger's 1936 essay "The Age of the World Picture." On the usurpation of Christian eschatology by modern political theologies, see Carl Schmitt's classic study, *Political Theology* (1922), and his *Roman Catholicism and Political Form* (1925); see also Löwith 1957 and Wolfe 2013b.

humanity's salvation. To that end, it had at least to equivocate on the role of divine grace, if not outright conflate its operation with the supposedly progressive course of history. While still bearing some formal resemblance to eschatology, the modern concept of utopia is no longer contingent on the theological virtues of hope and faith; and it is no accident that at the beginning of the seventeenth century, the question of grace was to emerge as the fulcrum of theological debate.[68] For by embracing a "decisionist" and autocratic ethos in the present and so asserting virtual dominion over all future historical time, political theology invariably "atrophies hope . . . [by] restating it in human, seemingly realist terms" and by supplanting both faith and politics with "deceptive surrogates."[69]

Rather than conceive death as mere annihilation and view the human person's descent into the *Sheol* as terminal and irreversible (as do Hobbes and his many existentialist heirs), Christian eschatology takes on faith that the human being's fragmented and disordered existence in this world—a sphere "of dereliction, isolation, loneliness, and thus abandonment to nothingness"—will be resolved in a realm beyond time.[70] From Origen until the threshold of the Reformation, theology (with very few exceptions) took it as a given that the *eschaton* could never be anticipated *in time*, let alone be predicted as a specific historical event. Following Luke's pronouncement that "the kingdom of God does not come with observation [*non venit regnum Dei cum observatione*]" (Lk 17:20), official church teaching consistently, and after 1260 categorically, rejected any Chiliastic (stadial) conception of history. The catalyst for this doctrinal clarification was the short-lived but conspicuous appeal of Joachim of Fiore (d. 1202), whose preaching had proposed the imminent completion of Christian, anagogical narrative. Effectively predicting that Christ's impending return would itself consummate and fulfill the direction of historical time to date, Joachim's views continued to divide the Franciscan order for decades after his death and remained a source of conflict within the order that was not resolved until, in 1257, John of Parma was replaced by Bonaventure as its new minister general. Beginning in the mid-1250s, eventually culminating in his late *Collationes in Hexaemeron* (1273), Bonaventure consistently pushes back against Joachim's chiliastic conception and unequivocally rejects the "the idea of a definitive, intra-historical fulfillment," affirming instead "the *im*possibility of an inner fulfillment of the world."[71]

---

68. Central here is the debate between the Port-Royal School (Saci, Nicole, Arnauld, Pascal) and the Jesuits; on the theological stakes of the debate, see Kolakowski 1995, 3–110; on its historical context, see Eire 2016, 660–90.

69. Ratzinger 1988, 59 (Ger. 2012, 85).

70. Ibid., 81–82 (Ger. 103–4); on Hobbes as the perhaps most paradigmatic instance of political theology, see Pfau 2013a, 185–213.

71. Ratzinger 1988, 213 (Ger. 215; emphasis mine); on Bonaventure's theology of history and his decisive rejection of Joachim, see especially Ratzinger's 1959 thesis (Ratzinger 2009, 559–90);

Yet even as they maintain that the eschaton per se falls altogether outside the order of time, theologians and contemplatives from the early Fathers through Bernard and Bonaventure to Julian and Nicholas of Cusa also insist that, obliquely, it already dwells with and among us. Within the temporal order of finite, human history, that is, the eschaton manifests itself in fragments, signs, and images—each of which, when apprehended as a "gift" (*donum*) opens up the possibility of epiphanic, intensely focused, extratemporal experience.[72] Each such instance is a figure of Christ, indisputably present, even as his meaning remains often unrecognized and never entirely fulfilled. To understand Christian eschatology is to experience the temporal "now" as something more than the merely formal line dividing past from future. Unexpectedly showing us the point "where we start from," as T. S. Eliot was to put it, the eschaton is latently present in experiential form, as the gift of meaning and love ("the unfamiliar name") offered to human life as it navigates the precarious sea of finite, distended time.[73] Eliot's repeated, careful placement of the adverb *now* throughout his *Four Quartets* recalls an analogous, though similarly perplexing, use of the word in the Gospel of John: "The hour is coming, and now is, when the dead shall hear the voice of the Son of God: and they that hear shall live [venit hora et nunc est quando mortui audient vocem Filii Dei et qui audierint vivent]" (Jn 5:25).[74] In his commentary on John, Aquinas flags "two strange occurrences [*duo mirabilia*]. One when [John] says that the dead will hear. The other, when he adds that it is through hearing that they will come to life again, as though hearing comes before life."[75] Yet if we understand the resurrection figuratively, as an "interior concept" (Aquinas), the passage begins to speak to us. Thus, John refers not only, literally, to the "now" of historical time presently inhabited by the human being *in statu praesentis vitae* but also, figuratively, to human existence *sub specie aeternitatis*, insofar as human existence becomes fully human and intelligible only when it has learned to see and examine

---

and Löwith 1957, 145–59. Already in St. Paul a chasm opens up between a view of the eschaton as *impending* within historical time and another view according to which its arrival can never be gauged in human, time-bound terms. The formation of the *ecclesia* and the gradual clarification of its principal tenets in theological reflection, starting in the second century and continuing to this day, naturally implies that the conception of an unfathomably distant eschaton ultimately prevailed.

72. As von Balthasar puts it, "Faith, hope, and charity pass through a fragmentary existence toward an as yet unfathomable completion. Hence they can only grow distrustful if their completeness is made known and offered to them in advance. For it is the fragmentary nature of man and world that attests to what is authentic. Just as a blind person will feel with expert hands for the sharp edges of shards, so the virtues are informed by the breaking points of existence as to the direction toward completion intended for them by God" (1963, 116; trans. mine).

73. Eliot 2015, 1:207 ("Little Gidding," line 9).

74. See Jn 5:25, 11:26, 16:17–18; Matt. 28:20; Lk 17:20 ff.; Acts 3:20 f.

75. Aquinas 2003, I:295. As von Balthasar notes, John's eschatology consistently emphasizes an understanding of the eschaton as always fully present, through Christ, in the present and, as such, furnishing us with concrete visions of the hoped-for consummation of distended, historical time.

itself in this way. And nowhere is that challenge more pronounced than in the dying person's struggle to redirect his vision away from finite, visible things and attachments and, instead, "to discern; to read, meditate, pray, contemplate, detach."[76] It is this shift from the anagogical to the eschatological image that now stands to be considered, with specific focus on how visuality informs the changing conception of dying in late medieval culture.

To begin with, let us take up two prominent figures, Julian of Norwich and Jan van Eyck, whose approach to contemplative writing and religious art, respectively, illustrates how at the threshold of the fifteenth century the image of the Man of Sorrows has become altogether central in preparing the dying person for her ultimate judgment. Against the backdrop of the plague, Northern European societies evolved new forms of lay piety that, while not competing with the Mass, let alone contesting the ecclesial and dogmatic foundations of religious culture, nevertheless supplemented it with more introspective forms of piety and also opened up more personal registers of expression. A key feature of this markedly inward conception of lay piety, often associated with the *devotio moderna* arising in Northern Europe during the fourteenth century, is an emphasis on the spiritual significance of suffering ("tribulation"). Even as the economic situation of a growing segment of the Northern European populace had notably improved in the aftermath of the plague—with grain prices falling and wages rising sharply in many regions—the memory of that cataclysmic event appeared to stand in eerie contrast to the superficially greater ease of late fourteenth-century life, particularly in the towns, where, by 1375, approximately one-fifth of the entire population resided.[77] It seemed as timely as ever for people to admonish themselves that "in the middle of life," however flourishing, "we are in death" (*in media vitae in morte sumus*).

First, though, it bears recalling the theological rationale for images (both mental and material) in liturgical and contemplative practice prior to the developments about to be considered. What had legitimated spiritual vision well into the late fourteenth century was not the image-object stored in the beholder's memory as a distinct and separate reality. Rather, the person encountering it, usually in an ecclesial space and liturgical context, tended to receive depictions of Christ's crucifixion and

---

76. Appleford 2014, 121.

77. On rising wages, declining prices of essentials, and improved dietary standards after 1375, see Dyer 2005, 128–39. Even as the economic aftermath of the plague showed "puzzling and contradictory trends[,] ... 'a time of economic decline ... and ... the golden age of the English peasantry,'" the structural realignment mainly favored the laboring classes: "The lords were weakened. Under pressure from the shortage of labour and tenants, and lower prices of the grain and wool on their estates, they abandoned direct management of agriculture, by leasing their demesnes. They also saw their jurisdictional power over peasants eroded, as serfdom withered away and private courts lost much power" (Dyer 2005, 8, 33).

eventual triumph anagogically, as prefigurations of her own hoped-for salvation. To behold such images was to be reminded of one's own status as *imago Dei*. Hence, the truth-value of the desired *imitatio* was not to be found within visible depiction itself but, instead, concerned the way that images might assist in their beholder's spiritual transformation or conversion. Rather than *represent* religious meanings, the depicted "image-object" (Husserl) sought to bring about a vision. We recall Marion's summary claim that "the icon does not result from a vision but provokes one. . . . [It] summons sight in letting the visible be saturated little by little with the invisible."[78] Functioning both as an objective correlative of inner vision and as mnemonic devices for keeping scriptural narrative present before the minds of the (mostly illiterate) faithful, images and the many sacred objects on which they are imprinted are infused with eschatological significance; they seek to mediate what, at least prior to the fifteenth century, is consistently envisioned as the faithful's longed-for ascent into an imageless realm. Yet even as the eschaton mediated by images continues to be understood as strictly aniconic, there is not only ample evidence that by "the twelfth century, images became more central to the practice of Latin Christianity," but that they were becoming increasingly wedded to particular material objects, "chalices and patens, Eucharistic doves and pyxes, croziers and combs, fans and censers," often adorned with narrative imagery and conspicuously on display during the celebration of the liturgy.[79] At the same time, the function of such images by and large still abides within the rationale that, long before, Gregory the Great had outlined in two widely quoted letters (AD 599) written to Serenus of Marseille, "Pictorial representation is made use of in Churches for this reason; that such as are ignorant of letters may at least read by looking at the walls for what they cannot read in books." Countermanding Serenus's indiscriminate destruction of images, Gregory had affirmed their supplemental value ("a picture is instead of reading") and, consequently, had enjoined the rogue bishop to instruct his congregation to view them rightly—namely, not by adoration as holy matter but as temporal conduits to their transcendent prototype: "For to adore a picture is one thing, but to learn through the story of a picture what is to be adored is another."[80]

While firmly opposed to Serenus's indiscriminate iconoclasm, Gregory's defense of religious imagery remained heavily qualified in at least two respects. First, by construing images as the "books of the illiterate" (*libri idiotarum*), he accepts visual matter only as a provisional expedient or substitute for essentially imageless,

---

78. Marion 1991, 17.

79. Lipton 2008, 256; see also Duffy 2005, 91–116.

80. Gregory the Great, *PNF* 13:23, 53 (Epistles, Bk. IX, no. 105; and Bk. XI, no. 13); on Gregory's letters to Serenus and to the recluse Secundinus, see Freedberg 1989, 162–64; and Besançon 2000, 149–51.

Figure 3.1. "Joseph and Potiphar's Wife," Vienna Genesis, sixth century. Vienna, Öster-reichische Nationalbibliothek, Cod. Theol. Grec. 31, fol. 16v

spiritual meanings that, ultimately, ought to be conveyed in the spoken or written word. From this follows the second point, namely, that in accordance with the Augustinian *ratio triplex* all religious imagery serves exclusively didactic, affective, or mnemonic purposes. In simplified form, the image conveys what the unlettered may otherwise fail to grasp; it is meant to help them cultivate the habit of empathetic vision and to revive the memory of biblical narrative that the illiterate could otherwise absorb only by hearing. Yet by the same token, the visible image remains fundamentally extraneous to the spiritual meanings it seeks to activate or reinforce; and here the affective and the mnemonic functions of images that Western Christianity had emphasized from late antiquity appear to be in growing tension with one another. In framing the image exclusively as the visible memorial of biblical narrative, Gregory posits that the depiction of an episode from scripture not only calls up a particular instant pictorialized, but the narrative in its virtual totality.

A case in point, roughly contemporaneous with Gregory the Great, would be the so-called Vienna Genesis, a Syriac illuminated manuscript containing portions of the Book of Genesis. The late Roman, naturalistic style employed throughout comes through in one of the best-preserved pages, featuring the story of Joseph and Potiphar's wife (Gn 37) (fig. 3.1). A twofold dynamic seems to be at work here, with scriptural narrative both sponsoring and, up to a point, consecrating the image that has been derived from it. Concurrently, that narrative's overall meaning is itself strengthened, indeed consummated, by the beholder's recognition of the particular "scene" or "moment" visualized, as well as its place within the narrative in question. Recognition of a visual motif and its metonymic embedding in sacred narrative thus cause *visus* and *memoria* to be fused into a phenomenologically distinct experience: "vision" (*visio*).[81]

Still, the ineffable capacity of images to conjure and focus complex narrative developments in a single instant already hints at their ontologically distinct and unique status. Well beyond recalling and elaborating an antecedent narrative, the visible image seeks to direct the beholder to the narrative's central meaning and, in so doing, appears imbued with a *presence* that temporally distended, narrative forms seem unable to achieve.[82] By impressing, and often overwhelming, the beholder with their affective charism, visualizations of scripture, particularly those dating from before the fifteenth century, far exceed the mnemonic function of mere retrieval sanctioned by the *ratio triplex*. Naturally, certain image motifs displayed that power more fully than others. Above all, the ubiquitous depictions of Christ on the cross and the orientation of liturgical action toward the Eucharist's commemoration of Christ's Passion tended to reinforce this association between visuality and dying. "Late medieval believers gazing on the Host," Duffy observes, "were often moved to reflect on the last moment when they would gaze on it, the hour of death. . . . It was believed that for those who did die suddenly, the mere sight of the Host that day would be accounted to them as housel. . . . Sight of the Host was thus linked instinctively with the solitary communion of the deathbed, and the lonely journey into the other world" that Christ's crucifixion and resurrection had everlastingly modeled for all Christians.[83] As we shall see, there is a quasi-liturgical quality to the way that dying in late medieval culture is being choreographed "around a threefold process of contrition, confession, and satisfaction," a process crucially centered on the dying person's visualization of the Man of Sorrows. Similarly, during Mass, the Liturgy of the Word "was immediately followed by the Veneration of the Cross, in which a crucifix with a veil draped over it was carried into the middle of the choir and dramatically unveiled as the priests sang *Ecce lignum crucis*."[84] This markedly visual character of sacramental and liturgical practice, unwaveringly focused on Christ's Passion, also

---

81. Belting's claim that "images contain moments from a narrative, although they themselves are not narratives," and that images are "comprehensible only through being recognized from the Scriptures" (1994, 10) seems excessively formalist. It loses sight of the phenomenology of memory, of how the act of remembering telescopes discrete moments in a temporally distended narrative into an affectively charged *presence*.

82. On images building on the passion narrative and miracle wrought by Christ, see Freedberg 1989, 168–75.

83. Duffy 2005, 120.

84. Lipton 2005, 1198.

informs the increasingly popular genre of small-sized religious paintings in the late fourteenth century, as well as the woodcuts that, a few decades later, will be featured in spiritual guidebooks for the dying. Overall, the surge of religious imagery both within ecclesial spaces and outside aimed to ensure the right kind of spiritual vision of those approaching the ultimate threshold and, thus, to "reduce time spent in purgatory."[85]

More than mastering the threshold of death itself, however, what mattered was preparing for it by constant, scrupulous self-examination in anticipation of the moment when one's soul was to find itself "face to face with God, stripped of all masks and disguises. . . . A person was to dispel self-delusion in the face of death," and integral to that quest was cultivating an accurate spiritual vision.[86] The source texts on which the late medieval Devout, either members of lay communities or tertiaries ("Brothers and Sister of Penance"), habitually drew as part of that effort tended to be the same: Augustine, Dionysius, Bernard of Clairvaux, and (to a lesser extent) Bonaventure. Yet whereas in all these writers the word *image* usually denotes a spiritual vision achieved in the form of *mental* imagery, starting around the middle of the fourteenth century the situation was to become more complicated. For at that point, contemplative practice and spiritual self-examination, both in everyday religious life and in extremis, tend to involve focused interaction with images and sacred artifacts in ways no longer constrained by the aniconicism of eleventh- and twelfth-century mystics like Meister Eckhart and Bernard. Jeffrey Hamburger speaks of a "discrepancy between the strict standards of 'imageless devotion' established in theoretical texts of the twelfth century . . . and late medieval practice," in which material images, often the private property of the more affluent faithful, increasingly shape religious practice as a subjective, inward experience.[87] Similarly, in her study of late medieval spiritual guidance books for the dying, Amy Appleford shows how these lay texts are "suggestive of a broader shift . . . toward a more interiorized, whether individual or small group, understanding of the ars moriendi."[88]

While such "growth of individualism" exemplified by "intense devotion to the Blessed Sacrament" can indeed be observed, both Eamon Duffy and John Van Engen have rightly cautioned against letting this shift obscure the abiding "unitive and cor-

---

85. Appleford 2014, 103, 122. As the author of *The Twelve Profits of Tribulation*, a thirteenth-century Latin treatise (*De duodecim utilitatibus tribulationibus*) preserved in six fifteenth-century translations, remarks, "Tribulacion is well necessary to the herte to make hym turne unto hym-self, & constreineth hym to seye with the prophet: *Reuertere reuertere*, . . . [Songs 6:13]" (quoted in Appleford 2014, 119).

86. Van Engen 2008, 296.

87. Hamburger 1998, 114.

88. Appleford 2014, 128.

porative dimension" of late medieval sacramental practice.[89] What seems clear, however, is that after 1350 the relationship between the narrative telos of medieval Christianity—the *visio beatifica* altogether central to Hugh and Richard of St. Victor, Bernard, and Bonaventure—and the image wherein that eschaton is rendered darkly visible has significantly changed. Prior to the late fourteenth century, there seemed to be no confusion as to what was taking place when the priest elevated the Host high above his head while repeating the words of institution: *Hoc est enim corpus meum*; and for the most part, Dominicans and Franciscans held to Aquinas's Aristotelian explanation that in the Eucharist the (invisible) substance is Christ and that the bread and wine are its (visible) accidents, which, for the duration of the sacramental action, "continue in this sacrament without a subject." Hence, in communion, "Christ's body is not received by being seen, but only its sacrament, because sight does not penetrate to the substance of Christ's body, but only to the sacramental species. . . . But he who eats, receives not only the sacramental species, but likewise Christ Himself Who is under them."[90] On Aquinas's account, which was to remain the lodestar for the doctrine of the Eucharist, "seeing" the Host is categorically distinct from "perceiving" the elevated bread and wine. For the faithful "see[] neither the unseeable substance nor the seeable accidents but an appearance substituted by God for the accidents in order to indicate the unseeable substance beneath."[91] Even so, Christ's own words (Lk 22:19) were bound to remain as intuitively perplexing to those attending Mass in the fourteenth century as (presumably) they had been to his disciples. How, that is, were the faithful to reconcile his "real presence" in the Eucharist, affirmed by the words of *institution*, with the fact that the raised Host was intuitively experienced as the visible image of Christ's body, that is, as a case of *substitution*?

---

89. Duffy 2005, 92. Duffy emphasizes the corporative and ecclesial ways in which religion was practiced (121–23, 131–54); likewise, Van Engen stresses "the institutional dimensions of community-building" and cautions against the hermeneutic prejudice built into the antinomy of "charisma and institution." In the study of late-medieval culture, the result is a "hidden or not-so-hidden narrative of cycles whereby institutions move from spirit to establishment to decline" (2008, 12–21). By contrast, Belting's contention that "mysticism was to bring about a private form of religion" and that "private salvation" [*sic*!] was the true subject matter of fifteenth-century religious painting and sculpture (1994, 411, 418) seems to overlook the mystics' enduring affiliation with and, in the case of anchoritic life, their spatial attachment to the church and the liturgy.

90. Aquinas, *ST* III.67–71, III.80–84 (quote from III.80 ad 4).

91. Bynum 2005, 213–14. It bears noting that Bynum's formulation echoes, almost verbatim, Heidegger's definition of the phenomenon, which "precisely does *not* mean that something shows itself" but, on the contrary, "means that something makes itself known which does not show itself. It makes itself known through something that does show itself. Appearing is a *not showing itself*. But this 'not' must by no means be confused with the privative 'not' which determines the structure of semblance. What does *not* show itself, in the manner of what appears, can also never seem" (1996, 26 [§7]).

As remains to be seen, during the fifty or so years separating Julian of Norwich's utterly committed deathbed vision of the crucified Christ from the tenuous gaze of van Eyck's Canon van der Paele, the relationship between divine reality and its image shifts from one of (spiritual) mediation to one of (epistemological) competition. The same change also registers as an increasingly literal understanding of eucharistic presence during the same period. Thus, "the perception of images underwent change once Christ's body in the present was invested, by the sacrament [of the Eucharist], with real presence. The Eucharist's advantage over the images as regards reality [*Realität*] was compensated for by the realism [*Realismus*] of the latter."[92] Still, within the tradition of mystical and contemplative writing to which we now turn, the pivotal moment of transubstantiation that, more than anything else, fused seeing and believing, the visible and the numinous, was not yet being doubted or openly mocked—as in some notorious cases the English Lollards had done. Indeed, "Lollardy was only possible because the appearance of bread in the Host cloaked the divine reality which was the true source of blessing. The Host did not look like the thing it was."[93]

For the most part, however, the pre-Tridentine Mass with its distinctive cadences, sounds, scents, and visual epiphanies remained uncontested well into the fifteenth century and, across Europe and England, allowed the faithful to assent to God's numinous reality by visible, symbolic means.[94] Above all, it is in the Eucharist that the polarity of *sacramentum* and *mysterium* is made visible. Changes to the liturgy, including the priest's turning his back to the laity while facing the altar during the Eucharist, implicitly associated the raised Host with the paneled paintings and "carved reliefs erected behind the altar (retables)," which the Synod of Trier (1310) had ordained to be placed behind or above every altar (fig. 3.2).[95] Whereas "*mysterium* mainly evokes the idea of depth and obscurity, it nearly always also evokes at the same time that of 'type' or 'symbol'; and as for *sacramentum*, that word hides as much as it reveals of the thing that it signifies[:] . . . 'it prefigures secretly', 'it

---

92. Belting 2006, 91; trans. mine.

93. Duffy 2005, 102, 110–12. On the theological underpinnings of the Eucharist, the *Corpus Mysticum*, that Duffy shows to have been the fulcrum of late -medieval piety, see de Lubac's eponymous study (2006, esp. 37–74).

94. Only in the later fourteenth century, a group of paintings appear depicting the so-called Gregory Mass, referring to how the Man of Sorrows had supposedly manifested himself to Pope Gregory the Great, who, while saying Mass, had prayed for a visible sign to convince those doubting the real presence of Christ in the Eucharist. Paintings depicting the Mass of St. Gregory, the legend of which had been widely disseminated in Jacobus de Voragine's mid-thirteenth-century compilation, the *Legenda Aurea*, surface mainly in the early sixteenth century, at which point the doctrine of transubstantiation has come under growing theological pressure; for a detailed discussion, see Bynum 2005.

95. Lipton 2008, 270.

Figure 3.2. Despenser retable, Norwich Cathedral, ca. 1382

prefigures mystically."[96] Aquinas thus characterizes the sacraments as "signs foretelling future glory [*signa prognostica futurae gloriae*]."[97] That the visible, sacramental sign could instantiate a dynamic of revelation and concealment without those terms hardening into an antinomy, and that Bonaventure's well-worn Pauline (Rom 1:20) formula *per visibilia ad invisibilia* could be taken as an action that "anticipates: *presigns, pre-figures, pre-demonstrates*," has much to do with the fact that prior to the fifteenth century *imago* and *visio* tended to be mainly conceived in inward, mentalistic terms.[98] No wedge had as yet been driven between the visible image and the spiritual contents it mediated.

A representative case is that of the thirteenth-century female mystic, Gertrude von Helfta (1256–1302), a reformed Benedictine nun whose writings appear strongly influenced by those of Bernard of Clairvaux. Many of the rhetorical features and theological concerns dominating in late fourteenth-century contemplative writing seem already in place in Gertrude's *Herald of Divine Love*, such as her longed-for fusion of Christ's tribulation on the cross with her own: "inscribe with your precious blood, most merciful Lord, your wounds on my heart, that I may read in them both your sufferings and your love." What initially seems but an expression of spiritual desire soon evolves into an imaginative vision experienced when, "during the middle of

---

96. De Lubac 2006, 47–48 (quoting Augustine and Rupert of Deutz). "Mystery is essentially an action. . . . It focuses less on the apparent sign, or rather the hidden reality, than on both at the same time: on their mutual relationship, union and implications" (51).

97. Aquinas, *ST* III.60.3.

98. The visible Host "is not simply oriented towards the past, dependent on Calvary. It is also oriented towards a future, which in turn depends on it. . . . [I]t has a double symbolism. It is a sacrament of memory but also a sacrament of hope" (de Lubac 2006, 66).

Lent, I was once more lying sick in bed. . . . The Lord . . . showed me, issuing from his left side as though from the innermost depths of his blessed heart, a stream of flowing water as pure as crystal and as solid. It proceeded to cover his adorable breast like a jewel. I saw that it was transparent, colored in hues of gold and rose, alternating in various ways." At times, the particularity of such visions prompts heretical inclinations, such as when, chastised by a vision of Christ ("I saw you opening with both hands the wound of your deified heart"), Gertrude finds herself commanded "(perverse like the Jews asking for a sign [Matt. 12:38]) to stretch forth my right hand. Then, contracting the aperture of the wound in which my hand was enclosed, you said: 'See, I promise to keep intact the gifts which I have given you.'"[99]

A pattern of concealment and disclosure seems to be unfolding as Gertrude, prompted by her spiritual visions, alternately imagines or seeks to touch the material image corresponding to these visions. As in Julian of Norwich's early *Vision of a Devout Woman*, it is specifically with the crucifix that the boundaries between spiritual vision and image-object appear blurred. Thus, when "holding a crucifix in her hand with devout attention," most likely featuring Christ's body in painted or sculpted form, the "delectable image" prompts both rapture and unease. On the one hand, it works on the beholder "like a burnished mirror," such that "one cannot look at a crucifix without being touched by God's grace." Yet this visceral power makes Gertrude "anxious to acquire an image of the holy cross," a desire from which she "refrained [only] for conscience's sake, because she feared that such an occupation might hinder her enjoyment of the interior gifts of God." A gravitational pull seems to emanate from the symbol of the faith, exposing "a person [to] take pleasure in the mere possession of a crucifix" and investing it with magical, talismanic powers. Yet in that case, the beholder will succumb to her "natural inclinations rather than striving to imitate the example of [the Lord's] passion."[100] Hence, if Gertrude's writings root "mystical phenomena in sensory experience and, more specifically, in images," such a fusion of religious culture "with a universal epistemology" risks draining visionary experience of its epiphanic uniqueness by "level[ing] distinctions between mystical, visionary, and visual experience."[101]

The desire to emulate Christ's life and passion required a constant balancing of spiritual vision and material visualization, of Christ's *imago* as the eschaton and its concrete depiction in the form of an image; and here, no less than in modern culture, the visual medium appears imbued with an agency of its own, thus threatening to

---

99. Gertrude 1993, 100, 107–8, 124–25.

100. Ibid., 210, 212–13. While reading Gertrude largely in sync with the Victorine School and the theology of Bonaventure, Hamburger (2000, 59) notes that in "Gertrude's visionary piety, however, *visibilia* have come to a far more predominant role."

101. Hamburger 2000, 60.

usurp the message. As Caroline Bynum has shown, Christianity had long featured images embossed on any variety of liturgical objects, as well as a wide array of relics and objects, a type of "holy matter" calculated to induce in the beholder a spiritual longing structurally cognate with prayer and, thus, exceeding the representational content of the particular image in question.[102] Woven into the timeless rhythms of the liturgy was a vast array of material objects: crucifixes, croziers, reliquaries, embossed covers of gospels and prayer books found in local churches, sumptuously ornamented shrines, polychrome sculptures incorporated into stone columns, elaborately wood-carved church doors, the prismatic marvel of stained-glass windows at matins and vespers, and a profusion of stone-carved capitals and ceiling frescoes adorning the great cathedrals. Absorbing the beholder in a veritable torrent of images featuring a familiar array of scriptural scenes and Christian motifs, they all served to arrest and absorb the gaze and spiritual attention of the faithful, and to induce in the celebrants of the Mass, or those arriving for quiet prayer, a state of "trance" (*excessus mentis*) not unlike the dream visions found in the prophetic books of the Old Testament.[103] Indeed, until the late fourteenth century, it appeared that material objects could serve as "image-carriers" (Husserl's *Bildträger*) without causing idolatrous confusion. Prior to the fifteenth century, that is, the words of admonition found on the wall of St. Mark's in Venice—"the image teaches God, but it is not itself God"—by and large express a shared understanding rather than a contested proposition.[104] Thus, the authority conceded to religious images was not thought to require independent verification of what they depict. Rather, their purpose was to instill in congregants a mental habit of focused and attentive (if affectively charged) vision, thereby enabling them to respond to the grace revealed *in* and *through* the "living" image itself.[105]

Still, a profusion of material images, either painted on wood panels or featured in increasingly lavish illuminated manuscripts of scripture or in the newly popular genre of the Book of Hours, seemed to vacillate uneasily between reinforcing the modern Devout's sought-after spiritual vision and materially interfering with it. On the one hand, the followers of the *devotio moderna* set up their way of life in an age when visual images enlivened the walls of churches, chapels, and shrines. Sacred paintings and sculptures were now becoming widely obtainable in commercial

---

102. Bynum 2011, esp. 125 ff.

103. On the affinity between pagan conceptions of dream visions (esp. those of Macrobius and Calcidius), Augustine's *visio intellectualis*, and the mystical *ekstasis* of medieval Christianity, see Newman 2005, 7–11.

104. Quoted in Lipton 2008, 259.

105. See Kartsonis 1998; and, on "images which come alive [and] are taken to be further instances of the kind of miraculous event that supports the verity of the Christian Faith" (Freedberg 1989, 299), see also Bredekamp 2010, 101–69.

markets, at the high end or low, not only for side altars, but an individual's private chambers. Devotion and the visual became so interlinked that the practice of devotion could hardly be imagined without the assistance of images designed to inspire and focus it. Yet this growing relationship between spiritual vision and material images also prompted concern that the practice of "image-less meditation, the goal for some earlier and contemporary mystical writers," was being undermined by a profusion of religious paintings and other commissioned artifacts and that their status as private property should become a substitute of sorts for the spiritual conversion identified as the true goal of lay piety.[106] Among the most prominent voices of the thousands who in the second half of the fourteenth century had embraced the "common life" in the Low Countries, the movement's founder, Geert Grote of Deventer (1340–84), took up precisely this issue.

Well educated and enjoying prospects of a successful clerical career, Grote at age thirty-five underwent a sharp spiritual conversion of exactly the kind longed for by adherents of the *devotio moderna*. Following several years of meditation and study at a Carthusian monastery and, by 1380, ordained as a deacon, Grote obtained a special license to preach and, to the growing dismay of the beneficed clergy at Utrecht (whose morals he regularly attacked in his sermons), developed a considerable following in that region. Around 1383, shortly before his death from the plague and at just about the same time as Julian of Norwich embarked on narrating her near-death experience in *A Vision of a Devout Woman*, Grote composed his "Sermon on Four Classes of Subjects Suitable for Meditation." Relevant to our purposes is specifically the fourth class of subjects, comprising "imagined and fictive things, received . . . as aids to our childishness, because our feeble imaginations are thereby helped." Echoing Gregory the Great, Grote initially frames images as mnemonic aids pure and simple. Within the spiritual life, what legitimates an image is not pictorial verisimilitude. On the contrary, images should formally differ from what they "serve to recall mentally for a moment, lest we become deceived in our actual sight by some image." Already lurking in the background is Grote's lingering suspicion that, due to its distinct ontology, an image may never be restricted to a purely supplemental function. Hence, even as he urges that "images should be taken for nothing other than signs and directed toward the signification of past events," Grote finds them infused with an ineffable charism that exceeds their official, subsidiary relation vis-à-vis scripture. Were it not for this presence, invariably marked by an element of excess, there would be no reason to suppose that images could allow "the past [to] be represented to and *more forcefully* impressed upon the present." By its very nature, an image infuses

---

106. Van Engen 2008, 300. "The intent [of the Devout] was not to immerse themselves in passion images, but to enter mentally into the passion, so it could overcome their passions, counter their trouble or despair, act as an antidote to anxiety or pain or evil" (301).

what it depicts with greater reality than the thing or object can attain as such. Neither copying its subject in purely mechanical fashion nor simply referring to it as a merely extraneous entity, the image instead effects what Gadamer calls "an increase in being" (*Zuwachs an Sein*); or, as Grote puts it, "things refer more fully to other things than do words to things."[107]

Grote's repeated, nominalist insistence that "all images are signs of particular things and have in themselves nothing universal" and that, consequently, "no knowledge consists in images," contradicts his claims elsewhere in this short sermon that images reinforce and deepen the laity's grasp of essential, spiritual truths: "Those images that stick more tenaciously to the mind also imprint all the *more forcefully* the spiritual realities signified through them."[108] As we had seen in other contexts, attempts to functionalize the image and hold it to a strictly subsidiary role vis-à-vis "pure Being" typically fail because the phenomenology of the image turns out to exceed the purposes for which they were invoked. In Grote's case, the situation is further complicated by the anti-Scholastic drift of his argument, a common trait of the *devotio moderna*. For the modern-day Devout, while often engaged in teaching, copying books, and "invok[ing] canon law to defend their way of life," were nevertheless deeply suspicious of Scholasticism and what they considered its overemphasis of purely verbal disputes. In its Scholastic forms, theology "meant idle speculation," and Grote for one "dismissed theologians as thinking carnally (*carnaliter*)" and prone to "intellectual self-satisfaction."[109] Yet in claiming that "the less the minds of . . . laymen are cluttered with letters, in my judgment, the more firmly, lastingly, and deeply they are bent toward and seized upon by other images," Grote finds himself caught between his anti-Scholasticism and a model of conversion bound up with the uncontainable charisma of images.

In the event, the only way to proceed here is by affirming the centrality of images while also stressing their provisional nature. Images, Grote writes, "are not to be left behind until faith and love have been wholly purified." Yet in time or, rather, at the threshold beyond historical time, the world of *visibilia* shall melt away altogether; and it is this eschatological expectancy that, on Grote's view (following

---

107. Van Engen, 1988, 99–102.

108. Van Engen 1988, 111, 113; emphasis mine. Grote's sermon reflects a broader shift in late medieval culture whereby "visions inspired by images . . . are distinguished, in part, by the degree to which they develop a self-conscious discourse on the status of images, imaginative experience, and their role in visionary perception" (Hamburger 2000, 48).

109. Van Engen 2008, 238. Early in his *De Imitatione Christi*, Thomas à Kempis thus asks, "Of what profit to you is it to dispute high things about the Trinity if you lack humility and thus displease the Trinity? Truly, high words do not make a person holy and just [Quid prodest tibi, alta de Trinitate disputare, si careas humilitate, unde displiceas Trinitati? Vere, alta verba non faciunt sanctum et justum]"; quoted in Van Engen 2008, 239.

Bernard and Bonaventure), must inform how the Devout interact with images. Hence, he writes, "we should not withdraw from images and the imagined in our new birth until Christ and spiritual understanding have again taken shape within us, until we are spiritual beings judging all things spiritually." Notably, "image" for Grote covers a wide spectrum that includes, but is by no means limited to, painting, sculpture, and such but also scriptural figuration, parables, and tropes of all kinds. As he observes in passing, "The sacraments [too] have a certain audible visuality," with the sign being "seen" in such a way as to obfuscate the fact that it is "the work of abstraction." Provided nothing of what is "visually signified . . . is signified as if it were visible through the sign," the beholder/listener may glimpse meanings beyond all visual or verbal mediation.[110] That is, image and word per se can only intimate a state of spiritual fullness from which, by dint of their medial character, they necessarily also detract. Invariably, and appropriately, they remind the beholder/listener of the distance between the image as a sensory presence operative in distended time and its ultimate fulfillment in a realm cleansed of all mediation. Hence, in theological and contemplative speech, images—far from begging to be reduced to some literal-historical sense—convey a heightened state of eschatological expectancy; both in their material-visual and textual-metaphoric forms, they gravitate toward their ultimate self-suspension, the point when their medial constitution will have been supplanted by the transparency of pure meaning ("Spirit").

DYING FROM "BODELYE" INTO "GASTELYE" SIGHT: JULIAN OF NORWICH SEES THE MAN OF SORROWS

Turning now to Julian of Norwich, we find her early work reflects the influence of two distinct, though not incompatible, traditions. On the one hand, there is the enduring appeal of an apophatic ("negative") theology reaching back at least to pseudo-Dionysius, and that is influentially extended by Bernard of Clairvaux. Of decisive influence on the emergent tradition of female mystical writing that begins with Elizabeth of Schönau's *Liber Viarum Dei* (ca. 1256) and is followed by Gertrude of Helfta, Elisabeth of Hungary, Mechthild of Magdeburg, and Mechthild von Hackeborn, apophaticism remains foundational to fourteenth-century contemplatives such as Bridget of Sweden and Julian of Norwich. Unfolding less in dissent from than parallel to the ongoing Scholastic disputes between the faculties in Paris and Oxford, the writers just mentioned appear far more concerned with the phenomenology of religious experience than with elaborating abstract, a priori definitions of its con-

---

110. Van Engen 1988, 109, 113, 115.

tents. Many of their writings show theological reflection and literary innovation to be fused in novel ways, unfolding as it were within the same epistemic and affective space, often imaginatively and sometimes uneasily. At the same time, by the middle of the fourteenth century, this inward-looking and mostly aniconic strand of contemplative writing converges with forms of lay piety associated with the *devotio moderna* that after 1370 is rapidly gaining in prominence, particularly in the lower Rhenish region, the Dutch countries, and northern France.

Though an anchoress and, as such, working with a different model of spiritual community than the one concurrently being developed across the Channel, Julian's work shares many of the rhetorical strategies and spiritual objectives dear to the Brothers and Sisters of the Common Life. That this should be so is, perhaps, not all that surprising considering the multiple crises that, in the second half of the fourteenth century, made the search for more effective forms of spiritual self-examination and self-description a matter of great urgency. To begin with, the church, weakened by the Schism (1378–1417), struggled to respond to the laity's surging interest in more personal forms of meditation, as reflected by the appeal of spiritual communities whose strict discipline often stood in vexing contrast to the material ease and slack discipline characterizing the lives of beneficed clergy and the episcopacy. Still, while Julian's chosen form of life as an anchoress exempted her from immediate supervision by the "Halye Kyrke," it did not conflict with established church doctrine and liturgical practice. Indeed, the scrupulous, searching tone that pervades her writings, to a degree rarely seen since Augustine's *Confessions*, undoubtedly has more to do with the profoundly unsettled times in which Julian found herself. First, there was the ongoing conflict between England and France, eventually christened the Hundred Years' War (1336–1453). Intervening barely a decade into that war was, of course, the cataclysm of the plague, which starting in 1347 continued to devastate regions across Europe for the next several decades and, in some areas, killed off 50 percent of the population. Close to the time of Julian's early text, there was the English Peasant Revolt, or "Great Rising" (1381), precipitated by a confluence of interminable war, plague, and high taxation. Finally, there was the Schism, which inevitably cast doubt on the theological probity and institutional authority of the church and its magisterium. It can hardly surprise, then, that these cumulative disasters should have intensified concerns both practical and speculative about death, dying, and last things.

Yet whereas theological debates over the relationship between finite existence and its redemption at the conclusion of historical time had heretofore been taken up mainly by a handful of highly educated scholars at Paris and Oxford, eschatological questions after 1350 tend to engage a much wider segment of the faithful. Indeed, while dutifully repeating the Platonic topos of "philosophy as care and concern with death" (*philosophia est cura et sollicitudo mortis*), as Roger Bacon puts it around 1240, neither philosophy nor Scholastic theology seem to engage death and dying with the same systematic fervor and probity that they visit on so many other topics. At most, Rolf Schönberger notes, "the topic of death broadly speaking departs the domain of philosophy without ever quite arriving in the province of thirteenth- and fourteenth-century theology."[111] That this should be so arguably has to do with the genres of writing on which philosophical and theological reflection predominantly rely. For the prevailing academic modes of syllogistic argumentation and scholastic *disputatio* seem ill fitted to the longing, felt with such urgency by the faithful, for an intuitive vision of the eschaton. Instead, it is in first-person visionary testimony and contemplative writing, often triggered by near-death or out-of-body experiences, that the question of eschatology, ever pressing and ineluctible, is being broached in late medieval culture. Well beyond scholastic debates engaging Joachim of Fiore's chiliastic, stadial conception of history, eschatological speculation pursued against the backdrop of the disasters just mentioned began to consume lay communities, particularly in the Low Countries, northern France, and England; and it is at this point that the expanded culture of meditation on death and redemption also takes on a conspicuously visual cast, both pictorial and verbal. Extreme aniconic speculation, such as Meister Eckhart's suggestion that the soul is capable "fully to transcend its created nature" and thus pass beyond the order of time, is firmly rejected by Bernard of Clairvaux on the grounds that "to lose yourself as though you did not exist and to have no sense of yourself, to be emptied of yourself (Phil. 2.7) and almost annihilated, belongs to heavenly not to human love."[112]

When censoring Meister Eckhart, the church had identified a total of twenty-eight propositions either heretical or verging on heresy. Of these, two specifically bear on our concerns here. The first conceives man's deification as a literal possibility ("We are transformed completely into God and changed into him [*convertimur in eum*] without any residue or distinction [*nulla est distinctio*]"). The second claim maintains the outright nullity of all created being: "All creatures are one pure nothing. I do not say that they are something ordinary or anything, but that they are one pure nothing [*quod sint unum purum nihil*]."[113] One can see how Eckhart's quasi-Gnostic disparagement of visible, embodied creation in the second of these two theses would lead to an equally literal view of "deification" that threatened to erase all distinction between man and God. In effect, Eckhart had proposed a theology with-

---

111. Schönberger 2002, 726; trans. mine. For a concise account of Aquinas's eschatological conception, see te Velde 2002.

112. Bernard 1987, 195 (*On Loving God* X.27). Bernard may also be referencing John's caveat that "we are now the sons of God; and it hath not yet appeared what we shall be. We know, that, when he shall appear, we shall be like to him: because we shall see him as he is" (1 Jn 3:2).

113. For the condemnation, see the papal bull *Dolentes Referimus* (aka the Constitution *In agro dominico*, published 27 March 1329), in Denzinger 2012, nos. 950–80 (quoting nos. 960 and 976).

out mediation, thereby voiding the concept of *analogia* cautiously outlined at the Fourth Lateran Council and thus draining the experience of distended time and embodied creation of all anagogical value and spiritual meaning. Yet, as the bishops pressing the case against Eckhart saw it, the point of faith and the church surely was not to promote unfettered, self-idolizing, metaphysical speculation. Rather, it was to help finite and fallible human beings cope with the fact that redemption fell outside the scope of things inaccessible to formal ratiocination or eschatological speculation. Hence, people needed guidance with regard to inhabiting creation *in the right way*, to sift finite, created being for its figural (specifically anagogical) significance, not repudiate it as a literal "nothing." To aspire to the *visio beatifica* meant to participate in, not reject, the life here below.

One way of doing so was by dying unto the world, figurally speaking, such as by joining a beguine or beghard community or by having oneself enclosed as an anchorite in a small cell, usually attached to a church. In the latter case, the spiritual life chosen resembled a living death, for which reason the priest, during the ceremony of enclosure, would administer extreme unction to the anchoress committing herself to seek "purity of heart" and no longer to look toward the world beyond her damp and tenuously illuminated cell.[114] As the unknown author of *Ancrene Wisse* (ca. 1220), the book of instruction for anchorites, had put it so eloquently, enclosure ("God's prison") was a way of integrating the reality of bodily death into one's spiritual life: "This is the delving: to be busily and eagerly always about it, with a constant yearning, with the heat of the hungry; to wade up out of sin; to creep out of the flesh."[115] Ever mindful that her embodied condition points toward death, Julian of Norwich distinguishes between fear of death, of which she has none ("for nothinge that I was aferde fore"), and her desire to continue in this life as long as God wills it, so as to be able to perform works on his behalf and, in so doing, "have the more knowinge and loving of God in the blisse of hevene."[116]

By the time Julian writes her *Vision of a Devout Woman*, sometime around 1383, much of Europe had been in the grip of the plague for a full generation. Increasingly, life in towns and in the country resembled the reality embraced by anchorites—a spatially confined and anguished existence riveted on death as the ubiquitous and seemingly inescapable reality. Unfolding over more than four decades, the cataclysm of the plague had forced Europe's population to confront dying as the ultimate

---

114. On those living on the margins of religious life (hermits, recluses, penitents, beguines, and beghards) in the twelfth and thirteenth centuries, see Simons 2008, 311–23; Savage and Watson 1991, 7–32.

115. Savage and Watson 1991, 88.

116. Julian of Norwich 2006, 65 (Sec. 2, lines 8–10). Henceforth, Julian's texts will be cited parenthetically as *V* (*A Vision Showed to a Devout Woman*) and *R* (*A Revelation of Love*), followed by section (or chapter) and line numbers as given by Watson and Jenkins.

spiritual test, both for the sufferer and for her community. No longer fitting into an organic and timeless cycle of death and renewal, the demise of yet another plague victim furnished those present with further troubling evidence of a crisis afflicting all of humanity and, possibly, betokening a definitive withdrawal of divine grace from the world as a whole. While not overtly linked with the plague, which continued to resurface throughout England, including in the year of Julian's near-death experience, the anchoress's *Vision* is remarkable for its unequivocal affirmation of divine grace and its affirmation of all suffering as "penance," to be willingly undergone and, by God's grace, to be endured. As the author of *Ancrene Wisse* had specified, "All you ever endure is penance, and hard penance, my dear sisters; . . . all you suffer is martyrdom for you in the most severe of orders, for night and day you are up on God's cross. . . . There is nothing for it then but to suffer gladly."[117] When interpreted as partial atonement for the inexpungable stain of sin, suffering is part of a divine plan, for which reason Julian will (rather controversially) characterize sin as "behovely"—that is, as fitting in with finite human existence rather than being a gratuitous and irredeemable stain on it.

Still, the bracing speed with which the plague depopulated large swaths of the countryside and towns across Europe and England severely tested such faith in the providential order of things. Following its rapid spread from Sicily northward, beginning in October 1347, the plague is estimated to have cut Europe's (and England's) population by as much as 50 percent.[118] In Julian's lifetime, both the plague's initial appearance in 1347 and its particularly virulent second wave starting in 1360 devastated all regions of the kingdom, with significant recurrences following in 1369, 1379–83, and 1389–93. Predictably, the pandemic also strained ecclesiastic and monastic structures, undermining spiritual discipline to the point that priests, especially nonbeneficed clergy, routinely refused to administer last rites to the dying. Those priests still prepared to do so also had to prepare the dying person's next of kin for the possibility of facing death on their own. Amid the incessant funereal peal of church bells, those seeking pastoral guidance during their final hours could draw on a new resource, the manual known as the *Ars Moriendi* initially circulating in Latin versions but soon translated into the vernacular (French, Dutch, German, and English). Conceived as a popular elaboration on the established church protocol gov-

---

117. Savage and Watson 1991, 176, 180.

118. For a recent, comprehensive account of the plague, including its regional impact across Europe, see Benedictow 2004, 342–79; on how to interpret the long-term decline or, in some regions, stagnation of population rates, see Hatcher 1977, 11–46. Plague-related mortality among the (beneficed) clergy ran around 45% (upwards of 48% in the Dioceses of Winchester and Norwich), though far lower (around 18%) among bishops; see the tables and maps in Benedictow 2004, 356–59.

erning assistance to the dying, the so-called *ordo visitandi*, versions of the *Ars Moriendi* first appear late in the fourteenth century. Following the "Treatise on the Right Order of Dying" (*Tractatus de bono ordine moriendi*, ca. 1390) by Johan van Mies in Prague, it is in the third part of Jean Gerson's *Opus Tripartitum* (1408) that this small book, subsequently disseminated across Europe under the title *De arte moriendi*, first surfaces. Promoted by the Council of Constance (1414–18), where Gerson, chancellor of the University of Paris since 1395, had played a decisive role, numerous vernacular translations of Gerson's treatise subsequently appeared in Germany, France, Germany, Bohemia, and Hungary; and over three hundred Latin and vernacular versions of the treatise still exist today.[119]

Greatly enhancing the book's enduring popularity are some eleven woodcuts that, after 1450, came to be routinely inserted into printings of it. Each of these images offered a visual aid to the priest and the dying person's relatives as to how they ought to choreograph the process of dying and offer comfort to those facing their final passage. The first five images depict devils alternately besieging the dying person's faith, hope, and patience or tempting her vanity and avarice. They are followed by five contrasting images that show angels rebuffing vices and temptations, as well as strengthening the soul's virtuous resolve in the face of death. Of this second grouping, the tenth woodcut, "Contra Avaritiam" (fig. 3.3), depicts the deathbed, with a crucifix figuring prominently behind the bed. Christ's and the Virgin Mary's downward lines of sight converge on the dying person, whose gaze appears less focused on the angel at the center of the image than on a transcendent beyond for which the angel is the metonym. As the tempting devil withdraws in defeat, another angel conceals the couple at the bottom left, lest their sight rekindle the dying person's attachment to worldly goods and so disrupt her spiritual vision. For the same reason, and possibly echoing Matthew 10:37–38, the woodcut shows how family members ought to be kept at the periphery of the dying person's vision (here in the upper left of the image), lest they interfere with her intense focus on the suffering of the crucified Christ. Altogether, the choreography of figures and sightlines underscores the nullity of all earthly attachments, which must be disavowed if the *visio beatifica* is to be attained.[120]

---

119. For a survey of primary texts in the *ars bene moriendi* tradition, see Rudolf 1957, esp. 56–112; Duffy 2005, 313–27; and Binski 1996, 29–50. On the way that the *Ars Moriendi* reconciles Christian eschatological speculation with sacramental practice, see Ariès 1991, esp. 95–110; and within fifteenth-century French culture, Male 1986, 348–55.

120. In support of the dying person's explicit separation from all earthly attachments, Rudolf (1957) points to a number of inscriptions on plate 10 (though not visible on the woodcut used here), including allusions to Matt 10:37 ("Whoever loves father and mother more than me is not worthy of me"); 14:29 (Peter to Christ: "Lord, save me!"); Lk 14:26 and 14:33 ("none of you can become my disciple if you do not give up all your possessions").

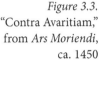

Figure 3.3.
"Contra Avaritiam,"
from *Ars Moriendi,*
ca. 1450

Precisely this spatial choreography, aimed at defeating sensory and material attachments of every kind and "the lust of the eyes" (1 Jn 2:16) in particular, had always
been at the heart of anchoritic life. The underlying paradox, then, is of human life
both ordered toward the eschaton of an ultimate vision and, to that end, committed
to overcoming the transient attachments of sight: "*Ostende mihi faciem tuam* (Canticles 2:14)—'Show your face to me and to no one else; look at me if you would have
clear sight with your heart's eyes. . . . ' In this way the Lord speaks to his spouse." Yet
quoting, as so often, Bernard of Clairvaux, the author of *Ancrene Wisse* also insists
that, "just as death came into the world through sin, so through the window of the
eye death has her entrance into the soul." Enjoying as part of her betrothal to Christ
two crucial "marriage-gifts: swiftness and the light of clear sight," the anchoress exemplifies what the dying should seek at the end of their life: namely, to renounce

"earthly speech [and] fleshly sights" and, thus liberated, enjoy "the clear sight of God's face."[121]

Yet roughly two centuries after *Ancrene Wisse*, the scene has changed. Its aniconism and Pauline antinomy between fleshly and spiritual sight, while not rejected, has itself become the premise for a new kind of image disseminated in the medium of the woodcut, a new technique for reproducing images, with the relatively coarse illustrations found in the *Ars Moriendi* being among the first of their kind to appear in Europe. That technology, in turn, is part of a wider shift whereby "ever more elaborate imaginings of the Crucifixion . . . characterized thirteenth-century devotions, . . . [including] visual features that were increasingly apparent in thirteenth-century art [such as] the sag of Christ's arms and consequent stretching of his torso and exposure of his rib cage."[122] This broad shift in religious and artistic culture registers most palpably in the eleventh and final woodcut (fig. 3.4). It depicts the telos of Christian life, the moment of the good death, as opposed to the dreaded event of an unforeseen death (*mors improvisa*) when, as Geert Grote writes around 1380, "the Lord [is] . . . like a thief that comes in the night" and the "calamity of death overtakes [sinners] in an instant."[123] A large number of angels and saints hover in the background, with one of them receiving the dying man's soul in the form of a child's body—a common late medieval motif also employed by Julian—even as various devils helplessly rage in the foreground.[124] Now, in the final moment of her life, the dying person is to be given images of her favored saints, and she is summoned to call upon the Virgin, as exemplified by the saints praying devoutly to Christ on the crucifix.

At the heart of this image, however, there lurks a telling ambiguity: Are we to take the saints depicted in the upper half of the woodcut in strictly allegorical fashion, that is, as figuring the inherently aniconic motif of supreme piety? Or, alternatively, does their physical presence to the eyes of the beholder (of the woodcut) confirm their real presence to the dying person's spiritual sight, as is the case when during Mass the Host is raised so as to allow the faithful to see Christ's body? Put in

---

121. Savage and Watson 1991, 70, 82–83; see also the text's poignant quotation of Jeremiah (*Lamentations* 3:51): "Alas, my eyes have robbed my soul" (*oculus meus depredatus est animam meam*) (71). See also Lipton, who notes that "the scribe [of *Ancrene Wisse*] turned especially to Cistercian sources when assembling prayers for the anchoresses" (2005, 1195).

122. Lipton 2005, 1196.

123. Grote, in Van Engen 1988, 81.

124. "And in this time I sawe a body lying on the erth, which body shewde hevy and feerfulle. . . . And sodeynly oute of this body sprong a fulle fair creature, a litille child, full shapen and formed, swif and lifly and whiter then the lilye, which sharpely glided uppe into heven" (*V* 64:24–28. Notably, in section 2 of Julian's *Vision*, the curate entering Julian's room ("to be ate mine endinge") is accompanied by a child, too (*V* 2:21).

Figure 3.4.
Final plate,
Ars Moriendi,
ca. 1450

another way: Are the figures in the upper half of this woodcut to be taken as *representations* of the saints or as images mediating their *real presence*? Most likely, it is a case of both-and. Thus, if "supernatural beings have invaded the bedroom," as Ariès puts it, they have done so as both correlates of empirical sight (*visus*) for those viewing the woodcuts and as real presences revealed to the *visio* of the dying person who here is notably depicted with his eyes already closed.[125] A key feature in both woodcuts, then, is the dyad of image and fulfillment, of the dying man (*moriens*) and the Man of Sorrows, with Christ on the cross affirming the former's capacity to face and master his own death. Insofar as he successfully attends to, and participates in, the

---

125. Ariès 1991, 108.

crucified Christ as his "focal image," the dying man "is in effect controlling the character of his own death, and so of his destiny."[126]

With "apocalyptic inspiration [having] disappeared" or, at least, retreated to the margins of popular conceptions of death, "the bedroom became a crowded battlefield centred on the last agonies of the man or woman in the bed." Not coincidentally, "the stages of this struggle were vividly resolved into striking images."[127] With remarkable theological probity and earnestness of expression, Julian of Norwich's *Vision of a Devout Woman* depicts the hour of death as a "judging and weighing" of the individual's soul rather than an affliction of mankind in general.[128] Julian's early text reflects a late fourteenth-century shift in the theology and iconography of dying inasmuch as both image and writing now depict a person's final hour as the pivotal, last judgment on the narrative arc of her life rather than an attempt to imagine her afterlife. What distinguishes the *ars moriendi* tradition is specifically this "separation of resurrection and judgment," as a result of which "the traditional interval between judgment . . . and physical death disappeared."[129] Instead, the moment of last judgment is now located in the very hour of one's death where the *moriens* confronts what T. S. Eliot calls the "intersection of timelessness with time."[130] As the culmination of the eschatological narrative that is a Christian life, the dying person (*moriens*) mobilizes all her powers of conscious attention so as to embrace death as the just and meaningful completion of her earthly existence. In closing the gap between death and the last judgment and thus absorbing the eschaton into the realm of human time, albeit as its culminating moment, the *ars moriendi* betrays the growing influence of a chiliastic conception of time controversially put forward by Joachim of Fiore. A century earlier, Bonaventure's attempt in his *Talks on the Six Days of Creation* (1273) to reconcile Joachim's heterodox views with with core tenets of Augustinian theology had hedged on the main issue. Thus, even as Bonaventure "rejects the view that with Christ the highest degree of inner-historical fulfillment is already realized so that there is nothing left but an eschatological hope for that which lies *beyond* all history," he nevertheless holds open the possibility of "a new salvation *in* history, *within* the limits of this time." A "new inner-worldly, inner-messianic hope" has begun to weaken the central Augustinian tenet, according to which "Christ is the

---

126. Binski 1996, 40.

127. Duffy 2005, 317.

128. Ariès 1991, 101.

129. Ibid., 107 f.; Ariès quotes Alberto Tenenti, who notes that in the *ars moriendi* tradition "the dying man attends his own drama as a witness rather than as an actor" (109). See also Duffy, who notes that the ritual aspect of dying and "the constantly reiterated concern to secure shrift and housel in the hour of death represents a strong lay conviction, and not merely the mechanical acceptance of ecclesiastical directives" (2005, 313).

130. Eliot 2015, 1:199 ("Dry Salvages," V, 18–19).

end of the ages." Instead, in "the Bonaventurian schema, Christ is the center of the ages."[131]

It is this ambiguous placement of the eschaton in relation to finite history—at the threshold between the time of "distention" and that of "attention," between distracted sight and spiritual insight—that furnishes the point of departure for Julian of Norwich. In what follows, we will restrict ourselves to her *Vision of a Devout Woman*, the so-called short text, now dated to approximately 1385, though copied and likely further revised as late as 1413.[132] Not much is known about Julian's life. Born in 1342 or 1343, she survived the plague. Her dialect appears to place her in the vicinity of Norwich, where in early adulthood she was likely a nun at the Benedictine Convent in Carrow, close to the church of St. Julian's in Conesford, Norwich. Subsequently enclosed at that church as an anchoress, though possibly only after 1385, Julian chose a life in direct obedience to God, not an abbess.[133] As already noted, the telos toward which the anchoress's contemplative life is ordered is the *visio beatifica*, to be definitively attained at the hour of her death. In pursuit of this vision, the anchoress adheres to a meticulously structured hourly regimen of prayer and reflection, a more rigorous version of St. Antony's and John Cassian's desert monasticism, though unlike her fourth-century forebears Julian would also have been actively communicating with and ministering to members of her parish.[134] On 8 May (or, perhaps, 13 May) 1373, it looked as though the anchoress Julian of Norwich, at age thirty, was finding her three most cherished wishes fulfilled: "the first was to have minde of Cristes passion. The seconde was bodelye syekenes. And the thrid was to have of Goddes gifte thre wondes" (*V* 1:1–2). Lying gravely ill and expected to die that day, Julian hopes that "bodelye syekenes" will cause her to experience Christ's passion not only by empathetic imagination, itself strengthened by long-standing habits of devotion, but, even beyond this, that "I might have sene bodilye the passion of oure lorde that he sufferede for me" (*V* 1:7–8). To be sure, the devotional practices of an anchoress, no less than those followed by nuns or laypersons, conform with magisterial

---

131. Ratzinger 1989, 13–14, 17; italics restored as in the German original (in Ratzinger 2009, 448).

132. See Barry Windeatt, in Julian 2015, xx–xxii.

133. "[Julian] is a common lay parishioner, attached to a parish church. But yet, in practical, pastoral reality, she is positioned at the margins of the ways of life of her fellow Christians, being neither religious nor secular, neither clerical nor yet an ordinary laywoman, professed but not a nun; she is canonically marginal just as the physical positioning of her cell is attached to, but remains outside, the main body of her parish church" (Turner 2011, 13).

134. The anchorite's personal and meditative search for a comprehensive theological understanding has prompted some critics to read Julian in direct opposition to the church and its magisterium. For a refutation of such appropriative readings of Julian, see Turner 2011, 70–75; on Julian's theology, which she was to develop in far greater detail in her later *Revelation of Love* (ca. 1395), see esp. Baker 1994, 64–106; Aers 2009, 133–71; and Turner 2011, 3–31, 103–34.

teaching, which for centuries had drawn on visual matter of all kinds, including "the paintinges of crucifexes that er made be the grace of God aftere the techinge of haly kyrke to the liknes of Cristes passion." This reference to "paintinges of crucifexes" has often been taken as evidence of Julian's wish "not to be associated with heretical Lollard hostility towards images," a hypothesis further strengthened by the fact that this particular phrase enters the short text only in its 1413 redaction.[135] Yet even as Julian unequivocally professes her belief in the passion narrative depicted on stained-glass windows and wall paintings of her Conesford church, her true goal is an unmediated vision ("withouten any meen" [*V* 1:14]) that no longer requires the beholder to decode and authenticate its referent but to be brought face-to-face with Christ himself: "I desirede a bodilye sight, wharein I might have more knawinge of bodelye paines of oure lorde oure savioure" (*V* 1:13–14).

Within the spiritual economy of the *imitatio Christi* pervading late medieval religious life, then, imitation is precisely *not* a case of mimetic realism. For the correlate of Julian's hoped-for vision does not consist in *simulating* Christ's suffering. Rather, echoing the three desires identified at the start of her text, Julian's three figural "wounds" (of contrition, compassion, and "wilfulle langinge to God" [*V* 1:40–41]) reinforce the intentionality underlying all anchoritic practice: namely, to merge with Christ to whom she prays (roughly five hours a day), whom she longs to see, and of whose perfection she longs to partake. Seen in the context of the finite, sinful human being's kenotic surrender to Christ's transcendent goodness, Julian's vision is emphatically not an instance of possession but, rather, a "gifte . . . come to my minde with contrition, frelye withouten any sekinge" (*V* 1:20–21). Sight here is eschatologically constituted in that its subject longs to merge, both physically and spiritually, with Christ's passion. Such longing, however, becomes possible only at the threshold of death, when Christ "lerede [taught] me that I shulde behalde the gloriouse asethe [atonement]" (*V* 14:9). As for her "wilfulle desire to hafe of Goddes gifte a bodelye syekenes," Julian views her own illness, suffering, and expected death ("wenande myselfe that I shulde die") in relation to the sacramental order of the *ars moriendi*, a relation she specifically embraces: "that I might in the sekenes take alle my rightinges [rites] of haly kyrke" (*V* 1:23–24). This sacramental dimension is crucial, for to ignore it would risk misconstruing Julian's vision as a purely idiosyncratic form of piety. There is nothing solipsistic about her argument, however, as Julian repeatedly insists that those in the throes of ultimate bodily suffering ever depend on the support and guidance of both their fellow Christians ("evencristen") and the community of saints and Christ manifested in "shewings" perhaps uniquely placed in reach of the dying.

---

135. See Windeatt, in Julian 2015, xxi.

Throughout Julian's writings, spiritual vision is inseparably entwined with the dying person's embodied consciousness. Its medium is the sufferer's very flesh. Subject to "alle manere of paines, bodelye and gastelye" (*V* 1:26), Julian experiences her physical being not as generically embodied but, specifically, as the self-sentiency of "this wreched fleshe" (*V* 3:17)—frail, vulnerable, and bound for pain and death. In its very infirmity, the flesh also furnishes the ground from which Augustine's and Bonaventure's corporeal sight may ascend to spiritual and, ultimately, intellectual vision. Yet as "bodelye sight" turns into "gastelye [spiritual] sight," the physiology of the suffering, enfleshed being is not transcended or sublated in Hegelian speculative fashion any more than the visible image is being repudiated. For even as Julian's "reflections developed in her 'vunderstanding,' 'in gostely syght,' she simultaneneously held 'the bodely syght' that her own text has so subtly set aside."[136] Likewise, illness and physical suffering insistently tether all vision to the sentient, perceiving person, understood as "flesh" (*Leib*) rather than mere "body" (*Körper*). Julian's insistence on the interdependency of illness and vision, of "bodelye" and "gasteleye" sight, thus confirms a key insight much later developed in modern phenomenology: "Flesh spiritualizes . . . [and] renders visible the bodies of the world that would remain, without it, in the night of the unseen."[137]

The fulcrum of Julian's early text—the moment from which all narrative momentum and theological reflection proceed—concerns the vision "shewed" during her near-death experience when she "wened nought tille have liffede tille daye" (*V* 2:3). Having lost sensation in her lower body,

> was I stirred to be sette upperightes, lenande with clothes to my hede, for to have the mare fredome of my herte to be ate Goddes wille, and thinking on him whiles my life walde laste. And thay that were with me sente for the person my curette [the parson, my curate] to be atte mine endinge. He come, and a childe with him, and brought a crosse, and be thane I hadde sette mine eyen and might nought speke. The persone [parson] sette the crosse before my face, and saide: "Doughter, I have brought the image of thy savioure. Loke thereupon, and com-

---

136. Aers and Staley 1996, 85.

137. Marion 2002b, 89. It bears noting that the body/flesh distinction correlates with that between the visible and the invisible. As Marion remarks, "Flesh and body are phenomenologically opposed all the more radically [in] that one has for its function to make appear in feeling, to the point that it remains invisible as such, while the other, having for its definition to appear as visible, is never in a position to make appear, or feel, or intend. The body appears, but flesh remains invisible" (88). Similarly, Solovyov notes that, unlike the body, flesh "breaks loose from its bounds. . . . [It] has ceased to be passive and is striving for independence and infinity, seeks to attract the spiritual power to itself" (2005, 42). For a theological meditation on the body/flesh antinomy, see Griffiths 2018, 1–56; and also ch. 2 above.

forthe the therewith in reverence of him that diede for the and me." Methought than that I was welle, for mine eyen ware sette upwarde into hevene, whether I trustede for to come. Botte nevethelesse I assended to sette mine eyen in the face of the crucifixe, if I might, for to endure the langer into the time of min endinge. (*V* 2:17–26)

If the crucifix is "the image of thy savioure," as the *ordo visitandi* has the curate put it, "image" here does not function substitutively; it does not "represent" the savior in the sense of some conventional imitation. Again, Husserl's tripartite distinction helps clinch the salient point: the material "image-carrier" (Husserl's *Bildt*räger) of the crucifix is positioned in such a way as to focus Julian's visual attention onto the "image-object" (*Bildgegenstand*) of Christ's body and face depicted on it. Yet the dying anchoress's visual concentration ultimately aims to fuse Christ's timeless *imago* with her own mental image of it. By itself, the crucifix does not depict its "original" at Calvary any more than the image of Christ on it "represents" God's son who "under Pontius Pilate suffered death and was buried." For the visible image here not only memorializes that historical occurrence of his death and resurrection, but, as experienced by Julian on her deathbed, embodies the eschaton as her reality, too ("mine eyen ware sette upwarde into hevene"). With its central dramatic tableau, then, Julian's text reflects how for the past century and a half "the accent [had] slowly shifted from love mysticism, in which the Eucharist was the emblematic trigger of union with the Beloved, to passion mysticism, in which the cross was the first and foremost focus of the visionary's affectionate gaze."[138]

Part of the difficulty of accurately capturing what is at stake in this deathbed vision stems from the hybrid character of the object presented to Julian's gaze. Thus, formally speaking, the cross belongs to the order of the symbol; yet at the same time, affixed to it, is the image of the crucified Christ, either in stacciato relief form or, more commonly, as sculpted onto a wooden cross (fig. 3.5). This "image-object" of the sculpted or painted Man of Sorrows thus is not yet the terminus for quotidian perception that it will be a generation after Julian, when the painted portrait begins to supplant the iconic face.[139] In Julian's text and the *ars moriendi* tradition that would likely have framed her near-death experience in 1373, the figure of the crucified Christ serves as the medium by means of which, and beyond which, Julian's gaze must pass toward her ultimately aniconic vision of Christ as eschaton. This aniconic vision is a case of assent rather than perception. For its true focus is what Husserl calls the "image-subject" (*Bildsujet*), the point where the meaning prefigured by the

---

138. Fraeters 2012, 188.
139. On the shift from the "true face" (*das echte Gesicht*) to the portrait bearing a resemblance to the face (*das ähnliche Gesicht*), see Belting 2014, 148–56; and esp. Belting 2006, 45–56, 89–101.

Figure 3.5.
Wooden crucifix,
ca. 1250, Tuscany.
London, Victoria and
Albert Museum

visible image is properly consummated. This ultimate fulfillment of the image in an ineffable, eschatological vision nonetheless can be realized only by means of the visible image. Tellingly, Julian on her deathbed is not looking *at* the crucifix but, instead, assents "to sette mine eyen *in the face of* the crucifixe." Facing imminent death, her unwavering attention is absorbed by the crucifix held in front of her, which in turn mediates the reality of "him that diede for the[e] and me." Consistent with the eschatological drama visualized in the woodcuts found in mid-fifteenth-century printings of the *ars moriendi*, Julian, during what are expected to be her final hours, maintains strict focus on the crucifix and does "nought assente to putte my saule in perille, for beside the crosse was . . . botte uglinesse of feendes" (*V* 10:52–53; emphasis mine).

It is this sacramental choreography, enabling the dying person's empathetic visualization of Christ's *face*, rather than a mere depiction of it, which throws into relief the nexus between dying, vision, and prayer. As *visus* (directed at the crucifix) turns into *visio* (of Christ's face), the anchoress experiences "a grete aninge [union] betwyx Criste and us" [*V* 10:44] and, consequently, an unprecedented level of self-recognition that in anchoritic life is always intimately entwined with prayer. Praying here means acknowledging one's temporally distended and incomplete condition. For once fullness of vision and self-recognition have been attained, prayer will no longer be called for: "when we see God we hafe that we desire, and then nedes us nought to praye" (*V* 19:51). Prayer thus confirms the subject's lingering temporal distance vis-à-vis what, in the hour of her death, she finds intuitively (if also ineffably) gifted in Christ's face. As Jean Chrétien notes, "A first description of prayer can situate it in an act of presence to the invisible, . . . [whereby] the [person] praying stands in the presence of a being which he believes but does not see and manifests himself to it." In praying, Julian petitions the invisible God that she may be seen by him, thereby putting her very being "thoroughly at stake, in all dimensions of [her] being." Uniquely, in prayer "an other [is] silently introduced into my dialogue with myself," thus nudging the subject praying to overcome its habitual "egocentrism."[140] Just as spiritual vision never claims epistemic dominion over the image, so prayer differs categorically from both propositional and performative speech. It is neither a case of spontaneous self-expression nor one of propositional utterance but, like vision, acknowledges a gift received. For, as Julian repeatedly notes, God himself is the ground of prayer by revealing to her that "I am grounde of thy beseking" (*R* 41:8). As Denys Turner puts it, "Prayer as beseking is the form in which [the] vision of divine providence intersects subjectively with our temporal experience so as to become a narrative through which we are inserted into that eternity. . . . Prayer is the collapsed unity of contemplative vision extruded across narrative sequence."[141]

Beginning in section 3 of *A Vision*, Julian's "bodelye sight," which thus far has been fixated on the visible crucifix, yields to a dramatic vision of the suffering Christ: "sodaynlye I sawe the rede blode trekille down fro under the garlande alle hate, freshlye, plentefully, and livelye, right as methought that it was in that time that the garlonde of thornes was thrystede on his blessede hede. . . . I conseyvede treulye and mightelye that it was himselfe that shewed it me, withouten any meen" (*V* 3:10–14). At first glance, the hermeneutics of this vision appear simple enough, suggesting that the mental image at issue is not a subjective projection but an objective "shewing" ("that oure lorde Jhesu . . . walde shewe me comforthe before the time of my temptation" [*V* 3:18–19]). Yet Julian herself appears startled by the fact that the vision,

---

140. Chrétien 2000, 149, 153; on the call-response dynamic of human speech, which is rendered explicit in prayer, see also Chrétien's outline of a phenomenology of prayer in Janicaud 2000, 147–75; on prayer in Julian's *Showings*, see Turner 2011, 135–66.

141. Turner 2011, 156.

which she takes to be uniquely granted to her as she lies dying, should conform so precisely to specific passages in the Gospels: "fulle gretlye I was astonned, for wondere and mervyle that I had, that he wolde be so homlye [intimate] with a sinfulle creature lyevande in this wreched fleshe" (*V* 3:16–17). In the event, she recognizes that her vision remains insubstantial and potentially deceptive unless she commits herself to discerning its theological import. Thus, while superficially the short text appears to reproduce "a conventional version of Christ's humanity, figured through the tortured, wounded, bleeding body on the cross, . . . her distinctive rhetorical strategies actually resist it, unravel it, estrange us from it. . . . [F]amiliar images are turned into theological reflections on the Trinity" in a distinctive confessional idiom that grows increasingly "analytic, rationally curious, abstract."[142]

Section 10 bears out that observation in more detail, for it is here that Julian recalls how "Criste shewed me a partye of his passione nere his dyinge," which left her overwhelmed by Christ's face: "drye and bludyelesse with pale dyinge . . . turnede more dede to the blewe [blue] / in the lippes, thare I sawe this foure colourse" (*V* 10:3–6). Are we to consider this vision of Christ's lifeless, broken body as but a feverish projection on Julian's part? Or, alternatively, ought we to read it as a retroactive dramatization, likely produced and embellished for the benefit of her "evencristene"? Put differently, are we looking at an empirically unverifiable occurrence or witnessing a sophisticated rhetorical performance? In the event, having to choose between a wholly uncritical acceptance of Julian's "shewings" and a hermeneutics of suspicion simply will not do. For to dismiss Julian's startlingly specific vision of the suffering Christ's face and body (especially in sections 3 and 10) as a mere retroactive invention would mean framing her writing in a skeptical epistemology not only alien to Julian's world but also bound to obscure the theological certitude that undergirds her entire narrative and is reflected in her countless assurances of having seen "sothly" and "in trothe." A critical framework that preemptively declares empirical ("bodelye") sight and intellectual ("gastelye") vision to be incommensurable will fail both Julian and us. For the deliverances of spiritual sight are continuous with, not opposed to, a hermeneutic practice that proceeds from and returns to them.

In fact, what we stand to learn from Julian is that neither blind faith nor peremptory skepticism leads to the understanding sought by Julian's *Vision*. Thus, what at the time of her expected death was "revealed" to her is not some determinate and indubitable theological knowledge. Rather, an integral feature of contemplative vision is to discern and unfold the spiritual meanings that they contain. Intuitive plenitude and hermeneutic labor are not opposed but complementary. Thus, Julian approaches her vision not as a case of inward and instantaneous certitude but as a cluster of arresting visual particulars calling for further study and reflection, for which reason

---

142. Aers and Staley 1996, 82.

she continually declines to own her experiences in either conceptual or empathetic fashion. Far from comporting with William James's definition of a "theopathic experience," Julian understands her "shewings" as a supreme instance of transcendent and ineffable givenness and, consequently, as both an ethical and a hermeneutic challenge. [143] As Mary Carruthers notes, for female mystics writing in the tradition of Bernard, "the use of . . . inventory *picturae* was a conscious rhetorical decision, in keeping with well-established conventions of oratory." Similarly, Aers and Staley consider the relationship of the reader to Julian's images, which "have been designed to emphasize their constructedness," altogether intellectual. If Julian's writings persistently "*draw attention to themselves*, her aim is not to evoke Christ's pain on Calvary, not to induce the affective responses we might have expected in a conventional meditation on the Crucifixion. . . . On the contrary, the reader is placed in a rather detached, speculative relationship to images," indeed becoming a participant in the "interactions of image, exegesis and reflection [that] discourages any affective identifications with the crucified body."[144]

Always, seeing is contiguous with understanding, not opposed to it. Merely to behold a "litille thinge" such as the hazelnut, visualize it as an image, and thus have "understandinge" of it as infused with complex theological meanings is all part of a single, unbroken chain of meditation that, to most of Julian's contemporaries, would have been known as the hermeneutic practice of *lectio divina*. Julian's reflections on what she has seen are themselves an extension of such seeing, not an attempt to overcome it. Thus, a turn of phrase such as "I sawe sothly," which recurs countless times, intimates a reciprocity between originary sight (*visus*) and eventual insight (*visio*), between something visually taken-in and its subsequently being intellectually taken-as. Throughout her writings, seeing, feeling, understanding, and knowing are contiguous and mutually reinforcing epistemic states—such that at times a single sentence may fuse sensory, affective, visionary, and ratiocinative states: "In this felinge, mine understandinge was lifted uppe into heven, and thare I sawe thre hevens" (*V* 12:6 f.). That the experiential datum of "bodelye sight" is not supplanted, let alone invalidated by more complex forms of "understandinge" to which it gives rise, has to do with the initial vision's overwhelming presence and richness. As Turner remarks, there is "no difference between . . . the meaning of 'see,' whether in its character as

143. "There is no English name for such a sweet excess of devotion, so I will refer to it as a theopathic condition" (James 1987, 312).
144. Carruthers 2006, 289; Aers and Staley 1996, 86. Likewise, Watson remarks on the "imagistic sparseness . . . largely untypical of the experiences of medieval women visionaries" (quoted by Aers and Staley 1996, 97 n. 29). See also Lipton, who notes how "both monastic and lay texts approach the crucifix through isolated parts, constructing religious meaning by way of fragmented visual experience" and framing "the power of vision [as] simultaneously inescapable and incomplete" (2005, 1202–3).

experience or from the standpoint of its truth-bearing properties wrung from that experience by much reflective labor."[145] Part of what makes Julian's writing so peculiarly challenging for contemporary readers is that modern skeptical and suspicious inquiry tends to develop its basic concepts in binary and disjunctive rather than integrative and complementary fashion. Their many differences notwithstanding, modern rationalist-deductive and empiricist-inductive epistemologies both premise a fundamental antinomy between sensory experience and cognitive certainty, between putatively "empty" data and the "warranted" propositions reason may venture about them only because it has willfully and peremptorily opposed itself to the order of appearance. Thus, the temporality undergirding modern epistemologies tends to be linear and supersessionist, such that raw experiential data come first, then are systematized, ordered, and ultimately supplanted by a set of "conclusions" reached by strictly anthropomorphic, conceptual means.[146]

This is not the place to revisit various incisive critiques directed at the premises of modern scientific method and at the scope of its presumed applicability, such as those advanced by Hans-Georg Gadamer, Michael Polanyi, John McDowell, or Charles Taylor. Suffice it to recall that for experiential data even to solicit an observer's scrutiny they must have come into view against the background of what Polanyi calls a "tacit dimension." Some "subsidiary awareness" of those background conditions must already be operative if a given phenomenon is to be experienced as literally remarkable, that is, as imbued with as yet unrealized significance rather than amounting to mere sensory "noise." As Polanyi puts it, "We can use our formulas only after we have made sense of the world to the point of asking questions about it and have established the bearing of the formulas on the experience that they are to explain." It is some such "tacit dimension" or "prejudgment" (Gadamer) that allows us to apprehend, say, a rich and perplexing visual phenomenon, as the kernel of insights as yet unrealized—in other words, to be approached as a potential conduit to further insight, which is to say, as a problem. "A problem," Polanyi remarks, "designates a gap within a constellation of clues pointing towards something unknown."[147] That Polanyi's formulation would have resonated with Julian's concept of "shewing" becomes apparent in the passage where she recalls how, while on her deathbed, God

---

145. Turner 2011, 78.

146. Though significantly modified by his successors (e.g., Hume, Kant), Descartes's rationalist framework continued to underwrite the competing epistemological frameworks of neo-Kantianism, positivism, and reductionism in the twentieth century. The main exception to the persistence of Cartesian axioms in modern epistemology is found in modern phenomenology, particularly as outlined by Husserl, Merleau-Ponty, and Marion, all of whom tend to situate their project in some proximity to classical metaphysics. For an overview of the phenomenological movement's metaphysical and theological underpinnings, see Baring 2019, 25–84, 183–210.

147. Polanyi 1969, 179, 171; see also Gadamer 2006, 268–336; and Pfau 2013a, 35–75, 584–90.

shewed me a litille thinge the quantite of a hasielle nutte, lygande [lying] in the palme of my hande, and, to my understanding, that it was as rounde as any balle. I lokede thereupon, and thought: "Whate maye this be?" And I was answered generaly thus: "It is alle that is made." I merveylede howe that it might laste, for me thought it might falle sodaynlye to nought for litille [being so small]. And I was answerede in mine understandinge: "It lasts and ever shalle, for God loves it. And so hath alle thinge the beinge thorowe the love of God." (*V* 4:7–13)

Seeing for Julian is essentially contiguous, if not outright synonymous, with interpreting the visible world as one would read any passage of scripture. The visible is to be received, not as a self-contained, inert, and self-evident *object*, but, rather, as an intuitively arresting *presence*. What accounts for the indisputable reality of the visible is the fact *that* it appears, regardless of *what* object or notion the appearance may point to. The certitude with which appearance is apprehended as such is not contingent on some separate act of verification or predication. Rather, precisely insofar as it is received as something continuously self-giving, rather than being owned by the subject in some representational form, the phenomenon must be honored as a gift. For the dynamic way in which a phenomenon is experienced enjoins the beholder to participate in it, to scrutinize it, and to seek to discern the reality that is being revealed, or made manifest, *through* the order of the visible and as such necessarily transcends it. To Julian, the "hasielle nutte" is not some inert *res extensa*; it is not literally self-evident but, rather, a figure of progressive understanding. It does not await the imposition of a concept but, precisely in accordance with *how* it appears to her, will prompt a series of questions and reflections. Nor is there anything solipsistic to this short meditation, for each reflective step (" . . . and I was answerede in mine understandinge") is articulated in writing for others rather than formed as an esoteric intellectual conception.

With good reason, Turner thus rejects "any attempt on our part to force some sharp positivist cleavage between the word 'see' as implying some immediacy of direct experience and the subsequent interpretation of that experience."[148] Attempts to subject Julian's writings to a hermeneutic of suspicion can only sow confusion. For whereas Cartesian "principles" and the Kantian "categories" seek to establish an absolute warrant for speaking of determinate *objects*, Julian's does not subject the reality of her experience to Pyrrhonist doubt or to epistemic dominion. Rather, she seeks to honor phenomenality as a gift and guidance, even with something as trifling as a "hasielle nutte." Thinking unfolds as an open-ended meditation on the visible world and what it may disclose about the source, God's love, whereby which all

---

148. Turner 2011, 80.

things are sustained in being. Hence Julian interprets the experience of the visible above all as a calling, that is, the distinctive call of the phenomenon to be sifted—humbly, patiently, and insistently—as a gift, to be cared for in open-ended and undesigning meditation. More than most of her readers, past or present, Julian continually struggles to comprehend what she has seen, and her writings present us with an increasingly complex transcript of that struggle. Yet even as she is deaf to the Siren's call of skepticism, which after all is not just a modern invention, Julian also avoids a naive, in tendency fideist, stance that would consider all "shewings" as de facto self-interpreting. Instead, her aim is patiently to understand how her "shewings" incrementally clarify her faith, whose experiential and intellectual substance is beyond all doubt even as its metaphysical grounds remain unfathomable. Hence, any mystical meaning located in Julian's writings "consists precisely not in some immediate datum of experience as distinct from its interpretation but, on the contrary, in the hidden meaning that can be known to be there, but in its ultimate significance inaccessibly so."[149]

In light of Julian's careful probing of the enigmatic bond between intuitive assent to and reflective understanding of her "shewings," it bears recalling the three complementary levels of hermeneutic practice, identified by Gadamer as the art of "understanding" (*subtilitas intelligendi*), "interpretation" (*subtilitas interpretandi*), and, crucially, "application" (*subtilitas applicandi*).[150] As in classical legal interpretation, Neoplatonist thought, and patristic exegesis, "understandinge" for Julian means participating *in* the fullness of appearance, rather than aspire to its speculative overcoming or naturalistic discrediting. Thus, the ultimate validation of the insights yielded by hermeneutic practice concerns not their formal correctness as propositions but the lived fulfillment of the meanings that such practice has revealed, that is, their "application" to the subject. For Julian, contemplating and reflecting on the vision unfolded in the opening sections of her short text thus can never be a function of subjective self-assertion or detached conceptual mastery. Rather, it is the meditative structure of the *lectio divina* that furnishes the template for continued inquiry and reflection. Such meditative *lectio* is no "private" pursuit, for the spiritual meanings unveiled are validated by their applicability not only to Julian's personal salvation, but, in equal measure, to the spiritual flourishing of the "evencristene" to whom Julian continually addresses herself. In affirming that "sothelye charite stirres me to

---

149. Ibid., 81.
150. Gadamer 2006, 306–7. Responding to Habermas's critique of *Truth and Method*, Gadamer affirms the essential bond between hermeneutics and Aristotelian *phronēsis*. As the foundation of all rational community, *phronēsis* must not be confused with the "procedural consciousness" (*Regelbewußtsein*) of modern method. Instead, the truth-claims of hermeneutics fundamentally aim to "bring into view prospects for knowledge [*Erkenntnischance offenzulegen*] that would otherwise go unrecognized" (Gadamer 1993b, 253, 263; trans. mine).

telle yowe it" (*V* 6:38), Julian confirms that unfolding for her fellow Christians the implications of her "shewings" is itself an integral component of their meaning.

The fact that Julian does not die, and that the eschaton of seeing God "face to face" is for the time being deferred, recalls the analogous predicament confronted by the early Christian communities of the first and second centuries. Given that Christ's apparently deferred return could not be anticipated with any certainty, it became necessary to rethink the relation between finite, historical time and the eschaton by embracing the church (Christ's body) and investing it with enduring hermeneutic and practical responsibility. Placing great ethical and interpretive burden on temporal and manifestly fallible human existence, the incalculably deferred eschaton came to be understood as "an event breaking into history, an event that transcends and is heterogeneous to it."[151] Finding themselves mired in distended, historical time, Christian communities thus began to evolve hermeneutic strategies by which to appraise and, if possible, legitimate the goods, practices, and goals ordering their finite, time-bound lives. Always, the task was to scrutinize the spiritual import of visible things and practices without allowing those particular goods to enter into competition with the eschaton or, in Pelagian or semi-Pelagian fashion, to claim ultimate agency in the drama of personal salvation. Ever cautious as to the deeper meaning of her deathbed recovery, Julian interprets it as both a gift and an obligation but never as "evidence" of her eventual salvation. Her writings thus put the time unexpectedly granted to her to spiritually legitimate use without claiming any privileged perspective for herself. Repeatedly confessing her sinfulness, and conceiving her "shewings" as a hermeneutic burden rather than private revelation, Julian seeks to fullfill her spiritual life by contemplating and sharing in writing what she has seen. What good there is in her vision—and Julian takes it to be altogether inexhaustible—can be honored only by imparting her "shewings" to a community of the faithful in an extended act of charity: "I was mekille [much] stirred in charite to mine evencristene, that thaye might alle see and knawe the same that I sawe" (*V* 7:8 f.). Contemplative writing, then, is never simply a matter of reporting on specific "shewings." Rather, it aims to sift their spiritual import and, in so doing, to acknowledge the "soverayne techare" and "blissede techinge of oure lorde" (*V* 6:38; 7:1).

Yet what, finally, is the knowledge to which her visions cumulatively direct her? Particularly in the shorter text, *Vision of a Devout Woman*, seeing and understanding tend to converge on the ultimate threshold moment of death. As Julian rivets her eyes on the crucifix in the hope of thus witnessing and participating in Christ's

---

151. Blumenberg 1983, 30–31; building on his critique of Karl Löwith's secularization thesis, Blumenberg distinguishes between historical time shaped by the eschaton's "immediate expectation" (*Naherwartung*) and the, in his view corrosive, effect on the sacred that makes itself felt when Christianity confronted a "longterm indeterminacy" (42–51).

Passion, her gaze fuses attention ("visemente"), understanding ("wittande"), and knowing ("knawande") into a single hermeneutic constellation. At this pivotal moment, which is the precise analogue of the eucharistic celebration during Mass, Julian no longer sees a material object, or a representation of what transpired on Calvary centuries ago, but the passion itself.

> I sawe with bodely sight the face of the crucifixe that hange before me, in whilke I behelde continuely a party of his passion: despite, spittinge, sowlinge of his body, and buffetinge in his blisfulle face, and many langoures and paines, ma than I can telle, and ofte changinge of coloure, and alle his blissede face a time closede in dry blode. (*V* 8:1–5)

Such attending-to and understanding what one sees requires extreme empathy: "I feled no paine botte for Cristes paines" (*V* 10:30–31), Julian remarks, intimating a parallel of sorts between Christ's suffering and her own. The dynamic structure of her vision thus prefigures "a grete aninge [union] betwyx Criste and us. For when he was in paine, we ware in paine" (*V* 10:44). Such empathetic vision extends well beyond the carefully circumscribed affective, mnemonic, and didactic functions stipulated by the Augustinian *ratio triplex*. For Julian and the thirteenth-century female mystics who precede her, "empathetic" vision does not consist in a sudden spike of subjective affect but, instead, transforms the beholder's very being.[152] Likewise, in Julian's text vision moves beyond the abstract quality of Neoplatonic "participation" (*methexis*) inasmuch as hers is a vision of Christ as *person* rather than as an ineffable, numinous being. Moreover, Julian not only finds her question concerning the role of human sinfulness answered by Christ's real presence during her deathbed vision, but "vision" is the only modality in which that answer can be tendered, and Christ's love was all that her vision was meant to convey: "For he wille that we be like to him in anehede [unity] of endeles luffe to oureselfe and to oure evencristen" (*V* 18:15).

Facing imminent death and finding herself profoundly unsettled by her vision ("I consayved a softe drede"), Julian is ultimately reassured by the knowledge that the full import of her vision will never fall solely within her dominion and responsibility. For in her vision itself, "oure lorde answerde me thus: 'I kepe the fulle sekerly'" (*V* 17:2–3). The phrasing here shows Julian firmly within an apophatic, mystical tradition, which means that Julian's vision can never *contain* but only ever *prefigure* the fullness of Christ's love. We recall de Lubac's clarification, "'Mystic, dogmatic, and solid speech' . . . does not establish him who holds it or who hears it within the mys-

---

152. Julian's rhetorical approach to visuality "actually prevents any affective identification and works to estrange us from the traditions of composition which may have made us think we are familiar with both the scene and the meditational mode" (Aers and Staley 1996, 89).

teries of the future age." Instead, such speech remains unequivocally within the order of distended, historical time, though also unwaveringly expectant of that order's eventual suspension. For Julian, the eschaton of the *visio beatifica* will only ever be partially manifested, beheld through a glass darkly, within the changeful "now" of finite existence. To affirm that "this shewed oure lorde me in the holehed of luffe [fullness of love] that we stande in, in his sight," and that "he luffes us nowe as wele whiles we ere here as he shalle do when we ere thare before his blissed face" (*V* 17:12–14) is not a case of epistemological overreach or metaphysical hubris. For Julian's unshakable certitude in approaching death is grounded in an awareness that the visualized "grete aninge [union] betwyx Criste and us" can take place only beyond death, in a realm utterly dissimilar from the world of Augustinian "memory time" ever prone to sin, error, and spiritual confusion. Like other contemplatives, followers of the *devotio moderna* and, ideally, the entire community of the faithful, Julian's life as an anchoress has had her prepare for, and as much as possible visualize, the decisive moment. The most emblematic goal of anchoritic practice is of course the same as for all of Julian's "evencristene," namely, to anticipate both intellectually and empathetically the transfiguration of death into eternal life as it is celebrated in the Eucharist and, again, in the quasi-sacramental structure of the *ars moriendi*.[153]

FROM IMAGELESS DEVOTION TO DEVOTIONAL PICTURES: ESCHATOLOGICAL CONFUSION IN VAN EYCK

Even as Christianity's framing of death within a sacramental order would continue to play a significant role in modernity's imaginary, the clarity and serenity evident on every page of Julian's writings show signs of atrophying just a generation after her death in 1416. By the early fifteenth century, Western Christianity's economy of salvation as articulated in thirteenth- and fourteenth-century mystical and contemplative writing, as well as the inventory of religious symbols and devotional images on which it had long relied, becomes increasingly unstable. As for the scope and legitimacy of symbol and image, long circumscribed by the apophatic tradition extending from Dionysius via Bernard and the Victorine School to the female mystics and contemplatives of Julian's time, the balance markedly shifts once devotional images are more widely available and the church's exclusive guardianship over their uses started to fray. Gradually, that is, Western Christianity grows more accepting of art images and less exacting as regards their theological legitimacy. By the early fifteenth century, the restrictive image concept formulated by pseudo-Dionysius and extended by

---

153. See Bynum 2006, 208–40.

Bernard, Bonaventure, all the way to Julian and Grote, appears to have lost much of its force. No longer confined to Bonaventure's formula (*per visibilia ad invisibilia*), the balance between Christianity's economy of salvation and the iconic forms tasked with mediating it appears to have tilted in favor of the latter. Increasingly, that is, doctrinal truth and eschatological expectancy appear enmeshed with, even dependent on, a more variegated and notably "realist" conception of religious art. If Gregory the Great had offered a qualified defense of the image—namely, as a mnemonic device meant to assist the illiterate masses—religious art turns out to flourish more than ever at a point when literacy, particularly in fifteenth-century towns and cities, is on the ascendant. What had been a relationship of supplementarity has evolved into one of dependency.

By 1400, new forms of lay piety, both in the private lives of the more affluent classes and in the tertiary spiritual communities associated with the *devotio moderna*, have spread across Northern Europe, often alongside, yet at times also in conflict with, the church. Within this new spiritual imaginary and its intensely personal forms of piety, painted images increasingly play a pivotal role. Often commissioned by wealthy individuals and commanding impressive prices in the new marketplace for art, this new type of religious painting not only stands well apart from the Italo-Byzantine style still dominant across much of Italy. The works of van Eyck, von der Weyden, Petrus Christus, or Memling, to name but a few, reflect also the emergence of inherently formal-aesthetic criteria that foreshadow the a-religious and eventually antireligious drift of Renaissance painting in the next century. What Bynum calls the "materialization and literalization of vision into object," whose earliest manifestations she traces back to around 1200, has come to flower in unprecedented and, as England's Lollards see it, scandalous ways some two hundred years later.[154] By then, a material culture of visuality and increasingly sumptuous and sophisticated religious painting has become steadily more detached from liturgical structures, affirming less the church's theological core tenets than the social status and political influence of bishops and abbots patronizing the artists commissioned to produce

---

154. Bynum 2011, 143; see also Dinzelbacher (2004), on how late medieval culture increasingly invests material objects with spiritual significance and, increasingly, found itself having to sustain and give concrete shape to devotional and liturgical practice. For a wealth of examples regarding the contested visual culture surrounding late medieval sacramental practice in East Anglia, see Duffy 2005, 63–68, who notes that in response to "the Lollard attack on the sacramental teaching of the Church," some forty baptismal fonts were commissioned in the 1460s, their octagonal form emphatically depicting the seven sacraments in what amounts to "an extremely precise and full form of catechetical teaching" (65 f.). See also Aston 1990, 104–54, who notes the strong link between the Lollards' iconoclasm and anticlericalism, as well as their insistence that the Decalogue's prohibition of images was not materially altered by Christ's incarnation as *imago Dei* "but remained as valid as it had ever been under the Jews—'For the same God is now, with the same commandment'" (120).

such works. Starting in the mid-thirteenth century and continuing until the Reformation, the status of the image and its relation to spiritual vision undergo significant change, almost a reversal.

Commenting, a century ago, on an obsessive visuality pervading religious life in late medieval Flanders and northern France, Johan Huizinga noted that "where faith rests on tangible images, it is hardly possible to make qualitative distinctions between the nature and degree of sanctity of the different elements of the faith. That God is to be worshipped and the saints merely venerated is not taught by the picture itself, and the difference is lost unless the church constantly warns about the necessary distinction." A seemingly omnipresent religious imagery left "no room between what was depicted, . . . the Trinity, the flames of hell, the catalog of saints—and faith in all this. There was no room for the question 'Is this true?'"[155] Though the apophaticism of Bernard's *Sermons on the Song of Songs* and St. Bonaventure's *Itinerarium* is never rejected outright, "the apparent opposition between the devotional image [*Andachtsbild*] and the imageless devotion" central to mystical theology has been greatly attenuated.[156] Indeed, already while Henry Suso and Meister Eckhart were formulating their strictly aniconic theologies, the concept of spiritual vision had begun to edge away from their strictly mentalistic conceptions. Paradoxically, their attempt "to affirm the value of the spiritual unmitigated by sensual perception" had the effect of reinvigorating the iconicity of religious experience that their writings sought to disavow: "Instead of providing evidence *for* aniconism, strictures on image making testify to exactly the opposite, namely the propensity . . . to make images and icons, and to figure the god in human form."[157]

Slowly yet inexorably, "the term 'image', originally a metaphor used for denoting a psychological concept, . . . assumed a concrete meaning applicable to pictorial art."[158] A new question thus arose, concerning "the way in which the act of looking itself enters into the problem of arousal," thereby revealing "a cognitive relation between looking and enlivening, and between looking hard, not turning away, concentrating, and enjoying on the one hand, and possession and arousal on the other."

---

155. Huizinga 1996, 189 f.; see also Ringbom 1969; Hamburger 1998, 111–48.

156. Ringbom 1969, 159. On the enduring centrality of commentaries on the *Canticles* for shaping late medieval debate over the status of vision and images, see Huizinga 1996, 227–29.

157. Freedberg 1989, 65, 60. "We in the West tend to dismiss the kinds of powers that were once called divine, all the more when we perceive the deployment of artistry and skill in working the object. But we do so because of our cultural prejudices in favor of what we think of as disinterested aesthetic judgment, and not because the god has departed from the image. The fact is that there is nothing in the history of response to suggest the possibility of complete disinterestedness of this kind. . . . If images were once, let us say, invested with lifelike and supernatural powers, it would surely be extravagant to suggest that any subsequent perception of a work of art could free itself of this history entirely" (74).

158. Ringbom 1969, 166.

Fundamentally, the question was about the agency of images that were no longer held to the *pro*visional function of mediating essentially apophatic truths. Instead, the painted image now served as a stimulant for anthropomorphic, affective forms of spirituality seemingly consummated in the very act of beholding. Instead of directing the viewer toward insights relative to which visual and verbal forms had previously stood in strictly anagogical relation, the religious "content" depicted by the new religious art image seemed to enthrall the beholder rather than enjoining an open-ended hermeneutic effort. Reinforcing this historical shift toward "arousal by sight of picture" is the unprecedented formal complexity, sumptuous coloration, and marked interest in verisimilitude of perspective and design of the artworks that after 1400 begin to proliferate in the great cathedrals and town churches, yet also in private residences and chapels not infrequently attached to them.[159] While transforming the very notion of sacred space, these art images also demanded a new level of aesthetic connoisseurship and where that was found wanting tended to be supplemented by elaborate inscriptions and by a new genre of writing: art historical commentary.[160] Nothing better reflects the extraordinary change wrought in barely two generations, roughly between 1385 and 1435, than this shift in the relation of image and text—from the devotional image of the Man of Sorrows eliciting patient and humble contemplation to religious art images now titled so as to ensure that their beholder may readily decode scriptural references and symbolic meanings and, thus, learn to appreciate the artist's painterly achievement. Yet knowledge that takes the form of learned philological commentary is inherently discursive and, thus, extrinsic to religious meanings no longer experienced but strictly referred or alluded to by the art image. Visual and spiritual cognition have begun to part ways.

Among the first to draw attention to the growing dependency of spiritual vision on material images and sacred objects starting in the later fourteenth century was Johan Huizinga. Yet his emphatically retrospective and nostalgic portrait of the "waning" Middle Ages naturally casts as a matter of decline and eventual decadence what fifteenth-century viewers in Northern Europe would more likely have experienced as a dramatic expansion of visual-cum-spiritual experience. On Hans Belting's magisterial account, the period between 1350 and 1490 is characterized by a growing awareness that received Italo-Byzantine styles are increasingly being displaced by new, more realist and more self-consciously symbolic forms of religious painting. A gap begins to open up between the spiritual and liturgical function of images, on the one hand, and their formal and hermeneutic intricacy as aesthetic artifacts, on the other.

---

159. Freedberg 1989, 325–26.

160. See Lipton (2008, 263–64), who provides numerous examples of literal readings not only forestalled by the formal and motivic complexity of images but also being positively discouraged as naive and misleading by abbots and theologians of the later twelfth century.

Naturally, the pace of these shifts tends to vary by region and local geography; for example, the hilltop locations of cities such as Siena and Orvieto rendered them less prone to new artistic influences than, say, a commercial center like Florence. Thus it would take several more decades before the old techniques and underlying theological principles informing Italo-Byzantine panel painting of, say, Buoninsegna or Lorenzetti, were regarded as outmoded. Still, as Cennini's systematic exposition in *Il Libro dell' Arte* (1390) suggests, by the end of the fourteenth century the late Italo-Byzantine style had already "taken on the appearance of deliberate archaism."[161] To make up for the style's fading authority, the religious paintings abiding within this older matrix continued to grow in size and feature increasingly lavish ornamentation. Concurrently, as Belting has shown, a culture of private devotional images takes shape, above all, in Flanders, the Rhineland, and Northern France—areas where religious life and practice are significantly transformed by the *devotio moderna*. These private images are distinguished by their small, pocket-sized formats or, in the case of the wealthy elite of commercial towns and cities and the aristocracy, become an integral feature of the relatively new, sumptuously illuminated genre, the Book of Hours.

In growing contrast to the multiple-viewpoint ("reverse-perspective") technique and the elongated faces and foreheads dominating the old Byzantine-influenced paintings, fifteenth-century religious art features increasingly realist ways of placing a moment from biblical narrative within landscapes or interiors of great spatial and symbolic complexity. Moreover, the increased availability of panel paintings, and, by the mid-fifteenth-century, woodcuts, further enhanced their commercial appeal as quasi-spiritual tokens to be acquired for private devotion: "Individual citizens did not want an image different from the public one so much as they needed one that would belong to them personally. They expected the image to speak to them in person."[162] The transition from an iconic to an image-based vision is characterized by "the increasingly important role of corporeal imagery in spiritual life."[163] In this development, extending from the late thirteenth through the fifteenth century, "the process of vision is detached from the process of reading [scripture]." As the new type of devotional image becomes a repository of scriptural allusions and increasingly

---

161. Belting 1994, 409.

162. Ibid., 409–10. An "act of duty," the acquisition of devotional images furnished its owner "not only a tool for devotion but a certification of the pious disposition they were to attain. Images became visible proofs of an inner life" (411). The function of Cennini's *Libro dell' Arte*, which for long stretches reads like a manual for artists eager to work within an established, Italo-Byzantine template, remains contested. Broecke suggests it was "intended as a spectacular display of . . . Cennino's knowledge and abilities, formed into a satisfying literary whole designed to impress the cutting-edge intellectuals of the Carrara court" (2015, 9).

163. Hamburger 1998, 121, 148.

fungible symbolic meanings, the power of biblical narrative and its truth claims appear increasingly dependent on the material image-object. Sara Lipton has remarked
on the "multiplication and diversification of subject matter, a trend towards emo-
tionalism and naturalism in style, and the introduction of religious art into urban
and bourgeois domestic spaces."[164] Aside from competing for the three-dimensional
realism that until now had been the exclusive province of sculpture, the rapid development of linear perspective observable in religious painting at the start of the
fifteenth century not only "integrates mystical theology with a universal epistemology . . . [but] also tended to level distinctions between mystical, visionary, and
visual experience."[165]

Arguably, the growing investment in images, less as conduits *to* than as tangible evidence *of* formerly ineffable, spiritual meanings, favors a realist conception
of art long exemplified by the medium of sculpture and, after 1430, also emulated
in painting by a new emphasis on verisimilar, three-dimensional spatial effects. As
"seeing came to define believing, the need to assert and safeguard auratic authenticity became ever more pronounced."[166] No longer, then, is the image legitimated by
an invisible, numinous truth that it seeks to mediate; and the quality of how it is experienced by the beholder consequently shifts from a stance of devout, prayerful attention to a highly self-conscious appraisal of its visible motifs. For an example, let us
consider van Eyck's *Virgin and Child with Canon van der Paele* (1434–36) (fig. 3.6), a
work that shows the phenomenology of religious images and their medial status to
have fundamentally changed. Here the act of devotion and prayer centered on the
image of the Madonna has itself become the painting's central motif; devotional vision is both realized *in* and (reflexively) authenticated *by* the image. Set within an
imaginary ecclesial space adapted to the unique choreography of figures, van Eyck's
painting combines extraordinary technical artistry of the kind "that appeals emphatically to the senses" with complex symbolic figures and motifs.[167] Meanwhile,
the painting's background is enlivened both by the pallid light visible through the
milky, diaphanous windows and by the spatial recesses stimulating a visual curiosity
that the image itself will never satisfy. Perhaps most striking about the choreography
of persons in the foreground is the complete absence of eye contact among any of
them. Thus, the devout and gravely ill Canon van der Paele, clutching his prayer
book, has just removed his eyeglasses in a gesture intended to present him as "fundamentally disconnected from the perceptible world." While suggesting his transition,

---

164. Lipton 2008, 266; see also Bynum 2011, 44–123.
165. Hamburger 2000, 60.
166. Ibid., 48–49. On the beholder's "oscillation between the painted and the imagined picture
[*Changieren zwischen gemaltem und imaginierten Bild*]," see Dinzelbacher 2004 (quote from 68).
167. Rothstein 2005, 52.

Figure 3.6. Jan van Eyck, *Virgin and Child with Canon Joris van der Paele*, 1434–36. Bruges, Groeningemuseum

either intended or momentarily achieved, from material perception (of the book in his hands) to spiritual vision, the gesture also "allud[es] to the fallibility of the senses more generally."[168] Likewise, none of the other figures appear to make eye contact, the sole exception being the infant Christ whose searching look is firmly trained on van der Paele.[169]

Meanwhile, the Virgin and Child so regally and realistically placed at the painting's center might may also be taken as a projection of the dying canon's inner vision, presumably informed by reflections on the Last Judgment. Whether we are to think of that vision as merely aspirational or as having been positively achieved depends, at least in part, on our knowledge of van der Paele's persona and the specific office with

---

168. Ibid., 50.

169. For discussions of the painting, see Lane 1991 (on van der Paele's illness); on van Eyck's realism, see Seidel 1991; Harbison 1991; and Rothstein 2005.

which the painting's title associates him. As a secular canon with allegiance to the church and the pope, van der Paele (ca. 1370–1443) enjoyed a privileged position that guaranteed him income from numerous prebends without any major service obligations. Deriving substantial worldly benefits from the church without rendering her significant service would likely have been perceived as "questionable on both political and intellectual grounds" by his contemporaries.[170] By capturing the lavish ornamentation of the church interior and St. Donatian's episcopal attire, van Eyck's painting hints at a sharp tension between the church as a space of conspicuous material wealth and the invisible eschaton to which the well-beneficed, albeit gravely ill canon appears to direct his prayerful attention at last. The antinomy between corporate-ecclesiastic and private-devotional objectives is accentuated by emblematic figures gazing in various directions without their eyes ever meeting, and it is further reinforced by an inscription referencing St. Donatian's rebirth and subsequent consecration as bishop: "SOLO P[AR]TV NON[VS] FR[ATRV]M MERS[VS] VIV[VS] REDIT[VR]. RENAT[VS] ARCH[IEPISC]O[PV]S PR[I]M[VS] REMIS CONSTI-TUVITVR."[171]

Fundamentally, van Eyck's painting features two distinct plateaus of meaning that operate in virtual simultaneity: a realistic one involving three men—St. Donatian, patron saint of the canon's church in Bruges, in full bishop's regalia earnestly appraising the canon, who in turn seems awkwardly placed next to the canon's name-saint, St. George. Their choreography, however, already suggests unresolved tensions between the Church Penitent and the Church Militant. The other plateau involves the eschaton of the Church Triumphant, embodied by the Virgin and Child, whose presence ought to be (and, perhaps, actually is) the true focus of the dying canon's spiritual vision. At the same time, the emphatically realist presentation of the Madonna and Child as the painting's central motif invites the beholder to authenticate at the level of empirical sight (*visus*) what the penitent canon sees or aspires to see by inward contemplation (*visio*). Hence Bret Rothstein views van der Paele "quite clearly in the company of the surrounding group," as confirmed by the visual detail of St. George's shadow falling across the canon's shoulder. Van Eyck "cleverly implies that the Virgin, Child, saints, and van der Paele are nothing less than physically present before us." Yet Rothstein's concession that the canon "does not see the group around him at all" inevitably complicates whatever spiritual message such pictorial

---

170. Harbison 1991, 55; "there is an edge to this painting" in that van Eyck seems "to imply that van der Paele wanted the best of both worlds, the institutional and the personal" (67, 69).

171. "The ninth brother from a single birth, he fell into the water and returned alive. Thus reborn, he was made the first Archbishop of Reims. He now enjoys the eternal glory of God." See Rothstein 2005, 64, 211 n. 47; another disquieting symbol is found in the figure of Cain slaying Abel, placed to the left of Mary's throne.

realism might be taken to convey.[172] For any notion of realism anchored in a verifiably shared perception begins to crumble if it is claimed that an image places "before us," in spatiotemporal simultaneity, a fifteenth-century canon, two saints who died more than a millennium earlier, and the Virgin and Christ child. More plausibly, one might hold that their visibility for beholders of van Eyck's canvas stems from the painting's stunning simulation of a three-dimensional ecclesiastic space. The picture's verisimilitude offers its viewers a perceptual crutch of sorts as they struggle to reconcile its material, visible aspect with its elusive "image-subject" (Husserl), in this case, the spiritual communion of saints, Virgin, and Child in which the canon seeks to participate.

A further complication, as Jeffrey Hamburger has noted, arises from the fact that van Eyck, evidently delighting in his consummate technical wizardry, paints his various reflections (including his own) on the armor of St. George.[173] Such conspicuous artistic feats as the painting of reflections (most famously realized in van Eyck's Arnolfini portrait) and the impressive smoothness of brushwork when it comes to capturing texture and color (e.g., the bishop's and the Virgin's robes, the mail in St. George's armor, the semitransparent glass panels in the background) are all the more remarkable given the novelty of van Eyck's medium, siccative oil on oak panel, which had been in use only since about 1410. And yet, while the superior luminosity and stunningly fine pigmentation of the new mixture allowed for unprecedented levels of painterly illusionism, it thereby also threatened to obscure the theological foundations of the devotional image (*Andachtsbild*). At the very least, van Eyck's pictorial realism seems to accept, if not positively reinforce, the viewer's "postlapsarian mental function, which necessarily relies on pictures as a consequence of spiritual blindness." Yet if this is the case, then Rothstein's conclusion that "we respond to the saint as though he is present before us" would appear precisely the wrong one to draw.[174] For in that case the beholder will be enthralled, indeed trapped, within van Eyck's illusory pictorial spaces and consequently barred from attaining the spiritual vision to which van der Paele, having taken off his eyeglasses, evidently aspires, perhaps in atonement for the rather parasitic worldly life he has led. Precisely the hypnotic power of van Eyck's pictorial realism prevents his viewers from remembering that the vision to which they ought to ascend can be attained only if they, too, remove their glasses.

The problem of realism and hyper-simulation is that it confounds the spiritual vision that it aims to authenticate. Once the perfection of illusory, three-dimensional

---

172. Rothstein 2005, 52–53.

173. "Van Eyck does more than merely call attention to his artistic wizardry or even to his presence in this picture. He also holds in check the illusion of unimpeded access to a realm of supernatural experience" (Hamburger 2000, 51).

174. Rothstein 2005, 58, 64.

space, material texture, and symbolic detail have become the overriding artistic objective, the painted image distracts from, and ultimately supervenes on, the mystic's
ideal of a strictly aniconic, spiritual vision. Whereas Bonaventure's *Itinerarium* had
conceived vision as an integral narrative sequence leading from three-dimensional,
visible "remnants" (*vestigia*) toward the aniconic vision of the *trinitas superessen-
tialis*, van Eyck's painting implicitly frames the visible and the invisible as locked
in an epistemological competition of sorts. Henceforth, the painted image depicts
the devotional and liturgical practices of socioeconomically distinct individuals in
three-dimensional space, with their attire and other symbolic detail attesting to their
worldly and temporal condition. With the telos of the mystic *visio beatifica* having
drifted out of sight, realist painting seeks to maximize the visibility of both what it
depicts and of itself qua picture. It "will always strive to present precisely those aspects that shine with a greater radiance. . . . [In it] only the visible remains entirely presented, without further promising anything else to see save what is offered
already." Anchored in linear perspective and realized on smoothly lacquered surfaces that conceal the material brushwork to which the painted image owes its existence, van Eyck's art of illusion transmutes the liturgically embedded and theologically grounded *eikōn* into a painterly artifact. Henceforth, religious painting's
"non-physical space, where the visible alone reigns, abolishes *l'invu* (the invisible by
default), and reduces the phenomenon to pure visibility."[175] Increasingly, then, the
devotional image evolves into a membrane of sorts, at once promising and obstructing access "to an impenetrable and incommensurable reality." As the mid-fifteenth-
century devotional image continues to evolve into a cultural commodity and status
symbol of sorts, earlier religious paintings are being recut so as to fit into expensively
ornamented tondo frames, thereby further blurring the boundary between their
owners' ostensive piety and affirmations of their socioeconomic status. The owner
thus could imagine that "to look into the expensively painted mirror [was] to see, not
himself, but the image of the suffering Christ," an equivocal dynamic on full display
in Cosimo Medici's image-saturated private chapel in the Palazzo Medici-Ricardi
(fig. 3.7).[176]

　　We begin to see the outlines of an emergent antinomy between theological and
aesthetic values as van Eyck's painting simultaneously presupposes and confounds
"the medieval notion that three-dimensional images . . . had a higher claim on reality

---

　　175. Marion 2002b, 63, 68.
　　176. Belting 1994, 422. Installed shortly after Cosimo's return from exile to Florence in 1434,
the chapel's rich ceiling ornamentation, costly marble floors (featuring the family emblems), and
sumptuous murals (by Gozzoli, a student of Fra Angelico) were completed only when Cosimo's
son, Piero, had the space expanded around 1460. The murals depict the journey of the Magi, whose
sumptuous presentation aligns with the worldly splendor of the Medici themselves; see MacGregor
2000, 37–41.

Figure 3.7. Chapel in the Palazzo Medici-Ricardi, ca. 1460

than a mere picture." Thus, the painter's depiction of Canon van der Paele reveals the way that the devotional image (*Andachtsbild*) has been profoundly altered in form and function by its self-conscious realization as an art image that already foreshadows Schiller's eventual concept of the "sentimental." For the beholder cannot possibly fail to notice "the degree to which the[se paintings] develop a self-conscious discourse on the status of images, imaginative experience, and their role in visionary perception."[177] Once again, the image reveals both its power and ambivalence, its precarious suspension between the iconic and the idolatrous, between what Marion identifies as "two manners of being, . . . not two classes of beings." In the case of the idol, the beholder's hermeneutic activity is wholly circumscribed by the visible image, such that whatever meaning is attributed to the (painted) image must admit

177. Hamburger 2000, 53, 48. As Belting observes, "The functions of devotion against that of true aesthetics were far apart from each other, but the painter makes this problem the real issue of his picture" (1989, 430).

of verification by some visible detail. A logic of strict immanence here supplants the earlier, mystical conception according to which the image can only mediate, but never unilaterally capture, an essentially apophatic knowledge. The result is a circular epistemology according to which the visible is forever in need of supplemental proof, even as the evidence adduced for that purpose must itself always satisfy the requirement of pure immanence and total visibility. Once visibility has been instituted as both the supreme type of evidence and as forever begging further verification, "image" (*eikōn*) and "idol" (*eidōlon*) become all but indistinguishable. For what defines the idol is how it "fascinates and captivates the gaze precisely because everything in it must expose itself to the gaze. . . . With its visibility, [the idol] fills the intention of the gaze, which wants nothing other than to see."[178] At issue is an "apparent opposition between the devotional image and the imageless devotion," between the image as preliminary scaffolding of a strictly numinous truth, or as the indispensable catalyst for attaining that truth in the form of a vision; or, as Hamburger formulates the central question, "Were the visions inspired by the art, or the art by the visions?"[179]

If, within the "new conception of the holy image, . . . the subjective moment exists within the image itself," and if thereby "the image has changed to the point where a private salvation becomes its real subject matter," the startling emphasis on its medial and material constitution threatens to compromise the theological justification of images that Byzantine monastics and clerics had formulated nearly seven centuries earlier.[180] By 1450, the phenomenology of image experience has decisively shifted, away from mystical contemplation and toward a type of connoisseurship aimed at reconciling the formal-technical, symbolic-motivic, and theological dimensions of the painted image—dimensions intuitively felt to be no longer in alignment. The metaphysical dimension of images and the spiritual quality of the gaze they institute has become palpably atrophied, just as the asceticism of anchoritic life and the *unio mystica* at the heart of Julian's writings (recalling the Byzantine ideal of *theōsis*) appear increasingly remote. Still, such loss of spiritual certitudes and the creeping secularity observable in a good deal of fifteenth-century religious painting not only did not go unnoticed at the time but gave rise to frantic attempts at reinjecting spiritual meaning into a world awash in excessive visuality and material ostentation. The result is a new concept of the art image as symbolic form whose metaphysical, specifically eschatological, import proves unstable in proportion as it has drifted away from its origins in Dionysian, apophatic theology and toward a worldview consumed with bringing all things to total, sumptuous visibility. A century ago, Huizinga char-

---

178. Marion 1991, 9–10; "The idol consigns the divine to the measure of a human gaze" (14).
179. Ringbom 1969, 159; Hamburger 1998, 115.
180. Belting 1989, 418, 416.

acterized late medieval Flanders and northern France as a "world perfectly pictured through [an] all-encompassing symbolism." No doubt aware of the shallow and increasingly formulaic productions of the symbolist movement that had only recently been supplanted by pictorial modernism, Huizinga concluded that the fifteenth-century fascination with embodying religious knowledge in lavishly colored and subtly allusive images had caused "the individual symbols [to be] turned into petrified flowers." What at first blush might have been taken as evidence of a prolific imagination, symbolism perilously "attaches itself to the intellectual function like a parasitic plant and degenerates into pure habit and a disease of thought."[181]

Anchored in the laws of linear perspective, three-dimensional space, and proto-historicist notions of realism (of textures and styles of dress, building designs, interior decor, etc.), fifteenth-century Flemish and northern German painting tends to encode spiritual meanings in a religious symbolism that, in time, reduces to little more than a familiar array of pictorial convention and self-conscious allusions to scripture. Aimed at recognition rather than revelation, the emergent symbolism appears to drift away from the anagogical image concept, which sought to orient the beholder toward numinous meanings with which it did not purport to coincide, and in which it participated only by refusing to limit itself to mere visibility. By contrast, late medieval symbolism's affiliation with new forms of pictorial realism aims at "the continuous transfusion of the feeling for God's majesty and for eternity into everything that can be perceived and thought." In this "polyphony of thought," where "anything with its individual qualities can be the symbol of yet other things," and where "highest things are symbolized by thousands of lower things," the crucial axiom of apophatic theology—namely, the ontological difference between divine Being and mundane beings—has effectively dropped out.[182]

Implicitly, the new symbolism that transforms fifteenth-century painting reflects the growing appeal of theological Nominalism, which (against the conception of *analogia* expounded by the Fourth Lateran Council) asserted the univocity of divine and finite being. Thus, pictorial symbolism treats the abundant diversity of mundane beings not only as legitimate expressions of, but as outright convertible with, the invisible God. To conceive of the visible and the numinous order as sharing in one and the same ontological substratum yielded a "new interest in nature" that, as Charles Taylor notes, "was not a step outside of a religious outlook, even partially; it was a mutation within this outlook."[183] In particular the Franciscans' stress on Christ's human nature as a legitimate object of devotion had, in time, "granted individual form a definitiveness which it had not possessed before." The result is "a daring

181. Huizinga 1996, 240.
182. Ibid., 239.
183. Taylor 2007, 95.

cosmic symbolism" that regards each discrete fact of nature as suffused with "inexhaustible expressiveness."[184] As so often, the shift in outlook is subtle and can easily be missed. We recall how in Julian's *Vision*, a thing as small and ephemeral as a "hasielle nutte" mediates the metaphysical truth that like "alle thinge, [it has] the beinge thorowe the love of God" (*V* 4:7–13). In its formal identity and continuity in time, each particular, visible thing may be understood as a reflection of the invisible source that sustains it in being. Yet by the same token, each particular thing can only *mediate* a numinous reality but never claim to coincide with it. As an image, then, Julian's "hasielle nutte" can only signify *per analogiam*. By contrast, the emergent symbolism presents us with a fundamentally new image concept, supposing each visible particular to be infused with *immediate and infinite significance*. The "consciousness of difference" that John of Damascus, or, in our time, Gadamer, regards as an altogether integral feature of the image has melted away. An early case in point would be the subtly individualized, late Italo-Byzantine style of Cimabue and Duccio. Here the balance between universal spiritual meanings and increasingly refined techniques for rendering human individuality visible gradually tilts in favor of the latter. Henceforth, the painted image's technical wizardry and symbolic complexity eclipse the transcendent meanings that an iconographic approach had sought to prefigure.

As symbolism supplants anagogy, its claim to instantaneous and authentic fullness of meaning dissolves the fruitful tension between Augustinian "memory time" and its eschatological fulfillment. By the late fifteenth and early sixteenth century, a finely spun system of symbolic equivalences has drained the underlying cosmological framework, the Great Chain of Being, of all eschatological meaning. As Arthur Lovejoy noted, it cannot surprise that "the notion of infinitesimal gradation . . . was hardly suitable to a program which was, after all, designed to bring man as speedily as possible to his supersensible felicity."[185] It would be a mistake, however, to suppose that the transmutation of the devotional image into a material art object and into private property had categorically shorn art of all religious or metaphysical significance and, instead, had set images and their experience on some irreversible, secular trajectory. For the *unio mystica*, whose evolution we have sketched thus far, and the eschatological orientation at its very heart were never something merely *notional* and, consequently, could not simply fade away. Mystical vision and eschatological hope cannot be "explained" (away) as a historically contingent theological formula about to be dispelled by the putatively "enlightened" modernity that lay ahead. For one thing, the eschaton must be understood as a comprehensive revelation that not only structures the threshold-event of death but also passes judgment on the entire narra-

---

184. Dupré 1993, 36. On the Nominalist underpinnings of the "realism" emerging in late thirteenth-century religious painting, see also Pfau 2013a, 160–82; Taylor 2007, 90–99.
185. Lovejoy 1964, 90.

tive of the life that has led up to that final moment. Indeed, the eschaton that is the vanishing point of a spiritual vision grounded in the three theological virtues is always latently present in this life, too. It furnishes the source of mental and spiritual energy absent which human life, however secular its material conditions and self-appraisal, would quickly cease to have any meaning whatsoever and, in due course, become positively unendurable. Put differently, the eschatological vision at the heart of Bernard's, Bonaventure's, and Julian's spiritual and exegetical narratives does not simply disappear outright. Rather, it is displaced and, at times, disfigured by an idolatrous gaze no longer capable of distinguishing between the material image presentation and its symbolic meaning and thus prone to conflating eschatological fulfillment with the pleasure of physical sight. In ways that from a normative theological standpoint ought to be considered almost entirely illicit, the Renaissance's quest for the formal and physical perfection of the image effectively substitutes itself for an earlier apophatic economy that had understood all images (pictorial and textual) to be both anagogically ordered toward the eschaton *and* at an infinite remove from it. To illustrate the persistence of eschatological vision in an avowedly post-, at times militantly anti-metaphysical, era, we will have to momentarily disrupt chronology and leap ahead to consider the interrelated crises of image and eschatology at the turn of the twentieth century.

AFTER SYMBOLISM: ESCHATOLOGICAL DESPAIR AND COUNTERFEIT DEVOTION IN TOLSTOY AND MANN

If "the bureau of eschatology had usually been closed during the nineteenth century," as Ernst Troeltsch remarked, it opened under new management and with considerable fanfare by the end of 1918. In the wake of World War I and the Spanish flu and for much of the twentieth century, questions of eschatology would become "the storm center" of theology, the central inspiration for writers as disparate as Barth, Bultmann, Heidegger, Przywara, Congar, Ratzinger, and von Balthasar, to name but a few.[186] No doubt, what precipitated this reengagement with eschatology and closely associated questions concerning death, time, and love was the slaughter of some 10 million soldiers in the trenches of the war, followed by another 40 million dead from the 1918–19 Spanish flu.[187] The sheer magnitude of suffering and death compressed into just five years seemed to defy all rational comprehension. Indeed,

---

186. Troeltsch, quoted in von Balthasar 1989a, 255. For a concise and lucid survey of the transformation of post–World War I philosophy and theology by eschatology (in Bultmann, Heidegger, Gogarten, Rosenzweig, et al.), see Wolfe 2019. Arguably, von Balthasar was the first to perceive and articulate this pattern, in the revised version of his *Apokalypse der deutschen Seele* (1939).

187. On the human and social costs of the Great War, see Stevenson 2004, 404–11.

it raised questions beyond the obviously pressing ones concerning moral responsibility for the utterly senseless, so-called Great War and the manifest failure of gov-
ernments to cope with the pandemic that, quite predictably, had descended on a
malnourished and resource-deprived global populace. What also became clear to a
generation of post–World War I writers such as Rilke, Scheler, Barth, Heidegger,
Przywara, T. Mann, T. S. Eliot, C. Dawson, and many others besides was that an entirely new language was needed in which to address pressing questions raised by the
late cataclysm. Evidently, the liberal-progressive optimism and spiritual compla-
cency that had dominated European political, intellectual, and religious culture
throughout the "long nineteenth century" had come abruptly to a close. Thus, virtually all of the competing explanatory frames that the long nineteenth century had
evolved—scientific naturalism, laissez-faire liberalism, various shades of socialism,
imperialism, nationalism, anarchism, symbolist decadence, as well as Leonine Catholicism and liberal Protestantism—had been swept away, along with an entire generation of youth, by successive mass slaughter, famine, pandemic, and revolution,
upheavals for which, in at least some instances, these ideologies themselves bore
considerable responsibility.

Along with millions of lives, what had been obliterated in the trenches was the
axiomatic meliorism undergirding virtually all those nineteenth-century grand narratives for which Hegel's (and Comte's) "reinterpretation of revelation as continuous
and progressive" had furnished the template. After 1914, a liberal-Protestant "explanation" of the Last Judgment as a "history-immanent event" and of God as no longer
"beyond history so as to irrupt into it . . . but [as] himself constituted in and through
history" seemed but a genteel fiction that was unceremoniously laid to rest in the
blood-soaked fields of Flanders and Eastern Prussia.[188] In the aftermath of the Hegelian, liberal-historicist framework, the most promising scheme to fill this conceptual
void was a spectral, existentialist vision advanced by Heidegger, though anticipated
just as forcefully (and with due horror) by Augustine long before: "God forbid that
there should be any truth in a doctrine threatening us with a true misery which is
never to end, but which is to be interrupted, often and without end, by intervals of
false blessedness."[189] Perhaps for the first time since the later Middle Ages, the question of human existence, of Dasein, or being-in-the-world, that Heidegger was to
formulate so ambitiously, was being posed in holistic ways that exceeded the brief of
modern specialized inquiry. From Barth's *Letter to the Romans* (1918/22), Max Scheler's *Of the Eternal in Man* (1921) Rilke's *Duino Elegies* (1922), Eliot's *The Waste Land*,
Thomas Mann's *Magic Mountain* (1924), and Heidegger's *Being and Time* (1927) to
Erich Przywara's *Analogia Entis* (1932) and Eliot's *Four Quartets* (1936–43), the

---

188. Wolfe 2017, 686–87.
189. Augustine 1998, 530 (XII.21).

metaphysical specter haunting intellectuals during the interwar years was, as Rilke put in 1925, that "this life suspended over the abyss should prove impossible [*daß dieses so ins Bodenlose gehängte Leben unmöglich sei*]."[190]

However different their rhetorical approach and the conclusions reached, the writers just named all understand themselves to be confronting a condition of pervasive eschatological doubt, even despair; and they concur that their holistic project necessitated a categorical break with the conceptualist and disciplinary models refined during the previous century: economics, sociology, historicism, neo-Kantianism, and classical-liberal political thought. Instead, in what may be conceived broadly as an Augustinian turn in early twentieth-century philosophy, theology, and the arts, renewed emphasis is placed on articulating how the human being experiences its existence and that whatever intellectual and spiritual orientation it is capable of, unfolds at an intuitive, preconceptual level rather than by drawing on inherited conceptual schemes and procedures that by the 1920s appear depleted and discredited, the spoiled fruit of a bygone era.

Having traced the concept of anagogical vision and eschatological hope from Augustine to Julian should put us on guard against naively embracing a hermeneutics of strict finitude and immanence, one whose deficiencies appear especially glaring where modern subjectivity confronts death. For once metaphysical commitments and eschatological hope have been abandoned, death is experienced as sheer negation and, consequently, as the loss of all meaning, as something that ought not to be at all. Such a view of death as the "greatest evil" (Hobbes) seemed inevitable given the shift, largely complete by the mid-seventeenth century, from an Aristotelian, teleological cosmology to the post- or anti-metaphysical notion of an aggregate "nature" under the exclusive jurisdiction of modernity's *homo faber*. Henceforth, "knowledge of nature serves the purpose of manufacture [*im Dienst des Machens*]," whereas "teleological thinking had constituted an empathic knowledge of nature, an attempt to understand nature as our equal [*Natur als unseresgleichen zu verstehen*]."[191] Once Gassendi, Hobbes, Mandeville, LaMettrie, Helvetius, Priestley, and others supplant classical teleology with mechanistic explanatory schemes fueled exclusively by

---

190. Rilke to Withold Hulewicz (13 November 1925), *RB* 2:374 (my emphasis).

191. Spaemann 2011, vol. 2, 105; remarking on philosophical naturalism's habitual confusion of teleonomy and teleology, Spaemann notes that truly "living [*lebendig*] is only a system that is a whole unto itself and that strives to be a whole [*das danach strebt, ein Ganzes zu sein*], rather than a system that merely presents itself as a whole to a living observer." Consequently, "if we ask where exactly it is decided whether to interpret life as something epiphenomenal or as something ontological-original, it seems to me that the answer will always depend on this: whether we consider life's teleology [*Finalität*] primarily in terms of self-preservation [*Selbsterhaltung*] or self-transcendence" (88). On the dismantling of final causation and teleological thinking in early modernity, see also Spaemann and Löw 2005, 81–121; Dupré 1993, 15–90; Pfau 2018a.

efficient causation, life—including human life—becomes but one more quality that may be predicated of certain material forms. Life is reduced from a mystery to an epistemological puzzle; it does not name the holistic reality of everything that "can be the case" (to borrow Wittgenstein's phrase) but, instead, is but another secondary quality predicated of certain classes of beings. Neither gift nor mystery, whatever remains puzzling about life is to be solved by reducing it to a finite set of somatic "states" begging biomechanical "explanation." No longer, that is, is life understood as an entelechy in which practical, technical, and contemplative knowledge (Aristotle's triad *phronēsis*, *technē*, and *theōria*) are fully integrated. Instead, with mechanist, monocausal explanatory schemes of modern naturalism proving either unable or unwilling to invest life with any meaning beyond that of sheer self-prolongation, death and dying are construed as sheer negation, an unwelcome challenge to the epistemological hubris of *homo faber*.

To be sure, this de-potentiation of life by naturalist and reductionist explanatory schemes also met with resistance, such as in Leibniz's metaphysical and Kant's more qualified, "critical" defense of teleology, both of which provided critical support for the Romantic idea of organic form that allowed life to be understood as a purposive narrative rather than a function of mechanically induced, discontinuous states. Still drawing on a teleological principle, Hegel's *Phenomenology of Spirit* (1807) appears to be the last major philosophical text to rely on an expressly Christian-eschatological understanding of death as the threshold separating finite and imperfect life from its intended sublation and completion. Here death is yet conceived as a threshold rather than a terminus, indeed as the source rather than occlusion of all meaning. Fueled by "the tremendous power of the negative, spirit [*Geist*] does not shrink from death. Rather, it is "the life that endures it and maintains itself in it. It wins its truth only when, in utter dismemberment [*Verwüstung*], it finds itself. . . . Spirit is this power only by looking the negative in the face and tarrying with it."[192] Hegel's qualified retention of an eschatological framework still resonates in the work of Georg Simmel, who in 1910 likewise demurs at the reductionist concept of death as sheer negation, that is, no more than the mythical fates capriciously severing the thread of life (*Parzenschnitt*). For to conceive death merely as something to be avoided, postponed, and denied not only leaves us with a stunted conception of death, but also of life, which on this view appears "only as a temporal approximation of death." What Heidegger in *Being and Time* will reformulate (without acknowledging his debt to Simmel) as "being-toward-death" is captured in the latter's 1910 essay as the existential situation whereby "the life that we use up as we approach death is used up to flee death."[193]

---

192. Hegel 1977, 19 (par. 32).
193. Simmel 2007b, 72, 75.

Such speculative rearguard actions notwithstanding, modern narrative is over-whelmingly anti-teleological and, more by naturalistic default than explicit reason-ing, appears largely indifferent to eschatological concerns. Or, more accurately, the protagonists of the modern novel from Stendhal's Julien Sorel to Tolstoy's Ivan Ilyich to Kafka's Joseph K. have casually embraced a naturalistic, wholly immanent con-ception of existence . . . until the end beckons. It is only in the face of imminent death that their negative faith is put to the test, one it usually fails, often spectacularly so, thus furnishing the occasion for modern, post-eschatological narrative. It is at this pivotal moment that the modern, "buffered" self (C. Taylor) confronts death as the ultimate, impenetrable mystery, a bastion of unintelligibility whose walls no amount of epistemic confidence and Enlightenment pathos can ever hope to breach. In the absence of a metaphysical framework and, consequently, bereft of all hope, the protagonists of modern narrative have moved from eschatological confusion of the kind we had seen lurking in van Eyck's depiction of Canon van der Paele to outright metaphysical despair. Paradigmatic of the modern individual's perplexity and horror in the face of death, and of the "transcendental homelessness" (Lukács) it exposes, is Tolstoy's *Death of Ivan Ilyich*. Unfolding with the economy of detail and stringent mastery of narrative so characteristic of Tolstoy's art, the story furnishes a profound diagnosis of the fundamental ailments of bourgeois modernity as a whole. It captures the frightful isolation of modernity's "buffered" individual, as an unbridgeable emo-tional chasm separates the dying Ivan from friends and family members: "'You see, he's dead, and I am not,' each of them thought or felt."[194] Along the way, Tolstoy's narrative also indicts the myopic, technocratic outlook of modern medicine, as Ivan's doctors "solve" his terminal condition by a mere "weighing of probabilities—a float-ing kidney, chronic catarrh, or appendicitis" (*TDI* 61). Yet above all, the process of dying exposes Ivan's own metaphysical perplexity. For as soon as he has grasped the terminal nature of his condition, Ivan finds himself ensnared "in continual de-spair. . . . It cannot be that I should die. It would be too terrible" (*TDI* 70). What leaves Ivan reeling is less his deteriorating physical condition than his utter inability to sum up his life as having served any purpose beyond the usual socioeconomic successes that identify him as the quintessential petit-bourgeois. Having made his middling career by judging others in court, Ivan now finds himself stunned and dis-mayed by what the impending, last judgment reveals about himself: "more terrible than his physical sufferings were his moral sufferings; . . . these were his chief tor-ment" (*TDI* 88). Inexorably, from behind personal grievances and moral anguish, metaphysical questions intrude into Ivan's consciousness, questions that, with a com-placency characteristic of the nineteenth-century bourgeoisie, he had long assumed to have been "solved" or "overcome" by decades of scientific progress. Learning

194. Tolstoy 2009, 40; henceforth cited parenthetically as *TDI*.

otherwise, Ivan weeps "over . . . his terrible loneliness, over the cruelty of people, over the cruelty of God, over the absence of God" (*TDI* 83).

While enjoying good health, Ivan, like his contemporaries, had considered death as nothing more than the final breakdown of somatic processes that, just as casually, nineteenth-century naturalism had pronounced as the only valid and adequate definition of life. Yet as the ultimate moment approaches, this conception of death as sheer negation—"a momentary shudder in a vacant room," as Eliot will later put it— confronts Ivan with the essential poverty of the modern, naturalist view of life as sheer animality.[195] Bereft of any metaphysical framework and any eschatological vision, Ivan not only reevaluates death but also his entire life leading up to it; and as he does so, deep reservoirs of rage and shame rise to the surface. Dying belatedly reveals to Ivan Ilyich the essential hollowness of the life that has preceded it, "easy, pleasant, merry, and always decent and approved by society" (*TDI* 51). Now, at the threshold of death, "it occurred to [Ivan] that what had formerly appeared completely impossible to him, that he had not lived his life as he should have, might be true" (*TDI* 88). Like the suffering that precedes it, and which, as Nietzsche puts it, a vainglorious, superficial modernity presumes to have abolished altogether, death for Ivan is the very distillation of meaninglessness, an enigmatic termination of the pointless agony that precedes it: "Three days of suffering, and then death" (*TDI* 45). Where a medieval contemplative such as Julian of Norwich approaches death with supremely focused, self-emptying prayer, all Ivan can summon is "a three-day ceaseless howling" of rage and despair, a continual scream (or, sometimes, a despondent murmur) of incomprehension that will resonate throughout modern fiction, such as in Rilke's *Malte Laurids Brigge* and Mann's *Magic Mountain* and *Doctor Faustus*.[196]

A living (and now dying) witness to the ultimate triumph of Schopenhauerian pessimism over Hegelian, liberal-Protestant progress narratives, Ivan Ilyich can respond to his eschatological despair with nothing but unremitting roars of despair. Uncomprehending rage, rather than articulacy and vision, has become the bourgeois's default response to death. Ivan's last days, spent in metaphysical bewilderment and spiritual anguish, illustrate how the subjects of post-1850 narrative respond to their incipient end; and those who do not meet their end with screams of uncomprehending rage find themselves engulfed by a mix of shame and perplexity. Not by accident, late nineteenth- and early twentieth-century fiction often compares human

---

195. Eliot 1967, 16.

196. Recounting for his cousin Hans Castorp the moment that a female patient faces her last hour, and likely alluding to Edward Munch's 1893 *The Scream*, Joachim Ziemssen reports: "The moment the priest sets a foot over the threshold, a hue and cry starts up inside, first a shriek like nothing you've ever heard, three or four times in a row, and then just screaming without a pause or break, like a mouth gaping wide open, I suppose, 'Ahhh-' and with such misery and terror and defiance in it that I can't describe it" (Mann 1995c, 52).

death to animals expiring in isolation, without dignity, and confounded by the aura of meaninglessness that death casts back on the entire trajectory of their life. "Like a dog," are the last words the dying Joseph K. hears, and "it was as though shame should outlive him."[197] Similarly, the cousin of Mann's protagonist in *The Magic Mountain*, Joachim Ziemssen, sensing death from tuberculosis to be imminent, feels "only shame and self-reproach," with the narrator musing how strange it is "that a creature feels ashamed . . . and slinks into its den to perish, convinced that it cannot hope to encounter any respect or reverence for its sufferings and death throes—and rightly so, for joyous birds on the wing show no honor to a sick comrade in their flock, but instead peck him angrily, disdainfully with their beaks."[198] More gently yet, though no less perplexed, the dying Consul Kröger in Mann's *Buddenbrooks* (1901) reflects on "his life and . . . life in general, which suddenly seemed so distant and strange—all that unnecessary, noisy hustle and bustle, in whose midst he had stood and which now was imperceptibly drawing away from him, a distant echo to which he turned an amazed ear." In the event, he finds only two words to summarize it all: "Curious. Curious [*kurios*]."[199]

Responding to the eschatological void at the heart of nineteenth-century liberal-secular culture, fin-de-siècle symbolism had sought to infuse existence once again with symbolic significance in ways that superficially resemble the late medieval religious art image. The narrative oeuvre of Oscar Wilde, Joris-Karl Huysmans, Maurice Maeterlinck, and Georges Rodenbach; the lyric productions of the *poètes maudits* (Verlaine, Rimbaud, Nerval) and their peers in Russia (Blok, Bely, Bryusov) and Germany (the young Rilke, Stefan George, Georg Trakl); and the painterly symbolism of Gustave Moreau, Arnold Böcklin, and James Ensor, to name but a few, pursue the same paradoxical objective: to supplant realism with verbal and pictorial forms aspiring to transcendent significance, yet all the while claiming total creative and intellectual control over the symbolic forms thus produced. "What distinguishes the Symbolism of our day from the Symbolism of the past," writes Arthur Symons in 1899, "is that it has now become conscious of itself." With decades of utilitarian and liberal-progressive thought having "starved [the] soul long enough in the contemplation and the re-arrangement of material things, [there] comes the turn of the soul; and with it comes . . . a literature in which the visible world is no longer a reality, and the unseen world no longer a dream." The fulcrum of this "revolt against exteriority, against rhetoric, against a materialistic tradition" is a symbolism that "speaks to us so intimately, so solemnly, as only religion had hitherto spoken to us, [and that]

---

197. Kafka 1990, 241. "'Wie ein Hund' sagte er, es war, als sollte die Scham ihn überleben" (trans. mine).

198. Kafka, closing sentence of *The Trial* (1990); Mann 1995c, 522 (trans. mine).

199. Mann 1993, 68.

becomes itself a kind of religion with all the duties and responsibilities of the sacred ritual."[200] Rather at odds with symbolism's highly self-conscious aesthetic, Symons's naive proclamation bears out von Balthasar's charge that symbolist art could only ever simulate transcendence and, ultimately, ended up worshipping its own technique as a "false divinity" of sorts.[201]

Untethered from all religious faith, dogma, and liturgical practice, symbolism's deceptively timeless image concept verges on the idolatrous by framing the symbol as an image contrived rather than received. The very fact that symbolism came and went in the space of just a couple of decades is a further indication of its aesthetic and epistemic hubris, to say nothing of the theological illiteracy of its main proponents. In fact, for the symbol to properly function as such, a metaphysical realism of sorts has to be presupposed rather than conjured by symbolic images, however ingeniously contrived. The reality that manifests *in* symbolic form must itself be (and be understood as) the numinous source *of* that symbol's authority. Or, as Gadamer puts it, "a symbol manifests the presence of something that really is at all times present [*stets gegenw*ärtig]. . . . For it is only because what is symbolized is present itself that it can be present in the symbol." Simply put: no symbol without metaphysics. For the symbol presupposes and in its form makes manifest an *antecedent*, numinous reality. It participates in that reality but can never autonomously "construct" it. Far from being the product of an individual artist's imagination, as is the case with the art image (*Kunstbild*), the symbol's power altogether originates in the numinous being whose timeless, real presence the symbol mediates—not by *referring to* it, or by arbitrarily *substituting itself for* it, but by *participating in* it.

> A symbol not only points to something; it represents it by taking its place. . . . [And] only because it thus presents the presence of what it represents is the symbol itself treated with the reverence due to the symbolized. A picture also represents, but through itself, through the increment of meaning [*durch das Mehr an Bedeutung*] that it brings. . . . Hence the picture is situated halfway between a sign and a symbol. Its representing is neither a pure pointing-to-something [*reines Verweisen*] nor a pure taking-the-place-of-something [*Stellvertretung*].[202]

Situated halfway between indication and substitution, the symbol's authority can originate neither in a contingent act of verbal definition nor in a fit of individual inspiration; its perceived meaning and significance is not the default of some extrinsic, cultural norm. Rather, the symbol's authority originates in a formal act of "institu-

---

200. Symons 1919, 3, 5.
201. Balthasar 1967, 224.
202. Gadamer 2006, 148.

tion" (*Stiftung*) that, as we saw in the previous chapter, ultimately harks back to the Byzantine rites of consecrating and naming the icon. Precisely this quasi-sacramental institution, however, has vanished in the case of the painted art image, for which reason its beholder's response will prove strictly contingent and subjective. By contrast, to properly recognize and respond to a symbol, which Gadamer notes "need not be pictorial [*bildlich*]," one must have been antecedently initiated into the metaphysical economy that authorizes the symbol in the first place. Yet in that case, the response accorded to the symbol is one of obligation, not taste. Its authority is a matter of "recognition" (*Anerkennung*) and "reverence" (*Verehrung*), with Gadamer's choice of the latter term clearly echoing John of Damascus's concept of "veneration" (*proskynēsis*) due to a holy icon.

Let us end this chapter with three snapshots from different phases of Thomas Mann's narrative oeuvre. In each case, the narrative at issue sheds a particular light on the twofold crisis, of eschatological thinking and the image, as it unfolds between roughly 1890 and 1925, from fin-de-siècle symbolism to early modernist imagism to post–World War I expressionism. Prior to 1914, Mann tends to stage the problem of symbolism mainly as a conflict between the authentic veneration of images and their voyeuristic possession. During this early period, the eschatological crisis underlying that conflict remains largely implicit, and it will move to the center of Mann's narrative art only with *The Magic Mountain* (1924), from which we will take our final example. Meanwhile, linking all three examples is their shared focus on the late medieval genre of the devotional image (*Andachtsbild*), a fact that underscores the unresolved and increasingly urgent eschatological questions vexing modern liberal-secular culture and unraveling the fragile psyche of Mann's protagonists.

We begin with an image of Mary cradling the infant Jesus, not a painting, as it turns out, but "a big sepia photograph, framed most tastefully in old gold . . . and placed on an easel in the center" of a Munich art dealer's display window around 1900: "The sacred figure was ravishingly feminine, naked, and beautiful. Her great sultry eyes were rimmed with shadow, and her lips were half parted in a strange and delicate smile."[203] Such is the scandalous premise of Thomas Mann's short story "Gladius Dei" (1902), though the scandal not only consists in the sexualized presentation of the Virgin, which predictably elicits lewd stares and blasphemous comments from the "carefree young men" with "loosely tied cravats" passing through Munich in its most decadent phase; it is further compounded by the fact that the image is a photograph, a "first-class reproduction," commercially sold for "seventy marks." Hence, even as its sumptuous gold frame conjures the aura of religious painting, the idolatrous image is not a unique original but a photographic reproduction

---

203. According to Reed (in Mann 2004, 119), the most likely inspiration for Mann's description of the Madonna is a painting by the Gabriel Cornelius von Max (1840–1915).

that, consequently, cannot be neutralized or contained. Finally, this being the main narrative premise, there is the scandal that to those passing by and gazing at it, the image with its "depraved flavor deliberately emphasized" has altogether ceased to be scandalous; it is just one more art object in a city awash with "facsimiles of modern paintings [and] gay sensuous fantasies in which the world of antiquity seems to have been brought back to life."[204]

Enter the story's protagonist, Hieronymus, a young monk of severe monastic discipline whose "face exactly resembled an old portrait once painted by a monk and now preserved in Florence." Evidently modeled on Girolamo Savonarola, the young seminarian is shocked by the photograph and, during the days that follow, finds himself haunted by it: "The picture of the Madonna went with him. Continually, even as he sat in his small hard narrow room or knelt in the cool churches, it stood before his outraged soul with its sultry, dark-rimmed eyes[,] . . . naked and beautiful. And no prayer could exorcise it." Confronted with a photograph that, in his view, utterly desecrates the devotional image of the Theotokos, Hieronymus finds his spiritual identity compromised by an image whose motif, half a millennium earlier, would have been the catalyst of earnest and focused prayer. Teeming with iconoclast and millenarian fervor, Hieronymus thus enters the art shop in order to inform its proprietor that the image's "exaltation and blasphemous idolatry of beauty is a crime," and to demand that it be removed from the display window "at once and for ever." Unfazed, the art gallery's worldly owner, who "in his leisure hours was writing a pamphlet on the modern movement in art," briefly trots out some boiler-plate counterarguments, less as prompts for an earnest dialogue than as rhetorical questions designed to foreclose on it: "Is it wrong to exhibit Madonnas? Is it wrong to paint them?" Barely dignifying that defense with a rejoinder ("You know very well that what has been painted there is vice itself, naked lust"), Hieronymus instead outlines his vision of the only theologically defensible end of art: a gigantic auto-da-fé to consume all the "vanities of the world: the artist's carnival costumes, the ornaments, vases, jewelry, and objets d'art, the naked statues, the busts of women, the painted revivals of paganism, the masterly portraits of famous beauties . . . all piled up into a great pyramid. . . . He saw them all piled up into a great pyramid, and he saw the multitude, enthralled by his terrible words, consign them to flames amid cries of jubilation." The only true end of art, he makes clear, will be one that consumes art in all of its manifestations. Put differently, the only viable eschatological image involves the total expurgation of all visible images and, this being the monk's strong implication, will

---

204. Mann 1988, 76–84. As Reed points out (Mann 2004, 107), Thomas Mann had entered a marginal "Savonarola" into his copy of the *Genealogy of Morals*, specifically at the start of Part 3, §11, where Nietzsche discusses "ascetic ideals." More generally, parallels between prewar Munich and Florence under Medici rule pervade Mann's work during the early 1900s.

issue in the destruction of the entire civilization that gave rise to them. Naturally, his millenarian visions—which a dozen years later will be fulfilled in the Great War—fail to persuade the art gallery's proprietor, who instead sees to it that Hieronymus will be unceremoniously thrown out of the store by a "malt-nourished, herculean and awe-inspiring" employee.[205]

In the event, the young Thomas Mann's concern with social satire and with dramatizing how readily ordinary social interactions may turn toward the grotesque (herein strongly echoing Dostoevsky and Nietzsche) also imposes limitations. For the comic and satiric approach glosses over the intractable question of how creativity and faith may be brought into alignment. "Gladius Dei" is but one of several attempts by the young Mann to reckon with what, already in 1902, he sensed was the dead end of symbolist decadence, a dilemma also explored in some of his other short fiction of that decade ("Tristan," "Wälsungenblut," "Schwere Stunde"). Both the story's satiric tone and the monk's grotesque presentation as a latter-day Savonarola suggest that the clash of a hedonistic, unrepentantly secular culture with an uncompromising iconoclast sensibility cannot be resolved in the terms in which it is here framed. Yet neither can the conflict simply be ignored. The grotesque contrast between Hieronymus's apocalyptic indictment of symbolism and decadence, on the one hand, and the commercial worldliness and nonchalant hedonism of prewar Munich, on the other, only highlights an insoluble, though likely also unendurable, antagonism at the heart of modern culture.

Written a decade later, Mann's *Death in Venice* (1912) traces the final disintegration and collapse of the Calvinist work ethic that Max Weber in 1905 had identified as the foundation of both modern *homo economicus* and the bourgeois intelligentsia (*Bildungsbürgertum*), both of which the novella portrays as being on the verge of disintegration. Right away, it bears noting that the impending demise of the ideal of *Bildung*, associated above all with the writings of Herder, Kant, and Goethe, is anything but a contingent mishap. In fact, Mann's novella exposes the unsound metaphysical and aesthetic foundations on which that very ideal had rested all along.[206] At age fifty, Mann's protagonist, Gustav von Aschenbach, is for all intents and purposes finished. His style, bereft of its onetime "immediate daring" (*unmittelbare Kühnheiten*), has become "fixed and exemplary, conservative, formal, even formulaic [sein Still wandelte sich . . . ins mustergültig-Feststehende, herkömmlich-Geschliffene, Erhaltende, Formelle, selbst Formelhafte]." Mann's decision to mimic his protagonist's arch diction throughout the narrative adds yet another layer of irony to a story defined by

---

205. Mann 1988, 85–88.

206. On the dual origins of nineteenth-century *Bildung* in Renaissance humanism and German pietism, see Herdt 2019, esp. 112–187; for a response, Pfau, https://syndicate.network/symposia /theology/forming-humanity/.

its protagonist's spiritual depletion, his idolatrous gaze, and his tragic failure of self-recognition. If von Aschenbach's "deep and fatigued gaze" (*diese Augen, müde und tief durch die Gläser blickend*) had once yielded inspired visions unfolding within, his expressive daring has for some time been supplanted by "an official and pedagogic element" (*etwas amtlich Erzieherisches*).[207] Putting an official stamp on the defeat of creative energy by bourgeois convention is von Aschenbach's recent elevation into the nobility, as well as the fact that snippets from his prose have lately been incorporated into school primers as exemplars of stylistic perfection. Simply put, the middle-aged author has crossed the threshold into the secular equivalent of the afterlife, that faux eternity known as fame. Clearly, von Aschenbach is also a foil for Mann, who by 1912 is casting about for new aesthetic strategies, sensing that the late symbolist idiom and decadent atmospherics pervading *Buddenbrooks*, as well as the social satire or grotesque psychological constellations of his early short fiction, fail to address the death spiral in which European bourgeois culture appears caught up. In the event, von Aschenbach responds to his depleted organic and aesthetic vitality by giving free rein at last to impulses whose repression over several decades had shaped his Protestant work ethic and austere public persona. It is precisely the type of response that Mann knows he cannot afford.[208]

With his creative and procreative life having run its course, von Aschenbach undergoes what is ambiguously called a "rebirth" (*Wiedergeburt*) that manifests itself above all in an "almost immoderate strengthening of his feeling for beauty [*übermäßiges Erstarken seines Schönheitssinnes*]."[209] What of late causes various sights and images to be so alluring to von Aschenbach is their implicit promise to release him from the serfdom of open-ended, unrelenting artistic labor. Hence the homoerotic charge of his vision reflects less a sexual than a metaphysical desire; *eros* here concerns a striving for absolute possession that, in one of the novella's numerous allusions to Plato's *Phaedrus*, von Aschenbach hopes to realize in the modality of physical sight no longer constrained by social and religious norms.[210] Step by step, von

207. Mann 1995b, 10 / 1981a, 571; henceforth cited with English pagination first and German second.

208. On the multilayered self-analysis that the novella affords Mann, see the commentary in the new *Große Frankfurter Ausgabe*, vol. 22, 360–72; see also Mann's probing analysis of his novella in his letter to Carl Maria Weber (4 July 1920), in Mann 1995a, 1:176–80. Reed 1996, 144–78, comments on Mann's faltering inspiration in early 1911 and, notably, on his difficulties with concluding the novella ("I can't find the conclusion. . . . My vitality is extremely low right now"), letter to H. Mann, 27 April 1912, in Mann 1998, 114.

209. Mann 1995b, 9–10 / 1981a, 570.

210. See esp. Plato 1997, 511–12 (*Phaedrus* 232a–233b) and Socrates's critique of erotic possession as a self-canceling proposition, ultimately denying the beloved's autonomous existence (239e–240e) who otherwise would be "disgusted in the extreme to see the face of that older man who's lost

Aschenbach descends into the lowest, sunless circle of his hybrid psyche as artist and bourgeois. With his disordered impulses and desires constantly enticing him to advance further, he confronts what Judith Wolfe has called an "eschatology without eschaton"—a movement *through* and wholly circumscribed *by* the horizon of distended time from which death alone furnishes definitive release.[211] No longer the threshold to eternity, death promises only to release modernity's "buffered self" (C. Taylor) from the fetters of bureaucratic humdrum and chronometric time. It merely concludes but cannot resolve the enigma of a purely immanent concept of existence that, on Georg Simmel's shrewd diagnosis, is at every moment defined by the certainty of death and its "form-giving significance" (*formgebende Bedeutung des Todes*). On this account, "each of life's steps is revealed [not] only as a temporal approximation of death, but is positively and a priori shaped through death as a real element of Life. . . . The life that we use up as we approach death is used up to flee death."[212]

The existential paradox of this simultaneously fugitive and death-seeking movement emerges in von Aschenbach's compulsive sea voyage from Pola to Venice, described as a quest for "the incomparable and unrelated" (*was er suchte, war das Fremdartige und Bezuglose*). While that formulation illustrates the protagonist's as yet tenuous grasp of his true destiny, his subsequent embarkation on the coffin-like gondola that is to take him to the Lido sharpens the point. The conveyance is reminiscent of "death itself, the bier, the drab funeral, and final, wordless ride [*es erinnert . . . an Bahre und düsteres Begängnis und letzte, schweigsame Fahrt*]."[213] Lacking all contour, "the murky dome" of the Adriatic Sea both bewilders and seduces von Aschenbach, not least because being adrift "in empty undifferentiated space[,] our senses lack the means to measure time as well."[214] Anticipating Mann's trope of seafaring as both an intended evasion of death and its de facto approximation,

---

his looks" (240d). "The truth of Aschenbach's passion is not mainly that it is homoerotic but that it is an all-consuming fantasy of possession . . . inspir[ing] him to seek after 'beauty itself'" (Goldman 1988, 201).

211. Wolfe 2013a, esp. 116–35; as Wolfe points out, "Heidegger's project in *Being and Time*" offers "a morally charged description of 'the human' as most vitally defined by the tension between ineluctable finitude and the equally persistent desire to transcend it." Yet in so doing, Heidegger's analysis tacitly relies on the latent insistence of metaphysics precisely for the purpose of continually disavowing it: "While Heidegger's analysis is a virtuoso *plaidoyer* for the ineluctable finitude of human existence, its pathos depends on the assumption of a desire to transcend finitude which the analysis itself cannot and does not attempt to account for" (133).

212. Simmel 2007b, 75.

213. Mann 1995b, 12 (trans. modified), 25 / 1981a, 573, 579.

214. Ibid., 14 / 576. "He loved the sea for deep-seated reasons: . . . because of his own proclivity—forbidden, directly counter to his life's work, and seductive for that very reason—for the unorganized, immoderate, eternal: for nothingness" (24 / 591).

Simmel had made the quintessentially Augustinian point that human beings tend to pursue death precisely by seeking to evade it: "By means of earning a living and enjoyment, work and rest, . . . we are like people who walk in the opposite direction of a moving ship: as they walk towards the south, the ground on which they are doing so is being carried to the north."[215] First published in the 1910 issue of *Logos*, Simmel's account, however unintentionally, also attests to the persistence of eschatological motifs at a time when Max Weber (a writer of great interest to Thomas Mann) had diagnosed the bourgeois European as thoroughly "disenchanted," dispirited, and organically depleted, though unflinching in his commitment to procedural and institutional life-forms, an efficient (if soulless) work ethic, and a flat-line, chronometric model of time circumscribing existence as a whole.[216]

At the heart of Mann's novella and ensuring its coherence as a narrative is a single image (*Standbild*) appearing in a variety of permutations and fusing two types of vision ordinarily considered incommensurable: voyeurism and devotion. In its most familiar iteration, the image centers on the figure of St. Sebastian, at once a metonym for the character of Tadzio and an allegory of the sheer transience of visible, physical beauty. Suffused with homoerotic overtones already observable in Mantegna's and Botticelli's late fifteenth-century versions, the figure of St. Sebastian initially enters the narrative in rather oblique fashion. Thus, early in the novella, von Aschenbach is taken aback by an inner experience that has apparently eluded him for quite some time, namely, the sudden shift from physical perception to inspired vision. As his languid eyes survey a Greek Orthodox churchyard adjacent to an eerily deserted square in the very heart of Munich, the stale and cliché-ridden, fin-de-siècle aesthetic of marble headstones and gold-plated lettering predictably fails to engage the writer. Soon, however, von Aschenbach's distracted, tired gaze passes beyond these mere clichés of eschatological hope and finds itself unaccountably detained by a figure whose distinctive posture evokes Renaissance depictions of St. Sebastian (an affinity, however, likely to register only during a second reading).

---

215. Simmel, 2007b, 74–75. As Eric Przywara already noted, the striking affinities between Simmel's 1910 essay and Heidegger's analysis of finitude and death in *Being and Time* (1927) make the absence of any mention of it in Heidegger's work more than a little surprising: "Is it not the case that this now forgotten, great thinker has anticipated our own present today: this either/or between Toynbee's optimistic philosophy of progress and Heidegger's philosophy of death? And all this, even though Simmel was the one whose *Logos* essay on 'The Metaphysics of Death' had anticipated all that Rilke and, following him, Heidegger, were to call 'being-toward-death'" (Przywara 1955, 1, 38; trans. mine).

216. While Weber's most dystopic version of that argument appears in *Science as Vocation* (1919), much of it is anticipated in his earlier *Protestant Ethic* (1905); on Max Weber and Thomas Mann, see Harvey Goldman's eponymous study (1988, 187–208). On the elegiac affect central to secular modernity—and on historicist method as the formal and institutional mechanism of knowledge as a form of "retrieval" undertaken in the absence of eschatological hope—see Pfau 2013a, 35–52, 402–13.

The unusual appearance of a man in the portico, close to the apocalyptic beasts which guard the staircase, . . . steered his thoughts into a completely different direction. Not very tall, thin, beardless and strikingly round-nosed, the man belonged to the red-headed type and had its milk-like and freckled skin. . . . The broad and straight-rimmed bast hat which covered his head gave him the air of the foreign and far-traveled. . . . [I]n the right hand [he held] a stick with an iron tip, which he had pushed diagonally into the ground and on which he, feet crossed, leaned with his hip. With his raised head, so that on his scrawny neck which stuck out from his sport shirt the Adam's apple projected forcefully and well-defined, he looked into the distance, with colorless, red-lashed eyes between which there were two vertical, definite furrows. . . . His demeanor . . . was that of cool survey, audacious, even wild; because, be it that he was grimacing against the brightness of the setting sun or that it was a more permanent physiognomic disfiguration, his lips seemed too short, the teeth were entirely uncovered, so that they, quite long and bare to the gums, gleamed white between his lips.[217]

The first of several such iconic figures, this memento mori precariously balances fossilized religious and depleted secular elements. Thus, von Aschenbach's alter ego, the stranger, is part dandy sporting "a yellowish sports suit" that will reappear on the figure of the inebriated, "faux youth" whose drunken displays on the boat from Pola to Venice fill von Aschenbach with horror. For now, however, the stranger's defiant pose, leaning aslant on a walking stick with ostentatious relaxation and beckoning von Aschenbach with his deathlike grimace (to reappear on the gondolier later in the story), recalls Mantegna's regal depiction of St. Sebastian while also anticipating Tadzio's classically sculpted presentation against the setting sun in the novella's penultimate paragraph: "He turned his torso, one hand at his side, and looked over his shoulder to the shore."[218]

Von Aschenbach's visual fixation on this figure triggers in him "a kind of roving unrest, a youthfully ardent desire for faraway places . . . new or at least unaccustomed and forgotten for so long." The novella's phrasing here—attributing to von Aschenbach a desire that "projects itself visually" (*seine Begierde ward sehend*)—nicely encapsulates both symbolism's core aspiration and its irremediable flaw.[219] Thus, Bernard's and Bonaventure's anagogical movement (*per visibilia ad invisibilia*) is now effectively inverted in that von Aschenbach's gaze aims to transpose an unfathomed eschatological longing into the finite realm and onto visible forms, to be

217. Mann 1995b, 6 / 1981a, 560.
218. Ibid., 61 / 640.
219. Ibid., 3 [trans. modified] / 562.

seized by his voyeuristic sensibility and then refashioned by his authorial persona. If nothing else, what renders such longing illicit is the fact that it originates in unacknowledged bourgeois despair; or, as Dante so succinctly puts it, "without hope we live in desire."[220] Indeed, fueling von Aschenbach's regression from *askēsis* into *hēdonē* is a desire to forestall self-recognition, yet also an unconscious longing for death as the only state capable of liberating him from the thralldom of desire itself. The unreal, essentially hopeless nature of such longing is reinforced by the fact that his mute idolatry of Tadzio's youthful body leaves the aging voyeur notably isolated. Not by accident, *Death in Venice* features only minimal dialogue, with von Aschenbach repeatedly characterized as "solitary" (*der Einsame*), "taciturn" (*der Schweigsame*), and "gazing" (*der Schauende*) forever transfixed by "images and impressions" (*Bilder und Wahrnehmungen*).[221]

Two other iconographic details bear pointing out, as both will recur throughout the novella. One concerns the detail of the stranger's "crossed feet" (*mit gekreuzten Füßen*), which is in keeping with the iconography of the Man of Sorrows in Western art, such as in Albrecht Dürer's well-known drawing of 1505 (fig. 3.8). The other detail concerns the stranger's iron-tipped walking stick (*mit eiserner Spitze versehener Stock*)—apprehended with telescopic accuracy by von Aschenbach—which again links him to the figure of the martyred, beautiful youth pierced by arrows. The devotional image of St. Sebastian is expressly introduced in the novella's second chapter, where we learn that a critic had attested von Aschenbach "an intellectual and youthful masculinity that grits its teeth in proud modesty and stands by calmly while its body is pierced by swords and spears." Most famously realized by Mantegna (fig. 3.9), the motif of St. Sebastian penetrated by iron-tipped arrows figures art itself as a type of secular martyrdom, a painstaking quest for the perfected, beautiful forms capable of concealing from the world their creator's "sapping of strength and biological decay."[222] Chiming with Nietzsche's aphorism, "no beautiful surface without a terrifying depth [*keine schöne Oberfläche ohne schreckliche Tiefe*]," the image here entwines the Augustinian motif of man's intrinsic corruption with some core tenets of

220. Dante 2002, 69. "Sanza speme vivemo in disio" (*Inferno* 4:42).

221. Mann 1995b, 19, 50 / 1981a, 625, 640.

222. Ibid., 8 / 568. "Die elegante Selbstbeherrschung, die bis zum letzten Augenblick eine innere Unterhöhlung, den biologischen Verfall vor den Augen der Welt verbirgt." Arguably the most acclaimed version of this motif of the martyr is Botticelli's *St. Sebastian* (1474), widely thought to have inspired Rilke's eponymous poem in *Neue Gedichte* (1907), *KA* 1:471. The sonnet's opening couplet ("Wie ein Liegender so steht er; ganz hingehalten von dem großen Willen") in turn anticipates the defiant posture of the stranger who, at noon on a deserted square in the heart of Munich, so unexpectedly arrests von Aschenbach's gaze. Rilke's identification of martyrdom with the destruction of physical beauty, reflected in the truncation of his sonnet by one line, also resonates with Mann's novella, though the focus in the latter locates martyrdom as much in the act of *creating* beauty as in its eventual destruction.

Figure 3.8.
Albrecht Dürer,
Christ on the Cross.
Vienna, Graphische Sammlung,
Albertina

modern nihilism.[223] Thus art may indeed temporarily conceal such depravity, and transient visions of pure beauty may for a while allow those who consume them, perhaps even the artist-creator himself, to be deceived about their irremediable, post-lapsarian condition.

Von Aschenbach is trapped in metaphysical limbo: unable to resign himself to the disenchanted sensibility of the Weberian, liberal-Protestant bourgeois who he has become, yet also terminally estranged from the metaphysical-realist framework that would allow him to grasp the visible world as infused with anagogical meaning. Instead, Mann's protagonist roams the visible world in search of the ultimate image (*Standbild*), one he hopes to capture in ekphrastic prose and to infuse with a pseudo-eschatological hope for definitive liberation from his twofold temporal bondage: the not-yet of Protestantism's ceaselessly prospecting work ethic and the no-longer of his

223. Nietzsche 1980, 7:159 (Entry #91, April 1871).

Figure 3.9.
Andrea Mantegna, *St. Sebastian*,
1456–59. Vienna,
Kunsthistorisches Museum

epigonal, artistic persona. Throughout the novella, the people von Aschenbach meets are either transposed into grotesque if also alluring doubles of his own disordered psyche (e.g., the "faux youth" on the boat, or the street entertainer in Venice); or they are voyeuristically sculpted as "a divine image" (*dieses göttliche Bildwerk*) by the protagonist's idolatrous gaze in an increasingly frantic attempt at forestalling self-recognition. Originating in eschatological despair, not hope, von Aschenbach's vision is a case of self-projection, and the image that correlates with it no longer manifests anything beyond itself but serves only to idolize the modern artist's creative martyrdom: "Because composure beneath blows of fate, graciousness in the midst of torment, does not signify mere endurance; it is an active achievement, a positive triumph, and the figure of St. Sebastian is its most beautiful symbol, if not in all of art, then at least in the type of art we are discussing." Mann's choice of the third-century saint as emblematic of the martyrdom of writing is significant; for more than his voyeuristic rapport with the visible world, von Aschenbach's true idolatry concerns the written word by means of which he hopes to shelter visible, embodied being—and ultimately himself—from the touch of time: "When you looked into this fictional world of Aschenbach's, you saw the elegant self-control that conceals the sapping of strength and biological decay from the eyes of the world up to the last minute."[224] It is the same gaze that, alighting on Tadzio's adolescent body, elicits a remarkable meditation.

> The severe and pure will, which, operating obscurely, had managed to bring this godlike image [*dies göttliche Bildwerk*] into the light of day—was it not . . . operative in him as well when, full of sober passion, he liberated from the marble block of language the slender form which he had seen in his mind and which he presented to the world as an icon and mirror of intellectual beauty?
>
> Icon and mirror! His eyes embraced the noble figure standing there by the edge of the blue, and in a rising wave of rapture he felt that as he looked he understood beauty itself, form as divine thought, the one, the pure perfection, which dwells in the mind, and of which a human image and analogue [*Abbild und Gleichnis*], slender and lovely, was offered here for worship [*zur Anbetung aufgerichtet*].[225]

In this final phase, a symbolist aesthetic reveals itself as a conspicuous instance of what W. J. T. Mitchell calls "ekphrastic hope," which Lessing's *Laokoön* had emphatically rejected as a brazen "invitation to idolatry: 'superstition loaded the [statues of] the gods with symbols." Yet in Mann's novella, the ekphrastic quest for "achieving vision, iconicity, or a 'still moment' of plastic presence through language" is no longer an expression of "hope" (theologically speaking) but, instead, reflects symbolism's underlying psychopathology of visual desire masking eschatological despair.[226] For even as it deplores the flatness of a postmetaphysical and postliturgical world on aesthetic grounds, the symbolist image no longer constitutes, as the liturgical symbol once had, a conduit toward the invisible logos. Opposing a realist

---

224. Mann 1995b, 8 / 1981a, 568.

225. Ibid., 36 / 606.

226. Mitchell 1994, 156. "Aschenbach has looked at everything—and lived his own life—as a symbol. He has finally come to *love* only symbols." Having utterly embraced and internalized the Protestant work ethic that Weber had diagnosed in 1905, Mann's protagonist is imprisoned in the virtual reality of his own authorial creation: "The tragedy is that *Aschenbach now lives completely in symbols*" (Goldman 1988, 203; emphasis mine).

aesthetic it (mistakenly) accused of having drained all revelatory power from the image, symbolism remained ensnared by its dialectical other, a photo-realist notion of mimesis variously repudiated as redundant, pedantic, or outright trivial. Hence, in sharp contrast to its onetime anagogical function, the post-Romantic symbol aspires to merge, both affectively and physically, with the "experience" of visibility pure and simple. Yet in so striving to coincide, without remainder, with a spurious transcendence for which it effectively substitutes itself, the symbolist image has surrendered its status as a "phenomenon" (*Erscheinung*) in the strict sense. Von Aschenbach's voyeuristic and ekphrastic fetishizing of Tadzio as "sculpture" (*Standbild*) and "ectype" (*Abbild*) shows postmetaphysical symbolism to remain trapped by misapprehending the eschaton as that final moment *in time* when the image has yielded to the beholder's total, if virtual, possession; and once that moment has been reached, the image's power of disclosing aniconic meanings beyond its own surface play of form, color, and light simply dissolves, exposing both its own nullity as idol and the insubstantiality of the desire to which it had owed its ephemeral splendor.

Here the written word no longer seeks to *fulfill* the image but, instead, aims to *simulate* visuality as a hermetic and ineffable experience. In the event, when von Aschenbach has finished casting the deliverances of his idolatrous gaze into a page and a half of meticulously crafted prose, "conscience accused him, as if after a debauchery."[227] What half a millennium earlier had been grasped as the anagogical relation between the strictly *provisional* status of the visible image and its numinous fulfillment has now been supplanted by an idolatrous longing for the total convergence of the verbal with the visual. Hence it cannot surprise to find representatives of fin-de-siècle symbolism (e.g., Huysmans, Rodenbach, Maeterlinck, Wilde) struggling with narrative form and plot. For their (ultimately unsuccessful) attempts to infuse every visible image or scene with transcendent significance ends up draining aesthetic form of all metonymic force and anagogical movement. The only remaining plot, which symbolism reiterates ad nauseam, concerns the moral and physical decay and eventual demise of its voyeuristic protagonists. In the absence of eschatological hope, narrative grinds to a halt or, at most, recycles the familiar story of a Dantean descent into progressively lower circles of depravity.[228] Yet *Death in Venice* does not simply deploy symbolist techniques, but, in focusing on von Aschenbach's idolatrous disfiguration of the devotional image, exposes symbolism as an insoluble aesthetic and moral dilemma.

---

227. Mann 1995b, 55 / 1981a, 608. "Ihm war, als ob sein Gewissen wie nach einer Ausschweifung Klage führe."

228. Prominent examples here would include Huysmans's *À rebours* (1884), Wilde's *Picture of Dorian Gray* (1890), and Rodenbach's *Bruges la Morte* (1892).

The final example of a devotional image unexpectedly surfacing in early twentieth-century Western Europe and revealing both the full scope of eschatological despair and its consequent crisis of narrative form is found in Mann's *Magic Mountain* (1924). A panoramic work that Mann had initially conceived as a "satyr play" (*Satyrspiel*) to supplement the tragic narrative unfolded in *Death in Venice*, the novel soon outgrew that purpose. Consciously employing Wagner's *Leitmotif* technique, Mann's nearly thousand-page novel weaves a number of archetypal images or Goethean *Urbilder* into an intricate and richly allusive tapestry of interacting motifs.[229] Of these, that of the Christian Pietà holds particular significance for a novel that, in the aftermath of the Great War and the collapse of nineteenth-century European culture, attempts to sift the debris—what Eliot, writing at the same time, calls "a heap of broken images"—for shards of eschatological hope.[230] Halfway through the novel, Mann introduces the character Leo Naphta whose intellectual and spiritual formation traces the evolution of European culture since the Enlightenment and foreshadows its impending self-destruction in the impending Great War. Born into eastern Galician shtetl culture and soon orphaned, he had successively embraced socialism, turned Jesuit, and now makes his appearance as a (terminally ill) nihilist. While encapsulating European modernity's successive ideological temptations, Naphta's intellectual peregrination is perhaps best understood as an attempt to cope with (or escape from?) a traumatic image stamped onto his psyche as a young child. As a young boy, Leo had returned home to find it set ablaze during an anti-Semitic pogrom in czarist Russia, with his father, Elijah, kosher butcher by trade, having been crucified to the door of the family's house.[231] Ever since, Naphta's tireless quest to understand or escape that haunting "primal image" (a Goethean *Urbild* if ever there was one) has shaped his identity as the quintessential cosmopolitan-fugitive European, thoroughly exposed to Enlightenment Europe's major ideologies, yet never truly at home in any of them. His quest for understanding or, barring that, for release in death will only end when, in an absurd duel he has provoked with his intellectual foil, the liberal-secular humanist Lodovico Settembrini, he commits suicide because his opponent, true to his humanistic principles, had refused to fire on him.

Of ascetic disposition and portrayed as "corrosively ugly" (*von ätzender Häßlichkeit*), Naphta arrives at his final destination, the Berghof sanatorium in Davos for

---

229. On the form-constituting function of images in *The Magic Mountain*, as well as on their transmutation by modern medial technologies, see Pfau 2005a and the secondary literature by Haupt, Downing, and Otis quoted there.

230. Eliot 2015, 1:55 ("The Waste Land," line 22).

231. Mann 1995c, 433 / 1981b, 617. "Mit Nägeln gekreuzigt, hatte man ihn an der Tür seines brennenden Hauses hängend gefunden."

Figure 3.10.
Pietà, ca. 1325.
Bonn, Rheinisches
Landesmuseum

those suffering (and mostly dying) from tuberculosis, with just one prized possession. It is an early fourteenth-century wooden sculpture, a pietà.[232] Upon visiting Naphta's flat in Davos-Dorf, rented from the tailor Lukaček (an allusion to Georg Lukács, on whom Naphta is widely thought to have been modeled), the novel's protagonist, Hans Castorp, finds his attention immediately drawn by the pietà, a sculpture bearing a strong formal resemblance to the genre of the "devotional image" (*Andachtsbild*) that, as we have seen, had steadily grown in popularity in fourteenth-century Northern Europe. As described in the novel, the sculpture is evidently modeled on the so-called Röttgen Pietà, the work of an anonymous artist and dated to about 1320 (fig. 3.10).

In the corner, to the left of the sofa and chairs, was a work of art: a painted wooden sculpture set atop a large pedestal draped in red, a profoundly terrifying

232. Ibid., 366 / 523. Naphta's "caustic" appearance, his "studied silence," and "pale gray eyes" link his severe physical appearance with that of Christ in the wooden pietà that will soon be introduced as his one prized possession.

work, a naïve pietà—very effective, almost grotesque. The Mother of God, her hood drawn up, her brows furrowed in agony, her mouth skewed and gaping in lamentation; the Man of Sorrows on her lap, a primitive figure, badly out of scale, the crudely fashioned body revealing an ignorance of anatomy, the drooping head studded with thorns, the face and limbs splattered and dripping with blood, thick globs of congealed blood at the wound in the side, nail marks on the hands and feet.[233]

What meaning, if any, can there be in a devotional image created some six centuries earlier and in religious and intellectual circumstances utterly different from the world inhabited by highly educated, moribund Europeans such as those assembled in Davos on the eve of World War I? Clearly, the Theotokos no longer amounts to a spiritual presence but, instead, will by default be appraised as an "artwork" (*Kunstwerk*); and seen in that light it predictably elicits a response of aesthetic perplexity rather than prayerful devotion: "I would never have thought that anything could be simultaneously so ugly—beg your pardon—and so beautiful," comments Hans Castorp upon seeing the sculpture in Naphta's otherwise sparse and somber apartment.[234]

Still, for all its naïveté, Castorp's remark captures the salient point: in its encounter with this sculpture the modern individual confronts the essential poverty and inadequacy of those Kantian formal-aesthetic categories—the beautiful, disinterested pleasure, taste, and so forth—that for more than a century had underwritten the bourgeois project of *Bildung*. If anything, more a case of Kant's dynamic sublime than of the beautiful, the pietà unsettles the beholder with its unfiltered message of extreme suffering and grief. Whereas "tribulacion" had held profound theological significance in thirteenth-century religious life, it was specifically the "abolition of suffering" that, according to Nietzsche (never far from Mann's mind), modern liberal-secular culture had embraced as its supreme "goal."[235] By contrast, for the motif

---

233. Ibid., 385 / 550. "Aber in dem Winkel links von der Sofagruppe war ein Kunstwerk zu sehen, eine große, auf rot verkleidetem Sockel erhöhte bemalte Holzplastik, —etwas innig Schreckhaftes, einer Pietà, einfältig und wirkungsvoll bis zum Grotesken: die Gottesmutter in der Haube, mit zusammengezogenen Brauen und jammernd schief geöffnetem Munde, den Schmerzensmann auf ihrem Schoß, eine im Größenverhältnis primitiv verfehlte Figur mit kraß herausgearbeiteter Anatomie, die jedoch von Unwissenheit zeugte, das hängende Haupt von Dornen starrend, Gesicht und Glieder mit Blut befleckt und berieselt, dicke Trauben geronnenen Blutes an der Seitenwunde und den Nägelmalen der Hände und Füße." Though Mann had likely seen the sculpture during his November 1920 visit to Bonn, the city's art museum having acquired it in 1912, his description is almost certainly based on a photograph.

234. Mann 1995c, 386 / 551.

235. As Nietzsche argues in *Beyond Good and Evil* (1887), modern liberal society's overriding concern with "well-being . . . is no goal; it looks to us like an end [*das ist ja kein Ziel, das scheint uns*

of the pietà to be intelligible at all, the suffering it so unsparingly presents must be understood as a threshold to be crossed rather than an obstacle to be avoided. Suffering is the price of admission to the eschaton of the *visio beatifica*. How seeing the pietà is experienced, its phenomenology, thus stands in sharp contrast to the covetous, homoerotic gaze with which von Aschenbach appropriates the St. Sebastian–Tadzio figure as an allegory of his personal martyrdom as a creative writer. Twelve years later and in the aftermath of the Great War and a pandemic, the last remnants of the symbolist aesthetic that *Death in Venice* had sought to scrutinize have been swept away as Mann discovers in suffering far more than a metaphor for a decaying culture. For one, the nature and profundity of suffering are no longer confined to corporeal and visible sensation, though Mann not only resists aestheticizing suffering but also refuses to intellectualize it as a strictly notional, if ineffable, occurrence.

Instead, even as suffering can be mediated or witnessed only by means of sight and images that necessarily emphasize its bodily nature, those beholding Naphta's wooden pietà intuitively grasp that to close in on the reality of suffering one must look beyond Christ's and Mary's tormented bodies and, consequently, beyond the visible image itself. This much the former Jesuit Naphta knows very well, not only at an intellectual level but also, given his traumatic biography, from experience. Responding to Castorp's impromptu remark, he thus notes that "we are dealing with beauty of the Spirit, not the flesh, which is basically stupid. And abstract, as well. . . . The beauty of the body is abstract. Only inner beauty, the beauty of religious expression, possesses true reality."[236] To be sure, Naphta understands that suffering cannot be reduced to a purely immanent, psychophysiological event, that it reaches deeper than physical pain and private anguish. Yet he is no longer able to translate this insight into action because he has lost the ability to *narrate* the story of his suffering and, as a result, cannot extricate himself from its grip. Hence, unable to envision peace, he seeks death. A "solution" that has gradually ripened in his mind since his boyhood trauma, death now appears the only conceivable telos for the nihilist intellectual who has lost both the capacity for transcending his suffering by means of narrative and the power and inner resolution to pray. More than his sparse social

---

ein ENDE!]." Consequently, modern culture's attempt "to abolish suffering" only renders "humanity . . . smaller," for it was precisely "the discipline [*Zucht*] of suffering . . . [that] has been the sole cause of every enhancement of humanity [*Erhöhungen des Menschen*] thus far" (Nietzsche 2002, 116–17 [#225]).

236. Mann here is almost certainly drawing on a passage in Heinrich von Eicken's *Geschichte und System der mittelalterlichen Weltanschauung* (1887), where the author argues that in foregrounding the ugliness of Christ's mangled body Christianity sought to distance itself from the physical perfection of the pagan gods in classical art; Eicken's characterization of the suffering body as *signum mortificationis* is also invoked verbatim by Naphta shortly afterward, as is a reference to Innocent III's *De miseria humanae conditionis*, a work also discussed by Eicken in the same context.

contacts, it is the unchanging and unsparing *imago* of the wooden pietà that confronts Naphta with his inability to embrace the *logos* as a source of revelation and redemption, and not just as a tool of dialectical mastery, an art in which he clearly excels. In the end, Naphta is—and knows himself to be—a failed mystic or (in late nineteenth-century parlance) a nihilist, modeled as much on Dostoevsky's Ivan Karamazov and on the tubercular and moribund Ippolít Teréntyev of *The Idiot* as on the historical figure of Georg Lukâcs. Bereft of the impersonal and searching devotional habit for which the fourteenth-century sculpture had once provided a visual focus, the onetime Jesuit Naphta instead finds his quintessentially modern, divided psyche mirrored back to him in his prized possession—a harsh reminder that the price for his antinomian construal of faith and knowledge is nothing less than the loss of eschatological hope. Returning to our argument's chronological order, we can explore how, half a millennium earlier, Nicholas of Cusa had offered one of the last and most comprehensive articulations of mystical vision, with the devotional icon playing a decisive role in integrating affective and intellectual forms of cognition.

4

THE MYSTICAL IMAGE

Platonism and Communal Vision in Nicholas of Cusa

Christian truth has, if I may say so, its own eyes with which to see; indeed, it seems to be all eyes. But it would be very disturbing, indeed, it would be impossible, for me to look at a painting or a piece of cloth if I discovered while looking at it that it was the painting or the cloth that was looking at me. And this is the case with the Christian truth; it is Christian truth that is observing me, whether I am doing what it says I should do. See, this is why Christian truth cannot be presented for observation or discoursed upon as observations.
—Søren Kierkegaard, *Practice in Christianity*

AT THE LIMITS OF RATIONAL THEOLOGY: MYSTICAL VISION IN NICHOLAS OF CUSA AND HIS INTERLOCUTORS

On 23 October 1453, Nicholas of Cusa, having served three conflict-laden years as bishop of Brixen in the Tyrol while trying to enforce a papal mandate for reforming his diocese, writes a short note to Kaspar Aindorffer, abbot of the Benedictine monastery at Tegernsee. In it he confirms that he is about to complete a treatise expounding his understanding of mystical theology, a point on which Aindorffer had requested clarification. He also assures the abbot that the manuscript will be sent as soon as it has been copied. Sometime after 15 January 1454, Aindorffer gratefully acknowledges receipt of the book and confirms that further copies of it have been prepared and are now being forwarded elsewhere, possibly to the abbey at Melk and to the Carthusian monastery at Aggsbach, about which more will soon be said. Though Guttenberg's experiments with movable type were already under way in this momentous year of 1453, which in May had also witnessed the end of the Byzantine Empire (which fifteen years earlier Nicholas had visited as a papal legate), Cusa's career up to his death in 1464 remains steeped in the culture of manuscripts, letters, and sermons, written and copied by hand and circulated by messengers rather than disseminated as printed matter. In the event, the treatise he had just completed, *De Visione Dei*—or, as he refers to it, *De Icona*—would prove his most enduringly popular work.[1]

As he writes the treatise, at age fifty-two, Nicholas of Cusa finds himself at the apex of his career, though also embattled on many sides. The son of a successful merchant from Kues (present-day Bernkastel-Kues) on the Moselle River, Nicholas of Kues (also Cusanus, Cryfftz, or Krebs) is himself a figure of many transitions and stark contrasts—a profound, contemplative thinker forever navigating between Athens and Jerusalem, yet also an administrator willing to use coercion and violence to enforce his draconian reform program for the church.[2] Nicholas's career, as a student of *artes liberales* at Heidelberg (1416–17) and of canon law at Padua where he takes his degree in 1423, a secretary of the archbishop of Trier, a young priest participating at the Council of Basel (1433–34), a papal legate to Germany (1440), and named cardinal in 1448 and bishop of Brixen in 1450, links his native Northern European world with that of northern Italy and, finally, Rome. Intellectually speaking, too, Nicholas—canon lawyer, philologist, mystical theologian, and mathematician extraordinaire—joins late Scholasticism with the emergent culture of humanistic learning and scientific experimentation soon known as the Italian Renaissance.[3] Already

---

1. Cusa, *De Visione Dei*, ed. J. Hopkins [henceforth cited parenthetically as *VD* following the 1985 Jasper Hopkins edition]. All other writings of Nicholas will be cited following the two-volume edition of his works prepared by Jasper Hopkins, with individual works cited with the following abbreviations (with Roman numerals and Arabic numbers identifying books and chapters, as applicable): *ADI* = *Apologia Doctae Ignorantiae* (1448); *AT* = *De Apice Theoriae* (1464); *DB* = *De Beryllo* (1458); *Comp.* = *Compendium* (1463); *DC* = *De coniecturis* (1441); *DI* = *De docta ignorantia* (1440); *DP* = *De Principio* (1459); *IM* = *Idiota de Mente* (1450); *NA* = *De li non aliud* (1462); *QD* = *De Quaerendo Deum* (1445); *TP* = *Trialogus de Possest* (1460); *VS* = *De Venatione Sapientiae* (1463).

2. On Cusa's career, see McGinn 2005, 432–83; Cusa 1997 (introduction by Bond, 3–190); Harries 2001, 24–30; and Hopkins's introduction in Cusa, *VD* 3–28.

3. Unsurprisingly, Nicholas's position at the very threshold of a scientific and soon schismatic modernity has compelled some readers to either see him as the last major representative of what Louis Dupré (1993) calls the "medieval synthesis" or, conversely, to appropriate him as a visionary figure presaging the *mathesis universalis* of Leibniz and of Kant's strictures regarding the metaphysical foundations of scientific inquiry. The backward-looking position is, perhaps, most fully developed by Blumenberg (1983, 343–60, 457–81), for whom Cusa is a key figure: "the question of the Cusan's 'modernity' promises to open up access to the problem of the legitimacy of the modern age" (577). While acknowledging signs in Cusa's oeuvre pointing to a "positivization of *curiositas*" (359),

while teaching canon law in Cologne (1426), Nicholas discovers pagan works (Pliny, Plautus) and takes a particular interest in Neoplatonist writings such as Proclus's commentary on Plato's *Parmenides* and the mystical theology of pseudo-Dionysius, whose putative status as a student of the apostle Paul Nicholas in his later years chose not to question, even after Lorenzo Valla in 1457 had definitively proven the writings of the "Areopagite" to have been written several centuries later. Finally, the North-South divide that defines so much of his career also shapes Nicholas's ecclesiological and theological writings, particularly during the two decades (1430–50) when the Conciliarist movement mounted a robust, if ultimately unsuccessful, campaign against papal supremacy. "Dedicated to solving problems of curial and monastic corruption and to the reform and regulation of devotional practices amongst believers," Conciliarism had a significant bearing "on the topic of mystical theology."[4] Hence it is that, following his first book, *De concordantia catholica* (1433), in which he had asserted the superior authority of the Council in Basel, Nicholas's decision to switch sides the next year and support the papal cause would never be forgotten by those with whom he later found himself disputing the finer points of mystical theology.

Support for Conciliarism ran particularly strong among adherents of the affective mysticism associated with the lay movement of the *devotio moderna* in the Low Countries, as well as those Hussites who, having survived the Hussite wars of the 1420s, had reached a settlement at the Council of Basel. Except for the relatively uneducated Vincent of the Carthusian monastery at Aggsbach, the others are all closely connected with the University of Vienna, a bastion of the Conciliarist reform movement that Nicholas had briefly supported at the Council of Basel (1431–45). In the event, and to the lasting irritation of Vincent in particular, Nicholas switched to

---

Blumenberg (1983) reads Cusa's work as an attempt "to grasp reality one more time in a consistently medieval fashion" (469) and as "combin[ing] traits of medieval piety with criticism of Scholasticism and a new power of disposition over the tradition of antiquity" (471). In this view, Blumenberg reacts above all against Cassirer's appropriative reading of Cusa as a modern, proto-Kantian (see Cassirer 1974, 21–72). Both Cassirer and, especially, Blumenberg underplay the metaphysical and theological dimensions of Nicholas's thought (what Blumenberg rather schematically terms "the medieval system" [476]); for a thorough critique of Blumenberg, see Hopkins's introduction to Cusa, *VD* 51–93. For a comprehensive theological reading of Nicholas, see Haubst 1991; and, for a critique of Cassirer's and Blumenberg's either/or approach, see Hoff 2013, xiv–xxvi. Offering a more capacious and integrative appraisal of Cusa's oeuvre, von Balthasar notes that "Cusa certainly provides a provisional sketch for the structure of the period—from the Renaissance to Hegel—which is just opening up, but in the best elements of his foundation outlives its collapse. His renewal of antiquity is more than renaissance: it is a retraining in the lost primordial articulations of human thought. . . . From the classical point of view (as philosophy of being) and from the modern point of view (as philosophy of mind and of freedom), Nicholas' effort of thought always serves the accomplishment of the *analogia entis*" (1991, 222).

4. Ziebart 2014, 147.

the papal side as early as 1434.[5] Still, his commitment to reforming the church remained undiminished, notwithstanding his support of the papacy after 1434. Though he had broken with the Conciliarist cause, Nicholas would prove himself an unyielding reformer of the church and, in the course of pressing the papal reform agenda, found himself entangled in sometimes violent conflict with intransigent religious communities. A case in point was Abbess Verena of Steuben, whose fierce resistance to Nicholas's reform efforts ultimately led to a conflagration in which in April 1458 his troops killed fifty of the abbess's armed men. He fared rather less well when, in his seemingly interminable conflict with Duke Sigismund as bishop of Brixen in the Tyrol, he had to escape several times to save his life. Political and monastic opposition against papal schemes for ecclesial reform at times merged. Thus, the Conciliarist (anti-papal) agenda was also championed by Carthusians, as well as some prominent intellectuals at the University of Vienna, all of them keen to safeguard forms of personal piety against what they regarded as arid and hyper-rationalist, late Scholastic speculation issuing from most of Europe's twenty-three universities.

Undoubtedly, the towering intellectual and political persona of Jean Gerson (1363–1429) had done much to focus early fifteenth-century discussions of mystical theology, in both its speculative and practical dimensions. As chancellor of the University of Paris and as the preeminent theologian at the Council of Constance in 1414–18, Gerson had long been dedicated to closing the growing gap between academic theology and popular piety and to restoring the study of theology at Paris "to a more modest, contemplative, monastic type of devotion."[6] Wary of the university's intellectual calcification and financial corruption, Gerson pointedly rejected Scholasticism's labyrinthine web of abstractions and distinctions. Yet he was no less outspoken when criticizing the purely affective and antirational spirituality then on the ascendant across northern France and the Low Countries and, a generation later, confronting Nicholas of Cusa in the irascible persona of the Carthusian Vincent of Aggsbach. Thus, in distinguishing between mystical theology (defined by love of what is good) and speculative theology (concerned with knowledge of what is true), Gerson did not present the two approaches as incommensurable or as outright

---

5. On the background of the disputants, see Ziebart 2014, 139–52; the principal documents of the South German theological debate about mysticism and Cusa's *De Visione Dei* can be found in Cusa 1998; on Cusa's mystical theology, its historical sources and hermeneutic strategies, see Dupré 1996, who particularly stresses Meister Eckhart's influence on Nicholas's writings.

6. Ziebart 2014, 148. Gerson's long letter to his former teacher, Pierre d'Ailly (1 April 1400), offers a diagnosis of what he thinks has long enfeebled academic theology fixated on "pointless teachings that are fruitless or superficial" and that spurn scripture; his long list of complaints is followed by a series of proposed remedial steps. Gerson 1998, 168–75; on Gerson, see also McGinn 2012, 86–95.

competitors. Indeed, excessive reading and purely affective devotion are equally liable to miss the true goal of contemplative silence: "They are deceived who want always either to read or to pray aloud or to receive devotional encouragement from those who speak to them. . . . [Instead], it is necessary 'in silence to await God's salvation' (Lam 3:26)" and to "grow accustomed to praying in spirit and in mind (1 Cor 14:15)."[7] While drawing a sharp distinction between speculative and mystical theology, Gerson conceded that the latter is experiential rather than analytic and that its phenomenology is one of affective love rather than explicit understanding. Yet while characterizing mystical theology as "irrational, mindless, foolish wisdom [*irrationalis et amens, et stulta sapientia*]," Gerson also granted that such spirituality nevertheless constitutes a type of wisdom insofar as it involves experiential knowledge of (and unreserved assent to) what is loved.[8] Indeed, even though "the erudite can know . . . more clearly than the simple believer," Gerson denied that he "can know . . . more truly and more sublimely."[9]

Of particular significance for our purposes is the emphatically aniconic nature of mystical theology. Thus, Vincent of Aggsbach rejects Gerson's identification of mystical theology with contemplation, maintaining that "mysticism" is literally concerned with the hidden God, whereas contemplation is by definition visual. When taken to an extreme, as Vincent will do, this position forecloses on any kind of mediation and attempts—not without troubling Gnostic overtones—to bypass the splendor of visible creation in favor of a direct relationship to the Creator. Such a strictly affective *devotio* involves no propositions, no rational argument, no explicit demonstrations. Instead, it rests on the ineffable, if incontrovertible charisma of an inner *experience* engaging all the spiritual senses.[10] Recalling Meister Eckhart (whose more controversial writings also impinge on Nicholas's oeuvre), such a concept of mystic vision always risks devolving into outright fideism, a form of devotion so exclusively generated and certified by the untutored believer as in effect to foreclose on the possibility of a *community* of the faithful and, by implication, subverting the liturgical and sacramental authority of the church. In time, Gerson's characterization of mystic theology as "irrational" (*amentium*) was to draw the ire of Vincent of Aggsbach who, following up on his 1453 polemic against Gerson with his *Impugnatorium Laudatorii Doctae Ignorantiae* (1454) against Nicholas of Cusa, conjures a three-

---

7. Gerson 1998, 322. In his polemical response to Gerson (*Tractatus cuiusdam Carthusiensis de Mystica Theologia*, 1453), Vincent of Aggsbach remains unpersuaded, charging Gerson with illicitly amalgamating Dionysius's radical model of mystical contemplation with Scholastic thought.

8. *Mystica Theologia Speculativa* 1402–3, 28th Consideration, quoted in Hopkins's introduction to *VD* 288 n. 13.

9. Hopkins, introduction to Cusa 1985 (*VD*), 10.

10. On the spiritual senses in late medieval piety and in Cusa, see the essays by McGinn and Green, in Gavrilyuk and Coakley 2012.

headed beast named "Gerchumar," a compound of *Ger*son, *C[h]u*sa, and *Ma*rquard Sprenger, prior of the Tegernsee monastery.[11] Just as Thomas Gallus (bishop of Vercelli) and Magister Albertus Magnus of Cologne had put forth competing affective and intellective readings of Dionysius's oeuvre in the first half of the thirteenth century, so once again the *quaestio difficilis*, as formulated by Hugh of Balma, resurfaces nearly two centuries later: "whether the soul in her *affectus* by means of aspiration and yearning can be moved into God without any of the intellect's cogitation leading the way or keeping her company."[12]

It is commonplace for those engaged in early and mid-fifteenth-century discussions of mystical theology to present their respective views mainly as a faithful exegesis of Dionysius's *Mystical Theology*, a text widely considered to have had an extraordinary impact on Western spirituality. So as to better gauge that work's bearing on the understanding of spiritual sight and mental imagery, let us briefly recall some of its basic claims. Dionysius's advice to Timothy is, "as you look for a sight of the mysterious things, . . . leave behind you everything perceived and understood, everything perceptible and understandable."[13] Recalling Moses's ascent of Mount Sinai, which had also inspired Gregory of Nyssa's influential *Life of Moses* in the fourth century, Dionysius conceives of mystical theology as an upward trajectory that pivots on shedding all attachments to conventional signs and visible being. Ultimately, to "leave behind every divine light, every voice, every word from heaven . . . [and] to "plunge into the darkness where . . . there dwells the One who is beyond all things" (*MT* 1000c) entails "an absolute abandonment of yourself" (*MT* 1000a). As Nicholas will also argue in *De filiatione Dei*, "We are called to become what we are, that is, the image of a plenitude that transcends all comparative determinations."[14]

Left unclear, however, is whether the resulting spiritual condition simply negates all knowledge or whether it instances positive knowledge in its own right. Thus, even as "Moses breaks . . . away from what sees and is seen and plunges into the truly mysterious darkness of unknowing" (*MT* 1001a), Dionysius still finds that ultimate state to involve a degree of self-awareness. What sight and other sense-based cognition forestall, and what the mystic seeks to attain, is not some purely affective state but a type of insight that transcends the opposition of reason and affect. As Dionysius

---

11. On Vincent's debate with Gerson and Cusa, see Ziebart 2014, 162 ff.; and Marion 2016, 305 ff.

12. Found in *The Roads to Sion Mourn* (*Viae Sion Lugent*), a work long attributed to Bonaventure but now known to belong to the Carthusian monk Hugh of Balma, as quoted in McGinn 2005, 450.

13. *Mystical Theology*, in Pseudo-Dionysius 1987, 133–42, 997b; henceforth quoted parenthetically as *MT*.

14. Hoff 2013, 13.

exclaims, "If only we lacked sight and knowledge so as to see, *so as to know,* unseeing and unknowing, *that which lies beyond all vision and knowledge*" (*MT* 1025a; emphasis mine). Drawing out this other dimension of knowing, beginning with *De docta ignorantia* and also in his correspondence with the monks at Tegernsee, Nicholas will emphasize how negative theology involves far more than simply expunging all lexical and visual particularity. If in mystical contemplation "we plunge into that darkness which is beyond intellect," the resulting "speechless and unknowing" (*MT* 1033b) state is something sui generis rather than simply arising, as it were by default, from the expurgation of all conceptual and discursive practice. More than a matter of sheer subtraction, mystical theology opens up on God's absolute presence and reality, which "is beyond assertion and denial. We make assertions and denials of what is next to it, but never of it, for it is . . . beyond every assertion, being the perfect and unique cause of things" (*MT* 1048b).

The decline and eventual defeat (in 1448) of Conciliarism, whose opposition to a central ecclesial authority made it a natural ally for the laity's growing investment in affective forms of piety, did not end the wide-ranging debate regarding the appropriate form and ultimate claims of mystical theology. Indeed, how to read and understand pseudo-Dionysius's *Mystical Theology* continued to be a subject of vigorous dispute, waged, among others, by the prior of the Carthusian monastery at Aggsbach, Vincent; the prior of the Benedictine monastery at Tegernsee, Marquard Sprenger; and the Munich-based theologian Bernard von Waging. Another significant interlocutor for Nicholas is Johannes Keck (1400–1450), whom Nicholas had come to know at the Council of Basel and whose subsequent work as a theologian at Tegernsee likely brought Nicholas into contact with that monastic community. In characteristically deferential language, the Tegernsee abbot, Caspar Aindorffer, writes to Nicholas on 22 September 1452, acknowledging that his monks have already been avidly copying various of Nicholas sermons on the topic of mystical theology, yet also requesting further clarification on this central point: "whether the pious soul is capable of attaining God without intellectual knowledge, without prior or concurrent reflection, solely by affective means or by the highest mental state, called 'synderesis,' moving and rushing toward Him in immediate manner."[15]

Hinting that this question will require a more comprehensive answer, eventually tendered in *De Visione Dei* a year later, Nicholas initially limits himself to just a few salient considerations. First, he stresses that love of God cannot be purely affective

---

15. "Est autem hec questio, utrum anima devota sine intellectus cognicione vel etiam sine cogitacione previa vel concomitante solo affectu seu per mentis apicem, quam vocant sinderesim, Deum attingere possit et in ipsum immediate moveri aut ferri" (Cusa 1998; von Kues, *Briefe und Dokumente,* 92, trans. mine; henceforth cited parenthetically as *KBD*).

because, as such, all love is a form of assent to a good that must to some extent be known: "what is loved or chosen as the Good [*sub racione boni diligitur seu eligitur*] is not loved altogether without knowledge of the good [*non diligitur sine omni cognitione boni*]. Hence the love with which one strives toward God contains knowledge [*cognicio*], even as one does not grasp what it is that one loves" (*KBD* 93). Second, it follows that where mystical theology is concerned, a different kind of knowledge is involved, one that does not venture explicit propositions about the nature of its object but, consistent with Anselm's *fides quaerens intellectum*, incrementally seeks to elucidate the certitude that is faith: "Because the simple faithful are led to their faith by the word, they are by means of this high knowledge of this world, with which they believe in God, elevated to friendship with God [cum hac altissima huius mundi sciencia, qua credunt Deo, rapiuntur in amiciciam Dei]" (*KBD* 95). Like Augustine and Anselm, Nicholas holds that "revelation completes the search for wisdom rather than canceling or overriding it. . . . [T]he application of reason to further the understanding of the truths revealed in faith . . . is a necessity."[16]

Reiterating his critique of a strictly noncognitivist understanding of love, Nicholas writes to Bernard of Waging (28 July 1455) that "those who claim that affect seizes exclusively upon the wholly unknown [*affectum in penitus ignotum ferri seu moveri*] contradict Aristotle who, in Book 3 of *De Anima*, remarks that affect can only move toward an object that is known, for it alone stimulates affect [*bonum enim apprehensum movet affectum*]" (*KBD* 183). He then directs his reader to a passage from *De Veritate* that bears quoting at some length because of the exemplary care with which Aquinas parses the claims of both an antirationalist and a strictly rationalist understanding of faith.

> No one can move toward God by any other motion unless at the same time he move with this motion of faith; for all other motions of the mind toward God the Justifier belong to the affections, whereas only the motion of faith belongs to the intellect. The affections, however, are moved toward their object only in so far as it is apprehended; for the apprehended good moves the affections, as is said in *The Soul*. Hence the motion of the apprehensive power is required for the motion of the affective, just as the mover needs to move actively for the mobile to be moved. In this way also the motion of faith is included in that of charity and in every other motion by which the mind is moved toward God. But because justice is completed in the affections, if man were turned toward God only with his intellect, he would not be coming into contact with God by the power that receives justice, his affections. Thus he could not be justified. It is therefore

---

16. McGinn 2005, 440.

required that not only the intellect be turned toward God but also the affec-tions.[17]

For Nicholas, the crucial error of a purely affective approach to mystical the-ology is to conceive faith and knowledge in purely antinomian ways and, in so doing, validate ignorance without recognizing that the darkness or cloud of unknowing into which mystical contemplation takes the believer involves a kind of intellectual discipline in its own right. Yet that seems to be the position of Vincent of Aggsbach, and to an extent of Hugh of Balma before him: namely, to posit "an (intellectually) impassable divide between human cognition and the 'supra-mental' cognition at-tained in mystical theology."[18]

Implicitly, Vincent's understanding of "mystical devotion as a radically personal and individual experience—a matter strictly between the devotee and God" under-mines all objective structures (sacramental, liturgical, ecclesial) in ways that already foreshadow Luther's conception some seventy years later of a wholly unmediated faith effectively guaranteeing the believer's salvation.[19] Such an approach ends up being turned into a fetish of sorts or creating surrogates for itself and investing faith itself with talismanic powers. Sobering as it may be, not every believer is, or should claim to be, a new St. Paul.

> If we know a simple, avid follower of Divine commandments and recognize him as a faithful Christian, we believe that he may be raptured into a state of vision [*eum ad visionem uti Paulus rapi posse credimus*], as was the case with Paul. Yet in this state of rapture many are deceived [*decipiuntur*] because they become at-tached to images and take their own fantastic vision as truth [*qui imaginibus in-haerent et visionem fantasticam putant veram*]. For truth is an object of intellect and is *not seen except as something invisible* [*non nisi visibiliter videtur*]. (*KBD* 95; emphasis mine)

To make sense of that last paradoxical phrase—which firmly pushes back against af-fective mysticism's self-idolization—is a central concern of this chapter. A first hint at

---

17. *De Veritate*, Q 28, A 4 (www.documentacatholicaomnia.eu/03d/1225-1274,_Thomas_Aquinas,_The_29_questions_on_Truth_(Mulligan_Translation),_EN.pdf; accessed 4 July 2020); the article is misidentified by Nicholas as Article 5. Aquinas is likely thinking of Augustine, *De Trinitate* X.1.3. Ziebart's insistence that Nicholas's "strong defense of the role of intellect [is] taken not from Neoplatonic sources but from the scholastic-Aristotelian tradition as articulated by Thomas" (2014, 171) seems unpersuasive, not least because it draws on a long-standing prejudice against Neoplatonism as inherently antirational.

18. Ziebart 2014, 187.

19. Ibid., 187, 184; for a brief discussion of Luther's conception of faith, see Pfau 2017b and the seminal study by Paul Hacker cited there.

what Nicholas may have in mind can be found in some letters written around the time that he was drafting *De Visione Dei*. Nicholas's correspondence with the monks at the Benedictine monastery at Tegernsee subsequent to his visit there in May 1452 clarifies his understanding of the image (*icon*) as the catalyst of what he calls "absolute vision," even as in the course of drawing closer to such vision the visible image will necessarily end up consuming and abolishing itself. In particular Nicholas's letter of 14 September 1453, written just as he was putting the finishing touches on *De Visione Dei*, sent a month later to the monks at Tegernsee, is a crucial document for understanding how he views the relation of mystical vision to the intellect and how such dynamic vision transforms and expands human cognition.

The letter is written against the background of fierce attacks that Vincent, prior at the Charterhouse of Aggsbach since 1435, had initiated against Nicholas starting in the early 1440s.[20] Unlike most other participants in the debate, the Carthusian Vincent had not studied at the university and, to judge by his writing, prefers a crudely polemical style. Having gradually distanced himself from Gerson's qualified Scholasticism and from the regional and intellectual Francophilia, which had inspired the young Cusa to sign his notes on Gerson's *Mystical Theology* with the Lotharingian "Nicholas of Treves," he now defends the wisdom of "not-knowing" and of unlettered, lay piety.[21] At the same time, Nicholas rejects a purely affective, as it were self-certifying, understanding of mysticism. For one thing, such a conception fails to heed Augustine's insight that "to say 'He loves to know the unknown' is not the same as saying 'He loves the unknown.' [For] it can happen that a man loves to know the unknown, but that he should love the unknown is impossible."[22] Merely to maintain that "darkness is found when everything has been withdrawn from God [*quando omnia a Deo auferuntur*], such that the one seeking is confronted by nothing rather than something," is to subscribe to a badly truncated idea of mystical contemplation. In fact, the "darkness" at issue will signify only if the faithful have entered into it in the proper way; and for that to happen it does not suffice "merely to occupy oneself with negative theology. For because negative theology only subtracts and does not positively affirm anything [*nihil ponat*] . . . it will not allow God to be seen

---

20. On Vincent's background and writings, see Ziebart 2014, 146–98. McGinn (2005, 453) characterizes him as a "literalist and something of a fundamentalist" who became a strict adherent of the affective interpretations of Dionysius's *Mystical Theology* developed by Gallus, Grossteste, and Hugh of Balma two centuries earlier. Similarly, Ziebart describes Vincent as "a stubborn, abrasive, and bitter old man." The fact that his incessant polemics eventually resulted in his censure and, ultimately, his deposition as prior would seem to confirm that appraisal. For a sample of Vincent's writing, from his 1454 *Impugnatorium Laudatorii*, see appendix 4 in Ziebart 2014, 295–96; and *KBD* 238–65.

21. See de Certeau 1987, 4.

22. Augustine 1991, 289 (*De Trinitate* X.1.3).

in unveiled form [*tunc per illam revelate non videbitur Deus*] but, rather, will suggest that He does not exist; conversely, if we seek for Him in positive terms, God will be found by imitation and veiled, but never unveiled" (*KBD* 96–98).

Not-knowing must itself be grasped as a form of knowledge, a practice of intellectual humility that signals the believer's growing receptivity to the sheer givenness of God in all creation. The intentionality in question can no longer be assimilated to notions of agency and epistemological dominion. Rather, "if the mind no longer comprehends, it is placed in the shadow [*umbra*] of non-knowing; and when it grasps the darkness, it is a sign that God is where he is seeking Him [quando sentit caliginem, signum est, quia ibi est Deus, quem querit]" (*KBD* 96). Such a progression from "shadow" into a "darkness" wherein individual being can no longer be misidentified with God recalls Dionysius's understanding of mystical vision as an ethos rather than an epistemological claim. The state to be aimed at, where "the confusion to which one rises without knowledge is certitude, and darkness is light[,] . . . can neither be taught nor known [*non potest nec tradi nec sciri*]." Nevertheless, "some kind of cognition has to be presupposed [*necesse est . . . premittere cognicionem qualemcumque*], since what is wholly unknown can neither be loved nor found; and if it were found, it would not be recognized [*non apprehenderetur*]" (*KBD* 98). Against Vincent of Aggsbach's critique of his *De docta ignorantia*, Nicholas affirms that, on his reading, Dionysius "did not at all want Timothy to ascend bereft of all knowledge [michi videtur nequaquam Dyonisium voluisse Thymoteum ignote debere consurgere] except in the way in which I have previously stated it, and not in the mode in which the Carthusian would have the affect leave behind the intellect."[23] In a subsequent letter to Aindorffer, Nicholas reiterates that "whoever has been recognized by God knows God; for nothing unknown can be loved [Qui a Deo cognitus est, hic Deum cognoscit, nichil enim incognitum amatur]" (*KBD* 110). The passage neatly encapsulates the coincidence of seeing and being seen for which Nicholas's early *De docta ignorantia* had furnished the conceptual template, yet which is now being deepened in significant ways.

In a development that will culminate in *De Visione Dei* and in his final work, "On the Summit of Contemplation" (*De Apice Theoriae*) from 1464, Nicholas thus refines his understanding of mystical theology in ways that avoid becoming trapped by (or between) the strict Aristotelianism of Johannes Wenck and the affective mysticism championed by Vincent of Aggsbach. In a polemical treatise directed against *De docta ignorantia*, Wenck had charged that Nicholas's "doctrine of learned ignorance completely abandoned the philosophy of Aristotle while maintaining the possibility of attaining knowledge of the divine beyond human limitations."[24] Con-

---

23. *KBD* 100; on this letter, see also Ziebart 2014, 160–63; and Beierwaltes 2017, 257–60.
24. See the discussion in Muratori and Meliadò 2020, 250–52.

versely, Vincent maintained that "learned ignorance illicitly *introduces* 'Aristotelian' metaphysics and philosophy into the divine realm of mystical theology."[25] Realizing that Wenck's and Vincent's critiques cancel one another, Nicholas clearly rejects them both. Instead, beginning with his *Apologia Doctae Ignorantiae*, in which he responded to Wenck, Nicholas begins to move beyond the paradigm of a *coincidentia oppositorum*, which remains conceptualist even as it seeks to demonstrate the inapplicability of any determinate concepts to God. To the dismay of committed Aristotelians such as Johannes Wenck, yet by now also parting ways with Jean Gerson's more guarded Scholasticism, Nicholas's *Apologia* (1449) maintains that what can be conceptually affirmed and what (once again by logical reasoning) is deemed to fall outside the scope of concepts reaches only up to "the walls of Paradise" but will never allow the mind to breach them. Early on in his *Apologia*, Nicholas thus notes that knowledge as understood by the "Aristotelian sect [*Aristotelica secta*]" is simply inapplicable to mystical theology. For in its propositional and syllogistic presentation such knowledge is only ever "exercised for disputing" and merely looks for a "victory of words" (*ADI* 6, 8). Even as it may conceptually affirm God's invisibility and the importance of negation, its verbal character leaves it unable to move where mystical theology seeks to take us: "to a rest and a silence where a vision of the invisible God is granted to us [ad vacationem et silentium, ubi est visio, que nobis conceditur, invisibilis Dei]" (*ADI* 8).

Whereas conceptual thinking accepts visible, particular being only as the temporary scaffolding *from* which to derive its abstract concept of form (*species*), Nicholas takes a more qualified approach. Thus, even as his conception of "form" (*eidos/species*) appears more indebted to Plotinus than to Aristotle, he firmly rejects Nominalism's unmediated concept of knowledge, according to which every "representation is a cognition, and to represent is to be that by means of which something is cognized [repraesentatio est cognitio et repraesentare est esse illud quo aliquid cognoscitur]," as Ockham argues. Once cognition is no longer indebted to the realism of forms but, instead, posits a direct correlation between particular being and its representation, the image inevitably is absorbed into a general economy of reference and signification. Thus, Ockham accords the image only a mnemonic function; it merely "represents that of which it is the image through an act of remembering."[26] In eliding the concept of form (*species*), which on the classical Platonist account images are meant to render visible, Nominalism has fundamentally denuded the image of its uniquely nonpropositional function. It is no longer viewed as an ontologically distinct medium, capable of unveiling or disclosing nonpropositional meanings. Instead, it now serves the strictly ancillary or supplemental function of indexing or

---

25. Ziebart 2014, 180; emphasis mine.
26. Ockham 1991, 257 (*Quodlibetal* IV, Q 3).

referring to singular entities putatively ascertained beforehand. As remains to be seen, the Nominalist framework is fundamentally congruent with (and arguably sponsors) the proto-Cartesian logic undergirding Leon Battista Alberti's development, in *De Pictura* (1435), of a linear, single-viewpoint perspective according to which the very reality of any object now depends altogether on the position the viewer assigns it in three-dimensional space. On this view, the image aspires toward an ideal of total visibility rather than mediating God's categorical invisibility. As we shall find, Nicholas clearly realizes that to embrace Alberti's theory of representation is to commit to an incipiently naturalist framework that no longer conceives of the invisible as the ontological source of all knowledge but, instead, as a temporary defect to be remedied by human, scientific means. At least implicitly, the perspectival theories developed by Alberto, Brunelleschi, and Ghiberti presage the stance animating the scientific revolution of the early seventeenth century: that of nature "perfecting" and, in time, obviating grace.

Paradoxically, the modern imperative of subjecting *all* being to *total* visibility also has a curiously disembodying effect on the world of things. For in placing the "object firmly in the 'outer world,'" Renaissance theories of art institute an essential "distance between 'subject' and 'object[,]' . . . between the eye and the world of things."[27] With object knowledge thought to depend on the observer's perspective, the goal naturally becomes maximizing the subject's perceptual dominion over phenomena by rendering them maximally visible and transparent. Hence, rational cognition is aligned with the geometric and mathematical laws governing perspectival seeing, which in turn means that the knowledge of phenomena is construed as a subjective achievement and, as such, has "become independent of their existence."[28] What initially is proffered as a geometric method meant to render each particular thing exhaustively and definitively visible gradually evolves into an absolute warrant for crediting visible being with reality in the first place. As spiritual vision is supplanted by verifiable sight, what legitimates the (mental) image is, precisely, that it can be *contained* as *this* visible particular and, thus, drain the phenomenal world of all intrinsic meaning. Once the Nominalist concept of *representation* has displaced that of manifestation, modern anthropocentric and perspectival cognition has instituted an ontological divide between the observer and reality that will find its fullest expression in Descartes's *Meditations*. As remains to be seen, early modern theories of perspectival representation are both the root cause of the chasm now said to separate mind and world, beholder and object, and a methodology devised to compensate for that dilemma ex post facto.

27. Panofsky 1968, 50–51.
28. Scheier 2010, 71.

By contrast, the Neoplatonist tradition, on which Cusa increasingly draws, posits form as the point of contact between *materia* and *ratio*, that is, as the medium in and through which the intrinsic order and intelligibility of the visible world reveals itself.

> Man measures his own intellect in terms of the power of its works; and thereby he measures the Divine Intellect, even as an original is measured by means of its image. Now, this knowledge [of the Divine Intellect] is symbolical knowledge. Yet, man has a very refined power-of-seeing through which he sees that the symbolism is a *symbolism* of the true Reality, so that he knows the true Reality to be a Reality that is not figurable by means of any symbolism.[29]

Truth is measured by way of the image, rather than vice versa, for as Nicholas observes elsewhere, "an actual existent is understood and not conceived [*sed actuale intelligitur et non concipitur*]" (*IM* 8, ¶108). At once a veil and a medium for a progressive unveiling of Being, the image in Nicholas's account retains its foundational role vis-à-vis reason (*logos*). As de Certeau puts it, "Seeing is the act through which *singularity coincides with totality*."[30] While no image can ever coincide with the divine *logos*, its concrete, charismatic presence reveals it to be "a symbolism of the true Reality [*veritatis aenigma*]." Nicholas's frequent choice of *aenigma* rather than *imago* reminds us that "image" neither involves the outright replication of perceptible being nor claims equivalence with the invisible *logos* that has brought forth all discrete beings. Hence, even as he adheres to the Platonic view that "beauty enlivens insofar as it is true [*inquantum vera, intantum vivificate*]," Nicholas qualifies it by stressing that "what pleases the eye is beauty inasmuch as it is discovered in a visible thing, that is, is found not *per se* but in otherness [*ubi non reperitur in se, sed in alio*], not in Truth but in its resemblance to Truth, in image and enigma [*non in veritate, sed in verisimilitudine et imagine aut aenigmate*]."[31]

Yet for this insight to take hold, the finite intellect must be tempered by wisdom and epistemic humility. We must recognize that "in our intellect all things are present in accordance with the intellect's mode of being [*secundum ipsius essendi modem sunt omnia*]." Referencing Proclus's *Six Books on the Theology of Plato*, Nicholas emphasizes the intellect's latent capacity for recognizing itself, not as the ultimate source

---

29. *DB* 6, ¶ 7: "Mensurat suum intellectum per potentiam operum suorum et ex hoc mensurat divinum intellectum, sicut veritas mensuratur per imaginem. Et haec est aenigmatica scientia. Habet autem visum subtilissimum, per quem videt aenigma esse veritatis aenigma, ut sciat hanc veritatem, que non est figurabilis in aliquo aenigmate."

30. De Certeau 1987, 23.

31. Sermo CCXXXI, quoted in Borsche 2010, 177.

of knowledge exercising dominion over all possible phenomena, but as *imago Dei*: "By means of its own intellectual wisdom [*per sapientiam intellectualem suam*] it makes concepts of Wisdom, which is free of all things, and concepts of wisdom that is contracted to all things" (*VS* 17, ¶49). For inasmuch as knowing is

> assimilation, the intellect finds all things to be within itself as in a mirror that is alive with an intellectual life. . . . And this assimilation is a living image of the Creator and of all things. But since the intellect is a living and intellectual image of God [*viva et intellectualis Dei imago*], who is not *other* than anything: when the intellect enters into itself and knows that it is such an image, it observes within itself what kind of thing its own Exemplar is. For, without doubt, the intellect knows that this Exemplar is its God, whose likeness the intellect is [*quale est suum exemplar in se speculator. Hunc enim indubie deum suum cognoscit, cuius est similtudo*].[32]

The measure of the intellect's wisdom is its ability and willingness to receive visible phenomena as authentic manifestations of the divine while also recognizing itself as the image that imperfectly mediates the fullness of the *logos*.

> God shines forth in creatures as the truth shines forth in an image [*Deus relucet in creaturis sicut veritas in imagine*]. Therefore, if anyone sees that the very great variety of things is an image of the one God, then when he leaves behind all the variety of all the images, he proceeds incomprehensibly to the Incomprehensible. For he is led into an ecstasy when he gazes in wonderment at this infinite Being which in all comprehensible things is present as in a mirror and in a symbolism [*hoc infinitum esse . . . quod in omnibus comprehnsibilibus est ut in speculo et aenigmate*]. (*ADI* 11)

As Hans Urs von Balthasar remarks, "The God whom Nicholas encounters in all things is no '*dieu des philosophes*.'" Rather, in Pauline fashion, for Nicholas "the hidden God [is] manifest in his creation. [Though] transcendent over the world, [He] is distant from no-one and wills to be sought longingly by all, always and through all things."[33] As Nicholas advances his defense of "learned ignorance" in the *Apologia*, it becomes apparent that "mystical seeing does not imply the objectifying effect that we commonly associate with visual activity."[34] Far from some mindless optical event or an expression of aimless, frivolous curiosity, seeing constitutes a form of intellection in its own right. Aristotelians such as Johannes Wenck, who would confine knowl-

---

32. *VS* 17, ¶ 50; see also *IM* 7, ¶¶ 99–100.
33. Balthasar 1991, 213.
34. Dupré 1996, 215.

edge strictly within the bounds of syllogistic reasoning and propositional assertions, "fail to notice that learned ignorance is concerned with the mind's eye and with apprehension-by-the-intellect [non enim advertit doctam ignorantiam versari circa mentis oculum et intellectibilitatem]—so that whoever is led to the point of *seeing* ceases from all discursive reasoning, and his evidence comes from sight. 'He bears witness to what he has seen'—as John the Baptist says of Christ [Jn 3:32]" (*ADI* 14; emphasis mine).[35]

For Werner Beierwaltes, there can be no question that Cusa is centrally "inspired by the Dionysian and Proclean framework, according to which the One or God is 'above, prior to, or beyond all opposition.'" Hence, *De Visione Dei* will "no longer simply identify the notion of a *coincidentia oppositorum* with absolute infinity itself. Rather, Nicholas now traces that notion back to its precondition, viz. of insight into the infinite [*Einblick ins Unendliche*]." Already by the mid-1440s, the framework of the *coincidentia oppositorum* is being replaced by a different model, "a no-longer-conceptual, no-longer-reified seeing [in ein nicht-mehr-begreifendes, nicht mehr gegenständliches Sehen]."[36] The limits of conceptualism, as drawn by apophatic theology, cannot in turn be articulated in conceptual form. For to do so is to confine negative theology within a logic of subtraction, which can never account for the anterior insight that compels apophaticism's seemingly endless cascade of negations.

> Every concept reaches its limit at the wall of Paradise [*Omnis enim conceptus terminatur in muro paradisi*]. Moreover, if anyone expresses any likeness and maintains that You are to be conceived in accordance with it, I know as well that this likeness is not a likeness of You. Similarly, if anyone recounts his understanding of You, intending to offer a means for Your being understood, he is still far away from You. For You are separated by a very high wall from all these [modes of apprehending]. For [this] wall separates from You whatever can be spoken of or thought of, because You are free from all the things that can be captured by any concept. Hence, when I am very highly elevated, I see that You are Infinity [*infinitatem te video*]. Consequently, You are not approachable, not comprehensible, not nameable, not manifold, and not visible. (*VD* 13, ¶ 52)

---

35. For a modern echo of Wenck's rejection of mystical experience, see Maritain's firmly Thomist account (1995, 282–295). While admitting "a natural 'spirituality' . . . and the existence of a natural 'contemplation,'" Maritain rejects the possibility of "an *authentic* and *properly so-called* mystical experience . . . which is not a counterfeit or illusion, and . . . bears on God Himself." For to admit "a genuine experience of the depths of God's being on the natural level" would be to blur the boundary separating our "natural intellectuality [with] . . . our intellectuality as it flows from grace." In the event, Maritain contends, the knowledge claimed by such mystical experience features "no *passion* of God suffered within the soul, no *contact* with God" but, instead, can claim "a knowledge always essentially from afar, even though affectively determined" (286–87, 289).

36. Beierwaltes 2017, 263.

The limits of conceptual knowledge must themselves be given in experiential form, that is, in an interior vision that cannot be mapped onto ordinary perception, a "seeing" no longer constrained by static objects or the notions derived from the perception of such objects. Nicholas's September 1453 letter to Aindorffer sketches the dialectic of seeing with which he will open *De Visione Dei*, "where by some painting [*quomodo ex ymagine*] . . . that simultaneously sees everything and each one [*omnia et singula videntis*] we are being led by a sensible experience into mystical theology, such that with complete certitude and infinite vision we intuit in simultaneity everything that we comprehend individually with all possible love and care [*quodam sensibili experimento ducamur ad misticam theologiam, ut certissime intueamur infinitum visum ita omnia simul videre, quod singulariter singula et omni amore et diligencia amplecti*]" (*KBD* 100). Self-recognition means having been seen by God as a being capable of seeing him, and being capable of such vision only *because* one has been seen by him.

THE RETURN OF NEOPLATONISM IN NICHOLAS OF CUSA'S SPECULATIVE THEOLOGY OF THE IMAGE

Whereas in Book 3 of *De docta ignorantia* Nicholas had unfolded the self-consummation of conceptual thought, his account of mystical theology in *De Visione Dei* some thirteen years later conceives finite being's relatedness to God's infinity phenomenologically, that is, in ways no longer hemmed in by a dialectic of affirmation and negation. As Nicholas writes to Aindorffer, "It seemed to me, that [Dionysius's] entire mystical theology consists in entering into absolute infinity, for infinity involves the coincidence of opposites . . . and nobody can see God mystically except in the darkness of this coinciding [*nemo potest Deum mistice videre nisi in caligine coincidencie*]" (*KBD* 100). In its alterity vis-à-vis all finite and oppositional being—where X^1 only ever *is* in virtue of its not being X^2, X^3, and so forth—infinity must be understood as "the creative positing and ground of all oppositionality, which is finitude's mode of being. . . . Time and again Cusa reiterates the foundational Neo-Platonist conception that 'infinity contains all, such that it belongs to none (*infinitas sic omnia est, quod nullum omnium*).' That is, infinity understood as the divine principle is the dynamic ground [*gründender Grund*] of each single being in its individuality and particularity; yet it also grounds the coherence of the universe's inherently relational unity."[37] Infinity thus is to be understood as the telos of all particular being, what Nicholas calls "the end that delimits all things [*finis omnia finiens*]" (*VD* 13, § 54),

---

37. Ibid., 270.

that wherein the naturally dispersed and "unfinished" (*in-finitum*) nature of each and every particular being will at last be resolved.

However obliquely, Nicholas's Neoplatonist conception of absolute infinity as absolute simplicity also responds to fourteenth-century Nominalism's univocal conception of being as sheer singularity and its rejection of the Aristotelian concept of species and universals that had been a particularly controversial feature of Aquinas's theology. Yet unlike a committed late Scholastic such as Johannes Wenck, Nicholas by the mid-fifteenth century draws on strands of Neoplatonist thought that, mediated by John Scotus Eriugena, Meister Eckhart, and, to a lesser extent, Bonaventure, had at last begun to blossom and transform the philosophical and theological language of his day. With its at times marked Neoplatonist overtones, the shift is especially palpable throughout *De Visione Dei*, such as when Nicholas identifies God's infinity as absolute simplicity: "Infinity is simplicity; contradiction does not exist apart from otherness. But in simplicity otherness is present without contradiction [*alteritas autem in simplicitate est sine contradictione*], because [in simplicity otherness is] simplicity itself. For whatever is predicated of absolute simplicity coincides with absolute simplicity, because in absolute simplicity having is being" (*VD* 13, ¶ 55). Passages such as this one show Nicholas to be particularly alert to how late medieval mysticism relates to the Neoplatonist legacy that, refocused by Dionysius into a Christo-centric vision, had been transmitted by John Scotus Eriugena, Hugh and Richard of St. Victor, and Bonaventure and that at the start of the fifteenth century begins to develop a much larger footprint in theological and intellectual debates, particularly in Italy.

Nicholas's frequent choice of philosophical dialogue and the Platonic *elegchos*— a process of questioning and refutation aimed at "resolv[ing] ambiguities into contradictions"—is typical of early Renaissance practice.[38] For a long time known mainly through Galen's summaries and subsequently promoted by Petrarch, who perceived strong connections between the cosmology of Plato's *Timaeus* and the Gospel of St. John, Platonist thought gains in resonance as a result of the writings and teaching of Byzantine scholar Manuel Chrysoloras. Having arrived in Florence in 1397, by 1402, Chrysoloras appears to have completed a first draft translation of Plato's *Republic* into Latin. By 1420, a translation of that work is for the first time made commercially available by Uberto Decembrio. A subsequent attempt by Georgios Plethon (d. 1450) to fuse various texts by Psellus and Proclus into what he proposed as a reconstruction of Platonic theology caused something of an uproar at the Council of Florence

---

38. Gaukroger 2006, 230; see also D'Amico (2010, 98), who remarks on the comprehensive list of Neoplatonist writers found in Nicholas's marginalia (Dionysius, Marius Victorinus, Scotus Eriugena, Honorius Augustodinensis, and Berthold of Moosburg's commentary on Proclus's *Elements of Theology*).

(1439–40). For it appeared to offer a serious, if scandalously pagan, alternative to Scholastic Aristotelianism. Though Marsilio Ficino's commentaries on Plato and Plotinus, as well as his *Theologia Platonica* (1469–74), would postdate Nicholas, the revival of Neoplatonism had already been gathering momentum during the cardinal's last years. Ironically, attempts by George of Trezibond (1395–1484) to warn his contemporaries against the repaganization of philosophy may have done more to promote Plato's writings than anything else prior to Ficino.[39]

Of particular consequence for our purposes are efforts by Cardinal Bessarion (1400–1472) to promote a Platonic approach that, at least implicitly, undermined Scholasticism's Aristotelian framework of inquiry based on the principle of analogy. Bessarion's Platonizing model comports with ongoing efforts to appropriate the writings of pseudo-Dionysius for strictly affective forms of mystical contemplation. In both cases, what prevails is "a kind of intuitive knowledge or wisdom which is a form of contemplative understanding."[40] Indeed, rather like the philosophy of Michael Polanyi in our time, the early Renaissance revival of Platonism is not actually *opposed* to a more formal scientific mode of inquiry long associated with Averroist Aristotelianism. Rather, in ways that also eminently characterize Nicholas writings, the Platonist revival aims to recover an underlying metaphysical or "tacit dimension" (Polanyi) against which the discrete phenomena addressed by scientific analysis stand forth, and from which they draw their concrete interest and potential significance. Hence, as Gaukroger remarks, "those who took up the Platonist option . . . saw their project in terms of an interpretation of nature, something that uncovers hidden truths, and is more like interpretation of a sacred text in which one seeks to uncover a hidden and unique truth than something to be pursued in terms of empirical investigation."[41] While that much seems true, it turns out that the principle of analogy is not, in fact, suspended but at most inflected by the rising Platonism of the mid-fifteenth century.

For Nicholas, resemblances of the Dionysian corpus with lately rediscovered Neoplatonist writings of Proclus as filtered by the informed translations and commentaries of John Scotus Eriugena and Albertus Magnus would have been striking enough to wonder privately about the official identification of Dionysius as one of St. Paul's converts (Acts 17:34). Having had access to Latin translations of Dionysius's works, as well as to Pietro Balbi's translation of Proclus's *Platonic Theology* and

---

39. On the Florentine Plato revival in the fifteenth century, see Gaukroger 2006, 88–101; Ficino began his study of Greek only in 1456 and did not embark on translating Plato's works, with funding from Cosimo de Medici, until six years later; on the rediscovery of Platonic texts in the fifteenth century, see Dupré 1993, 42–60. On Nicholas's involvement in the fifteenth-century revival of Platonism, see Muratori and Meliadò 2020, 248–79.

40. Gaukroger 2006, 91.

41. Ibid., 233.

Commentary on Parmenides, Nicholas, in his overall philosophical and theological approach, shows these two strands of speculative thought merging into a single, foundational constellation.[42] This is apparent, even though Nicholas does not appear to have had firsthand knowledge of Plotinus's writings. As we have seen, Plotinus was able to show that the One, though invisible, is nevertheless so diffused throughout all of creation as to be mediated, to a greater or lesser extent, by all visible being. Furthermore, when conceived as a gradated, hierarchical order, creation furnishes a prima facie template for the ascent toward a contemplative seeing that participates in the One. Plotinian resonances are found throughout Nicholas's oeuvre, such as when in *De Coniecturis* (1442) he specifies that "the entire power of our mind ought to focus on refining the concept of oneness, for the entire multitude of things knowable depends on the knowledge of oneness; and in all knowledge oneness is whatever is known." Hence it is that "form [descends] into what-is-formable (since form is distinct and, therefore, a oneness) [*forma est discretiva, quare unitas*]" (*DC* 10, ¶ 44).

In parsing the concept of divine being in his later *Trialogus de Possest* (1460), Nicholas draws on a quintessentially Plotinian trope when noting that "God is [the] sun," albeit "not in the same way as is the visible sun [*modo essendi quo hic sol est*]." For divine Being is not circumscribed by any particular quiddity, even as it encompasses each and every entity and form of being. Rather, "He is the Form for all things [*omnibus forma*], since He is the efficient, the formal . . . and the final cause" (*TP*, ¶ 12). Tellingly, though, Nicholas develops the trope of the sun in ways that set his panentheist position firmly apart from any pantheist views that might arise due to its markedly Platonic overtones.[43] As the living, generative principle of forms (*forma formarum*), God is the noncontingent Being in which all "possibility" and all "actuality" (*posse + esse*: hence, *Possest*) coincide. Hence, "forms exist more truly and more vitally [*verius et vivacius*] in the Form of forms than in matter" (*TP*, ¶ 13). Nicholas does not assert God's substantive identity *with* the sun but thinks God is the source that allows sun and light to bring what is possible into actuality. His sight is

---

42. As Beierwaltes (1998b, 132–33) notes, there had been multiple translations of Dionysius's writings beginning with Hilduin of St. Denis in the ninth century. Nicholas is known to have had access to them as evidenced by Codices Nos. 43–45 in his Bernkastel-Kues library; he also annotated extensively Albertus Magnus's commentary on the Areopagite's works. Nicholas references Proclus's Parmenides commentary in *NA* 20, ¶ 92. The Neoplatonist filiations of Nicholas's thought emerge perhaps most fully at the beginning of *De li non aliud* (early 1462), where two of his interlocutors—Abbot John of Vigevius and Pietro Balbi of Pisa—are said to be engaged in translating Proclus's writings; see Muratori and Meliadò 2020.

43. Late in *De Possest*, Nicholas specifically pushes back against a certain (mis)understanding of Creation as an emanation of forms in time: "For only if the created thing is seen to have been eternally present in the Creator's invisible power can it be understood to have emanated from the Creator. . . . It is necessary that the Creator be all the things which are possible to be [*opportet omnia creabilia actu in eius potestate esse*]" (*TP*, ¶ 73).

essentially creative, giving rise to the "actuality of every possibility" (*actus omnis potentiae*). Hence, the "I am I-who-am" (Ex 3:14), God's very name, "leads the one-who-is-speculating beyond all the senses, all reason, and all intellect unto a mystical vision [*in mysticam visionem*], where there is an end to the ascent of all cognitive power and where there is the beginning of the revelation of the unknown God" (*TP*, ¶ 15).

While Dionysius's apophatic (negative) approach to theology remains in place and virtually unchanged in much of Nicholas's writing, it is not the final horizon toward which Nicholas takes "mystical vision" to be ordered. Being "unlimitable and unboundable, . . . inconceivable . . . [and] also ineffable," God is beyond all predication. He is also, therefore, beyond the reach of the intellect, which cannot understand "unless [it] becomes like the intelligible object [*nisi enim intellectus se intelligibili assimilet, non intelligit*]" (*TP*, ¶ 17). When, later in the conversation (*TP*, ¶¶ 54–57), one of his interlocutors develops an elaborate simile for God's Being in relation to the world of visible particulars, Nicholas does not deny that "many symbolisms guide us [*aenigmata multa nos ducant*]" but cautions that "there is no end of symbolisms, since no symbolism is so close that there cannot always be a closer one. Only the Son of God is the image of the substance of the Father ['*figura substantiae*' *patris*]" (*TP*, ¶¶ 54, 58). The qualification and shift in terminology are revealing here. As the source of all actuality and possibility, God is nevertheless absolutely distinct from any of their conceivable manifestations. Hence, whatever "symbolisms" (*aenigmata*) human beings may devise in an attempt to grasp God must formally acknowledge their intrinsic heteronomy vis-à-vis God. Whereas every conceivable image also veils the Being it would mediate, thereby pointing to an ultimate "darkness" of human intellectual and affective striving, only Christ's image coincides with the *Possest* that is God.

Nicholas's choice of "figura" rather than "imago" as the antonym of the *aenigmata* wrought by human hands recalls the term's patristic provenance, that is, *figura* as a truly anagogical image sustained by faith in its eventual fulfillment. For Augustine in particular, *figura* comes into play where the temporal economy of image qua similitude has been suspended. As Auerbach notes, *figura* "removes the concrete event from time . . . and places it into the perspective of timeless eternity." Though it cannot coincide with what it foretells, *figura* nevertheless is only intelligible as such in relation to Truth rather than contingent historical events. It is an *imitatio veritatis*. A new opposition surfaces in late patristic writing, "namely between *figura* and *historia*." Whereas history (or *littera*) names a literal or, we might now say, empirical and determinate event, "*figura* is the same meaning or event, but seen from the perspective of the future fulfillment hidden within it, and this fulfillment is *veritas*, or truth. *Figura* thus appears as the middle term between *littera-historia* and *veritas.*"[44] Both Platonists and patristic writers had maintained that, by its very nature, an image seeks to overcome its "contracted" status as mere similitude and to become properly *figura*. Likely following Proclus, Nicholas affirms that even "though reason and logic deal only with the images of forms [*circa imagines formarum tantum versatur*]," nevertheless the human mind "attempt[s] to see things theologically, as these things transcend the meaning of a name . . . turn[ing] attention toward Exemplars and Ideas [*sed res ultra vim vocabuli theologice intueri conantur et ad exemplaria et ideas se convertunt*]" (*IM* 2, ¶ 66). Being necessarily tethered to some particular thing of determinate form, no visible image can ever mediate absolute Being with the finite intellect.

And yet, as Nicholas frequently points out, by its very nature the visible image cannot be reduced to a discursive or referential function any more than it ought to be credited with accomplishing some mystical fusion of finite and divine being. Confined to the realm of determinate, actual particulars, the intellect "cannot attain to the proportion between the possibility and the actuality. For we have no common medium [*nullum medium commune*] by which to attain to the relationship, since the possibility is infinite and indeterminate, whereas the actuality is finite and determined" (*TP*, ¶ 42). Referencing his earlier *De Visione Dei*, Nicholas admits that, in order to think how "the One which is essentially *in* all things *is* all things, . . . more lucid symbolisms [*clariora aenigmata*]" (*TP*, ¶ 58) are required. Hence, every speculative image, simile, or symbol must in its very composition encompass and acknowledge the divine economy within which it operates and vis-à-vis which it will necessarily fall short. Precisely this metaphysical qualification, however, the image is uniquely suited to meet; for "we cannot without images see this negative presupposition [*negativam praesuppositum*] more simply and more truly [*Hoc nulla alia via absque phantasmate simplicius et verius videri potest*]" (*TP*, ¶ 67).

The point resurfaces in Nicholas's late *De Venatione Sapientiae* (1463), where he affirms that "those things which exist but are not all that which they can be made to be are never constant, and they perish. Therefore, they imitate [*imitantur*] perpetual things but will never attain them" (*VS* 3, ¶ 8). All circumscribed matter thus both temporarily instantiates and ultimately falls short of, reveals and veils, the divine archetype (*forma formarum*) of which it is an image. It cannot do otherwise since Nicholas considers all determinate (actual) being is subject to the "distension" (*diairesis* and *diastasis*) of time, as Plotinus and Augustine had done long before him, echoing Plato's characterization of time as "a moving image of eternity" (*Timaios* 37d5). In foregrounding its constitutive difference vis-à-vis its archetype, an image

---

44. Auerbach 2014, 88, 91. The phrase "imitation of truth" is from Gaudentius of Brescia, quoted in Auerbach 2014, 89.

throws into relief the dialectical bond between identity and difference, the One and the many. As is the case in Plotinian contemplation, this dialectical structure governs human thought not merely in the sense of an external, formal procedure or method, but, beyond that, it embodies "the essential dynamic structure internal to thinking itself."[45] Nicholas sees the play of identity and difference as a dialectical unfolding of the One *within time*. Whatever can be *for* an intellect, and thus is capable of eliciting reflection and expression, belongs to the temporal order. At the same time, thought by its very nature aspires to overcome the temporal and material constitution of its objects, that is, seeks to grasp their form and, in so doing, to ascend or, rather, return to the One. "Of all things," Nicholas writes, "there is only a single Cause, which creates the possibility of everything's being made. This Creating Cause both precedes all possible-being-created and is also its telos [*illa omne posse fieri praecedat sitque ipsius terminus*]" (*VS* 7, ¶16).

As is specifically revealed by the phenomenology of the image that Nicholas develops in *De Visione Dei* and extending from there, via the Cambridge Neoplatonists all the way to Goethe and Schelling, the metaphysical premise of an all-encompassing One (*hen*) is the indispensable foundation for any subsequent dialectic of identity and difference. Hence Plotinus's One and Cusanus's God as the *coincidentia oppositorum* are not to be confused with a concept of self-identity said to operate *within* that polarity. As Nicholas stresses, God understood as the "Not-Other [*non aliud*] does not merely signify 'sameness' [*li idem*]" or a strictly formal self-identity in the way those terms tend to be ascribed to a finite entity. Rather, God as the "Not-other" precedes all nameable things: "and so, although God is named 'Not-other' because He is not *other* than any other, He is not on this account the same as any other [*non est idem cum aliquo*]" (*VS* 14, ¶ 41). Not being "other-to" any particular being, God is wholly immanent in the world. At the same time, in virtue of being "not-other-to" any particular being, God also cannot be identified with any *one* of them. Hence God's Being relates to finite beings neither qua sameness nor qua indifference but, instead, as the One wherein transcendence and immanence coincide. It

---

45. Beierwaltes [1985] 2016, 15. As Muratori and Meliadò point out, Nicholas's exposure to a Platonist-inflected reading of Aristotle's *Metaphysics* likely began during his studies at the University of Cologne, which probably included his attending lectures by Heymeric of Campo, whose *Compendium divinorum* (1420–22) argued for the centrality of Proclus's *Elements of Theology*, first translated by Gerald of Cremona in the twelfth century, as completing (along with Boethius's *De hebdomadibus*) Aristotle's *Metaphysics*. Heavily drawing on Dionysius and Proclus, the early fifteenth-century "Albertist" school, as it became known, saw "the ideal structure of human science . . . rooted in the emanative pattern of the universe" and unfolding as a "gradual procession of multiplicity from the One." Rather than contest Aristotelianism outright, Heymeric's objective was to "reinterpret Aristotelian logic in a strongly realist sense as the key to expounding the order of the universe and to revealing the common rational foundation of theological, cosmological, and anthropological investigation" (Muratori and Meliadò 2020, 256–57).

is this nuanced and profound conceptual framework undergirding Nicholas's philosophical theology that also presents an alternative to Heidegger's antinomian construction of Being and beings, as well as classical metaphysics' alleged "forgetfulness of Being" (*Seinsvergessenheit*), from Socrates all the way into the twentieth century.

For divine Being to manifest itself in time, all individual (circumscribed) being must be approached not just as a self-contained, empirically observable singularity, but as an image mediating its invisible source: "All things, because they exist, bear witness of God that He exists [*Omnia enim, quia sunt, et deum, quia est, attestantur*]" (*VS* 12, ¶ 31; *DC* I, ¶ 12). This manifestation is principally apprehended in the form of an interior, mental image, which late in his career Nicholas variously conceives in terms of "intuition," "meditation," and "speculation." While originating in a concrete, optical experience, the "intuiting" of which Nicholas speaks posits *visibilia* as conduits toward God, that is, toward the invisible, "actualized potentiality" (*possest*) that manifests itself in them. The Trinitarian view of Christ as "the image [*eikōn*] of the invisible God" (Col. 1:15) at all times undergirds Nicholas's conception of the image and interior vision. Thus, the One, here introduced as the ultimate *source* of all number ("every number . . . actually can be made from the potency of oneness"), that is, God himself, is not to be understood numerically. Instead, "the actuality of a number that is made or that will be made is subsequent to that eternal Actuality [*aeternum actus*], as an image is subsequent to its original [*sequitur ut imago veritatem*]."[46] Furthermore, if the relation of *visibilia* to *invisibilia*, of perceptible forms to light, is essentially analogical, it also follows that the image cannot be assimilated to the propositional structure of "representation." Likewise, light itself is neither substance nor *accidens*, and hence is not fungible with color, which always presupposes light. Rather, "corporeal light" figures the light of the mind (*lux intellectualis*). On this analogy, "God the Father of things is a Light inaccessible by any cognition [*lucem omni cognitione inaccessibilem*], [and] . . . all things are reflected brightnesses of this Light—to which reflections the mental seeing [*visus mentis*] is related as perceptual seeing is related to sunlight.[47] In other words, light is the ontological condition of visibility that allows things to manifest themselves in all their formal and chromatic particularity. Consequently, light itself can never be "elucidated" by reference to further *visibilia*.

Hence, too, the image stands in an essential relation to Truth (*veritas*), as a presence unconditionally given rather than contingently asserted or, put differently, as a case of metaphysical disclosure rather than propositional correctness. Never confined to, let alone identified with, the representation of a particular referent, truth

---

46. *VS* 13, ¶ 37; the formula returns verbatim in *AT* 20.

47. *Comp.* 1, ¶ 2. On Cusa's strictly theological (nonempirical) and metaphoric use of light and color, see Borsche 2010.

unfolds inasmuch as the beholder of finite being recognizes herself as participating in an anterior, transcendent order that Husserl was to call the pre-predicative. Or, as Nicholas puts it, "the mind's power to see exceeds its power to comprehend." For the "mind's simple vision [*simplex visio mentis*]" (*AT* 10–11) is exclusively concerned with intelligible things and, thus, with itself: "What the mind sees are intelligible things, and they are [ontologically] prior to sensible things. Hence, the mind sees itself [*videt igitur mens se*]" (*AT* 24). As the correlate of a "mental vision" that, following the principle of analogy, strives to apprehend sensible things solely as manifestations of antecedent (invisible) Being, the "image" (*imago*) no longer has any affiliation with the finite economy of empirical reference or discursive meaning. For, once it is grasped as a function of "mental vision," the image cannot be framed as the correlate of some appropriative *perception* passing "through" and ultimately asserting dominion over the visible by resolving it into an abstract concept. Instead, mental vision is steeped in an ethos of humility, an awareness that the only knowledge it can ever yield is one of *analogia*, a knowledge infinitely more dissimilar than similar vis-à-vis the divine source of the visible.

More emphatically than Husserl's notion of a pre-predicative "intuition of essence" (*Wesensschau*), Nicholas understands mental vision as supra-predicative, a form of intuitive seeing that fundamentally exceeds the reach of words. Both in his philosophical breviary, the 1463 *Compendium* (esp. ¶¶ 1–3), and in *De Venatione Sapientiae* (ch. 33) of the same year, Nicholas offers a concise sketch of his philosophy of language, specifically as it relates to "mental vision" (*visio mentalis*):

> By nature a thing exists before it is knowable. Therefore, neither the senses, the imagination, nor the intellect attains unto the mode-of-being [*essendi modum*], since the latter precedes all these. Now, all the things that are arrived at by whatever manner of knowing signify only that antecedent mode-of-being. And, hence, they are not this reality itself but are likenesses, forms, or signs of it [*similitudines, species aut signa eius*].

Reflecting his deep-seated realist commitments, Nicholas affirms the need for an "intermediary which, without ceasing to be the object, would be capable of becoming the subject" of knowledge. What is required, then, is "something by which the object can coincide with our intellect without being itself destroyed, and without our intellect ceasing to be what it is."[48] For Aquinas that something is found in the con-

---

48. *Comp.* 1, ¶ 1. Nicholas's theory of language is marked by a strong if implicit reaction against the Nominalism of his day. As he writes in 1450, "Whoever thinks that in the intellect there can be nothing that is not present in reason also thinks that in the intellect there can be nothing that was not first in the senses. And he must maintain that a thing is nothing except insofar as it is captured

cept of species. Yet while at first glance Nicholas's terminology exhibits greater plasticity and visual concreteness (e.g., "likenesses, forms, or signs"), Étienne Gilson concedes that, for Aquinas, too, "it is almost impossible to speak of [species] except as if the species were an image, an equivalent or substitute for the object." However, we may say that object and form, thing and likeness, converge in the medium of the "image" only if their relation is understood as one of hypostatic union rather than analytic disjunction. Hence, Gilson continues,

> it is important to understand that the species of an object is not one being and the object another. It is the very object under the mode of species; that is, it is still the object considered in action and in the efficacy it exerts over a subject. Under this condition only can we say that it is not the species of the object that is present in thought, but the object through its species. . . . The whole objectivity of human knowledge depends in the last analysis upon the fact that it is not a superadded intermediary, or a distinct substitute which is introduced into our thought in place of the thing. It is, rather, the sensible species of the thing itself which, rendered intelligible by the agent intellect, becomes the form of our possible intellect.[49]

For Nicholas, this Thomist epistemology of intelligible forms—which Gilson characterizes as a kind of image—is fundamentally presupposed where he takes up the question of how the word makes explicit a prediscursive, intuitive grasp of the object, as mediated by the notion of *species*. Since the relation of a word to its object depends on how the latter was antecedently "conceived [*concepit*], it is not the case that words are precise and thus that a thing cannot be named by a more precise word." Quoting Plato's Seventh Letter (342a–e) and pseudo-Dionysius's *Divine*

---

by a name. . . . He would deny that forms considered in themselves and in their true nature, as separated [from matter], exist otherwise than as entities-of-reason; and he would hold Exemplars and Ideas to be of no account." Conversely, to admit "that in the mind's intellect there is something that was neither in the senses nor in reason—viz., the exemplifying and incommunicable true nature of the forms that shine forth in perceptible things—[is] also [to] say that, by nature, exemplars precede perceptible things, even as an original [precedes] an image [of itself]." Neoplatonism, however, does not dispute the inherent value and meaningfulness of different types of conceptual analysis; it only rejects their claim to be wholly self-originating and self-sufficient. For "there is only one, most simple Infinite Form, which in all things shines forth as the most adequate Exemplar of each and every formable thing. Thus, it will be altogether true that there is not more than one independently existing Exemplar, or Idea, of things. And, indeed, no one's reason can attain unto this Infinite Form. Hence, the Ineffable [Form] is not grasped by any names imposed by reason's operation" (*IM* 1, ¶¶ 64–67). For a detailed and wide-ranging account of Nicholas's theory of language, see Casarella 2017, esp. 252–71; and, on the "theosemiotic" of the *Compendium*, 254–72.

49. Gilson 1956, 227–28.

Names (*DN* 4:11), Nicholas points out that the concept can never capture "the thing's essential form [*ratio essentiae rei*], which precedes each thing." Difference and dissension (*dissensio*) can manifest themselves "only in the words variously assigned to things" but never in the "substantifying forms of things [*substantifica ratione rerum*]." Hence, in his pursuit of divine Wisdom, the eponymous huntsman of Nicholas's treatise will "refuse to predicate of God human words according to their human assignment" (*VS* 33, ¶¶ 97–98).

Following pseudo-Dionysius, Nicholas approaches "language [as] a medium that can only be brought into relation to the truth by taking itself as provisional and tending continually toward the point of its self-suspension." Though Hans Blumenberg cannot bring himself to embrace Nicholas's ideal of epistemological humility, he does acknowledge that "Cusa's quasi-experimental procedure of continually renewed testing of the boundary of transcendence" pivots on validating silence as the very apex of mystical theology rather than as the symptom of an intellectually defective condition. As was the case for Plotinus and Meister Eckhart among others, there is, in "Cusa's procedure[,] . . . an essential difference between muteness and falling silent."[50] At the limits of the domain governed by discursive speech, concepts, syllogisms, and propositions, a metaphysical space opens up—a space of elective and considered silence; and it is here that Nicholas locates the opening for a spiritual sight concerned not with individual beings and the conceptual schemes that human ingenuity imposes on them but with their unfathomable "ground of being." For only when "no knowledge of the mode-of-being" is claimed can "we have mental sight [*visum mentalem*] that looks unto that which is prior to all cognition. Hence, if someone endeavors to find in [the realm of] cognition that which he sees in the foregoing [mental] way, he strives in vain, just as would someone who attempted to touch with his hand a *color*—something which is only *visible*. Therefore, the mind's sight is related to that mode-of-being in something like the way that perceptual sight is related to light."[51]

In sharp contrast to a wholly illusory and illegitimate notion of transcendence, such as will underwrite the naturalist and skeptical epistemologies of Hume, Feuerbach, Renan, and Nietzsche, Nicholas knows better than to misconstrue God's transcendence as but the antonym of human finitude and immanence. Instead, following the Neoplatonist tradition we have been tracing, Nicholas understands divine transcendence as the very source that both contains and reconciles those very antinomies. As he had so programmatically formulated it in *De docta ignorantia* (1440),

---

50. Blumenberg 1983, 490.

51. *Comp.* 2; see also *AT* ¶¶ 8–11. Behind this framework stands the patristic concept of *theophany*, which Nicholas derives above all from Dionysius. See also *DC* II/17: ¶ 177; and *VS* 9, 15.

because "there is no comparative relation of the infinite to the finite, . . . opposing features belong only to those beings which can be comparatively greater and lesser." Being beyond all quantity, God ("the maximum") "is the measure [*metrum et mensura*] of all things," and as such is simultaneously "in each thing and in no thing [*quomodo maximum est in qualibet re et in nulla*]."[52] Or, to recall two neologisms fashioned later on, Nicholas speaks of God as the unconditional "possibility-of-being-made" (*posse fieri*) and the wholly "non-Other" (*non-aliud*)—that is, as the Being relative to which no actual or potential being could ever stand in a relation of alterity and opposition. As the *non aliud* and *actus purissimus* (*VS* 9, ¶ 25), God cannot be identified *with* anything nor be named *as* anything.

As Nicholas continues to emphasize, the mental image and the "absolute vision" toward which it points human sight both serve a vital function. Thus, the image furnishes the medium through which participation in the One becomes possible for finite beings and their "contracted" intellects. Since an image is "always the image *of* something, an ectype of the proto- or archetype [*des Vor- oder Urbildes*], it simultaneously resembles and differs from the latter." In its very being, then, an image "is 'dependent' on a ground by which it is constituted. And only insofar as an image formally establishes and legitimates itself in relation *to* its constituting ground, by participating in it, will it be capable of imitation or representation." It is this oscillation of sameness and difference that explains why "the image is not something static and fixed but inherently dialectical and dynamic. . . . Similarity and dissimilarity, identity and difference, that is, do not oppose one another *within* the image [*im Bild nicht gegeneinander stehen*]; rather, they are fused within it as co-agents [*zu einem Miteinander-Wirken verbunden*]. . . . [Thus], the 'realization of the image' is above all a liberating of a *positive* potential within it, . . . such that reality encompassed in the image [*bildhafte Wirklichkeit*] occasions a movement of both return and ascent: from the many images to the One archetype [*zum Einen Ur-Bild*]."[53] Such a view naturally presupposes that the image be understood not as a finite artifact but as a *medium*, such that visible things are apprehended as manifestations of the divine *logos* rather than as the contingent fruit of human making. As Nicholas so programmatically affirms in Pauline terms (cf. Col 1:15, Rom 1:20, 1 Cor 13:12): "visible things are truly images of invisible things, and from created things the Creator can be knowably seen as in a mirror and a symbolism [*quasi in speculo et in aenigmate*]."[54]

---

52. *DI* 3, ¶ 9; 4, ¶ 12; 17, ¶ 50.

53. Beierwaltes [1985] 2016, 76–78; as Nicholas writes, "since the eligible and desirable End is the Good, this *per se* Good will be the Cause of all things, since all things are turned toward their own Cause and seek it [*omnia ad suam causam conversa ipsam appetent*]" (*VS* 8, ¶ 20).

54. *DI* I–II, ¶ 30. Nicholas's considerable debt to John Scotus Eriugena, a pivotal figure in the transmission of Dionysius's writings, cannot be pursued here. In his *Periphyseon* (III.4) we can see

Still, all particular, visible being is only ever a fleeting and contingent instantiation of its form, a mere "likeness of its exemplar [*similtudinem exemplaris*]."
Because God is both "Not-Other" and yet wholly distinct from (though never the
contrary of) his creation, the very notion of similitude is always constrained by an
infinitely greater dissimilitude: "Though every image seems to be a likeness of its exemplar, yet, apart from the maximum image, which in unity of nature is that which
its exemplar is, there is no image so similar or so equal to its exemplar but that it
could be infinitely more similar and more equal" (*DI* 11, ⁋ 30). By definition, then,
"all likeness is imperfect" such that "if a similarity is posited, a greater similarity can
always be posited *ad infinitum*." Nicholas's position naturally rules out a correspondence theory of truth, for "truth is not attained by means of likenesses" (*ADI* 28).
Scattered throughout his oeuvre, passages such as these echo almost verbatim the
formula with which the Fourth Lateran Council (1215) had rejected Joachim of Fiore's construal of the Trinity as a merely numerical unity, a definition judged to have
ignored (or denied) the infinite dissimilarity between God and creation.[55] Beginning
with *De docta ignorantia*, Nicholas's entire philosophical theology is framed by the
conception of the visible, phenomenal world as relating to God analogically.

Though centrally rooted in Catholic thought, this framework of the *analogia entis*, as it later came to be elaborated by Erich Przywara and Gottlieb Söhngen,
is already hinted at in Anaxagoras's Fragment 21a, "What appears makes visible
what is hidden [*opsis ton adelon: ta phainomena*]." The gnomic line points to an all-
encompassing analogy between the visible and that which, though invisible per se,
nevertheless has structured all phenomena in such a way as for them progressively
to reveal to us the (divine) source of their being and their (potential) intelligibility.
Indeed, analogy must have been presupposed wherever inferential knowledge is
being pursued. For scientific inquiry even to get under way, it must have posited
causal relationships governing the internal structure and, thus, rendering it stable,
observable, and potentially intelligible. The very premise that visible phenomena
may disclose to us the invisible, noncontingent laws of their being rests on the ontological premise of an analogy linking absolute Being and contingent beings; hence,

---

Eriugena's considerable anticipation of what, half a millennium later, finds expression in Nicholas's view of visible nature as theophany, that is, as the self-revelation of creation's hidden, divine
ground in the form of "images" (*aenigmata*), a "veil" (*vellum*), or a "mirror" (*speculum*) of visible,
determinate things. On Eriugena and Cusa, see also Beierwaltes 1998b, 142–50; and, on Eriugena
in particular, Beierwaltes [1985] 2016, 337–67; on Nicholas's acceptance of Eriugena's etymological
association of "God" and "sight" (*theō/theorō*, in *Periphyseon* 425c), see D'Amico 2010, 98–105.

55. "Between Creator and creature there can be remarked no similarity so great that a greater
dissimilarity between them cannot be seen [inter creatorem et creatura non potest tanta similitudo
notari, quin inter eos maior sit dissimilitudo notanda]."

the intelligibility of the latter cannot be reduced to whatever properties the finite intellect happens to ascribe to them.[56]

The metaphysical framework known as *analogia entis* is tentatively outlined early in Aquinas's *Summa Theologiae* (*ST* I.13), where Thomas distinguishes between a strictly apophatic and a kataphatic way of understanding language in relation to the divine. Navigating between an extreme, Dionysian apophaticism, according to which "no name belongs to God in the same sense that it belongs to creatures" (*ST* I.13.5), and the obverse position, asserting that names apply in the same (univocal) way to both God and finite things, Aquinas outlines his view of analogical predication. Having affirmed that "no name is predicated univocally of God and creatures" *and*, conversely, that "neither . . . are names applied to God and creatures in a purely equivocal sense"—in which case "nothing could be named or demonstrated about God at all"—Aquinas insists on a tensioned *relation* between the two, which must not be misconstrued as an outright *antinomy*. Relation here must be taken in the sense of a nondualistic "distinction," not to be confused with a "separation, for separated from their source, creatures would perish." Simply put, language "must be able to span 'the distinction' of creatures from creator without collapsing it."[57] Instead, "whatever is said of God and creatures, is said according to the relation of a creature to God [*secundum quod est aliquis ordo creaturae ad Deum*] as its principle and cause." Not only, that is, does the principle of analogy allow us to speak rationally, albeit mediately, about God; doing so also proves foundational for our knowledge of finite beings. Indeed, for Aquinas "the notion of analogy . . . belongs to the common practice of language," considering that by its very nature a word (*nomen*) throws into relief a being without claiming to coincide with it substantially.[58] What allows

---

56. See Hans Diller, who has remarked on the fundamental difference in procedure, whereby an "analogy provides us with a fully realized parallel" between an observable event and its underlying causal mechanism, and "a sign [which] merely indicates an essentially unknown process or state" (1932, 20). Still, for us to take a phenomenon *as a sign*, as begging hermeneutic scrutiny, already presupposes an underlying, invisible *ratio* to which the particular sign (*Zeichen*) bears a necessary ("lawful") relationship as an *analogon*. On this issue, see also Hadot 2006, 29–36; on the disappearance of the *analogia* framework in modern natural theology, see Hanby 2013, 150–85.

57. Burrell 2005, 87, 78. Burrell stresses the influence of Dionysius on Aquinas's "breakthrough to *esse*," as well as Aquinas's reliance on Neoplatonism's paradigmatic view of relation as consummated in "participation" (87). Te Velde concurs, remarking how for Aquinas "analogy is clearly of a Neoplatonic origin; it is intrinsically connected with the idea of a causal hierarchy, with the notion of participation, and with the 'descent' of the effect from the cause" (2006, 110); see also Burrell 2008, 63–77.

58. Te Velde 2006, 109. "Any name signifies a thing under a certain *ratio* [i.e., a certain concept—T. P.] according to which a thing is known and conceived *as* such and such. The way it is conceived and accordingly signified reflects the way in which the perfection falls within our experience, even if the perfection as conceived under its *ratio* does not intrinsically depend on the conditions of

language to signify being is an underlying *ratio* or concept that must be kept logically distinct from the thing it helps us understand. For "every creature represents Him, and is like Him so far as it possesses some perfection; yet it represents Him not as something of the same species or genus, but as the excelling principle of whose form the effects fall short [*sicut excellens principium, a cuius forma effectus deficient*]" (*ST* I.13.2). In analogical predication, "the limits of a determinate genus are transcended towards something that lies outside that genus. . . . Analogy thus enables one to establish semantic connections between different genera without denying the boundaries between those genera."[59]

Yet for analogical predication to furnish a plausible *via media* between univocal and equivocal uses of language, respectively, a metaphysical foundation must already be presupposed, that is, a noncontingent, timeless "analogy of being" (*analogia entis*). For Aquinas, "being" (*esse*) cannot be reduced to yet another finite predicate such as, say, "round," "white," or "healthy." Instead, it furnishes the transcendent condition of possibility (to hazard a Kantian turn of phrase) on which all formal predication and discursive knowledge rest. Put differently, being "is not restricted to a category (*genus*)." For meaningful statements about genera and species to be possible, their plurality "must be reduced to a unity which itself cannot be expressed by a common univocal predicate. . . . 'Being' is, thus, not a common predicate by which the essence is signified in a most abstract and universal manner, but it signifies each particular thing as related to being, which is common to all things."[60] It bears stressing that this ultimate predicate of "being" has not in turn been abstracted *from* particular existents. What analogy points *to*—God as containing all possible perfections *simpliciter*—is not simply another distinct entity or genus. On the contrary, the reality of each particular thing becomes itself intelligible only insofar as its specific degree of perfection is traced back, *per analogiam*, to the transcendent being that is its source. As Aquinas puts it, "Our intellect, since it knows God from creatures, in order to understand God, forms conceptions proportional to the perfections flowing from God to creatures, which perfections pre-exist in God unitedly and simply, whereas in creatures they are received and divided and multiplied" (*ST* I.13.4).

Just as is the case with Nicholas's theological concept of spiritual or "absolute" vision, so perfection terms such as "wisdom," "love," or "goodness" cannot be ade-

---

experience" (106). Even as "the *ratio* [say, of divine goodness] does not represent adequately to the human mind the *res*, goodness, as it is in God, . . . we still have access to the thing signified because of the way we know God indirectly from creatures" (Hütter 2019, 12; see also 400).

59. Te Velde 2006, 111; see also his extended discussion of the "analogy of being" (115–21).

60. Ibid., 117; note, however, that *esse*, while not fungible with other predicates, "is not a univocal expression in spite of its substantive form." In fact, "Aquinas did not even look for such a baseline" but, instead, "displays a consistency more akin to fidelity than to logical completeness" (Burrell 2008, 66). Conversely, it would also be a mistake to think of analogy in terms of metaphor.

quately understood within the confines of ordinary discourse. On the contrary, "as regards what is signified by these names, they belong properly to God, and more properly than they belong to creatures." Yet when it comes to "their mode of signification [*modus significandi*], . . . they do not properly and strictly apply to God; for their mode of signification applies to creatures" (*ST* I.13.3). The principle of analogy, then, allows us to distinguish between the purely *lexical* reach of names, steeped in past usage (*modus*) and their moral or *aspirational* dimension. After all, language is not simply a structure concerned with the replication of meanings but, crucially, with orienting speakers and listeners toward participating in the fullness of meaning implied by perfection terms. Hence, "it makes sense to use words like 'wise' beyond their accustomed ken. For these terms embody a structure of assessment (*res*) besides an inherited history of uses (*modus*)."[61] Echoing Neoplatonism's conception of all visible being as the expression of "order" (*kosmos*), the analogy of being is the metaphysical condition that allows us to understand the totality of all particular, finite, and distinct beings (genera, species, and particulars), as these subsist within an all-encompassing and integrative framework and also as seeking to express that framework by attaining the perfection of their given form. It is this integrative aspect of analogical predication that prompts Aquinas to speak of it as a "mode of community of idea [*iste modus communitatis medius est*], . . . a mean between pure equivocation and simple univocation. For in analogies the idea is not, as it is in univocal, one and the same, yet it is not totally diverse as in equivocals" (*ST* I.13.5).

The only conceivable metaphysical alternative to the *analogia* principle would likely involve positing a quasi-Gnostic conflict between the self-sufficient divine *logos* and embodied, visible, and infinitely dispersed and discontinuous matter incessantly (if vainly) striving to usurp God's place. Such a view ends up construing specific phenomena as so many idols ensnaring the beholder, who thus is left pining for a totalizing grasp of the *logos* that, it is argued, can be attained only by rejecting all forms of mediation; and precisely this is happening during the first half of the fifteenth century. Beginning with theories of linear, single-viewpoint perspective that are being developed during Nicholas's lifetime, the Neoplatonist model of kenotic and participatory vision is being challenged by anthropocentric modes of seeing in which a hermetic subject unilaterally asserts dominion over a world of disaggregated "objects." As it happens, the modern Florentine conception of a universe rendered wholly transparent for the individual observer may have been unwittingly prepared for by the exaggerated stress on unmediated vision found in the affective mysticism of writers like Vincent of Aggsbach. Both a strictly affective mystical vision and an anthropocentric ideal of linear, single-viewpoint perspective seem animated by the

---

61. Burrell 2008, 77.

same ideals of total immediacy and transparency. Consequently, both will reject the framework of the *analogia entis* and Nicholas's conception of mystical theology as "learned ignorance."[62] Indeed, it is in Nicholas's oeuvre that, "for the last time in the Catholic realm . . . the fundamental articulations of the historical revelation remain enclosed within the . . . paradox of the *analogia entis*," which involves "not simply the harmonious rhythm of 'contraries' but, as with John Eriugena, the coincidence of opposites." In Pauline fashion, Nicholas thus conceives of "the hidden God [as] manifest in his creation. [Though] transcendent over the world, [he] is distant from no-one and wills to be sought longingly by all, always and through all things."[63] To be sure, to maintain that "the notion of the 'world as image' [*Welt als Bild*] always implies the causal dependency of the phenomenal cosmos on the intelligible cosmos" must not obscure the fundamentally different ways in which Neoplatonism and Christianity conceive the One and God, respectively, to relate to visible creation.[64] Only in the latter case will the material realm be understood as issuing from God's free and deliberate act (a *logismos* or a case of *boulēsis*).

What sets emanation and creation apart from one another is that with emanationism—and with modern emergentist theories (Mill, Broad, Alexander) that are its descendants—all visible being is "relative being in all its plurality, is the aggregate" of the absolute *pan* but, by the same token, is marked by an apparitional, unreal, wholly contingent quality. Yet, as Bulgakov points out, "if the relative is only an illusion, then the question arises again: Whose illusion? Is it possible to think it completely outside of and apart from the Absolute?" Responding to this paradox, Bulgakov argues that the Judeo-Christian concept of creation holds not only, with emanation-

---

62. Though Nicholas never opposes the (supposedly irrational) world of experience to God's inscrutable *logos*, his early writings exhibit a marked tension between mental image and sensuous appearance, with the latter being coded as inferior. As Kreuzer (2010, 89 f.) notes, Nicholas gradually moves away from that scheme.

63. Balthasar 1991, 211–13; Cuozzo's extreme stipulation that "there can be no analogy or relation between the finite and the infinite" (2005, 188) would, if accepted, drain Nicholas's metaphors, similes, and examples—such as in *De Beryllo*—of all significance; the point is raised with more circumspection by Dupré (1996, 210), who notes that a "radically Neoplatonic" position of this kind can be found in Meister Eckhart, even as the latter's "call for a gradual 'decreation'" also exposes a tension within Neoplatonism: "for if God remains above all names and the creature *qua creature* totally differs from divine nature, then, in the final analysis, creaturehood retains no function in the deification process." As Dupré goes on to show (210–12), Nicholas here follows the Flemish mystic John of Ruusbroec (1293–1381), who had rejected Eckhart's (in tendency Gnostic) line of argument.

64. Beierwaltes [1985] 2016, 84 n. 24; Dupré (1996, 216) is right to note, however, that "Christian Neoplatonists have persistently experienced problems in keeping their versions of the doctrine of creation sufficiently distinct from any kind of emanationism" and that Cusa responds to that dilemma by insisting "that each mind is created singularly and individually [*factum autem semper est singular et implurificabile, sicut omne individuum*]" (*VS* 37, ¶ 109).

ism, that "the world is real in its divine foundation insofar as its being is *being in the Absolute*," but also that "the world is posited at the same time *outside* the Absolute, as the self-existent relative. . . . The concept of creation is therefore *broader* than that of emanation." In the latter, the visible world appears to oscillate between radical necessity and utter fortuitousness, with its discrete manifestations appearing wholly other, indeed unrelated to the Absolute *from* which their various forms had to separate and *to* which, for the duration of their visible existence, they bear no essential relation.[65] By contrast, given that nothing can be logically anterior or phenomenally exterior to God, who is wholly self-causing (*causa sui*), creation has to be understood as an absolutely free act; it cannot be "explained" as a quasi-naturalist case of self-generation or emanation. Whereas "the philosophical God is essentially self-centered, thought simply contemplating itself, the God of faith is basically defined by the category of relationship." Admittedly, some of Nicholas's writings remain precariously close to the Neoplatonist conception of "the supreme being . . . as absolute, enclosed autarchy."[66]

Missing from Nicholas's writing, then, is a fully developed conception of how this supreme being is mediated in the finite order of history and its evolving conceptions of God, something already attempted by Bonaventure and altogether central to Hegel's idealism. It is this impersonal and seemingly ahistorical outlook that causes the Neoplatonist concept of emanation to stand in ambiguous relation vis-à-vis the Christian concept of creation. We recall how Plotinian emanationism involves a primordial "partitioning" (*diastasis*), a dynamic conception of the One as it externalizes and shares itself in the myriad time-bound forms and conceptions that constitute "world."[67] As Blumenberg contends, the "fundamental Platonic equivocation, [namely,] that the world is indeed the reproduced image of Ideas but cannot attain the perfection of the original," is resolved by Neoplatonism, which views the world categorically "as the great failure to equal its ideal model." From here it is still a step, though on Blumenberg's reading not a big one, to the Gnostic view according to which "the world is the labyrinth of the *pneuma* gone astray." According to Blumenberg, Christianity's reclamation of creation as benevolent came at a steep price, namely, the Augustinian conception of original sin according to which mankind bore "guilt . . . for the condition in which he found the world," compounded by

---

65. Bulgakov 2012b, 183–84. "In the opposition of creation and emanation, the principal debate is not about God but about the world, not about the divine foundation of the world, but about its creaturely nature."

66. Ratzinger 2004, 147–48.

67. "By 'world' is meant not simply the physical stuff of the cosmos, but all that constitutes the domain of the livable and the affirmable space, whether human relations, . . . social institutions, . . . and religions" (O'Regan 2014, 100).

"renunciation of any attempt to change for his benefit, through action, a reality for the adversity of which he had himself to blame."[68]

Though overdrawn and overly abstract at times, Blumenberg's thesis highlights the persistence of Gnostic motifs that were to haunt theology and philosophy starting in late antiquity and would periodically resurface well into the modern era. Regardless of whether the visible world is conceived as the product of the Gnostics' demiurge, or as the emanation of the Plotinian One, or as the creation of Christianity's triune god, an ontological chasm seems to be the price paid for there being something rather than nothingness. Yet is such partitioning or "sundering" (as Blake calls it) of Being into multifarious, visible forms an act of divine generosity? Or, conversely, does it betoken a fateful declension, a lapse of eternal Being into the chaos of transient forms that those living amidst the debris will henceforth struggle to fit into a coherent narrative form, what they call history? It is this metaphysical ambiguity forever haunting the visible world—a case of divine self-disclosure or self-betrayal?— that prompted Blumenberg to read Cusa as a prominent figure in the narrative drama of philosophical modernity as constituted by its prolonged struggle with the legacy of Gnosticism.[69]

Starting in the early modern period, the resurgence of "Gnosticism had made acute the problem of the world," and threw into relief the way that a legitimation of the visible world, a "*cosmodicy* [was] conditional on *theodicy*."[70] As the "world" appeared to be in need of a metaphysical legitimation, a "world-picture" (Heidegger's *Weltbild*), everything depended on the epistemic form and spiritual motives informing *how* human beings looked upon the world. One of Cusa's remote descendants, once again confronting this basic dilemma, is William Blake, who warrants brief consideration here. Though not a Gnostic, Blake considered it imperative to confront head-on the metaphysical ambiguity of creation; and he did so by refashioning both image and word in pointedly anti-mimetic ways that bear significant resemblance to the Byzantine icon theorists of the eighth and ninth centuries. His oeuvre is unique in this regard in that it fuses a pointedly anti- or premodern aes-

---

68. Blumenberg 1983, 128, 136. Following von Harnack, he goes on to argue that "to retrieve the world as the creation from the negative role assigned to it by the doctrine of its demiurgic origin, and to salvage the dignity of the ancient cosmos for its role in the Christian system, was the central effort all the way from Augustine to the height of Scholasticism" (130). O'Regan's account of Gnosis in relation to Neoplatonism and modern thought seems far more nuanced and probing than Blumenberg's provocative, albeit overly schematic, reading.

69. As noted above, Plotinus's relationship to Gnosticism is at times ambiguous (see above, 105–9); on the decisive, albeit oblique role played by Marcionite Gnosis in the constitution of philosophical modernity, see Blumenberg 1983, 127–43; for a conceptual blueprint of Valentinian Gnosis and its reverberations in nineteenth-century theology and philosophy, see O'Regan 2001, 99–136; on the persistence of Gnostic motifs in Hegel, see O'Regan 2014.

70. Blumenberg 1983, 142.

thetic with a sharply antinomian version of Christianity, one that he felt was routinely betrayed by Georgian England's Church-and-State mentality and Anglicanism's
middle-brow, mostly lackluster theology. Ever intent on dismantling expressive conventions and philosophical abstractions, Blake's rewriting of *Genesis* in his *Book of
Urizen* (1794) seems at first glance to adhere to a Gnostic view of creation as a cosmic miscarriage and divine misadventure:

> Sund'ring, dark'ning, thund'ring
> Rent away with a terrible crash
> Eternity roll'd wide apart
> Wide asunder rolling
> Mountainous all around
> Departing; departing: departing;
> Leaving ruinous fragments of life
> Hanging frowning cliffs & all between
> An ocean of voidness unfathomable.[71]

As so often in Blake's illuminated books, the ratio of image and word in this
rewriting of the Creation story (fig. 4.1) proves tantalizingly asymmetrical and ambiguous. Thus, Blake's illumination of the above lines gives us a calm and collected
Urizen who, eyes closed, opens up for us the luminous book of nature of which it is
ultimately impossible to say whether it will end up affirming or betraying his inward,
creative vision. To be sure, in Blake's iconography the bound book, unlike the infinity
of the scroll, inevitably delimits divine and infinite creation within the compass
of human, "contracted" vision, as Nicholas calls it. Still, Blake's serene iconography
hardly comports with the anarchic "terrible crash" so histrionically evoked in the poetry. Instead, with its dual, two-column layout in the manner of contemporary Bible
printing, Blake's illuminated *Book of Urizen* purposely vacillates between viewing
creation as God's disastrous, self-willed contraction into embodied form and, conversely, rapturously greeting the luminous visible forms wrought by this act of pri-
meval creation—forms that invite the beholder to participate in the divine, creative
vision that brought them forth.

If Urizen realizes his divinity by drawing boundaries (as intimated by the pun on
Urizen / horizon), the resulting "fragments of life," described as "ruinous" in the text,
are, in fact, visualized in a sumptuous and absorbing chiaroscuro. Thus, as creative
vision is translated into visible creation, poetic vision into resplendent imagery, the

---

71. *The (First) Book of Urizen*, 1794, pl. 5, *BPP* 73; on creation, prophesy, and eschatology in
Blake's *Book of Urizen*, see Tannenbaum 1982, esp. 201–24; on Blake's emulation of scripture, see
McGann 1986.

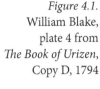
Figure 4.1.
William Blake,
plate 4 from
The Book of Urizen,
Copy D, 1794

narrative of Urizen's violent, catastrophic birthing of the cosmos is illuminated with an abundance of light and color that not only surpasses the abstract language of that narrative, but whose resplendent visuality celebrates the very creation that the story anathemizes in quasi-Gnostic fashion. Put differently, Blake's *Book of Urizen* appears to stage the triumph of the visible, and of color in particular, over a culture of ratiocination and abstraction that would expunge image and vision for good. As Walter Benjamin was to observe in an early fragment, "Where color provides the contours, objects are not reduced to things but are constituted by an order consisting of an infinite range of nuances." Just as children's naive wisdom prompts them to "elevate [color] to a spiritual level," so Blake's book, fashioned for the finite and never fully cleansed perceptions of fallible human beings, invites its reader to access divine infinity through the "bound" realm of visible and polychrome forms.[72]

Still, even as Neoplatonist emanationism appears to institute a fundamental *division* between the numinous One and the visible many, this is not the same as positing an outright *opposition* between *logos* and *hylē*, Being and matter. For, however much the world appears to be dispersed into manifold, finite beings, it

> does not degenerate into a diffuse, aimless array of contradictions, nor into some caricature of the archetype [*Zerrbild des Ur-Bildes*] that would constitute—as a radical dualism of the Gnostic variety maintains—a mere perversion of all positive predicates adhering to the first Principle. Instead, the empirical world preserves within its own realm and in a unique modality [*auf eigentümliche Weise*] what it has received from the intelligible domain. Hence, even as we may speak

---

72. Benjamin 1996, 50–51 ("A Child's View of Color," ca. 1914–15).

of two discrete worlds, their difference [*Verschiedenheit*] is nevertheless "relativized," not only because of an equivalent relationship between the two but also an active *participation* [*Teilhabe*] of the phenomenal in the intelligible world is being maintained. . . . For every singular being there is, within the realm of the intelligible, its founding idea.[73]

Crucial for understanding the *analogia* model, then, is that visible phenomena are not only formally related to the invisible as the metaphysical source of their existence. For in their distinctive mode of appearance they also actively participate *in* their divine source and, indeed, visibly mediate it for the finite intellect. The figure of the circle, understood as "an entity of reason," for example, is not only formally compatible with its rational form or *eidos* but also actively unveils the latter: "a perceptible circle partakes, with a degree of otherness, of the oneness of the conceptual circle." Even as the latter remains in its very essence "unimpartible" (*incommunicabilis*), its visible, embodied instantiation in a particular and therefore "other" modality does not categorically estrange it from its founding idea. Conversely, the essentially "incommunicable" character of pure Being must not be reduced to an ontological void. As Nicholas points out, that the essential form "cannot be partaken of as it is [in itself] is not due to a defect on its part but is due to the fact that it is partaken of by something *other* and, hence, is partaken of *otherwise* [Non est igitur, uti est, imparticipabile suo defectu, sed quia in alia participatur, hinc et aliter]" (*DC* 11, § 54; emphasis mine). The Platonic concept of "participation" (*methexis*) here reappears as the phenomenological correlate of the metaphysical framework known as *analogia entis* that, as we continue to find, posits an essential and meaningful, albeit limited, "resemblance" (*similitudo*) between divine Being and contingent beings.

With his thinking "deeply rooted in the analogical rationality of the Middle Ages," Nicholas of Cusa likewise regards all *visibilia* as the indispensable medium facilitating access to *intelligibilia*.[74] While a crucial part of this process of mediation, "forms" are not, however, inferred *from* visible things but instead are recognized as the ontological *cause* of their visibility. Thus, even as it invites the beholder to participate in its intelligible form, each visible thing also unveils and mediates the metaphysical grounds of its existence. Nicholas's proto-phenomenological concept of seeing as participation, elaborated in chapters 1–17 in *De Visione Dei*, confirms the

---

73. Beierwaltes [1985] 2016, 85; emphasis mine. See also Kreuzer, who remarks how in Cusa "the universe of the creature is 'image'" and how "intellection is that activity whereby images received in the form of creaturely life are being assimilated." Sight is always "In-Sight" (*Einsicht*), "a becoming conscious of the mirroring wherein the universe of creaturely images—including the image of mind itself—can be seen and intuited" (2010, 89–93).

74. Hoff 2013, 92.

presupposition that individual being and form are ontologically related, that is, are part of a single, divine economy that encompasses both identity and difference. That individual being can never fully coincide with the real form of which it is a fleeting manifestation must not be attributed to the supposedly lapsed nature of material being, as Gnosticism had claimed. Rather, it arises from the fact that the individual thing and its *eidos*, beings and Being, unfold in ontologically distinct, albeit analogically related domains. Hence such distinctness or "otherness" ought to be taken in an adverbial rather than predicative sense. For what sets particular being apart from its form is *how* rather than *what* it is—that is, being considered as *actus* rather than as a separate *quiddity*. Thus, *what* a particular thing is cannot be conclusively ascertained simply by juxtaposing it, in a cascade of negations or formal discriminations, to myriad other particular beings. Instead, positive knowledge of a particular thing pivots on identifying the intrinsic law that governs and shapes it over time, which is to say, the *form* that a particular being imperfectly instantiates. As we shall see, it is this fundamentally Neoplatonist insight that much later prompts Goethe to replace Linné's static taxonomy of species with an account of how, over the course of its differential development, a given organism dynamically instantiates its archetypal form (*Urbild*) as a kind of "dynamic order" (*bewegliche Ordnung*). Anticipating such a framework, Nicholas notes how the very hypothesis that "all things are that which they are by partaking of the One" is brought home for us precisely by their distinctive way of manifesting themselves: "in each and every thing . . . the One shines forth in its own way [*in omnibus et in quolibet suo quidem modo resplendent*]. Therefore, you have need of no other consideration than that you seek out the identity that is present in the diversity of the things which you are to investigate [*identitatem inquiras aut in alteritate unitatem*]. For then you will see [*intueberis*], in the otherness of contracted beings, the 'modes,' as it were, of Absolute Oneness."[75] Let us now turn to the work in which Nicholas unfolds this argument most fully.

REAL PRESENCE OR ARTISTIC SIMULACRUM:
CUSA'S *DE VISIONE DEI* AND ALBERTI'S *DE PICTURA*

Written in the momentous year 1453, which saw the siege and fall of Constantinople (29 May and, a few months later, the end of the Hundred Years' War, *De Visione Dei* opens with Nicholas offering a set of instructions to the addressees of his treatise. Responding to the Benedictines at Tegernsee Abbey, who had asked him for clarifica-

---

75. *DC* II.1, ¶ 71; see also *NA* 10, ¶ 36. As Hoff notes, what distinguishes the *analogia* framework is that it "not only appreciates abstract, interchangeable values but also the singular and unique" (2013, 68).

Figure 4.2.
Rogier van der Weyden,
The Justice of Trajan, 1450,
textile copy of painting (detail).
Bern, Historical Museum

tion on the nature of mystical vision, Nicholas begins with a visual catechesis of sorts, instructing the monks how to look at a Christ icon that, wrought to his specifications, had been included along with the manuscript of his new book. While the various icons referenced by Nicholas, including the one sent to Tegernsee, are all lost today, his detailed description of the one commissioned for his Benedictine contacts closely resembles a number of extant artworks. Nicholas mentions Rogier van der Weyden, whose experimentation with an "omnivoyant" gaze is preserved in a textile copy of his painting, *The Justice of Trajan* (fig. 4.2), thought to have been made in 1450 and to have been located in Brussels, where Nicholas may well have seen it during his tour of the Low Countries in 1451–52.[76] The icon shows a face, almost certainly meant to be Christ's, that will lock onto the beholder's gaze regardless of the latter's spatial location. As per Nicholas's account, the icon's formal composition follows the standard frontal presentation of the Christ icon found on Byzantine coins manufactured under Justinian II in AD 691–92, which in turn recalls the

76. See Stock 1989, 52; Belting 2011b, 221–38.

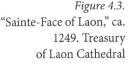

Figure 4.3.
"Sainte-Face of Laon," ca.
1249. Treasury
of Laon Cathedral

mid-sixth-century Pantocrator icon at St. Catherine's Monastery in Sinai.[77] More particularly, Nicholas's reference to the "Veronica in my chapel at Coblenz," close to his native Bernkastel, taps into the popular legend of Christ's face imprinted on the cloth handed to him by Veronica at the Sixth Station of the Cross, a legend that had taken hold in Western Christianity during the twelfth century as part of a surging popular fascination with Christ's passion.

Corresponding to the Eastern Church's much older, legendary Edessa Mandylion—also lost but "preserved" in a number of alleged replicas—the *vera icon*'s authority derives from the notion, widely accepted as fact, that the image in question was "not wrought by human hands" (*acheiropoiēton*). Such is the case with the so-called Holy Face of Laon (fig. 4.3), whose documented, lively history begins in 1249 when Jaques de Pantaléon (later Pope Urban IV) offered it to his sister, abbess of the Cistercian convent of Montreuil-en-Thiérache.[78] Serving as the template for many twelfth-century murals, the icon's neckless face of Christ effectively simulates the

---

77. See above, ch. 2, fig. 8. For a detailed formal and theological discussion of this icon, see Constas 2014, 37–98; on the theological arguments of both iconodules and iconoclasts, Schönborn 1994, 147–78; Tsakiridou 2013, 193–223; Mondzain 2005, 67–117; and Pelikan 2011, 67–98.

78. Belting 2006, 45–85; quote from 84. Subsequently transferred to the convent Montreuilles-Dames near Laon and framed in a silver reliquary, the icon was sheltered from being melted down along with the entire reliquary during the French Revolution in 1792. Since 1807, it has been in the treasury of Laon Cathedral; see Evans 2004, 174–75.

Figure 4.4.
Copy after Jan van Eyck,
Salvator Mundi, 1438–40.
Bruges, Groeningemuseum

true image of Christ as legend claimed it had been preserved on the cloth (*mandylion*) handed to him by Veronica. Insofar as it was thought to "offer not a picture of the Mandylion, but the Mandylion itself," the icon was approached fundamentally as a relic, not an image.[79] Capitalizing on the anagrammatic relation between this unique image (*vera icon*) and its human recipient (*Veronica*), the image in question constitutes no artificial sign but an unmediated presence, no contingent product but a transcendent gift (*donum*)—Christ handing over his *imago* much like he passed the bread and the chalice at the Last Supper on the preceding night. Between 1438 and 1440, Jan van Eyck is known to have worked on what Hans Belting calls "a portrait of the Christ icon," an oil-on-panel image likely to have formed part of a diptych and preserved in three copies (fig. 4.4). By drawing on the already "authenticated" Veronica icon, van Eyck's image offers itself as both a painterly artifact or portrait and a real presence or "lifelike" (*au vif*) face. Consequently, the artist's role is twofold: the

---

79. Closely related is the Eastern Orthodox icon of Veliky Ustiug, dated 1447, which notably features the omnivoyant gaze that some six years later becomes the focus of Nicholas's treatise. The iconography here "is based on the legend of Abgar, the king of Edessa, who . . . sent the painter Ananias to Christ, asking him to paint a portrait of Christ in the hope that looking upon it would cure the king of disease" (Evans 2004, 175).

"inventor" whose name we find inscribed on the Bruges copy of van Eyck's icon and the "witness" who has simultaneously *conceived* and *received* the image as both spiritual vision and visible presence.[80]

Possibly inspired by van Eyck's work, which he may have studied during his 1451 mission to the Low Countries, Nicholas remarks how "among human works I have not found an image more suitable to our purpose than the image of someone omnivoyant, so that his face, through subtle pictorial artistry, is such that it seems to behold everything around it" (*VD* Introd., 2). From the outset, then, Nicholas establishes that the *imago Dei* is not a painting but a presence, not a portrait but a face, not a commentary-dependent artifice but a manifestation enjoining the beholder to detach herself from her singular, "contracted" viewpoint. In framing the encounter with the icon thus, Nicholas echoes the central claims of Byzantine iconodules of the ninth century, in particular the patriarch Nikephoros and Theodore the Studite. On their account, far from "'circumscribing' [Christ's] divine nature," the icon depicts the face of Jesus, "the *prosōpon*, the person of the Word. In the icon, we see neither a divine nor a human *nature*, but rather the face of the *person* of Jesus who is God and man."[81] It is this focus on the face and, thus, on Christ's presence as a *person* that accounts for the depth and force of Nicholas's subsequent argument. For the face is not experienced as merely "portrayed," but, always, as *looking* at the beholder. Belting likewise points out that "the way Christ gazes at us is still abstract, like an icon—it is an 'absolute gaze.'"[82] Hence some readers of *De Visione Dei* have construed the work's title mainly as a *genitivus subjectivus*: "for the central focus is God's vision of us, not ours of God."[83] Far from a naturalistic and unilateral dominion over the empirically visible, seeing presupposes being-seen by God, whose eternal, "absolute gaze" is embodied by the icon, just as the icon's gaze always already falls on the beholder before the latter's "contracted" sight can focus on the icon.

Insofar as the beholder attends to the infinity that is the face of the other (as Levinas famously calls it) she will recognize herself as created by God's "absolute vision" (*visio absoluta*); and it is this "being-seen" (*videri*) that the icon mediates for

---

80. See the discussion of the "true" and "alike" faces in Belting 2014, 148–56.

81. Schönborn 1994, 176.

82. Belting 2011b, 225. As Archbishop Damianos puts it, icons of saints, likewise, constitute "*living* images . . . evoking their perpetual presence and providing Christians constantly with visual paradigms of their attainment of *theosis*" (Evans 2004, 338). See also Freedberg (1989), who notes how the "living" image "provokes empathy" (231) and who cautions against anthropological attempts to assimilate the topos of the living image to some notion of primitive animism (284), urging instead that the "countless miracle legends in which images are said to move, speak, weep, strike out, and eat" must be taken seriously as "historical testimony to cognitive fact" (291).

83. Bond 2002, 185; likewise, D'Amico notes how, in Nicholas's treatise, "the possibility of all human vision [*Schau*] presupposes God's absolute vision" (2010, 106).

the finite, human viewer. Inasmuch as "in our sight of Him, God sees Himself," the result is a generative, not a reproductive, concept of mental vision: "*visio absoluta* is productivity; seeing is creating."[84] Anterior to whatever epistemological purposes it may serve, vision constitutes a metaphysical event. To attend to visible forms is not to "register" them in seemingly neutral and occasional fashion but, rather, to *witness* their self-manifestation. Things appear not just *for* a beholder at her choosing. Rather, they primordially manifest themselves *to* the human being's "contracted" sight, such that prior to claiming epistemic agency the beholder will have been the addressee of being in its self-disclosure. Hence, in contrast to the contingent utility of ambient objects (what Heidegger calls the sheer "being-to-hand" [*Zuhandenheit*]), the icon operates on a different ontological plateau and in an essentially twofold manner. For not only does it involve "the appearance '*of* something,'" but within and by means of this visible appearance "something makes itself known that does *not* show itself."[85]

Such a "self-showing" (*sich-selbst-Zeigen*) that is also simultaneously an unveiling of something not visible per se also implies that coming face-to-face with the icon will ideally issue in a moment of self-recognition rather than some value-neutral apperception. Furthermore, the icon's utterly specific way of facing and focusing the beholder's gaze implicitly "leads" (in the pedagogical sense of *manuducere*) her toward apprehending within the order of the visible the transcendent source of its very being. The very disclosure of the visible, insofar as it progressively concentrates finite human vision, mediates God's "uncontracted" or "absolute" sight in spatiotemporal form. In unusually charged, almost rapturous diction, Nicholas thus affirms that intrinsic to human vision is this consciousness of being-sought-out by the visible appearance and the invisible source of its being that it mediates. Hence, seeing necessarily implies our "being-seen" (*videri*), that is, for the beholder to be called upon by the charisma of the visible and, thus, to find one's ethical and intellectual being jointly affirmed by the antecedent reality of God's absolute sight. For "where Your eye is present Your love is also present.... Your seeing is loving.... Your seeing is Your being. I exist because You look upon me [*ideo ego sum quia tu me respicis*]" (*VD* 4:11).

And yet, no matter how much the human gaze may take itself to be spiritually attuned to the divine being that is its ultimate ground or source, sight always remains confined within the realm of similitude. Once again affirming the framework of the *analogia entis* as the outer perimeter of all human knowledge, Nicholas thus concedes, "I know, however [*scio autem*], that the capability which conduces to union is

---

84. Beierwaltes 1988, 100; D'Amico 2010, 98.
85. Heidegger 1996, 26 (§ 7).

only likeness; but incapability results from unlikeness." To whatever extent finite sight succeeds in becoming insight, it will have embraced—more fully though still imperfectly—visible being as an imperfect manifestation of God's "maximal goodness, which cannot fail to impart itself to whatever is capable of receiving it." As Nicholas consistently emphasizes, finite, contracted sight ought to be impelled by a longing for greater similitude with the absolute sight that mediates itself through its visible creations. All contracted sight ought to adequate itself to what is ultimately invisible: "If by every possible means I make myself like unto Your goodness, then according to my degree of likeness [*gradus similitudinis*] thereto I will be capable of receiving truth" (*VD* 4:12). Hence, the apotheosis of finite, contingent sight is a state of contemplative insight, which successfully balances the partial similitude against visible being's infinite dissimilitude vis-à-vis God: "I presently contemplate eternal life in a mirror, an icon, a symbolism, because eternal life is only Your blessed gaze, by which You never cease looking upon me most lovingly—even to the point of beholding the intimate recesses of my soul" (*VD* 4:13). Far from betraying or detracting from God's "absolute" sight, the mediation that prompts Nicholas to speak of human "contracted" sight as a type of mirror, icon, or symbolism is indispensable to, indeed properly constitutive of, the overall economy of spiritual sight.

Let us consider the icon accompanying the manuscript that Nicholas had sent to the brethren at Tegernsee. Though enlisted for creative theological purposes in *De Visione Dei*, painting a human gaze that is at all times focused on each and everyone is far from novel, indeed harkens back to the illusionist technique already found in Roman mural painting. Starting in the thirteenth century, the "all-seeing image" (*figura cuncta videntis*), which as Lawrence Bond maintains is actually not all that difficult to achieve, undergoes a revival of sorts in the Tyrol region. By the early fifteenth century, it has been technically perfected and is being adapted for more individualized depictions of the human face than are found in Eastern iconography.[86] Nicholas's instructions to the monks, which aim "to elevate you . . . through a devotional exercise [*per quondam praxim devotionis*] unto mystical theology" (*VD* Introd.:5), situate the icon within the relatively new genre of the *imago pietatis*, an image of smaller size typically made to the specifications of an individual and designed to induce in the beholder a state of focused and sustained spiritual self-examination. Drawing on Belting's early work on this genre, Alex Stock situates the "devotional image [*Andachtsbild*] . . . between the didactic function of images de-

---

86. Stock 1989, 51; Bond 2002, 181. On Eastern iconographic techniques and the way that they engage the spiritual senses, see Evans 2004, especially the contributions by Archbishop Damianos and Georgopoulou. As Damianos notes, the "corporeal immobility and measured stance" that defines the Orthodox icon is "but a visual reminder and a reflection of the perfect union of body and soul achieved by [the subject's] inner disposition of *psuchía*, 'stillness'" (338).

picting scenes from Biblical narrative and the hieratic images of Christ and the saints."[87]

Perhaps the version closest to the panel that Nicholas enclosed with his manuscript is the Christ icon painted by van Eyck around 1438, now extant in three copies from his workshop. Consistent with the core axioms of Byzantine image theory, the image in question ought not to be approached as the portrait of a historical individual. It does not "represent" the historical figure of Jesus but, instead, asks the beholder to meet Christ in whom "dwelleth the fullness of the Godhead bodily" (Col 2:9), that is, to form a mental image and spiritual vision of Christ by assenting to the unconditional and inexhaustible presence of the icon's gaze. To ensure the beholder's attention, the icon has been purged of all secondary features. There are no elements of narrative *istoria*, no attempts at simulating a perspective on background scenery, and no symbolic objects of the kind beginning to enter early fifteenth-century religious and portrait painting. Instead, the meaning that eventuates in the exchange of the icon's and the beholder's gaze transcends temporal concerns, something underscored by the fact that the one instance of an omnivoyant gaze encountered by Nicholas and still known today centers on the motif of Justice. As "an absolute presence and a generality of presence, outside any context . . . a timeless and unlocated face," van der Weyden's *visio facialis* reminds us of the hiatus separating the kind of justice vicariously achieved in private settlements and political compromises from the timeless virtue of *Iustitia*.[88]

Capitalizing on the otherworldly effect of the omnivoyant gaze that he had occasion to study in various contemporary images, Nicholas emphasizes the icon's "experimental" (*experimentaliter*) function, thus parting ways with the mnemonic and affective rhetoric that had begun to dominate a great deal of late fourteenth- and fifteenth-century religious painting. Initially characterizing the icon he had commissioned for the brethren at the Tegernsee monastery as simply "a sort of likeness [*quadam similitudine*]," Nicholas soon subordinates the icon's material and representational aspect—what Husserl calls "image-carrier" (*Bildträger*) and "image-object" (*Bildgegenstand*)—to the incontrovertible, visual presence it institutes, Husserl's "image-subject" (*Bildsujet*).[89] Thus, throughout much of *De Visione Dei*, the

---

87. Stock 1989, 54; see also Belting, 1981, 3–46; and my discussion of van Eyck's *Virgin and Child with Canon van der Paele* (1435) below.

88. "In *De Visione Dei* one sees God through and, therefore, beyond image and icon—not merely by means of an icon but by passing through the image and moving from a meditation to a contemplation of the infinite, incomprehensible God beyond all concepts, figures, and imaginings" (Bond 2002, 182, 184). See also Beierwaltes, who characterizes Cusa's icon as an "intellectual figure [*Denkform*]" (1988, 95), and Stock, who reads *De Visione Dei* as a "philosophical prayer [*philosophisches Gebet*]" (1989, 60).

89. See Husserl 2005, 20–22 (§ 9); and the discussion below, ch. 8.

image (*eicona*) altogether merges with the presence it renders visible: Christ's "face" (*facies*). Even so, the spiritual power being communicated by Christ's face can be realized only if the beholder relinquishes any notion of seeing as a taking-possession-of and as exercising dominion over what is transparently visible. Appropriately, Nicholas's exegesis is not focused on the image per se but on the quality of the gaze it institutes, a gaze whose spiritual meaning will be fulfilled only if and when it succeeds in detaching itself from the icon's material scaffolding. For the true locus of *visio* is a function of *how* rather than *what*; that is, it concerns not the "object" seen but the spiritual self-awareness that the gaze induces in the beholder. As Nicholas points out, "It is not the essence of sight that sight beholds one object more than another." Rather, "sight's perfection [*perfectionis visus*]" inheres in its capacity to "behold each and everything at once." This, then, is "absolute sight, . . . [which] excels all the acuity, swiftness, and power" of actual sight. Nicholas also calls it "abstract sight [*abstractum visum*]" because it has been "mentally . . . freed from all eyes and organs [*absolvi ab omnibus oculis et organis*]" (*VD* 1:6).

For the benefit of the Tegernsee brethren, Nicholas thus "encloses a panel [*tabellam*] that I was able to acquire. It contains the figure of an omnivoyant [individual]; and I call it the 'icon of God' [*figuram cuncta videntis tenentem, quam eiconam dei appello*]" (*VD* Introd.:2). He instructs the monks to

> hang this icon somewhere, e.g., on the north wall; and you brothers stand around it, at a short distance from it, and observe it. Regardless of the place from which each of you looks at it, each will have the impression that he alone is being looked at by it. To the brother who is situated in the east, it will seem that the face is looking toward the east; to the brother in the south, that the face is looking south. . . . First of all, then, marvel at how it is possible that [the face] behold each and every one of you at once. For the imagination of the brother who is standing in the east does not at all apprehend the icon's gaze that is being directed toward a different region, viz., toward the west or the south. (*VD* Introd.:3)

Finding the "icon's gaze moved unmovably" as he changes his position, a monk may eventually "ask the approaching brother whether the icon's gaze moves continually with him" and, being told that the icon's gaze moves both with him and in the opposite manner, "he will believe his fellow-monk." Paradoxically, then, the icon realizes a spiritual community precisely by instilling in each of its members a sense of being the sole and constant focus of its gaze, "as if [the icon] saw only this person and nothing else."[90] Not only does the icon's omnivoyant gaze stand in as a figure for

---

90. Bond 2002, 192; see also Cuozzo 2005, 190; and de Certeau, who notes how "it is an oral testimony (the *revelatio revelatoris*) that alone makes it possible to 'believe' what escapes sight. . . . [T]he image henceforth 'requires' discourse" (1987, 13).

God's absolute vision; it also enjoins each individual viewer to acknowledge the partial and incomplete deliverances of his gaze: "It shows me that I am not in control of the space of my visual perceptions. As soon as I listen to someone who is looking at a shared focus of attention from a different viewpoint I start to appreciate that something is invisible to me."[91] The material icon furnishes the heuristic device that allows Nicholas to illustrate for his readers this "absolute" or "abstract" sight and, by extension, to show mystical theology to issue in a type of spiritual cognition. No longer tethered to a particular object or referent but, instead, reflexively doubling back on itself, mental vision ultimately aims at the total suspension of visibility, visuality, and at expunging all naturalistic conceptions and concerns associated with worldly existence. It is "this return movement of the image into the ground . . . in which the transition from unmediated sensory experience to reflexive intellectual activity takes place." What von Balthasar identifies as "the image's renunciation of itself, by which it waives any claim to be a reality existing and important for its own sake, . . . [a] renunciation of its own unreality" and an affirmation of itself as "purely subservient to reality" goes to the very heart of Nicholas's mystical theology.[92] For, as Nicholas points out, it is precisely through their interaction with the icon or, rather, with the gaze that the icon models for them that the Tegernsee brethren are to be "led . . . into most sacred darkness [*in sacratissimam obscuritatem manuducere*]" (*VD* Introd.:1–2).

Such leading the beholder by the hand (*manuducere*) toward the fullness of inner, mental vision places *De Visione Dei* on the border between catechesis and speculative theology. Nicholas's treatise, that is, "seems to join a western and Benedictine spirituality of *lectio* to a Byzantine spirituality of gazing. Cusanus's icon becomes text; his text and the reader become icons."[93] Yet more than John of Damascus, Theodore the Studite, or Photios, Nicholas's phenomenology of image consciousness resists construing the relationship of the icon and its beholder in affective terms. We recall how, in his sermon (AD 867) celebrating the restoration of icons to St. Sophia in Constantinople, Photios relishes how "even in her images . . . the Virgin's grace delights, comforts, and strengthens us." Evidently favoring the more visceral, affective power of sight, image and word in Photios's account ultimately compete for the same epistemological space. Thus, the deeds of the martyrs and saints "are conveyed both by stories and by pictures, but it is the spectators rather than the hearers who are drawn to emulation."[94] In the event, Nicholas's intellectual objective is to establish the

---

91. Hoff 2013, 105–6.

92. Balthasar 2001, 147.

93. Bond 2002, 182–83. As de Certeau notes, "The gaze fixed on the spectator also has the cultural value of a miracle," thus situating Nicholas's spiritual exercise "in an aura of mystery and secrecy which is enriched by a hundred other stories of devotion" (1987, 12).

94. Photios, Homily XVII, in Mango 1958, 290, 294.

complementarity of word and image on the grounds that, by its very nature, every image aspires to an invisible reality, just as the spiritual meaning of the spoken word can only be fulfilled in a condition of contemplative silence. For Nicholas, sight does not so much construct as respond to an anterior visible reality. Or, as Beierwaltes puts it, "seeing attests to a foundational visibility that beckons sight [*eine principielle Sichtbarkeit, die des Sehens bedarf*]. Seeing, that is, comes alive in a sensuously differentiating reflection [*sinnlich-differenzierende Reflexion*]."[95]

In focusing on the quality of the gaze that the icon models for its beholder, Nicholas frames the icon as a medium for catechesis rather than as a painting inviting the beholder to exercise visual dominion over a simulated, three-dimensional space. Thus, for "sight to apprehend distinctly that which is visible, two paths of light [must] meet." Far from being some naturalistic occurrence, seeing constitutes an essentially intellectual act; it "takes interest in the sensation and pays attention to it in order to discriminate. Accordingly, the spirit in the eye does not discriminate but rather in that spirit a higher spirit [*spiritus altior*] accomplishes the discriminating" (*QD* 2:33). By stressing the icon's capacity for guiding the beholder toward contemplative, mental vision, Nicholas implicitly rejects modern, scientific theories of linear perspective and the single-viewpoint approach to painting that are being developed during the first half of the fifteenth century by artists, mathematicians, and architects such as Brunelleschi, Ghiberti, Piero della Francesca, Biagio Pelacani, and, most famously, Leon Battista Alberti. Tellingly, the proponents of a new theory of vision, and of a modern approach to painting premised on it, do not so much reject as simply ignore earlier iconic and Italo-Byzantine techniques for which the illusion of three-dimensional space seemed to be of little or no concern. Yet Nicholas's catechesis of the Tegernsee monks on properly seeing and responding to the all-seeing Christ icon clearly implies that something of crucial value will be lost if the concept of mental vision is supplanted by a realist framework of linear perspective and if interior vision is displaced by a naturalistic and anthropocentric model of sight. As Nicholas fully realizes, the position set forth by Alberti in *De Pictura* (1435), and later amplified by Piero della Francesca's *De prospectiva pingendi* (ca. 1474), implicitly sacrifices the ideal of progressive spiritual ascent mediated by an iconic vision (*visio mentalis*) to a notion of empirical sight (*visus*) that seeks to achieve instantaneous and total dominion over the realm of the visible. The Neoplatonist metaphysics of light has contracted into a strictly naturalist conception of sight, which in turn is being pared down to optical laws.

Dedicated (in its Italian version) to Brunelleschi, Alberti's compact treatise *De Pictura* (1435), "the first modern manual for painters," accomplishes a paradigmatic

---

95. Beierwaltes 1988, 94.

shift that Belting has characterized as the "transformation of the post-Islamic *theory of vision* into the *theory of pictures*."[96] A manifesto of the modern scientific method that predates Bacon's *Novum Organon* by almost two centuries, *De Pictura* is not, however, without precedents. Intent on conceptualizing pictorial space in strictly quantitative terms, Alberti draws on Biagio Pelacani's earlier efforts in *Quaestiones Perspectivae* (ca. 1390), which in turn was indebted to Vitrivius's theory of architecture. With its tripartite "progression through rudiments, practice and ends" Alberti's didactic treatise also appears "deeply influenced by Roman treatises on rhetoric."[97] It is, as its author notes, the work of "a pure mathematician" (I.1), and its sole purpose is to outline the kind of technique needed to take control of three-dimensional space. The objective is, simply put, to "master illusion, where the word 'mastery' [means] . . . to be able to produce convincing representations of the world as we see it but also to have understood the logic of these illusions."[98] Inasmuch as for Alberti painting aims simply to reconstitute, or simulate, the perspectival logic governing ordinary perception of objects in space, it follows that for him "painting and sculpture are cognate arts" (II.27). Indeed, the idea of a manual for condensing the techniques required for simulating three-dimensional, sculptural effects on a two-dimensional plane had been suggested to Alberti by artworks wrought by Masaccio and Donatello during the 1420s in Florence and Siena, respectively.[99]

Throughout *De Pictura*, Alberti's main concern rests with the mimetic correctness of material sight. The object of painting is no longer to transport the beholder spiritually but to affirm visible space by means of a perspectivally correct placement of objects in it. The latter are subject strictly to the beholder's perspectival control over a given field of vision. In focusing on the techniques required for simulating three-dimensional space and subjecting it to the "central ray" of the human individual, *De Pictura* makes clear that for Alberti, perspective has become "a system and not just an intention." As a result, "the term 'forms' consign[s] objects to the changing conditions of perception."[100] Stating that "we are not writing a history of painting like Pliny, but treating of the art in an entirely new way" (II.26), Alberti is openly dismissive of older theories and debates, such as those concerning the nature of vision (extromission vs. intromission), which he considers "quite without value for our

---

96. Grafton 2000, 113; Belting 2011a, 147.

97. Alberti 2004, 19; on Alberti's self-conscious view of painting as a rhetorical art, see Grafton 2000, 116–24: "Often, . . . he wrote as if he saw himself not as a painter or a practical man but as an orator, using verbal skills to comment on a world of visual practice that was not his own" (119).

98. Harries 2001, 69.

99. Masaccio's *Holy Trinity* in Santa Maria Novella and the Brancacci Chapel, Florence (1425), and Donatello's first bronze *stiacciato* relief sculpture, *The Feast of Herod*, in the Baptistery in Siena (1427). See also Grafton 2000, 112–21.

100. Belting 2011a, 136.

purposes."[101] The entire speculative tradition concerned with hidden links between sight and vision, eye and soul, has simply ceased to be of any interest. Indeed, as Karsten Harries notes, "Alberti's art is incompatible with . . . spiritual perspective. A God-centered art gives way to a human-centered art."[102] No more than "an animate mirror" (I.6), the eye of the painter has achieved dominion over three-dimensional space at the expense of the beholder's spiritual self-awareness.

Such a model of vision wherein the seer seeks to exercise total control over the realm of the visible without himself being exposed to sight and the vicissitudes of self-recognition not only looks ahead to Bentham's Panopticon. It is already observable in New Testament narratives, such as the parable of Zacchaeus (Lk 19:1–11). Feeling ill at ease amidst a crowd of onlookers that, he suspects, may be hostile to him, Zacchaeus instead chooses to climb a tree so as to see Jesus while remaining himself unseen. In ways that he may not yet realize, Zacchaeus thus "seeks" (*zēteō*) Jesus who, in turn, "seeks and saves" (Lk 19:10) those who are lost. Being a man "little of stature" who paradoxically craves both invisibility and recognition, the tax collector and proverbial rich man (*plousios*) Zacchaeus is loathed by his people who, for their part, vocally demur at Jesus's willingness to acknowledge and "joyfully" receive this social pariah. Even more than the disdain of the whole community (*pantes*), however, Zacchaeus dreads being seen and acknowledged by Jesus and thus being confronted with his own covetousness. In the event, the parable ends with Zacchaeus's conversion and pledge henceforth to honor the good of distributive justice. While initially choosing observation over participation, spectatorship over self-recognition (like so many other figures in the Gospels), Zacchaeus at last relinquishes his heretofore uninvolved, merely curious, isolated point of view. His conversion and eventual acceptance by his native community begins with Zacchaeus asking to be seen by Jesus, not only for who he is, but also for who, once acknowledged and illumined by Jesus's gaze, he may yet become: "Behold [*Idou*], Lord, the half of my goods I give to the poor; and if I have taken any thing from any man by false accusation, I restore him fourfold" (Lk 19:8).[103]

By contrast, Alberti's implicitly secular theory of vision pivots on the premise of an inwardly and outwardly detached spectator who, unlike Zacchaeus, will never surrender his furtive gaze from a hidden vantage point. Instead, *De Pictura* presents us with a defiantly anthropomorphic framework whose sole aim it is to ensure the spectator's dominion over three-dimensional space, like "another God."[104] Once

---

101. On medieval theories of vision developed by Alhazen, Grosseteste, Witelo, and Roger Bacon, see Lindberg 1976, esp. 48–121; and Belting 2011a, 129–35.

102. Harries 2001, 85.

103. On this episode, see Constas 2014, 30–31.

104. The phrase translates as *un altro iddio*, found at the opening of Part II of the Italian version of Alberti's treatise, *Della Pittura*.

the eye is construed as simply "an animate mirror" (I.6), the painted image no longer serves to mediate a numinous, invisible truth and, as a matter of principle, suspends all inquiry into the spectator's potential for self-recognition and spiritual transformation. For Alberti, an "image" (*pictura* or, sometimes, *simulacrum*) is the product of an exclusively human, innerworldly ingenuity. Pointedly excluded from his definition is any type of nonphysical, or mental, image.[105] Framed exclusively as an objective, quantifiable artifact, the perspectively "correct" picture instead attests to the superior craftsmanship of its maker and, by extension, invites the beholder to share in the painter's glory and dominion over the visible: "The function of the painter is to draw with lines and paint in colors on a surface any given bodies in such a way that, at a fixed distance and with a certain, determined position of the centric ray, what you see represented appears to be in relief and just like those bodies." What Alberti conceives primarily as a perfection of technical skill, moreover, aims expressly at increased social recognition: "The aim of the painter is to obtain praise, favour, and good-will for his work" (III.52). Thus, the medieval concept of *ars* (skill), which builds on Aristotle's *technē*, has effectively been supplanted by "notions of 'theory' and 'method.'" As a result, "*visio*—vision—was coming to mean not only *the act of seeing* but also *what was seen*, . . . [and] 'form' (*specie*) and 'resemblance' (*similitude*) are linked to individual objects in optical theory."[106] Alberti's unqualified embrace of Protagoras's maxim that "man is the scale and measure of all things" (I.18) positions him at the cusp of an epochal shift such that (as Belting puts it with a nod to Heidegger) "the gazing subject occupies a position in that he takes possession of the world as a picture."[107] Likewise, Alberti's choice of a personal emblem, the "winged eye" (fig. 4.5) with its Ciceronian inscription, "what next" (*quid tum*), truly captures the modern "thinker who emphasize[s] not contemplation but striving, laboring, producing."[108] On every page of *De Pictura* we encounter this distinctly modern, confident striving to appropriate in scientific, methodical fashion the visible world, definitive knowledge of which had until recently been deemed the exclusive province of an omniscient and omnivoyant God.[109]

Epochal though Alberti's position appears, it is not without precursors of its own. Thus, that God, whose creative, absolute vision Alberti's mathematization of

---

105. See Bredekamp 2010, 34, who quotes Alberti's *De Statua* (*On Sculpture*), § 1.

106. Belting 2011b, 151; see also his discussion of Ghiberti's and Piero della Francesca's mathematization of perspective (150–59).

107. Belting 2011b, 211. As Heidegger had put it, "The fact that the world becomes picture at all is what distinguishes the essence of the modern age" (1977, 129). On the implications of this shift, see Pfau 2013a, 21–26.

108. Harries 2001, 68.

109. On this emblem, see Bredekamp 2010, 331–33, who remarks on the emblem's fusion of optic and haptic functions; imaged objects seem to attract the eye with such force as to pull it out of its socket and cause it to fly toward them.

Figure 4.5.
"Winged Eye,"
personal emblem of
Leon Battista Alberti.
Washington, DC,
National Gallery of
Art, Samuel H. Kress
Collection

perspective would seek to usurp, had been conceived in theologically problematic ways as early as the early thirteenth century.[110] Specifically, Alberti's deiform concept of perception—namely, as a "central ray" extending unimpeded through transparent space so as to (re-)create finite, perceptible objects—inadvertently replicates the inscrutable God of fourteenth-century Voluntarist theology. Indeed, in transposing God's absolute vision into a totalizing account of empirical sight, *De Pictura* responds to Voluntarism's central premise of a divine *ratio* separated from man by an ontological chasm. The only way for the human intellect to cope with this state of affairs was to disaggregate God's unfathomable creative power (*potentia absoluta*) from its concrete manifestation in the order (*potentia ordinata*) of the visible world. Increasingly, that is, emphasis shifted away from mystical contemplation to naturalistic explanation, from approaching the visible world as manifesting God's unfathomable *logos* to methodically aggregating and scrutinizing all observable, secondary causes and, in so doing, instrumentalizing them for human ends. As Louis Dupré notes, whereas "in earlier Scholasticism, God did not surrender his sovereign power to secondary causes," later Nominalists such as Ockham, Biel, and Autrecourt posited "the idea of an independent order of secondary causes [that] gradually led to a

---

110. As Hoff points out, "The freemasonic symbolism of the detached all-seeing eye did not emerge *ex nihilo* or without precursors. It was consistent with the representationalist ontology of the late medieval Franciscan tradition" (2013, 78).

conception of nature as fully equipped to act without special divine assistance."[111] Alberti's methodical conceptualization of linear perspective and of the image as a strict facsimile of ordinary perception capitalizes on this bifurcation of grace and nature, transcendence and immanence, primary and secondary causation, as it had begun to unfold during the previous century. By contrast, Aquinas's *visio beatifica* and, as remains to be seen, Nicholas's "view[ing] with inner eyes the truth which is pointed to by the painting" (*VD* 10:40) locates sight within a Neoplatonist economy of "participation" (*methexis*).

One may be tempted, then, to situate Alberti in a genealogy of modern thought extending from Ockham's divine command ethic via Alberti to the Enlightenment (Masonic) symbol of the all-seeing eye to Bentham's Panopticon and, eventually, to the anthropomorphic theologies of Feuerbach, Strauss, or Renan. Yet this distinctly modern lens must not be allowed to eclipse an older, Christian-Platonist genealogy whose resurgence in mid-fifteenth-century Italy clearly leaves its imprint on Nicholas of Cusa's later writings, beginning with *De Visione Dei*. At the very least, we must not suppose that the preoccupation with divine omnipotence that pervades fourteenth-century Nominalist and Voluntarist theology, and that extends to the Enlightenment's masonic symbolism of the all-seeing eye, had altogether foreclosed on Neoplatonism's dynamic model of the spiritual vision, as elaborated from Gregory of Nyssa and Maximus the Confessor all the way to contemplative mystics such as Julian of Norwich, Catherine of Siena, and Nicholas's widely read contemporary, Thomas à Kempis.[112] By contrast, Alberti's relationship to the Platonist and mystical concept of vision is, if anything, confused and at times curiously imperceptive. Let us consider two instances that throw into relief the self-deluded modernity of *De Pictura*.

First, there is Alberti's invocation of the myth of Narcissus who, as Ovid tells it, had fallen in love with his own reflection (*Metam.* III:402–36). The shift from St. Luke, reputedly the first painter of icons, to the mythical figure of Narcissus is revealing, not least because Alberti identifies the latter as "the inventor of painting [whose] tale . . . fits our purpose perfectly. [For] what is painting but the act of embracing by means of art the surface of the pool" (II.26). Alberti's telling stipulation that "the painter is not concerned with things that are not visible" (II.36) and that "painting aims to represent things seen" (II.30) effectively contracts all vision to empirical sight

---

111. Dupré 1993, 177–78. Similarly, Taylor notes that Ockham's rejection of "the realism of essences" entailed a shift whereby "the meaning of being is relative not just to a vision of the world but also to an understanding of the stance of the agent in the world" (2007, 97).

112. On the problematic legacy of Ockham's divine command ethic, see Aers 2009, 25–54, who notes how, "as usual, [Ockham] seems more interested in exploring what God's freedom allegedly could have performed than in exploring what God has actually revealed and done in Christ with humanity" (40); see also Dupré 1993, 121–44; Taylor 2007, 90–99; Pfau 2013a, 160–82.

and assimilates the concept of the image to its concrete, painted instantiation. Once confined to an economy of strict verisimilitude, the painted image merely *recon*stitutes, and furnishes visible evidence for, objects taken to exist prior to and independent of their material realization as painting. No longer, that is, does the image mediate the unknown and invisible according to a metaphysics of analogy. Effectively precluding any prospect of discovery and spiritual ascent, Alberti instead conceives of painting as a facsimile intended to duplicate a finite perception and, in so doing, reconfirm existing conceptions of reality: "Through painting, the faces of the dead go on living for a very long time" (II.25), Alberti assures his reader, content to claim a strictly mnemonic function for the image. Yet to put it thus once more begs the central question, namely, whence images derive this very power of (re)animating the beings they depict.[113]

Precisely this single-minded commitment to mimetically duplicating the deliverances of empirical sight and bringing them under the beholder's geometrical dominion turns out to have strangely disembodying side effects. Just as Narcissus "loves a bodiless dream" (*spem sine corpore amat*), so Alberti's ideal of linear, single-viewpoint perspective, being likewise animated by a desire for total possession of visible appearance, effectively prizes appropriation of the visible object over knowledge of its form. Here it bears noting how Ovid's story recalls Socrates's utter dismantling, in the *Phaedrus*, of Lysias's proposed definition of love as total possession. As Socrates points out, to equate love with dominion traps both lover and beloved in an inexorable downward spiral that renders both increasingly unreal. For "he who is ruled by desire and is a slave to pleasure will inevitably desire to make his beloved as pleasing to himself as possible" and, consequently, strives to render the beloved "always . . . weaker and inferior" (238e–239a). The logical outcome is the utter decreation of the beloved as a person who, having been denuded of all reality and presence by the lover's covetous gaze, ends up being consigned to a shadowy, deathlike state.

It is telling that, in sharp contrast to Cusa, Alberti can speak in any detail only about the method employed in *producing* painting but, throughout *De Pictura*, has virtually nothing to say about any actual paintings. He cannot respond to the painted image because it opens up no new vistas, reveals nothing but, at most, attests to the formal correctness of the technique governing its production. The status of the painted image is no longer that of a medium but strictly that of a material object, appraised exclusively as regards its fungibility with the linear geometry organizing everyday perception. Inasmuch as painting aims exclusively to simulate on two-dimensional planes what has been visibly experienced in spatial perception, a successful implementation of perspectival technique effectively paralyzes the beholder,

---

113. On Alberti's perplexity in the face of the image's revivifying power, see Freedberg 1989, 44–45; Belting 2011a, 78.

rendering her inexpressive, if not outright mute. Just so, when bending over an unclouded "pool, limpid and silvery," to quench bodily thirst, Ovid's Narcissus lapses into catatonic self-absorption, having now succumbed to "another thirst" (*sitim sedare cupit, sitis altera crevit*). As a result of mistaking "what is only a shadow" for a body (*corpus putat esse, quod unda est*), the optical acuity of Narcissus's gaze grows in inverse proportion to his comprehension of what presents itself to his sight.

> As he drank he saw before his eyes
> A form, a face, and loved with leaping heart
> A hope unreal [*spem sine corpore amat*] and thought the shape was real.
> Spellbound [*adstupet*] he saw himself, and motionless
> Lay like a marble statue staring down.
> He gazes at his eyes, twin constellation,
> His hair worthy of Bacchus or Apollo,
> …
> All he admires that all admire in him,
> Himself he longs for, unwittingly,
> Praising is praised, desiring is desired,
> And love he kindles while with love he burns.
> How often in vain he kissed the cheating pool
> And in the water sank his arms to clasp
> The neck he saw, but could not clasp himself!
> Not knowing what he sees [*quid videat, nescit*], he adores the sight;
> That false face fools and fuels his delight.[114]

By identifying the art of painting with the figure of Narcissus, Alberti betrays a remarkable lack of hermeneutic awareness. To be sure, Ovid's youth seems an apt emblem for the kind of illusionist aesthetic outlined in Alberti's short treatise. Yet Ovid's retelling of the myth also means to show how the twin fantasies of total visibility and total possession come at a fatal cost. For to instrumentalize the image merely in order to secure the beholder's desire for total self-possession means to denude sight of any generative dimension. Moreover, as the story of Narcissus also suggests, to see but one's reflection or "twin constellation" entails not knowing *what* one sees and, by extension, for the beholder to be barred from all self-recognition. Drained of all anagogical power, Alberti's image forestalls any narrative progression from sight to knowledge and, instead, leaves its beholder, like Narcissus, marooned in cognitive limbo. Such an appraisal sharply contrasts with how, little more than a century earlier, Canto 30 of Dante's *Purgatorio* had portrayed Narcissus as the very

---

114. Ovid 1986, III, lines 414–29.

embodiment of sinful self-idolization. Having merged with his reflection, and as a result unable to distinguish between mirror and icon, Narcissus's idolatrous persona prevents him from grasping his paralyzed condition. At once a prefiguration and indictment of Alberti's pictorial modernity, Dante's decision to place Narcissus within an eschatological framework reveals Ovid's youth as fatally ensnared by illusions of creaturely permanence and Pelagian self-perfection.[115]

Among the many paradoxes running through the Narcissus story in the *Metamorphosis*, we witness a youth losing touch with his temporal existence precisely by seeking to embrace himself in the shadowy reality of the image. Consigned to a strictly mirroring function, as mere *reflection*, the image ceases to exist as such. It has been stripped of the most elemental criterion that, as John of Damascus had pointed out, allows us to speak of an image (*eikōn*) in the first place: its difference vis-à-vis its prototype. In misidentifying Ovid's Narcissus as an unwitting innovator rather than as the spiritual failure portrayed by Dante, Alberti embodies modernity's misguided attempt to lay claim to the world solely as picture. For once it is accepted that "images merely simulate meaning, they can only mean themselves." The result is a curious merger of idolatry and iconoclasm, since "only a reality that can solely subsist in the image protects the latter from being confused with reality." Put differently, once the economy of mimesis has been supplanted by the technical ideal of total simulation, "images have been denuded of our faith that they amount to more than images; consequently, we no longer need to reject them. Idolatry thus mutates into iconoclasm in a new key. . . . The abuse of images has meanwhile become invisible."[116]

Unable to distinguish between the image understood as a generative *medium* and a mere simulacrum or mirror reflection that leaves the beholder spiritually and cognitively paralyzed, Narcissus no longer *sees* an image at all. Instead, "spellbound, he saw himself, and motionless / Lay like a marble statue staring down." We recall Gadamer's caveat that, however "tied to the original represented in it," "presentation" (*Darstellung*) is always "more than a copy. That the representation is a picture—and not the original itself—does not mean anything negative, . . . but rather an autonomous reality." It is precisely this ontological difference separating image from what is depicted that makes it possible for the beholder to achieve self-recognition *in* and *by means of* the image: "What is pictured . . . comes to presentation in the represen-

---

115. Admonished by Beatrice not to pine for his now-absent pagan guide (Virgil) but to look upon her, Dante signals for the reader his comprehension by emphasizing the changed quality of his gaze. No longer is it directed at an affirmation of familiar reality but, instead, refocuses on the Marian vision of Beatrice: "'I truly am Beatrice / How did you dare approach that mountain? Do you not know that here man lives in joy?' / I lowered my eyes to the clear water. / But when I saw myself reflected, *I drew them back / toward the grass*, such shame weighed on my brow." (Dante 2003, XXX, lines 73–78; emphasis mine).

116. Belting 2006, 15, 22, 26, 29.

tation [*daß es in der Darstellung zur Darstellung kommt*]. . . . By being presented it experiences, as it were, an *increase in being* [*einen Zuwachs an Sein*]."[117] That Alberti should have seized on the mythical figure of Narcissus as the embodiment of modern pictorial realism reveals the extent to which *De Pictura* has lost sight of the basic difference between image and mirror, between the medium that actively "presents" (*darstellen*) a meaningful subject and *pictura* as but a facsimile of the visible object.

Related to this constellation and especially germane to our purposes is a second motif in *De Pictura*, namely, Alberti's advice on painting the human face. It, too, is approached as but a "composition of . . . surfaces large and small" (II.35). Again, what dominates is a quest for three-dimensionality, a pictorial simulation of sculpture-like effects that Alberti had found exemplified by Donatello's bronze *stiacciato* reliefs, such as his *Feast of Herod* (1427) in the Siena Baptistery (fig. 4.6). The real presence of the human face, and the possibility of the image mediating a person whose gaze has the potential to arrest and transform the beholder, has been subordinated to the narrative exigencies of *istoria*. On Nicholas's account, the gaze of the Christ icon enfolds the contemplative viewer in love: "Where Your eye is present Your love is also present. . . . Your seeing is loving" (*VD* 4:11). Indeed, the contemplative gaze is itself drawn forth by the icon's seeing: "I look most attentively only unto You (You never turning the eyes of my mind away), because You embrace me with a steadfast look [*quia tu me continua vision amplecteris*]" (*VD* 4:12). By contrast, Alberti takes meaning to be objectively and dramatically realized only *within* the image rather than arising from the beholder's interaction with it. Spectatorial rather than relational in kind, meaning in *De Pictura* inheres strictly in the *sensation* of verisimilitude rather than at the level of contemplation and reflection. It is less achieved than confirmed by the beholder who judges a painting based on its conformity with everyday spatiotemporal perception. For his part, Nicholas takes the Christ icon to model an absolute presence, at once exclusive to each being and encompassing of all: "You who are the Absolute Being of all things [*absolutum esse omnium*] are present to each thing as if You were concerned about no other thing at all" (*VD* 4:10). In this metaphysical framework, true agency rests with the icon, which thus precludes anything like the quest for perspectival dominion that fuels Alberti's representationalism.

Unsurprisingly, *De Pictura* consistently foregrounds the image's formal and spatial contiguity with the world it aims to capture by means of geometric perspective. Rejecting the iconic, frontal presentation of the face in Italo-Byzantine images and demurring at that style's "excessive use of gold" (II.49), Alberti voices a strong preference for relief-like spatial effects: "In painting I would praise . . . those faces which seem to stand out from the pictures as if they were sculpted" (II.46). Both remarks

117. Gadamer 2006, 135.

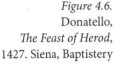

Figure 4.6.
Donatello,
The Feast of Herod,
1427. Siena, Baptistery

attest to Alberti's concern with safeguarding pictorial illusion against being ruptured by the conspicuous two-dimensionality and liberal use of gold so characteristic of the Italo-Byzantine style. Yet this older tradition of applying gold leaf to depictions of Christ and the saints was meant to underscore the icon's proximity to the relic, thereby reinforcing its status as an object of veneration rather than a product of human ingenuity. Moreover, the icon's "coat of gold and jewels expressed the mentality of an agrarian society under feudal rule, in which gold was valued not merely as an item of exchange but as an expression of power and prestige."[118] In contrast, for Alberti the human face is assumed to share in the same spatiotemporal order as any other being, including its beholder. It has become an object inter alia, indeed a simulacrum, and, as such, it lacks all transformative, spiritual agency. No longer looking back at the beholder, the painted face instead is conceived as a particular arrangement of colored planes where "grace and beauty must above all be sought" (II.35). As such, it is but one more instance of human physiology, the body that throughout *De Pictura* furnishes the Protagoran "natural measure" for the proper calibration of single-viewpoint, linear perspective.[119]

---

118. Belting 1994, 301–2; see also Harries 2001, 84–85.

119. Harries 2001, 75; Alberti's "painter reduces experience to momentary, monocular vision and places us on a flat earth. The perspectival art of Alberti subjects what it presents to a human measure that has itself been subjected to the demand for ease of representation" (77).

"SEEING AND BEING-SEEN COINCIDE":
VISUAL CATECHESIS AND COMMUNION IN *DE VISIONE DEI*

Returning to Nicholas of Cusa, we find his *De Visione Dei* not only participating in a complex debate over the nature of mystic contemplation but also taking up the status of the (painted) image and the competing intentionalities to which it may give rise: Is it to be construed as an artifact (*pictura*) wrought by human ingenuity and fostering a presumption (or illusion?) of total control over finite, three-dimensional space? Or ought we to think of the image instead as a medium giving rise to a contemplative vision where one's seeing unveils one's being-seen by God, respectively? In pondering these matters, Nicholas reveals his deep-seated Neoplatonic allegiances, already hinted at in the alternate titles of his 1453 treatise. Variously referred to as *De Visione Dei* or as *De icona*, the treatise (in evident contrast to Alberti's *De Pictura*) frames the icon as instituting and shaping a transcendent vision. Even so, Nicholas does not reject outright the modern conception of the image as a man-made "object." Rather, he insists that the image is by definition more than, indeed is ontologically distinct from, the contingent deliverances of empirical sight. It does not simulate quotidian perception or simply mirror empirically visible being. Conversely, the icon does not purport to represent the ("as yet") invisible God any more than it means to negate outright the telos of the *visio Dei*. Whereas Alberti unequivocally states that "the painter is not concerned with things that are not visible" (II.36), Nicholas's icon is specifically and uniquely designed to lead its beholder into the "absolute darkness" of God, the *non-Other* (*non aliud*).[120] As noted before, Nicholas, unlike the Romantic-era Platonism of Schelling's *Bruno* or Coleridge's *Philosophical Lectures*, does not conceive of God's transcendent darkness as diametrically opposed to, let alone as negating, the immanent order of the visible. Rather, the *non aliud* of the Cusan God encompasses all binaries, including those of the visible and the invisible, the finite many and the transcendent One.

When approached as the conduit toward a mental vision that transcends, but does not negate, the visible world, Nicholas's icon first and foremost enjoins its beholder to engage in spiritual and intellectual self-examination. Whereas Alberti's painting (*pictura*) abides within a matrix of anthropomorphic and potentially narcissistic "sight," Nicholas's icon mediates the ontologically distinct yet analogically related orders of the visible and the invisible. Hence the true telos of mental vision is self-recognition, not self-affirmation, contemplative thinking rather than naturalistic mirroring. As Nicholas writes elsewhere, "Plato is said to have painted [*pinxisse*]

120. For Alberti "only that remains invisible which has not yet been rendered sufficiently visible" (Belting 2006, 13).

now and then, which, we believe, he would never have done if it was detrimental to thinking [*nisi quia speculatione non adversabatur*]" (*IM* 1:54).[121] Thinking, he insists, truly comes into its own only in this speculative sense, namely, as the mind's motion toward self-transcendence, rather than as conceptually predetermined ("interested") computation. So understood, thinking not only is compatible with pictorialization, as Plato had already conceded, but its ascending movement unfolds as a dialectic between absolute and contracted (perspectival) vision.

Central to that dialectic is the constant quest of finite, "contracted" sight to surpass itself in the contemplation of the source that has brought forth and forever sustains all contingent, visible being. Hence, if mental sight seeks to "encompass all modes of seeing . . . in such a way that it encompasses each mode" (*VD* 2:8), such "absolute sight" (*absoluta visio*) must not be construed as some distant and likely unattainable telos. On the contrary, it is the *conditio sine qua non* for all contingent, empirical sight: "all contracted sight exists through Absolute Sight and cannot at all exist without it" (*VD* 2:8). For in the absence of divine being, finite sight would have nothing to see: "You are present to each and every thing—just as *being*, without which things cannot exist, is present to each and every thing" (*VD* 2:10). Whatever concept of image and vision one espouses reveals first and foremost one's "natural attitude" (Husserl's *natürliche Einstellung*) toward the unconditional givenness of creation. It opens up a sphere of intuitive "knowing [*Wissen*] that has nothing of conceptual thinking in it and only changes into a clear intuiting when attention is turned toward [it], and even then only partially and mostly in a very imperfect manner."[122]

Nicholas here extends arguments first developed in his earlier, short treatise *On Seeking God* (*De Quaerendo Deum*) from 1445. As he points out there, we must not misconstrue the operation of a given sense as having been "caused" by the object that that sense uniquely apprehends. Thus, sight delivers our sensation of colors but is not itself "found in the visible world." Rather, sight as such belongs to the order of *invisibilia*, and "no name among all the names that can be named in the realm [of visible things] befits sight" (*QD* 1:22). Precisely because it is able to convey to us a particular kind of *awareness* (of sensible things), any given sense already surpasses the order of the sensible. Hence, sight (*visus*) cannot itself be grasped in terms of visualization of particular forms and colors, just as the intellect "is not found in the realm of rational things, for the intellect is as the eye, and rational things are as colors" (*QD* 1:25). Each sense furnishes, as Kant will later put it, a particular condition of possibility for our knowledge of a sensible object. As such, in their joint operation our multiple senses do not generate a welter of disjointed data. On the contrary, they unveil the spatiotemporal identity of a given appearance and, in their synthetic, integrative operation, affirm its reality as *one* thing, not many. The new desk made of pine found in my office *smells* of resin; its coat of varnish still *feels* moist; the drawer underneath it *sounds* hollow when I knock against it; and I *see* the same desk as being of a light golden-brown. The deliverances of each sense thus are a priori and integrally ordered toward "a unified sensorium [*ad sensum communem*]" (*QD* 1:24), which is to say, they must be understood as acts of intelligence rather than as wholly disjointed data.

As Garth Green has shown, Nicholas "inherits and synthesizes the Aristotelian doctrine of the common sense (*sensus communis*) and inner senses (*sensus interiores*) with the Origenist doctrine of the spiritual senses (*sensus spirituales*)." Whereas Aquinas had rejected the very notion of a "spiritual sense" in the way that Origen had posited it in *Contra Celsum* (1.48), Nicholas's theological aesthetics synthesizes the "double inheritance" of the Origenist-Augustinian view, which holds that spiritual knowledge is possible independent of sensible particulars, and the Aristotelian-Thomist view, according to which all human intellect arises from concrete sensible particulars. Yet rather than posit "a second, spiritual sensorium" alongside empirical cognition, Nicholas uncovers "a hidden theological significance within the shadows of the physical sensorium."[123] His point of departure for such a synthesis is provided by Aristotle's stipulation that the five senses do not simply operate in isolation, but, instead, draw on "a common sensibility [*aisthēsis koinē*] which enables us to perceive them non-incidentally."[124] The point is brought home when, at the start of *De Quaerendo Deum*, Nicholas notes that a supersensible dimension inheres in the very etymology of the Greek word for "seeing." As he observes, when St. Paul in his letters refers to God as *Theos*, he was clearly not identifying God's essence, which is categorically impossible. Rather, "*Theos* is the name of God only insofar as God is sought, by human beings, in this world." As it turns out, such spiritual and intellectual seeking is etymologically coded into the sensible act of seeing; for *Theos*, the name for God, "is derived from *theoro*, which means 'I see' and 'I hasten.' . . . Therefore, the seeker ought to hasten by means of sight [*currere igitur debet quaerens per visum*], so that he can attain unto God, who sees all things" (*QD* 1:19).

As the source of light, God at once enables and elicits sight, for "light is a medium between spiritual natures and material natures. . . . [It] brings forms [*figurae*] to sight, so that in this way the form [*forma*] of the sensible world ascends unto reason and unto the intellect and, by means of the intellect, attains its end in God" (*QD* 2:37). Light is not a contingent, material appearance, the *lux corporealis* "whose opposite is darkness." Rather, it is the ontological condition for both being and appearance. Nicholas calls it the "most simple and infinite light, in which darkness is infinite

---

123. Green 2012, 210–14.
124. Aristotle 1984, 1:676 (*De Anima* III, 425a28).

light [*infinita lux*] . . . and that this infinite light always shines in the darkness of our ignorance [*semper lucet in tenebris nostrae ignorantiae*] but the darkness cannot comprehend it (*DI* I:86). An Aristotelian-Thomist epistemology grounded in sensible particulars thus is nested within a Platonist teleological framework. In time, though, Nicholas will take a more critical view of Aristotle and, in his later writings, will foreground the Platonist framework as the only one truly capable of elucidating spiritual (mystical) vision as positively arising from (though never opposed to) sensible knowledge.[125] Sensation cannot be reduced to a causal relationship between finite entities and finite human agents; for its phenomenology reveals how, by dint of such materially concrete acts of visual experience, "we are drawn unto the unknown God . . . who cannot be apprehended in any other way than by His revealing Himself. Moreover, He wills to be sought [*quaeri vult*]" (*QD* 3:39). Precisely because spiritual vision is teleologically embedded in empirical sight, to see, properly speaking, means to prevent the idolatrous proclivities of empirical perception from yeilding to a form of Augustinian *curiositas*, which in contrast to legitimate studiousness is intent on appropriating and dominating its visible objects.[126] For like any fantasy of total possession such seeing inexorably ends up negating the reality of what is seen and, consequently, can never issue in genuine "thinking" (*speculatio*).

  If seeing is to be understood not only as conducive to thinking but also as positively instantiating thought, eye and mind must let themselves be guided by the visible rather than seeking to consume it. Hence, mental vision precisely does *not* negate or simply overleap the realm of empirical, visible things. Rather, in a sense much later echoed by Heidegger's notion of "equanimity" (*Gelassenheit*), such vision unfolds in sympathetic communion *with* the visible. Such a "simple and relaxed" stance neither rejects the methods devised by human epistemic curiosity nor allows the subject to become enslaved to them. Rather, it ensures our openness to what at once pervades technology and is hidden by it. The "equanimity vis-à-vis things" (*Gelassenheit zu den Dingen*) that defines the contemplative intellect does not reject em-

---

125. See *De Beryllo* (1458), where Nicholas critiques Aristotle's disjunctive approach, which prevents him from admitting that "a coincidence of contraries . . . precedes duality. But out of fear of admitting that contraries are present at the same time in the same thing," Aristotle ended up "posit[ing] in matter a certain inchoateness of forms. . . . For this reason, all those philosophers [*hoc omne philosophi*]"—a description that surely includes Aristotle's Dominican heirs—"failed to arrive at the Spirit, who is the Beginning-of-Union [*principium connexionis*]," whereas "the Platonists did so" (*DB* 26:41).

126. See Augustine, *Conf.* 10.35.54; and his pointed quote of "the lust of the eyes" (*concupiscientia oculorum / hē epithumia tōn ophthalmōn*) (1 Jn 2:16). As Paul Griffiths notes, "The deepest contrast between curiosity and studiousness has to do with the kind of world that the seeker for and professor of each inhabits. The curious inhabit a world of objects, which can be sequestered and possessed; the studious inhabit a world of gifts, given things, which can be known by participation, but which, because of their very natures, can never be possessed" (2009, 22).

pirical sight and the techniques aimed at enhancing and controlling the visibility of things. Instead, it is precisely within the Aristotelian-Thomist domain of concrete, sense-based perception and the techniques devised for the refinement of the "data" resulting from it that Nicholas locates the point of departure for a mystical vision. In strikingly similar language, Heidegger's *Gelassenheit* thus is characterized by our "stand[ing] at once within the realm of that which hides itself from us, and hides itself just in approaching us." It is the "realm of mystery" (*Geheimnis*); and what Nicholas calls contemplative (mental) vision involves precisely this "stance [*Haltung*] . . . which enables us to keep open to the meaning hidden in technology, *openness to the mystery*" (*Offenheit für das Geheimnis*).[127]

For "seeing" (*visio*) to be more than sight, without thereby negating it, it must *face* Being rather than dominate it. It is this "facing" that the icon enclosed with Nicholas's treatise seeks to model for the Tegernsee brethren: "I stand before the image of Your Face, my God—an image which I behold with sensible eyes. And I attempt to view with inner eyes the truth which is pointed to by the painting [*oculis interioribus intueri veritatem, que in pictura signatur*]" (*VD* 10:40). Mental vision, it must be stressed again, is not the negation of "bodily sight" but its typological fulfillment. Thus, when affirming that "the invisible Truth of Your face I see not with the bodily eyes which look at this icon of You but with mental and intellectual eyes [*sed mentalibus et intellectualibus oculis*]" (*VD* 6:19), Nicholas is establishing a distinction, not an opposition. For his iconic model of seeing as *facing* premises that the "object" seen is not constituted by our sight but anterior to it. In seeing and attending to it, we thus come face-to-face with a reality that has all along awaited our turning towards it: "Your eyes are always upon me" and "You never close Your eyes" (*VD* 5:17, 15). The finite subject's "contracted" gaze thus is but a belated and necessarily incomplete response elicited by God's timeless presence: "Your seeing is Your working" (*VD* 5:18).

Two aspects of Nicholas's treatise still remain to be considered. First, there is his repeated characterization of sight as a specular event, with the (mental) image functioning like a mirror of sorts. Yet in contrast to Alberti's anthropocentric and self-referential gaze, Nicholas maintains that specular and finite sight, far from granting the beholder unilateral and total dominion over a field of vision, alerts her to its partial and incomplete nature: "For the eye is like a mirror; and a mirror, however small, figuratively receives into itself [*figurative recipiat*] a large mountain and all that is on the surface of the mountain. . . . Nevertheless, by means of the mirroring eye our sight sees only and particularly that to which it turns; for the power of the eye can be

---

127. Heidegger elaborates on this concept of *Gelassenheit* in his eponymous 1955 memorial lecture at his native Meßkirch; quotes from Heidegger 2014, 22–24 (German); and 1966, 54–55 (emphasis mine).

determined by the object only in a particular way" (*VD* 8:32). The epistemological humility voiced in that last phrase implicitly repudiates Alberti's model of the eye as an autonomous and unfettered agent asserting unconditional ownership over all visible, external reality. For Nicholas, "contracted" sight is instead the medium enabling the finite human individual to participate in the Triune God mirrored in all creation: "I presently contemplate eternal life in a mirror, an icon, a symbolism [*in speculo, in eicona, in aenigmate*], because eternal life is only Your blessed gaze, by which You never cease looking upon me most lovingly" (*VD* 4:13). Never merely a volitional and anthropomorphic occurrence, human sight rests on the metaphysical presupposition of God's continuous presence, which alone guarantees the formal reality of *what* is seen and, thus, ensures that empirical sight (as opposed to mindless gazing) can participate in the real, that is, issue in knowledge: "Your seeing is Your being. I exist because You look upon me. And if You were to withdraw Your countenance from me, I would not at all continue to exist" (*VD* 4:11). In God, then, "seeing and being-seen coincide."[128]

Still, being by its very nature always incomplete and prone to distortion, finite sight can never outright merge with God's absolute vision. Situated on an ontologically distinct plane, the "contracted" gaze instead finds its own spiritual condition mirrored back by God's face. The fulfillment of the finite gaze and the mental images it yields does not issue in symbolic or cognitive dominion over the realm of visible things but, rather, in a moment of spiritual self-recognition. For "whoever looks angrily unto You will find Your Face likewise to display anger. Whoever looks unto You joyfully will find Your face likewise to be joyous. . . . For just as the bodily eye, in looking through a red glass, judges as red whatever it sees, and as green whatever it sees if looking through a green glass, so each mental eye, cloaked with contraction and affection, judges You . . . according to the nature of the contraction and the affection" (*VD* 6:20). In a lengthy apostrophe toward the end of his treatise, Nicholas recapitulates the entire economy of empirical sight and mental vision.

> My God, when You seem to me as if You were formable prime matter, because You receive the form of each one who looks unto You, You elevate me, so that I discern the following: viz., that the one who looks unto You does not bestow form upon You; rather, he beholds himself in You, because he receives from You that which he is. And so, that which You seem to receive from the one who looks unto You—this You bestow, as if You were a living Mirror-of-eternity [*speculum*

---

128. *VD* 10, ¶ 43; see also *Theological Complement*, 14. As de Certeau (1987, 8) notes, in Nicholas's texts, the mirror functions as "the instrument for the passing (*transsumptio*) from one kind of 'seeing' to the other. Mounted inside the texts, . . . the mirror is to the visual what the illuminatory 'word' is to the verbal."

aeternitatis vivum], which is the Form of forms. When someone looks into this Mirror, he sees his own form in the Form of forms, which the Mirror is. And he judges the form [*iudicat formam*] seen in the Mirror to be the image [*esse figuram*] of his own form, because such would be the case with regard to a polished material mirror. However, the contrary thereof is true, because in the Mirror of eternity that which he sees is not an image but is the Truth, of which the beholder is the image [*quia id quod videt in illo aeternitatis speculo non est figura sed veritas, cuius ipse videns est figura*]. Therefore, in You, my God, the image is the Truth and Exemplar of each and every thing that exists or can exist. (*VD* 15:67)

"Image" (*figura*) here does not stand for an artifact on the order of Alberti's *pictura* but for a mediating agency that positively transforms the beholder ("You elevate me"); it transfigures the beholder, enabling him to grasp his true being for the first time ("he receives from You that which he is") and to achieve spiritual self-recognition by "judg[ing] the form seen in the Mirror to be the image [*esse figuram*] of his own form."

At the heart of Nicholas's reflections here is a twofold reversal: the icon is recognized as a "mirror" (*speculum*), and the spectator is reconstituted as the "image" (*figura*) reflected back onto himself by the icon-mirror.[129] To be sure, Nicholas's characterization of the icon as a mirror cannot be taken literally. Yet neither is it simply a rhetorical conceit. Instead, it attests to the icon's distinctive ontology. We recall Gadamer's incisive account of the image (*Bild*) as situated "halfway between . . . *pure indication* [*Verweisung*: also, "reference"], which is the essence of the sign, and *pure substitution* [*Vertreten*], which is the essence of the symbol." By its very nature, an image always exceeds the sign's strictly referential function. Even so, like the sign, an image "must first draw attention to itself. It must be striking." Yet unlike the sign, the image "does not disappear in pointing to something else but, in its own being, shares in what it represents [*hat in seinem eigenen Sein teil an dem, was es abbildet*]." As Gadamer continues:

> a picture points to what it represents [*Verweisung auf das Dargestellte*] only through its own content. By concentrating on it, we too come into contact with what is represented. The picture points by causing us to linger over it [*indem es verweilen läßt*], for . . . its ontological valence consists in not being absolutely different from what it represents but sharing in its being. We saw that what is

---

129. See Hoff (2013, 122), who notes how Nicholas's patristic image of the "living mirror (*speculum vivum*) . . . invert[s] the anthropocentrism of Alberti's proto-modern account of perspective perception."

represented comes into its own in the picture [*das Dargestellte kommt im Bilde zu sich selbst*]. It experiences an increase in being [*Seinszuwachs*]. But that means that it is there in the picture itself.[130]

We can accept Gadamer's account and apply it to Nicholas's discussion of the icon, albeit with this crucial qualification: being a mirror, the image yielded by the icon always also reflects the beholder himself. For it is he, not Christ, who stands to undergo "an increase in being." Hence, Gadamer's observation that, notwithstanding other crucial differences, the image to an extent retains the referential function of the sign (*Zeichen*) needs to be amended. For insofar as it transforms the beholder's spiritual being, Nicholas's icon constitutes a "holy sign." Its function is essentially sacramental, not naturalistic, in that it unveils a real presence rather than furnishing a mimetic representation. As such, "the Trinitarian mirror and its created image cannot relate to each other like two mutually reflexive principles that determine each other dialectically." Rather, "the absolute mirror remains unaffected by the temporal change of creation . . . because the eternal image of the triune God *is* already everything that the creation actualizes through temporal change."[131]

Nicholas's icon, then, is neither confined to the realm of finite, historical existence nor does it purport to transcend that domain outright. Instead, while materially concrete and formally specific in its presentation, the icon also participates within a divine, sacramental economy and, as such, renders that economy visible. The point can be clarified by juxtaposing Nicholas's icon to Walter Benjamin's conception of the dialectical image, which opens access to a timeless moment in which the totality of historically determinate existence congeals and effectively surpasses itself. As Benjamin writes, the dialectical image "is that wherein what has been comes together in a flash with the now to form a constellation. In other words, image is dialectics at a standstill." It would be a mistake, however, to read Benjamin's claim that dialectical "images not only . . . belong to a particular time" but also "attain legibility only at a particular time" as affirmation of a strictly historicist and immanent viewpoint. In fact, much to the distress of his more orthodox Marxist friends, Benjamin understands dialectics as fundamentally ordered toward the revelation of *transcendent*, not historically contingent, meanings. Hence, the image at the fulcrum of this dialectic cannot be reduced to a coefficient of the historical forces attendant on its origination. In fact, "while the relation of the present to the past is purely temporal, the relation of what-has-been to the now is dialectical: not temporal in nature but figural [*bildlich*]." The true locus of the image, for Benjamin no less than for Nicholas

---

130. Gadamer 2006, 145–46.
131. Hoff 2013, 122–23.

of Cusa, is neither determined by purely historical and material forces nor does it fall altogether outside of history. Rejecting as wholly incommensurable an antinomian view of immanence and transcendence, which he finds exemplified in German Romanticism, Benjamin bluntly states that a "resolute refusal of the concept of 'timeless truth' is in order."[132] Still, what prompts this rejection is not some doctrinaire Marxist-historicist framework but, rather, a pointedly Messianic conception wherein the dialectical image marks the irruption of Truth into the order of immanent life, as happens in a "flash" or "caesura in thought." Made manifest through a serendipitous "constellation" of historical forces and tensions even as it transcends them, Benjamin's concept of truth bears conspicuous resemblance to the Christian idea of grace—unpredictably revealed, not claimed, a gift, not an achievement, requiring endless hermeneutic patience and commitment for its import to be discerned.

Though Nicholas does not operate with an explicit concept of historical time, his view of the image's revelatory entwining of finitude and transcendence, the visible and the invisible, resonates with Benjamin's conceptual schema. Understood as a holy sign, Nicholas's icon situates the act of beholding within the order of "liturgical action," which in turn "requires a community in which to exist." To be in the presence of such a holy sign, or icon, thus shows that the experience of grace—where "seeing and being-seen coincide" (*VD* 10:44)—is essentially liturgical and communal: "Grace is not just the most intimate inwardness of a single individual in which all other persons have no place." Rather, it involves "a genuine opening of the individual to the demands of existence with others and as a whole."[133] The icon's spiritual transformation of the individual beholder thus cannot be separated from its liturgical and communal dimension. We recall how in his instructions to the Tegernsee brethren Nicholas had intimated the icon's capacity for bringing about *communio* insofar as it prompts each beholder to compare his visual experience with his fellow monk. It creates a community of trust. Having learned that the "icon's gaze moves continually with" each beholder, "he will believe his fellow-monk" (*VD* Introd.: 4). Insofar as contemplation of the icon gives rise to a liturgical community, it implicitly works against the establishment of an idolatrous gaze. Moreover, not only does "the gaze of the other exclude the possession of an image," but it catechizes the individual into embracing, and understanding himself as properly constituted by, a spiritual community: "The itinerary of a single silent man pursued by [the icon's] gaze is transformed into the genesis of an association."[134]

Meanwhile, the spiritual deepening experienced by each individual beholder also explains why, when remarking on the icon's capacity for inducing self-

---

132. Benjamin 1999, 462–63 (Convolute N2a,3; and N3,1–2).
133. Ratzinger 1987, 48.
134. De Certeau 1987, 18–19.

recognition, Nicholas's preferred term is *figura* rather than *imago*. Thus, insofar as the beholder recognizes his spiritual being as positively constituted by the icon's gaze, he will learn to take measure of the distance between the self-image with which he approached the icon and the fuller being that he will become as a result of having contemplated it. *Figura*, then, names this distance between our temporal being and its spiritual fulfillment; and it is Nicholas's contention that only mystical contemplation is capable of bridging that distance. Not coincidentally, his sharp juxtaposition, in the passage quoted above, of *figura* and *veritas* aligns rather precisely with an argument famously developed in Erich Auerbach's eponymous essay on *figura*. As Auerbach there notes, in pre-Christian, Roman thought, *figura* almost exclusively denotes tangible, three-dimensional objects—sculptures, buildings, and so forth—or, perhaps, a visual duplicate of them. Thus, in Ovid, the word evidently means a "copy," and, similarly, in Vitruvius it tends to signify "an architectural and three-dimensional shape or, at most, the copy or outline of such a shape." So far, then, *figura* does not yet carry any "sense of illusion or transformation." Even as a semantic shift of sorts "from form to portrait" begins to announce itself in Pliny's *Natural History* (ch. 35), the truly momentous change is only wrought by early patristic theology.[135] Rejecting Marcion's Gnostic opposition between the ineffable *demiourgos* believed to have wrought of visible, material being and the god who will redeem that creation, Tertullian specifically deploys *figura* as prophesying the ultimate reconciliation of the two realms.

Hence, even as it remains forever distinct from truth (*veritas*), *figura* in Tertullian's writings no longer stands in outright conflict with it. Instead, as a complex event or text demanding patient exegesis, *figura* positively anticipates its own, numinous fulfillment, and eschatological Truth. Hence, for Tertullian, "shadowy similarities in the structure of events . . . are often enough to make the *figura* recognizable." Emphasizing Tertullian's "realism," which he contrasts with Origen's spiritualism, Auerbach notes how in order for the spiritual significance of material, visible realities to come into view, the latter must not be discredited as merely apparitional or "shadowy" beings. The realm of *figura* is never one of mere semblance but, instead, prefigures Truth. As Tertullian had noted, far from being unreal, "carnal things always come first as examples of things spiritual [*qua semper carnalia in figuram spiritualium antecedent*]."[136] Taking a further, crucial step, Augustine clarifies that anagogical (prefigurative) meaning does not supersede, let alone invalidate, the image's material foundation. Far from betraying the spiritual meaning encoded in it, a "true" image always prepares the formal and material ground for a process of ongoing, spiritual cognition. That is, when considered in its specific modality as *figura*, the

135. Auerbach 2014, 74, 78–79.
136. Quoted in Auerbach 2014, 82.

icon safeguards hermeneutic practice against any idolatrous collapsing of the visible image with its transcendent referent.

Conversely, *figura* also precludes demoting the image to a merely abstract (allegorical) sign that nowise shares *in* but merely points *to* ineffable, transcendent being. Both visibly and intelligibly, that is, *figura* is the phenomenological correlate of what patristic and Scholastic writing understand by intercession or mediation.[137] It claims no separate being for itself but, instead, unfolds both intuitively and intellectually how material being, though infinitely dissimilar from divine being, nevertheless participates in it. Discussing Revelation 20:10, Augustine in *De Civitate Dei* notes that "when this world passes away, this will not come about by the utter destruction of things, but by their transformation [*mutatione namque rerum non omni modo interitu, transibit hic mundus*]. This is why the apostle [1 Cor 7:31 f.] says: 'For the figure of this world passeth away. . . . It is, then, the figure, not the nature, that passeth away.'"[138] The relation between *figura* and Truth, in turn, is sustained by the literal-historical meaning of the event or text that is being scrutinized with regard to its prophetic potential. All three—*littera, figura*, and *veritas*—thus constitute a single reality seen from different perspectives. As Auerbach puts it, if "*historia* . . . is the literal meaning or the event to which it refers, *figura* is the same meaning or event, but seen from the perspective of the future fulfillment hidden within it, and this fulfillment is *veritas*, or truth." Hence, *figura* fundamentally differs from the "magical powers" ascribed to the symbol: "*Figura* must always be historical."[139]

This takes us to the second and final point to be considered. Crucially, the very possibility of *figura* and figural exegesis, which following their consolidation in Augustine's writings would shape exegesis and epistemology for the next millennium in the West, presupposes an ontological link between temporal being and divine eternity, between history and metaphysics. Considering the lasting impact of fourteenth-century Nominalism on subsequent philosophical theology, Nicholas stands out for, among other things, his embrace of a metaphysic of *analogia* developed in particularly incisive ways in his later work. This analogical framework posits "that the world is itself invested with meaning, ethical purpose, and intelligibility, of which it cannot be rationally divested. . . . However, the world invested with such meaning, purpose, and intelligibility is itself suggestive of a higher and more mysterious, Logos, or

---

137. On this claim, see ch. 2 above, 145–84.

138. Augustine 1998, 998 (XX, 14).

139. Auerbach 2014, 91, 99. See also Freedberg (1989), who in his otherwise sympathetic account of Gadamer's concept of the image criticizes him for momentarily lapsing "into the usual prejudice of associating what he called 'picture magic' with the prehistory of the picture." Crucial for Freedberg is to guard against investing images with "magical" powers—less a coherent position than a concession that we have left behind intellectual argument for purely affective claims—while at the same time acknowledging "the supernatural effectiveness of images" (80).

reason, that underlies the creation and has given it being out of love."[140] That said, linking Nicholas with a metaphysics of *analogia* requires some additional explanation. To begin with, only a handful of explicit references to the notion of *analogia* can be found in Nicholas's oeuvre. Moreover, given that many of his writings espouse a holistic metaphysics of Being with distinctly Neoplatonist underpinnings, one might well suppose that Nicholas's thought is fundamentally at odds with the concept of *analogia*. Yet on closer inspection this turns out not to be the case. To begin with, we find Nicholas time and again appraising all creaturely being as the "unfolding" (*explicatio*) or "contraction" (*contractio*) of the triune God. Hence, created (contingent) being becomes intelligible only (and precisely) insofar as it participates in absolute Being, even as it remains ontologically distinct from the latter due to its temporal and "contracted" appearance. The very concept of participation thus rests on a metaphysics of analogy that mediates and harmonizes the two orders of being.[141] Precisely because the *non aliud* of absolute Being is the source of finite, "contracted" existence, it can never be outright incommensurable with finite being, even as it remains forever ontologically distinct from it. Ultimately, it is only with the Christian concept of the *analogia entis* that the ontological presupposition of the Platonist-Neoplatonist idea of participation came to be fully worked out.

In Nicholas's early work, the concept of analogy surfaces in the more restricted, Scholastic sense of an *analogia proportionalis*, that is, as a quantitative "proportionality" between divine (absolute) knowledge and the finite, "contracted" scope of the human intellect. Yet even then, the objective is never speculatively to *infer* God from finite beings as apprehended by the human intellect. Rather, Nicholas seeks "to understand the nature and operation of the intellectual soul [*Geist-seele*] as an *image of God* in light of an antecedent intuition of God."[142] Knowledge of God is never of the order of a methodical extrapolation, logical inference, or syllogistic conclusion. Hence, as early as in his 1440 treatise *On Learned Ignorance*, Nicholas distinguishes between a purely mathematical concept of analogy as quantitative proportionality and the metaphysical concept of an "analogy of participation" (*analogia participationis*) linking created and divine being.[143] As he notes, "because the infinite escapes all proportion, the infinite as infinite is unknown. But since proportion expresses agreement in some one point and also expresses otherness, it cannot be understood from

---

140. White 2011, 27. What the ontological framework of *analogia* categorically excludes is the possibility that visible being could intelligibly manifest itself without being indexed to an anterior concept of form. Not until the scientific revolution of the seventeenth century did such a "rendering accidental the relation of each thing to its own form" become conceivable (Hanby 2013, 355).

141. Haubst 1991, 233.

142. Ibid., 237.

143. It bears pointing out that several centuries later this very distinction will resurface in Kant's account of the mathematical and dynamic sublime; see *Critique of Judgment*, §§ 25–29.

number" (*DI* 1:3). All finite, particular, and quantifiable being thus remains on-tologically distinct from divine being, which alone exhibits absolute unity and for that reason must also never be treated as a numerical concept.[144] As Nicholas had argued early on, "Unity, or *ōntas* so to speak, comes from the Greek *ōn*, which in Latin is called *ens*, and unity is, as it were, being [*Et est unitas quasi entitas*]. In fact, God is the being of things, for God is the form of being [*forma essendi*] and therefore is being [*entitas*]" (*DI* I:22). There being "no proportion between the infinite and the finite, . . . a finite intellect cannot precisely attain the truth of things by means of like-ness" (*DI* 1:9–10).

That being so, the question naturally arises, what would justify claiming an ana-logical relation between two realms already described as ontologically (or "infi-nitely") distinct? After all, how can we claim that "every image seems to be a likeness of its exemplar" if, at the same time, we concede that "there is no image so similar or so equal to its exemplar but that it could be *infinitely* more similar or more equal" (*DI* I:30; emphasis mine)? Does the theological postulate of analogy in the face of "infi-nite" dissimilarity not merely obfuscate an absolute chasm separating the image from its archetype, "contracted" being from divine *Unitas*? The resolution of this formal-logical tension has to be found in a phenomenological account of how finite, visible being is experienced, which is to say, in Nicholas's Platonist concept of participation. As so often, it is pseudo-Dionysius who points the way, such as in this key pas-sage from *On the Divine Names*, also quoted by Nicholas: "We cannot know God in his nature. . . . But we know him from the arrangement of everything, because every-thing is, in a sense, projected out from him, and this order [*diataxeōs*] possesses cer-tain images [*eikonas*] and semblances [*homoiōmata*] of his divine paradigms."[145] To be sure, "divine oneness is identity, that is impartible, inexplicable, and—as it is [in itself]—unattainable [*inattingibilem*]" (*DC* 11:54). To suppose that the intellect, through the operation of its senses, may participate in God's "inexplicable identity" becomes a defensible claim only if we understand the finite agent to have no sepa-rate, let alone anterior being *apart from such participation*. Being constituted by God's absolute sight, all human, "contracted" perception is possible and intelligible only as a response to the former; as Nicholas puts it, "Created minds do not receive into themselves the ray of Divine Light as if by their nature they *preceded* their par-taking [of the Divine Light]. Rather, the intellect's partaking of that unimpartible, most actual Light [*incommunicabilis ipsius actualissimae lucis*] *constitutes* the [re-spective] quiddity of created minds. Therefore, the actuality of our intelligence con-sists in its partaking of the Divine Intellect" (*DC* 11:56).

---

144. Paraphrasing Augustine (*De Trinitate* 6.7), Nicholas remarks that "when you begin to count the Trinity you depart from the truth" (*DI* 1:57).

145. Pseudo-Dionysius 1987, 108 (*DN* VII:3; *PG* 869d).

Not only, then, is the finite agent's participation in divine oneness mediated by the senses; but the fact that in a given instance of perception our various sense data are synthetically configured as pertaining to *the same* object also implies a distinct intellect whose operation is not contingent on such data but, on the contrary, constitutes an anterior, "common sensibility [*aisthēsis koinē*]," as Aristotle had formulated it. Hence, Nicholas also distinguishes between the essentially intellectual nature of sight (*visio*) and its contingent instantiation as a perceptual act (*visus*): "Sight is partaken differently by various acts-of-sight, just as, also, the diversity of the acts-of-sight is contained concordantly in the oneness of absolute sight [*visio absoluta*]" (*DC* 11:55).

At first glance, Nicholas's perspectival theory would seem to echo Alberti's account of a linear, single-viewpoint perspective. For our capacity to apprehend visible being is necessarily defined by our unique line of sight. Yet as Nicholas is quick to point out, precisely this awareness of our perspectival situation leads us to acknowledge "the defect that characterizes the falling away from preciseness," that is, from absolute sight. Self-enclosed, perspectival vision is not something to be perfected (as Alberti would have it) but to be overcome. For merely to abide within it leaves the beholder isolated and bereft of a communal vision whose outlines have already come into focus in the intellect's comparison of contracted and absolute sight. The latter, which is God's exclusive domain though also the goal of all human striving, enfolds *all* aspects of the visible and, as such, also encompasses every other conceivable perspective on it. Finite sight, then, instills in us the knowledge of the intrinsic deficiency, or incompleteness, of any given "act-of-sight." Anticipating the opening argument of *De Visione Dei*, Nicholas thus remarks how, under the penumbra of "defective" sight, "you contemplate the face not as it is [in itself] but in its otherness [*quoniam faciem ipsam non . . . sed in alteritate*], according to your eye's angle, which differs from [that of] all the eyes of other living beings" (*DC* 11:57).

There is, however, one exception, one instance in which the duality of contracted, perspectival sight and absolute vision appears to be resolved—namely, in the contemplation of the omnivoyant icon at the heart of *De Visione Dei*. It alone is capable of modeling for us a perfection of sight, and its continuity with mystical insight, that ordinary, sense-based perception could never achieve, a temporary fusion of sensory *visus* and contemplative *visio*. The apotheosis of humility, such seeing becomes inseparable from being-seen. Where the beholder truly comes face-to-face with the icon, she will partake of the divine gaze, albeit still only *by analogy*; for "every concept of face is less than Your Face, O Lord, and . . . in all faces the Face of faces is seen in a veiled and symbolic manner [*velate et aenigmate*]" (*VD* 6:21–22). Analogy sets fundamental limits to the extravagant claims of a strictly affective mysticism, a model from which Nicholas had expressly distanced himself in his writings and a state that, by his own admission, he had never experienced. Yet insofar as mystical vision draws the beholder closer to the all-encompassing reality of the divine gaze, the "likeness" between contracted and absolute sight does not betoken any defect. On the contrary, modeled on the patristic concept of *figura*, the "likeness" of finite, "mental sight" (*visio mentalis*) to God's *visio absoluta* carries with it eschatological implications. For it is in contemplative experience—where "seeing and being seen coincide"—that the finite individual experiences herself as teleologically ordered toward the fullness of God's absolute vision. As Nicholas remarks, "I know that the capability which conduces to union is only likeness; but incapability results from unlikeness. Therefore, if by every possible means I make myself like unto Your goodness, then according to my degree of likeness thereto I will be capable of receiving truth" (*VD* 4:12).

The distinctive phenomenology of iconic vision thus resides above all in its capacity to let us gently pass beyond visible things, in humble recognition of their—and our—finitude. To do so is not to devalue, let alone repudiate, the material world. Rather, iconic vision arises from the recognition that the visible world is meant to bring about a knowledge of forms, not things: "Your face I see not with the bodily eyes which look at this icon of You but with mental and intellectual eyes. This Truth is signified by this contracted shadow-like image [*in umbra hic contracta*]" (*VD* 6:19). Echoing Nicholas half a millennium later, von Balthasar likewise speaks of a "return movement of the image into the ground, of the phenomenal appearance into the essence, [which] is also the context in which the transition from unmediated sensory experience to reflexive intellectual activity [*reflektierender Geist*] takes place." Still, it would be a mistake "to interpret this process as if the pure essence supplanted the image, or, in noetic terms, the pure concept superseded sense perception." On the contrary, the phenomenalization of essence in appearance—as Plato's *Sophist* had already shown—"was never superfluous. . . . On the contrary, the appearance was really required for the revelation of the essence; it was the light of the essence, made possible its truth, and enabled its emergence from the night of concealment."[146]

At this late point in Nicholas's mystical theology, "the appearance's task is no longer to reveal by appearing in its own right and by directing all eyes to, and keeping them focused on, itself as a kind of stand-in for the essence. Rather, it now has to reveal by stepping back, by making itself superfluous, by effacing itself, in order to direct attention, no longer to it, the appearance, but only to the essence itself." We will encounter the same pattern time and again, including in the late poems of Hopkins, Rilke, and Eliot. What von Balthasar calls the image's self-renunciation, though "transfiguration" might be an equally apt term, had in turn been modeled for

---

146. Balthasar 2001, 147.

Nicholas in the writings of Plotinus, pseudo-Dionysius, or, close to his own time, the contemplative writings of those associated with the *devotio moderna*.[147] It is this pattern of an eventual shift from bodily to spiritual sight, from the visible picture to the mental image, that structures most of Nicholas's treatises and dialogues. In seeking to articulate the phenomenology of visual experience in the medium of *writing*, that is, we find that the ultimate depth and poignancy of the image includes *its self-suspension as strictly visible appearance*. For the plenitude of meanings compressed into the visible image will remain inaccessible as long as our focus is merely on the circumscribed thing it renders visible and on the formal and material techniques employed to do so. Instead, as Nicholas points out, our engagement of the visible world is ultimately animated by a desire for a vision that can neither be definitively realized by the visible image nor ever unfold entirely independent of it. Just as bodily sight is intrinsically ordered toward mental vision, so the latter finds its fulfillment in an apophaticism that is neither the negation of the visible nor its imperfect anticipation but, instead, its consummation: "Since [our eye] seeks to see a light which it cannot see, it knows that as long as it sees something, this is not the thing it is seeking. Therefore it must pass beyond all visible light [*transilire debet omnem lucem*] into . . . darkness [*in caligine*]" (*VD* 6:22).[148]

147. Ibid.
148. On Nicholas's notion of mystical vision as "entering into darkness," see Haubst 1991, 341–48.

Part II

THE IMAGE IN THE ERA
OF NATURALISM AND THE
PERSISTENCE OF METAPHYSICS

5

THE SYMBOLIC IMAGE
Visualizing the Metamorphosis of Being in Goethe

A chaos of heterogeneous substances, such as our Milton has described, is not only an impossible state, but it is palpably *impossible. It presupposes, moreover, the thing it is intended to solve, and makes* that *the effect which had been called in as the explanatory* cause. *The requisite and only serviceable fiction, therefore, is the representation of CHAOS as one vast homogeneous drop! In this sense it may be even justified, as an appropriate symbol of the great fundamental truth that all things spring from, and subsist in, the endless strife between indifference and difference. The whole history of Nature is comprised in the specification of the transitional states from the one to the other.*

—Samuel Coleridge, *Theory of Life*

RETHINKING "DIFFERENCE": DEVELOPMENT, TRANSFORMATION, AND GOETHE'S LAW OF BEING

Toward the end of his study of Nicholas of Cusa, Johannes Hoff draws a distinction between Nicholas's "apophatic account" of transcendence and what he calls an "aporetic account." The latter, advanced by early German Romanticism, Fichte, Novalis, and Hölderlin in particular, construes transcendence as the antonym of finite, visible being. As Hoff notes, "The early Romantics reduced Kant's preconception of God . . . to the nullity of a neutral ontological principle, namely, to the bare existence as an irreducible 'X' that unites what is torn apart." Concluding, with Kant, that this numinous deity eludes all determinative knowledge, the Romantics further maintained that the "Absolute" cannot be known by analogy and that immanence and transcen-dence are wholly incommensurable; and indeed both the Platonic concept of participation and the Neoplatonist and Scholastic concept of *analogia* had, by the late eighteenth century, been either sidelined or openly repudiated. The culmination of a process that had been unfolding since the rise of late Scholastic Nominalism, in particular Fichte's antinomian framing of visible and numinous being, not only "reduce[d] the Absolute to a neutralized *formal* principle." It also risked depriving finite, visible things of ever being more than what they contingently *appeared* to be: ephemeral, particular entities bereft of intrinsic form, agency, and significance. The real had been reduced to a function of contingent human "positing" (*Setzung*), and whatever knowledge there was to be of finite beings inhered in quasi-conceptual properties ascribed *to*, not discovered *in*, them.

By the same token, to deny that the "Absolute" could ever enter into any relation whatsoever with the order of immanence, late Enlightenment skeptics such as Hume, naturalistic thinkers like Priestley, and speculative idealists like Fichte appeared on the verge of repeating the cardinal error of Eleatic philosophy. Like Parmenides, that is, they defined transcendence or the "Absolute" in strictly formal-logical fashion as a hermetically sealed totality, thereby denying it any capacity for manifesting or revealing itself in the order of finite being. With the metaphysical concepts of *analogia* and participation thus suspended, both the numinous Absolute and the order of visible being appeared strangely drained of texture, meaning, and agency. In fact, Hoff remarks, once "we no longer know *what* it is that we are talking about, then we are also no longer justified in drawing conclusions about its *existence*."[1] Conceived as wholly other and incommensurable, God has turned into an abstraction, a void, and, ultimately, an *absence*.

While this line of argument and its troubling conclusions are unfolded in particularly explicit form by Kant and Fichte, their antinomian construal of immanence and transcendence had been prepared for by a long line of Enlightenment skeptics, of both a materialist and a rationalist kind. Building on the antimetaphysical line of argument variously advanced by Hobbes, Shaftesbury, Mandeville, and the French Encyclopedists, it was Hume whose *Dialogues concerning Natural Religion* (1779) had, in the figure of Philo, given particularly witty and charismatic expression to this view. To be sure, more than Kant and Fichte, Novalis and Hölderlin wrestled not only with Hume's corrosive and relentless skepticism but also with the arid formalisms and theological minimalism of the early Fichte. Yet, in the event, the early Romantics' "solution" to this dilemma was to confine the immanence-transcendence

---

1. Hoff 2013, 128.

antinomy exclusively to the sphere of human subjectivity where, as they sought to demonstrate, it played out as a dialectic of "feeling" (*Gefühl*) and "reflection."[2] Novalis's *Fichte-Studies* shows the enigma of transcendence to persist where Fichte thought to have solved it, namely, in the formal-logical operation of "positing" (*Setzung*) that would originate both an absolute "I" and "non-I." Likewise, Hölderlin also recognizes that a dialectic of "positing" and "reflection" alone cannot encompass and explain the reality of Being, which, as he would note, is never a closed system but in its essence an "opening" (*das Offene*). With luminous imagery and stunning sound patterning drawn in part from classical Greek prosodic technique, Hölderlin's late elegies and "patriotic songs" (*Vaterländische Gesänge*) thus mourn the modern self's profound estrangement from its transcendent source.[3] Still, it seemed that even a qualified reclamation of transcendence or the "Absolute" such as early German Romanticism pursues it came at the expense of its phenomenology. However "posited" or "inferred," that is, Romantic transcendence appears abstract, remote, and notional.

Long weary of abstract theological and philosophical speculation, Goethe felt no less uneasy about the tendency of his Romantic contemporaries to spin purely verbal edifices of thought; and their hyper-self-conscious framing of such speculative pursuits in a rhetoric of "wit" or "irony" did not, in his view, remedy that shortcoming. A telling example would be Friedrich Schlegel's breezy assertion that "an idea is a concept perfected to the point of irony, an absolute synthesis of absolute antitheses."[4] While much of what follows in this Athenaeum fragment (#121) is often suggestive, though hardly conclusive, Schlegel's opening characterization of the idea as a "concept" (*Begriff*) marks the precise point on which, as we will see, Goethe was not prepared to follow his Romantic contemporaries. As he saw it, the idea stands ontologically apart from the order of concepts insofar as it is a function of intuition, not ratiocination. In a sense yet to be considered, an idea can be *seen*. Hence, Goethe follows a fundamentally different route by conceiving the mind-world relation in Neoplatonist terms and by reclaiming the *analogia* principle that, some three centuries earlier, had framed Cusa's philosophical theology.[5] As he remarks in *Maxims and Reflections* (1810), "Each existing thing is an analogue of every other thing [*ein*

---

2. Having "rejected Spinoza's rational limitations that rendered God wholly immanent, . . . the Frühromantiker [early Romantics] began to synthesize a position from [Spinozan immanentism and Platonic realism] wherein all individual being, including the self, inhered and participated in absolute being, which itself transcended immanence" (Hampton 2019, 6–7).

3. On Fichte and Novalis, see Pfau 2005b, 27–74; Pinkard 2002, 131–71; Frank 2011, 39–54, 151–76. On Hölderlin's understanding of self-consciousness and its transcendent "ground," conceptions evidently steeped in the Pietist culture of his native Svabia, see the letters from his time at the Tübingen seminary (1788–93), in Hölderlin 1943–86, vol. 6, i:41–96; and his poetry of the same period, esp. "Hymn to Immortality" (*Hymne an die Unsterblichkeit*), 1/i:116–19).

4. Schlegel 1991, 33.

5. Hoff 2013, 128.

Analogon alles Existierenden]; for which reason all being strikes us simultaneously as distinct and related [*gesondert und verknüpft*]." What makes analogy such a valuable principle, then, is the way it at once elicits and restrains our reflective involvement with appearances: "Analogy does not intrude, does not seek to prove anything; . . . it has this advantage, that it does not definitively conclude [*nicht abschließt*] and, indeed, does not seek anything ultimate."[6] As Goethe will argue time and again, insofar as we abide with the appearances nature puts before us, we not only maintain a level of epistemic humility that befits all human beings, but, paradoxically, also come to understand better both the phenomenon before us and the intuitive grounds from which our all intellectual activity springs.

Following his early attachment to the *Sturm und Drang* (Storm and Stress) movement, itself an offshoot of the broader current of sentimentalism ushered in by Rousseau, Goethe by the mid-1780s was searching for a more capacious and more objective outlook, one that will show the "formation" (*Bildung*) and "development" (*Entwicklung*) of human subjectivity to be correlated with its active and focused, visual encounter with the natural world. Looking back upon this recalibration of his artistic persona in 1817, Goethe recalls being appalled by Wilhelm Heinse's "use of creative art to refine and adorn sensuality and illogical methods of thinking," yet also by Schiller's *Robbers*, of whose "ethical and dramatic paradoxes . . . I had been endeavoring to purify myself."[7] Beginning with his extended journey through all of Italy (1786–88), Goethe embarked on new forms of scientific study and writing that he would continue to develop for more than three decades.[8] During the months following his return from Naples to Rome in late October 1787, Goethe seemingly embraced a new vocation of sorts, namely, a "part-time art student." As he writes to Duke Carl August in Weimar, "In these one and a half years of solitude I have found myself again; but as what—As an artist! [*Künstler*]."[9] In the event, what prompted Goethe's statement was not some inflated self-image as a great painterly talent but, rather, the realization that only now had he learned what it means to see—namely, an involved and continuous visualizing of form. A similar revelation was to inspire

6. Johann Wolfgang von Goethe, *Werke*, ed. Erich Trunz (Hamburger Ausgabe); henceforth cited as *GHA* with volume number followed by page number and, here, followed by Trunz's numbering of aphorisms in *Maximen und Reflexionen*. Thus, *GHA* 12:368 (#23, 25–26). As Hoff remarks, Goethe "scales back and investigates *both* the existence *and* the essence of this principle [Kant's numinous X] analogically through the reality of its symbolic manifestations in nature and history" (2013, 128).

7. The remarks open Goethe's reminiscence ("Propitious Encounter") about the beginnings of his botanical studies and writings in the late 1780s; Goethe 1952, 215 (henceforth cited parenthetically as *EM*).

8. On the immense variety of influences absorbed and projects conceived during this journey, see Boyle 1991, 415–530.

9. Quoted in Boyle 1991, 491.

Rilke's quest for an objective, visual poetics around 1907, prompted in that case by his revelatory encounter with the work of Cézanne. For his part, when experimenting with drawings of the human form and close-up study of its anatomy, Goethe realized that until now he had "averted [his] eyes from it as if from the light of the sun."[10] The Plotinian trope of the sun is telling, suggesting a vastly expanded artistic ambition that seeks to home in not only on the concrete reality of visible forms but also on the very source that renders them distinctly visible to begin with.

What in his botanical writings Goethe calls "seeing the form" involves a focused and attentive apprehension of organic form manifesting itself as gradual and purposive internal "transformation" (*Umwandlung*), that is, as an entelechy rather than a product of contingent, externally induced "alteration." On this account, *what* the attentive observer sees at any given moment will only ever be a partial and fleeting manifestation of the "law of form," which remains invisible as such even as it can be visually apprehended in its discrete phases. Conversely, if in keeping with much seventeenth- and eighteenth-century empiricist study, "one assumes that all causality is external causality, the investigator need not take appearances to be fundamental." Those cultivating such an approach "must first discredit the given before they can reinterpret it through reductionist logic." It is this "separating the content of experience from the activity of consciousness" that Goethe categorically rejects.[11] In his botanical writings, his numerous aphorisms on science and experience, and his novelistic depiction of the modern individual's progressive formation and self-cultivation (*Bildung*) through a notably practical engagement with the objective world, organic and intelligent (human) life is conceived as a process of ceaseless internal (formal) differentiation. In conscious opposition to mechanistic accounts of perception advanced by modern empiricism, Goethe revives a Neoplatonist dialectic of the visible and the invisible that, thus far, I have traced in the preceding three chapters. As he summarizes his conclusions in *Maxims and Reflections* (1810), "The supreme task is to understand that everything factual is itself already theory. The blueness of the sky already reveals [*offenbart*] for us the basic law of chromaticism. We ought not to search for anything *behind* the phenomena. For they themselves are the doctrine." Intellection is inseparable from the visual experience of a given phenomenon, since what elicits reflective thought in the first place is a given thing's distinctive way of manifesting itself: "Whoever has a phenomenon before his eyes, frequently already thinks beyond it; by contrast, whoever is merely told of a phenomenon doesn't think at all."[12]

---

10. Ibid., 489. As regards Rilke's analogous transformation from a late Romantic poet to a proponent of a "new factuality" (*neue Sachlichkeit*), see ch. 8, below.

11. Brady 1998, 89–90.

12. *GHA* 12:432 (#488, 504).

Insofar as it arrests and engages our visual and intellectual attention, a phenomenon always manifests the transcendent *logos* in some particular form. The realm of appearance, then, is never a random concatenation of inert, "dumb" matter but, on the contrary, constitutes an order whose symbolic significance can be traced in the way it phenomenalizes itself as sensory form. For Goethe, appearance is essentially symbolic: "Symbolism transforms an appearance into an idea, an idea into an image, and this it does in such a way as for the idea contained in the image to remain infinitely efficacious [*wirksam*] and unattainable." The symbolic, then, is the moment "where the particular represents the universal, not as a dream or shadow, but as the living and instantaneous revelation of the unfathomable [*als lebendig-augenblickliche Offenbarung des Unerforschlichen*]."[13] While Goethe would always reject conceiving this *logos* in terms of Revelation and a personal God, the Platonism undergirding his theory of art and knowledge is palpable and, with time, grows only more pronounced: "We call an idea that which at all times manifests itself [*zur Erscheinung kommt*] and, consequently, presents itself to us as the law of all appearance [*Gesetz aller Erscheinungen*]." Though invisible per se, the law governing all phenomena is also unveiled or mediated by them. Indeed, the fact that appearances are susceptible of theoretical scrutiny at all implicitly confirms that a single, all-encompassing truth manifests itself in and through them. As Goethe puts it, "The idea is eternal and it is one [*ewig und einzig*]," and "Truth is deiform [*das Wahre ist gottähnlich*]; it does not appear in unmediated form but must be inferred from its manifestations."[14] Around 1800, this Platonist framework resurfaces in scientific and cultural contexts profoundly altered as the result of the closely entwined rise of post- or antimetaphysical conceptions of rationality and the scientific revolution of the seventeenth century.

---

13. *GHA* 12:470 (#749, 752); on Goethe's conception of the symbolic, which he pointedly associates with concrete sensory experience (contrasted with allegory's inherently abstract mode of signification), see Adams 1983, 47–58; on the Romantic symbol's conceptual bearings, see Halmi 2007, 1–26. The affinities between Goethe's understanding of the symbol and Coleridge's famous definition of it in his *Statesman's Manual* (1816) are palpable and have often been remarked; see also De Man 1983, 187–228.

14. *GHA* 12:366 (#10, 11, 13); "Whoever would disavow nature as a divine organ might as well deny all revelation [*leugne gleich alle Offenbarung*]," and "'Nature conceals God [*verbirgt Gott*]!' But not from everyone" (365, #2, 3). As Simmel remarks, for Goethe, mind and nature are "parallel expressions of the divine Being that evolves in Nature in the external dimension with the same reality as within the soul, the internal dimension. This way, Nature retains its unconditional, external, more perceptible reality without relinquishing her essential unity with the human heart—without first needing to be transformed, as with Kant, into a representation within the latter" (2007a, 167). Hampton's emphasis on the Platonic underpinnings of early German Romanticism also applies to Goethe's thinking during the 1780s and 1790s: "Platonism provided the Romantics with the philosophical insights that would allow them to take two seeming philosophical extremes and begin to synthesise a new position wherein all individual being, including the self, inhered and participated in absolute being" (2019, 125).

Arguably the most significant change involves the growing emphasis on "presentation" (*Darstellung*), that is, on no longer visualizing form as a passive, though attentive, beholder, but giving active and objective expression to it in some medium or other, be it poetry, scientific prose, or indeed drawing. "Seeing" in the age of Goethe no longer constitutes a garden-variety instance of "perception" mechanistically imprinting sensory data on an otherwise neutral or "blank" consciousness. Rather, Goethe takes consciousness as always conscious-of some phenomenon or other. That is, a dynamic, imaginative, and reciprocal engagement with a given natural phenomenon gradually crystallizes both the *eidos* manifesting itself in particular, visible being and the observer's own creative and intellectual potential.

In his botanical writings, which beginning around 1787 would extend for more than three decades, Goethe thus establishes a strong link between a markedly formalist conception of plant life and a concurrent progression toward greater complexity of awareness that unfolds within the intelligence of the observer. Noting that his "botanical education resembled to a certain degree the course of botanical history itself," insofar as it shows him to have "progressed from superficial observation to useful application," Goethe recognizes that observer and object share in one and the same *logos*. As patient, undeviating sight issues in objective insight, the observer's intelligence undergoes the same differential growth as the organism with which it is concerned. "Seeing" not only generates a differentiated "image" (*Bild*) of its visible correlate, but, concurrently, effects a "development" (*Bildung*) and deeper levels of self-recognition on the part of the observing intelligence. What by 1790 Goethe begins to formulate under the heading "metamorphosis" appears entwined with a more wide-ranging cultural ideal of self-origination, self-organization, and organic flourishing that German culture from the late eighteenth to the early twentieth century tends to subsume under the master trope of *Bildung*, one whose ineffable, organic or process-like nature resists conceptual scrutiny and, in the case of Goethe in particular, accounts for his lifelong distrust of pure "theory." Inevitably, then, we confront the challenge of how to distill the conceptual outlines of a dynamic practice recurrently characterized by its proponents as altogether elemental: an all-encompassing Law of Being or Life rather than a particular (falsifiable) method of knowing.

As it turns out, a final, brief glance back at Nicholas of Cusa is warranted here. For not only does Nicholas signally anticipate Goethe's analogical framing of nature as the dynamic manifestation of an overarching, divine "law" (*Gesetz*) or Platonic *logos*. He also draws a conceptual implication of cosmological theory from Plotinus and Proclus all the way to the threshold of the modern era, before being eclipsed by mechanist explanatory schemes variously elaborated by Boyle, Hobbes, and their eighteenth-century descendants. To close in on that implication, let us turn to a passage in *De Visione Dei* in which Nicholas foreshadows Goethe's conception of the mental image (*Urbild*). His example is a nut tree whose dynamic, ceaselessly self-differentiating development aptly encapsulates the gestational (and in tendency metaphysical) character of human vision, at once finite and partial, yet, in its particular dynamism, exhibiting its deiform nature.

> Turn[ing] toward this large and tall nut tree, whose beginning I seek to see. And with the sensible eye I see that it is large, spacious, colored, laden with branches, with leaves, and with nuts. Then with the mind's eye I see that this tree existed in its seed not in the manner in which I here behold it but potentially. I consider attentively this seed's admirable power, wherein were present the whole of this tree, all its nuts. . . . I see that this tree is a certain unfolding of the seed's power and that the seed is a certain unfolding of Omnipotent power. (*VD* 7, 23–24)

To "see" here means to apprehend the form or idea of which the visible tree is a conspicuous, albeit partial manifestation. On this model, the "seed" (*semine*) is no more the efficient cause of the resulting nut tree than that tree "causes" us to perceive it. For properly to "see" the nut tree as such is not simply to perceive it in its contingent three-dimensionality. Rather, it is to grasp its teleological constitution, as having fully realized its invisible form as it had been contained in the tree. The visible tree thus enables the beholder to participate in the form or idea (*eidos*), to have a mental image of the archetype that has manifested itself in the tree before us. Now, the very interplay between the "sensible eye" (*oculo sensibili*) and the "mental eye" (*oculo mentis*) of which Nicholas speaks is conceivable only on the metaphysical premise of *analogia*. For only if mind and world are ontologically configured as formally commensurable and ontologically coordinated is it possible for human intuition to blossom into cognition or, as Nicholas puts it, to "behold, intellectually, oneness in otherness."

Still, just as Goethe will argue in *Maxims and Reflections*, such an "analogy of participation" can only take the form of a tacit supposition; it does not constitute a conceptual claim or formal proposition, for it itself undergirds all conceptual activity in relation to the external world. After all, in every act of cognition for which there is an intuitive foundation, mind must have already, albeit tacitly, presupposed such an analogy. Put differently, when attending to its very mode of operation, mind finds itself to have engaged the sensible world not as its diametrical other but in the modality of *participation*. It discovers itself to be sharing, ontologically speaking, in the very order of being that also includes organic beings and inorganic matter. For Nicholas, as for Goethe writing some three and a half centuries later, the mind-world relation is more intimate and more immediate than the series of productive "negations" through which Hegelian dialectics seeks to resolve the impasse of Cartesian dualism. Thus, Nicholas's passage rests on a basic analogy between the visible growth of the nut tree and the mind's ascent from sight to insight. Seeing and thinking are, for Nicholas no less than for Goethe, part of a single dynamic process; and, as Nicholas had argued early on, to grasp that nexus constitutes itself a higher kind of seeing.

> If you want to behold, intellectually, oneness in otherness, then pay very careful attention [*diligentissime adverte*] also to the following: viz., that for oneness to proceed into otherness is, at the same time, for otherness to return into oneness. . . . As regards form: the more one and the more perfect each form is, the more its proceeding [into otherness] is otherness's returning [into its oneness]. (*DC* I:53)

With unmistakable Plotinian overtones, Nicholas here sets up one of the most incisive accounts of knowledge as "participation" since Plato introduced the concept of *methexis* in the *Parmenides*. The discussion proves especially valuable for our purposes because it foreshadows Goethe's later take on the perennial question of the many and the one, in particular his contention that the "variety" and "differentiation" exhibited by organic life-forms is intelligible only because, in their very mode of self-manifestation, these beings reveal to us the ontological *relatedness* and, ultimately, the oneness of all being rather than its terminal heterogeneity.

As Nicholas unequivocally states, in all perception we "see adequately and very clearly that oneness is identity that is unimpartible, inexplicable, and—as such—unattainable [unitatem esse ipsam identitatem incommunicabilem, inexplicabilem atquae, uti est, inattingibilem]." A visible circle, Nicholas notes, can always be imagined as more precise than it currently presents itself. Yet that its pure form should be "unimpartible" does not constitute a defect but, instead, "is due to the fact that it is partaken of by something *other* and, hence, is partaken of *otherwise*" (*DC* 11:54). By its very nature, our sensible and intellectual participation in phenomena presupposes an underlying, ontological difference; that is, "inexplicable identity is unfolded variously and differently in otherness [*varie differenter in alteritate explicatur*]. For example, sight is partaken of differently by various acts-of-sight, just as, also, the diversity of the acts-of-sight is contained concordantly in the oneness of absolute sight [*visibilium varietas in unitate visus concordanter complicatur*]." By its very nature, sense-based cognition always unfolds "in terms of otherness-of-variation [*in alteritate variationis*]" (*DC* 11:55).

While this much may seem standard Platonist fare, Nicholas now adds a reflection that will resurface and pay considerable dividends in Goethe's scientific writings. For as he points out, to participate in forms, which is to say, in "the ray of Divine Light," is not something done by finite minds already in existence. On the contrary, it is only through such participation that the human intellect constitutes itself in the first place: "The intellect's partaking of that unimpartible, most actual light *constitutes* the [respective] quiddity of created mind. Therefore, the actuality of our intelligence consists in its partaking of the Divine Intellect [*Actualitas igitur intelligentiae nostrae in participatione divini intellectus exsistit*]" (*DC* 11:56). This insight is brought home for us, Nicholas maintains, every time that an act of sense perception is tempered by our rational awareness of the inevitable "falling away from preciseness." Put differently, all intuition is simultaneously validated and qualified by reflection, which can never be the ground and source of theoretical certainty per se but remains at the level of a basic "surmise" (*coniectura*). Only by turning "toward the root from whence the senses' discrimination flows, . . . namely, toward reason," will sight ever become insight. Yet in so turning, mind also becomes "conjecturally" aware of the ontological divide separating it from the contingent deliverances of empirical sight. For in reflecting on its visual intake of, say, the face of Pope Eugene IV, the mind discovers that it has not seen that face absolutely but only "in its otherness, according to your eye's angle, which differs from [that of] all the eyes of other living beings" (*DC* 11:57). It thus grasps the difference of the many and the one as both constitutive of, and as a constraint on, all sense perception. Having attained that insight, the beholder also learns to embrace the very notion of "difference," not as sheer heterogeneity, but as revealing the ontological nexus between the one and the many: "Since whatever can be partaken of is partaken of only with a degree of otherness," it follows that the One that "is unfolded in otherness" will be experienced only successively, as "changeable," that is, as "a mode-of-power" differentially unfolding an "unpartakeable oneness" in time (*DC* 11:58).

Before we can proceed to explore Goethe's conception of organic life as a dynamic *imago*, we need to tarry a little longer with this foundational philosophical category of difference. Once we think of "difference" less as betokening heterogeneity and incommensurability—that is, as a figure of *negation*—and more as intuition's first step toward *integration*, the term acquires a fundamentally new valence. It then emerges, as Nicholas's account of participation had already demonstrated, as the load-bearing concept for all sense-based cognition. Any account of Romantic *Bildung*, particularly as Goethe develops the concept in his botanical writings and in *Wilhelm Meister's Apprenticeship* (1796), must build on this integrative, in essence Platonist, understanding of difference as the dialectical bond of being with non-being, as relatedness rather than heteronomy, as typological rather than antinomian, and as the foundation for a model of knowledge qua participation rather than anchored in some version of dualism. As we saw, this conception of an "internally differentiated One" (*to hen . . . diapheromenon auto heautō*), first unfolded as a musical trope in Plato's *Symposium* and then developed in the *Parmenides* and the *Sophist* as a full-fledged dialectic of being and non-being, outlines the ontological condition for any knowledge whatsoever.[15] "Difference," Michel Henry notes, "is the essence of unity. . . . It is the essence of a presence which is obtained through the mediation of phenomenological distance." Precisely here, in the internal differentiation of Being into visible appearance—whose essential form, the image, only ever has being relative to the being from which it differs—consciousness finds itself participating in Being. "Consciousness itself is nothing other than the alienation of Being, namely Being as such. The becoming-other of Being is identical to its bursting-forth in the phenomenal condition of presence. *This phenomenal dimension of presence is consciousness itself.*"[16] For Goethe no less than for Nicholas and the Neoplatonist tradition on which he draws, absolute "form" only ever reveals itself as a spatiotemporally differentiated presentation of a given thing's spatial aspects and temporal phases and, precisely in its dual form as an *appearing-of* and an *appearing-for* (consciousness), reveals the ontological bond between mind and world. It is at this fascinating border region, where the domains of Neoplatonism, Romantic aesthetics, organicism, and modern phenomenology abut one another, that we begin to understand difference as *essentially* integrative rather than analytically disjunctive.

As hinted above, to conceive difference as the visible exfoliation of a thing's form in time requires us to distinguish more precisely between the claims of organicism and those of dialectics, the philosophical framework to which it bears marked affinity. Whereas the principal medium of dialectics is the "concept" (*Begriff*), organicism of the kind found in Goethe, Schelling, and Coleridge pivots on the (in origin Platonic) "image," which renders the archetypal "form" (*eidos*) of all being intuitively present for us. In implicit contradistinction to Hegel's abstract conception of intellectual work, Goethe will later remark that "thinking is more interesting than knowing, but not more [interesting] than intuiting" (*Denken ist interessanter als Wissen, aber nicht als Anschauen*); and he prizes integrative, intuitive knowing more highly than any analytic fragmenting of the phenomenon at hand: "Knowing is based on discerning what is to be differentiated [*Kenntnis des zu Unterscheidenden*], scientific knowledge on what is not to be differentiated [*Anerkennung des nicht zu*

---

15. See above, ch. 1, 79–92. Plato writes, "What Heraclitus had in mind, though his mode of expression certainly leaves much to be desired, . . . [is] 'the one being at variance with itself is in agreement with itself like the attunement of a bow or lyre'" (*Symposium* 187a). In his novel *Hyperion*, consciously modeled on the *Symposium*, Hölderlin famously takes up Plato's formulation, itself attributed to Heraclitus, and renders it as "das Eine in sich selbst Unterschiedene," thus emphasizing how the "understanding" (*Verstand*) finds its ground in the "divine *hen diapheromenon heautō*, the ideal of beauty espoused by reason in its striving" (Hölderlin 1943–86, 3:83); Hölderlin truncates the Heraclitean phrase to *hen diapheron heautō*.

16. Henry 1973, 72, 78.

Unterscheidenden]." Hence, "a thinking man errs more especially when he inquires into cause and effect: both of these together make up the indivisible phenomenon."[17]

Here it bears recalling that the concept of difference acquired central importance as a result of the critique of Aristotelian ontology pioneered by thirteenth- and fourteenth-century Franciscans (Duns Scotus, Ockham, Autrecourt, et al.).[18] Inadvertently, a dispute initially confined to Scholastic theology laid the groundwork for the gradual bifurcation of theology and philosophy, particularly with regard to questions subsequently compartmentalized as the province of epistemology. Thus, in Ockham the Scholastic concept of a "thing" (*res*) loses its status as an ontological "category" (*praedicamentum*) and, instead, is defined as a free-floating singularity defined, above all, by its sheer dissimilarity vis-à-vis other beings. As a Nominalist epistemology begins to take hold, "things" formerly defined by their participation in substantial forms are now construed as discrete "objects" (*objecta*). To know such an object pivots on identifying and classifying it as a disembedded singularity rather than as the "concreation" of substantial form and the transcendent *logos* that had originated it.[19] Inasmuch as Nominalist epistemology commutes *res* into *obiectum*, the latter is no longer viewed as a dynamic and self-disclosing agent but, instead, as an inert, seemingly dumb *res extensa*. For theological reasons that cannot be explored in detail here, this conceptual shift effectively abandons the Aristotelian-Thomistic doctrine of substantial form wherein being and act are fundamentally convertible. On that account, knowing a given thing meant attending to its agent character (*operatio*), that is, to the way it actively manifests the substantial form which, as a "concreated" thing, it embodies in necessarily partial and imperfect form.

Nevertheless, in virtue of its "participation" in the substantial form of which it is a "concreation," each particular thing occupies a stable position within a providential

---

17. *GHA* 12:398 (#242), 407 (#305), 446 (#591).

18. See Ockham 1991, esp. 1:13 (on the singularity of cognition); 2:19 (on the body as contingent on referentiality); 3:12 (on the conceptual status of all thought); 4:23–25 (on the contingency of substance on determinate quantity and quality). On the origins of modern scientific thought in the Nominalist (Franciscan) critique of Aristotelian and Thomistic "substantial form," see Dupré 1993, 15–90; Taylor 2007, 90–99; Buckley 2004, 25–47; Blumenberg 1983, 126–79; Gillespie 2007, 19–43, 170–246. On eighteenth-century empiricism and the particularization of knowledge, see Dupré 2004, 18–44; Cassirer 1951, 37–92; Adorno and Horkheimer 1972, 3–42, esp. 22–23.

19. On Aquinas's conception of form, see *ST* I.45.8: "The form of a natural body is not subsisting, but is that by which a thing is. . . . [I]t does not belong to forms to be made or to be created, but to be concreated [Non enim considerabant quod forma naturalis corporis non est subsistens, sed quo aliquid est . . . formarum non est fieri neque creari, sed concreata esse]." On form in Aquinas, see McCabe 2008, 41–50; on its rejection by fourteenth-century Nominalism, see Dupré 1993, 167–89; on Aquinas's "'non-subject-centered' approach to human experience . . . as the actualization of intellectual capacities by potentially significant objects, according to the axiom '*intellectus in actu est intelligibile in actu*' [our intellectual capacities actualized *are* the world's intelligibility realized]," see Kerr 2002, 26–33, 46–51; quote from 27.

and timeless order (*kosmos*). Consequently, the meaning and value of a given thing (*res*) pivots on its differential relatedness to many other things, which Aquinas acknowledges when remarking "on the marvelous connection of things [*mirabilis rerum connexio*]."[20] Yet beginning with Ockham and culminating in Lockean empiricism, "difference" of form takes on a strictly *disjunctive* sense, now signifying the incommensurability of discrete beings. As Goethe, and alongside him Schiller and Hölderlin, also realized, "in a world without a framework of participation, there was no longer a structure to mediate between the divine absolute and contingent reality."[21] The name of that structure, *analogia*, begins to fade as philosophical inquiry gradually embraces an immanent conception of knowledge whose insistence on the verifiability of perception and the demonstrability of propositions can no longer accommodate, or even understand the rationale for, a *visio intellectualis* that from pseudo-Dionysius and Maximus the Confessor to Bernard, Bonaventure, and Cusa had framed knowledge as an active and searching response to the givenness of the real rather than as a kind of conceptual dominion.

Starting with fourteenth-century Nominalism and hitting its stride in the rationalist and mechanist explanatory schemes of Gassendi, Descartes, Hobbes, and their Enlightenment heirs, this contemplative tradition of knowledge is gradually being supplanted by a model of inquiry that regards individual being as but an inert entity, subject to mechanical explanation, and thus as a logical puzzle to be solved by the formal-syllogistic parsing that, beginning with Peter Ramus, extends all the way to Carnap, Russell, and Quine in our time.[22] In its modern sense as *determinatio*, knowledge of natural beings thus is no longer understood to originate in a moment of intuition but, instead, as the product of a logical sequence of highly particular propositions ventured "about" isolated problems or "objects." It bears recalling in this context that whereas the word *obiectum* in classical and medieval cosmology "did not denote a thing, . . . [for] things were subjects of their own actualization in being, in attributes, in processes, and in the realizations of their potentialities," its valence undergoes a decisive shift by the start of the seventeenth century.[23] Henceforth, to know a thing means to isolate it as *obiectum* and to "explain" it as a product of so-called

---

20. On the Aristotelian-Thomist view of the cosmos, and some of the conceptual tensions lurking within this framework, see Lovejoy 1964, 67–98; for the quote from Aquinas, see *Summa Contra Gentiles*, II:68.

21. Hampton 2019, 17.

22. On the Franciscan's (Nominalist) rejection of the Dominicans' attempt to "bridge theology and natural philosophy" by, among other means, "the discovery of natural analogies to transcendent truths," see Gaukroger 2006, 80–87 (quote from 80); on the subsequent disaggregation of primary (divine) and secondary (natural) causation, see Dupré 1993, 167–79; for a discussion of Ramus and Peter of Spain and their legacy of formalist (and notably probabilistic) analysis, grounded not in "truth at all, but [in] confidence or trust," see Ong 1983, 53–91; quote from 65.

23. Buckley 2004, 94.

secondary (material and efficient) causes said to operate independently of how this "object" is experienced. On this account, knowledge of objects is represented in acts of formally correct, abstract predication, the procedure championed by Francis Bacon as introducing the "method, order, and process of connecting and advancing experience."[24]

Once the focus of scientific inquiry was placed on the material and efficient interaction between singular objects, rather than on the dynamic process whereby a given object formally constituted itself as a specific thing to begin with, the inevitable result was what Husserl calls the "mathematization" of reason, which no longer understands itself as participating in an antecedently given "order" (*kosmos*) of things but as granting (or denying) objects reality insofar as they conform (or fail to conform) to modern reason's quantifying predeterminations. While remarking on the consequent, "monstrous contrast between the repeated failures of metaphysics and the uninterrupted and ever-increasing wave of theoretical and practical successes in the positive sciences," Husserl also notes that the breathtaking advances of modern scientific rationality had come at a cost that modern science would never be able to cover. For by instituting an ontological chasm between object and reason, between inert (mindless) *res extensa* and a mind intent on determining being by means of quantitative and causal determination, modern inquiry wrought a dissociation of sensibility, as Eliot had famously called it a few years before Husserl. The determinability of being qua "object" pivots on its ontological "separateness" from the *logos*. In a searching formulation that also chimes with Eliot's trope of "dissociation," Husserl asks, "Should reason and being be *separated* where reason, as knowing, determines what is?"[25]

Not until the later eighteenth century, and then prompted by a resurgent interest in Platonist thought (in the writings of Bishop Berkeley and the Dutch philosopher Frans Hemsterhuis, as well as of Herder, Hölderlin, and Goethe), is the Nominalist understanding of difference as sheer heterogeneity and incompatibility of mind and world, and of one thing from another, being qualified and, in some crucial respects, rejected.[26] This Plato-inspired revival of an integrative and holistic concept of being,

---

24. Bacon 2000, 81.

25. Husserl 1970, 11 (§ 5), trans. modified; emphasis mine. "Ist Vernunft und Seiendes zu trennen, wo erkennende Vernunft bestimmt, was Seiendes ist?" In his 1921 essay "The Metaphysical Poets," Eliot had noted that "in the seventeenth century a dissociation of sensibility set in, from which we have never recovered." At stake is "the difference between the intellectual poet and the reflective poet. Tennyson and Browning are poets, and they think; but they do not feel their thought as immediately as the odour of a rose." By contrast, Eliot remarks, "a thought to Donne was an experience; it modified his sensibility" (Eliot 2015, vol. 1, 380).

26. On the reception and inflection of Platonic thought, particularly the *Timaeus* and *Phaedrus*, in the writings of Hölderlin, see his verse narrative, *Hyperion*, and several of his shorter essays, including "Das Werden im Vergehen" (Becoming within Passing-Away), "Über das Gesetz der

which by 1800 is well under way, (re)conceptualizes the idea of form, both organic and human, as the self-generation (*epigenesis*) and intrinsically purposive development of organic being in time, with each stage at once formally distinctive yet inseparably entwined with all other stages, both preceding and succeeding it. Early German Romanticism's term of art for this dynamic conception of form is *Bildung*. No longer is the visible world construed in terms of "preformationism," that is, as a static inventory of inert and dissimilar entities such as Carl Linné (1707–78) had sought to aggregate within a comprehensive, abstract taxonomy of botanical species.[27] Linné's taxonomic ordering of observable reality suffered from his apparent inability to articulate how he had arrived at the specific categories for classifying botanical forms. His nomenclature of "funguses, algae, mosses, ferns, grasses, palms, *and plants*" perplexes given his inability to distinguish between these six genera and the umbrella term "plant," introduced as it were by default: "Plants is the designation of the rest, which cannot be included in the families above."[28] Furthermore, Linné's specification of botanical categories ("Every plant-name must consist of a generic name and a specific one") risks a kind of Nominalist hyperinflation by generating ever new names as further morphological differences reveal themselves.[29]

Writing at the end of the century, Kant (discussing teleological reason in his third *Critique*), Johann Friedrich Blumenbach (1752–1840), and Goethe all reject Linné's taxonomic approach, mainly because it fails to attend to the dynamic and teleological constitution of organic form. On their competing account, whose philosophical underpinnings in Plotinus and Nicholas of Cusa we have already considered, the very intelligibility of all visible particulars pivots on our apprehending their respective form, or *eidos*. For that to happen, and for a given thing's form to be grasped as actively manifesting the *logos* of which it is a temporal instantiation, the observer must learn to interpret the ceaseless interplay of identity and difference, and of the one and the many, as manifesting an underlying, timeless order. Hence Goethe repeatedly notes that true knowledge must never be reduced to an

---

Freiheit" (The Law of Freedom), and "Urtheil und Seyn" (Judgment and Being); for a discussion of Hölderlin's debt to Platonic thought, see Beiser 2002, 375–406.

27. On the emergence and consolidation of the eighteenth-century "life sciences" into various branches of modern biology, see Nyhart 1995, 1–64, who offers an excellent discussion of morphology and formalist biology between 1800 and 1850; and Steigerwald 2019, 323–89. On the institutionalization of the natural sciences, see Cahan 2003, 291–328; and Robert Richards's essay ("Biology") in Cahan 2003, 16–48. The process of disciplinary specialization, as well as institutional and professional consolidation, correlates with the demise of natural theology or arguments from design after 1800; on that topic, see Thompson 2007, esp. 138–73; Gould 2002, 116–36, 170–96. On the metaphysical and ethical costs associated with the rise of modern objectivity, see Dupré 1993, 65–92; Pfau 2007.

28. Linné 2003, 51.

29. Ibid., 170.

anthropomorphism but, on the contrary, demands of the observer a certain self-suspension and epistemic humility. For inasmuch as knowing is inseparable from intuiting (*Anschauen*), something different is required than subsuming the individual object under general concepts of our own devising: "Where feeble intellects go wrong in their thinking is that they proceed immediately from the single factor to what is general, whereas it is only in totality that what is general can be sought."[30] Whereas the merely "general" and abstract concept loses interest in the individual thing once it has been satisfactorily classified, totality itself is only ever revealed by a being's distinctive mode of appearance. As a phenomenon, which is to say as *actus*, individual being *participates in* totality and, indeed, positively unveils it. Yet it will do so only when considered as a form actively constituting itself rather than as the objective product of extrinsic, mechanical forces; and here our intellectual habits often interfere, privileging as they do the fixed and determinate object as a self-contained, observer-independent reality: "Reason is ordered toward what's in a state of becoming; understanding toward what's fully determined [Die Vernunft ist auf das Werdende, der Verstand auf das Gewordene angewiesen]."[31]

For Goethe, then, "cognition is not a proposition about what is perceived but an activity that actualizes the perception. *Each act of seeing is necessarily an act of understanding.* . . . We do not perceive and then bring forward a concept to understand. We focus our understanding to bring forth a perception."[32] What in a Goethean turn of phrase Michael Polanyi calls the "structural kinship of the arts of knowing and doing" thus delineates two fundamentally distinct ways of relating to visible particulars.

> We can be aware of them uncomprehendingly, i.e., in themselves, or understandingly, in their participation in a comprehensive entity. In the first case, we focus our attention on the isolated particulars; in the second, our attention is directed beyond them to the entity to which they contribute. In the first case therefore we may say that we are aware of the particulars *focally*; in the second, that we notice them *subsidiarily in terms of their participation in a whole*. [However], focal and subsidiary awareness are . . . not *two degrees* of attention but *two kinds* of attention given to the same particulars.[33]

For Goethe, the first type of ("focal") awareness characterizes Linné's approach and accounts for its overall weakness. For as a result of his eagerness to assimilate the

---

30. *GHA* 12:433 (#490).
31. *GHA* 12:438 (#538).
32. Brady 1998, 88.
33. Polanyi 1969, 126, 128.

data yielded by focal awareness to his taxonomic system, Linné "interpreted too narrowly," such as when equating "outer and inner bark, the wood and the pith, as equally functioning parts, equally alive and essential."[34] In so failing to grasp morphological differences as intrinsically purposive and, hence, as manifesting an integral, organic form, Linné committed what, for Goethe, is the cardinal sin of modern analysis—namely, to stray from the dynamic phenomenon by absorbing it into a static nomenclature. Linné effectively failed "to grasp that everything factual is *eo ipso* theory. The blue of the sky reveals for us the law of chromaticism. We must guard against wanting to seek anything *behind* the phenomena. They themselves are what they teach [Man suche nur nichts hinter den Phänomenen. Sie selbst sind die Lehre]."[35] Reflecting his lifelong debt to Goethe, von Balthasar in his late *Theo-Logic* echoes Goethe's aphoristic observation in particularly incisive ways. As he notes, the order of phenomena is imbued with significance in an altogether essential manner, rather than by ascription. Indeed,

> significance is [itself] an irreducible phenomenon. It requires an appearing surface upon which a non-appearing depth expresses and indicates its presence. The surface is, so to say, loaded with the whole sense contained in this depth, yet it does not come apart at the seams. What is contained in the hidden center presses outward, as is nicely conveyed by the word "ex-pression." As we have already observed, this by no means involves a mechanical reproduction of the inside on the outward surface. The image holds the significant content; it would therefore be futile to hunt behind it for the archetype, as if the vision of the archetype would render the signification of its derivative image superfluous and rob it of its force.[36]

Any proper science of forms thus must let itself be guided by the particular way in which a particular being's form actively and visibly manifests itself over time. In claiming that *how* a given thing dynamically manifests itself for the observer will determine *what* we can know about it, Goethe's approach distinctly foreshadows the project of modern phenomenology as worked out by Husserl around 1906–7 and others following in his wake.

Subtly amalgamating Platonic form (*eidos*), Aristotelian teleology (*entelecheia*), and Ovidian metamorphosis, Goethe's botanical writings of the late 1780s both revive and repurpose the ancient conception of nature-as-process and Scholasticism's concept of being as act. The empiricist, in origin Nominalist, understanding of

---

34. *EM* 75.
35. *GHA* 12:432 (#488).
36. Balthasar 2001, 139.

difference as static and disjunctive thus is being challenged by a dynamic and integrative conception of difference as the organizing principle of all organic life: "transformation" (*Verwandlung*). Goethe categorically rejects the assumption, well established since the days of Hobbes and Newton, that "all causality is external causality, [and that] the investigator need not take appearances to be fundamental."[37] As the genetic presentation of plant development in his *Metamorphosis of Plants* shows, which Goethe subsequently restates in epigrammatic form in *Maxims and Reflections*, scientific inquiry must always unfold as an observer's attentive and sympathetic tracing of the phenomenon's dynamic presentation as exemplified in the "continual transformation" of the plant's foliar structure. "We are well advised," Goethe remarks, "not to tarry in the realm of abstraction. What is esoteric tends to cause harm by seeking to become exoteric. Life is best taught by what is living."[38] No longer, then, is the self-identity of a thing grounded in the Newtonian idea of an inert "substance." Rather, it comes to be "seen" as an internally differentiating and self organizing process. "Difference," we might say, turns into a verb; where the Nominalists and their empiricist heirs had located the identity of an object in its strict "incommensurability" (*Verschiedenheit*) with other entities, organicist and dialectical thinking derives the identity of a thing, and the "law" governing its form, from the progressive differentiation that characterizes its very mode of appearance, which in turn is reflexively appraised by the observing intellect.

Goethe's momentous insight revives crucial aspects of Aristotelian and Thomistic thought that had largely been eclipsed by modernity's rejection of final causes and substantial forms in favor of instrumental or efficient models of reason. What drives the late eighteenth-century reappraisal of "difference" is the following question: How are mind and world ontologically configured *before* their relation comes to be viewed as an epistemological problem? It is this question that brings into focus the role of mental imagery and intuitive cognition as *originary* or *constitutive* acts, as opposed to the secondary and derivative status accorded them by Cartesian dualism and post-Lockean empiricism. As remains to be seen in greater detail, the question also shaped Husserl's early phenomenological writings, and it resurfaces in particularly concentrated form yet again in Heidegger's late meditation on the problem of identity and difference, specifically where he ponders Parmenides's gnomic pronouncement that "the same <is> thinking as well as being" (*to gar auto noein esti te kai einai*). What, Heidegger asks, are we to make of this constitutive "belonging together" of mind and

---

37. Brady 1998, 89.
38. *GHA* 12:432 (#487). See Halmi's discussion of the Romantic symbol as a comprehensive response to the rise of the mechanistic framework during the previous century, which "reduced phenomena to a handful of real properties, whether visible or not, and reconstructed the universe hypothetically from those properties according to uniform and mathematically specifiable principles" (2007, 35).

world? After all, it would appear that "we lack the foundation for determining anything reliable about the *belonging* together of man and Being" and thus are "confined within the attempt to represent the 'together' . . . as a coordination [*Zuordnung*] and to establish and explain this coordination either in terms of man or in terms of Being."[39] While obviously a being, "just like the stone, the tree, or the eagle," man's "distinctive feature lies in this, that, as the being who thinks, he is open to Being, face to face with Being." Crucially, then, "difference" (which by definition belongs to the domain of thinking) must not be "applied" to the mind/world relation since that very relation itself constitutes not an a posteriori synthesis of discrete entities but, instead, precedes all analytic or reflexive discrimination: "We stubbornly misunderstand this . . . *belonging* together of man and Being as long as we represent everything only in categories and mediations."[40] There is no warrant for modern Reason's peremptory disaggregation of mind and world, simply because the notion of difference that permits any such parsing is itself a primordial and constitutive feature of mental activity to begin with.

Most troubling to Heidegger is how the chasm that modern conceptualism has instituted between reason and its supposed other, the "world," which, in a revealing turn of phrase, J. G. Fichte will call the "non-I" (*nicht-Ich*), has caused thinking to be conflated with "representation." For the modern subject to recover the identity of mind and world—that is, their ontological "belonging together"—it is imperative that we "move away from the attitude of representational thinking [*vorstellendes Denken*]."[41] Goethe's far more concrete and practical response to the same problem warrants close examination, not least because, unlike Hegel in his own time and Heidegger a century later, Goethe does not take it for granted that a theoretical dilemma will necessarily have to be remedied by further theoretical argument. Instead, what distinguishes Goethe's scientific writings from those of virtually all his peers, with the notable exception of Alexander von Humboldt, is their insistently concrete and practical character. In subtly understated language, Goethe's botanical writings cannily anticipate modern phenomenology by establishing an unfailingly concrete and dynamic model of what it means to be in the presence of phenomena or, simply, to "see." His contention that "all truth is only ever formed and visually

---

39. Heidegger 1969, 30; see also McDowell's (1996) influential discussion of "how conceptual capacities are drawn on *in* receptivity, not exercised *on* some supposedly prior deliverances of receptivity." Against Donald Davidson's view of experience as a strictly "extra-conceptual impact on sensibility," McDowell argues that, logically, we have no choice but to affirm that "the conceptual contents that are most basic . . . are already possessed by impressions themselves" (1996, 9–10).

40. Heidegger 1969, 31–32.

41. Ibid., 32. For a discussion of Heidegger's critique of the representational model of thinking, see his "The Age of the World Picture" in Heidegger 2002, 57–85; and my discussion in Pfau 2013a, 21–27.

apprehended" hints at his decisive break with the Kantian model of apperception that accompanies the synthesis of sensory data in what remains a heavily compartmentalized, not to say baroque, architecture of the mind.[42] For Goethe, seeing is not mere "experience" (*Erfahrung*) but an "event" (*Ereignis*) that has much in common with ancient "contemplation" (*theōria*), "wonder" (*thaumazein*), and "revelation" (*parousia*). What Goethe calls *Ereignis*—the word so momentously placed at the end of *Faust II* ("Alles Vergängliche / Ist nur ein Gleichnis / Das Unzulängliche / Hier wird's Ereignis")—is anterior to the category of efficient causation that had largely come to be viewed as the *only* paradigm of rationality since the scientific revolution of the seventeenth century.[43]

Moreover, his deictic emphasis on the here and now ("Hier *wird's Ereignis*") also hints at a revelatory, higher kind of knowing that can eventuate only as the coincidence of empirical sight and symbolic vision. Notably, Goethe's foregrounding of the event character of beauty as self-manifesting and instantaneously arresting reflects an (in origin Protestant) reluctance to invest the beautiful with transcendental significance, precisely because it is inherently bound up with manipulable, visible appearance. As von Balthasar notes, "From the standpoint of Protestantism, beauty has to be transferred wholly to the sphere of event [*Ereignis*]" because, from that perspective, "any kind of regularity, of immanence which is seen as a perduring, inherent *qualitas*, as Being-in-repose, as *habitus*, as something that can be manipulated, is already by that very fact identified with demonic corruption."[44] In the event, Goethe's deep Platonist filiations allow him to overcome Protestantism's peremptory qualification of the aesthetic "event" as finite, contingent, and self-consuming. Indeed, more conspicuously than in his literary oeuvre, it is in the domain of scientific inquiry that Goethe recognizes the intrinsic purposiveness and efficiency of natural forms as attesting to the transcendent status of beauty.

It bears considering, at least briefly, how Goethe's concept of the event will be echoed by the later Heidegger, who specifically links *Ereignis* with a strictly nonproprietary practice of "seeing" or "beholding." For both, "event" recalls us to a prediscursive encounter between mind and world, seemingly unmediated by the "scaffolding" (*Ge-Stell*) that pervades all of modern technological rationality. "Event" names the space of where a primordial "belonging together" of mind and world un-

---

42. "Alle Wahrheit zuletzt wird nur gebildet, geschaut" (*GHA* 1:211).

43. *GHA* 3:364. English: "All things corruptible / Are but a parable; Earth's insufficiency / Here finds fulfillment" (Goethe 1959, 288).

44. As von Balthasar continues, on this (Protestant) "assumption . . . the world of the beautiful originally belongs to man, and it is he who determines its content and boundaries. The native country of the beautiful would then be the world or, at most, 'Being' itself, but only in so far as Being is not divine but 'creaturely'. In scholastic terms, therefore, we could say that beauty is an attribute of 'predicated' and not of 'transcendental Being'" (1982, 67, 69).

folds, or "eventuates"—not as a subjective "experience" (*Erlebnis*) but as the founding reality absent which there could be neither any experience nor any propositions ventured about it.

> Within the scaffolding there prevails a strange ownership and a strange appropriation. We must experience simply this owning in which man and Being are delivered over to each other, that is, we must enter into what we call *the event of appropriation*. <The word "event" we take from autochthonous language. Event means literally to bring-into-view, that is, to behold, that is, to draw close to oneself *qua* looking, to appropriate.> . . . What we experience in the frame as the constellation of Being and man through the modern world of technology is a prelude to what is called the event of appropriation. This event, however, does not necessarily persist in its prelude. For in the event of appropriation the possibility arises that it may overcome the mere dominance of the frame to turn it into a more original appropriating.[45]

Heidegger's "event" is the moment where thinking experiences itself as more than a belated synthesis and appropriation of supposedly mindless, perceptual data; and to close in on this "more-than" requires a phenomenological turn of sorts. Mind recognizes its reciprocal involvement with the ambient world, one whose appearances are structured in ways that conform to, indeed elicit and refine, the subject's conceptual powers. This coincidence of thinking and perceiving (*noein*) must not be confused with Kantian "apperception," however, for the event in question is not exclusively subject centered. Rather, Heidegger contends, to think is by definition *to act on an already existing relation*, to respond to the call of the phenomenon in its primordial givenness, which begins with the beholder recognizing herself as ontologically entwined with the phenomenal world. Both the phenomenon's givenness and its capacity to instill in the beholder an awareness of this "belonging together" of mind and world recall Aquinas's notion of creation as gift (*donum*), which by its very nature enjoins the recipient to honor and care for it.

For Heidegger, this intimate bond linking seeing and thinking, intuitive and conscious awareness of the world, shines through in the etymological connection

---

45. Heidegger 1969, 36–37; the text in angular brackets is omitted in Stambaugh's translation; the full German passage reads as follows: "Im Ge-Stell waltet ein seltsames Vereignen und Zueignen. Es gilt, dieses Eignen, worin Mensch und Sein einander ge-eignet sind, schlicht zu erfahren, d.h. einzukehren in das, was wir das Ereignis nennen. Das Wort Ereignis ist der gewachsenen Sprache entnommen. Er-eignen heißt ursprünglich: er-äugen, d.h. erblicken, im Blicken zu sich rufen, an-eignen. . . . Was wir im Ge-Stell als der Konstellation von Sein und Mensch durch die moderne technische Welt erfahren, ist ein Vorspiel dessen, was Er-eignis heißt. Dieses verharrt jedoch nicht notwendig in seinem Vorspiel. Denn im Er-eignis spricht die Möglichkeit an, daß es das bloße Walten des Ge-Stells in ein anfänglicheres Sein verwindet" (Heidegger 1978, 24–25).

between "event" (*Er-eignis*) and "bringing-into-view" (*Er-äugen*). Yet once the event character of "seeing" as a kind of envisioning has been forgotten and empiricism and mechanist theories of perception have resolved seeing into a simple mirroring of isolated particulars, "difference" becomes sheer heterogeneity, and scientific inquiry no longer understands itself as premised on an anterior coordination of mind and world. The concept of difference now serves only to arrange ever more elaborate taxonomies of the kind associated with Linné. Paradoxically, the latter's inflationary tabulation of formal differences (of genera, species, subspecies, etc.) has a numbing effect on those lingering over Linné's actuarial tables. Untethered from all consideration of being and process, difference reduces to mere "indifference." Or, as Heidegger will eventually observe, unable to name Being itself, modern reason in reducing difference to sheer heterogeneity surrenders its deliberative and prudential dimension. Instead, it devolves into a quasi-algorithmic, computational form of "reckoning" (as Hobbes likes to call it) whose essence, according to Heidegger, is crystallized in the idea of technology as "scaffolding" (*Ge-Stell*).

While Heidegger may think of Hegel as the quintessential representative of modern metaphysics and its "forgetfulness of Being" (*Seinsvergessenheit*), the latter's writings often draw close to the notion of event that Heidegger has in mind. Extending Hölderlin's speculative interest in Heraclitus's idea of a "self-differentiating One" (*to hen diapheromenonn auto heautō*), Hegel's project does not seek to reconcile mind and world in the way that Kant's "transcendental synthesis" attempts to reconcile the order of appearances with that of understanding (*Verstand*). Instead, Hegel dispenses altogether with the representationalist paradigm of knowledge, what he calls "picture-thinking," which aims to reproduce the correspondence of mind and its object in propositional form. Instead, Hegel's *Phenomenology* rethinks the "difference" between reason and its objects as a temporal process whereby an as yet unrealized "unity" (*Einheit*) between them is gradually revealed and restored. On this dialectical account, "difference" no longer betokens absolute "opposition" (*Gegensatz*) and incommensurability. Rather, it is experienced in temporal and historical form as an ongoing process of "mediation" (*Vermittlung*). Hence, simply to have thought beings as "different" (*verschieden*) already means to have apprehended them as standing in some "relation" (*Beziehung*) to one another. Profoundly indebted to Plotinus, Hegel thus views difference as the way in which the finite intellect is engaged in the labor of "mediation, which is nothing but self-sameness [understood] as its own movement [*die Vermittlung ist nichts anders als die sich bewegende Sichselbstgleichheit*]."[46]

Hegel extends a claim first advanced by Schelling vis-à-vis Fichte and Kant: namely, that as the principal tool of the understanding, the "concept" (*Begriff*) does

---

46. Hegel 1977, 11 (German: Hegel 1952, 21).

not operate in radical separation from being (*Sein*) but, instead, is fundamentally on a continuum with it. The concept is the subject's principal tool for making explicit how it has been participating *in* being all along; and in the process of conceptual thinking the subject furthermore comes to recognize itself as continually "self-forming" (*bildend*). For the young Schelling, the central challenge is "to explain the absolute correspondence of the object and the representation, of being and cognition." That neither Cartesian rationalism nor Lockean empiricism accepted this challenge confirms modern epistemology's misguided embrace of a "representationalist" model of knowledge, which tacitly presupposed that mind and world had *already* established contact. Here philosophical inquiry could advance further only "under *one* condition, [namely] if there existed a being capable of an intuition of itself, that is, simultaneously representing and represented, or intuiting and intuited." Each intuitive act that is directed outward at the world of appearances thereby also constitutes an act of "self-inspection" (*Selbstanschauung*) and, consequently, also of "self-limitation" (*Selbstbeschränkung*). It is only through the dialectic of intuitive and reflective commerce with the world of appearances that mind becomes self-aware as a temporally evolving and distinct being. Inasmuch as "every *act of the soul* is also a determinate *stage of the soul*," all discrete acts of intuition incrementally produce the history of self-consciousness: "The history of the human spirit will prove none other than the history of the different *stages* [*Zustände*] in passing through which spirit progressively attains an intuition of itself, [which is] pure self-consciousness."[47] Far from a correlate of a "representation" or proposition formulated by a timeless and hermetic consciousness, it is this intuition of external phenomena that establishes the conditions under which self-consciousness and self-recognition become possible in the first place.

Schelling's early critique of vestiges of dualism in Kant and of Fichte's overly schematic and formalist concept of idealism helped prepare for Hegel's dialectical dismantling of empiricism's notion of "sense certainty" (*sinnliche Gewissheit*) in chapter 1 of the *Phenomenology*. As Hegel there demonstrates, modern philosophy's inability to grasp the true nature of dialectical thinking stems from its widespread and erroneous understanding of the "concept" as but the static representation of an equally static and alien reality. To the extent that our intellectual armature presupposes the ontological separation of mind and world, he contends, we have not yet

---

47. Schelling 1994, 77–78, 90. As Pinkard notes, "When we reflect . . . on the conditions under which we can know something about a world independent of us, we necessarily break apart items that are originally at one with each other, and we arrange those items in some kind of order. Thus, we separate 'representations' from the objects that they seem to represent, and we then wonder how it is that they are supposed to be brought back together. . . . Unless there were already a *pre-reflective* unity of thought and being, reflection could not do its work, without our already 'being in touch' with things" (2002, 177–78).

understood what a "concept" properly is. Hence, what Hegel defines as the "labor of the spirit" (*Arbeit des Geistes*) "consists not so much in purging the individual of an immediate, sensuous mode of apprehension . . . but rather in just its opposite, in freeing determinate thoughts [*Gedanken*] from their fixity. . . . [For] fixed thoughts have the 'I', the power of the negative, or pure actuality, for the substance and element of their existence." To explicate the intrinsic "dynamism" (*Bewegung*) of thought is the great task of speculative philosophy: "Thoughts become fluid when pure thinking . . . recognizes itself as a moment, or when the pure certainty of self abstracts from itself — not by leaving itself out, or setting itself aside, but by giving up the *fixity* of its self-positing. . . . Through this movement the pure thoughts become *notions* [*Begriffe*], and are only now what they are in truth, self-movements [*Selbstbewegungen*], circles, spiritual essences, which is what their substance is."[48] The reappraisal of "difference" just sketched thus asks that we understand seeing as far more than a contingent encounter with raw perceptual data and that we grasp visual experience instead as a symbolic event, that is, as *Darstellung* rather than trivially contingent "representation."

And yet, even as Hegel's dialectic loosens the grip of representationalist "picture-thinking" and reduces the emphasis on a "pure" conceptualism typical of modern epistemology, his own deep-seated rationalism still constrains the experience of natural being *as a phenomenon* in ways that Goethe, for one, cannot accept. Thus, beginning with the *Phenomenology* (1807) and continuing through his lectures on aesthetics in the early 1820s, Hegel construes thinking as progressively distancing itself from the contingent, "sensuous" (*sinnlich*) consciousness in which it had originated and ultimately supplanting it altogether in the medium of the concept. Though Hegel is careful not to negate or disparage sensuous experience outright, the focus of his phenomenology is on how, in its interaction with "external" matter, consciousness ultimately consummates itself as a reflected totality. Hence the communally valid self-awareness that Hegel calls "spirit" necessarily *transcends* and ultimately *comprehends*, or "internalizes" (*erinnern*), all its previous instantiations—with Hegel's *Erinnerung* evidently indebted to Plato's notion of *anamnesis*. What Hegel calls the "labor of the spirit" (*Arbeit des Geistes*) can be accomplished only by gradually absorbing sensuous particularity into consciousness and reappraising contingent appearance solely for its conceptual yield. By its very nature, mere "sight"—or, rather, "gazing" (*Schauen*), as Hegel calls it — will always fall short of reflexive, conceptually

---

48. Hegel 1977, 19–20 (German: Hegel 1952, 30–31). Taylor characterizes consciousness as quasi "bi-polar: it is consciousness *of* something; and this means that its contents are not just inert, but bear on something outside. As a knowing subject my thoughts, perceptions, etc., are also knowledge *claims*" (1975, 135); see also Pinkard's detailed reading of how, early in the *Phenomenology*, Hegel shows that "the *representationalist* picture of knowledge . . . fails to fulfill the goals it sets for itself" (1996, 21).

determinate insight. For though not altogether bereft of conceptual import, the act of seeing proves distressingly inarticulate because, as Hegel never tires to insist, the "articulation of form" (*Ausbildung der Form*) can only ever be realized in the medium of speculative concepts: "Truth has only the concept as the element of its existence [*an dem Begriffe allein das Element ihrer Existenz zu haben*]."[49] It is precisely on this point, the subordination of the visual to the abstract and of the symbolic to the conceptual, that Goethe begs to differ.

"SEEING THE IDEA": INTUITING ACTUALITY AND POTENTIALITY IN *THE METAMORPHOSIS OF PLANTS*

In Goethe's writings, seeing does not involve passively receiving a contingent material reality; nor can it be reduced to verifying and representing contents already known. It belongs to the order of the "event" (*Ereignis*) rather than "experience" (*Erlebnis*). In the course of it, the seeing subject is transformed by its visual interaction with a dynamic phenomenon, one properly seen only insofar as the observer resists the temptation of exercising epistemic dominion over it. To see means to participate in Being as a self-giving phenomenon rather than prejudge it as inert *res extensa*. More than Nicholas or Dionysius before him, Goethe emphasizes the dynamic nature of the phenomenon, effectively stipulating that it can only be visualized on account of its active, self-manifesting nature. Throughout his botanical writings, Goethe understands seeing as the intellectual intuition of a symbolic form, a mode of cognition that Kant, for one, had declared to be impossible, yet that had always been an integral feature of the Neoplatonist tradition from Plotinus to Nicholas. The subject of such *visio mentis* or *visio intellectualis* participates in appearance as symbolic form and gradually recognizes such form as the specific, visible manifestation of the very law of being. Unlike the object knowledge that Lockean empiricism had anchored in some strictly nonconceptual sensation, intuition for Goethe relates to phenomena precisely by visualizing them as progressively manifesting, in their structured and progressive unfolding, the *logos* to which they owe their very being. To see for him means to apprehend the sensory, not as a mere prelude to conceptuality, but as *inviting us to visualize, and thus participate in, the order of the intelligible itself*. Intuition does not simply anticipate conceptuality any more than it is to be reduced to the conceptual. In fact, the space of intelligibility opened up by mental vision (*visio mentalis*) is not coextensive with conceptuality but, on the contrary, constitutes its very

---

49. Hegel 1977, 7 (German: Hegel 1952, 16); on the paradoxes of "sense-certainty" and their first speculative resolution in "perception" (*Wahrnehmung*) in the *Phenomenology*, see Pinkard 1996, 20–34; and Taylor 1975, 140–47.

foundation. Insofar as intuition (*Anschauung*) fuses apperception and cognition, it allows the individual to participate, albeit only *per analogiam*, in the *logos* as it manifests itself in some specific, visible form.

Concurrently, each act of intuition also brings the beholder's intellectual and ethical persona into sharper focus. If "the highest gift we have received from God and Nature is life itself, the monad's rotation around its own axis, . . . a second grace [*eine zweite Gunst*] involves experience [*das Erlebte*], the becoming aware and intervention [*Eingreifen*] of the monad in the external domains, whereby it recognizes itself as an internally boundless and externally limited being. . . . The third [gift] concerns what, in active practice, we oppose as word and letter [*als Handlung und Tat, als Wort und Schrift*] to the external world."[50] It is this reciprocity of call and response, of the phenomenal world as a kind of "favor" (*Gunst*) eliciting and cultivating (*bilden*) the beholder's growing powers of intuition and reflection, that is at the center of Goethe's scientific and literary pursuits throughout the 1790s and beyond. Reacting against "the development of the sciences whose techniques of objectivation could not accommodate his concept of a morphology of nature," Goethe became increasingly critical of modern science's disaggregation of nature into discrete and unrelated singularities and its consequent failure to grasp nature as an ontologically given reality rather than a product of human conceptual or material intervention.[51] By now, it should be clear that the present reading parts ways with recent attempts at "demystifying" both Goethe's concept of natural form as primordially given and his concept of the symbolic forms, variously scientific or lyric, in which natural form is to be rendered intelligible for us.

Two examples will suffice to demarcate the fundamental divergence of approach. Not coincidentally both appeared within a year of one another and set about to dismantle the putative, and quintessentially Goethean, "myth" of natural form as self-originating. Helmut Müller-Sievers has offered a sharply critical appraisal of "self-generation" (*epigenesis*), which he dismisses as "an imposition" because it gives credence to the idea of "mundane origination," a notion he deems inauthentic, indeed a conceptual fraud, from the very outset. On his dogmatically antirealist account, epigenesis "generates ideologies by suggesting that their origin be natural." Fundamentally, Müller-Sievers's argument aims to expose the very concept of nature as pure ideology and, consequently, to repudiate each and every institution premised on nature as ontology, including love, marriage, and indeed human language. Tellingly, Müller-Sievers's discussion of Goethe focuses almost exclusively on *Elective Affinities* while largely bypassing the botanical writings in which Goethe's concept of nature as a dynamic entelechy is being developed. Naturally, a critic intent on con-

---

50. *GHA* 12:396–97 (#227–29).
51. Breidbach 2006, 61.

firming dystopian conclusions he has presumably reached beforehand ("Marriage is impossible," a mere function of "intrigue and accidentality, . . . and love does not mediate between these two spheres") will find it easier to press his case against nature in the context of human agents and institutions.[52] For his hermeneutic of suspicion is rather more difficult to sustain if one were to shift his focus to where Goethe for one had always placed it: namely, in the domain of organic life and the phenomenology of its experience. For it is the study of natural forms that, if anything, Goethe thought could yield a reliable account of self-generation. Whether the epigenetic logic of organic life can plausibly account for the production and replication of human social and cultural forms and institutions, however, remains a far more tangled and ambiguous question that, to judge by the *Elective Affinities* or his *Roman Elegies*, Goethe tackled with fitting, deeply considered irony.

Analogous to Müller-Sievers's critique of epigenesis, David Wellbery has sought to unmask the "primordial orality" of Goethe's lyric oeuvre as a historically contingent instance of myth-making. Echoing Wilfrid Sellar's antirealist critique of the "myth of the given," Wellbery insistently questions the mythic self-presence at the heart of Goethe's lyric voice, portraying it as an ingenious case of cultural autoproduction. Summing up his reading of "Mahomet's Gesang" (1772), Wellbery views that early lyric as conjuring up a "heavenly Origin, the flow of originary liquidity downward from the mountains, communication of the divine to all who dwell within the compass of its historical law. The *force* of orality carries the life of nature into the cultural domain and thereby establishes the identity of a historical subject, a *Volk*."[53] Still, inasmuch as any act of hermeneutic suspicion requires a legitimate target, and not a straw man, the "force" suffusing lyric speech suggests that more is at work than sheer contrivance and performative skill. In fact, the enduring power of Goethe's lyrics cannot be reduced to a historically contingent recalibration of lyric form as the "phonocentric myth" of a "subjective presence-to-self in the immediacy and transparency of the *s'entendre parler*."[54] More accurate, it seems, would be to understand the charismatic presence of Goethe's lyric voice as having been discerned within, and distilled from, language itself. That is, his poetic voice "finds" and "actualizes" realities that manifest the transcendent *logos* underwriting the possibility of significant utterance no less than the formal coherence of visible, natural phenomena. Thus, the

---

52. Müller-Sievers 1997, 5, 122.

53. Wellbery 1996, 192 (first emphasis mine).

54. Ibid., 205, referencing Derrida's early critique of Husserl's phonocentrism in *Speech and Phenomena*. The skeptical epistemology undergirding Wellbery's reading also informs de Man's earlier influential critique of the Romantic symbol, which he argues reflects a general "temptation . . . for the self to borrow, so to speak, the temporal stability that it lacks from nature, and to devise strategies by means of which nature is brought down to a human level while still escaping from "the unimaginable touch of human time" (de Man 1983, 197).

"primordial orality" of which Wellbery speaks does not catch the lyric poet in some illicit act of auto-production and self-mystification. Rather, lyric speech originates in the recognition that the world of natural appearance and the visceral attunement it elicits in the beholder jointly attest to an underlying, timeless *logos*. The *source* of Goethe's "primordial orality" is not itself an origin retroactively produced; it is not an ingenious contrivance but, on the contrary, reflects a heightened responsiveness to the call of the phenomenon, whose symbolic significance lyric speech seeks to affirm, refine, and communicate.

Let us now return to consider how Goethe's botanical theories reject the mechanistic and abstract epistemologies that had dominated the study of nature since the later seventeenth century. Most troubling to Goethe is how these frameworks preclude our grasping the primordial connection between an intelligent observer and organic life and, as a result, frame the study of nature as a laborious reconstruction of discrete "objects" in terms of efficient and material causation. What had faded from view was a deeper understanding of (natural) being as thing (*res*) and act (*actus*), as a process of continual differentiation, variation, and transformation that in his botanical writings Goethe captures under the heading "metamorphosis" and in his poetic oeuvre, as a primordial, self-constituting, and unconditioned lyric voice. Throughout his far-flung botanical writings, Goethe time and again insists that to understand the development of an organism means to grasp its constituent parts as the differentiated manifestation of a single morphological template. Organicism implies that we assume a fundamental homology whereby seemingly distinct features of a complex organism can be visualized as manifestations of a single idea. Rather than posit the substantive heterogeneity of parts, "difference" in this new, simultaneously concrete and speculative sense enables the gifted observer to access the dynamic and teleological constitution of living forms.

Differentiation thus lies at the very root of Goethe's lifelong commitment to morphology as the only justifiable method for the study of life, be it in the domain of biology, psychology, or aesthetics. In his 1817 preface to a new edition of *The Metamorphosis of Plants* (first published in 1790), Goethe notes that "when we study forms, the organic ones in particular, nowhere do we find permanence, repose, or termination. We find rather that everything is in ceaseless flux. This is why our language makes such frequent use of the term 'Bildung' to designate what has been brought forth and likewise what is in the process of being brought forth." Beyond the two distinct meanings of *Bildung* here identified, there is yet another manifestation of it, namely, "a drive [*Trieb*] to recognize living forms as such, to understand their outwardly visible and tangible parts in relation to one another, to lay hold of them as indicia of inner parts."[55] In what may be a fragment of a larger poem on natural pro-

---

55. *GHA* 13:55 / *EM* 23.

cesses, the hexametric "Metamorphosis of Animal Life" (Metamorphose der Tiere), Goethe again identifies the organism's pattern of continual self-differentiation as the very law of organic form:

Dieser schöne Begriff von Macht und Schranken, von Willkür
Und Gesetz, von Freiheit und Maß, von beweglicher Ordnung

[This beautiful notion of power and limits, of spontaneity
And law, of freedom and measure, of dynamic order.][56]

In its basic outline, this conception of organic life as unceasing and purposive self-organization appears to have first occurred to Goethe during his Italian journey of 1787. First published in 1817 as part of some autobiographical miscellanies in his journal *Zur Morphologie*, Goethe's short reminiscence of his "propitious encounter" (*Glückliches Ereignis*) with Schiller sometime around 1788–89 centers on a conversation about the status of method in scientific inquiry. Cued by Schiller's misgivings about the "mangled methods of regarding Nature [*eine so zerstückelte Art die Natur zu behandeln*]," Goethe had launched into "a spirited explanation of my [Goethe's] theory of the metamorphosis of plants with graphic pen sketches of a symbolic plant. He listened and looked with great interest, with unerring comprehension, but when I had ended, he shook his head, saying, 'That is not an empiric experience, it is an idea.' . . . Controlling myself, I replied, 'How splendid that I have ideas without knowing it, and can see them before my very eyes.'"[57] Momentarily stung by the gravity of Schiller's objection, Goethe realizes that to formulate a compelling account of organic development requires a far more explicit notion of what it means to relate to phenomena or, simply, to "see" an idea.

Goethe's vexed conversation with Schiller recalls similar difficulties that Socrates encounters when trying to explain to Parmenides how individual, "many" things partake of one form. "Each form as a whole [*holon to eidos*]—one thing—is in each of the many." Assuming that there is just one order of being, Parmenides naturally assumes that form's oneness will be fragmented into the many insofar as it inheres in

---

56. *GHA* 1:203 (trans. mine); first printed in 1820, the date of composition of "Metamorphosis of Animals" is rather uncertain; Trunz proposes near-contemporaneity with Goethe's closely related didactic poem, "Metamorphosis of Plants," written in June 1798, though a diary entry of 10 November 1806 has been construed as evidence of a far later composition of "Metamorphosis of Animals," a poem whose strictly hexametric form also differs considerably from the elegiac distich employed in "Metamorphosis of Plants" (see *GHA* 1:616–19).

57. *GHA* 10:540–41/*EM* 217; for a discussion of this pivotal exchange and on Goethe's inception of metamorphosis as a template for studying the development of living forms, see Brady 1998, 83–111; Miller 2002, 45–77; Holland 2009, 19–55; Breidbach 2006, 17–20.

many discrete beings: "'So, being one and the same, it will be at the same time, as a whole, in things that are many and separate; and thus it would be separate from itself.'—'No it wouldn't,' Socrates said." Instead, by way of analogy he recommends thinking of form as the spatiotemporal totality of "one and the same day, [which] is in many places at the same time and is none the less not separate from itself. If it's like that, each of the forms might be, at the same time, one and the same in all."[58] Not only does the particularity of each individual thing not contradict the timeless self-identity of its form, but it is only on account of the latter that we are able to participate in a given phenomenon with genuine understanding. As Goethe was to remark in his *Italian Journey*, "How could I recognize that this or that form was a plant if all were not built on the same model."[59]

Undergirding Goethe's botanical theorizing, then, is the possibility of mental imagery and an interior vision—a *visio intellectualis* that, some important differences notwithstanding, comports with how Plotinus and Nicholas of Cusa had conceived of it long before. Crucially, for Goethe as for his illustrious predecessors, such mental imagery must comport with the process character of the "thing" (*res*) as it dynamically discloses itself rather than construct an "object" in an instantaneous synthesis of perceptual and conceptual values. The internal differentiation that defines plant life demands a quasi-phenomenological type of perceptual intelligence, one that undergoes a correlative *Bildung* as it responds to the evolving appearances of organic life. In a short essay of 1823, Goethe notes how his method of "concrete thinking" (*gegenständliches Denken*) ultimately refers back to but also qualifies the ancient precept of self-knowledge (*gnōthi seauton*) that, from the Stoics all the way through Descartes and Kant, had anchored the project of philosophical rationalism. As regards the latter's quarantining of intuition from reflection, Goethe demurs: "The great and important-sounding advice, 'Know thyself,' always appeared to me to be open to question, as a ruse of conspiring priests intent upon confusing the laity with unattainable ideals, upon seducing them from active life to dangerous introspection. Man knows himself only insofar as he knows the world, becoming aware of it only within himself, and of himself only within it. Each new subject, well-observed, opens up within us a new vehicle of thought."[60] In this element of adventitious self-recognition arising from humble, inductive seeing—contrary to the *libido dominandi* that fuels post-Cartesian, deductive rationalism—we can still trace the outlines of Nicholas of Cusa's catechetical understanding of iconic vision. An incremental

---

58. Plato, *Parmenides* 131a–b; see also *Rep.* Bk. 5, where Socrates shows that to be truly "awake" means to grasp the form and concrete being as both distinct *and* related. The one who properly knows reality must "believe in the beautiful itself, can both see it and the things that participate in it and doesn't believe that the participants are it or that it itself is the participants" (476c).

59. *GHA* 11:266 / Goethe 1989, 214.

60. *GHA* 13:38 / *EM* 235–36.

and reciprocal process of exchange between observer and phenomenon, Goethe's concept of seeing recalls a type of epistemic humility all but expunged from natural philosophy and philosophy during the previous century and a half.

Before drawing additional implications from Goethe's incidental remarks on the art of botanical observation, let us scrutinize Goethe's central proposition of a "symbolic plant" and his provocative claim that by means of it he could "see [ideas] before my very own eyes." The notion of an archetypal or symbolic plant (*Urpflanze*) initially surfaces in Goethe's account of his stay at Padua, which included a first visit to Europe's oldest botanic garden on 27 September 1786.[61] As he notes:

> Many plants can stay outdoors even in the winter, . . . [and] it is agreeable and instructive to wander amidst vegetation that is foreign to us. We eventually think no more at all about plants we are accustomed to, like other long familiar objects; and what is observation without thought? Here in this newly encountered diversity that idea of mine keeps gaining strength, namely, that perhaps all plant forms can be derived from one plant. Only in this way would it be possible truly to determine genera and species.[62]

Not to be confused with Charles Darwin's later notion of "one common ancestor," Goethe's *Urpflanze* does not hypostatize a primal organism *inferentially*, that is, on the basis of intermediate forms extracted from the geological record. In fact, Goethe's botanical studies unfold in almost complete indifference to his own concurrent geological research or that of professional stratigraphy. Instead, what prompts Goethe's hypothesis of an archetypal *Urpflanze* is his dissatisfaction with the mechanical, Linnéan taxonomy of species based on a single arbitrary physiological trait that often led to the peculiar attribution of a given species to a genus with which it has nothing in common except the one criterion that governs the taxonomic process.[63] His basic critical concerns with Linnéan taxonomy aside, Goethe's far more

---

61. See Boyle 1991, 423.

62. *GHA* 11:60 / Goethe 1989, 53–54.

63. On Linné, whose main work, *Systema Naturae* (1st ed. 1735), while influential throughout the remainder of the century, was already assailed by Buffon's *Histoire Naturelle* (1749–67), see Grene and Depew 2004, 72–74. For an account of Goethe's emergent interest in Linné, botany, and (via Herder) the transmutation of species, see Richards 2002, 375, 383–400. Above all, Goethe credits Rousseau for having suggested to him "a method more progressive and less removed from the senses than the one pursued by . . . Linné." As Goethe writes, Linné's taxonomical approach, in which a man is "expected to commit to memory a ready-made terminology, a certain number of words, and bywords, with which to classify any given form . . . always seemed to me to result in a kind of mosaic, in which one completed block is placed next to another, creating finally a single picture from thousands of pieces; this was somewhat distasteful to me" (*GHA* 13:158, 160–61 / *EM* 157, 159–60); on that passage, see Brady 1998, 92–93. For fine introductions to Goethe's concepts of morphology and the *Urphänomen*, see Boyle 1991, 592–97; Steigerwald 2002.

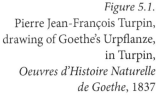

Figure 5.1.
Pierre Jean-François Turpin,
drawing of Goethe's Urpflanze,
in Turpin,
*Oeuvres d'Histoire Naturelle
de Goethe*, 1837

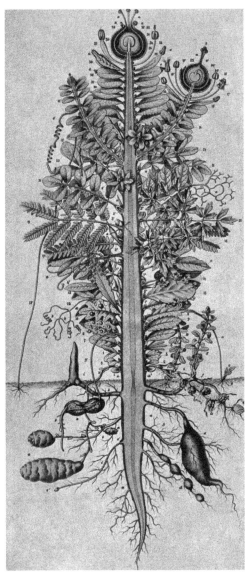

pressing objective is to recover the ontological unity of "thinking and seeing" that Plato had probed long before in the *Parmenides*. A subsequent entry (17 April 1787) in his *Italian Journey* finds Goethe musing on the opulent vegetation of Palermo and recalling his "old fanciful idea [*alte Grille*]": "Might I not discover the primordial plant [*Urpflanze*] amid this multitude? Such a thing must exist, after all!"[64] Even if Goethe would much later express bemusement at his youthful expectation of actu-

---

64. *GHA* 11:266 / Goethe 1989, 214.

ally finding the primordial plant, or idea, materializing before him, his hopes were not altogether unfounded. In fact, at every stage of its formation, a given plant does realize *some* aspect of that idea, which presumably gave the French botanist Pierre Jean François Turpin (1775–1840) the scientific and aesthetic confidence to produce a woodcut of what the young poet had claimed to see with his very eyes (fig. 5.1).

Most famously, Goethe's letter to Herder, written from Naples on 17 May 1787, identifies the two principal traits governing Goethe's botanical theory: its economy and its susceptibility to imaginative extension and variation.

> The chief point, where the germ is lodged, I have discerned quite clearly and beyond doubt. The rest I can also already see as a whole, with only a few points still remaining to be captured more distinctly. The archetypal plant [*Urpflanze*] as I see it will be the most wonderful creation in the whole world, and nature herself will envy me for it. With this model, and the key to it, one will be able to invent plants without limit to conform, that is to say, plants which even if they do not actually exist nevertheless might exist and which are not merely picturesque and poetic visions and illusions, but have inner truth and logic. The same law will permit itself to be applied to everything that is living.[65]

Recalling insights first gathered in 1787 and published only in 1816, Goethe's observations would powerfully resonate in the introduction to Alexander von Humboldt's *Kosmos* (1845). Remarking how "in the midst of this immense variety, and this periodic transformation of animal and vegetable productions, we see incessantly revealed the primordial mystery of all organic development," Humboldt expressly recalls Goethe, with whom he had begun an intensive exchange of ideas about plant biology, geology, and the laws of life following their first meeting in March 1794. In all its diversity, he writes, we find revealed "that same great problem of *metamorphosis* which Goethe has treated with more than common sagacity, and to the solution of which man is urged by his desire of reducing vital forms to the smallest number of fundamental types." Like Goethe, Humboldt also stresses the reciprocal and dynamic interaction between the observer and natural phenomena: "Nature . . . whether considered as the universality of all that is and ever will be, . . . or as their mysterious prototype, reveals itself to the simple mind and feelings of man as something earthly, and closely allied to himself."[66]

Rejecting from the outset the notion "that the plant forms around us are . . . predetermined," Goethe later recalls being attracted by a diametrically opposed view that posits a structural correlation between botanical knowledge and the plant's

---

65. *GHA* 11:323–24 / *EM* 14.
66. Humboldt 1997, 41, 83.

mode of appearance as a dynamic, differentiating process. Thus, he finds himself enthralled by the sheer dynamism of organic life, "a happy mobility and flexibility, enabling [plants] to adapt themselves to the many conditions throughout the world, and to be formed and reformed in accordance with them."[67] To be sure, Goethe's formalism does not altogether reject the functionalist hypothesis of adaptive development; he merely opposes the more extreme view, advanced by Lamarck, that contingent environmental factors will *unilaterally* determine a plant's morphology and, in effect, alter its developmental trajectory in real time.[68] Characterized by both its conceptual frugality and its imaginative potential, Goethe's botanical theory holds that any given plant species develops by differentially realizing a single organic form: the leaf. In a sequence of paragraphs, Goethe's most comprehensive botanical text, the *Metamorphosis of Plants*, thus construes plant life as a trajectory of increasing morphological complexity. Presented in classical, almost Linnéan fashion, as a series of short, at times aphoristic paragraphs, Goethe's *Attempt to Elucidate the Metamorphosis of Plants* (1790) draws on an already rich array of carefully preserved and described specimens whose total number, by the time of Goethe's death, would exceed eighteen thousand.[69] As Goethe proceeds to detail, in the course of its developmental trajectory a given plant species differentially exfoliates a single *Gestalt* whose archetypal status Goethe gradually seeks to distill—not *infer*—through a series of precise empirical observations and descriptions. Seed-leaves [*Samenblätter*], roots, stem, branch, corolla [*Krone*], nectarines, calyx [*Kelch*], petals, fruits, and style [*Griffel*] all refer back to a single morphological template. Conceived as a process of "unceasing transformation" (*fortwährendes Umbilden*), all plant life thus unfolds as the continual metamorphosis of a single archetypal *Gestalt* or *Idee* for which the leaf furnishes the most compelling formal paradigm.[70]

I should immediately clarify that Goethe's "leaf" (*Blatt*) must "not be taken literally as the actual reduction of all serial diversity to the actual form of a stem leaf. Such a reading would contravene the Platonic character of archetypes in formalist theory. The 'leaf' represents an abstract generating principle from which stem

---

67. *GHA* 13:163 / *EM* 161–62.

68. Thus, in §30 in his *Metamorphosis of Plants*, Goethe acknowledges how "abundant nutriment retards the flowering of a plant and that moderate, or indeed scanty, nutriment hastens it" (*GHA* 13:72–73 / *EM* 42). See also the remarks in the later, autobiographical recollections of his botanical research ("Geschichte meiner botanischen Studien"), where Goethe appears to concede a more significant adaptive relation between plant development and environmental conditions (*GHA* 13:161 / *EM* 160); see also Richards 2002, 445; and Gould 2002, 288–89, who also sees Goethe's formalism as open to functionalist considerations.

69. Pörksen 2001, 203; on the genesis of Goethe's 1790 essay, see Boyle 1991, 592–97.

70. *GHA* 13:60 / *EM* 27; Goethe's concept of *Gestalt* (organic form) greatly influenced von Balthasar's understanding of it as the form "that transcends and comprehends both the knower and the known, and for that reason resists being reduced to either" (Schindler 2004, 167).

leaves depart least in actual expression."[71] Instead, the study of plant life thus resolves itself for Goethe into a rigorous forensic description of how the morphological core unit of the "leaf" (*Blatt*) generates variational differences over time and, in so doing, achieves a fuller, more complex expression that will eventually allow us to identify it as a specific plant. Jochen Bockemühl breaks down the developmental process into four discrete activities: (1) "shooting," when the leaf's apiculus extends away from the growing point"; (2) "articulating," when the tip "begins to move in several different directions"; (3) "spreading," when "the points of articulation begin to move away from each other"; and (4) "stemming," when "the stalk at the base of the leaf extends itself."[72] Echoing Ernst Cassirer's observation that mythical consciousness is above all distinguished by its "intensity," Bockemühl thus notes how the leaf, being the central module of Goethe's entire botanical theory, challenges the observer to participate in the phenomenon in a very specific manner: "It is crucial to emphasize that this increasing ideality is not an increasing abstraction. The greater ideality of the last two levels [i.e., the four generative activities just identified and the regulative movements of separating/interpenetrating and fusing/inversion] is not a function of their remoteness from the phenomena but, rather, of the degree of intensity with which we participate mentally in the phenomena."[73] In a drawing during his early botanical researches, Goethe offers a visual aid for this process in which the ideal can neither be framed as an antonym of empirically observable facts, nor as gratuitously abstracting from them (fig. 5.2).

Here, then, we are returned to the changing conception of "difference" in late eighteenth-century philosophy and the life sciences. That is, we find differentiation holding a constitutive function in Goethe's ontological view of life as manifesting itself in some dynamic, self-differentiating form or other: "whatever becomes appearance, must differentiate itself so as to appear at all [*was in die Erscheinung tritt, muß sich trennen, um nur zu erscheinen*]."[74] This process of differentiation,

---

71. Gould 2002, 285; see also Bockemühl, who notes that Goethe's temporal conception of form allows it to become manifest in, rather than conflict with, the particular phases of organic life: "Each individual now appears to be coming from something as well as passing to something else, and by so doing *represents*, to our mind, *more than itself*, since each form can no longer be separated from its before or after. . . . Viewed in the context of movement, the forms reveal what their stasis conceals, and they no longer seem unlike" (1998, 106).

72. Bockemühl 1998, 116.

73. Ibid., 127; see also Breithaupt, who remarks, "For Goethe the act of perception is the act of objectivity as such [*Akt der Gegenständlichkeit selbst*]. The perception of the object has the same structure as the object itself: the splitting up of the particular and the universal into a dynamic of reciprocity" (2000, 75). For David Wellbery, this "tension between finitude and infinity, the contingent and the necessary," is the defining characteristic of Romanticism's endogenous (self-generating) understanding of form (Wellbery 2012, 19).

74. *GHA* 13:561.

Figure 5.2. Johann W. von Goethe, drawing of leaf development, 1790

meanwhile, is characterized by two traits that, according to Goethe, define the *Bildung* of organic forms as a subtly agonistic "becoming" (*Werden*) and "metamorphosis" (*Umbildung*), with form continually oscillating between "polarity and intensification" (*Polarität und Steigerung*).[75] Likewise, as regards a given plant species' morphological complexity, variational differences, and occasional irregularity, Goethe posits two additional operative principles, rendered by Stephen Jay Gould as "the refinement of sap" and "cycles of expansion and contraction." Progressing from "cotyledon to flower," such "refinement" or "intensification" organizes all morphological differences along a linear, goal-oriented trajectory as, for example, in the gradated foliar structure of the sunflower. At the same time, Goethe, like Lamarck, also responds to "empirical data of greater complexity and messiness," for which reason he introduces a second principle, cyclical rather than sequential in kind.[76] His "cycles of expansion and contraction" thus seek to account for both the modification of the archetypal leaf (as pistil, stem leaf, calyx, etc.) and more contingent phenomena,

---

75. *GHA* 13:48; "tension is the seemingly indifferent state of an energized being that is utterly ready to manifest, differentiate, and polarize itself [der indifferent scheinende Zustand eines energischen Wesens in völliger Bereitschaft, sich zu manifestieren, zu differenzieren, zu polarisieren]" (*GHA* 12:369 (# 31).

76. Gould 2002, 287.

Figure 5.3. Perfoliate Rose, watercolor commissioned for Goethe's *Metamorphosis of Plants*, likely painted by a pupil of the Weimar drawing school, ca. 1790

such as peculiar digressions, excentric formations such as a perfoliate rose whose blossom is penetrated by its own stem (fig. 5.3).[77]

As Ronald Brady and Olaf Breidbach have noted in their detailed accounts of Goethe's plant morphology, the archetypal plant of which Goethe begins to speak in 1787 "was probably a general plan—rather than an ancestral species—from its inception." For Goethe postulates "(1) the 'general homology' of all appendicular organs of the shoot; (2) a generalized plan for the underlying organ; (3) by repetition and transformation of the underlying organ, a generalized plan for the whole shoot."[78] In short, the "idea" of an archetypal plant is neither an abstraction from the empirical processes of plant development nor a hypothesis ventured prior to the actual observation of organic growth. Rather, as it constitutes itself in the very act and event of intuitive vision, the mental image or "idea" of a single *Gestalt* (the leaf) comes into focus as the concrete framework absent which there could be no knowledge of a given plant's progressive, internal differentiation. Put differently, Goethe's botanical theory rests on the premise that "seeing the form," contrary to empiricism's

77. *GHA* 13:78; see also Richards 2002, 447–49. Aside from Blumenbach and the young Alexander von Humboldt, the latter of whom first meets Goethe in Weimar in 1794, the principal source for Goethe's concept is undoubtedly Kant's discussion of teleological thinking in the *Critique of Judgment*, esp. §§ 62–78.

78. Brady 1987, 269; see also Breidbach 2006, 207–67.

prevailing view of perception as an unmediated, garden-variety occurrence, involves a highly specific set of skills. "His understanding of morphology" pivots on a "mode of cultivated perception that he regarded as at once a seeing and a knowing."[79] Indeed, as Polanyi has noted, "There is a close analogy between the *elucidation of a comprehensive object* and the mastering of a skill, . . . a structural kinship of the arts of knowing and doing."[80]

As we have already seen, Polanyi's distinction between focal and background awareness presupposes an interior, as it were mental, image integrating and organizing relevant particulars either "uncomprehendingly, . . . in their participation in a comprehensive entity," or by directing our attention "beyond them to the entity to which they contribute." The main point here is to understand focal and subsidiary vision as complementary and reciprocal, that is, not as "*two degrees* of attention but [as] *two kinds* of attention given to the same particulars."[81] Polanyi's distinction confirms that, in preferring an inductive mode of inquiry to the Enlightenment's abstract and taxonomic approach to the life sciences, Goethe is not simply inverting the latter's deductive procedures. Rather, "the process of inductive discovery is in fact an oscillation between movements of analysis and integration in which, on balance, integration predominates." For such integration to happen, knowledge is "better described as a process of knowing." It pivots on our capacity for "comprehending unspecifiable entities," whose full significance has yet to reveal itself. This "tacit dimension," as Polanyi calls it, implies an essential continuity, indeed a homology of sorts, linking the successive apprehension of significant detail in the phenomenal world with its progressive integration by the observer's intellect. To see thus means prima facie to have an "intimation" of a reality that "may yet reveal itself to our deepened understanding in an indefinite range of unexpected manifestations."[82]

What has thus far been explored under the heading of the mental image presupposes an ontological bond between the visible "many" phenomena and the invisible "one" (the form or *eidos*) that these phenomena progressively reveal, thereby manifesting themselves to the observer as (potentially) significant entities. That no single phenomenon can reveal the fullness of the idea, being only ever a partial and imperfect instantiation of it, also explains why the observer will be able to grasp the nexus between *eidos* and appearance only at the level of analogy. Even so, the fact that the act of observing is experienced as a meaningful shuttling back and forth between

---

79. Steigerwald 2019, 251.
80. Polanyi 1969, 125. For a fuller discussion of knowledge as "skill," see Polanyi 1962, 49–65.
81. Polanyi 1969, 127–28.
82. Ibid., 130, 132–33. Within twentieth-century philosophy, perhaps no work bears closer resemblance to Goethe's understanding of knowledge as the convergence of a "dynamic order" (*bewegliche Ordnung*) in the phenomenal world with the subject's progression from intuitive to reflexive (self-)awareness than Alfred North Whitehead's *Process and Reality* (1929).

focal and subsidiary awareness, between instances of highly particular awareness and increasingly expansive acts of integration, confirms that objective manifestation and subjective comprehension are grounded in one and the same underlying *logos*. As Polanyi remarks elsewhere, "If we are to identify . . . the presence of significant order with the operation of an ordering principle, no highly significant order can ever be said to be solely due to an accidental collocation of atoms." Indeed, what is strictly random could never emerge as a correlate of significant perception, much less of focal awareness.[83]

In the final section (§120) of his *Metamorphosis of Plants*, Goethe appears to anticipate central tenets of Polanyi's metascientific argument as he attempts to furnish a more precise definition of the "leaf." For the leaf is not only some instantaneously visible detail, a correlate of our focal awareness, but also furnishes the integrating principle confirming the intrinsic purposiveness of form. Only where this principle informs our subsidiary awareness can our discrete perceptual acts coalesce into a meaningful sequence. As Goethe observes, "It is self-evident that we ought to have a general term with which to designate this diversely metamorphosed organ and with which to compare all manifestations of its form. At present we must be content to train ourselves to bring these manifestations into relationship in opposing directions, backward and forward. For we might equally well say that a stamen is a contracted petal, as that a petal is a stamen in a state of expansion."[84] Goethe's "leaf" thus is neither a heuristic abstraction (on the order of the Kantian "schema") nor merely a "simplification of foliar members." "All empirical forms are, for [Goethe], equally particularized, and his general organ can be general only by lacking such particularity. His *leaf* accomplishes this requirement *by having no form at all*."[85] To make better sense of this seemingly paradoxical entity—at once concrete, dynamic, yet devoid of all particularity—we will have to press further our inquiry into what for Goethe it means to "see" in the realm of science and poetry.

The catalyst impelling the entire process of metamorphosis is a self-originating, "formative drive" (*Bildungstrieb*) first proposed by Blumenbach: "a kind of Newtonian force for the biological realm . . . [that] did not exist apart from its material constituents but could not be explained in terms of those elements."[86] Readily seized

83. Polanyi 1962, 35. "Randomness alone can never produce a significant pattern, for it consists in the absence of any such pattern" (37).

84. *GHA* 13:101/*EM* 77.

85. Brady 1998, 272.

86. Lenoir 1982, 20–21; on Blumenbach's theory and its reception and development by Herder and Kant, see also Richards (2002, 216–37), who rejects Lenoir's emergentist interpretation of the "formative drive" as "implausible." As we shall see, to characterize the *Bildungstrieb* as "an emergent property" is to premise one's interpretation of organic form on an incoherent metaphysics that tacitly considers potentiality to be ontologically prior to actuality.

upon by Kant in part 2 of his *Critique of Judgment*, Blumenbach's teleological conception of organic life as an emergent and self-regulating phenomenon also made a strong impression on Goethe, who was to acknowledge the centrality of the *Bildungstrieb* in his eponymous essay of 1817–18. Still, Goethe insists that simply to institute "a *nisus formativus*, . . . a vigorous activity effecting formation," is to remain unproductively fixated on "words that merely beg the question." What is needed is a framework that will encompass both the continually evolving relationship between dynamic form objectively presented by nature and the process whereby the beholder's visual apprehension of such form causes her to undergo an analogous development (*Bildung*). As Diderot had mused as early as 1753, already hinting at the decline of mechanist theories, "Could so-called living matter not simply be matter which moves itself?" By the early 1780s, Alexander von Humboldt's and Blumenbach's hypothesis of an "internal fire breaking the bonds of chemical affinity and preventing the elements from being joined to one another, [what] we call a vital force." or "formative drive," had laid the groundwork for Goethe's concept of organic life as an internally conditioned, teleological process of continuous self-transformation.[87] As he claims, "in considering an organic entity, unity and freedom of the creative urge are incomprehensible without the concept of metamorphosis." Ever wary of attempts to identify ultimate causes by a mere tweaking of scientific nomenclature, Goethe instead focuses on the objectively given phenomenon. Scientific study, he maintains, must at all times attend to "ideal archetypes giving necessity to the transformation of form through a disciplined perception, the pure phenomena that could be represented through images."[88]

In an introductory essay on morphology from 1806 (first published in 1817), Goethe thus dwells on the modular logic of organic development that, over the next century and a half, was to become a central feature of formalist analysis, not only in biology, but also in the study of literary genres (Jolles, Propp), as well as, notably, in the formalist analysis of classical music that, not coincidentally, crystallized in response to the oeuvre of Goethe's most eminent musical contemporary, Beethoven.[89] Whereas close observation of plant growth reveals that "what has just been formed is instantly transformed [*umgebildet*]," botanical study can respond to such fluidity

---

87. *GHA* 13:32 / *EM* 233; Diderot and Humboldt, quoted in Gaukroger 2016, 75, 101. On Kant's and Kielmeyer's "teleomechanical" inflection of Blumenbach's notion of a "formative drive," see Lenoir 1982, 17–53.

88. Steigerwald 2002, 311.

89. The central role of modularity within formalist analyses of Beethoven's middle- and late-period instrumental music gradually emerges in the work of Joseph Marx, Eduard Hanslick, Heinrich Schenker, Fritz Cassirer, and Rudolf Rèti. On the striking affinities between biological formalism and its equivalent in classical music, what Arnold Schönberg was to call "developing variation" (*Entwicklungsvariation*), see Subotnik 1991, 15–41; Rosen 1998, 403–48; Pfau 2015.

only by subdividing the body of a given plant organism. Yet as it does so, it "finally come[s] to such beginnings as have been labeled 'similar parts' [*Similarteile*]." Goethe is concerned not merely with noting the apparent resemblance of discrete parts, but with identifying, on that basis, "a higher law of the organism." After all, the true goal of empirical observation is not to disaggregate parts but to "see and understand" (in the rich sense of Parmenides's *noein*) morphological difference as the expression of the fundamental principle that "all is leaf" (*Alles ist Blatt*).[90]

Lurking behind Goethe's gnomic remark is a by now familiar metaphysical implication, namely, that the relationship between the One and the many does not constitute an antinomy. Rather than conceive of manifold being as strictly incommensurable with the One, Goethe sees natural form in all its diversity and dynamism as both participating in the One and, indeed, a partial and fleeting manifestation of it. More than the concurrently unfolding projects of the Jena Romantics, which sooner or later tilt toward abstract speculation, Goethe's concept of metamorphosis reflects what Alexander Hampton calls "the search for a language of transcendence in an age of immanence."[91] For unless human thought wishes to dispense with ontology altogether and commit to a strictly immanent view of being—an aspiration more easily voiced than fulfilled—it follows that the *logos* that finds dynamic expression *in* the visible world cannot be thought as competing *against* finite being. Rather, the transcendence of the One must be thought as the "non-other" (Cusa's *non aliud*) of the many, that is, as substantially encompassing all manifold existence and precisely thereby guaranteeing its material being and formal specificity. What in Cusa is worked out with unprecedented explicitness and conceptual rigor still informs Goethe's theory of life, albeit now mainly as a constant implication: namely, that the relationship of transcendence and immanence is one of complementarity rather than antinomy. The notion had first suggested itself to Goethe during his Italian journey of 1787.

> Each living creature is a complex, not a unit; even when it appears to be an individual, it nevertheless remains an aggregation of living and independent parts, identical in idea and disposition, but in outward appearance identical or similar, unlike or dissimilar. These organisms are partly united by origin; partly they discover each other and unite. They separate and seek each other out again, thus

---

90. Goethe 1887–1919, pt. II, 7:282.

91. Hampton 2019, 55. For David B. Hart, any coherent understanding of the *logos* proceeds, "like Plotinus, as though the Father were the One from whom difference departs in successive stages of noetic contemplation and psychic dissemination," that being, incidentally, also William Blake's position in *The Book of Urizen* (1794). For the "Trinity is not a Neoplatonic dégringolade of the divine into the lower orders of being, or a monad progressively distorted into multiplicity" (2004, 185).

bringing about endless production in all ways and in all directions. . . . That a plant or even a tree, though it appears to us as an individual, consists purely of detached parts resembling both each other and the whole—of this fact there is no doubt.[92]

As the basic module organizing how a given plant undergoes continuous morphological change or differentiation over time—and so properly constituting its specificity as a *type*—Goethe's leaf anticipates trends in contemporary biology to explain "*how* individual forms are made," something that neither Darwinian evolution nor the great synthesis of the 1930s and 1940s had been able to explain. For Darwin, the *form* of a given species is of interest mainly insofar as its minute variations, as traced in the long *durée* of the geological record, may help explain why some varieties of a species are still around while others have vanished. To the evolutionary theorist, form matters primarily in an actuarial sense, as the substratum of minute morphological differences that, in entirely adventitious manner, furnish the material basis on which natural selection operates, thereby allowing us to explain why some forms persist over time whereas others have been expunged from the geological record. Far from being engaged as a distinct reality and presence per se, form on such an account signifies only in an aggregate sense, that is, as a statistically significant sample of iterations exhibited by a given species as it undergoes natural selection over time.[93]

Yet to take that view risks losing sight of the reality and presence of concrete, visible being, the actual natural organism intuitively engaging the observer and allowing her to proceed, inductively, to understanding the reality and integrity of *this* form and *this* species. Echoing Goethe's botanical theory, Sean B. Carroll thus insists that "key to understanding form is *development*, the process through which a single-celled egg gives rise to a complex, multi-billion-celled animal."[94] "Development" here encapsulates two aspects, "formation" (*Bildung*) and "transformation" (*Metamor-*

---

92. *GHA* 13:56–57 / *EM* 24.

93. As Ernst Mayr, himself a central figure in the "great synthesis" puts it, that disciplinary shift fused the inquiries of "two factions, on the one side the experimental geneticists, mostly interested in the mechanism of evolution and studying variation within a population as well as the achievement and maintenance of adaptation, and another faction consisting of the naturalists, systematists, and paleontologists, primarily interested in the study of biodiversity, that is, species, speciation, and macroevolution. In the years 1937 to 1947, a synthesis of the two fields was achieved owing to a mutual understanding of each other's views. The result was the so-called evolutionary synthesis, actually very much of a return to classical Darwinism, evolution as variation and selection" (Plenary address delivered at the 51st Annual Meeting of the American Institute of Biological Sciences, Washington, DC, 22 March 2000, https://academic.oup.com/bioscience/article/50/10/895/234040; accessed 7 July 2020.

94. Carroll 2005, x.

phose). Goethe's theory posits both to be continually operative and wholly entwined, thus defining not only the objective (natural) world of plant and animal life, but, correlatively, the sensory-cum-intellectual development of the beholder. So understood, development fills in a major blind spot of evolutionary biology in its dominant, Darwinian realization. For as such, evolutionary thinking had only ever sought to explain morphological differences *functionally*, namely, as arising from chance variation and natural selection, and hence ascertainable only a posteriori through the aggregation of myriad samples spanning vast expanses of geological time. Yet in so framing the question, Darwinian evolutionary theory lacked both the interest and the conceptual armature for explaining how *this or that particular form* is generated. Differentiation here signifies only "dissimilarity" (from other plant variants) and is not understood as the intrinsic principle that allows a particular organic being to constitute itself, actively, in the here and now. Insofar as natural selection operates with a purely disjunctive understanding of morphological difference, it can only ever hypothesize, on strictly actuarial grounds, why some forms are still with us whereas others have gone extinct. One is bound to conclude that functionalism continually presupposes, rather than supplants, formalism.

As Carroll points out, whereas "every animal form is a product of two processes—development from an egg and evolution from its ancestors," Darwinian thought largely took for granted the former and focused its aggregative reasoning on variations such as could be read off the copious, if uneven, array of specimens from successive geological periods.[95] Fundamentally "ignorant of the relationship between genes and form," toward which Gregor Mendel's research was already pointing, Darwin and Huxley arguably had to proceed as they did since "the puzzle of how a simple egg gives rise to a complex individual stood as one of the most elusive questions in all of biology."[96] Only recently, then, has a new area of inquiry comparing developmental genes between species arisen "at the interface of embryology and evolutionary biology—evolutionary developmental biology, or 'Evo Devo' for short." Contemporary work in the emergent field of Evo Devo thus focuses on the minute processes whereby genetic information is translated into, or realized as, a specific organic form; its overall concern thus lies with "how complexity is constructed from a single cell."

As it happens, this relatively new area of inquiry exhibits some striking conceptual affinities with Goethe's morphological approach to development two centuries earlier. Given that "only a tiny fraction of our DNA, just about 1.5 percent, codes for the roughly 25,000 proteins in our bodies" and another 3 percent are "regulatory"— that is, determining "when, where, and how much of a gene's product is made"—it

---

95. Ibid., 4.

96. On Darwin's reluctance to engage Mendel's papers on heredity, even as he declared that "variation is the base of all," see Browne 2002, 2:200–206.

comes as no surprise that any given organism is preponderantly comprised of modular parts rather than heterogeneous components.[97] Through a series of examples, Carroll illustrates the logic of "modular design," such that in the case of a butterfly wing what at first glance might strike the observer as a chaotic and asymmetrical design turns out, upon closer inspection, to be "built of repeating motifs." From primitive trilobites of the Cambrian and Silusian strata to millipedes, snake skeletons, or the bone structure of the human hand, the new field of Evo Devo furnishes genetic confirmation for a discovery, attributed to the British biologist William Bateson (1861–1926), "that many large animals were constructed of repeated parts, and many body parts themselves were constructed of repeated units." When scrutinizing a given limb structure in diverse species, or even across multiple genera, advanced comparative anatomy will thus reveal "*serial homologs*, structures that arose as a repeated series and have become differentiated to varying degrees in different animals."[98] Carroll here refers to observations first made by the paleontologist Samuel Wendell Williston (1851–1918), who, in 1914, declared it to be "a law in evolution that the parts in an organism tend toward reduction in number, with the fewer parts greatly specialized in function."[99]

A full century earlier, osteological research had already drawn Goethe's attention to the modular logic underlying skeletal structures, in part because such a hypothesis allows him "to create series of formal differentiations [*Serien von Formdiversifizierungen*]" and to grasp "complexity as variation [*Vielfalt als Variation zu begreifen*]." As Goethe had put it, "Becoming is simply the exfoliation of what is possible, rather than the creation of the new."[100] Likewise, modern evolutionary developmental biology seeks to establish a strong causal link between the apparent economy of modular design (something that Goethe had already observed in his *Metamorphosis of Plants*) and the broader field of evolutionary genetics. If, as Carroll puts it, "modularity, symmetry, and polarity are nearly universal features of animal design," then

97. Ibid., 6–12.

98. Carroll 2005, 21, 26, 29; the notion of organisms connected by a "functional analogy" of their basic blueprint surfaces in a variety of nineteenth-century biologists, including Étienne Geoffrey de St. Hilaire, who in 1818 speaks of "a principle of connections" and a "principle of composition," and Richard Owen, who in 1848 defines functional similarity as *analogy* and standard party identity as *homology* (quoted in Brady 1987, 257–300, 258–59). Likewise, Darwin speaks of a common phylum whose persistence, throughout the variations effected by descent, heredity, and selective transmission, is legible in the "mutual affinities of organic beings" (Darwin 2006, 450).

99. Quoted in Carroll 2005, 33. Curiously, John Ruskin anticipates this argument almost verbatim in *Modern Painters II* (1846): "As we rise in order of being, the number of similar members becomes less, and their structure commonly seems based on the principle of the unity of two things by a third, as Plato states it [referencing *Timaeus* 31a]" (*RCW* IV, 96).

100. Quoted in Breidbach 2006, 29–30, 69; on the pioneering arguments of Caspar Friedrich Wolff (1734–94) concerning the modularity and differential logic of developmental processes in organic nature, see Breidbach 2006, 87–93.

any longitudinal study of how species diversify requires that one begin by studying the genetic rules that govern the "development," or *Bildung*, of discrete organisms.[101]

Given the close affinities between the life sciences and aesthetic models of auto-poiesis around 1800, it hardly comes as a surprise that Goethe's notion of a modular, "dynamic form" (itself subject to apprehension by a science of morphology) should in due course have been echoed by a branch of literary studies focused specifically on the emergence and internal organization of literary forms and genres. Vladimir Propp's *Morphology of the Folktale* (1928) may be the best-known attempt to identify a modular depth structure of some thirty-one "functions" and seven character ar-chetypes (or "actants" in Greimas's parlance). What we call and experience as story (*récit*) thus arises from the various combinations, emphases, and interrelations into which these narrative modules can enter. Another study, more subtle in approach though less resonant in Anglo-American criticism, is André Jolles's *Simple Forms* (*Einfache Formen*), published in 1930. For Jolles, the central question is "how lan-guage, without surrendering the role of SIGNIFICATION (*Bedeutung*), may simultane-ously become FORM [*Gebilde*]." Concentrating on a number of familiar and compact genres (legend, heroic poem, myth, riddle, fairy tale, etc.), Jolles traces the genesis of "simple forms" by observing "how the same phenomenon will repeat itself in en-riched form [*wie eine selbe Erscheinung . . . sich anreichernd wiederholt*] at another level, and how an identical, form-giving and delimiting power, operating at continu-ously higher levels, will control the system [of literary genre] as a totality."[102] Offering as a first illustration of this model the simple form of hagiographic narrative, Jolles emphasizes that modularity here cannot be reduced to a mechanical *accumulation* of traits required for sainthood (specific actions, consistently superior conduct, mira-cles, etc.). Rather, the narrative case for sainthood becomes compelling, in much the same way that the prosecution of a crime does, only if the discrete features give rise to a coherent *imitatio*. That is, the modules or topoi constituting the building blocks of the case to be made must coalesce into a compelling symbolic form or *Gestalt*. Only in the resulting, condensed narrative form does the hagiographic vita become a significant *imago* of the saint to whom it refers; and for it to do so it "has to unfold in such a way that . . . in it the life in question occurs again. It is not sufficient for the vita to offer a neutral inventory of events and acts, but it must allow them to consti-tute themselves as form [*diese in sich zur Form werden lassen*]."[103]

On Jolles's account, the full significance of form thus can never be grasped by some positivistic or historicist method for the simple reason that, as a condition of its

---

101. Carroll 2005, 34.

102. Jolles 1965, 9; on the intricate connection of poetic form to late eighteenth-century theo-ries of plant and and animal organisms, see Gigante 2009, 1–48.

103. Jolles 1965, 39–40.

very *emergence*, form "shatters the historicity of its components and now saturates them with the value of imitability." Drawing on physiological metaphors, particularly from the realm of osteology, Jolles thus notes how the sheer recurrence of certain "motifs" or "topoi" (words he deploys with some unease) shows language—along with its narrated, modular events—"gradually calcifying [*erhärtet*] into a first type of literary form." Going beyond Propp's morphology of the folktale, Jolles rejects what he considers structuralism's arbitrary schemes of literary classification in favor of a genetic view of form as a modular, self-organizing, and intrinsically significant (symbolic) reality. In ways that recall Goethe's dismissal of Linné's abstract taxonomy, Jolles thus insists that literary form constitutes itself in much the same way that a living organism generates its eventual *Gestalt* based on an internal causality that is the very law of its being, which is to say, not as a mechanical assembly of heterogeneous parts, but as a sequence of transformations occurring within the linguistic material itself. Guided by the intellect, language "names, is generative, creative, interpretive [*benennend, erzeugend, schaffend, deutend*] and, thus, generates a form [*bildet eine Gestalt*]; having issued from life, form also continually feeds back into life; for this no artwork is needed." One is struck by the continuities between Jolles's account of genre as "simple form" and the terminology ("modular design," "serial homologs," "polarity") employed by Carroll as he seeks to complement evolutionary accounts of species development with an equally precise model for the emergence of particular organic forms. Thus, Jolles's distinction between a "simple form" and its specific realization in a given *récit* (*gegenwärtige einfache Form*) echoes both Goethe's concept of a "dynamic form" whose identity is bound up with its ceaseless internal transformation and Carroll's insight into the way that modularity guarantees both the stability and efficiency of biological forms.[104]

We can now return to the relationship between an objective, visible form undergoing continuous internal differentiation and the mental image wherein Goethe's beholder progressively visualizes the idea made manifest by a given organic form. In this process, the observing intellect and its phenomenological correlate, a particular dynamic form, mutually constitute one another. Corresponding to each phase of a plant's becoming is a distinct "qualitative phase" in the observer's conscious awareness. No specific manifestation of form captured as a mental image will ever prove definitive; yet neither are any of its manifestations to be considered merely appari-

---

104. Ibid., 44, 47, 50. However unwittingly, both Jolles's and Carroll's theories (of literary and biological form, respectively) rest on the Aristotelian-Thomistic concept of form as "species" or *forma substantialis*, actualized qua "operation," as opposed to the Nominalist understanding of form as sheer singularity (*haecceitas*). That is, both Jolles and Carroll invest form with agency, conceived as an actively self-constituting reality rather than something merely predicated, ex post facto, of verbal or biological "matter." On this issue, see below, ch. 6, 542–47.

tional. Rather than reject the concrete "leaf" as a mere chimera, let alone break down its various stages into incidental and distinct "parts," Goethe instead identifies metamorphosis as the fundamental law governing all of organic life. On his view, the substantial form to which he assigns the heuristic name "leaf" (*Blatt*) furnishes the enduring *and* concrete substratum for a process of continuous internal differentiation whereby a plant realizes its very being, as it were exfoliating itself in progressively fuller ways. As the formal template enabling the observer to visualize the modular design of organic beings, the leaf holds unique significance within Goethe's botanical research. For it allows the truly observing eye to "see" an idea and, hence, genuinely "see" for the first time. Put differently, the leaf is simultaneously an actual physical entity *and* the reflex of a universal law governing all organic production.

Insofar as Goethe's organic form is actualized as a process of ceaseless internal differentiation, it remains firmly grounded in a metaphysical realism that conceives being as a composite of act and potency. Thus, Aristotle posits that "the proximate matter and the form are one and the same thing, the one potentially, the other actually. . . . [E]ach thing is a unity, and the potential and the actual are somehow one." Echoing that insight, Goethe will maintain that the potentiality of a thing entails its self-actualization, and that, "where the source of the becoming is in the very thing which suffers change," potentiality and actuality are fused in a single being or entelechy, such that "in this state [the seed] is already potentially a man."[105] For Goethe, "entelechy, a being that is perpetually in operation [*ein Wesen, das immer in Funktion ist*]," most aptly captures the way in which actuality and potentiality converge in organic form.[106] As he puts it in his didactic poem, *The Metamorphosis of Plants* (1798), "a love poem with erotic overtones . . . inspired by Erasmus Darwin's *Loves of Plants*" and written for a mostly female audience:[107]

> . . . wie nach und nach sich die Pflanze
> Stufenweise geführt, bildet zu Blüten und Frucht.
> Aus dem Samen entwickelt sie sich, sobald ihn der Erde
> Stille befruchtender Schoß hold in das Leben entläßt,
> Und dem Reize des Lichts, des heiligen, ewig bewegten,
> Gleich den zärtesten Bau keimender Blätter empfiehlt.
> Einfach schlief in dem Samen die Kraft; ein beginnendes Vorbild
> Lag, verschlossen in sich, unter die Hülle gebeugt,
> Blatt und Wurzel und Keim, nur halb geformet und farblos.[108]

---

105. Aristotle 1984, 2:1650–51; 1656–57 (*Met.* 1045b18–20; 1049a10–16; 1049b3–10).

106. *GHA* 12:371 (#44).

107. Steigerwald 2019, 264.

108. *GHA* 1:199. "How the plant / Burgeons by stages into flower and fruit, / Bursts from the seed so soon as fertile earth / Sends it to life from her sweet bosom, and / Commends the unfolding

Unlike nineteenth-century "emergentist" theories, Goethe does not entertain the notion that the very reality and being of the plant is itself the mere *product* or *effect* of potentiality, as though the latter existed somehow apart from it. In this respect, too, his conception of metamorphosis rests on classically realist foundations. For as Aristotle notes in his *Metaphysics*, actual being itself will always be the ontological foundation for all potentiality.

> It is clear that actuality is prior to potentiality. . . . For nature is in the same genus as potentiality; for it is a principle of movement—not, however in something else but in the thing itself *qua* itself. To all such potentiality, then, actuality is prior both in formula and in substance. . . . For from the potential the actual is always produced *in an actual thing*, e.g., man by man.[109]

Potentiality, that is, does not impose form on matter from without but draws out what is always already present in actual being. This it will do in virtue of the fact that any given being is of a particular kind, or species, and hence is imbued with final causality. By contrast, to construe potentiality as an unconstrained self-actuation and, thus, to elevate it over actuality, as Heidegger will later do, strikes Goethe no less than Aristotle as intuitively implausible and conceptually incoherent.[110] Remarking on the "perfection" reached by the leaf, Goethe's poem continues:

> Und so erreicht es zuerst die höchst bestimmte Vollendung
> Die bei manchem Geschlecht dich zum Erstaunen bewegt.
> Viel gerippt und gezackt, auf mastig strotzender Fläche,
> Scheinet die Fülle des Triebs frei und unendlich zu sein.
> Doch hier hält die Natur, mit mächtigen Händen, die Bildung
> An und lenket sie sanft in das Vollkommenere hin.[111]

---

of the delicate leaf / To the sacred goad of ever-moving light! / Asleep within the seed the power lies, / Foreshadowed pattern [*Vorbild*], folded in the shell, / Root, leaf, and germ, pale and half-formed" (Miller 2009, 1).

109. *Met.* 1049b20. Aquinas likewise "has no use for sheer vacant possibility. It is always the possibility *of* some existing thing" (McCabe 2008, 43).

110. As David Bentley Hart remarks, in "elevating possibility over actuality," Heidegger merely sidesteps the essential question of metaphysics, namely, "How is it that either possibility or actuality *is*? Whence comes the 'is' in 'it is possible'?" Ultimately, "Heidegger, by thinking of possibility as 'higher' than actuality, is really only transposing his terms; he is thinking of the possible *as* the actual" (2017, 17–19).

111. *GHA* 1:199–200. "At length attaining preordained fulfillment. / Oft the beholder marvels at the wealth / Of shape and structure shown in succulent surface— / The infinite freedom of the growing leaf. / Yet nature bids a halt; her mighty hands, Gently directing it toward a higher perfection" (Miller 2009, 2; trans. modified).

Unbeknownst to Goethe, his other major precursor here is Aquinas, who, like Aristotle, holds that there is no such thing as matter without form, no potentiality that is not already premised on a prior actuality. There simply cannot be such a thing as "formless existence" or some wholly undetermined "nothing-in-particular." At the same time, while building Christian *sacra doctrina* on a realist metaphysical base, Aquinas has to confront the fundamental divergence between the Aristotelian view that substance and actuality express the eternity of the world and the notion of divine creation ex nihilo as revealed in scripture. If "it is impossible that any being should be presupposed" prior to the "emanation of universal being from the first principle" (i.e., God), how then are we to understand the phrase "ex nihilo" in a positive sense? Aquinas rejects the widespread misconstrual of ex nihilo as being, somehow, the (material? efficient?) *cause* of created being. Basic logic precludes such argumentation. For "when anything is said to be made from nothing," the *ex* in the phrase "ex nihilo" "does not signify the material cause," as (re)introducing such a cause would obviously contradict the very notion of ex nihilo. Rather, he notes, the phrase must be taken to signify an intrinsic "order [*non designat causam materialem, sed ordinem tantum*]; as when we say, 'from morning comes midday.'" Just as God's absolute being has originated, encompasses, and forever sustains both the potentiality and the actuality of the world, rather than being their efficient cause, so material and finite being unfolds in visible form what it had eternally been in the divine mind. Yet *for us*, this metaphysical state of affairs can reveal itself only in the time-bound world of visible (ontic) being, which is to say, only *per analogiam*. For Aquinas, the overarching objective is to "consider not only the emanation of a particular being from a particular agent, but also the emanation of all being from the universal cause, which is God, . . . which we designate by the name of creation." To succeed in this endeavor does not mean to behold the divine source of particular being per se, which human cognition cannot do. Rather, it is to participate in the "perfection" (*Vollendung*) of visible being by witnessing how it achieves its inner telos over time: "Changes receive species and dignity, not from the term 'wherefrom,' but from the term 'whereto.'"[112]

It is precisely in their teleological constitution that natural beings allow us to grasp temporal change as a meaningful sequence rather than as random and unintelligible mutation. Hence Aquinas conceives "change" as transformation, not alteration, that is, as realizing the potentiality of a given being and, thus, rendering it "more perfect and excellent. . . . [G]eneration is simply nobler [*nobilior*] and more excellent than alteration, because the substantial form is nobler than the accidental form."[113] Whereas in alteration the forces of change are understood to be extrinsic to

---

112. *ST* I-45 A1.
113. *ST* I-44 A8.

the being in question, generation and transformation understand these "accidents and forms . . . [to be] 'con-created' [*concreata*]." That is, to explain natural form as a mere assembly of heterogeneous parts begs the question, not least because the provenance of those parts remains elusive. For Aquinas, "creation does not mean the building-up of a composite thing [*rei compositae*] from pre-existing principles; but it means that the 'composite' is created so that it is brought into being at the same time with all its principles."[114] In contrast to the pointedly aniconic idea of mystic *visio* advanced by Meister Eckhart, Aquinas acknowledges that what actuates and develops our intellect is our continuing, sensory appraisal of the world. If "all knowledge comes by the form [*omnis cogitatio est per formam*]," "sight"—both intellectual and sensible—becomes the moment where form "appears," constituting itself as an "event" much in the way that Heidegger's etymological conjunction of "event" and "beholding" (*er-eignen/er-äugen*) means to draw out. As Aquinas puts it, "Two things are required both for sensible and for intellectual vision—viz., the power of sight and the union of the thing seen with the sight. For vision is made actual only when the thing seen is in a certain way in the seer [unio rei visae cum visu, non enim fit visio in actu, nisi per hoc quod res visa quodammodo est in vidente]."[115]

The Aristotelian and Thomistic underpinnings of Goethe's understanding of organic form as dynamically self-manifesting are striking, even as his intellectual moorings prevent him from recognizing these deep conceptual genealogies. Goethe's indebtedness, however inadvertent, to an Aristotelian-Thomist metaphysics, highlights for us a crucial link between classical realism and modern phenomenology's attempt to rearticulate the ontological nexus between mind and world, something we will have occasion to consider later on. For now, brief consideration of Merleau-Ponty's theory of perception will have to suffice as regards intimating some striking affinities between Goethe's "concrete thinking" (*gegenständliches Denken*) and mid-twentieth-century phenomenology. Recalling the pre-Socratic idea of an ontological "coordination" of mind and world, Merleau-Ponty in his 1946 address to La Société française de philosophie remarks that "meaning and signs, the form and matter of perception, [are] related from the beginning and that, as we say, the matter of perception [is] 'pregnant with its form.'" Perhaps alluding to Kant's acute difficulties with grounding the synthesis of apperception in the "Transcendental Deduction" of his first *Critique*, Merleau-Ponty stresses the preconceptual and nondiscursive origins of the mind-world relationship: "The synthesis which constitutes the unity of the perceived objects and which gives meaning to the perceptual data is not an intellectual synthesis." For whereas "an intellectual act would grasp the object either as possible or as necessary, . . . in perception it is 'real'; it is given as the infinite sum of

---

114. *ST* I-45 A4; see McCabe 2008, 7–15.
115. *ST* I-12 A2.

an indefinite series of perspectival views in each of which it is given but in none of which it is given exhaustively."[116]

Perception thus conforms to the temporal structure of beings in a double sense. First, perception unfolds as a series of contiguous perspectives, what Husserl calls "adumbrations" (*Abschattungen*), on visible form.[117] Second, perception is itself temporally constituted in that its visible correlate, the phenomenon, is objectively experienced as a ceaselessly self-differentiating, time-bound reality. While that is evidently true in the case of entelechies, such as plants or animals unfolding the very law of their being over time, it also holds true for inanimate beings, which likewise constitute themselves for the observer only as a temporal succession of "adumbrations." In all cases, the reality of a thing is not a function of ascription or predication but, being logically anterior to any positings (*Setzungen*) and verbal definitions, inheres in its ceaselessly self-manifestation as *form*. Both form and observing intelligence are mutually constitutive, even if their ontological, preconceptual belonging-together elude the "natural attitude" (*natürliche Einstellung*) and can only be drawn out in a phenomenological reflection.

To speak of the "preconceptual" here is another way of formulating the axiom of philosophical realism, according to which "the world does not consist of facts but of things concerning which there are facts."[118] It is this manifestation of being anterior to human perceptual and discursive involvement that will prompt Husserl to remark that "appearances do not themselves appear to us; rather, they are experienced" (Die Erscheinungen selbst erscheinen nicht, sie werden erlebt).[119] Substantially anticipated by Goethe, Husserl's insight revives the originally Scholastic claim that the reality of the "thing" (*res*) inheres in its operation (*omnis res sit propter suam operationem*), where, consequently, the engaged beholder and that which is beheld share in the same dynamic principle. "A certain fittingness of world to mind" (*convenientia*

---

116. Merleau-Ponty 1964, 15. As Steigerwald notes, the ambition of Goethe's botanical project "was to eliminate the subjective elements he contended were leading contemporary art and science astray and to provide an objective vision of science in their stead, an intuition of *Urphänomene* on the basis of a disciplined perception" (2002, 314). A fuller discussion of Goethe's scientific writings in relation to modern phenomenology would have to include Franz Brentano's critique of "perception" and his pioneering account of intentionality, as well as Husserl's discussion of "attentiveness" (*Aufmerksamkeit*) and his discrimination between the material substratum of an intentional act and its "quality" (*Logical Investigations* V, §§ 19–20).

117. Husserl introduces the concept of *Abschattung* (adumbration) in his 1907 lectures *Ding und Raum* (*Thing and Space*), §§ 14, 21–22, with special emphasis on the "continuity" (*Stetigkeit*) linking each perceptual stage to those preceding and succeeding it; see the discussion of Husserl below.

118. McCabe 2008, 17.

119. Husserl 2001, II:83 (German: Husserl 1980, II:350 [5th Investigation, § 2]); trans. modified.

entis ad intellectum) thus yields what Fergus Kerr calls a radically "non-interiorist account of the self," one that no longer involves a hermetic Cartesian *cogito* protractedly wrestling with medium-sized dry goods. Instead, "action, activity, inward and external, is the normal manifestation of being." What Goethe shares with modern phenomenology is this visceral discomfort with modes of conceptualization that are not immediately guided by the dynamic structure of appearance. Reflection must not conquer phenomena but alert us to the way that reality and meaning cannot, at least not without great loss, be separated from its phenomenalization. Put differently, the real is not what we may predicate of it. Rather, it discloses itself as "a constantly reassembling network of transactions, beings becoming themselves in their doings, . . . always already in relation, self-revealing in [their] own unique proper way, acting reacting, and interacting."[120]

As Goethe never ceases to insist, only by attending to organic life in its dynamic unfolding can the beholder grasp the deep nexus between perceiving and thinking; for after all, "What is observation without thought?" In a particularly fine aphorism, Goethe characterizes this fusion of observation with thought wrought by the insistent self-giving of the phenomenon: "There is a delicate empiricism which enters into the closest union with its object and is therefore transformed into an actual theory [Es gibt eine zarte Empirie, die sich mit dem Gegenstand innigst identisch macht und dadurch zur eigentlichen Theorie wird]."[121] Such an observation confirms Goethe's as a precursor of modern phenomenolog as it will be developed in the work of Brentano, Husserl, and the early Heidegger. We recall the latter's stringent characterization of "phenomenon" in *Being and Time*, in particular his remarks on the ambivalent meaning of *phainesthai* ("to bring into daylight"). Specifically, where the verb surfaces in the middle voice ("that within which something can become manifest, visible in itself"), it appears to cut through the antinomy of deception and revelation, mere semblance and ineffable being.

> Only because something claims to show itself in accordance with its meaning at all, that is, claims to be a phenomenon, *can* it show itself *as* something it is *not*, or *can* it "only look like." . . . One speaks of "appearances or symptoms of illness." What is meant by this are occurrences in the body that show themselves and in this self-showing as such "indicate" something that does *not* show itself. Appearance, as the appearance "of something," thus precisely does *not* mean that something shows itself; rather, it means that something makes itself known which does not show itself. It makes itself known through something that does show

---

120. *ST* I.105.5; Kerr 2002, 32, 148–49.
121. *GHA* 12:435 / Goethe 1998, 75.

itself. Appearing is a *not showing itself*. But this "not" must by no means be confused with the privative not which determines the structure of semblance. What does *not* show itself, in the manner of what appears, can also never seem.[122]

The observer here participates in the phenomenon in such a way that the event of seeing opens access to the *eidos* of Being itself. While Heidegger himself does not wish to foreground the Platonist implications of his argument here, his characterization of "phenomenon" bears an unmistakable affinity to the concept of "mental vision" (*visio mentalis*) as we have traced it in Plotinus, Cusa, and Goethe. Precisely because the phenomenon does not "refer to" or otherwise "signify" but only mediates the real as a "not-showing-itself" by means of what *does* appear, it cannot be discredited as mere semblance. To put it in positive terms, the observer's intelligence takes shape and becomes progressively more self-aware insofar as it successively apprehends, visualizes, and understands each fleeting presentation of a given thing as manifesting its underlying substantial form, which remains necessarily invisible per se.

Related to Goethe's "reoccupation" of the most significant premodern concept of knowledge is his association of "phenomenon" with its etymological roots, *light* and *darkness*. The word *phenomenon* appears most frequently in the context of Goethe's *Theory of Colors* and in his vast correspondence related to that project. As he remarks, "The phenomenon appears to me as a universal that will disclose itself under specific conditions, such as when in the course of prismatic experiments a pure light displaces the appearance to the dark margins."[123] Science's principal challenge, then, is to articulate the phenomenon's deep structural logic and how the observing intelligence itself is implicated in it. A number of aphorisms from *Maxims and Reflections* make a compelling case for Goethe as a precursor of twentieth-century phenomenological thought. Noting how "the phenomenon is not detached from the observer, but intertwined and involved with him," Goethe is keen to avoid any hint of Cartesian dualism when reflecting on the event character of sensory experience: "Everything factual is already theory: to understand this would be the greatest possible achievement. . . . Don't go looking for anything beyond phenomena: they are themselves what they teach, the doctrine"; and again, "He who has a phenomenon before

---

122. Heidegger 1979, 25–26 / Heidegger 1996, 29.

123. Letter to T. J. Seebeck (21 January 1816): "So erscheint mir das Phänomen als ein allgemeines überall verborgen liegendes, unter gewissen Umständen hervortretendes, wie denn bey den prismatischen Versuchen ein reines lichtes Bild die Erscheinung an die dunklen Ränder drängt" (Goethe 1887–1919, pt. IV, vol. 26, 228. For a discussion of Goethe's creative reciprocity of sight and phenomenon in *The Theory of Colors* and his elegiac poem "Metamporphosis of Plants" (1798), see Tantillo 2007; Crawford 2007.

his eyes is often already thinking beyond it; whoever only hears talk of it, thinks nothing at all [Wer ein Phänomen vor Augen hat, denkt schon oft drüber hinaus; wer nur davon erzählen hört, denkt gar nichts]."[124] The challenge for science thus is to understand that it is only ever involved with "objects" at the level of "phenomenon." Consequently, it must at all times stay focused on the dynamic process whereby phenomena make their "appearance" and so show themselves to be constitutively entwined with an observing intelligence. Ultimately, "seeing" the objective world as phenomenon is, for Goethe, at once a radically deductive and inductive process; for it to deliver anything, "we must focus the mind as well as the eye and conceptualize to perceive. The perceiver is also a thinker in a manner that usually escapes notice, and what is thought in this manner is also seen—that is, the resultant image is an instance of our conceptual category."[125]

FROM INTUITION TO SYMBOLIC FORM: METAMORPHOSIS, GENRE,
AND SYMBOL IN OVID AND GOETHE

It now becomes clear how, for Goethe, in its continual self-differentiation, a given plant discloses its archetype (*Urbild*, *Urpflanze*), or "idea," in a far more concrete sense than Schiller could conceive. Key to any genuine "grasping" of the phenomenon as the manifest "truth" of a being is what Goethe calls "intuition" (*Anschauung*). Whereas Kant's *Critique of Pure Reason* (1781) defines intuition as the basic sensory apprehension of an as yet unorganized set of data by the "reproductive imagination" (later echoed by Coleridge's notion of "fancy"), Goethe understands it as the active fusion of the sensory and the cognitive in a mental image: "The pure phenomenon, as the concrete instantiation of ideas, as the immediate relation of the ideal and the real, is symbolic."[126] To intuit a natural phenomenon is to apprehend a distinctive and complex organizational pattern in visual form. Yet such insight into the form (*eidos*) of organic life as manifested in a given natural phenomenon is not an act of cognition unilaterally accomplished by the subject. Rather intuition involves a moment of holistic *recognition*, with the progression from sight to insight positioning the beholder as responding to the call of the phenomenon. For unless a pattern of some kind is already in place at the moment of "seeing," no meaningful perception could have occurred.

Not to be confused with mere gazing or object-perception, "seeing" in the Goethean sense reappraises the modern object as *phenomenon*, that is, as a mani-

---

124. *GHA* 12:435 (#512); 432 (#488); 434 (#504) / Goethe 1998, 155, 77, 155.
125. Brady 1998, 97.
126. Steigerwald 2019, 258.

festation of life "acting" (*agens*). This is not the place to expand on the aesthetic implications of Goethe's understanding of phenomenon and what, with his approval, the anthropologist Heimroth in 1823 labeled Goethe's "concrete thinking" (*gegenständliches Denken*). Still, it bears noting that in a letter of September 1800, Coleridge is pursuing a strikingly similar course of inquiry, pondering whether "an action bearing all the semblance of pre-designing Consciousness may yet be simply organic, & whether a series of such actions are possible—and close on the heels of this question would follow the old 'Is Logic the Essence of Thinking?' in other words—Is thinking impossible without arbitrary signs? &—how far is the word 'arbitrary' a misnomer? Are not words &c parts & germinations of the Plant? And what is the Law of their Growth?" What was to be a lifelong pursuit for Coleridge, namely, "to destroy the old antithesis of Words & Things, elevating, as it were, words into Things, & living Things too," delineates the agenda for a Romantic poetics very similar to the philosophical poetics of Novalis and Schlegel.[127] Subsequently, in a Notebook entry of April 1804, Coleridge muses on how "looking" at a phenomenon finds the beholder searching for a symbolic language that will allow the individual to discern an eternal truth within a particular object.

> In looking at objects of Nature, while I am thinking, as at yonder moon dim-glimmering thro' the dewy window-pane, I seem rather to be seeking, as it were *asking*, a symbolical language for something within me that already and forever exists, than observing any thing new. Even when that latter is the case, yet still I have always an obscure feeling as if that new phaenomenon were the dim Awaking of a forgotten or hidden Truth of my inner Nature/It is still interesting, as a Word, a Symbol! It is *logos*, the Creator![128]

With strong Platonist overtones, though also exhibiting a distinctly new, phenomenological bent, Coleridge reflects on how, prior to all conceptuality, our apprehension of visible form sifts the phenomenon for a "symbolical language" by which to account for the ineffable convergence of sight and insight, intuition and recognition. This symbolic language, in turn, attests to a metaphysical bond linking, "always and forever," the realm of visible forms with the "hidden Truth of my inner nature." Once the experience of a given phenomenon registers as a kind of "recollection" (*anamnēsis*), human language not only ventures propositions about visible reality per se, but thereby hears itself as an echo of the *logos*. As Coleridge puts it in another entry, "The moment we conceive the divine energy, that moment we co-conceive the *logos*." Ultimately, all epistemic commerce with the visible world identifies the

---

127. Coleridge 1956–1971, 1:625–26 (Letter 22 September 1800).
128. Coleridge 1961, #2546; emphasis mine.

moment when "the redeemed & sanctified become finally themselves Words of the *Word*—even as articulate sounds are made by the Reason to represent Forms, in the mind, and Forms are a language of the notions—*verba significant phaenomena, phaenomena sunt quasi verba noematum (tōn noumenōn)*."[129] For both Coleridge and Goethe, knowledge is framed as an essentially Platonic dialectic of active participation *in* and intuitive recognition *of* the phenomenon as bearing witness to the primordial coordination of mind and world.

That said, the dynamic narrative of *Bildung* so unfolded should not be confused with emergentist theories that, several decades later, John Stuart Mill will advance in his *System of Logic* (1843). Neither Goethe nor Coleridge thinks of our knowledge of phenomena as originating in some primal, amorphous welter of chemical ("heteropathic") causes whose concurrence Mill claims produces emergent properties. Nor do they subscribe to a model of natural science that involves tabulating and conceptualizing raw, and intrinsically meaningless, physical "data" only after the fact, as it were, and by a subject fundamentally unrelated to them. On the contrary, like Coleridge, Goethe never tires to emphasize that for sight to amount to more than erratic, mindless gazing, it must involve a moment of sudden recognition, a flash of *insight* whereby the beholder discovers herself to be in the presence of a meaningful structure rather than amorphous matter. Goethe calls it an *aperçu*, a moment at once speculative and concrete that will register as an "awakening" or as a "conversion of sense [*Sinnesänderung*]." Telling here is the fusion, within that last compound noun, of a sensory and an intellectual dimension. Thus, even as an *aperçu* involves the beholder suddenly becoming "conscious of a great maxim, which is always an operation of the mind akin to genius [das Gewahrwerden einer großen Maxime, welches immer eine genialische Geistesoperation ist]," this moment of disclosure is wholly bound up with the act of seeing.[130] It hardly surprises, then, that the term *aperçu* should occur with particular frequency throughout Goethe's *Theory of Colors*. Raising the stakes in one such instance, Goethe insists that "everything in science depends on what is called an *aperçu*, a becoming aware of what truly constitutes the ground of appearance; such a realization will bear fruit ad infinitum."[131]

As described in this passage, the Goethean *aperçu* bears close resemblance to what in his third *Critique* Kant develops under the heading "aesthetic idea," which

---

129. Ibid., #2445 (February 1805).

130. *GHA* 10:89 / Goethe 1949, 603. In *Maxims and Reflections*, Goethe remarks, "Alles wahre Aperçu kommt aus einer Folge und bringt Folge. Es ist ein Mittelglied einer großen, produktiv aufsteigenden Kette" (*GHA* 12:414 [# 365]). Wellbery sees Goethe advancing "the epistemological figure of a systematically disciplined intuitive attention that conforms to and finally produces out of itself the formal regularity in question" (2012, 16).

131. *GHA* 14:98.

likewise "occasions much thought, without however any definite thought, i.e., any *concept*, being . . . adequate to it; it consequently cannot be completely compassed and made intelligible by language."[132] Both notions involve the sudden convergence of our sensory and intellectual faculties in a productive (albeit strictly formal) relation. Hence, what Kant refers to as the "conformity" or "attunement" (Übereinstimmung, *Zusammenstimmung*) between the sensory and intellectual faculties of cognition amounts to a formal condition that enables what he calls "knowledge in general" (*Erkenntnis* überhaupt).[133] It is only when this condition has been met and ratified by an act of reflective judgment that the project of subjective cognition and its eventual, intersubjective "communicability" (Kant's *Mitteilbarkeit*) can get under way. Yet unlike Kant, Goethe does not hold that the fortuitous convergence of the subject's sensory and intellectual capacities relationship is ratified in an explicit act of reflective judgment. Rather, the "event" (*Ereignis*) of concrete "seeing" and thinking (*gegenständliches Denken*) issues in an intuitive recognition, an *aperçu*, that confirms for the observer that she is in the presence of a meaningful, dynamic form rather than an ephemeral and contingent "object." The specific object in view is but the conduit for the form, which can never appear as such but, instead, discloses itself as a mental image, or *aperçu*.

Anticipating Heidegger's definition of the phenomenon, "seeing" for Goethe means recognizing within a given appearance the law that has generated and now gives shape to the organic being that appears. Yet unlike Heidegger, Goethe also maintains (as Nicholas of Cusa had done before him) that the very possibility of an intuitive and significant response to natural phenomena presupposes a metaphysics of analogy. For the phenomenon that registers in intuition and is "stabilized" (as Arnold Gehlen will put it) by some type of mental image can yield "insight"—that is, the *aperçu* of an underlying law—only if we posit an ontological relatedness between the order of appearance and the order of being. Were it not for that analogy, contingent sight could not grasp empirical beings as entelechies, that is, as manifesting an intrinsic purposiveness. Raw perception of a given form would never advance to the point where form is understood as an entelechy. Instead, the beholder would incessantly contrive more proper names for each species, subspecies, and variety—a project animated by the irrational expectation that a strictly disjunctive notion of difference as *negation* will somehow, eventually, yield *positive* knowledge of plant life.

In maintaining, against Linné, that "each existing thing is an analogue of every other thing" and that consequently "all being strikes us simultaneously as distinct

---

132. Kant 1951, 157 (§ 49).

133. For a fuller discussion of judgment and its reliance on a phenomenology of "voice" (*Stimme*) and "mood" (*Stimmung*), see Pfau 2005b, 33–45.

and related [*gesondert und verknüpft*]," Goethe holds a fundamentally different view of the natural world.[134] His characterization of the plant's successive development as "*vegetative growth*, by development of stems and leaves; and next, through *reproduction*, which is completed in the formation of flower and fruit," outlines a dynamic incompatible with a Neoclassical aesthetic committed to imitation (*mimēsis*) of discrete and invariant objects.[135] As Goethe notes, any science that adheres to a naively mimetic framework is doomed to fail; in this regard, "physics is worst off. . . . Its hypotheses and analogies are but concealed anthropomorphisms, parables, and such. By means of these [physicists] believe [themselves] to be stating the phenomenon itself, rather than attending to the conditions under which the phenomenon appears."[136] No matter how finely granulated a mere looking-at appearances becomes, it can never issue in knowledge but, instead, will expire in an unreflected, mimetic doubling of the phenomenon itself—a kind of hypersimulation yielding little more than exhaustive, literal descriptions and taxonomies.

By contrast, when tracing the progressive differentiation of, say, the ordinary field buttercup (*Ranunculus acris*) through its successive developmental stages, Goethe's observer visually participates in a process of infinitely subdivided transitional moments. Logically speaking, "the movement we are *thinking* would, if entirely phenomenal, be entirely continuous, leaving no gaps. Thus, as gaps narrow the impression of movement is strengthened." Ultimately, then, there is no underlying object that undergoes variational or teleological change. Rather, change itself is the only reality, and as such it "demands difference, and [as] continuous change, continuous difference." Inasmuch as any discrete visualization of a given plant isolates an "arrested stage, or *Gestalt*, it is an abstraction. It is held in arrest by our sensible experience, but when we attempt to detect the relation between stages, we must dissolve that condition in the mind." As Brady continues:

> Were someone to remark, when viewing such a series, that 'they are all the same thing,' the meaning of the statement would seem immediately apparent. But no single schema can generalize upon the series, for each schema, being itself a type of *Gestalt*, will be closer to one stage of the series than it is to the others. This is very apparent with the leaves, but it holds true of the vertebrae as well. . . . It might seem counter-intuitive to speak of movement, rather than an object mak-

---

134. *GHA* 12:368 (#23).
135. *GHA* 13:99 / *EM* 76.
136. Diary entry from April 1817: "Die Physik dagegen ist am übelsten dran . . . ihre Hypothesen und Analogien sind versteckte Anthropomorphismen, Gleichnißreden und dergleichen. Dadurch glauben sie das Phänomen auszusprechen, anstatt, daß sie sich um die Bedingungen bekümmern sollten, unter welchen es erscheint, da sie denn gar bald das wahre mit den Händen greifen könnten" (Goethe 1887–1919, pt. III, vol. 6, 32–33).

ing the movement, as generative, but between the forms and their movement there is only one possibility. We must remember that no single *Gestalt, qua Gestalt,* can generate a movement between forms. We detect the movement through the differential between forms, but no one form can give us this. The movement, on the other hand, is a continuity which must contain, in order to be continuous, multiple *Gestalts.* Thus the movement is not itself a product of the forms from which it is detected, but rather the unity of those forms, from which unity of any form belonging to the series can be generated.[137]

To understand the metamorphosis of plants, it is crucial for the observer focused on the organic growth of a particular species to resist the temptation to formulate laws based on abstractions. For Goethe, the "law" governing metamorphosis is not to be construed as an independent and abstract causal force. Neither should it be viewed as a purely heuristic notion, an expedient schema mobilized so as to furnish some ex post facto explanation of the changes exhibited by organic matter. Rather, change—which, again, must be understood as intrinsic *transformation* rather than contingent *alteration*—holds ontological status because it is inseparable from the very being that exhibits change. "Idea and existence," von Balthasar writes, "indicate the mysterious orientation of all becoming [*alles Werdenden*] to be more than itself: everything finite is ekstatic [*alles Seinde ist ekstatisch*]."[138] Hence, if it is illogical to speak of change taking place *between* stages, it is also impermissible to posit a separate and invariant substratum that supposedly holds constant through the process of change. Change, in Goethe's theory, is not visited on antecedently given matter. Rather, it positively *realizes* the form absent which we cannot even speak of matter. Moreover, in so doing, change allows the observer to participate, qua mental vision, in the reality of a given, substantial form. Visualization here is the *only* viable mode of grasping a specific organic being; and attempts to trace its internal and continuous transformation back to an efficient cause or "vital force" (*Lebenskraft*), supposedly slumbering within organic matter itself, add no explanatory value. For leaving aside the fact that such a strictly hypostatized force could never be verified or falsified, the concept permits us to conjecture only *why* a given organism undergoes change but never to account for the morphological specificity, or pattern, exhibited by such change.

What distinguishes Goethe's morphological science is this genial capacity of "seeing" in every actual manifestation of natural form its underlying potentiality: "The morphologist not only 'sees' that two distinct configurations are still 'the same,' but is made aware, by the same faculty, of nascent potentials that seem to arise from

---

137. Brady 1987, 276–79.
138. Balthasar 1998, 1:416.

every juxtaposition." Forever in transition, the individual leaf consequently "*represents*, to our mind, more than itself. . . . Its full import can appear *within sensible conditions* only through continuous transformation—through change."[139] To reiterate: taken as phenomenon, Goethe's leaf visually realizes the idea of the whole of (plant) life, the deep and imageless truth that, while unable to appear *as such*, accounts of the leaf's formal mode of appearance must necessarily seize upon it in some concrete guise or *Gestalt*. Whereas ordinary empirical inquiry will separate "the living thing . . . into its elements, but one cannot put these elements together again," Goethe's overarching concern is to "recognize living forms as such, to understand their outwardly visible and tangible parts in relation to one another, and to lay hold of them as indicia of the inner parts [*ihre* äußern *sichtbaren greiflichen Teile . . . als Andeutungen des Innern aufzunehmen*]."[140]

Yet the ultimate significance of this proto-phenomenological model of visual cognition that is being worked out in Goethe's botanical writings rests with how it in/forms and cultivates the observer's intelligence. Hence, for the mental image of form qua metamorphosis to be fully consummated, some adequate, symbolic form of presentation (*Darstellung*) is required. If morphology is "only to present and not to explain," that is, to stage the *Urphänomen* as a self-manifesting reality or presence, rather than subject to causal explanation, the proper object of *Darstellung* does not concern the imitation of some object "out there."[141] Rather, what begs to be drawn out in symbolic form is specifically the founding "intuition" (*Anschauung*) wherein the observer gains access "to the conditions under which the phenomenon appears" in the first place. Where Kant's transcendental method partitions knowledge into the theoretical and the practical reason, thereby instituting a division he would later struggle to overcome in his third *Critique*, Goethe's approach remains fundamentally committed to the classical (in origin Aristotelian) framework according to which *epistēmē* and *praxis* are inextricably entwined. Science for Goethe pivots on the kind of *hermeneutic* skill (in the Aristotelian sense of *technē*) required to bring empirical discernment and reflective judgment into productive alignment. Any meaningful engagement with the objective, natural world involves a continuous shuttling back and forth between intuition and reflection, sight and insight. Concurrently, in order to remain at all times in closest possible contact with a particular natural phenomenon, scientific inquiry must ceaselessly guide and "cultivate" (*bilden*) the observer's powers of intuition, attention, and intellection. Hence, the true measure of knowledge is none other than the observer's ability to translate mental vision into in-

---

139. Brady 1987, 282, 285.

140. *GHA* 13:5 / *EM* 23.

141. *GHA* 13:120 / *EM* 88. "Urformen, as pure phenomena, present the lawful relationships of empirical phenomena, not their causes" (Steigerwald 2019, 255).

tuitive comprehension and, ultimately, into a symbolic "presentation" of the natural phenomenon at issue.

Crucially, for Goethean metamorphosis to prove more than a hypothesis, its seemingly inscrutable, mythic efficacy must be cashed out in aesthetic form. An objective verbal correlative is needed that will make explicit the dynamic character and metaphysical significance of images first crystallized by intuitive vision without rendering them inert, abstract, or gratuitously speculative. Perhaps no writer had modeled such dynamic form better for Goethe than Ovid, whose abundantly visual style in his *Metamorphoses* (ca. AD 8) had so vividly dramatized self-transformation as the omnipresent, mythical form organizing all visible being. With its imagery forever nudging us to visualize connections, associations, linkages, and morphological shifts of all sorts, Ovid had alighted on metonymy as the formal device fusing together event and meaning, story (*mythos*) and plot—that is, the temporal and the symbolic. Premising that the ultimate aim of all symbolic presentation, whether verbal or pictorial, is to reveal visible reality as a pattern of ceaseless transformation, Ovid's poetry identifies intrinsic *change* (not extrinsic alteration) as the shared foundation of both narrative and visual art. Proposing to tell "of bodies changed to other forms . . . In one continuous song from nature's first / Remote beginnings to our modern times," he thus frames transformation, in all its alternately sudden, creeping, freakish, or splendid manifestations, as the very essence of being.[142] Throughout the "continuous song" of his *Metamorphoses* what perplexes is not the hypothesis of things (material, organic, animate, or human) initially appearing *dissimilar* but, on the contrary, that seemingly discrete entities reveal themselves as transient manifestations of an underlying, integrative, and significant form. Ultimately, all being appears imbued with an inscrutable propensity to change its shape without the interference of external causes and in so doing reveal itself as the fleeting manifestation of an ideal, albeit invisible, form.

In the *Metamorphoses*, then, the Heraclitean principle of flux no longer operates as an unstable relation *between* discrete things. Instead, self-induced, formal differentiation now appears as the very essence of beings whose formal presentation, though forever transient, is now grasped as wholly contiguous and purposive. This shift from a disjunctive and random to an integrative and purposive understanding of difference is altogether central to the narrative and figural art of the *Metamorphoses*. For Ovid, transformation is not simply a mythic conception, but turns out to be intricately entwined with the shifting and multilayered process of aesthetic presentation (*Darstellung*). A fine example of metamorphosis as both an ontological principle and a premise for narrative art can be found in Ovid's frequent use of transformative

---

142. Ovid 1986, bk. 1, lines 1–5.

puns and other types of wordplay. As Garth Tissol has shown in great detail, "Though the reader receives Ovid's version of a tale together with the echoes of other versions that it calls to life in the memory, at the same time Ovid's own version may cause the reader's judgment to undergo many revisions. Ovid perceived in narrative structure, no less than in wit, an opportunity to embody metamorphosis and flux."[143]

Implicitly, then, Ovid's consciously *literary* project addresses the specter of a chasm opening up between the noumenal and the phenomenal long before the two realms were expressly disaggregated by Descartes. Yet what captivates Ovid's reimagining of classical mythology is not some abstract notion of being and its potential quarantining from the order of appearance. On the contrary, the central objective of his *Metamorphoses* is to imagine the material and phenomenal world as a welter of things palpably, albeit inscrutably, *related*, which the poem's many stories tease out in unfailingly concrete and often playful language. For Ovid no less than for Goethe, it is the coalescence of the archetypal and ectypal, of ontology and phenomenology, that furnishes the impetus for scientific study and, as a result, invests the study of natural forms with a strong narrative momentum. "Change" in the physical universe will necessarily reproduce itself as the ongoing formation (*Bildung*) of an observing intelligence constituting itself through a continual feedback loop of sight and insight. Hence, for Goethe, any observable material change reveals the observer's complex response to the event of transformation: first, by learning to interpret seemingly disparate appearances as formally contiguous points of reference; and, second, by seeking to capture change in symbolic (narrative) form, thereby vindicating both the temporal constitution of all appearance and the supratemporal unity of observing consciousness.[144]

A couple of passages in the *Metamorphoses* throw into relief the originality and pivotal influence of Ovid's narrative art on Goethe the scientist. The story of Daphne, relentlessly pursued by Jupiter and imploring her father, Peneus, to shelter her from the Olympian god's feral sexuality is particularly apposite. For it shows that the ultimate goal of metamorphosis is not to exchange one appearance for another but, rather, for Daphne to escape her ephemeral and vulnerable condition of visi-

---

143. Tissol 1991, 88. Likewise, in their classical commentary, Haupt and Ehwald remark on "Ovid's exaggerated rhetoric, which intensifies, expands, and transforms what it has received" (quoted in Tissol 1991, 115).

144. Breidbach 2006, 55–56. Among the Romantics, it is arguably Shelley who most fully embraces Ovid's central notion of "omnia mutantur, nihil interit" (everything changes, nothing dies); see his famous opening lines in "Mont Blanc" or his shorter lyrics, especially "The Cloud" and "Ode to the West Wind." With regard to the latter, Wasserman notes how "each stanza of the poem's *terza rima* contains an unused, unfulfilled line that, like a seed in the grave, upon the completion, or 'death,' of its own stanza gives birth to the rhyme of the next" (Wasserman 1971, 245). On Shelley and contemporary debates in the life sciences, see also Gigante 2009, 154–207.

bility by attaining her true telos of invisibility, that is, to transcend the realm of contingent appearance for that of enduring, substantial form.

> And then she saw the river, swift Peneus,
> And called; "Help, father, help! If mystic power
> Dwells in your waters, change me and destroy
> My baleful beauty that has pleased too well.'
> Scarce had she made her prayer when through her limbs
> A dragging languor spread, her tender bosom
> Was wrapped in thin smooth bark, her slender arms
> Were changed to branches and her hair to leaves;
> Her feet but now so swift were anchored fast
> In numb stiff roots, her face and head became
> The crown of a green tree; all that remained
> Of Daphne was her shining loveliness.
> And still Apollo loved her; on the trunk
> He placed his hand and felt beneath the bark
> Her heart still beating[145]

Impelling Ovid's dramatic account of cross-species transformation is Daphne's desire for shelter from Apollo's sexual predations and, thus, retaining control over her future progeny (fig. 5.4). Since such shelter cannot be obtained in three-dimensional space, and since the object of contest is her very body, nothing less than transcending her embodied, visible condition will do. Daphne's transformation into an alien physical shape thus proves less invasive than if, sexually violated, she were to give birth to offspring from which she would be profoundly alienated. Yet the most compelling aspects of Ovidian metamorphosis are the myriad sensory particulars, the visceral power of detail, and the way in which images reveal his underlying grasp of embodied being as a kaleidoscope of perceptible qualities continually reconfiguring themselves.

A long tradition of readers has thus viewed Ovid's approach to epic form as one of "clever pastiche" and his overall art as "letting each detail catch his reader's attention without ever arresting it." Yet as the Daphne episode shows, "variety was never an unsophisticated or simple thing," since the motif of the "determined virgin courted by the passionate god" is itself repeatedly transformed in the course of Ovid's narrative. Far from offering up "epic [as] a façade, [Ovid] gradually subtracts and adds motif-elements so that in the end he has, in fact, substituted one complete motif for

---

145. Ovid 1986, 1:537–52.

Figure 5.4. "Apollo and Daphne" mosaic, third century. Princeton University Art Museum

another."[146] Embedded in an irresistibly propulsive syntax, the discrete images that capture Daphne's metamorphosis do not merely evoke specific physical parts (leaves, roots, bark, branches, etc.), but, crucially, unveil a startling isomorphism of her human body with the Lauraceae tree. Thus, she is not so much transfigured into something "else" but, in a deeper sense that can be captured only figurally, merges with a form to which she has always borne a latent kinship. Itself a veritable archetype of continuous organic development, the Lauraceae tree does not "differ" from her in the sense of being a wholly separate and incompatible entity. Rather, it embodies nature as forever metastasizing and, hence, as something in which Daphne has always latently shared and to which she now returns. In its modular structure, Ovid's narrative presents the laurel tree (one of some 30 to 50 genera and about 2,000 distinct species) as bearing a marked formal affinity to the human body; and for one to

146. Otis 1966, 77–79.

morph into the other is not to *alter* but to *preserve* its continually altering and internally differentiating essence.

There is, of course, no shortage of examples from literary history to show how compelling an artistic premise Ovid created. By transposing the immediacy of mythic consciousness into the sensory *and* self-conscious "event" of the creative act, metamorphosis throws into relief the question of *Darstellung* or *poïësis* that was to occupy countless poets and aestheticians, particularly during the (long) Romantic period. We encounter it in Milton's *Paradise Lost*, Coleridge's "Christabel," Beethoven's late variations, Keats's "Lamia," Wagner's *Tristan & Isolde*, Kafka's *Metamorphosis*, Richard Strauss's *Tod und Verklärung, Metamorphosen*, and *Daphne*, and in Schoenberg's austere realization of form as *Entwicklungsvariation*. In all these cases, a series of transformations comprising literary or musical narrative both preserves and discerns the nature of its protagonist or core motif. In all its dimensions—as material instantiation, phenomenal apprehension, and symbolic presentation—metamorphosis fuels a process of *Bildung* that Goethe was to characterize as "perpetual transfiguration" (*fortwährendes Umbilden*).[147] In the final book of the *Metamorphoses*, Ovid sets forth a more general conception of transformational change.

> the soul
> Roams to and fro, now here, now there, and takes
> What frame it will, passing from beast to man,
> From our own form to beast and never dies.
> As yielding wax is stamped with new designs
> And changes shape and seems not still the same,
> Yet is indeed the same, even so our souls
> Are still the same for ever, but adopt
> In their migrations every-varying forms.

---

147. *GHA* 13:60. Few artists explore the aesthetic potential of metamorphosis more profoundly than Wagner and R. Strauss. What, in a letter to Matilde Wesendonck (29 October 1859), Wagner refers to as his art "of the most subtle, most gradual transition" (*Kunst des feinsten, allmählichsten Übergangs*) in *Tristan und Isolde*, pivots on his proto-Modernist use of chromaticism. In drawing on the mythic power of metamorphosis at every turn, Wagner's richly polyphonic score mobilizes the formal device of "chromatic alteration." By this principle, "a note that impinges on its neighbour as a chromatic passing note or as a suspension began as a variant or chromaticization of a diatonic degree—that is, as an 'alteration.' . . . The chromaticism of *Tristan* relies for its expressive effect on the listener's awareness of deviation from the diatonic background of the chord—that is on his awareness of the 'alteration': the musical expression is inseparable from the divergence from the norm" (Dahlhaus and Deathridge 1984, 119–20); see also Scruton 2004, 75–118. Likewise, a transformational logic also organizes much of Wagner's *Ring*, such that any number of motifs (Rhinemaiden-, Wotan-, Valhalla-, Siegfried-motif et al.) are variationally derived from the circular leitmotif of the ring. For a discussion of "transfiguration" (*Verwandlung*) in the oeuvre of Richard Strauss, see Gilliam 2003.

Bury a prize bull, slain for sacrifice,
And from the rotting flesh—a well-known fact—
Bees everywhere are born, flower-loving bees,
Which like their parent range the countryside,
Work with a will and a hope for work's reward.
A charger in his grave will generate
Hornets. If you remove the bending claws
Of a beach-crab and sink the rest in sand,
A scorpion will crawl from the buried part,
Tail curved to strike. And grubs, as country folk
Observe, whose white cocoons are wrapped in leaves,
Emerge as butterflies that grace a grave.
. . . . . .
These creatures all derive their first beginnings
From others of their kind.
. . . . . .
So—lest I range too far and my steeds lose
Their course—the earth and all therein, the sky
And all thereunder change and change again.
We too ourselves, who of this world are part,
Not only flesh and blood but pilgrim souls,
Can make our homes in creatures of the wild
Or of the farm. These creatures might have housed
Souls of our parents, brothers, other kin[148]

Most clearly, the shift toward a more abstract thinking of difference is reflected by Ovid's use, in the first passage, of simile ("As yielding wax is stamped . . . ") and, in the final long passage, of metonymy. Both tropes throw into relief the mythical principle of "the one that differs within itself," which by then Ovid has traced extensively in many stories. As his self-conscious aside ("lest I range too far . . . ") makes clear, the *Metamorphoses* does not claim to produce myth but, instead, to cast in fitting aesthetic form the invisible mythic principle that subtends and organizes all visible being. What Ernst Cassirer notes about Schelling's late *Philosophy of Mythology* (1842) holds true also for the *Metamorphoses*: "The phenomenon which is here to be considered is not the mythical content as such but the significance it possesses for human consciousness and the power it exerts on consciousness. The problem is not the material content of mythology, but the intensity with which it is experienced,

---

148. Ovid 1986, 15:166–74, 362–73, 393–94, 460–67.

with which it is *believed*—as only something endowed with objective reality can be believed."[149] Vividly captured in the metonymic sequencing (bull, charger, crab, etc.) of carcasses forever generating new forms, the transformations that past myths had ascribed to the violent caprice of the Greeks' anthropomorphic gods turns out to be no less observable, indeed predictable, in the quotidian cycles of natural life and death.[150]

For Ovid and Goethe, the artistic objective is fundamentally the same: to visualize life as a continuous process comprising infinitely subtle transitions, to be captured in a correspondingly rich and vivid mode of aesthetic "presentation" (*Darstellung*) that avoids reducing life to something merely abstract and notional. The objective is neither to disavow the mythic principle of metamorphosis nor to subject it to dialectical mastery, but to render it visible by distilling it from its myriad transient manifestations. For while it continues to perform its subterranean work, the mythic principle of metamorphosis as yet "lacks the category of the ideal. For here 'image' does not represent the 'thing'; it *is* the thing; it does not merely stand for the object, but has the same actuality, so that it replaces the thing's immediate presence."[151] What is needed, then, is for the sheer particularity and contingency of metamorphosis to be afforded aesthetic "presentation" (*Darstellung*), that is, for its otherwise invisible, mythic principle to attain objective, visible presence in the medium of the image. For Arnold Gehlen, "presentation" (*Darstellung*) thus lays bare one of the basic "anthropological roots of art" in that it "transposes" seemingly contingent and ephemeral occurrences "into the category of preservation and continuity [die *Überführung* in die Kategorie des Beisichbehaltens und der Dauer]." In this regard, he maintains, image-based, intuitive modes of understanding far surpass abstract-deductive forms of ratiocination: "The tremendous superiority of presentation [*Darstellung*] over the concept" has to do with the fact that "the former takes the specificity of the object as its point of departure and invests it with continuity; by contrast, the concept merely 'means' something and evaporates unless it is sustained by some external support." Thus, "by capturing the real in the image, we transcended it in the direction of immanence [man transzendierte (das Wirkliche), es im Bilde darstellend, ins Diesseits]."[152]

Clearly inspired by Ovid's *Metamorphoses*, Goethe's botanical theory remains significant not only for its dynamic understanding of natural form but also for

---

149. Cassirer 1955, 5.

150. Richards (2002, 375 n.) notes that, as early as 1786, Goethe had begun to study the apparent generation of minute organisms (*infusoria*) when exposed to light and the way organic matter appeared to generate living organisms that, over the course of days, would undergo further transformation.

151. Cassirer 1955, 38.

152. Gehlen 2004, 63.

showing all sensory experience to be intimately entwined with the aesthetic process of *Darstellung*. As Goethe notes in his *Theory of Color* (§ 751):

> We never sufficiently reflect that a language, strictly speaking, can only be symbolical and figurative, that it can never express things directly, but only, as it were, reflectedly [*nur im Widerscheine*]. This is especially the case in speaking of qualities which are only imperfectly presented to observation, which might rather be called powers than objects, and which are ever in movement throughout nature. They are not to be arrested, and yet we find it necessary to describe them; hence we look for all kinds of formulae in order, figuratively [*gleichnisweise*] at least, to define them.[153]

Just as the myth of Daphne had exemplified long before, Goethe understands internal differentiation as the very essence of life—a continuous "becoming other in order to remain itself."[154] It is not merely a chemical churning of matter or the sum total of photosynthesis, circulation, respiration, digestion, and so forth. Rather, as an intrinsically concrete and "appearing" form, life continually solicits our active participation as observing and representing (*darstellende*) intelligence.

This last consideration also makes clear that knowledge, for Goethe, does not so much aim at a determinate representation (*Vorstellung*) of Cartesian *res extensae* situated in Newtonian space; nor does it involve an apperceptive synthesis and accumulation of "data" to be "applied" or otherwise "expended" in the pursuit of some contingent objective. The "idea" at the heart of Goethean organicism, and the dynamic image yielded by his intuitionist approach to scientific knowledge, is not fungible with the order of concepts. An idea does not predicate something "about" a discrete "object" but, instead, takes shape as a beholder participates, by means of mental or intellectual vision, in a given thing's self-manifestation. Intuition is a mode of accessing the real as it manifests itself in the "dynamic order" (*bewegliche Ordnung*) of organic being. In evident contrast to conceptual and discursive knowledge, symbolic (intuitive) vision does not break with the order of appearance but, instead, lets itself always be guided by it, responds to the call of the phenomenon, and, in so doing, participates in the *logos* that encompasses both being and appearance.[155] Now,

---

153. *GHA* 13:491–92 / Goethe 1967, 300. In his introduction to that work, Goethe remarks on how, struggling for adequate terminology for this most elusive of phenomena (light), observers have fashioned "a symbolical language . . . which, from its close analogy, may be employed as equivalent to a direct and appropriate terminology" (*GHA* 13:316 / Goethe 1967, xix).

154. Brady 1987, 286.

155. For Goethe, "seeing" is a mode of "cognizing, . . . not a proposition about what is perceived but an activity that actualizes the perception. *Each act of seeing is necessarily an act of understanding.* . . . We do not perceive and then bring forward a concept to understand. We focus our

if the image (be it visual or verbal) arising from such intuitive vision is experienced as imbued with symbolic significance, the question that had previously arisen in fifteenth-century religious painting once again presents itself: How are we to understand the relation of image to symbol, and how are we to appraise Goethe's particular inflection of that relationship?

Throughout the far-flung Neoplatonist tradition, exemplified thus far by Plotinus, Nicholas of Cusa, and now Goethe, the image is invested with symbolic significance insofar as it mediates a transcendent dimension manifesting itself in the order of the visible. What the symbol allows intuitive vision (*visio mentalis*) to access is the convergence of two ontologically distinct orders in a single, specific phenomenon. A visible, time-bound, and three-dimensional thing elicits our focused and searching sensory-cum-intellectual participation. As Goethe was to remark to Eckerman, where that occurs, the experience of the thing as it phenomenally gives itself to the observer brings about a recognition. For von Balthasar, this sudden transfiguration of sheer phenomenality into a distinctive *Gestalt* effects in the beholder a "retrospective remembering and *ana-mnesis* of what has been seen—*conversio ad phantasma (verissimum!)*—[that] constitutes the basis of understanding anything."[156] Sight turns into insight as the phenomenon is experienced as visibly mediating the "gentle law" (*das sanfte Gesetz*)—itself numinous and hence invisible—*of* which the specific thing seen is a transient manifestation and *to* which it owes its very being. It is this *coincidentia oppositorum* (Cusa), this convergence or "falling-into-one" (*symballein*) of contingent being and its transcendent source, that causes the phenomenon to be experienced as saturated with symbolic meaning.

Consequently, it would be a category mistake to construe the symbol itself as but another object inter alia. More accurately, where sensory experience appears suffused with symbolic significance it is intuitively grasped as enabling the beholder to participate both in the visible phenomenon and, by means of it, in its numinous source. It is precisely *in* and *by means of* the realm of the visible that the student of a natural phenomenon is able to intuit its *eidos* or, in Aristotelian terminology, grasp it as an entelechy. While "seeing the idea," as Goethe had put it in conversation with Schiller, means indeed to participate in the *logos*, the relation remains strictly one of analogy. Mindful of the ultimate "mystery" (*Geheimnis*) linking *logos* and *kosmos*, God and nature, Goethe's scientist "acquiesces and forms concepts that seek to stand in analogy to the origins of being [bescheiden wir uns und bilden Begriffe, die

---

understanding to bring forth a perception" (Brady 1998, 88). Breithaupt notes that "above all, the aim of Goethe's Phenomenology is to preserve the openness of the phenomenon and to prevent its mortification by the definitively objective [Offenhalten des Phänomenalen, die Verhinderung der Mortifikation durch das endgültige Objective]" (2000, 78).

156. Balthasar 1982, 30.

analog jenen Uranfängen sein möchten]." For the very possibility of scientific in-quiry posits "that idea and experience can, indeed must, be analogues [daß Idee und Erfahrung analog sein können, ja müssen]."[157] Hence, Goethe's scientific and poetic oeuvre rests on this ontological framework of an *analogia entis*, just as its phenome-nology centers on the symbol. Still, even as natural phenomena enable the observer to achieve intuitive knowledge of their intrinsically purposive form, the *eidos* thus apprehended is not itself identical with the transcendent *logos* to which it owes its very being. Rather, it enables the finite intellect to participate in the *logos* by analogy insofar as the symbol presupposes—and qua image visibly claims—"a primordial metaphysical kinship" (*metaphysische Urverwandtschaft*) with *logos*. It follows, as Gadamer has demonstrated, that the symbol, at least for Goethe, must never be re-duced to an aesthetic category or rhetorical form. Rather, because it manifests "a general tendency toward [significant] meaning [allgemeine Richtung auf das Bedeu-tende, das er in allen Erscheinungen sucht]," the symbol for Goethe is "not so much an aesthetic experience as an experience of reality [*Wirklichkeitserfahrung*]."[158]

It is this analogical relationship that explains why image and symbol hold such a crucial, mediating function in Goethe's scientific and aesthetic theories. Belonging to a domain fundamentally different from that of discrete objects or particular modes of signification, Goethe fundamentally rejects the view subsequently taken by Hegel and a great deal of modern critical thought—namely, that the symbol forms part of the Enlightenment's exhaustive taxonomy of "artificial" signs. Far from thinking of it as but another historically contingent "sign" (*Zeichen*), as Hegel will claim in his *Aesthetics*, Goethe views the symbol as altogether foundational for human culture of any kind, and indispensable to human cognition, intuitive, empirical, or specula-tive.[159] In his characteristically expansive and forthright manner, Goethe remarks in

---

157. *GHA* 13:31.
158. Gadamer 2006, 64, 66. Von Balthasar speaks of analogy as "the ultimate formula of Goethe's worldview" ([1937–39] 1998, 1:436–37). On Romantic literary and philosophical conceptions of the symbol, see Halmi 2007, 1–26, 63–98. Halmi views "the theorization of the symbol in the Romantic period . . . as an attempt, however illogical and methodologically dubious in itself, to foster a sense of harmony of the human mind with nature," possibly motivated by a desire to "reduc[e] anxiety about the place of the individual in bourgeois society" in the aftermath of the French Revolution (2007, 24). Yet Goethe cannot easily be fitted into such an explanatory scheme, seeing as he resists a narrowly *aesthetic* and *theoretical* view of the symbol. In fact, his appraisal of the symbolic as an *Urphänomen* grounded in a Platonist metaphysics cannot be encompassed by a strictly historicizing account unless, of course, we invest such a contextualizing and functionalist method with a quasi-metaphysical authority of its own. Not only does Goethe not reject "analogically for ontologically based symbolism," as Halmi suggests (2007, 93), but in time the principle of analogy came to be understood as a key implication of an Aristotelian, realist ontology.
159. "Now the symbol is *prima facie* a *sign*." Yet whereas "in a *mere sign* the connection which meaning and its expression have with one another is only a purely arbitrary linkage," in the case of the symbol "its externality comprises in itself at the same time the content of the idea which it

an 1818 letter that "everything that happens is a symbol, and, in fully represent-ing itself, it points to everything else."[160] As part of "a general tendency toward mean-ing that [Goethe] seeks in all phenomena," the symbol sets the conditions under which knowledge of whatever kind (intuitive, representational, predicative, or purely formal) becomes possible in the first place.[161] Wherever mind responds to the sheer givenness of being qua phenomenon, symbolic or intuitive vision establishes the very parameters for predicating being per se (e.g., "This object in the distance is an elm tree") or ascribing specific properties to it (e.g., "This laurel tree is budding"). In evident contrast to Hegel's historicizing account, Goethe demurs at attempts to de-limit the symbol as a strictly premodern mode of signification within a general sys-tem of semiotics and, thus, as a passing episode in a general history of aesthetics.

Hence it would be a category error to construe the symbol as properly "realized" (*verwirklicht*) only in the realm of the conceptual and the discursive. Let us tarry a little longer with the obverse Hegelian and, eventually, neo-Kantian approach, which frames image and symbol exclusively as something *made*, not given, which is to say, as a product of human reason rather than as arising from an elemental, intuitive re-ceptivity to the *logos*. A representative case of such an anthropocentric approach and its ultimately aniconic concept of rationality is found in Ernst Cassirer's discussion of the symbol as a specific type of human expressivity. What is true of language in gen-eral "holds equally true for the hermetic world of images and signs, which includes the realms of myth, religion, and art [*der mythischen, der religiösen, der künstlerischen Welt*]. There is a mistaken, albeit persistent tendency to gauge the content and the 'truth' contained by these realms based on what they contain by way of *being* [*was sie an Dasein in sich schließen*], rather than according to the force and cohesiveness of expression itself [*Kraft und Geschlossenheit des Ausdrucks selbst*]."[162] A product of human "expression" (*Ausdruck*) originating in an intuitive (mental) vision of being in its sheer givenness, the symbol seizes upon being and, on Cassirer's neo-Kantian account, refashions it for strictly immanent ends. Thus construed by Cassirer as a product of finite, human "making" (*facere*), the symbol constitutes a quantum leap

---

brings into appearance" (Hegel 1975, 1:304–5; see also his introduction to symbolic art, 303–22). As Gadamer notes, Hegel's historicizing approach rests on the premise of a "disproportion between image and meaning" in any "particular art form." And yet, what distinguishes the symbolic image is "less the disproportion than the coincidence of image and meaning." Unlike Kant, Goethe, and Schelling, Hegel's account cannot credit the symbol with unveiling what, in his view, is the exclusive province of the concept (*Begriff*), namely, to give definitive expression to the premise "that the finite and the infinite genuinely belong together [*eine innere Zusammengehörigkeit von Endlichem und Unendlichem*]" (Gadamer 2006, 67–68).

160. Goethe, Letter to Schubart, 3 April 1818, quoted in Gadamer 2006, 66.
161. Gadamer 2006, 66.
162. Cassirer 1983, 176.

in the quintessentially modern project of individual self-fashioning and bringing the entire visible world under rational and scientific dominion. And yet, such a conception of the symbol as the harbinger of an anthropocentric, in tendency secular and wholly immanent, modernity fails to acknowledge the symbol's origins in Christian thought of late antiquity. In fact, the function of the symbolic image in the premodern era is essentially the obverse of the one foregrounded by Hegelian and neo-Kantian thought. In its religious and, more specifically, its liturgical function, the symbol mediates the human community's vertical relationship to a creator-God who is invisible and transcendent.

An integral feature of apophatic theology, the symbol had for more than a millenium been grounded in a stance of epistemic humility: "The Transcendent is clothed in the terms of being, with shape and form on things which have neither, and numerous symbols are employed to convey the varied attributes of what is an imageless and supra-natural simplicity."[163] Among the most influential expositors of an apophatic theology that would eventually be upended by the Quattrocento, pseudo-Dionysius never fails to insist that the symbol is not made but received; it is not a human contrivance but a reality unveiled, a divine gift and accommodation: "The Word of God makes use of poetic imagery[,] . . . not for the sake of art, but as a concession to the nature of our own mind."[164] Moreover, the limitations of the human intellect thus accommodated are not historically contingent; they cannot be overcome by some Hegelian dialectic but, instead, are woven into the fabric of our very being. The unchanging rationale for all symbolism, "for creating types for the typeless, for giving shape to what is actually without shape," arises from the human being's epistemic limitations and finitude. Hence, the symbol is not a historically contingent technique of signification but, instead, constitutes the eternal source on which all abstract knowledge depends and from which, however unwittingly, it must draw. Intuitive (mental) vision and the symbolic presentation to which it gives rise constitute, in Dionysius's account, the very foundation on which abstract, conceptual thought builds; and it is precisely because "we lack the ability to be directly raised up to conceptual contemplations" that it would be illogical to credit abstract thought with the capacity to take possession of and ultimately expunge its own symbolic foundations. Instead, symbols simultaneously descend on the finite subject in the form of intuitive vision, providing "our own upliftings that come naturally to us" and prevent, by dint of their essential dissimilarity from the divine *logos*, the subject from conflating the order of (symbolic) appearance with the invisible reality that it medi-

---

163. Pseudo-Dionysius 1987, 52 (*DN*, 592B).
164. Ibid., 148 (*CH*, 137B).

ates: "it is the protective garb of the understanding of what is ineffable and invisible to the common multitude."[165]

By contrast, in Cassirer's argument the symbol is circumscribed by a neo-Kantian Enlightenment narrative and its Pelagian faith in the "immanent frame" of scientific rationality. It purports to bring all being under exclusively human, scientific dominion and rejects any suggestion that knowledge might rest on presuppositions beyond its control, that the intuitive vision in which finite cognition originates and to which it responds is itself a case of ineffable, transcendent givenness. Hence, Cassirer stipulates, wherever we speak of a "symbolic content . . . the image has ceased to be something merely received from without [*ein bloß von außen Empfangenes*]; it now has turned into something formed from within [*ein von innen her Gebildetes*] in which the elemental principle of free creativity [*das Grundprinzip freien Bildens*] prevails." Having mastered the art of active, symbolic self-expression, "consciousness is no longer contented with *having* a sensuous content but, instead, *generates* it out of its own resources [*aus sich heraus erzeugt*]."[166] While rightly stressing the dynamic character of the symbol, Cassirer equates that dynamism with the finite individual's autonomous production of meaning, which in turn he frames in exclusively conceptual terms. Tellingly, he is prepared to speak of a symbol only if it no longer engages the visible world "in the manner of dead images on a tablet [*wie tote Bilder auf einer Tafel*]" but, instead, "penetrates [being] with the phonetic gestalt of the word [*mit der Lautgestalt des Wortes durchdringen*]." In pointedly anti-Aristotelian and post-metaphysical language, Cassirer characterizes the "image" (*Bild*) as per se lifeless and mute, impassively awaiting its liberation by the human "form-giving act" (*des Bildens* or *Bildgestaltung*). By contrast, where the world is apprehended in its sheer phenomenal givenness in the medium of the image, Cassirer only sees the opaque handiwork of a Gnostic demiurge of sorts, that is, a primitive or "mythic consciousness governed and paralyzed by demonic compulsion" (*dämonischer Zwang*).[167]

While Cassirer's humanistic inflection of the neo-Kantian program frequently draws on Kant and Goethe as its main intellectual forebears, he not only overlooks Goethe's well-documented "disinclination towards epistemology," but, on a key point,

---

165. Ibid., 149 (*CH*, 140A); 283 (Letter IX, 1105C).

166. Cassirer 1983, 176–77. Georg Simmel's juxtaposition of Kant and Goethe in his eponymous 1916 essay reaches different and more persuasive conclusions. For Simmel, Goethe does not endorse Kant's project of "elevat[ing] our sense of the value and the interconnectedness of the world as a whole into the sphere of abstract concepts." Instead, "Goethe seeks the unity of the subjective and objective principles, of nature and mind, within their appearances" (Simmel 2007a, 162–63).

167. Cassirer 1983, 178, 183, 188. "The intellectual framework of modern idealism was needed so as definitively to overcome the Aristotelian-Scholastic concept of species" and the "mimetic theory [*Abbildtheorie*]" in which, so Cassirer maintains, it remains mired (184).

also parts ways with Kant.[168] At issue is Kant's famous discussion of the beautiful as a symbol of the good in § 59 of the *Critique of Judgment*. There he speaks of *hypotyposis*, a "sensible illustration . . . [that] is either *schematic*, when to a concept comprehended by the understanding the corresponding intuition is given, or . . . *symbolic*." Underwriting that distinction is Kant's insight that the symbolic is *eo ipso* incommensurable with discursive and conceptual reason. For the symbol alone is capable of supplying "an intuition" not governed by a rational concept but, instead, offering an "indirect presentation [*indirekte Darstellung*] . . . in which the expression [furnishes] merely a symbol for reflection."[169] By emphasizing the "indirect" nature of this presentation, Kant acknowledges that the relationship of symbol to concept is not deictic but analogical. The symbolic image presents us with a visible analogue for the reflection that gives birth, as it were, to the concept itself. Kant's repeated characterization of the symbol as "analogous" to the "form of reflection" that yields conceptual ("schematic") cognition attests to his lingering awareness that the symbol's metaphysical underpinnings also extend, *by analogy*, to the domain of conceptual reflection. As Gadamer points out, Kant "does justice to the theological truth that had found its scholastic form in the *analogia entis* and keeps human concepts separate from God."[170] Yet precisely this metaphysical analogy of sensible intuition and abstract reflection has disappeared in Cassirer's account, in which the symbol no longer inhabits a distinct ontological position but, supposedly lodged in competition for the same epistemic space as the concept, will inevitably be expunged by the latter.

Beyond that, Cassirer's argument becomes entangled in further paradoxes and contradictions. Thus, he all but ignores the distinction between allegory and symbol, an integral if complicated feature of Romanticism's critical turn *against* Enlightenment rationalism, and which for that reason alone cannot simply be absorbed into a neo-Kantian explanatory scheme. Whereas allegory remains grounded in preestablished rhetorical patterns and a quasi-conceptual inventory of emblems, the "symbol is not related by its meaning to another meaning, but its own sensory existence *has* 'meaning.'"[171] Furthermore, in characterizing mythical thinking as a sphere defined by the "indifference of image and thing" (*Indifferenz von Bild und Sache*), Cassirer presupposes, though notably does not prove, that cognition can only ever take conceptual form. By the same token, his hypothesis of a primitive and opaque "mythical-magic concatenation" (*Verflechtungszusammenhang*) wherein thing and image appear indistinguishable—an iconoclast position that John Damascene had already refuted in the eighth century—would, if true, make it logically impossible to speak of

---

168. Simmel 2007a, 164.
169. Kant 1951, 197–98 (§ 59).
170. Gadamer 2006, 65.
171. Ibid., 63.

images at all. Cassirer's decision to do so anyway reveals the hidden pathos of his post-Kantian idealism.

All along, that is, the quest for a truly immanent, rigorously conceptual and anthropomorphic epistemology remains dependent on primitive, mythical, and insufficiently autonomous modes of representation, which it then proceeds to dismantle; and here the image, which Cassirer construes as the talismanic and "magical" precursor of a modern, scientific worldview, proves vitally important. Sounding rather more Hegelian than Kantian, Cassirer thus constructs an emancipatory narrative, which traces the gradual "liberation" of symbolic and, eventually, conceptual meanings from a supposedly primitive and static agglomeration of mythic images: "Belief in the magic efficacy of words and images . . . had formed the basic element of a mythical world-view. Gradually, however, there unfolds within that framework an emancipation and liberation [*Loslösung und Befreiung*] to the extent that the world of myth yields to that of religion." Fast-forwarding several millennia, Cassirer now posits a direct causal link between the prohibition of images and the emergence of a "new monotheistic consciousness *wherein the animating, spiritual power of the image has been extinguished* [*daß die beseelende, die geistige Kraft des Bildes wie verloschen ist*] and all meaning and significance has withdrawn into another, purely intellectual sphere and, thus, reducing the being of the image [*vom Sein des Bildes*] leaves behind but the empty, material husk [*das leere materielle Substrat zurückläßt*]."[172]

Beyond the paradoxes already identified, Cassirer's reading, however eloquently presented and imbued with a secular-humanist pathos of the best kind, ultimately rests on the assumption of a postmetaphysical, strictly immanent conception of reason. Yet what underwrites the concept of the symbolic, and not only at some conjectural (mythic) beginning of human history but throughout all of it up to and including our present moment, is what Gadamer calls its "metaphysical background." In contrast to the contingent, rhetorical constitution of allegory, the symbol arises from an intuitive understanding that "it is possible to be led beyond the sensible to the divine. For the world of the senses is not [pace Cassirer] mere nothingness and

---

172. Cassirer 1983, 188–89; emphasis mine. For Sperber, the "cryptological view of symbolism" that would quarantine the symbol from the order of sign and concept, exposes a "semiological illusion" endemic to much post-Enlightenment thought. Yet to posit that symbolic form and semantic content can be successfully disaggregated, and that the symbol is to be superseded by abstract, conceptual forms of knowledge is to overlook that such "semiologism is one of the bases of *our* ideology." Precisely this "motivation" to construe the interpretation of symbols as effectively *overcoming* their imagistic character "is not meta-symbolic . . . but must itself be interpreted symbolically." Consequently, when "interpret[ing] a symbol with an associated idea, one should not substitute the second term of the association for the first, but rather consider them together" (1975, 37, 47). Likewise, Freedberg criticizes a tendency to characterize (and thereby dismiss?) "the identity of the picture and what is pictured" in terms of "picture-magic" (1989, 79–80).

darkness but the outflowing and reflection of truth."[173] Hence, for Cassirer to distinguish between "the image as such and the intellectual, imageless truth that it seeks to present [*der bildlosen Wahrheit, die es darstellen will*]," is to suppose that philosophical knowledge can somehow (yet how?) definitively supplant the image, even as the latter unveils the very being to which reflection lays claim in abstract, conceptual form.[174] Indeed, if the iconic deliverances of intuitive vision truly permitted their residue-free translation into a purely conceptual domain, rational cognition would thereby find itself deprived of its very raison d'être.

Ultimately, modern Reason's self-conception as a progress narrative inexorably moving toward a totality of all "warranted" (verifiable) acts of predication exhibits a fundamentally ambivalent pattern, rather akin to Freud's *fort-da* game in which an object of interest is compulsively made to appear and then again disappear. For human reason to take itself as steadily advancing—with a sense of autonomy and confidence grounded in the idea of a universal scientific method—toward a comprehensive solution to the mystery of being, it must both isolate its various objects of inquiry and, simultaneously, forget how those objects had first come to its attention. That is, a strictly procedural and immanent mode of reasoning will have to elide, or disavow, those moments of intuitive vision in which the intrinsically ordered, symbolically significant character of reality had first revealed itself. Only in consequence of this elision or forgetting can modern discursive rationality proclaim itself as substantially identical with the *logos*.

Still, apologists of a strictly immanent, secular, and procedural rationality are likely to challenge the above account with a barrage of questions. What justification, they may ask, do we have for exempting intuition and symbol from being subject to rigorous conceptual scrutiny and its eventual verdict? If Goethe diverges from the Hegelian and neo-Kantian view of image and symbol—namely, as mere anticipations of transparent and definitive conceptual insight—why should his position not be dismissed as merely eccentric and, thus, irrelevant to modernity's dominant systemic and procedural notion of reason? What warrant could there possibly be for crediting intuitive vision with the power of grasping, in the medium of the symbolic image, the convergence of the particular and its idea? Does such an argument not manifestly fail to provide the required extrinsic criterion of its falsifiability? And how indeed *could* it be verified, if not once again in terms of the very scientific framework whose authority it so summarily contests? Evidently, the question is of a quasi-juridical nature. How are we to appraise the respective authority of concept and image, which is to say, of propositional (discursive) and intuitive (symbolic) cognition, without relying on one of these modes as we seek to adjudicate their competing

---

173. Gadamer 2006, 64.
174. Cassirer 1983, 189.

claims? Simply to persist in juxtaposing the claims advanced by the incommensurable frameworks of realism and conceptualism will evidently not resolve the central issue. Instead, we must show how one of them is logically incoherent, which is to say, *fails on its own terms* rather than those advanced by the competing epistemic paradigm.

As a first step in that direction, it helps to point out that thought itself "is born not out of the emptiness of self-production, . . . [but] is reflected out of the mass of experience, out of *experience*, which is in no way a freely posited object of thought but rather one forcibly given."[175] Sergius Bulgakov's observation not only resonates with arguments concurrently being developed by Husserl in his early phenomenological writings; it also resonates with Goethe's understanding of symbol and image as unveiling an "inexhaustible" and "unfathomable" antecedent reality.

> Symbolism transfigures an appearance into an idea, and the idea into an image; this it does in such a manner as for the idea contained in the image to remain forever efficacious and unattainable [*unendlich wirksam und unerreichbar*] and, even when articulated in languages to remain ineffable [*selbst in allen Sprachen ausgesprochen, doch unaussprechlich bliebe*]. . . . True symbolism obtains, where the particular is represented as the universal, not as dream or shadow, but as a living and instantaneous revelation of the unfathomable [*als lebendig-augenblickliche Offenbarung des Unerforschlichen*].[176]

Whereas Cassirer frequently aligns his position with Goethe's but, in so doing, inevitably gives his reading an idealist slant, Goethe himself always stresses the immense fecundity of the symbolic image. The symbol's "infinitely efficacious" and "unfathomable" presentation (*Darstellung*) of an idea, while occasioning much reflection and discourse, can never be depleted or superseded by it. Ever in the position of a respondent to the fullness of the symbolic, rather than its putative origin, human language cannot possibly exhaust the imagistic riches woven into intuition. As Goethe notes, "Word and image are correlates forever seeking . . . and balancing one another [*sich immerfort suchen . . . sich immerfort balancieren*]."[177]

---

175. Bulgakov 2012b, 106.

176. *GHA* 12:470–71 (#749, 752); see also Goethe's often-quoted letter to Schiller (16 August 1797), in which he remarks on certain experiences of certain "fortuitous objects" (*glückliche Gegenstände*) whose symbolic character is not contingent on a poetic or otherwise aesthetic treatment. Instead, their very mode of appearance shows them to "encapsulate a certain totality" (*eine gewisse Totalität in sich schließen*). These "symbolic" objects reveal that, in everyday life no less than in an encounter with art, acts of visual perception not only issue in contingent "representations" of matter, but, beyond that, can unveil a charisma or "presence" at the heart of appearance itself (Goethe 1987, 439–40); on this letter and Goethe's theory of the symbol, see Berndt 2012.

177. *GHA* 12:493 (#907).

Like Coleridge and Goethe profoundly indebted to the Platonic tradition, though a century later also cognizant (and wary) of its Hegelian appropriation, Bulgakov emphasizes the substantive, rather than rhetorical, fusion of the particular and the universal in the symbol. As he notes, to speak of an antinomy of the abstract and the concrete makes sense only within the domain of discursive and conceptual reason. By contrast, "the real relationship between ideas and prototypes, between genus and species and individuals, is expressed in the fact that in ideas both the general and the individual exist as one thing. . . . In its idea the genus exists both as one and as the fullness of all its individuals, in their unrepeatable particularities, with this unity existing not only *in abstracto* but also *in concreto*." Simply put, the symbolic and the conceptual are not two *alternative* ways of approaching and framing visible appearance. Rather, the conceptual presupposes the symbolic. For if it were not for this fundamental "participation of concepts in ideas," this coincidence of the particular and the universal, concepts would prove indistinguishable from proper names; absent such participation, that is, a concept could never bring about the kind of "summation and generalization" that constitutes its epistemic authority. Indeed, Bulgakov insists, it is precisely "by the fact of their existence [that concepts] testify to the 'mental vision' of the ideal essences of being. . . . *Participation* in ideas (*methexis*) is proper to general concepts."[178]

When Goethe, in a letter to Schiller, portrays himself as "following the calm and cool path of observation, of mere seeing [*den ruhigen und kalten Weg des Beobachtens, ja des bloßen Sehens*]," the underlying ethos is neither one of Cartesian detachment *from* the phenomenon nor is it one of mystic transport *beyond* it.[179] Instead, the undesigning and attentive visualization of natural form that Goethe advocates adapts itself to the dynamic structure of the phenomenon as it gives itself to the observer; and as it does so, an intuition, or symbolic image, throws into relief the form or *eidos* of the visible thing, thus preparing the ground for its eventual conceptualization. Hence, for Goethe, seeing does not reduce to a mundane type of behavior but, on the contrary, constitutes an act and, potentially, a significant "event." Still, intuitive vision and the symbolic forms it unveils cannot capture Being per se. It can issue only in an *image*, which, as we have seen above, is by definition a *medium* rather than an essence and, as such, allows the beholder to participate in the reality of forms without, however, being able to "represent" them per se. The Platonic concept of "participation" (*methexis*) thus appears inseparable from that of mediation. Hence, in

---

178. Bulgakov 2012a, 236–38; see also 223, where Bulgakov comments on Aristotle's misreading of Plato (in *Metaphysics* XIII and XIV and I, ch. 9). Aristotle's "confusion of ideas and concepts" exhibits striking parallels to Cassirer's problematic view of the symbol, including Goethe's understanding of it.

179. Goethe 1987, 439.

understanding Goethe's concept of symbolic form as *participating in* real being, we are precisely not investing it with any claim to immediacy that Enlightenment thinkers and their neo-Kantian descendants worked so hard to discredit. Instead, being forever mediated by the symbolic *image*, intuitive vision can access the ontological source of visible (natural) forms only *per analogiam* but can never claim substantive identity with it.

Crucially, Goethe resists the lure of pantheism no less than the Gnostic tendencies that reverberate in post-Reformation natural theology and in the categorical disjunction of matter and meaning by eighteenth-century empiricism. What prompted Goethe's instinctive distrust of the disjunctive and detached ethos informing any taxonomic approaches to nature as a "System," such as we find them in Locke, Linné, La Mettrie, d'Holbach, and Priestley, is one conspicuous casualty: none of them acknowledge the phenomenon of beauty. And yet, while engaging with natural forms, Goethe's beholder experiences herself as subject to a transformation no less profound than is exhibited by the visible phenomena themselves. Moreover, the fact that, time and again, the "event" of seeing is found to realign the observer's affective and cognitive persona suggests that all interactions with the visible, natural world unfold under the penumbra of Plato's three transcendentals. Prompted by Kant's "Analytic of the Beautiful" in his third *Critique*, Goethe understands this distinctive convergence of affect and knowledge—ratified by the "aesthetic-reflective judgment" and phenomenalized by a "feeling of disinterested pleasure"—as the most salient feature of intuitive vision. To see the form with intuitive clarity is to witness the essential continuity between the beautiful and the true; it is to find the contingent deliverances of one's gaze to be always already transcendentally *in/formed*. Hans Urs von Balthasar, whose philosophical theology builds on his early studies of German classicism, and Goethe's oeuvre in particular, states the salient point with characteristic verve.

> The form as it appears [*erscheinende Gestalt*] to us is beautiful only because the delight that it arouses in us is founded upon the fact that, in it, the truth and goodness of the depths of reality [*Tiefenwahrheit und Tiefengutheit*] are manifested and bestowed, and this manifestation and bestowal reveal themselves to us as being something infinitely and inexhaustibly valuable and fascinating. The appearance of the form, as revelation of the depths, is an indissoluble union of two things. It is the real presence of the depths, of the whole of reality, *and* it is a real pointing beyond itself to these depths.[180]

---

180. Balthasar 1982, 118; von Balthasar's most comprehensive discussion of Goethe is found in vol. 1 of his *Apokalypse der deutschen Seele*, first published in 1937 (reprint 1998, 407–514). On the strong founding presence of Goethe for von Balthasar's theological aesthetics, see

Yet still within Goethe's lifetime, this integrative and metaphysical framework came under such pressure that, by 1830, it appeared increasingly difficult to visualize natural forms both as verifiably "real" and as symbolic forms. A fork in the road has been reached once visualization and the images to which it gives rise are no longer being credited with transcendental, symbolic significance. Thus, as the natural sciences begin to exfoliate into various empirical disciplines and subfields, their rapidly expanding social and institutional cache also effect a profound shift in post-Hegelian aesthetics, away from avowed or, at least, acknowledged metaphysical filiations and toward an in tendency naturalistic program of literary and pictorial realism. It is this shift and its hidden tensions that now stand to be considered.

Nichols (2006, 98–108), who notes that the latter's overriding concern was with "Goethe's ontology" and, in particular, his morphology disclosing that ontology "in ever-differentiated images" (99); on von Balthasar's theological poetics and his redemptive account of beauty, see also Carpenter 2015, 40–81.

6

THE FORENSIC IMAGE

Paradoxes of Realism in Lyell, Darwin, and Ruskin

And yet in that utter visibility
The Stone's alive with what's invisible:
Waterweed, stirred sand-grains hurrying off,
The shadowy, unshadowed stream itself.
All afternoon, heat wavered on the steps
And the air we stood up to our eyes in wavered
Like the zigzag hieroglyph for life itself.

Strange how things in the offing, once they're sensed,
Convert to things foreknown;
And how what's come upon is manifest
Only in light of what has been gone through.
Seventh heaven may be
The whole truth of a sixth sense come to pass

—Seamus Heaney, *Seeing Things*

"THE EYE, UNASSISTED BY ANY ART":
LYELL AND DARWIN ON VISUALIZING NATURAL FORMS

Mid-nineteenth-century literary and pictorial realism has long been understood as a postmetaphysical development, fueled by a naturalism committed to discarding

479

transcendent presuppositions such as inform Goethe's, Schelling's, and Coleridge's concept of the symbolic.[1] In one respect or another, the three constitutive features of the Romantic symbol—its organic structure (*heautonomy*), its avowed capacity to reconcile opposites (*syntheticism*), and its unification of meaning and being (*tautegory*)—appear to be either suspended or expressly rejected by realism.[2] Instead, the word *réalisme* makes its first appearance in France in 1826 and by the mid-1830s spreads rapidly, with growing emphasis on social reform and democratic movements: "Realism stood for an exact and unedited representation of nature, for truth and contemporaneity," and particularly in France it "represented a material approach to the world, to some even a pictorial equivalent to positivism."[3] Both in France and in Germany, starting in the 1830s, increased stress on the social efficacy of art causes literary and pictorial art to downplay, at times outright disavow, the formal-aesthetic traditions associated with Romanticism and Idealism and to reject the putative autonomy of the art forms associated with them. In Germany, the school of "young German" (*Jungdeutsche*) poets, Wienbarg, Laube, and Herwegh (aptly dubbed "the iron lark" by Heine), consciously distinguishes its own politically and socially engaged poetics from both Weimar classicism and the flights of Romantic sublimity successively attempted in Jena, Heidelberg, Munich, and Vienna. A common trait of this shift is its pointedly antireligious and antimetaphysical tenor, for which writings by Germany's "left Hegelians" (Feuerbach, Strauss, Bauer, Stirner) and their French counterparts (Fourier, Proudhon, Considérant) had laid crucial theoretical foundations.

As one would expect, the emergence of a "realist" conception of the art image unfolds in stages. Thus, while stipulating that "the art of painting must consist only in the representation of objects that are visible," Courbet, as late as 1861, remains wary of the instrumentalization of realism for sociopolitical ends. As he insists, "Art is entirely individual and . . . each artist must rely solely on the talent arising from his own inspiration and his own study of tradition."[4] Already a few years earlier, Proudhon enlisted Courbet's art, which he regarded with mixed feelings, to press his case for a post-Romantic, indeed post-aesthetic art exclusively legitimated by its so-

---

1. On literary realism, see Jameson 2013, 15–26; Lukács 1977; Sengle 1971, 1:257–83; on pictorial realism, see Fried 1990, 223–90.

2. On these three essential features of the symbol and, more controversially, of symbolic language, see Whistler 2013, 22, 37–47.

3. Hemingway 2007, 105; yet as Hemingway points out, drawing on Roman Jakobson's classic essay "Realism in Art," the reality effect to which, say, Courbet's realism hinges on deforming received notions of verisimilitude, which in the case of Courbet involved employing "vigorous brushwork" techniques that stress "the material quiddity of things" and, in so doing, "affirm the social reality of what he depicts" (110). For a detailed account of Courbet's approach, see Fried's discussion of *Burial at Ornans* (1849), in Fried 1990, 111–47.

4. Quoted in Taylor 1987, 347.

cial and political functionality: "Art—having become rational and reasonable, critical and judicious, marching abreast with [Comte's] *positive philosophy, positive politics*, and *positive metaphysics* . . . — . . . can no longer serve to foster tyranny, prostitution, and pauperism. As an art of observation, and no longer of inspiration, it would have to lie to itself and deliberately destroy itself, which is impossible." Maintaining in the spirit of Auguste Comte and Hyppolite Taine that "art is henceforth incorruptible," Proudhon's *Concerning the Principle of Art and Its Social Purpose* (1857) signals a rupture within pictorial realism itself as the image's fidelity to the visible is being supplanted by its political instrumentalization.[5]

By midcentury, the ideological co-optation of art extends across Western Europe all the way to Russia. There eminent critics such as Belinsky and Herzen also promote an aesthetics committed to addressing social and political concerns; hence, as Belinski puts it, artworks "no longer require any more poetry and artistry than necessary" but, instead, should pursue their didactic ends "entirely without poetry and artistry."[6] Looking back in 1881 on the aesthetic realism and positivist social thought of the midcentury, Vladimir Soloviev rejects such an outlook, noting that the "attempt to copy phenomena of . . . reality slavishly [and], just as slavishly, to serve the topic of the day" was bound to fail on both counts. Thus, a realism of mere detail, what he calls "the unsuccessful pursuit of only apparently real details," will cause the "reality of the whole [to be] lost." Furthermore, a realist program singlemindedly consumed by Chernyshevsky's (and later Lenin's) famous question, "What is to be done?," is bound to expire in an aesthetic transactionalism of sorts. For in conceiving of reality as the sum total of known and verified facts passively awaiting the imprint of human desires and projects, aesthetic and philosophical inquiry invariably lose sight of the "enlightening and regenerative power" that would allow art and humanity to advance from what is to what should be, from merely registering the "evils of life" to actually "correcting" them.[7]

Few writers sensed more keenly realism's susceptibility to ideological abstractions and its consequent instrumentalization than George Eliot. Ever on guard against instances of "the artistic mind, which looks for its subjects into literature instead of life," she frames realism as the art of attentive and correct vision and, hence, as the very paradigm of inductive cognition. As such, realist art must at all times resist "the splendid conquests of modern generalization" and, instead, must approach its subject in the spirit of "natural history." Her position is given programmatic expression

---

5. Ibid., 394.

6. Quoted in Frank 2010, 113; edging beyond left-Hegelian positions toward militant radicalism and anarchism, a new generation of critics constituting itself by the mid-1850s around Chernyshevsky, Dobrolyubov, and the journal the *Contemporary* altogether rejects any art that does not serve expressly didactic, protorevolutionary purposes.

7. Soloviev 2003, 4, 21–22.

in an 1856 review essay, where Eliot summarily declares that "the greatest benefit we owe to the artist, whether painter, poet, or novelist, is the extension of our sympathies." The essential task of all art is to enable us to *see* the real rather than attenuate it by a ready-made inventory of abstract conceptions. To content oneself with visually reconfirming our notions and preconceptions of the real is, ultimately, to fail as a human being; for genuine seeing such as literary and pictorial realism means to instill in its audience "surprises even the trivial and the selfish into that attention which is apart from themselves."[8] Among those who understood the centrality of an attentive vision capable of "exten[ding] our sympathies" was John Ruskin. For her part, Eliot, reviewing volume 3 of *Modern Painters* in 1856, praises Ruskin for impressing on his readers, in exceptionally vivid and accessible prose, the realist ideal: "The truth of infinite value that he teaches is *realism*—the doctrine that all truth and beauty are to be attained by a humble and faithful study of nature, and not by substituting vague forms, bred by imagination on the mists of feeling, in place of definite, substantial reality. The thorough acceptance of this doctrine would remould our life."[9]

As remains to be seen, Ruskin's lifelong project of a kind of aesthetic catechesis of mid-Victorian culture begins, in *Modern Painters I* (1843), with sustained and profound reflections on the metaphysical underpinnings of even the most elemental, visual apprehension of reality. For where we properly *see* a fact we find ourselves participating in reality as an *event*, as the moment where the deceptively "obvious" construction of the real as sheer fact ends up being unmasked, when Shelley's "veil of familiarity" is stripped away and natural phenomena are visualized, as it were for the first time, in their incomprehensible presence and inexhaustible fecundity. For Ruskin as for his Romantic precursors, properly to see the real can never be reduced to an act of methodical verification and epistemic dominion but, instead, entails an unveiling of the true along the lines of what Plato famously means by "recognition" (*anamnēsis*). Notably, in Britain such a conception of realism did not unfold as part of a left-liberal and, in time, socialist political program such as dominates on the continent. Rather, the evolution of a distinctively British realist aesthetics is closely linked to the rise of empirical, inductive science that gets under way in the 1820s. Thus, Ruskin's post-Romantic, realist aesthetic initially appears fueled less by a push for social reform—a project largely associated with his late works—mainly because that impetus had to some extent been defused by the Reform Acts of June 1832.

Undoubtedly, this rapprochement of aesthetic production with the natural sciences is fueled by a concurrent pivoting of scientific inquiry toward an inductive and empirical approach that during the 1830s bears particular fruit in the fields of plant

---

8. "The Natural History of German Life," in Eliot 1990, 108–9, 111.
9. Eliot 1990, 367.

and animal biology, as well as geology. John Ruskin's stipulation that "every class of rock, earth, and cloud, must be known by the painter, with geologic and meteorologic accuracy" and that "the highest art . . . seizes th[e] specific character" of each natural entity points to this growing alignment of aesthetics with scientific inquiry.[10] The image that is constituted by a certain type of forensic vision becomes part of a complex economy of evidence, particularly in the emergent fields of biology and geology. Yet what end is being served by such rigorous empirical fidelity to the real? To answer that question we, too, must proceed inductively by tracing the new conception of nature and its visualization as it emerges in Lyell and the young Darwin, followed by a fuller consideration of Ruskin's spectacular first monograph, volume 1 of *Modern Painters*, published in 1843 when he was barely twenty-four years old. Such an initial, brief foray into Lyell and the young Darwin of the notebooks will shed further light on Ruskin's preoccupation in *Modern Painters I* with painting's unwavering preoccupation with attending to the real, which is to say, to the "specific" nature of pictorial truth—which he takes pains to distinguish from both random particularity and empty generalization.

Widely regarded as the founding text of modern geological science, Charles Lyell's three-volume *Principles of Geology* (1830–33) proved influential not least because of its author's uncompromising insistence on close empirical observation and fieldwork. Born in 1797 into a family of wealthy and conservative Scottish Tory landholders, young Charles was educated at Exeter College, Oxford. The reigning curriculum at the time heavily favored Anglo-Protestant teachings of natural theology, as represented by William Buckland's Bridgewater treatise on genealogy and mineralogy and, especially, by William Paley's eponymous 1802 textbook and his earlier *Evidences of Christianity* (1794), works bound to impress on Lyell how readily scientific inquiry and religious teaching could come into conflict. For decades, controversy between traditional, literal accounts of Creation and geological and botanical study had been defused, at least in part, by classifying scientific practice—the collecting and selling of specimens gathered and studied with the aid of homemade scientific instruments—as a lower-middle-class amateur pursuit. Fieldwork was a

---

10. Ruskin 1904, III, 32, 38 (henceforth cited as *RCW*); see also Ruskin's prefatory critique of pictorial generalization, whose wording recalls Blake's equally vehement critique ("to Generalize is to be an Idiot"), though as we shall see Ruskin would demur at Blake's follow-up ("to Particularize is the Alone Distinction of Merit" [1982, 641]). As Ruskin notes, "It is just as impossible to generalize granite and slate, as it is to generalize a man and a cow. An animal must be either one animal or another animal: it cannot be a general animal, or it is no animal; and so a rock must be either one rock or another rock; it cannot be a general rock, or it is no rock. . . . Every attempt to produce that which shall be any rock, ends in the production of that which is no rock" (*RCW* III, 34); Ruskin reiterates his concern with the "pursuit of ideal form" and the "peculiar virtues and duties of every species of being, down even to the stone . . . [and] ideality of granite and slate" in *Modern Painters II* (*RCW* IV, 173).

menial pursuit, fueled by the collector's individual curiosity rather than lofty professional goals, and as such it was carefully quarantined from abstract speculation of the kind pursued by university-educated gentlemen. Having first been introduced to his future field of study when reading Blakewell's *Introduction to Geology* in 1816 and attending Buckland's lectures in mineralogy the following year, Lyell appears to have concluded that the conflict between natural theology and increasingly popular hypotheses concerning "former worlds" predating God's six-day creation could not be resolved as long as the earth sciences had not yet been put on a firmly inductive footing.[11] His embrace of Whig reform politics effortlessly translated into a quest for a new approach to science based on observation and the study of material, "true" causes. Yet doing so required threading multiple needles. To begin with, Lyell had to distinguish his own empirical approach from Enlightenment materialism and mechanism, explanatory models whose reductionist tendencies remained tainted by the atheism and political radicalism of the French Revolution. Beyond that, Lyell's attempt to put geological inquiry on a solid empirical footing and to spell out its inductive methods had to be sheltered from the radical claims of Lamarckian transmutation. Finally, he had to find a way out of the "bold and sweeping generalizations" of his precursors, such as the "Neptunist" theory held by Abraham Werner at the Mining Academy in Freiberg, whose speculative habits, as Lyell demurred, had caused him to embrace "imaginary causes" and to "torture the phenomena of distant countries . . . into conformity with his theoretical standard."[12]

Lyell deftly navigated these shallows by balancing his Whig political sympathies with the religious and political conservatism of moderate Tory circles, from which he never entirely broke free.[13] His conciliatory approach was signaled above all by the decision to publish *Principles of Geology* with the upscale and highly reputable house of John Murray, as well as by his careful placement of review essays in the conservative *Quarterly Review*. The strategy paid off, shielding as it did the more explosive implications of Lyell's geological research from politically motivated attacks and,

---

11. On Lyell's early intellectual formation, see Klaver 1997, 18–26.

12. Lyell 1997, 10–12.

13. On Lyell, see Secord 2015, 138–72; and his introduction to Lyell 1997; see also Klaver 1997, 27–33, who notes that Lyell's uniformitarian views may have been significantly indebted to George H. Toulmin (1753–1817). Rudwick remarks on the often-inconsistent application of Lyell's uniformitarian and nondirectionalist views of geological history, as well as on Lyell's frequent "distortion and oversimplification of the theories of his predecessors"; see Rudwick 1970, 10. Similarly, Porter comments on the "polemical significance of Lyell's history," noting that "while Lyell's history of the earth is uniformitarian, his history of geology is *catastrophic*: a succession of Gargantuan figures, great for their . . . baneful influence, paraded before the reader without law or cause" (1976, 92, 97). Oldroyd points out that Lyell effectively conflates "scientific" geology with the "uniformitarian" views to which he is committed, any anticipation of which he habitually downplayed in his predecessors (in Cahan 2003, 90–91).

instead, drawing praise for the "wholesome and beneficial effect upon the mind" of *Principles*. Writing in the *Spectator* (14 January 1832), a reviewer heaped effusive praise on Lyell as the long looked for "enlightened geologist" who, having found a way to interpret nature's "sermons in stones and tongues in brooks," had made a vital contribution to the moral formation of his readers: "Vanity shrivels into nothingness; wrongs are forgotten, errors forgiven, prejudices fade away; the present is taken at its real value, [and] virtue is tried by an eternal standard."[14] Above all, it was Lyell's shrewd decision to draw on the established, commonsense tradition of Lockean empiricism that allowed him to avoid controversy while nudging geological inquiry away from the deductive and speculative habits of an older "natural philosophy" and toward a rigorously inductive and observation-based scientific practice. Newton's insistence that true knowledge of nature depended on identifying *verae causae*, "true causes," observable in actual operation is key here; and it is this premise that not only transformed the role of visualization in the emergent disciplines of geology and biology, but, by the early 1840s, also ushered in a new phase in the emergent aesthetics of pictorial realism. Increasingly, realism became synonymous with a procedural notion of "objectivity," one that "attempts to eliminate the mediating presence of the observer" and, thus, put a premium on a purely factual "seeing *that*" unadulterated by any interpretive "seeing *as*."[15]

As Lyell himself never tired to assure his readers, henceforth only facts and observable causes were to ground scientific knowledge, which consequently will no longer indulge in flights of speculation or fanciful deductions. In Lyell's "book of facts" (as the *Scotsman* newspaper referred to *Principles of Geology*), fact and visibility have become fully convertible; what is to count as a fact must be susceptible to being aggregated and visualized in graphs, sketches, full-fledged drawings, maps, and so forth. Fieldwork conducted during his extensive travels is now considered the indispensable foundation for all scientific inquiry. The same ethos will also animate Ruskin as he composes the first volume of *Modern Painters* a decade later and, even more so, the Pre-Raphaelites for whom "working out of doors rather than from memory [proves] crucial to the purpose of divesting the mind of convention and verifying everything by reference to the motif."[16] The artist must paint only what can be seen; and for that to happen, art and its empirical objects must always share a specific location. With the authority of deductive reasoning fading fast by the 1830s, visualization becomes the very foundation of scientific practice; and the images it yields now serve primarily forensic purposes. As a result, currently observable phenomena are scrutinized as evidence of past geological developments that, by a

---

14. Lyell 1997, xv.
15. Daston and Galison 1992, 82–83.
16. Allison Smith, in Staley and Newell 2004, 17.

far-flung chain of causal relationships, had resulted in Earth's present aspect. As Secord points out, "It was the visibility of modern causes that made them the *only* legitimate basis of explanation."[17] A couple of years later, the general enthusiasm for "discriminating stones" and the "dreams of the geologist" and his "rock-inspired eyes" had already left the sixteen-year-old John Ruskin touring the Jura mountains of Switzerland mesmerized by the undulating motion of eons visible in the landscape whose "solid mountains wave and twist" (*RCW* II, 407–8).

To visualize some particular aspect of a complex rock formation is to be presented with a "time capsule" of sorts. Underlying Lyell's claim that the present, visible aspect of the Earth serves as our conduit to the discovery of the laws of stratification—ever in operation and ever invisible per se—is his hypothesis of uniformitarianism, which more than anything set his *Principles* apart from the geological speculations of his precursors (Werner, Cuvier, Buckland). James Hutton's thesis "that all past changes on the globe had been brought about by the slow agency of existing causes" converted Earth's inexhaustible wealth of visible phenomena into potential evidence for grasping its history. At the same time, "a geologist who rejects cosmological [First] causes" now has to learn, as it were for the first time, how properly to visualize and interpret this evidence.[18] If for Lyell the present has become the key to the past, making effective use of that key will require a fundamentally new culture of forensic seeing. Each visible phenomenon furnishes the geologist with a bridge between two incommensurable temporal plateaus: his own, anthropomorphic (or "historical") time and a previously unimagined scale of geological time— what Hans Blumenberg distinguishes as "biographical and cosmic time" (*Lebenszeit* and *Weltzeit*).

Concurrently, Lyell also frames geological study as a process of reading the earth's crust "as a book . . . written in characters of the most striking and imposing kind," as "legible characters" and "ancient memorials of nature . . . written in a living language."[19] Given their frequent use, such tropes have prompted some readers to consider "narrative [as] clearly an essential part of *Principles*."[20] Yet this claim ought to be taken with caution considering that narrative necessarily presupposes directionality, which Lyell (and following him, Darwin) consistently denies. Hence, it is visual rather than narrative imagination that anchors the modern naturalist's forensic practice. Even so, Lyell acknowledges, the scientist is confronted by a persistent asymmetry between quotidian perception and its deep conceptual implications, a

---

17. Lyell 1997, xxi.

18. Lyell 1997, 17 (vol. 1, ch. 4).

19. Lyell, *Principles*, ch. 20, quoted in Klaver 1997, 43.

20. Ibid., 46; see also Beer, who remarks how "'reading' . . . implies narrative order and diverse relations between material and period of telling, sujet and fabula" (1983, 39).

tension bound to leave "the imagination . . . first fatigued and overpowered by endeavouring to conceive the immensity of time required for the annihilation of whole continents by so insensible a process."[21] Thus, while having vastly expanded the evidentiary role of visible (geological) matter, Lyell also realizes that the eerily "tranquil deposition of sedimentary matter and the slow development of organic life" (*LPG* 24) has unsettled the very concept of the image produced by the geologist's patient observation. Henceforth, visible phenomena can no longer be grasped as static realities in the present. Rather, they must be appraised as traces of an invisible past, "organic remains" inviting the expert's forensic gaze to detect in them the "true causes" of past geological development. In principle, then, everything "out there" to be seen by the geologist is less some contingent and innocuous present aspect than holographic evidence of unfathomably complex and ongoing geological developments that extend into the farthest recess of Earth's past. Frequently overlooked, though for our purposes highly significant, is the following: the image as it incrementally constitutes itself through focused and sustained observation, provided that such practice is itself guided by an inductive approach to science, is not merely a *product*, but just as much the *catalyst* of scientific insight. To clarify why and how this should be so, we need to follow Lyell's argument a bit further.

Chapter 5 of *Principles* finds Lyell considering how to read presently observable data. What may an observer legitimately premise when studying geological phenomena? What presuppositions, if any, may permissibly guide inductive reasoning? In the event, he acknowledges that no science, however rigorously inductive, can dispense with basic (in origin Aristotelian) categories or what he calls "fixed and invariable laws and . . . the undeviating uniformity of secondary causes" (*LPG* 27). In fact, not only *may* scientific observation posit the uniformity or constancy of causal forces, but where this metaphysical presupposition is abandoned no meaningful knowledge could ever be expected. Though primarily intended to guide empirical practice, Lyell's uniformitarian axiom holds profound metaphysical implications. For underlying it is the Aristotelian-Scholastic premise that being and truth are convertible, an ontological supposition to which we shall return in due course. To close in on what is at stake, it helps to remind ourselves that within Lyell's uniformitarian

---

21. *LPG* 16–17. This is not the place to retrace the science/theology divide and the momentous debate on human evolution (kicked off by Lamarck's theory of species "transmutation"); as Secord has shown, Lyell's professed agnosticism regarding progressive, "directional" models of geological "deep time" allowed him to side-step the Lamarckian controversy. Indeed, though privately committed to "free[ing] the science from Moses" (Letter, quoted in Rudwick 1970, 10), Lyell's actual publication carefully threads the needle when it comes to characterizing the antinomy between geological research and Protestantism's literal creation theology, and nowhere more so than where the origins of man are concerned. Likewise, he is coy about identifying by name the "French naturalists" who first claimed a correlation between geological stratigraphy and the systematic gathering and dating of fossil remains (*LPG* 23–24).

and inductive framework to "see" means less to look *for* something than learning to become receptive to the *non-event* character of geological time as manifested in deceptively static, previously overlooked geological phenomena. Lyell writes that while "man observes the annual decomposition of crystalline and igneous rocks, and may sometimes see their conversion into stratified deposits, . . . he cannot witness the reconversion of the sedimentary into the crystalline but subterranean fire" (*LPG* 33). Neither nineteenth-century science nor literature in its realist and naturalist guise operate any longer with an anthropomorphic concept of the "event" but, instead, seek to uncover the truth of being as it is encoded in essentially stable and inconspicuous processes. To suppose that at any point in geological time "the uniformity of the action of subterranean forces" could have been suspended and that "Nature had been at any former epoch parsimonious of time and prodigal of violence" is to reason "contrary to analogy" (*LPG* 38).

With his passing reference to "analogy," a term of whose Scholastic provenance he would likely have been surprised to learn, Lyell is advancing an elemental claim. Simply put, what makes natural phenomena intelligible or, rather, calculable is that they are the product of forces continually in operation and therefore mostly invariant in strength except when checked by a counterforce. Were it not for this premise of strict continuity of process and coherence of form, visible phenomena could never *actually* be understood, indeed could not even be apprehended as *potentially* intelligible. It is this insight that explains the consistent stress, in the writings of Lyell, Darwin, and Ruskin, on the "organization" of natural forms. Thus, as remains to be seen, Ruskin is also preoccupied with "the ever-increasing revelation of the phenomena of the physical universe as the eye learns to read them: the art and the science of aspects." Indeed, his praise of Turner, "the only painter who has ever drawn a mountain, or a stone; no other man ever having learned their organization," could just as plausibly be applied to Lyell and the young Darwin.[22] It is this premise of the manifest organization of visible being, that is, the coherence and recurrence implied by the very concept of form, that accounts for Lyell's reference to the principle of analogy. What the very specificity of visible being qua form thus presupposes is the tacit dimension of the *logos*, itself the ontological premise of the convertibility of *ens* and *verum*, of the material and formal coherence of visible things and our knowledge of them, of phenomena and cognition. Absent this premise of a transcendent, all-encompassing *logos* phenomena could never be grasped as meaningful and significant facts. Put in Scholastic terms, only insofar as a particular entity has being, prop-

---

22. Ball 1971, 67; *RCW* III, 252; Ruskin's exposure to early nineteenth-century geology was mainly filtered through Buckland, whose Bridgewater treatise and evangelically inflected lectures at Christ Church College, where Ruskin attended his lectures, consistently emphasized the providential and benevolent character of nature; see Hewison 1976, 21–29.

erly speaking, can it also be cognized as a medium of truth. By contrast, where a modern, "mechanistic ontology" proclaims, in the face of the *visible* reality of forms, that "external matter remains essentially outside of meaning, . . . a true *adaequatio rei ad intellectum* [proves] permanently impossible."[23]

Meanwhile, for Lyell, who admittedly shows no inclination to speculative detours of the sort just taken, the implications of the "analogy" to which he makes passing reference are of a strictly practical nature. The question that presents itself to him concerns the enigmatic power of visible phenomena to unveil realities or "laws" that are invisible per se and yet can evidently be discerned within geological formations. How can it be that *what* is seen has the capacity, by dint of its specific "aspect" or "image," to direct the scientist to truths at once irrefutable and yet *in*visible? Acknowledging the strange capacity of material sight to extend into abstract insight, Lyell muses on the paradox that something as limited as perception should nevertheless prove indispensable for, and capable of giving rise to, complex scientific understanding:

> The first and greatest difficulty . . . consists in our habitual unconsciousness that our position as observers is essentially unfavourable, when we endeavour to estimate the magnitude of the changes now in progress. In consequence of our inattention to this subject, we are liable to make the greatest mistakes in contrasting the present with former states of the globe. . . . We are called upon, in our researches into the state of the earth, as in our endeavours to comprehend the mechanism of the heavens, to invent means for *overcoming the limited range of our vision*. We are perpetually required to bring, as far as possible, within the sphere of observation, things to which the eye, *unassisted by any art*, could never obtain access. (*LPG* 31, 33; emphasis mine)

To develop a comprehensive understanding of geological history, science must first overcome perception's confinement within a strictly anthropomorphic time scale. A decade before Ruskin's *Modern Painters I*, Lyell already shows early Victorian visual and scientific culture to pivot on a coherent set of forensic visualization and inductive reasoning. As Ruskin will write in 1843, "Every class of rock, earth, and cloud, must be known by the painter, with geologic and meteorologic accuracy" (*RCW* III, 38). Just so, Lyell insists that in order to see the slow, albeit inexorable progression of geological time, and hence to grasp it as more than a logical inference, a new technique (taking Lyell's "art" in the Aristotelian sense of *technē*) of visualization

---

23. Hanby 2013, 204; Hanby's sharp critique of Darwin posits, correctly it seems to me, "that science generally and evolutionary biology particularly are constitutively and inexorably related to metaphysics and theology" (186).

is required. While recognizing the inadequacy of empiricism's anthropomorphic model of perception, Lyell is not willing to cede geology to deductive reasoning and speculation of the kind Locke had termed "complex ideas."[24] Rather than relying on concepts derived from elaborate and error-prone chains of inference, geological knowledge must be visualized and, thus, be experienced as intuitively evident. In contrast to most of his peers, Lyell's program "for overcoming the limited range of our vision" thus carries significant implications for the way scientific and aesthetic practice of the late 1830s and 1840s recast the nature and objectives of visual experience.[25] Henceforth, the act of seeing shall unfold as a patient, microscopic, and undesigning visualization of raw, seemingly unfiltered phenomena. By Lyell's logic, which is substantially embraced by Darwin and Ruskin, the image is as much the *product* as it is the *source* of visual practice; and its forensic and evidentiary function would seem to displace, if not obviate outright, the symbolic and speculative import that had been at the heart of Romantic visual culture.

As has often been remarked, Lyell's "program of perceptual reform," driven by massive detail and abundant verbal and visual imagery, proved enormously influential for the young Charles Darwin for whom Lyell's "*Principles* . . . is all about seeing."[26] The young Darwin acknowledges as much in a letter (29 August 1844), remarking, "I always feel as if my books came half out of Lyell's brain & that I never acknowledge this sufficiently. . . . It altered the whole tone of one's mind & therefore that when seeing a thing never seen by Lyell, one yet saw it partially through his eyes."[27] Lyell's work could not have appeared at a more auspicious time for Darwin, who eagerly awaited the third and final volume of *Principles* while voyaging on the HMS *Beagle* and conducting first research expeditions into the interior of Argentina. Lyell's methodological prescriptions and his uniformitarian framework offered invaluable guidance to the young Darwin as he struggled to grasp the causal forces that could have brought forth botanical and geological phenomena of such abundance and complexity as he encountered in South America's coastal and interior zones. Throughout his 1,740 days spent at sea and on distant lands, Darwin was stunned by

---

24. Locke 1975, 163–66 (*Essay* bk. II, ch. 12).

25. As Rudwick notes, "Although [Lyell's] scientific colleagues readily accepted a vast time scale on the intellectual level, Lyell seems to have recognized that it was their scientific *imagination* that needed transforming" (1970, 11).

26. Lyell 1997, Introduction, xx.

27. Darwin 2008, 87. Regarding Lyell's influence on Darwin, see Browne 1995, 186–90, 444–47. A month earlier, in what Janet Browne calls "the strangest letter of his life" (1995, 446), Darwin had instructed his wife, Emma, that, in the event of his death, Lyell would be the best choice for editing and publishing all his unpublished manuscripts. In the spring of 1859, Darwin asks Lyell's advice concerning ongoing negotiations about the publication of his *Origin of Species*; and in that book Darwin famously credits Lyell with "having produced a revolution in natural science" (Darwin 2006, 629) and, crucially, in the conception of evolutionary time.

the profusion and "novelty of the vegetable forms," yet also disoriented by his evident unpreparedness when it came to accounting for the meaning of what he saw. Writing to his father early during his journey, from Bahia, Brazil, Darwin admits, "It is utterly useless to say anything about the Scenery.—it would be as profitable to explain to a blind man colours, as to a person, who has not been out of Europe, the total dissimilarity of a Tropical view.—Whenever I enjoy anything I always either [*sic*] look forward to writing it down either in my log Book (which increases in bulk), or in a letter."[28]

As the sheer copiousness of South American flora overwhelms Darwin the budding naturalist, Darwin the collector realizes that the number of samples he is so assiduously gathering and shipping home to England in a steady stream of crates will prove unsatisfactory. "I am afraid," he writes to his Cambridge professor, John Henry Henslow, "[my collection] is very small.—but I have not been idle & you must recollect that in lower tribes, what a very small show hundreds of species make." Likewise, Darwin admits that, having "endeavoured to get specimens of every variety of rock, & hav[ing] written notes upon all," his sampling of geological specimens will be found "too small."[29] Confronted with both an overabundance of natural forms and, paradoxically, sample sizes inadequate to explain the myriad species of plants, minerals, and fossils, Darwin defaults to writing as the best expedient. In his letters, diaries, and, starting in 1836, his notebooks, the pattern followed tends to be the same: what begins as a meticulous recording of particular forms encountered gradually mutates into focused morphological description and discrimination of varieties, followed by initially tentative questions about the causal impact of geological and climatic conditions on their development and distribution. The genre of the notebook in particular appears the ideal medium for Darwin's "interweaving of description, causal explanation, and reports of occasional experimental inquiries."[30] For it allows the naturalist to preserve a record of visual experience, capturing the forms of such experience in prose (and sometimes in sketches) ranging from a mere aide mémoire to forensic description, tentative hypotheses, and outlines for more continuous prose to be written in the future.

Whereas Alexander von Humboldt, during his South American travels some thirty-five years earlier, could rely on the support of his gifted collaborator and draftsman, Aimé Bonpland (1773–1858), Darwin's on-site researches unfolded by and large as a one-person undertaking. Lacking a learned fellow observer as well as

---

28. Darwin 2008, 21, 23 (8 February–1 March 1832).

29. Ibid., 26 (23 July–15 August 1832); thinking back on his specimen gathering on the Galápagos Islands, Darwin recalls how he "determined to collect blindly every sort of fact, which cd bear anyway on what are species" (85 [11 January 1844]).

30. Sloan 2003, 29.

any expertise in drawing, Darwin defaults to informal writing (correspondence, diaries, notebooks) as the medium best suited for preserving, sifting, ordering, and conceptualizing natural forms of astonishing diversity and strangeness. As for the Augustinian view that memory is indispensable to cognition, Darwin sounds a skeptical note, writing in his *Journal of Researches* (1839): "Let the collector's motto be, 'Trust nothing to the memory,' for the memory becomes a fickle guardian when one interesting object is succeeded by another still more interesting."[31] Not to be confused with the diaries and field notebooks that Darwin kept on hand while exploring coastal and interior terrains in the Southern Hemisphere, the notebooks that he began in 1836 while returning from Mauritius to England are his first attempts at sifting his specimen and field notes, and ever so tentatively beginning to venture hypotheses about the temporal sequence of specific forms, causal relationships between forms and their environment, patterns of geographic distribution, and such.[32] Hence the notebooks serve principally to mediate Darwin's cautious advance from sight to insight, from detailed description of morphological and transhistorical affinities among various species to venturing a complex theory concerning the development of organic forms over vast expanses of geological time. Being the first in a series that extends until 1844, the so-called Red Notebook covers the period from May 1836 to January 1837. Assembled during the long sea voyage from Mauritius via the Cape of Good Hope back to England, at a point when "the most exotic parts of the voyage were over," this particular notebook served mainly "as a storehouse for references."[33] Yet already at this early point, two subtly related issues increasingly guide Darwin's thinking, both of which have significant bearing on the realist turn, starting in the 1830s, toward a forensic and naturalistic model of visual cognition: speciation and holism.

The first of these concerns, apparent in Notebook B (begun in July 1837) has to do with how to conceptualize a species. At what point does a "variety" become a "species"? Are real, ontological factors in play or, conversely, might it all be a matter of "how [one] looked at it?"[34] In the event, the famous case of the Galápagos finches is but one of countless such perplexities. For Darwin, the elusive transition from

---

31. Darwin 1987b, 469. On Darwin's notebooks, see Browne 1995, 364; and Hodge, who specifically remarks on the growing move from concrete empirical to "highly theoretical, abstract, and general" (2003, 44).

32. The entries in these field notebooks tend to be disjointed, since Darwin did not take more than one such book with him on any given excursion. It was not until the final leg of his return to England (May–October 1836) and during the exceptionally productive phase of his studies in Cambridge, when he could draw on the sizable collection of specimens that had been accumulating there, that Darwin began to sift, order, and conceptualize the profusion of geological, botanical, and animal specimens and accumulated notes.

33. Browne 1995, 327; Darwin 1987, 19.

34. Browne 1995, 359.

variety to species shows that the reality of a given species is inseparable from its origination or (in his awkward makeshift phrase) its "non-creation." As Hodge has shown, Darwin parts ways with Lyell (and also Paley) in Notebooks B and D on the question of speciation. To Lyell's stipulation that species arose independently of one another and that, though susceptible of change, their varieties could "never deviate far enough to be called a separate species," Darwin responds (in the margins of his copy of *Principles*), "If this were true, adios theory."[35] Instead, Darwin reconsiders Lamarck's transmutationist theory, albeit from a rigorously inductive, empirical perspective that precludes all generalizing about what "Nature *wanted*, . . . *had to*, . . . *had need*," expressions frequently found in Lamarck and, at times, infusing his argument with an aura of magic.[36] For Darwin, the pressing question is how adaptive diversification might play out "over an unlimitedly long run . . . from the earliest life of all up to the arrival in recent times of man himself."[37]

Gradually, that is, Darwin came to understand the intricate spatiotemporal logic of speciation, with geographic distribution and patterns of heredity intricately balanced so as to ensure a more or less stable number of species and varieties. Tentatively summing up his discoveries in Cambridge in the summer of 1837, Darwin notes how "the young of living beings, become permanently changed or subject to variety" and how "every animal has tendency to change."[38] As Étienne Gilson points out, for Darwin no less than for Aristotle, "the order of the living is the order of motion, . . . which has in itself the principle of its own change."[39] And yet that still leaves unexplained why some species maintain their identity over vast stretches of time while others succumb to strong variation and, eventually, transmutation in relatively quick succession. Darwin was never able to resolve altogether his perplexity on this count, so succinctly stated in his notebooks: "Those species which have long remained are those—?Lyell?—which have wide range and therefore cross & keep similar. But this is difficulty; This immutability of some species."[40] Underlying the puzzling, uneven pace of speciation is a related, equally perplexing question. For if the diversification of *some* varieties issues in a new species, does that new form

---

35. Quoted in Browne 1995, 366.

36. Gilson 1984, 55; "[Darwin] undertook right from the beginning to demonstrate that there had been a 'transmutation of species', a term . . . much more appropriate to his thought than that of evolution" (61). In a letter to J. D. Hooker (11 January 1844), Darwin admits, "I am almost convinced (quite contrary to opinion I started with) that species are not immutable. Heaven forfend me from Lamarck nonsense of a 'tendency to progression' 'adaptations from the slow willing of animals' &c,—but the conclusions I am led to are not widely different from his" (Darwin 2008, 85).

37. Hodge 2003, 44–45.

38. Darwin 1987, 3, 16 (Notebook B).

39. Gilson 1984, 5.

40. Darwin 1987, Notebook B, 170; quoted parenthetically in this chapter as *DN* B, followed by page number.

preserve or displace its ancestor? As Darwin tentatively puts it, "If *species* generate 'other *species*', their race is not utterly cut off" (*DN* B, 72).

As has often been noted, Darwin's most famous book never actually made good on its title, saying next to nothing about the *origin* of species in its speculative, indeed metaphysical sense. Looking back on his epoch-making book in 1871, Darwin summarizes its main intention: "I had two distinct objects in view, firstly, to shew that species had not been separately created, and secondly, that natural selection had been the chief agent of change, though largely aided by the inherited effects of habit, and slightly by the direct action of the surrounding conditions."[41] To be sure, Darwin had succeeded in overturning Lyell's doctrine of the separate creation of species. Yet his arguments in this regard rely on an ex post facto logic, presupposing as they do that species are always already in existence, thereby causing the very meaning of species to appear increasingly uncertain as his argument develops. The question that was to consume Darwin once he had returned to England in October 1836 was "not how it comes about that there are species, but only how a species can give birth to another."[42] Indeed, at any given point in time, a given species may either be looked upon as a solid, distinct class of being or as an emergent (or "well-marked") variety of some antecedent species.

Nevertheless, Gilson's conclusion that Darwin had only a muddled or shifting understanding of species does not quite get to the heart of the matter. For the concept of species, far from being something the modern scientist could unilaterally establish by definition, actually amounts to a presupposition absent which Darwin's project of deriving the laws of organic development from empirical observation could never even get under way. Thus, if the empirical data obtained by fieldwork are to become intelligible at all, they must have been already filtered through the normative idea of a species. To see how this is the case, let us recall that it was Darwin's dissent from his "transmutationist" predecessors, Lamarck in particular, that led him to seek an alternative concept of species, free of philosophical and cultural assumptions about "separate creation," "progressive development," and such. Maintaining furthermore that "it is absurd to talk of one animal being higher than another," Darwin effectively disaggregates speciation from any directional conception of geological time, for which reason he would later on resist speaking of "evolution," a concept whose prospective certitude made him uneasy. Instead, he opts for the retrospective certainty of "descent with modification." As he laconically remarks about the early entries in Notebook B, "The above speculations are applicable to non progressive development" (*DN* B, 44). Even so, it would be a category error to conclude—as Dar-

---

41. *The Descent of Man*, in Darwin 2006, 863.
42. Gilson 1984, 96; "at no time did Darwin undertake to clarify the issue of the origin of species . . . in the sense of the origin of the *existence* of species" (168; emphasis mine).

win eventually did—that within his theory of natural selection "species" is something merely notional, an inference drawn from a welter of particular, empirical observations. In fact, as an *idea* in the classical, Platonic sense of an ontological reality, "species" always already grounds and directs the young Darwin's morphological study of organisms as they are revealed in the geological record. Thus, even as a given species is instantiated only *through* empirical particulars, it is the very idea of it that renders these particulars visible and intelligible in the first place. Speaking of the Galápagos finches, Darwin could thus write with consternation that "no two naturalists agree on any fundamental idea that I can see."[43]

Still, when carried out with due attention to the morphology of individual specimens and pursued over numerous generations as permitted by an uneven geological record, such study reveals natural forms (varieties, subspecies, and species alike) to exhibit only ever a provisional stability. For one thing, Darwin would eventually hold that the intelligibility of a given natural form can never be disentangled from the local conditions as they prevailed at the time of its existence. Once other factors or "principles" such as heredity and sexual selection were added to his strictly algorithmic "species *concept*," it naturally followed that speciation and contingency had to be regarded as two sides of the same coin. Pervasive contingency was the price paid by any functionalist conception of natural form. Unsurprisingly, in developing his theory of natural selection and descent with modification, Darwin had decisively exposed the basic mistake at the heart of natural theology in the age of Paley, namely, its assumption that all species ought to be considered fixed and ahistorical. Yet that assumption in turn was nested within another, equally fallacious premise, namely, that species is a generic and abstract notion rather than a reality in the classical, Aristotelian sense of a *forma substantialis*. In fact, it is in the nature of species, properly understood as a *specific* form, that it allows us to grasp and order a dynamic welter of visible phenomena in the first place.

At first blush, Darwin's own account had decisively broken with Paley's idea of the ahistorical, "independent creation" of multiple species, that is, diverse and distinct forms of life having originated independently rather than as a complex sequence of historical "descent." And yet, as Michael Hanby notes, Paley would "determine what Darwin *sees*—or wants to see—in looking at living beings" because Darwin "largely accepts Paley's conflation of nature and artifice, . . . with its deep roots in Newtonian mechanics." The resulting "fusion of *technē* and *logos* reduces truth to *factum* (the made), in much the same way that Vico's *New Science* (1725) supplants a metaphysics of "creation" with a historical process of "making." Even so,

---

43. 30 July 1837 (Darwin 2008, 63). In time, Darwin was to surrender these vestiges of metaphysical realism and commit himself instead to a concept of the "organism [as] a 'natureless' artifact artificially related to its own form" (Hanby 2013, 209).

attempts to reduce biological forms to a contingent historical sequence "is contradicted not only by the lived lives of organisms but by the structure of cognition."
Indeed, for our purposes it matters that the "cognition" (of species) begins in and is
circumscribed by our *visual* apprehension of phenomena as distinctly bounded
"forms."[44] What Goethe and Darwin both refer to as "seeing the idea" invests form
with ontological standing. For only inasmuch as form is visually apprehended as
having (noncontingent) being can it be raised to the status of the intelligible.

Inevitably, Darwin finds himself confronting the Platonic paradox of the One
and the many, a problem his academic training and intellectual temperament left
him ill prepared to recognize, let alone solve. As the Russian mathematician and
theologian Pavel Florensky was to observe early in the twentieth century, if "knowledge exists only where *hen* expands to include *polla*, forming *hen kai polla* (the one
and the many), there has to be something in the way that we perceive diverse instances of the same species that permits, or rather compels, judging them as such.
"For a general judgment is a unique act of thought, not an accumulation of many
judgments." Realism, in other words, is not predicated *of* discrete phenomena as they
register in perception. Rather, their ontological reality allows them to so register in
the first place. As he continues to wrestle with the elusive concept of species, Darwin
comes up (albeit often unwittingly) on a simple yet inescapable question: "What real
processes and things, what objects, of knowledge, must exist if there are to be general
concepts about them?"[45] At least in part, Darwin's predicament stems from the fact
that in his fieldwork he adheres, for good reason, to a rigorously empirical, descriptive procedure. Concepts, including that of species, may crystallize *from* a vast array
of particular acts of observation and description. Yet because such a procedure tends
to disaggregate, not unify, it ends up foregrounding, not the specificity, but the *singularity* of the visible phenomena to which it attends. At the same time, the realism
of empirical (nominalist) description remains aimless unless its profusion of data
serves some underlying integrative end. Ultimately, all "realist theories come out of a
sense of the kinship of all being, a sense of the non-absolute isolation of things, moments, and states, which is due not to their mechanical mixing, or to the fuzziness of
their definition, but to their inner kinship and unity." In Platonic terms, "not only is
hen nonexclusively *hen*, but it is also *polla* and even *pan*."[46] The procedural rationality
of "realist" description or pictorialization presupposes a *logos*, that is, a metaphysical
realism not contingent on man-made definitions and institutions but incrementally

---

44. Hanby 2013, 199–203, 189; Darwin mistakenly assumes that species "are fundamentally a matter of taxonomy." What Hanby calls "Darwin's nominalism" is at bottom the result of his
"conflation of being and history, [which] follows logically from the prior conflation of nature and
artifice" (202).

45. Florensky 2020, 13.

46. Ibid., 24.

(if only ever partially) unveiled by countless acts of focused visualization and description.

Darwin's "species problem," as it has become known in the precincts of evolutionary biology, is fundamentally the result of an inattention pervading the very discipline he helped found to *the ways in* which phenomena *come into view*, namely, through acts of undesigning, attentive visualization rather than top-down conceptualization. What Michael Hanby diagnoses as the "denial of the ontological primacy of form," a denial whose Nominalist origins I have discussed elsewhere, effectively meant that, in Darwin's later work, "species" exists only as a "species *concept*" and not, or no longer, as the correlate of visual cognition.[47] Modern evolutionary biology, and perhaps modern science more widely, thus appears consumed with "know-how" rather than "know-what," to recall Hans Jonas's distinction. It categorically refuses to venture pronouncements on the reality, the very being of the entities it studies. Such questions are now deemed unpardonably speculative, for to answer them would be to leave behind the tight chain of successive inferences and to credit, as classical metaphysics had done, our senses with the power of apprehending reality *in* appearance. Hence it is that, in time, Darwin ceases to have any serious interest in "organisms *as such*, but only insofar as they can plausibly be accounted for by natural selection." No longer a reality that is visually apprehended, "modern species are mere 'species *concepts*,' . . . functional entities, organizing members of a class, not ontological entities expressing an intrinsic nature common to those members." Underlying this purely notional and abstract view of species as the carbon that fuels evolutionary history, a view Darwin had fully embraced by the time he published his *Origin of Species*, is the antimetaphysical assumption "that species members have no ontological identity in excess to this history."[48]

That said, my present purpose is not to retrace the admittedly fascinating tale of how, in the course of Notebook B, Darwin began to formulate some first, tentative thoughts about natural selection and adaptive diversification brought about by the intricate workings of sexual selection as it unfolds within a slowly changing geological setting and in the face of ecological contingencies ranging from changing climates to random occurrences such as "seed blown into desert" (*DN* B, 209e).[49]

---

47. Ibid., 203; on the effects of late Scholastic Nominalism on modern thought, see Pfau 2013a, 163–71, 420–31.

48. Hanby 2013, 206–7.

49. By coincidence, Darwin's image of windblown seed destined for oblivion in an indifferent environment resurfaces in Tennyson's despondent question about the bearing of it all on mankind: "And he, shall he, / Man, her last work, who seemed so fair, / Such splendid purpose in his eyes / . . . / Be blown about the desert dust, / Or sealed within the iron hills?" *In Memoriam*, Canto LVI, lines 8–20. Tennyson's point of reference for his poem, published in 1850, is not Darwin but Lyell's *Principles of Geology* and Robert Chambers's *Vestiges from the Natural History of Creation*

Rather, the main point to be established is why Darwin's concept of species cannot be reduced to a mere hypothesis or inference or a merely emergent property of organic matter but, instead, shows natural form to be a real existent. For what allows a natural being to be experienced as distinctly visible phenomenon is, precisely, its real species character, the *form* that allows it to stand forth against the background "noise" of unorganized percepts; were it not for the form of the species manifesting itself in the particular, the latter could not even be recognized as a distinct being and source of potential insight. To be sure, natural forms in Darwin's theory are understood to have taken their present aspect only as a result of contingent material forces extending far back in geological time. Nevertheless, a "functionalist" narrative drawing on the aleatory interplay of heredity, chance variation, adaptation, and so forth already presupposes a concept of specific agent forms that, logically, can be neither wholly contingent nor wholly abstract. For the term "species" to signify anything, it must be instantiated, however variably, by real existing entities that, were it otherwise, could never even be visualized as objects of potential inquiry.

Simply put, functionalism presupposes realism because it is premised on formally distinctive, or *specific*, agents capable of realizing a given set of functions. There can be no function without agency, just as there can be no agent without a specific form. Hence, the formal integrity (not to be misconstrued as immutability) of the concept of species, understood *as a reality* rather than a hypothesis or inference, proves indispensable for the life sciences as they seek to navigate between the Scylla of random and meaningless particularity and the Charybdis of empty, unverifiable generalization. If anything, the latter is even more unpardonable in a scientist, with Darwin "look[ing] at a strong tendency to generalize as an entire evil."[50] Perhaps no contemporary of the young Darwin articulates the salient distinction better than Ruskin in the first volume of *Modern Painters*:

> It is carelessly and falsely said that general ideas are more important than particular ones; carelessly and falsely, I say, because the so-called general idea is important, not because it is common to all the individuals of that species, but because it separates that species from everything else. It is the distinctiveness, not the universality of the truth, which renders it important. And the so-called particular idea is unimportant, not because it is not predicable of the whole species, but because it is predicable of things out of that species. It is not its individuality, but its generality, which renders it unimportant. So then truths are important just in proportion as they are characteristic; and are valuable, primarily,

---

(1844), the latter being arguably the most successful attempt to popularize proto-evolutionist theories for a broad Victorian readership.

50. Letter to J. D. Hooker, 11 January 1844 (Darwin 2008, 84).

as they separate the species from all other created things; secondarily, as they separate the individuals of that species from one another. (*RCW* III, 152)

Just as the "general" overleaps all *detail*, whereas the "specific" builds on it, so the mere particular is identifiable as such only in contradistinction to the general, which paradoxically causes the two notions to merge and, thus, to be equally unhelpful for a genuine understanding of form. If a species were something static and immutable, the concept itself would effectively be assimilated to the general and the abstract. In that case, species (or "form" in its Aristotelian-Thomist sense) would be something merely notional rather than discernibly real, a probable inference rather than a palpable presence. With good reason, then, Ruskin insists that the "specific" must *eo ipso* be "distinctive."

This crucial qualification not only affirms that a given species is necessarily realized within a determinate spatiotemporal setting but also posits that it *stands forth* as a distinctive reality within that setting. The specific, the *species* or *form* that permits its particular instantiations to be known, constitutes their reality. Hence, the idea of a species cannot be explained away as a mere coefficient of historically contingent, material forces. Where we speak of a species, having discerned the specific character of being, the form in question can never be construed as a random particularity or an empty generality. Rather, in the order of being, the specific—being real, not merely notional—is anterior to both. In the event, Gilson's critique of Darwin ("one sees . . . how indeterminate the idea of species remains in his mind") would be valid only if we were to invest the concept of species with a timeless fixity.[51] Yet the main point of Darwin's theorizing is, of course, to show that species is a *dynamic* reality— not a static notion abstracted only after the fact from aggregated individual samples. Conversely, to assume that "species" serves an exclusively heuristic purpose—as Darwin, in his notebooks and subsequent writings, hypothesizes concerning "the buddings and splittings in the tree of species branchings, when one ancestral species has a dozen descendant species"—also will not suffice.[52] For such an understanding of species as a (quasi-Kantian) *regulative idea* can only issue in an anthropomorphic, ex post facto concept of particular objects *already* given in experience. It cannot, however, explain how it is that objects of such incontrovertible phenomenal distinctness or quiddity should discernibly manifest themselves for the observer to begin with.

Here again Ruskin's caveat that "it is the distinctiveness, not the universality of the truth, which renders it important" offers a valuable hint. For his observation

---

51. Gilson 1984, 172.

52. Hodge 2003, 48–49; as the summary continues: "In the greater multiplying of species in the diversifying descent of a large group, a class, say, rather than a mere genus, there will be vastly more extinctions, and so more gaps in character, within and between such groups."

shows that reality—and, consequently, an aesthetic realism committed to depicting it—is not fungible with abstract or generalizing notions superimposed on it by a detached observer-scientist. Rather, the true locus of reality is found in the *specific*, the *species character* whereby a given phenomenon stands out distinctly against the background of various other entities and, only on that condition, can (in Husserl's terminology) "constitute itself" in the observing consciousness. The specificity (or quiddity) of a thing and its phenomenality are convertible because both are, ontologically speaking, real rather than purely notional; and the real must logically precede any inference drawn *from* appearances, as well as any hypothesis ventured *about* them. Instead, the real shines through in the incontrovertible givenness and presence of phenomena—that is, not as some hypostatized substratum of appearance but as the event of manifestation itself. We recall Goethe's caveat that "we ought not to search for anything *behind* the phenomena. For they themselves are the doctrine."[53] Ultimately, Darwin's and Ruskin's understanding of natural form as specific, distinctive, and dynamic returns us to a Scholastic position according to which the reality of things is inseparable from their *quidditas*. As Joseph Pieper puts it:

> Every existing being is *aliquid*. This statement is not as plain and definitely not as tautological as it may at first appear. The common translation of *aliquid* with "something" would be quite misleading here. For the meaning of *aliquid*, explained already in medieval etymology (we may add, correctly, for once), is the same as *aliud quid*, "something other, something apart." Every existing thing is "something apart," which means: something distinguished and separated from all other things, something with its own identity. This transcendental concept of *aliquid* . . . thus opens an illuminating approach to reality, illuminating as much in breadth as in depth: all that exists, exists as form; all form in turn is defined by its delimitation. . . . The transcendentals *ens, res* and *unum* regard the intrinsic reality of all that is, as distinct from *aliquid*, which implies an essential relatedness of every being to another being.[54]

Lest we drift into the realm of purely abstract speculation, of which Scholasticism is so often accused, let us recall that "quiddity," which tethers the contingent appearance of a particular entity to the reality of its species, manifests itself not as a concept but as a visible presence—an image. A species must have been *seen* before it can be known. As Gilson points out to his fellow philosophers who, he suspects, have never laid eyes on even a single barnacle in their lives, "Darwin's entire doctrine rests

---

53. *GHA* 12:432 (#488).
54. Pieper 1989, 33–34.

upon thousands of facts, . . . of which he cites but a small sample."[55] Darwin, whose patience when scrutinizing seemingly unremarkable organisms for minute variations bordered on the angelic, had understood from the start that scientific understanding begins in, and remains forever entwined with, the art of seeing. Responding to Hooker, he thus notes "how painfully (to me) true is your remark that no one has hardly a right to examine the question of species who has not minutely described many."[56]

Still, as Aristotle had pointed out long before, there is no clear-cut answer as to the method that scientific inquiry into natural forms ought to adopt: "Ought we . . . to begin by discussing each separate substance—man, lion, ox, and the like—taking each kind in hand independently of the rest, or ought we rather to lay down the attributes which they have in common in virtue of some common element of their nature"? The specialist no doubt will incline to the former approach, by "starting straight off with the particular species." And yet such an approach not only creates redundancies, but, it appears, presupposes a concept of species: "If we deal with each species independently of the rest, we shall frequently be obliged to repeat the same statements over and over again, . . . [producing] frequent repetitions as to the characters, themselves identical but recurring in animals specifically distinct."[57] Meanwhile, the generalist's preference for determining a given species by cross-referencing its morphological and behavioral attributes with other species (say, quadrupeds or ruminants) risks blurring the boundaries between species and genera. By shifting the focus from a formalist to a functionalist concept of species, which is to say, by homing in on speciation as a dynamic process, Darwin would seem to have found a way around Aristotle's methodological quandary. And yet the study of particular phenomena that, since Aristotle, had defined specialized inquiry already presupposes that a given entity has manifested itself to the scientist in its distinctive and visible *specificity*. The species character of a particular being thus *is* its reality, that is, the ontological trait absent which a thing could never *appear* as distinctive and potentially knowable to begin with. Understood as the quiddity of a thing, species is not simply another attribute or secondary quality, but, instead, the real condition under which a thing constitutes itself as a distinctly visible form.

We can now briefly consider the second feature that, as noted above, frames Darwin's functionalist understanding of natural forms: holism. As is well known, Darwin's formation as a "philosophical naturalist" was greatly influenced by three contemporary scientists: Charles Lyell, John Herschel, and Alexander von Humboldt. Herschel's *Preliminary Discourse on the Study of Natural Philosophy* (1830)

---

55. Gilson 1984, 166.
56. 10 September 1845 (Darwin 2008, 93).
57. Aristotle 1984, 994–95 (*Parts of Animals* 639a15–639b5).

proposed a valuable account of "active" inductive reasoning, and it did much to alert Darwin to hidden presuppositions when it came to identifying facts, formulating causal relationships, and defining criteria for what constitutes evidence; and the crucial impact of Lyell's *Principles* on the young Darwin has already been considered. For his part, Lyell had been greatly inspired by Humboldt's essay on rock stratification (*Geognostical Essay on the Superposition of Rocks*), published in 1822, which prompted the young Lyell to travel to Paris and seek out Humboldt's acquaintance. Another of Humboldt's many publications, his 1817 essay *The Isothermal Lines and the Distribution of Heat on the Earth* had fascinated both Lyell and Darwin with its first scientific attempt to understand global climate patterns.[58] Meanwhile, Humboldt's early and groundbreaking work, *Personal Narrative of Travels to the Equinoctial Regions of the New Continent* (1806), a work that turned its author into a celebrity across Europe, illustrated for Darwin that any functionalist account of natural forms necessarily had to take a wide view of the multitude of factors conceivably impinging on speciation and descent with modification.

Except for Darwin himself, no other nineteenth-century naturalist could rival the scope and daring of Humboldt's explorations. From Berlin to Paris, London, St. Petersburg, and Rome, European high society was enthralled by vivid accounts of Humboldt's countless feats, including his ascent of the Chimborazo, an inactive volcano in the Andes standing at 21,000 feet; his multiyear exploration of the remotest parts of the Oronoco River; his conversations with Napoleon, Bolívar, Jefferson, and other political celebrities; at sixty years of age, his 1829 travels to the Altai Mountains in Russia's far east, which included a forbidden excursion into Mongolia.[59]

Published in 1845, the first volume of Humboldt's magnum opus, *Cosmos* (1845), attempts to outline a truly all-encompassing "physical description of the earth." For

58. As early as 1800, some 200 miles south of Caracas at Lake Valencia, Humboldt had first formulated his theory of human-induced climate change, noting the correlation between human-induced changes in vegetation (deforestation) and shifting rainfall patterns and how indeed "everything is interaction and reciprocal" (Wulf 2015, 57–59).

59. In the event, Humboldt did not quite scale the Chimborazo but had to turn back at 19,000 feet; see Wulf 2015, 51–110, 201–16. Arguably the most famous scientist of his century, Humboldt's global fame was evident when the centenary of his birth, in September 1869, was being commemorated with celebrations and speeches in Buenos Aires, Mexico City, Moscow, Alexandria (Egypt), San Francisco, Charleston, Cleveland (where some 8,000 people assembled), Pittsburgh (with 10,000 in attendance, including President Ulysses S. Grant), and New York City (featuring a crowd of 25,000 in Central Park); in Humboldt's hometown, Berlin, some 80,000 braved torrential rains, with all offices and agencies closed for the day in tribute. Capes, waterfalls, ocean currents, rivers, and mountains around the world are named after Humboldt, as well as some 100 species of animals and 300 plant species. Rachel Carson's great environmental classic, *Silent Spring* (1962), is one of countless works inspired by Humboldt's pioneering insight into the interconnectedness of ecosystems.

his part, Darwin, strongly influenced by Humboldt's earlier publications, had in his notebooks embarked on a similar quest for a "comprehensive and holistic science[,] . . . a general philosophy of nature in which [he] sought to integrate the land, sea, forest and landscape, encountered in a holistic experience of nature reminiscent of Humboldt's own reflections."[60] In what was to become the *Summa* of an astounding career, Humboldt's five-volume *Cosmos: A Sketch of a Physical Description of the Universe* (1845–62), first presented as a series of lectures in Berlin, drew for his large and mesmerized audience a seemingly all-encompassing portrait of the physical world.[61] A true product of the German Enlightenment, Humboldt never once invokes God as Creator of the universe, nor does he use the term "creation" (*Schöpfung*), a decision quickly "corrected" by his English translators. Arguably the most fascinating portion of his encyclopedic treatise spanning astronomy, geology, oceanography, climatology, and hydrography, as well as the geographic distribution of innumerable plant and animal species, is Humboldt's lengthy introduction and justification of his project in volume 1. In it, Humboldt advances two claims of particular relevance for the concurrently emerging movement of pictorial realism. First and foremost, he emphasizes the need to achieve a holistic vision of the cosmos. Nature writing must capture what is intuitively apparent to any sensitive observer just as much as what draws the scientist's expert gaze: "The spontaneous impressions of the untutored mind lead, like the laborious deductions of the cultivated intellect, to the same intimate persuasion, that one common, lawful and hence eternal chain encompasses all of nature." Reflecting the profound influence of Goethe's symbolic worldview on his intellectual formation, Humboldt time and again remarks on how, when contemplating an infinitely variegated yet intertwined natural world, "the mind is penetrated by the same sense of the grandeur and vast expanse of nature, revealing to the soul, by a mysterious inspiration, the existence of laws that regulate the forces of the universe." Nature, when "submitted to the process of thought, is unity in diversity

---

60. Sloan 2003, 24, 33. On Humboldt's impact on Darwin, see also Wulf 2015, 217–34. From Rio de Janeiro, Darwin writes: "formerly admired Humboldt, I now almost adore him; he alone gives any notion, of the feelings which are raised in the mind on first entering the Tropics" (to J. D. Henslow, 18 May–16 June 1832); and to his father: "If you really want to have a (notion) of tropical countries, *study* Humboldt. — Skip th(e) scientific parts & commence after leaving Teneriffe.— My feelings amount to admiration the more I read him" (8 February–1 March 1832). By September 1839, Humboldt writes to Darwin at length, praising the latter's recently published *Journal of Researches*.

61. Published in a print run of 20,000 copies in April 1845, the first volume of *Kosmos* sold out within a couple of months; immediately reprinted, the work was also quickly translated into English, Dutch, Italian, French, Danish, Polish, Swedish, Spanish, Russian, and Hungarian; published between 1845 and 1849, the three competing English translations of volume 1 alone sold over 40,000 copies. Still, there being no copyright provisions for translations, Humboldt received no royalties from any of them; see Wulf 2015, 245, 248 n.

of phenomena; a harmony, blending together all created things, however dissimilar in form and attributes; one great whole (*to ōn*) animated by the breath of life."[62]

The challenge of scientific prose, which Humboldt believes had not been met thus far, is to achieve a level of eloquence and vividness that evokes the "breath of life [*Hauch des Lebens*]" with which, mysteriously, an intuitive and holistic vision of the natural world is imbued. Still, attempts to reconstitute the visual experience of nature in the medium of writing risk widening the gap between mind and world. What makes this endeavor so challenging is that holism must not devolve into a mere abstraction but, instead, ought to be realized as a quasi-intuitive experience, indeed, as an event of a cosmic rather than anthropocentric kind. While "external nature may be opposed to the intellectual world, . . . [and] nature may be opposed to art," Humboldt insists that juxtapositions of this kind should never result in "separat[ing] the sphere of nature from that of mind, since such a separation would reduce the physical science of the world to a mere aggregation of empirical specialities." On the contrary, "the external world has no real existence for us beyond the image reflected within ourselves [*indem sie sich in uns zu einer Naturanschauung gestaltet*] through the medium of the senses. As intelligence and forms of speech, thought and its verbal symbols are united by secret and indissoluble links, so does the external world blend almost unconsciously . . . with our ideas and feelings."[63] Yet this "earnest endeavor to comprehend the phenomena of physical objects in their general connection, and to represent nature as one great whole, moved and animated by internal forces," is intended not only as a synoptic view of present conditions but also as a diachronic account.

It is this second feature of Humboldt's project, the attempt to capture the vestiges of deep geological time in what he calls "nature-painting" (*Naturgemälde*), that links his simultaneously intuitive and forensic approach to the work of Darwin and Ruskin in England. Every visible aspect, every image of the natural world, is at once an integrative canvas and a holograph of time. It not only displays "organic matter . . . continually undergoing change and being dissolved to form new combinations" but also "reveals at every phase of its existence the mystery of its former conditions." Undoubtedly inspired by the comparative linguistic analyses of his brother Wilhelm, Humboldt hazards an analogy between the sedimentation of geological and organic matter, on the one hand, and the historical growth of languages, on the other: "In tracing the physical delineation of the globe, we behold the present and the past reciprocally incorporated, as it were, with one another; for the domain of nature is like that of languages, in which etymological research reveals a successive development

---

62. Humboldt 1997, 24, 25, 27 (trans. modified).
63. Ibid., 76.

by showing us the primary condition of an idiom reflected in the forms of speech in use at the present day."[64]

It is this historical depth that the attentive observer can intuit in the visible aspect of surface forms and phenomena of both nature and culture. Their charismatic appeal, Humboldt maintains, stems from the way that the reality that presents itself *to* sight is felt to be far richer and more complex than can actually be visualized. What is intuited, and what the scientist's forensic vision and prose descriptions subsequently seek to distill, is the previously unforeseen and overlooked. Humboldt's *Naturgemälde* in prose maps rather well onto Jean-Luc Marion's concept of the saturated phenomenon. In its excessive visibility, phenomenal nature "has stopped presenting itself to our look as an object that we would produce." Instead, "the visible that saturates it, and without which it could not rise up from itself, overflows on us." Such phenomena produce an excess of meaning "that cannot be granted a univocal sense in return," even as every one of these meanings is "equally legitimate and rigorous."[65] For Lyell, Darwin, and Humboldt, it is this peculiar excess of the visible world—"peculiar" because the phenomenon's material abundance and historical complexity can be readily felt *and* just as easily overlooked—that challenges the writer of science to do justice to the sheer abundance of natural phenomena, with each natural thing exhibiting an unimaginably complex filiation with other forms, as well as a quasi-holographic, temporal dimension. As Humboldt puts it, "Whether it is domes of trachyte, cones of basalt, lava streams . . . or white deposits of pumice, *their form is their history*."[66]

Two richly evocative and panoramic descriptions of the Andes, by Humboldt and Darwin, as well as a famous painting by Frederick Church (inspired by Humboldt's prose), illustrate the remarkable fusion of lyric and forensic elements as a new generation of naturalists seek to capture the physical world in a prose that, in turn, bears strong affinities with mid-nineteenth-century pictorial realism. The first of these passages, from Humboldt's immensely successful *Personal Narrative of Travels*, published in 1806 and translated by Helen Maria Williams (whose picturesque accounts of the French Revolution a decade earlier had earned her a considerable readership), seeks to convey the abundance and strangeness of life in the rain forest along the Oronoco River.

> The beasts of the forest retire to the thickets; the birds hide themselves beneath the foliage of the trees, or in the crevices of the rocks. Yet, amid this apparent silence, when we lend an attentive ear to the most feeble sounds transmitted by

64. Ibid., 7, 27, 72.
65. Marion 2002b, 74, 112.
66. Humboldt 1997, 72; emphasis mine.

the air, we hear a dull vibration, a continual murmur, a hum of insects, that fill, if we may use the expression, all the lower strata of the air. Nothing is better fitted to make man feel the extent and power of organic life. Myriads of insects creep upon the soil, and flutter round the plants parched by the ardour of the Sun. A confused noise issues from every bush, from the decayed trunks of trees, from the clefts of the rock, and from the ground undermined by the lizards, millipedes, and cecilias. There are so many voices proclaiming to us, that all nature breathes; and that, under a thousand different forms, life is diffused throughout the cracked and dusty soil, as well as in the bosom of the waters, and in the air that circulates around us.[67]

As Andrea Wulf points out, the passage clearly inspired one of Darwin's most famous paragraphs, the one concluding *On the Origin of Species* ("It is interesting to contemplate an entangled bank"). If anything, Humboldt's writing is more sensuous, more lyrical, not least because in order to allow his readers to achieve an imaginative vision of a scene so distant and strange he focuses less on what can be seen than on what can be heard. The "power of organic life" must be felt as a ceaseless hum and murmur, an eternal symphony filling the air. Whereas attempting an outright description of the landscape would risk turning the natural world into a static picture at a distinct remove from the beholder, the unceasing soundscape of insects, birds, lizards that is echoed by the gently swaying trees reinforces the image of nature as a ceaselessly active and infinitely variegated whole. With this soundscape resonating in the observer's very body, the naturalist becomes a participant in the scene, indeed a physical part of it, as it were by default. Notably, life for Humboldt is not a surface phenomenon always readily seen but, instead, is a reality constituted by all our senses and encompassing everything, from the subterranean ("diffused throughout the cracked and dusty soil") to the ambient waters and the air. It is the boundless diffusion of life itself that allows the naturalist to feel and grasp the cosmos as a truly three-dimensional and cohesive presence, with geological time adding a fourth dimension. The composite effect is one of limitless, form-giving power (*dynamis*), a word that also holds great significance in the writings of Humboldt's brother, Wilhelm, and, likewise, in the closing lines of Shelley's "Mont Blanc." There Shelley comments on a power that, far from being observer-dependent, properly constitutes sight as imaginative participation: "the power is there / The still and solemn power of many sights, / And many sounds, and much of life and death." And yet, inevitably, "the secret strength of things / Which governs thought, and to the infinite dome / Of heaven is as a law" will always remain at least partially invisible and ineffable.[68]

---

67. Humboldt, quoted in Wulf 2015, 234 n.
68. Shelley, "Mont Blanc," lines 127–41.

The second passage to be considered, once again attentive to the holistic and deep-temporal character of the natural world, is found late in *Voyage of the Beagle*, with Darwin describing a group of travelers struggling upward to the Peuquenes ridge in the Cordilleras. At an altitude of 13,000 feet, the struggle for life, or at least for air, is viscerally felt; indeed, in the earlier, diary version of the passage Darwin specifically remarks that "the labor of walking is excessive, & breathing deep & diffi-cult; & it is nearly incomprehensible to me how Humboldt (& others subsequently) have reached 19,000 feet."[69] Having reached the midpoint of his ascent, Darwin pauses to view the ambient landscape from what, on Alberti's conception of linear perspective, would likely be the optimal vantage point.

> When about halfway up, we met a large party with seventy loaded mules. It was interesting to hear the wild cries of the muleteers, and to watch the long de-scending string of the animals; they appeared so diminutive, there being nothing but the black mountains with which they could be compared. When near the summit, the wind, as generally happens, was impetuous and extremely cold. On each side of the ridge, we had to pass over broad bands of perpetual snow, which were now soon to be covered by a fresh layer. When we reached the crest and looked backwards, a glorious view was presented. The atmosphere resplendently clear; the sky an intense blue; the profound valleys; the wild broken forms; the heaps of ruins, piled up during the lapse of ages; the bright-coloured rocks, con-trasted with the quiet mountains of snow; all these together produced a scene no one could have imagined. Neither plant nor bird, excepting a few condors wheel-ing around the higher pinnacles, distracted my attention from the inanimate mass. I felt glad that I was alone: it was like watching a thunderstorm, or hearing in full orchestra a chorus from the Messiah.[70]

Compared to Humboldt's earlier prose, Darwin's description seems more in line with the somewhat mannered tradition of the English picturesque style of the late eighteenth century, which here is only momentarily punctured by a more sublime note characteristic of Wordsworth's high Romantic idiom. Contributing to this im-pression is the passage's concluding reference to Handel's *Messiah*, which probably ought to be read as a concession to the religious sensibilities of his mainstream An-glican readers rather than as expressing genuine religious sentiments; after all, the simile ("it was like watching a thunderstorm") that sets up the allusion to Handel's oratorio appears somewhat incongruously superimposed on a description that, just a few lines earlier, had remarked on the "intense blue" and "glorious view" of the scenery. Still, the passage's alternation between picturesque beauty and Romantic

69. Darwin 1987, 266.
70. Darwin 2006, 284–85.

sublimity also bears some affinity to Wordsworth's *Prelude*, not published until 1850, though completed by 1805. Thus, Darwin's "wild broken forms" and "heaps of ruins" recall Wordsworth's famous evocation of a "soulless" Alpine landscape, overwhelming the beholder with the dizzying sight of "woods decaying, never to be decay'd, / . . . stationary blasts of waterfalls, / . . . torrents shooting from the clear blue sky."[71]

In both cases, a visually overwhelming experience stands in for a power that is incontrovertibly operative, potentially menacing, and ever unfathomable. For Wordsworth, that power furnished a visible analogue for the soulless, all-devouring legacy of the French Revolution, which under its principal heir, Napoleon Bonaparte, threatened to erase all of Europe's political, religious, and cultural traditions. In Darwin's case, the power is, rather more literally, that of nature as a lawful and implacable process unfolding in complete separation from, and indifference to, human history. The asymmetry between geological and human time scales is palpably visualized by the string of "diminutive" muleteers arduously and precariously working their way up into a nonhuman sphere of snow and ice. Still, Darwin's later style, such as his masterful concluding paragraph to *On the Origin of Species*, far more effectively conveys the interest encoded in the natural world. In both the above passage and in the justly famous conclusion to his most celebrated work, Darwin deploys the epithet "interesting" ("It was interesting to hear the wild cries of the muleteers . . . " / "It is interesting to contemplate an entangled bank . . . "). Yet only in the latter passage is Darwin able to clinch, in language at once forensic and lyrical, the true source of such interest. For by 1859 he appears to have realized that the true "grandeur in this view of life" stems from its dynamic, not its scenic, character and that what stands to be visualized is not what is already plainly self-evident but, rather, the visible in all its specificity and reality.[72]

The limitations of a strictly "scenic" approach to visualizing and comprehending the natural world in all its formal and sensuous abundance are particularly

---

71. Wordsworth 1979 (1805 version), bk. VI, lines 454, 557–61.

72. "It is interesting to contemplate a tangled bank, clothed with many plants of many kinds, with birds singing on the bushes, with various insects flitting about, and with worms crawling through the damp earth, and to reflect that these elaborately constructed forms, so different from each other, and dependent upon each other in so complex a manner, have all been produced by laws acting around us. These laws, taken in the largest sense, being Growth with reproduction; Inheritance which is almost implied by reproduction; Variability from the indirect and direct action of the conditions of life, and from use and disuse; a Ratio of Increase so high as to lead to a Struggle for Life, and as a consequence to Natural Selection, entailing Divergence of Character and the Extinction of less improved forms. Thus, from the war of nature, from famine and death, the most exalted object which we are capable of conceiving, namely, the production of the higher animals, directly follows. There is grandeur in this view of life, with its several powers, having been originally breathed by the Creator into a few forms or into one; and that, whilst this planet has gone circling on according to the fixed law of gravity, from so simple a beginning endless forms most beautiful and most wonderful have been, and are being evolved" (Darwin 2006, 760).

Figure 6.1. Frederic Edwin Church, *Heart of the Andes*, 1859. New York, Metropolitan Museum of Art

evident in one of the most celebrated nineteenth-century landscape paintings, Frederic Edwin Church's monumental *The Heart of the Andes*. A pupil of Thomas Cole, founder of the Hudson River School, Church (1826–1900) first presented his vast canvas (5 x 10 feet) at a specially arranged studio on Broadway in New York in May 1859, during the very week that Humboldt, whose *Cosmos* (in its English translation of 1849) had been the main inspiration behind Church's painting, died in Paris and only a few months before Darwin's *On the Origin of Species* was published. During its initial three-week showing, *Heart of the Andes* (fig. 6.1) drew some twelve thousand people. Insured for $10,000 and, soon after its initial showing, sold for that amount (the highest price commanded by any American artwork to date), the painting also proved a lucrative business proposition for the organizers of its exhibition; a steel engraving commissioned at the time of its exhibition fetched another $6,000. Given its immense size, the painting required viewers to stand back at a considerable distance to take in its overall panoramic effect. At the same time, in order to appreciate the countless details of flora and fauna, viewers at the original exhibition were provided with opera glasses. In addition, two guidebooks broke down the canvas into sections (sky, snow dome, road and left foreground, etc.) and, in the other instance, retraced Humboldt's and Church's travels that had provided the inspiration and empirical foundation for the painting, respectively. As Avery notes, these guidebooks also provide "a measure of the literalism and literariness of the painting itself."[73]

---

73. Avery 1993, 35.

Fascinated by Humboldt's travels and writings, Church had embarked in 1853 on the first of two journeys to South America (mainly Colombia and Ecuador) in order to take notes and produce sketches and preliminary studies for a series of paintings of actual or, in the present case, idealized South American landscapes. Notably, these preliminary works include not only grand vistas but also highly technical drawings of foliage, large-leafed plants, and deciduous trees.[74] Though not a botanist and likely unfamiliar with many of the plants he encountered, Church nevertheless drew them with "enough accuracy that one can . . . apply at least family names to the most prominent." Similar to his Pre-Raphaelite contemporaries in England, Church approached painting as creating facsimiles of perception, that is, as the art of minutely recording, rather than symbolically condensing, a visual scene. At the same time, in contrast to Humboldt's unflinchingly secular outlook, Church's strong Calvinist background is plainly evident in *Heart of the Andes*, which involves the viewer in a visual pilgrimage on the model of Bunyan's *Pilgrim's Progress* that first comes to rest at the wooden cross in the painting's center-left foreground and, eventually, at the church near the painting's center, or "heart." Even so, the panoramic or scenic approach to pictorial space lacks any unifying device, and the transition from the massive trees in the foreground, particularly on the right side, to the middle range of the painting suggests Church's struggle with the laws of perspective. Instead of a single, integrative visual grammar, the canvas presents the viewer with myriad visual details—various kinds of foliage, birds sitting on scrubs, exotic ferns, and flowers of various alluring color in the foreground. As Avery puts it, then, "with *The Heart of the Andes*, the question 'What does one see?' must yield to 'What can one find?'"[75]

Notwithstanding its initial popularity, Church's *Heart of the Andes* ultimately remains an instructive failure, for the same reasons that Darwin's picturesque genre piece in *The Voyage of the Beagle* seems so palpably inferior to the lyrical summation that concludes *On the Origin of Species*. In both instances, pictorial and descriptive realism resolves itself into accumulating details and rendering them transparently, indeed oppressively, visible. The gimmick of providing viewers in New York with opera glasses so as to study these details one by one confirms what the critic writing for the *Crayon* (a short-lived art journal dedicated to promoting Ruskin's aesthetic philosophy) also demurred: Church's painting lacked "unity and repose" precisely because "every square inch of the canvas [is] covered with nature's statistics." Another reviewer, writing for the *Century*, likewise found Church's "facility of characterization and expression" to render his paintings as but "a combination of objects" seemingly drained of any symbolic significance.[76] What a critic in the *Albion* referred

---

74. For a discussion of Church's preparatory sketches and studies, see Avery 1993, 19–31.
75. Ibid., 35, 10.
76. Quoted in Avery 1993, 37–38.

to as Church's "Barnumesque and altogether objectionable" tendency of "resorting to a showman's device" highlights a dilemma that, several years before, had also prompted Ruskin's unease when sifting the implications of the new Pre-Raphaelite school's photorealist conception of painting. The unflattering comparison with P. T. Barnum's distinctive blend of business and showmanship seems fitting, if also stinging, not least because, unlike any other American painting, *The Heart of the Andes* would be continuously on tour in the same places also featuring Barnum's extravaganzas. Thus, between 1859 and 1861, the painting was to be exhibited in London and, back in the United States, in Boston, Philadelphia, Baltimore, Cincinnati, Chicago, and St. Louis.

Echoing the caveat of the critic writing for the *Albion* that "artifice does not fraternize with Art," a writer in the *New York Evening Post* demurs at Church's "attempt to mingle the real with the ideal. . . . A picture is a picture, and not an actual scene, and all attempts to make it any thing more than a picture belong to the cosmoramic and dioramic order of art."[77] Like Darwin's early diaries and the first of his notebooks (the so-called Red Notebook), Church's painting lacks a clear focal point, a shortcoming that exposes pictorial realism's inherently confused image concept; and it is John Ruskin whose writings embody mid-nineteenth-century aesthetic realism's struggle to formulate a coherent theory of the image, just as Darwin had struggled to articulate exactly what he meant by "species," since at every step of his far-flung empirical research the reality of species appeared to have been already presupposed. Simply put, both Ruskin and Darwin confront the fact that aesthetic and scientific cognition, and their underlying naturalistic axioms, remains haunted by ontological commitments associated above all with classical Aristotelian-Thomist realism and its origins in Plato's doctrine of ideas.

SPECIFICITY—DISTINCTIVENESS—TRUTH: VISIBILITY AS EVENT IN *MODERN PAINTERS I* (1843)

Born in 1819, the son of a Scots wine merchant and an intensely pious Protestant mother, John Ruskin was schooled largely in his upper-middle-class home.[78] It was followed by a rather indifferent academic career at Christ Church College, Oxford (1836–41), with the one highlight consisting in Ruskin's being awarded the Newdigate Prize in poetry. Meanwhile, his family's ample means allowed Ruskin to take

---

77. Quoted in Avery 1986, 60.

78. On Ruskin's family background, the grandfather's suicide prompted by bankruptcy, social disgrace, and mental disorder, and his father's tenacious and ultimately successful efforts at rebuilding the family's financial and social reputation, as well as his domineering mother, see Hewison 1976, 14–16; and the more detailed account in Hilton 1985, 1–40.

breaks from his studies for extended travels through Italy and Switzerland (in 1835 and 1840–41, respectively), reminiscent of the eighteenth-century "grand tour," and thereby to deepen his somewhat irregular education in the arts. As Ruskin comments in 1844, he had been "allowed, at a time when boys are usually learning their grammar, to ramble on the shores of Como and Lucerne." While his aesthetic peregrinations may have had "a most unfortunate effect, of course, as far as general or human knowledge is concerned," they yielded a "most beneficial effect on that peculiar sensibility to the beautiful in all things that God has made, which it is my present aim to render more universal" (*RCW* III, 669). As early as 1836, Ruskin was taking a passionate and decidedly partisan interest in J. W. M. Turner's late and increasingly controversial works. Fueled by "black anger in which I have remained pretty nearly ever since" (*RCW* XXXV, 217), he drafted a vehement response to a derisive review of three of Turner's paintings that had appeared in *Blackwood's Edinburgh Magazine*. Though the seventeen-year-old author was ultimately persuaded to hold off mailing his jeremiad, the central arguments of what was to be volume 1 of *Modern Painters* already emerge here with characteristic gusto.

What captivated Ruskin, and what so bewildered early Victorian critics still mired in the neoclassical aesthetics of Joshua Reynolds and the Royal Academy (of which Turner, too, had long been a member), is Turner's insistent foregrounding of medium over subject, of the infinitely complex interaction of color and light that, in his late paintings, defies neoclassical expectations of a sharply delineated and readily identifiable subject. Looking back on his youthful effusions in his 1885 autobiography, *Praeterita*, Ruskin remarks that what drew him to Turner "was almost wholly the pure artistic quality . . . whatever the subject." Budding artistic discernment and Oedipal rebellion may have gone hand in hand when, as Ruskin recalls around 1840, "[I] saw clearly that my father's joy in Rubens and Sir Joshua could never become sentient of Turner's microscopic touch" (*RCW* XXXV, 254, 256). That "touch" already dominates his unpublished polemic against John Eagles, the well-known art critic writing for *Blackwood's*. Discussing one of the pieces the reviewer had found objectionable, Turner's *Mercury and Argus* (1836), Ruskin focuses on "what real artists and men of feeling and taste must admire, but dare not attempt to imitate. . . . Many-coloured mists are floating above the distant city" and the "sea whose motionless and silent transparency is beaming with phosphor light, . . . emanates out of its sapphire serenity" (*RCW* III, 638–39).

It is this novel attention to the *how* rather than *what* of pictorial realism that proves of consuming interest to the young Ruskin.[79] Turner's art, he will maintain,

---

79. Quoting *Modern Painters I* (*RCW* III, 92), Wettlaufer concurs with Ruskin's appraisal of art as "a form of experience where the *how* of perception/reception is as important as the *what*. . . . The artist's goal then is not to reproduce the actual scene, but the *experience* of that scene, the mental state provoked" (1994, 215–16).

does not so much abandon realism as deepen and expand its scope by drawing attention to visual phenomena that, while seemingly beyond the scope of neoclassical mimesis, are nonetheless real and distinctly observable—dissolving shapes, unfurling mists, fluctuations of light, and subtle gradations of color. Prompted by his early encounter with Turner, yet in any event responsive to precisely those phenomena that Turner's late work also seeks to capture, Ruskin's diary entries from his 1840–41 tour of Switzerland and Italy already feature bursts of his charismatic prose style, one whose luminous impressionism and forensic crispness was to make *Modern Painters I* (1843) a major publishing event and draw the admiration of writers such as Charlotte Brontë and George Eliot.[80] An entry from Chamonix, 26 June 1842, illustrates the convergence of personal and art critical writing at the time.

> When I woke at 6 past three, its form was scarcely distinguishable through morning mist, which in the lower valley hung in dense white flakes among the trees along the course of the Arve. There were heavy white clouds over the Pavillon, relieved against a threatening black ground which reached the horizon. The outline of the snow was throughout indistinct with what I thought were wind avalanches, but I believe they must have been evaporating moisture, blowing towards Cormayeur. As the dawn grew brighter, a brown group of cloud formed near the Dome du Goûter—not on it, but in the sky, blowing also towards Cormayeur. Presently the black threatening part of the horizon grew luminous, and threw out the clouds, before white, as grey masses from its body, gradually disappearing itself into the ordinary light of pure horizon. A few minutes afterwards the first rose touched the summit, the mist gradually melting from the higher hills, leaving that in the valley arranged at the top in exquisitely fine, horizontal, water-like cirri, separated by little intervals from its chief mass. The light lowered to the Tacul and Dome, and such intense fire I never saw. The colour is deeper in the evening, but far less brilliant; a quarter of an hour afterwards, when it had touched the Aiguille du Goûter, it began to diminish on the summit, which then looked feeble and green beside the Tacul and Aiguille du Goûter. (*RCW* III, xxvii)

Though vivid and evocative, Ruskin's prose is no straightforwardly descriptive or "scenic" affair, mainly because its markedly temporal dimension destabilizes the

---

80. "I have only had instinct to guide me in judging of art; I feel now as if I had been walking blindfold—this book seems to give me eyes. I do wish I had pictures within reach by which to test the new sense. Who can read these glowing descriptions of Turner's works without longing to see them?" (Brontë, quoted in *RCW* III, xxxix). As Ball remarks, Ruskin's prose "enthrones the world of nature in all its colour and detail with such energy of presentation that it amounts to a revaluation of descriptive writing" (1971, 55).

Neoclassical view (famously set forth in Lessing's *Laokoön* [1766]) of the pictorial as spatial and therefore static. Instead, Ruskin's prose presents visual aspects in continuous flux: shifting mists punctured by oblique shapes, clouds forever reorganizing themselves, diffusive light breaking through partial obstructions, growing in radiance and intensity, and so forth. The focus, indeed the principal interest and drama of Ruskin's prose, arises from the way it foregrounds the highly unstable conditions under which visible forms manifest themselves and, consequently, enliven the act of seeing itself. Rather than aspiring to ekphrastic dominion over putatively static objects by "simply enumerating them," Ruskin's prose aims at "translating visual effects."[81] The writing here participates in the dynamism of the phenomena themselves; there is an *accelerando* quality to the passage, as the visual field appears to organize itself at an increasing pace; an ineffable, previously unimagined revelation appears to be at hand ("part of the horizon grew luminous") as the visible field progressively reveals its true specificity ("the first rose touched the summit, the mist gradually melting"). So as to home in on the phenomenology of visual experience, Ruskin foregrounds *how* visible particulars give themselves to sight, how they shape the act of seeing, not qua "objects," but as a focused "intentionality" (Husserl) and "quality of attention" (S. Weil). Stress is placed on the pregnant detail, a term not to be confused with contingent particularity but understood, instead, as unveiling the *specific* nature or quiddity of the visible. The protorealist quality of Ruskin's style stems from his unflagging attention to the phenomenology of visual experience; his is a realism of the image as an emergent correlate of seeing, that is, the realist image understood as a formal coming-to, an *advent*, and, phenomenologically speaking, a pure event.

Characteristic of Ruskin's early prose is a fundamental shift, away from conventional notions of pictorial and descriptive realism and its aesthetics of simulation and toward a naturalistic style that seeks to foreground the highly fluid *conditions* of vision. Some of his harshest criticisms are reserved for a bland and generic ideal of mimetic truth, such as is reflected in Reynolds's "frequent advice . . . to neglect specific form in landscape, and treat its materials in large masses, aiming only at general truths; the flexibility of foliage, but not its kind; the rigidity of rock, but not its mineral character."[82] The essence of painting, Ruskin insists, is in fact the obverse, for "every herb and flower of the field has its specific, distinct, and perfect beauty; it has its peculiar habitation, expression, and function. The highest art is that which seizes

---

81. Helsinger 1982, 22.

82. *RCW* III, 28. For Gombrich, *Modern Painters* is "perhaps the last and most persuasive book in the tradition that starts with Pliny and Vasari in which the history of art is interpreted as progress toward visual truth" (1972, 14). As Ball puts it, "Ruskin puts forward the proposition that stating facts is not a prosaic, but a challenging imaginative activity. In his practice he demonstrates that

this specific character, which develops and illustrates it, which assigns to it its proper position in the landscape, and which, by means of it, enhances and enforces the great impression which the picture is intended to convey" (*RCW* III, 33). Indeed, wherever painting neglects the specificity of what the eye sees, it either gravitates toward mindless particularity ("the numbered hairs and mapped wrinkles of Denner" [*RCW* III, 32]) or to generic abstractions of the kind found in Canaletto's "servile and mindless imitation, [which] imitates nothing but the blackness of the shadows," and which leaves Venice's buildings and stones bereft of "their architectural beauty [and] their ancestral dignity; for there is no texture of stone nor character of age in Canaletto's touch; which is invariably a violent, black, sharp, ruled penmanlike line, as far removed from the grace of nature as from her faintness and transparency. . . . He professes nothing but coloured daguerreotypeism" (*RCW* III, 215).

Yet how is painting to capture the specific in ways that will enable, indeed compel, the beholder to grasp it? Is it possible to "see" a species as such or, as Goethe had suggested to an incredulous Schiller, to "see an idea"? What, in other words, is the phenomenology of the *specifically* visible? A passing reminiscence found in *Praeterita* offers some hints. Looking back on his life's work after some four decades, Ruskin recalls seeing, in the spring of 1842 on the road to Norwood, "a bit of ivy round a thorn stem, which seemed, even to my critical judgment, not ill 'composed.'" Notably, in deciding to "make a light and shade pencil study of it," Ruskin does not attempt to evoke the thorn as a botanical object but, instead, responds to the composition that had elicited his visual attention to begin with. What could easily have remained a fleeting perception of some miscellaneous flora evolves into a conversion experience of sorts; for "when it was done, I saw that I had virtually lost all my time since I was twelve years old, because no one had ever told me to draw what was really there" (*RCW* XXXV, 311). The passage offers a near-perfect anticipation of Wittgenstein's oft-quoted injunction, "Don't think, but look!," as well as the philosopher's new understanding of conceptuality as learning to see "family resemblances" rather than covering up the visible with uniform and abstract notions. To follow this suggestion is to realize that "you won't see something that is common to *all*, but . . . a complicated network of similarities overlapping and criss-crossing: similarities in the large and in the small."[83] It is in just this sense that Ruskin keeps stressing the priority of what is specifically visible over intellectual abstraction or generalization.

---

there is a poetry of statement and that a religious vision can be stimulated by its 'singular veracity,' feeding on the wonder of the fact as it is, rather than transforming it into a psychological symbol" (1971, 63). See also Nichols 2016, 46–71; and, on Ruskin's impassioned, "post-picturesque" defense of Turner, Teukolsky 2009, 28–34; on Ruskin's late self-criticism of his early, exuberant style, see his 1877 notes for lectures titled "Readings in 'Modern Painters'" (*RCW* XXII, 514–15).

83. Wittgenstein 2009, 36 (#66).

Specificity (*species* or *forma*) here emerges as the core feature of knowledge; and by its very nature it belongs to the order of experience rather than inference.

Though Ruskin's output of drawings and paintings is small, some of his studies exhibit exceptional skill and precision, always enlisted in the service of distilling what is specific from the contingently particular while avoiding any slippage into empty generalization. Among his best-known and technically most accomplished studies in this regard is *Gneiss Rock, Glenfinlas* (1853) (fig. 6.2). Intended for inclusion in volume 3 of *Modern Painters* and produced while joining John Everett Millais during an outing in Perthshire (today's Stirling Council Area), Ruskin's drawing impressively conveys the laminated, slatelike texture of the steeply descending rock formation. What he later described as "an old drawing of the *Modern Painters* time" could have been finished, except that "the weather broke; and the stems in the upper righthand corner had to be rudely struck in with body-colour." Still, Ruskin was satisfied that "the mass of this rock is carefully studied with good method," the artist having been keen for "these last thirty years to do one bit of rock foreground completely, with its moss and lichen inlaying" (*RCW* XIII, 524). The attention to petrological detail is indeed almost unprecedented, with the possible exception of Dürer's 1495 sketch of a rock quarry whose unusual mixture of black chalk and watercolor had yielded similar detail of texture and structure. For his part, Ruskin in volume 4 of *Modern Painters* would devote an entire chapter to "slaty crystals" (*RCW* VI, 146–55), in which his characteristic blend of obsessive and perspicuous writing is on full display. A metamorphic rock composed of quartz, feldspar, or orthoclase, gneiss there is described "as the very type of perfect rocks." Unlike granites, which "are too far removed," and unlike the lower rocks that tend to have "the look of dried earth about them," there is in gneiss "nothing petty or limited in the display of their bulk." It stands forth and is "calculated especially to attract observation, and reward it." It is the very substance of earth triumphant, "peeping out among the hedges or forests: but from the lowest valley to the highest clouds, all is theirs—one adamantine dominion and rigid authority of rock" (*RCW* VI, 150–51). Where the beholder succeeds in grasping the distinctness and specificity of a natural form, a truth will have manifested itself. As Ruskin had already written in 1843, "It is the distinctiveness, not the universality of the truth, which renders it important." Consequently, "truths are important just in proportion as they are characteristic; and are valuable, primarily, as they separate the species from all other created things" (*RCW* III, 152).

A decade later, the point had taken, with a critic in the *Art Journal* confirming "how completely dependent all the beauties of landscape are on great geological phenomena," an insight linked specifically to the advent of photography. The reviewer goes on to note that as a result of new scientific insight into "the physical differences in rocks" it has at last become evident how "each rock gives its own peculiar charac-

Figure 6.2. John Ruskin, *Gneiss Rock, Glenfinlas*, 1853. Oxford, Ashmolean Museum of Art

ter to the landscape which it forms."[84] The attention to geological detail often found in Pre-Raphaelite painting is particularly evident in John Brett's *The Glacier of Rosenlaui* (1856) and William Dyce's *Pegwell Bay, Kent* (1858) (fig. 6.3). Francis Palgrave, principal art critic of the *Saturday Review*, was unnerved by the unwavering facticity of Dyce's painting, which appeared bereft of all "feeling for the poetry of the dying

---

84. Anonymous writer, *Art Journal* (1855): 275.

Figure 6.3. William Dyce, *Pegwell Bay, Kent*, 1858. London, Tate Gallery

day." What another critic likewise bemoaned as the painter's habit of "compil[ing] mere facts together, by dint of mere hard-staring eyes," does indeed unsettle, though less because of a lack of poetic sentiment than because Dyce's naturalism speaks a truth incompatible with, and uncontainable by, sentimental or Romantic literary convention.[85] It is less the absence of established sentiment than the emergence of a new *kind* of emotion that bewilders the mid-Victorian eye. For the same kind of dispassionate, forensic visual attention bestowed on mineralogical detail also extends to the human figures casually sampling rocks. In their haphazard and pointedly unsocial placement across the monochrome shore, human beings mirror the miscellaneous distribution of rocks and shells in this antediluvian world, tenuously hovering at the very margins separating land from the sea out of which most life-forms were thought to have emerged. Adding to this effect is the painting's quasi-photographic and documentary feel with its narrowly gauged pallet of sepia and brown tones, which subtly assimilates human existence to a mute and indifferent geological reality and leaves the amateur collectors looking flattened and forlorn in this unfathomable world of rocks and shells.[86]

---

85. Quoted in Flint 2000, 202.
86. On Dyce's painting, see Staley and Newell 2004, 188.

In reappraising the visible as an event, and visualization as an intentional act rather than as passive "recipiency" (as Coleridge had called it), Ruskin for the first time understands that the phenomenology of sight is logically anterior to, and infinitely richer than, an act of perception. For it does not confine itself to identifying and verifying previously known and seemingly inert entities but, instead, apprehends the visible world as a distinctive, specific, and wholly unique spatiotemporal event. As Aquinas had maintained long before, being is self-manifestation, or, in Thomist language, *esse* and *actus* are convertible. Specifically, this event character of the image as constituted by an undesigning, attentive, and minutely responsive seeing also shows how deeply pictorial and metaphysical realism are entwined. For where a visible aspect or image captures the beholder's attention with its incontrovertible, charismatic givenness, reality is unveiled not as an inert *object* but as a pregnant *fact*, imbued with seemingly numinous energy. No mere correlate of passive experience or detached perception, the visual encounter with being is experienced as an intrinsically significant event rather than as an empty "occurrence." Put differently, the visible for Ruskin is a gift, a richly textured and absorbing presence that positions the beholder as the addressee of an image rather than as the owner of a perception. Inasmuch as to see is, properly speaking, to witness being in its self-manifestation, pictorial realism thus reopens ontological questions that the rise of modern epistemological theories had occluded for the previous two centuries. Having rejected metaphysical realism outright, the modern accounts of the mind-world relation successively advanced by Bacon, Descartes, and Hobbes proved uninterested in, yet also incapable of, accounting for why the phenomenal world is so often experienced not as inert and uniform *res extensa* expiring in flat-line objectivity but as a richly textured presence involving the beholder and the phenomenal world in an open-ended and transformative dynamic of call and response.

In a wide-ranging essay, Lorraine Daston and Peter Galison comment on the changing culture of "objectivity" in the nineteenth century, when authors valued pictures above all because they "served the cause of incorruptibility: they would check the impulse to infuse observation with a pet theory, and endure as facts for tomorrow's researchers."[87] Yet the popular slogan "truth to nature" fueling a new phase in the understanding of scientific objectivity—for example, in medicine, geography, and biology—is premised on an anti- or, in any event, post-metaphysical ethos that may hold true, up to a point, for Lyell and Darwin, yet that seems clearly inapposite to Ruskin's aesthetic theories. As Daston and Galison note, the new scientific concept of the image as a "working object" (e.g., "atlas images, type specimens, or laboratory processes") presupposes that these "working objects are not yet concepts, much less

---

87. Daston and Galison 1992, 86.

conjectures or theories; they are the materials from which concepts are formed and to which they are applied." The main challenge, of course, was *how* properly to select and fashion such images, since any conceivable choice was bound to prejudge the nature of the object under investigation and, hence, to introduce bias into the entire research program. Insofar as "nineteenth-century objectivity aspired to the self-discipline of saints," enjoining the observer of natural phenomena to exercise maximal restraint and to "foreswear judgment, interpretation, and even the testimony of one's own senses," the initial encounter of eye and world seemed to present an insurmountable obstacle. For where (scientific) knowledge should eventuate, the event of seeing must have already taken place; and what allows a phenomenon to stand out against a background of visual miscellany and sheer "noise" of disjointed optical data is its very reality and specificity, that is, its conspicuously textured and distinctive *form*. The form of a thing must have manifested itself, as an "event," *prior* to any attempt to predicate certain "properties" of it; for absent this event (or *advent*) of form the eye could never achieve "focal awareness" (Polanyi) of a given phenomenon and, thus, seek to venture propositions about it.

Yet Ruskin's scientific contemporaries no longer operate within a realist ontology in which *ens* and *verum* are convertible and which thus invites us to respond to the visible as the event of the *logos* manifesting itself. At the same time, their post-metaphysical stance comes at a price. Thus, the "selection of 'typical', 'characteristic', 'ideal', or 'average' images" now presents modern inquiry with a seemingly insoluble methodological dilemma or, alternatively, with a temptation, namely, to decide unilaterally what objects and images shall henceforth be considered representative, a decision that naturally says far more about the hubris of Western scientific culture than about the objects themselves.[88] By contrast, Ruskin understood that the image is never a heuristic expedient or value-neutral "working object" but an event wherein truth and being become jointly and visibly manifest in the medium of the image. "Nothing can atone for want of truth," Ruskin writes (*RCW* III, 137), and where there is truth it involves nothing less than the specificity of the visible, and not just "the stamp of the real [for] eyes that have been taught the conventions (e.g., sharp outlines versus soft edges)."[89] Pictorial truth, then, is a coefficient of its composite medium (tone, color, chiaroscuro, space) and its specific object (clouds, rocks, ferns, etc.); and this holds equally true for "natural" phenomena and painting. In both cases, visualization of the phenomenon as it is "being-given" (Marion's être *donné*) is logically anterior to perception. To be sure, what the subject consciously knows of is the objective correlate of a perception rather than that of "intuition" or "apprehension," which Husserl terms *Anschauung* and *Auffassung*, respectively. Pure "eidetic

---

88. Ibid., 82–83, 85–87.
89. Ibid., 93.

intuition" falls below the threshold of conscious awareness, even as it establishes contact with the phenomenon *of* which the subject may subsequently form a (conscious) perception.

As an example, we may think of a situation where I (mis)identify a person slowly approaching me in the distance as a dear friend before realizing that it is a stranger. Yet precisely the fact that I am able to revise an initial (mis)perception by taking "a second look" confirms that perception cannot be the ultimate ground of knowledge but, instead, interprets an anterior, unconditionally given phenomenon. To revise my initial, mistaken perception in light of the progressively more distinct appearance of the person approaching me is to become aware of an elemental difference between intuition and perception. That it is possible at all for us to revise our perceptions confirms that, logically speaking, we have not properly seen at all until and unless we have allowed the phenomenon to register in intuition unfiltered by any perception, conception, or naming—that is, simply *in the way that it visibly gives itself*. "Our perceptions, our judgments, our whole knowledge of the world can be changed, crossed out, Husserl says, but not nullified." Rather, they will be supplanted by "other perceptions, other judgments more true, *because we are within being and because there is something*."[90] The negation of a specific perception, far from nullifying the phenomenon that it was meant to elucidate, only attests to the superior fecundity of the phenomenon itself, that is, to the unique event character of the visible and intuition.

As Jean-Luc Marion notes, "event" here needs to be understood as that which "*precedes its cause* (or its causes)," and which consequently cannot be assimilated to a deterministic matrix of cause and effect. Thus, the event of the visible, its sheer unadulterated phenomenality, unveils "the temporal privilege of the effect." It shows that, in the order of cognition, "all knowledge begins by the event of the effect," that is, some distinctive and specific manifestation that irresistibly arrests our gaze and demands our visual attention and participation. Quoting Charles Péguy on his generation's event par excellence, the Great War ("one feels that one is in the midst of the event itself and its aging. / Nothing any longer pretties up and disguises its aging"), Marion offers a characterization of the event whose phenomenology also, and not coincidentally, accounts for the enduring appeal of pictorial realism: "The event, looked at in the eye of its storm, arises and accomplishes itself when nothing more comes to pass—nothing identifiable by or identifiable with one or several causes . . . when the thing itself, after the fashion of an avalanche[,] . . . collapses by *itself*, puts *itself* into motion, decides for itself and by itself, without cause or reason."[91]

Slumbering within the realist conception of the image as the "emancipation of the event from cause" is a potentially traumatic force that, half a century later, would

---

90. Merleau-Ponty 1968, 128; emphasis mine.
91. Marion 2002a, 165, 168, 170, 171.

shape the jarring imagism of high modernist writing in the wake of the Great War such as we find in Woolf, Musil, Kafka, and David Jones. Marion's reference to Péguy chimes with the artist-writer David Jones's *In Parenthesis* (1937), where "the tedious flow" of soldiers eating, tending to their equipment, and officers dispensing routine orders is brutally eclipsed by an incoming artillery strike,

> some approaching violence—registered not by the ear nor any single faculty— an on-rushing pervasion, saturating all existence. . . . Out of the vortex, rifling the air it came—bright, brass-shod, Pandoran; with all-filling screaming the howling crescendo's up-piling snapt. The universal world, breath held, one half second, a bludgeoned stillness. Then the pent violence released a consummation of all burstings-out; all sudden up-rendings and rivings-through—all taking-out of vents—all barrier-breaking—all unmaking, Pernitric begetting—the dissolving and splitting of solid things.[92]

The event here is one of total, unfathomable rupture, mercilessly "up-rending" the visible and familiar order of things, for which reason Jones's language revolves around the sense of hearing, not sight. Put differently, what accounts for the event character of sensory "apprehension"—taking that term in its double sense of sensory uptake and elemental dread—is the consummation of the image, the "barrier-breaking" when visibility is eclipsed by an imageless reality, which the order of visible things can only ever intimate but never definitively embody. Built around gerund forms that conjure an aura of overwhelming force unattributable to any known subject or source, Jones's language consummates a development already under way in Turner's late style and made explicit by Ruskin. It is the shift from a conception of mimesis pledged to replicating stable, visible objects to one concerned with the event of visibility as such, a shift that ultimately results in the realist image's self-consummation.[93] Paradoxically, the "event" is simultaneously over- and underdetermined, for which reason it cannot be assimilated to the domain of the concept. It is marked by an "excess" whereby our visual experience of a "saturated phenomenon"— Marion's term of art, notably echoed by Jones's shell strike, "saturating all existence"— becomes a witnessing of what is essentially nonrepeatable, unique, and intelligible only *per analogiam*. Hence, Marion argues, the event unveils a wholly transcendent

---

92. Jones 2003, 24.

93. It hardly needs to be pointed out how closely entwined this emergent understanding of the image as "event" is with modern trauma theory, first pioneered in Freud's *Beyond the Pleasure Principle* (1920) and, further, in *Moses and Monotheism* (1938); on the Romantic origins of trauma theory, see Pfau 2005a, 191–306; for competing psychoanalytic and clinical models of traumatic experience, see Caruth 1996, 11–25; and for a discussion of shell shock and traumatic memory, Leys 2000, 83–119.

"possibility," one whose truth cannot be causally derived from antecedent factors, which is to say, a "possibility" in the nondeterministic sense of a phenomenon visibly accomplishing itself in ways both unprecedented and unforeseeable. Where we speak of an event, "possibility is first exercised not in relation to an essence in order to foresee an actuality, but, in an exactly inverse sense, by *an ascent toward form* that delivers an unpredictable landing and provokes a fait accompli, in the end freeing the incident 'outside essence.'"[94]

In passing, it is instructive to juxtapose Marion's account of the visible as event to Darwin's and Lyell's inductive approach to natural phenomena discussed above. When looking at forms at once unfamiliar and distinctive, unique and specific, Darwin found himself repeatedly musing on precisely this oblique event character of the natural world. At first glance, the tranquillity of life on Darwin's "tangled bank" would seem to belie the magnitude of transformations wrought over millions of years; and yet it is precisely by attending to the myriad visible forms of life that those transformations begin to reveal themselves. With their consistent stress on the uniformitarian nature of organic life and its inherent tendency to remain in a state of equilibrium, Lyell and Darwin seem intent on draining biological and inanimate reality of all possibility—that is, the possibility of things being otherwise than they are. At first blush, then, natural selection leaves no conceptual space for what is called the event, that is, for the conspicuous, unprecedented, and/or unpredictable alteration of a prevailing state. Thus, embracing speciation as an event and rupture would have meant relapsing either into the original event of Creation (as in Paley's argument from design), which by the 1850s still commanded strong allegiance in mainstream Anglo-Protestant circles, or into a "catastrophist" account of massive geological upheaval (such as Georges Cuvier had advanced). At the same time, Darwin also found Lamarckian transmutation wanting, mainly because of its failure to produce tangible evidence and a causal warrant for how various species should have come to be or persist in being into the present. Darwin's theory of natural selection, then, seeks to attenuate the event character of speciation by diffusing it into an algorithm composed of "chance variation," sexual selection, heredity, and ecological contingency. On the other hand, each of these factors, when considered in isolation, may well be understood as an "event" in the way Marion conceives of it. Hence, the appeal of Darwin's theory, its scientific respectability, is ensured only if none of these factors, *taken by themselves*, are ever invested with decisive causal force. Instead, all of them must be understood as being in perpetual, joint, and oblique operation; and only on that condition can they be credited with having brought about the diversity of species and their continual transformation and redistribution. For Darwin, as for Lyell, it is a "uniformitarian" model of time that "explains" or, rather, masks the *event* of

---

94. Marion 2002a, 170–73; last emphasis mine.

speciation by redescribing and attenuating it as an inconspicuous, if also implacable, *process* known as natural selection.

A similar dialectic of the event as the moment where a visible scene throws into relief unfathomably complex transformations, and in so doing reveals the image's inherent drift toward transcending the bounds of sheer visibility, also informs Turner's mature, "inveterately didactic" style of the 1830s.[95] If Ruskin's emblematic style in *Modern Painters I* seeks to emulate the immediacy of the visual, Turner's late style appears to pursue the inverse, though equally catechetical, objective: to conduct in his paintings an "interrogation about how visual imagery conveys meaning and how a viewer comprehends the art of painting . . . [whose] ultimate and encompassing aim . . . was to teach the viewer *how* to look into paintings (and not just at them) in order to understand the significance of art as a form of communication."[96] Pervading these pioneering works, which furnished the central inspiration for Ruskin's *Modern Painters I*, was Turner's experimentation with luminous orange-yellow sunsets and fine chromatic transitions, such as we find in *The Burning of the House of Lords and Commons* (1834) (fig. 6.4) and his Claude Lorrain–inspired *Regulus* (1837). In particular, the first of two canvases depicting the fire in Parliament looks ahead to Turner's increasingly abstract use of color in *The Slave Ship* (1840) and "*Light and Color (Goethe's Theory)—the Morning after the Deluge—Moses Writing the Book of Genesis.*" The latter painting, known to have been inspired by Goethe's *Theory of Colors* (1810; first translated into English in 1840), startles with its total protomodernist subordination of mimetic convention to colorist effect.

Meanwhile, Turner's dramatic rendition of the 16 October fire in Parliament captures a sensational event widely felt to befit a superannuated political system unresponsive to the changing demographic, industrial, and social realities of post-Napoleonic Britain. In the wake of the first Reform Act of 1832, whose modernizing effects were gradually beginning to register across the country, the year 1834 had begun with Robert Owen founding the Consolidated Trades Union, followed by the formal abolition of slavery across most of the British Empire and the launching of the navy's first steam-powered warship. The biggest such conflagration since the great London fire of 1666, the burning of Parliament was immediately found to hold symbolic significance. To many, Guy Fawkes's wish for a "Parliament full, free and frequent" and the expurgation of "old corruption" seemed to have come true at last, a perception acknowledged obliquely by Turner's decision to incorporate large, indistinct crowds of onlookers both in the foreground and cramming the flanking structure of Westminster Bridge. Mirroring the beholder of the painting itself, the

95. Wettlaufer 1994, 210.
96. Kathleen Nicholson, quoted in Wettlaufer 1994, 209–10.

Figure 6.4. Joseph William Mallord Turner, *The Burning of the House of Lords and Commons,* 1834. Philadelphia Museum of Art

indistinct mass of spectators in the foreground adds a three-dimensional quality to the painting while also enhancing its overall dramatic effect. Here, then, Turner's stunning exploration of light and color—enhanced by his experimentation with megilp, a fast-drying oil mixture appreciated for its superior transparency and luminous, glossy effects—allows the painting to reinforce the widely felt significance of its subject matter.

No such sensationalism, however, informs the historical and pictorial event of Turner's *Fighting Téméraire Tugged to Her Last Berth to Be Broken Up, 1838,* first exhibited in spring 1839 (fig. 6.5). Subtly balancing mimetic and abstract elements, the scene of an old line ship of Trafalgar fame being towed away by a steam-powered tugboat presented itself in ready-to-paint fashion to Turner, who just then happened to be returning from a trip to Margate. Another artist, W. F. Woodington, sculptor of the reliefs at the base of Nelson's column in Trafalgar Square, also witnessed the scene and noted Turner rapidly sketching it in anticipation of the eventual painting, "ready, as it were, for the easel: a historical fact in an observed natural setting."[97]

97. Wilton 1987, 202.

Figure 6.5. Joseph William Mallord Turner, *The Fighting Téméraire Tugged to Her Last Berth to Be Broken Up*, 1838. London, National Gallery

Completed and exhibited at the Royal Academy of the Arts in May 1839, the sizable canvas (35 x 47 inches) drew widespread praise at a time when Turner's eccentric personality and artistic direction had begun to vex and unsettle critics and viewers alike. For once, there were none of the hostile reactions that three years earlier had prompted the young Ruskin's vehement defense of Turner against seemingly obtuse and openly hostile Tory establishment critics. Writing for *Fraser's Magazine*, W. M. Thackeray raved about Turner's singular achievement as a colorist in *The Fighting Téméraire*: "When the art of translating colours into music or poetry shall be discovered, [this painting] will be found to be a magnificent ode or piece of music."[98] Though verging on the grandiose, Thackeray's praise astutely notes the painted image's gravitational pull toward another medium wherein the event character of Turner's unique fusion of light and color may be reconstituted. Also among those mesmerized by the five new Turner paintings at the Royal Academy's spring 1839 exhibition was the twenty-year-old John Ruskin, who took up Thackeray's challenge of discovering the "art of translating colours," a phrase that happens to capture the

---

98. Quoted in Wilton 1987, 207.

central intent of *Modern Painters I* uncommonly well. As Ruskin would later argue, meeting that challenge was also a way of defending the aura of the individual artwork and sheltering the emotional integrity of the viewer's response from being diluted by the crowded and commercialized setting of the modern gallery, which had become the default venue for the encounter with images.[99]

In the event, Turner's extraordinary gifts as a colorist and a master of chiaroscuro effects, as well as his ability to show how color and light shape our visual apprehension of texture (of clouds, water, steam, wood, metal, cloth, etc.), made *The Fighting Téméraire* a particularly rewarding subject for Ruskin. Exemplary of Ruskin's attempt at "translating" the encounter with Turner's quintessential modernity into luminous prose aimed at drawing out the truth value of such visual experience is his long chapter, "The Truth of Colour." From the outset, Ruskin is intent on sidelining the affective categories so central to much Romantic art criticism: "I am not talking about what is sublime, but about what is true. . . . My business is to match colours, not to talk sentiment." While Ruskin's ultimate criterion of "truth" remains elusive, this much is certain: truth does not allow for any substitution; it cannot be "represented" by any individual perception or particular object but, instead, is itself the metaphysical condition allowing visible things to be experienced as distinctive, specific, and significant phenomena in the first place. Put differently, for Ruskin truth is never something constructed but only ever something revealed; and as such it is wholly incommensurable with artifice. It is not a correlate of finite "making" (*facere*) but, instead, manifests an anterior, transcendent "creating" (*creare*). An intrinsic property of being that can never be secured in propositional form, truth is attainable only qua participation: "Truth is only to be measured by close comparison of actual facts; we may talk for ever about it in generals, and prove nothing. We cannot tell what effect falsehood may produce on this or that person, but we can very well tell what is false and what is not" (*RCW* III, 283). Ruskin's unflagging commitment to exposing painted falsehood is an indispensable preparatory step toward retrieving the image, stripping away as it does aesthetic conventions and accumulated bad habits of seeing, much as the restoration of old masterworks seeks to expunge accumulated grime and the incompetent touch-up work of past ages.

As for the scene that Turner witnessed in 1838, its symbolic significance was palpable: the old order of wood and wind power nudged into oblivion by the new era of coal, steel, and steam; the maritime heroism of Trafalgar supplanted by the feats

---

99. On the growing divide between the aura of the painted image and its commercialized setting, see Siegel 2000, 167–89. In his July 1857 lecture, "The Political Economy of Art," Ruskin thus mused on "the subtle balance which your economist has to strike: to accumulate as much art as to be able to give the whole nation a supply of it, according to its need, and yet to regulate its distribution so that there shall be no glut of it, nor contempt" (*RCW* XVI, 60–61).

of modern engineering; the forces of nature no longer harnessed but, in the form of fossil fuels and iron ore, consumed, and so forth. Yet in Turner's *Fighting Téméraire* this epochal shift of the sun setting on the old heroic order unfolds against the backdrop of an abundantly textured and chromatically rich evening sky. It is this symbolic timing that infuses an otherwise mundane fact (one ship being towed by another) with iconic significance. In drawing the beholder's attention to the symbolic power of light and color, Turner's image suggests that, however momentous it may otherwise appear, man-made, linear history will remain ever circumscribed by the imperturbable rhythms and cycles of natural time. Indeed, were it not for its poignant timing at sunset, the event so luminously captured by Turner would never have registered at all but, instead, would have been absorbed by the banal order of the merely factual and, thus, faded into instant oblivion. This is not to say, however, that the scene's symbolic significance is not something artificially constructed. Rather, it is the condition absent which an otherwise factual occurrence could never have been intuited as a significant event to begin with. Put differently, the scene could never have been produced as a *painting* if it had not first revealed itself as an *image*; and what allows, indeed compels, Turner to visualize the trivially factual as a symbolic event is, above all, the drama of color and light that made the original scene so conspicuously visible. An avid reader of Plato (a matter to be considered shortly), Turner would undoubtedly have concurred with Socrates's claim that "vision could certainly never see anything that has no color."[100]

Though always subordinate to light and shade, color is a basic phenomenological constituent of the visual. Its operation is logically anterior both to any mimetic intention on the painter's part and to any potential identification of what Husserl calls the "image-object" (*Bildgegenstand*) on the beholder's part. Likewise, Ruskin premises from the outset that the plenitude of nature's hues and shades cannot be represented or simulated by any art ("no gorgeousness of the pallet," Turner's included, "can even reach . . . the ordinary effects of daylight"). Hence, as the following rapturous passage makes clear, the order of natural phenomena must be understood as the *source*, not the object, of the artist's mimetic aspirations.

> But it is a widely different thing when nature herself takes a colouring fit, and does something extraordinary, something really to exhibit her power. She has a thousand ways and means of rising above herself, but incomparably the noblest manifestations of her capability of colour are in these sunsets among the

---

100. Plato 1997, 655 (*Charmides* 168e). While the claim may seem perplexing to modern readers accustomed to black and white photography or pencil drawings, it is fundamentally valid. For in such media, color is positively *withheld* from the thing pictorialized, at least in cases of representational art.

high clouds. I speak especially of the moment before the sun sinks, when his light turns pure rose-colour, and when this light falls upon a zenith covered with countless cloud-forms of inconceivable delicacy, threads and flakes of vapour, which would in common daylight be pure snowwhite, and which give therefore fair field to the tone of light. There is then no limit to the multitude, and no check to the intensity, of the hues assumed. The whole sky from the zenith to the horizon becomes one molten mantling sea of colour and fire; every black bar turns into massy gold, every ripple and wave into unsullied shadowless crimson, and purple, and scarlet, and colours for which there are no words in language, and no ideas in the mind, things which can only be conceived while they are visible; the intense hollow blue of the upper sky melting through it all, showing here deep, and pure, and lightless; there, modulated by the filmy formless body of the transparent vapour, till it is lost imperceptibly in its crimson and gold. (*RCW* III, 285–86)

Characteristic of the rapturous tone so often encountered in *Modern Painters I*, the above passage fuses the visionary with the catechetical. The prose, that is, seeks to guide the Victorian eye to richer, more immersive habits of visualization. At the same time, Ruskin's prose style nudges the reader toward the realization that what causes visual phenomena to be experienced as so profoundly saturated and absorbing is that they mediate essentially *invisible* meanings. Undergirding the distinctive prose style of *Modern Painters I* is what W. J. T. Mitchell calls the "ekphrastic hope" of closing the gap between the discursive and the intuitive, notional and real assent, the temporality of the word and the spatiality of the image—a gap that in the wake of Lessing's *Laokoön* was widely considered to be unbridgeable. The goal of ekphrastic hope, Mitchell notes, is "the overcoming of otherness, . . . of achieving vision, iconicity, or a 'still moment' of plastic presence through language." For Ruskin, ekphrasis is the structural principle fueling the production of an altogether new kind of prose. Far from an occasional performative feat on the order of Homer's "Shield of Achilles" or Shelley's "On the Medusa of Leonardo da Vinci," Ruskin's prose turns Horace's *ut pictura poiesis* into a structural principle that shows ekphrasis to be "paradigmatic of a fundamental tendency in all linguistic expression." Yet that tendency is not simply to attain to the same degree of vividness and conspicuous visibility as painting or, for that matter, photography. Rather, the true telos of "ekphrastic hope" is to realize the ultimate intention, the "image-subject" (*Bildsujet*), as Husserl calls it, that the visible image can only *point toward* but never actually attain.[101] Ekphrastic hope seeks to make manifest in the medium of the word a fullness of meaning that can be

---

101. Mitchell 1994, 156.

mediated only by the objectively visible image, yet which, being a case of mediation, can never be adequately realized within the order of the visible. Ekphrasis, that is, aims to liberate the plenitude of iconic vision, first adumbrated by the visible image, from the medial constraints of sheer visibility.

More than anything, Ruskin's ekphrastic prose aims to reconstitute what Husserl will later call the "absolute givenness" (*absolute Gegebenheit*) of the phenomenon as a superabundant reality. The revolution that Ruskin brings about in art criticism stems above all from his uncompromising shift away from the objects of painting and questions of pictorial verisimilitude and toward the act and experience of seeing itself. The true genius of Turner's mature style, Ruskin insists, lies in the way it prompts the adult mid-Victorian eye—so cultured, educated, and steeped in aesthetic and social convention—to remember the primal drama and meaning of visual experience, which consists not in identifying particular objects but in participating in their creative self-manifestation. A visible instance of grace, the painted image ultimately operates on a metaphysical rather than representational plateau. For it unveils the real in all its dynamic, abundant givenness from the superficies of man-made conventions, notions, and disembodied certainties. "How seldom," Ruskin muses, do "people think of looking for a sunset at all, and how seldom, if they do, they are in a position from which it can be fully seen, the chances that their attention should be awake, and their position favourable" (*RCW* III, 286).

The mimetic function of painting, its realism, is inseparably entwined with the image's ontological status as a medium. Echoing arguments first advanced by the Byzantine iconodules a millennium earlier, Ruskin understands that an image is constituted by its ontological difference from the reality it mediates. Speaking of Turner's astonishing gift for evoking the chromatic spectrum of the sky, and by extension of spatial distance and gradually dissolving textures, Ruskin concedes "that wherever in brilliant effects of this kind, we approach to anything like a true statement of nature's colour, there must yet be a distinct difference in the impression we convey, because we cannot approach her light" (*RCW* III, 289). What painting ought to recall for us is the ontological divide separating numinous reality and the still overwhelming phenomenology of its experience, however partial and incomplete.

> All such hues are usually given by her with an accompanying intensity of sunbeams which dazzles and overpowers the eye, so that it cannot rest on the actual colour, nor understand what they are; and hence in art, in rendering all effects of this kind, there must be a want of the ideas of imitation, which are the great source of enjoyment to the ordinary observer; because we can only give one series of truths, those of colour, and are unable to give the accompanying truths of light; so that the more true we are in colour, the greater, ordinarily, will be the

discrepancy felt between the intensity of hue and the feebleness of light. (*RCW* III, 289)

Ruskin's "all-consuming desire to make his readers *see*" and his lifelong "program of perceptual and cultural reform" have often been remarked on.[102] Yet an often-overlooked feature of his aesthetic catechesis of the Victorian eye concerns the epistemic and moral humility said to inform aesthetic production and response. Paradoxically, that is, Turner's superiority as a colorist revolves not only around "the dazzling intensity . . . of light which he sheds through every hue" but also his realization that such "vividness of pure colour" must be used "only where nature uses it, and in less degree" (*RCW* III, 291). Hence, rather than seeking to reconstitute a specific historical scene, the spectacular chromaticism of Turner's sunset and the subtle dramaturgy of ambient colors focuses the beholder's gaze on the primal event of visibility. The painted image is not so much proffered as the material simulacrum of a particular event but, instead, subtly condenses the irreversible flow of historical time into symbolic form.

In an early fragment from 1914, already alluded to earlier, Walter Benjamin remarks on color's elemental freedom from all lexical convention and referential constraint: "color absorbs into itself by imparting[,] . . . surrendering itself" and submerging the eye in the primal event of appearance, of the visible as incontrovertibly real. A case of pure manifestation, color exists on a different ontological plateau from concrete (ontic) being; it is neither something particular nor something notional, neither a singularity nor an abstraction. Hence, Benjamin muses, "where color provides the contours, objects are not reduced to things but are constituted by an order consisting of an infinite range of nuances." It is this primal quality of color that prompts Benjamin to link the experience of color to the unfettered visual imagination of young children, who as yet inhabit a paradisiacal state unconcerned with reified, objective, and named entities. Color, he goes on to remark, "lacks multiplicity, because it is undefined and exists only in perception." As he puts it in another fragment of the same year, "color is single, not as a lifeless thing and a rigid individuality but as a winged creature that flits from one form to the next." The paradox of

---

102. Helsinger 1982, 5; Wettlaufer 1994, 212; as Helsinger notes, inasmuch as for Ruskin "seeing is a temporal and often a linguistic activity . . . his verbal art teaches perceptual skills" ultimately geared "to combine seeing with reading" (1982, 3); likewise, Ball remarks on "Ruskin's exaltation of fact and the capacity to see it" and on his concern with training the eye to "learn [the object's] organization" and, in so doing, "recognizing the comprehensiveness of its self-expression" (1971, 69). Several of Ruskin's letters (reprinted in *RCW* III, 665–71) show him to have been quite conscious and deliberate in formulating the project of *Modern Painters I* as one of aesthetic-cum-religious catechesis.

color inheres in the fact that its phenomenology (the quality of its experience) is incontrovertible and real even as it cannot be assimilated to any preexisting conceptual grid. Benjamin's speculative musing that "color is something spiritual, something whose clarity is spiritual," echoes a point altogether central to *Modern Painters I*: namely, that in color the per se invisible presence of light, itself the transcendent source of all visibility, manifests itself as an event;[103] and it is this capacity of color to render manifest the metaphysical underpinnings of pictorial truth that prompts Ruskin's profound, albeit often obsessive, discussion of color in Turner's mature oeuvre.

So as to gauge the wider significance of Ruskin's account of color and tone as the very sources of truth, at the level of both visualization and artistic representation, let us recall the obverse case of Kant's *Critique of Judgment* (1790). For Kant, color (and, likewise, sound) can never furnish the "determining ground" of aesthetic-reflective judgment simply because of its infinitely textured and chromatically nuanced material constitution. Instead, "mere color" must be consigned to the realm of "simple sensation" (*lediglich Empfindung*), and it has "a *right* to be regarded as beautiful only in so far as [it is] *pure*." Given Kant's formalist concept of aesthetic value, the sensation of color and sound inevitably fails the key test, namely, to further "with certainty" (*mit Gewißheit*) his philosophical goal of "universal communicability" (*allgemeine Mitteilbarkeit*). Drawing on the writings of the mathematician Leonhard Euler (1707–83), Kant briefly entertains the possibility of mind perceiving the hypostatized, "isochronous vibrations" that make up color not only "by sense," but also "perceiving by reflection the regular play of impressions." If it were possible to demonstrate the strictest mathematical lawfulness to be operative within matter itself ("which," Kant hastens to add, "I very much doubt"), then indeed color and sound could be credited with holding cognitive value. Yet given Kant's twin conditions—first, that materiality is essentially contingent and irregular; and second, that aesthetic judgment must categorically eschew all material contingency—sensation can never be the source of but only ever an obstacle to cognition. For, as Kant rightly posits, sensation is irreducibly complex, textured, and, as such, unlikely to be contained by "pure" concepts of any kind. Hence his definition of a "pure sensation" (*reine Empfindung*) is cast in terms such as could never be met by any actual sensation: "'pure' in a simple mode of sensation means that its uniformity [*Gleichförmigkeit*] is troubled and interrupted by no foreign sensation."[104]

---

103. Benjamin 1996, 48, 50; see also the discussion of Plotinus on light and color above, ch. 1, 108–11.

104. Kant 1951, 59–60 (§ 14); conceivably, the straight lines, rigid geometry, and flat, uniform colors of Canaletto—Ruskin's bête noire—had they ever made it to Königsberg, would have met with Kant's approval.

Kant's chimera of "pure sensation" also explains the recurrent slippage, found throughout his "Analytic of the Beautiful," from the visible "line" (or "outline") to a strictly notional realm of "form."[105] What, then, animates his utopian quest for a kind of sensation purged of all contingency, and for an ideal "form" (*Form*) seamlessly instantiated by "appearance" without any admixture of "semblance"? In Hegelian terms, what accounts for philosophy's persistent dream of *Erscheinung* without *Schein*, that is, of achieving knowledge at once "absolute" yet immanent, conceptually autonomous yet supposedly "absolved" of all transcendent presuppositions? It is modern philosophy's untiring quest for total conceptual self-sufficiency, which is to say, for a strictly anthropomorphic lifeworld that everywhere and at all times exhibits only the determinative imprimatur of *homo faber*. And yet, Kant's considered study of eighteenth-century empiricism and materialism runs too deep for him ever to lose sight of the fact that any quest for "pure" knowledge already presupposes a realm of contingent appearances and experiences whose anterior givenness rational inquiry now seeks to resolve into "lawful" representations and concepts. Kant's *fort-da* game with material sensation, then, is not a momentary blunder in an otherwise tidy logical demonstration. Rather, his preoccupation with those "sensations" that most resist the Enlightenment's immanent conception of "pure" knowledge exposes the dialectical nature of his entire philosophical project. For to know the world, on Kant's account, not only requires quarantining and overcoming its initial manifestation in contingent sense perception; it also entails having to live with the fear that this very project will remain forever incomplete and, indeed, may collapse at any point as a result of its incompletion. The latter point, first flagged by Schopenhauer and subsequently elaborated by Nietzsche as "the blight that lies dormant in the womb of theoretical culture" and the unwarranted "optimism lurking within the essence of logic" was eventually writ large by Heidegger and, in a different key, by Adorno and Horkheimer.[106]

What animates and so relentlessly impels Kant to suspend the world's sheer givenness, to devalue its nature as manifestation and "appearance" (*Erscheinung*), and, ultimately, to exclude from nature, as it were *per definitionem*, whatever cannot be assimilated to a conceptual grid of man's own devising is modernity's most elemental fear: that reason (*logos*) should turn out to be, and ever has been, a transcendent gift rather than an immanent tool, a grace received and participated in rather than an instrument employed in purely pragmatic and adventitious fashion. Steeped

---

105. For a fuller discussion of Kantian aesthetics in relation to image theory, see Pfau 2021.

106. See Schopenhauer's critique of causality, conceptualism, and representation in *The World as Will and Representation* ([1818] 1969, 112–39 [§§ 23–26]); Nietzsche resumes and extends this critique in his *Birth of Tragedy* (1872 [quote from Nietzsche 1993, 87]); see also Heidegger's *Metaphysical Foundations of Logic* (1928); Adorno and Horkheimer 1972, 43–80.

in a Calvinist environment of strictness similar to the Pietist culture from which for much of his life Kant sought to extricate himself, Ruskin takes a nearly obverse view. Visible and richly textured forms inspire "awe," not fear, and they are beautiful because their very being is essentially convertible with truth—understood as something experientially revealed rather than claimed in propositional form. The ultimate goal of visual culture is to participate in the visible as the symbolic conduit to a numinous truth rather than to bring it under the dominion of conceptual schemes of strictly anthropomorphic provenance. As Ruskin was to put it in the final volume of *The Stones of Venice* (1853), the visible image is always "pro-visional," which is to say, constitutes an ephemeral manifestation whose full import can never be adequately realized in the domain of visible things. For its true significance resides in its symbolic powers of intimation rather than syllogistic demonstration.

> For even if the symbolic vision itself be not terrible, the scene of what may be veiled behind it becomes all the more awful in proportion to the insignificance or strangeness of the sign itself; and, I believe, this thrill of mingled doubt, fear, and curiosity lies at the very root of the delight which mankind take in symbolism. It was not an accidental necessity for the conveyance of truth by pictures instead of words, which led to its universal adoption wherever art was on the advance; but the Divine fear which necessarily follows on the understanding that a thing is other and greater than it seems; and which, it appears probable, has been rendered peculiarly attractive to the human heart, because God would have us understand that this is true not of invented symbols merely, but of all things amidst which we live; that there is a deeper meaning within them than eye hath seen, or ear hath heard; and that the whole visible creation is a mere perishable symbol of things eternal and true. (*RCW* XI, 182–83)

What in *Modern Painters I* is but the germ of an intuition has, a decade later, evolved into an essentially metaphysical position. At this point, Ruskin—who "belongs with the great tradition of Western metaphysical realism"—posits, first, that being necessarily transcends its phenomenalization and, second, that being finds its most adequate manifestation in visible forms which, unlike man-made concepts, acknowledge the excess of being over its partial and imperfect manifestation ("a thing is other and greater than it seems").[107] Considering Ruskin's deep immersion in Scottish Presbyterianism and its unflinchingly literal approach to scriptural interpretation, it cannot surprise that metaphysical and speculative inquiry should by and large have felt alien to him. Even so, his core insight into the relation between the visible and the invisible, arising from a decade-long empirical study of painting's for-

---

107. Nichols 2016, 52.

mal and material particularity, is fundamentally of a piece with classical metaphysics and speculative theology. By conceiving the entire realm of visible things as essentially a realm of mediation, that is, of *figura* (*typos*), Ruskin also shows himself to have moved away from his Calvinist beginnings and to have embraced a far more nuanced, metaphysically informed hermeneutic of creation. Thus, to the extent that things have reality, their very visibility points toward the invisible source that imbues them with the specificity of *form*, which in turn is the ground of their potential intelligibility and, concurrently, positions visible being in a relation of analogy to the divine *logos* itself. As Ruskin puts it, "The whole visible creation is a mere perishable symbol of things eternal and true" (*RCW* 11, 183). That is, there "must be a true and real connection between that abstract idea and the features of nature as she was and is" (*RCW* III, 26). It is this metaphysical realism undergirding Ruskin's aesthetic that now stands to be considered in more detail.

THE TRUTH *IN* AND *BEYOND* THE IMAGE: THE METAPHYSICAL FOUNDATIONS OF RUSKIN'S AESTHETICS

Ruskin's early conception of pictorial realism has two distinct, albeit related, focal points: first, the material nature of the medium (color, tone, light, chiaroscuro, etc.); and, second, how proper handling of the medium enables art to capture the specific character of the object and, thus, unveil its truth-value. Still, at this early point in his career, Ruskin vacillates as to the proper locus or source of pictorial truth. At times, *Modern Painters I* hews close to a narrowly mimetic, quasi-photorealist concept of the image. On this view, the truth of painting inheres exclusively in painting's mimetic fidelity to what is manifestly visible rather than to a subject idea (Husserl's image-*sujet*) that the painting itself—understood as medium rather than object—seeks to make manifest in its own right. Where this line of argument prevails, the young Ruskin will often appear oddly inattentive to the symbolic dimension of painting. His obsessive tabulation of formal and material choices that, in his view, render earlier landscape art (e.g., that of Claude, Poussin, or Salvatore Rosa) decidedly inferior to Turner's all but ignores the symbolic dimension of the art image, that is, its underlying concern with what Husserl will later term the "truth of disclosure," in contradistinction to a narrowly mimetic "truth of correctness."[108]

---

108. Wettlaufer's claim that, already for the young Ruskin, "painting and poetry have identical ends, while the means—images or words—are merely vehicles to be exploited and ultimately transcended" seems to overstate her case; and to speak of Ruskin's "continuing efforts to discount the material sign in favor of its symbolic import" (1994, 213) disregards a great deal of writing in *Modern Painters I*, a work preoccupied like no other with the formal and material particulars of the painted image.

This is not the place to trace the evolution of *Modern Painters* and Ruskin's later style, which as early as 1846 appears to have shed much of its late Romantic exuberance and, already in *Modern Painters II*, aspires to a tone of "high moral authority," somewhat in the manner of Richard Hooker. Novel in this regard is Ruskin's anti-utilitarian program of a "theocentric humanism" that views all of art, not just its religious forms, as "constitut[ing] a high moral and spiritual endeavor."[109] Let us instead consider a long paragraph from the "Conclusion" to volume 1 of Ruskin's *Modern Painters* (1843), which illustrates both the affinity of Ruskin's early aesthetics with the rise of inductive science and his growing awareness of the intricate link between visualization and cognition. At the same time, this summation also reveals Ruskin's fundamentally different take on the ultimate goal of visual culture—namely, to achieve an experiential rather than inferential relation with truth that far surpasses his scientific contemporaries' aspiration toward conceptual and methodological correctness.

> From young artists nothing ought to be tolerated but simple *bonâ fide imitation* of nature. They have no business to ape the execution of masters; to utter weak and disjointed repetitions of other men's words, and mimic the gestures of the preacher, without understanding his meaning or sharing in his emotions. We do not want their crude ideas of composition, their unformed conceptions of the Beautiful, their unsystematized experiments upon the Sublime. We scorn their velocity; for it is without direction: we reject their decision; for it is without grounds: we contemn their composition; for it is without materials: we reprobate their choice; for it is without comparison. Their duty is neither to choose, nor compose, nor imagine, nor experimentalize; but to be humble and earnest in following the steps of nature, and tracing the finger of God. Nothing is so bad a symptom, in the work of young artists, as too much dexterity of handling; for it is a sign that they are satisfied with their work, and have tried to do nothing more than they were able to do. Their work should be full of failures; for these are the signs of efforts. They should keep to quiet colours, greys and browns; and, making the early works of Turner their example, as his latest are to be their object of emulation, should go to Nature in all singleness of heart, and walk with her laboriously and trustingly, having no other thoughts but how best to penetrate her meaning, and remember her instruction; rejecting nothing, selecting nothing, and scorning nothing; believing all things to be right and good, and rejoicing always in the truth. (*RCW* III, 623–24)

---

109. Nichols 2016, 77–78.

Particularly striking about this passage is its curious blend of Romantic and anti-Romantic topoi. Echoing the Romantics' concern with spontaneity, Ruskin rejects any lingering affiliation art may yet have with self-conscious rhetoric and artifice ("too much dexterity of handling") and with a neoclassical concept of imitation ("weak and disjointed repetitions of other men's words"). Likewise, his injunction that the artist "should go to Nature in all singleness of heart" has a distinctly Wordsworthian ring to it. Yet at the same time, Ruskin discourages premature flights of originality and, instead, urges young artists to make Turner's early works "their object of emulation." While it remains unclear whether such discipleship is truly compatible with "tracing the finger of God" in nature herself, Ruskin certainly discourages Romanticism's more abstract and speculative tendencies, which in his view jeopardize the principal requirement of all art—namely, to trace the organization and composition of the visible world "laboriously and trustingly, . . . rejecting nothing, selecting nothing, and scorning nothing."

Just how are we to understand Ruskin's much-quoted closing injunction? To answer the question is to discover what the somewhat contradictory prescriptions in the above passage already suggest: namely, that pictorial realism of the kind Ruskin is urging cannot be realized in the exclusively immanent terms in which it is here advanced. As should be clear by now, metaphysical implications do not melt away simply because a realist aesthetic and its underlying naturalistic axioms would have them do so. In fact, the very quest for a purely immanent conception of knowledge and aesthetic form is liable to remain tinged by precisely those transcendent implications that it would disavow. Their insistence within an immanent, realist aesthetic, however, is not merely a function of pictorial realism inadvertently and dialectically retaining a transcendent (symbolic) dimension precisely by its efforts to negate them. Rather, the transcendent implications of the (realist) image actually constitute an integral, ontological feature of all human cognition and representation. To the question, "Can the image and aesthetic form generally be conceived in strictly immanent terms?," the answer has to be an unequivocal "No." Yet to show why that is the only possible answer, we must trace realism's purely immanent concept of the image to the point where it can be shown to fail, necessarily and on its own terms. That is, we will have to consider how the post-Romantic image, itself the product of a shift from the symbolic to the forensic, leaves realist aesthetics entangled in a fundamental antinomy. What is that antinomy?

For now, only a provisional answer can be ventured, and it runs something like this: though obviously a highly complex and somewhat fractured aesthetic development, nineteenth-century pictorial and literary realism posits that what can be seen, observed, and described will unveil its significance and, ultimately, its truth in strictly immanent fashion, free of any transcendent presuppositions or aspirations. According to the more extreme logic of pictorial realism cultivated by the Pre-Raphaelites, visible phenomena are no longer analogues of truth but, materially and immediately, purport *to be* that truth. Pre-Raphaelite aesthetics no longer frames pictorial form in symbolic terms, that is, as a formal conduit *to* a truth that lies beyond the visible. Rather, the visible and the true are (idolatrously) taken to be wholly convertible and immanent. Yet, as John of Damascus had pointed out a millennium earlier in his refutation of iconoclast arguments, to elide the ontological difference between the image (*eikōn*) and the numinous truth that it mediates is to dissolve the very concept of an image.[110] The question thus becomes, Where an image claims to represent, without difference or residue, a slice of visible reality, does it thereby constitute an instance of truthful representation or, rather, a case of hypersimulation and, ultimately, of visual deception and idolatrous substitution?

Clearly aware of the uncertain status of the image within a regime of pictorial realism that he himself is urging, the young John Ruskin remarks on "a kind of pleasurable surprise, . . . exactly the same in its nature as that which we receive from juggling," felt in the presence of a "work . . . seen to resemble something which we know it is not." When presented with a verisimilar "imitation," the beholder's consciousness is caught up in a back-and-forth movement of pictorial illusion and conceptual unmasking, a dialectic that, Ruskin claims, will affectively register as a kind of "gentle surprise" and pleasure.

> Now two things are requisite to our complete and most pleasurable perception of this: first, that the resemblance be so perfect as to amount to a deception; secondly, that there be some means of proving at the same moment that it is a deception. The most perfect ideas and pleasures of imitation are, therefore, when one sense is contradicted by another, both bearing as positive evidence on the subject as each is capable of alone; as when the eye says a thing is round, and the finger says it is flat: they are, therefore, never felt in so high a degree as in painting, where appearance of projection, roughness, hair, velvet, etc., are given with a smooth surface, or in wax-work, where the first evidence of the senses is perpetually contradicted by their experience. (*RCW* III, 101)

Pictorial realism's central antinomy—that is, of the image understood as either *homologous with* or *analogous to* truth—plays out as the spectator's vacillation between a state of visual illusion and its reflective exposure as such. It is by no means obvious, however, that the beholder of a realist painting will necessarily derive "pleasure" from the fact that "the first evidence of the senses is perpetually contradicted by their experience." In fact, to construe the relation between perception and reflec-

---

110. See above, ch. 2.

tion in antinomian fashion would deprive the beholder of the conceptual resources needed for advancing from (visual) perception to (intellectual) conception. Instead, to the extent that the painted image is meant to simulate rather than depict reality, it risks foreclosing on art's most elemental objective, namely, to unveil truth in a manner that can be intuitively grasped. Thus, in an 1820 letter, John Constable determined that the recent invention of the diorama fell outside the province of art, for "art pleases by *reminding*, not by *deceiving*."[111] And merely to have proven "that it is a deception," as Ruskin notes, is hardly the same as to have attained access to pictorial truth. Rather, such disillusionment tends to produce a sense of resignation, leaving the beholder merely "undeceived / Of that which, deceiving, could no longer harm."[112]

In the event, Ruskin concedes that the mind, when presented with pictorial hypersimulation, can only ever attain a critical, or reactive, knowledge. For it "does not dwell on the suggestion, but on the perception that it is a false suggestion: it derives its pleasure, not from the contemplation of a truth, but from the discovery of a falsehood" (*RCW* III, 108). Already at this early point in his career, then, Ruskin understands that deception or simulation is far from an adequate framework for pictorial realism. For one thing, "imitation can only be of something material, but truth has reference to statements both of the qualities of material things, and of emotions, impressions, and thoughts." Indeed, once it is acknowledged that "there is a moral as well as material truth" (*RCW* III, 104), the question inevitably arises as to how these two truths are related. Are we to consider them as steps in a speculative sequence, with the physiology of sight furnishing the necessary condition for an eventual, superior kind of moral insight? Alternatively, does the fact that, in one instance, the intellectual movement is one of dissent from material "deception" and, in the other, of assent to a moral truth suggest that Ruskin is developing incommensurable conceptions of pictorial truth? His passing observation that "the senses are not usually . . . cognizant, with accuracy, of any truths but those of space and projection" (*RCW* III, 105) would speak in favor of the latter, that is, an antinomian conception of the image as giving rise to either notional *dissent* (a deception exposed as such) or "real assent," as Newman will later conceive of it.[113] What prompts Ruskin to favor the

---

111. Quoted in Gombrich 1972, 38.

112. Eliot 2015, 1:187 ("East Coker," lines 86–87).

113. For Newman, whose thinking in this regard, like Ruskin's, is heavily indebted to Locke, "real assent" arises from intuitive experience: "an image derived from experience . . . is stronger than an abstraction, conception, or conclusion." Hence, the true force of an image resides in its realizing a *presence*, and not just a concept of verisimilitude or resemblance. For if, as Newman argues, "resemblance exists only in the cases of notional assent, when the assent is given to notions," the resulting mental state is, perhaps, one of "certainty" based on inferential reasoning but never one of "certitude." Notional assent, then, is properly produced not by our experience but only by our

latter, antinomian view is above all his unease with the modern concept of imitation as a quasi-mechanical replication (or simulation) of the visible: "We shall see, in the course of our investigation of ideas of truth, that ideas of imitation not only do not imply their presence, but even are inconsistent with it; and that pictures which imitate so as to deceive, are never true" (*RCW* III, 108).

Paradoxically, a reductive understanding of imitation as sheer illusionism or hypersimulation actually triggers a chain of reflections that unravels the purported realism of such productions. Inevitably, an unreflected (photorealist) conception of truth as outright replication results in the image's formal and intellectual bankruptcy, an outcome Ruskin finds supremely embodied in the "miserable, virtueless, heartless mechanism, . . . the servile and mindless imitation[s]" of Canaletto. Ironically, the latter's utter artistic failure is most effectively exposed by comparison with photography, the medium that his "coloured daguerreotypeism" (*RCW* III, 215) had so unwittingly and imperfectly anticipated. Once we "plac[e] portions of detail accurately copied from Canaletto side by side with engravings from the daguerreotype," Ruskin observes, it becomes apparent that what the new medium delivers is signally lacking in the paintings themselves. His deep investment in the most rigorous fidelity of painting to nature notwithstanding, Ruskin as early as 1843 is already beginning to formulate his critique of a photorealist ideal that, a decade later, will cause him to question the Pre-Raphaelites' aesthetic axioms and goals.

Delivered in November 1853, Ruskin's lecture on Pre-Raphaelitism anticipates T. S. Eliot's famous claim about the "dissociation of sensibility" some seventy years later. As Ruskin formulates it, "A change took place, about the time of Raphael, in the spirit of Roman Catholics and Protestants both; and that change consisted in the *denial* of their religious belief, at least in the external and trivial affairs of life, and often in far more serious things" (*RCW* XII, 139). The shift from "ancient religious" to "modern and profane" art must be understood as absolute, for where metaphysics is concerned, "there is no question of degree. . . . He who offers God a second place, offers Him no place" (*RCW* XII, 142–43). At first glance, Ruskin's claims appear to reverse his strong claims, in *Modern Painters I*, for the superiority of modern painting, Turner's art in particular, over that of the "ancients." Yet that valuation begins to look far less clear-cut once we recall that already in 1843 Ruskin's overarching concern is with pictorial truth as the very foundation of moral truth. Such a view appears fundamentally continuous with his claim, in the 1853 Edinburgh lecture, that prior to Raphael, "the entire purpose of art was moral teaching," whereas in modern art the stress falls altogether on "finish of execution . . . rather than thought, and [on] beauty

---

interpretation of an image; see Newman 1979, 49, 51; for a fuller discussion of Newman's theory of "apprehension" and (real and notional) assent, see Richardson 2007, 47–66.

rather than veracity" (*RCW* XII, 145, 150). Nowhere does the transcendental home-lessness of modern art emerge more clearly than in its confused notion of mimesis, as is evident in the quintessentially modern genre of historical painting. Such hankering after *past* achievements, Ruskin notes, would have struck the ancients as "ridiculous." "What," he asks, "do you suppose our descendants will care for our imaginations of the events of former days? Suppose the Greeks, instead of representing their own warriors as they fought at Marathon, had left us nothing but their imaginations of Egyptian battles" (*RCW* XII, 151). Once a merely technical concern with mimetic correctness has supplanted the goal of pictorial truth, art has effectively lost its proper object. Echoing similar arguments found in Schiller's lectures, *On Naïve and Sentimental Poetry* (1795), Hegel's lectures on aesthetics (1821–29), and Heine's lectures, *On Religion and Philosophy in Germany* (1833), Ruskin considers modern painting to be trapped in a profane and epigonal worldview.

Fixated on "working everything, down to the most minute detail, from nature, and from nature only," and insisting that every "background [be] painted to the last touch," the Pre-Raphaelite school, Ruskin argues, had effectively lost sight of painting's medial dimension and, consequently, of the image's constitutive participation in the being that it makes visible. Sharply critical of John Brett's *Val d'Aosta*, which had been on display at the Royal Academy in 1859, Ruskin in his "Academy Notes" of that same year argues that the painting's exhaustive rendering of detail prevents it from being "a noble picture." For it is "wholly emotionless," rendering truth so dispassionately objective that no attachment to it could possibly be formed: "I cannot find from it that the painter loved, or feared, anything in all that wonderful piece of the world. There seems to me no awe of the mountains there—no real love of the chestnuts or the vines. Keenness of eye and fineness of hand as much as you choose; but of emotion, or of intention, nothing traceable" (*RCW* XIV, 236). No longer the conduit to an invisible truth, the Pre-Raphaelite image is reduced to a formally correct facsimile of visible particulars. Due to its "laborious finish" (*RCW* XII, 159), such art has lost its integrative, holistic function and, as a result, has ceased to communicate with the beholder in potentially transformative ways. What, then, is occluded when the painted image is conceived as but a simulacrum of the real, and when "the relation of invention to observation, and composition to imitation" (*RCW* XII, 161), has shifted so decisively in favor of the latter? Though less a conceptual thinker than a singularly perceptive artist-critic, Ruskin as early as *Modern Painters I* had begun to outline his answer to this question at the very heart of realist aesthetics. As became progressively clearer to him, to inquire into the proper ratio between art's formal-technical means and its ultimate, invisible ends is to find pictorial realism implicated in a metaphysical realism whose moorings extend all the way back into classical and Scholastic thought.

The central point comes into focus as Ruskin remarks on what he takes to be the categorical difference between painting and sculpture, effectively denying that the latter still constitutes an imitation: "The moment we come to marble, our definition checks us, for a marble figure does not look like what it is not: it looks like marble and like the form of a man, but then it *is* marble, and it *is* the form of a man. It does not look like a man, which it is not, but like the form of a man, which it is. Form is form, *bona fide* and actual, whether in marble or in flesh—not an imitation or resemblance of form, but real form" (*RCW* III, 101). Whether the transition from appearance to form can be as readily mapped onto the medial difference between painting and sculpture as Ruskin suggests seems doubtful, not least because since the mid-fourteenth-century discovery of linear perspective, painting had increasingly, and often very effectively, sought to emulate three-dimensionality and a spatial sense of form. Still, Ruskin's main insight remains valid and important, namely, that form and the beholder's grasp of it is the true telos of all representation (*mimēsis*). It is form, not appearance, that constitutes the true locus of knowledge and that, consequently, can never be a correlate of "imitation or resemblance" but only of cognition. As Joseph Pieper puts it:

> "Form" stands for that which gives a thing its identity, which makes it what it is. The "form" of a thing is its intrinsic identifying imprint [*was den Dingen von innen her ihre Prägung gibt*], so that every thing is what it is through the "form" it has. For a thing to have knowledge, then, means to carry in itself the identity (*quidditas*) of some other being or thing, and not only its "image" but indeed its "form." A being's ability to know, therefore, is its ability to transcend its own delimitations, the ability to step out of its own identity and to have "also the form of the other being," which means: to *be* in the other being.[114]

Paradoxically, then, the most rigorous concept of verisimilitude destines the image for self-consummation in the domain of pure form. That is, it allows the image to move beyond its contingent, temporal concern with resemblance by enabling its

---

114. Pieper 1989, 37. I take Pieper's argument to be congruent with what Therese Cory has recently elaborated as the "formal constituent view" of intelligible form in Aquinas. On this account, "the species fulfills its cognitive task precisely in being a form in the ordinary sense, by doing no more and no less than any ordinary form does." Form (*species*) is not a "psychological device" on the order of "'a representation,' 'concept,' 'formal sign,' 'x in intentional being,'" and so forth. Instead, "the species is distinctive in the manner that any form is distinct from any other: namely, by the kind of being it instantiates. What makes species distinctively cognitive forms is that they instantiate a distinctively cognitive—mental, i.e., conscious—kind of being. Mental being is a distinctive kind of real being, and so is color, or heat, or life, or any other" (Cory 2020, 264); see her lucid account of the "metaphysical role" served by Aquinas's concept of species, exemplified by the botanical species "fern," as the ontologically real point where being and knowing converge (279–91).

beholder to recognize the noncontingent truth of pure form. To put the matter in theological terms, a positive (*kataphatic*) investment in visible representations is grounded in an anterior (*apophatic*) knowledge of forms beyond the reach of human predication. Thus, even as appearance and the real, the orders of mediation and truth, can never outright coincide, they turn out to be inextricably entwined within the finite intellect.

As should be apparent by now, Ruskin's remarks bear considerable affinity to Plato's discussion of the image in Book 7 of the *Republic*. We recall how Socrates and Glaucon, while continuing to sift the implications of the allegory of the cave, ponder the central question concerning the kind of dialectics that links visible entities to the realm of ideas. Remarking on "the song that dialectic sings," Socrates insists on a fundamental analogy between perception and cognition: the path toward the "intelligible . . . is imitated by the power of sight." In scrutinizing visible things, from "animals" to "stars, and, in the end, the sun itself," empirical sight persists "until [it] grasps the good itself with understanding itself, . . . reaches the end of the intelligible, just as the other reached the end of the visible."[115] Insofar as dialectics enables human beings to claw their way out of Plato's cave and "into the sunlight," they will rejoice in their "newly acquired ability to look at divine images in water and shadows of the things that are, rather than, as before, merely at shadows of statues thrown by another source of light that is itself a shadow in relation to the sun." Crucially, this ascent toward the light of truth does not entail renouncing visible things per se. Instead, the image is reappraised as no longer an "imitation by copying or replication" but, rather, as an "imitation [*mimēsis*] by depiction."[116] The kind of archetypal (rather than ectypal) seeing that is the goal of Platonic dialectics continually avails itself of the "craft" (*technē*) of material sight, which "has the power to awaken the best part of the soul and lead it upward to the study of the best [*ariston*] among the things that are."[117] A lifelong student (and amateur translator) of Plato's dialogues, Ruskin, in *Modern Painters II* (1846), expressly invokes the Platonic distinction between sensory apprehension and speculative reflection: "Now the mere animal consciousness of the pleasantness I call Æsthesis; but the exulting, reverent, and grateful perception

---

115. Plato 1997, 1147–48 (*Rep.* 532a).

116. Wiesing 2010, 106; as Wiesing points out, Plato's *mimēsis* is a genus "refer[ring] to all kinds of imitation" (108); it may encompass either the sense of "copying" or that of "presentation [*Darstellung*]" and, as I argue here, associates these two possibilities as a dialectical sequence. See also Gadamer, who points out that "the complete separation of a world of the ideas from the world of appearances would be a crass absurdity." Indeed, it would be a mistake to consider this "separation" (*chōrismos*) as an ontological state of affairs to be overcome, as it were after the fact, by Platonic dialectics: "The chorismos is not a doctrine that must first be overcome. Rather, from beginning to end, it is an essential component of true dialectic" (Gadamer 1986, 16, 19–20); see above, ch. 1, 63–79.

117. Plato 1997, 1148 (*Rep.* 532c).

of it I call *Theoria*. For this, and this only, is the full comprehension and contemplation of the Beautiful as a gift of God" (*RCW* IV, 47). Only where being is subject to "contemplation," which receives it as a "gift" and, thus, as a conduit to the invisible giver, will the true and the real have become convertible and essentially one with being itself.

In its fullest articulation, which is found in Part I of Aquinas's *De Veritate*, Plato's argument will be taken to mean that "being cannot be known without the true [*ens non potest intellegi sine vero*], for it cannot be known unless it agrees with or conforms to the intellect."[118] This is not to say, however, that Aquinas considers the truth of things to be itself observer-dependent. Rather, he simply affirms that a thing's actual being and its potential intelligibility (for a finite intellect) are ontologically fungible. How so? Precisely because "truth in creatures is found in . . . things themselves and in intellect [*in rebus ipsis, et in intellectu*]" (*DV* I.6), truth is never contingent on finite acts of predication; it cannot be reduced to yet another secondary quality (e.g., texture, shape, color) such as we may ascribe to a given thing. On the contrary, to venture intelligible claims about visible things at all, truth must already "inhere in things themselves." Yet in what sense can this be the case? At issue here is Aquinas's distinction between truth predicated of things in "a primary and a secondary sense." The latter concerns the human agent's intellect, the arbiter of contingent truth and falsehood to the extent that it conforms (or fails to conform) itself to the thing in question: "A thing is not called true . . . unless it conforms to the intellect." Yet in so discerning and predicating the truth of a thing, the finite intellect already depends on that thing's *being* truth in a more elemental, "primary sense," by which Aquinas means that a thing has been created as a distinctive and cohesive form by God's creative vision. Hence, truth is the ultimate measure of all being, of its reality; and it is so in the twofold sense of the genitive construction. Being truth-infused, a thing possesses reality precisely insofar as it correlates with God's transcendent, creative vision. That vision is its true measure, for only "the divine intellect . . . measures [but] is not measured." Conversely, insofar as a thing is real or truth-infused, it furnishes the finite mind with the measure required for drawing out a given thing's reality and intelligibility. Yet this it can only do in medial form, that is, only by means of mental images and, subsequently, in concepts of its own devising. Hence Aquinas's reminder that "our intellect is measured, and measures only artifacts, not natural things [*non mensurans res quidem naturales, sed artificiales tantum*]" (*DV* I.2).

---

118. Aquinas, *De Veritate* I.1.ad 3, www.documentacatholicaomnia.eu/03d/1225-1274,_Thomas _Aquinas,_The_29_questions_on_Truth_(Mulligan_Translation),_EN.pdf (accessed 11 July 2020; cited in the text below as *DV*). See also Aristotle 1984, 2:1570 (*Metaphysics* II.1.993b30): "The principles of eternal things must be always most true; for they are not merely sometimes true, nor is there any cause of their being, but they themselves are the cause of the being of other things, so that as each thing is in respect of being, so is it in respect of truth."

Referencing Aristotle, Aquinas specifies that precisely those "natural things from which our intellect gets its scientific knowledge in turn measure our intellect [*res naturales . . . mensurant intellectum nostrum*]." They will do so because their (potential) intelligibility is an ontological feature of natural beings. Indeed, it is impossible to conceive a thing (*res*) that we would credit with actual being while also denying it all intelligibility. For were that the case, the thing in question could not even manifest itself for us as a specific entity. Hence, for Plato and Aristotle no less than for Aquinas, insofar as there is being, the visible things in which it has assumed specific form will be *specifically* experienced as truth-bearing or truth-infused. Their reality does not depend on the beholder's veridical judgment; it is not subject to "warranted assertibility." For it is by dint of its ontological constitution as an appearance, either actually or potentially intelligible, that a given thing points to an anterior and abiding presence (the Scholastic *archetypus intellectus*) to whose continuing creative presence it owes its being and upon which all finite knowledge of it depends: "Things are themselves measured by the divine intellect, in which are all created things—just as all works of art find their origin in the intellect of the artist" (*DV* I.2). Pieper's summation of Aquinas's argument bears quoting in full here.

> Truth is predicated of every being inasmuch as it has being. And this truth is seen as actually residing *in* all things, so much so that "truth" may interchangeably stand for "being." And further, the truth of all things is coextensive with the very being of all things; for there is no being at all that would not, by necessity, also be true. All this, then, has some immediate implications: every being, as being, stands in relation to a knowing mind. This relational orientation toward a knowing mind represents the same ontological reality as the very being of a thing. "To be," therefore, means the same as "to be oriented toward a knowing mind." The realm of "being as such," finally, does not extend beyond the realm of all that is oriented toward a knowing mind, so that no existing being is without such relational orientation. Nothing can be perceived as "being" and not at the same time as "true." For no real "being" can be perceived without implying that it relates or "conforms" to the knowing mind.[119]

This is not the place to rehearse in detail the sudden abrogation of this framework in seventeenth-century philosophy; a few statements, typically blunt and peremptory in their rejection of Aristotelian and Scholastic realism, will have to suffice. With Bacon's *Novum Organon* having pointed the way, Hobbes for one will no longer even entertain, let alone dialogically engage, the possibility that truth might be an

119. Pieper 1989, 35.

intrinsic property of being. In his customary, apodictic style, he thus states that "truth consists of predication, and not in things as such [*veritas enim in dicto, non in re consistit*]."[120] The point is echoed by Spinoza, whose reluctance to engage Scholasticism's realist ontology may well have been a result of his having been almost entirely unfamiliar with that tradition: "Altogether in the wrong," he writes, "are those who consider truth to be a property of being." For Spinoza, it is altogether axiomatic that things are, as he puts it, "mute" and that truth and knowledge are the exclusive province of human discursive practice.[121] No longer found *in* but only ever imposed *on* being, truth is conceived in strictly notional and anthropocentric terms. Writing in 1710, Vico thus draws the inevitable conclusion, namely, that human knowledge is a synthetic "doing" (*coagere*) of sorts. Rather than respond to its object, it veritably produces it, a finite activity that by default renders "the true and the made convertible."[122] By the time he revises his *Critique of Pure Reason* (1787), Kant outright dismisses the core axiom of Scholastic realism—which he reformulates as *quodlibet ens est unum, verum bonum*—as but an ossified and irrational creed of "the Schoolmen." For Kant, these "transcendental predicates are, in fact, nothing more but logical requirements and criteria of knowledge" that, "as so often happens, ha[d] been wrongly interpreted."[123]

In the decades following, however, the pendulum begins to swing back as Romantic writers such as Novalis, Schelling, Goethe, and Coleridge find a purely immanent perspective on being, shorn of all metaphysical presuppositions, to expire in a skepticism at once parasitical on the anterior givenness of the world and ever intent on negating it. Thus, for Ruskin, who early in his career was heavily influenced by Wordsworth, rejecting out of hand the ontological convertibility of being and truth appears counterintuitive and implausible.[124] Indeed, the very project of a purely im-

---

120. Hobbes 1845, 1:31.

121. Spinoza, quoted in Pieper 1989, 17.

122. The argument is most fully developed at the outset of Vico's early *De antiquissime Italiorum sapientia* (1710), though later reiterated in his *New Science* (1725); see Palmer's introduction to the earlier text (Vico 1988, 17–34; quote from 18); for a Hegelian interpretation of that principle in Vico's magnum opus, see Hösle 2016, 46–51.

123. As Kant continues: "the criterion of the possibility of a concept (not of an object) is the definition of it, in which the unity of the concept, the truth of all that may be immediately deduced, and finally, the *completeness* of what has been thus deduced from it, yield all that is required for the construction of the whole concept" (Kant 1965, 118–19 [*Critique of Pure Reason*, B 114–15]). For Pieper, it is "clear that Kant explicitly denies truth to be a property of being as such" (1989, 19; trans. corrected); for a discussion of the earlier passages by Hobbes and Spinoza, see Pieper 1989, 15–20. Still, it ought to be noted that Kant's condescending treatment (in §12 of the 1787 text of the first *Critique*) may owe much to the way that the proposition had been flattened and indeed rendered "tautological" by Christian Wolff.

124. On Wordsworth's influence on the young Ruskin, particularly that of *The Excursion* (1814), see Hewison 1976, 16–23; on Ruskin's gradually more critical view of Wordsworth, particularly in

manent aesthetic strikes him as an impossible undertaking unless we acknowledge that the reality of appearance is necessarily grounded in a metaphysical realism of forms. Ruskin, who during his work on *Modern Painters I* was also engaged in the continued study of Plato's dialogues and who late in life made it a habit to translate a passage of scripture or of Plato every day, conceives of painting as a realist art precisely insofar as the resulting image *participates in*, rather than unilaterally produces, the Platonic form of things.[125] As he puts it in his preface to the second edition of *Modern Painters I* (1844), "There is an ideal form of every herb, flower, and tree, it is that form to which every individual of the species has a tendency to arrive, freed from the influence of accident or disease" (*RCW* III, 28). While pictorial mimesis does not, of course, claim to render these forms visible per se, it positions the image (both visualized *in* and painted *from* nature) as a conduit to the reality of the forms themselves. Conversely, "there is no access to being at all except insofar as it manifests itself. . . . Appearance and being can neither be separated from each other, nor can they ever be simply identified."[126] Such, we recall, had been Plato's decisive insight, arduously worked out as the progression from the iconoclasm of *Republic* 10 to the concept of image as "participation" (*methexis*) in the *Parmenides* and the *Sophist*.

Properly understood, every image is a window onto the reality of forms, with which it cannot ever coincide, to be sure, yet relative to which it stands in vivid analogical relation by dint of its charismatic self-manifestation or *Gestalt*: "Whatever depth of gloom may seem to invest the objects of a real landscape, yet a window with that landscape seen through it will invariably appear a broad space of light as compared with the shade of the room walls." Quoting the *Phaedrus* ("someone . . . trained not in full sunlight but in dappled shade" [239c]), Ruskin insists on "the necessity, if a picture is to be truthful in effect of colour, that it should tell as a broad space of graduated illumination." Whereas Claude, Poussin, and their neoclassical heirs managed to produce only a "patchwork of black shades," Turner "has translated the unattainable intensity of one tone of colour, into the attainable pitch of a higher one: the golden green, for instance, of intense sunshine on verdure, into pure yellow, because he knows it to be impossible, with any mixture of blue whatsoever, to give faithfully its relative intensity of light; and Turner always will have his light and shade right, whatever it costs him in colour" (*RCW* III, 284). Still, even the most consummate art image remains but a pale shadow of nature's "colouring fit." When it comes to its relation vis-à-vis natural appearances, the realist image is a debtor, not a proprietor,

---

Modern Painters III (1856), see Helsinger's sensitive reading (1982, 41–60); see also Nichols 2016, 364–67.

125. See diary entries for November 1843, quoted in Wedderburn and Cooke's introduction (*RCW* III, xx).

126. Schindler 2004, 177.

since its very possibility depends on the infinite range and splendor of visible natural phenomena, and "no gorgeousness of the pallet can reach even these. But it is a widely different thing when nature herself takes a colouring fit, and does something extraordinary, something really to exhibit her power. She has a thousand ways and means of rising above herself, but incomparably the noblest manifestations of her capability of colour are in these sunsets among the high clouds" (*RCW* III, 285). What follows is yet another rapturous evocation of the chromatic richness, the inexhaustible spectrum of textures, of light variously refracted, and of continually shifting atmospheric qualities that Ruskin finds most vividly displayed at sunset.

It is this quest for the utmost fidelity to visible phenomena whose enigmatic splendor mediates their numinous source that points to a central paradox of pictorial realism. On the one hand, its forensic conception of the image, which as we saw is greatly indebted to the rise of inductive methods in the emergent fields of geology and biology, appears to hold that truth is indeed a property of things and, as such, can be ascertained only by bracketing the observer's subjective and psychological disposition. Yet at the same time, pictorial realism also posits that visible phenomena do not so much disclose or unveil a truth but, instead, embody that truth in strictly immanent form. What threatens to drop out in the latter conception is the concept of *analogia*, such that all that remains is but an array of "correct" painterly techniques— of tone, of color, of chiaroscuro, of space, of skies, of clouds, of earth, water, and so on. As a result, pictorial truth cannot "be discerned by the uneducated senses" (*RCW* III, 140) but requires a comprehensive aesthetic education such as Ruskin ended up acquiring and refining over the better part of his career. In the event, for the Ruskin of *Modern Painters I* truth vacillates between an intrinsic (ontological) property of things and a strictly observer-dependent attribute, that is, between subjective idealism and metaphysical realism.

On the one hand, the truth of things appears no longer intrinsic to their very being but, instead, as a contingent function of predication and ascription. Considered from this perspective, aesthetic realism is by definition incommensurable with philosophical realism. And yet, throughout *Modern Painters I* and even more in Ruskin's discussion of Pre-Raphaelite art, a strictly immanent conception of the image such as mid-nineteenth-century realism seeks to develop becomes entangled in incoherent and contradictory claims. Far from being the immanent, sociopolitical program as which mid-nineteenth-century pictorial "realism" has been construed, its underpinnings remain inevitably those of an Aristotelian and Thomist metaphysical realism. Indeed, it is the considerable merit of Ruskin to have become progressively aware, during the decade following the spectacular 1843 debut of *Modern Painters I*, of these underpinnings and to have adjusted his conception of art and image accordingly. Just as Lyell's and Darwin's intellectual formations pivoted on rejecting abstract, deductive, and perilously speculative habits of scientific argument, so Ruskin's conception of pictorial truth demanded the expurgation of all generic ideals and schematic practices from the art of drawing and painting. A first step in that direction meant rejecting Joshua Reynolds's neoclassical approach, whereby an aesthetic ideal would invariably distort the empirically visible world. For Ruskin, who not coincidentally is fond of citing Locke's *Essay concerning Human Understanding* in his early writings, the question of painting is, ultimately, a de jure question.[127] Should an inherited set of aesthetic conventions predetermine what can be seen and, consequently, depicted? Or is the truth of the visible world to be the first and final arbiter of the image, such that what legitimates painting is not its impact on historically contingent "taste" but, rather, its truth-value? What causes neoclassical, picturesque, and Romantic-sublime aesthetic ideals to fail Ruskin's test is that, wittingly or not, they end up becoming a Procrustian bed of sorts that disfigures the specificity and truth of the visible world. The picturesque, in particular, presented "a false vision of nature" by construing visible forms as mere stage decor for a strictly scenic and superficially idealized conception of form.[128] Yet, as Ruskin never tires to emphasize, the world cannot be captured in painting unless it has been properly seen: "All the great men *see* what they paint before they paint it—see it in a perfectly passive manner,—cannot help seeing it if they would; whether in their mind's eye, or in bodily fact, does not matter; very often the mental vision is . . . clearer than the bodily one" (*RCW* V, 114). As Ruskin will later write at the outset of *Elements of Drawing* (1857), "I am nearly convinced that, when once we see keenly enough, there is very little difficulty in drawing what we see; but, even supposing that this difficulty be still great, I believe that the sight is a more important thing than the drawing" (*RCW* XV, 13).

For the early Ruskin, "any discovery of 'laws' in the universe was only arrived at by the development of close study of natural detail. The laws are not beyond or

---

127. Wedderburn and Cooke remark on Ruskin's copious reading of Locke, which may have also inspired his characteristically obsessive, not to say baroque, "classifications, divisions, and marginal summaries" throughout *Modern Painters*; see *RCW* III, xix; Teukolsky notes how Ruskin's early writing "abounds with this rhetoric of empiricism," which at times makes *Modern Painters I* read like a study in the "comparative anatomy of painting-specimens" (2009, 35). Still, within a few years, not least because of his unease with the aesthetic program of the Pre-Raphaelites, Ruskin significantly qualifies his empiricist allegiances; notably, his occasional references to (daguerrotype) photography in *Modern Painters* are consistently negative and, as we saw in his remarks on Canaletto, frequently disparaging. As Ackerman points out, "By mid-century, as the aesthetic of the Sublime waned with that of the Picturesque, some of the best photographers did produce prints that reflected that tradition in painting and printmaking." Technological advances, such as the "wet collodion process" that reduced exposure time and increased the transparency and precision of lights and shadows on the negative, allowed early photography, pioneered by William H. F. Talbot, Gustave Le Gray, and Roger Fenton, to outstrip the photorealist ideal of painting almost as soon as the Pre-Raphaelites formulated it as an aesthetic ideal (Ackerman 2003, 91); on Nichols's reading, "Ruskin does not regard the 'sublime' as more than a mode of the beautiful" (2016, 58).

128. Hewison 1976, 46.

behind the facts but within them."[129] Hence, visible *being* evolves into a significant *fact* insofar as its mode of appearance, and its consequent visualization, allows the beholder or painter to grasp and articulate its specific form. What Robert Hewison calls Ruskin's "determinedly non-speculative, non-analytical approach" shows visualization to be intrinsically cognitive. To visualize a phenomenon, or cluster of phenomena, is no mere sensory act. Far more than the laying of material or thematic foundations for painting, seeing "is an act of determination about the certainties in the external world."[130] Ruskin's impassioned advocacy of Turner in the first volume of *Modern Painters* shows him to be an heir not only of Romanticism but also of an empiricist tradition that, extending from Locke through Priestley, had continued to shadow Romantic aesthetics even, or perhaps especially, in its most exalted, sublime flights. Patricia Ball is surely right to note how Ruskin's aesthetics, at times almost to the exclusion of everything else, "upholds the place of fact, especially natural fact, in art, and the duty of the artist to respect it totally."[131] Still, while such a characterization of Ruskin's aesthetics puts us on the right track, the concept of fact in his oeuvre no longer carries the self-evident meaning that it had held in early eighteenth-century British empiricism. For what Ruskin calls a "fact" involves a great deal more than mere sensible matter contingently perceived and categorized by an otherwise blank consciousness. Instead, "fact" for Ruskin refers to a natural appearance arresting the beholder with its unique organization; it is the moment when being, by virtue of its distinctive structure, engages the observer, holds his attention, and enables him to grasp and articulate a truth. Put differently, in Ruskin's account a fact is the *real* cause of perception even as, concurrently, perception is the *ideal* cause of what comes to be called a fact. The "highest landscape painting," Ruskin writes in the preface to the second edition of *Modern Painters*, must "be based on perfect cognizance of the form, functions, and system of every organic or definitely structured existence which it has to represent" (*RCW* III, 35).

Where Ruskin speaks of a "fact" the word *truth* is sure to follow, as indeed it does in the long passage quoted above. "Fact" names the moment where being is found to have truly accomplished itself, as *factum* in the participial sense, having revealed itself to the observing consciousness as an intrinsically significant appearance; and to grasp or know a fact is to have become aware of its specific form through acts of sustained visual attention. Seeing here *is* knowing, not a prelude to it. To put the matter thus is to premise an ontological coordination of mind and world absent which there could never be a realist aesthetic of the kind Ruskin seeks to unfold. Much later, in

---

129. Ball 1971, 57.
130. Hewison 1976, 21; Teukolsky 2009, 40.
131. Ball 1971, 62.

his autobiographical work *Praeterita* (1885–89), Ruskin thus remarks how "the woods, which I had only looked on as wilderness, fulfilled I then saw, in their beauty, the same laws which guided the clouds, divided the light, and balanced the wave. 'He hath made everything beautiful, in his time,' became for me thenceforward the interpretation of the bond between the human mind and all visible things" (*RCW* XXXV, 315).

As so often happens, however, the continuity asserted ("became henceforth") by the autobiographical voice airbrushes a prolonged interlude of religious doubt and disbelief during the late 1850s and 1860s.[132] Still, the young Ruskin was firmly persuaded of an ontological "bond" between mind and the visible world, and hence also of mind's indelible (if also ineffable) connection to a numinous (divine) creator. That said, *Modern Painters* is by no means a work of religious speculation, as is apparent by Ruskin's frequent insistence on the primacy of the phenomenal over the cognitive. As he notes, "Although it is possible to reach what I have stated to be the first end of art, the representation of facts, without reaching the second, the representation of thoughts, yet it is altogether impossible to reach the second without having previously reached the first" (*RCW* III, 136). In putting it thus, Ruskin echoes Goethe's injunction that "we ought not to search for anything *behind* the phenomena. For they themselves are the doctrine." Just so, Ruskin premises that whatever "laws" could be shown to operate within the natural world "are not beyond or behind the facts but within them."[133] Likewise, Goethe's neo-Platonic conception of form as "reality" in the strong, metaphysical sense still resonates in Ruskin's comments on the "exquisite and complex symmetries" exhibited by the foliar structure of trees; his discussion "Leaf Aspects" in the fifth and final volume of *Modern Painters* (1860) culminates in the quintessentially Goethean affirmation that "if you can paint *one* leaf, you can paint the world" (*RCW* V, 52).

For Ruskin, it follows that the "image," properly understood, should never be tainted or manipulated: "The skill of the artist, and the perfection of his art, are never proved until both are forgotten. The artist has done nothing till he has concealed himself; the art is imperfect which is visible. . . . The power of the masters is shown by their self-annihilation. It is commensurate with the degree in which they themselves appear not in their work" (*RCW* III, 22–23). Though plain enough as such, the argument for an aesthetic committed to disavowing its very mode of production masks a deeper, in part psychological, ambivalence. Art must not only conceal its

---

132. Even as Ruskin's Christian belief "was shaken by a combination of scientific discovery and biblical criticism," he not only arrived at an "allegiance to what he called 'Catholic,' although not Roman, Catholic Christianity [but] even in his most doctrinally agnostic moments, the essentially religious temper of his mind endured" (Nichols 2016, 48).

133. *GHA* 12:432 (#488); Ball 1971, 57.

status as artifice, but, in so doing, must expunge the artist's very persona, a claim certainly borne out in Ruskin's case by his well-documented dread of introspection. As regards the objective and conceptual status of the painted image, Ruskin's emphatic rejection of material contrivance and self-conscious pictorial rhetoric of any kind is consistent with pictorial realism's "repudiation of drama which involved an almost total rejection of conflict, opposition, and contrast" that Michael Fried has diagnosed in Courbet's oeuvre starting in the 1840s.[134] Similarly, Fredric Jameson has remarked on realism's constantly attempted "symbiosis of . . . storytelling with impulses of scenic elaboration, description." The latter, he suggests, masks an "affective investment, which allows [realism] to develop towards a scenic present which . . . secretly abhors the other temporalities which constitute the force of the tale or récit in the first place."[135]

What accounts for such a retreat, in both literary and pictorial realism, from drama and "other temporalities," as Jameson calls them? A first, tentative answer would have to take note of the coincidence, during the 1840s and 1850s, of an end-of-history *mentalité* fueled, on the one hand, by the theoretical optimism of Hegel and Comte and, on the other, by the growing hegemony of naturalistic explanatory frameworks in the sciences. One result of these dominant conceptual schemes is the displacement, which I have explored elsewhere, of the category of action by that of behavior.[136] The excessively familiar plot lines unfolded by Dickens, Balzac, Flaubert, G. Eliot, and Tolstoy—featuring characters whose lust for money, inheritance, professional success, and social ascendancy and, above all, hunger for any kind of stimulation (gambling, adulterous sex) mask an incipient despair over their personally and statistically insignificant existence—strongly suggests that life has lost its classical, dramatic purpose and narrative dynamism. George Eliot's famous reference to the "many Theresas" of her own time, who unlike their famous forebear Teresa of Ávila "found themselves no epic life where there was a constant unfolding of far-resonant action," hints at the apparent demotion of life and being to a mostly actuarial value. All that remains is, "perhaps, a life of mistakes, the offspring of a certain spiritual grandeur ill-matched with the meanness of opportunity; perhaps a tragic failure which found no sacred poet and sank unwept into oblivion."[137]

With its focus on undramatic and unremarkable phenomena, mid-nineteenth-century realism stands in apparent continuity with the typically nameless and miscellaneous figures that prove of fleeting interest to the usually detached and sometimes uncomprehending poet-narrator of Wordsworth's *Lyrical Ballads*. Yet whereas

---

134. Fried 1990, 227.
135. Jameson 2013, 11.
136. Pfau 2013a, 343–50, 374–83.
137. Eliot 2004, 31.

the genre of the ballad still presupposes a fundamentally intact culture of memory and storytelling, midcentury realist narrative takes a darker turn in which Eliot is something of an outlier. Thus, her plea that "the greatest benefit we owe to the artist, whether painter, poet, or novelist, is the extension of our sympathies" can be viewed as a rearguard action against naturalistic patterns of behavior, ranging from the trivial or whimsical to the grandiose and the positively feral. Echoing Wordsworth's preface to *Lyrical Ballads*, Eliot's review of Wilhelm Riehl's *Die bürgerliche Gesellschaft* (1851) acknowledges that "many disintegrating forces have been at work on the peasant character, and [that] degeneration is unhappily going on at a greater pace than development." As a class, the peasantry seems to be merging with the bourgeoisie, being "more dependent on ready money than formerly." Modern life, she laments, appears "founded on generalizations and statistics," fueled by a general view "that all social questions are merged in economical science," and convinced that "the relations of men to their neighbours may be settled by algebraic equations."[138] The overall impression here is of lived human existence not so much changing as losing its texture and devolving into a mere simulation of life. Eliot's own realism above all seeks to tabulate the root causes of modern life's steady advance into unreality and, where possible, to counter it at the level of plot. To that end, following Wordsworth and Ruskin, she redirects her descriptive and narrative focus onto the material shape, specific sentiments, and local habits of rural England—a domestic ethnography or Geertzian, "thick description" *avant la lettre* designed to unmask the pernicious abstractions and generic patterns of behavior threatening to merge the reality of mid-Victorian life with its sociological description and actuarial tabulation.

A similar project of reconstructing vision as an ethic of attention to the local, the specific, and the true also informs the pictorial realism of the Pre-Raphaelite school whose close-up paintings of rocks and flowers expressly reject neoclassicism's linear organization of visual space, such as we encounter it in the *coulisses* of Claude Lorrain and the studied symmetries of Nicholas Poussin, vestiges of which still survive in the landscapes of Gainsborough and Constable. As a result of their "almost total rejection of conflict, opposition, and contrast both thematically and structurally," Courbet, Menzel, and the Pre-Raphaelite school (John Brett, William Holman Hunt, Rosa Brett, John Inchbold) derive the image's organization from the specificity of natural forms (and social conventions) as they present themselves ready-made to these painters. In the case of the Pre-Raphaelites, the result is a type of image "more aptly . . . described as 'nature studies' than landscapes."[139] Rosa Brett's *Thistles* (1860) provides a fine case in point (fig. 6.6). Here the landscape has itself become once

---

138. "Natural History of German Life" (*Westminster Review*, July 1856), in Eliot 1990, 110–12, 121.

139. Fried 1990, 227; Staley and Newall 2004, 29.

Figure 6.6. Thistles, 1860, Rosa Brett (1829–1882). Tate. Photo © Tate.

again background, as it had been in late fifteenth-century religious painting, a genre perhaps alluded to by the faint contours of a country church now dwarfed by the painting's eponymous plant. Meanwhile, Brett's choice of a flower so unglamorous, the pictorial equivalent of George Eliot's unwept-for Theresas, shows how a new, realist aesthetic will allow the thistle's distinctive texture and form—captured with microscopic accuracy, accentuated by the distribution of bright greens, and dominating our visual frame—to reorganize both the pictorial space and the beholder's habits of visual attention. Brett's thistles exemplify what, in his visual catechesis of the Victorian middle class, Ruskin never tired to emphasize, namely, that the true goal of painting rests with "the expression of the specific not the individual, but the specific characters of every object, in their perfection. There is an ideal form of every herb, flower, and tree, it is that form to which every individual of the species has a tendency to arrive, freed from the influence of accident or disease. Every landscape painter should know the specific characters of every object he has to represent, rock, flower" (*RCW* III, 27).

Unsurprisingly, the Pre-Raphaelite artists during their early years had embraced Ruskin's *Modern Painters* as their most authoritative and comprehensive point of reference. For as Ruskin had so forcefully argued, to ensure truth in painting required first and foremost sheltering the image from all dramatic gestures and self-conscious artifice. For the painted image to have integrity and convey truth, it had to function solely as the *medium* for a truth attainable only where the painted image captured visible phenomena with forensic accuracy. Such truth therefore ought never be *intended* as a pictorial statement or proposition. Ruskin's blunt admonition that "the picture which is looked to for an interpretation of nature is invaluable, but the picture which is taken as a substitute for nature had better be burned" (*RCW* III, 12) makes clear that a painting should but reconstitute the image originally revealed in focused and attentive visualization.[140] Understood as an objective facsimile of visual experience, the painted image should neither add to nor omit anything from its founding intuition. Still, even as the realist image's mimetic commitments would seem to preclude any interpretive surfeit, Ruskin—like John of Damascus a millennium earlier—is well aware of the ontological difference between the image and what it depicts. Hence, his insistence that "we should use pictures not as authorities, but as comments on nature, just as we use divines not as authorities, but as comments on the Bible" (*RCW* III, 45 n.) acknowledges that pictorialization can never positively *claim* but only *assent to*, and *illuminate*, a transcendent reality that is neither reducible to nor in conflict with visible things but, instead, is the very condition of their being. Hence, no picture can ever be the duplicate of, or substitute for, the double event of phenomenalization and intuition to which it owes its existence. Rather, in seeking to cast that event in objective form, pictorialization yields a kind of nonpropositional knowledge, not claimed in syllogistic form, but unveiled in the distinctive medium of the image whose unique power and purpose it is to transmute the visible into the revealed.

---

140. *RCW* III, 12. As Ruskin was to put it much later, in *The Eagle's Nest* (1872), "Through the whole of following life, whatever power of judgment I have obtained, in art, which I am now confident and happy in using, or communicating, has depended on my steady habit of always looking for the subject principally, and for the art, only as the means of expressing it" (*RCW* XXII, 153).

In the event, the young Ruskin's strict biblicism, and the murky, middlebrow Protestant theology that had supplanted it during his middle years, prevented him from sifting the metaphysical implications of the image. To do so would have required a level of philosophical and theological training he neither received nor sought, even as many of his more searching formulations come tantalizingly close to grasping the salient point. No such limitations, however, impinge on a supremely talented young poet and gifted draftsman of the next generation, Gerard Manley Hopkins, whose quest for establishing a strong link between visual experience and theologically informed faith owes a good deal to Ruskin's oeuvre while also surpassing it in some crucial respects; and it is to Hopkins that we now turn.

7

THE SACRAMENTAL IMAGE
G. M. Hopkins

The presence of beauty in the world is the experimental proof of the possibility of incarnation.

—Simone Weil, *New York Notebook*

*Art. It is the triumph of art to lead to something other than itself:
to a life which is fully conscious of the pact between the mind and the world*

—Simone Weil, *Pre-War Notebook*

"ALL MY EYES SEE, WANDERING ON THE WORLD": HOPKINS ON PARTICULARITY AND PRESENCE

On 23 February 1877, with his final examinations in moral theology looming just ahead, Gerard Manley Hopkins resumes his quest for expressing his religious faith in a language far more intuitive and imagistic than the neo-Thomist formulas with which his Jesuit teachers have been inundating him. A letter of that date, written to his mother for her birthday, finds Hopkins implicitly contrasting "the most wearisome work" of reviewing "moral theology over and over again" and an array of arresting natural phenomena forever riveting his attention to the splendors of the Welsh landscape surrounding St. Beuno's Seminary. Hopkins mentions the "sharp frost with bitter north winds" and a total eclipse of the moon, "dazzling bright and the shadow brown." Also enclosed as a birthday present in the letter he sends to his mother on March 3, the day he passes his exams, are "two sonnets I wrote in a freak the other day"—"God's Grandeur" and "The Starlight Night."[1] Having resumed writing poetry in spectacular fashion with "The Wreck of the Deutschland" in December 1875, following "the slaughter of the innocents" (*HCW* III:423) more than seven years earlier when, on 11 May 1868, he had burned all his juvenilia, Hopkins had produced barely ten poems since. Of the lyrics immediately following "The Wreck of the Deutschland," some are experimental (e.g., written in Welsh, a language Hopkins is avidly studying at the time), while others seem of an occasional, commemorative and somewhat conventional cast ("The Silver Jubilee," "Penmaen Pool").

Only one short, seven-line lyric titled "Moonrise, June 19, 1876" stands out among these incidental productions. It exhibits that distinctive Hopkinsian fusion of alliterative, rhythmic, and lexical effects that brings into focus "the prized, the desirable sight, unsought" of the Welsh landscape. Paradoxically, it is the nocturnal scene's pale and ephemeral aspect ("not-to-call night | in the white and the walk of the morning") that causes it to arrest and imprint itself on Hopkins's vision.

> The móon, dwíndled and thínned to the frínge | of a fíngernail héld to the cándle,
> Or páring of páradisáïcal fruit, | lovely in wáning but lústerless[2]

Arresting here is the image's oscillation between a faintly translucent object of marginal visibility ("dwíndled and thinned") and a simile ("páring of páradisáïcal fruit") hinting at an impending *parousia* of sorts. The distinction at issue here maps onto what Husserl will call "the difference between content that is experienced and the object that appears."[3] Still, even as phenomenon and object, the content experienced and the objective reality that funds it are not conflated, neither are they divided, but they are held in delicate equipoise in the beholder's consciousness. Thus, Moel Maenefa, a prominent mountain rising to almost 950 feet and located just behind St. Beuno's Seminary, is imaged as a palpable energy barely contained by optical laws: "A cusp still clasped him, a fluke yet fanged him | entangled him, not quite utterly." For the mountain to come into view is less a case of objective exposure than of elicit-

---

1. Letters, in Hopkins 2006– , I:261–63 (henceforth cited parenthetically as *HCW* followed by volume and page number); see also White 1992, 266–69.

2. Hopkins 1986, 121; henceforth cited parenthetically as *HMW*.

3. Husserl 2005, 12 (de[r] Unterschied zwischen dem Inhalt, der 'erlebt' wird, und dem Gegenstand, der erscheint [2006b, 14, §5]).

ing the observer's participation and, thereby, unveiling the "páradisáïcal fruit" that has slumbered all along within the beholder's consciousness. Objective vision and self-revelation, the visible aspect and its invisible meaning, attainable only insofar as it is "unsought," appear fully enmeshed. Captivated and transformed, Hopkins thus remarks on how the nocturnal scene "Parted me leaf and leaf, divided me, | eyelid and eyelid of slumber" (*HMW* 121).

Still, these incidental seven lines of poetry only hint at the unprecedented visual, metaphoric, and prosodic creativity that was to burst forth some eight months later, beginning with the two sonnets Hopkins sends to his mother in late February 1877. Anyone unacquainted with Hopkins's biography and, perhaps, unaware of his decision to convert to Catholicism and to embark on the Jesuit novitiate in September 1868, might initially read the title, "God's Grandeur," and perceive the lines following as a standard sonnet, firmly rooted in the tradition of Ruskinian aesthetics and its underlying framework of "natural theology" that, in its canonical formulation by William Paley, continued to shape mainstream Anglo-Protestantism's outlook on God and creation throughout the nineteenth century. Already the sonnet's first line, however, makes clear that we are in the presence of a different voice, profoundly shaped by metaphysical concerns and intent on repurposing the sonnet form so as to articulate a religious metaphysic in far more startling and compelling ways than the discourse of academic theology.

> The world is charged with the grandeur of God.
> It will flame out, like shining from shook foil;
> It gathers to a greatness, like the ooze of oil
> Crushed.
>
> (HMW 128)

With its blunt, opening declaration that "the world is *charged* with the grandeur of God," the poem at once parts ways with the framework of natural theology. Continuously elaborated from John Ray to William Paley, natural theology had established itself as a *via media* of sorts for Britain's lettered classes, the scientific corollary of Anglicanism itself, that "golden mean between men who believe too much and men who believe too little," as Newman was to put it in 1870.[4] On this view, the world is but an inventory of things exhibiting more or less sophisticated "design" and, when taken as divine "contrivances," inviting the diligent naturalist to draw, time and again, the inference of an underlying first cause: God. Yet if, as Paley had repeatedly insisted, "a contriver is still necessary," the natural theologian's quest is strictly epistemological in kind and yields little more than a repetition of the same basic inference.

---

4. Newman 1979, 253.

God is to be inferred *from* "the complexity, subtlety, and curiosity of the mechanism" precisely because, for Paley, God is *not* a manifest presence *in* creation.[5] Seen as a vast array of "instruments" and "mechanisms," the world of natural theology is not a charged presence but the fossilized enigma of primary causation. At best, natural theology presents the observer with "an interesting uncertainty," as Hopkins puts it in an 1883 letter to his liberal-Protestant friend, Robert Bridges, who had professed doubt about the central mysteries of the faith, the Incarnation in particular. In his response, Hopkins ventures to clarify that

> you do not mean by mystery what a Catholic does. You mean an interesting un-
> certainty; the uncertainty ceasing, interest ceases also. This happens in some
> things; to you in religion. But a Catholic by mystery means an *incomprehensible
> certainty*: without certainty, without formulation there is no interest. . . . The
> clearer the formulation, the greater the interest. At bottom, the source of interest
> is the same in both cases, in your mind and in ours; it is the unknown, the re-
> serve of truth beyond what the mind reaches and still feels to be behind. But the
> interest a Catholic feels is, . . . of a far finer kind than yours. Yours turns out to be
> a curiosity only; the curiosity satisfied, the trick found out (to be a little profane),
> the answer heard, it vanishes at once. But you know there are . . . some resolu-
> tions of suspensions so lovely in music that even the feeling of interest is keenest
> when they are known. . . . [Here] knowledge leaves the mind swinging; poised,
> but on the quiver. And this might be the ecstasy of interest, one would think. So
> too of the Incarnation. (*HCW* II:619; emphasis mine)

"God's Grandeur" is Hopkins's way of drawing the reader into this "incomprehensible certainty" of a world charged with presence rather than encountered as an epistemological puzzle of sorts. Foreshadowing the eponymous *Herrlichkeit* of Hans Urs von Balthasar's monumental work on theological aesthetics, Hopkins's "grandeur" names a perceptible splendor, a manifestation of abundant fullness and fecundity. "Grandeur" here does not indicate a sublime abstraction but a concrete manifestation; it does not stand for an invisible, omnipotent agent but, to the attentive

---

5. Paley 1802, 21–32. On Paley's religious epistemology and its enduring institutional influence on Victorian religious and scientific thought, including at Cambridge and Oxford, see Thompson 2007, 232–65; Gould sees Paley's oeuvre as presenting "a subtle, coherently reasoned brief for an adaptionist natural theology" (2002, 266). On growing criticism of Paley in the 1840s, see Secord 2000, 93, 338, 350; see also Pfau 2012. Paley's framework seems to lurk behind J. Hillis Miller's wildly inaccurate claim that in Hopkins's writings, "neither within nor without is God anywhere directly present to me. He exists only as a necessary deduction from my discovery of myself as the most highly pitched entity in the creation" (1975, 273).

beholder, discloses an infinitely variegated array of distinctively "charged" forms. Its medium is not the concept but the image, not some enigmatic First Cause but a "charged" presence. Moreover, the "charge" in question not only involves the abundance with which God continues to infuse all creation; it is also an injunction, a charge issued to each finite human being *in* the world to witness and respond to what is experientially given by learning to see the visible as the revealed.

Though unmistakably Catholic, Hopkins's cosmology departs from Suárez's manualist Thomism, then dominating Jesuit teaching, especially as regards its rigid parsing of primary and secondary causation. Formulated in the "dispiriting" intellectual climate at St. Beuno's Seminary during the 1870s and 1880s, when "Suarez and Suarez only was taught," Hopkins's reservations are not merely aesthetic, though they are that, too; for though Suárez is "a man of vast volume of mind," Hopkins finds him to be "without originality or brilliancy[;] he treats everything satisfactorily, but you never remember a phrase of his."[6] Yet the main issue here concerns Suárez's problematic departure from Aquinas's account of "double causation," in which God and creature are both fully efficacious according to their respective natures. By contrast, post-Reformation Thomism tends to deny creatures any causal agency of their own. The result is a version of natural theology conceived as a prima facie demonstration or, rather, deduction of God's existence. In an apparent misconstrual of *Summa Theologiae* I.2 A3, the manualist approaches created nature as an epistemological challenge to be met by explanatory schemes that begin to resemble the Cartesian and Newtonian projects of monocausal, immanent *demonstration* of something otherwise held in doubt. Thus, to the Scholasticism of the early modern period, creation presents itself increasingly as an *explanandum* rather than as divine manifestation. Indeed, insofar as it is no longer conceived as a fully realized form, creation verges on the wholly notional and abstract, a mere concept approximating Baius's "pure nature." Insofar as it mutates into an epistemological puzzle rather than being experienced as a presence and source of metaphysical certitude, the concept of nature becomes a free-floating abstraction seemingly devoid of any phenomenology and untethered from any concept of the supernatural.[7]

Quietly merging with a naturalistic strand of argument previously introduced into late Scholastic theology, Descartes's skeptical epistemology ignores a crucial

---

6. Hopkins 1959b, 292 (henceforth cited parenthetically as *SDW* followed by page number); *HCW* I:503.

7. Notably, the "separation of the natural and the supernatural into two independent orders of reality" arose from within late Scholasticism, rather than being perpetrated (as is often thought) by Cartesian rationalism. On Baius's concept of *natura pura*, see de Lubac 2000a, 1–30; quote from xii.

qualification found in Aristotle. The latter had emphasized that the aim of all knowledge-by-demonstration can only ever be "the conclusion in which a proper accident is predicated of a certain subject." Yet as Aristotle had also stressed, by its very nature "demonstrative knowledge presupposes prior knowledge of the *subiectum*," which is to say, a preconceptual certitude *that* the subject exists (*an sit*) and an intuitive grasp of *what* it is (*quid est*).[8] By contrast, a strictly rationalist approach suspends and, ultimately, discredits the reality of experience for lack of a conceptual warrant. It thus holds the presence of the given phenomenon hostage, to be ransomed by the ex post facto certainty of what syllogistic demonstration *concludes* to be true. The result is a cramped view of reality as a network of efficient causal relationships that can be ascertained and validated only in syllogistic form. None other than Aquinas already foresaw that such a framework was destined to impoverish knowledge, noting that "to detract from the perfection of creatures is to detract from the perfection of divine power. But, if no creature has any active role in the production of any effect, much is detracted from the perfection of the creature."[9] As we shall see, Hopkins's theo-poetics is premised on a conception of the thing as dynamic form, as agency (*actus*) rather than inert object.

Perhaps alluding to Psalm 71:19, Hopkins's opening declaration, "The world is charged with the grandeur of God," thus ought not to be construed as a proposition in need of demonstration.[10] Rather, it names a metaphysical reality that registers as "certitude" in the observer's consciousness. The line affirms an unconditional givenness or grace and acknowledges the "charge" in creation in which we participate always and everywhere, "for Christ plays in ten-thousand places" (*HMW* 129). It is not in the realm of the spectacular and the (Romantic) sublime but in the startling particularity of nature all around us that man "faces" these "graces." Hopkins's decision (in "As kingfishers catch fire") to end rhyme *graces*, *faces*, and *places* attests to his incarnational view of inconspicuous, everyday natural phenomena. In some respects, Hopkins is the heir to the early Wordsworth's poetics of the ordinary. Echoes of "I wandered lonely as a cloud" and various other lyrics from Wordsworth's *Poems in Two Volumes* (1807), particularly the subsection titled "Moods of My Own Mind," seem palpable in Hopkins's tribute to "wind-wandering, weed-winding bank" (*HMW* 142), his affirmation of "the weeds and the wilderness" (*HMW* 153), or the glad repose in the opening lines of the late poem "Ashboughs" (1887):

---

8. Te Velde 2006, 40.

9. *Summa Contra Gentiles*, III.69.15 (https://isidore.co/aquinas/english/ContraGentiles3a .htm#69; accessed 16 July 2020); see also Kerr 2002, 17–51, esp. 44–45; and, on the misconstrual of Aquinas's "Five Ways" (*quinquae viae*), te Velde 2006, 37–63.

10. K. Hart (2017, 12) proposes Ps. 71:19 as an intertext, referencing the Douay-Rheims version.

Not of all my eyes see, wandering on the world
Is anything a milk to the mind so, só sighs deep
Poetry to it, as a tree whose boughs break in the sky.
(*HMW* 177)

Yet Hopkins's paeans to "sweet Earth . . . with leavès throng / And louchèd low grass" (*HMW* 156) serve fundamentally different ends from those intended by Wordsworth's often generic-sounding evocation of "the common range of visible things." For inevitably, the latter ends up affirming the speaker's exemplary sensibility, such as in *The Prelude* where Wordsworth, not at all bashful, recalls how "In Nature's presence stood, as I stand now, / A sensitive and a creative soul."[11] Where Wordsworth's poetics of the ordinary draws on images of divinity and transcendence, it typically does so in order to complete its theodicy of the Romantic individual.

A very different, almost diametrically opposed dynamic informs Hopkins's kenotic stance and with its stress on the unassuming particularity or "inscape" of what is visibly given, such as in the miscellaneous, indeed eccentric, imagery in the opening lines of "God's Grandeur." Why, after all, should God's grandeur be found, of all things, in the "shining from shook foil" and the "ooze of oil / Crushed"? A first inkling of an answer has to do with the fact that both images resist being absorbed into an abstract matrix of causation. What distinguishes them is their peculiar visual and tactile quality, evocative of a familiar and distinctive sensory experience rather than begging causal explanation. Commenting on his simile of "shook foil" in an 1883 letter to Robert Bridges, Hopkins notes, "My sonnet might have been written expressly for the image's sake." Yet what lends purpose to the image is not some clever conceit ("I do not mean by foil set-off at all") but its visual immediacy—a sensation that is *eo ipso* also a (re)cognition, a knowledge not begged but abundantly delivered in sensuous form: "I mean foil in its ~~literal~~ sense of leaf or tinsel, and no other word whatever will give the effect I want. Shaken goldfoil gives off broad glares like sheet lightning and also, and this is true of nothing else, owing to its zigzag dints and creasings and network of small many cornered facets, a sort of fork lightning too" (*HCW* II:559). Hopkins's decision to strike out "literal" and his insistence that "no other word whatever" will provide the desired "effect" show that "image" here is neither a rhetorical device nor a case of circumlocution. Rather, "shining from shook foil" discloses the truth of a unique phenomenon, its "inscape," precisely by steering clear of notions of resemblance and an aesthetic of imitation. The image is true only insofar as it achieves consubstantiality with the experience of the unique being *of* which it is the image. Effectively merging the experience of visualization and reading, Hopkins's imagery—eccentric on account of its objects' sheer ordinariness—

---

11. Wordsworth 1979, 74 (*The Prelude* [1805], bk. 2, line 182; and bk. 11, lines 256–57).

asks us to linger over the optical phenomenon. An attentive beholder thus may come to apprehend within a "network of many cornered facets" an infinitude of small-scale illuminations, each one a prefiguration of the theo-drama of an ultimate, perfected vision that shall absorb and reconcile them all.

Meanwhile, the second simile, "like the ooze of oil / Crushed" teems with salvific connotations, olive oil serving medicinal purposes yet also applied at the sacrament of extreme unction. An earlier version of the line ("like an oozing oil / Pressed") likely alludes to Micah 6:15 ("thou shalt tread the olives, but thou shalt not anoint thee with oil"). Fittingly, the minor prophecy is invoked precisely as the sonnet transitions from the fullness of God's presence and grandeur to its betrayal by human beings fixated on material gain only. Micah 6:9–16 tells of God reprimanding the city's Israelites for their dishonest trading practices ("Shall I count *them* pure with the wicked balances and with the bag of deceitful weights?"). For Hopkins, commerce not only tends to involve deceit within a community, but its unceasing fixation on production and profits inevitably dulls awareness of creation's inherent splendor. Mackenzie's commentary quotes Richardson's *Dictionary* (1858 ed.), which defines trade as "a way or course *trodden*, and *retrodden*, passed and repassed."[12] Where creation is thus devalued, God will inevitably fare the same way.

> Why do men then now not reck his rod?
> Generations have trod, have trod, have trod;
> And all is seared with trade; bleared, smeared with toil;
> And wears man's smudge and shares man's smell: the soil
> Is bare now, nor can foot feel, being shod.

By redeploying, in line 6, the "short, light, tripping, and trifling" (*HCW* I:491) iambic cadence so prevalent in the English sonnet, Hopkins foregrounds man's constant, unrepentant de-creation of God's grandeur through the gruesome monotony of industrialized labor with its inevitable dulling of the senses and degrading of attention. The "smudge" of the repeated diphthong ("bleared, smeared . . . wears . . . shares . . . bare") captures how the distinctive and vivid particularity of created nature, including human beings, is forever being degraded. The motif reappears elsewhere, perhaps most strongly in "The Caged Skylark," with its reference to how "Man's mounting spirit in his bone-house, mean house, dwells . . . in drudgery, day-labouring-out life's age." Six years earlier, Hopkins had remarked that "England . . . is itself in great measure founded on wrecking" and that its economic and class system ("this iniquitous order") was causing "the greatest and most necessary part of a very rich nation to live

---

12. MacKenzie 2008, 54.

a hard life without dignity, knowledge, comforts, delight, or hopes in the midst of plenty—which plenty they make."[13] However shocking to Robert Bridges, the tenor of "God's Grandeur" and Hopkins's critique of an industrial utilitarianism destined to degrade both human and natural form continues to resonate throughout his oeuvre, perhaps most prominently in "Binsey Poplars" (1879) and in "Ribblesdale" (1883). Here, "sweet Earth" seems doomed, like Philomela, to bear mute witness to the violence perpetrated against her, and to find no human voice rising in her defense. The particulars with which it is filled ("leaves throng / And louchèd [slouched] grass") stand in for the voice that would protest creation's desecration: "no tongue to plead, no heart to feel, / . . . Thou canst but be, but that thou well dost." Ecological devastation is also, and especially, spiritual desecration where unchecked economic interests "reave both our rich round world bare / And none reck of world after." To Hopkins, the human voice—and uniquely that of poetry—substitutes its articulacy for the mute eloquence of natural forms that comprise creation as a whole: "And what is Earth's eye, tongue, or heart else, where / Else, but in dear and dogged man?" (*HMW* 156–57). The relation of man and nature is of symbiosis rather than appropriation, of "earnest expectation . . . for the manifestation of God," as St. Paul puts it (Rom. 8:19) in a passage Hopkins had chosen as the epigraph for "Ribblesdale."

And yet even as by the early 1880s Hopkins's lyrics wind up on a note of "care and dear concern," his poetics never devolve into outright despair. This is readily apparent in "God's Grandeur" with its affirmation of how amid all this wintry desolation ("the soil / Is bare now") finite beings may yet participate in creation's grandeur by cultivating an undesigning attention and creative responsiveness to the abundant givenness of the visible world. For, as Hopkins will put it a few years later, "He has created us for bliss and He will give it, or the failure will be ours" (*SDW* 194). The failure to grasp the fullness of what is visibly and gratuitously given is not inevitable but contingent, a consequence of the mind having embraced false goods and yielded to wayward desires. The temporally distended, at times distracted, ways in which visual experience of nature unfolds does not unravel creation per se and for good. Rather, creation tends to be occluded by human beings' self-inflicted lapse into mechanical doing and its attendant, selective blindness. Hence, as Kevin Hart rightly stresses, the sestet does not follow "in the spirit of contrast" but of contiguity: "*And for all this*" rather than "*But for all this.*"[14] The affirmation of a metaphysical plenitude impervious to human de-creation commences with Hopkins reclaiming the visible world by retracing in minute verbal and iconic form our *experience* of that

---

13. *HCW* I:210. Nearly two decades later, the church establishment would echo Hopkins's view, such as in Cardinal Manning's express support of striking East London dockworkers in 1889 and, more guardedly, in Leo XIII's 1891 encyclical, *Rerum Novarum*.

14. K. Hart 2017, 17.

world. To that end, the generic conventions of sonnet writing must be suspended or disrupted, just as the experience of what Marion calls the saturated phenomenon can eventuate only if and when it exceeds and disrupts the epistemological and aesthetic frames by which we would possess it. Just so, "various devices [are] successfully employed to make up for the short-coming" of what Hopkins considers the "tripping" and "trifling" pattern of mid-Victorian sonnet writing.[15]

> And for all this, nature is never spent;
> There lives the dearest freshness deep down things;
> And though the last lights off the black West went
> Oh, morning, at the brown brink eastward, springs—
> Because the Holy Ghost over the bent
> World broods with warm breast and with ah! bright wings.

Though doubtful in our own times of likely irreversible, human-engineered ecological devastation, Hopkins's credo that "nature is never spent" pivots on a fundamental analogy between the ceaseless fecundity of nature and inexhaustible, divine grace. As Anne Carpenter remarks, "Grace illuminates natural beauty—not for the sake of rendering it unnatural, but to bring it to its fullness."[16] Likewise, Earth's rotation shows what Hopkins later calls "our rich round world" (*HMW* 157) to be forever moving toward light, as "morning, at the brown brink eastward, springs—." A fine instance of "sprung rhythm" and, more particularly, of what Hopkins calls "rising rhythm" (*HCW* I:414), the line's stress on the final word ("springs—") conveys not only the certainty of renewal but also the intuitive certitude with which renewal is experienced, namely, as a spiritual *event* rather than as a mere astronomical and chronometric fact. Likewise, Hopkins's scrupulous placement of the final exclamation ("ah!") *within* the final phrase ("and with ah! bright wings"), rather than before it, avoids the impression of stodginess in the sonnet's unmistakably Miltonic last two lines.[17]

In his Notebooks of 8 August 1872, Hopkins evokes the same *Gestalt* of the globe's curvature and its palpable material and metaphysical cohesion: "From the

---

15. *HCW* I:491. "As in the creation of the world, the less perfect depends upon the more perfect in order of intention, so does the rhythm of the poem depend upon the meaning of the argument" (Ward 2002, 152). Ward's reading of stress distribution in the poem's first line does not convince, however; I would suggest "The **world** is **charged** with the **grand**eur of **God**."

16. Carpenter 2015, 181.

17. "So also I cut myself off from the use of ere, o'er, wellnigh, what time, say not (for *do not say*), because, though dignified, they neither belong to nor ever cd. arise from, or be the elevation of, ordinary modern speech. For it seems to me that the poetical language of an age shd. be the current language heightened, to any degree heightened and unlike itself, but not . . . an obsolete one. This is Shakespeare's and Milton's practice and the want of it will be fatal to Tennyson's Idylls and plays, to Swinburne, and perhaps to Morris" (*HCW* I:365).

high-road I saw how the sea, dark blue with violet cloud-shadows, was warped to the round of the world like a coat upon a ball" (*HCW* III:532), a phenomenon again remarked on two years later: "The sea striped with splintered purple cloud-shadows. I marked the bole, the burling and roundness of the world" (*HCW* III:587–88). The characteristically precise, almost forensic observation informs the sonnet's closing image of "the Holy Ghost over the bent / world broods." Alluding, furthermore, to Milton's Spirit, which "from the first / Wa'st present, and with mighty wings outspread / Dove-like sat'st brooding on the vast abyss / and mad'st it pregnant," Hopkins's final lines fuse literal and proper meaning in a single *figura*.[18] That is, the Holy Spirit conceived as a dove signifies only if the latter's tactile ("with warm breast") and visual ("and with ah! bright wings") qualities are apprehended as divine manifestation rather than contingent appearance. For the literal image to *mean*, or make "pregnant" (as Milton puts it), rather than merely *be*, it must be infused with the Holy Spirit *of which* it is the image. It is an *image* in contradistinction to any notion of mere imitation (*mimēsis*), that is, the embodiment rather than a derivative of a "presence-laden" thing that can be unveiled only in the medium of the image.[19] Even more than Milton's dove, Hopkins's "Holy Ghost" is no mere rhetorical device, neither allegorical sign nor Romantic symbol. Rather, it is an image in the Latin sense of *figura* (Gk. *typos*) because "it does not disappear in pointing to something else but, in its own being, shares in what it represents."[20] For its logic is one of consubstantiality (*homoousia*) rather than derivation (*homoiousia*) or substitution, of an essential disclosure rather than contingent illustration.

Awareness of this fundamental distinction had allowed Basil of Caesarea to reject, some fifteen hundred years before Hopkins, various Arian and semi-Arian speculations that construed the Holy Spirit as but a "subordinate agent" or "local approximation" of God.[21] Against such views, Basil maintains that it is only after having been "purified" from the stain of original sin and having "come back again to his natural beauty, and as it were [having] cleaned the Royal Image and restor[ed] its ancient form" that the human being beholds the Holy Spirit. It is a vision that sin had only temporarily obscured, though never definitively expunged. Making his case

---

18. Milton, *Paradise Lost* I:19–22.

19. Ballinger 2000, 146. As Sobolev observes, "The act of sensuous perception simultaneously becomes the act of transcendence" (2011, 55); yet it is misleading to argue that, as regards things, "Hopkins tries to achieve the unmediated perception of their simple being, of the uniqueness and unity of the forms of nature" (58). Mediation is not an impediment to *theōsis* but, on the contrary, its condition of possibility.

20. Gadamer 2006, 146. Gadamer situates the image (*Bild*) "halfway between . . . *pure indication* [*Verweisung*], which is the essence of the sign, and *pure substitution* [*Vertretung*], which is the essence of the symbol" (145).

21. *PNF* 8:3–5, 15–16 (*Of the Holy Spirit*, chs. 2 and 9).

against the *pneumatomachi*, Basil strikes a hymnal note that at times prefigures the closing lines of "God's Grandeur." Thus, the Holy Spirit,

> like the sun, will by the aid of thy purified eye show thee in Himself the image of the invisible, and in the blessed spectacle of the image thou shalt behold the unspeakable beauty of the archetype. . . . Just as when a sunbeam falls on bright and transparent bodies, they themselves become brilliant too, and shed forth *a fresh brightness* from themselves, so souls wherein the Spirit dwells, illuminated by the Spirit, themselves become spiritual, and send forth their grace to others.[22]

To see "the unspeakable beauty of the archetype" and to apprehend the sheer givenness of the phenomenon as "the image of the invisible" is not, however, to invest everyday "intuition" (Husserl's *Anschauung*) with magical powers. Rather, it means reclaiming a dimension within the phenomenon anterior to its reification as "perception," a dimension that surpasses the finitude of ordinary intuition, which restricts the phenomenon to what can be predicted or verified after the fact. Beyond an anthropomorphic framework that posits in advance the convertibility of experience with the order of (scientific) discourse, there always remains "the possibility of an unconditioned and irreducible phenomenon that . . . does not amount to 'telling tales.'" Indeed, it is in the domain of what Marion calls the "saturated phenomenon" that "intuition would give *more, indeed immeasurably more*, than intention would ever have intended or foreseen."[23] Where the event of the phenomenon supplants the facts anticipated by perception, *intuition merges with contemplation*. Here, the order of the visible is apprehended as one of disclosure, the unveiling of an inexhaustible and "incomprehensible certainty" (*HCW* II:619), rather than as an epistemological challenge to be met on preestablished, anthropomorphic terms.

Recalling the opening of "God's Grandeur," Hopkins's unfinished treatise on Ignatius's *Spiritual Exercises*, written during the Long Retreat during his tertianship in November 1881, reflects on the Holy Spirit specifically under the heading "Contemplation." As he writes, "Contemplation of the Holy Ghost sent to us through creatures . . . shown *in operibus*" shows the Spirit to be "uncreated grace and the sharing by man of the divine nature and the bestowal of himself by God on man. . . . *All things therefore are charged with love, are charged with God and if we know how to touch them give off sparks and take fire, yield drops and flow, ring and tell of him*" (*SDW* 195; emphasis mine). No doubt, Hopkins would have endorsed von Balthasar's assessment that "the elimination of aesthetics from theology and from the whole Christian life . . . has meant, broadly, the expulsion of contemplation from the act of

---

22. *PNF* 8:3–5, 15–16 (*Of the Holy Spirit*, ch. 9) (emphasis mine).
23. Marion 2008, 25, 32.

faith, the exclusion of 'seeing' from 'hearing', [and] the removal of the *inchoatio visionis* from the *fides*.[24] In a similar vein, having identified several distinctive phenomena, the sonnet "Spring" appears to fuse their Edenic abundance in a single synoptic question:

> Nothing is so beautiful as Spring—
> When weeds, in wheels, shoot long and lovely and lush;
> Thrush's eggs look little low heavens, and thrush
> Through the echoing timber does so rinse and wring
> The ear, it strikes like lightnings to hear him sing;
> The glassy peartree leaves and blooms, they brush
> The descending blue; that blue is all in a rush
> With richness; the racing lambs too have fair their fling.
> What is all this juice and all this joy?
>
> (*HMW* 130–31)

"The Starlight Night" sums up the infinitude of earthbound and cosmic phenomena as "all a purchase, all . . . a prize" (*HMW* 128); likewise, "Pied Beauty" paraphrases its opening panoply of highly particularized things as "all things counter, original, spàre, strange" (*HMW* 133).

Such synoptic phrasing raises conceptual and theological issues to which we must now turn. For if "*all* things" constitute essential ("charged") manifestations of God, then of what consequence is it to speak of *this* unique thing, *here* and *now*, rather than apprehending it as the contingent instantiation of its species, or as the random product of causes that might just as plausibly have brought forth something else entirely? Does each thing's formal identity, material specificity, and spatio-temporal actuality—that is, its inscape—constrain or enhance its capacity to manifest God? Should we read "God's Grandeur" and, even more so, poems such as "The Windhover," "Pied Beauty," or "Spring" as implying that each thing's distinctive inscape holds a unique position within the Great Chain of Being? Or are we to take the specificity of each given thing as evidence of its own, unique perfection and, thus, as equivalent to all other things, each perfected in its own way? In some probing remarks from late 1881, Hopkins insists that the particularity of finite beings does not preclude their perfection. To be sure, "nothing finite can exist of itself," but every being is "limited and determined to particular dates of time and place." Yet such exhaustive determinacy is not a defect but a form of perfection, indeed (as we shall

---

24. Balthasar 1982, 70 / Balthasar 1961, I:65. Firmly resisting this "de-aestheticization" [*Entästhetisierung*], Hopkins's "poems . . . preserve the stance of a keenly contemplative rather than a dramatic involvement" (Ball 1971, 107).

see), the very way that its essence manifests itself. Thus, to the extent that a thing's formal and material constitution reveals it to be *this* and *only* this, it "has a great perfection, a great stress, and is more distinctive and higher selved, than anything else I see. . . . To be determined and distinctive is a perfection" (*SDW* 124). Perfection thus is precisely *not* an abstract quality, nothing notional or generic, but, on the contrary, inheres in the utmost particularity of a being.

Yet, if this is so, then how are we to understand the "all" in some of the passages quoted above. If, as C. S. Lewis was to quip, "the *Romance of the Rose* could not, without loss, be rewritten as *The Romance of the Onion*," what then does it mean that "Christ plays in ten-thousand places"? Ontologically speaking, is each particular inscape, in addition to being a unique manifestation (not just a symbol) of God, to be considered as incommensurable or as fungible with all others? We appear to be caught between two distinct and equally problematic conceptual scenarios: either to take the "all" in Hopkins's various affirmations that all things "are charged with the grandeur of God" to imply their equivalence and interchangeability (in which case, his theo-poetics would seem open to charges of pantheism); or, conversely, to take each thing as an image manifesting God in a wholly unique and partial manner. As it happens, the conceptual tension has a long history, reaching at least as far back as Gregory of Nyssa's interpretation of "the Platonic 'idea' in terms of the Aristotelian and Stoic notion of the 'universal' (*katholou*), which meant both the dominant unity and ground of the being of all individuals categorized under it as well as their collective, final reality." This line of argument was to be expanded by Maximus the Confessor (AD 580–662), who "saw the basic structure of the world as a dynamic tension between universal (*katholou*) and particular (*kath' hekaston*) being."[25] While commenting on pseudo-Dionysius, Maximus had further shown how God's infinity cannot be understood as a composite, since "nothing that is divisible . . . or composite . . . could possibly be infinite, for it is neither simple nor single, nor numberable or numbered."[26] Of relevance here is Maximus's insight that God's infinity and indivisibility cannot be understood as numerical *singularity*. For insofar as God categorically and utterly exceeds all category-based knowledge, his monad-like character must not be taken as an *instance* of number but as the ineffable *source* of plurality, that is, of all created being in its inexhaustible diversity. The divine name (attribute) of infinity is logically anterior to the antinomy between pantheism's accumulative and synoptic "all" and a mysticism that would apprehend God in the sheer singularity of a given inscape. What stands to be avoided, then, is the either/or of a naive

---

25. Balthasar 2003, 116.

26. Maximus 2014, 301 (*Ambiguum* 10, 1184C). "The Godhead is above and beyond all division, addition, and every part and whole (since it is devoid of quantity), and all existence according to place, and every concept that defines it in terms of how it exists" (1185D).

pantheism that would read Hopkins's "all" as the sheer accumulation of particularities and a naive mysticism that, "somehow," collapses every singular inscape with the transcendent God whom it manifests. A more integrative, albeit differentiated, understanding of Hopkins's inscape as an *imago Dei* is needed, and what follows is a step-by-step attempt to develop such a conception.

A METAPHYSICAL REALISM WITHOUT ABSTRACTION: INSCAPE AND CERTITUDE IN SCOTUS AND HOPKINS

How such questions are to be answered, and what a given answer would imply for understanding Hopkins's theo-poiesis of a world filled with "all things, counter, original, spàre, strange," things *dis-"charged"* into so many images, depends on the philosophical and theological contexts invoked in formulating it. In drawing on a wide array of biographical and textual evidence, Hopkins scholarship has long situated his poetic and theological writings in the context of Scotus, Ignatius, Ruskin, and, to a lesser extent, Newman.[27] While yielding valuable connections, this approach has also caused a great deal of interpretive work to stay within the orbit of influence study. Particularly as regards Scotus, numerous scholars have made a strong and erudite case for Hopkins's debt to the Franciscan Scholastic, which here can be rehearsed only in compressed form. By now, a consensus of sorts has emerged to the effect "that the path to an analysis of Hopkins' theological aesthetics runs through his interpretation and possible assimilation of Scotist doctrine."[28] And yet the most engaging and revealing aspect of hermeneutic practice concerns not tracing influences but scrutinizing their inflection and transformation by an emergent voice. Too often, we risk framing putative sources as quasi-efficient causes rather than as sources eliciting in the writer responding to them forms of hermeneutic scrutiny that, in turn, prepare for the creative discernment of previously unmapped semantic spaces—a movement comprising dialogue and dissent toward what Hölderlin and Rilke call "the open" (*das Offene*).

What draws Hopkins to Scotus, then, is less an eagerness to emulate the latter's theological vision than an array of questions and terms that will enable him to formulate a poetics for which there is no obvious literary or aesthetic precedent. Beginning in 1872 and culminating during his seminary years at St. Beuno's in Wales (1874–77), Hopkins's use of Scotus is not only wholly affirmative but also highly selective. For the Franciscan Scholastic's theory of knowledge, and little else besides,

---

27. On Hopkins and Scotus, see Ballinger 2000, 103–50; Devlin 1950; Pomplun 2015; Ward 2002, 158–97; White 1992, 275–84; Young 1989–90.

28. Ballinger 2000, 106 f.

maps with uncanny precision on theories Hopkins had begun formulating during his final year at Oxford (1867) and the year immediately following.[29] For Hopkins as a reader of Scotus, intellectual discovery and poetic self-recognition are intimately entwined. His initial exploration of Scotus leaves him "flush with a new stroke of enthusiasm . . . [such that] when I took in any inscape of the sky or sea I thought of Scotus."[30] That Hopkins values Scotus's writings for their seeming confirmation of theological and philosophical speculations he had been pursuing for half a decade is rendered more interesting yet because central to the Franciscan friar's epistemology is the proposition that knowledge involves a progressive drawing-out of intuitive cognition. Rejecting Henry of Ghent's skepticism concerning the possibility of "natural knowledge" (*cognitio naturalis*), Scotus maintains that "a reasoning process presupposes a knowledge of the simple thing towards which one reasons [*ad quod discurritur*]." Consequently, "a thing which is true can be known before its truth is known."[31] Quoting Augustine (*De Trin.* XV.12), Scotus stresses that knowledge begins not in doubt, but, on the contrary, springs from the certitude that phenomena registered by the senses are real, even as the constructions we put upon them may be inadequate or wrong: "There is certitude that I see even when the illusion is in the organ itself. . . . Through our bodily senses . . . we learn the heavens, the earth, the sea and all that are in them. . . . We have certitude [*certitudo*]." To the adherents of radical skepticism, who in response to any proposition brought before them maintain "that nothing is self-evident," Scotus's rejoinder will be that they have effectively placed themselves outside the sphere of reason: "I will not argue with you for it is clear that you are a quibbler [*protervus*]."[32]

For Scotus, "the sensible thing outside causes a confused sense image [*causat phantasma confusum*]." That the material source of cognition furnishes but an "intuitive" or "confused knowledge" (*cognitio intuitiva* or *cognitum confuse*) does not entail subsequent error or deception. Rather, such sentient beginnings attest to the

---

29. See "The Probable Future of Metaphysics" (Hilary Term, 1867) and "Notes on Greek Philosophy," especially the self-contained essay on Parmenides (February 1868) in which the concept "inscape" is first developed (*HCW* IV:287–321). See also Thomas 1968; Ballinger 2000, 106–9 nn. 9–11.

30. *HCW* III:532 (Journals, 4 August 1872); writing to Robert Bridges in February 1875, Hopkins assures his friend, "I do not afflict myself much about my ignorance [of Hegel]," and reports having "put back Aristotle's Metaphysics in the library some time ago feeling that I could not read them now and so probably should never. After all I can, at all events a little, read Duns Scotus and I care for him more even than Aristotle and more *pace tua* than a dozen Hegels" (*HCW* I:242).

31. Scotus 1987, 23, 99.

32. Ibid., 112, 105, 119. For Hopkins, the point was brought home by J. H. Newman's *An Essay in Aid of a Grammar of Assent* (1870), a work on which he had proposed to write a commentary. Newman politely declined, "because I do not feel the need of it" (*HCW* II:571); see letters from Newman to GMH of 27 February and 26 April 1883.

knower's preconceptual, albeit focused, awareness of a given appearance's distinctive character. For "the senses are not a cause but merely an occasion of the intellect's knowledge."[33] Hence, the very capacity of mind (*intellectus*) to respond in attentive and focused ways to what is phenomenally given presupposes the concurrent existence and operation of what Scotus calls *formalitates*, "aspects of a thing perceived that are separable realities and yet do not violate the unity that makes that entity a single thing."[34] Scotus also speaks of a *species specialissima*, something "immediately given in sensation" that allows knowledge, literally, *to take shape* as the "awareness of a general pattern of sense-qualities before we are aware of any particular individual."[35] This awareness of what Hopkins as early as 1868 calls "inscape" first manifests itself in a mental image, that is, in "a refined energy accenting the nerves" (*HCW* IV:307). Scotus calls it a *phantasma*; Husserl will call it the "absolute givenness in apprehension" (*absolute Gegebenheit in der Auffassung*); Marion will speak of "the happening phenomenon" as the "event" of the visible "accomplish[ing] an originary givenness," in contradistinction to the "object" that is but "a fallen [*déchu*] phenomenon, because it appears as always already expired [*échu*]."[36] In each case, what is at stake is the instance when mind and world first enter into contact in such a way as for the visibly given phenomenon to reveal within consciousness a primal orientation toward and an incipient convergence with the phenomenon. Finding itself commensurable within the thing that it apprehends, "the mind turns to it, not as to the object, nor as to anything representing the object, but so as to intensify its own likeness to the object."[37]

Already during his studies at Balliol College and long before his cursory readings in Scotus's *Opus Oxoniense* allowed him to put the matter in more technical terms, Hopkins appeared deeply preoccupied with homing in on this intriguing fusion of perceptual and spiritual cognition, both of which he takes to originate in our apprehension of the distinctive formal organization or inscape of a particular appearance (something he would later find echoed in Scotus's notion of *formalitas*). Two journal entries from 1869 and 1872 illustrate the way in which perceptual consciousness crystallizes as the beholder's active participation in and transformation by the phenomenon.

---

33. Scotus 1987, 128, 108.

34. Ward 2002, 162.

35. Devlin 1950, 196; see also Sobolev's remark, "Hopkins' descriptions of singular physical objects exemplify the doctrine of inscape not because these objects embody unique designs, but—on the contrary—because they exist as variations of endlessly repeatable patterns" (2011, 89). On Scotus and Hopkins, see Ward's detailed and lucid discussion (2002, 159–97); Ballinger 2000, 103–50; Young 1989–90; Pomplun 2015; Muller 2003, 74–100.

36. Husserl 1991, §3; Marion 2002b, 30–53, quotes from 38, 36.

37. Scotus, quoted in Devlin 1950, 118.

On the 9th there was snow but not lying on the roads. On the grass it became a crust lifted on the heads of the blades. As we went down a field near Caesar's Camp I noticed it before me *squalentem*, coat below coat, sketched in intersecting edges bearing "idiom" all down the slope: —I have no other word yet for that *which takes the eye or mind in a bold hand or effective sketching or in marked features or again in graphic writing*, which not being beauty nor true inscape yet gives interest and makes ugliness even better than meaninglessness.

Ground sheeted with taut tattered streaks of crisp gritty snow. Green-white tufts of long bleached grass like heads of hair or the crowns of heads of hair, each a whorl of slender curves, one tuft taking up another—however these I might have noticed any day. I *saw the inscape freshly, as if my eye were still growing*, though *with a companion the eye and the ear are for the most part shut and instress cannot come.* . . . All the world is full of inscape and chance left free to act falls into an order as well as purpose: looking out of my window I caught it in the random clods and broken heaps of snow made by the cast of a broom."[38]

What Hopkins thus characterizes as our responsiveness to a thing's "inscape" first manifests itself as a mental image—a *phantasma*, as Maximus the Confessor had put it in the seventh century, or a *cognitio confuse,* as Scotus was to argue at the beginning of the fourteenth. We should note the dynamic and transformative nature of vision (". . . as if my eye were still growing"), which for Hopkins involves attending in a sustained manner to the texture and structure of a phenomenon that precisely because it was not purposely sought can also not be second-guessed as regards its sheer reality vis-à-vis the beholder. Likewise, where Scotus discusses "insight of something existing, as it exists" (*visio existentis ut existens*) or "insight into existing nature" (*visio naturae existentis*), his concern is with the advent of the image as pure, unconditional "self-showing," albeit in a sense far more open to metaphysics than Heidegger's *sich-selbst-Zeigen*.[39] Not only does this advent of a phenomenon or *formalitas* alert us to a fundamental "commensurability" (*convenientia*) of mind and world prior to all inference, abstraction, and conceptualization; but that mind and world appear teleologically ordered toward one another can also be understood as an unconditional good or, in theological parlance, as an instance of grace.

---

38. *HCW* III:483, 544, 549; emphasis mine. Hopkins's passing stress on solitude as a condition for receptiveness to instress will be echoed in the second of Claudel's *Five Great Odes*: "Why do you listen alone? / Because only alone do I submit to a divine measure, the perfect measure, holy, free, all-powerful, creative! [Pourquoi donc seul l'entends tu? Parce que seule soumise à une mesure divine! / Parce qu'elle n'est tout entière que mesure même, / La mesure sainte, libre, toute-puissante, créatrice!]" (Claudel 1967, 247 / 2020, 53).

39. Heidegger 1996, 28–31 (§7).

This "pre-predicative" knowledge (as Husserl will later call it) affirms the consubstantiality of essence and activity, such that "what the mind knows is identical
with what the mind *is*."[40] What Scotus calls "the first act" of knowing or "insight into
existing nature" and "insight into something existing *as it exists*" stands in sharp contrast to conceptualism. For the latter can never capture the unique "thisness" (*haecceitas*) of an appearance but, being keen to move *beyond* the phenomenon's sheer
particularity, merely extrapolates general traits from it. To isolate what Scotus identifies as the first act of cognition is essentially the same operation as Husserl's "phenomenological reduction," which likewise aims to bring into focus nothing more,
nor less, than the totality of an appearance (*Erscheinung*) as a unique, pre-predicative
event without abstracting from it an "appearing object" (*erscheinender Gegenstand*),
let alone predicating anything about it. Hence Hopkins's passing remark, "To me
there is no resemblance" (*SDW* 123) of things in the natural world; and even though
in some late letters he dismisses "unstrung hysterical creatures" such as "crazy Blake"
(*HCW* II:821), Hopkins would undoubtedly have endorsed the London printmaker's
assertion that all "General Knowledge is Remote Knowledge, [that] it is in Particulars that Wisdom consists" and that "to generalize is to be an idiot."[41]

Strictly speaking, then, Scotus, Hopkins, and Husserl all agree that "to perceive
is not to judge or think that we perceive."[42] For the main goal is to attend to the phenomenon that "shows itself" only when engaged in a strictly nonproprietary and
nondeterminative manner. For inasmuch as for Scotus "insight" (*visio*) does not as
yet extend "into the individuality of any particular thing [*visio naturae existentis sine
visione singularitatis*], . . . the sensing mind is not aware of any individual as such but
it is directly aware of nature as a real entity, and yet of nature as permeated with a
certain individuality [Sensus no per se sentit singulare, tamen sentit naturam extra
animam primo, sed ut coniunctam singularitati necessario]."[43] As for Parmenides,
Plotinus, and Augustine, Scotus's epistemology rests on an ontology that posits Being
as anterior to all individual acts of knowledge. The metaphysical reality of all forms
and their teleological orientation toward intelligibility is always presupposed by any
discursive and conceptual sifting of our perceptions. Though always grounded in the
apprehension of sense data, knowledge does not construct, let alone impose, sense
on the putatively inchoate deliverances of our sensory apparatus. Instead, Scotus
conceives of knowledge as our participation in divine (uncircumscribed) Being as
mediated by created (circumscribed) being, which discloses itself to our senses in the

---

40. Devlin 1950, 124–25.
41. Blake 1982, 560, 641.
42. Romano 2015, 63; for a programmatic statement of the "phenomenological reduction,"
see Husserl 1991, §§3–8; on the notion of the "pre-predicative" and its logical entanglements, see
Romano 2015, 66–88. On Husserl's conception of the image, see also ch. 10, below.
43. Quoted in Devlin 1950, 120.

sheer givenness of unique and distinctive appearance: "In the present life no concept representing reality is formed naturally in the mind except by reason of those factors which naturally motivate the intellect . . . [viz.,] the active intellect, the image or the object revealed in the sense image [illa sunt phantasma vel objectum relucens in phantasmate et intellectus agens]."

Indeed, this anteriority of the *logos* vis-à-vis individual acts of cognition is evident in the way that concrete knowledge unfolds. For, as Scotus insists, all "reasoning [*discursus*] presupposes a knowledge of the simple thing towards which one reasons." Hence, sensory-cum-discursive understanding does not unilaterally construct the world by conceptual means of its own devising but, instead, recognizes itself as a participant in the transcendent order of the *logos*. It makes explicit, *discloses*, or *unveils* the intrinsic coherence of that which appears and, in so doing, shows the intellect and the phenomena it engages to be teleologically ordered toward one another. As Scotus puts it, "No concept could arise in virtue of the active intellect and the sense image that is not univocal but only analogous with, or wholly other than, what is revealed in the sense image. . . . No object will produce a simple and proper concept of itself and a simple and proper concept of another object unless it contains this second object essentially or virtually."[44] As we have seen already and will soon have occasion to explore further, Scotus's condition ("unless it contains this second object . . . virtually") delineates the sphere of the image as ontologically dependent on an anterior being and yet, as a case of what Gadamer calls "presentation" (*Darstellung*), investing its source with a distinctive presence unattainable for logical and propositional cognition.

Scotus's term of art for the mind's pre-predicative awareness of, and orientation to, the identity and integrity of the phenomenon—which is always more than mere "resemblance" and, thus, can never be dismissed as mere "semblance"—is *cognitio habitualis*. He opposes it to the discretionary judgments of *cognitio activa*, which yield a determinative and necessarily abstract concept and, by their very nature, are susceptible of error. Now, the intuitive and the real converge in what Scotus calls "little forms" (*formalitates*), "organizing relations within a single object . . . not separable from one another" but certainly varied in that "a thing potentially has as many *formalitates* as there are truthful ways of looking at it." Understood as *formalitas*, the

---

44. Scotus 1987, 22–23; Muller's claim that Scotus's belief in a univocity of being "allowed Hopkins to view nature as a core of pent-up divine energy" (assuming that this is indeed Scotus's position) has the unfortunate effect of turning Hopkins into a neo-Romantic committed to "theories of an organic universe of interrelated substance and spirit" (2003, 94). Though Hopkins may never have fully considered the implications of Scotus's univocalist arguments, the latter's rejection of the *analogia entis* framework leaves only two alternatives: that of a "theopanism" that collapses all immanence into a transcendent god or a pantheism that diffuses such a god into ontic being. As we shall see below, Hopkins rejects both options.

image "is not the spinning of fictions but the serial revelation of the actual structure of truth, in the only way it can be perceived by temporal creatures."[45] It follows that the image or *phantasma* as which a phenomenon registers in the observer cannot be assimilated to the conceptual objectives of a philosophical system. The correlate of this image is neither some primordial object nor a mere projection. Rather, Scotus's *phantasma* reflects a state of absolute (nonrepresentational) certitude wherein mind finds itself to be wholly entwined with world; in time, such a position will be revived in more qualified language not only by continental phenomenology but also by John McDowell's critical realism.[46] Notably, the kinds of images abounding in Hopkins's journals do not *refer* to anything, nor are they premised on some antecedent concept now being fulfilled by a particular intuition.

To understand the underlying dialectic of Hopkins's writings on nature, metaphysics, and theology after 1868, we must recall the broader intellectual and theological culture with which he finds himself increasingly at odds. Militating against Hopkins's view of nature's inscapes as bona fide manifestations of their divine source is the prevailing scientific culture of mid-Victorian England, which posits that scientific knowledge of nature requires nothing less than the complete rejection of metaphysical realism. As he puts it, the dominant model of "science is atomic, not to be grasped and held together, 'scopeless,' without metaphysics: this alone gives meaning to laws and sequences and causes and developments" (*HCW* IV:288). Hopkins evidently rejects the majority view, which during the previous decade had been exemplified by Darwin's *Origin of Species* (1859) and which he characterizes in terms remarkably similar to Stephen Jay Gould's "punctuated equilibrium." On this account, "nature is a string all the differences in which are really chromatic but certain places in it have become accidentally fixed." As a result, an antimetaphysical naturalism or "atomism like a stiffness or sprain seems to hang and hamper our speculation." Against this model, Hopkins calls for a "new Realism" (*HCW* IV:289), insisting that in order to appraise particular natural entities at all ("notes on a scale"), there must be "certain forms, wh. have a great hold on the mind and are always reappearing and seem imperishable, . . . [and which] are inexplicable on the theory of pure chromaticism and continuity—the forms have in some sense or other an absolute existence."[47] Yet Hopkins also realizes that philosophical and theological arguments marshaled "against the grain of popular thought" have usually "come out too abstract, unpregnant, and inefficient." Hence, even as the prevailing naturalism will likely have to be confronted by "some shape of the Platonic ideas" (*HCW* IV:290),

---

45. Ward 2002, 189–90.

46. See McDowell 1996, 3–23.

47. *HCW* IV:290. Later, in his 1880 writings on Ignatius, Hopkins concedes that "the form of the whole species is nearer being a true Self than the individual," albeit only as fruits of human, conceptual ingenuity: "But these universals are finite only" (*SDW* 128).

Hopkins is firmly on guard against the propensity of these "ideas" to turn once again into mere abstractions, seemingly unrelated to the particularity of the phenomenal world and destined to resemble the arid conceptualism they would oppose.

It is here that Scotus's writings turned out to anticipate Hopkins's attempts to formulate a Realism that does not conceive "essence" as an abstraction or species-like universal but, on the contrary, as a visible and intelligible being of the utmost determinacy and particularity. Central to Scotus's epistemology, and reappearing in Hopkins's writings and Husserl's phenomenology, is the premise that all things, regardless of their contingent appearance and unique attributes, share the predicate of Being (*esse*). By definition invisible per se, this ontological substratum not only funds and sustains all finite being, but is also thrown into vivid, albeit fleeting relief by the distinctive phenomenology of each finite being. Each particular entity is not just a spatiotemporal something but, by its very mode of appearing, may also be apprehended as a particular manifestation of its source. For Hopkins to assert that "nothing finite can exist of itself . . . I myself cannot be selfexistent" (*SDW* 124–25) is to confirm "that ontology is the horizon of his poetics."[48] Summarizing Scotus's conception of *formalitas*, Louis Dupré remarks that "what distinguishes one being from another—the *forma individualis*—is itself a form, rather than being a mere quantification of a universal *species* singularized by the principle of indeterminacy (*material signata quantitate*) as Aquinas had proclaimed. The singularity of the individual adds a *formal* characteristic to the universal forms of genus and species. Individuality, then, far from being a mere sign of contingency, constitutes the supreme form."[49] More than anything else in the *Opus Oxoniense*, what so appealed to Hopkins was Scotus's grasp of individual form as the perfection of determinacy rather than as a random product of *in*determinacy in the manner of Lyell and Darwin. As he had put it, "to be determined and distinctive is a perfection" (*SDW* 124). Two questions now arise. First, what specific warrant might there be for Hopkins to take this view? That is, in what way might a given thing's mode of appearance, its phenomenology, warrant ascribing to it an "essence" that is other (and more) than an abstraction? Second, assuming the case for a Realism of nonabstract essences can be made, is it more than so much idiosyncratic speculation on Hopkins's part? Are there, in addition to Scotus's precursor role, also philosophical and/or theological voices that have advanced a similar position in the wake of Hopkins?

---

48. Sobolev 2011, 54.

49. Dupré 1993, 38–39; by contrast, Aquinas sees the concept (*verbum mentis*) originating "through the so-called *species*," which to a certain extent "separates the natural being from the ideal one." Here Dupré quotes *Summa contra Gentiles* I:53, where Aquinas specifies that "an external thing does not exist in our intellect according to its own nature; rather, it is necessary that its *species* be in our intellect" (103). Both Scotus and, following him, Hopkins disagree.

Regarding both of these questions, let us briefly consider Claude Romano's trenchant account of what he calls "an essentialism without essences," a philosophical position he develops by way of expanding on an often overlooked feature of Husserl's alleged Platonism in *Ideas I* (1913). There Husserl advances, in addition to the essentialism of properties and abstract concepts, an alternative conception of essence as strictly tied to the contingent individual entity. The case begins with Husserl putting pressure on the notion of "contingency" (*Zufälligkeit*) and showing that it signifies only in relation to a determinate state of affairs or "factualness" (*Tatsächlichkeit*). Far from denoting randomness, then,

> contingency . . . is constrained by virtue of being correlated with a *necessity* [*korrelativ bezogen auf eine Notwendigkeit*] that does not refer to the mere factual obtaining of a rule governing the coordination of spatiotemporal facts but instead has the character of the *necessity of an essence* [*Wesensnotwendigkeit*] and is thus correlated to the *universality of an essence*. When we said that each fact "in keeping with its own essence" could be otherwise, we already expressed thereby *that it just is part of the sense of everything contingent to have an essence and thus an eidos that is to be grasped purely*, and this [*eidos*] stands then under *truths of essences at various levels of universality* [*Wesens-Wahrheiten verschiedener Allgemeinheitsstufe*]. An individual object is not merely in general an individual one, a *This here!* A "once and only" object. Fashioned as such and such "in its very self" it has *its own kind of being*, its complement of *essential* predicables that must pertain to it (as "the entity as it is in itself" [*als Seiendem, wie es in sich selbst ist*]), so that other secondary, relative determinations can pertain to it.[50]

As soon as one recognizes this necessity of "predicates necessary to a thing's being what it is," the concept of essence ceases to be understood in terms of generality, abstraction, and universality, as the prevailing tradition of reading Plato had long maintained. Instead, Romano argues, "essence . . . answers the [Aristotelian] question *ti esti?*—namely the set of predicates that define the *to ti en einai*, the 'what' that the thing 'is' or better, the 'what it is to be [that thing]', or yet again the 'what it is [for that thing] to be the thing it is [it was]—what Latin expresses as *quidditas*." As Aristotle had noted, essence is also "about the thing and not only about the predicates. . . . Since individual objects can have an essence as well as general [predicable] properties, the individual essence, that is, the set of predicates necessary for an individual to be the *individual* it is, distinct from all other individuals falling under the same

50. Husserl 2014, 10 (§2).

genus, must be distinguished from the generic essence."[51] The latter can specify only the *kind* or *species* under which the individual is subsumed. Its province is thus one of logical, though not essential, necessity.

Scotus will reiterate the point when maintaining against Henry of Ghent that "we must look beyond all our ideas of attributes or quasi-attributes, in order to find a quidditative concept to which the former may be attributed." And only a "sense image [*phantasma*] that is not univocal but only analogous with, or wholly other than, what is revealed in the sense image" can "motivate the intellect" to engage in conceptual activity.[52] It is only through the primal charism of the image, and never through the modal relationships enshrined in Aristotelian categories, that a thing's essence discloses itself—bearing in mind that essence here does not abstract from or stand in as a mere allegory for being but, on the contrary, names a thing's spatiotemporal singularity (*haecceitas*) and indubitable sensory presence to an observing consciousness. Likewise, Husserl's insistence, early on in his *Ideas I*, that "generality of essence" (*Wesensallgemeinheit*) not be conflated with "eidetic necessity" (*Wesensnotwendigkeit*) shows that modal logic alone will not suffice to understand the real essence of being. Consequently, "the pair necessary/contingent does not coincide with the pair essential/accidental, because the mention of essence introduces an extralogical element, an element of *relevance* of the property under consideration, . . . [one] having no equivalent from the point of view of modal logic. The truth of the proposition that attributes an essential property (or that attributes a property essential) is not necessary *in an unqualified way*; it is necessary *by virtue of the identity of the object*." While it is *necessary* for Frodo, my Yorkshire terrier, to belong to a set (the genus dog and the species terrier), it is not *essential* for this particular dog, little Frodo, "to belong to any sets whatsoever."[53]

What may seem a rather recondite, technical quibble thus far turns out to hold great significance, as recent attempts to qualify the jurisdiction of modal logic have shown.[54] For not only does Husserl demonstrate that essence and necessity are not convertible. He effectively reverses the traditional view according to which essence is to be defined modally, that is, in terms of Aristotelian categories. Overturning that assumption, Husserl's concept of an "essential [or eidetic] necessity" (*Wesensnotwendigkeit*) pivots on a radical concretion or "particularization" (*Besonderung*) of individual being, which thus not only cannot be reduced to logical modalities, but in effect furnishes their ontological warrant in the first place. It is here that we are presented with "Husserl's central intuition: all essential attribution of a property gives

51. Romano 2015, 203–4.
52. Scotus 1987, 19, 22.
53. Romano 2015, 204–5.
54. See the discussion of Kit Fine's "Essence and Modality" (1994), in Romano 2015, 207–14.

rise to a necessary truth, nowise to a truth that is necessary *in an unqualified way*, but to a truth that is necessary by virtue of the identity of the object in question."[55]

For Hopkins, this particularized, essential necessity is modeled by Scotus's conception of *formalitas* and *haecceitas*. In the strict sense of an essential singularity, Scotus's "individual form" (*formalitas*), we recall, "adds a *formal* characteristic to the universal forms of genus or species."[56] Yet we now also see that the essential necessity of the individual thing is not fungible with, indeed is not of the same *kind* as, formal essences such as genus and species. Rather, it is an essence wholly inseparable from the material thing's spatiotemporal instantiation as "this here" (Husserl's *dieses Da*; Scotus's *haecceitas*). Indeed, "from Husserl's point of view, a material essence does not *have* an essence in the same way in which it *is* an essence." Consequently, predication cannot circumscribe Being; and a material essence that a thing *has*, and in virtue of which it is what it is, must be seen as logically anterior to any quality predicated of it. Understandably worried that this insight might in turn undergo reification, Romano speaks of "an *adverbial* conception of essence: there are no essences as ideal objects, but things are *essentially* such and such."[57] Yet as soon as the central point has been established, the phenomenological question naturally arises: How is it that this "essential necessity" (*Wesensnotwendigkeit*) of an individual thing discloses itself to consciousness? What is the quality of its experience, its phenomenology? Of consuming interest to Hopkins in his *Journals* and the great sonnets of the late 1870s is precisely this sense of contingency as denoting an individual thing's supreme determinacy or essence, as well as how its abundance or "excess" (Marion) strikes and in/ forms the beholding consciousness: "the form penetrates, the prepossession flushes the matter" (*HCW* IV:307).

In several short essays on Greek philosophy, written in 1868, Hopkins had first mapped the questions that his encounter with Scotus's *Opus Oxoniense* some four years later would allow him to address in more consistent terms. Having taken a rare "double-first" in Classics and "Greats" (*Humaniores Majorae*) from Oxford's intellectual powerhouse, Balliol College, the recent graduate and Catholic convert is retracing his readings in classical philosophy in search of a vocabulary that, in time, will culminate in his conceptions of inscape and instress. As for whether "abstractions exist apart in any way fr. the concrete," Hopkins notes that "the idea . . . is not the abstraction, ~~it is~~ indeed it is as much the concrete as the abstract and exists before

---

55. Romano 2015, 207–8.

56. Dupré 1993, 38–39. As Sobolev notes, "Hopkins' 'aesthetic of particularity' should be called, in more precise terms, the theology of particularity" (2011, 58).

57. Romano 2015, 209, 211. Likewise, "Hopkins spurns the distinction between essence and existence. He is not concerned with the universal, but with wording and thus poetically inscaping an individual thing in a particular moment of time" (Ballinger 2000, 196).

the universal has been abstracted from the particulars." An idea both anticipates actual experience and, in retrospect, synthesizes the quality of that experience: "it was never true while the things lasted, though now it is the true, in fact, the only, way of ~~lookin~~ thinking of them" (*HCW* IV:304). For Hopkins, what encapsulates the idea's prismatic and luminous quality is the Plotinian trope "of the sun in broken water, where the sun's face being once crossed by the ripples each one carries an image down with it as its own sun; and these images are always mounting the ripples and trying to fall back once again" (*HCW* IV:305). As in the countless descriptions filling his notebooks, as well as some probing letters sent to the editors of the journal *Nature*, Hopkins's forensic precision shows him firmly on guard against the hazard of "unpregnant and inefficient" abstraction. Wherever they happen to fall on the spectrum from the descriptive to the expressive, words are inherently capable of denoting a "thing and not a relation."[58]

Yet for that to happen, the word must be imbued with what Hopkins calls a "prepossession of feeling," by which he appears to mean the word's elemental bond with a given phenomenon as the correlate of pure "apprehension," the fulcrum of our "focal awareness" (Polanyi). Husserl will speak of "pure apprehension" (*reine Auffassung*) wherein consciousness attends to the phenomenon as a distinctive, charismatic presence without framing it conceptually as a perception. As such, the word, especially the poetic word, is ontologically distinct from the domain of concepts, for it does not aim to convert the phenomenon into a perception in the Wittgensteinian sense of a *taking-X-as-Y*. Rather, the word's most elemental function is that of letting something appear, "to 'give it a name,' to come out with something, to word or put a thought or thing."[59] Where the word unveils, rather than naming or labeling, an appearance, it will allow the latter to fill, inform and, potentially, transform the beholding consciousness. To the extent that an appearance brings about the apprehension of a thing's essence, it does so in the modality of an image whose significance pivots on our receiving it just as it gives itself, and to do so in an "abiding" manner, by "enjoy[ing] a single thought: we may call it contemplation" (*HCW* IV:306-7).

Held in focus by contemplation, "the image is a likeness to the primordial form in that it has the 'stress' of the latter in itself."[60] Or, as Hopkins puts it, the image is an instance of "prepossession" and of the mind's "foredrawing act" (*HCW* IV:306, 315); it captures a "brute beauty"—such as we encounter in the distinctive *Gestalt* of the Windhover's movements—as yet unaffected by rhetorical and cultural surfeit. What

---

58. These are the letters of 16 November 1882, 15 November 1883, and 30 October 1884 (*HCW* II:549, 637, 686–88).

59. *HCW* IV:315. Hopkins here introduces the Greek *phantizesthai*, the middle infinitive form that ultimately derives from *phainō* ("to bring to light, to make appear" [Liddell and Hart]).

60. Balthasar 1986, 393.

merges such appearance into an image is its intuitive hold on the observer, that is, its capacity to trigger what Hopkins, and eventually Husserl in his Fifth *Logical Investigation*, calls "attentiveness" (*Aufmerksamkeit*): "to see, ... *to attend to, to take heed of, and to contemplate* ... [and] Thirdly, *to watch and consider*. ... When continued or kept on the strain the act of [memory] is attention, advertence, heed, the being *ware*, and its habit, knowledge, the being *aware*" (*SDW* 174). In this dynamic, the term "prepossession" appears to denote the sheer plenitude and event-like character of visibility, of the inscaped phenomenon arresting and (temporarily) filling the beholding consciousness.

> The further in anything, as a work of art, the organisation is carried out, the deeper the form penetrates, the prepossession flushes the matter, the more effort will be required in apprehension, the more power of comparison, ~~wh.~~ the more capacity for receiving that synthesis of (either successive or spatially distinct) impressions wh. gives us ~~the prepossession in~~ the unity with the prepossession conveyed by it. ... But some minds prefer that the prepossession they are to receive shd. be conveyed by the least organic, expressive, by the most suggestive way. By this means the prepossession and the definition, uttering, are distinguished and unwound, wh. is the less sane attitude. (*HCW* IV:307–8)

"Prepossession," then, is a *phenomenological* concept and, as such, not subject to the requirements of modal logic. It posits that the very way that a phenomenon is apprehended, indeed, its capacity to be focally apprehended at all, discloses the essential nature of the thing *of* which it is the appearance. For if it is only in virtue of its unique mode of appearance that a thing has being; and only in response to its anterior and unique givenness can a thing's being become an object of epistemological inquiry or, for that matter, doubt.

Quoting Parmenides, Hopkins thus affirms "that all things are upheld by instress and are meaningless without it." Echoing the Scholastic postulate regarding the convertibility of being (*esse*) and act (*actus*), Hopkins effectively asserts that we can access the world of things only insofar as it actively divulges itself to us and, consequently, only by responding to the specific manner of that disclosure. There can be no epistemology without an anterior phenomenology. Hence, Parmenides's "*esti* may roughly be expressed by *things are* or *here is truth*. ... I have often felt ... the depth of an instress or how fast the inscape holds a thing that nothing is so pregnant and straightforward to the truth as simple <u>yes</u> and <u>is</u>. 'Thou couldst never either know or say/ ~~a thing that~~ what was not, there wd. be no coming at it.' ~~No~~ There wd. be no bridge, no stem of stress between us and things to bear us out and carry the mind over" (*HCW* IV:313). Regarding Parmenides's apparent likening of Being to a perfectly rounded sphere, Hopkins thus notes how its formal integrity and self-identity are inseparable: "Not-being is here seen as want of oneness" (*HCW* IV:315), neither disclosing anything nor concealing that which (on a genuinely phenomenological view) cannot appear per se. Once the phenomenological reduction has suspended all consideration of a thing's accidental attributes and qualities and focused us on its sheer and indubitable presence, the latter refers us back to a single substratum (for lack of a better word) *of which* a given appearance is one among many possible ones. Phenomenological inquiry discloses how the identity of a thing is preconceptually given by virtue of the fact that, in its distinctive mode of appearance, the saturated phenomenon elicits the beholder's quest for a unified organizational schema, a pre-conceptual *image* or *form* (*eidos*). For only that can appear which is truly identical with itself, a "one"—not in any monolithic sense, to be sure, but inasmuch as it is im-bued ("instressed") with the type of organized, structured agency that Hopkins calls inscape.

Yet because it can appear only on that condition, the saturated phenomenon also depends on our participation in it. Appearing and beholding are two inseparable di-mensions of a single event, much like *figura* (*typos*) and its fulfillment condition the allegorical and anagogical interpretation of scripture. Of relevance here is Scotus's refutation of a central claim underpinning Henry of Ghent's epistemological skep-ticism. That things of which we have sensory awareness appear mutable does not, as Henry and (much later) Descartes would have it, invalidate the knowledge we form of them: "for it is not precisely this *mutability* in the object that causes the knowl-edge; [rather] it is the *nature* of this mutable object that does so, and this nature is immutable."[61] Mutability is itself an essential, not accidental, feature of all kinds of things encountered in nature. Things exhibit transformative change; their form is an entelechy manifested by their continuous internal *transformation* (as Goethe had so influentially argued) and hence cannot be grasped by mechanist categories of acci-dent and alteration. Indeed, the transformational, agent character of natural things is not what stands to be explained (*explanandum*). On the contrary, its visible mani-festation furnishes the very source and guide for any understanding we could ever hope to attain of their being. Scotus's *formalitas* and Hopkins's *inscape* are attempts to identify the dynamic phenomenology of natural beings absent which an observer could hardly achieve the focal awareness (Polanyi) required for entering into an epi-stemic relationship to a particular thing. Thus, Hopkins's world is neither an aggre-gation of so many inert objects nor a kaleidoscope of random apparitions. Rather it is filled with things that, each in its own way, are distinguished by a unique mode of action. It is a world of almost primal animism—von Balthasar speaks of a *Urwelt* as opposed to mid-Victorians' customary notion of landscape as *Kulturlandschaft*—a world in which beauty and terror, grace and suffering, are not antonyms but two

---

61. Scotus 1987, 116.

sides of the same coin. For the lethal indifference of the "wind's burly and beat of en-dragonéd seas" (*HMW* 116) draws on the same primal energy as the visually mes-merizing play of kingfishers catching fires; dragonflies drawing flame; a swirling pool of water giving off "a wíndpuff-bónnet of fáwn-fróth"; a windhover's "hurl and glid-ing"; the skylark's "sweetest spells"; and the "rinse and wring" of the thrush's song striking the ear "like lightening"[62] (*HMW* 129–32).

Each thing has agency, indeed will manifest its *form* precisely by exhibiting a dis-tinct pattern of transformation. To cover one's eye at sunset so as not to have one's eye "blunted" by the sun itself is to encounter minute shifts of color and light inten-sity: "Today I inscaped them together and made the sun the true eye and ace of the whole, as it is. It was all active and tossing out light" (*HCW* III:484). And insofar as its reality is convertible with its mode of agency, each thing is also subject to change—albeit not in the sense of contingent alteration but of purposive transformation. In-deed, change is the ontological condition absent which a thing could never manifest itself as *this active being*. Far from amounting to some static and generic object, each thing participates in the ontological order of creation by manifesting itself dynami-cally. As Scotus puts it, "Something can be represented under an immutable aspect, even if that which does the representing is something mutable in itself."[63] Far from invalidating a given thing's self-identity and continuity, mutability affirms the reality and formal specificity of a thing as bound up with its "act" or "operation" (*actus*). The interdependence of form and act is given quasi-programmatic expression in the octet of "As kingfishers catch fire" (1877):

> As kingfishers catch fire, dragonflies draw flame;
> As tumbled over rim in roundy wells
> Stones ring; like each tucked string tells, each hung bell's
> Bow swung finds tongue to fling out broad its name;
> Each mortal thing does one thing and the same:
> Deals out that being indoors each one dwells;
> Selves—goes itself; *myself* it speaks and spells,
> Crying *Whát I dó is me: for that I came.*
>
> (*HMW* 129)

The poem's intricate sound patterning, built around alliteration and internal rhyme ("rim" and "ring" / "hung" and "swung" / "selves" and "spells") embodies what it also

---

62. *HMW* 129–32. Balthasar 1986, 359 / German orig. 1984, II.2, 725. For an excellent discus-sion of von Balthasar's reading of, and debt to, Hopkins's incarnational poetics, see Carpenter 2015, 162–82.

63. Scotus 1987, 116, 117.

advances in quasi propositional form: namely, that even as each thing is wholly unique in its mode of operation it is also interconnected with all other things. The world is an ensemble of inscapes, related rather than isolated, complementary rather than incommensurable, and dynamic rather than static. Hence, even as "each word for Hopkins is a node or pattern of linguistic energy," what makes it pregnant with meaning is its formal and material contiguity with other words, a resemblance often coded into a given word's phonetic and rhythmic pattern. The etymological speculations that pervade Hopkins's early diaries illustrate this contiguity and complementarity of words no less than things.[64] Hence his contention that "any two things however unlike are in something like" (*SDW* 123). That a thing's inscape should prompt us to distinguish it from that of another already intimates their relatedness. In Hopkins's sonnet, moreover, inscape is nothing notional but, on the contrary, is a case of being positively manifesting itself as *actus*: "Each thing . . . / Deals out" its being, and "each hung bell's / Bow . . . fling[s] out broad its name." No mere assertion or conclusion of speculative inquiry, as critics tracing Scotus's influence on Hopkins often imply, *haeceitas* in Scotus and "inscape" in Hopkins names what phenomenology has more recently explored under the heading of "givenness," "perceptual faith," and "the essence of manifestation."[65] Hence, though distinctness of inscape is of crucial importance, its true relevance does not rest with its epistemological import but with its phenomenological status as the manifestation or disclosure, qua visible thing, of God; and it is for this reason that viewing Hopkins strictly through the lens of Scotus proves a constraint.

> I say móre: the just man justices;
> Keeps grace: thát keeps all his goings graces;
> Acts in God's eye what in God's eye he is—
> Chríst—for Christ plays in ten thousand places,
> Lovely in limbs, and lovely in eyes not his
> To the Father through the features of men's faces.
>   (*HMW* 129)

---

64. See Hopkins's sifting of "cling, clam, clem, meaning starve, . . . clammed to death . . . perhaps distantly akin to *claudere*, close, kleis, clasp, etc, and cleave," or his tracing of "Flick, fillip, flip, fleck, flake . . . connected with *fly, flee, flit*, meaning to fly off" (*HCW* III:118–19, 126). J. Hillis Miller's otherwise engaging discussion of inscape as sound patterning (1975, 279–87) is marred by some capricious assertions, such as that "the meaning is there only as a necessary support for the pattern" and that inscape in Hopkins "means just the opposite of the Scotist *haecceitas*" (282). Ward offers a helpful corrective here, noting that "as in the creation of the world, the less perfect depends upon the more perfect in the order of intention, so does the rhythm of the poem depend upon the meaning of the argument." Still, the question remains, "Can words mean not ideas of things but *things*?" (2002, 152, 171).

65. Marion 2002a, 7–70; Merleau-Ponty 1968, 95–129; Henry 1973, 164–218.

Hopkins's poetic practice seeks to sustain a thing in what Husserl was to call its initial "pure apprehension" (*reine Auffassung*) without immediately proceeding to categorize and label it. What distinguishes his poetic vision is the way it tarries with the sheer givenness of the phenomenon and, thus, forestalls the reification of "appearance" (*Erscheinung*) into "perception" (*Wahrnehmung*) and its consequent assimilation to a matrix of lexical, epistemic, and cultural norms. It is this understanding of Hopkins's theo-poetics as essentially contemplative, as a quasi-liturgical witnessing and participating in the revealed image, that has at times been eclipsed by an at times too narrow focus on Hopkins's debt to Scotus's epistemology. The remainder of this chapter is an attempt to recalibrate the relationship between the conceptual and the contemplative dimensions of Hopkins's poetry. Mediating between them is the acheiropoietic *image*, which it should be remembered is not a mimetic contrivance but the manifestation of inscaped, dynamic being summoning its beholder to quasi-liturgical participation in the sacramental order of natural phenomena understood as gifts. It is this metaphysical and liturgical dimension of the image in Hopkins's writings to which we must now attend. To do so is to move beyond Scotus's epistemological framing of individual form, and the certitude of its apprehension qua image, that the Franciscan Scholastic had so influentially modeled for Hopkins.

Far from static derivatives of monolithic Being, individual forms in Hopkins's writings phenomenalize themselves as dynamic agents in Euclidian space, and their apprehension by an observing consciousness is principally mediated, not by a concept, but by the image. As an image, a thing's nonabstract essence (Scotus's *formalitas*; Hopkins's inscape) is wholly bound up with its mode of manifestation, which is the only way that Being may disclose itself to finite, time-bound minds. Conversely, were it not for this transcendent, noumenal substratum, all appearance would prove randomly apparitional. It could not be grasped as a phenomenon *sensu strictu*, simply because it would not be legible as the appearance *of* anything and, hence, could not even properly begin to engage the mind *as* a phenomenon. It follows that appearance is not a simple *punctum* but a layered manifestation of Being, no random "occurrence" but an event whose significance crystallizes when the observer grasps what is visible as the formally particular unveiling of something invisible. We recall Heidegger's succinct characterization of appearance, which "as the appearance 'of something,' . . . precisely does *not* mean that something shows itself; rather, it means that something makes itself known which does not show itself. It makes itself known through something that does show itself. Appearing is a *not showing itself*."[66] Being licenses the phenomenon's "self-showing," its categorical "givenness," and in so doing reveals itself as its source. As Marion puts it, "Being withdraws from beings because

---

it gives them."[67] "Inscape" not only ensures that each phenomenon becomes properly visible as the correlate of our "focal awareness."[68] It also affirms that the world so constituted is one of abundant manifestation whose sheer givenness we experience as the event, or advent, of the gift presented by a giver who has concealed himself in the gift now revealed as present to "a givee who does indeed receive it, but without being able to repay it."[69]

Phenomenality, in other words, cannot be thought as either randomly apparitional or straighforwardly transparent. Rather, in its very essence it formally unveils the very Being that is its source. It is *essentially* manifestation. Yet as such it remains incomplete until the observing consciousness responds to the phenomenon at hand by transposing it into the medium of the poetic word. Writing to Dixon in 1878, Hopkins remarks how "to every form perceived by the mind belongs, of the nature of things, admiration." And while there are countless "things and phenom events, phenomena of all sorts, that go without notice, go unwitnessed," there is ample cause to "regret this want of witness in brute nature." Thus, the attentive, unprepossessing gaze institutes, certainly *ought* to institute, a relation of reciprocity such that "what you look hard at seems to look hard at you" (*HCW* I:305, 504). For Jean-Louis Chrétien, too, "visible beauty calls for spoken beauty," such that (with Chrétien here quoting Levinas) "the 'epiphany' comes in the Saying of the one who receives it."[70] While remarking that Hopkins "is more confined to the fact when he sketches or considers pictures," Patricia Ball concurs with John Piper's earlier assessment that "it would be a mistake . . . to think of the visual arts as Hopkins' true medium, for 'he thought about painting only in poetic terms,' and the life of his imagination dwells in 'the brilliance and freshness' of his verbal art."[71] Indeed, if the young Hopkins still entertains "a more rational hope . . . of doing something—in poetry and painting" (*HCW* I:65) in part as a result of his fascination with the Pre-Raphaelite movement, his in-

---

67. Marion 2002a, 36.

68. The concept is Michael Polanyi's, whose account of the multiple levels involved in what we call perception rests on the underlying distinction between "focal" and "subsidiary awareness," which he insists "are definitely *not two degrees* of attention but *two kinds* of attention given to the *same* particulars." In the first case, "we focus our attention on the isolated particulars; in the second, our attention is directed beyond them to the entity to which they contribute, . . . [that is], we notice them *subsidiarily in terms of their participation in the whole*" ("Knowing and Being," in Polanyi 1969, 128). As Polanyi realizes, subsidiary awareness in particular is deeply enmeshed with an apophatic, mystical tradition. See Polanyi 1962, 55–65, 195–202.

69. Marion 2002a, 87.

70. Chrétien 2004, 11; quote from Levinas's *Otherwise than Being* in Chrétien 2004, 30.

71. Ball 1971, 129; on Hopkins and the visual arts, see Phillips 2008; on Hopkins and Ruskin, without doubt the preeminent influence on the former's understanding of the visual arts, see White 1992, 68–79; and Ballinger 2000, 25–59. See also appendix I to Humphrey House's edition of Hopkins's *Journals and Papers*, 453 ff., which reproduces most extant drawings by Hopkins.

terest in the visual arts fades markedly after 1868. Eventually, his journal entries and sonnets approach "inscape" as calling for the audible (poetic) word, which not only receives but assents to the acheiropoietic image's revelatory powers.[72]

Hence, the poetic word must be structured in such ways as not merely to *refer to* the *acheiropoieton* but positively to take up into itself and embody the very inscape in whose apprehension it originated. It is here that Hopkins, while still a student at Balliol College, begins to reflect on poetic diction as "speech only employed to carry the inscape of speech for the inscape's sake." Strictly speaking, all poetry stands in an a posteriori relation to the inscape, which "must be dwelt on." The word thus bears grateful witness to the uniqueness of inscape, which in turn "must be understood as so standing by itself that it could be copied and repeated." Conceived as a kind of "repetition" that structurally mirrors, and so renders explicit, the visual phenomenon by which it was summoned, poetic speech is an "*oftening, over-and-overing, aftering* of the inscape." Unlike referential and determinative discourse, verse ought to be apprehended first and foremost as "spoken sound, not spoken words." It is "speech couched in a repeating figure . . . employed to carry the inscape of spoken sound." It is the often-neglected particularity of sound patterning that causes Hopkins to remind Robert Bridges repeatedly to read his, Hopkins's, verse "not slovenly . . . with the eyes but with your ears . . . as I always wish to be read" (*HCW* I:296, 355). Yet even as the poetic word's soundscape ultimately stands "over and above meaning, at least the grammatical, historical, and logical meaning," it is not bereft of all semantic dimension.[73] Instead, poetic meaning arises from a structural coordination of formal elements, that is, from an ensemble of sensory values rather than from the lexical value of its constituent terms. Hopkins's overriding principle here is that of parallelism, which he specifies can be of "two kinds," the diatonic and the chromatic. In the first case, "the opposition is clearly marked," whereas in the latter case it involves "gradation, intensity, climax, tone, expression (as the word is used in music), ~~light~~ *chiaroscuro*" (*HCW* IV:120–21).

In his remarkable college essay, "On the Origin of Beauty: A Platonic Dialogue," dated May 1865, the barely twenty-one-year-old Hopkins construes beauty as "a mixture of regularity and irregularity." Beauty, that is, does not answer to a preexisting formal template but, instead, presents us with a *Gestalt* that, although "so irregular that no law cd. be traced in it," echoes that shape internally. Hence, in the case of an irregularly shaped leaf, there does appear to be "a law or regularity" after all provided "the other side exactly agreed with" it. This "comparison of things with themselves" simultaneously produces "a sense of symmetry and the violation of it, [which

---

72. On Hopkins's interest in the Pre-Raphaelites, see the essay by Norman White, in Thornton 1975, 89–106.

73. "Poetry and Verse," in Hopkins 1959a, 289.

is] preferable to pure symmetry." Received as "two things seen by the light of each other," beauty thus constitutes itself as a "relation." Breaking with Romantic expressivism, Hopkins thus locates beauty not, at least not principally, in subjective "Pathos" but in an objective, "structural unity" (*HCW* IV:141–45, 152–53).

What now ensues is Hopkins's first delineation of a prosodic theory that in time he will elaborate as "sprung rhythm." Of central importance is his contention that conventional prosodic schemes, based on syllable counts, inevitably flatten out and distort the unique pitch value of sounds. Thus "the accentual sequence (which we call a trochee) in odours is the same as in sweet or in sicken, but the foot is not exactly like them simply because it is made of a different word." Lamentably occluded by the antinomy of utter shapelessness and strict determinacy is the province of perceptible beauty, which is to say, "regularity or likeness tempered by irregularity or difference." All aesthetic form is organized, Hopkins contends, on "the common principle . . . of parallelism," which may operate by contiguity or contrast, chromaticism or diatonism (*HCW* IV:152–54, 158). Between these early, Plato-inspired aesthetic speculations and Hopkins's formulation of "sprung rhythm" in the later 1870s falls his encounter with Scotus; indeed, considered as a formal principle, sprung rhythm may justly be regarded as the apotheosis of Scotus's concept of *formalitas*. The idea "long haunting my ear," Hopkins writes in 1878, is of a verse that "consists in scanning by accents or stresses alone, without any account of the number of syllables." Or, most elementally, this is the "essence of sprung rhythm: one stress makes one foot, no matter how many or few the syllables" (*HCW* I:317, 345). Though Hopkins admits detecting scattered instances of sprung rhythm in earlier poets (Shakespeare, Milton, Campbell, Dyer), the technique had never before been implemented with any consistency. Yet Hopkins considers it a "more natural principle than the ordinary system, much more flexible and capable of much greater effects," so much so that by contrast "all English verse, except Milton's, almost, offends me as 'licentious'" (*HCW* I:317, 281).

What, then, is it that prompts this seemingly eccentric formal preoccupation? "Why do I employ sprung rhythm at all? Because it is the nearest to the rhythm of prose, that is the native and natural rhythm of speech, the least forced, the most rhetorical and emphatic of all possible rhythms." As such, sprung rhythm combines "opposite and, one wd. have thought, incompatible excellences, markedness of rhythm . . . and naturalness of expression" (*HCW* I:280–82). What Hopkins values is sprung rhythm's capacity for modeling the cadence, pitch, and rhythm of the poetic word in accordance with the singular perceptual experience that draws forth speech in the first place. Designed to bring the word into maximal conformity with the "happening phenomenon" (Marion) to whose call it responds, sprung rhythm is not an arbitrary formal contrivance superimposed on ordinary speech. Rather, it aims to repristinate the word so that it can once again respond, authentically and fully, to the unique call encoded in the visible, phenomenal world. Far from belonging to the province of mere artifice—what the young Hopkins had critiqued as "pure Parnassian"—poetry seeks to purify the word.[74] Consequently, it must eschew all established prosodic regularities and rhetorical conventions.

If Hopkins's preoccupation with sprung rhythm coincides with his diminishing interest in drawing, this is so because his focus has increasingly shifted from the draftsman's replication of things in their sheer objective otherness as ordained, say, in Ruskin's *Elements of Drawing* (1857). Instead, Hopkins seeks to capture the way phenomena begin to constitute themselves in the beholder's consciousness, not as "objects," but as formally unique natural images (*acheiropoietai*). Sprung rhythm facilitates this overall aim, namely, "design, pattern or what I am in the habit of calling 'inscape,' [which] is what I above all aim at in poetry" (*HCW* I:334). Poetry, then, is not the goal but the medium whose formal shaping necessarily serves metaphysical ends; and to home in on these ends, it is imperative that we extend our inquiry beyond Hopkins's well-documented biographical and intellectual preoccupation with Ruskin's aesthetic and Scotus's epistemological concerns.

"HEAVEN'S SWEET GIFT": APOPHATIC BEAUTY IN PSEUDO-DIONYSIUS AND HOPKINS

It is no accident that Hopkins's exploration of verbal structures irreducible to strict symmetries should have coincided with his intensive study of Platonic dialogue.[75] His teacher, the widely revered and controversial Benjamin Jowett, was deeply committed to the Socratic method of teaching and its aim of "self-realisation on the intellectual level," in sharp contrast to what Oxford Don and Rector of Lincoln College Mark Pattison lamented as "the tyranny of the examination system." The latter, Pattison wrote in his *Suggestions on Academical Organisation* (1868), appeared to consist of little more than an unrelenting imperative of memorization, which in his view

---

74. In an 1864 letter to Benjamin Baillie, Hopkins distinguishes poetry of genuine "inspiration" from another "kind I call Parnassian. It can only be ~~written~~ spoken by poets, but is not in the highest sense poetry. It does not require the mood of mind in which the poetry of inspiration is written." While "great men, poets I mean, have each their own dialect as it were of Parnassian," they are also trapped by it. They can see things in this Parnassian way and describe them in this Parnassian tongue, without further effort of inspiration." Hopkins's prime examples are Tennyson and Wordsworth, with the latter having written "an 'intolerable deal' of Parnassian" (*HCW* I:68–69).

75. Starting with the 1863 Easter term, Hopkins listens to Benjamin Jowett's university lectures, "On the Style and Philosophy of Plato" and "Plato's Republic." He subsequently attends lectures on Greek rhetoric (Demosthenes, Thucydides), attends Jowett's lectures on Sophocles and Plato (Lent and Easter terms, 1864), and beginning with the 1865 Lent term until Michaelmas 1866, has tutorials every term on Plato and Greek composition, all but one with Jowett; see *HCW* IV:40–50.

"ha[d] destroyed all desire to learn."[76] Implicitly opposed to the university's stress on systematization and memorization, Hopkins's extended study of Plato under Jowett's direction had confirmed for him the superiority of "Platonism[,] . . . that philosophy wh. never cd. be a system" (*HCW* IV:129). At once improvisatory and profound, colloquial and speculative, Platonic dialogue provides Hopkins with the archetype of a form unconstrained by social, cultural, and rhetorical convention and, thus, formally matched as closely as possible to the ideational process it embodies. Hopkins would never cease to admire Plato's "spiritual insight into nature," finding it far superior to "the strictly poetical insight and inspiration of our poetry." For even as the imaginative vision found in modern verse is "of the finest, finer perhaps than the Greek, . . . its rhetoric is inadequate—seldom first rate."[77]

At the same time, other developments complicate this picture. Thus, even as the freshman Hopkins explores the aleatory rhetoric and cosmological certitudes of Platonic dialogue, he is increasingly attracted by the ultra–High Church voices of Henry Perry Liddon (1829–90), vice principal of St. Edmund Hall, and Edward Pusey (1800-1882), Regius Professor of Hebrew and canon of Christ Church. Avowed opponents of the progressive Jowett, Liddon and Pusey represent the last flourishing of the Tractarian movement, in which Pusey had participated since its beginnings in 1833. Shortly after arriving at Balliol in April 1863, Hopkins is introduced to Liddon's Sunday lectures on Paul's first epistle to the Corinthians, no doubt intended as a counterpoint to Jowett's liberal-secular teachings. Tertullian's ancient query ("What indeed does Athens have to do with Jerusalem?") appeared to fit Oxford's intellectual polarization in the early 1860s with uncanny precision. Unsurprisingly, the institutional and religious fault lines almost from the outset fracture the highly gifted, budding classicist's allegiances during his freshman year. Thus, as Pusey and Liddon captivate new students in their lectures and through the sacrament of auricular confession (while also seeking to have Jowett convicted of heresy), the young Hopkins begins to supplement his study of Plato's works with various extracurricular materials.[78] In marked contrast to the conventional reading habits of his middle-class up-

---

76. White 1992, 94; Pattison, quoted in *HCW* IV:74–75.

77. *HCW* II: 800. The late epistolary comment echoes Hopkins's early passion for Plato: "I get more and more sympathetic with 'the true men' as agst. the Sophistik, Philistine, Doctrinaire, Utilitarian, Positive, and on the whole Negative . . . and prefer to err with Plato" (*HCW* I:175). Even during his dark and depressing days in the "wretchedness and gloom" of Dublin, he seeks to lift his spirits by revisiting the dialogues and, as he puts it, "unsphering the spirit of Plato" (*HCW* II:752).

78. On the "Ecclesiastical storm" (Jowett) sweeping over Oxford in the 1860s, fueled by the publication of *Essays and Reviews* (1860), see Shea and Whitla 2000, 28–46. Jowett's contribution to that volume ("On the Interpretation of Scripture") was to be one of the exhibits in an unsuccessful attempt, led by Pusey in 1863, to have Jowett convicted of heresy. For a discussion of responses to the volume, see Shea and Whitla 2000, 106–26 (on Jowett's hermeneutic theories) and 775–817

bringing in Hampstead—mainly a diet of middlebrow magazines (*Punch, The Times, the Quarterly Review, Cornhill Magazine,* among others)—Hopkins's early diary entries at Balliol show him reading, or intending to read more controversial fare. It includes Newman's *Tracts for the Times,* Pusey's sermons and lectures, *Essays and Reviews,* Villari's *Life of Savonarola,* Liddon's *Tracts,* and an article on the *Filioque* that may well have directed him to an 1853 monograph, *Subjects relating to the 'Orthodox' or 'Eastern-Catholic' Communion* by William Palmer, brother of his tutor, Edwin Palmer (*HCW* III:277–80, 286). Jesuit and other Catholic periodicals (the *Tablet,* the *Chronicle, Letters and Notices,* the *Month*), as well as the mainstream Anglican *Church Times* also engage Hopkins at Balliol.

Much has been made of the influence exerted in person and print by charismatic intellectuals and theologians on the fastidiously self-scrutinizing young poet in whose mind, as he would much later put it, "selfwrung, selfstrung, sheathe- and shelterless | thoúghts agáinst thoughts ín groans grínd" (*HMW* 175). What seemed an impossible proposition to Hopkins almost as soon as he arrived at Balliol was Oxford's standard regimen of conventional socialization and mainstream intellectual avocations—a middle-of-the-road finishing school for the mid-Victorian middle class destined for humdrum lives as civil servants and Anglican clergymen. Instead, readings, writings, thoughts, and observations, for Hopkins, inexorably led to questions of a decidedly speculative and metaphysical cast. Thus, notebook entries from 1865 (MS. CL II.69) show him agonizing over his "disrespectful feeling towards Jowett—Languor at lecture" or, perhaps with greater detachment, remarking in May 1866 on "[Walter] Pater talking two hours agst. Xtianity" (*HCW* III:299, 363). Such entries hint at his growing disenchantment with the varieties of agnosticism that Jowett, Pattison, Pater, et al. were offering.

Arguably the most lasting publication to emerge from the Tractarian movement had been Pusey's monumental *Library of the Fathers,* a subscription effort that resulted in fifty-one volumes beginning with Augustine's *Confessions* (published in 1838) and concluding, in 1885, with Cyril of Alexandria's commentary on the Gospel of John. By the time of Hopkins's arrival at Balliol, the project had become a core reference for anyone with serious Anglo-Catholic sympathies.[79] Pusey's theology in particular is thoroughly steeped in his lifelong study of patristic theology, St. John Chrysostom above all, who with some fifteen volumes is disproportionately well represented in Pusey's *Library of the Fathers.* Yet as Peter Nockles has shown, from

---

(on the heresy trial). On Liddon's growing influence over Hopkins, see Higgins introduction in *HCW* IV:11–16; White 1992, 51–67; on the distinctly Victorian nature of Hopkins's Catholicism, see Muller 2003, 8–26.

79. Brittain (1988, 20-45) considers the Tractarians' comprehensive *ressourcement* of Anglicanism and Pusey's panentheism to have significantly shaped Hopkins's Christology and sacramental vision.

its very beginnings, "there was a tension [evident in Newman's conception of a *via media*] between on the one hand the need to prove himself a sound Anglican, and on the other hand his growing conviction that the Fathers went beyond Anglican teaching."[80] If Tractarianism's attempt at recovering the apostolic tradition in its full scope had sought to put High Church Anglicanism on a firmer footing, it ended up exposing its theological incoherence, to say nothing of Anglo-Protestantism's vexed legacy of Erastianism. Writing in 1845, Newman had remarked on the "utter incongruity between Protestantism and historical Christianity" and, to remedy Anglicanism's difficulties, proposed a sophisticated account of tradition qua "development" that would draw on "the testimony of our most natural informant concerning doctrine and worship of Christianity, viz. the history of eighteen hundred years."[81] Two decades after Newman's spectacular conversion, Hopkins—in close contact with Newman during the critical months leading up to that step—appears to have recognized the unsustainability of the Anglican *via media* and to have resolved the matter for himself rather more quickly.

Yet in what follows, the goal is not to retrace Hopkins's rather swift, albeit agonizing, conversion; nor, for that matter, to contextualize, and so assimilate, Hopkins to an array of undoubtedly influential and impressive Anglo-Catholic and Catholic personae—preeminently Newman, Pusey, Liddon, and, more distantly, Scotus and Ignatius. Instead, what stands to be explored are the rich theological implications of Hopkins's journals and nature sonnets, which exhibit a marked convergence with the cosmology, Christology, and sacramental vision of post-Nicaean theology. To that end, the remainder of this discussion puts Hopkins in conversation with writers to whom, in all probability, he would have had only very limited (if any) exposure, such as pseudo-Dionysius and Maximus the Confessor. Doing so requires paying careful hermeneutic and exegetical attention to the habits of perception, and to the theopoetic insights encoded in the very *form* of Hopkins's writings. More than the propositions and affirmations one might hope to glean from his descriptive prose and lyric forms, it is their medial quality that explains why witnessing the world's givenness in the written word is, for Hopkins, the only plausible way toward a fully em-

---

80. Nockles 1994, 109–27; quote from 113.

81. Newman 1989, 8, 29; in his 1851 *Lectures on the Present Position of Catholics in England*, Newman adopts a more strident tone, particularly when indicting the establishment character of English Protestantism: "[It] is the religion of the throne . . . grafted upon loyalty; and its strength is not in argument, not in fact, . . . not in an apostolical succession; not in sanction of Scripture—but in a royal road to faith, in backing up a King, whom men see, against a Pope whom they do not see." It is also an intellectually complacent faith, suited to a people "impatient of inquiry, so careless of abstract truth, so apathetic to historical fact, so contemptuous of foreign ideas, [that it] will *ex animo* swear to the truth of a religion which indulges their natural turn of mind, and involves no severe thought or tedious application" (Newman 2000, 62–63). On Newman's concept of tradition, see Pfau 2017b.

bodied Christology. Hence, access to the great poetry of 1875 and beyond is opened less by the early poetry, much of which treads along fairly conventional lines that Hopkins emphatically repudiated when deciding, in May 1868, to burn his juvenilia (the "slaughter of the innocents"). Instead, it is in his notebooks that Hopkins seeks to transpose his undesigning and attentive perception of natural phenomena into the medium of writing. With often microscopic precision, his entries distill a given phenomenon's *formalitas* or inscape and, in so doing, apprehend it as a particular manifestation and revelation of the *logos* that pervades and constitutes the cosmos as a whole.

While on the Isle of Man in August 1873 for the second time in a year, Hopkins is preoccupied with seascapes on this ancient and largely uncultivated island. If Scotus's *Commentary on the Sentences* had made for exhilarating reading during the previous retreat there, this time it is Matthew Arnold's poems, which the seminarian "read . . . with more interest than rapture, . . . for they seem to have all the ingredients of poetry without quite being it" (*HCW* I:226). Still, if "Dover Beach" fails to engage and inspire the young seminarian in 1873, the isle's ambient seascapes prove all the more absorbing, captivating Hopkins's gaze during both sojourns with an infinite variety of tactile and visual forms. One of his few preserved pencil drawings (fig. 7.1) from his visit to Shanklin, Isle of Wight (1866), already foreshadows what, in characteristically sensuous and evocative turns of phrase, resurfaces in his notebook entries of August 1872. There Hopkins speaks of "dimpled foamlaps, . . . the dance and swagging of the light green tongues or nipples of waves," and the challenge of taking in the "sea, dark blue with violet cloud-shadows, [and] . . . the scaping from the break and flooding of the wave. . . . The eyes have before them a region of milky surf but it is hard for them to unpack the huddling and gnarls of the water and law out the shapes and the sequence of the running" (*HCW* III:532–35). A year later, the journals mention "painted white cobbled foam tumbling over the rocks and combed away off their sides again, . . . [and] foam exploding and smouldering under water, mak[ing] a chrysoprase green." While passing the mill-hamlet of Balaglas in the glen, Hopkins finds himself absorbed by the "chromatic" beauty and infinite gradation of both color and texture: "The rock is limestone, smooth and pale white, not rough and gritty, and without moss, stained red where the water runs and cut smoothly and vertically hewed by the force of the brook into highwalled channels with deep pools. The water is so clear in the still pools it is like shadowy air and in the falls the white is not foamed and chalky, as is so clear in the still pools it is like shadowy air and in the falls the white is not foamed and chalky, as at Stonyhurst, but like the white of ice or glass. . . . I saw and sketched as well as I could."[82] Hopkins's writing appears a verbal

---

82. *HCW* III:556. Though a competent draftsman, Hopkins was "no better at drawing than other members of his household who shared his goals and training" (Bump, in Thornton 1975, 73).

Figure 7.1. Gerard Manley Hopkins, *Shanklin, Isle of Wight*, 1866

facsimile of John Everett Millais paintings, much admired by Hopkins's brother Arthur and young Gerard himself, who was clearly inspired by Millais's "hypersensitive, microscopic eye for detail." Yet compared to the Pre-Raphaelite filigree work observable in a sketch Hopkins had produced on the Isle of Wight seven years earlier (see fig. 7.1), to say nothing of the luxuriant verbal precision found in his 1873 notebook entry, the later sketch seems trifling (fig. 7.2).[83]

Carrying both visual (Ruskinian) and spiritual (Ignatian) overtones, Hopkins's notebook writings amount to a kind of mental discipline, as indeed all focused composition must be. Yet in marked contrast to the harsh Jesuit practices aimed at disciplining and mortifying the self in Victorian England, there is a very different,

---

83. Bump, in Thornton 1975, 83; gradually, Hopkins grew "less interested in a finished picture than in noting certain effects of shading and perspective" (74).

Figure 7.2.
Gerard Manley
Hopkins,
*Sketch from
Isle of Man*,
1873

affirmative and celebratory quality to these nature descriptions.[84] Evocative of a more Platonist strand in Western Catholicism and Eastern Orthodox teaching, Hopkins's notebooks give us a self not to be broken and expunged but, instead, to be emptied of all distractions so as to cultivate its spiritual senses. The proper aim of *askēsis* is a

---

84. White (1992, 171–85) details the range of disciplinary measures that were a routine feature of the novitiate: exam beads designed to "help you keep count of the number of times you fell into a fault," subsequently to be tabulated in a little gray book; use of "disciplines," the nickname for scourges encircled by barbed wire; chains to be fastened to the upper part of the right leg and worn for several hours, "their spikes gripping the thigh muscles"; elaborate regimes of punishment, such as being made to "crawl around under the tables and kissing the toes of those already seated"; Thomas (1969, 41 n.) quotes R. F. Clarke, an Oxford graduate and convert who joined the Jesuits just three years after Hopkins. Clarke's "Training of a Jesuit" (*Nineteenth Century* xl [August 1896]) recalls a military officer testifying that army discipline was easier to bear than that of the novitiate.

self-emptying (*kenōsis*) rather than fastidious self-abnegation, which by an inescapable dialectic, as Hopkins appears to have realized after 1866, ends up magnifying the self's sinfulness and opacity to the point that they become omnipresent and insurmountable. Hence, the discipline of eye and mind—no less than discipline of body, with which Hopkins's journals show him struggling so acutely during his first two years at Balliol—must always be understood as a means toward a higher end; and that transcendent end is to participate, in the most focused sensory-cum-intellectual ways possible, in the incarnate God through his creation. As Lesley Higgins remarks, "'Composition of place' was key in his imaginative life; the diaries were an opportunity to re-experience places in his own terms, in words and drawings, and thus convert them into felt experiences" (*HCW* III:45). As Hopkins's drawing of sea and land clashing on the Isle of Man (dated 12 August 1873) suggests (see fig. 7.2), sketching had for the most part become a mnemonic device to enable the verbal sculpting and, eventually, theo-poetic contemplation of his sonnets rather than a medium of genuinely independent standing. As such, attentive visualization and sketching (verbal or graphic) also has an expiration date in that the phenomenon's momentary excessive presence cannot be sustained indefinitely; as early as 1863, Hopkins thus notes how "for a certain time I am astonished at the beauty of a tree, shape, effect etc, then when the passion, so to speak, has subsided, it is consigned to my treasury of explored beauty, and acknowledged with admiration and interest ever after, while something new takes its place" (*HCW* I, 43).

Twelve years later, Hopkins takes the crucial step by embracing, with his master's tacit approval, what he had always known to be his other true vocation: the writing of poetry. And even though Liddon and Pusey would regard any Oxford student's conversion to Rome a lamentable event, their Tractarian efforts at a *ressourcement* of High Church Anglicanism ensured that the Jesuit's severe discipline could not, in the end, prevent Hopkins from giving poetic voice to a far richer and affirmative conception of Christianity. Reflecting his extensive study of the Fathers, Pusey's discussion of the real presence of Christ in the Eucharist, strongly affirmed by Hopkins during his Balliol years, is phrased in ways that "affirm the sacramental character of the cosmos." As Pusey writes, "The world is full of types, and it were probably true to say that everything is a type if we could but realize it."[85] For Hopkins, an attentive visual encounter with natural phenomena is modeled on the Eucharist, a communion that lifts the beholder out of chronological time and, paradoxically, consummates his life by "unselving" him.

---

85. Brittain 1988, 31; Pusey, quoted from 33.

I kiss my hand
To the stars, lovely-asunder
Starlight, wafting him out of it; and
Glow, glory in thunder;
Kiss my hand to the dappled-with-damson west:
Since, though he is under the world's splendour and wonder,
His mystery must be instressed, stressed;
For I greet him the days I meet him, and bless when I understand.

(*HMW* 111)

The call-and-response structure of the visible world, doubly honored by an un-designing gaze and the poetic transcription of its yield, carries with it strong over-tones of spiritual renewal: "unless you refresh the mind from time to time you can-not always remember or believe how deep the inscape in things ~~goes~~ is" (*HCW* III:504). Herein Hopkins echoes Liddon's worry that "man has lived so long in the Temple of Nature that he forgets its sacramental, its mysterious character." Referenc-ing Clement of Alexandria, Liddon expressly affirms Christ as the "Author and ar-chetype of all existing beings" and as "the archetypal form after which the creatures are modeled. . . . He is the producer and sustainer of all created existence."[86]

At the same time, Liddon and Pusey firmly resist any pantheist tendencies to which such arguments might easily give rise. Instead, they all hold that "creation's participation in the life of Christ is by grace, not by identity[;] . . . the relationship is sacramental, not pantheistic." In the Eastern Church, the distinction, formulated preeminently by St. Gregory Palamas, is between God's essence and His energies.[87] The underlying question is whether and how a strictly apophatic theology can be reconciled with an aesthetic that, as Liddon had put it, traces God in all of creation in a twofold manner: "The *eikōn* is indeed originally God as unbegun, unending re-flection of Himself in Himself; but the *eikōn* is also the Organ whereby God, in His Essence, reveals Himself to His creatures. . . . Christ is the End of created things as well as their immediate Source." Quoting Paul (Col. 1:17), Liddon concludes, "It

---

86. Quoted in Brittain 1988, 47, 49 f.

87. Dating back to Basil of Caesarea and Gregory of Nyssa, "the doctrine of the energies, inef-fably distinct from the essence, is the dogmatic basis of the real character of all mystical experience. God, who is inaccessible in His essence, is present in His energies 'as in a mirror,' remaining invisible in that which He is; 'in the same way we are able to see our faces, themselves invisible to us in a glass,' according to a saying of St. Gregory Palamas (Sermon on the Presentation of the Holy Virgin in the Temple). Wholly unknowable in His essence, God wholly reveals Himself in His energies, which yet in no way divide His nature into two parts—knowable and unknowable—but signify two different modes of the divine existence, in the essence and outside of the essence" (Lossky 1997, 85).

follows naturally that the *plērōma*, that is to say, the entire cycle of the Divine attributes, considered as a series of powers or forces dwells in Jesus Christ; and this not in any merely ideal or transcendental manner, but with the actual reality which men attach to the presence of material bodies which they can feel and measure through the organs of sense."[88] Among the theological writers of late antiquity, few wrestle in a more sustained way with the tension between strict apophaticism and a Christ manifested in "the actual reality which men attach to the presence of material bodies" than pseudo-Dionysius and Maximus the Confessor; and it is to the first that we must once more turn.

Bringing Dionysius into conversation with Hopkins is not a case of demonstrable influence but of instructive, transhistorical convergence.[89] The few extant attempts to link Hopkins to patristic writers have for the most part relied on circumstantial (mainly biographical) evidence and conjecture.[90] By contrast, the dialogic reading of Hopkins with Dionysius and, below, with Maximus the Confessor, is grounded in a considered exegesis of their respective writings. The objective, then, is not to argue for the earlier writer's "influence" and the latter's "debt" but to stage a cross-historical and mutually illuminating conversation between their writings. That late patristic and sixth- and seventh-century Byzantine theological writings offer ample precedent for Hopkins's markedly visual theo-poetics can be gleaned from John Meyendorff's summary characterization.

> Because the concept of *theologia* in Byzantium, as with the Cappadocian Fathers, was inseparable from *theoria* ('contemplation'), theology could not be—as it was in the West—a rational deduction from "revealed" premises, . . . [which] represented for the Byzantines the lowest and least reliable level of theology. The

---

88. Liddon 1867, 322–24.

89. Almost nothing is known about the writer known today as pseudo-Dionysius. The myth flagged by the prefix holds that the "Areopagite" was converted to Christianity around AD 50 in Athens, supposedly as a result of hearing a sermon by early Christianity's most famous convert, St. Paul. That legend presumably served to place Dionysius's theological voice and persona in close proximity to apostolic Christianity and to present his voice as a direct "creation" of Paul's witness. In fact, Dionysius's arguments, such as his discussion of the creed in its post-Chalcedonian form and his evident familiarity with patristic writings, place him firmly in the late fifth and first half of the sixth century, which prompted some (e.g., Stiglmayr) to identify him as the patriarch of Antioch, Severus (465–538). While this hypothesis has since been rejected, a colloquy held in 532 between orthodox adherents of Chalcedon and "Severians" clinging to a miaphysite Christology happens to be the first time that the Corpus Areopagiticum is mentioned. A key figure in extricating Dionysius from the miaphysites trying to claim him is John of Scythopolis (writing around 530). On the many textual and genealogical tangles, see Pelikan's introduction in pseudo-Dionysius 1987, 11–46.

90. Brittain (1988, 10) speculates that "Keble's *Tract 89* may have helped to put Hopkins in touch with . . . Irenaeus's thought." Marucci's *The Fine Delight That the Fathers Taught* (1994) does not engage with patristic writings at all.

true theologian was *the one who saw and experienced the content of his theology*;
and this experience was considered to belong not to the intellect alone (although
the intellect was not excluded from its perception), but to the "eyes of the Spirit,"
which place the whole man—intellect, emotions, and even senses—in contact
with divine existence.[91]

Meyendorff goes on to remark on "the reluctance of the Byzantine Christian mind
to reduce theology to one particular form of human appropriation—the intellectual," and he emphasizes that "Scripture and the Church's magisterium cannot be
considered as the only 'sources' of theology."[92] It is this integrative and comprehensive framework, in which metaphysical meanings do not compete with but, instead,
are instantiated in sensory, and particularly in visual forms, that makes Hopkins
resonate with a conception of the "spiritual senses" whose strongest representatives
in early Christianity would include Gregory of Nyssa, pseudo-Dionysius, and Maximus the Confessor.[93]

Even so, the strict apophaticism of a pseudo-Dionysius might be thought to
conflict with Hopkins's acutely visual and sensuous poetics and its seeming aestheticization of the inscaped God. This fundamental tension, which we have seen reappear time and again throughout this book, is succinctly formulated at the start of von
Balthasar's trilogy.[94]

> Are we objectively justified in restricting the beautiful to the area of inner-
> worldly relationships between 'matter and form', between 'that which appears
> and the appearance itself', justified in restricting it to the psychic states of
> imagination and empathy which are certainly required for the perception and
> production of such expressional relationships [*die seelischen Zustände der Ein-
> bildungskraft und der Gestimmtheit*]? *Or:* May we not think of the beautiful as
> one of the transcendental attributes of Being as such, and thereby ascribe to the
> beautiful the same range of application and the same inwardly analogous form
> that we ascribe to the one, the true, the good?

The majority of the Fathers, he continues, "regarded beauty as a transcendental
and did theology accordingly," such that "contemplation . . . is the flashing anticipation of eschatological illumination." Even pseudo-Dionysius, "after all, the father of

---

91. Meyendorff 1983, 8–9; emphasis mine.

92. Ibid., 11. Gavrilyuk (2012, 96) rightly insists that *theoria* covers a considerable semantic
spectrum, from "contemplation" to "reflection" to "observation" and "perception."

93. On Gregory of Nyssa's seminal role in joining theological and aesthetic reflection, and
on his conception of beauty as "fittingness" and "gratuity" (not the same as Kantian "disinterestedness"), see Carnes 2014, 45–60.

94. Balthasar 1982, 36-37 / 1961, 35.

the strictest negative theology," had affirmed "the necessity of religious symbols for sense-endowed humanity."[95] His apophaticism is never far off, however, such as when demurring at Gregory of Nyssa's seeming identification of beauty "as a name for a radically transcendent God."[96] Asks the Areopagite, "How can we speak of the divine names? How can we do this if the Transcendent surpasses all discourse and all knowledge, if it abides beyond the reach of mind and of being, if it encompasses and circumscribes, embraces and anticipates all things while itself eluding their grasp and escaping from any perception, imagination, opinion, name, discourse, apprehension or understanding?"[97] With its elongated, anaphoric structure, the passage affirms that God's radical transcendence will always be the ontological premise, and never a mere conclusion of Dionysian theology. For the overriding concern here is how finite, sinful, and fallible human beings may yet relate to the divine without equivocating, let alone purporting to overleap, the ontological difference between finitude and transcendence. God's being is "at a total remove from every condition, movement, life, imagination, conjecture, name, discourse, thought, conception, being, rest, dwelling, unity, [and] limit" (DN 593C–D). The first and last objective of theology, then, will be praise, not knowledge, of God; and because such praise can approach "this divinely beneficent Providence" only through its visible correlates, "you must turn to all of creation" (DN 593D). To the question, "How do we know him?," the answer will therefore be that "we know him from the arrangement of everything, because everything is, in a sense, projected out from him, and this order possesses certain images and semblances of his divine paradigm" (DN 869D). Hence, while "transcending all" and therefore "rightly nameless," God encompasses and unifies the names of everything within the finite ("ontic") realm: "yet he has the names of everything that is" (DN 596C).

In Dionysian fashion, Hopkins's "Pied Beauty" seeks to circumscribe God with a cascade of names taken, seemingly at random, from an infinite scale of qualities and intensities. At the same time acknowledging the imperfect relation that all names bear to the divine essence, Hopkins's appropriately foreshortened, "curtal" sonnet ends abruptly with the blunt enjoinder that human speech will only ever stand in a provisional or analogous relationship to the ineffable source of all being and that consequently an authentic relationship to the creator must be one of praise, not knowledge.

---

95. Ibid., 38–39 / 1961, 36–37.
96. Carnes 2014, 45.
97. All citations of the pseudo-Dionysian corpus follow the marginal pagination in *The Complete Works*, which corresponds to vol. 3 of the *Patrologia Graeca* edition of pseudo-Dionysius's writings. In addition, the English titles are given in abbreviated form, thus: *Divine Names = DN; Mystical Theology = MT; Celestial Hierarchy = CH; Ecclesiastical Hierarchy = EH; Letters = EP [Epistolae]*. Cited here: *DN* 593A.

All things counter, original, spare, strange;
Whatever is fickle, frecklèd (who knows how?)
With swift, slów; sweet, sóur; adazzle, dím;
He fathers-forth whose beauty is past change:
                Práise Hím.
                (*HMW* 133)

Striking here is the rapid-fire listing of qualities, which oscillate between an objective "name" predicated of a particular thing and that of so many vivid, albeit ephemeral sensations flooding the beholder's consciousness. Putting it thus hints at the tension between a sensible world awash in countless, diversely textured qualities that present us with a kaleidoscopic, if notably unstable, beauty, and the enigmatic source of him who "fathers-forth [and] whose beauty is past change." Yet as the terse, double-stressed injunction ("Práise Hím") makes plain, the tension is not ours to resolve. For any attempt to do so will expire either in a hyper-Augustinian suspicion of the aesthetic or in a pantheist aestheticization, and consequent dissolving, of God's transcendence.

Placing increased stress on the Cappadocian understanding of "negative" theology, pseudo-Dionysius had conceived the apophatic stance above all as a safeguard against an idolatrous (or, in any event, pantheist and pagan) outright identification of God either with purely intellectual concepts or with God's material creation. Viewed as a kind of *katharsis* or "inward purification" and a rejection of anthropomorphic ways of "form[ing] concepts about god," apophaticism "excludes all abstract and purely intellectual theology." Reflecting insight into the limits of a purely ratiocinative approach, Dionysian apophaticism is not one theological option among others but the only coherent stance *from* which to approach God and creation. That said, it would be a mistake to think of apophatic (or "negative") theology as simply opposing the claims of cataphatic (or "positive") theology. On the contrary, far from disputing the presence of God *in* all things, apophaticism means to safeguard against identifying God *with* the order of the visible. "Everything," pseudo-Dionysius writes, "is, in a sense, projected out from [God], and this order possesses certain images and semblances of his divine paradigms." The restrictive, or "negative," aspect only comes into play insofar as theology needs to maintain a sharp distinction between the (divine) *source* and its infinitely ramified manifestations: "God is therefore known in all things and as distinct from all things."[98] Consequently, the theophanies or created energies in which God manifests himself to finite beings will prove legitimate, indeed vitally important, as long as they are apprehended as "images . . . intended to

---

98. *DN* 869D–872A. "According to the Areopagite, we do not know God away or apart from the senses, but precisely through them" (Ivanovic 2020, 78).

guide us and to fit our faculties for the contemplation to that which transcends all understanding."[99] Far from trapping the human intellect in a rigid dualism that would proscribe visual contact with creation, negative theology positively legitimates and enjoins it. As pseudo-Dionysius puts it:

> Many scripture writers will tell you that divinity is not only invisible and incomprehensible, but also 'unsearchable and inscrutable'.... And yet... [it] is not absolute incommunicable to everything. By itself it generously reveals a firm transcendent beam, granting enlightenments proportionate to each being, and thereby draws sacred minds upwards to its permitted contemplation, to *participation* and to the state of becoming like it. (*DN* 558C–D; emphasis mine)

As discussed above (ch. 1), Plato's neologism of "participation" (*methexis*) is seminal for "bring[ing] out the logical connection of the many to the one, the thing 'in common,' a connection that was not implied in mimesis." Whereas mimesis "refers to the existence of what is imitated or represented, . . . *methexis* refers to coexistence with something."[100] It counters the thesis of a radical split (*chōrismos*) between the world of ideas and that of appearances, a central feature of Aristotle's critique of Plato. If one follows Gadamer by reading the crucial passage in the *Parmenides* (128b–134e) as Plato's way of "reduc[ing] such an understanding of the *chōrismos* to absurdity," then the only logical alternative is to understand Plato's "ideas [as] ideas *of* appearances . . . that do not constitute a world for itself." The supposed Platonic dualism, a cosmos divided into deficient sensory experience and pure, immutable ideas, respectively, is not at all Plato's position. Rather, the notion of such a "split" (*chōrismos*), far from being a doctrine to be contested, is "from beginning to end . . . an essential component of true dialectic."[101]

It is in this sense of a dialectical tension that pseudo-Dionysius conceives of "participation" as an underlying spiritual narrative of sorts whose subject advances through a cosmos organized as an infinitely gradated hierarchy. Whereas the "celestial hierarchy . . . is something out of this world," the spatiotemporal extrusion of God's creative powers has produced a "human hierarchy . . . pluralized in a great variety of perceptible symbols [*aisthētōn symbolōn*] lifting us upward hierarchically until we are brought as far as we can be into the unity of divinization" (*EH* 373A). Commenting on this passage, Ernst Kitzinger in a landmark essay notes that "to pseudo-Dionysios, the entire world of the senses in all its variety reflects the world of the spirit. Contemplation of the former serves as a means to elevate ourselves toward

---

99. Lossky 1997, 37–40.
100. Gadamer 1986, 11–13.
101. Ibid., 16–17, 20.

the latter."[102] Hence, "the more a thing participates in the one infinitely generous God, the closer one is to him and the more divine one is with respect to others" (*DN* 817B–C). To participate in divine Being is a matter of "rising up, as we do, from obscure images to the single Cause of everything, rising with eyes that see beyond the cosmos to contemplate all things" (*DN* 821B). It adumbrates an indispensable, practical dimension of the human intellect whose ultimate goal, for pseudo-Dionysius no less than Gregory of Nyssa, is that of "divinization" (*theōsis*).

Yet such an ascent is plausible only on the premise that the movement of temporal, finite being is itself suffused with the *logos* toward which it strives. Thus, *methexis* is not some dubious amalgamation of wholly distinct levels of being. Rather, it stakes an ontological claim that at once affirms these levels (of archetypal and ectypal being) as distinct, hierarchically ordered, and analogically related. Put differently, Plato's theory of participation posits that the sensory experience of visible things as distinct, organized forms implicitly puts the beholder in touch with the *logos* that accounts for the intelligibility of a given thing as a specific "this." When Hopkins writes that "what you look hard at seems to look hard at you" (*HCW* III: 504), he means to affirm that to see is to be in the presence of something whose very intelligibility shows it as being ordered toward the beholder. Phenomenality is not an accidental quality of being. Things not only *are* and, now and then, also *appear*. Rather, their being is inseparable from their appearing *to* us, arresting and engaging our attention as manifestations, and in so doing revealing mind and world to be ordered toward one another. It is this ontological reciprocity of phenomenon and beholder in a call-and-response dynamic (to be taken up shortly) that Plato's neologism of *methexis* had first identified. Absent that ontological premise, all talk of divinization would be nothing more than an elaborate anthropomorphism or naive idealism. Indeed, as Erich Przywara has painstakingly shown, Plato himself had already construed the relation of archetype and image as one of

> "unconscious coincidence" of a "grace from above." For as much as the archetypes can be said to be "instantiated within nature," nevertheless, in its essence, the real not only goes "towards the above" but comes "from above." . . . For the *paradeigmata* are not "abstract paradigms," which first attain "figural concrete reality" in the *eikones*; rather, the *eikones* are "icons"—that is, in their figural

---

102. Kitzinger 1954, 138. Ladner sees Dionysius "mov[ing] farther away from the genuinely Platonic relation between images and ideas," something evidenced by the near-total absence of the terms *idea* and *eidos* in the writings of the Areopagite. Aside from the more technical *eikōn*, the term "truly characteristic for Dionysios . . . is the term *proorismos*, a noun related to the Paulinian verb *proorizein*, which means 'to mark out providentially" and "signif[ying] God's foreknowledge and pre-definition of things He was to create" (Ladner 1953, 9); Lossky (1997, 23–43) concurs.

content they are the radiance of what lies beyond the heavens: figurality (*eikas-thenai*) as participation (*methexis*).[103]

Far from anathemizing material nature, Dionysian contemplation engages corporeal being strictly as an image mediating for the beholder that being's very source. Material forms are not only both real and figural, but they owe their very reality to the transcendent being toward which, as *eikones*, they orient the beholder. As pseudo-Dionysius writes:

> It is quite impossible that we humans should, in any immaterial way, rise up to imitate and to contemplate the heavenly hierarchies without the aid of those material means capable of guiding us as our nature requires. . . . [Hence] the source of spiritual perfection provided us with perceptible images of these heavenly minds, . . . reveal[ing] all this to us in the sacred pictures of the scriptures so that he might lift us in spirit up through the perceptible to the conceptual, from sacred shapes and symbols to the simple peaks of the hierarchies of heaven. (*CH* 121C–124A)

Based on this concept of participation, which asserts that the sensory and the eidetic, the finite and the transcendent, are not incommensurable but integral components of a dialectic of parts and whole, we can identify four areas of significant convergence between pseudo-Dionysius's theology and Hopkins's theo-poetics.

1) A first one concerns the complete absence of apologetics from their respective writings. As von Balthasar remarks about pseudo-Dionysius, "Why engage in controversy? To do so is only to descend to the level of one's attacker."[104] While that need not necessarily be the fate of *all* apologetics, as Newman's *Apologia* had powerfully illustrated for his contemporaries, Hopkins among them, the latter consistently eschews apologetics in favor of capturing, in the most exacting lyric iconography, God's indisputable presence in the world. As Hopkins so categorically puts it in his Ignatian commentary, "The first faculty directed towards God is the sense of God's *presence*[,] the second that of His *essence*" (*SDW* 175). Having minutely described the inscape of the bluebell ("mixed of strength and grace"), Hopkins concludes, "I do not think that I have even seen anything more beautiful than the bluebell I have been looking at. I *know* the beauty of our Lord *by* it" (*HCW* III:489; emphasis mine). Rather than being coveted for hedonistic, "private" enjoyment, the beautiful "is the cause of harmony, of sympathy, of community" (*DN* 704A). Dionysius's language here has strong Neoplatonist overtones, notwithstanding some fundamental differ-

---

103. Przywara 2014, 241.
104. Balthasar 1984, 149.

ences between Plotinian and Dionysian thought.[105] Likewise, and in sharp contrast to the aestheticism of mid-Victorian culture (e.g., the Pre-Raphaelite movement), Hopkins understands beauty and the image mediating it as a source of metaphysical certitude. It is, as Husserl will say, *Evidenz*, or, in von Balthasar's phrasing, "the beautiful carries with it an evidence of unmediated illumination [*Evidenz . . . , die unmittelbar ein-leuchtet*]." As the fulcrum of an "incomprehensible certainty" (*HCW* II:619) rather than an "interesting uncertainty" (*HCW* II:619), and unlike garden-variety perceptible objects, the image cannot be viewed with indifference but effects in the beholder something akin to what Newman calls "real assent."

2) Von Balthasar's passing observation that "there is hardly another theology so thoroughly pervaded by aesthetic categories as that of the Areopagite" opens up a second area of convergence between Dionysius and Hopkins. Taking us well beyond the epistemological questions that Scotus had so influentially modeled for Hopkins is the issue of "beauty." Echoing Plato's pun (*Cratylus* 416c) on "calling" (*kalein*) and "beauty" (*kalos*), pseudo-Dionysius identifies beauty as a calling, a summons that we must meet: "Beauty 'bids' all things to itself (whence it is called 'beauty') and gathers everything into itself."[106] Hopkins's late sonnet, "To what serves mortal beauty?" (1885), likewise frames beauty, not as a quasi-mechanical cause of pleasure, but as a call or summons.

> To what serves mortal beauty | dangerous; does set danc-
> ing blood the O-seal-that-so | feature, flung prouder form
> Than Purcell tune lets tread to? | See: it does this: keeps warm
> Men's wits to the things that are; | what good means—where a glance
> Master more may than gaze, | gaze out of countenance.
> Those lovely lads once, wet-fresh | windfalls of war's storm,
> How then should Gregory, a father, | have gleanèd else from swarm-
> ed Rome? But God to a nation | dealt that day's dear chance.
> To man, that needs would worship | block or barren stone,

---

105. On Dionysius's rejection of Origenist and other seemingly Platonist versions of dualism, see Meyendorff 1983, 12 and 27 ff., 37–41. Ivanovic (2010, 17–21) identifies four distinct areas in which Dionysius's divergence from Plotinus is especially significant: (1) the contraction of Plotinus's "emanating hypostases" (the One; Intelligence; Soul) into attributes of a single, personal God; (2) the shift from Plotinus's view of the cosmos arising from necessity to one created by providential, Divine love; (3) the affirmation, in Dionysius, of God as continuously present to and involved with his cosmos rather than being its abstract, first cause; and (4) the sharper conception of the soul's enduring distinctness in its "return" (*epistrophē*) to God, as opposed to the Plotinian notion of an outright "reamalgamation."

106. *DN* 701D. Chrétien (2004, 7, 16 f.) recalls the etymological connection of *kalein* and *kalon*, quoting among others Ulrich of Strasbourg's commentary on Dionysius, as well as John Scotus Erigena's (Dionysius-inspired) *Periphyseon*.

Our law says: Love what are | love's worthiest, were all known;
World's loveliest—men's selves. Self | flashes off frame and face.
What do then? how meet beauty? | Merely meet it; own,
Home at heart, heaven's sweet gift; | then leave, let that alone.
Yea, wish that though, wish all, | God's better beauty, grace.

(*HMW* 167)

To call up both the beauty of mortals and the transience of beautiful forms, "mortal beauty" is also, always, to place oneself in mortal danger. For "beauty | dangerous" moves and unsettles the beholder with its "face feature-perfect"—as an earlier draft reads for what in the final version becomes the "O-seal-that-so | feature." Beauty is not something merely seen as any other object. Rather, it is something we "face," unsettling our sense of self with an infinity of ethical implications that Levinas finds embodied in "the face of the other." It allows us to "see" that the presence of a perfected form, "the things that are," inherently divulges "what good means."

Hopkins's unusual choice of the Alexandrine for this sonnet, similar to Hölderlin's unrivaled exploration of hexametric form for complex dialectical purposes, accommodates more complex syntactic and propositional phrasing than the compressed organization of his earlier sonnets. The ultimate, ethical purpose of visible, embodied beauty is one of transformation and conversion. Hopkins recalls Bede's account of how Pope Gregory the Great dedicated himself to converting England to Christianity, prompted to do so by a group of prisoners he encounters in Rome: "Those lovely lads, wet-fresh | windfalls of war's storm." Though evidently mortal, their beauty far surpasses the pagans' "worship [of] block or barren stone." The encounter, and the papal mission it helps crystallize, is unthinkable except as a gift, an instance of "grace" (line 14) experienced as "that day's dear chance." Bede's story of Pope Gregory, arrested by the call embodied in the faces of Rome's young prisoners, models for us an invisible, spiritual meaning ("what good means") asking to be realized in every encounter with another human being. When apprehended as the event of a call, rather than as an object, beauty grants the beholder access to a domain where desire (including, especially, desire *for* beauty) and self-interest have no place. Here, as Hopkins puts it, "self | flashes off frame and face." Hence, the poem's central question ("What do then? How meet beauty?") concerns ethics, not aesthetics.

Hopkins's closing answer ("merely meet it") might seem a bit evasive at first glance. Yet it gains in force once we place stress, as the line asks to be read, on "meet"—that is, as assenting and responding to beauty as a visible summons, an ethical challenge met time and again by Christ in Galilee and, in this instance, confronting Pope Gregory. Finding himself suddenly confronted with the face of the subaltern other, a prisoner, the pope not only finds his persona and office involved in a strange people's conversion but, as a result, also undergoes a conversion in his own right. Jean-Louis Chrétien has written insightfully about beauty as the fulcrum of the beholder's ethical and spiritual condition. "Things and forms," he observes, "do not beckon us because they are beautiful in themselves. . . . Rather, we call them beautiful because they call us and recall us. . . . They beckon our gaze, but also beckon our voice."[107] While Chrétien does not make the point explicit, it follows that to face beauty is, phenomenologically speaking, not at all the same as to perceive an object. For the latter will only ever be experienced and conceptualized on a spectrum ranging from aversion to indifference to desire. Objects do not have an addressee, whereas for Hopkins (as for Chrétien) beauty is conceivable only as a calling. Even if the beholder-addressee of beauty's call should fail, perhaps fail utterly, to respond to what is gratuitously and superabundantly given to her, that failure would still be an event, unlike the non-event of sheer indifference with which perception may simply pass over its object. For "He has created us for bliss and He will give it, or the failure will be ours" (*SDW* 194).

As with Gregory the Great, inexplicably detained by the faces of Rome's pagan prisoners, a momentary look reaches into his soul deeper than an interested or covetous gaze ever could: "where a glance / Master more may than gaze, | gaze out of countenance." The result of the encounter with beauty is one of conversion—again, not just that of pagan England but of the pope. As Chrétien puts it, "The in-itself of beauty is to be for-the-other, aimed at gathering the other back to itself." Gregory the Great's *metanoia* is an instance of "beauty addressing us, call[ing] us to ourselves, to truly become ourselves. . . . Beauty intends us for what in our being bears promise."[108] The call of the image not only elicits an articulate response, but unveils within the respondent a capacity for so responding that would otherwise have gone unrecognized. To find oneself as the addressee of a phenomenon's call is to experience what Hopkins calls "instress," which "demands from the observing subject 'an answering stress,' so that it might be understood by a kind of ontic sympathy through which the subject can speak a word that corresponds to the thing understood."[109] Hence, to respond to the phenomenon of beauty is, first and foremost, a case of "real assent" (Newman). It is to say "yes" not only to the phenomenon but to the possibility of having oneself unveiled in the first place by the encounter with beauty. Again, Chrétien: "Every initiative on my part only perpetuates an immemorial yes"; or, in Hopkins's haunting fusion of metaphysical affirmation and self-abnegation early in "The Wreck of the Deutschland" (stanza 2): "Dost thou touch me afresh? / Over again I

---

107. Chrétien 2004, 3, 9.
108. Ibid., 13.
109. Carpenter 2015, 163–64.

feel thy finger and find theé // I did say yes / O at lightning and lashed rod."[110] Poetry's creative word is a response to the call that created it to begin with: "The Word's every call . . . is always creative," in the sense that God "calls into being what is not" (*kalountos ta mē onta hōs onta* [Rom 4:17]). It is a response that will be forever "exceeded by that which calls forth this response, . . . that which is unheard-of in my voice, that which has acquiesced on my behalf before my voice begins to become audible and which alone makes it speak, makes it repeat a 'yes' that it has never said a first time."[111] Hopkinsian sprung rhythm is meant to capture to the utmost this visual participation in, and response to, the "charged" world.

3) Another issue pervading the Corpus Areopagiticum with significant bearing on Hopkins concerns the quasi-liturgical, and specifically eucharistic, function of his images. Like Plato long before him, so pseudo-Dionysius regards images and symbols as both indispensable and fragile, mediating as they do an "ascent from the lower to the higher, not a progress from the outer to the inner."[112] In their symbolic-metaphysical sense, as opposed to the lingering paganism of Roman mimetic painting, images are the fulcrum of Dionysius's speculative theology. Complementing his mystical approach, which "reaches union with God, but is beyond all knowledge, in an exit from oneself (*extasis*)," the speculative approach "starts from our experience of being, and, following the images of creatures, goes back to their divine model."[113] Even so, there is the constant temptation of conflating the image with that toward which it can only ever point, and of human "beings push[ing] beyond the reasonable limits set to their vision and . . . imagin[ing] that they can actually gaze upon those beams which transcend their power of sight" (*EH* 400A). Aside from some general guidelines for the exegesis of verbal imagery, laid down in Dionysius's ninth epistle (*EP* 1104C–1105B), the principal safeguard against such hubris is the liturgy, described at great length in the *Ecclesiastical Hierarchy* as an initiation into seeing properly—which is to say, not referentially but symbolically: "the symbolic tradition . . . strips the postulant of his former life, deprives him of the very last attractions of this world." Among Hopkins's lyrics, few capture this liturgical dimension of an attentive and self-emptying vision as fully as his 1877 sonnet "Hurrahing in Harvest."

> Summer ends now; now, barbarous in beauty, the stooks rise
> Around; up above, what wind-walks! what lovely behaviour
> Of silk-sack clouds! has wilder, willful-wavier

---

110. Ibid., 19; and *HMW* 110.

111. Chrétien 2004, 19, 22, 25 f.; in Chrétien's concise formulation: "That which gives us voice alters it" (26).

112. Gavrilyuk 2012, 98.

113. Boulnois 2020, 103.

Meal-drift moulded ever and melted across skies?
I wálk, I lift up, I líft úp heart, éyes,
Down all that glory in the heavens to glean our Saviour;
And, éyes, héart, what looks, what lips yet gáve you a
Rapturous love's greeting of realer, of rounder replies?
And the azurous hung hills are his world-wielding shoulder
Majestic—as a stallion stalwart, very-violet-sweet!—
      These things, these things were here and but the beholder
Wánting; whích two whén they ónce meet
The heart rears wings bold and bolder
And hurls for him, O half hurls earth for him off under his féet.

(HMW 137)

One is reminded of Iris Murdoch's Platonist observation that "we use our imagi-nation not to escape the world but to join it."[114] The sonnet offers us a phenome-nology of a transcendently "charged" world coalescing into a richly textured image, with the poem's irregular, "sprung" rhythms designed to trace a "rapturous" amalga-mation of perceptual, emotive, and reflexive values. We witness the unique conver-gence of mind and world that Husserl was to call "image consciousness"—at once unpredictable, irresistible, and suffused with transcendent significance. Yet the motif of the harvest also ensures that the image so evocatively unfolded in the sonnet's octet will not simply be consigned to the domain of the miraculous and ineffable. Instead, alluding to Christ's earthly presence, the speaker affirms that "these things were here." The beholder thus is to grasp the timeless rhythms of agrarian life and work as both *eikōn* and *typos* (*imago* and *figura*), as both visible appearance and theophany, as what was "here" and is destined to return. Unlike Proust's unsought-for *mémoire involontaire*, triggered by our chance encounter with some miscella-neous object or sensation, Hopkins's visual epiphanies hinge on our receptivity to the providential dimension of visible things in their incontrovertible and abundant givenness: "these things were here and but the beholder / Wánting."

It is above all the modern, verificationist model of perception and generically preestablished poetic conventions of taste (what Hopkins, in his early critique of Tennyson, calls "Parnassian") that will cause the beholder to appear "wánting"— that is, inadequate or altogether absent.[115] Poetry here is not to be confused with

---

114. Murdoch 1970, 88.

115. *HCW* I:67–73. Both in Wordsworth and in Tennyson, the evolution of a distinctive and recognizable style causes the infinite particularity and charisma of things to vanish under the poet's preestablished gaze or what Hopkins calls "too essentially Wordsworthian, too persistently his way of looking at things" (*HCW* I:71).

subjective, versified "expression" but is "speech for the inscape's sake."[116] The sonnet's protomodernist, defamiliarizing imagery ("silk-sack clouds" / "meal drift") ensures that the total image, "barbarous in beauty," will not expire in polite Englishness. Instead, Hopkins's sonnet completely fuses the event of beholding and the act of affirming the reality of what is so beheld. As Kevin Hart puts it, "The entire poem is set in the mode of *how*, not *that* or *what*."[117] The second quatrain's *accelerando* pattern and increasing frequency of stressed syllables highlights the speaker's real assent to the incontrovertible and absorbing reality of the visible scene ("I walk, I lift up, I lift up heart, éyes" and "And, éyes, héart, what looks, what lips yet gave you a / Rapturous love's greeting of realer, of rounder replies?"). Harvesting the scene as materially real and present evidence, as *figura*, demands that the language steer clear of all subjective affect. With good reason, Jean-Luc Marion thus insists that "the gaze would see absolutely nothing if evidence remained a mere subjective impression, an effect of consciousness, in short, an idolatrous mirror where the mind refers to itself an impression that impresses only it."[118]

Implicitly, then, Hopkins's sonnet rejects as false the choice between Romantic sublime transport and Ruskinian dispassionate objectivism; the title's precise wording ("Hurrahing *in* Harvest," not *at*, *during*, or *after*) hints that the acheiropoietic image is apprehended neither as a sublime, transcendent experience nor as a correlate of Darwinian, forensic naturalism. Instead, sonnets like "Hurrahing," "The Windhover," or "As Kingfishers catch fire" offer a phenomenological description of the beholder's attentive and active participation in the sheer givenness of the visible; only so can the visible function as both image and *figura* rather than as some strictly intramundane perception. Indeed, the figural completion of the visible is not to be sought in some unspecified beyond but unfolds precisely within the intricately constructed or "inscaped" domain of the sonnet. In sharp contrast to the Wordsworthian sublime or Keatsian, objective ekphrasis (e.g., "To Autumn"), "Hurrahing in Harvest" unfolds as an Ignatian spiritual exercise.[119] The poem's meditative *operatio* centers on the speaker's quest for bearing articulate witness to his transformative encounter with the unconditional givenness of the Real *in* and *as* an image. Hence it is the *world*, and not some mystical beyond, that (to quote another of Hopkins's epigrammatic openings) is "charged with the grandeur of God."

If Hopkins's nature sonnets amount to a literary tour-de-force in the way they distill transcendent meanings from the sprung rhythms of visual experience, their

---

116. "Poetry and Verse," in Hopkins 1959a, 289; see also Hopkins's earlier draft (while at Balliol College), "Poetic Diction" (*HCW* I:120–22).

117. K. Hart 2017, 29.

118. Marion 2002a, 20.

119. On Hopkins's sonnets in relation to Ignatian spiritual exercises, see Ballinger 2000, 61–102.

insight proves unpredictable, an instance of grace divulged only to the solitary in-dividual; as Hopkins remarks in his journals, "With a companion the eye and the ear are for the most part shut and instress cannot come" (*HCW* III:544). To the extent that inscape is visually consummated as something unconditionally given and "not imposed outwards from the mind," its apprehension is not subject to the will and its rhetorical armature. "Hurrahing in Harvest" is strictly about witnessing, rather than identifying with, the visible as it discloses itself. Merely to witness the event of in-scape thus eschews both affective identification and propositional thought. For by its very nature conceptual thought abstracts from and so attenuates the charisma of what is phenomenally given. For ratiocination serves as a buffer for a subject anxious to know beforehand whither it is tending; it is inherently risk-averse, intent on main-taining distance between the beholder and the self-giving phenomenon. By contrast, Hopkinsian vision attends to the "running instress by which we identify or, better, test and refuse to identify with our various suggestions / a thought which has just slipped from the mind at an interruption" (*HCW* III:519). Such seeing opens up on a fundamentally different mode of being in the world, an openness and receptivity to phenomena whose abundant givenness prefigures the beholder's spiritual flourish-ing. As Hopkins's sonnets of the late 1870s show time and again, such responsive-ness to inscape is not a case of passivity but, on the contrary, a kind of sensory-cum-spiritual action. To see here is to embrace the phenomenon's intrinsic patterns ("in-scape") and its sheer cohesiveness ("instress").

To close in on this alternate type of intentionality—attentive yet undesigning, re-sponsive though not passive—it bears recalling that a strictly conceptual and propo-sitional outlook on the phenomenal world could never by itself move the subject to action but only give rise to some type of "reaction" or "behavior." For authentic, intel-ligible action arises from internal motivation rather than external (efficient) cau-sation. As such, genuine action unsettles modernity's "buffered self" by originating within it the kind of transformative change that cannot be mapped onto the strictly notional or experientially familiar. As Maurice Blondel puts it, "We do not act, if we do not draw from ourselves the principle of our action, if this principle does not surpass past experiences, if we do not sense in it something else, if we do not make of it a kind of transcendent reality. One is never interested in one's own acts unless they are mixed in with some passionate ideology. . . . We die, as we live, only for a be-lief."[120] Inasmuch as its source and telos originate in a *vision* of the good rather than in a *movement* prompted by subjective desire or aimed at formal correctness, all

---

120. Blondel 1984, 114; elsewhere, Blondel speaks of action as an all-pervading "system of spontaneous or willed movements, a setting of the organism into motion, a determinate use of one's vital strengths, in view of some pleasure or interest, under the influence of a need, an idea or a dream" (36). For a fuller discussion of action, see Pfau 2013a, 316–19, 395–98.

action is essentially spiritual and, hence, ought not be confused with the physical implementation of some contingent interest or objective. So understood, action seeks
to infuse meaning not as something superimposed but as visibly disclosed and as-
sented to.[121] Unlike the Romantic sublime with its claim to a private and ineffable
revelation, image and vision in Hopkins's poetics serve to realize a quasi-liturgical
community. Thus, his sonnets operate with a rhythmic conception of time as *presence* ("Summer ends *now*") rather than Romantic recollection; and to see is to understand oneself as the addressee of a transcendent gaze ("I lift up, I líft úp heart, éyes")
rather than the owner of a sublime experience.

Hopkins's beholder is, thus, always also the one seen, sought out, and transfixed
by the inscaped phenomenon that arrests his gaze. Hopkinsian "inscape" thus appears structurally cognate with the "responding icon" in the Byzantine liturgy, which

> manifests its protoype alive and capable of presence, thought, will, action, inter-
> action, and dialogue with the viewer. The reality of the prototype is projected
> onto the icon, which then responds as a live image with a soul, and operates as
> the seal and guarantee of the prototype. . . . The divinization of man (*theōsis*) to
> which the image thus contributes requires the active participation of the faithful,
> who addresses it and pays his devotions to it as he would if he were able to ad-
> dress the prototype directly.[122]

Likewise, von Balthasar speaks of the liturgy, particularly in Dionysius's writings, as the "bridge" between history and fulfillment, Old and New Covenant. The
liturgical image is modeled on the Incarnation that it celebrates; raised to "a liturgical potency" that Dionysius calls "theo-mimesis" (*theomimēton* [CH 165B]), the
visible no longer conflicts with revelation, even as it cannot ever coincide with it: "In
the Church's liturgy the Platonic dialectic of the image is to a certain extent stilled."[123]
Enjoining the celebrant to surrender of all false attachments, the liturgy's "symbolic
tradition . . . stands him naked and barefoot to face westward" and, having so freed
him, turns him "to face eastward." To see here is to aspire to a state of self-emptying
(*kenōsis*) and to apprehend material things as images (*eikonas*), which in turn are
conceived as symbolic intimations of "sacred things" (*hiera*), with the whole of the
liturgy being the supreme symbol. Not only is the Eucharist (*mystērion synaxeōs*) an

---

121. As Murdoch puts it, "Any artist will readily understand [how] the idea of a patient, loving
regard, directed upon a person, a thing, a situation presents the will not as unimpeded movement
but as something much more like 'obedience'" (1971, 39).

122. Kartsonis 1998, 65–66; see also Florensky 1996, 51–69; Constas 1997, 54–86.

123. Balthasar 1984, 176, 183.

image of the divine, but every image, properly seen, is enfolded by an incarnational, sacramental logic. Hence, "those who are stone deaf to what the sacred sacraments teach, also have no eye for the imagery" (*EH* 432C). It bears pointing out that pseudo-Dionysius, herein clearly distancing himself from the Platonic tradition, "does not express the soul's progress towards God in terms of increasing interiority" or self-knowledge.[124] On the contrary, the movement of *theōsis* originates in the gift that is the encounter with visible creation. Hence, pseudo-Dionysius echoes the long-standing association of light and vision with the sacramental order, which since Justin Martyr had identified light as the condition for spiritual vision.

Conversely, no amount of discursive explanation can ever compensate for the failure to apprehend transcendent meaning in images: "That is why so many continue to be unbelieving in the presence of explanations of the divine mysteries [*tōn theiōn mystēriōn logois*], for we contemplate them solely by way of the perceptible symbols [*aisthētōn symbolōn*] attached to them" (*EP* 1104B). Hence, pseudo-Dionysius never tires to stress that to those outside the faith, the visible world will never divulge its symbolic import. For not only does "the ordered arrangement of the whole visible realm make known the invisible things of God [*tōn aoratōn tou theou*]" (*EP* 1108B), as he affirms quoting Romans 1:20; but such mediation by the images embedded in scripture and the symbolic acts of the liturgy also shelters the visible world from being distorted by the uninitiated and profane. Indeed, the symbol "is the protective garb of the understanding of what is ineffable and invisible to the common multitude" (*EP* 1105C). Learning to see, or what pseudo-Dionysius calls "the holy journey to the heart of the sacred symbols" (*EP* 1108C), requires sustained pedagogical effort. Lest image and symbol should tempt the beholder into conflating them with the invisible and unknowable God, "the way of negation" is "more suitable to the realm of the divine." Indeed, "positive affirmations are always unfitting to the hiddenness of the inexpressible" (*CH* 141A).

Yet what are we to understand by such "dissimilar shapes," considering that pseudo-Dionysius's apophatic framework by definition cannot conceive of any presentation resembling the divine. The concern, it turns out, is not ontological but of a practical-pedagogical kind. Thus, pseudo-Dionysius favors symbols and images whose artless and inconspicuous nature will not "mislead someone into thinking that the heavenly beings are golden or gleaming men, glamorous, wearing lustrous clothes," and so forth (*CH* 141B). By preferring "humble forms [*aischra morphōmata*] to represent the divine" and "images drawn from the world" (140B–C), he makes a case, at least implicitly, for the acheiropoietic image, which is not made but "found" or, more precisely, which "finds" and calls to the beholder rather than being fash-

---

124. Ibid., 197.

ioned in accordance with established aesthetic and rhetorical conventions.[125] Such an image falls categorically outside the conceptual reach of modern aesthetics and, to the extent that its metaphysical implications are taken seriously, exposes the notion of aesthetic autonomy as a metaphysical aberration. By contrast, the acheiropoietic image, in arresting the beholder, gives evidence of what Merleau-Ponty calls "the *logos* that pronounces itself silently in every sensible thing."[126] Or, as Hopkins puts it in an 1873 journal entry, "all the world is full of inscape: and chance left free to act falls into an order as well as purpose \\ looking out my window I caught it in the random clods and broken heaps of snow made by the cast of a broom" (*HCW* III:549).

Hopkins's notebooks ought to be read as such an attempt at disciplining the eye to the point that the visible divulges its underlying, ordering principle or *logos* and, in so doing, can be apprehended as an incarnation of the divine. A metonymic sequence of sorts thus proceeds from plainly visible, if seemingly random, entities. At some point, some formal trait will "arrest" Hopkins's attention, such as when "my eye was suddenly caught by the scaping of the leaves that grow in allies and avenues: I noticed it first in an elm and then in limes. They fall from the two sides of the branch or spray in two marked planes" (*HCW* III:477). At this point, when in Paul Claudel's words, "the eye listens," inscaped phenomena assert a kind of agency over the beholder or, as Hopkins puts it, "'carve out' one's thought with painful definiteness."[127] A pattern begins to emerge, a "regularity" that, while still at Balliol, Hopkins had shrewdly distinguished from "absolute uniformity" and, anticipating the idea of "inscape," had defined as "a mixture of regularity and irregularity" or of "symmetry and change" (*HCW* IV:139–41). The eye is now attuned to a kind of "organisation," which reveals itself by looking at an ensemble of phenomena of the same *kind* or species— oak and elm leaves, clouds, ice crystals, or, perhaps, the "composition of the crowd in the theatre, all the heads looking one way thrown up by their black coats relieved only by white shirt-fronts etc: the short strokes of eyes, nose, mouth, repeated hundreds of times I believe it is wh. give the visible law: looked at it in any one instance it flies.—I cd. find a sort of beauty in this" (*HCW* III:366). Inscape is the pattern exhibited by the ensemble as a whole and, eventually, reconstituted in Hopkins's poetry as a pattern of sound.

---

125. Sobolev's claim that "Hopkins never explains the meaning of a landscape or the reason why he has chosen it" (2011, 46) fails to consider that, in fact, the landscape or, rather, the particular "inscaped" being "has found" Hopkins. The difference is that between a Romantic aesthetics of production (or "expressivism") and a theo-poetics of "attention."

126. Merleau-Ponty 1968, 208; elsewhere, with reference to modern painting, Merleau-Ponty affirms that "there is a system of equivalences, a Logos of lines, of lighting, of colors, of reliefs, of masses—a conceptless presentation of universal Being" (1964, 182); see my discussion of Merleau-Ponty, Cézanne, and Rilke below.

127. Paul Claudel, quoted in Chrétien 2004, 9; Hopkins, *HCW* III:360.

It bears pointing out that, for pseudo-Dionysius, symbol "does not negate the difference between the symbol and the symbolized. [Instead, it] represents what they have in common. . . . For something to reveal God and to be the body of the revelation, it must, in some way, be similar to God." At the same time, considering that God is wholly transcendent to all being and all modes of predication, the symbol can achieve such "similarity" only in an analogical sense. It does not embody, let alone represent, God's perfection but, instead, encapsulates in distinctive, visible form "a set of properties, peculiarities, and highly positive qualities . . . [that] have to be perfect in all aspects and representable (i.e., in words and colors)—ideal targets of the possible perfection of the visible world."[128] As pseudo-Dionysius puts it, "The very same things are both similar and dissimilar to God" (*DN* 916A). Still, Dionysian theology, while it does not conceive of created beings interchangeably, nevertheless will grant them only provisional significance. Material things are ultimately self-consuming, to be sublated into the domain of the image, itself a higher (medial rather than material) scaffolding whose sole value rests with pointing toward a truth beyond all appearance. For Tsakiridou, all divinization (*theōsis*) ultimately pivots on things shedding and overcoming their material particularity: "Discarnation is a precondition for divinization." Thus, pseudo-Dionysius's "theology compresses beings within a hierarchical order in which their uniqueness and individuality is gradually eliminated." Thus, the image supervenes on its material correlate and, as such, proves more real as a "verbal icon" than as a visible object.[129] In this regard, pseudo-Dionysius reflects his deep Neoplatonic roots, from which— as Plotinus's rejection of individual portraiture shows—springs the notion that particularity in the visual realm necessarily obscures "the pure idea of the absolute." If the Platonic approach consistently tilts toward "the devaluation of individual likeness," it will have to disclaim any essential bond between the *eikōn* and the transcendent God toward which it seeks to orient the beholder's vision.[130] As pseudo-Dionysius notes, it was paradoxically the early church's "burning and generous urge to secure uplifting and divinization [*theōsis*] for their subordinates" that led to a use of "images derived from the senses [*aisthētais eikosi*]" and ended up dispersing "something united [into] a variegation and plurality. Of necessity, they made human what was divine" (*EH* 376D–377A).

---

128. Ivanovic 2010, 51–52. To assimilate similarity and imitation, as Ivanovic proposes to do, is a logical mistake. For in circular fashion it defines the image by its (putative) resemblance to its referent rather than as a distinct form of "presentation" (*Darstellung*) inducing in the observer an equally distinctive intentionality or "image-consciousness" (Husserl's *Bildbewusstsein*). If Jane and Jill are twins, they bear a resemblance to one another; yet neither ought therefore to be considered the image of the other.

129. Tsakiridou 2013, 168–69.

130. Belting 1994, 132. On Dionysius's Platonism, see Boulnois 2020, 102–8.

Again, von Balthasar captures the essential tension that pervades literary, philo-sophical, and theological writing as soon as it confronts the transcendent impli-cation of images: "It is the greatness of man and his tragedy to embrace both with-out being able to bring them into a final synthesis: to be immersed in the aesthetics of the world of images and at the same time to have irresistibly to dissolve all images in the light of the imageless [*alle Bilder unaufhaltsam in das Bildlose aufklären zu müssen*]."[131] It is here, too, that the significant convergence of pseudo-Dionysius's mystical theology and Hopkins's theo-poetics reaches its limit. For in the strict and immutable hierarchical order of the Dionysian cosmos, each thing's "activity seems confined to how a thing receives and reflects the divine light," thus imparting to "theophany an abstract and detached quality . . . that favors its intellectual experi-ence."[132] Unlike what we find in Hopkins's great sonnets, the Areopagite's Chris-tology remains too attenuated, his cosmology too Plotinian with its (proto-Hegelian) rhetoric of supersession and dematerialization, where "things give way to pictures, pictures to words, word to concepts and concepts to ideas, until all substantive form disappears leaving the intellect free to perceive 'that which lies beyond sight and knowledge.'"[133]

THE VISIBLE AS MANIFESTATION AND *ANALOGIA*:
MAXIMUS AND HOPKINS ON CONTEMPLATION

The attempt by Irenaeus—and, following him, Gregory of Nyssa and Basil the Great—to integrate the natural world into a comprehensive divine economy finds a particularly fulsome expression in the writings of Maximus the Confessor (AD 580–663).[134] As "the most world-affirming thinker of all the Greek Fathers," Maximus re-

---

131. Balthasar 1984, 179 (trans. modified).

132. Tsakiridou 2013, 172.

133. Ibid., 173; quote from *MT* 1025A. Tsakiridou may be overstating Dionysius's Plotinian and Origenist debt; for, as von Balthasar notes, Dionysius does not follow Plotinus's framework of a "world-soul" and the ultimately pantheist logic of emanations (1984, 160–61), and the Dionysian, triune God cannot be conceived by a Plotinian "simplification" or reduction to "the One" but re-mains wholly transcendent to *any* operation of the finite intellect; cf. Balthasar 2003, 29–56.

134. For accounts of Maximus's dramatic and long life, see Louth 1996, 3–18; Blowers and Wilken's introduction to Maximus 2003, 13–43; Balthasar 2003, 74–80. As the latter points out, "What makes Maximos a genius is that he was able to reach inside, and open up to each other, five or six intellectual worlds that seemingly had lost all contact; he was able to bring out of each a light that illumined all the rest. . . . He was a contemplative biblical theologian, a philosopher of Aristotelian training, a mystic in the great Neoplatonic tradition of Gregory of Nyssa and Pseudo-Dionysios the Areopagite, an enthusiastic theologian of the Word along the lines of Origen, a strict monk of the Evagrian tradition, and—finally and before all else—a man of the Church" (57). Uniting all these features is the Christological theme, which "in Maximos' conception of the universe . . .

gards "'contemplation of nature' (*theōria physikē*) and of the structures of meaning (*logoi*) hidden within it" as "a necessary step, a kind of initiation, into the knowledge of God."[135] The Origenist view of material creation as a Fall, a point on which Origen partly concurs with the Gnostics whom he otherwise opposes, yet also the Platonism pervading much of pseudo-Dionysius's writings, have faded, even as the latter's strict apophaticism remains central to Maximus's thought. Concurrently, he seizes upon the Chalcedonian formula of the simultaneous ontological presence of a divine and a human nature, of two wills "indivisibly" (*adiairetōs*) and "unconfusedly" (*asynchytōs*) united in Christ, as the template for his theological anthropology and his cosmology. In each domain of inquiry, the intellectual and the sensible (material) principle are at once distinct, complementary, and productively entwined: "Mighty indeed is the relationship of intelligible beings to the objects of intellection, as is that of sensible beings to the objects of sense, and thus man, fashioned of soul and sensible body, . . . is both contained within these divisions and contains them."[136]

This "circumincession" (*perichōrēsis*) of distinct natures in divine Being—introduced by Maximus and, as he repeatedly insists, impossible to grasp in terms of number and addition—becomes the conceptual template, not only for the incarnation, but for all domains of theological inquiry.[137] As von Balthasar notes, "The christological synthesis . . . far from being an exception . . . finds confirmation of a sort in the most general laws of being." Maximus's theology thus concludes five centuries of often-polarized theological debate, much of it dominated by the enduring and divisive legacy of Origenism and its sharp, at times Gnostic, division between perfect spiritual and fallen material being. If Plato's "divide" (*chōrismos*) of the idea and its material instantiation had been taken as absolute, a case of terminal incommensurability rather than mediated by a dialectics of "participation" (*methexis*), "Maximos' eyes look for God in both realms of the world, in sense and intellect, earth and heaven. . . . Only the closure of the two, the growing reciprocity that forms the world as a whole, becomes for him the place where the Transcendent appears, visible precisely in this burgeoning immanence as the One who is wholly other."[138]

---

corrects Neoplatonic mysticism, confirms the Aristotelian metaphysics, and prevents the Origenist-monastic strain from becoming simple escapism" (66).

135. Balthasar 2003, 61.

136. Maximus's writings are cited parenthetically, as follows: *A = Ambigua*, followed by volume and page number; *MSW = Selected Writings*; *CMC = On the Cosmic Mystery of Christ*. Thus, for the above passage, *A* 10:1153A–B.

137. See Thunberg 1995, 23, who defines *perichōrēsis* "as a divine permeation into the human nature" and as implying "the aspect of reciprocity within a divine-human relationship" (28); Maximus had developed this drawing on Gregory Nazianzen's use of *perichōrousōn* (in Epistle 101).

138. Balthasar 2003, 67, 84–85.

Here we first encounter the argument—central much later to G. M. Hopkins's rehabilitation of image and "inscape"—that the material world not only is not merely the correlate of mundane perception, but, in fact, can never even be properly realized in that contingent modality. For quotidian perception proceeds by subsuming that which gives itself to be seen under some abstract scheme of classification or other; and in so foreclosing on the specificity and presence of what is seen, perception not only drains the phenomenon of its charismatic presence but also prevents the beholder from becoming aware of their profound relatedness to the visible world. The dominant ethos here is one of prevarication, distance, and containment. Maximus resists (Neo)Platonism's and Origenism's suspicion of the material world's multifarious and dynamic appearance, a suspicion that, in its very attempt at safeguarding God's transcendent purity, effectively "overleaps the reality of His creation."[139] As he strives to rethink the relation between the visible and the invisible, Maximus conceives of that relation neither antithetically nor as some undifferentiated amalgamation. Instead, he draws on the Chalcedonian framework of a divine *oikonomia*, a "mutual ontological presence (*perichōrēsis*) [that] not only preserves the being particular to each element, to the divine and the human natures, but also brings each of them to its perfection in their very difference."[140] As Maximus puts it in *The Church's Mystagogy*, it is God's force that "leads all beings to a common and unconfused identity of movement and existence, no one being originally in revolt against any other or separated from him by a difference of nature or of movement[,] . . . not by dissolving or destroying them or putting an end to their existence. Rather it does so by transcending them and revealing them, as the whole reveals its parts" (*MSW* 186). "Being" (*ousia*) and "Person" (*hypostasis*)—that is, what is subject to *perception* and to *recognition*, respectively—should be understood in generative, productive relation with one another.

Von Balthasar speaks of a "tension within the world between the intellectual and phenomenal realms, the world of thought and the world of sense [die innerweltliche Spannung zwischen geistig-intelligibler und sinnlich-phänomenaler Welt]," and of a "twofold, incomprehensible, and irreversible self-opening [*Teilgabe*] of this unity to both the world as a whole and the world in all its particulars."[141] As Maximus puts it:

The whole spiritual world seems mystically imprinted on the whole sensible world in symbolic forms, for those who are capable of seeing this. . . . And again,

---

139. Ibid., 48 (trans. modified). On Maximus, see also Louth 1996, 3–77; on Maximus's cosmological framework, see Balthasar 2003, 137–77; Thunberg 1995, 50–93; Florovsky 1987, 208–53; Tsakiridou 2013, 167–92; on Maximus's conception of the "spiritual senses," see esp. Aquino 2012, 104–20.

140. Balthasar 2003, 63–64.

141. Ibid., 84, 86.

"The invisible realities [*aorata*] from the creation of the world have been perceived [*kathoratai*] and are recognized through things he has made," says the divine Apostle [Paul, Rom. 1:20]. And if we perceive what does not appear by means of what does, as the Scripture has it, then much more will visible things be understood by means of invisible by those who advance in spiritual contemplation. Indeed, the contemplation of intelligible things by means of visible realities is spiritual knowledge and understanding of visible things through the visible. (*MSW* 189)

To Maximus, the pivotal passage from Paul implies at least two things: first, that there is an indelible nexus between what is phenomenally given and its transcendent source, between *visibilia* and *invisibilia*; and second, this very nexus itself is not the fruit of enthusiastic projection or esoteric speculation. Rather, it arises from a specific form of visual attention of which humans are uniquely capable. In the *Ambigua* (ca. AD 632), Maximus specifically insists that the operation of the "senses [be] informed by reason," thereby "allowing no room for sensation to operate independently of the reins of reason, nor allowing reason itself to range beyond the simplicity of the intellect." In sharp contrast to modern epistemology's disjunctive account of sensory and intellectual functions, Maximus's integrative vision is premised on—and conducive to our apprehension of—a cosmic order. Thus, "the mediating power of reason conducts the forms and figures perceived by the senses toward their manifold inner principles [*logoi*], and concentrates the manifold diversity of the principles that are in beings . . . into a uniform, simple, and undifferentiated intuition." Whoever succeeds at that "has acquired a true impression (as much as is humanly possible) of their creator, sustainer, and originator" (*A* 15:1216B). Echoing what von Balthasar has influentially characterized as Maximus's "cosmic liturgy," Hopkins speaks of the two dimensions of "God's utterance of himself." Thus, this "utterance . . . in himself is God the word, outside himself is this world. This world then is word, expression, news of God. Therefore its end, its purpose, its purport, its meaning, is God and its life or work to name and praise him" (*SDW* 129).

Maximus's commitment to negative (apophatic) theology is unwavering. Yet inasmuch as the task of theology is to "make manifest what is hidden by means of an apophatic negation," it must find a way of engaging the reality and presence of the visible, created world that does not confine it to a merely sensory *effect* of an absent, divine cause but attests to God as the "eternally active creator [*aei . . . energeian . . . Dēmiourgos*]" (*A* 70:1080D).[142] Neither pagan (Quintilian) rhetoric nor a

---

142. Fagerberg calls this the paradox of "apophasis and revelation" (2009–10, 229), an early version of which can be found in Gregory of Nazianzen's understanding of the Godhead as "at once earthly and heavenly, tangible and intangible, comprehensible and incomprehensible" (Epistle CI in *PNF* 7:439).

strictly figurative adumbration of the divine *plērōma* will do; for by its very nature apophatic theology is incommensurable with ordinary acts of referential or syllogistic predication—a view that Maximus takes over from the Cappadocians (esp. Gregory Nazianzen) and pseudo-Dionysius the Areopagite. Instead, "leaving aside every capacity to picture the truth by means of figures and signs," those engaged in contemplation are to be "lifted up in silence by the power of the Spirit from written words and visible things to the Word Himself. . . . [F]or when the letter is desired only for itself, it tends to kill the indwelling Word, . . . just as the beauty of creatures, when not beheld for the glory of their Creator inevitably deprives beholders of their rational devotion to the Word" (*A* 10:1129C–1132A).[143]

The image (*eikōn*), an integral component of Maximus's theology, is not to be confused with a rhetorical or expressive technique such as is deployed for contingent, pragmatic reasons. Far from some artifice fashioned by a subject who enjoys independent spiritual standing, the image prima facie unveils and delineates the scope and direction of spiritual reflection. Where contemplation is concerned, only the *eikōn* has agency, moving as it may the human being engaged in its contemplation: "From the same source whence we received our being, we should also long to receive being moved, like an image [*eikōn*] that has ascended to its archetype, corresponding to it completely, in the way an impression corresponds to its stamp" (*A* 7:1076C). For Maximus, the image uniquely entwines the singular source (*logos*) of the cosmos and "the marvelous physical phenomena that we see, which are naturally interconnected, so that the harmonious web of the universe is contained within it like the various elements in a book." Thus God "leads us to a unitary idea of the truth, allowing Himself to be seen *by analogy* through visible things" (*A* 10:1129A).

In its abundant and inexhaustible givenness as a focal point of visual attention, each and every created form functions simultaneously as an image (*eikōn*) of the divine *logos* and as a figure (*typos*) of a fullness (*plērōma*) and rational order (*cosmos*) fleetingly indexed by our contemplation of visible forms. "There is," remarks Andrew Louth, "something intensely visual about Maximos's reflections," a point echoed by Tsakiridou, who notes how in Maximus "the very faculties that ordinarily deny and obscure [Christ]—the senses[—] . . . now assist in his revelation."[144] Paradoxically, Maximus insists that apophatic theology positively demands a distinctive kind of vi-

---

143. Earlier, Maximus elaborates on his commitment to apophatic reflection: "No argument will ever be able to demonstrate the simultaneous interdependence of being and what transcends being or of the diverse species or concepts (*logoi*) and the *logos*" (*A* 7:1081B). Early in the twentieth century, Pavel Florensky reaffirms Maximus's distinction as that between the image of ascent, an aesthetic technique, or "mere mechanism constructed in accordance with the moment of its psychic genesis" and "the descending image [that] incarnates in real images the experience of the highest realm" (1996, 45).

144. Louth 2004, 73; Tsakiridou 2013, 175.

sion attainable for finite human beings: "Creation itself—stripped of the soiled pre-conceptions of those who till then believed they saw it clearly, but who in fact were deceived and bound to sense-perception alone—now appearing in the variety of different forms that constitute it, all declaring the power of the Creator Word, in the same way that a garment makes known the dignity of the one who wears it" (*A* 10:1128C). Indeed, "those who are capable of seeing" not only take in what is phe-nomenally apparent; they also achieve the kind of sustained quality of "attention" (a word much later put to similar use by Simone Weil and Iris Murdoch) that allows them to apprehend the visible as *real* in an incarnational sense, that is, as far more than the sum of its mundane, discrete aspects. Such attentive, spiritual seeing simul-taneously constitutes a noetic act whereby the Real enters into a complex economy of meaning. Yet this meaning, for Maximus, can be of different kinds. Thus, an appear-ance may prompt an observer to embed it in a frame of seemingly equivalent phe-nomena—a "taking of X as Y" such as is said to underlie Wittgenstein's language games. Yet Maximus also sees another possibility, one largely eclipsed by the strictly horizontal perspective of modern epistemology. As he puts the choice made by the beholder: "The mind which is settled in the contemplation of visible realities searches out either the natural reasons of things or those which are signified by them, or else it seeks the cause itself" (*MSW* 46). Beyond isolating "natural reasons" of finite, visible matter by laterally cross-referencing it with analogous phenomena, we may also engage the world as it comes into visibility.

When approached not as a circumscribed object but as *manifestatio*, as the full-ness of an image rather than a finite perception begging causal explanation, the visible appears in a different light. It now unveils for the beholder an anagogical di-mension, appearing not as object but manifesting itself as *figura* anticipating the phenomenon's ultimate redemption. It is real in the dual sense of materiality phe-nomenalized as "sight" (*visus*) and as "insight" (*visio*), as a finite, embodied thing in-timating—albeit in strictly analogical form—its hoped-for, typological fulfillment. In crediting "visible things" with giving real presence to "those which are signified by them," Maximus notably does *not* view their function as analogous to pagan sym-bols, nor as allegorical schematizations of a numinous, transcendent order. Rather, *figura* impresses on the beholder/reader the coinherence of what is phenomenally given with its as yet unconsummated, spiritual significance. As Auerbach remarks in his eponymous essay on *figura*, referencing Dante's supreme realization of this model, "The literal meaning and historical reality of a character do not contradict that figure's deeper meaning. Rather, they figure it. Historical reality is not annulled by this deeper meaning."[145] In fact, the "future fulfillment or *veritas*" integral to *figura*

145. "*Figura*," in Auerbach 2014, 111.

must itself become phenomenally distinct; there is nothing notional or abstract about it. With his nuanced retreat from the Platonism of pseudo-Dionysius and his careful avoidance of the pantheist and emanationist framework found in Plotinus and, in attenuated form, still lingering on in pseudo-Dionysius, Maximus helped lay the groundwork for the Byzantine iconodules' defense of images by providing a rich theological rationale for the ultimate "inseparability of image (*eikōn*) and the idea (*ennoia*) in the eikon."[146] For he shows that any devaluation of created, particular, and visible being ends up leveling the distinction between mundane perception and a revelatory image consciousness, a distinction echoed much later by Husserl as the distinction between the truth of correctness and the truth of disclosure.[147] In its absence, all talk of God gravitates toward the purely notional and the abstract. For Maximus and a host of writers who, wittingly or not, are his heirs (Goethe and Hegel among them), there can be no knowledge without mediation, just as the image is utterly misconstrued when treated as a substitute for, or a derivative of, mundane "object-perception" (*Dingwahrnehmung*). In fact, the very possibility of perception presupposes the "pure apprehension" (*reine Auffassung*) of the visual phenomenon prior to and independent of taking it *as* a particular thing—as Husserl and those building on his account of image consciousness (Merleau-Ponty, Marion, Alloa) were to argue.[148]

Perhaps no poem of Hopkins instantiates more poignantly the way in which the natural phenomenon is apprehended as an acheiropoietic image, and in turn is grasped by the beholding consciousness as a visible *figura* (*typos*) of the incarnate *logos*, than "The Windhover," considered by Hopkins to be "the best thing I ever wrote" (*HCW* I:362) and among the most widely anthologized poems in the English language. The sonnet's power stems above all from the way that its highly particular and ecstatic visuality and luxuriant soundscape are presented as truly *essential to* a knowledge of Christ, albeit not *identical with* him. The kestrel is both a contingent natural being and, given its spatiotemporal determinacy as *this* bird seen at St. Beuno's on 30 June 1877 executing distinctive patterns of flight and motion, it also has an essential quality in the way Husserl and Romano define it. It is this fusion of the contingent and the essential that draws Hopkins's attention and invites him to see the kestrel as an *acheiropoieton* manifesting the source in which all being originated, as well as "the terminus of [God's] providence" (*CMC* 124) to which it seeks to return. The motional trope of "hovering" thus aptly situates *this* bird and *this* beholder in a communion of sorts, inhabiting at once a physical place and a spiritual state. Both,

---

146. Pelikan 2011, 3.
147. Husserl 1977, 120–27 (§§44–45).
148. See below ch. 8.

that is, hover between heaven and earth—rather like the eponymous "Ashboughs" whose "talons sweep / The smouldering enormous winter welkin."

"The Windhover"
(to Christ our Lord)

I caught this morning morning's minion, king-
dom of daylight's dauphin, dapple-dáwn-drawn Falcon, in his riding
Of the rólling level úndernéath him steady áir, and striding
High there, how he rung upon the rein of a wimpling wing
In his ecstasy! then off, off forth on swing,
As a skate's heel sweeps smooth on a bow-bend: the hurl and gliding
Rebuffed the big wind. My heart in hiding
Stirred for a bird,—the achieve of, the mastery of the thing!
Brute beauty and valour and act, oh, air, pride, plume, here
Buckle! AND the fire that breaks from thee then, a billion
Times told lovelier, more dangerous, O my chevalier!
No wónder of it: shéer plód makes plough down síllion
Shine, and blue-bleak embers, ah my dear,
Fall, gáll themsélves, and gásh góld-vermílion.

(*HMW* 132)

What dominates is the sense of a beginning, a dawn revelation (with "morning" conspicuously repeated in opening line) that features the kestrel's temporal being "in his ecstasy" yielding to the "king- / dom" for which the bird itself is the figure. Thus, "daylight's dauphin" functions typologically by mediating between the kestrel's natural being and the figure of Christ to whom the sonnet, uniquely in this regard among Hopkins's poems, is dedicated. The Windhover's very being is consummated by this mediation. It does not belong to the order of objects but, instead, is pure "act" and *energeia*, a distinctive pattern of movements fused into a single *Gestalt* by the poem's end-rhymed "riding," "striding," and "gliding." Movement is one of the ways in which, as Maximus had argued, an essence discloses itself insofar as the movement in question exhibits a distinctive pattern: "All things move in either a linear, circular, or spiral manner. All motion, in other words, unfolds in simple and composite patterns" (*A* 7:1072B). At once effortless yet teeming with energy, utterly controlled yet free, the soaring kestrel transfixes the beholder with its very "achieve" and its aura of a supernatural, "brute beauty." Ultimately, the bird's sheer "mastery of the thing"—fully realizing in its action what it was created to be—embodies Christ's perfection. Even so, Hopkins also reminds us that, compared to the splendor of the kestrel's morning daylight, Christ's is a fire "a billion / Times told lovelier, more dangerous."

"Hiersein ist herrlich!" (*Being here is glorious*), Rilke will write in his seventh Duino elegy. With far greater metaphysical confidence, Hopkins's sonnet conveys such "splendor" (echoed by the eponymous *Herrlichkeit* of von Balthasar's trilogy), albeit not in the form of a proposition asserted, but as the event of sheer being witnessed in all its "brute beauty and valour and act." Hence, the poet's "heart in hiding" seeks not simply to participate in but to merge with the Christ icon visibly figured by the kestrel in flight—a merging given audible expression by the internal rhyme of the octet's final line ("stirred for a bird"). To see and to know is also to love, to "stir for" that which is seen.[149] As Maximus puts it, "From God come both our general power of motion (for He is our beginning), and the particular way that we move toward Him (for He is our end)." To see is to be summoned by that which gives itself to be seen, to "be moved intellectively . . . [and to] become a knowing intellect. But if it knows, it surely loves that which it knows; and if it loves, it certainly suffers an ecstasy toward it as an object of love." Such a movement, like that of Hopkins's bird as "off forth on swing," will intensify and "greatly accelerate its motion" (*A* 7:1073C). The kestrel's ecstasy is transferred onto the beholder who is moved to see, *in* and *by means of* the bird, what nevertheless remains *beyond* all vision and, as Maximus had put it, will have "sanctified his sense with uncontaminated images" (*MSW* 131). Gently correcting Origen's premise of material creation as a declension of sorts, Maximus posits that "we are able conjecturally to derive an image—not of that participation in goodness which existed long ago and fell to corruption—but that of which the worthy shall partake in the age to come; and I say an 'image' because what we hope for is beyond all images, surpassing vision and hearing and understanding, according to Scripture."[150]

---

149. In more caustic fashion, Keats formulates this placing of the human animal among other animals in an 1819 letter: "The greater part of Men make their way with the same instinctiveness, the same unwandering eye from their purposes, the same animal eagerness as the Hawk—the Hawk wants a Mate, so does the Man—look at them both set about it and procure on in the same manner—they get their food in the same manner—The noble animal Man for his amusement smokes his pipe—the Hawk balances about the Clouds—that this the only difference of their leisures. This it is that makes the Amusement of Life—to a speculative Mind. I go among the F[ie]lds and catch a glimpse of a stoat or a fieldmouse peeping out of the withered grass—the creature hath a purpose and its eyes are bright with it. I go among the buildings of a city and I see a Man hurrying along—to what? The creature has a purpose and his eyes are bright with it" (Keats 1891, 236).

150. *A* 7:1076A. Elsewhere, Maximus distances himself more firmly from Origenism's negative view of visible and sensible matter: "In applying itself to visible things the mind knows them in accordance with nature through the medium of the senses, so that neither is the mind evil, nor is natural knowledge, nor the things, nor the senses, for these are all works of God" (*MSW* 48).

Characteristic of many of Hopkins's nature sonnets, "The Windhover" mobilizes the formal division of the Petrarchan sonnet into octet and sestet so as to move from a particular image to what transcends the visible realm altogether. In this case, the pivot is located in the enigmatic "Buckle" of line 10. It marks the turning point where the visible is supplanted by the knowledge that it can only ever be *figura* (*typos*) *for*, but never essentially coincide *with*, that toward which it points. A great deal of philological detective work has been lavished on the meaning of "Buckle" here. Indeed, the allusions and associations variously imputed to the word may be seen to enrich the word's twofold meaning: (1) a turn, loop, or bell curve–like swerve indicating that an apex has been reached and is now followed by a downward motion; and (2) the link between two distinct, though not opposed domains—in this instance those of finite appearance and transcendent truth, respectively.[151] At the same time, Hopkins's unusual choice to capitalize the conjunction ("Buckle! AND") emphasizes that these two domains of being are distinct yet related. Thus, the image of the kestrel points to—but nowise merges with—the transcendent and ineffable God, "the fire that breaks from thee then, a billion / Times told lovelier, more dangerous." The relationship between inscaped natural being and "Christ our Lord," the image and the source of all being, respectively, remains one of analogy. We are not presented with a Gnostic scenario in which the visible competes with (or, rather, against) the invisible for the same epistemological space. Nor, for that matter, does Hopkins's sonnet construe (in Dionysian fashion) the visible image as some strictly provisional scaffolding, to be superseded by its ineffable divine referent. Instead, as the poem's dedication makes clear, the kestrel's Christocentric dimension is honored precisely by keeping both dimensions in productive tension and balance. In so doing, the poem avoids an outright collapsing of immanence into transcendence, or vice versa, and instead presents visible being in tensioned relation to its transcendent source. As Hopkins will later put it in his commentary on Ignatius, "His presence is a reality, though invisible," and "Though God gives us His Word and Image, the Word and Image has with it the divine substance" (*SDW* 194).

Joining the two realms, the "buckle" correlating visible, inscaped being with the ineffable, triune God (thereby fusing octet and sestet into a poetically and theologically coherent statement) is the underlying framework of *analogia*. As Maximus writes, the God who has "wisely inscribed [the marvelous physical phenomena that we see] and is ineffably inscribed within them, is rendered legible when He is read by

---

151. MacKenzie (2008, 72–73) references several interpretations, including the function of "buckle" in the art of falconry; its presence as a D-shaped fetterlock on the heraldic badge of the House of York; and its meaning of an arc of electric light, "dangerous" as well as full of color, described in period handbooks on electricity.

us, communicating to us solely the concept that He exists, and not what He is, . . . allowing Himself to be seen *by analogy* through visible things [*analogōs . . . dia tōn horatōn*] as their *Creator*."¹⁵² As Przywara will put it almost fifteen hundred years later, "The sphere of creatureliness . . . 'has' (ontically) being and (noëtically) truth (goodness, beauty) in such measure as it is related, beyond itself, to this latter, super-ordinated sphere. That is to say: *analogy* is established *as a participatory being-related-above-and-beyond*."¹⁵³ Now, depending on whether this carefully wrought model of the *analogia entis* is kept in view or not, the intentionality underlying our engagement of visible being will typically be one of two kinds: either an idolatrous gaze will reify a given phenomenon into an anthropomorphic perception, which in turn human desire seeks to appropriate as an object; or an undesigning, attentive gaze may apprehend the natural phenomenon as an "image" (*eikōn*) capable of mediating, in strictly analogical form, the *logos* that is at once its source and its end. On this latter understanding, the icon instantiates what Maximus already outlines as the analogy of being: "All things are related to Him without being confused with Him, who is the essential and personally distinct Logos of God the Father" (*A* 7:1077C). Long before Aquinas and, in the twentieth century, Erich Przywara, Hans Urs von Balthasar, and Gottlieb Söhngen were to conceive the *analogia entis* as the metaphysical foundation for Catholic theology, Maximus affirms (with pseudo-Dionysius) that created or "circumscribed" beings or *logoi* are never convertible with divine Being or *logos*. Where Scotus much later will equivocate on this crucial point, Maximus categorically affirms that "it is not possible for the infinite and the finite to exist simultaneously on the same level of being" (*A* 7:1081B). For him, as for Hopkins, *logos* and *logoi* are analogically related, and "the Word . . . is concealed within beings" (*A* 6:1068B). For that reason, created being never merely *is* but, in its actlike, dynamic manifestation, solicits the human beholder's participation in what Hopkins calls "bidding." As an inscaped appearance whose intrinsic coherence and formal determinacy not only betoken *existence*, but constitute a palpable *presence*, a natural

---

152. *A* 10:1128D. In *Ad Thalassium* 60, Maximus again draws on the concept of analogy as he offers this programmatic statement about spiritual knowledge: "It is impossible for rational knowledge (*logos*) of God to coexist with the direct experience [*peira*] of God, or for conceptual knowledge (*noēsis*) of God to coexist with immediate perception (*aisthēsis*) of God. By 'rational knowledge of God' I mean the use of the analogy of created beings [*tēn ek tōn ontōn analogian*] in the intellectual contemplation of God; by 'perception' I mean the experience through participation, of the supernatural goods" (*CMC* 126).

153. Przywara 2014, 212–13. As Anne Carpenter (2015, 176) remarks, "Univocity destroys particularity, while analogy upholds it." For only the latter can relate "unique things to a supremely unique object—God" without either opposing them as incommensurables or conflating them to the point of indistinctness.

being such as Hopkins's kestrel is simultaneously the *imago* of its transcendent source, which it mediates for the beholder.[154] Maximus's warrant for this additional stipulation has to do with the fact that, as Przywara was to put it, "creaturely potentiality does not, of itself, place limits on God, but rather receives its limits from God."[155]

Though he does not cast the matter in terms of *analogia*, Hopkins nevertheless holds the same view. Thus, while not denying "that there is a universal really, and not only logically," he points out that ultimately both "the species and individual in the brutes," though distinct from one another, must neither be confused with nor disaggregated from the *logos* whom they manifest. Where Maximus suggests a distinction between one (divine) *logos* or Word and multiple *logoi*, Hopkins likewise affirms with regard to "the form of the whole species [that] these universals are finite only. . . . God is so deeply present to everything, that it would be impossible for him *but for his infinity* not to be identified with them." Conversely, "were it not for God's infinity he could not be so intimately present to things" (*SDW* 128; emphasis mine). It is God's unconditional, intimate presence *to* and non-identity *with* created things that the poem's closing tercet captures so brilliantly.

> No wónder of it: shéer plód makes plough down síllion
> Shine, and blue-bleak embers, ah my dear,
> Fall, gáll themsélves, and gásh góld-vermílion.

The shift from the octet's motional tropes to brilliant colors ("blue-bleak embers / gásh góld-vermílion) brings home the *analogia* framework in uniquely vivid and particular ways. Rapturously addressed ("O my chevalier!"), Christ's wound, or "gash," shifts the visual focus to his blood. The warm crimson of Christ's blood prefigures the earthly fecundity of plowed fields, reinforced by the end rhyme of "síllion" and "vermilion." Likewise, the rhythmic labor of breaking the dark soil into symmetrical furrows ("sillions") polishes the steel plow, which thus reflects the radiance ("Shine") of God who, in Przywara's searching formulation is both "*in-and-beyond*" (*inund-über*) finite, material being.[156] Inasmuch as "God infinitely transcends all

---

154. As Benedict XVI categorically put it in his Regensburg Address of 2005, "The faith of the Church has always insisted that between God and us . . . there exists a real analogy, in which—as the Fourth Lateran Council in 1215 stated—unlikeness remains infinitely greater than likeness, yet not to the point of abolishing analogy and its language" (Ratzinger 2007, 137–38).

155. Przywara 2014, 222. Quoting Aquinas (*De potentia*, q. 1 a. 5), Przywara affirms that "no potentiality of the creature . . . is able by its enactment to exhaust this act that is interiorly related to itself" (222).

156. A formal metaphysics thus must not only stipulate "that the divine absolute as it appears 'from' the creaturely can be only 'beyond (everything creaturely)' [*Gott über Geschöpf*]. On the

things which participate or are participated," created beings can only be a figure or image of God by having formally inscribed within them what the Fourth Lateran Council had stipulated as the "greater dissimilarity" qualifying the analogical relation between finite and transcendent being. Or, as Maximus puts it, "All visible things need a cross, that is, a capacity which holds back the participation in what is active in them according to sense" (*MSW* 137, 140). For Maximus, this caveat extends not only to visible things but also to the spoken and written word, including scripture, whose meaning is consummated not in the modality of literal reference but in that of spiritual significance: "We must necessarily take thought for the 'body' of Holy Scripture, which is far superior to its 'garments,' by which I mean its inner meanings, which are divine and exalted" (*A* 10:1132B).

At the same time, the concept of *analogia* safeguards against the stigmatization of material nature's visible forms as inherently fallen, the illicit fruit of creation, which the Gnostics and, to a certain extent, Origenists had regarded as an ontological miscarriage of sorts. In fact, the ongoing process of spiritual formation not only does not anathematize material creation, but positively enjoins the beholder to approach it by cultivating an intentionality wherein the senses and the mind are fully integrated with one another. Hence, Maximus repeatedly warns against an idolatrous gaze that, by exclusively reveling in sight as a "bodily sensation," fails to "put to death *the mind of the flesh* [*to phronēma tēs sarkos*]" (*A* 10:1149A). The allusion to Romans 8:6 chimes with Maximus's caveat that "the beauty of creatures, when not beheld for the glory of their Creator, inevitably deprives the beholders of their rational devotion to the Word" (*A* 10:1129D–1132A). Yet this spiritualist outlook in no way contradicts Maximus's overarching commitment to "spiritual contemplation [*kata theōrian*]" (*A* 21:1244B) anchored in sensory participation and mediated by "the eyes of the soul [*tēs psychēs ta ommata*]" (*CMC* 107). The soul can attain its true end only insofar as it is embodied and capable of integrating material sight and spiritual vision. As he puts it, all "intelligible things are the soul of sensible things, and sensible things are the body of intelligible things[,] . . . and both make up one world as body and soul make up one man, [and] neither of these elements joined to the other in unity denies or displaces the other according to the law of the one who has bound them together" (*MSW* 196). Indeed, the ultimate goal of a spiritual life, "deification" (*theōsis*), is attainable only *through and by means of* sensory knowledge, which as "spiritual contemplation" or "noetic perception" (*aisthēsis noētikē*) keeps similarity and dissimilarity—of creation to creator—in the tensioned balance that a metaphys-

---

contrary, this 'beyond' is 'beyond' in the fullest sense only when the appearing of the divine absolute is not bound in any way intrinsically to this 'from (the creaturely)' [*von . . . aus dem Geschöpflichen*] but instead presides independently over the manner of its own appearing" (Przywara 2014, 161).

ics of analogy implies: "The symbolic contemplation of intelligible things by means of visible realities is spiritual knowledge and understanding [*pneumatikē epistēmē kai noēsis*] of [in]visible things through the visible."[157]

For Maximus, then, "the interpretive process is a deeper perception of the higher meaning in and through the literal." Distinct yet complementary, sensory (image-based) knowledge and intellection correspond "to the difference between the logos of nature and the *tropos* of virtue."[158] Yet this difference, again in accordance with the principle of *analogia*, must not be construed as an outright contradiction of incommensurables. In fact, Maximus (as pseudo-Dionysius a century earlier) holds that there cannot be any conceptual knowledge of God without sensory knowledge, which belongs to the order of what Bertrand Russell terms "knowledge by acquaintance." Sense-based cognition is the indispensable and enduring guide for the movement toward deification (*theōsis*). Its utter concreteness and specificity—as sensory awareness of a thing's essential *thisness*—constitutes both its greatest liability and greatest advantage. Sensory awareness, that is, remains always fraught with the risk of a purely immanent, desirous gaze mired in the transient pleasure (*hēdonē*) of its very occurrence. Still, it is precisely the concrete quality of sensory participation in the visible that allows it to serve as the linchpin for an education in the virtues, a form of spiritual practice whereby inclination is cultivated as a right habit and, eventually, as a virtue. Echoing Gregory of Nyssa's *Life of Moses*, Maximus thus positions the spiritual senses within an economy of deification: "The mind who . . . is instructed in true knowledge through the contemplation of created beings, receives a hidden and mystical commission from God invisibly to lead out of the *Egypt* of the heart—that is, from [the realm of] flesh and sense—divine thoughts of created beings, in the manner of the Israelites." As it advances on "the road of the virtues" (*CMC* 106), the subject by cultivating its spiritual senses discovers how "the virtues reorder the passions, and thereby enable the intellect to see properly and move towards divine likeness." For Maximus, this progression provides a theodicy of the senses as spiritual and also, from the perspective of finite, human existence, reveals their "transformative dimension."[159] In a carefully conditional turn of phrase, Maximus thus affirms that "if the soul, in drawing on its own powers, makes proper use of the senses, singling out the manifold principles of beings, and being able wisely to transfer to itself the whole of what it sees—in which God is concealed and silently proclaimed [*en hō kekryptai theos siōpē kēryttomenos*]—it will have succeeded in cre-

---

157. *MSW* 189. The Greek text may be corrupt here: *tōn horomenōn . . . dia tōn aoratōn*, as its literal meaning ("of visible things *through the invisible*") makes little or no sense; further misleading is the printed translation ("of visible things through the visible").

158. Aquino 2012, 110.

159. Ibid., 115.

ating by the mind's power of free choice a superlatively beauteous and spiritual world within itself" (*A* 21:1248C).

Ballinger's claim that "in Scotus, Hopkins discovered that sensation could be a kind of 'spiritual sense'" and, consequently, glimpsed "the possibility of making poetry a theology," though it risks overstating Scotus's influence, is fundamentally correct. For it hints at how Hopkins's theo-poetics rehabilitates a conception of the spiritual senses that had been integral to Cappadocian and Byzantine theology and had culminated in Maximus's cosmic theology.[160] The conjunction emerges in particularly luminous, sound-patterned imagery in the curtal sonnet usually titled "Ashboughs."

> Not of all my eyes see, wandering on the world,
> Is anything a milk to the mind so, só sighs deep
> Poetry to it, as a tree whose boughs break in the sky.
> Say it is áshboughs: whether on a December day and furled
> Fast or they in clammyish láshtender combs creep
> Apart wide and new-nestle at heaven most high.
> They touch heaven, tabour on it; how their talons sweep
> The smouldering enormous winter welkin! May
> Mells blue and snowwhite through them, a fringe and fray
> Of greenery: it is old earth's groping towards the steep
> Heaven whom she childs us by.
>
> (HMW 177–78)

Alliteration ("milk to the mind"—"new-nestle"—"May / Mells"—"fringe and fray") and intricate patterns of sound and rhythm ("clammyish láshtender"—"smouldering enormous") produce quasi-tactile, at times intimate effects. The poetic word, which in Hopkins should always be approached as a correlate of hearing as much as of sight, here works to effect a near-total fusion of the particular image of ashboughs and the consciousness that is filled and ordered by it. Bringing home the "close relationship between being, knowing, and wording" so characteristic of Hopkins's poetry, the ashboughs that are the focal point of the eleven-line meditation constitute at once a particular *thing*, a distinct *sensation* of that thing, an image-*object* (the ash as a natural entity) arising from that sensation, and, finally, an "image-subject" (Husserl's *Bildsujet*) that is invisible per se.[161] As regards the latter, the ashboughs' distinc-

---

160. Ballinger 2000, 149; on Maximus's concept of the spiritual senses, see Aquino 2012, 104–20.

161. Ballinger 2000, 192.

tively inscaped *figura*—mediating the invisible through the visible—is accentuated by the way the ash's branches are described as "groping towards the steep / Heaven," "their talons sweep[ing]" the sky. In an 1872 notebook entry, Hopkins had remarked on the peculiar inscape of the ash tree, whose "combs are not wiry and straight but rich and beautifully curved" (*HCW* III:533). Yet in the lyric, the visual presentation of the ashboughs is not another natural phenomenon subject to ekphrastic tracing but, instead, an instance of complex figural speech hinting at the complementarity between the visible and its numinous fulfillment, such that the ashboughs' very inscape "sighs deep / poetry to" and is veritable "milk to the mind." As the beholder's eyes, "wandering on the world," respond to the call of the visible by attending to its inscape, they witness the transfiguration of object into agent. Both for Maximus and for Hopkins, "communion rather than mere participation is the key. . . . Beings are to be perceived and thought from their own standpoint, in the terms they pose by being what they are."[162] Initially "furled fast," the ashboughs are gradually apprehended in their full dynamism. Thus, the beholder's eye and spirit ascend, they "creep / Apart wide," effectively shifting from *res* to *figura*, from merely being to actively manifesting their transcendent source.

Some four decades after Hopkins, Paul Claudel will independently develop a strikingly similar conception of the lyric image. For Claudel, too, the verbal icon responds to the strict uniqueness and integrity of each visible, "inscaped" phenomenon, which it receives as a quasi-sacramental gift (*donné*), and to whose incomprehensible certainty and presence poetic, figural speech bears witness. In the last of his *Cinq Grandes Odes*, "La Maison Fermée" (1908), Claudel remarks how, in the aftermath of ephemeral, worldly passion, he is filled only with

> the longing
> To know God in his fixity and to find truth by attention,
>   and each thing, which is all others, recreating it
>   in my own thought by its intelligible name.
> . . . . . .
> My God, who have *made all things to be given*,
>   give me desire to the measure of your mercy,
>   so that I may given in turn what is given to me
>   to those who can receive it.
> . . . . . .
> To me, also, *every figure and form, every image of nature*
>   *has been given*, not as beasts for hunting and devouring,

---

162. Tsakiridou 2013, 180.

but so that I may gather them and make them present again
in my spirit, each serving me to understand the others—[163]

Hopkins's "inscape" and Claudel's "figures of nature" are visible sacramental tokens
"made . . . to be given" and to resonate in finite consciousness. Each inscaped phenomenon imparts focus and definition ("instress") to the beholder's consciousness
and, in turn, is completed "in my thought by its intelligible name." What Husserl,
writing at the same time, calls "eidetic intuition" becomes in Claudel's ode the epiphanic drama of daily rebirth, when "the spirit opening its eyes, / beginning once
again the day, find[s] each thing in its place / in the great workshop of consciousness
[l'esprit qui oeuvre les yeux / Recommençant sa journée et qui trouve chacque chose
à / sa place dans l'immense atelier de la connaissance]." Like Hopkins, Claudel rejects
the Cartesian view of consciousness as unilaterally reconstituting an otherwise unstable and deceptive world of appearances in rational and abstract form. Instead,
even as it actively constitutes the world of distinct things, consciousness (connais-
sance) also finds itself being "born" (Co-Naissance) by its intuitive receptivity and responsiveness to the phenomenal world as it so inexhaustibly gives itself.[164] Bearing witness to the myriad ways that the world's "saturated" or "inscaped" phenomena
resonate in the articulate world-inner-space that is consciousness (Rilke will call it
Weltinnenraum), the poetic word, for both Hopkins and Claudel, uniquely attests to
the irresistible and inexhaustible grace of the Real: "The created word . . . by which all
things / created are given over to mankind [La parole créée est cela en qui toutes choses créées sont faites à l'homme donnables]."[165]

What we find compressed into Hopkins's unpredictable patterns of "sprung
rhythm," alliteration, and sound patterning and what infuses the expansive syntax
and lavish parataxes of Claudel's prosody (the so-called verset Claudélien) is one and
the same reality. As we saw earlier, drawing on Husserl, Romano characterized that
reality as an "essentialism without essences." It demands a wholly unique mode of
(poetic) speech that can present us with "the set of predicates necessary for an indi-

---

163. " . . . [le] désir / De connaître Dieu dans sa fixité et d'acquérir la vérité / par l'attention et
chaque chose qui est toutes les autres / en la recréant avec son nom intelligible dans ma pensée. / . . .
O mon Dieu, qui avez fait toutes choses donnables, / donnez-moi un désir à la mesure de votre misé-
ricorde! / Afin qu'à mon tour à ceux-là qui peuvent le recevoir / je donne en moi cela qui à moi est
donné. / . . . Et moi aussi, toutes les figures de la nature m'ont été / données, non point comme des bêtes
que l'on chasse / et la chair à dévorer, / Mais pour que je les rassemble dans mon esprit, me / servant
de chacune pour comprendre tous les autres" (Claudel 1967, 280–81 / 2020, 94–95; my emphasis).
164. See "Traité de la Co-Naissance au Monde et de Soi-Même," Part II of Claudel's L'Art poétique (Claudel 1967, 149–204).
165. Claudel 1967, 281 / 2020, 95.

vidual to be the *individual* it is, distinct from all other individuals falling under the same genus" and, thus, sheltered from being confused with the Scholastic conception of a "generic essence."[166] No longer, then, can the iconicity of the visible be entrusted to received conventions of poetic expression and aesthetic judgment. Rather, the Hopkinsian, multiply instressed line with its fusion of intricate sound patterning, syntactic innovation, sprung rhythm, and startling enjambment must be read as responding to "a being's particular act of expression at any given moment of its existence . . . [when it] puts forth a 'voice' or 'image' of its nature." Iconicity gives being as event, as manifestation, and in so doing allows us to glimpse how "a being's subsistence is entirely determined by its essence, [how] it becomes iconic to itself in the sense that it encompasses (outlines) in its particular acts of existence its own nature and in so doing exists perspicuously and conspicuously to itself. Iconicity in this context is not mere likeness (and verisimilitude). It is an act of self-realization: a being's *performance* is its truth. Neither is *enargeia* mere vividness. It is an act of self-circumscription: a being's dynamic possession of its truth."[167]

As Tsakiridou's characterization of the icon ("an act of self-circumscription") implies, the principle of *analogia* sets limits to what the finite, individual being and its image can do. They can only ever intimate a presence that necessarily remains beyond vision, though they may do so with such force and specificity that inscape will be experienced not only as a factual appearance, but, more important, as manifesting the transcendent source *of* which it is the image and *in* which it enjoins us to participate. Yet only if the phenomenon is received in all its sensory specificity, and only if its felt sensuous quality is held in consciousness as uniquely *this*, will the visible event and its numinous significance, fact and value, be experienced as mutually constitutive rather than as logical antonyms. Such is the case in Hopkins's springtime revelation of the sky descending through the ash's "talons," and it suffuses the lyric meditation with an oblique eschatological dimension. Thus, as the ash tree's "clammyish láshtender combs" puncture the "enormous winter welkin," the monochrome visible scene is about to be displaced by a kaleidoscope of chiaroscuro effects and mezzotints, an abundance about to be revealed that no image could ever contain: as "May / Mells blue and snowwhite through them, a fringe and fray / Of greenery." For all earthbound, temporally distended experience there necessarily remains an ultimate dissimilarity between the deliverances of the senses and the metaphysical meanings that they can delineate only in partial and strictly analogous form. For Hopkins no less than for Maximus, it is through the operation of the spiritual senses that finite consciousness becomes aware of a "mysterious tension between similar

---

166. Romano 2015, 204.
167. Tsakiridou 2013, 188.

and dissimilar, corresponding to the tension between God in us and God [beyond] us" that for Przywara defines the *analogia entis*.[168] As Maximus puts it:

> The senses of the body, according to the more divine principle that is appropriate to them, are said to be the elements for the powers of the soul, gently guiding them into actualization through the perceptions of the inner principles of beings. . . . For this reason some have even called the senses [*tas aisthēseis*] paradigmatic images of the powers of the soul [*paradeigmatikas tōn psychikōn dynameōn eikonas*], since according to a certain mystical principle, every sense along with its respective organ . . . of sense perception has been given primordially and naturally an *analogous* power of the soul. . . . [T]he sense of sight, or the eye, is the image of the intellect [*tou . . . nou estin eikōn hē opsis*]. . . . In accordance with the law of God, who created all things in wisdom, the soul is naturally conveyed by the vehicle, as it were, of the senses, which it sets in motion by its own powers [*dia tōn autēs dynameōn kai pros ta aisthēta poikilōs diabibazomenē*], and by means of which it is variously transported through the sensible world. (*A* 21:1248A–C; emphasis mine)

In what may well be regarded as Hopkins's apotheosis of the spiritual senses that had defined his earlier nature poetry, "Spelt from Sibyl's Leaves" (1886) is also a farewell to his visual theo-poetics. In the sonnet's programmatic declaration, earth's "dapple is at an end," extinguished by the twilight of nightfall. What succeeds it is an incipient, mystical passage into the dark night of the soul: "lét life wind / Off hér once skéined stained véined variety." Reminiscent of a thoroughgoing, aniconic mysticism found in Meister Eckhart and St. John of the Cross, Hopkins's late sonnet appears to break decisively with the lyrics written roughly a decade earlier. What in a letter he describes as "the longest sonnet . . . ever made, longest by its own proper length, namely by the length of its lines," concludes his long-standing preoccupation with a sacramental poetics of visible nature—inscaped, instressed, and profoundly absorbing in its inexhaustible particularity. By contrast, the present sonnet opens with an evocation of dusk that foreshadows a final, eschatological darkness, as "Evening strains to be time's vást, ' womb-of-all, home-of-all, hearse-of-all night, . . . / óur night ' whélms, whélms, ánd will end us."

Not by accident, the sonnet's anguished farewell to the *acheiropoietai* of Hopkins's nature sonnets involves a pivot from the essential concreteness of visual phenomena to the more speculative deliverances of sound. In the letter to Bridges in

---

168. Przywara 2014, 554 (trans. John Betz); this text also contains a superb discussion of Przywara's account of the *analogia entis* in response to dialectical Protestant theologians (Barth, Gogarten, Thurneysen).

which he also encloses a fair copy of "Spelt from Sibyl's Leaves," Hopkins thus places heightened stress on the way that, perhaps uniquely, the medium of sound and the event of the word—listened-to as spoken—may break through the strictly analogical relation that at once links the order of the visible *to* and separates it *from* its divine source. This late sonnet, Hopkins writes, like "all my verse, . . . is, as a living art, should be, made for performance." Though profoundly steeped in and responsive to visual experience, lyric meaning now pivots above all on the dynamic range and ineffable modulations of sound that mediate the intelligible word. Transposed into writing, all circumscribed and spatiotemporally bounded inscape at last submits to an apophaticism with which its concrete, sensory charism had always stood in some tension. Inasmuch as hearing is the spiritual sense least prone to reification by an idolatrous gaze, it consummates the spiritual sense of vision—a type of "sublation" (*Aufhebung*) that, we have found, repeatedly emerges as the ultimate telos of transposing the visible into the medium of the word. Hence, as Hopkins stipulates in a letter to Bridges, reading this "longest sonnet" is preeminently an aural event: "Its performance is not reading with the eye but loud, leisurely, poetical (not rhetorical) recitation, with long ~~pauses~~ rests, long dwells on the rhyme and other marked syllables, and so on. This sonnet shd. almost be sung . . . *tempo rubato*."[169]

> Earnest, earthless, equal, attuneable, ' vaulty, voluminous, . . . stupendous
> Evening strains to be time's vást, ' womb-of-all, home-of-all, hearse-of-all night.
> Her fond yellow hornlight wound to the west, ' her wild hollow hoarlight hung
>   to the height
> Waste; her earliest stars, earl-stars, ' stárs principal, overbend us,
> Fíre-féaturing heaven. For earth ' her being as unbound, her dapple is at an
>   end, as-
> tray or aswarm, all throughther, in throngs; ' self ín self steepèd and páshed—
>   quite
> Disremembering, dísmémbering, ' áll now. Heart, you round me right
> With: Óur évening is over us; óur night ' whélms, whélms, ánd will end us.
> Only the beak-leaved boughs dragonish ' damask the tool-smooth bleak light;
>   black,
> Ever so black on it. Óur tale, O óur oracle! ' Lét life, wáned, ah lét life wind
> Off hér once skéined stained véined varíety ' upon áll on twó spools; párt, pen,
>   páck

---

169. *HCW* II:841–42. On Hopkins's late preoccupation with musical effects, see Michael Suárez's introductory discussion in *HCW* VII:38–43; on his unsuccessful attempts at composition and apparent lack of talent as a singer, see White 1992, 410–18.

Now her áll in twó flocks, twó folds—black, white; ' right, wrong; reckon but,
    reck but, mind
But thése two; wáre of a wórld where bút these ' twó tell, each off the óther; of a
    rack
Where, selfwrung, selfstrung, sheathe- and shelterless, ' thóughts agaínst
    thoughts ín groans grínd.

(*HMW* 175)

The focus is on the experience of "vaulty, voluminous" space rather than on any
particular thing within it. Faintly offset by "the beak-leaved boughs" whose somber black stands at slight tonal variance with "the tool-smooth bleak light," the scene
points to the representational minimalism of Gerhard Richter's *Waldstück* (Forest
Piece) (1965) (fig. 7.3). Dissolving the visible world's chromatic richness and particularity of all *Gestalt*, dusk marks the moment when time appears to separate from
space. Adrift in a sea of monochrome phantasmagoria, the gaze falters. Sounding
an unfamiliar Gnostic note, Hopkins's late sonnet presents life as fundamentally divided into fallen, earthbound existence and an ineffable transcendence: "áll on twó
spools . . . / áll in twó flocks, twó folds—black, white." The transitional time of "equal,
attuneable" evening intimates a metaphysical transfiguration so definitive as to preclude any return from it. There will be no dawn and no future sights. Hopkinsian,
inscaped being awaits its final interment as "Evening strains to be time's vást, ' womb-
of-all, home-of-all, hearse-of-all night."

    As it shifts beyond the sensuous concreteness of visible things, a now-vertical
gaze finds itself enveloped by "stárs principal, [that] overbend us" and imminently
consumed by a "Fíre-féaturing heaven." Perched at the very threshold of the visible,
phenomena can no longer be named but, instead, throw into relief the epistemic and
moral darkness ("ever so black") that enfolds "life, wáned." All that remains is to
be "wáre [aware/wary] of a wórld where bút these twó tell, each off the óther," a world
in which Ignatian discipline and "the worm of conscience [of] mind gnawing and
feeding on its own most miserable self" (*SDW* 243) have vanquished, seemingly for
good, the spiritual sense of sight. Here we find ourselves at the threshold of Hopkins's
despondent final years in Dublin (1884–89); years of confinement in a gray, notoriously unhealthy, and economically declining city; years of bare life spent "Among
strangers" and "at a third remove" (*HMW* 166), that is, lived out in terminal estrangement from family, from England with its familiar patterns of sociability and its
natural beauty; years, finally, consumed with the interminable labor of grading thousands of Latin exams in the dank, crumbling, poorly lit spaces of Dublin's faltering
University College. It is beyond the scope of this discussion to trace further Hopkins's descent into "the fell of dark," into "black hours," and into a despondency that
leaves the poet "Pitched past pitch of grief" (*HMW* 166–67).

Figure 7.3. Gerhard Richter, *Waldstück* (Forest Piece), 1965. Nürnberg, Neues Museum, Staatliches Museum für Kunst und Design

There can be no doubt that the darkness of these late sonnets reflects compre-hensive despair more than spiritual hope and that the night that "will end us" reveals the shadow side of apophaticism—that of a God abiding in immeasurable numinous darkness rather than made manifest, *per analogiam*, by inscaped forms. Hence, the charismatic call of visible beauty, though still intermittently heard, is now increas-ingly experienced as a torment that Hopkins wishes to see definitively, even violently expunged, such as in an 1885 fragment in which he welcomes the wind and hail that will "May's beauty massacre . . . Bid joy back, have at the harvest, [and] keep Hope pale" (*HMW* 167). As with other writers already considered, and as remains to be seen in the case of Rilke, the *analogia* principle that for a while had allowed Hopkins to invest visible phenomena with revelatory power while also safeguarding against their quasi-pantheist conflation requires an aesthetic and intellectual balancing act that imaginative writing—and the fictive personae it conjures—can sustain only for so long. Perhaps it was inevitable that the luminous plenitude of Hopkins's nature sonnets and the metaphysical certitude they adumbrate proved to be short-lived, yielding but a handful of spectacular poems. As they seek to render charismatic visual experiences in the uniquely compressed form of sprung rhythm, Hopkins's lyric inscapes mark the last time that the lyric word stands in expressly contiguous relation to transcendence. Henceforth, high modernist epiphany of the kind found in Rilke, Mann, Proust, Joyce, and Woolf, perhaps even the late Eliot, will be a rather more muted and prevaricating affair, with its proponents for the most part anxious to avoid both the robust metaphysical affirmations and the outright existentialist despair that bookend Hopkins's mature oeuvre.

8

THE EPIPHANIC IMAGE

Husserl—Cézanne—Rilke

Anita . . . had arrayed various large-caliber questions against me: 'Do you believe in God?'—'Do you believe in life after death?'—My dear! I did not respond with Augustinian confessions but, instead, hedged my bets [ganz abwartend]. More than ever I am baffled by this impatience of mind, which overleaps everything in order to ask in this manner. . . . Down below, right next to the poplar that's in plain view, this poplar for beginners, something is blossoming (a plum-tree? a cherry-tree?); and on the road just beyond it, and again in the space above, a bird repeats a two-note sequence. . . . This it is which should occupy us; this we should give as an answer to such large questions, should look up and say whatever we see: doesn't it contain everything—far more than our interpretations and speculations?
—Rilke, letter to Nancy Wunderly-Volkart, 26 March 1920

CAPTURING THE "PRE-PREDICATIVE": ON THE MODERNISM OF HUSSERL'S 1905 LECTURES

Following prompts by some of its major representatives, modernism has long been viewed as an aesthetic meditation on the broader aspirations and limits of philosophical modernity. In their preferred genre, the manifesto, the movement's principal theoreticians (Pound, Lewis, Marinetti, Mayakovsky, Schoenberg, et al.) all seem to voice a suspicion that modernity "had not been modern enough"; that it was time to "set fire to the old hypocrisies" (Woolf) of moral and intellectual autonomy that the Enlightenment had bequeathed the nineteenth-century bourgeoisie; and that only a thorough shift "from philosophy, primarily, but also from science and religion to art as the leading or 'legislating force' could remedy the ennui and lack of orientation that had so indisputably overtaken much of European culture."[1] Most of the aesthetic programs surfacing after 1900 offer their distinctive variation on a shared and overriding theme: the repudiation of bourgeois conceptions of art that for the preceding half century or longer had been formally and institutionally enshrined as pictorial realism, poetic symbolism, and the formal hierarchies organizing tonal music. All these techniques had allowed the nineteenth-century bourgeoisie to instrumentalize aesthetics as a highly adaptive system of formal discriminations and symbolic values and, in so doing, legitimate itself as the politically and economically dominant class. While this general outlook (an often-exaggerated construction of modernism as the emancipation *from* inherited cultural and aesthetic norms and practices) has much to recommend it, it does not tell us much about the movement's actual objectives. As we shall see, modernism's iconoclastic response to the formal choices and aesthetic practices of nineteenth-century culture is, to a considerable extent, prompted by a desire to retrieve and redeem phenomena long neglected or positively obscured by a bourgeois aesthetic that after 1900 appears depleted and hidebound.

Notably, the quintessential modernist slogan, "Make it new!," appears to target less the message than, at least initially, the medium of art. The question now pressing is whether the experience of art's foundational elements—sound, rhythm, and color in particular—might yet be cultivated by new aesthetic techniques or whether modernism's attempt to lay bare the constitution of reality in experience ultimately compels a definitive break with the inherited, variously Kantian and Hegelian, projects of philosophical aesthetics. To an unusual degree, modernism's attempt to access the dynamics of appearance as such seems to pervade all the arts. We encounter it in the disorienting and haunting cascade of pitches opening Schoenberg's *Drei Klavierstücke* (1909) whose jagged soundscapes tantalize the listener with intimations of a musical form that never quite comes into focus. Such atonal experiments are early stages in Schoenberg's programmatic "emancipation of dissonance" from a centuries-old, normative system of key relationships that had demanded the eventual, successful "resolution" (*Auflösung*) of all dissonance into a supervening hierarchy of tonal values. By refusing to abide within that matrix, Schoenberg drives a sharp wedge between event and meaning, between sound as sheer appearance and the complex melodic and harmonic symmetries that, Schoenberg contends, had for centuries supervened on the primal event of "sonority" (*Klang*) itself. After all, "harmony is not a

---

1. Pippin 1999, 6, 29.

natural attribute of sound but a way of giving significance to sound."[2] Paradoxically, Schoenberg's attempted retrieval of *Klang* from the historical accretions of listening expectations and the inherited constraints of form and harmony would issue in a serialism that accords an unprecedented and determinative role to abstraction. Still, what matters for now is the principal and representative aim of his early (atonal) modernism: to disentangle the raw phenomena of sound and pitch from any abstract formal schemata and to allow their materiality to achieve full presence as such. Similarly, Futurists such as Marinetti, Mayakovsky, and Wat (who preferred the label "Dadaist") for a brief but intensely charged period exulted in "the idea of words being liberated" from all referential meaning or normative constraint and, instead, being reduced to a purely sonorous, quasi-somatic status. At last, so the proposition ran, "words were things and you could do whatever you liked with them."[3]

An analogous preoccupation with the primal drama of appearance and sensation also informs pictorial modernism. One may think of the scandalous nude females of Manet's *Déjeuner sur l'herbe* (1863) and *Olympia* (1865), or the maid in *The Bar at Folies Bergère* (1882) looking directly at the painting's beholder. Hovering between the dissociated and the defiant, their unwavering gaze disrupts the illusionist covenant that had underwritten the bourgeois ideal of representational art. Insofar as the unsparing candor of Manet's paintings emphasizes "the flat surfaces on which they were painted," the relation between the object depicted and its spatial situatedness within the ambient, so-called real world crumbles. Not least because of the rise of democratic forms and institutions, painting's role, established since the Renaissance, of furnishing the truly representative forms appeared to have reached a dead end. As Arnold Gehlen puts it, "At last, there no longer appeared to be a pure being or state [*irgendein bloßes Dasein und Sosein*] that was affectively experienced as exemplary [*vorbildlich*]. . . . The time had finally come for painting to attempt and ground itself . . . out of its own art-resources [*aus den eigenen Kunstmitteln*]," color, tone, planes, density of pigmentation, patterns of brush strokes, and so forth.[4] By "abandon[ing] in principle the representation of the kind of space that recognizable objects can inhabit," pictorial modernism ended up "convert[ing] theoretical possibilities into empirical ones."[5] The widening gap then grows more pronounced

---

2. Rosen 1996, 25. Yet Rosen also acknowledges the dialectical tension in which atonal music must abide vis-à-vis inherited forms: "The powerful emotional force of Schoenberg's music would . . . become intelligible only against an inherited background of traditional harmony, and would itself be an incoherent system, dependent on a musical culture it was intent on destroying" (27).

3. Wat 1977, 5.

4. Gehlen 2016, 57–58.

5. Greenberg 1995, 86–87, 92. On Manet and a Hegelian approach to pictorial modernism, see Pippin 2014, 27–62.

in the peculiar "flatness" of Cézanne's depopulated landscapes and otherworldly still lifes, "undistracted by an interest in virtuoso illusionism" such that by 1900 it is almost exclusively color, not line, that "is called upon to do the work of linear perspective."[6]

In passing, we note how in early modernist painting the exfoliation of an object's discrete aspects in Picasso's and Braque's early Cubist experiments aligns rather accurately with Husserl's concept of "aspectual seeing" (*Abschattung*; also *Gestaltabschattungen* or *Farbenabschattungen*). Not coincidentally, in elaborating the experiential (not spatial) operation of *Abschattung* Husserl draws a sharp distinction "between being as experience and being as thing."[7] There is also the lurid intensity of primary colors that rendered the works of Fauvists ("wild beasts") such as Matissse and H. Rousseau so shocking to viewers and critics when first displayed at the Salon d'Automne in 1905. The modernist painter "is not satisfied to be a cultured animal but takes up culture from its inception and founds it anew." Fundamentally, this means that the artwork records an experience rather than pictorializing an idea and that "'conception' cannot precede 'execution.'"[8] Here, too, the disruptive effect is such that "whereas one tends to see what is in an Old Master before one sees the picture itself, one sees a Modernist picture as a picture first." Emphatically antisculptural, modernist painting after 1905 appears to pursue a "purely optical experience" undiluted by extrinsic, "tactile associations" and no longer dependent on the simulation of three-dimensionality by means of linear perspective. Still, for Clement Greenberg, it is misleading to construe pictorial modernism as aiming at a categorical break with inherited techniques. For modernism's principal struggle is not with this or that precursor aesthetic but with the far more elemental paradox—confronted long before by Byzantine iconophiles and, again, by Russian icon theorists at the very time that modernism surged to prominence in Western Europe's capitals. That paradox, simply put, is that "the essential norms or conventions of painting are at the same time the limiting conditions with which a picture must comply in order to be experienced as a picture."[9]

Closely related to the Postimpressionist revolution in painting is modernism's unsparing critique of late nineteenth-century symbolism. "All over Europe," Hugh Kenner writes, "poets had decided that effects were intrinsic to poetry, and were aiming at them by deliberative process." In what "we have learned to call . . . 'Symbolist' . . . the Romantic effect has become a structural principle, . . . a systematized

6. Danchev 2012, 293 (quoting David Sylvester), 305.
7. Husserl 2014, 73 ("Ein grundwesentlicher Unterschied tritt also hervor zwischen SEIN ALS ERLEBNIS und SEIN ALS DING" [Husserl 2009, 87, §42]).
8. Merleau-Ponty 1993, 69.
9. Greenberg 1995, 85, 89. On Byzantine and Russian icon theory in relation to high modernism, see Nelson 2007, 160–61; Florensky 1996, 33–98; Antonova 2010, 29–62.

suggestiveness" characterized, perhaps less in its original French and Belgian instantiation (Verlaine, Mallarmé, Laforgue, Maeterlinck) than in its "domesticated" English forms (Pater, Symons), by a "passionate attention to transient effects."[10] Particularly in pre–World War I Russia, symbolism becomes the target of a withering critique on account of its hazy and artificial conception of the image, with Osip Mandelstam in particular demurring at "the refined prolixity" of this distinctly Western movement. All of reality is on the verge of being dissolved into a vague system of pseudovisual associations bereft of intrinsic value and clarity: "None of the [Symbolists'] images is interesting in itself: the rose is a likeness of the sun, the sun is a likeness of a rose. . . . Images are gutted like scarecrows and packed with foreign content. . . . Perception is demoralized. Nothing is real, genuine." In this "epoch of pseudo-Symbolism," the poetic word has been reduced to a simulacrum of visual effects, a technique that ends up defrauding both image and word.[11]

For the young generation that comes of age by 1910 (H.D., Eliot, Pound, Akhmatova, Mandelstam, among others), the restoration of the visual and the verbal revolved around achieving a compression of lyric form and understanding that word and image are linked in an ontological sense rather than by aesthetic and social convention. As Pound writes, "An image is a radiant node or cluster, . . . a VORTEX from which, and through which, and into which, ideas are constantly rushing. . . . An *image* is real because we know it directly." Never more decisive than when wielding his red pen to prune the poetry of his contemporaries, Ezra Pound's instructions to H.D. nicely capture Imagism's new ethos of compression: "Objective— no slither—direct—no excess of adjectives. etc. No metaphors that won't permit examination.—It's straight talk."[12] Ultimately, what stands to be reclaimed from the morass of discursive and aesthetic convention is the word itself, understood as the "logos" that positively unveils and manifests a reality rather than a deluge of words merely pointing toward the real or, what's worse, substituting itself for it. As Mandelstam will write in the early 1920s, "There is essentially no difference between a word and an image. An image is merely a word which has been sealed up, which cannot be touched. An image is inappropriate for everyday use, just as an ikon lamp would be inappropriate for lighting a cigarette. But such sealed-up images are also

---

10. Kenner 1971, 130, 133, 182.

11. Mandelstam 1979, 121, 129 ("On the Nature of the Word"); see also "A Letter about Russian Poetry," where Mandelstam characterizes "Russian Symbolism [as] no more than a belated form of naïve Westernization transferred into the realm of esthetic perception and poetic technique" and characterized by a "regeneration of intense individualism and hypertrophy of the creative 'I' which confused its boundaries with the newly discovered boundaries of the world of passion" (157); by 1923, Mandelstam notes that "almost nothing remains of early Symbolism, swollen as it was from the dropsy of great themes" (171).

12. Quoted in Kenner 1971, 174.

very necessary."[13] The cigarette here stands as a metaphor for purely private, bourgeois concerns, for the "I" as a self-possessed agent "still engaged in the daylight world of reality, of representation." It is this Archimedean center of consciousness—self-possessed and enclosed in a cocoon of aesthetic taste and social convention—that the modernist lyric dislodges by staging for its audience "a conflict within the function of language as representation and within the conception of language as the act of an autonomous self."[14]

In some important respects, it turns out, modernist art and the emergent discipline of phenomenology appear to be pursuing the same goal. Animating both projects is less some iconoclastic opposition to inherited aesthetic and philosophical practice than an attempt to open up a level of experience that had categorically eluded their precursors. What is being sought is not a crisper articulation of meanings already identified by different formal means but a new language capable of accessing a level of experience categorically inaccessible to the epistemological and aesthetic framework of the long Enlightenment. By shifting focus from the *what* to the *how* of experience, the languages of modernist art and phenomenology confront a challenge previously identified by the early Romantics as a fundamental human predicament: how to overcome the myriad ways in which discursive and aesthetic protocols obscure the event character of phenomena as such, thereby making it all but impossible to capture the *quality* of an experience without its putative content having already been predetermined and reified as a particular kind of object.

It is no accident that, starting around 1905, both Husserl and Rilke should have found their mature voice by learning to scrutinize the *image* (*Bild*) as the medium anterior to all perception and conceptualization of an "object." For both, it is the image that, by arresting and focusing our gaze, first unveils things in their incontestable presence qua "appearance" (*Erscheinung*) and, as Husserl would put it in 1907, in their "absolute givenness" (*absolute Gegebenheit*). Reflecting a pervasive linguistic skepticism (*Sprachkrise*) explored in the writings of Mauthner, Hoffmannsthal, Schnitzler, Mach, Kraus, and others, the poetic and phenomenological explorations of Rilke and Husserl after 1903 aim to access the reality of things (*Dinge/Sachen*) as they manifest themselves in a prediscursive space (*Raum*). As Rilke writes in 1903, "Most events are beyond articulation; they exist in a space that no word has ever entered [die meisten Ereignisse sind unsagbar, vollziehen sich in einem Raume, den nie ein Wort betreten hat]."[15] Paradoxically, it is the precipitous action of language, of

---

13. Mandelstam 1979, 128.
14. De Man 1983, 171.
15. Rilke, *Kommentierte Ausgabe*, 4:514 (17 February 1903, trans. mine); henceforth cited parenthetically as *KA*. See also Antje Büsgen's insightful discussion of Rilke in relation to the visual arts: "Rilke's orientation toward the visible and his project of learning-to-see is indeed grounded in a pronounced skepticism about language" (Büsgen 2013, 136).

naming, that threatens to eclipse any awareness of experience as a distinctive and dynamic unveiling of things in this pre-predicative "space" (*Raum*). Between 1902 and 1914, Rilke is consumed with the project of reclaiming, both *in* and *by means of* the (poetic) image, reality as an epiphanic event. His conception of sight as the most elemental type of "insight" (*Einsehen*), namely, into a reality accessible solely through the medium of the image, exhibits striking parallels to Husserl's early outlines of phenomenology; and it anticipates by some twenty years Husserl's distinction between "the truth of correctness" and the "truth of disclosure."[16] We will soon return to the strong metaphysical, indeed numinous, implications of Husserl's "reduction" and to his essentially mystical concept of an "eidetic intuition" onto which it opens.

In his 1902 monograph on Rodin, while alluding to the errant figures of Dante's *Commedia*, Rilke praises the sculptor for his unrivaled ability to effect a "quiet redemption of things" (*des Dingseins leise Erlösung*). The act of "creation" (*Schaffen*) consists first and foremost in such a redeeming or "resurrecting" (*auferstehen*) of beings—people no less than things (*Dinge*)—whose expressive potential remains as yet unrealized (*KA* 4:424–25). To do so requires, of the poet no less than the phenomenologist, a quasi-religious cultivation of humility, patience, and silence: "Everything is gestation and then birthing. To let each impression and each embryo of a feeling come to completion, entirely in itself, in the dark, in the unsayable, the unconscious, beyond the reach of one's own understanding, and with deep humility and patience to wait for the hour when a new clarity is born . . . this alone is what it means to live as an artist: in understanding as in creating."[17] Such focused, undesigning expectancy, which waits for an impression to realize itself *within* consciousness, yet without the interference of will or desire (a central motif of Rilke's *Letters to a Young Poet*), proves remarkably consistent with the concept of a "transcendental reduction" that Husserl begins to outline in his 1907 *The Idea of Phenomenology* and in his 1907 lectures published as *Thing and Space* (*Ding und Raum*). The objective here is a *metanoia* of sorts, a conversion of philosophical attention whereby "we look *at*

---

16. Husserl 1977, 120–27 (§§ 44–45). The privileged role of sight in Husserl has often been remarked but will, for present purposes, simply be taken as a given in the way formulated, for example, in *Ideas I*: "*Immediately seeing—not merely sensory, experiential seeing,* but *seeing in general, i.e., any kind of consciousness that affords [something] in an originary fashion*—is the ultimate source of legitimacy of all rational claims [Das unmittelbare 'Sehen', nicht bloß das sinnliche, erfahrende Sehen, sondern DAS SEHEN ÜBERHAUPT ALS ORIGINÄR GEBENDES BEWUSSTSEIN WELCHER ART IMMER, ist die letzte Rechtsquelle aller vernünftigen Behauptungen]" (Husserl 2014, 36 / 2009, 43 [§19]).

17. Rilke 1984, 23–24 (letter of 23 April 1903); henceforth cited parenthetically as *RB*, with translations from the letters mine). "Jeden Eindruck und jeden Keim eines Gefühls ganz in sich, im Dunkel, im Unsagbaren, Unbewussten, dem eigenen Verstande Unerreichbaren sich vollenden lassen und mit tiefer Demut und Geduld die Stunde der Niederkunft einer neuen Klarheit abwarten: das allein heißt künstlerisch leben: im Verstehen wie im Schaffen" (*KA* 4:521).

what we normally look *through*." In Husserl's more technical idiom, we must learn to suspend "doxic modalities" and to neutralize "the intentionalities we now contemplate."[18] Yet as he presses ahead with this new type of investigation, Husserl appears increasingly disconcerted by the distinct prospect that something as unruly as "phantasy" (*Einbildungskraft, Phantasie*) and its principal medium, the "image" (*Bild*), may prove indispensable to phenomenology's attempt at healing the Cartesian rift between mind and world.[19]

Throughout his 1905 lectures, *Phantasie und Bildbewußtsein* (Phantasy and Image-Consciousness), Husserl takes pains to distentangle image from perception and the act of "pictorialization" (*Verbildlichung*) from that of perception. Rather than proffer formal-aesthetic discriminations between different *kinds* of images, Husserl's focus in these lectures is squarely placed on the specific intentionality and noetic work that consciousness performs as it interacts with visual phenomena. On his account, the image does not belong to the order of objects but to that of intentional acts, albeit acts that are not so much deliberately performed as they are "stimulated" (*erregt*) by our primal encounter with phenomena.[20] Constitutive of an image, Husserl argues, is thus not a set of formal-aesthetic criteria such as are presupposed wherever there is talk of some formal resemblance between image and object. Rather, the reality and presence of the image is bound up with what Husserl calls "primitive image-consciousness" (*primitives Bildbewußtsein*).

What matters here is to bring explicitly to consciousness that imaging has meaning only through a peculiar consciousness, that having a resembling content does not mean the same thing as apprehending an image. On the contrary, what resembles something turns into an image of it only through the unique and absolutely primitive image-consciousness.[21]

It is this stress on the "primitive" (putatively prediscursive and preconceptual) dynamics of image-consciousness that connects Husserl's early phenomenology with attempts by his modernist contemporaries to home in on the most elemental con-

---

18. Sokolowski 2000, 49–50; on Husserl's development between his *Logical Investigations* (1901) and his *Ideas I* (1913), see Baring 2019, 39–84.

19. On the key question—"Is a disclosure of reality possible where mind and world would no longer appear in opposition to one another, but as two sides of a single whole"?—see Fischer 2015, 15–68; quote from 21.

20. Alloa 2011b, 196.

21. Husserl 2005, 18 / 2006b, 19 (§8). "Hier kommt es darauf an . . . , daß die Bildlichkeit erst Sinn hat durch ein eigenes Bewusstsein, daß einen ähnlichen Inhalt haben nicht soviel heisst, wie ein Bild auffassen, sondern dass Ähnliches für Ähnliches zum Bild erst wird durch das eigenartige und schlechthin primitive Bildlichkeitsbewußtsein."

stituents of art: sound, color, and spatial form. For the phenomenological project of a rigorous description of intentional acts, just as for the antibourgeois "primitivism" of modernist painting, music, or poetic "imagism," concerns with mimetic "correctness" that had been the legacy of nineteenth-century realism play at most a subordinate role. As Cézanne observes about himself, "I am a primitive, I have a lazy eye.... If a head interests me, I make it too big."[22] Henceforth, what qualifies a given presentation as an image is not its formal resemblance (or reference) to some other entity. Rather, being brought forth by what Husserl names "phantasy," the image enables consciousness to synthesize a multitude of aspects into a formal unity, an "object." The primal *apprehension* of as yet unorganized visual data can advance to the bona fide "perception" of an object only because phantasy "pictorializes" (*verbildlicht*) the phenomenon in its aspectual, sensuous givenness; only an image can salvage phenomena from the merely apparitional and enable us to visualize them as manifestations of being. Put differently, what is fundamentally at issue is not an image apprehended *as X* but X apprehended *as an image*. From a certain, common-sense perspective, Husserl's programmatic call for philosophy to "return to things themselves" may well be taken to reflect his discomfort not only with the dualist turn of modern philosophy but also with the superficial aesthetic forms and distinctions devised by modern thought so as to mediate and reconcile the rift between mind and world.

At the same time, an uneasy, quasi-iconoclast strain often surfaces in Husserl's writings, particularly when the drift of his phenomenological analyses hints at a scenario in which phantasy and images seem to operate independently of, if not outright anterior to, the *logos* or *ratio* of philosophical inquiry as such. Still, rigorous philosophical inquiry must by its very nature consider the possibility that its declared objects of inquiry may end up supervening on its method or, put differently, that the phenomena examined may have equal or greater agency than the *cogito* committed to their analysis. At the very least, that is, mind and world, consciousness and phenomenon, appear pervaded by one and the same *logos*. Such, in any event, seems to be the premise of Husserl's 1904–5 lectures, *Phantasy and Image-Consciousness*. For as he studies the peculiar intentionality and dynamism of phantasy and "image-consciousness" (*Bildbewußtsein*), he comes to recognize in them the very embodiment of the "transcendental attitude" (*Einstellung*) that he had only begun to formulate in his *Logical Investigations* (1901/2). By their very nature phantasy and image-consciousness resist any confusing of the "sensuous content . . . that is experienced" with the "object of the phantasy" (man verwechselt den sinnlichen Inhalt, der in der Phantasievorstellung erlebt ist, . . . mit dem Gegenstand der

---

22. Quoted in Danchev 2012, 74.

Phantasie), at which Husserl so often demurs in his precursors.[23] Precisely because phantasy and image-consciousness operate anterior to, and independent of, any external, perceptual object, they demand a painstaking phenomenological description of the very acts of "pictorialization" (*Verbildlichung*) and "representation" (*Vorstellung*), which in turn requires approaching these noetic acts "independently of believing or not believing, of doubting or wishing."[24] Constitutive of what Husserl calls "phantasy" (*Phantasie*), "pictorialization" (*Verbildlichung*) reveals a type of intentionality not fungible with forms of ordinary consciousness, such as interpretation, verification, critique, or any variety of syllogistic modes. Instead, even though it is grounded in a physical (*leibhaft*) object perception, the content of "image-consciousness" (*Bildbewußtsein*) remains inaccessible to the "natural attitude" (*natürliche Einstellung*) of everyday conscious life.

What Husserl calls "apprehension" (*Auffassung*) presents consciousness with data that by definition can neither be doubted nor discredited as mere illusion or deception. For any distinction between "presence in the flesh" (*Leibhaftigkeit*) and "presence in belief" (*Glaubhaftigkeit*) arises only at the level of perception. Seen from the angle chosen by Alfred Stieglitz in 1903, the Flatiron Building in Manhattan will appear as no more than a facade; yet as the viewpoint shifts, that initial appraisal, however believable at first, will be corrected. Yet what makes that correction possible is another sensory apprehension rather than some peremptory (Cartesian) distrust in the phenomenal world. This tells us, Husserl argues, that we are always able to maintain a logical distinction between perception and its object: "The perception of a surface is not a surface; and yet an object does appear in the perception, and this appearing object is characterized as a surface."[25] Where images are concerned, however, this distinction turns out to have no jurisdiction. For an image is never the correlate of a contingent "psychological attitude" but, on the contrary, amounts to an "absolute phenomenological datum, which we behold [*ein absolutes phänomenologisches Datum, auf das wir hinblicken*]." Under the "phenomenological reduction," the focus of analysis has categorically shifted from quotidian "object-perception" (*Dingwahrnehmung*) to the "reduced lived experience of perception" (*Erlebniswahrnehmung*), and the latter is by definition "incompatible with disbelief and doubt."[26] For the impulse of doubt or the methodical skepticism arrayed against possible error can enter the scene only *after* the passage from apprehension to perception has been

---

23. Husserl 2005, 7 / 2006b, 9 (§ 3).

24. Husserl 2005, 10 / 2006b, 12 (§ 4); as Husserl elaborates, "The apprehension content by itself, of course, is not yet a perceptual interpretation, which is only something added to it [Der Auffassungsinhalt für sich ist ja noch keine wahrnehmende Deutung, die kommt erst dazu]" (2005, 11 / 2006b, 13 [§ 5]).

25. Husserl 1997, 13, 14 / 1991, 15–17 (§§ 5–6).

26. Husserl 1997, 19 / 1991, 21 (§ 8; trans. modified).

completed. Doubt, analysis, and critique, that is, can work on "appearance" (*Erschei-nung*) only after it has been "perceived," that is, has been either identified, or named, or interpreted in the form of an explicit proposition.[27] Yet at that point, the very domain of phenomenology has already been overleaped, or, rather, prejudged. For phenomenological description is not concerned with "apprehension *contents*" (*Auf-fassungsinhalte*) but with "apprehension *characteristics*" (*Auffassungscharaktere*): "In phantasy, to be sure, the object itself appears (insofar as it is precisely the *object* that appears there) but it does not appear as present [*gegenwärtig*]. . . . It is only re-presented [*vergegenwärtigt*]."[28]

Husserl's searching formulations alternately mask and reveal a "tension be-tween the image as a purely reproductive mode and as an original way of accessing the essence [*Wesenheit*] that remains inaccessible to perception."[29] Thus, to claim that "perceptual appearance" (*Wahrnehmungserscheinung*) and "phantasy" (*Phantasie-erscheinung*) differ from one another in the same way as original and image raises some tantalizing questions.[30] Which of the two constituent terms, we ask, corre-sponds to the original and the image, respectively? Might it not be the case that "per-ceptual appearance" is itself a derivative of an initially unfiltered image-apprehension? After all, as Husserl had already pointed out, by its very nature perception comprises a determinate "content" (*Inhalt*). We can speak of a "perception" (*Wahrnehmung*) only where we have already taken an "appearance" as X (rather than Y or Z). Put dif-ferently, perception always confers a certain nominal fixity on a given "appearance" (*Erscheinung*). Yet such a "taking-as" can determine only a selection of the total phe-nomenon; only some particular "aspect" (*Abschattung*) is being "rendered sensible" (*versinnlicht*) and "evident" at any given moment, whereas all other possible "as-pects" of the phenomenon are in play only virtually, namely, through the diaphanous medium of the "image" (*Bild*).[31] If this is the case, then is the image not ontologically prior to the specifiable and determinate "content" (*Inhalt*) foregrounded by a given act of perception? And would it not furthermore follow that philosophy through the ages was mistaken when taking perception to be the "original" and the image as its derivative?[32]

---

27. As Husserl observes elsewhere, "It is evident that the essence of the reduced lived experi-ence of perception is incompatible with disbelief and doubt [Das Wesen der reduzierten Erleb-niswahrnehmung ist evident unverträglich mit Unglauben und Zweifel]" (1997, 19 / 1991, 22 [§ 8]).

28. Husserl 2005, 18 / 2006b, 18 (§ 8).

29. Alloa 2011b, 205.

30. Husserl 2005, 8 / 2006b, 10 (§ 4).

31. Husserl's repeated attempts to exclude symbol and phantasy from preserving those aspects of a perception not presently experienced seem forced and ultimately unconvincing; see esp. *Ding und Raum* §§ 17–18, pp. 54–56.

32. These questions continue to engage Husserl in later works, esp. his *Ideas* (1913). For a lucid exposition of the tangled relationship between perception and phantasy, see Alloa 2011b, 179–216.

That this conclusion had not previously been drawn, Husserl maintains, has to do with rationalism's habit of beginning inquiry with a set of principles or "positings" (*Setzungen*), rather than proceeding descriptively by scrutinizing the composite nature of "experience" (*Erfahrung*), in particular, how it comprises discrete intentional acts of "apprehension" (*Auffassung*) whose progressive synthesis in consciousness undergirds all "object-perception" (*Gegenstandswahrnehmung*). Beginning with his *Logical Investigations*, Husserl thus rejects all psychologizing approaches to epistemology, including that of his onetime teacher Franz Brentano, on account of their failure to distinguish between the phenomenalization of specific contents and those contents themselves: "Whoever (in company with a great many psychologists) sees only the contents and closes his eyes to the objectivation, to the difference between the content that is experienced and the object that appears, naturally gets into the most severe difficulties [Wer, mit sehr vielen Psychologen, nur die Inhalte sieht und vor der Objektivierung, vor dem Unterschied zwischen dem Inhalt, der 'erlebt' wird, und dem Gegenstand, der erscheint, die Augen verschliesst, kommt natürlich in die ärgsten Verlegenheiten]."[33] The overarching concern of his 1905 lectures *Phantasy and Image-Consciousness* thus rests with mapping this elemental, pre-linguistic realm of sheer "apprehension" that constitutes itself as the distinct form of consciousness known as *Bildbewußtsein*: "In phantasy, to be sure, the object itself appears (insofar as it is precisely the *object* that appears there), but it does not appear as present. It is only re-presented; it is as though it were there, but only as though. It appears to us in *image* [In der Phantasie erscheint der Gegenstand zwar insofern selbst, als eben ER es ist, der da erscheint, aber er erscheint nicht als gegenwärtig, er ist nur vergegenwärtigt, es ist gleichsam so, als wäre er da, aber nur gleichsam, er erscheint uns im BILDE]."[34]

Even prior to unfolding his "transcendental reduction" or *epoché* in his 1907 lectures, *The Idea of Phenomenology*, Husserl's analyses of image and image-consciousness effectively point toward that concept as the centerpiece of his entire undertaking. For once quarantined from claims about their determinate contents, phantasy and image emerge as the very foundation for perception. While the latter may seem a case of receptivity rather than agency, what Husserl calls "apprehension" (*Auffassung*) belongs very much to the order of an act. As mediated by the image, which itself is generated in phantasy, all sensory apprehension (auditory no less than visual) unfolds as an *active* synthesis. Far from being a case of passive "recipiency" (as Coleridge calls it), sight works actively through the self-giving phenomenon by synthesizing its temporally discrete aspects. That some such pro-visional synthesis is part of the act of sight already emerges in the physiology of eye movement. For "how

---

33. Husserl 2005, 12 / 2006b, 14 (§ 5).
34. Husserl 2005, 18 / 2006b, 18 (§ 8).

could the movement of the eyes not blur things if movement . . . were only a reflex? If it did not have its antennae, its clairvoyance? If vision were not prefigured in it?"[35] Sight not only sees, but proleptically foresees the totality of the being whose discrete aspects it successively takes in. It is this primal *actus* that, in *Ideas I* (1913), Husserl calls "the principle of all principles: that each intuition affording [something] in an an originary way is a legitimate source of knowledge, that whatever presents itself to us in 'Intuition' in an originary way (so to speak, in its actuality in person) is to be taken simply as what it affords in itself there [daß jede originär gebende Anschauung eine Rechtsquelle der Erkenntnis sei, daß alles, was sich in der 'Intuition' darbietet, einfach hinzunehmen sei, als was es sich da gibt, aber auch nur in den Schranken in denen es sich gibt]."[36]

Yet unlike his Romantic precursors, Fichte and Schelling in particular, Husserl recognizes that "intuition" (*Anschauung*) is essentially temporal in nature. Recalling the ideal of sustained contemplation cultivated in late medieval mysticism, intuition synthesizes successive aspects into a coherent vision of the whole. Moreover, like any synthesis, this original, "giving" (*gebende*) intuition also posits the ontological complementarity of consciousness and phenomenon, that is, presupposes that mind and world are teleologically ordered toward one another. For the phenomenon will be actualized only insofar as consciousness apprehends it as imbued with a latent, as yet unrealized, significance. It follows that not everything visible is subject to the kind of active synthesis involved in "seeing." In what sense, then, is sight to be understood as a *synthetic* act? For Husserl, the answer has to do with the fact that all "perception" depends on the ongoing fusion of the specific aspect that presents itself to consciousness right now with other "aspects" (*Abschattungen*) either apprehended previously or yet to come into focus. Thus, every visual phenomenon consists of a number of discrete aspects extruded into a temporal sequence. Whether our gaze traverses a landscape, traces the cues of a classical painting, or takes in the shifting presentation of a Rodin sculpture as we encircle it, seeing unfolds as a continual oscillation between present and latent aspects, all of which must be synthesized as aspects *of the same* phenomenon.[37] What Husserl calls intentionality (*consciousness-of-X*) therefore can never be reduced to a present *punctum* but, instead, has consciousness reconcile a present and manifest aspect with those previously taken in and others anticipated with growing confidence.

---

35. Merleau-Ponty 1993, 124.

36. Husserl 2014, 43 / 2009, 51 (§ 24); on this "principle," see Marion 2002a, 21–25; on the concept of the *epoché*, see Sokolowski, 2000, 47–51; Zahavi 2003, 43–53. Against his empiricist and neo-Kantian detractors, such as Rickert, Husserl would always maintain that the *epoché* and, more generally, "his phenomenology, instead of denying the world, merely clarified its meaning" (Baring 2019, 58).

37. See Sokolowski 2000, 17–21; Alloa 2011b, 183–88.

Yet for that to happen, as Husserl had already observed in his *Logical Investigations*, the latent aspects must be pictorialized or *"illustrated* in the nuclear content of the percept [*im Kerngehalt der Wahrnehmung verbildlicht*]."[38] Emerging from the shadows of a merely derivative, quasi-parasitical function to which Husserl's early writings often seek to confine it, the image here reconciles the cascade of "appresentations" of which any object perception is comprised. As it turns out, the image is foundational *to* perception rather than a derivative *of* it; or, as Emanuel Alloa puts it, "the iconic already corrodes the original perception." This being so, it stands to reason that the image also plays a pivotal role in what, in Husserl's somewhat arid nomenclature, is known as the *epoché* and the "transcendental reduction," the latter arguably being the Archimedean point of his transcendental phenomenology.[39] When mediated by the diaphanous image and its corresponding image-consciousness, a given "thing" (*Ding*) is initially apprehended as a distinctive *Gestalt* or "inscape" (as Hopkins christens it). Thus shorn of all contingency and background noise, the very being of a thing is indeed "quietly redeemed" in the medium of the image, very much in the sense of what Rilke so poignantly calls *des Dingseins leise Erlösung*.[40] To elucidate and bring home the meaning of *epoché*—albeit in a sense that ultimately exceeds Husserl's philosophical objectives—turns out to be the indispensable and distinctive function of the image as it mediates between mind and world. Were it not for the medium of the image, it would be impossible for a temporal sequence of "aspects" (*Abschattungen*) to be synthesized as a unified "thing." Bearing considerable resemblance to Kant's "schematism," "phantasy" and "image" prove indispensable for the transcendental synthesis whereby discrete phenomenal qualities are apprehended as manifestations of a single entity, such that the act of visual apprehension may pass over into one of bona fide perception.

---

38. Husserl 2001, II:220 / 1980, pt. II/2, 56 (VI, § 14). In his attempt to disentangle "signitive" and "intuitive" intentions, the former correlating with perceptions and the latter with images, Husserl realizes that images preserve those "aspects" (*Abschattungen*) not currently focused on by perception: "the elements of the invisible rear side, the interior, etc., are no doubt subsidiarily intended in more or less definite fashion, symbolically [*sie sind durch das primär Erscheinende symbolisch angedeutet*], but are not currently part of the intuitive, i.e., of the perceptual or imaginative content, of the percept [*selbst fallen sie gar nicht in den anschaulichen . . . Gehalt der Wahrnehmung*]." Absent such mediation and reconciliation of both visible and occluded aspects by a symbolic presentation or image, "there would only ever be one percept [*so gäbe es . . . für jeden Gegenstand nur eine einzige Wahrnehmung*]" (ibid.).

39. Alloa 2011b, 187 (trans. mine); as Sokolowski points out, the term "reduction" is often misconstrued as taking us "'back' to what seems to be a more restricted viewpoint, one that simply targets the intentionalities themselves." Yet reduction for Husserl involves not a diminution of scope or contents but, rather, a "leading back" (consistent with the Latin root *re-ducere*) to a domain logically anterior to that of perceptions, propositions, doubt, and detachment (Sokolowski 2000, 49).

40. *KA* 4:424.

Yet to put it thus is to invest image and image-consciousness with an epiphanic, indeed metaphysical, significance that, even more than Rilke, Husserl seems reluctant to acknowledge. Still, he concedes that what the *epoché* asks of philosophy—"as little understanding as possible, as much pure intuition as possible [*möglichst wenig Verstand, aber möglichst reine Intuition*]"—bears more than a passing resemblance to the *visio intellectualis* of the mystics: "we are here reminded of the speech of the mystics when they describe the intellectual act of seeing [wir werden in der Tat an die Rede der Mystiker erinnert, wenn sie das intellektuelle Schauen . . . beschreiben]." Indeed, a fundamental task of phenomenology is to reclaim an experiential domain "that contains no discursive knowledge. The whole trick here is to let the seeing eye have its say [*rein dem schauenden Auge das Wort zu lassen*] and to exclude all transcendent reference that is interwoven with seeing, those things that are ostensibly given or thought along with what is seen."[41] What Husserl calls the phenomenon's "absolute givenness" (*absolute Gegebenheit*) constitutes itself in the event of "beholding" (*Schauen*).[42] To call it an *event*, in contradistinction to the empirical act of "perception" (*Wahrnehmung*), is to acknowledge such an elemental beholding as the very ground enabling consciousness to enter into an intentional relation with the world and integrate its discrete perceptions into a comprehensive system of knowledge. Husserl's concept of such a primal "beholding" (*Schau*) hovers between the Latin *visus* and *visio*, between the aspectual (contingent) apprehension of a thing and its dawning recognition as intrinsically real and significant. Hence, "beholding" is not a variant of "perception" (*Wahrnehmung*) but, rather, its precondition. In such *visio* or *Schau*, the phenomenal world reveals itself as *logos*, as a source of truth; starting in 1907, Husserl speaks of this visual apprehension of the thing's pre-predicative reality mediated by an image as an "eidetic intuition" (*Wesenserschauung*).[43]

Still, the question remains whether such "pure vision" (*reine Schau*), however quarantined from any positing of a being external to it, is fundamentally *responsive to* or, instead, properly *constitutive of* the phenomenon's givenness. Sensing that he is about to stray from phenomenology as a descriptive undertaking into metaphysics proper, Husserl pulls back, electing instead to "disregard the metaphysical purposes of the critique of knowledge and attend solely to the *task of clarifying its aims* [Sehen wir von den metaphysischen Abzweckungen der Erkenntniskritik ab, halten wir uns rein an ihre Aufgabe]."[44] Likewise, in his next set of lectures, *Thing and Space* (*Ding und Raum*), he again equivocates on the decisive question of where, ultimately, phenomenological agency is located in consciousness or in the world of things actively

---

41. Husserl 1999, 46–47 / 1950, 62.

42. "This looking involves an absolute givenness" (*In diesem Schauen ist . . . eine absolute Gegebenheit*), which Husserl also terms "evidence" (*Evidenz*): 1997, 9, 11 / 1991, 11, 13.

43. Husserl 1997, 25 / 1991, 28 (§ 10).

44. Husserl 1999, 19 / 1950, 23 (emphasis mine).

manifesting themselves. Is "experiential objectivity . . . self-constituting" or "self-manifesting"? Or, alternatively, does such objectivity presuppose an antecedent reality that merely "comes to givenness" (*zur Gegebenheit kommen*) in experience?[45] Considering that Husserl's phenomenological project rests on the postulate that all transcendent reality has its primal ground and bearer [*Urgrund und Träger*] in . . . consciousness," a great deal evidently depends on whether the "originary presentive intuition" of the world in consciousness is creative or merely reproductive.[46]

All these perplexities reopen the question concerning the status of the image in Husserl, specifically its numinous dimension, which modern epistemology and aesthetics had either tabled indefinitely or positively obscured. To say that the image "presents the subject but is not the subject itself [Das Bild macht die Sache vorstellig, ist aber nicht sie selbst]," hints at its capacity to *unveil* real being rather than represent or illustrate preestablished notions in some allegorical and emblematic manner.[47] By way of clarifying that point, Husserl introduces a tripartite distinction between (1) the "material scaffolding" (*Bildträger*), canvas, frame, siccative oil colors, and so on, required for realizing an image as a visible entity in space; (2) the image-object (*Bildobjekt*), that is, the entity visibly depicted in the image; and (3) the "image subject" (*Bildsujet*) or prototype, which, while not visible per se, can be mediated in and through the image. As we saw early on, the prototype does not coincide with the visible image, nor can it be grasped independent of it. Hence, in image-consciousness seeing and ideation, intuition and perception, are experienced as essentially entwined, though never identical: "For I do not look at painting as one looks at a thing, fixing it in its place. My gaze wanders within it as in the halos of Being. Rather than seeing it, I see according to it or with it."[48] Merleau-Ponty's formulation alerts us to the unique fusion of embodied and interpretive seeing. It is this coincidence of taking-in the visible image and taking it *as* the conduit toward Being itself—at once mediated in the image and yet forever transcendent to it—which prompts Husserl to speak of image-consciousness as a unique kind of experience.

> What does actually exist there, apart from the "painting" [*Gemälde*] as a physical thing, the piece of canvas with its determinate distribution of color pigments, *is* a certain complex of sensations that the spectator contemplating the painting experiences in himself [*in sich erlebt*], as well as the apprehension and meaning

---

45. Husserl 1997, 7, 131 / 1991, 8, 154 (§§ 2, 44); Husserl's diction here seems unsure: *das Sich-Konstituieren—das Sich-Beurkunden könnte ich auch sagen* (ibid.).

46. Husserl 1997, 34 / 1991, 40 (§ 13).

47. Husserl 2005, 20 / 2006b, 20 (§ 8). On "pictorial difference" as evidence of the unique mode of being (*Seinsweise*) of images, see Gadamer 2006, 130–52; Freedberg 1989, 54–81; Alloa 2013.

48. Merleau-Ponty 1993, 126; for Cézanne, "interpretation should not be a reflection distinct from the act of seeing" (66).

that he bases on this complex so that the consciousness of the image occurs for him. . . . What is added is the apprehension that interprets the content [*den Inhalt deutet*], conferring on it the relation to something objective [*ihm gegenständliche Beziehung verleiht*].[49]

Ever reluctant to take even minor speculative leaps, Husserl in the next two sections (§§ 9–10) subjects the concept of apprehension to a step-by-step phenomenological description. It is at such moments that the proximity of phenomenology to ordinary language philosophy, however unrecognized by Husserl even in his late phase, seems most palpable. Thus, his rigorous account of how discrete material elements are being "apprehended" (*aufgefasst*), "experienced" (*erlebt*), and "interpreted" (*gedeutet*) shows noetic and linguistic distinctions to be inextricably entwined. In the event, all these discrete, subsidiary features of "apprehension"—ranging from the rudimentary and sensuous to higher forms of focalized interpretation—converge in this: that for consciousness to visually "apprehend" a multiplicity of aspects as manifestations of a single, unified entity, a synthesis of these aspects must have already been achieved. Yet since no perceptual or conceptual determinations have as yet been ventured about the phenomenon, such a synthesis must itself be a product of "phantasy," whose fruits are made manifest for consciousness by the "image" (*Bild*).

Though he has not yet confronted the Platonist underpinnings of his transcendental phenomenology, as he will in *Ideas I* (1913), the early Husserl already senses that insofar as a thing can ever "appear" (*erscheinen*), it will have been mediated *for*, not *by*, consciousness. Hence, far from being a function of finite, conscious positing, being is inseparable from the dramatic and revelatory structure of appearance; it is an event. Just as Plato had demonstrated in the *Parmenides* and the *Sophist* that being cannot be thought independent of its self-manifestation, Husserl insists that being must be consummated, or "realized," as appearance. Yet all appearing *of* something is also an appearing *to* someone, to consciousness; and for that to happen, a primal, creative act of "phantasy"—mediated by the image—must respond to the "absolute givenness" of the phenomenon *as* it has given itself. Precisely because Husserl understands visual apprehension to be "a creative act" (*Schöpfung der Natur*), he insists on subjecting phantasy and image-consciousness to rigorous analysis. Their operation has to be broken down into a sequence of minute, metonymic steps, each of which in turn serves to confirm the veracity of Husserl's descriptive nomenclature. Yet to proceed in this way is to invite more fundamental questions yet. Can the enterprise of phenomenology as a "rigorous science" (*strenge Wissenschaft*) ever amount to more than a scrupulous tracing of the structure of appearance? Does even the most rigorous forensic and value-neutral description of experience not already presuppose the

_____

49. Husserl 2005, 23–24 / 2006b, 24 (§ 10).

very *logos* it hopes to unveil? Moreover, in parsing the structure of appearance and its apprehension in consciousness, are the phenomenologist's words, categories, and concepts not already infused with meanings and *qualia* endemic to our so-called natural attitude? Conversely, even if the phenomenologist were to succeed in circumnavigating, or, at least, properly entering into, this hermeneutic circle, what would be gained by doing so? Can descriptive phenomenology ever truly hope to catch up with, let alone declare epistemic dominion over, the structure of appearance? Or are such aspirations perhaps misguided, and should phenomenological inquiry instead content itself with participating in—rather than trying to determine—the *logos* as it manifests itself in the very structure of appearance?

The central aim of Husserlian, transcendental phenomenology is to think *according to* the pure "appresentation" of the visible world as it unfolds in "image-consciousness" (*Bildbewußtsein*). Phenomenological inquiry here is not pledged, as it were a priori, to overcoming our intuitive contact with phenomena by conceptual or discursive means. On the contrary, it takes seriously the possibility that only an image can accomplish the synthesis of a thing's aspects in consciousness and, in so doing, establish the conditions for bona fide object perception and cognition. Not coincidentally, the image in Husserl's early writings operates in ways strikingly analogous to the "transcendental schematism" of Kant's first *Critique*, described there as "an art concealed in the depth of the human soul, . . . as it were [*gleichsam*], a monogram of pure *a priori* imagination."[50] In the latter case, the very possibility of knowledge would rest on an irreducibly metaphysical foundation: the "image" (*eikōn*) itself would then have to be analogically related to (though never outright identical with) being. Just as in the tradition extending from the later Plato all the way to Nicholas of Cusa and Goethe, *logos* encompasses both, the reality of being and of appearance (not to be confused with mere semblance). Yet to an unusual degree, Husserl's own idiom also reflects the extent to which his philosophical objectives pivot on "metaphors, images, and figural expressions . . . provid[ing] possibilities for articulating and expressing intuitions that are given to sense experiences, ones for which a clear conceptual language cannot be found." Far from a makeshift solution or tactical expedient, such mining of language's "productivity and formative qualities" attests to an indelible link between our discursive *logoi* and the metaphysical *logos* that is their ineffable source.[51]

While Husserl in his 1904–5 lectures is not yet ready to pursue the metaphysical implications just outlined, he does concede that phantasy is an integral feature of all apprehension. For it alone credits what consciousness "apprehends" with containing more than is immediately apparent. Phantasy anticipates that the order of "appear-

50. Kant 1965, 183 (A 141–42).
51. McGillen 2021, 29–30.

ance" (*Erscheinung*), far from being one of transient "semblance" (*Schein*), is itself cohesive and potentially revelatory. Far from confabulating meaning, it intuitively discerns, within the givenness of the phenomenon, a cohesive structure or inscape and, thus, grasps the phenomenon itself as partially manifesting the invisible *logos* that had brought it forth. While an ontological difference always remains between the temporal order of appearance and the ideality of its meaning, the two domains are nevertheless constitutively related. The time-bound act of visual apprehension and the synthesis of its several aspects thus converge in a sensory-cum-intellectual act that Husserl calls "vision" (*Schau*). Yet even as he grants consciousness the capacity for apprehending the visible phenomenon *and* pictorializing its intrinsic organization, Husserl does not espouse a kind of "intellectual intuition" such as Fichte, Novalis, and the early Schelling had postulated. On the contrary, he insists on a "certain mediacy of representation" (*eine gewisse Mittelbarkeit des Vorstellens* [PB §11, p. 26]) within image or phantasy presentation that is notably missing in ordinary "perceptual presentation" (*Wahrnehmungsvorstellung*) and Romantic, intuitionist models of "immediate" cognition. The medium that prompts him to speak of such "mediality" is, of course, the image in the way I am here exploring it.

Still, merely to stipulate that all apprehension of phenomena is mediated does not solve anything. For just as an "appearance" presupposes a consciousness capable of distinguishing between appearance-*of* and appearaing-*as* (i.e., in the guise of) something, so, too, with the image. For if an image is to synthesize the multiplicity of "aspects" that make up the phenomenon and "make present" (*darstellen*) the single, unified "thing" underlying them, a unique kind of intentionality is required that generates the image *in* and *through* which the objective world can be so apprehended. Husserl calls it "phantasy," and he maintains that where it is at work

> something objective appears. . . . However, no one considers this appearance to be an appearance of the object itself. Certainly no one takes this faint, fluctuating appearance—now rising fleetingly to the surface, now disappearing, its content changing in so many ways as it does so—to be the appearance of the object, of the palace itself, for example; rather, one takes it to be the representation [*Vorstellung*] of the object, a re-presentation [*Vergegenwärtigung*], a pictorialization [*Verbildlichung*]. But mark my words, one does not thereby mean the appearance as it is actually given. One does not perchance look at it as it is and appears, and say to oneself: This is an image. Rather, one lives totally [*lebt man ganz und gar*] in the new apprehending that grounds itself on the appearance: *in the image* one sees the *subject* [*im* BILDE *schaut man die* SACHE *an*]. The image-consciousness has a tinction that confers on it a signification that points beyond its primary object [über seinen primären Gegenstand hinausweisende Bedeutung]: the characteristic of representation according to resemblance. . . . Hence I do not

bring about a mere perception [*Ich vollziehe also nicht eine blosse Wahrnehmung*].[52]

Crucially, image-consciousness does not consist of "differentiating and juxtaposing" (*Unterscheiden und Beziehen*) an image with the "perceptual object" (*Wahrnehmungsgegenstand*) *of* which it is the image. Rather, what we call an image is "immediately felt" to be such (*das Bild fühlt sich unmittelbar als Bild*) and, thus, cannot be resolved into an strictly diaphanous appearance. In fact, Evan Thompson notes, the act of seeing involves more than "attending to features of what there is to see. . . . I can also attend to how seeing feels, to what the activity of seeing is like for me, and to the ways it feels different from freely imagining and from remembering. In attending to experience in this way, I can become aware of features I do not normally notice (attend to), precisely because they usually remain implicit and prereflective."[53] It is this alternative intentionality, focused on the *how* rather than *what* of "sight" (*Schau*), that ultimately prompts Husserl to ponder the essential relatedness of phantasy, image, and subject. By its very nature, that is, image-consciousness neither conflates nor disaggregates image and object. Rather, as Husserl has already shown, for consciousness to enter into a noetic relation with a given object, phantasy must have fashioned a mental image that synthesizes the multiple "aspects" of the phenomenon as it is being experienced.

Furthermore, image-consciousness implies a latent awareness that the image generated by "phantasy" is essentially bound up with the thing whose appearance it synthesizes even as it remains at an ontological remove from it. Echoing observations already found in John of Damascus and other iconophiles, Husserl thus reiterates that

> if the appearing image were absolutely identical phenomenally with the object meant, or, better, if the image appearance [*Bilderscheinung*] showed no difference whatsoever from the perceptual appearance [*Wahrnehmungserscheinung*] of the object itself, a depictive consciousness [*Bildlichkeitsbewusstsein*] could scarcely come about. This is certain: A consciousness of difference must be there, even though the subject does not appear in the proper sense [ein Bewusstsein von Differenz muss vorhanden sein, obschon das Sujet im eigentlichen Sinn nicht erscheint].[54]

Paradoxically, my awareness that what I apprehend is an image, and hence distinct from the thing depicted in the image, in no way diminishes the latter's power. On the

---

52. Husserl 2005, 27 / 2006b, 28 (§ 12).
53. Thompson 2008, 404.
54. Husserl 2005, 22 / 2006a, 22 (§ 9).

contrary, it reinforces the very charism of an image, its ineffable capacity to endow being with presence. Unlike the concept, an image can induce and sustain a heightened "focal awareness" (to recall Michael Polanyi's term), thus enabling the beholder to sense within a given appearance a significance well beyond what is plainly visible. Similarly, Arnold Gehlen remarks on a holistic knowledge that can be realized only in the medium of the image, a knowledge that proves scarcely attainable, and definitely not sustainable, by strictly discursive or conceptual means. Hence,

> the immense expressive force of Neolithic cave painting stems from its ability to convey to us the conception of an entire world, a world that could not be brought to make itself accessible by any other means. Herein lies the enormous superiority of presentation [*Darstellung*] vis-à-vis the concept; the former takes up the very being of its object, stabilizes and fixes it in time, and in so doing stabilizes the world itself for consciousness. By contrast, the concept merely "means" something and evaporates unless it is kept alive by external supports.[55]

Anticipating some aspects of Gehlen's anthropology of images, Husserl navigates between the Scylla of Romantic expressivism and the Charybdis of analytic scientism that will credit the image with reality only insofar as it can be assimilated to the order of objective, verifiable propositions. By contrast, an "image-subject" (*Bildsujet*) for Husserl is an inherently significant meaning inseparable from our experience of the phenomenal world and accessible solely through the medium of the image (though never identical with it). Crucially, then, the "noëma" that corresponds to image-consciousness must be "experienced" (*erlebt*) rather than conceptualized or inferred. The image has being and reality precisely because, anterior to all protocols of proof or doubt, it is experienced as engaging and, potentially, transforming the beholder. The dynamic, then, is not that of a neutral observer confronting an object but a beholder recognizing herself as the addressee of an image. The very fact that visible phenomena may draw the beholder in, rather than diffidently abiding in "objective" distance from her, confirms that both are always already enclosed and mutually attuned within the same (pre-Newtonian) space of pure experience. The observer "feels that she is the sensible coming to itself, and that in return the sensible is . . . an extension of her own flesh." Striking a heightened, personal tone, Merleau-Ponty specifies that at the level of pre-predicative experience, "fact and essence can no longer be distinguished, . . . being no longer being *before me*, but surrounding me and in

55. Gehlen 2004, 63 (trans. mine). For Gehlen's comprehensive engagement with pictorial modernism, see *Zeitbilder* (1st ed. 1960), esp. pt. I (Gehlen 2016, 5–77); and, for a critique of Gehlen's sociological and anthropological functionalizing of the image, see Gadamer's review ("Begriffene Malerei?"), in Gadamer 1993a, 305–14.

a sense traversing me, and my vision of Being not forming itself from elsewhere, but from the midst of Being."[56]

Thus, the intentionality that correlates with the experience of the visible is never one of preemptive or gratuitous doubt but of assent to an indubitable and significant presence. As Husserl had so poignantly formulated it, "we see the meant object *in* the image, or *out of* it the intended object looks toward us [in das Bild schauen wir den gemeinten Gegenstand hinein, oder aus ihm schaut er <zu> uns her]."[57] Husserl's curiously equivocal remark recalls a G. M. Hopkins remark in one of his notebook entries: "What you look hard at seems to look hard at you." Closer to Husserl's own time, Cézanne is reported to have observed that "the landscape . . . becomes conscious in me. . . . I'll be the subjective conscience of this landscape."[58] Indeed, it is a key trait of images that they do not ask their beholder analytically to distinguish between the (visible) "presentation" and the (invisible) "sujet" mediated *by* and *as* image: "The appearing image thing does not awaken a new presentation that otherwise would have nothing to do with it [Das erscheinende Bildding weckt nicht eine neue Vorstellung, die sonst mit ihm nichts zu tun hätte]." For Husserl, then, the image is not fungible with any discursive form; it does not belong to the order of "reference" (*Verweis*) any more than it presents its *sujet* in merely allegorical fashion (*analogisches Symbol*). Still, to see the image is to apprehend not only the "subject" (*Sache*) depicted in it but also the image *as such*. For, as Husserl insists, "if the conscious relation to something depicted is not given with the image, then we certainly do not have an image. This conscious relation, however, is given through that specific consciousness belonging to the re-presentation of what does not appear in what does appear [durch jenes eigentümliche Bewusstsein der Vergegenwärtigung eines Nicht-Erscheinenden im Erscheinenden]."[59]

Rather than rely on the deceptive primacy of the "natural attitude" (*natürliche Einstellung*) that prompts a great deal of aesthetic theory to treat the image as a derivative of an antecedent "object-perception" (*Dingwahrnehmung*), Husserl and, more consistently yet, Rilke hold that the image uniquely opens access to the reality of things in their numinous, radiant, and timeless being. As Aquinas (whose affinity

---

56. Merleau-Ponty 1968, 114; his remarks build on the early Husserl, particularly his 1907 lectures, *Ding und Raum*, in which Husserl develops the notion of the "reduction" whereby one distinguishes between the "absolute givenness" of "perception" (*Wahrnehmung*) and its being reflectively taken *as* something (§§ 7–10); on the secondary and inapposite role of philosophical reflection and epistemological skepticism vis-à-vis the phenomenal world, see Merleau-Ponty 1968, 3–49.

57. Husserl 2005, 31 / 2006b, 32 (§ 8); trans. modified.

58. Hopkins *HCW* 3:504; Cézanne, as reported by Joachim Gasquet, in Doran 2001, 111.

59. Husserl 2005, 31, 32 / 2006b, 32, 33 (§ 8); this last insight, Heidegger will argue in *Being and Time* (§ 7), ultimately extends beyond the image to anything that can be properly classified as a "phenomenon" (Heidegger 1996, 25–34).

to transcendental phenomenology was to be of enduring interest to Edith Stein, one of Husserl's preeminent students) stresses, the being of a thing is its *actus*, its sheer fecundity, the way it opens itself up to participation, thereby tacitly transforming the consciousness drawn into its orbit. Gadamer will later remark that, when mediated by the image, the world of things undergoes "an increase in being" (*einen Zuwachs an Sein*).[60] Sight and insight, raw "apprehension" (*Auffassung*) and focused "interpretation" (*Deutung*), appear to have merged in the image, which thus enbles us to "see" (*schauen*) the *logos* encapsulated within the phenomenon. What Husserl in 1905 calls the "image-subject" and what the Byzantine iconophiles call the "prototype" is experienced as self-manifesting rather than something being merely "referred to." This *sujet* discloses itself *through* and *as* an image, with the latter mediating a knowledge not "owned" but gratuitously received, not conceptually "determined" (*bestimmt*) but intuitively "experienced" (*erlebt*). Recalling Plato's concept of knowledge as "participation" (*methexis*), Husserl argues that "in order to present the object we are supposed to immerse ourselves *in* the image [um uns den Gegenstand vorstellig zu machen, sollen wir uns IN das Bild hineinschauen]."[61] It bears recalling here that "thing" (*Gegenstand*) is not to be confused with the inert, medium-sized dry goods that it denotes in the British empiricist tradition. Rather, a "thing" for Husserl is self-manifesting, a presence experienced as imbued with significant meaning.[62] As Husserl puts it, the image uniquely presents us with a "second object [*Gegenstand*]"

> that is intended in a quite singular way. No appearance corresponds to it. It does not stand before me separately, in an intuition of its own; it does not appear as a second thing in addition to the image [*er erscheint nicht als ein zweites neben dem Bild*]. It appears in and with the image, precisely because the image representation arises. If we say that the image represents the subject, the subject is not

---

60. Gadamer 2006, 135; Gadamer's programmatic statement here bears quoting more fully: "Considered aesthetically, however, the image has its own being [*hat das Bild im ästhetischen Sinne des Wortes ein eigenes Sein*]. This being as presentation [*Darstellung*], as precisely that in which it is not the same as what is represented, gives it the positive distinction of being a picture as opposed to a mere reflected image [*gegenüber dem bloßen Abbild*]. . . . This kind of image is not a copy, for it presents something which, without it, would not present itself in this way. It says something about the original [Ein solches Bild ist kein Abbild, denn es stellt etwas dar, was ohne es sich nicht so darstellte. Es sagt über das Urbild etwas aus]" (2006, 135 / 1975, 133; trans. modified).

61. Husserl 2005, 37 / 2006b, 36 (§ 15).

62. To put it thus is to stress phenomenology's perennially contested affinity with metaphysics and theology, such as has been elaborated by Michel Henry, Jean-Louis Chrétien, and Jean-Luc Marion. Yet even in Heidegger (e.g., in § 7 of *Sein und Zeit*) and in the late writings of Merleau-Ponty, the essential nexus between the visible image and the invisible to which it summons the beholder remains an integral feature of understanding the nature of the image, and indeed of the phenomenon as such.

for that reason intuited in a new presentation; rather it is intuited only in the characteristic that makes the appearance of the object functioning as an image felt by our consciousness, by our perceiving, precisely as an image representation [nur intuitiv in dem Charakter, der die Erscheinung des als Bild fungierenden Gegenstandes eben für unser Bewusstsein . . . als Bildrepräsentation fühlbar macht].[63]

At this point a summary of Husserl's understanding of image and image-consciousness is in order.

(1) Since everyday perception comprises a temporal sequence of "aspects" (*Abschattungen*), their synthesis, which makes object-perception (*Gegenstandswahrnehmung*) possible, originates in an intuition (*Anschauung*) and its formal correlate, an "image" (*Bild*) wrought by an act of imagination or "phantasy."

(2) Every image, however, also requires a material foundation, that is, presupposes the kind of scaffolding (oil, tempera, canvas, wood panel, etc.) for its support. This "image-support" (*Bildträger*) allows for the presentation of the visible "image-object" (*Bildgegenstand*), which is apprehended in ways categorically different from ordinary, spatiotemporal perception. Corresponding to what is visibly depicted (*dargestellt*), "the physical image awakens the mental image, and this in turn presents something else, the *sujet* [Das physische Bild weckt das geistige Bild, und dieses wieder stellt ein anderes: das Sujet vor]."[64] Now, this relation between the physical and the mental image originates neither in an act of inference nor an instance of mechanical causation. Rather, the visible image is the *medium* through which being is able to constitute itself *in* and *for* consciousness, it being understood that medium and being remain ontologically distinct from (though not opposed to) one another.

(3) To credit the image with a unique "presence" also means that its apprehension is not governed by inner-time consciousness in the way that this is the case with successive, "aspectual" object perception. Instead, since "the space of phantasy is categorically distinct from the domain of perception [*das Phantasiefeld ist völlig getrennt vom Wahrnehmungsfeld*]," the image is situated on the ontological plane of the *nunc stans* rather than in the temporal "present" of a particular perceptual phase that is instantaneously displaced by further "aspects" (*Abschattungen*).[65]

---

63. Husserl 2005, 29 / 2006b, 30 (§ 13).

64. Husserl 2005, 30 / 2006b, 30 (§ 14).

65. Husserl 2005, 53 / 2006b, 51 (§ 24); Husserl's view of the image *sub specie aeternitatis* stands in fundamental continuity with the later Plato and Neoplatonist figures such as Nicholas of Cusa and Goethe.

Hence, the image's absolute (nontemporal) presence, the simultaneity of every-thing it contains, is integral to its very mode of being or *Seinsweise* (Gadamer). For the "sujet" mediated by it is a totality and ideality, much like the "prototype" in the writings of Gregory of Nyssa, John of Damascus, Nikephoros, and other iconodules. As Husserl notes, the present of the image "is a *different* present, an-other time determination [<Es> ist im aktuellen Jetzt nicht, sein "gegenwärtig" ist ein anderes, eine andere Zeitbestimmtheit]."[66]

(4) Insofar as phantasy is constitutively involved in how consciousness first "appre-hends" (*auffassen*) a phenomenon, the image wrought by phantasy is integral to the syntheses that issue in a fully developed object perception. Unlike hallucina-tion, however, an image cannot be confused with real being. For in the absence of a "grounding appearance" (*fundierende Erscheinung*) with which it interacts, "there would be nothing that could serve as an image to re-present [*vergegen-wärtigen*] something else."[67] Whereas the concept serves to *determine* the phe-nomenon and, thus, assimilate it to a grid of preexisting aims and purposes, the image responds to the way that a phenomenon *gives* itself. Instead of reifying the phenomenon as a specific "object," the image allows it to manifest itself and reveal itself as imbued with *logos*-like reality and presence.

(5) An instance of the "equanimity" that the later Heidegger explores under the heading *Gelassenheit*, the image suspends all instrumental and appropriative re-lations between consciousness and object. Yet even as it invites consciousness to tarry with the "apprehension characteristics" of pure appearance, the image—though indispensable for the disclosure of being—remains ontologically sepa-rate from it. Echoing the dialectical relationship between being and non-being in Plato's late writings, Husserl thus insists that "the image must be *clearly* set apart from reality [*Das Bild muss sich klar von der Wirklichkeit scheiden*]; that is, set apart in a purely intuitive way, without any assistance from indirect thought. We are to be taken out of empirical reality and lifted up into the equally intuitive world of imagery. Aesthetic semblance [*Schein*] is not sensory illusion [*Sinnen-trug*] . . . and aesthetic effects are not the effects of annual fairs [*Jahrmarktsef-fekte*]."[68]

(6) Image-consciousness exemplifies an elemental (prediscursive) mediation of mind and world that, after 1907, Husserl will continue to elaborate under the heading "epoché" or "reduction." Now, because it is never a derivative of perception, the

---

66. Husserl 2006b, 116 n. 2 (Supplemental text No. 2; trans. mine).
67. Husserl 2005, 43 / 2006b, 41 (§ 19).
68. Husserl 2005, 44 / 2006b, 43 (§ 19). As Alloa notes, "a path suggests itself, between pure givenness and active representation," one letting "what appears present itself in its being" (2011b, 204 f.; trans. mine).

image is incommensurable with emblematic, allegorical, or otherwise referential forms, all of which presuppose a preexisting code. Whereas symbolic, emblematic, and allegorical depictions achieve uptake only in relation to preexisting discursive and conceptual frameworks, the image can never be assimilated to a matrix of representation, substitution, or illusion: "Whoever immerses himself purely in an image, whoever lives in its imaging, has the re-presentation of the object in the image itself [Wer sich rein in ein Bild hineinschaut, der lebt in der Bildlichkeit, er hat im Bild selbst die Vergegenwärtigung eines Objekts]."[69]

More problematic, however, is the manner in which Husserl's intuitionist approach appears to drive a wedge between sight and cognition. By restricting phantasy and image to mere *pre*conditions for perceptual and discursive knowledge, he considers them to be all but immune to acts of conceptualization. Likewise, Husserl's phenomenological approach bypasses all manner of formal-aesthetic categories (e.g., illusion, simulation, perspectivalism), conceptions of style (realism, impressionism, cubism, abstract expressionism, etc.), and indeed any number of conceptual lenses through which one might seek to approach the image. For Husserl, the entire methodological inventory of the previous two centuries (epistemological skepticism, historical hermeneutics, or theories of empathetic cognition) habitually employed to clarify the deliverances of everyday perception is strictly inapplicable where our response to images is at stake. For when subjected to a rigorous phenomenological description of its experience, the image no longer feeds off, bears on, or otherwise competes with ordinary object-perception; and precisely because all object "positings" (*Setzungen*) have been strictly bracketed in this type of analysis, the image can also never be construed (and thus dismissed) as an instance of sheer projection, hallucination, or outright deception. Its reality as a correlate of intentional awareness is neither less than nor in any way contingent on any object or entity "really existing" out there. Indeed, "intentionality is not merely a feature of our consciousness of actually existing objects, but also something that characterizes our fantasies, our predictions, our recollections, and so forth."[70] If anything, we have seen that the image

---

69. Husserl 2005, 38 / 2006b, 37 (§ 16). For Husserl, the image-*sujet* is never intended or otherwise "referred to" but, on the contrary, self-disclosing. As such, an image unveils within the thing *of* which it is the image some poignant meaning or "insight." What is disclosed is thus never some preexisting referent or state of affairs now merely being pictorially or symbolically invoked. As Husserl repeatedly stresses throughout his 1905 lectures, the image is not to be conflated with the symbol or the sign (§ 25, pp. 54 f.; § 40, pp. 84 f.); hence Gadamer situates the image between the pure "indication" (*Verweisung*) that defines the sign and the pure "substitution" (*Vertretung*) that is effected by the symbol; see Gadamer 1975, 144–48.

70. Zahavi 2003, 19.

holds a unique position in Husserl's early phenomenology in that it mediates an intentional object by synthesizing the countless visual "aspects" of which perceptual consciousness of an object is comprised.

Still, Husserl's restriction of image-consciousness to a purely intuitive level remains problematic or at least underdeveloped. For one thing, he does not distinguish between the production of mental and art images. For even if the image originates in a prediscursive, intuitive type of vision, it nevertheless also feeds on an inherited pictorial grammar and rhetoric, a complex and evolving inventory of aesthetic styles and valuations, and a historically grown array of visual habits, all of which in turn reflect culturally specific norms. Overall, Husserl seems insufficiently mindful of the beholder's hermeneutic entanglement in antecedent visual experiences, aesthetic norms, and cultural practices. The question of whether Husserl's transcendental reduction is bound to expire in an unchecked intuitionism, as Heinrich Rickert was to charge, or whether phenomenology's "bracketing" (*Ausklammern*) of all transcendent "positings" (*Setzungen*) is philosophically legitimate and viable remains, for the time being, open. To answer it, we will have to shift from a more immanent study of Husserl's writings between 1904 and 1907 to cognate developments in some of his modernist contemporaries, in particular Cézanne's late works and Rilke's evolution of a "concrete" (*sachlich*) and pointedly visual idiom between 1903 and 1908, for which the former's Postimpressionist style turns out to have provided crucial inspiration.

DINGWERDUNG AS EPIPHANY: RODIN, CÉZANNE, AND RILKE'S VISUAL POETICS OF 1907

In a letter to Hugo von Hofmannnsthal, dated 12 January 1907, Husserl hazards a sweeping analogy between phenomenology's transcendental "attitude" (*Einstellung*) and what he calls a "strictly aesthetic" perspective. The phenomenological method, he notes,

> requires a standpoint that categorically differs from the "natural" [attitude] as regards objectivity; such a stance is closely related to the perspective in which your art as a purely aesthetic [attitude] places us. To intuit a purely aesthetic artwork unfolds by altogether suspending any existential attitude of the intellect [Die Anschauung eines rein ästhetischen Kunstwerkes vollzieht sich in strenger Ausschaltung jeder existenzialen Stellungnahme des Intellekts]. . . . Or, rather, the artwork transposes us (compels us, as it were) into a position of purely aesthetic significance from which all other [existential] considerations have been

excluded [in den Zustand rein ästhetischer, jene Stellungnahmen ausschlie-
ßender Bedeutung].⁷¹

Still, Husserl's notion of a "strictly aesthetic" perspective vacillates between a
fin-de-siècle conception of Symbolist art with which Hofmannsthal is strongly associated and an avant-garde aesthetic aimed at capturing the raw phenomenality of
things. Notably, and strikingly cognate with Husserl's concept of *epoché*, Hofmannsthal has just begun to drill beneath the cultural strata of mid-nineteenth-century
bourgeois realism (Balzac, Flaubert, Tolstoy), naturalism (Hauptmann, Zola, Hardy),
and, most recently, the verbal clutter of fin-de-siècle symbolism that had been so
central to his own aesthetic formation, as well as that of his early modernist contemporaries (Laforgue, Mallarmè, Maeterlinck, early Eliot and Rilke). Characteristically
reticent, however, Husserl in his January 1907 letter does not hazard an opinion as to
whether the objectives of phenomenology and modernist aesthetics, however analogous their aims, are equally well positioned to succeed.

In fact, for phenomenology's deeper purposes to be not only *asserted* as a project,
but descriptively and expressively *realized*, forms of verbal creativity are required
that go well beyond the mostly arid terminology to which Husserl adheres throughout his career. Rilke's stunningly inventive and untiring exploration of lyric and epistolary form nudges the phenomenological project of a "return to things themselves"
(*zu den Sachen Selbst*) toward what, beginning with his monograph on Rodin, he
calls "the quiet redemption of the being of things" (*des Dingseins leise Erlösung*) (*KA*
4:424–25). In the event, the attempt to retrieve our apprehension of things in their
prediscursive givenness, goes well beyond Husserl's technical nomenclature. For
such a retrieval seeks ultimately to *redeem* the reality and integrity of the world of
things, a quest about whose ethical and implicitly normative dimensions Rilke becomes more articulate as he leaves behind him a sentimentalizing Catholicism associated above all with his mother, as well as the often-mannered symbolism of his
early poetic efforts. In striking analogy to Husserl's "reduction," Rilke's poetic practice after 1903 involves forms of reflection that manifestly suspend or disable any
hermeneutic frames conventionally associated with a "natural attitude." Beginning
with lyrics eventually included in his *New Poems* (*Neue Gedichte*) of 1907–8, some
written as early as 1903, Rilke experiments with a mode of writing wholly outside the
orbit of Symbolist or sentimentalizing rhetoric and unallied with any established aesthetic movement or school. Centered on moments of focused visualization, the lyric

---

71. Husserl 1994, 7:133 (trans. mine); on Husserl's letter, and on the significance of Hofmannsthal's *Kleine Dramen*, a book the celebrated young poet had gifted to Husserl, for the latter's
1906–7 breakthrough in formulating his phenomenological method, see the discussion in de Warren 2021.

image is being reconceived as a form of participation, akin to Plato's theory of *methexis*, in the very being of things. As such, it appears immune to the hermeneutics of suspicion that a poetry steeped in late Romantic expressive conventions inevitably calls forth: "Things alone speak to me[,] . . . things that are perfect. They referred me to prototypes, to the moved, living world, *seen simply as such and without interpretation* as the occasion for things [nur die Dinge reden zu mir, . . . alle Dinge, die vollkommen sind. Sie wiesen mich auf die Vorbilder hin; auf die bewegte lebendige Welt, *einfach und ohne Deutung gesehen* als Anlaß zu Dingen]."[72] For Rilke, particularly after 1905, lyric form bears articulate witness to the event of having seen; it mediates our prediscursive, preeminently visual encounter with the phenomenal world of "things" (*Dinge*), not objects.

Pivotal for this turn was Rilke's well-known immersion in the visual arts, particularly between 1902 and 1914, which has been the subject of some probing scholarship.[73] The true significance of a few preeminent artists for Rilke, above all Rodin and Cézanne, stems less from their artistic creations than from what these works divulge about their approach to art and its ultimate aims. Whereas Rilke's early writings on visual art, especially his short monograph *Worpswede* and minor pieces written between 1898 and 1901, tend to ring overly sentimental and diffuse, they occasionally offer glimpses into what will become the poet's fundamental concern after 1904. Thus, in the short essay "Impressionism" (1898), Rilke credits the arts with "striving for the simplest and most elemental means" (*diesem Hindrängen der Künste zu den einfachsten, elementaren Mitteln*) (*KA* 4:133). Another early piece finds Rilke distinguishing the realm of effects and meanings from the sheer being of things. As he remarks, "The essence of beauty is found not in its effect but in its being [daß das Wesen der Schönheit nicht im Wirken liegt, sondern im Sein]" (*KA* 4:116), and "a thing is not inferior to a word, a scent, or a dream [daß ein Ding ist nicht schlechter als ein Wort oder ein Duft oder ein Traum]" (*KA* 4:127). He sharpens the point in his 1902 essay "On Landscape," noting how, if things are to become accessible to undesigning apprehension, "someone has to come from afar to tell us what surrounds us," which means "sensing landscape no longer thematically [*nicht mehr stofflich empfinden*] . . . but objectively [*gegenständlich*]" (*KA* 4:213). Similarly, in an essay of 1907, Rilke recalls how a decade earlier Jens Jacobsen's books had first impressed on him the need for an "unselective beholding" (*unwählerisches Schauen*) (*KA* 4:652).

Prior to Rilke's momentous encounter with Cézanne's oeuvre, it was mainly Rodin who impressed the young poet with his post-Romantic understanding of art

---

72. Rilke 1991, 1:153 (8 August 1903; trans. and emphasis mine; henceforth cited parenthetically as *RB*).

73. See esp. Antje Büsgen's survey of Rilke and the visual arts (in Rilke 2013, 130–50); on Rilke and Cézanne, see Meyer 1963, 244–86; Jamme 1992; Fischer 2015, 69–169.

as "arising in non-purposive ways from beholding and working" (*absichtslos aus Schauen und Arbeit entsprang*) (*KA* 4:213). Aside from Georg Simmel's article in *Berliner Tageblatt* (29 September 1902), which Rilke knew, the poet's long essay, written in typical breathless fashion in less than a month, is among the first pieces to draw the German-speaking world's attention to the sculptor's oeuvre.[74] For Rilke and Simmel, Rodin's sculptures embody, with unrivaled perfection and classical objectivity, various paradigmatic situations of human existence. The epitome of the modern artist, Rodin pioneers a new aesthetic in which the artwork constitutes itself as the tangible record of the artist's intensely focused visual encounter with his subject. Crucial for Rilke's own artistic development is Rodin's capacity for objective and absorptive beholding, an act seemingly shorn of both sentimental embroidery and reflective distance. Rodin's oeuvre reveals to Rilke that seeing is the very essence of creativity, not a prelude to it. As Rilke would eventually find confirmed in the work of Cézanne, Rodin's sculptures celebrate no other enigma but that of visibility. Yet to do so demands nothing less than for the beholder to embark on the "unfamiliar and arduous path of simple seeing" (*das einfache Schauen*) (*KA* 4:430). For as it opens itself to, and absorbs, the infinitely variegated play of aspects that comprise the body's total surface, the beholding consciousness experiences itself as continuous with its object. Beholder and thing appear to share one and the same phenomenological space— what Rilke will later call *Weltinnenraum*.

In even more pronounced ways than is the case in (two-dimensional) painting, sculpture reveals to Rilke what Merleau-Ponty will later identify as the beholder's "degree zero of spatiality. I do not see it according to its exterior envelope; I live it from the inside; I am immersed in it. After all, the world is around me, not in front of me."[75] As it beholds or "apprehends" embodied form, simply by tracing its inexhaustible variety of aspects and the constant shifts and redistribution of light, shade, and color, consciousness experiences itself as co-creator of the thing. Insofar as the act of beholding does not seek to prepossess, name, or reflect on the phenomenon, it instantiates a nonpropositional truth in the sense that Aquinas defines truth as the "adequation of thing and intellect" (*adaequatio intellectus et rei*).[76] When understood as the source of sight and insight, rather than as an *explanandum* begging for reflec-

---

74. *KA* 4:403–513; see also Rilke's letters to his wife and onetime student of Rodin, Clara Westhoff (*RB* 1:126–59).

75. Merleau-Ponty 1993, 127, 138.

76. *De Veritate* 1:1. Aquinas introduces this formal definition—which applies to both the process and the product of cognition—as already established and then proceeds to offer an exegesis of it: "In this conformity is fulfilled the formal constituent of the true, and this is what the true adds to being, namely, the conformity or equation of thing and intellect. As we said, the knowledge of a thing is a consequence of this conformity; therefore, it is an effect of truth, even though the fact that the thing is a being is prior to its truth."

tive and detached comprehension, a thing not only gives itself without making any demands, but in its very self-sufficiency qua appearance it also unveils an inner completeness and determinacy. Hence, Rilke notes, it came to pass that as Rodin steadily "advanced on his eccentric path, everything accidental began to recede and one law led him toward another." In attending to the intricate play of "surfaces" (*Oberflächen*), Rodin found them "to consist of an infinitely varied encounter of light with the thing itself" (*KA* 4:421). Like Husserl, that is, Rodin had alighted on the difference between objective and perceptual contents. Consequently, his sculptures do not posit object-type entities, "poses or groups, or compositions. Rather, there were an infinite number of living surfaces [*lebendige Flächen*]." Rodin's aesthetics reduces to a phenomenology of the human form itself, "more dispersed, greater, more mysterious and eternal [*zerstreuter, größer, geheimnisvoller und ewiger*]. The human being had become a cathedral, and there were many thousands such cathedrals, each differing from all the others and each one alive" (*KA* 4:412).

Rilke's claim that things can be apprehended, under the artist's contemplative gaze, in their undiluted and unfiltered phenomenality, is not just another aesthetic or epistemological assertion. Rather, it presupposes a certain ontology. Defaulting to theological concepts, Rilke seeks to intimate the outlines of that ontology by framing the primal encounter of beholder and thing in terms of revelation and grace (*Offenbarung, Gnade*). As he mulls over Rodin's gnomic promise to him, "Tu auras la grâce des grandes choses [You will have the grace of great things]" (*KA* 4:406), Rilke gradually realizes that the origin of creativity lies not in "doing" but in "receiving": "it is not the making of forms that I must learn from [Rodin], but rather a profound collectedness for the sake of such making [nicht bilden muß ich lernen von ihm, aber tiefes Gesammeltsein um des Bildens willen]." To cultivate creative sight requires quasi-monastic forms of concentration, with the act of beholding and capturing the visible world being the modern equivalent of Benedict's motto of *orare et laborare*: "that the innermost, secret chamber of my heart should become my workplace, cell, and refuge; and that all these monastic stirrings in me should found an order, for the sake of my labor and devotion [daß all dieses Mönchische in mir klostergründend würde, um meiner Arbeit und Andacht willen]."[77] Once apprehended by the eyes of an artist and transfigured into a sculpture or an image, the thing in question is being redeemed from its vagrant, indeterminate position in mundane space. It will become "somehow inviolable, sacrosanct [*unantastbar . . . sakrosankt*], and immune to contingency and time. . . . The image required its own, secure space. . . . It had to be inserted into the quiet permanence of space and its great laws [mußte seinen eigenen, sicheren Platz erhalten, . . . eingeschaltet werden in die stille Dauer des Raumes und

---

77. To Lou Andreas-Salomé (10 August 1903), *RB* 1:155, 157.

seiner großen Gesetze]."[78] Tentatively adumbrated in such passages is Rilke's growing sense that seeing and the distinctive kinds of nonpropositional knowledge it yields cannot be framed as an encounter of subject and object. Rather, as Alloa puts it (referencing Merleau-Ponty), "any theory of perception can rise above reifying dualisms only by becoming ontology—otherwise, it would contradict its ambition to undo the anthropocentric privilege—since the sensible 'is precisely that medium in which there can be *being* without it having to be posited.'"[79]

To sculpt the human form is nothing more, or less, than to maintain the utmost fidelity to how it has been seen. The artwork itself simply traces the act of creation that had taken place in the focused and sustained beholding of the thing or body itself. Commenting on Rodin's first major work, the unglamorous yet utterly absorbing *Man with the Broken Nose* (1863–64), Rilke remarks that the sculptor "had made him just as God had formed original man, without any other intention than to create life itself, unnamed life [ohne die Absicht, etwas anderes zu wirken als das Leben selbst, namenloses Leben]" (*KA* 4:433). Far from deteriorating into a dystopian naturalism, however, Rodin's preoccupation with the infinitely variegated presentation of things and bodies does not drain them of "life"—a word as crucial in Rilke's aesthetics as it had been for the late Nietzsche. For "whether something can become a life [*ein Leben werden kann*] does not depend on great ideas but, rather, on whether the latter can be turned into a craft [*Handwerk*], something practiced daily that stays with us until the very end" (*KA* 4:458). As practice, art studies and sculpts every aspect of the body until we have learned to grasp the inner determinacy of its visible surfaces and, thus, have positively the "gesture" (*Gebärde*) that positively ensouls a body. In capturing the human form in its utmost, visible concreteness, Rodin's oeuvre accomplished what Rilke calls "the birth of gesture" (*die Geburt der Gebärde*) (*KA* 4:419), and it is precisely through the specificity of gesture and posture that Rodin's bodies become conduits to the soul. Inasmuch as Rodin conceives the human body as the medium or form of the soul, he echoes (however unwittingly) not only Aristotle's *De Anima* but also his contemporary, Cézanne. Traversing the Louvre and ex-

---

78. *KA* 4:410–11; echoing his more expansive characterization of Rodin's creative process in a letter to Andreas-Salomé (8 August 1903): "When creating an artwork his task is to fit the thing more intensively, firmly, and a thousand times more perfectly into the expanse of space [*in den weiten Raum einzufügen*]. . . . A thing is determined; an art-thing [*Kunst-Ding*] must be more determined yet; sheltered from all contingency, cleansed of all opacity, lifted out of the order of time and handed over to space, it has become permanent, capable of eternity [*der Zeit enthoben und dem Raum gegeben, ist es dauernd geworden, fähig zur Ewigkeit*]" (*RB* 1:149). See also Gadamer's observation that, with the rise of "the modern industrial and administrative state and its functionalized spaces" having made it evident that "we no longer have any room for pictures," it has once again become apparent that "images are not just pictures but need space" (*daß Bilder nicht nur Bilder sind, sondern Platz heischen*) (2006, 132).

79. Alloa 2017, 80.

pressing discontent at the "fleshless" figures of Cimabue and Fra Angelico, the irascible Provençal is reported to have exclaimed: "I'm with Taine, and what's more, I'm a painter. I'm a sensualist. . . . You don't paint souls. You paint bodies; and when the bodies are well painted, dammit, the soul—if they have one—the soul shines through all over the place."[80]

What Rodin imparted to Rilke was, above all, this possibility of the phenomenon's aesthetic salvation, of rescuing the thing—not by transcending its embodied, visible particularity but, on the contrary, attending to it with the utmost insistence. What renders the artist's sight genuinely creative is precisely this refusal to look away from (or beyond) the phenomenon, this insistence on honoring it in its utter "thereness," as Rilke will call it, and in so doing to shelter it from being asphyxiated in a web of social, discursive, and aesthetic convention. Unlike quotidian object-perception, aesthetic contemplation involves a *participating in* reality and appearance, "thing" (*Ding*) and "image" (*Bild*), by conceiving them not as static antinomies to be resolved by conceptual means but honoring them as integral manifestations of an all-encompassing *logos*. For as long as it has not yet been framed by established techniques of representation and interpretation, the visible phenomenon still has agency; and it is art alone that allows us to access the dynamic thing before discursive and conceptual activity has caused it to calcify as but another inert object. Hence, the formal completeness of sculpture or painting, and the integrity of aesthetic "presentation" (*Darstellung*) more generally, can never be gauged by the material completeness of the object that it depicts. Already the "partially visible trees found in impressionist painting," Rilke notes, had taught late nineteenth-century viewers that "an aesthetic whole [*künstlerisches Ganzes*] does not have to coincide with an ordinary object-totality [*Ding-Ganzes*], but that independent of it new kinds of unity may constitute themselves within the image, new syntheses, configurations and proportions [*neue Einheiten, neue Zusammenschlüsse, Verhältnisse und Gleichgewichte*]" (*KA* 4:421).

In commenting on Rodin's *Man with the Broken Nose* (fig. 8.1), Rilke appears intensely aware of the infinitely variegated, "aspectual" nature of beholding Rodin's sculptures, which for that reason appear to have at least as much agency as the observer. At every instant, the beholder of Rodin's bust is presented with a new aspect of the subject's "tormented expression," all of which cumulatively unveil a "fullness of life" (*Fülle von Leben*) while also confirming Rodin's unique ability to fuse the strictest particularity and universality.

---

80. From Joachim Gasquet's recollections of Cézanne (1921), quoted in Danchev 2012, 103; specifically in Rodin's nudes, Rilke finds an analogous "incurvation into the interior [*dieses Sich-nach-innen-Biegen zurück in die eigene Tiefe*]." About Rodin's *La Méditation* (1886), he comments, "Never before has the human body been so configured by its interiority, has been so curved by its own soul [*Niemals ist ein menschlicher Körper so um sein Inneres versammelt gewesen, so gebogen von seiner eigenen Seele*]" (*KA* 4:420).

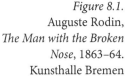

Figure 8.1.
Auguste Rodin,
*The Man with the Broken
Nose*, 1863–64.
Kunsthalle Bremen

On this face, there are no symmetrical surfaces, nothing is repeated, no space remains empty, mute, or indifferent. . . . Holding this mask and turning it, one is
surprised by the continuous change of aspects [*über den fortwährenden Wechsel
der Profile*]. . . . Yet it is not from its incomparable sculpting [*aus der unverglei-
chlichen Durchbildung*] alone that an impression of beauty arises. It stems from
the impression of equipoise, of all the animate surfaces balancing one another
[*des Ausgleichs aller dieser bewegten Flächen untereinander*], from the recognition that all these excitations pulsate within the thing itself and also terminate
there [*daß alle diese Erregungsmomente in dem Dinge selbst ausschwingen und zu
Ende gehen*]. (*KA* 4:416)

Yet even where Rodin's "initial inspiration arises from a thematic proposition [*vom
Stofflichen*]," say, in some "ancient myth, a passage of poetry, a historical scene or a
real-life personage," the same inexorable pull toward an ineffable and impersonal
revelation can be observed. Under Rodin's hands, Rilke finds, any subject matter is
gradually transposed "into something concrete and nameless [*immer mehr in Sachli-*

ches und Namenloses]."[81] Yet this transformation is, precisely, *not* accomplished by some kind of abstractive reflection such as would specify a given appearance by naming it or investing it with ideal meaning. Instead, "we find that [art] cannot move beyond surfaces, cannot ever enter into a thing's interior; that, instead, all it can accomplish is to produce a surface that in a determinate way is wholly continuous [*auf eine bestimmte Weise geschlossen*] and never accidental[,] . . . just this surface and nothing else [*nur diese Oberfläche, —sonst nichts*]" (*KA* 4:457–58).

With astonishing precision, Rilke here anticipates what, half a century later, Merleau-Ponty will call "perceptual faith," that is, a state of complete certitude regarding the primal reality of appearance and our embodied, spatiotemporal bond with it. Moreover, such "faith" affirms that whatever philosophical reflection may add to the experience of seeing will itself have been guided *by* the appearance in question and therefore cannot logically claim to "overcome it." For Merleau-Ponty, "it is therefore the greatest degree of belief that our vision goes to the things themselves. . . . [We] must seek in the world itself the secret of our perceptual bond with it. It must use words not according to their pre-established signification, but in order to state this prelogical bond. It must plunge into the world instead of surveying it."[82] By staging the objective drama of the body's infinitely variegated and exhaustively determined "surfaces," Rodin's sculptures transform the phenomenology of seeing; that is, they confront consciousness with the fact that, at least temporarily, it is utterly defined by the act and experience of beholding (*Schauen*). In Rodin's drawings no less than his sculptures, Rilke finds "nothing dramatized, nothing intentional, no trace of a name [nichts Dargestelltes, nichts Gemeintes, keine Spur von einem Namen]" but only an invitation to a wholly "non-intentional" (*absichtslos*) beholding and participating in the thing as it generously manifests itself in its innumerable aspectual presentations (*KA* 4:464).

Rilke's frequent emphasis on the "nameless" and "non-intentional" character of "beholding" (*Schau*) shows his emerging poetics to bear more than a passing affinity to the mystic idea of silent contemplation. Silence here signifies in a wholly positive sense; it "is not the exile of speech," not a case of speech deferred or suppressed. Rather, it furnishes an indispensable condition absent which the phenomenon could never properly reveal itself. Put positively, it is "the silence of listening . . . when even the word is presented in silence, without losing any of its vitality, in reading" and also in seeing. Inasmuch as "silence . . . runs alongside hope," it shows the act of attentive listening or beholding to be imbued with a metaphysical expectancy.[83] To behold the

---

81. *KA* 4:430; for the painter, "revelations . . . seem to emanate from the things themselves" (Merleau-Ponty 1993, 129).

82. Merleau-Ponty 1968, 28, 38–39.

83. Sarah 2017, 80–81, 61; see also Merleau-Ponty's "Indirect Language and the Voices of Silence" (1993, 76–120).

phenomenon is not to appropriate it in sensory fashion but to witness the thing as it discloses and reveals itself. Such silent witnessing of being in its very act of phenomenalization, or self-manifestation, discovers reality to be at once complete in itself and yet utterly "open" (*offen*) to us. The silence in question differs categorically from the negative "not-yet" of reflective, discursive, and conceptual speech eager to intrude on the event of appearance and purloin it from itself. For Rilke, silence is integral to the very being of things; it is "a silence . . . that surrounds things; things that are not coerced in any form whatsoever [eine Stille; die Stille, die um Dinge ist. Der zu nichts gedrängten Dinge]."[84]

Enthralled early on by the plasticity of language in Dante's *Commedia*, Rodin had begun to visualize embodied, human existence in ways rarely before captured by sculpture. On Rilke's telling of it, Rodin read key passages in the *Commedia* as having been "formed rather than written [*nicht geschrieben, sondern geformt*]" (*KA* 4:413). If it was poetry that made Rodin a truly accomplished sculptor, a curiously inverse logic was to ensure that Rodin's sculptures (along with Cézanne's paintings) would help Rilke become the mature poet of the *New Poems* (1907–8). Writing to his wife, Clara Westhoff—herself a sculptor who in 1900 had apprenticed with Rodin—in March 1907, Rilke encourages her

> to seize with quick motion this and that, fleeting phenomena, aspects, sudden flashes of revelation [*rasch Vorübergehendes, Einblicke, kurze aufblitzende Aufschlüsse*] that may only last a second. . . . Trivial matter that often gains significance due to a fleeting intensity of our seeing [*durch eine vorübergehende Intensität unseres Sehens*]. . . . Beholding [*das Anschauen*] is such miraculous business, and we know so little about it; in it, we are turned altogether outward, and yet just when we appear to be so the most things begin to take place within us that have longingly waited to be themselves unobserved; and just as they unfold within us, self-contained and strangely anonymously, without our involvement—their significance crystallizes in the exterior thing. . . . Of late, I have often found some face touching me, say, in the morning as it unfolds here [in Capri]; there has already been lots of sunshine, much light, and when suddenly in some passageway you are presented with a face, then due to the contrast one sees its very being with such distinctness of nuance that the fleeting impression is involuntarily magnified into the symbolic.

"More than ever," he concludes, "I wish for someone who could paint, seriously paint" (*RB* 1:247). Half a year later, that someone presented himself in the rooms of

---

84. *KA* 4:455; the word "silence" (*Stille*) figures prominently throughout Rilke's oeuvre (some 500 times).

the Salon d'Automne, where Rilke discovered some fifty paintings by Paul Cézanne, who had died the previous year. Still, as usually happens when an artist draws key inspiration from another medium, engagement with that other art form is liable to wane as the artist's own aesthetic objectives begin to consolidate. Thus, the Rodin monograph marks the apex of Rilke's writing about the visual arts, such that by mid-October 1907, though still enthralled by Cézanne's paintings, Rilke realizes that he does not actually wish to write *about* painting. In fact, "as always when I fall into the error of writing about art, it was valid more as a personal and provisional insight than as a fact objectively derived from the presence of the pictures."[85] For his true project, already under way for some time, involves capturing, in the medium of poetry, our visual contact with things as they constitute themselves in an "apprehension" (*Auffassung*) and, in so doing, transform our very sense of being in the world.

As far as Rilke is concerned, Cézanne's purpose was achieved once the painter had enabled the poet fully to articulate his poetic conception of "factual articulation" (*sachliches Sagen*): "I can tell how much I've changed by the way Cézanne challenges me now [Daran wieviel Cézanne mir zu tun gibt, merk ich, wie sehr ich anders geworden bin]." Moreover, having just received the proofs for his *Neue Gedichte*, he finds in these poems confirmation of "an instinctive tendency toward the same factualness [in den Gedichten sind instinctive Ansätze zu ähnlicher Sachlichkeit]." By 18 October 1907, Rilke has grown weary of writing about Cézanne, realizing that it is not so much painting as such that has preoccupied him but, rather, "the turning point in these paintings which I recognized because I had just reached it in my own work [es ist die Wendung in dieser Malerei, die ich erkannte, weil ich sie eben in meiner Arbeit erreicht hatte]."[86] Moreover, in embracing Cézanne's congenial aesthetic, Rilke takes many of his cues from the painter Émile Bernard, whose "Souvenirs sur Paul Cézanne" (published in the *Mercure de France* in two installments on 1 and 16 October 1907) Rilke's letters to Clara at times echo verbatim.[87] Even so, the fifty paintings by Cézanne displayed at the Salon d'Automne exactly one year after the painter's death made a profound impression on Rilke, who remarks on having spent as much as two hours in front of individual paintings (*KA* 4:612 / 38).

---

85. *KA* 4:616–17; Rilke's letters on Cézanne are henceforth cited parenthetically, followed by page reference to their English translation (Rilke 2002); here pp. 45, 47, 49.

86. *KA* 4:622/57; "Rilke's alertness to visual phenomena consistently served purposes of his own artistic and poetic self-determination." Moreover, his steadily improving ability of "existentially and sujet-focused seeing appeared to liberate him from the restrictions of classical aesthetics and ensured his perceptual openness vis-à-vis all manner of being" (Büsgen 2013, 132-35).

87. See Herman Meyer's scrupulous philological account of "Rilkes Cézanne Erlebnis" (1963, 244-86); the text of Bernard's "Memories of Paul Cézanne" and letters exchanged between the two painters can be found in Doran 2001, 25-79; for an extensive and rich discussion of Rilke and Cézanne, see also Fischer 2015, 69-169.

What so absorbs Rilke in Cézanne's art is above all the primal givenness and charism of color, which intimates a numinous order of being anterior to all object-perception and reference. Rilke's observations to that effect were to be echoed by Roger Fry, whose searching monograph on Cézanne, published the year after Rilke's death, speaks of the painter's "desperate search" for a "reality [that] no doubt lay always behind this veil of color, [a reality] different, more solid, more dense, in closer relation to the needs of the spirit." For Fry, color is "the most fundamental quality and the primary inspiration" in all of Cézanne, "the one quality . . . [that] remains supremely great under all conditions," and Cézanne's frequent observations on *sensations colorantes* and the smell, sound, or feel of color—such as remarking to Gasquet on "the pure blue scent of pine"—suggest that, like his contemporary Alexander Scriabin, he may have been susceptible to synesthesia.[88] A generation later, Heinrich Petzet, having prepared the first edition of Rilke's *Letters on Cézanne* (1952) at the urging of Martin Heidegger, likewise speaks of color in Cézanne as a "numinous essence" (*numinose Wesenheit*). Color is the pictorial *Urphänomen*, the absolute datum and inexhaustible wellspring of all pictorialization. Writing to his student and admirer Émile Bernard, he reflects on

> the stubbornness with which I pursue the *realization* of that part of nature that falls before our eyes and gives us the picture . . . to give the image of what we see. . . . The *sensations colorantes* that create light are the cause of abstractions that do not allow me to cover my canvas, nor to pursue the delimitation of objects when their points of contact are subtle, delicate; the result of which is that my image or painting is incomplete.[89]

Rilke, who had read Bernard's 1904 and 1907 essays on the painter, embraces and extends this self-characterization. Focusing almost exclusively on the primary datum of color, Rilke takes Cézanne's notion of *réalisation* in strict etymological fashion as the phenomenological project of *Dingwerdung*, that is, as the "self-constitution" of things in the apprehending consciousness prior to any positing or reification of the appearance in question. Pushing back against his Impressionist contemporaries, "Cézanne wants to represent the object, to find it again behind the atmosphere." Yet his departure does not involve, as one might have expected, a reaffirmation of line and outline but, on the contrary, pivots on his infinitely subtle modulation of color, tones, "a progression of chromatic nuances across the object, a modulation of colors which stays close to the object's form and to the light it receives."[90] More than any-

---

88. Fry 1927, 13; Danchev 2012, 219.
89. Cézanne 2013, 355 (23 October 1905).
90. Merleau-Ponty 1993, 62.

thing, it is Cézanne's discernment of color that enthralls Rilke: "The good conscience of these reds, these blues, their simple truthfulness, it educates you." Cézanne, he marvels, has taken color "personally, as no one has ever used color before, simply for making the object [wie kein Mensch noch Farbe genommen hat, nur um das Ding damit zu machen. Die Farbe geht völlig auf in dessen Verwirklichung]." As perceptive as they are, Rilke's observations on Cézanne the colorist also prove completely oblivious to the painter's influential destabilization of linear perspective. Instead, he quite single-mindedly insists "that it is color which constitutes the art of painting" (*daß es die Farbe ist, die die Malerei ausmacht*). Particularly in the painter's late works, Rilke detects an impersonal and dispassionate idiom free of "any preferences or biases or fastidious predilections" such as to render reality "so incorruptibly reduced . . . to its color content that it resumed a new existence in a beyond of color, without previous memories [die so unbestechlich Seiendes auf seinen Farbeninhalt zusammenzog, daß es in einem Jenseits von Farbe eine neue Existenz, ohne frühere Erinnerungen, anfing]" (*KA* 4:623 / 58).

Time and again, Rilke remarks on how color endows a thing with phenomenality and presence, with a primal thereness untouched by considerations of how the thing in question might fit into a world of discursive means and practical ends. Anticipating Alex Danchev's remark that "a Cézanne portrait is more a thereness than a likeness," Rilke remarks about Cézanne's apples that "they cease to be edible altogether, that's how thing-like and real they become [bei Cézanne hört ihre Eßbarkeit überhaupt auf, so sehr dinghaft wirklich werden sie, so einfach unvertilgbar in ihrer eigensinnigen Vorhandenheit]."[91] By focusing the beholder's attention on a thing's visible surface, color induces consciousness to immerse itself in the thing's sheer phenomenality, untroubled by how it may be contextually embedded in the world. Again, color opens the path toward a mode of visual apprehension not (yet) attenuated by hermeneutic perplexities of any kind. It is, Rilke writes, "as if these colors could heal one of indecision once and for all [*als ob diese Farben einem die Unentschlossenheit abnähmen ein für allemal*]" (*KA* 4:616 / 45). Cézanne's irregular planes of color operate in much the same way as the infinitely varied surfaces of Rodin's sculptures, with their continually shifting aspects detaining the beholder's gaze and, ever so slowly, manifesting the very being of the sculpted thing itself. A prime instance of Husserl's concept of "aspectual" form (*Abschattung*), the infinite gradation of surface and color in Rodin's and Cézanne's work opens access, in the medium of appearance, to what lies beyond all appearance. Rilke speaks of Rodin's "knowledge of the *one* surface whereby the whole world was offered up to art—offered up but not yet handed over [Wissen von der *einen* Oberfläche, mit welchem dieser Kunst die ganze Welt angeboten war. Angeboten, noch nicht gegeben]" (*KA* 4:460).

---

91. Danchev 2012, 293; Rilke, *KA* 4:608 / 30.

If Rodin's sculptures "consisted of innumerable encounters of light with a thing, each one of which turned out to be different and remarkable [bestand aus unendlich vielen Begegnungen des Lichtes mit dem Dinge, und es zeigte sich, daß jede dieser Begegnungen anders war und jede merkwürdig]" (KA 4:411), Rilke finds the same aesthetic principle at work in Cézanne, albeit in far more intensive form yet. Two brief case studies may help illustrate the dynamic. In Cézanne's 1899 *Portrait of Ambroise Vollard* (fig. 8.2), the first art dealer to have taken an interest in the painter's work and author of an early biography (1914), the departure from the covenant of verisimilitude that had long governed classical portraiture could hardly be more striking. Tonally, Cézanne restricts himself almost entirely to a spectrum of brown and gray. Likewise, having been purged of any objects or emblems, the pictorial space recalls late Byzantine iconography's singular focus and severity of line. What symbolic force may slumber within the image must be found in the intricate, camouflage-like pattern of brown tones and the subject's brooding and impenetrable posture. Fundamentally, however, Cézanne's concern is "to give the image of what we see, forgetting everything that has appeared before us" or, as he writes to Louis Leydet, "to give sufficient form to the sensations we experience through contact with nature."[92] If it seems that the painter's focus had narrowed to only those things that truly elicit and hold his attention, another friend confirms as much. Recalling Cézanne's work habits while engaged in his portrait of Vollard, Joachim Gasquet recalls how "during many sessions, Cézanne seemed to make only a few brushstrokes but never ceased to devour the subject with his eyes."[93] In his 1914 biography of Cézanne, Vollard himself also remarks on the painter's manic obsession with capturing and memorizing the configuration of shades and colors, which made the process of sitting for him excruciating and slowed down the actual painting to just a few brushstrokes in several hours: "After a hundred and fifteen sessions, Cézanne abandoned my portrait to return to Aix. 'I'm not discontent with the front of the shirt' . . . were his last words."[94]

For Cézanne, visual attention presupposes the absolute stillness of his objects, for which reason he found apples (less prone to change during the weeks that it takes him to complete a canvas) rather more congenial subjects than flowers or human beings. Even paper flowers are found wanting: "These sacred hussies change their tone

---

92. Cézanne 2013, 355, 332 (to Émile Bernard, 23 October 1905; to Louis Leydet, 17 January 1904).

93. Quoted in Cachin 1996, 422. As Cézanne's acquaintance, the painter Maurice Denis, noted during the countless sessions while Vollard was sitting for his portrait, the painter time and again complained that his subject's slight shift in posture "had made him lose the *line of concentration*" (422); Denis was also the first to remark on Cézanne's "perpetual nervous *inquiétude*" (quoted in Danchev 2012, 14).

94. Cachin 1996, 422–23.

Figure 8.2. Paul Cézanne, *Portrait of Ambroise Vollard*, 1899. Cambridge, MA, Fogg Art Museum, Harvard University

sooner or later."[95] By contrast, human subjects proved notoriously frustrating for the irascible Provençal: "Wretch! You're changing the pose. I say to you, . . . remain still as an apple. Does an apple fidget?"[96] Such fastidiousness reveals a fundamentally new aim. For Cézanne, the object of pictorialization is no longer to depict an object or

---

95. Danchev 2012, 79.
96. Gasquet, quoted in Cachin 1996, 422.

person but, rather, its particular aspect *as he sees it*. Remarking on Cézanne's "real gift, the extraordinary sensibility of his reaction to actual vision of no matter what phenomenon," Fry regrettably blurs the psychological concept "reaction" with the phenomenological category "experience."[97] While the former is essentially contingent, the main point of painting (and, for Rilke, of lyric writing) is precisely to circumnavigate such contingency and the entire aesthetic program of expressivity, subjectivity, and so forth. Instead, painting for Cézanne means to transcribe how a given phenomenon constitutes itself in visual experience *prior* to being identified as a particular entity in social space and historical time. Inasmuch as the subjects of a portrait, or the apples, drapes, and vases of a still-life, are being painted simply as visible things, in their incontrovertible "thereness," their pose and form often appear awkward, their bodies but a composite of shapes slightly askew and uncomfortably frozen in time. Cézanne's Vollard portrait confirms as much with its subject appearing somber and inscrutable, looking downward in striking departure from conventional portraiture.

As our gaze lingers, further oddities emerge, such as the strange greenish and gray specks on the forehead, the left arm's awkward angularity, and a raised right leg not just obscuring but positively eclipsing the left hand. A dense mass of tangled and cross-cutting lines and chromatically shifting planes (*taches*) creates the overall impression of an unfinished portrait. Its hieratic subject appears self-contained and brooding, an ineffable presence that simultaneously elicits our interest and defeats it with an aura of terminal inaccessibility. Crucially, Vollard's eyes are not just invisible but positively missing within their clearly delineated sockets. Meanwhile, the infinite gradation of brown and gray tones, as well as the minimalist, seemingly unfinished background, further estrange us from any realist covenant. One is disoriented by countless irregular planes of brown and gray whose cumulative effect seems to be a blurring of boundaries between person and thing. Early on, Roger Fry had remarked on the "Byzantine austerity of design" and his "instinctive, though as yet unconscious, bias towards severe architectural dispositions," which impresses on the beholder the ineffable and potentially volatile otherness of Cézanne's subjects.[98] Some of the portrait's recessive and muted interiority emerges again in Picasso's 1910 portrait of Vollard (fig. 8.3), which manifestly capitalizes on the proto-Cubist tendencies found in Cézanne's earlier work, even as their overall effect now seems far more controlled, less a quest for psychological depth than a technically self-assured performance.

---

97. Fry 1927, 31.

98. Fry 1927, 20, 26. As Danchev observes, Braque and Picasso were among the first to notice how, in an apparent departure from Renaissance linear perspective, Cézanne collapses horizontal into vertical lines, with "color . . . called upon to do the work of linear perspective" (2012, 305).

Figure 8.3.
Pablo Picasso,
Portrait of Ambroise Vollard,
1910.
Moscow, Pushkin State
Museum of Fine Arts

By contrast, Cézanne's Vollard portrait leaves us with a saturated yet enigmatic presence that defeats our visual expectations by exceeding them, that is, by severing any nexus between this image and what has been previously seen. Confronting us, instead, in "its very excess, without the security of the concept," Cézanne's late portraits are instances of what Marion calls "saturated phenomena." Reminiscent of Augustine's distinction between *veritas lucens* and *veritas redarguens*, this type of phenomenon does not simply appear *to* and demonstrate something *for* its beholder but, instead, "remonstrates with the one who receives it."[99] It is this insistent focusing of the beholder on the phenomenality of things, rather than on their objective and conceptual status, that renders "a Cézanne portrait . . . more a thereness than a likeness."[100] Structurally cognate with Husserl's "reduction," it suspends the beholder's natural attitude of quotidian perception and, instead, focuses her visual attention on the very dynamics and textures governing appearance. As Rilke was to sum up

99. Marion 2008, 140; see also Marion 2004, 24–45.
100. Danchev 2012, 293.

his impressions of the retrospective at the Salon d'Automne, Cézanne did not paint "'look at me' but 'here it is.'" Yet as soon as perception supplants this timeless state of pure apprehension, "one judges [the thing] instead of saying it [*man beurteilt es, statt es zu sagen*]."[101]

For Cézanne, this state of pure, undesigning attention is the phenomenological ground zero of what he calls *réaliser* and *realization*. As he writes to his student Émile Bernard, "In order to make progress in realization, there is only nature, and an eye educated by contact with it. It becomes concentric by dint of looking and working. I mean that in an orange, apple, a ball, a head, there is a culminating point, and this point is always the closest to our eye, the edges of objects recede towards a center placed at eye level."[102] Regarding this curious equation of orange, apple, and [human] head, Giacometti in 1957 noted that "Cézanne blew sky high [traditional portraiture] by painting the head as an object. He said as much: 'I paint a head like a door, like anything else.' As he painted the left ear, he established a greater rapport between the ear and the background than between the left ear and the right ear, a greater rapport between the colour of the hair and the colour of the sweater than between the ear and the structure of the skull."[103] To a neighbor in Aix, Cézanne remarked on "how a man or woman resembled a cylinder," echoing his widely quoted remark that one should "treat nature in terms of the cylinder, the sphere, and the cone, everything put in perspective, so that each side of an object, of a plane leads to a central point."[104]

The act of visualization for Cézanne and, by 1907, also for Rilke pivots on completely expunging, or at least suspending, our preoccupation with subjective sentiment and nominal reference. The emergence of the visible thing, its gradual self-disclosure, supplants the drama of meaning. As a result, the dense and unfathomable quality that pervades not only his landscapes but also his portraits (e.g., Vollard, Gasquet, Geffroy, Vallier, and even his wife, Marie-Hortense) enthralls and disturbs in equal measure. Both in their looming proximity and their infinite distance vis-à-vis the beholder, the subjects of Cézanne's portraits do not give us a specific, known individual. Rather, we are confronted with the bewildering and humbling fact that *there is* someone, a being, with whom we share a lived space and who, nevertheless,

---

101. Ibid., 317; Rilke, *KA* 4:616 / 46. "Cézanne did not want to separate the stable things which we see and the shifting way in which they appear; he wanted to depict matter as it takes on form" (Merleau-Ponty 1993, 63).

102. Cézanne 2013, 342 (to Émile Bernard, 25 July 1904). As Alloa puts it, "Art is not an alternative to the natural world but an intensification of its operations" (2017, 65).

103. Cézanne 2013, 343.

104. Ibid., 334–35. Likewise, David Sylvester sees the overriding objective of Cézanne's mature style to consist in "concentrat[ing] all his attention on achieving the most precise and complete sensation of a human presence." Yet this he paradoxically "achieves . . . because he was also undistracted by an interest in virtuoso illusionism" (quoted in Danchev 2012, 293).

Figure 8.4.
Paul Cézanne,
*Mme. Cézanne in a
Red Armchair*, 1877.
Boston, Museum
of Fine Arts

remains inscrutably other. Anticipating Merleau-Ponty's observation that "Cézanne's people are strange, as if viewed by a creature of another species," Rilke comments on the "animal alertness" and "untiring, objective wakefulness in the unblinking eyes" in *Madame Cézanne in a Red Armchair* (1877) (fig. 8.4). The gaze, he muses, is fully equivalent to that of Cézanne the painter, whose "unimpeachably accurate" habit of seeing neither "presumes superiority" (überlegen *anzusehen*) nor claims to "interpret" (*auszulegen*) his subject.

As Rilke saw so clearly, Cézanne's art unfolds in a domain anterior to that of interest, interpretation, and symbolic closure. "Interpretation should not be a reflection distinct from the act of seeing."[105] Instead, the ethical space opened up by Cézanne's unflinchingly engaged, impersonal gaze is one of sheer equivalence with his subject, and thus of wonder at the latter being indeed so indisputably and unfathomably present; it is the gaze of the utmost "humble objectivity, with the unquestioning, matter-of-fact interest of a dog who sees himself in a mirror and thinks: hmm, there's another dog" (*KA* 4:633 / 74–75). Throughout his letters to Clara of October 1907,

---

105. Merleau-Ponty 1993, 66.

Rilke remains preoccupied by the fact that Cézanne's human subjects exist on the same plane as his apples, "so very thing-like and . . . stubborn thereness" (*so sehr dinghaft . . . in ihrer eigensinnigen Vorhandenheit*) (*KA* 4:608 / 30). Having "so incorruptibly contracted reality to its color content," which he weighs "on the scales of an infinitely responsive conscience" (*eines unendlich beweglichen Gewissens*), Cézanne has unearthed within human consciousness a new stratum of awareness, a quality of attention utterly bound up with the reality of the being across from it. Immune to any sentiment, desire, or context-dependent meaning, "this limitless objectivity, this categorical refusal to meddle refuses in an alien unity, . . . strikes people as so offensive and comical in Cézanne's portraits. . . . they start missing the interpretation, the judgment, the superiority" (*KA* 4:623/58).

As Rilke's epistolary processing of his Cézanne experience winds down, he at last formulates the central question: Can the insights opened up by Cézanne's Post-impressionist concept of the painted image be transferred to the medium of poetic language and, if so, might doing so conceivably transform the latter? It is not the image as artifact, let alone as material token of some prevailing ideal of "beauty," that engages Rilke. Rather, the goal is to transpose into the written word *how* consciousness apprehends a thing in its very givenness and presence and, thus, to "transfigure things into the indestructibility of the written word."[106] Struggling to convey to Clara the viewing experience of Cézanne's 1877 portrait of his wife ("words seemed more inadequate than ever"), Rilke nevertheless maintains that what the painting means to tell us ought to be conveyable in speech: "if one could only look at such a picture as if it were part of nature . . . it ought to be possible to express its existence somehow [dann müßte es als ein Seiendes auch irgendwie ausgesagt werden können]" (*KA* 4:631 / 73) (see fig. 8.4). The very attempt of capturing the phenomenology of the image in *writing* reveals some fundamental truths about visual cognition. Thus, with the retrospective at the Salon d'Automne about to close, a seemingly hypnotized Rilke returns one last time "to look up a violet, a green or certain blue tones which I believe I should have seen better, *more unforgettably*." And yet, even as "the great color scheme of the woman in the red armchair is becoming as irretrievable in my memory as a number with very many digits," the experience of the image as a whole appears to have ineradicably nested in the poet's consciousness: "In my feeling, the consciousness of their presence has become a heightening [in meinem Gefühl ist das Bewußtsein ihres Vorhandenseins zu einer Erhöhung geworden] which I can feel even in my sleep; my blood describes it within me, but the naming of it passes by

---

106. Jamme 1992, 388; on difficulties framing Rilke's transposition of object perception into language in phenomenological terms, see Müller 1999. Luke Fischer (2015), though more sanguine about such a project, largely eschews Husserl's conception in favor of Merleáu-Ponty's; see my discussion below.

somewhere outside [aber das Sagen geht irgendwo draußen vorbei] and is not called in" (*KA* 4:630 / 70).

What Cézanne had taught Rilke was this ontological priority of seeing over perception, and of "saying" (*Sagen*) over "expression." Henceforth, his poetic program stipulates that, "first, artistic perception has to surpass itself to the point that even something horrible, something that seems no more than disgusting *is*, and is *valid*, along with everything else that is [das Seiende zu sehen, das, mit allem anderen Seienden, *gilt*]." Revealing significant, if incidental, affinities with the aims of Husserl's phenomenology, what Rilke calls the "trend toward plainspoken truth [*die ganze Entwicklung zum sachlichen Sagen*]" (*KA* 4:624 / 60) seeks to rehabilitate the poetic word for the sake of capturing the reality, presence, and numinous integrity of things. A decade and a half later, Rilke's *Sonnets to Orpheus*—in which the sense of hearing has by and large supplanted that of vision—acknowledge both the splendor and impermanence of sight: "Far be from him who beholds any trace of regret [Fern von dem Schauenden sei jeglicher Hauch des Bedauerns]."[107] Sonnet 11 (in part 2 of the cycle) offers perhaps the most exemplary formulation of what might be called the self-immolation of visual and proprietary experience.

> Sei allem Abschied voran, als wäre er hinter
> dir, wie der Winter, der eben geht.
> Denn unter Wintern ist einer so endlos Winter,
> daß, überwinternd, dein Herz überhaupt übersteht.
> Sei immer tot in Eurydike -, singender steige,
> preisender steige zurück in den reinen Bezug.
> Hier, unter Schwindenden, sei, im Reiche der Neige,
> sei ein klingendes Glas, das sich im Klang schon zerschlug.
> Sei - und wisse zugleich des Nicht-Seins Bedingung,
> den unendlichen Grund deiner innigen Schwingung,
> daß du sie völlig vollziehst dieses einzige Mal.
> Zu dem gebrauchten sowohl, wie zum dumpfen und stummen
> Vorrat der vollen Natur, den unsäglichen Summen,
> zähle dich jubelnd hinzu und vernichte die Zahl.[108]

---

107. *KA* 2:262; on the aniconic turn of Rilke's later oeuvre, and its increasingly abstract and multiperspectival concept of space, see Gerok-Reiter 1993, esp. 497–501.

108. *KA* 2:263-64. "Be ahead of all parting, as though it already were / behind you, like the winter that has just gone by. / For among these winters there is one so endlessly winter / that only by wintering through it will your heart survive. // Be forever dead in Eurydice—more gladly arise / into the seamless life proclaimed in your song. / Here, in the realm of decline, among momentary days / be the crystal cup that shattered even as it rang. // Be—and yet know the great void where all things begin, / the infinite source of your own most intense vibration, / so that, this once, you may give it your perfect assent. // To all that is used-up, and to all the muffled and dumb / creatures in the

By 1922, Rilke has come to embrace a fundamentally aniconic position, not least because he regards all visual commerce with being to be inevitably tainted by proprietary desires of some kind or another. Our gaze never quite allows being to unfold in toto, to manifest itself through an infinity of aspects, without our prioritizing one of them and, thus, absorbing and instrumentalizing a given phenomenon for some subjective scheme or other. Cézanne's great gift consisted in intimating, still in pictorial form, a wholly objective (*sachlich*) take on the world to which we should all aspire. Fusing aesthetic and ethical concerns, his oeuvre had allowed Rilke to formulate a poetic program that, beginning with the radically impersonal gaze of *Neue Gedichte* (1907/8) ultimately leads him to the threshold of a strictly "imageless sight" (*bildloses Sehen*), as Annette Gerok-Reiter so felicitously terms it. The self-suspension of the image coincides with that of the beholder: "be the crystal cup that shattered even as it rang. // Be—and yet know the great void where all things begin." The fusion of these two stances, however, can be accomplished only in the medium of the (poetic) word, and only if language itself undergoes a profound transformation.[109] The word must be freed from the shackles of aesthetic convention and its preestablished codes of beauty and mundane reference. Beauty is not the declared aim but an inevitable entailment of a quasi-phenomenological turn in modernist poetics. Already while writing on Rodin, Rilke had insisted that "beauty cannot be manufactured" (*daß man Schönheit nicht machen kann*) but can only ever be witnessed and borne. To advance to a poetics in "saying the thing" (*sachliches Sagen*) is to recognize that "we can only create propitious or sublime conditions for what, on occasion, inclines to linger with us: an altar and fruit and a flame. Everything else lies beyond our powers [Man kann nur freundliche oder erhabene Umstände schaffen für Das, was manchmal bei uns verweilen mag: einen Altar und Früchte und eine Flamme—Das Andere steht nicht in unserer Macht]" (*KA* 4:457). Coded into this strictly negative characterization is the prospect of a form of lyric writing fundamentally cognate with Husserl's transcendental "perspective" (*Einstellung*). Its sole focus is the intentionality wrought by the event of "appearance" (*Erscheinung*), that is, the unfathomable fullness of a thing as the correlate of "apprehension" (*Auffassung*).

Throughout his letters and prose writings from 1903 until about 1914, Rilke frequently frames this poetic ideal of *sachliches Sagen* with images and allusions to religious life and the sacred, though largely shorn of doctrinal and denominational specificity. He praises van Gogh's capacity for infusing the most mundane things with a sacred dimension: "or a garden, or a park, which is seen and shown with the same utter lack of prejudice or of pride; or simply, things, a chair for example, of

---

world's full reserve, the unsayable sums, / joyfully add your*self*, and cancel the count" (Rilke 2009, 159).

109. Gerok-Reiter 1993, 500.

the most ordinary kind: and yet, how much there is in all this that reminds one of the 'saints' [*wieviel ist in alledem von den 'Heiligen'*] he promised himself and resolved to paint at some much later time" (*KA* 4:601/17). Beyond Cézanne's "devotion . . . lies the beginning of sainthood [*hinter dieser Hingabe beginnt . . . die Heiligkeit*]" (*KA* 4:624 / 61). Elsewhere, Rilke likens the artwork's synoptic, life-sustaining power to prayer: "therein lies the enormous aid the work of art brings to the life of the one who must make it [*die ungeheure Hülfe des Kunstdings für das Leben dessen, der es machen muß*],—that it is his epitome, the knot in the rosary at which his life says a prayer, the ever-returning proof to himself of his unity and genuineness [*daß es seine Zusammenfassung ist; der Knoten im Rosenkranz, bei dem sein Leben ein Gebet spricht, der immer wiederkehrende, für ihn selbst gegebene Beweis seiner Einheit und Wahrhaftigkeit*]" (*KA* 4:594 / 4).

At the same time, Rilke's conception of the lyric as "plainspoken" (*sachlich*) views consciousness as utterly absorbed and transformed by the way phantasy is operative in the process of apprehension. Rilke's *New Poems* time and again move beyond Husserl's visual trope of *Evidenz* and his postulate of "a perfect synthesis of fulfillment where an . . . existence-positing intention is adequately fulfilled by a corresponding perception."[110] Located not so much *beyond* as *within* the event of visual apprehension, Rilke's lyrics begin precisely where the phenomenon exceeds what consciousness can anticipate or preview, where it moves beyond "adequation" between what is foreseen and what is given in intuition. Particularly the most compressed lyrics in *New Poems*, centered on some seemingly quotidian thing or being, both hark back to Kant's notion of the dynamic sublime and also foreshadow Marion's notion of a phenomenon "saturated with intuition, . . . a phenomenon in which intuition would give *more, indeed immeasurably more*, than intuition ever would have intended or foreseen." Precisely because of this "excess of intuition, and thus of givenness, over the intention, the concept, and the aim," such phenomena are not mastered by but, on the contrary, transformative of consciousness. Their "experience" (*Erlebnis*) is not governed by an anterior and firmly established subject. Rather, like Prince Myshkin's shattering encounter with Holbein's *Dead Christ*, the phenomenon's very experience unsettles and reconfigures what seemed a self-possessed subjectivity. Yet even as such a phenomenon "cannot be aimed at, . . . cannot be borne," its experience ought not be construed as an extraordinary psychological state. At issue is not some "limit case, an exceptional, vaguely irrational, in short, a 'mystical' case of phenomenality." Rather, it confirms a potential slumbering within the fundamental, "operative definition of the phenomenon."[111] Platonic "wonder" (*thaumazein*) and the Kantian "sublime" must not be "explained" (away) as epistemological states of emergency. For

---

110. Zahavi 2003, 32.
111. Marion 2008, 32–35, 45.

what is truly wondrous is not that some things appear conspicuous and strange but that things appear at all.

Insofar as modernist conceptions of art have parted ways with both classical aesthetics and Romantic expressivism, the artwork is neither a "making" (*facere*) in accordance with an antecedent intention nor a case of ex nihilo "creation" (*creare*) grounded in Romantic notions of originality and inwardness. Rather, art seeks to reconstitute the primal experience of the phenomenal world as it gives itself *to* and is constituted *in* (but not *by*) consciousness. The resulting artwork is a transcript, a record of an experience whose epiphanic fullness exceeds all antecedent intention and, thus, leaves consciousness itself profoundly altered. Precisely because the founding category is that of "experience," rather than intention, the artist ought to desist from all meta-reflections about art, poetry, form, and aesthetic goals. With evident approval, Rilke thus recalls (by way of Émile Bernard's reportage) Cézanne's frequent claims that "talking about art is virtually useless. Work that leads to progress in one's own *métier* is sufficient recompense for not being understood by imbeciles."[112] Just as Rilke had previously been taken with Rodin's "dark path of purposeless labor [*der dunkle Weg seiner absichtslosen Arbeit*]" (*KA* 4:467), so in his letters on Cézanne he once again recalls "that Rodin does not 'think about' his work but remains within it: within the attainable." Precisely "this humble path he trod within the real [*seinen demütigen, geduldigen, ins Wirkliche gestellten Weg*]" allows him to respond to the excess of the visible: "In art, you can only abide within the 'well done', and insofar as you do so it increases and surpasses you again and again [Man kann nur im 'Gekonnten' bleiben in der Kunst, und dadurch, daß man darin bleibt, nimmt es zu und führt immer wieder über einen hinaus]" (*KA* 4:596 / 7–8). Both in his letters on Cézanne and, far more richly yet, in his *Neue Gedichte*, Rilke delineates an artless, seemingly unselfconscious concept of vision.

While it seems an exaggeration to characterize it as "almost rabidly anti-literary," Rilke's lyric practice does indeed seek to fortify the poetic word against the distractions posed by discursive speech and aesthetic convention alike.[113] His attempted repristination of the word thus constitutes a crucial step toward pinpointing the phenomenological origin (or *Selbst-Konstituierung*) of the mind-world relationship. Quarantined from all discursive entanglements, lyric speech may forge a path from what Husserl calls "evidence" to a bona fide epiphany, that is, from the sheer apprehension of what is given in appearance to "insight" (*Einsicht*) into its actual being. Yet for such a project to amount to more than a mystical intuitionism, it has to be remembered that perception, for Rilke no less than for Husserl, is by definition a temporal event whose syntheses depend on the operation of phantasy. To clinch the

---

112. Cézanne 2013, 339; see also 336.
113. Meyer 1963, 259.

point, a brief return to Husserl's 1907 lectures, *Thing and Space*, is in order. Conceding that his examples of perception thus far have been something of an "idealizing fiction," Husserl notes that, just as a thing is always "apprehended" (*aufgefasst*) in time so consciousness, too, undergoes more or less continuous mutation. Considered as a temporal sequence, all apprehension involves a continual synthesizing of "fulfilled" (*erfüllte*) intentions with aspects as yet unfulfilled (anticipated) and awaiting future confirmation or correction. Rather than being grounded in a stable and instantaneously "evident" intuition, perception continually transcends what is manifestly (*leibhaft*) given to it. Consequently, "any perception of a thing involves a certain movement beyond what is encompassed by appearance proper [Nun gehört zu jeder Dingwahrnehmung ein gewisses Hinausgehen über das in eigentliche Erscheinung Fallende]." What's more, such a "reaching-beyond may well turn out to be mere misapprehension [dieses Hinausgreifen kann sehr wohl ein sich Vergreifen sein]."[114]

It is at this point that Husserl's and Rilke's paths sharply diverge. For Husserl, what "fulfills" an intention is the phenomenon's adequation to it, its intrinsic "evidence." By contrast, for Rilke and most modernists, the adequation of mind and world, consciousness and the phenomenon, is a dynamic, often disruptive event that ultimately resists containment by any conception extrinsic to it. For Rilke, all "intuiting" (*Anschauen*) is an excess of appearance, its saturation with an epiphanic presence impossible to contain by any known discursive and conceptual technique. To his credit, Husserl acknowledges an ineluctable dynamism at the heart of phenomena, a gravitational pull made manifest by the fact that they cannot be apprehended instantaneously—as the concept of "intuition" (*Anschauung*) might suggest—but exfoliate into countless aspects that await their synthesis in consciousness. Crucially, once perception is understood as inherently temporal, its synthesis requires not only the operation of phantasy but, along with it, a key trope of metaphysical realism: teleology. For the temporal sequence of a thing's aspectual presentations to issue in a coherent perception, it "must be governed by a certain teleology [Die Erscheinungsreihe ist durchherrscht von einer gewissen Teleologie]."[115] A book read backwards, a melody listened to in reverse, will not amount to a meaningful or "fulfilled" (*erfüllte*) intention. For the sequential aspects of an object-presentation to be synthesized into a meaningful whole, whatever feature happens to be apprehended right now furnishes not merely its own "evidence" but simultaneously foreshadows aspects yet to be apprehended.

---

114. Husserl 1991, 86, 96 / 1997, 73, 81 (§§ 26, 29).

115. Husserl 1991, 103 / 1997, 86 (§ 30), p. 103. As Husserl puts it elsewhere, "to understand knowledge is to clarify generally the teleological interconnections of knowledge [die TELEOLOGISCHEN ZUSAMMENHÄNGE der Erkenntnis zu genereller Klärung zu bringen]" (Husserl 1950, 57 / 1999, 43).

Any succession of discrete "aspects" (*Abschattungen*) synthesized in perception thus pivots on "another, denser and more tightly woven play of intentions and fulfillment [ein anderes, engeres und hier eingeflochtenes Spiel von Intentionen und Erfüllungen]." Put differently, the very coherence of what is evidently given in intuition demands that consciousness synthesize all "presentations" (*Darstellungen*), including those of aspects either no longer or not yet present. For "the consciousness of givenness is not completed *per se*, is not categorically valid, but points beyond itself; it intimates what is properly intended [es weist über sich hinaus; es ist Andeutung für das eigentlich Gemeinte]." All perception of a thing hinges on a synthesis of sorts, that is, on an image mediating present ("fulfilled") intentions with those that have either faded from view or have yet to come into focus. As Husserl remarks elsewhere, "Pure vision [*das Schauen*] extends beyond the temporal punctum of the 'now', and . . . is capable of intentionally fixating that which no longer is [*das jetzt nicht mehr seiende*]." Indeed, from a phenomenological standpoint, "perception and imagination are entirely equivalent—the same essence can be seen in both [für die Wesensbetrachtung rangiert Wahrnehmung und Phantasievorstellung ganz gleich, aus beiden ist dasselbe Wesen gleich gut herauszuschauen]."[116] If our apprehension of an appearance is to issue in a bona fide perception, every discrete aspect must be imbued with an "intimation" (*Andeutung*) of the fullness that is ultimately and properly "intended" (*gemeint*). This implies (to Husserl's acute vexation) that phantasy must generate an image capable of "supporting intentions that point in the direction of the more complete presentation [es trägt Intentionen, die in Richtung auf vollkommenere Darstellungen weisen]."

Husserl's deictic (and notably dynamic) turn of phrase (*weisen*) shows how profoundly consciousness is enmeshed with "presentation" (*Darstellung*) and its constitutive "medium"—the image: "and these intentions refer to [the object] through the intervention of presentations which by their very essence are mediating" (und sie weisen darauf [auf den Gegenstand] hin durch das Medium der ihrem Wesen nach vermittelnden Darstellungen).[117] As they smooth the passage from apprehension to perception, phantasy and its proper medium, the image, reveal cognition and

---

116. Husserl 1950, 68/1999, 50. Husserl emphatically restates the main point: "Imagination . . . not only functions in the same way as perception in the consideration of essence; it also seems that *singular* things are *given* in it, even given with evidence [Phantasie fungiert aber nicht nur für die Wesensbetrachtung gleich der Wahrnehmung, sie scheint auch in sich selbst SINGULÄRE GEGEBEN-HEITEN zu enthalten, und zwar als wirklich evidente Gegebenheiten]" (69 / 50).

117. Husserl 1991, 107 / 1997, 90 (§ 32); yet again, Husserl hedges on whether this type of mediation is even conceivable without phantasy: "Whether phantasy plays a role or not, . . . still the significance is there, and in its essence resides the 'reference' to possible fulfillment in the explicating presentational continuity [Ob die Phantasie mitspielt oder nicht . . . Bedeutung ist da, und in ihrem Wesen liegt der 'Hinweis' auf mögliche Erfüllung in der explizierenden Darstellungskontinuität]" (108 / 91).

creativity to be inextricably woven together. For the early Husserl at least, our grasp of appearances necessarily rests on something more than what Kant had termed the "reproductive imagination." Once again, Wordsworth's suggestive formulation "the mighty world / Of eye, and ear,—both what they half create, / And what perceive" resurfaces as Husserl confronts the fact that a strict replication of the visible, what he calls pure "appresentation" (*Appräsentation*) without "presentation" (*Darstellung*), would be empty and meaningless.[118] We are a long way off from what, beginning with his *Ideas I* and culminating in his *Cartesian Meditations*, Husserl will term the "passive synthesis" of consciousness with "absolute givenness," a notion critiqued incisively by Jean-Luc Marion.[119] The question of whether the "synthesis" of noësis and noëma is passive-receptive or dynamic-creative has a decisive bearing on the role that phantasy and image play in the apprehension of any appearance.

Once again, we find ourselves confronting the old Platonic question, namely, whether the image is essentially constitutive or merely derivative of Being. Where Husserl is concerned, answering the question depends largely on how we understand his concept of the *epoché*, a task greatly complicated by Husserl's often-ambiguous formulations. Thus, in his *Ideas*, Husserl's diction slips from a strictly heuristic characterization of *epoché* as incidentally "suspending" (*aussetzen*) any positing of real entities external to consciousness toward purposely "decommissioning" that very thesis (*wir "schalten sie aus"*).[120] Either way, it turns out that the contingent nature of the external world, the "bracketing" of which supposedly enables the project of transcendental phenomenology itself, ultimately resurfaces in the noëma itself. For inasmuch as phantasy, image (*Bild*), and presentation (*Darstellung*) facilitate the constitution of the phenomenon *in* and *for* consciousness, the *external* contingency that the phenomenological reduction means to quarantine for the time being resurfaces as the *internal* contingency of creative phantasy without which there would be no perception in the first place. All apprehending of things in their "absolute givenness" pivots on a creative dimension that appears to be woven into the very texture of human consciousness. Put differently, Husserl's notion of "immediate evidence"— that is, "the givenness that categorically rules out all meaningful doubt"—turns out to be indissolubly entwined with an epiphanic dimension. As Hans Urs von Balthasar had observed, the "irreality of the factual world [*Tatsachenwelt*], with which phenomenology avowedly was not concerned, returns within the *epoché* [*Klammer*] as the irreality of the noëma itself." For the intimate filiation of noësis and noëma is

---

118. Wordsworth and Coleridge 2002, 113 ("Tintern Abbey," lines 105–7).

119. Marion's *Being Given* offers arguably the most scrupulous discussion of the concept of "givenness" in phenomenology (2002a, 7–70), including its function within the broader economy of Husserl's "reduction" (14–27).

120. Husserl 2009, 63 (§ 31). "We place it as it were [*gleichsam*] 'out of action,' we 'suspend it,' we 'bracket it' [*klammern sie ein*]" (Husserl 2014, 54).

such "that active-noëtic operations always end up transforming the noëma and contribute to its constitution [daß aktiv-noëtische Operationen jeweils das Noëma verändern und zu seinem Aufbau beitragen]."[121] It is this creative dimension, dealt with equivocally at best in Husserl's early writings and gradually sidelined in his later writings, that features prominently in Rilke's mature lyric works, particularly in his *Neue Gedichte* (1907), to which we now turn.

SELF-CONSUMMATION OF THE LYRIC IMAGE: FROM VISUAL TO SPATIAL EPIPHANY, 1907–1914

Published in December 1907 and November 1908, the two volumes comprising Rilke's *New Poems* (of which the second carried the dedication *À mon grand ami Rodin*) proved a major success, with more than 36,000 copies sold in Rilke's lifetime. While also including numerous works of narrative poetry, which will not be considered here, the lyrics featured in this collection break decisively with the Impressionist and Symbolist conception of "expressive lyricism" (*Stimmungslyrik*). Rather than focus on "great things and thoughts," Rilke writes, his objective henceforth will be to explore "inconspicuous [*das Unscheinbare*], even ugly subjects" and to accede to their "indescribable demands." In so doing, the artist, "who by his very nature will in many respects always remain a spectator, will in that role experience life in its *entirety*, that is, the world as a whole" (*KA* 1:902). Echoing Husserl's outline of a phenomenology of perception in *Thing and Space* of the same year, Rilke's reconstitution of lyric form as *Dinggedicht* bears significant affinity to Husserl's *epoché*. He, too, proceeds by disembedding a given "thing" and suspending any "positing" (*Setzen*) of it as an objective reality independent of its mode of appearance. Contextual determinants are largely stripped away, except for those manifestly enmeshed with the principal thing as it registers in intuition. Some of the "things" taken up in these poems involve natural entities (a panther, a gazelle, or a blue hydrangea), while others fall in the category of artifacts or artistic performances involving human beings ("Archaic Torso of Apollo," "Spanish Dancer," "Cathedrals," etc.). Still, such categorizing misses the salient point—previously made by Cézanne ("I paint a head like a door")—namely, that prior to all perception, naming, and classifying there is the elemental reality of the thing as it unconditionally gives and constitutes itself in appearance. As a first example, let us consider Rilke's 1906 "The Rose Window" ("Die Fensterrose").

Da drin: das träge Treten ihrer Tatzen
macht eine Stille, die dich fast verwirrt;

---

121. Balthasar 1998, 3:117 (trans. mine).

und wie dann plötzlich eine von den Katzen
den Blick an ihr, der hin und wieder irrt,
gewaltsam in ihr großes Auge nimmt,—
den Blick, der, wie von eines Wirbels Kreis
ergriffen, eine kleine Weile schwimmt
und dann versinkt und nichts mehr von sich weiß, .
wenn dieses Auge, welches scheinbar ruht,
sich auftut und zusammenschlägt mit Tosen
und ihn hineinreißt bis ins rote Blut -:
So griffen einstmals aus dem Dunkelsein
der Kathedralen große Fensterrosen
ein Herz und rissen es in Gott hinein.[122]

The poem's main formal conceit involves reversing the order of subject matter and simile. Thus, the first eleven lines develop an intricate image of two kinds of gazes, human and feline, and their abrupt and unfathomable encounter. A recurrent focus of Rilke's middle period, this sudden meeting of two ontologically distinct spheres foregrounds two kinds of seeing: a human gaze vacillating between distraction and desire, a gaze "that keeps straying [*irrt*]" and, on the other hand, the cat's eye—hypnotic, invasive, and all but devouring of its human counterpart.[123] Most of the poem explores the dramaturgy of these two types of gaze while withholding the "thing" or "noëma" that is their proper correlate. Instead, the first eleven lines thoroughly dismantle the anthropocentric gaze and its presumed Olympian self-sufficiency, which had established itself as *the* paradigm of human cognition in the writings of Alberti, Brunelleschi, and other leading scientists of the fifteenth-century Florentine Renaissance. In Rilke's poem, the human being's illusion of optical and epistemic prowess is suddenly shattered; it abruptly "drowns" (*versinkt*), being consumed by the deceptively inferior "thing" on which the human gaze had so casually alighted just moments before.

---

122. *KA* 1:465–66. "In there: the lazy pacing of their paws / creates a stillness that's almost dizzying; / and as one of the cats then suddenly / takes the gaze that watches it carelessly // and snatches it into its own great eye,- / and that gaze, as if caught in a whirlpool's / circle, for a little while stays afloat / and then goes under and is lost to oblivion, // when this eye, which apparently rests / opens and slams shut with a roaring / and yanks it all the way into the blood –: // thus in olden times out of the darkness / the cathedral's great rose windows / would seize hearts and drag them in to God." (Rilke 2001a, 53; trans. modified).

123. See Fischer's discussion of Rilke's interest in the biological research of Jakob von Uexküll (2015, 231–53), with whom the poet was personally acquainted. Uexküll's quasi-phenomenological approach to the distinctive "organization" (*Bauplan*) of animals, and their embeddedness in a specific "biotope" (*Umwelt*), resonates in numerous lyrics of Rilke's middle period.

As is often the case in Rilke's *Dinggedichte*, the lyric statement pivots on a reversal of sorts. Suddenly enfeebled and paralyzed, the human gaze finds its presumptive dominion over the visible world challenged by a being whose very otherness threatens to consume and utterly transform the beholder, as when the cat's eye "slams shut with a roar / and tears [him] all the way inside the blood [*und ihn hineinreißt bis ins rote Blut*]." In the compact phenomenological meditation unfolded by Rilke's lyric, the "thing" in question is utterly transformed, stripped of its solid and inert otherness (*entdinglicht*), and reconstituted as an agency of unfathomable power.[124] In its inexplicably dynamic and charismatic presentation, the thing—which, again, is present only as a phenomenon registering in visual experience—triggers a "reversal" (*Umschlag*) typically signaled by some conspicuously placed adverb (*plötzlich, auf einmal, doch, aber*).[125] Only now that the lyric has staged the defeat of the Cartesian gaze—so methodically diffident in its outlook on the phenomenal world, and so suffused with epistemic hubris—does Rilke unveil the poem's true subject for which everything until now had served as a simile. The original, iridescent "eye" turns out to be the kind found in great medieval cathedrals, such as in Chartres (also featured in Rilke's "L'ange du meridien") and in Strasbourg (fig. 8.5). Whereas modernity can experience the sudden dismantling of its anthropocentric model of vision only as catastrophic annihilation, "formerly" (*einstmals*) the reversal of "seeing" (*videre*) into "being-seen" (*videri*), as Nicholas of Cusa had put it, had been embraced as the spiritual consummation of earthly existence. Moreover, in framing the entire lyric statement within a single syntactic structure (and thus dissolving the sonnet form's traditional reliance on strong contrasts), Rilke reinforces the sense that vision, rather than constituting a discretionary *act* firmly governed by subjective intention, tends to evolve into an inescapable and overwhelming *event*.[126] "Artworks," he writes, "are always the result of having-been-in-danger [*des in-Gefahr-Gewesenseins*], of having taken experience to its very limit. . . . The farther we proceed, the more proper, personal, and unique the experience turns out; finally, the artifact [*Kunstding*] is the necessary, irrepressible, and if possible definitive expression of that uniqueness.

---

124. The term *Entdinglichung*, a "derealization" of sorts, is Ulrich Fülleborn's, quoted by Müller, in Engel 2013, 300; this transposition of ephemeral things into the "indestructible medium of the word" will be a central concern of the *Duino Elegies* (1922); see Jamme 1992 (quote from 388); Pfau 2018b.

125. See Engel's commentary (*KA* 1:915); Müller, in Engel 2013, 296–318; Fischer 2015, 215–98.

126. On the face of it, the sonnet form, traditionally meant to express a particular subjective state or feeling, would seem inapposite to Rilke's project of a *Dinglyrik*. Yet Rilke reshapes the form, largely dissolving its traditional Petrarchan bifurcation, while also eschewing its highly self-conscious, Shakespearean inflection. Instead, the form's rhyme scheme is subordinate to expansive syntactic form; enjambment becomes the norm; and in some cases (including "The Rose Window" and "Roman Fountain") a single syntactic unit spans the entire lyric.

Figure 8.5.
Rose Window,
Strasbourg Cathedral

Therein lies the immeasurable contribution of the artifact to an individual's mastery of his life—that it is his summa [*seine Zusammenfassung*], the bead in the rosary, where life says a prayer, the eternally valid proof he is granted of his unity and truth [*Beweis seiner Einheit und Wahrhaftigkeit*]" (*RB* 1:259).

Still, as the qualifying temporal adverb *formerly* (*einstmals*) suggests, the modern individual's capacity for intuitive vision, and for letting itself be guided and shaped by such vision, appears greatly atrophied. The whole point of the poem, after all, is to illustrate for us, in the simile of the feline eye transfixing the human being, what it was like, long ago, for celebrants at Mass to find themselves enthralled by the splendor of sunlight breaking through a cathedral's stained-glass rose window— a spiritual experience that, it is implied, has all but vanished by the start of the twentieth century. What, then, is the relation between simile and original, between the rose window that "formerly" mediated the absolute certitude, timelessness, and mercy of God's transcendent gaze and its simile, the hypnotic, vaguely menacing gaze with which a cat's eyes may so unexpectedly transfix some hapless human being? Put differently, is it plausible to speak of an epiphanic experience without a metaphysics? Or can the former only reinforce our sense of terminal estrangement from the certitudes of metaphysical realism and the eschatological plenitude that the rose window formerly mediated for those gathered in medieval cathedrals? Can the epiphanic still carry meaning in an era dominated by naturalistic epistemologies and strictly immanent forms of explanation and cognition?

While by 1907 Rilke's view of Christianity proves deeply skeptical, if not outright dismissive, his preoccupation with the potentially numinous implications of visual phenomena—such as had preoccupied Christian theology for some fifteen hundred years—seems to grow only more pronounced. Indeed, Rilke seems convinced that the visible is a profoundly meaningful gift rather than a mere aggregate of value-neutral objects and that by affording visual experience the phenomenological scrutiny it so richly deserves we find the "thing" in question to have agency and to be making a positive claim on the beholder: "Our dear God has placed us in the midst of things not for the purpose of selecting [*nicht um auszuwählen*] but to practice *receiving* [*das Nehmen . . . zu betreiben*] thoroughly and magnificently" (*RB* 1:224). His "perceptual faith" (Merleau-Ponty) is on full display in "Blaue Hortensie" (Blue Hydrangea) of July 1906:

> So wie das letzte Grün in Farbentiegeln
> sind diese Blätter, trocken, stumpf und rauh,
> hinter den Blütendolden, die ein Blau
> nicht auf sich tragen, nur von ferne spiegeln.
>
> Sie spiegeln es verweint und ungenau,
> als wollten sie es wiederum verlieren,
> und wie in alten blauen Briefpapieren
> ist Gelb in ihnen, Violett und Grau;
>
> Verwaschnes wie an einer Kinderschürze,
> Nichtmehrgetragnes, dem nichts mehr geschieht:
> wie fühlt man eines kleinen Lebens Kürze.
>
> Doch plötzlich scheint das Blau sich zu verneuen
> in einer von den Dolden, und man sieht
> ein rührend Blaues sich vor Grünem freuen.[127]

Lacking a direct article, the title of Rilke's poem evokes the kind of caption given to a painting. Indeed, at first glance the sonnet reads like an ekphrasis of a (painted or real?) blue hydrangea. Yet soon we realize that the descriptive focus is placed not on

---

127. *KA* 1:481. "These leaves are like the last green / in the paint pots, dried up, dull, and rough / behind the flowered umbels whose blue / is not their own, only mirrored from far away. // In their mirror it is vague and tear-stained, / as if deep down they wished to lose it; / and as with [old] blue writing paper / there is yellow in them, violet and gray; // washed out as on a child's pinafore, / no longer worn things, which nothing can befall: / how one feels a small life's shortness. // But suddenly the blue seems to revive / in one of the umbels, and one sees / a touching blue's rejoicing in green" (Rilke 2001a, 97).

the "thing" per se but on its experience as an image. Whereas ekphrasis is typically conceived of as a sophisticated verbal conjuring or simulating of an actual or painted object, the descriptive approach of Rilke's *New Poems* recalls older, inherently spiritual modes of ekphrastic writing such as Paulus Silentiarius's or Patriarch Photios's descriptions of the visual and spiritual impact made by the restored mosaics in Hagia Sophia on their sixth- and ninth-century beholders, respectively. Likewise, for Rilke it is only insofar as lyric form can successfully identify significant aspects within the beholder's *response* that the visible thing in question constitutes itself. Phenomenality and being appear all but convertible, albeit with this important, Postimpressionist qualification that for Rilke, and also for the guarded modernism of the Acmeist and Imagist movements, any subjective impression is always indexed to a noncontingent "thing" (*Ding*) on whose ontological givenness and reality it cannot supervene. To further close in on Rilke's compressed, ephemeral lyric utterance, it helps to draw a heuristic distinction between its phenomenological and rhetorical dimensions. At its most elemental level, Rilke's poem aims to capture how color is "apprehended" (*aufgefasst*) and how its utter specificity registers in consciousness. That is its phenomenological objective, and that is where a reading of the poem ought to begin.

Now, it so happens that the phenomenon of color prompts Husserl, writing in the same year as Rilke, to rethink the concept of givenness as a matter of degree and temporal progression rather than as an absolute and instantaneous occurrence. Speaking of "coloration" of, say, a geometric form, Husserl notes that color admits of an "increase or decrease of the fullness of the givenness" (*Steigerung oder Minderung der Gegebenheitsfülle*). Yet such intensification is not merely adventitious but is built into the very intentionality of "color consciousness" (*Farbbewußtsein*). In seeing a particular tone of color, we mentally envision its ideal fulfillment: "we are not at all content with the incomplete" chromatic tone but, on the contrary, receive it as "an intimation of what is properly intended" (*Andeutung für das eigentlich Gemeinte*). The visible color "bears intentions that point in the direction of the more complete presentations" (*vollkommenere Darstellungen*) of "the 'object itself' as that would come to givenness."[128] Husserl's observation chimes with the later Cézanne's well-known penchant for reapplying color so as to arrive at progressively denser pigmentation and fuller saturation of a specific shade. The greater or lesser saturation of our "apprehension" (*Auffassung*) of color, and the resulting color-consciousness, shows that seeing is not a passive intaking of data but an active visualizing and, as such, is inextricably entwined with cognition.

In responding to the visible, consciousness thus appears imbued with an indelible expectancy, a "thoroughgoing intention" (*eine durchgehende Intention*) toward a

---

128. Husserl 1991, 106–7 / 1997, 89–90 (§ 32).

"telos" of the utmost plenitude of appearance as such, "where nothing more is missing [das Ziel . . . wo in Hinsicht der Gegebenheitsfülle nichts mehr zu vermissen ist]." We can see why Husserl consistently warned against conflating a given appearance with the thing itself. For the visible amounts to an "intimation" of a reality of which it typically falls short, yet which can be anticipated and pursued by consciousness only on the basis of an actual appearance. To be conscious means not only to *receive* but also to *complete* the phenomenal world. All presentations "by their very essence are mediating" an as yet unrealized, perhaps never entirely attainable, total givenness (sie weisen darauf hin durch das Medium der ihrem Wesen nach vermittelnden Darstellungen).[129] Insofar as a given "appearance" arrests, focuses, and sustains our "attention" (*Aufmerksamkeit*) it is experienced as infused with value; it is inherently "deserving of notice" (*merk-würdig*) because we intuit that a given phenomenon holds meanings begging our hermeneutic scrutiny: "The first appearance to arise is already significance [*Die erste auftauchende Erscheinung ist schon Bedeutung*], and it already signifies givenness. Nevertheless, it will still be interpreted in some direction [*auf etwas gedeutet werden*]." Precisely this temporal, nascently teleological quality of seeing and visualizing, this movement or "play of intention and fulfillment" (*dieses Spiel von Intention und Erfüllung*), also lies at the very heart of Rilke's poem.[130]

Perhaps most striking about Rilke's poem is the way in which a process as seemingly timeless as the apprehension of color is shown to be suffused with a highly complex temporal dimension. From the first line, the salient point is that, like all visible matter, color inevitably *fades*, thereby rendering the passage of time *visible*. If the poem's title evokes associations of vibrant, luminous organic life, the first lines seemingly defeat any such expectations. Color here manifests itself less as a visual than as a tactile sensation, little more than a calcified, chromatically ambiguous substance that remains at the bottom of a color pan. "Dry, dull and rough," its brittle texture hints at a onetime saturation that is no longer visible. Paradoxically, it is precisely the living hydrangea whose matte petals, "tear-stained and vague" (*verweint und ungenau*), evoke an aura of depletion and loss rather than fullness and presence. Instead of manifesting "blue" as a visible plenitude, they evoke its Platonic *eidos* only as something that, perhaps, once was but now appears altogether irretrievable. If Husserl's phenomenological account of "color-consciousness" conceives, say, the color blue as a Platonic *eidos* awaiting its fulfillment in the unspecified future, Rilke's similes tend to locate such plenitude in an irretrievable past. We hear echoes of Schiller's naive/sentimental distinction, that is, of the paradoxical fact that the integrity of sen-

---

129. Ibid.; it is a common mistake, Husserl notes, to consider "the pre-empirical color as one with (or as only un-essentially different from) the quality itself, the objective color" (1991, 117 / 1997, 98 [§ 34]).

130. Husserl 1991, 107–8 / 1997, 90–91 (§ 32).

sation associated with Schiller's "Naïve" can register in consciousness only as something lost and irretrievable, an impression reinforced by Rilke's emotionally tinged neologism *verweint* ("tear-stained") and the hydrangea's association with childhood ("washed out as on a child's apron"). The blue's fullness subsists only in a kind of Proustian, involuntary memory referring the beholder to a past whose connection to the present appears to have been decisively ruptured ("no longer worn things, which nothing can befall").

Yet like all great art—which arguably more than philosophical prose is oriented toward an imagined addressee—Rilke's lyric also seeks to bring about moments of recognition in the reader. In the event, the experience of loss, the encounter with colors that have irretrievably faded, is more than a matter of subtraction. Not to be reduced to a contingent absence, loss instead appears an integral feature of all human, time-bound existence. As Rilke comments in a letter to his wife, "We are also attached to *this*: to this fading and its tender, somewhat plaintive nuances. . . . We shall finally succeed to let everything contained in life's hands be valid, and to do so with an expectant, willing, as yet somewhat amateurish sense of justice [wir hängen auch daran: an diesem Welksein und an des Welkseins zarten, ein wenig klagenden Nuancen. . . . Wir kommen dazu, in des Lebens Händen alles gelten zu lassen in abwartender, in williger, noch ein wenig anfängerhafter Gerechtigkeit]" (*KA* 1:942). Rilke's unfailing alertness to riches contained in even the most ephemeral things and states of consciousness helps put us on guard against a strictly antinomian reading of the final tercet. It is here that the poem's rhetorical objective, namely, to deploy images and similes so as to trigger fleeting moments of recollection and self-recognition in the reader, emerges most fully.

Still, what at first blush seems a decisive "reversal" (*Umschlag*)—"But suddenly . . . "—is not a case of some transcendent power supervening, in Romantic-speculative fashion, on the material deficiencies of immanent existence. On the contrary, the agency for such "renewal" once again resides, not *beyond*, but *in* the phenomenal world: "But suddenly the blue seems to revive in one of the umbels." The closing lines, and indeed the poem as a whole, have received an inordinate amount of attention from readers advocating or contesting the viability of phenomenological interpretations of *New Poems*. Wolfgang Müller for one deems Rilke's lyric oeuvre fundamentally incommensurable with Husserl's phenomenological reduction as defined in *Ideas* (1913). Thus he rejects Käthe Hamburger's construal of "Blue Hydrangea" as a prime example of Husserl's "eidetic intuition" (*Wesenserschauung*) whereby consciousness lays claim to an object's essence without venturing any actual predications about it.[131] Instead, he maintains, the valence of the poem's blue "remains

---

131. See Hamburger 1966, 179–268; and, for a critique of her reading of "Blaue Hortensie," Müller 1999. Against Müller, Fischer rightly notes that, even as "Rilke does not perform the

contextually determined" and, in contrast to Husserl's eidetic intuition, does not categorically exclude "inessential" and "imperfect" elements. Drawing attention to the way that, in the poem's closing tercet, the abrupt rejuvenation of color and color-consciousness arises from a concrete and contingent moment of perception, Müller contends that any affinity between Rilke and Husserl is decidedly *not* to be found in the concept of the phenomenological reduction and the "eidetic intuition" it means to lay bare.[132] Drawing on Merleau-Ponty rather than Husserl, Luke Fischer concurs, observing that what links Rilke's poetry to phenomenology is a concept of "knowing, not [as] an imposition of meaning from a detached point of view, but [as] an understanding *out of* lived events."[133]

Yet to distinguish between "a phenomenology of the everyday" and a "phenomenology of the exceptional," even if the two states in question are to "be regarded as parts of a spectrum," remains unsatisfactory.[134] For it obscures the founding and form-giving premise of Rilke's *Neue Gedichte*: that the exceptional already slumbers *in* and erupts *from within* the ordinary rather being superinduced on it as a consequence of external or internal contingencies. To disaggregate the quotidian from the sublime and to posit them as distinct qualities or essences not only distorts an altogether central aspect to Rilke's lyric oeuvre during his middle years; it also misconstrues Husserl's development of transcendental phenomenology between 1906 and 1913. For starting with *The Idea of Phenomenology* (1906), Husserl, too, understands "intuition" (*Anschauung*) to involve an irruption of the epiphanic into the realm of "evidence" (*Evidenz*) such that the act of intuition and my consciousness of it are altogether fused. Moreover, having previously shown how all intuition pivots on the creative role of phantasy and its constitutive medium, the image, Husserl finds himself repeatedly confronted with (and often vexed by) the indelible, "pre-predicative" nexus between "ordinary perception" (*Wahrnehmung*) and "creative vision" (*Phanta-*

---

phenomenological reduction [in "Blaue Hortensie"] in a *Husserlian* manner, that does not mean that Rilke's procedure is not phenomenological" (2015, 217).

132. Müller 1999, 225–27. See Husserl's programmatic characterization of eidetic intuition early in *Ideas I*: "The intuition of an essence [*Wesensanschauung*] is consciousness of something, an 'object,' a something on which it focuses and which is 'itself given' in the intuition. . . . Every possible object or, to put it logically, *any subject of possible, true predications*' has precisely *its* ways, prior to all predicative thinking, of coming into view, a view that presents it, intuits it, at times even encountering it as it is 'itself in person,' 'apprehending' it. Thus, discernment of an essence *is* an intuition, and, if it is discernment in the exact sense and not a mere and perhaps vague envisaging, then it is an intuiting that affords the essence *in an originary way*, apprehending it in its selfhood 'in person.' [Wesenserschauung IST also Anschauung . . . im prägnanten Sinn und nicht eine bloße und vielleicht vage Vergegenwärtigung, [sondern] . . . eine originärgebende Anschauung, das Wesen in seiner "leibhaften" Selbstheit erfassend]" (Husserl 2009, 15 / 2014, 13 [§ 3]).

133. Fischer 2015, 65.

134. Ibid., 41 f.

sie), between the visible and the invisible. It is here that his phenomenological project comes face-to-face with the same metaphysical entanglements that also inform a good deal of modernist poetics.

Thinking through the numinous implications of intuition, however, has proven a challenge for which the antimetaphysical pathos animating much literary criticism since the 1960s has left that discipline exceedingly ill prepared. Thus, while acknowledging "the nearly ubiquitous presence" of the epiphanic in Rilke's *Neue Gedichte*, Müller is quick to circumnavigate such metaphysical concerns by characterizing intuition as altogether context-dependent and by defining the epiphanic as a strictly formal-aesthetic development ("a concept of modern poetics").[135] More cautiously, Fischer insists "that an invisible of *things* and the *world* attains a more perfect visibility *in* the work of art" and that the "invisible is revealed through a deep attentiveness to the exterior or visible," thus potentially allowing the beholder to "discern an epiphanic significance in it."[136] This rings true as far as it goes, though we ought to stress that for Rilke a work of art is less the source of epiphanic vision than a response to it, that is, an acknowledgment and articulation of its anterior reality and indisputable presence. In the event, the tercet concluding "Blaue Hortensie" offers a fine case in point: "Doch plötzlich scheint das Blau sich zu verneuen / in einer von den Dolden, und man sieht / ein rührend Blaues sich vor Grünem freuen" (But suddenly the blue seems to revive / in one of the umbels, and one sees / a touching blue's rejoicing in green). The suggestion, though advanced in rather tenuous phrasing, is that the revivifying of a richly saturated and pigmented blue is intuitively evident and, thus, cannot be dismissed as but a case of illusion or projection.[137] Still, we must ask, is it finally the color that is objectively "moving" (*rührend*), or is it the beholder who is subjectively moved in intuition? To translate the closing line's "rührend" as "touching" resolves the ambiguity in favor of the latter, thereby giving a misleadingly sentimental slant to the poem's conclusion. To do so is to posit a

---

135. Müller 1999, 226. There is no time here to explore the theological origins of the epiphanic in patristic, mostly Eastern writing (e.g., Epiphanius, *Contra Haereses*, II.1, ch. 27; Gregory of Nazianzen, *Oration* 38) and, eventually, also in the West (e.g., Gregory the Great, *Sermon* 34). Suffice it to say that the complementary relationship between Nativity and Epiphany, the event of Christ's birth and its subsequently being witnessed (adoration of the Magi) and sacramentally affirmed (Jesus's baptism), bears an intriguing affinity to Husserl's dual accreditation of the phenomenon as both "embodied" (*leibhaft*) and "credible" (*glaubhaft*); see *Thing and Space* (§§ 5, 9).

136. Fischer 2015, 135, 145.

137. Green's choice of "revive" is a necessarily imperfect rendering of the neologism *verneuen*, which Rilke evidently preferred over the more (or too) obvious *erneuern* or *verjüngen*. Yet as so often, the prefix *ver-* also connotes some perceptual or cognitive misadventure, a deception, illusion, or gratuitous projection, a possibility further kept open by the auxiliary use of "seems" (*scheint sich . . . zu verneuen*").

supervening affectivity for which there no longer appears to be any phenomenal correlate—in Husserlian terms, to conceive of a noësis without any noëma.

Neither Rilke nor Husserl, however, appears disposed to accept such a scenario. In fact, Rilke not only insists that inner and outer experience must be precisely aligned and that inner states wholly bereft of an objective phenomenological correlate are at the very least dubious; he also holds that the (in origin Romantic) distinction between mundane and sublime experiences ought to be jettisoned altogether. Instead, what Rilke calls "the felicitous coalescence of fulfillment and intuition in a poem [was in einem Gedicht . . . an Gelingen und Einsicht glücklich zusammenkommt]" involves an "always being-able-to [was man immer 'können' kann]." It thus depends far more "on understanding, reflection, insight, experience . . . than those momentous upheavals of the inner life that are beyond anyone's influence." At the heart of intuitive seeing, then, are "not exaltations [nicht Exaltationen], certainly not those, for otherwise they could never effect something so indescribably real within the mind [sonst könnten sie nicht so unbeschreiblich Reales im Geistigen durchsetzen]" (RB 1:478, 379). Defining of modernist epiphany is a thing's unfathomable capacity for initiating a vision (Schau) that unveils the very being of which the thing itself is a manifestation; and it is in the modality of an image that this unveiling takes place. As Rilke puts it in an early letter, "all things are there in order to become images for us in some manner [alle Dinge sind ja dazu da, damit sie uns Bilder werden in irgendeinem Sinn]."[138] The artwork, whether poem or painting, responds to, and actively works through, the intuitive vision resulting from a thing having manifested itself qua image.

Particularly the non-narrative poems of Rilke's middle period appear consumed with capturing the phenomenology of the thing-become-image by decisively disentangling the lyric image from any residual affiliations with classical rhetoric and its schematization of affective states—a development whose beginnings in German literature are often traced to Goethe's Sesenheim lyrics of 1772.[139] Not only do Rilke's New Poems extend this disengagement of poetry and rhetoric; they also predate by at least half a decade the "Imagism" of H.D., Pound, Lowell, and Williams, in particular the emphasis placed in various "imagist" manifestos of 1912 and 1913 on treating a given "thing" with the utmost directness and, to that end, rejecting any words that do not demonstrably contribute to the presentation of a thing. Likewise, Rilke foreshadows the Russian school known as "Acmeism" that, also beginning in 1912, had begun as a rejection of Symbolism's perceived vagueness and exaggerated affectivity. For young poets such as Akhmatova, Mandelstam, and Zenkevich, the aim of poetry was precision and palpability rather than conjuring states of opaque and transient inspi-

---

138. RB 1:41 (27 May 1899).
139. For the most detailed study of that shift, see Campe 1990, 487–554.

ration. Navigating between the political utopias and iconoclast fervor of the Futurists and the perceived bankruptcy of Symbolist tradition, Imagism, Acmeism, and Rilke's (Baudelaire-inspired) poetics of "concrete saying" (*sachliches Sagen*) all seek to restore the image to its originary (Platonic) function—namely, as medium rather than as a form of subjective self-expression or objective reference.

In a letter from 1907, Rilke remarks on the unique capacity of images to stabilize the relationship of consciousness (*unser Inneres*) vis-à-vis the world of things: "We place images outside ourselves; we seize every opportunity to image a world; we surround our interiority with one thing after another [Wir stellen Bilder aus uns hinaus, wir nehmen jeden Anlaß wahr, weltbildend zu werden, wir errichten Ding um Ding um unser Inneres herum]."[140] Animating his poetics is the central premise that, in Marion's formulation, "the icon does not result from a vision but provokes one. The icon is not seen, but appears. . . . [It] summons sight in letting the visible be saturated little by little with the invisible."[141] Marion's thesis comports with Rilke's poetic stance, provided we understand the (lyric) image not as an ex post facto artifact but as mediating an intuitive, and potentially epiphanic, vision. Hence, pace Müller, Rilke's poetry does not produce epiphanic images. Rather, it is inexorably led toward them by tracing how a given thing, in our intuitive and richly aspectual experience of it, is focused and synthesized unpredictably by the medium of the image. Inasmuch as "the epiphany is of something only indirectly available, something the visible object can't say itself but only nudges us towards," the image that mediates it should not be thought of as a discrete entity, let alone a rhetorical trope.[142] Rather, it coordinates the event of manifestation itself, which is to say, the advent of an intuition that, wholly exceeding the scope of the concept, "overflows with many meanings . . . each equally legitimate and rigorous, without managing either to unify them or organize them."[143]

A concluding look at the final poem in Rilke's *Neue Gedichte* (1907), "Die Rosenschale," will help pull together various strands of the present argument: (1) the structural function of "image" (*Bild*) and creative "presentation" (*Darstellung*) for a phenomenology of intuition and presentation (*Anschauung*; *Darstellung*); (2) the

---

140. *RB* 1:233 (20 January 1907). Rilke's remark is strikingly echoed by Arnold Gehlen's characterization of "presentation" (*Darstellung*) as a "transcending into this world" (ein Transzendieren ins Diesseits, aus der fließenden Zeit heraus in die Dauer, vermittelt durch ein Bild: das Göttliche gibt es nicht abstrakt, nur als Anschauliches, Leibhaft-Gewordenes, selbst Lebendiges) (2004, 62).

141. Marion 1991, 17.

142. Taylor 1989, 469; modernist "images are not simply introduced as simile or metaphor to characterize a central referent. . . . [Rather] from the Symbolists on, there has been a poetry which makes something appear by juxtaposing images. . . . The epiphany comes from between the words or images, as it were, from the force field they set up between them, and not through a central referent which they describe while transmuting" (465–66).

143. Marion 2002b, 112.

decisive shift from the natural attitude positing the reality of the object perceived to a phenomenology of manifestation, that is, of Being unveiled qua appearance; (3) the reciprocal "constituting" of appearance and consciousness; and (4) modernism's understanding of epiphanic meaning as something embedded *in* the structure of (visual) experience rather than being predicated ex post facto of ostensibly separate, mundane phenomena. By way of illustrating two fundamentally opposed forms of visual cognition, the poem opens with a jarring contrast between ferocious physical violence in the world of human affairs and the imperturbable presence of a "bowl of roses" whose manifest, if unfathomable, "thereness" suspends an outside world denatured and blinded by rage and violence.

> Zornige sahst du flackern, sahst zwei Knaben
> Zu einem Etwas sich zusammenballen,
> das Haß war und sich auf der Erde wälzte
> wie ein von Bienen überfallnes Tier;
> Schauspieler, aufgetürmte Übertreiber,
> rasende Pferde, die zusammenbrachen,
> den Blick wegwerfend, bläkend das Gebiß
> als schälte sich der Schädel aus dem Maule.
>
> Nun aber weißt du, wie sich das vergißt:
> Denn vor dir steht die volle Rosenschale,
> die unvergeßlich ist und angefüllt
> mit jenem Äußersten von Sein und Neigen,
> Hinhalten, Niemals-Gebenkönnen, Dastehn,
> das unser sein mag: Äußerstes auch uns.[144]

Verging on an Abstract Expressionism that Rilke would never quite embrace, the opening image presents human beings entangled, convulsed, and disfigured by ineffable aggression. In aspect little more than a contorted, nearly indecipherable *Gestalt*,

---

144. *KA* 1:508–9. "You've seen caged anger flare, seen two boys / roll themselves up into a knot / of pure hatred, writhing on the ground / like an animal attacked by bees; / you've seen the actors, giant exaggerators, / careening horses crashing down, / flinging their eyes away, baring their teeth / as if their skulls were peeling through their mouths. // But now you know how such things vanish: / for before you stands the full bowl of roses, / which is unforgettable, and wholly filled / with that utmost of being and bending, / of offering up, beyond power to give, of *presence*, / that might be ours: *our* utmost as well" (Rilke 2001a, 161). The description recalls Rilke's description of Rodin's groups of human bodies "touching everywhere, clinging together like animals, their jaws locked, . . . chains of bodies, arabesques and tendrils [*Er schuf Körper, die sich überall berührten und zusammenhielten wie ineinander verbissene Tiere, . . .* Ketten von Leibern, Gewinde und Ranken]" (*KA* 4:427).

the combatants have been reduced to a mere "something" (*ein Etwas*), denatured by inexplicable rage (*Zornige sahst Du flackern*), and they have notably "discarded" their power of sight (*den Blick wegwerfend*). In a brilliant and disturbing *prolepsis*, the combatants' embodied being is captured in all its transience, as the skull seems to protrude through a barely enfleshed face (*bläkend das Gebiss / als schälte sich der Schädel aus dem Maule*).

No less startling is the shift from disordered and fragmented perception to consciousness becalmed by and focused on the poem's eponymous object. Such an about-face is not, however, wrought by an act of will. Rather, as the oddly reflexive turn of phrase (*wie sich das vergißt*) suggests, the refocusing of the gaze is brought about by the imperturbable presence of the rose bowl so indelibly etched into consciousness (*unvergeßlich*). "Filled to the utmost with being and inclining" (*angefüllt mit jenem Äußersten von Sein und Neigen*), the bowl restores order to three-dimensional space without in the least reducing it, as merely contingent, ambient things might be expected to do. Instead, its "reality" and "effectivity" arises from the way that its qualities appear wholly enmeshed with the beholding consciousness: its self-focused radiance (*Sich-bescheinendes*), its delicacy (*viel Zartes*), its plentiful interiority (*lauter Inneres*), and its silent, open-ended self-disclosure (*Aufgehen ohne Ende*).

> Lautloses Leben, Aufgehn ohne Ende,
> Raum-brauchen ohne Raum von jenem Raum
> zu nehmen, den die Dinge rings verringern,
> fast nicht Umrissen-sein wie Ausgespartes
> und lauter Inneres, viel seltsam Zartes
> und Sich-bescheinendes—bis an den Rand:
> ist irgend etwas uns bekannt wie dies?[145]

The last line's ambiguous query ("is anything known to us as / like this?") can be taken either as a rhetorical question pointing to something *unprecedented* or as affirming the familiarity between consciousness and this thing as *incomparable*. Indeed, it may be precisely the profound intimacy of consciousness with its object that accounts for the uniqueness of this visual experience. As the boundaries between consciousness and its intentional object dissolve, three-dimensional, New-tonian space and the spatiotemporal nature of eidetic intuition appear no longer fungible but ontologically distinct. Whereas the former is grasped by quantification and division, the latter exhibits absolute continuity (*ohne Raum / von jenem Raum*

---

145. *KA* 1:509. "Life lived in quietness, endless opening out, / space being used without space being taken / from the space adjacent things diminish, / outline just hinted at, like ground left blank / and pure within-ness, much so strangely soft / and self-illuminating—out to the edge: / do we know anything like this?" (Rilke 2001a, 161).

zu nehmen, den die Dinge rings verringern). In a letter from 1919, Rilke recalls another such epiphany, which likewise had filled, indeed expanded, phenomenological space rather than subtracting from it: "once, on Capri, as I was standing in the garden underneath olive trees, the call of a bird, which had me close my eyes, was simultaneously within and outside of me, as in a single, continuous space of perfect extension and clarity [auf Capri einmal, als ich nachts im Garten stand, unter den Ölbäumen, und der Ruf eines Vogels, über dem ich die Augen schließen mußte, war gleichzeitig in mir und draußen wie in einem einzigen ununterschiedenen Raum von vollkommener Ausdehnung und Klarheit]."[146]

It is here that Rilke moves well beyond Husserl by focusing on the ineffable fullness of aural and visual experiences that fuse consciousness and thing in a continuous, nongeometric space (*Raum*). Fullness here does not refer merely to the multiplicity of "aspects" (*Abschattungen*) that prevent an object's spatiotemporal complexity from being taken in at once. At issue is not fullness as sheer quantity, as many-sidedness and epistemological constraint of a perception dispersed into countless aspects. Rather, fullness refers to a numinous radiance that accounts for the epiphanic structure of appearance, that is, as the event of manifestation, which does not beg causal explanation but whose splendor will cause the beholding eye to alternate between gazing with stunned absorption and closing its lids in self-protection.

> Und dann wie dies: daß ein Gefühl entsteht,
> weil Blütenblätter Blütenblätter rühren?
> Und dies: daß eins sich aufschlägt wie ein Lid,
> und drunter liegen lauter Augenlider,
> geschlossene, als ob sie, zehnfach schlafend,
> zu dämpfen hätten eines Innern Sehkraft.
> Und dies vor allem: daß durch diese Blätter
> das Licht hindurch muß. Aus den tausend Himmeln
> filtern sie langsam jenen Tropfen Dunkel,
> in dessen Feuerschein das wirre Bündel
> der Staubgefäße sich erregt und aufbäumt.
> Und die Bewegung in den Rosen, sieh:
> Gebärden von so kleinem Ausschlagswinkel,

---

146. *RB* 1:702 f. (14 January 1919); the letter may not be altogether reportage, seeing as it closely echoes a passage from the 1913 fragment, "Ein Erlebnis" (... da ein Vogelruf draußen und in seinem Innern übereinstimmend da war, indem er sich gewissermaßen an der Grenze des Körpers nicht brach, beides zu einem ununterbrochenen Raum zusammennahm) (*KA* 4:668); for a discussion of that fragment, see below.

daß sie unsichtbar blieben, liefen ihre
Strahlen nicht auseinander in das Weltall.[147]

In metaphorically associating eyelids and petals, Rilke thematizes the relation between vision and the diaphanous medium of the image through which eye and object may absorb and contain each other's energy. The petals occlude the innermost being of the rose "as though they had to sleep / tenfold, to quench a visionary power" (*als ob sie . . . zu dämpfen hätten eines Innern Sehkraft*). Conversely, as the petal "opens itself like an eyelid" (*sich aufschlägt wie ein Lid*), it positively elicits the very light that renders it visible to the human gaze. Both lid and petal owe their function and being to this light, which wholly transcends their order of being, yet which can register in consciousness only when refracted by the membrane of lid and petal. Rilke's imagery recalls the Plotinian conception, subsequently incorporated into Christian eschatology (e.g., in Bernard, the Victorine School, and Bonaventure), according to which visible being is both a manifestation of its transcendent source and, for the beholder, the conduit back to that source. All seeing is a motion *through* and *by means of* the visible toward the invisible—*per visibilia ad invisiblia*. The medium both enables and "filters," unveils and conceals, insofar as "through these petals / light must penetrate" (*daß durch diese Blätter / das Licht hindurch muß*). For being is only ever manifested by means of, yet never reducible to, a specific appearance. Possibly alluding to Plato's allegory of the cave (*Rep.* 514a–520a), Rilke thus depicts the petals as filtering light, just enough for the stamen in the depth of the chalice to erupt into a riotous, "tangled bunch" (*das wirre Bündel*). Recalling the poem's opening image of violent struggle, the efflorescence of the roses attests to their ineffable longing for participation in the very fullness (*plērōma*) from which they have sprung.

Rilke's lyric account of intuition appears "liberated from phenomenological stricture" of the kind Husserl so insistently places on perception. This stricture or "phenomenological prejudice would dictate in advance that, in the event of manifestation and in the indiscerptibility of phenomenon and perception, one may not and cannot see a light exceeding them as an ever more eminent phenomenality: not merely an object's hidden sides, or the interplication of the visible and the invisible in one another, but the . . . incandescence of the infinite simplicity that grants world

---

147. *KA* 1:509. "and like this: that a feeling arises, / because flower-petals touch flower-petals? / And this: that one opens like an eye, / and beneath it lie eyelid after eyelid, / all tightly closed, as if through tenfold sleep / they might curb an inner power of sight. / And this above all: that through these petals / light must pass. From a thousand skies / they slowly filter that drop of darkness / in whose fiery glow the tangled mass / of stamens bestirs itself and grows erect. // And the movement in the roses, look: / gestures from vibrations so minute / that they'd remain invisible, did not / their rays fan into the universe" (Rilke 2001a, 163).

and knower one to the other."[148] As had already been modeled for Rilke by Cézanne, the "infinite simplicity" enfolding thing and beholder is conveyed most poignantly by the incontrovertible givenness and presence of color. In "The Bowl of Roses," it returns in the form of an allusion to Botticelli's *Birth of Venus*, the goddess standing erect in her shell, blushing and turning against the backdrop of those white petals, expansive, open, and mirroring the beholder's unsettled gaze with a fusion of beguiling innocence and erotic longing. Rilke's concept of *Dingwerdung* pivots on an understanding visual experience as fundamentally an act of witnessing, not appropriation. Its phenomenology presupposes that the beholder is capable of letting the thing in question simply unveil itself by disembedding it from all spatiotemporal determinants ("coat, burden, . . . mask"). Yet to quarantine the eidetic intuition of a given thing from all ambient contexts is no longer a defensive maneuver or a matter of simple subtraction. On the contrary, it is premised on the beholder's infinite responsiveness to the *how* rather than the *what* of appearance, that is, to how something as mundane as a bowl of roses can manifest itself so utterly as to enable us to suspend (or "bracket" in the spirit of Husserl's *epoché*) anything that would interfere with our intuition of its essence.

> Sieh jene weiße, die sich selig aufschlug
> und dasteht in den großen offnen Blättern
> wie eine Venus aufrecht in der Muschel;
> und die errötende, die wie verwirrt
> nach einer kühlen sich hinüberwendet,
> und wie die kühle fühllos sich zurückzieht,
> und wie die kalte steht, in sich gehüllt,
> unter den offenen die alles abtun.
> Und *was* sie abtun, wie das leicht und schwer,
> wie es ein Mantel, eine Last, ein Flügel
> und eine Maske sein kann, je nach dem,
> und *wie* sie's abtun: wie vor dem Geliebten.[149]

This infinite fragility of the thing held suspended in visual experience here extends into a series of chromatic transitions of color and texture—of a fruit's yellow outside to its fuller, orange-red nectar within; of an ineffable rose color (Venus blush-

---

148. K. Hart 2017, 36.
149. *KA* 1:509–10. "Look at that white one, blissfully opened, / and standing there amidst its spread of petals / like a Venus balanced on her seashell; / and the blushing one, which as if flustered / turns across to one that is cool, / and how the cool one aloofly withdraws, / and how that cold one stands, wrapped in itself, / among the open ones, that shed everything. / and *what* they shed: how it can be / at once light and heavy, a cloak, a burden, / a wing and a mask—it all depends—/ and *how* they shed it: as before a lover" (Rilke 2001a, 163).

ing?) suspended between the bitter aftertaste of lilac and the opal whiteness of a porcelain cup "containing nothing but itself" (*die nichts enthält als sich*); of a batiste covering beneath whose linen texture one can fathom the "breath-warm" gown discarded for a bath in a forest's morning shade: "and that cambric one, is it not a dress, / in which the shift still clings, soft and breath-warm / both of them cast off together / in the morning shadows of the old woodland pool? [Und die batistene, ist sie kein Kleid, / in dem noch zart und atemwarm das Hemd steckt, / mit dem zugleich es abgeworfen wurde / im Morgenschatten an dem alten Waldbad?]."[150] Infinitely nuanced, the primal phenomena of color and texture give rise to equally unique and distinctive inner states. Indeed, every sensation is teleologically ordered to do just that, "to bring about a feeling" (*daß ein Gefühl entsteht*), to "transform" the phenomenon "into a handful of inwardness" (*in eine Hand voll Innres zu verwandeln*). It is *within* the phenomenon as it constitutes itself through its richly aspectual experience in consciousness, rather than *beyond* it, that Rilke locates the epiphanic. Persistently troubling Husserl's early phenomenology, the constitutive role that phantasy and image—creative agency and its medium—hold for perception is writ large by Rilke as the productive tension between evidence and epiphany, between the thing given in pure intuition and the numinous potentialities therein revealed.

The object-ontology undergirding Rilke's lyric epiphanies notably differs from Romanticism's subjective-expressive approach to the epiphanic and its roots in the Kantian, dynamic sublime. As Charles Taylor observes, an epiphany in Pound, Rilke, Eliot, Proust, and other modernists "is of something only indirectly available, something the visible object can't say itself but only nudges us towards." For Pound and, as we have seen, for Rilke, too, the image thus constitutes a vortex that concentrates "otherwise diffuse" energies into "an instant of time." The result is a fundamentally new concept of aesthetic work, one whose epiphanic dimension no longer rests with individual "words or images or objects evoked, but [arises] between them." Instead of an "expressive relation" unifying word and thing, poetic speech by its very disruption "of clearly defined images" establishes an "epiphanic field."[151] Taylor may be underestimating here the degree to which later Romantics such as Shelley (in "Mont Blanc" or "Ode to the West Wind") and Keats ("To Autumn") anticipate a more guarded, post-expressivist aesthetic. Still, his concept of an "epiphanic field" delineated in a "matter-of-fact" (*sachlich*) poetic *statement* (*Aussage*), rather than being claimed in subjective "expression" (*Ausdruck*), captures a salient aspect of Rilke's transition from the "middle period" of his *New Poems* to the post-Imagist style of the *Duino Elegies* and his *Sonnets to Orpheus*. Already in the closing stanza of Rilke's

---

150. *KA* 1:510 / 2001a, 163.
151. Taylor 1989, 469, 474, 475–77.

"Die Rosenschale," the poem that concludes part I of *New Poems*, a notably impersonal and subtly interrogative syntax nudges us beyond the visible; the phrasing here intimates a metaphysical, more specifically teleological, link between the phenomenal world of things and their "quiet redemption" (*leise Erlösung*) within a human interiority (*Innres*). Such inwardness, it turns out, is both constituted and becalmed (*sorglos*) by its visual encounter with something as ephemeral and diaphanous as a bowl of rose blossoms.

> Und sind nicht alle so, nur sich enthaltend,
> wenn Sich-enthalten heißt: die Welt da draußen
> und Wind und Regen und Geduld des Frühlings
> und Schuld und Unruh und vermummtes Schicksal
> und Dunkelheit der abendlichen Erde
> bis auf der Wolken Wandel, Flucht und Anflug,
> bis auf den vagen Einfluß ferner Sterne
> in eine Hand voll Innres zu verwandeln.
> Nun liegt es sorglos in den offnen Rosen.[152]

The "transformation" of the world "out there . . . into a handful of inwardness," which here coincides with nightfall and the eclipse of visibility ("darkness of the evening earth . . . and the vague influence of distant stars") hints at the increasingly tenuous relationship between the poetic word and the visible world in Rilke's oeuvre after 1910. As in G. M. Hopkins's late work, we once again observe a quasi-gravitational pull of the visual toward its own self-suspension and consummation in a kind of aniconic idiom that, in Rilke's case, proceeds to situate experience and cognition in a literally otherworldly space that marks an important threshold in the evolution of modernist epiphanic writing.

In a short prose piece of January 1913, titled "An Experience" (*Erlebnis I*) and arguably one of Rilke's more overtly "phenomenological" writings, the unidentified, third-person narrator recalls being comfortably "reposed" (*eingeruht*) against a tree and feeling so "utterly immersed in nature [*völlig eingelassen in die Natur*]" as to "abide in a state of almost unconscious contemplation [*daß er so . . . in einem beinah unbewußten Anschauen verweilte*]." Faint echoes of Rousseau's fifth *Reverie* pervade the writing as we learn how human, embodied consciousness finds itself utterly at

---

152. *KA* 1:510. "And aren't all that way: simply self-containing, / if self-containing means: to transform the world outside / and wind and rain and the patience of spring / and guilt and restlessness and muffled fate / and the darkness of the evening earth / out to the roaming and flying and fleeing of the clouds / and the vague influence of distant stars / into a handful of inwardness. // Now it lies carefree in these open roses" (Rilke 2001a, 165).

tuned to ambient space, indeed, enveloped in it as in a cocoon of sorts: "he felt as though he had never been filled by more subtle movements; his body was being treated like a soul [*sein Körper wurde gewissermaßen wie eine Seele behandelt*]." Foreshadowing Merleau-Ponty's phenomenology of bodily experience, Rilke's short prose piece frames consciousness in starkly anti-Cartesian fashion. Breaking with the visual approach of *New Poems*, Rilke here unfolds a new kind of phenomenological poetics. More than ever, consciousness here no longer abides within modernity's dominant epistemological matrices of rationalism and empiricism but, for all intents and purposes, has ceased to be the quasi-Archimedean center of experience. Nor for that matter does consciousness any longer claim optical dominion over the visible world in the manner of Alberti and his Renaissance successors. Instead, insofar as at certain epiphanic moments consciousness finds itself as enfleshed and at one with what Rilke elsewhere calls "the contiguous world" (*die verbundene Welt*) (*KA* 2:112), empirically visible matter seems at once closer and more distant.

The paradox is brought home in his 1914 poem titled "Wendung" (Volte-Face), which offers a diagnostic and highly self-conscious account of Rilke's turn away from the sharply focused Imagism of *New Poems*. A note appended to a first draft of the poem's opening lines tells us that henceforth "this wearying looking-outside-myself shall be replaced by a loving quest for inner plenitude [*daß dieses leerzehrende aus mir hinausschaun abgelöst werde durch ein liebevolles Bemühen um innere Fülle*]" (*KA* 2:503); and a letter to Lou Andreas Salomé, written the same day as the poem's first draft, confirms Rilke's growing unease with an "intellectual appropriation of the world that so utterly relies on the eye [*geistige Aneignung der Welt, wo sie sich so völlig des Auges bedient*] as has been the case with me." The visible world, and the "incessant outward-striving [*diese ununterbrochene Hinaussüchtigkeit*]" threatens to disperse the self and, ultimately, to render it atrophied, "an almost impalpable inner being [*jenem mir selbst kaum mehr erreichbaren inneren Dasein*]"[153] (*KA* 2:504). Rilke's choice of an epigraph for the poem, from a collection of aphorisms by Rudolf Kassner, reinforces the sense of his bidding farewell to the primacy of the visual that until recently had so shaped most of his lyric output: "The path from inwardness toward greatness leads through sacrifice [*Der Weg von der Innigkeit zur Größe geht durch das Opfer*]." What follows is a poem of renunciation that clearly anticipates the elegiac tone of his late work.

Unsurprisingly, Rilke's shift from the crystalline visuality of *New Poems* toward a more abstract and idealized model of inwardness—a shift once again unfolding in

---

153. *KA* 2:504. As early as 1912, while in Ronda, Spain, Rilke acknowledges that he "may have been too forceful in his commerce with concrete impressions, having lingered before them too long [*als ob ich den Eindrücken gegenüber zuviel Gewalt anwendete . . . ich bleib zu lang davor*]" (*KA* 2:506).

intriguing parallel to Husserl's increasingly Platonist reorientation in *Ideas I* (1913)—also entails a marked change in his conception of lyric form. Henceforth, Rilke's poems appear internally far more discontinuous, and they often present themselves as a montage of highly compressed images, sporadically recurring motifs, and micro-narratives rendered in ineffably allusive verse and in irregular, tenuously connected stanzaic units.[154] Poetic meaning no longer originates in a particular thing's focused visualization. Instead, we are presented with sudden convergences, fleeting personifications, spatial figures of experience, and enigmatic tropes that, as Arnold Gehlen was to observe about Abstract Expressionism, render Rilke's modernist lyric increasingly "commentary-dependent" (*kommentarbedürftig*). "Wendung," thus tantalizes with cryptic references to "creatures . . . wandering into his open gaze," and to birds that "flew straight through it" (*Tiere traten getrost in den offenen Blick . . . Vögel durchflogen ihn grad*); we learn of "flowers that reflected [his gaze] back into him, enlarged as in children" (*Blumen / wiederschauten in ihn / groß wie in Kinder*). However, what Husserl concurrently develops under the heading of "eidetic intuition" has ceased to be experienced as a gift. Instead, the inscrutable "contemplative" power said to have been supernaturally bestowed on some unspecified individual (*daß ein Schauender sei*) is experienced as a burden that threatens to drain its subject of all inwardness: "Watching for how long? / How long now, inwardly deprived, / Beseeching, from the ground of his gaze? [Schauend wie lang? / Seit wie lange schon innig entbehrend, / flehend im Grunde des Blicks?]." The world now appears but a hypertrophic inventory of things, at once inescapable and yet terminally alien. If it is a mirror, it has of late become a "mirror evaded" (*im gemiedenen Spiegel*). For the "things" (*Dinge*) that forever press upon consciousness in their mute and insistent visibility ultimately threaten to leave the lyric "eye" terminally bereft of love and "withhold any further consecration" (*verwehrten ihm weitere Weihen*). As Rilke now understands, there is—and as a matter of metaphysical necessity there has to be—"a limit to gazing. / And the world more fully contemplated / Wants to thrive in love" [Denn des Anschauns, siehe, ist eine Grenze. / Und die geschautere Welt / will in der Liebe gedeihen]."[155]

---

154. On Rilke's late style, see Anthony Stephens, in Engel 2013, 384–404. Rilke's montagelike handling of lyric form in his later poetry, including the *Duino Elegies*, seems to anticipate what, in the "Epistemo-Critical Prologue" to his *Origin of German Tragic Drama*, Walter Benjamin will elaborate as an aesthetic of fleeting and adventitious "constellations." On the broader contours of the modernist lyric, see Friedrich 1956, 140–213; de Man 1983, 166–86; and the large compendium of essays published by the Poetik und Hermeneutik working group (Iser 1966), especially the contributions by Henrich (on lyric form and Hegelian modernity), Preisendanz (on Trakl), Striedter (on Russian post-Symbolist lyric), and Iser (on Imagism and Eliot's *Waste Land*).

155. *KA* 2:100–101 / 2001b, 202–6 (trans. modified).

The poem's eponymous "volte-face," programmatically stated in the last stanza, is prompted by the realization that "The work of vision is done, / Now do heart-work / On the forms in you that you've caught: since you've / Overpowered them: but still don't know them [Werk des Gesichts ist getan, / tue nun Herz-Werk / an den Bildern in dir, jenen gefangenen; den du / überwältigtest sie: nun aber kennst du sie nicht]" (*KA* 2:102). As is also the case in Husserl's *Ideas*, Rilke's poetics after 1913 exhibits a Platonizing, even faintly Augustinian, bent, reminiscent of the *Confessions* (III.6.11), where God is said to be closer to us than we are to ourselves: "higher than my highest and more inward than my innermost self" (*interior intimo meo et superior summo meo*). As already intimated in Rilke's short prose piece, "Experience I" (1913), the visible world has receded, such that "all things appeared at once more distant and more true, perhaps a function of [the poet's] gaze, which no longer pointed ahead but seemed to dissolve out there, in the open [es mochte dies an seinem Blick liegen, der nicht mehr vorwärts gerichtet war und sich dort, im Offenen, verdünnte]" (*KA* 4:668). Yet this dissolution of the focalized gaze and the consequent self-suspension of the visible image is no longer experienced as a loss. On the contrary, as the classical (empiricist) model of perception appears increasingly attenuated, Rilke's prose also hints at a sharply intensified sense of contiguity between mind and ambient space. What characterizes enfleshed consciousness is its infinite receptivity, its nascent self-awareness as pure *medium*, so much so that the subject of experience "initially could not quite determine the sensorium through which he had received such a delicate and ample communication [daß er in den ersten Augenblicken den Sinn nicht recht feststellen konnte, durch den er eine derartig feine und ausgebreitete Mitteilung empfing]" (*KA* 4:667).

In the companion piece, *Erlebnis II*, Rilke further distinguishes between the *res extensa* of an inanimate "body" (*Körper*), a term manifestly inadequate for his purposes, and the innately *animated* nature of "flesh" (*Leib*). Said to have occurred on Capri at some unspecified point in time, the experience was distinguished by the way "the bird call outside and in his interior appeared wholly congruent [zusammenstimmend war]. . . . Back then, he closed his eyes that in his noble experience he should not be distracted by the contour of his flesh [um . . . durch den Kontur seines Leibes nicht beirrt zu sein]" (*KA* 4:669). Half a century later, Rilke's lyric prose will be echoed by Merleau-Ponty's similarly daring, late style in *The Visible and the Invisible*. Rejecting "the age-old assumptions that put the body in the world and the seer in the body, or, conversely, the world and the body in the seer as in a box," Merleau-Ponty imagines the moment when we cross the "frontier of the mute or solipsist world," the boundary separating propositional from experiential truth. It arrives when, "in the presence of other seers, my visible is confirmed as an exemplar of a universal visibility." At that moment, "we reach a second or figurative meaning of vision, which will be the *intuitus mentis* or idea, a sublimation of the flesh, which will be mind or thought."[156] Just so, what accounts for the experimental character of Rilke's prose here is the underlying premise that in "experience" (*Erlebnis*), strictly speaking, our conception of the world as an aggregate of discrete and distinctly visible things will be found to dissolve. What supplants it is an altogether different kind of mind-world relation, a kind of holistic attunement of enfleshed human consciousness to a different, non-Euclidian space that "is no longer [the] epistemological space of physics and geometry." Rather, in this "space of attunement [*gestimmter Raum*], which is no longer concerned with practical and logical aims and purposes," what unfolds is a "rich and profound mode of being wherein the human properly becomes itself [*das den Menschen erst zum Menschen macht*]."[157] In this space of pure intuition, sight and insight, sensation and cognition, phenomenal and intellectual being, appear wholly entwined. No longer are "space" (*Raum*) and the material and organic beings within it experienced as distinct realities but a spatialized sense of being continually impinges on human, enfleshed consciousness and, indeed, is positively constitutive of it.

Rilke's term for this space of pure experience, found in a poem of August 1914, is *Weltinnenraum*, a neologism rendered as "worldinnerspace" by Judith Ryan and widely taken to signal a break with the focalized visuality of *New Poems* and, instead, hinting at the speculative and obliquely metaphysical thrust of Rilke's later poetry. Drawing on Louis Binswanger's phenomenologically inspired work, David Wellbery explores the concept of lyric "attunement" (*Stimmung*) and the virtual space of *Dasein* it seeks to pry open. What distinguishes Rilke's *Weltinnenraum*—this space of attunement that Wellbery calls *der gestimmte Raum*—is that here "the foundation of purposively directed action is suspended. No longer . . . are aims and objectives at issue but, instead, 'a purposeless, though nonetheless rich and profound *Dasein*.'" Not coincidentally, the notion of such an aesthetic mood or attunement bears a striking formal resemblance to Husserl's concept of the *epoché*. For both concepts are premised on the total suspension or "bracketing" of any "positings" (*Setzungen*) of a reality transcendent to "experience" and, thus, lacking a phenomenological warrant. Furthermore, just as the phenomenon in its "absolute givenness" is the sole correlate of "experience" (*Erlebnis*), so the post-Symbolist notion of *Stimmung* so central to the modernist lyric of Trakl, Rilke, Eliot, and Mandelstam among others is distin-

---

156. Merleau-Ponty 1968, 138, 145. As Alloa points out, for the late Merleau-Ponty "art is no longer to be sought in works but rather in an amplification of the sensible bonds that connect us to the world. These bonds will henceforth be called 'flesh.' . . . Flesh is neither a sentient being nor an object sensed in itself, but that *through which* something sensible is sensed, its operative medium" (Alloa 2017, 65, 68). On flesh and its haptic character, see also Griffiths 2018, 1–12.

157. Binswanger 1955, 200; the essay ("Das Raumproblem in der Psychopathologie") dates from 1932. "I propose the term *space of attunement* [*gestimmter Raum*], . . . wherein human existence [*das menschliche Dasein*] abides . . . in some specifically tempered [*jeweils gestimmtes*] manner" (205).

guished by a palpable "indifference of inner and outer. . . . One no longer moves *in* space, but the entire spatial complexion has become dynamic [*der ganze Raumkomplex bewegt sich*]. . . . Space becomes an autonomous semantic medium."[158] It bears recalling the one, widely quoted lyric passage in which Rilke's concept of *Weltinnenraum* actually appears.

> Durch alle Wesen reicht der *eine* Raum:
> Weltinnenraum. Die Vögel fliegen still
> durch uns hindurch. O, der ich wachsen will,
> ich seh hinaus, und *in* mir wächst der Baum.
>
> Ich sorge mich, und in mir steht das Haus.
> Ich hüte mich, und in mir ist die Hut.
> Geliebter, der ich wurde: an mir ruht
> der schönen Schöpfung Bild und weint sich aus.[159]

Falling below the threshold of categorial definition, Rilke's *Weltinnenraum* can ultimately be mapped only in a non-narrative, lyric form. For only in the ludic exploration of the word *as a medium*, rather than as an inventory of distinct conceptions, is it possible to unearth the phantasmagoric underpinnings of what modern thought all too confidently homogenizes under the heading "experience." A fusion of inner and outer into a single experiential complex, *Weltinnenraum* is a prediscursive, non-Euclidian space of experience in its most elemental sense. The locus of "experience" here is not some black-box type, Cartesian *cogito* waxing skeptical about unstable appearances. Rather, the term signifies the primal, haptic quality of enfleshed consciousness as it makes contact with the ambient world; and by "world" we should no longer think of some contingent empirical "scene" to be confronted and mastered by the subject's stereoscopic gaze but, rather, a reality *sensed* as wholly contiguous with embodied consciousness itself.

Rilke's spatialized phantasmagoria of birds "fly[ing] through us still" and of a "tree [that] will rise *inside* me" presents this "worldinnerspace" as a domain logically anterior to all discrete perception, identification, and representation of

---

158. Wellbery 2011, 159, 161; on the Romantic origins of "mood" or "attunement" (*Stimmung*), see Pfau 2005b, esp. 1–74, and the literature by Nussbaum, Terada, Leyss, Caruth, Reddy, and others engaged there.

159. *KA* 2:113. "One single space pervades all beings here: / an inner world-space. Silently, the birds / fly through us still. Oh, I who want to grow, / can gaze outside: a tree will rise *inside* me. // I'm anxious, and a house abides within me. / I'm careful, and my safety has no fears. / My love, who I become: inside me dwells / the image of all beauty, streaming tears" (trans. David Young, https://archive.cortlandreview.com/features/13/summer/young.php; accessed 27 July 2021).

objects; this is a space of pure "intuition" (*Anschauung*), unmarked by the divisions that Cartesian rationalism and Lockean empiricism had instituted between mind and world. Hence, "experience" in both Husserl's phenomenological and Rilke's poetic modernism is no longer fungible with what modern epistemological frameworks, from Bacon to Kant, call "experience" (*Erfahrung*) and its rendering as objective "representation" (*Vorstellung*). More plausibly, we may think of *Erlebnis* as a post-liturgical revelation, as the primordial manifestation of Being wherein the ontological coordination of mind and world is intuitively grasped. Rilke's description of what he calls "experience" (*Erlebnis*) closely resembles Heidegger's phenomenological account of *Dasein* as "thrownness" (*Geworfenheit*), as always already "being-in-the-world" (*in-der-Welt-sein*) and, in certain epiphanic moments, experiencing this indelible continuity of inner and outer space. What remains to be considered, then, is the metaphysical status of the "event" (*Ereignis*), that is, the moment when the post-Euclidian domain of Rilke's *Weltinnenraum* registers as a distinct experience; and here phenomenology has offered two sharply divergent appraisals, one of stridently existentialist character (Heidegger) and the other cautiously theological in orientation (Marion).

Arguably more influenced by Rilke than he is prepared to acknowledge, Heidegger takes up and develops further this notion of the "event" in his 1936 *Contributions to Philosophy*. Impervious to causal determinations of any kind, the "event" marks *Dasein*'s primordial contact with the real, or "Beyng" or, in Heidegger's somewhat esoteric parlance, "the leap into beyng" (*der Sprung in das Seyn*), an instance of pure "origination" (*Ursprung*).[160] As the trope of a "leap" (*Sprung*) suggests, however, the metaphysical status of the event remains unfathomable. It is by definition a leap into "the open" (*das Offene*), a trope first introduced by Hölderlin and subsequently adopted and developed by the later Rilke and by Heidegger. For Heidegger in particular, it is impossible to ascertain whether the event, this "leap into being," constitutes a decisive turn toward or away from the God of metaphysics. In this "event," does God (or do "the gods") turn toward finite *Dasein* or, instead, withdraw from it for good. While it is impossible for *Dasein* to ascertain "whether in the event the remaining absent or the intrusion of the god decides for humans or against them [ob im Ereignis der Ausbleib oder der Anfall des Gottes sich für ihn oder gegen ihn entscheidet]," this much is intuitively clear: "event" stands for a moment of crisis (Grk. *krinō* = to put asunder, choose) where the status *Dasein* is about to be "decided."

Heidegger's account of "event" (*Ereignis*) is paradoxical insofar as this moment of primordial decision (*Ur-Sprung, Ent-scheidung*) turns out to be both vitally important and forever unknowable for *Dasein*. The event, so Heidegger, delineates "the

---

160. "Heidegger has a habit of not quoting the decisive authors precisely where, in his oeuvre, they truly speak" (Balthasar 1998, 3:195 n.).

time-space of the highest decision [*der Zeit-Raum der höchsten Entscheidung*]."[161] It is in this post-Euclidian "time-space" (*Zeit-Raum*) that truth "eventuates" and, so Heidegger claims, confronts *Dasein* with the full scope of its ontological incertitude. The latter is not a willed condition; it is not the fruit of methodical (Cartesian) skepticism, a philosophical procedure devised in the futile hope to escape from an all-encompassing incertitude allegedly visited on humankind by Descartes's spectral, "deceiving God" (*dieu trompeur*). Rather, by "event" Heidegger has in mind *Dasein*'s intuitive experience of the gods as "absconding" (*die Flucht der Götter*), a predicament that cannot be remedied but, instead, "must be witnessed and endured" (*muß erfahren und augestanden werden*). Hence, if "this event is the truth of beyng [*dieses Ereignis ist die Wahrheit des Seyns*]," what it impresses on *Dasein* is nothing less than its own, terminal indiscernibility: "Beyng as event—hesitant denial (refusal) [*Das Seyn als Ereignis—zögernde Versagung als* (*Verweigerung*)]."[162] Heidegger's concept of the event, then, consists in the wholescale rupturing and dismantling of the entire Neoplatonic and Christian metaphysics traced throughout this book. It returns us to a primitive apophaticism and a radically aniconic state wherein the image (*eikōn*) is no longer medium for, let alone a visible conduit to, the invisible God.

Yet Heidegger's characterization of the event as a type of ontological prevarication (a "hesitant denial and refusal") also throws into relief some stark differences between his own and Rilke's understanding of both "experience" (*Erlebnis*) and "event" (*Ereignis*). A fuller account of those differences, which would sensibly focus on the *Duino Elegies* and which I have sketched elsewhere, ought to begin by taking note of Rilke's far greater trust in the plasticity of language, and in the poetic word's inexhaustible responsiveness to the epiphanic fullness of the "happening phenomenon" (Marion), that is, appearance as the "event" of manifestation. Even as Rilke's later poetry leaves behind the visual and imagistic approach dominating in *New Poems*, his constructive orientation of lyric speech toward the "open" (*das Offene*) remains undiminished. There is no question for Rilke that the central, indeed the sole, purpose of the poetic word is to seek and close in on the parameters of *Dasein* in the modality of a "statement" (*Aussage*) that eschews both the (to him) oppressive definiteness of Aristotelian-realist "universality" and the vagaries of Romantic "expressivism" (*Ausdruck*).

Though more attenuated than the crystalline visual epiphanies found in *New Poems*, Rilke's later lyrics, from 1910 all the way to the *Sonnets to Orpheus* (1922), nevertheless attest to an unshakable faith in the poetic word's inexhaustible fecundity and responsiveness to the "superabundant being / [that] wells up in my heart"

---

161. Heidegger 1989, 9, 26, 24/ 2012, 10, 23, 21. On Heidegger's (partially hidden) debt to Rilke, see Balthasar 1998, 3:193–315; Pfau 2018b.

162. Heidegger 1989, 27, 29/2012, 24, 25.

(Überzähliges *Dasein / entspringt mir im Herzen*) (*KA* 2:229/59). Ever alert to the epiphanic possibilities that may unpredictably manifest themselves within the virtual domain of *Weltinnenraum*, Rilke's language does not content itself with ruminating and monotonously restating *Dasein*'s opacity and (alleged) metaphysical abandonment. This is not to deny that the late Rilke is acutely conscious of, and burdened by, a kind of metaphysical destitution endemic to modern life. Much of his later poetry features human voices "straining so hard against the strength of night," and oppressively aware of being adrift in a "disobedient world / full of refusal [*aufgelehnte Welt / voll Weigerung*]." Indeed, this depleted and recalcitrant world seems infinitely removed from the gods' "abundance of being" (Überfluß *von Dasein*). Yet even then, Rilke captures God's disembodied and eternally mute beauty in images whose charismatic presence seems all the more haunting: "Nothing is so mute / as a god's mouth. Beautiful as a swan / gliding over eternity's depthless surface / the god dives and guards his pure white [Nichts ist so stumm / wie eines Gottes Mund. Schön wie ein Schwan / auf seiner Ewigkeit grundlosen Fläche: / so zieht der Gott und taucht und schont sein Weiß]" (*KA* 2:50).

Insofar as intuition and image remain its ultimate and indispensable medium, the poetic word continues to participate in and reinforce our sense of the real as something forever self-manifesting, a palpable presence rather than a case of aniconic and apophatic negation. On both logical and phenomenological grounds, lyric speech cannot flourish where *Dasein* has been reduced to a mere "faltering" (*Versagung*) and an outright "refusal" (*Verweigerung*) of meaning. "And yet," Rilke insists, the world "breathes the space / in which the stars revolve [*Und atmet doch den Raum, / in dem die Sterne gehen*]."[163] The real here is neither something unilaterally "posited," nor is it definitively suspended in the spirit of modern existentialism's negative (and notably self-certifying) certitudes. Instead, the real remains an irrepressible presence, something "yet breathing" (*und atmet doch*) rather than Heidegger's generic abyss of "being." Indisputably self-manifesting, the real has presence; it is an "event" whose meanings—intuited, felt, seen—far exceed any matrix of cause and effect. As Marion notes, "The event *precedes its cause* (or causes), . . . having once come forward without any condition." It is characterized by "unrepeatability," "excessiveness," and an unfathomable "possibility [that] exceeds the preceding situation."[164] For Rilke, too, what he calls *Erlebnis* falls outside the spatiotemporal matrix of Kantian *Erfahrung* and, thus, cannot be assimilated to some preestablished web of historical, psychological, or mechanical causation.

Hence, too, an "event" that cannot be confined within any known form of causation will prove incommensurable with narrative form. Only the lyric's imagistic con-

---

163. *KA* 2:50 / 1995, 113.
164. Marion 2002a, 165–72; see also Marion 2002b, 30–53.

stitution seems capable of revealing our embodied and unfathomable embeddedness in the world, understood as a non-Euclidian space whose experience cannot be accounted for in terms of object-perception, representation, and communication. Where knowledge and discourse are to take hold, some primal seeing and feeling must first have eventuated—some mutual attunement of mind and world in which agency can never belong to just one side of the divide.

It is this unflinching insight into modern life's ontological precarity and indiscernibility, that is, into *Dasein* as forever "exposed on the cliffs of the heart [*Ausgesetzt auf den Bergen des Herzens*]," which ultimately compels Rilke's break with the visual certitudes of *New Poems*. What takes its place is a new, arguably more tentative but nevertheless hopeful, idiom characterized by highly compressed and ephemeral, phantasmagoric images and by a far greater reliance on interrogative syntax punctured by subjunctive and hortative locution.

> Durch den sich Vögel werfen, ist nicht der
> vertraute Raum, der die Gestalt dir steigert.
>
> . . .
>
> Raum greift aus uns und übersetzt die Dinge:
> daß dir das Dasein eines Baums gelinge,
> wirf Innenraum um ihn, aus jenem Raum,
> der in dir west. Umgieb ihn mit Verhaltung,
> Er grenzt sich nicht. Erst in der Eingestaltung
> In dein Verzichten wird er wirklich Baum.[165]

We detect here a distinctly new poetic ethos that seeks to chart a middle passage between postmetaphysical agnosticism (not to be confused with modern epistemological skepticism) and a faint eschatological hope. Attending to the real here means shifting one's stance from that of a subjective beholder or even impartial observer to one of undesigning, absorbed witnessing. The highest aim is to be wholly responsive to the myriad ways in which being accomplishes itself, an event to which—pace Heidegger—sentient and intuitive *Dasein* cannot possibly be indifferent. If mind and world are to be grasped as a single contiguous reality, *Dasein* must once more grant

---

165. *KA* 2:363. "The familiar space through which birds hurl themselves / is it not what intensifies the *Gestalt* for you? . . . Space reaches out of us and transposes things: / so that you may accomplish the being of a tree / envelop it with innerspace, drawing on that space / that lies within you. Surround it with restraint. / It does not delimit itself. Only when fitted / to your renunciation will it truly become tree" (Rilke 1995, 173). Notably, this late poem of 1924 recalls the magnificent opening poem of Rilke's *Buch der Bilder* (1901): "With your eyes . . . you lift very slowly one black tree / and place it against the sky: slender, alone. / And you have made the world [Mit deinen Augen . . . hebst du ganz langsam einen schwarzen Baum / und stellst ihn vor den Himmel: schlank, allein. Und hast die Welt gemacht]" (*KA* 1:257).

the world of visible things the phenomenological space that, in truth, it has always occupied. Hence, any distinction drawn between consciousness and its "environment" (*Umwelt*), particularly when it hardens into an antinomy and lasting estrangement, can be remedied only if mind invites hydrangeas, apples, and trees into its "innerspace" (*Innenraum*), not as "objects" unilaterally owned in perception but as self-manifesting "images" (*Bilder*). Then, yet only then, can reality be salvaged, not only from its nominalist construal as as an aggregate of so many discrete "objects," but also from its bland mystification as Heideggerian "beyng." Only then can the real be intuitively witnessed as the utterly concrete and vivid event of pure manifestation. For the late Rilke, the consummation of the real thus demands an act of "resignation" (*Verzichten*), the suspension of all desire for making, depicting, representing, or otherwise taking possession of the real. Where the real manifests itself, human flourishing hinges on the cultivation of a type of *kenōsis*, of ascetic "restraint" and, ultimately, "resignation" intimated in the Rilke's metonymic shift from *Verhaltung* to *Verzichten*.

Like his modernist peers, Rilke has decisively broken with the faux metaphysics of fin-de-siècle Symbolism. At the same time, he cannot embrace an existentialism that repackages metaphysical despair as an intellectual triumph of sorts; for doing so would mean the death of art, if nothing else. Yet neither is Rilke any longer able to see the world as the true and impassible *imago* of its divine creator, as Florensky, Bulgakov, or, by the early 1930s, the young von Balthasar so eloquently argue. Instead, and in far more guarded fashion, Rilke's lyrics frame epiphanic vision not as an "act" of claiming but strictly as the "event" of receiving; and what has been received, this at once unfathomable and inexhaustible gift of a world abounding with visible, self-manifesting things, can only be honored by lyric speech understood as impersonal "statement" (*Aussage*) rather than subjective "expression" (*Ausdruck*). What is called for, in other words, is a poetics of intimation most fittingly realized in a Postimpressionist lyric idiom that foregrounds a stance of "restraint" and "resignation." Rilke's guarded epiphanies do not renounce numinous reality but, in pointedly fragmentary lyric forms, keep it in play as the ultimate source, which modern existence can neither categorically disavow (skepticism) nor definitively possess (positivism). Resembling the archaeologist who tirelessly works to reassemble shards of a vase whose integrity he intuits, yet which he knows can never be restored to sight in its former plenitude, Rilke's lyrics seek to recover in textual form images of a reality only ever encountered in fissured and damaged form. Inaugurating a stance that has shaped artistic and intellectual practice to this day, his modernism attempts to capture the splendor of being (*Hiersein ist herrlich*) by gathering its image fragments in the medium of the lyric word. Lyric speech (*Aussage*) thus unfolds as ascetic discipline rather than romantic release, that is, as a post-Ignatian spiritual exercise in epistemic restraint and metaphysical resignation. For those taking themselves to inhabit a terminally postmetaphysical age, Rilke's qualified retention of image and vision may well prove the only way to carry on without relinquishing art (and by extension hope) or, conversely, acquiescing in art's instrumentalization and consequent trivialization for political ends.

WORKS CITED

Ackerman, James S. 2003. "The Photographic Picturesque." *Artibus et Historiae* 24.48: 73–94.

Adams, Hazard. 1983. *Philosophy of the Literary Symbolic*. Tallahassee: Florida State University Press.

Adorno, Theodor. 1997. *Aesthetic Theory*. Trans. and ed. Robert Hullot-Kentor. Minneapolis: University of Minnesota Press.

Adorno, Theodor, and Max Horkheimer. 1972. *Dialectic of the Enlightenment*. Trans. John Cumming. New York: Continuum.

Aers, David. 2009. *Salvation and Sin: Augustine, Langland, and Fourteenth-Century Theology*. Notre Dame, IN: University of Notre Dame Press.

Aers, David, and Lynn Staley. 1996. "The Humanity of Christ: Reflections on Julian of Norwich's *Revelation of Love*." In *The Powers of the Holy*. University Park: Pennsylvania State University Press.

Aksit, Ilhan. 2012. *Hagia Sophia: The History and the Architecture*. Istanbul: Aksit Yayincilik.

Alberti, Leon Battista. 2004. *On Painting*. Trans. Cecil Grayson. Harmondsworth: Penguin.

Alexander, Paul J. 1952. "Hypatius of Ephesus: A Note on Image Worship in the Sixth Century." *Harvard Theological Review* 45.3: 177–84.

Alloa, Emmanuel. 2011a. "Darstellen, was sich in der Darstellung allererst herstellt: Bildperformanz als Sichtbarmachung." In *Bild-Performanz*, ed. Ludger Schwarte, 33–58. Zurich: Diaphanes.

———. 2011b. *Das durchscheinende Bild: Konturen einer medialen Phänomenologie*. Zurich: Diaphanes.

———. 2013. "Visual Studies in Byzantium: A Pictorial Turn *avant la lettre.*" *Journal of Visual Culture* 12.1: 3–29.

———. 2015. "The Most Sublime of All Laws: The Strange Resurgence of a Kantian Motif in Contemporary Image Politics." *Critical Inquiry* 41: 367–89.

———. 2017. *Resistance of the Sensible World: An Introduction to Merleau-Ponty.* Trans. Jane Marie Todd. New York: Fordham University Press.

Anonymous. "Geology: Its Relation to the Picturesque." *Art Journal* 17 (1855): 275–76.

Antonova, Clemena. 2010. *Space, Time, and Presence in the Icon: Seeing the World with the Eyes of God.* Burlington, VT: Ashgate.

Apollonio, Carol. 2009a. "Dostoevsky's Religion: Words, Images, and the Seed of Charity." *Dostoevsky Studies* 13: 23–35.

———. 2009b. *Dostoevsky's Secrets: Reading against the Grain.* Evanston, IL: Northwestern University Press.

Appleford, Anne. 2014. *Learning to Die in London, 1380–1540.* Philadelphia: University of Pennsylvania Press.

Aquinas, Thomas. 2003. *Commentary on John.* Lander, WY: Aquinas Institute.

Aquino, Frederick D. 2012. "Maximus the Confessor." In *The Spiritual Senses: Perceiving God in Western Christianity*, ed. Paul L. Gavrilyuk and Sarah Coakley, 104–20. Cambridge: Cambridge University Press.

Ariès, Philippe. 1991. *The Hour of Our Death.* Trans. Helen Weaver. New York: Oxford University Press.

Aristotle. 1984. *The Complete Works of Aristotle.* 2 vols. Ed. Jonathan Barnes. Princeton, NJ: Bollingen.

Aston, Margaret. 1990. *England's Iconoclasts: Laws against Images.* Oxford: Oxford University Press.

Auerbach, Erich. 2014. *Time, History, and Literature: Selected Essays of Erich Auerbach.* Ed. James L. Porter. Princeton, NJ: Princeton University Press.

Augustine. 1991. *The Trinity.* Trans. Edmund Hill, O.P. Hyde Park, NY: New City Press.

———. 1993. *Sermons.* In *The Works of Saint Augustine*, Part III/7. Trans. Edmund Hill, O.P. La Rochelle, NY: New City Press.

———. 1997. *On Christian Teaching.* Trans. R. P. H. Green. Oxford: Oxford University Press.

———. 1998. *The City of God against the Pagans.* Trans. R. W. Dyson. Cambridge: Cambridge University Press.

———. 2001. *Confessions.* Trans. Philip Burton. New York: Knopf.

———. 2002. *On Genesis.* Trans. Edmund Hill, O.P. Hyde Park, NY: New City Press.

Avery, Kevin J. 1986. "'The Heart of the Andes Exhibited: Fredric E. Church's Window on the Equatorial World." *American Art Journal* 18.1: 52–72.

———. 1993. *Church's Great Picture, the Heart of the Andes.* New York: Metropolitan Museum of Art.

Back, Frances. 2002. *Verwandlung durch Offenbarung bei Paulus: Eine religionsgeschichtlich-exegetische Untersuchung zu 2 Kor 2, 14–4, 6.* Tübingen: Mohr Siebeck.

Bacon, Francis. 2000. *The New Organon*. Ed. Lisa Jardine and Michael Silverthorne. Cambridge: Cambridge University Press.

Baker, Denise. 1994. *Julian of Norwich's Showings: From Vision to Book*. Princeton, NJ: Princeton University Press.

Ball, Patricia. 1971. *The Science of Aspects: The Changing Role of Fact in the Work of Coleridge, Ruskin and Hopkins*. London: Athlone.

Ballinger, Philip A. 2000. *The Poem as Sacrament: The Theological Aesthetic of Gerard Manley Hopkins*. Louvain: Peeters Press.

Balthasar, Hans Urs von. [1937–39] 1998. *Apokalypse der deutschen Seele: Studien zu einer Lehre von letzten Haltungen*. 3 vols. Reprint. Einsiedeln: Johannes Verlag.

———. 1961. *Herrlichkeit: Eine theologische Ästhetik*. 3 vols. Einsiedeln: Johannes Verlag.

———. 1963. *Das Ganze im Fragment*. Einsiedeln: Johannes Verlag.

———. 1964. "Revelation and the Beautiful." In *Explorations in Theology*, vol. 1, trans. A. V. Littledale, 95–126. New York: Herder and Herder.

———. 1967. *A Theological Anthropology*. London: Sheed & Ward.

———. 1982. *The Glory of the Lord: A Theological Aesthetics*. Vol. 1, *Seeing the Form*. Trans. Erasmo Leiva-Merikakis. San Francisco: Ignatius Press.

———. 1984. *The Glory of the Lord*. Vol. 2, *Studies in Theological Style: Clerical Styles*. Trans. Andrew Louth et al. San Francisco: Ignatius Press.

———. 1985. *Theologik: Wahrheit der Welt*. Einsiedeln: Johannes Verlag.

———. 1986. *The Glory of the Lord*. Vol. 3, *Studies in Theological Style: Lay Styles*. Trans. Andrew Louth et al. San Francisco: Ignatius Press.

———. 1989a. *Explorations in Theology I: The Word Made Flesh*. San Francisco: Ignatius Press.

———. 1989b. *The Glory of the Lord*. Vol. 4, *The Realm of Metaphysics in Antiquity*. Trans. Brian McNeil et al. San Francisco: Ignatius Press.

———. 1991. *The Glory of the Lord*. Vol. 5, *The Realm of Metaphysics in the Modern Age*. London: T. & T. Clark.

———. 1997. *Présence et pensée*. Paris: Beauchesne.

———. 2001. *Theo-Logic: The Truth of the World*. San Francisco: Ignatius.

———. 2003. *The Cosmic Liturgy: The Universe according to Maximus the Confessor*. Trans. Brian E. Daley, S.J. San Francisco: Ignatius Press.

Barber, Charles. 1993. "From Transformation to Art: Art and Worship after Byzantine Iconoclasm." *Art Bulletin* 75, no. 1: 7–16.

———. 2002. *Figure and Likeness: On the Limits of Representation in Byzantine Iconoclasm*. Princeton, NJ: Princeton University Press.

———. 2010. "Defacement." *Yearbook for Comparative Literature* 56: 104–15.

Barber, Tabitha, and Stacy Boldrick. 2013. *Art under Attack: Histories of British Iconoclasm*. London: Tate Publications.

Baring, Edward. 2019. *Converts to the Real: Catholicism and the Making of Continental Philosophy*. Cambridge, MA: Harvard University Press.

Barrell, John. 1980. *The Dark Side of the Landscape: The Rural Poor in English Painting, 1730–1840*. Cambridge: Cambridge University Press.

Barth, Karl. 1968. *The Epistle to the Romans*. Trans. Edwin C. Hoskyns. London: Oxford University Press.

———. 2004. *Church Dogmatics*. Part II/1. Trans. T. H. L. Parker et al. London: T. & T. Clark.

Bätschmann, Oskar, and Pascal Griener. 1997. *Hans Holbein*. London: Reaktion Books.

Baxandall, Michael. 1972. *Painting and Experience in Fifteenth-Century Italy*. Oxford: Oxford University Press.

Beck, H. G. 1975. *Von der Fragwürdigkeit der Ikone*. Heft 7. Munich: Sitzungsbericht der Bayrischen Akademie der Wissenschaften.

Beeley, Christopher A. 2012. *The Unity of Christ: Continuity and Conflict in Patristic Tradition*. New Haven, CT: Yale University Press.

Beer, Gillian. 1983. *Darwin's Plots: Evolutionary Narrative in Darwin, George Eliot, and Nineteenth-Century Fiction*. Cambridge: Cambridge University Press.

Beierwaltes, Werner. [1985] 2016. *Denken des Einen*. Frankfurt: Klostermann.

———. 1988. "'*Visio Facialis*': Sehen ins Angesicht—Zur Koinzidenz des endlichen und unendlichen Blicks bei Cusanus." *Bayerische Akademie der Wissenschaften* 1: 90–124.

———. 1998. *Platonismus im Christentum*. Frankfurt: Klostermann.

———. 2001. *Das Wahre Selbst: Studien zu Plotins Begriff des Geistes und des Einen*. Frankfurt: Klostermann.

———. 2003. "Das Verhältnis von Philosophie und Theologie bei Nicolaus Cusanus." *Mittelungen und Forschungsbeiträge der Cusanus-Gesellschaft* 28: 65–102.

———. 2017. *Catena Aurea: Plotin, Augustinus, Eriugena, Thomas, Cusanus*. Frankfurt: Klostermann.

Beiser, Frederick. 2002. *German Idealism: The Struggle against Subjectivism, 1781–1801*. Cambridge, MA: Harvard University Press.

Bell, Peter N. 2009. *The Political Voices from the Age of Justinian*. Liverpool: Liverpool University Press.

Belting, Hans. 1980–81. "An Image and Its Function in the Liturgy: The Man of Sorrows in Byzantium." *Dumbarton Oaks Papers* 34–45: 1–16.

———. 1981. *Bild und Publikum im Mittelalter*. Berlin: Gebr. Mann Verlag.

———. 1994. *Likeness and Presence: A History of the Image before the Era of Art*. Chicago: University of Chicago Press.

———. 2006. *Das echte Bild: Bildfragen als Glaubensfragen*. Munich: C. H. Beck.

———. 2011a. *An Anthropology of Images: Picture, Medium, Body*. Princeton, NJ: Princeton University Press.

———. 2011b. *Florence and Baghdad: Renaissance Art and Arab Science*. Trans. Deborah L. Schneider. Cambridge, MA: Belknap Press of Harvard University Press.

———. 2014. *Faces: Eine Geschichte des Gesichts*. Munich: C. H. Beck.

Benedictow, Ole J. 2004. *The Black Death, 1346–1353: A Complete History*. Woodbridge: Boydell.

Benjamin, Walter. 1996. *Selected Writings, vol. 1, 1913–1926*. Trans. and ed. Marcus Bullock and Michael W. Jennings. Cambridge, MA: Belknap Press of Harvard University Press.

———. 1999. *The Arcades Project*. Trans. Howard Eiland and Kevin McLaughlin. Cambridge, MA: Belknap Press of Harvard University Press.

Bernard of Clairvaux. 1895. *Cantica Canticorum: Eighty-Six Sermons on the Song of Solomon*. Trans. and ed. Samuel J. Eales. London: E. Stock.

———. 1987. *Selected Works*. Trans. and ed. Gilian Rosemary Evans. New York: Paulist Press.

Berndt, Frauke. 2012. "The Myth of Otherness: Goethe on Presence." *Goethe Yearbook* 19: 49–66.

Besançon, Alain. 2000. *The Forbidden Image: An Intellectual History of Iconoclasm*. Chicago: University of Chicago Press.

Binski, Paul. 1996. *Medieval Death: Ritual and Representation*. London: British Museum Press.

Binswanger, Ludwig. 1955. *Ausgewählte Vorträge und Aufsätze*. Vol. 2. Bern: Francke.

Blake, William. 1982. *The Complete Poetry and Prose*. Ed. David Erdman. New York: Anchor.

Blondel, Maurice. [1893] 1984. *Action: Essay on a Critique of Life and a Science of Practice*. Trans. Oliva Blanchette. Notre Dame, IN: University of Notre Dame Press.

Bloom, Allan. 1968. *The Republic of Plato*. Translated and edited with an interpretive essay by Allen Bloom. New York: Basic Books.

Blumenberg, Hans. 1983. *The Legitimacy of the Modern Age*. Trans. Robert M. Wallace. Cambridge, MA: MIT Press.

Bockemühl, Jochen. 1998. "Transformations in the Foliage Leaves of Higher Plants." In *Goethe's Way of Science: A Phenomenology of Nature*, ed. David Seamon and Arthur Zajonc. Albany: SUNY Press.

Bocken, Inigo, and Harald Schwaetzer, eds. 2005. *Spiegel und Portrait: Zur Bedeutung zweier zentraler Bilder im Denken des Nicolaus Cusanus*. Maastricht: Uitgeverij Shaker.

Boehm, Gottfried, ed. 1994. *Was ist ein Bild?* Munich: Fink.

Bonaventure, St. 1882–1903. *Opera Omnia*. 11 vols. Quaracchi Edition. Florence: Ad Claras Aquas, 1882–1902.

———. 1996. *On the Reduction of Arts to Theology*. Trans. Zachary Hayes, O.F.M. St. Bonaventure, NY: Franciscan Institute.

———. 2002. *Itinerarium Mentis in Deum*. Trans. Zachary Hayes. St. Bonaventure, NY: Franciscan Institute.

———. 2005. *Breviloquium*. Ed. Dominic Monti, O.F.M. St. Bonaventure, NY: Franciscan Institute.

Bond, H. Lawrence. 2002. "The 'Icon' and the 'Iconic Text' in Nicholas of Cusa's *De Visione Dei* I–XVII." In *Nicholas of Cusa and His Age: Intellect and Spirituality*, ed. Thomas M. Izbicky and Christopher M. Bellitto, 177–97. Leiden: Brill,

Borsche, Tilman. 2010. "Das Bild von Licht und Farbe in den philosophischen Meditationen des Nikolaus von Kues." In *Videre et videri coincidunt: Theorien des Sehens in der ersten Hälfte des 15. Jahrhunderts*, ed. Wolfgang C. Schneider et al., 163–81. Muenster: Aschendorff Verlag.

Boulnois, Olivier. 2020. "The Concept of Theology." In *Christian Platonism: A History*, ed. Alexander Hampton and John Peter Kenney, 101–21. Cambridge: Cambridge University Press.

Boyle, Nicholas. 1991. *Goethe: The Poet and the Age.* Vol. 1. Oxford: Oxford University Press.

Brady, Ronald. 1987. "Form and Cause in Goethe's Morphology." In *Goethe and the Sciences: A Reappraisal,* ed. Frederick Amrine and Francis J. Zucker, 257–300. Dodrecht: D. Reidel.

———. 1998. "The Idea in Nature: Rereading Goethe's Organics." In *Goethe's Way of Science: A Phenomenology of Nature,* ed. David Seamon and Arthur Zajonc, 83–111. Albany: SUNY Press.

Brandwood, Leonard. 1990. *The Chronology of Plato's Dialogues.* Cambridge: Cambridge University Press.

Bredekamp, Horst. 2010. *Theorie des Bildakts.* Frankfurt: Suhrkamp.

———. 2011. "In der Tiefe der Künstlichkeit: Das Prinzip der bildaktiven Disjunktion." In *Sehen und Handeln,* vol. 1, *Actus et Imago,* ed. Horst Bredekamp, 207–24. Berlin: Akademie Verlag.

Breidbach, Olaf. 2006. *Goethes Metamorphosenlehre.* Munich: Fink.

Breithaupt, Fritz. 2000. *Jenseits der Bilder: Goethes Politik der Wahrnehmung.* Freiburg: Rombach.

Brenk, Beat. 2005. "Visibility and (Partial) Invisibility of Early Christian Images." In *Seeing the Invisible in Late Antiquity and the Early Middle Ages,* ed. Giselle de Nie et al., 139–83. Turnout: Brepols.

Brittain, Timothy. 1988. "Logos, Creation, and Epiphany in the Poetics of Gerard Manley Hopkins." PhD dissertation, University of Virginia.

Broecke, Lara. 2015. *Cennino Cennini's "Il Libro dell'Arte": A New Translation and Commentary and Italian Transcription.* London: Archive Publications.

Brown, Peter. 1973. "A Dark-Age Crisis: Aspects of the Iconoclastic Controversy." *English Historical Review* 88.346: 1–34.

Browne, Janet. 1995. *Charles Darwin: Voyaging.* Princeton, NJ: Princeton University Press.

———. 2002. *Charles Darwin: The Power of Place.* Princeton, NJ: Princeton University Press.

Brubaker, Leslie, and John Haldon. 2001. *Byzantium in the Iconoclast Era, c. 680–850: The Sources.* Aldershot: Ashgate.

———. 2011. *Byzantium in the Iconoclast Era, c. 680–850: A History.* Cambridge: Cambridge University Press.

Brunson, Molly. 2016. "Dostoevsky's Realist *Paragone*: Word, Image, and Fantastic Ekphrasis in *The Idiot.*" *Slavic and East European Journjal* 60.3: 447–70.

Buckley, Michael. 2004. *Denying and Disclosing God: The Ambiguous Progress of Modern Atheism.* New Haven, CT: Yale University Press.

Bühl, Gudrun, ed. 2008. *Dumbarton Oaks: The Collections.* Washington, DC: Dumbarton Oaks Research Library and Harvard University Press.

Bulgakov, Sergius. 2012a. *Icons and the Name of God.* Trans. Boris Jakim. Grand Rapids, MI: Eerdmans.

———. 2012b. *Unfading Light: Contemplations and Speculations.* Trans. Thomas A. Smith. Grand Rapids, MI: Eerdmans.

Burckhardt, Sigurd. 1956. "The Poet as Fool and Priest." *ELH* 23: 279–98.

Burrell, David B., C.S.C. 2005. "Analogy, Creation, and Theological Language." In *The Theology of Thomas Aquinas*, ed. Rik van Nieuwenhove and Joseph Wawrkykow, 77–98. Notre Dame, IN: University of Notre Dame Press.

———. 2008. *Aquinas: God & Action*. Scranton, PA: University of Scranton Press.

Büsgen, Antje. 2013. "Bildende Kunst." In *Rilke-Handbuch*, ed. Manfred Engel, 130–50. Stuttgart: J. B. Metzler.

Bynum, Caroline. 2005. "Seeing and Seeing Beyond: The Mass of St. Gregory in the Fifteenth Century." In *The Mind's Eye: Art and Theological Argument in the Middle Ages*, ed. Jeffrey F. Hamburger and Anne-Marie Bouché, 208–40. Princeton, NJ: Princeton University Press.

———. 2011. *Christian Materiality: An Essay on Religion in Late Medieval Europe*. New York: Zone Books.

Cachin, François. 1996. *Cézanne*. Philadelphia: Philadelphia Museum of Art.

Cahan, David, ed. 2003. *From Natural Philosophy to the Sciences*. Chicago: University of Chicago Press.

Calvin, John. 2011. *Institutes of Christian Religion*. 2 vols. Ed. John T. McNeill. Louisville, KY: Westminster John Knox Press..

Camille, Michael. 2000. "Before the Gaze: The Internal Senses and Late Medieval Practices of Seeing." In *Visuality Before and Beyond the Renaissance*, ed. Robert S. Nelson, 197–223. Cambridge: Cambridge University Press.

Campe, Rüdiger. 1990. *Affekt und Ausdruck: Zur Umwandlung der literarischen Rede im 17. und 18. Jahrhundert*. Tübingen: Niemeyer.

Carnes, Natalie. 2013. "Making, Breaking, Loving, and Hating Images: Prelude to a Theology of Iconoclasm." *Logos* 16.2: 17–34.

———. 2014. *Beauty: A Theological Engagement with Gregory of Nyssa*. Eugene, OR: Cascade Books.

Carpenter, Anne A. 2015. *Theo-Poetics: Hans Urs von Balthasar and the Risk of Art and Being*. Notre Dame, IN: University of Notre Dame Press.

Carroll, Sean. 2005. *Endless Forms Most Beautiful: The New Science of Evo Devo*. New York: Scribner.

Carruthers, Mary. 2006. "Moving Images in the Mind's Eye." In *The Mind's Eye: Art and Theological Argument in the Middle Ages*, ed. Jeffrey Hamburger and Anne-Marie Bouché, 287–305. Princeton, NJ: Princeton University Press.

Caruth, Cathy. 1996. *Unclaimed Experience: Trauma, Narrative, and History*. Baltimore: Johns Hopkins University Press.

Casarella, Peter. 2017. *Word as Bread: Language and Theology in Nicholas of Cusa*. Muenster: Aschendorff Verlag.

Cassirer, Ernst. 1951. *Philosophy of the Enlightenment*. Trans. Fritz C. A. Koelln and James P. Pettegrove. Princeton, NJ: Princeton University Press.

———. 1955. *The Philosophy of Symbolic Forms*. Vol. 1. Trans. Ralph Manheim. New Haven, CT: Yale University Press.

———. [1922] 1974. *Das Erkenntnisproblem in der Philosophie und Wissenschaft der neueren Zeit*. Darmstadt: Wissenschaftliche Buchgesellschaft.

———. 1983. *Wesen und Wirkung des Symbolbegriffs*. Darmstadt: WBG.

Cennini, Cennino. 2015. *Il Libro dell' Arte*. Trans. and ed. Lara Broecke. London: Archetype Publications.

Certeau, Michel de. 1987. "The Gaze of Nicholas of Cusa." *Diacritics* 17.3: 2–38.

Cézanne, Paul. 2013. *The Letters of Paul Cézanne*. Trans. and ed. Alex Danchev. Los Angeles: Getty Museum.

Chenavier, Robert. 2012. *Simone Weil: Attention to the Real*. Notre Dame, IN: University of Notre Dame Press.

Chrétien, Jean-Louis. 2000. "The Wounded Word." In *Phenomenology and the Theological Turn*, ed. Dominique Janicaud, 147–75. New York: Fordham University Press.

———. 2004. *The Call and the Response*. Trans. Anne A. Davenport. New York: Fordham University Press.

Clark, Stephen R. L. 2016. *Plotinus: Myth, Metaphor, and Philosophical Practice*. Chicago: University of Chicago Press.

Clark, Stuart. 2009. *Vanities of the Eye: Vision in Early Modern European Culture*. Oxford: Oxford University Press.

Claudel, Paul. 1967. *Œvres poétique*. Ed. Jacques Petit. Paris: Éditions Gallimard.

———. 2020. *Five Great Odes*. Trans. Jonathan Geltner. Brooklyn, NY: Angelico Press.

Coakley, Sarah. 2012. "Gregory of Nyssa." In *The Spiritual Senses: Perceiving God in Western Christianity*, ed. Paul L. Gavrilyuk and Sarah Coakley, 36–55. Cambridge: Cambridge University Press.

Coleridge, Samuel Taylor. 1956–71. *The Collected Letters of Samuel Taylor Coleridge*. 6 vols. Ed. Leslie Griggs. Oxford: Clarendon Press.

———. 1961. *The Notebooks of Samuel Taylor Coleridge*, vol. 2 (1804–8). Ed. Kathleen Coburn. Princeton, NJ: Bollingen.

Constas, Nicholas. 1997. "Icons and the Imagination." *Logos* 1.i: 114–27.

———. 2014. *The Art of Seeing: Paradox and Perception in Orthodox Iconography*. Alhambra, CA: Sebastian Press.

Cory, Therese Scarpelli. 2020. "Aquinas' Intelligible Species as Formal Constituents." *Documenti e studi sulla tradizione filosofica medievale* 31: 261–309.

Crawford, Heide. 2007. "Poetically Visualizing *Urgestalten*: The Union of Nature, Art, and the Love of Woman in Goethe's 'Die Metamorphose der Pflanzen.'" In *The Enlightened Eye: Goethe and Visual Culture*, ed. Evelyn K. Moore and Patricia A. Simpson, 279–88. Amsterdam: Rodopi.

Cuozzo, Gianluca. 2005. "Bild, *visio*, und Perspektive." In *Spiegel und Portrait*, ed. Inigo Bocken and Harald Schwaetzer, 177–95. Maastricht: Uitgeverij Shaker.

Cusa, Nicholas. 1985. *Nicholas of Cusa's Dialectical Mysticism: Text, Translation, and Interpretive Study of "De Visione Dei" by Jasper Hopkins*. Minneapolis: Arthur J. Banning Press.

———. 1997. *Selected Spiritual Writings*. Trans. H. Lawrence Bond. New York: Paulist Press.

———. 1998. *Nikolaus von Kues: Briefe und Dokumente zum Brixner Streit*. Ed. Wilhelm Baum and Raimund Senoner. Vienna: Turia & Kant.

———. 2001. *Complete Philosophical and Theological Treatises of Nicholas of Cusa*. 2 vols. Trans. Jasper Hopkins. Minneapolis: Arhur J. Banning Press.

————. [Kues, Nikolaus von]. 2002. *Philosophisch-theologische Werke*. 4 vols. Ed. Karl Borman. Hamburg: Felix Meiner.

Cushman, Jennifer. 2002. "Beyond Ekphrasis: *Logos* and *Eikon* in Rilke's Poetry." *College Literature* 29.3: 83–108.

Dahlhaus, Carl, and John Deathridge. 1984. *The New Grove Wagner*. New York: Norton.

D'Amico, Claudia. 2010. "Die Produktivität der *visio absoluta* bei Cusanus: Die Vorgänge im mittelalterlichen Neuplatonismus." In *Videre et videri coincidunt: Theorien des Sehens in der ersten Hälfte des 15. Jahrhunderts*, ed. Wolfgang C. Schneider et al., 97–110. Muenster: Aschendorff Verlag.

Danchev, Alex. 2012. *Cézanne: A Life*. New York: Pantheon.

Dante Alighieri. 2002. *Inferno*. Trans. Jean Hollander and Robert Hollander. New York: Anchor.

————. 2003. *Purgatorio*. Trans. Jean Hollander and Robert Hollander. New York: Anchor.

Danto, Arthur C. 1982. "Depiction and Description." *Philosophy and Phenomenological Research* 43.1: 1–19.

Darwin, Charles. 1987a. *Charles Darwin's Notebooks, 1836–1844*. Ed. Paul H. Barrett et al. London: British Museum and Cambridge University Press.

————. 1987b. *Works of Charles Darwin*. Vol. 3. Ed. Paul H. Barrett and R. B. Freeman. New York: New York University Press.

————. 2006. *From So Simple a Beginning: The Four Great Books of Charles Darwin*. Ed. Edward O. Wilson. New York: Norton.

————. 2008. *Origins: Selected Letters of Charles Darwin, 1822–1859*. Ed. Frederick Burkhardt. Cambridge: Cambridge University Press.

Daston, Lorraine, and Peter Galison. 1992. "The Image of Objectivity." *Representations* 40: 81–128.

de Lubac, Henri. 2000a. *Augustinianism and Modern Theology*. Trans. Lancelot Sheppard. New York: Herder & Herder.

————. 2000b. *Medieval Exegesis*. 3 vols. Trans. E. M. Macierowski. Grand Rapids, MI: Eerdmans.

————. 2006. *Corpus Mysticum: The Eucharist and the Church in the Middle Ages*. Trans. Gemma Simmonds, C.J. Notre Dame, IN: University of Notre Dame Press.

De Man, Paul. 1983. *Blindness and Insight*. Minneapolis: University of Minnesota Press.

Denzinger, Heinrich. 2012. *Enchiridion Symbolorum definitionum et declarationum de rebus fidei et morum*. San Francisco: Ignatius Press.

Derrida, Jacques. 1982. *Margins of Philosophy*. Trans. and ed. Alan Bass. Chicago: University of Chicago Press.

Descartes, René. 1677. *Opera Philosophica: Editio Ultima*. n.p.

————. 2017. *Meditations on First Philosophy*. Ed. John Cottingham. Cambridge: Cambridge University Press.

Desmond, William. 2012. *The Intimate Strangeness of Being: Metaphysics after Dialectic*. Washington, DC: Catholic University of America Press.

Devlin, Christopher. 1950. "The Image and the Word." *The Month* 2: 114–27; 3: 191–202.

DeWarren, Nicolas. 2021. "The Virtuous Philosopher and the Chameleon Poet: Husserl and Hofmannsthal." In *Phenomenology to the Letter: Husserl and Literature*, ed.

Philippe P. Haensler, Kristina Mendicino, and Rochelle Tobias, 263–82. Berlin: De Gruyter.

Didi-Huberman, Georges. 2005. *Confronting Images: Questioning the Ends of a Certain History of Art*. University Park: Pennsylvania State University Press.

Diller, Hans. 1932. "ΟΨΙΣ ΑΔΗΛΩΝ ΤΑ ΦΑΙΝΟΜΕΝΑ." *Hermes* 67.1: 14–42.

Dinzelbacher, Peter. 2004. "Religöses Erleben vor bildender Kunst in autobiographischen und biographischen Zeugnissen des Hoch- und Spätmittelalters." In *Images of Cult and Devotion*, ed. Søren Kaspersen, 61–88. Copenhagen: Museum Tusculanum Press.

Doran, Michael, ed. 2001. *Conversations with Cézanne*. Trans. Julie L. Cochran. Berkeley: University of California Press.

Dostoevsky, Fyodor. 1987. *Selected Letters of Fyodor Dostoevsky*. Trans. and ed. Joseph Frank and David I. Goldstein. New Brunswick, NJ: Rutgers University Press.

———. 2001. *The Idiot*. Trans. Larissa Volokhonsky and Richard Pevear. New York: Knopf.

Downey, Glanville. 1957. "Nikolaos Mesarites: Description of the Church of the Holy Apostles at Constantinople." *Transactions of the American Philosophical Society* 47.6: 855–924.

Duffy, Eamon. 2005. *The Stripping of the Altars*. New Haven, CT: Yale University Press.

Dupré, Louis. 1993. *Passage to Modernity*. New Haven, CT: Yale University Press.

———. 1996. "The Mystical Theology of Nicholas of Cusa's *De visione dei*." In *Nicholas of Cusa on Christ and the Church*, ed. Gerald Christianson and Thomas M. Izbicki, 205–20. Leiden: Brill.

———. 2004. *The Enlightenment and the Intellectual Foundations of Modern Culture*. New Haven, CT: Yale University Press.

Dyer, Christopher. 2005. *An Age of Transition? Economy and Society in England in the Later Middle Ages*. Oxford: Oxford University Press.

Eire, Carlos M. N. 2016. *Reformations: The Early Modern World, 1450–1650*. New Haven, CT: Yale University Press.

Eliot, George. 1990. *Selected Essays, Poems and Other Writings*. Ed. A. S. Byatt and Nicholas Warren. Harmondsworth: Penguin.

———. 2004. *Middlemarch*. Ed. Gregory Maertz. Peterborough, ONT: Broadview Press.

Eliot, T. S. 1967. *The Family Reunion*. New York: Harcourt, Brace & Company.

———. 2015. *The Poems*. 2 vols. Ed. Christopher Ricks and Jim McCue. Baltimore: Johns Hopkins University Press.

Ellenbogen, Josh, and Aaron Tugendhat, eds. 2011. *Idol Anxiety*. Stanford, CA: Stanford University Press.

Epictetus. 1995. *The Discourses*. Trans. Robin Hard. New York: Everyman.

Evans, Helen C., ed. 1997. *The Glory of Byzantium: Art and Culture of the Middle Byzantine Period, 843–1261*. New York: Metropolitan Museum of Art Publications.

———. 2004. *Byzantium: Faith and Power, 1261–1557*. New York: Metropolitan Museum of Art Publications.

Evdokimov, Paul. 1990. *The Art of the Icon: A Theology of Beauty*. Trans. Fr. Steven Bigham. Redondo Beach, CA: Oakwood.

Fagerberg, David W. 2009–10. "Liturgy as Icon of the Theological Imagination." *Louvain Studies* 34: 227–48.

Farrer, Austin. 1948. *The Glass of Vision: The Bampton Lectures for 1948*. n.p.: Dacre Press.

Felski, Rita. 2015. *The Limits of Critique*. Chicago: University of Chicago Press.

Fischer, Luke. 2015. *The Poet as Phenomenologist: Rilke and the New Poems*. London: Bloomsbury.

Flint, Kate. *The Victorians and the Visual Imagination*. Cambridge: Cambridge University Press, 2000.

Florensky, Pavel. 1996. *Iconostasis*. Trans. Donald Sheehan and Olga Adrejev. Crestwood, NY: St. Vladimir's Seminary Press.

———. 2004. *Beyond Vision: Essays on the Perception of Art*. London: Reaktion Books.

———. 2020. *The Meaning of Idealism: The Metaphysics of Genus and Countenance*. Trans. and ed. Boris Jakim. Brooklyn, NY: Semantron Press.

Florovsky, George. 1950. "Origen, Eusebius, and the Iconoclastic Controversy." *Church History* 19, no. 2: 77–96.

———. 1987. *The Byzantine Fathers of the Sixth to Eighth Century*. Vaduz, Liechtenstein: Notable & Academic.

Foxe, John. 1563. *Acts and Monuments* [*The Book of Martyrs*]. 1st ed. London.

Fraeters, Verle. 2012. "*Visio*/Vision." In *The Cambridge Companion to Medieval Mysticism*, ed. Amy Hollywood and Patricia Z. Beckman, 178–88. Cambridge: Cambridge University Press.

Frank, Joseph. 2010. *Dostoevsky, a Writer in His Time*. Princeton, NJ: Princeton University Press.

Frank, Manfred. 2011. *The Philosophical Foundations of Early German Romanticism*. Trans. Elizabeth Millán-Zaibert. Albany: SUNY Press.

Freedberg, David. 1989. *The Power of Images: Studies in the History and Theory of Response*. Chicago: University of Chicago Press.

———. 1995. "Holy Images and Other Images." Review of Belting, *Likeness and Presence*. www.researchgate.net/publication/264039807_Holy_Images_and_Other_Images.

Frei, Hans. 1980. *The Eclipse of Biblical Narrative: A Study in Eighteenth- and Nineteenth-Century Hermeneutics*. New Haven, CT: Yale University Press.

Fried, Michael. 1988. *Absorption and Theatricality: Painting and Beholder in the Age of Diderot*. Chicago: University of Chicago Press.

———. 1990. *Courbet's Realism*. Chicago: University of Chicago Press.

Friedrich, Hugo. 1956. *Die Struktur der modernen Lyrik von Baudelaire bis zur Gegenwart*. Berlin: Rowohlt.

Fry, Roger. 1927. *Cézanne: A Study of His Development*. New York: Macmillan.

Gadamer, Hans-Georg. 1975. *Wahrheit und Methode*. 2nd ed. Tübingen: J. C. B. Mohr.

———. 1976. *Philosophical Hermeneutics*. Trans. David E. Linge. Berkeley: University of California Press.

———. 1983. *Dialogue and Dialectic: Eight Hermeneutical Studies on Plato*. New Haven, CT: Yale University Press.

———. 1986. *The Idea of the Good in Platonic-Aristotelian Philosophy*. Trans. P. Christopher Smith. New Haven, CT: Yale University Press.

———. 1987. *Hegel, Husserl, Heidegger*. Tübingen: J. C. B. Mohr.

———. 1991. *Platon im Dialog*. Tübingen: J. C. B. Mohr.

———. 1993a. *Kunst als Aussage*. Tübingen: J. C. B. Mohr.

———. 1993b. *Wahrheit und Methode: Ergänzungen, Register*. Tübingen: J. C. B. Mohr.

———. 2006. *Truth and Method*. Trans. Joel Weinsheimer and Donald G. Marshall. New York: Continuum.

———. 2007. *The Gadamer Reader: A Bouquet of the Later Writings*. Trans. and ed. Richard E. Palmer. Evanston, IL: Northwestern University Press.

Gatrall, Jefferson A. 2004. "The Icon in the Picture: Reframing the Question of Dostoevsky's Modernist Iconography." *Slavic and East European Journal* 48.1: 1–25.

Gaukroger, Stephen. 2006. *The Emergence of a Scientific Culture: Science and the Shaping of Modernity, 1210–1685*. Oxford: Clarendon.

———. 2016. *The Natural and the Human: Science and the Shaping of Modernity, 1739–1841*. Oxford: Oxford University Press.

Gavrilyuk, Paul L. 2012. "Pseudo-Dionysius the Areopagite." In *The Spiritual Senses: Perceiving God in Western Christianity*, ed. Paul L. Gavrilyuk and Sarah Coakley, 86–103. Cambridge: Cambridge University Press.

Gavrilyuk, Paul L., and Sarah Coakley, eds. 2012. *The Spiritual Senses: Perceiving God in Western Christianity*. Cambridge: Cambridge University Press.

Gehlen, Arnold. 1978. *Der Mensch: Seine Natur und Stellung in der Welt*. 12th ed. Wiesbaden: Akademische Verlagsgesellschaft Atheanion.

———. 2004. *Urmensch und Spätkultur*. 6th rev. ed. Frankfurt: Klostermann.

———. 2016. *Zeit-Bilder, und andere kunstsoziologische Schriften*. Frankfurt: Klostermann.

Gerok-Reiter, Annette. 1993. "Perspektivität bei Rilke und Cézanne: Zur Raumerfahrung des späten Rilke." *Deutsche Vierteljahresschrift* 67: 484–520.

Gerson, Jean. 1998. *Early Works*. Trans. and ed. Brian Patrick McGuire. New York: Paulist Press.

Gertrude von Helfta. 1993. *The Herald of Divine Love*. New York: Paulist Press.

Gigante, Denise. 2009. *Life: Organic Form and Romanticism*. New Haven, CT: Yale University Press.

Gillespie, Michael A. 2007. *The Theological Origins of Modernity*. Chicago: University of Chicago Press.

Gilliam, Brian. 2003. "Ariadne, Daphne, and the Problem of *Verwandlung*." *Cambridge Opera Journal* 15: 67–80.

Gilson, Étienne. 1956. *The Christian Philosophy of St. Thomas Aquinas*. Trans. L K. Shook, C.S.B. New York: Random House.

———. 1965. *The Philosophy of St. Bonaventure*. Paterson, NJ: St. Anthony Guild Press.

———. 1984. *From Aristotle to Darwin and Back Again: A Journey in Final Causality, Species, and Evolution*. Trans. John Lyon. San Francisco: Ignatius Press.

Goethe, Johann Wolfgang von. 1887–1919. *Werke*. Weimarer Ausgabe. 143 vols. Ed. Hermann Böhlau et al. Weimar: Hermann Böhlau.

———. 1949. *Poetry and Truth from My Own Life*. Trans. Robert Oswald Moon. n.p.: Public Affairs Press.

———. 1952. *Botanical Writings*. Trans. and ed. Bertha Mueller and Charles J. Engard. Honolulu: University of Hawaii Press.

———. 1959. *Faust: Part Two.* Trans. Philip Wayne. Harmondsworth: Penguin.

———. 1967. *Theory of Colours.* Trans. Charles Lock Eastlake. London: F. Cass & Co.

———. 1981. *Werke.* Hamburger Ausgabe. 14 vols. Ed. Erich Trunz. Munich: Beck.

———. 1987. *Der Briefwechsel zwischen Goethe und Schiller.* Ed. Emil Staiger. Frankfurt: Insel.

———. 1989. *Italian Journey.* Trans. Robert R. Heitner, ed. Thomas P. Saine and Jeffrey L. Sammons. New York: Suhrkamp.

———. 1998. *Maxims and Reflections.* Trans. Elizabeth Stopp. Harmondsworth: Penguin.

Goldman, Harvey. 1988. *Max Weber and Thomas Mann: Calling and the Shaping of the Self.* Berkeley: University of California Press.

Gombrich, Ernst. 1972. *Art and Illusion.* Princeton, NJ: Bollingen.

Gordon, Peter. 2014. "Contextualism and Criticism in the History of Ideas." In *Rethinking Modern European Intellectual History,* ed. Darrin M. McMahon and Samuel Moyon, 32–55. New York: Oxford University Press,

Gosetti-Ferencei, Jennifer Anna. 2007. *The Ecstatic Quotidian: Phenomenological Sightings in Modern Art and Literature.* University Park: Pennsylvania State University Press.

Gould, Stephen J. 2002. *The Structure of Evolutionary Theory.* Cambridge, MA: Belknap Press of Harvard University Press.

Grafton, Anthony. 2000. *Leon Battista Alberti, Master-Builder of the Italian Renaissance.* Cambridge, MA: Harvard University Press.

Green, Garth W. 2012. "Nicholas of Cusa." In *The Spiritual Senses,* ed. Paul L. Gavrilyuk and Sarah Coakley, 210–23. Cambridge: Cambridge University Press.

Greenberg, Clement. 1961. "Cézanne." In *Art and Culture: Critical Essays,* 50–58. Boston: Beacon Press.

———. 1995. "Modernist Painting." In *The Collected Essays and Criticism,* vol. 4, 85–93. Chicago: University of Chicago Press.

Greer, Rowan A. 2001. *Christian Life and Christian Hope: Raids on the Inarticulate.* New York: Crossroad.

Grene, Marjorie, and David Depew. 2004. *The Philosophy of Biology: An Episodic History.* New York: Cambridge University Press.

Griffiths, Paul. 2009. *Intellectual Appetites: A Theological Grammar.* Washington, DC: Catholic University of America Press.

———. 2016. *The Practice of Catholic Theology: A Modest Proposal.* Washington, DC: Catholic University of America Press.

———. 2018. *Christian Flesh.* Stanford, CA: Stanford University Press.

Hadot, Pierre. 1993. *Plotinus: or, The Simplicity of Vision.* Trans. Michael Chase. Chicago: University of Chicago Press.

———. 1995. *Philosophy as a Way of Life.* Trans. Michael Chase. Oxford: Blackwell.

———. 2006. *The Veil of Isis.* Cambridge, MA: Harvard University Press.

Hahn, Cynthia. 2000. "*Visio Dei:* Changes in Medieval Visuality." In *Visuality Before and Beyond the Renaissance,* ed. Robert S. Nelson, 169–96. Cambridge: Cambridge University Press.

Halmi, Nicholas. 2007. *The Genealogy of the Romantic Symbol*. Oxford: Clarendon.

Hamburger, Jeffrey. 1998. *The Visual and the Visionary: Art and Female Spirituality in Late Medieval Germany*. New York: Zone Books.

———. 2000. "Seeing and Believing: The Suspicion of Sight and the Authentication of Vision in Late Medieval Art and Devotion." In *Imagination und Wirklichkeit*, ed. Klaus Krüger and Alessandro Nova, 47–69. Mainz: Philipp von Zabern Verlag.

———. 2012. "Mysticism and Visuality." In *The Cambridge Companion to Medieval Mysticism*, ed. Amy Hollywood and Patricia Z. Beckman, 277–93. Cambridge: Cambridge University Press.

Hamburger, Jeffrey F., and Anne-Marie Bouche, eds. 2005. *The Mind's Eye: Art and Theological Argument in the Middle Ages*. Princeton, NJ: Princeton University Press.

Hamburger, Käthe. 1966. *Philosophie der Dichter: Novalis, Schiller, Rilke*. Stuttgart: Kohlhammer.

Hampton, Alexander J. B. 2019. *Romanticism and the Re-Invention of Modern Religion*. Oxford: Oxford University Press.

Hanby, Michael. 2013. *No God, No Science: Theology, Cosmology, Biology*. Oxford: Wiley-Blackwell.

Harbison, Craig. 1991. *Jan van Eyck: The Play of Realism*. London: Reaktion Books.

Harries, Karsten. 2001. *Infinity and Perspective*. Cambridge, MA: MIT Press.

Hart, David Bentley. 2004. *The Beauty of the Infinite: The Aesthetics of Christian Truth*. Grand Rapids, MI: Eerdmans.

———. 2013. *The Experience of God: Being, Consciousness, Bliss*. New Haven, CT: Yale University Press.

———. 2017. *The Hidden and the Manifest*. Grand Rapids, MI: Eerdmans.

Hart, Kevin. 2017. *Poetry and Revelation: For a Phenomenology of Religious Poetry*. London: Bloomsbury.

Hatcher, John. 1977. *Plague, Population and the English Economy, 1348–1530*. London: Economic Society.

Haubst, Rudolf. 1991. *Streifzüge durch die Cusanische Theologie*. Muenster: Aschendorff Verlag.

Heath, J. M. F. 2013. *Paul's Visual Piety: The Metamorphosis of the Beholder*. Oxford: Oxford University Press.

Hegel, Georg F. W. 1952. *Phänomenologie des Geistes*. Ed. Johannes Hoffmeister. Hamburg: Meiner.

———. 1970. *Enzyklopädie der philosophischen Wissenschaften*. 3 vols. Ed. Eva Moldenhauer and Karl Markus Michel. Frankfurt: Suhrkamp.

———. 1975. *Aesthetics: Lectures on Fine Art*. 2 vols. Trans. T. M. Knox. Oxford: Clarendon.

———. 1977. *Phenomenology of Spirit*. Trans. A. V. Miller. New York: Oxford University Press.

Heidegger, Martin. 1966. *Discourse on Thinking*. Trans. John M. Anderson and E. Hans Freund. New York: Harper & Row.

———. 1967. *Wegmarken*. Frankfurt: Klostermann.

———. 1969. *Identity and Difference*. Trans. Joan Stambaugh. New York: Harper & Row.

———. 1977. "The Age of the World Picture." In *The Question Concerning Technology and Other Essays*, trans. William Lovitt, 115–54. New York: Harper & Row.

———. 1978. *Identität und Differenz*. Pfullingen: Neske.

———. 1979. *Sein und Zeit*. Tübingen: Niemeyer.

———. 1980. *Holzwege*. Frankfurt: Klostermann.

———. 1989. *Beiträge zur Philosophie*. Frankfurt: Klostermann.

———. 1996. *Being and Time*. Trans. Joan Stambaugh. Albany: SUNY Press.

———. 2002. *Off the Beaten Track*. Trans. and ed. Julian Young and Kenneth Haynes. Cambridge: Cambridge University Press.

———. 2012. *Contributions to Philosophy: Of the Event*. Trans. and ed. Richard Rojcewicz and Daniela Vallega-Neu. Bloomington: Indiana University Press.

———. 2014. *Gelassenheit: Heideggers Meßkircher Rede von 1955*. Freiburg: Karl Alber.

Hellman, John. 1982. *Simone Weil: An Introduction to Her Thought*. Eugene, OR: Wipf & Stock.

Helsinger, Elizabeth K. 1982. *Ruskin and the Art of the Beholder*. Cambridge, MA: Harvard University Press.

Hemingway, Andrew. 2007. "The Realist Aesthetic in Painting: 'Serious and committed, ironic and brutal, sincere and full of poetry.'" In *Adventures in Realism*, ed. Matthew Beaumont, 103–24. Oxford: Blackwell.

Henry, Michel. 1973. *The Essence of Manifestation*. Trans. Girard Etzkorn. The Hague: Martinus Nijhoff.

———. 2009. *Seeing the Invisible: On Kandinsky*. New York: Continuum.

Herdt, Jennifer. 2019. *Forming Humanity: Redeeming the German Bildung Tradition*. Chicago: University of Chicago Press.

Heroes, Walter. 2004. *Der Weg der Anschauung: Landschaft zwischen Ästhetik und Metaphysik*. Zug, Switzerland: Graue Edition.

Hewison, Robert. 1976. *John Ruskin: The Argument of the Eye*. Princeton, NJ: Princeton University Press.

Hilton, Timothy. 1985. *John Ruskin: The Early Years, 1819–1859*. New Haven, CT: Yale University Press.

Hobbes, Thomas. 1845. *Opera Philosophica Quae Latine Scripsit*. Vol. 1. London: Longman.

Hodge, Jonathan. 2003. "The Notebook Programmes and Projects of Darwin's London Years." In *The Cambridge Companion to Darwin*, ed. Jonathan Hodge and Gregory Radick, 40–68. Cambridge: Cambridge University Press.

Hoff, Johannes. 2013. *The Analogical Turn: Rethinking Modernity with Nicholas of Cusa*. Grand Rapids, MI: Eerdmans.

Hölderlin, Friedrich. 1943–86. *Sämtliche Werke*. Ed. Friedrich Beissner and Adolf Beck. Stuttgart: Cotta.

Holl, Karl. 1923. "Die Entstehung der Bilderwand in der griechischen Kirche." In *Gesammelte Aufsätze zur Kirchengeschichte*, vol. 2, 225–37. Tübingen: J. C. B. Mohr.

Holland, Jocelyn. 2009. *German Romanticism and Science*. New York: Routledge.

Hollywood, Amy. 2008. "Mysticism and Transcendence." In *The Cambridge Companion to Christian Mysticism*, ed. Amy Hollywood and Patricia Z. Beckman, 297–307. Cambridge: Cambridge University Press.

Homer. 1996. *The Iliad*. Trans. Robert Fagles. Harmondsworth: Penguin.

Hopkins, Gerard Manley. 1959a. *The Journals and Papers of Gerard Manley Hopkins*. Ed. Humphrey House. London: Oxford University Press.

———. 1959b. *The Sermons and Devotional Writings of Gerard Manley Hopkins*. Ed. Christopher Devlin. London: Oxford University Press.

———. 1986. *Gerard Manley Hopkins: The Major Works*. Ed. Catherine Phillips. Oxford: Oxford University Press.

———. 2006–. *The Collected Works of Gerard Manley Hopkins*. 8 vols. Ed. Lesley Higgins et al. Oxford: Oxford University Press.

Hopkins, Robert. 1998. *Picture, Image, and Experience*. Cambridge: Cambridge University Press.

Hösle, Vittorio. 2016. *Vicoäs: New Science of the Intersubjective World*. Trans. and ed. Francis R. Hittinger IV. Notre Dame, IN: University of Notre Dame Press.

Hugh of St. Victor. 1962. *Selected Spiritual Writings*. Trans. Aelred Squire, O.P. New York: Harper & Row.

Huizinga, Johan.1996. *Autumn of the Middle Ages*. Trans. Rodney J. Payton and Ulrich Mammitzsch. Chicago: University of Chicago Press.

Humboldt, Alexander von. 1997. *Cosmos*. Trans. E. C. Otté, ed. Nicolaas A. Rupke. Baltimore: Johns Hopkins University Press.

Hume, David. 2007. *A Treatise of Human Nature*. Ed. David F. Norton and Mary J. Norton. Oxford: Oxford University Press.

Husserl, Edmund. 1950. *Die Idee der Phänomenologie*. In *Husserliana: Gesammelte Werke*, vol. 2, ed. H. L. van Breda. The Hague: Martinus Nijhoff.

———. 1970. *The Crisis of the European Sciences and Transcendental Phenomenology*. Trans. David Carr. Evanston, IL: Northwestern University Press.

———. 1977. *Formal and Transcendental Logic*. Trans. Dorion Cairns. Dordrecht: Martinus Nijhoff.

———. 1980. *Logische Untersuchungen*. Tübingen: Max Niemeyer.

———. 1991. *Ding und Raum: Vorlesungen 1907*. Ed. Karl-Heinz Hahnengress and Smail Rapic. Hamburg: Meiner.

———. 1994. *Briefwechsel*. Vol. 7. Ed. Karl Schuhmann. Dordrecht: Kluwer.

———. 1997. *Thing and Space*. Trans. Richard Rojcewicz. Dodrecht: Kluwer.

———. 1999. *The Idea of Phenomenology*. Trans. Lee Hardy. Dodrecht: Kluwer.

———. 2001. *Logical Investigations*. Trans. J. N. Findlay. London: Routledge.

———. 2005. *Phantasy, Image-Consciousness and Memory*. Trans. John Brough. Dordrecht: Springer.

———. 2006a. *Basic Problems of Phenomenology*. Dordrecht: Springer.

———. 2006b. *Phantasie und Bildbewußtsein: Vorlesungen 1904/05*. Ed. Eduard Marbach. Hamburg: Meiner.

———. 2009. *Ideen zu einer reinen Phänomenologie und phänomenologischen Philosophie* (1913). Ed. Elisabeth Ströker. Hamburg: Meiner.

———. 2014. *Ideas for a Pure Phenomenology and a Phenomenological Philosophy.* Trans. Daniel O. Dahlstrom. Indianapolis, IN: Hackett.

Hütter, Reinhard. 2019. *Bound for Beatitude: A Thomistic Study in Eschatology and Ethics.* Washington, DC: Catholic University of America Press.

Imdahl, Max. 1968. "Vier Aspekte zum Problem der ästhetischen Grenzüberschreitung in der bildenden Kunst." In *Die nicht mehr schönen Künste*, ed. Hans-Robert Jauß, 493–505. Munich: Fink Verlag.

———. 1980. *Giotto—Arenafresken.* Munich: Fink Verlag.

Iser, Wolfgang, ed. 1966. *Immanente Ästhetik, ästhetische Reflexion: Lyrik als Paradigma der Moderne.* Munich: Fink.

Ivanovic, Filip. 2010. *Symbol and Icon: Dionysius the Areopagite and the Iconoclastic Crisis.* Eugene, OR: Cascade Books.

———. 2020. "Pseudo-Dionysius and the Importance of Sensible Things." In *Pseudo-Dionysius and Christian Visual Culture, c. 500–900*, ed. Francesca Dell'Acqua and Ernesto Sergio Mainoldi, 77–87. Cham: Palgrave Macmillan.

Jackson, Robert L. 1966. *Dostoevsky's Quest for Form: A Study of His Philosophy of Art.* New Haven, CT: Yale University Press.

James, William. 1987. *Varieties of Religious Experience.* In *Writings, 1902–1910.* New York: Library of America.

Jameson, Fredric. 2013. *The Antinomies of Realism.* New York: Verso.

Jamme, Christoph. 1992. "Der Verlust der Dinge: Cézanne—Rilke—Heidegger." *Deutsche Zeitschrift für Philosophie* 40: 385–97.

Janicaud, Dominique, et al., eds. 2000. *Phenomenology and the "Theological Turn."* New York: Fordham University Press.

Jensen, Robin. 2005. *Face to Face: Portraits of the Divine in Early Christianity.* Minneapolis, MN: Fortress Press.

John of Damascus. 1958. *Writings.* Ed. Frederick H. Chase Jr. Washington, DC: Catholic University of America Press.

———. 2003. *Three Treatises on the Divine Images.* Trans. and ed. Andrew Louth. Crestwood, NY: St. Vladimir's Seminary Press.

Johnson, Galen. A. 2013. "On the Origin(s) of Truth in Art: Merleau-Ponty, Klee, and Cézanne." *Research in Phenomenology* 43: 475–515.

Jolles, André. 1965. *Einfache Formen.* Tübingen: Max Niemeyer.

Jonas, Hans. 1954. "The Nobility of Sight." *Philosophy and Phenomenological Research* 14.4: 507–19.

———. 1961. "Homo Pictor und die Differentia des Menschen." *Zeitschrift für philosophische Forschung* 15.2: 161–76.

Jones, David. 2003. *In Parenthesis.* New York: New York Review of Books.

Julian of Norwich. 2006. *The Writings of Julian of Norwich.* Ed. Nicholas Watson and Jacqueline Jenkins. Philadelphia: University of Pennsylvania Press.

———. 2015. *Revelations of Divine Love.* Ed. Barry Windeatt. Oxford: Oxford University Press.

Kafka, Franz. 1990. *Der Proceß*. Frankfurt: Fischer.

Kandinsky, Wassily. 1977. *On the Spiritual in Art*. Trans. M. Sadler. New York: Dover.

Kant, Immanuel. 1951. *Critique of Judgment*. Trans. J. H. Bernard. New York: Hafner Press.

———. 1965. *Critique of Pure Reason*. Trans. Norman Kemp Smith. New York: St. Martin's Press.

Kartsonis, Anna. 1998. "The Responding Icon." In *Heaven on Earth: Art and the Church in Byzantium*, ed. Linda Safran, 58–80. University Park: Pennsylvania State University Press.

Kasper, Walter, et al., eds. 1993–2001. *Lexikon für Theologie und Kirche*. 10 vols. Freiburg: Herder Verlag.

Keats, John. 1891. *Letters of John Keats to His Family and Friends*. London: MacMillan.

Kennedy, Robert P. 2003. "The *Confessions* as Eschatological Narrative." In *A Reader's Companion to Augustine's Confessions*, ed. Kim Paffenroth and Robert P. Kennedy, 167–84. Louisville, KY: Westminster John Knox Press,

Kenner, Hugh. 1971. *The Pound Era*. Berkeley: University of California Press.

Kerr, Fergus. 2002. *After Aquinas: Versions of Thomism*. Oxford: Blackwell.

Kessler, Herbert L. 2000. *Spiritual Seeing: Picturing God's Invisibility in Medieval Art*. Philadelphia: University of Pennsylvania Press.

Kierkegaard, Søren. 1991. *Practice in Christianity*. Trans. and ed. Howard V. Hong and Edna H. Hong. Princeton, NJ: Princeton University Press.

Kirk, G. S., J. E. Raven, and M. Schofield, eds. 1983. *The Pre-Socratic Philosophers*. Cambridge: Cambridge University Press.

Kitzinger, Ernst. 1954. "The Cult of Images in the Age before Iconoclasm." *Dumbarton Oaks Papers* 8: 83–150.

———. 1995. *Byzantine Art in the Making*. Cambridge, MA: Harvard University Press.

Klaver, J. M. I. 1997. *Geology and Religious Sentiment: The Effect of Geological Discoveries on English Society and Literature between 1829 and 1859*. Leiden: Brill.

Koerner, Joseph Leo. 2002. "The Icon as Iconoclash." In *Iconoclash*, ed. Bruno Latour and Peter Weibel, 164–213. Cambridge, MA: MIT Press.

———. 2004. *The Reformation of the Image*. Chicago: University of Chicago Press.

Kolakowski, Leszek. 1995. *God Owes Us Nothing*. Chicago: University of Chicago Press.

Kostenec, Jan, and Ken Dark. 2011. "Paul the Silentiary's Description of Hagia Sophia in the Light of New Archeological Evidence." *Byzantinoslavica* 3: 88–105.

Kreuzer, Johann. 2010. "Das Bild und sein Sehen bei Nikolaus von Kues." In *Videre et videri coincidunt: Theorien des Sehens in der ersten Hälfte des 15. Jahrhunderts*, ed. Wolfgang C. Schneider et al., 81–96. Muenster: Aschendorff Verlag.

Krieger, Murray. 1967. "*Ekphrasis* and the Still Movement of Poetry; or, *Laokoön Revisited*." In *The Poet as Critic*, ed. Frederick P. W. McDowell, 3–26. Evanston, IL: Northwestern University Press.

Ladner, Gerhard B. 1953. "The Concept of the Image in the Greek Fathers and the Byzantine Iconoclastic Controversy." *Dumbarton Oaks Papers* 7: 1–34.

Lane, Barbara G. 1991. "The Case of Canon van der Paele." *Notes in the History of Art* 9.2: 1–6.

Latour, Bruno, and Peter Weibel. 2002. *Iconoclash: Beyond the Image Wars in Science, Religion, and Art.* Cambridge, MA: MIT Press.

Lenoir, Timothy. 1982. *The Strategy of Life: Teleology and Mechanics in Nineteenth-Century German Biology.* Chicago: University of Chicago Press.

Levinas, Emmanuel. 1987. "Reality and Its Shadow." In *Collected Philosophical Papers,* 1–14. Trans. Alphonso Lingis. Dordrecht: Martinus Nijhoff.

Leys, Ruth. 2000. *Trauma: A Genealogy.* Chicago: University of Chicago Press.

Liddon, Henry Perry. [1867]. 1908. *The Divinity of our Lord and Saviour Jesus Christ.* Reprint. New York: Longmans, Green & Co.

Lindberg, David C. 1976. *Theories of Vision from Al-Kindi to Kepler.* Chicago: University of Chicago Press.

Linné, Carl. 2003. *Linnaeus Philosophia Botanica.* Trans. and ed. Stephen Freer. Oxford: Oxford University Press.

Lipton, Sara. 2005. "'The Sweet Lean of His Head': Writing about Looking at the Crucifix in the High Middle Ages." *Speculum* 80: 1172–1208.

———. 2008. "Images and Their Uses." In *The Cambridge History of Christianity: Christianity in Western Europe c. 1100–c. 1500,* ed. Miriam Rubin and Walter Simons, 254–82. Cambridge: Cambridge University Press.

Locke, John. 1975. *An Essay Concerning Human Understanding.* Ed. Peter H. Nidditch. Oxford: Clarendon.

Lossky, Vladimir. 1997. *The Mystical Theology of the Eastern Church.* Crestwood, NY: St. Vladimir's Seminary Press.

Louth, Andrew. 1996. *Maximus the Confessor.* New York: Routledge.

———. 2002. *St. John Damascene: Tradition and Originality in Byzantine Theology.* Oxford: Oxford University Press.

———. 2004. "Beauty Will Save the World: The Formation of Byzantine Spirituality." *Theology Today* 61: 67–77.

———. 2005. "'Truly Visible Things Are Manifest Images of Invisible Things': Dionysios the Areopagite on Knowing the Invisible." In *Seeing the Invisible in Late Antiquity and the Early Middle Ages,* ed. Giselle de Nie et al., 15–24. Turnout: Brepols.

Lovejoy, Arthur O. 1964. *The Great Chain of Being.* Cambridge, MA: Harvard University Press.

Löwith, Karl. 1957. *Meaning in History.* Chicago: University of Chicago Press.

Lukâcs, Georg. 1977. "Realism in the Balance." In *Adorno, Benjamin, Bloch, Brecht, Lukâcs: Aesthetics and Politics,* ed. Fredric Jameson, 28–59. New York: Verso.

———. 1978. "Narrate or Describe?" In *Writer and Critic, and Other Essays,* trans. and ed. Arthur Kahn, 110–48. London: Merlin Press.

Lyell, Charles. 1997. *Principles of Geology.* Ed. James Secord. Harmondsworth: Penguin.

MacGregor, Neil. 2000. *Seeing Salvation: Images of Christ in Art.* New Haven, CT: Yale University Press.

MacIntyre, Alasdair. 1990. *Three Rival Versions of Moral Enquiry.* Notre Dame, IN: University of Notre Dame Press.

MacKenzie, Norman H. 2008. *A Reader's Guide to Gerard Manley Hopkins.* Philadelphia: St. Joseph's Press.

Macrides, Ruth, and Paul Magdalino. 1988. "The Architecture of Ekphrasis: Construction and Context of Paul the Silentiary's Poem on Hagia Sophia." *Byzantine and Modern Greek Studies* 12: 47–82.

Maguire, Henry. 1996. *The Icons of Their Bodies: Saints and Their Images in Byzantium.* Princeton, NJ: Princeton University Press.

Mainoldi, Ernesto Sergio. 2020. "Reassessing the Historico-Doctrinal Background of Pseudo-Dionysius' Image Theory." In *Pseudo-Dionysius and Christian Visual Culture, c. 500–900*, ed. Francesca Dell'Acqua and Ernesto Sergio Mainoldi, 1–45. Cham: Palgrave Macmillan.

Mainstone, Rowland J. 1988. *Hagia Sophia: Architecture, Structure and Liturgy of Justinian's Great Church.* New York: Thames and Hudson.

Male, Emile. 1986. *Religious Art in France: The Late Middle Ages.* Princeton, NJ: Princeton University Press.

Mandelstam, Osip. 1979. *Critical Prose and Letters.* Trans. and ed. Jane G. Harris and Constance Link. Woodstock, NY: Ardis Publishers.

Mango, Cyril, trans. and ed. 1958. *The Homilies of Photius, Patriarch of Constantinople.* Cambridge, MA: Harvard University Press.

Mann, Thomas. 1981a. "Der Tod in Venedig." In *Frühe Erzählungen.* Frankfurt: Fischer.

———. 1981b. *Der Zauberberg.* Frankfurt: Fischer.

———. 1988. *Death in Venice and other Stories.* Trans. David Luke. New York: Bantam Books.

———. 1993. *Buddenbrooks.* Trans. John E. Woods. New York: Vintage.

———. 1995a. *Briefe.* 3 vols. Ed. Erika Mann. Frankfurt: Fischer.

———. 1995b. *Death in Venice.* Trans. Stanley Applebaum. New York: Dover.

———. 1995c. *The Magic Mountain.* Trans. John E. Woods. New York: Vintage.

———. 1998. *The Letters of Heinrich and Thomas Mann.* Trans. Don Reneau. Berkeley: University of California Press.

———. 2004. *Frühe Erzählungen, 1893-1912.* Vol. 2/ii of *Grosse Kommentierte Frankfurter Ausgabe.* Commentary by Terence Reed. Frankfurt: Fischer.

Marion, Jean-Luc. 1991. *God without Being.* Trans. Thomas A. Carlson. Chicago: University of Chicago Press.

———. 2002a. *Being Given.* Stanford, CA: Stanford University Press.

———. 2002b. *In Excess: Studies of Saturated Phenomena.* Trans. Robyn Horner and Vincent Berrand. New York: Fordham University Press.

———. 2004. *The Crossing of the Visible.* Trans. James A. K. Smith. Stanford, CA: Stanford University Press.

———. 2008. *The Visible and the Revealed.* Trans. Christina M. Gschwandtner. New York: Fordham University Press.

———. 2015. *Negative Certainties.* Trans. Stephen E. Lewis. Chicago: University of Chicago Press.

——— 2016. "Seeing, or Seeing Oneself Seen: Nicholas of Cusa's Contribution in *De visione Dei.*" *Journal of Religion* 96.3: 305–31.

Maritain, Jacques. 1953. *Creative Intuition in Art and Poetry.* New York: Meridian.

———. 1995. *The Degrees of Knowledge.* Trans. Gerard B. Phelan. Notre Dame, IN: University of Notre Dame Press.

Marsengill, K. 2015. *Portraits and Icons: Between Reality and Spirituality in Byzantine Art.* Turnhout: Brepols.

Maslov, Boris. 2012. "The Limits of Platonism: Gregory of Nazianzus and the Invention of *theôsis.*" *Greek, Roman, and Byzantine Studies* 52: 440–68.

Maximus [the Confessor]. 1985. *Selected Writings.* Trans. George C. Berthold. New York: Paulist Press.

———. 2003. *On the Cosmic Mystery of Jesus Christ: Selected Writings from Maximus the Confessor.* Trans. Paul M. Blowers and Robert Louis Wilken. Crestwood, NY: St. Vladimir's Seminary Press.

———. 2014. *On Difficulties in the Church Fathers: The Ambigua.* 2 vols. Trans. and ed. Nicholas Constas. Cambridge, MA: Harvard University Press.

McCabe, Herbert. 2008. *On Aquinas.* New York: Continuum.

McDowell, John. 1996. *Mind and World.* Cambridge, MA: Harvard University Press.

McGann, Jerome. 1986. "The Idea of an Indeterminate Text: Blake's Bible of Hell and Dr. Alexander Geddes." *Studies in Romanticism* 25.3: 303–24.

McGillen, Michael. 2021. "Husserl's Image Worlds and the Language of Phenomenology." In *Phenomenology to the Letter: Husserl and Literature*, ed. Philippe P. Haensler, Kristina Mendicino, and Rochelle Tobias, 23–44. Berlin: De Gruyter.

McGinn, Bernard. 2005. *The Harvest of Mysticism in Medieval Germany.* New York: Herder & Herder.

———. 2012. *The Varieties of Vernacular Mysticism, 1350–1550.* New York: Herder & Herder.

McGregor, Neil. 2000. *Seeing Salvation: Images of Christ in Art.* London: BBC Worldwide.

McInroy, Mark. 2014. *Balthasar on the Spiritual Senses: Perceiving Splendour.* Oxford: Oxford University Press.

Meerson, Olga. 1995. "Ivolgin and Holbein: Non-Christ Risen vs. Christ Non-Risen." *Slavic and East European Journal* 39.2: 200–213.

Merleau-Ponty, Michel. 1964. *The Primacy of Perception.* Trans. James M. Edie. Evanston, IL: Northwestern University Press.

———. 1968. *The Visible and the Invisible.* Trans. Alphonso Lingis. Evanston, IL: Northwestern University Press.

———. 1993. *The Merleau-Ponty Aesthetics Reader: Philosophy and Painting.* Evanston, IL: Northwestern University Press.

———. 2010. *The Phenomenology of Perception.* Trans. Colin Smith. London: Routledge & Kegan Paul.

Meyendorff, John. 1983. *Byzantine Theology: Historical Trends and Doctrinal Themes.* New York: Fordham University Press.

Meyer, Herman. 1963. *Zarte Empirie: Studien zur Literaturgeschichte*. Stuttgart: Metzler.

Miller, Clyde Lee. 1996. "God's Presence: Some Cusan Proposal." In *Nicholas of Cusa on Christ and the Church*, ed. Gerald Christianson and Thomas M. Izbicki, 241–49. Leiden: Brill.

Miller, Elaine P. 2002. *The Vegetative Soul: From Philosophy of Nature to Subjectivity in the Feminine*. Albany: SUNY Press.

Miller, Gordon. 2009. *The Metamorphosis of Plants: Johann Wolfgang von Goethe*. Cambridge, MA: MIT Press.

Miller, J. Hillis. 1975. *The Disappearance of God: Five Nineteenth-Century Writers*. Cambridge, MA: Harvard University Press.

Mitchell, W. J. T. 1984. *Iconology: Image, Text, Ideology*. Chicago: University of Chicago Press.

———. 1994. *Picture Theory*. Chicago: University of Chicago Press.

Mondzain, Marie-José. 2005. *Image, Icon, Economy: The Byzantine Origins of the Contemporary Imaginary*. Trans. Rico Franses. Stanford, CA: Stanford University Press.

More, Sir Thomas. [1529] 1927. *The Dialogue Concerning Tyndale*. n.p.: Eyre & Spottiswoode.

Morgan, David. 2015. *The Forge of Vision: A Visual History of Modern Christianity*. Berkeley: University of California Press.

Mörike, Eduard. 1997. *Sämtliche Werke*. 2 vols. Darmstadt: Wissenschaftliche Buchgesellschaft.

Muller, Jill. 2003. *Gerard Manley Hopkins and Victorian Catholicism*. New York: Routledge.

Müller, Wolfgang G. 1999. "Rilke, Husserl, und die Dinglyrik der Moderne." In *Rilke und die Weltliteratur*, 214–35. Bonn: Artemis und Winkler.

Müller-Sievers, Helmut. 1997. *Self-Generation: Biology, Philosophy, and Literature around 1800*. Stanford, CA: Stanford University Press.

Muratori, Cecilia, and Mario Meliadò. 2020. "Northern Renaissance Platonism from Nicholas of Cusa to Jacob Böhme." In *Christian Platonism: A History*, ed. Alexander Hampton and John Peter Kenney, 246–79. Cambridge: Cambridge University Press.

Murdoch, Iris. 1970. *The Sovereignty of Good*. New York: Routledge.

———. 1997. *Existentialists and Mystics*. Ed. Peter Conradi. Harmondsworth: Penguin.

Natorp, Paul. 2004. *Plato's Theory of Ideas: An Introduction to Idealism*. Trans. Vasilis Politis and John Connolly. Baden-Baden: Sankt Augustin.

Nelson, Robert. 2007. "To Say and to See: Ekphrasis and Vision in Byzantium." In *Later Byzantine Painting: Art, Agency, and Appreciation*, 143–68. Aldershot: Ashgate.

Newman, Barbara. 2005. "What Did It Mean to Say 'I Saw'? The Clash between Theory and Practice in Medieval Visionary Culture." *Speculum* 80: 1–43.

Newman, John Henry. 1979. *An Essay in Aid of a Grammar of Assent*. Ed. Nicholas Lash. Notre Dame, IN: University of Notre Dame Press.

———. 1989. *An Essay on the Development of Christian Doctrine*. Ed. Nicholas Lash. Notre Dame, IN: University of Notre Dame Press.

———. 2000. *Lectures on the Present Position of Catholics in England.* Notre Dame, IN: University of Notre Dame Press.

Nichols, Aidan, O.P. 2006. *Scattering the Seed: A Guide through Balthasar's Early Writings on Philosophy and the Arts.* Washington, DC: Catholic University of America Press.

———. 2016. *All Great Art Is Praise: Art and Religion in John Ruskin.* Washington, DC: Catholic University of America Press.

Nietzsche, Friedrich. 1980. *Sämtliche Werke.* 15 vols. Ed. Giorgio Colli and Mazzino Montinari. Munich: dtv.

———. 1993. *The Birth of Tragedy.* Ed. Michael Tanner, trans. Shaun Whiteside. Harmondsworth: Penguin.

———. 2002. *Beyond Good and Evil.* Trans. and ed. Judith Norman and Rolf-Peter Horstmann. Cambridge: Cambridge University Press.

Noble, Thomas F., S.J. 2009. *Images, Iconoclasm, and the Carolingians.* University Park: Pennsylvania State University Press.

Nockles, Peter B. 1994. *The Oxford Movement in Context: Anglican High Churchmanship, 1760–1857.* Cambridge: Cambridge University Press.

Nussbaum, Martha. 1994. *The Therapy of Desire: Theory and Practice in Hellenistic Ethics.* Princeton, NJ: Princeton University Press.

Nyhart, Lynn K. 1995. *Biology Takes Form: Animal Morphology and the German Universities.* Chicago: University of Chicago Press.

Ockham, William. 1991. *Quodlibetal Questions.* Trans. Alfred J. Freddoso and Francis Kelley. New Haven, CT: Yale University Press.

Oldroyd, David R. 2003. "The Earth Sciences." In *From Natural Philosophy to the Sciences,* ed. David Cahan, 88–128. Chicago: University of Chicago Press,

Olds, Clifton. 1996. "Aspect and Perspective in Renaissance Thought: Nicholas of Cusa and Jan Van Eyck." In *Nicholas of Cusa on Christ and the Church,* ed. Gerald Christianson and Thomas M. Izbicki, 251–64. Leiden: Brill.

Ong, Walter. 1983. *Ramus: Method and the Decay of Dialogue.* Cambridge, MA: Harvard University Press.

O'Regan, Cyril. 2001. *Gnostic Return in Modernity.* Albany, NY: SUNY Press.

———. 2014. *The Anatomy of Misremembering: von Balthasar's Response to Philosophical Modernity.* Notre Dame, IN: University of Notre Dame Press.

Origen. 1869. *The Writings of Origen.* Trans. Frederick Crombie, D.D. The Ante-Nicene Library, vol. 10. London: T. & T. Clark.

———. 1872. *The Writings of Origen.* Vol. 2. Trans. Frederick Crombie, D.D. The Ante-Nicene Library, vol. 23. London: T. & T. Clark.

———. 1984. *Origen: Spirit and Fire, a Thematic Anthology of His Writings.* Ed. Hans Urs von Balthasar. Washington, DC: Catholic University of America Press.

Ostrogorsky, Georg. 1929. *Studien zur Geschichte des byzantinischen Bilderstreits.* Breslau: M. & H. Marcus.

Otis, Brooks. 1966. *Ovid as Epic Poet.* Cambridge: Cambridge University Press.

Ouspensky, Leonid. 1992. *Theology of the Icon.* 2 vols. Trans. Anthony Gythiel. Crestwood, NY: St. Vladimir's Seminary Press.

Ovid. 1986. *Metamorphoses*. Trans. A. D. Melville, ed. E. J. Kenney. New York: Oxford University Press.

Paley, William. [1802] 1890. *Natural Theology*. London.

Panofsky, Erwin. 1968. *Idea: A Concept in Art Theory*. Trans. Joseph J. S. Peake. Columbia: University of South Carolina Press.

———. 1997. *Perspective as Symbolic Form*. Trans. Christopher Wood. New York: Zone Books.

Parry, Kenneth. 1996. *Depicting the Word: Byzantine Iconophile Thought of the Eighth and Ninth Centuries*. Leiden: Brill.

Pascal, Blaise. 1954. Œuvres *complètes*. Ed. Jacques Chevalier. Paris: Gallimard.

Patočka, Jan. 2002. *Plato and Europe*. Trans. Petr Lom. Stanford, CA: Stanford University Press.

Patterson, Richard. 2013. "Word and Image in Plato." In *Presocratics and Plato: Festschrift at Delphi in Honor of Charles Kahn*, 429–55. Zurich: Parmenides.

Pelikan, Jaroslav. 1977. *The Christian Tradition: A History of the Development of Doctrine*. Vol. 2. Chicago: University of Chicago Press.

———. 2011. *Imago Dei: The Byzantine Apologia for Icons*. Princeton, NJ: Princeton University Press.

Pentcheva, Bissera V. 2006. "The Performative Icon." *Art Bulletin* 88.4: 631–55.

———. 2017a. *Hagia Sophia: Sound, Space, and Spirit in Byzantium*. University Park: Pennsylvania State University Press.

———. 2017b. "Vital Inbreathing: Iconicity beyond Representation in Late Antiquity." In *Icons and the Liturgy, East and West*, ed. Nicholas Denysenko, 56–73. Notre Dame, IN: University of Notre Dame Press.

Pfau, Thomas. 1997. *Wordsworth's Profession: Form, Class, and the Logic of Romantic Cultural Production*. Stanford: Stanford University Press.

———. 2005a. "From Mediation to Medium: Aesthetic and Anthropological Dimension of the Image (*Bild*) and the Crisis of *Bildung* in German Modernism." *Modernist Cultures* 1.2: 140–81. Special issue *Medium and Message in German Modernism*, ed. Thomas Pfau.

———. 2005b. *Romantic Moods: Paranoia, Trauma, and Melancholy, 1790–1840*. Baltimore: Johns Hopkins University Press.

———. 2007. "The Philosophy of Shipwreck: Gnosticism, Skepticism, and Coleridge's Catastrophic Modernity." *MLN* 122.5: 949–1004.

———. 2010. "All Is Leaf: Difference, Metamorphosis, and Goethe's Phenomenology of Knowledge." *Studies in Romanticism* 49.1: 3–41.

———. 2012. "William Paley." In *The Encyclopedia of Romantic Literature*, ed. Frederick Burwick, vol. 2, 974–79. Oxford: Wiley-Blackwell.

———. 2013a. *Minding the Modern: Intellectual Traditions, Human Agency, and Responsible Knowledge*. Notre Dame, IN: University of Notre Dame Press.

———. 2013b. "Rehabilitating the Image: With Some Reflections on G. M. Hopkins." *Yearbook of Comparative Literature* 59: 117–47.

———. 2015. "Beethoven's Heroic 'New Path': Organic Form and Its Consequences." *Andererseits* 4: 1–13.

———. 2017a. "Faith against Reason: Reflections on Luther's 500th." *Andererseits: A Journal of Transatlantic Studies* 5: 1–11.

———. 2017b. "Tradition." In *The Edinburgh Critical History of Nineteenth-Century Theology*, ed. Daniel Whistler, 219–46. Edinburgh: Edinburgh University Press.

———. 2017c. "Varieties of Non-Propositional Knowledge: Image, Attention, Action." In *Judgment & Action: Fragments toward a History*, ed. Vivasvan Soni and Thomas Pfau, 269–301. Evanston, IL: Northwestern University Press.

———. 2018a. "From Classical Teleology to Romantic *Bildung*." In *A Companion to Early German Romantic Philosophy*, ed. Elizabeth Millán and Judith Norman, 142–72. Amsterdam: Brill.

———. 2018b. "'Superabundant Being': Disambiguating Rilke and Heidegger." *Modern Theology* 35.1: 1–20.

———. 2021. "Kantian Aesthetics as 'Soft' Iconoclasm." *Logos: A Journal of Catholic Thought and Culture* 24.3: 69–88.

Phillips, Catherine. 2008. *Gerard Manley Hopkins and the Victorian Visual World*. Oxford: Oxford University Press.

Photios. 1958. *The Homilies of Photius, Patriarch of Constantinople*. Trans. and ed. Cyril Mango. Cambridge, MA: Harvard University Press.

Pieper, Joseph. 1989. *Living the Truth: The Truth of All Things and Reality and the Good*. San Francisco: Ignatius Press.

———. 2002. *Darstellungen und Interpretationen: Platon*. In *Werke*, vol. 1. Hamburg: Meiner.

———. 2006. *Schriften zur Philosophischen Anthropologie und Ethik*. Hamburg: Meiner.

Pinkard, Terry. 1996. *Hegel's Phenomenology: The Sociality of Reason*. New York: Cambridge University Press.

———. 2002. *German Philosophy, 1760–1860: The Legacy of Idealism*. New York: Cambridge University Press.

Pippin, Robert. 1999. *Modernism as a Philosophical Problem*. 2nd ed. Oxford: Blackwell.

———. 2014. *After the Beautiful: Hegel and the Philosophy of Pictorial Modernism*. Chicago: University of Chicago Press.

Plato. 1997. *Complete Works*. Ed. John M. Cooper. Indianapolis, IN: Hackett.

Plotinus. 1967. *The Enneads*. Trans. A. H. Armstrong. Loeb Classical Library. Cambridge, MA: Harvard University Press.

Podro, Michael. 2010. "Literalism and Truthfulness in Painting." *British Journal of Aesthetics* 50.4: 457–68.

Polanyi, Michael. 1962. *Personal Knowledge: Towards a Post-Critical Philosophy*. Chicago: University of Chicago Press.

———. 1969. *Knowing and Being*. Ed. Marjorie Grene. Chicago: University of Chicago Press.

Pomplun, Trent. 2015. "The Theology of Gerard Manley Hopkins: From Duns Scotus to the Baroque." *Journal of Religion* 95.1: 1–29.

Pörksen, Uwe. 2001. "Die Selbstüberwachung des Beobachters." *Goethe-Jahrbuch* 118: 203.

Porphyry. 2014. *On Abstinence from Killing Animals*. Trans. Gillian Clark. London: Bloomsbury.

Porter, James I. 2010. "Plato and the Platonic Tradition: The Image beyond the Image." *Yearbook of Comparative Literature* 56: 75–103.

Porter, Roy. 1976. "Charles Lyell and the Principles of the History of Geology." *British Journal for the History of Science* 9.2: 91–103.

Poster, Carol. 1998. "The Idea(s) of Order of Platonic Dialogues and Their Hermeneutic Consequences." *Phoenix: Journal of the Classical Association of Canada* 52.3–4: 282–98.

Post-Nicene Fathers. 2012. 14 vols. Ed. Philip Schaff and Henry Wace. Peabody, MA: Hendrickson Publishers.

Price, Richard, and Mary Whitby. 2009. *Chalcedon in Context: Church Councils 400–700*. Liverpool: Liverpool University Press.

Proclus. 1963. *The Elements of Theology*. 2nd ed. Trans. and ed. E. R. Dodds. Oxford: Clarendon.

Przywara, Erich. 1955. *In und Gegen: Stellungnahmen zur Zeit*. 2 vols. Nürnberg: Glock und Lutz.

———. 1996. *Analogia Entis: Metaphysik, Ur-Struktur und All-Rhythmus*. Einsiedeln: Johannes Verlag.

———. 2014. *Analogia Entis: Metaphysics, Original Structure and Universal Rhythm*. Trans. and ed. John Betz and David Bentley Hart. Grand Rapids, MI: Eerdmans.

Pseudo-Dionysius (the Areopagite). 1987. *The Complete Works*. Trans. Colm Luibheid. New York: Paulist Press.

Rabens, Volker. 2013. *The Holy Spirit and Ethics in Paul*. 2nd rev. ed. Tübingen: J. C. B. Mohr.

Rajan, Tilottama. 2002. *Deconstruction and the Remainders of Phenomenology*. Stanford, CA: Stanford University Press.

Ratzinger, Joseph (Benedict XVI). 1987. *Principles of Catholic Theology*. Trans. Mary Frances McCarthy, S.N.D. San Francisco: Ignatius Press.

———. 1988. *Eschatology: Death and Eternal Life*. Trans. Michael Waldstein. Washington, DC: Catholic University of America Press.

———. 1989. *The Theology of History in St. Bonaventure*. Trans. Zachary Hayes. San Francisco: Franciscan Herald Press.

———. 1993. *The Meaning of Christian Brotherhood*. San Francisco: Ignatius Press.

———. 2000. *The Spirit of the Liturgy*. Trans. John Saward. San Francisco: Ignatius Press.

———. 2004. *Introduction to Christianity*. Trans. J. R. Foster and Michael J. Miller. San Francisco: Ignatius Press.

———. 2007. *The Regensburg Lecture*. Ed. James V. Schall. South Bend, IN: St. Augustine's Press.

———. 2009. *Offenbarungsverständnis und Geschichtstheologie Bonvaenturas*. Freiburg: Herder.

———. 2012. *Auferstehung und Ewiges Leben*. Freiburg: Herder.

———. 2013. *Joseph Ratzinger in Communio.* Vol. 2, *Anthropology and Culture,* ed. David L. Schindler and Nicholas J. Healy. Grand Rapids, MI: Eerdmans.

Reed, T. J. 1996. *Thomas Mann: The Uses of Tradition.* Oxford: Clarendon.

Richard of St. Victor. 2012. *On the Apocalypse of John.* Trans. and ed. A. B. Kraebel. In *Interpretation of Scripture,* ed. F. T. Harkins and F. van Liere, 327–70. Turnhout: Brepols.

Richards, Robert. 2002. *The Romantic Conception of Life: Science and Philosophy in the Age of Goethe.* Chicago: University of Chicago Press.

Richardson, John Adkins. 1995. "On the 'Multiple Viewpoint' Theory of Early Modern Art." *Journal of Aesthetics & Art Criticism* 53.2: 129–37.

Richardson, Lawrence. 2007. *Newman's Approach to Knowledge.* Leominster: Gracewing.

Ricoeur, Paul. 1984. *Time and Narrative.* Trans. Kathleen McLaughlin and David Pellauer. Chicago: University of Chicago Press.

Rilke, Rainer Maria. 1984. *Letters to a Young Poet.* Trans. Stephen Mitchell. New York: Vintage.

———. 1991. *Briefe in zwei Bänden.* Ed. Horst Nalewski. Leipzig: Insel.

———. 1995. *Ahead of All Parting: The Selected Poetry and Prose of Rainer Maria Rilke.* Trans. and ed. Stephen Mitchell. New York: Modern Library.

———. 1996. *Werke: Kommentierte Ausgabe.* 4 vols. Ed. Manfred Engel and Ulrich Fülleborn. Leipzig: Insel.

———. 2001a. *New Poems: A Revised Bilingual Edition.* Trans. Edward Snow. San Francisco: North Point Press.

———. 2001b. *The Poetry of R. M. Rilke.* Trans. and ed. A. S. Kine. Luxembourg: PiT Press.

———. 2002. *Letters on Cézanne.* Trans. Joel Agee. New York: North Point Press.

———. 2009. *Duino Elegies & Sonnets to Orpheus.* Trans. and ed. Stephen Mitchell. New York: Vintage.

———. 2013. *Rilke-Handbuch: Leben—Werk—Wirkung.* Ed. Manfred Engel. Stuttgart: J. B. Metzler.

Ringbom, Sixten. 1969. "Devotional Images and Imaginative Devotions." *Gazette des Beaux-Arts* 73: 159–70.

Romano, Claude. 2015. *At the Heart of Reason.* Trans. Michael B. Smith and Claude Romano. Evanston, IL: Northwestern University Press.

Rosen, Stanley. 1996. *Arnold Schoenberg.* Chicago: University of Chicago Press.

———. 1998. *The Classical Style.* Rev ed. New York: Norton.

Rothstein, Bret L. 2005. *Sight and Spirituality in Early Netherlandish Painting.* New York: Cambridge University Press.

Rudolf, Rainer. 1957. *Ars Moriendi: Von der Kunst des heilsamen Lebens und Sterbens.* Cologne: Böhlau Verlag.

Rudwick, Martin J. S. 1970. "The Strategy of Lyell's Principles of Geology." *Isis* 61.1: 4–33.

Ruskin, John. 1903–12. *The Works of John Ruskin.* 39 vols. Ed. E. T. Cook and Alexander Wedderburn. London: George Allen.

Safran, Linda, ed. 1991. *Heaven on Earth: Art and the Church in Byzantium.* University Park: Pennsylvania State University Press.

Sahas, Daniel J. 1986. *Icons and Logos: Sources in Eighth-Century Iconoclasm*. Toronto: University of Toronto Press.

Salteren, George. 1641. *A Treatise against Images and Pictures in Churches*. London: Wm. Lee.

Sarah, Robert Cardinal. 2017. *The Power of Silence*. San Francisco: Ignatius Press.

Savage, Anne, and Nicholas Watson. 1991. *Anchoritic Spirituality: Ancrene Wisse and Associated Works*. New York: Paulist Press.

Scheier, Claus-Artur. 2010. "Albertis Narziss und der 'Cartesianismus' von 'De Pictura.'" In *Videre et videri coincidunt: Theorien des Sehens in der ersten Hälfte des 15. Jahrhunderts*, ed. Wolfgang C. Schneider, et al., 67–80. Muenster: Aschendorff Verlag.

Scheler, Max. 1921. *Vom Ewigen im Menschen*. Leipzig: Verlag der neue Geist.

Schelling, Friedrich W. J. 1994. *Idealism and the Endgame of Theory: Three Essays by F. W. J. Schelling*. Trans. and ed. Thomas Pfau. Albany: SUNY Press.

Schindler, D. C. 2004. *Hans Urs von Balthasar and the Dramatic Structure of Truth*. New York: Fordham University Press.

———. 2008. *Plato's Critique of Impure Reason*. Washington, DC: Catholic University of America Press.

Schlegel, Friedrich. 1991. *Philosophical Fragments*. Trans. Peter Firchow. Minneapolis: University of Minnesota Press.

Schneider, Wolfgang C., et al., eds. 2010. *Videre et videri coincidunt: Theorien des Sehens in der ersten Hälfte des 15. Jahrhunderts*. Muenster: Aschendorff Verlag.

Schnitzler, Norberg. 2010. "Visual Turn" im Mittelalter? Ein Paradigmenwechsel in der Naturwissenschaft und seine Folgen für die Theologie." In *Videre et videri coincidunt: Theorien des Sehens in der ersten Hälfte des 15. Jahrhunderts*, ed. Wolfgang C. Schneider et al., 311–31. Muenster: Aschendorff Verlag.

Schönberger, Rolf. 2002. "Von der *meditatio mortis* zur *ars moriendi*: Das Problem des Todes im Denken des Jean Gerson." In *Ende und Vollendung: Eschatologische Perspektiven im Mittelalter*, ed. Jan A. Aertsen and Martin Pickavé, 721–34. Berlin: De Gruyter.

Schönborn, Christoph. 1994. *God's Human Face: The Christ Icon*. Trans. Lothar Kraut. San Francisco: Ignatius Press.

Schopenhauer, Arthur. 1969. *The World as Will and Representation*, vol. 1. Trans. E. F. J. Payne. New York: Dover.

Schroeder, Frederic M. 1992. *Form and Transformation: A Study in the Philosophy of Plotinus*. Montreal: McGill-Queen's University Press.

Scotus, John Duns. 1987. *Philosophical Writings*. Ed. Allan Wolter, O.F.M. Indianapolis, IN: Hackett.

Scruton, Roger. 2004. *Death-Devoted Heart: Sex and the Sacred in Wagner's "Tristan and Isolde."* Oxford: Oxford University Press.

Secord, James. 2000. *Victorian Sensation*. Chicago: University of Chicago Press.

———. 2015. *Visions of Science: Books and Readers at the Dawn of the Victorian Age*. Chicago: University of Chicago Press.

Seidel, Linda. 1991. "The Value of Verisimilitude in the Art of van Eyck." *Yale French Studies*, 25–43.

Sengle, Friedrich. 1971–80. *Biedermeierzeit: Deutsche Literatur im Spannungsfeld zwischen Restauration und Revolution 1815–1848*. 3 vols. Stuttgart: Metzler.

Shaftsbury, Anthony Third Earl of. 2001. *Characteristicks of Men, Manners, Opinions, Times*. Indianapolis, IN: Liberty Fund.

Shea, Victor, and William Whitla, eds. 2000. *Essays and Reviews: The 1860 Text and Its Reading*. Charlottesville: University of Virginia Press.

Shiner, Larry. 2011. *The Invention of Art: A Cultural History*. Chicago: University of Chicago Press.

Siegel, Jonah. 2000. *Desire and Excess: The Nineteenth-Century Culture of Art*. Princeton, NJ: Princeton University Press.

Simmel, Georg. 1995. *Aufsätze und Abhandlungen, 1901–1908*. Frankfurt: Suhrkamp.

———. 2007a. "Kant and Goethe: On the History of the Modern *Weltanschauung*." *Theory, Culture & Society* 24.6: 159–91.

———. 2007b. "The Metaphysics of Death" (1910). *Theory, Culture & Society* 24.7–8: 72–77.

Simons, Walter. 2008. "On the Margins of Religious Life: Hermits and Recluses, Penitents and Tertiaries, Beguines and Beghards." In *The Cambridge History of Christianity*, vol. 4, ed. Miri Rubin, 311–23. Cambridge: Cambridge University Press.

Simpson, James. 2010. *Under the Hammer*. New York: Oxford University Press.

———. 2019. *Permanent Revolution: The Reformation and the Illiberal Roots of Liberalism*. Cambridge, MA: Harvard University Press.

Sloan, Phillip R. 2003. "The Making of a Philosophical Naturalist." In *The Cambridge Companion to Darwin*, ed. Jonathan Hodge and Gregory Radick, 17–39. Cambridge: Cambridge University Press.

Smith, A. Mark. 1981. "Getting the Big Picture in Perspectivist Optics." *Isis* 72.4: 568–89.

Sobolev, Dennis. 2011. *The Split World of Gerard Manley Hopkins*. Washington, DC: Catholic University of America Press.

Sokolowski, Robert. 2000. *Introduction to Phenomenology*. New York: Cambridge University Press.

———. 2005. "Visual Intelligence in Painting." *Review of Metaphysics* 59.2: 333–54.

Soloviev, Vladimir S. 2003. *The Heart of Reality: Essays on Beauty, Love, and Ethics*. Trans. and ed. Vladimir Wozniuk. Notre Dame, IN: University of Notre Dame Press.

Solovyov, Vladimir. 2005. *The Justification of the Good*. Trans. Nathalie A. Duddington, ed. Boris Jakim. Grand Rapids, MI: Eerdmans.

Spaemann, Robert. 2011. *Schritte über uns hinaus*. 2 vols. Stuttgart: Cotta.

Spaemann, Robert, and Reinhard Löw. 2005. *Natürliche Ziele: Geschichte und Wiederentdeckung des teleologischen Denkens*. Stuttgart: Cotta.

Sperber, Dan. 1975. *Rethinking Symbolism*. Cambridge: Cambridge University Press.

Staley, Allen, and Christopher Newall. 2004. *Pre-Raphaelite Vision: Truth to Nature*. London: Tate Publishing.

Steigerwald, Joan. 2002. "Goethe's Morphology: *Urphänomene* and Aesthetic Appraisal." *Journal of the History of Biology* 35: 291–328.

———. 2019. *Experimenting at the Boundaries of Life: Organic Vitality in Germany around 1800*. Pittsburgh, PA: University of Pittsburgh Press.

Stevenson, David. 2004. *Cataclysm: The First World War as Political Tragedy*. New York: Basic Books.

Stock, Alex. 1989. "Die Rolle der 'Icona Dei' in der Spekulation 'De Visione Dei.'" In *Das Sehen Gottes nach Nikolaus von Kues*, ed. Rudolf Haubst, 50–68. Trier: Paulinus-Verlag.

Subotnick, Rose R. 1991. *Developing Variations: Style and Ideology in Western Music*. Minneapolis: University of Minnesota Press.

Symons, Arthur. [1899] 1919. *The Symbolist Movement in Literature*. New York: E. P. Dutton.

Szlezàk, Thomas A. 1993. *Platon Lesen*. Stuttgart: Frommann-Holzboog.

Talbot, Alice-Mary, ed. 1998. *Byzantine Defenders of Images: Eight Saints' Lives in English Translation*. Washington, DC: Dumbarton Oaks Library.

Tannenbaum, Leslie A. 1982. *Biblical Tradition in Blake's Early Prophecies: The Great Code of Art*. Princeton, NJ: Princeton University Press.

Tantillo, Astrida. 2007. "The Subjective Eye: Goethe's *Farbenlehre* and Faust." In *The Enlightened Eye: Goethe and Visual Culture*, ed. Evelyn K. Moore and Patricia A. Simpson, 265–77. Amsterdam: Rodopi, 2007.

Taylor, Charles. 1975. *Hegel*. Cambridge: Cambridge University Press.

———. 1989. *Sources of the Self: The Making of the Modern Identity*. Cambridge, MA: Harvard University Press.

———. 2007. *A Secular Age*. Cambridge, MA: Harvard University Press.

Taylor, Joshua C. 1987. *Nineteenth-Century Theories of Art*. Berkeley: University of California Press.

Teukolsky, Rachel. 2009. *The Literate Eye: Victorian Art Writing and Modernist Aesthetics*. New York: Oxford University Press.

Te Velde, Rudi. 2002. "Christian Eschatology and the End of Time according to Thomas Aquinas." In *Ende und Vollendung: Eschatologische Perspektiven im Mittelalter*, ed. Jan A. Aertsen and Martin Pickavé, 595–604. Berlin: De Gruyter.

———. 2006. *Aquinas on God: The "Divine Science" of the Summa Theologiae*. Aldershot: Ashgate.

Theodore of Stoudios, St. 1981. *On the Holy Icons*. Trans. Catherine P. Roth. Crestwood, NY: St. Vladimir's Seminary Press.

Thiessen, Gesa Elsbeth. 2004. *Theological Aesthetics: A Reader*. Grand Rapids, MI: Eerdmans.

Thomas, Alfred, S.J. 1968. "Was Hopkins a Scotist Before He Read Scotus?" In *Scotismus Decursu Saeculorum, de doctrina Ioannis Duns Scoti*, 617–29. Rome: Cura Commissionis Scotisticae.

———. 1969. *Hopkins the Jesuit: The Years of Training*. London: Oxford University Press.

Thomas, Keith. 2006. "Art and Iconoclasm in Early Modern England." In *Religious Politics in Post-Reformation England*, ed. K. Ficham and P. Lake, 16–40. London: Boydell.

———. 2007. *Before Darwin: Reconciling God and Nature.* New Haven, CT: Yale University Press.

Thompson, Evan. 2007. *Mind in Life: Biology, Phenomenology, and the Sciences of Mind.* Cambridge, MA: Harvard University Press.

———. 2008. "Representationalism and the Phenomenology of Mental Imagery." *Synthese* 160: 397–415.

Thornton, R. K. R. 1975. *All My Eyes See: The Visual World of Gerard Manley Hopkins.* Sunderland, UK: Ceolfrith Press.

Thunberg, Lars. 1995. *Microcosm and Mediator: The Theological Anthropology of Maximus the Confessor.* 2nd ed. Chicago: Open Court.

Tissol, Garth. 1991. *The Face of Nature: Wit, Narrative, and Cosmic Origins in Ovid's "Metamorphoses."* Princeton, NJ: Princeton University Press.

Tolstoy, Leo. 2009. *The Death of Ivan Ilyich and Other Stories.* Trans. Richard Pevear and Larissa Volokhonsky. New York: Vintage.

Tsakiridou, C. A. 2013. *Icons in Time, Persons in Eternity: Orthodox Theology and the Aes thetics of the Christian Image.* Farnham: Ashgate.

Turner, Denys. 2011. *St. Julian of Norwich, Theologian.* New Haven, CT: Yale University Press.

Tyndale, William. 1531. *An Answer unto Sir Thomas More's Dialogue.* London.

Van Asselt, Willem, et al., eds. 2007. *Iconoclasm and Iconoclash.* Boston: Brill.

Van Engen, John, ed. 1988. *Devotio Moderna: Basic Writings.* New York: Paulist Press.

———. 2008. *Sisters and Brothers of the Common Life: The Devotio Moderna and the World of the Later Middle Ages.* Philadelphia: University of Pennsylvania Press.

Vernant, Jean-Pierre. 1991. *Mortals and Immortals: Collected Essays.* Ed. Froma I. Zeitlin. Princeton, NJ: Princeton University Press.

Vico, Gianbattista. 1988. *On the Most Ancient Wisdom of the Italians.* Trans. and ed. L. M. Palmer. Ithaca, NY: Cornell University Press.

Ward, Bernadette W. 2002. *World as Word: Philosophical Theology in Gerard Manley Hopkins.* Washington, DC: Catholic University of America Press.

Wasserman, Earl R. 1971. *Shelley: A Critical Reading.* Baltimore: Johns Hopkins University Press.

Wat, Aleksandr. 1977. *My Century.* Trans. and ed. Richard Lourie. New York: New York Review of Books.

Watson, Nicholas. 2006. Introduction to *The Writings of Julian of Norwich*, ed. N. Watson and J. Jenkins, 1–59. University Park: Pennsylvania State University Press.

Wawrykow, Joseph. 2005. "Grace." In *The Theology of Thomas Aquinas*, ed. Rik van Nieuwenhove and Joseph Wawrykow, 192–221. Notre Dame, IN: University of Notre Dame Press.

Weil, Simone. 1977. *Simone Weil Reader.* Ed. George A. Panichas. Wakefield, RI: Moyer Bell.

———. 1999. *Gravity and Grace.* Trans. Emma Crawford and Mario von der Ruhr. New York: Routledge.

Weitzmann, Kurt. 1979. *The Age of Spirituality: Late Antique and Early Christian Art, Third to Seventh Century.* New York: Metropolitan Museum of Art.

Wellbery, David E. 1996. *The Specular Moment: Goethe's Early Lyric and the Beginnings of Romanticism*. Stanford, CA: Stanford University Press.

———. 2011. "Der Gestimmte Raum: Von der Stimmungslyrik zur absoluten Dichtung." In *Stimmung: Zur Wiederkehr einer ästhetischen Kategorie*, ed. Anna-Katharina Gisbertz, 157–76. Munich: Fink.

———. 2012. "Romanticism and Modernity: Epistemological Continuities and Discontinuities." In *Romanticism and Modernity*, ed. Thomas Pfau and Robert Mitchell, 13–28. New York: Routledge.

Wettlaufer, Andrea K. 1994. *In the Mind's Eye: The Visual Impulse in Diderot, Baudelaire and Ruskin*. Amsterdam: Rodopi.

Wetzel, James. 2013. *Parting Knowledge: Essays after Augustine*. Eugene, OR: Cascade Books.

Wheeler, Michael. 1999. *Ruskin's God*. Cambridge: Cambridge University Press.

Whistler, Daniel. 2013. *Schelling's Theory of Symbolic Language: Forming the System of Identity*. Oxford: Oxford University Press.

White, Norman. 1992. *Hopkins: A Literary Biography*. Oxford: Oxford University Press.

White, Thomas Joseph, O.P., ed. 2011. *Analogia Entis: Invention of the Antichrist or the Wisdom of God?* Grand Rapids, MI: Eerdmans.

Wiesing, Lambert. 2010. *Artificial Presence: Philosophical Studies in Image Theory*. Trans. Nils F. Schott. Stanford, CA: Stanford University Press.

Williams, Rowan. 2008. *Dostoevsky: Language, Faith and Fiction*. New York: Continuum.

Wilton, Andrew. 1987. *Turner in His Time*. New York: Harry N. Abrams.

Witte, Bernd. 2008. "Bilder und Texte: Über die Urszene der Visualität, Das Bildverbot und das Bild in der Literatur." *Rivista di Letterratura e Cultura Tedesca* 8: 29–40.

Wittgenstein, Ludwig. 2009. *Philosophical Investigations*. 4th rev. ed. Trans. G. E. M. Anscombe et al. Oxford: Wiley-Blackwell.

Wolf, Gerhard. 2002. *Schleier und Spiegel: Traditionen des Christusbildes und die Bildkonzepte der Renaissance*. Munich: Fink.

Wolfe, Judith. 2013a. *Heidegger's Eschatology: Theological Horizons in Martin Heidegger's Early Work*. Oxford: Oxford University Press.

———. 2013b. "Messianism." In *The Oxford Handbook of Theology and Modern European Thought*, ed. Nicholas Adams, George Pattison, and Graham Ward, 301–24. Oxford: Oxford University Press.

———. 2017. "Eschatology." In *The Oxford Handbook of Nineteenth-Century Christian Thought*, ed. Joel D. S. Rasmussen et al., 676–96. Oxford: Oxford University Press.

———. 2019. "The Eschatological Turn in Modern German Philosophy." *Modern Theology* 35.1: 55–70.

Wolterstorff, Nicholas. 2008. "Beyond Beauty and the Aesthetic in the Engagement of Religion and Art." In *Theological Aesthetics after von Balthasar*, ed. Oleg V. Bychkov and James Fodor, 119–33. Burlington, VT: Ashgate.

Wordsworth, William. 1979. *The Prelude: 1799, 1805, 1850*. Ed. Jonathan Wordsworth et al. New York: Norton.

Wordsworth, William, and Samuel Taylor Coleridge. 2002. *Lyrical Ballads and Related Writings*. Ed. William Richey and Daniel Robinson. New York: Houghton Mifflin.

Wulf, Andrea. 2015. *The Invention of Nature*. London: Murray.

Yeats, William Butler. 1997. *The Collected Works of W. B. Yeats*. Vol. 1. New York: Scribner.

Young, R. V. 1989–90. "Hopkins, Scotus, and the Predication of Being." *Renascence* 42.1–2: 35–50.

Zahavi, Dan. 2003. *Husserl's Phenomenology*. Stanford, CA: Stanford University Press.

Ziebart, K. M. 2014. *Nicolaus Cusanus on Faith and the Intellect: A Case Study in 15th-Century Fides-Ratio Controversy*. Leiden: Brill.

Zuckert, Catherine H. 2009. *Plato's Philosophers: The Coherence of the Dialogues*. Chicago: University of Chicago Press.

INDEX

rationalism, 46, 83n38, 143, 278n146, 421–22, 428, 652, 713, 718
ratio triplex, 210, 250–51, 282
realism: Alberti and, 379; Aristotle and, 99; Darwin and, 496–98; development of, 479–81, 552–53; Hopkins and, 577–78; iconography and, 162–63, 172, 175; imitation and, 52, 271; Kant and, 546; metaphysics and, 52, 184, 245, 303–4, 445, 479–82, 496; modernity and, 106, 208, 237, 333, 379, 482–83, 485, 553; naturalism and, 479–80; Ruskin and, 52, 482, 499–500, 512–15, 520, 534–42, 546–48; symbolism and, 295, 303–4; truth and, 52; van Eyck and, 290–92
reason. See *logos*
recollection. *See* remembering
Reform Acts of June 1832, 482
Reformation, 7, 222, 246, 285
Regulus (Turner), 524
remembering: Aristotle and, 96, 230; Bonaventure and, 238; Goethe and, 453, 467; Hegel and, 422; Neoplatonism and, 467; Plato and, 35–36, 76, 96, 230, 238, 422, 453, 482; Romanticism and, 614; Ruskin and, 482
Renaissance, 37, 55, 120, 208, 297, 323, 334, 643, 695
representation. *See* imitation
Republic (Plato), 29, 32, 64, 66, 68, 70–79, 89–91, 120–21, 339, 543–44, 547
"Ribblesdale" (Hopkins), 565
Richard of St. Victor, 222–23, 235–36, 253, 339
Richards, Robert, 437n86
Rickert, Heinrich, 653n36, 667
Riha Paten, 166, *167*
Rilke, Rainer Maria: *analogia* and, 30, 639–40; artistic creation and, 38, 647, 668–72, 697–701, 705–15; beauty and, 688; color and, 678–79, 699–702; contemplation and, 174, 673; ekphrasis and, 699; epiphany and, 711, 720–22; hermeneutics and, 47; iconography

and, 185; image as medium and, 54, 646–47, 654, 662–63, 705, 709, 717, 720–23; influences on, 192, 669–73, 677–79, 683–89, 718; intuition and, 14, 17, 647, 691, 697, 702–4, 709–11, 714–18, 720; *logos* and, 673; matter and, 715; modernity and, 690, 720–23; painting and, 677–78, 684–86; participation and, 669; phenomenology and, 647, 668, 675, 678–81, 686–91, 699–715; pre-predicative experience and, 54, 647, 702–3; Romanticism and, 711; symbolism and, 704–5, 716–17; transformation and, 40; truth and, 647; vision and, 403, 647, 670–72, 675–76, 687–88, 695–99, 709, 715–16
Rilke, Rainer Maria, works: "An Experience," 712; "Blaue Hortensie," 698, 703; "The Bowl of Roses," 710; *Buch der Bilder*, 721n165; "Die Rosenschale," 705, 712; *Dinggedichte*, 54, 696; *Duino Elegies*, 298, 696n124, 719; *Erlebnis II*, 715; "Experience I," 715; "Impressionism," 669; *Malte Laurids Brigge*, 302; *Man with the Broken Nose*, 672–73, *674*; *Neue Gedichte*, 54, 312n222, 668, 677, 688–89, 690, 694, 702–6, 712–13, 719; "On Landscape," 669–70; "The Rose Window," 694–95; *Sonnets to Orpheus*, 687, 711, 719; *Weltinnenraum*, 54, 634, 670, 716–18, 720; "Wendung," 713–14; *Worpswede*, 669
Ripa, Caesare, 23
Robbers (Schiller), 402
Rodin, Auguste, 54, 647, 668–77, 679–80, 690
Roman Elegies (Goethe), 425
Romano, Claude, 14n23, 575n42, 579–81, 624, 634–35
Romanticism: *analogia* and, 400; Enlightenment and, 472; Hegel and, 42–43; intuition and, 15; modernity and, 400; participation and, 400; phenomenology and, 38, 646; remembering and,

THOMAS PFAU

is the Alice Mary Baldwin Professor of English at Duke University, with a secondary appointment on the Duke Divinity School faculty. He is the author, editor, and translator of twelve books, including *Minding the Modern: Human Agency, Intellectual Traditions, and Responsible Knowledge* (University of Notre Dame Press, 2013, 2015).

CPSIA information can be obtained
at www.ICGtesting.com
Printed in the USA
LVHW072016200422
716750LV00009B/297